Lancashire

First published in 1997 by

Philip's, a division of
Octopus Publishing Group Ltd
2-4 Heron Quays, London E14 4JP

Third colour edition 2004
First impression 2004

ISBN-10 0-540-08658-4 (pocket)
ISBN-13 978-0-540-08658-0 (pocket)

Printed and bound in Spain
by Cayfosa-Quebecor

Contents

III **Key to map symbols**

IV **Key to map pages**

VI **Route planning**

X **Administrative and Postcode boundaries**

1 **Street maps** at 2⅔ inches to 1 mile

226 **Street maps** at 1⅓ inches to 1 mile

244 **Index** of towns and villages

247 **Index** of streets, hospitals, industrial estates, railway stations, schools, shopping centres, universities and places of interest

Digital Data

The exceptionally high-quality mapping found in this atlas is available as digital data in TIFF format, which is easily convertible to other bitmapped (raster) image formats.

The index is also available in digital form as a standard database table. It contains all the details found in the printed index together with the National Grid reference for the map square in which each entry is named.

For further information and to discuss your requirements, please contact Philip's on 020 7644 6932 or james.mann@philips-maps.co.uk

Key to map symbols

22a	**Motorway** with junction number
	Primary route – dual/single carriageway
	A road – dual/single carriageway
	B road – dual/single carriageway
	Minor road – dual/single carriageway
	Other minor road – dual/single carriageway
	Road under construction
	Tunnel, covered road
	Rural track, private road or narrow road in urban area
	Gate or obstruction to traffic (restrictions may not apply at all times or to all vehicles)
	Path, bridleway, byway open to all traffic, road used as a public path
	Pedestrianised area
DY7	**Postcode boundaries**
	County and unitary authority boundaries
	Railway, tunnel, railway under construction
	Tramway, tramway under construction
	Miniature railway
Walsall	**Railway station**
	Private railway station
South Shields	**Metro station**
	Tram stop, tram stop under construction
	Bus, coach station

	Ambulance station
	Coastguard station
	Fire station
	Police station
	Accident and Emergency entrance to hospital
H	**Hospital**
	Place of worship
i	**Information Centre** (open all year)
P	**Parking**
P&R	**Park and Ride**
PO	**Post Office**
	Camping site
	Caravan site
	Golf course
	Picnic site
Prim Sch	**Important buildings, schools, colleges, universities and hospitals**
River Medway	**Water name**
	River, weir, stream
	Canal, lock, tunnel
	Water
	Tidal water
	Woods
	Built up area
Church	**Non-Roman antiquity**
ROMAN FORT	**Roman antiquity**
94 / 164	**Adjoining page indicators and overlap bands** The colour of the arrow and the band indicates the scale of the adjoining or overlapping page (see scales below)

Acad	**Academy**	Inst	**Institute**	Recn Gd	**Recreation Ground**
Allot Gdns	**Allotments**	Ct	**Law Court**	Resr	**Reservoir**
Cemy	**Cemetery**	L Ctr	**Leisure Centre**	Ret Pk	**Retail Park**
C Ctr	**Civic Centre**	LC	**Level Crossing**	Sch	**School**
CH	**Club House**	Liby	**Library**	Sh Ctr	**Shopping Centre**
Coll	**College**	Mkt	**Market**	TH	**Town Hall/House**
Crem	**Crematorium**	Meml	**Memorial**	Trad Est	**Trading Estate**
Ent	**Enterprise**	Mon	**Monument**	Univ	**University**
Ex H	**Exhibition Hall**	Mus	**Museum**	W Twr	**Water Tower**
Ind Est	**Industrial Estate**	Obsy	**Observatory**	Wks	**Works**
IRB Sta	**Inshore Rescue Boat Station**	Pal	**Royal Palace**	YH	**Youth Hostel**
		PH	**Public House**		

■ The small numbers around the edges of the maps identify the 1 kilometre National Grid lines

■ The dark grey border on the inside edge of some pages indicates that the mapping does not continue onto the adjacent page

The scale of the maps on the pages numbered in blue is 4.2 cm to 1 km • 2⅔ inches to 1 mile • 1: 23810

0 ¼ ½ ¾ 1 mile
0 250 m 500 m 750 m 1 kilometre

The scale of the maps on pages numbered in green is 2.1 cm to 1 km • 1⅓ inches to 1 mile • 1: 47620

0 ¼ ½ ¾ 1 mile
0 250m 500m 750 m 1 kilometre

Key to map pages

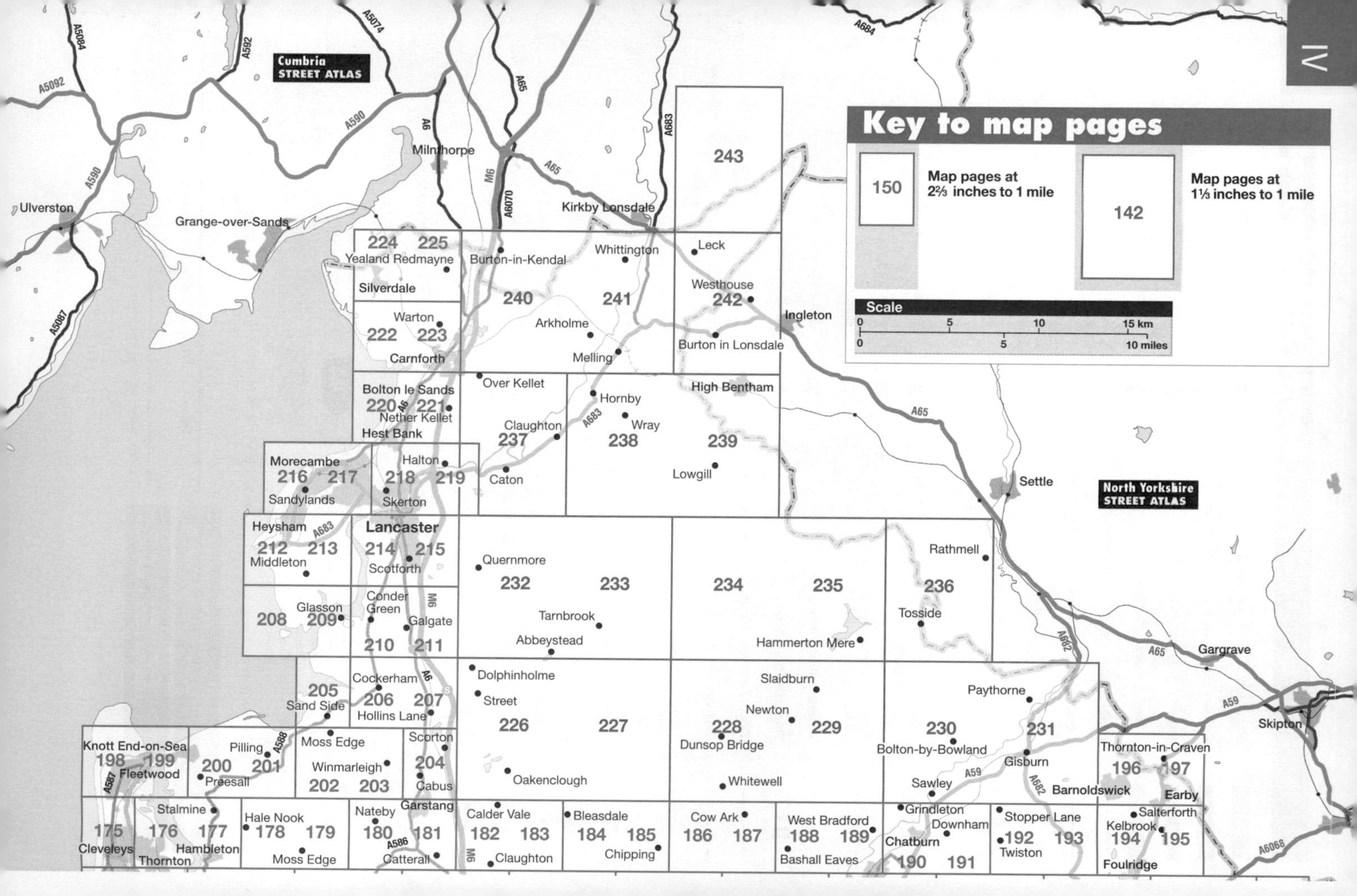

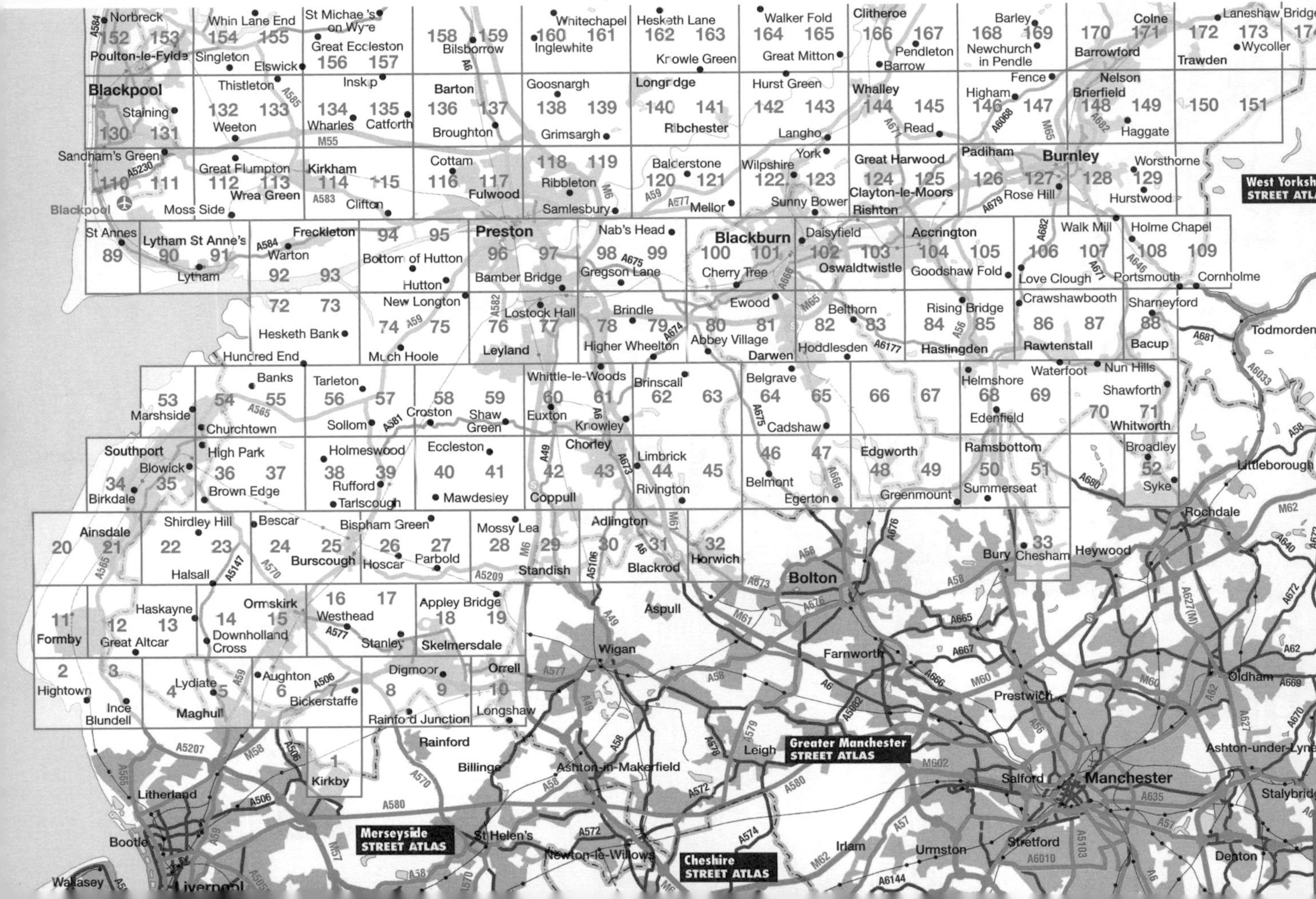

Norbreck 152 153 Poulton-le-Fylde
Whin Lane End 154 155 Singleton Elswick
St Michael's on Wyre Great Eccleston 156 157
158 159 Bilsborrow A6
Whitechapel 160 161 Inglewhite
Hesketh Lane 162 163 Knowle Green
Walker Fold 164 165 Great Mitton
Clitheroe 166 167 Pendleton Barrow
Barley 168 169 Newchurch in Pendle
170 Colne 171 Barrowford
172 173 174 Laneshaw Bridge Wycoller Trawden

Blackpool Staining 130 131
Thistleton 132 133 Weeton A585
Inskip 134 135 Wharles Catforth M55
Barton 136 137 Broughton
Goosnargh 138 139 Grimsargh
Longridge 140 141 Ribchester
Hurst Green 142 143 Langho
Whalley 144 145 Read A671
Higham 146 147 Fence A6068 M65
Nelson Brierfield 148 149 Haggate A682
150 151

Sandham's Green 110 111 A5230 Blackpool
Great Plumpton 112 113 Wrea Green Moss Side
Kirkham 114 115 Clifton A583
Cottam 116 117 Fulwood
118 119 Ribbleton Samlesbury M6
Balderstone 120 121 Mellor A59 A677
Wilpshire 122 123 York Sunny Bower
Great Harwood 124 125 Clayton-le-Moors Rishton
Padiham 126 127 Rose Hill A679
Burnley 128 129 Worsthorne Hurstwood

West Yorkshire STREET ATLAS

St Annes 89
Lytham St Anne's 90 91 Lytham
Freckleton 92 93 Warton A584
94 95 Bottom of Hutton Hutton
Preston 96 97 Bamber Bridge
Nab's Head 98 99 Gregson Lane A675
Blackburn 100 101 Cherry Tree A666
Daisyfield 102 103 Oswaldtwistle
Accrington 104 105 Goodshaw Fold
Walk Mill 106 107 Love Clough A682 A671
Holme Chapel 108 109 Portsmouth Cornholme A646

72 73 Hesketh Bank Hundred End
New Longton 74 75 Much Hoole A59
76 77 Lostock Hall Leyland A582
Brindle 78 79 Higher Wheelton A674
Ewood 80 81 Abbey Village Darwen
Belthorn 82 83 Hoddlesden A6177 M65
Rising Bridge 84 85 Haslingden A56
Crawshawbooth 86 87 Rawtenstall
Sharneyford 88 Bacup
Todmorden A681 A6033

53 Marshside
54 55 Banks Churchtown A565
Tarleton 56 57 Sollom A581
58 59 Croston Shaw Green
Whittle-le-Woods 60 61 Euxton Knowley A6
Brinscall 62 63
Belgrave 64 65 Cadshaw A675
66 67
Helmshore 68 69 Edenfield Waterfoot
Nun Hills Shawforth 70 71 Whitworth

Southport Blowick 34 35 Birkdale
High Park 36 37 Brown Edge
Holmeswood 38 39 Rufford Tarlscough
Eccleston 40 41 Mawdesley
Chorley 42 43 Coppull A49 A673
Limbrick 44 45 Rivington
46 47 Belmont Egerton A666
Edgworth 48 49 Greenmount
Ramsbottom 50 51 Summerseat A680
Broadley 52 Syke
Littleborough A58

Ainsdale 20 21 A565
Shirdley Hill 22 23 Halsall A5147
Bescar 24 25 Burscough A570
Bispham Green 26 27 Hoscar Parbold
Mossy Lea 28 29 Standish M6 A5209
Adlington 30 31 Blackrod A5106 A6 M61
32 Horwich
Bury 33 Chesham Heywood
Rochdale M62 A640 A672

11 Formby
Haskayne 12 13 Great Altcar
Ormskirk 14 15 Downholland Cross
16 17 Westhead Stanley A577
Appley Bridge 18 19 Skelmersdale
Aspull Wigan A49
Bolton A673 A676 A58 M61
Farnworth A665 A667 A666

2 Hightown 3 Ince Blundell
Lydiate 4 5 Maghull A59
Aughton 6 7 Bickerstaffe A506
Digmoor 8 9 Rainford Junction
Orrell 10 Longshaw A577
Prestwich M60 A6 A5082 A56
Oldham A62 A669 A627(M)

1 Kirkby
Rainford Billinge
Ashton-in-Makerfield A58
Leigh A579 A578
Greater Manchester STREET ATLAS
Salford Manchester A635 M602
Ashton-under-Lyne A627 A670
Stalybridge

Litherland Bootle Wallasey Liverpool A5207 M58 A565
A580 A570
Merseyside STREET ATLAS
St Helen's
Newton-le-Willows A572 A574
Cheshire STREET ATLAS
Irlam Urmston Stretford Denton M62 A57 A6144 A6010 A5103 A6

Route Planning

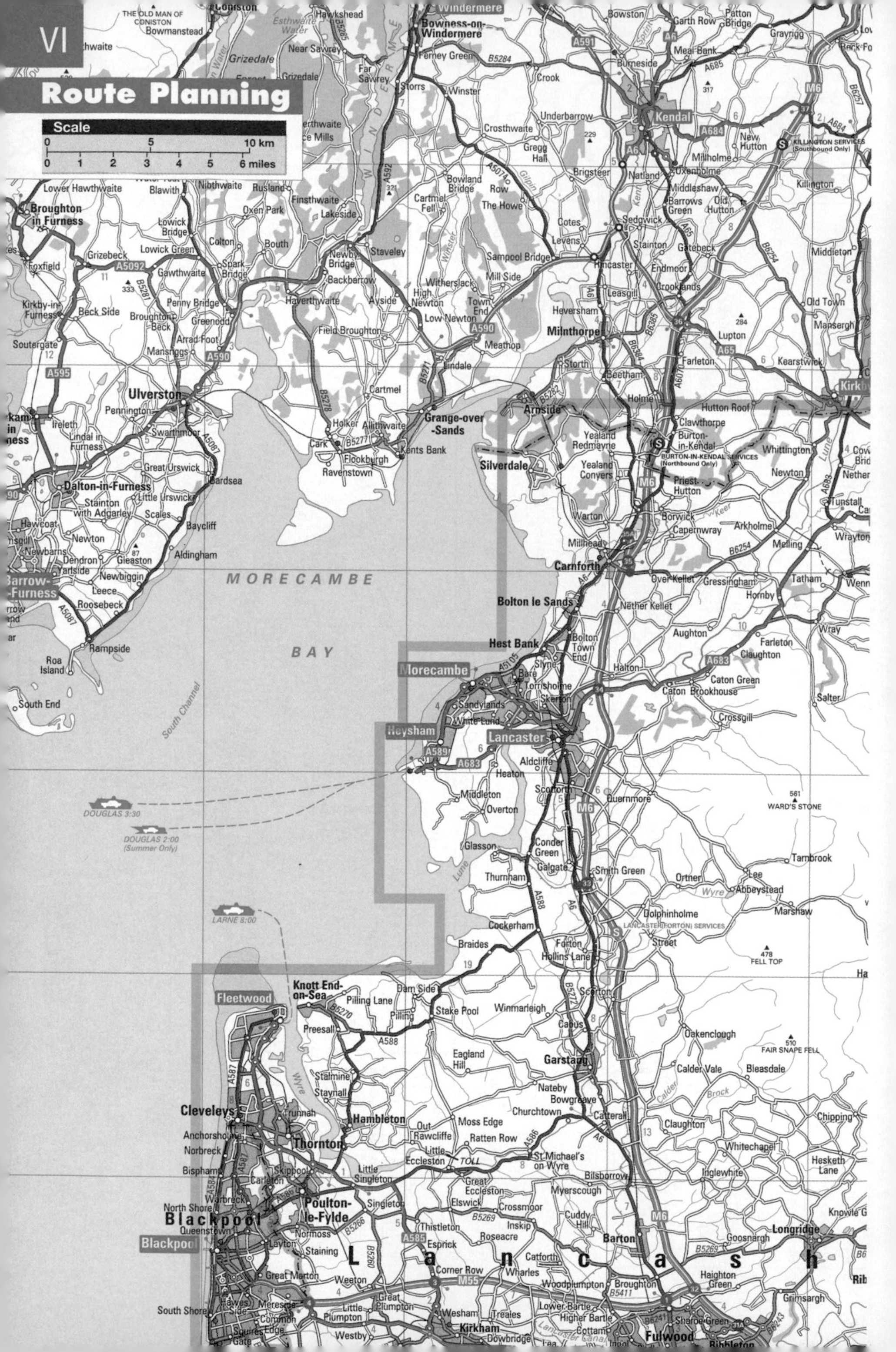

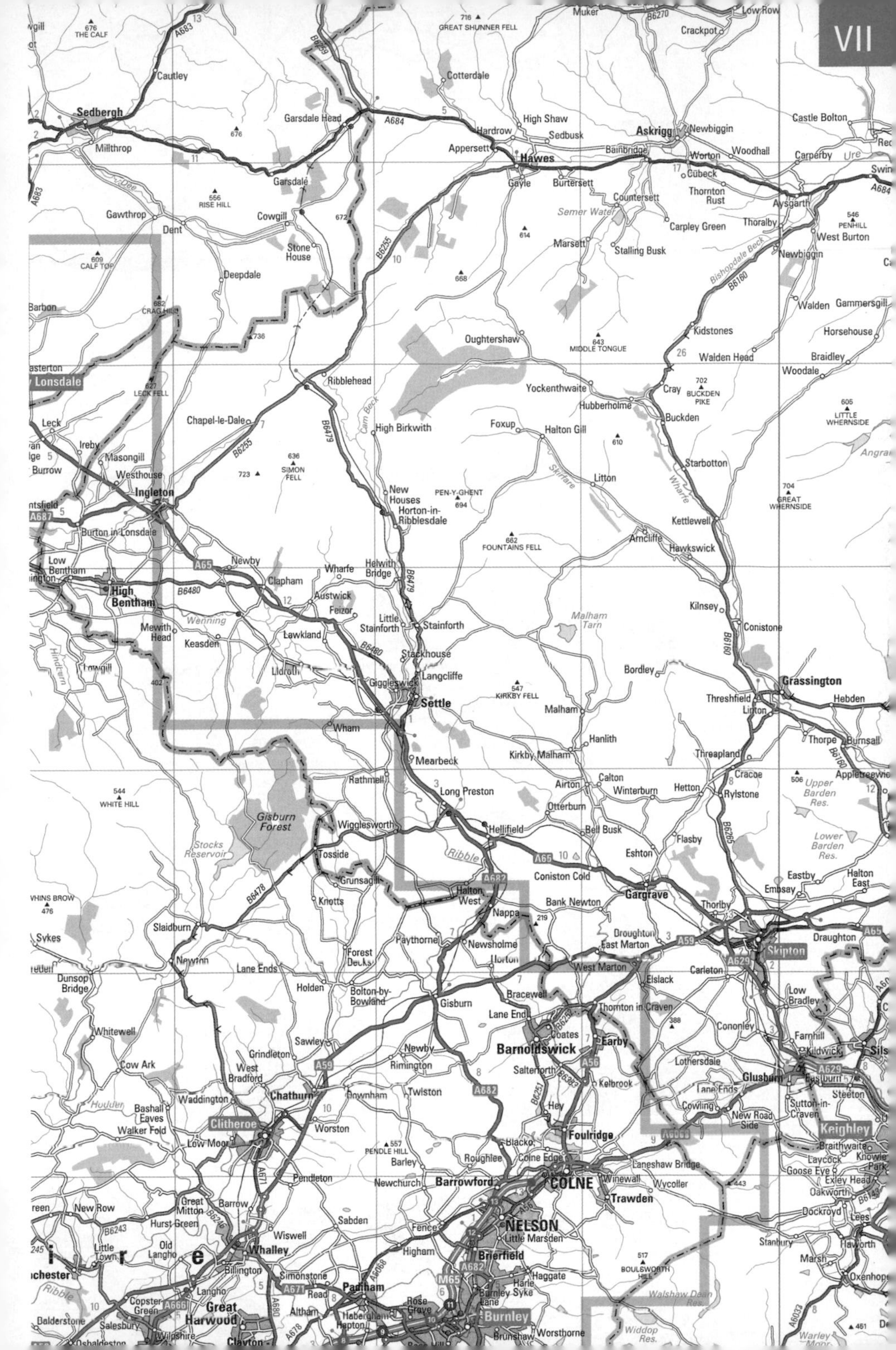

VII
THE CALF
GREAT SHUNNER FELL
Muker
Low Row
Crackpot
Cautley
Cotterdale
Sedbergh
Garsdale Head
A684
High Shaw
Hardrow
Sedbusk
Askrigg
Newbiggin
Castle Bolton
Millthrop
Appersett
Hawes
Bainbridge
Worton
Woodhall
Carperby
Ure
Garsdale
Gayle
Burtersett
Cubeck
Thornton Rust
Aysgarth
RISE HILL
Countersett
Semer Water
Gawthrop
Cowgill
Carpley Green
Thoralby
PENHILL
West Burton
Dent
Marsett
Stalling Busk
Newbiggin
CALF TOP
Stone House
Bishopdale Beck
Deepdale
B6160
Walden
Gammersgill
Barbon
CRAG HILL
Kidstones
Horsehouse
Oughtershaw
MIDDLE TONGUE
Walden Head
Braidley
Woodale
Casterton
Lonsdale
LECK FELL
Ribblehead
Yockenthwaite
Cray
BUCKDEN PIKE
LITTLE WHERNSIDE
Hubberholme
Buckden
Chapel-le-Dale
Cam Beck
High Birkwith
Foxup
Halton Gill
Leck
Ireby
Masongill
Westhouse
B6255
B6479
SIMON FELL
Skirfare
Litton
Starbotton
Wharfe
Angram
Burrow
Ingleton
New Houses
Horton-in-Ribblesdale
PEN-Y-GHENT
GREAT WHERNSIDE
A687
Burton in Lonsdale
FOUNTAINS FELL
Arncliffe
Hawkswick
Kettlewell
Low Bentham
A65
Newby
Wharfe
Helwith Bridge
High Bentham
B6480
Clapham
Austwick
Feizor
Little Stainforth
Stainforth
Malham Tarn
Kilnsey
Conistone
Wenning
Mewith Head
Keasden
Lawkland
Stackhouse
Lowgill
Hindburn
Lldroth
Giggleswick
Langcliffe
Bordley
Grassington
KIRKBY FELL
Settle
Malham
Threshfield
Linton
Hebden
Wham
Hanlith
Thorpe
Burnsall
Mearbeck
Kirkby Malham
Threapland
Cracoe
Appletreewick
WHITE HILL
Rathmell
Long Preston
Airton
Calton
Winterburn
Hetton
Rylstone
Upper Barden Res.
Gisburn Forest
Otterburn
Wigglesworth
Hellifield
Bell Busk
Flasby
Stocks Reservoir
Tosside
Ribble
Eshton
B6265
Lower Barden Res.
Coniston Cold
Eastby
Halton East
WHINS BROW
Grunsagill
Knotts
A682
Halton West
Bank Newton
Gargrave
Embsay
B6478
Nappa
Thorlby
Sykes
Slaidburn
Paythorne
Newsholme
Droughton
East Marton
A59
Draughton
Skipton
Newton
Forest Becks
Horton
West Marton
Carleton
A629
Dunsop Bridge
Lane Ends
Holden
Bolton-by-Bowland
Gisburn
Bracewell
Elslack
Low Bradley
Lane End
Thornton in Craven
Cononley
Farnhill
Whitewell
Sawley
Coates
Barnoldswick
Earby
Kildwick
Grindleton
Newby
Rimington
Salterforth
A56
Lothersdale
Glusburn
Eastburn
Cow Ark
West Bradford
Kelbrook
Lane Ends
Steeton
Waddington
Chatburn
Downham
Twiston
Cowling
New Road Side
Sutton-in-Craven
Hodder
Bashall Eaves
Hey
Keighley
Clitheroe
Worston
Foulridge
Walker Fold
Low Moor
PENDLE HILL
Blacko
Braithwaite
Barley
Roughlee
Colne Edge
Laneshaw Bridge
Laycock
Goose Eye
Exley Head
Pendleton
Newchurch
Barrowford
COLNE
Winewall
Wycoller
Trawden
Oakworth
Great Mitton
Barrow
New Row
B6246
B6243
Hurst Green
Wiswell
Sabden
Fence
NELSON
Little Marsden
Dockroyd
Lees
Old Langho
Little Town
Whalley
Higham
Brierfield
Stanbury
Haworth
BOULSWORTH HILL
Marsh
Billington
Simonstone
A6068
A682
M65
Haggate
Harle Syke
Oxenhope
Ribble
Langho
A671
Read
Padiham
Burnley Lane
Walshaw Dean Res.
Copster Green
A666
Great Harwood
Altham
Rose Grove
Habergham Eaves
Hapton
Burnley
A6033
Balderstone
Salesbury
Wilpshire
Clayton
A678
Brunshaw
Worsthorne
Widdop Res.
Warley Moor

Cleveleys
Anchorsholme
Norbreck
Bispham
North Shore
Blackpool
Queenstown
Blackpool
Hambleton
Thornton
Out Rawcliffe
Little Eccleston
Moss Edge
Ratten Row
St Michael's on Wyre
Catterall
Claughton
Chipping
Whitechapel
Inglewhite
Hesketh Lane
Little Singleton
Great Eccleston
Bilsborrow
Carleton
Poulton-le-Fylde
Singleton
Elswick
Myerscough
Crossmoor
Inskip
Cuddy Hill
Barton
Longridge
Goosnargh
Knowle Green
Normoss
Thistleton
Roseacre
Layton
Staining
Esprick
Lancashire
Great Marton
Weeton
Corner Row
Catforth
Wharles
Woodplumpton
Broughton
Haighton Green
Grimsargh
South Shore
Hawes Side
Mereside
Marton Moss
Squires Gate
Great Plumpton
Little Plumpton
Wesham
Kirkham
Treales
Lower Bartle
Higher Bartle
Cottam
Ingol
Fulwood
Sharoe Green
Ribbleton
Cadley
Lancaster Canal
Westby
Dowbridge
Lea Town
Moss Side
Wrea Green
Newton
Scales
Clifton
Preston
Samlesbury
Higher Ballam
Ansdell
St Annes
Lytham St Anne's
Fairhaven
Lytham
Warton
Freckleton
Ribble
Bottom of Hutton
Higher Penwortham
Walton-le-Dale
Hutton
Middleforth Green
Bamber Bridge
Higher Walton
Coup Green
Gregson Lane
Hoghton
Longton
New Longton
Lostock Hall
Farington
Walmer Bridge
Hesketh Bank
Becconsall
Much Hoole
Midge Hall
Leyland
Clayton Green
Brindle
Higher Wheelton
Hundred End
Broadfield
Clayton-le-Woods
Whittle-le-Woods
Wheelton
Banks
Tarleton
Bretherton
Euxton
Crossens
Marshside
Sollom
Croston
Ulnes Walton
Shaw Green
Churchtown
Mere Brow
Yarrow
Eccleston
Chorley
White
Southport
Holmeswood
Blowick
Rufford
Tarlscough
Mawdesley
Heskin Green
Charnock Richard
Weld Bank
Birkdale
Brown Edge
Snape Green
Bescar
Coppull
Hillside
Scarisbrick
New Lane
Bispham Green
Wrightington Bar
Adlington
Ainsdale-on-Sea
Ainsdale
Shirdley Hill
Pinfold
Liverpool
Burscough
Burscough Bridge
Parbold
Hill Dale
Dangerous Corner
Mossy Lea
Coppull Moor
Woodvale
Halsall
Shevington Moor
Standish
Blackrod
Newburgh
Appley Bridge
Shevington Vale
Red Rock
Barton
Haskayne
Ormskirk
Boars Head
Haigh
Freshfield
Formby
Westhead
Stanley
Dalton
Roby Mill
Shevington
Beech Hill
Aspull
Downholland Cross
Gathurst
Marylebone
Little Altcar
Great Altcar
Aughton Park
Blaguegate
Skelmersdale
Digmoor
Orrell
Up Holland
Wigan
Westhoughton
Pemberton
Hightown
Ince Blundell
Lydiate
Aughton
Stanley Gate
Royal Oak
Bickerstaffe
Rainford Junction
Higher End
Goose Green
Ince in Makerfield
Platt Bridge
Maghull
Lunt
Barrow Nook
Crawford
Longshaw
Bryn Gates
Little Crosby
Melling Mount
Rainford
Billinge
Abram
Bryn
Crank Wood
Thornton
Netherton
Sefton
Great Crosby
Melling
Kirkby
Crank
Garswood
Chadwick Green
Ashton-in-Makerfield
Moss Bank
Belfast 8:00
Douglas 4:00 (Winter Only)
Dublin 7:45
Crosby Channel
Waterloo
Seaforth
Litherland
Aintree
Southdene
Orrell
Fazakerley
Knowsley
Denton's Green
Haydock
Golborne
Lowton
Dublin 3:45 (Mar-Nov)
Douglas 2:30
Bootle
New Brighton
Walton
Norris Green
Gillar's Green
St Helens
Eccleston
Blackbrook
Broad Oak
Collins Green
Peasley Cross
Newton-le-Willows
Liscard
Egremont
Kirkdale
Merseyside
Anfield
West Derby
Thatto Heath
Sutton
Wallasey
Everton
Longview
Prescot
Eccleston Park
Rainhill
Sutton Leach
Burtonwood
Winwick
Leasowe
Moreton
Meols
Seacombe
Poulton
Bidston
Liverpool
Knotty Ash
Roby
Huyton
Whiston
Sutton Manor
Clock Face
Burtonwood Services
Houghton Green
Fearnhead
Rainhill Stoops
Bold Heath
Warrington
Claughton
Edge Hill
Wavertree
Childwall
Netherley
Tarbock Green
Cronton
Barrow's Green
Great Sankey
Upton
Greasby
Grange
Birkenhead
Toxteth
Dingle
Mossley Hill
Gateacre
Farnworth
Appleton
Penketh
Warrington
Woodchurch
Frankby
Tranmere
Rock Ferry
Prenton
West Kirby
Woolton
Hough Green
Ditton
Widnes
Higher Walton
Caldy
New Ferry
Aigburth
Allerton
Halewood
Grassendale
Thurstaston
Irby
Thingwall
Bebington
Storeton
Port Sunlight
Pensby
Barnston
Brimstage
Garston
Hunt's Cross
Hale Bank
Runcorn
Moore
Keckwick
Daresbury
Speke
Hale
Halton
Bromborough
Liverpool John Lennon
Liverpool Airport
Heswall
Thornton Hough
Eastham Ferry
Eastham
Mersey
Weston
Halton
Norton
Preston Brook
Preston on the Hill
Dutton
Gayton
Raby
Sutton Weaver
Aston
Dones Green
Parkgate
Hinderton
Willaston
Hooton
Childer Thornton
Ellesmere Port
Newtown
Frodsham
Neston
Overpool
Weaver
Toll
M6
M55
M65
M61
M58
M57
M62
M53
M56
A6
A583
A584
A585
A565
A570
A59
A5209
A577
A580
A58
A49
A57
A5058
A562
A561
A5300
A557
A533
A552
A553
A540
A41
A56
A50
B5269
B5260
B5266
B5259
B5411
B5248
B5249
B5246
B5195
B5193
B5205
B5204
B5192
B5137
B5136
B5356

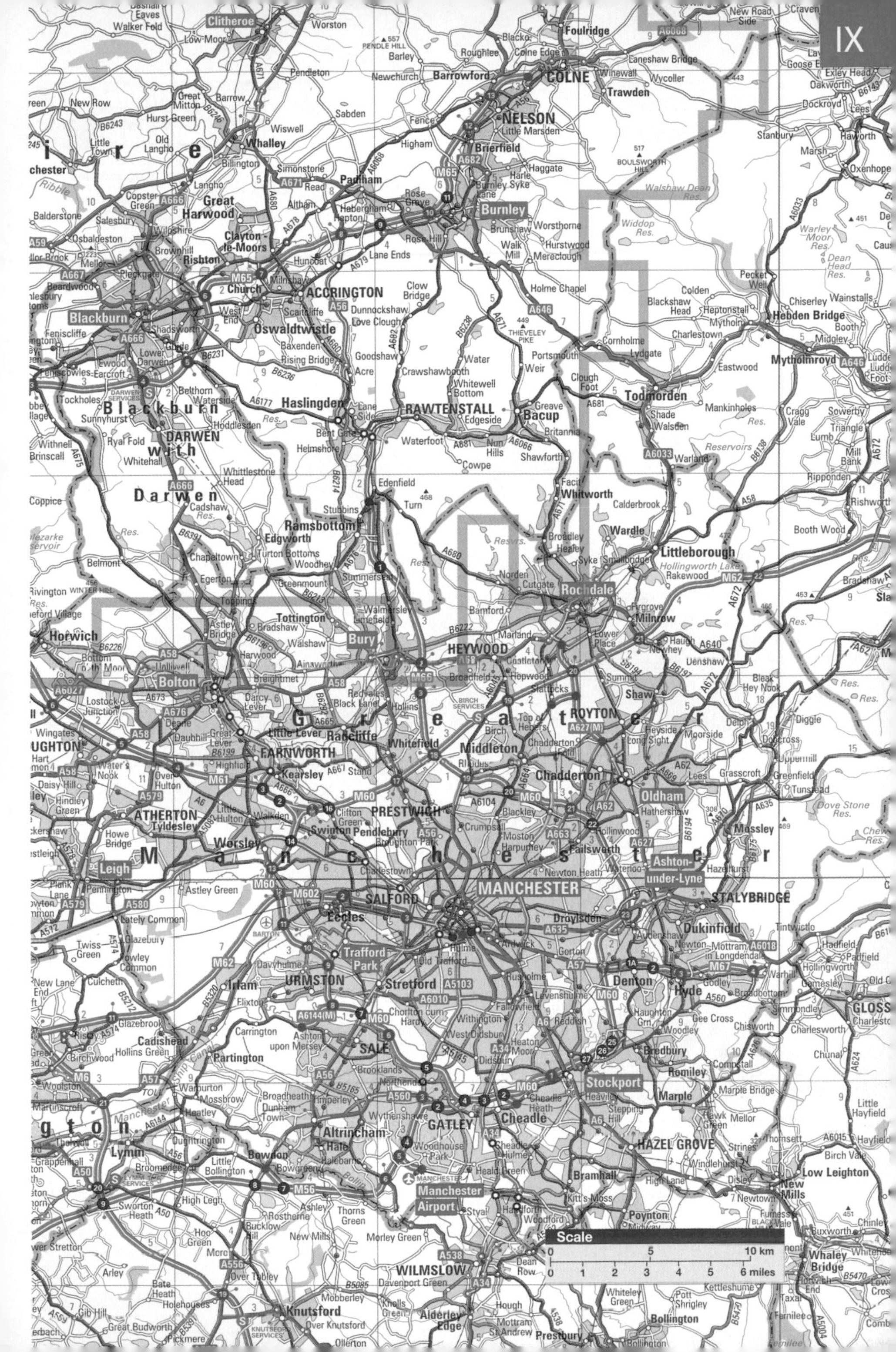
Clitheroe
Worston
PENDLE HILL
Foulridge
New Road Side
Craven
Walker Fold
Low Moor
Barley
Roughlee
Blacko
Colne Edge
Laneshaw Bridge
Pendleton
Newchurch
Barrowford
COLNE
Winewall
Wycoller
Exley Head
Oakworth
Trawden
Great Mitton
Barrow
New Row
Sabden
Dockroyd
Lees
Hurst Green
NELSON
Little Marsden
Fence
Wiswell
Stanbury
Haworth
Whalley
Higham
Brierfield
Little Town
Old Langho
BOULSWORTH HILL
Marsh
Oxenhope
Billington
Simonstone
Haggate
Padiham
Harle Syke
Read
Walshaw Dean Res.
Langho
Copster Green
Great Harwood
Burnley
Balderstone
Salesbury
Altham
Habergham
Rose Grove
Hapton
Worsthorne
Widdop Res.
Warley Moor Res.
Osbaldeston
Wilpshire
Clayton-le-Moors
Brunshaw
Mellor Brook
Brownhill
Rishton
Rose Hill
Lane Ends
Walk Mill
Hurstwood
Mereclough
Dean Head Res.
Mellor
Huncoat
Beardwood
Pleckgate
Church
Milnshaw
ACCRINGTON
Clow Bridge
Holme Chapel
Pecket Well
Colden
Blackshaw Head
Heptonstall
Chiserley
Wainstalls
Hebden Bridge
Blackburn
Scaitcliffe
Dunnockshaw
Love Clough
West End
Oswaldtwistle
Shadsworth
THIEVELEY PIKE
Mytholm
Charlestown
Booth
Midgley
Feniscliffe
Guide
Baxenden
Rising Bridge
Goodshaw
Acre
Water
Portsmouth
Cornholme
Lydgate
Mytholmroyd
Eastwood
Lower Darwen
Ewood
Feniscowles
Earcroft
Crawshawbooth
Weir
Clough Foot
Todmorden
Tockholes
Belthorn
Waterside
Haslingden
Whitewell Bottom
Greave
Bacup
Blackburn with Darwen
Sunnyhurst
Hoddlesden
RAWTENSTALL
Edgeside
Lane Side
Shade
Walsden
Mankinholes
Cragg Vale
Sowerby
Triangle
Britannia
Ryal Fold
DARWEN
Bent Gate
Waterfoot
Nun Hills
Shawforth
Reservoirs
Lumb
Withnell
Brinscall
Whitehall
Helmshore
Warland
Mill Bank
Cowpe
Whittlestone Head
Ripponden
Edenfield
Facit
Whitworth
Coppice
Turn
Rishworth
Cadshaw
Calderbrook
Stubbins
Ramsbottom
Wardle
Booth Wood
Edgworth
Broadley
Healey
Littleborough
Chapeltown
Turton Bottoms
Syke
Smallbridge
Hollingworth Lake
Rakewood
Woodhey
Belmont
Norden
Cutgate
Rochdale
Greenmount
Summerseat
Rivington
WINTER HILL
Egerton
Bradshaw
Toppings
Walmersley
Limefield
Bamford
Firgrove
Milnrow
Heptonstall
Tottington
Astley Bridge
Bury
Marland
Lower Place
Haugh
Newhey
Denshaw
Horwich
Walshaw
HEYWOOD
Harwood
Castleton
Hopwood
Bolton
Breightmet
Ainsworth
Broadfield
Slattocks
Summit
Shaw
Bleak Hey Nook
Lostock Junction
Darcy Lever
Redvales
Black Lane
Hollins
BIRCH SERVICES
Top of Hebers
ROYTON
Greater Manchester
Diggle
Deane
Birch
Heyside
Long Sight
Moorside
Delph
Wingates
Daubhill
Great Lever
Little Lever
Radcliffe
Whitefield
Middleton
Chadderton Fold
Dobcross
Westhoughton
Hart Common
Water's Nook
Highfield
FARNWORTH
Uppermill
Over Hulton
Kearsley
Stand
Rhodes
Chadderton
Grasscroft
Greenfield
Daisy Hill
Lees
Oldham
Tunstead
Hindley Green
ATHERTON
Tyldesley
Little Hulton
Walkden
Clifton
Swinton
Pendlebury
PRESTWICH
Blackley
Hathershaw
Dove Stone Res.
Howe Bridge
Crumpsall
Hollinwood
Mossley
Worsley
Broughton Park
Moston
Harpurhey
Failsworth
Leigh
Charlestown
Newton Heath
Waterloo
Ashton-under-Lyne
Hazelhurst
Pennington
Astley Green
MANCHESTER
STALYBRIDGE
SALFORD
Eccles
Droylsden
Dukinfield
Tintwistle
Lately Common
BARTON
Ardwick
Audenshaw
Hadfield
Padfield
Glazebury
Hulme
Gorton
Newton
Mottram in Longdendale
Twiss Green
Trafford Park
Old Trafford
Hollingworth
Fowley Common
Davyhulme
Rusholme
Warhill
New Lane End
Culcheth
Irlam
URMSTON
Stretford
Levenshulme
Denton
Hyde
Godley
Gamesley
Flixton
Fallowfield
Broadbottom
GLOSSOP
Chorlton cum Hardy
Withington
Reddish
Haughton Grn.
Simmondley
Charlestown
Glazebrook
Risley
Cadishead
Carrington
Ashton upon Mersey
West Didsbury
Gee Cross
Woodley
Chisworth
Charlesworth
SALE
Heaton Moor
Bredbury
Birchwood
Hollins Green
Partington
Didsbury
Chunal
Brooklands
Compstall
Romiley
Northenden
Stockport
Woolston
Warburton
Mossbrow
Broadheath
Timperley
Heaviley
Marple
Marple Bridge
Little Hayfield
Martinscroft
Dunham Town
Wythenshawe
Cheadle
Cheadle Heath
Stepping Hill
Mellor
Heatley
Altrincham
GATLEY
Hawk Green
Thornsett
Hayfield
Warrington
Thelwall
Lymm
Oughtrington
Hale
Woodhouse Park
Cheadle Hulme
HAZEL GROVE
Strines
Birch Vale
Grappenhall
Broomedge
Little Bollington
Bowdon
Bowgreen
Halebarns
Windlehurst
Low Leighton
LYMM SERVICES
Heald Green
Bramhall
High Lane
Disley
New Mills
MANCHESTER
Manchester Airport
Kitt's Moss
Newtown
High Legh
Styal
Handforth
Poynton
Furness Vale
Swarton Heath
Rostherne
Ashley
Thorns Green
Woodford
Lower Stretton
Bucklow Hill
New Mills
Morley Green
Hoo Green
Mere
Scale
10 km
6 miles
Dean Row
Whaley Bridge
Arley
Over Tabley
WILMSLOW
Davenport Green
Kettleshulme
Bate Heath
Mobberley
Whiteley Green
Pott Shrigley
Holehouses
Knolls Green
Gib Hill
Knutsford
Alderley Edge
Hough
Bollington
Taxal
Over Knutsford
Mottram St Andrew
Great Budworth
Pickmere
KNUTSFORD SERVICES
Ollerton
Prestbury
Fernilee
Combs
Ribble
Res.
Resvrs.
Rooley Moor
Manchester Ship Canal
Bollin
M65
M66
M61
M60
M62
M602
M56
M6
M67
A59
A666
A56
A58
A6
A34
A57
A635
A6010
A5103
A560
A627(M)
A6144(M)

Major administrative and Postcode boundaries
County and unitary authority boundaries
District boundaries
Postcode boundaries
Area covered by this atlas
Scale
0
5
10
15 km
0
5
10 miles
Cumbria
North Yorkshire
Lancashire
Lancaster
Wyre
Ribble Valley
Pendle
Blackpool
Fylde
Preston
Hyndburn
Burnley
South Ribble
Chorley
Blackburn with Darwen
Rossendale
West Lancashire
Calderdale
Bradford
Rochdale
Bolton
Bury
Oldham
Wigan
Salford
Sefton
St Helens
Manchester
Tameside
Liverpool
Knowsley
Warrington
Trafford
Stockport
SD
SJ
LA10
LA7
LA5
LA6
LA4
LA1
LA2
LA3
BD24
BD23
BD22
BB7
BB18
BB9
BB8
BB12
BB10
BB6
BB1
BB11
BB2
BB5
BB4
BB3
OL14
OL13
OL12
OL10
BL10
BL7
BL8
BL9
BL6
HX7
FY7
FY6
FY5
FY2
FY3
FY1
FY4
FY8
PR3
PR2
PR1
PR4
PR5
PR25
PR26
PR6
PR7
PR9
PR8
L40
WN1
WN2
WN6
WN8
WN5
WA11
L37
L39
L38
L31
L29
L33
Silverdale
Burton-in-Kendal
Carnforth
Burton in Lonsdale
High Bentham
Hornby
Morecambe
Caton
Heysham
Lancaster
Overton
Glasson
Galgate
Dolphinholme
Tosside
Slaidburn
Dunsop Bridge
Gisburn
Barnoldswick
Earby
Fleetwood
Pilling
Scorton
Garstang
Chipping
Cleveleys
Hambleton
Great Eccleston
Bilsborrow
Clitheroe
Colne
Trawden
Poulton-le-Fylde
Nelson
Longridge
Whalley
Blackpool
Padiham
Great Harwood
Burnley
Kirkham
Fulwood
Mellor
Preston
Blackburn
Holme Chapel
Lytham St Anne's
Warton
Accrington
Bamber Bridge
Walmer Bridge
Haslingden
Bacup
Leyland
Darwen
Banks
Tarleton
Brinscall
Croston
Eccleston
Chorley
Whitworth
Southport
Belmont
Ramsbottom
Adlington
Burscough
Ainsdale
Horwich
Parbold
Bury
Standish
Haskayne
Ormskirk
Formby
Aughton
Skelmersdale
Orrell
Hightown
Maghull
30
40
50
60
70
80
90
400

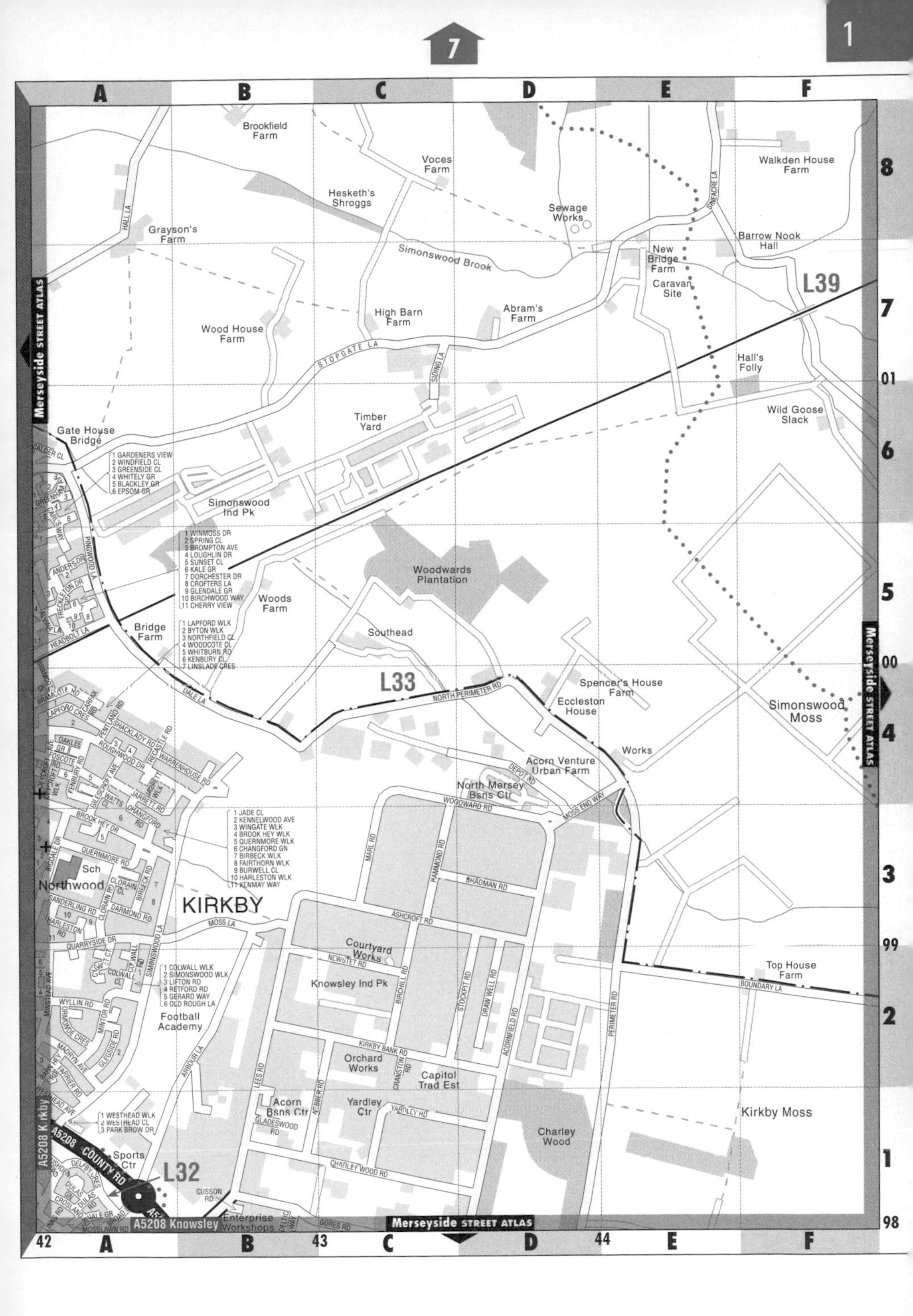
7
A
B
C
D
E
F
Brookfield Farm
Voces Farm
Walkden House Farm
Hesketh's Shroggs
Sewage Works
Grayson's Farm
HALL LA
Simonswood Brook
New Bridge Farm
Barrow Nook Hall
SINEACRE LA
Caravan Site
L39
Wood House Farm
High Barn Farm
Abram's Farm
STOPGATE LA
SIDING LA
Hall's Folly
Wild Goose Slack
Timber Yard
Gate House Bridge
1 GARDENERS VIEW
2 WINDFIELD CL
3 GREENSIDE CL
4 WHITELY GR
5 BLACKLEY GR
6 EPSOM GR
Simonswood Ind Pk
1 WINMOSS DR
2 SPRING CL
3 BROMPTON AVE
4 LOUGHLIN DR
5 SUNSET CL
6 KALE GR
7 DORCHESTER DR
8 CROFTERS LA
9 GLENDALE GR
10 BIRCHWOOD WAY
11 CHERRY VIEW
Woodwards Plantation
Woods Farm
PINGWOOD LA
HEADBOLT LA
Bridge Farm
1 LAPFORD WLK
2 BYTON WLK
3 NORTHFIELD CL
4 WOODCOTE CL
5 WHITBURN RD
6 KENBURY CL
7 LINSLADE CRES
Southead
L33
NORTH PERIMETER RD
DALE LA
Spencer's House Farm
Eccleston House
Simonswood Moss
Works
Acorn Venture Urban Farm
DEPOT RD
North Mersey Bsns Ctr
WOODWARD RD
MOSS END WAY
1 JADE CL
2 KENNELWOOD AVE
3 WINGATE WLK
4 BROOK HEY WLK
5 QUERNMORE WLK
6 CHANGFORD GN
7 BIRBECK WLK
8 FAIRTHORN WLK
9 BURWELL CL
10 HARLESTON WLK
11 KENMAY WAY
MARL RD
HAMMOND RD
BRADMAN RD
Sch
Northwood
KIRKBY
MOSS LA
ASHCROFT RD
Courtyard Works
NEWSTET RD
Knowsley Ind Pk
BIRCHILL RD
STOCKPIT RD
DRAW WELL RD
ACORNFIELD RD
PERIMETER RD
Top House Farm
BOUNDARY LA
1 COLWALL WLK
2 SIMONSWOOD WLK
3 LIFTON RD
4 RETFORD RD
5 GERARD WAY
6 OLD ROUGH LA
Football Academy
ARBOUR LA
KIRKBY BANK RD
Orchard Works
Capitol Trad Est
CRANSTON RD
LEES RD
Acorn Bsns Ctr
Yardley Ctr
YARDLEY RD
GLADESWOOD RD
Kirkby Moss
Charley Wood
1 WESTHEAD WLK
2 WESTHEAD CL
3 PARK BROW DR
Sports Ctr
L32
A5208 COUNTY RD
A5208 Kirkby
CHARLEY WOOD RD
CUSSON RD
A5208 Knowsley
Enterprise Workshops
GORES RD
Merseyside STREET ATLAS
42
43
44
98
99
00
01
1
2
3
4
5
6
7
8

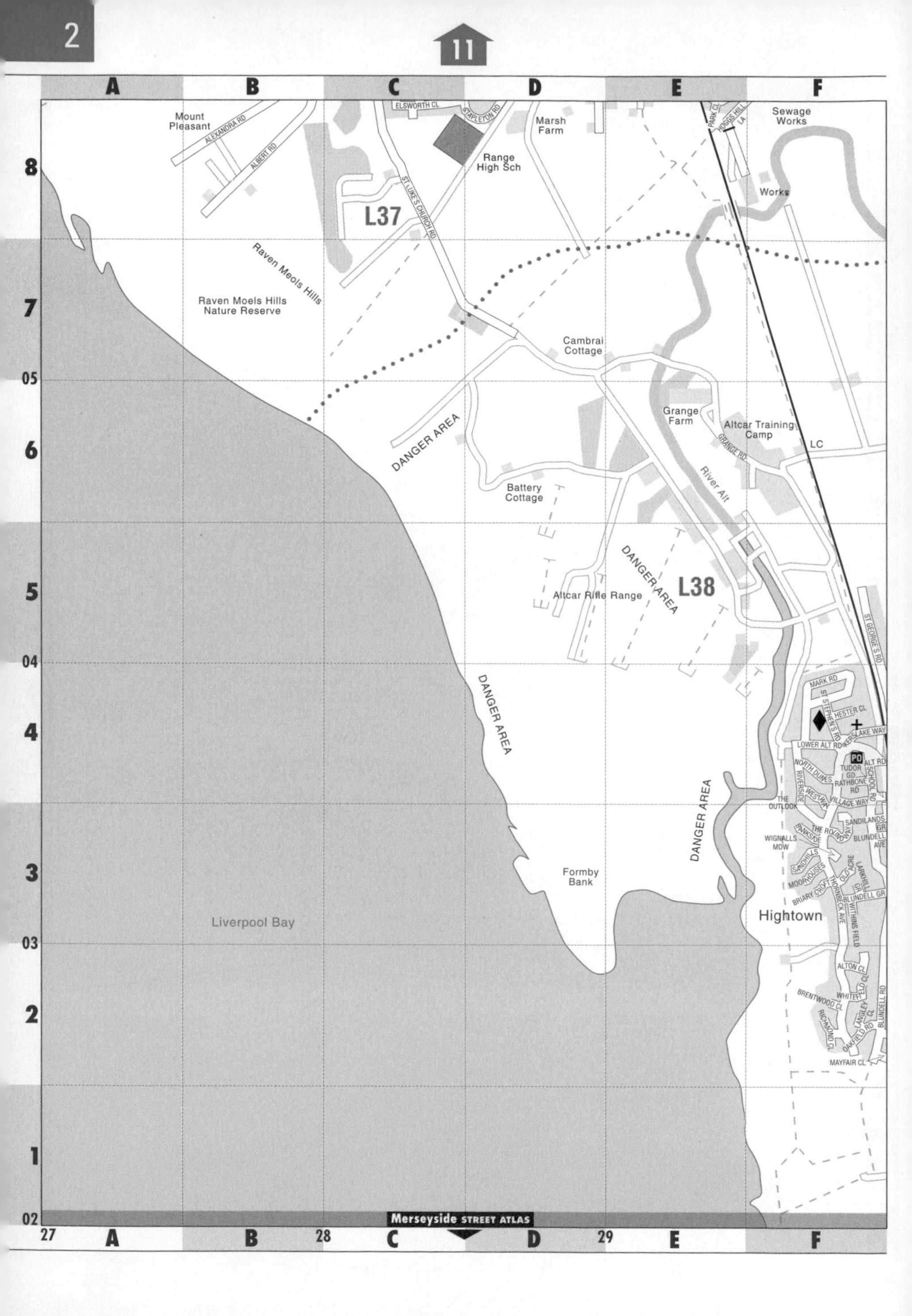

11
A
B
C
D
E
F
Mount Pleasant
ALEXANDRA RD
ALBERT RD
ELSWORTH CL
STAPLETON RD
Marsh Farm
Range High Sch
PARK CL
HOGGS HILL LA
Sewage Works
Works
ST LUKE'S CHURCH RD
L37
Raven Meols Hills
Raven Moels Hills Nature Reserve
Cambrai Cottage
DANGER AREA
Grange Farm
Altcar Training Camp
GRANGE RD
LC
River Alt
Battery Cottage
Altcar Rifle Range
L38
ST GEORGE'S RD
MARK RD
ST STEPHEN'S RD
HESTER CL
LOWER ALT RD
ALT RD
NORTH DUNES
TUDOR GD
RATHBONE RD
SCHOOL RD
RIVERSIDE
WEST WAY
VILLAGE WAY
THE OUTLOOK
SANDILANDS
THE ROUND WAY
WIGNALLS MDW
BANKSIDE
BLUNDELL AVE
SANDHILLS
MOORHOUSES
OLD ACRE
LARKHILL
BRIARY CROFT
THORNBECK AVE
BLUNDELL GR
WITHINS FIELD
Formby Bank
Hightown
Liverpool Bay
ALTON CL
BRENTWOOD CL
WHITEFIELD CL
RICHMOND CL
LANGLEY CL
OAKFIELD RD
BLUNDELL RD
MAYFAIR CL
8
7
05
6
5
04
4
3
03
2
1
02
27
28
29

12
4

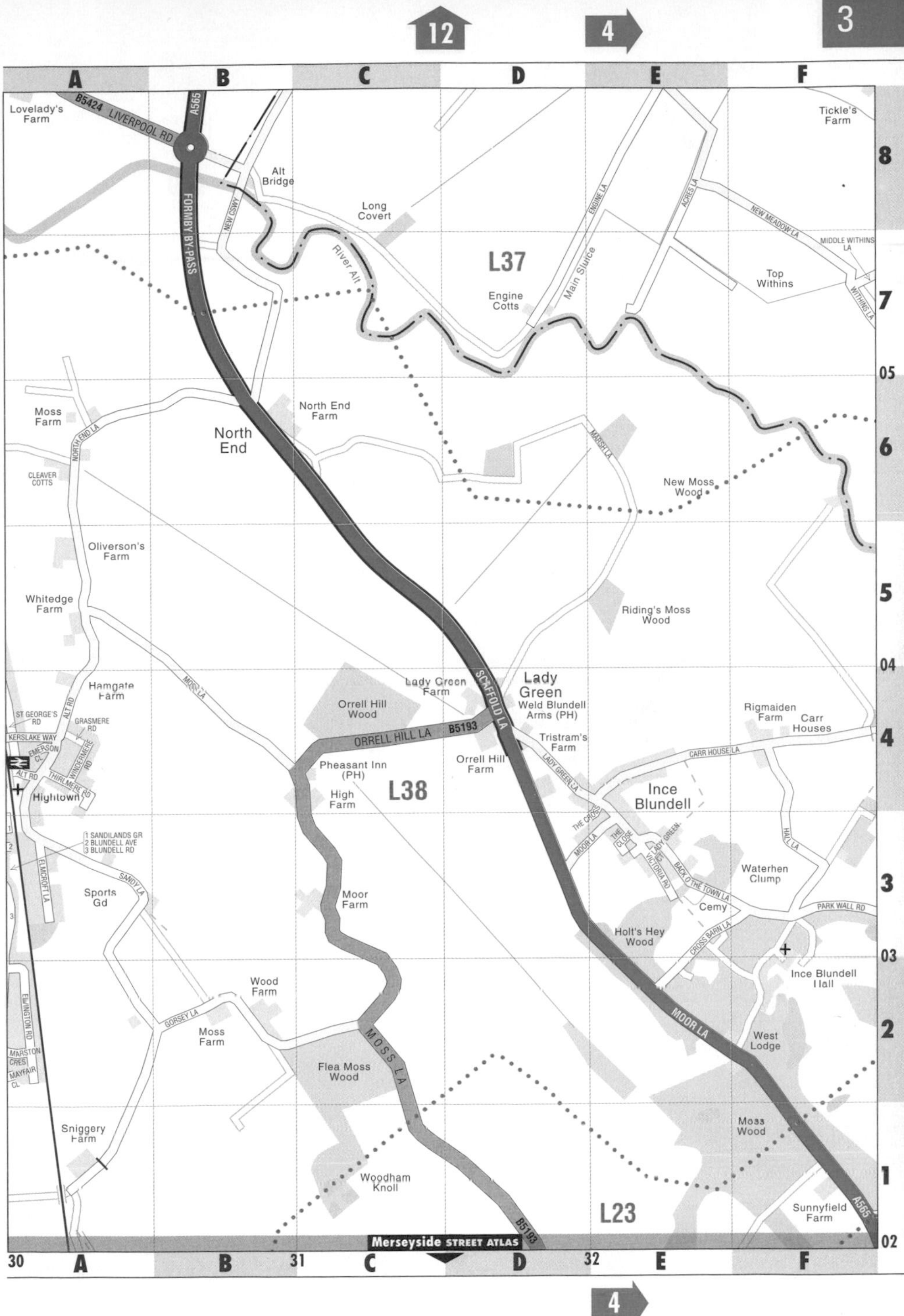
A
B
C
D
E
F
8
7
05
6
5
04
4
3
03
2
1
02
30
31
32
Lovelady's Farm
B5424 LIVERPOOL RD
A565
FORMBY BY-PASS
Alt Bridge
Long Covert
NEW CSWY
River Alt
L37
ENGINE LA
Main Sluice
Engine Cotts
ACRES LA
NEW MEADOW LA
MIDDLE WITHINS LA
Top Withins
WITHINS LA
Tickle's Farm
North End Farm
North End
Moss Farm
NORTH END LA
CLEAVER COTTS
MARSH LA
New Moss Wood
Oliverson's Farm
Whitedge Farm
Riding's Moss Wood
Hamgate Farm
MOSS LA
Lady Green Farm
SCAFFOLD LA
Lady Green
Weld Blundell Arms (PH)
Orrell Hill Wood
ST GEORGE'S RD
ALT RD
GRASMERE RD
KERSLAKE WAY
EMERSON CL
WINDERMERE RD
THIRLMERE RD
Hightown
ORRELL HILL LA
B5193
Tristram's Farm
Rigmaiden Farm
Carr Houses
CARR HOUSE LA
Pheasant Inn (PH)
Orrell Hill Farm
LADY GREEN LA
L38
High Farm
Ince Blundell
THE CROSS
MOOR LA
THE CLOSE
LADY GREEN CT
VICTORIA RD
BACK O'THE TOWN LA
HALL LA
Waterhen Clump
1 SANDILANDS GR
2 BLUNDELL AVE
3 BLUNDELL RD
ELMCROFT LA
SANDY LA
Sports Gd
Moor Farm
Cemy
PARK WALL RD
Holt's Hey Wood
CROSS BARN LA
Ince Blundell Hall
Wood Farm
GORSEY LA
Moss Farm
MOSS LA
MOOR LA
West Lodge
ELLINGTON RD
MARSTON CRES
MAYFAIR CL
Flea Moss Wood
Moss Wood
Sniggery Farm
Woodham Knoll
L23
Sunnyfield Farm
A565

4

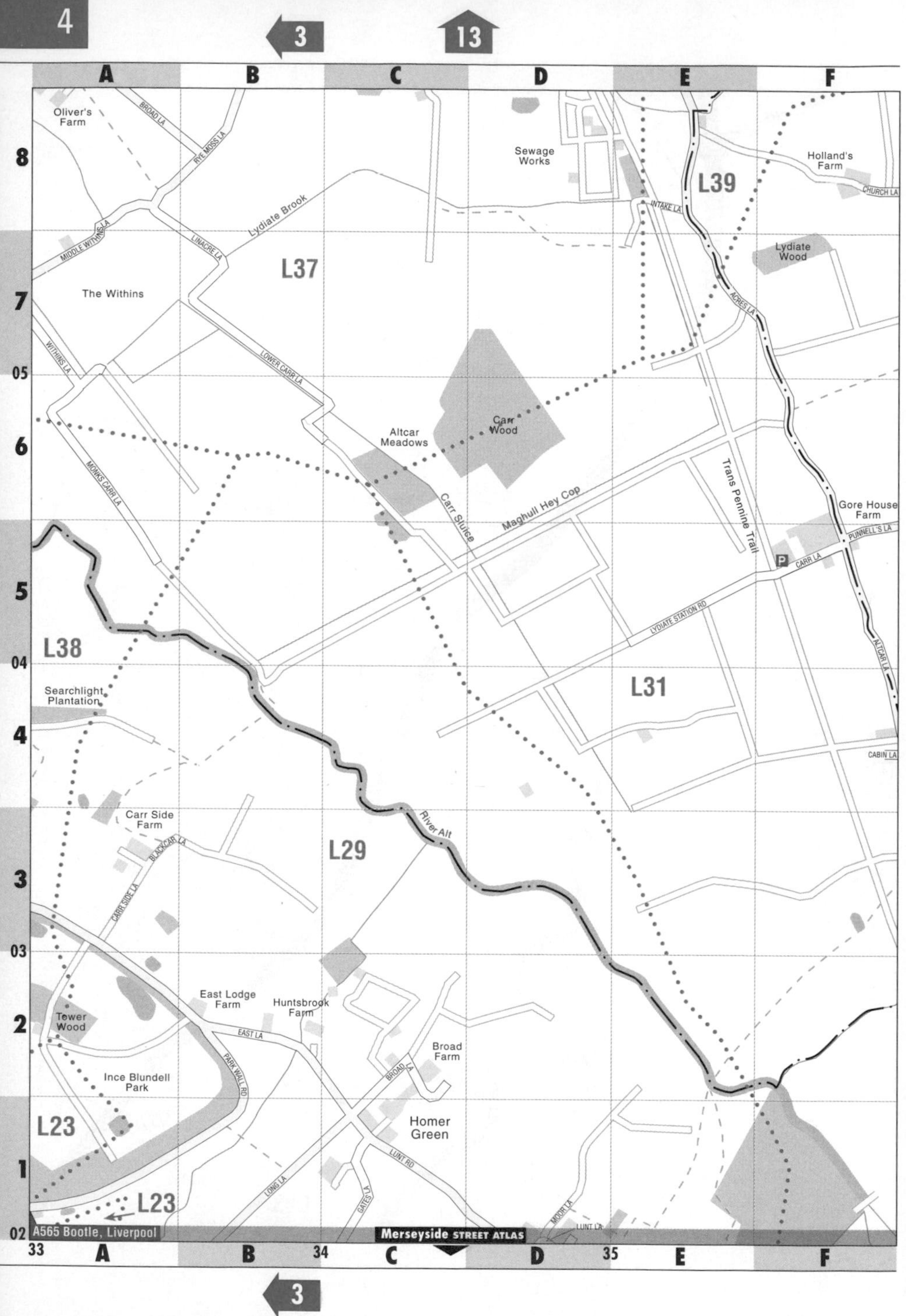
3
13
A
B
C
D
E
F
8
7
05
6
5
04
4
3
03
2
1
02
33
34
35
Oliver's Farm
BROAD LA
RYE MOSS LA
Lydiate Brook
Sewage Works
INTAKE LA
L39
Holland's Farm
CHURCH LA
MIDDLE WITHINS LA
LINACRE LA
L37
Lydiate Wood
The Withins
ACRES LA
WITHINS LA
LOWER CARR LA
Altcar Meadows
Carr Wood
MONKS CARR LA
Carr Sluice
Maghull Hey Cop
Trans Pennine Trail
Gore House Farm
PUNNELL'S LA
CARR LA
LYDIATE STATION RD
ALTCAR LA
L38
Searchlight Plantation
L31
CABIN LA
Carr Side Farm
BLACKCAR LA
River Alt
L29
CARR SIDE LA
East Lodge Farm
Huntsbrook Farm
Tower Wood
EAST LA
PARK WALL RD
Broad Farm
BROAD LA
Ince Blundell Park
L23
Homer Green
LUNT RD
LONG LA
GATES LA
MOOR LA
LUNT LA
L23
A565 Bootle, Liverpool
Merseyside STREET ATLAS

3

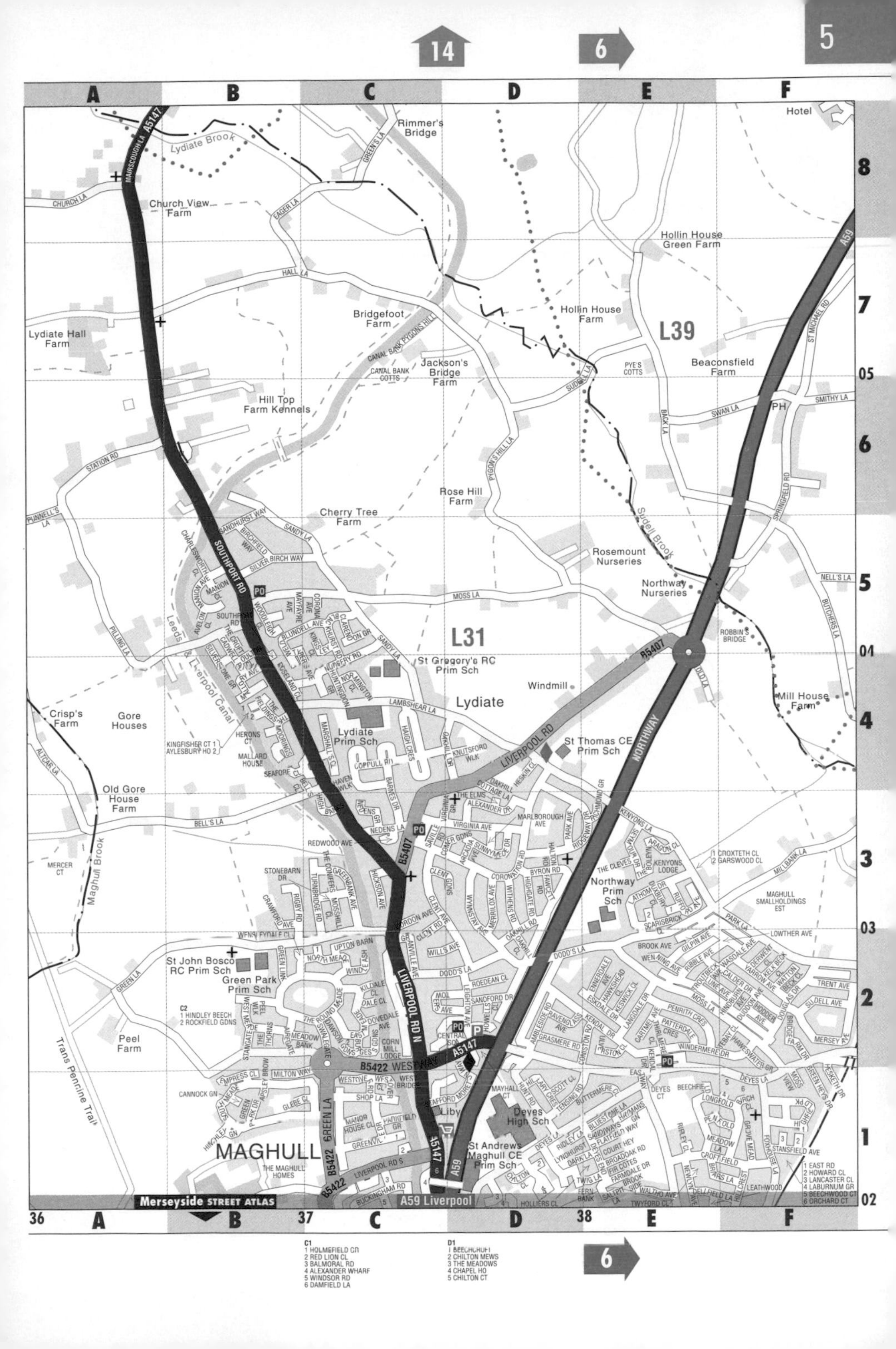
5
14
6
A
B
C
D
E
F
8
7
05
6
5
04
4
3
03
2
1
02
36
37
38
Rimmer's Bridge
Hotel
Lydiate Brook
MAINSCOUGH LA
A5147
CHURCH LA
Church View Farm
EAGER LA
GREEN'S LA
Hollin House Green Farm
HALL LA
Bridgefoot Farm
Hollin House Farm
Lydiate Hall Farm
L39
CANAL BANK
PYGONS HILL
Jackson's Bridge Farm
CANAL BANK COTTS
PYE'S COTTS
Beaconsfield Farm
SUDELL LA
Hill Top Farm Kennels
SWAN LA
BACK LA
SMITHY LA
PH
A59
ST MICHAEL RD
STATION RD
PYGON'S HILL LA
Rose Hill Farm
SPRINGFIELD RD
PUNNELL'S LA
Cherry Tree Farm
Sudell Brook
SANDHURST WAY
SANDY LA
BIRCHFIELD WAY
SILVER BIRCH WAY
Rosemount Nurseries
SOUTHPORT RD
PO
Northway Nurseries
NELL'S LA
MOSS LA
L31
Leeds & Liverpool Canal
ROBBIN'S BRIDGE
PILLING LA
BUTCHERS LA
St Gregory's RC Prim Sch
B5407
Windmill
Mill House Farm
Crisp's Farm
Gore Houses
LAMBSHEAR LA
Lydiate
Lydiate Prim Sch
LIVERPOOL RD
NORTHWAY
St Thomas CE Prim Sch
KINGFISHER CT
AYLESBURY HO
MALLARD HOUSE
HERONS CT
KNUTSFORD WLK
COPPULL RI
Old Gore House Farm
ALTCAR LA
SEAFORE CL
BELL'S LA
HAVEN WLK
HIGH BANKS
NEDENS GR
BARNES DR
OAKHILL COTTAGE LA
THE ELMS
ALEXANDER DR
MARLBOROUGH AVE
KENYONS LA
VIRGINIA AVE
PARK AVE
RIDGEWAY
RICHMOND GR
ARAGON CL
KENYONS LODGE
THE CLEVES
THE BOLEYNS
1 CROXTETH CL
2 GARSWOOD CL
MILLBANK LA
REDWOOD AVE
COMER GDNS
SUNNYMEDE DR
HALTON RD
BYRON RD
MERCER CT
Maghull Brook
STONEBARN DR
THE CONIFERS
GREENBANK AVE
HICKSON AVE
CORONATION RD
Northway Prim Sch
MAGHULL SMALLHOLDINGS EST
CLENT AVE
HIGHGATE RD
FAWCETT
RUFFORD
CRAWFORD AVE
RIGBY RD
TURNBRIDGE RD
MOSSHILL CL
GORDON AVE
CLENT RD
MERRILOX AVE
WITHENS RD
WYNSTAY AVE
OAKHILL RD
ATHOL DR
SCARISBRICK CL
PARK LA
LOWTHER AVE
WENSLEYDALE CL
UPTON BARN
GREEN LINK
NORTH MEADE
WINDLE ASH
WILLS AVE
DODD'S LA
BROOK AVE
GILPIN AVE
WENNING AVE
RIBBLE AVE
WASDALE AVE
DERWENT CL
St John Bosco RC Prim Sch
Green Park Prim Sch
GREEN LA
KILDALE CL
DALE CL
LIVERPOOL RD N
ROEDEAN CL
SANDFORD DR
ENNERDALE AVE
HAWKSHEAD CL
ESKDALE DR
KESWICK CL
LANGDALE DR
PENRITH CRES
MOSS LA
CALDER DR
YARROW AVE
TRENT AVE
SUDELL AVE
C2
1 HINDLEY BEECH
2 ROCKFIELD GDNS
WEST MEADE
PEEL WLK
THE THORNS
THE ROUND MEADE
DOVEDALE AVE
LEIGHTON AVE
AMBLESIDE RD
RAVENGLASS AVE
KENDAL DR
PATTERDALE CRES
Peel Farm
STANGATE
MEADOW BANK
DAWSON GDNS
CORN MILL LODGE
CENTRAL SQ
P
GRASMERE RD
CONISTON RD
WINDERMERE DR
HAWESWATER GR
BRIDGE FARM DR
MERSEY AVE
Trans Pennine Trail
B5422 WESTWAY
A5147
EMPRESS CL
MILTON WAY
WESTOVER CL
WEST BRIDGE
MAYHALL CT
DEYES LA
DEYES CT
BEECHFIELD
CANNOCK GN
GLEBE CL
SHOP LA
STAFFORD MOAT
Deyes High Sch
LONGFOLD
BIRCH CL
HESKETH DR
Liby
MANOR HOUSE CL
BUTTERMERE CL
BLUESTONE LA
HAYMANS GR
FLATFIELD WAY
GREENVIEW
St Andrews Maghull CE Prim Sch
RIDLEY LA
LYNDHURST
DARK LA
COURT HEY
BROADOAK RD
FIR COTES
FARMDALE DR
MEADOW LA
CROFTFIELD
STANSFIELD AVE
MAGHULL
GREEN LA
B5422
THE MAGHULL HOMES
LIVERPOOL RD S
CHILTON CL
TWIG LA
BROOK SIDE
BRIARS LA
LEATHWOOD
1 EAST RD
2 HOWARD CL
3 LANCASTER CL
4 LABURNUM GR
5 BEECHWOOD CT
6 ORCHARD CT
BUCKINGHAM RD
A59 Liverpool
FERN BANK
SALTPIT LA
HOLLIERS CL
TWYFORD CL
WALTHO AVE
DELLFIELD LA
Merseyside STREET ATLAS
C1
1 HOLMEFIELD GR
2 RED LION CL
3 BALMORAL RD
4 ALEXANDER WHARF
5 WINDSOR RD
6 DAMFIELD LA
D1
1 BEECHCROFT
2 CHILTON MEWS
3 THE MEADOWS
4 CHAPEL HO
5 CHILTON CT

5
15

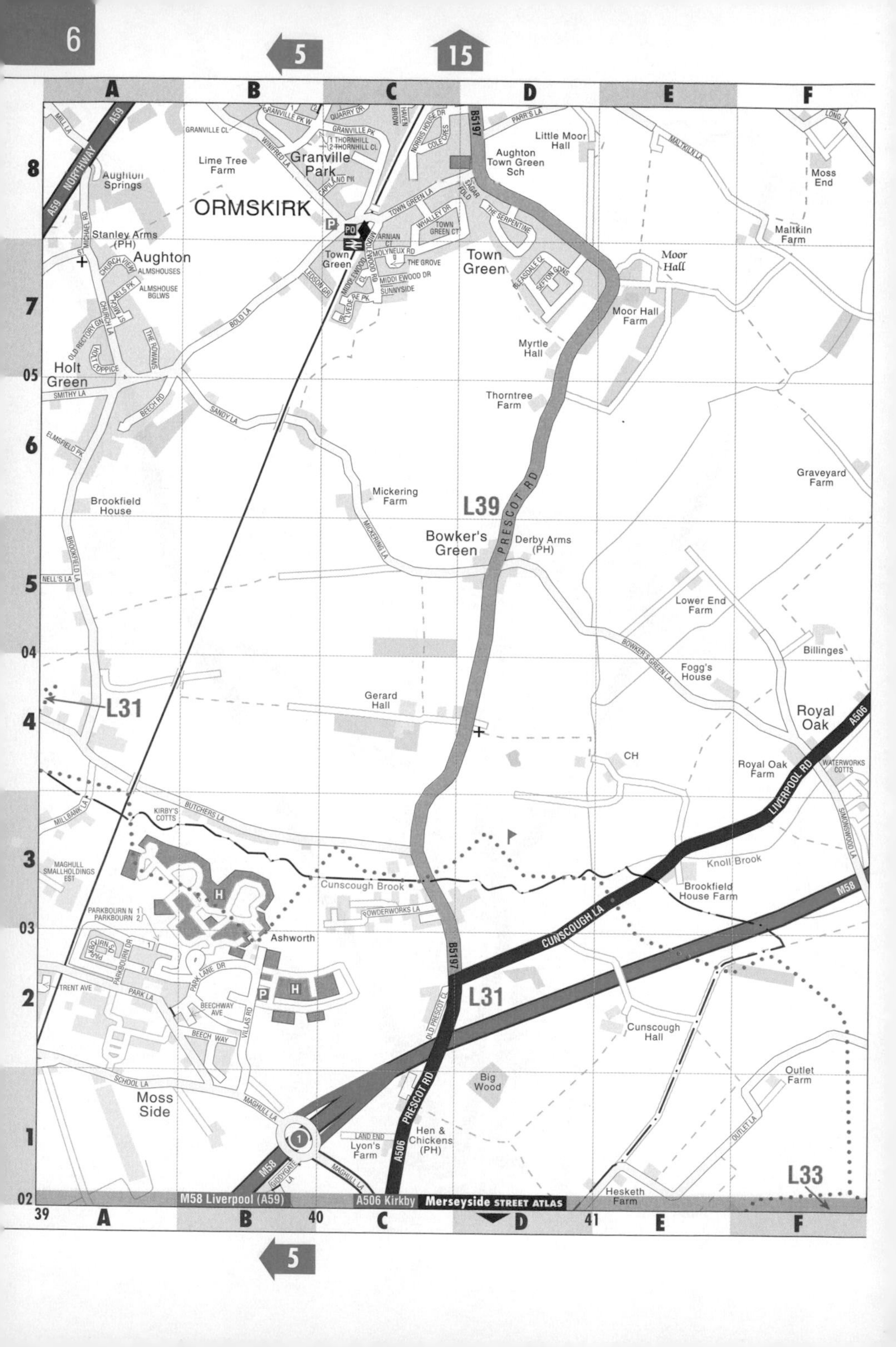
ORMSKIRK
Granville Park
Lime Tree Farm
Aughton Springs
Stanley Arms (PH)
Aughton
Town Green
Little Moor Hall
Aughton Town Green Sch
Moss End
Maltkiln Farm
Moor Hall
Moor Hall Farm
Myrtle Hall
Thorntree Farm
Holt Green
Brookfield House
Mickering Farm
Graveyard Farm
L39
PRESCOT RD
Bowker's Green
Derby Arms (PH)
Lower End Farm
Billinges
Fogg's House
Gerard Hall
Royal Oak
Royal Oak Farm
CH
L31
Knoll Brook
Cunscough Brook
Brookfield House Farm
Ashworth
CUNSCOUGH LA
LIVERPOOL RD
M58
A506
B5197
Cunscough Hall
Big Wood
Outlet Farm
Moss Side
Hen & Chickens (PH)
Lyon's Farm
Hesketh Farm
L33
MAGHULL SMALLHOLDINGS EST
BUTCHERS LA
SANDY LA
BOLD LA
MICKERING LA
BOWKER'S GREEN LA
SCHOOL LA
MAGHULL LA
PARK LA
VILLAS RD
POWDERWORKS LA
A59 NORTHWAY
M58 Liverpool (A59)
A506 Kirkby
Merseyside STREET ATLAS

5

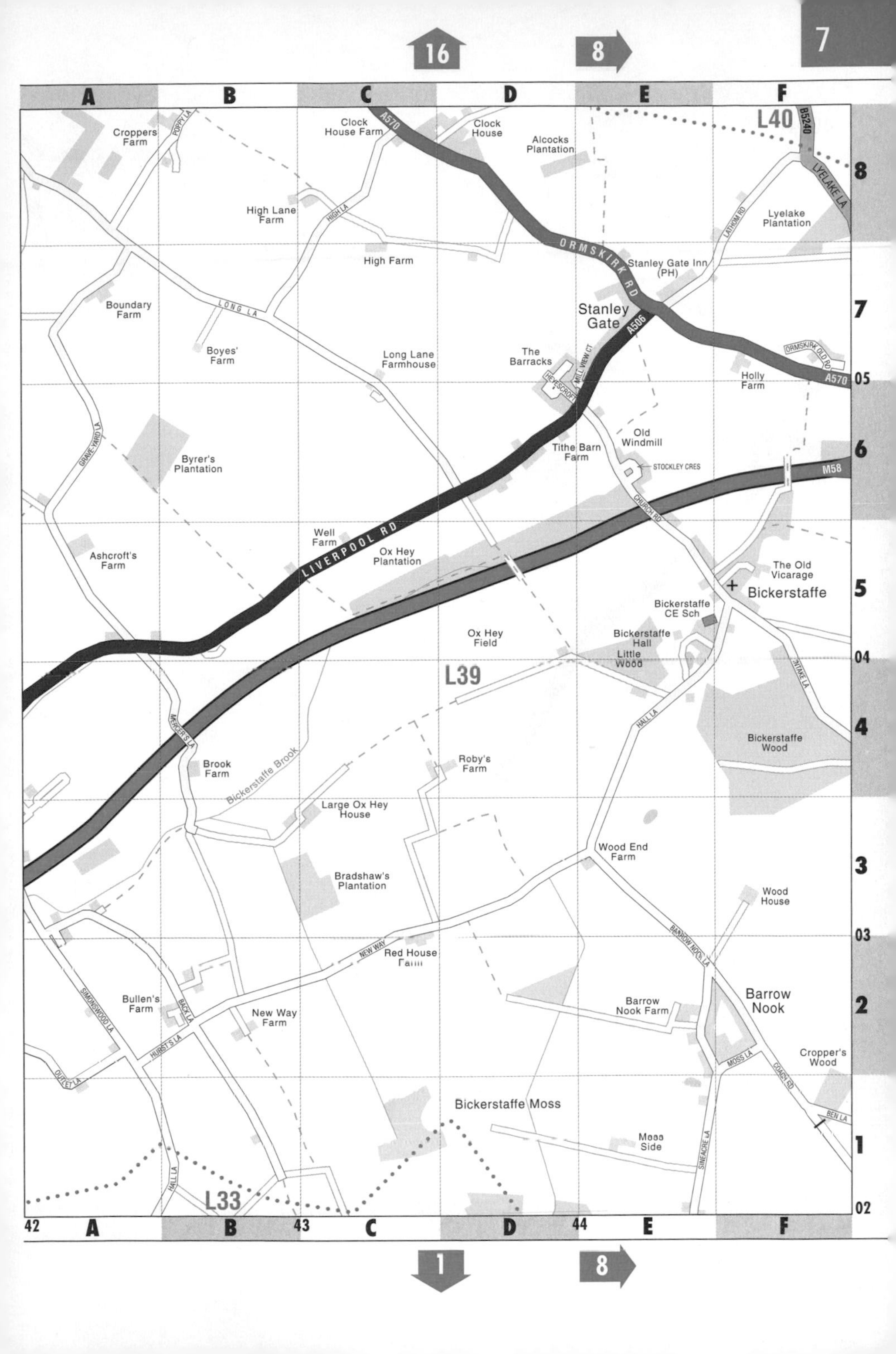
16
8
Croppers Farm
Clock House Farm
Clock House
Alcocks Plantation
L40
High Lane Farm
High Farm
Lyelake Plantation
Stanley Gate Inn (PH)
ORMSKIRK RD
Boundary Farm
LONG LA
Stanley Gate
Boyes' Farm
Long Lane Farmhouse
The Barracks
Holly Farm
Old Windmill
Tithe Barn Farm
Byrer's Plantation
STOCKLEY CRES
M58
Well Farm
LIVERPOOL RD
Ox Hey Plantation
Ashcroft's Farm
The Old Vicarage
Bickerstaffe
Bickerstaffe CE Sch
Bickerstaffe Hall
Ox Hey Field
Little Wood
L39
Bickerstaffe Wood
Brook Farm
Roby's Farm
Bickerstaffe Brook
Large Ox Hey House
Wood End Farm
Bradshaw's Plantation
Wood House
Red House Farm
Bullen's Farm
New Way Farm
Barrow Nook Farm
Barrow Nook
Cropper's Wood
Bickerstaffe Moss
Moss Side
L33
1
8

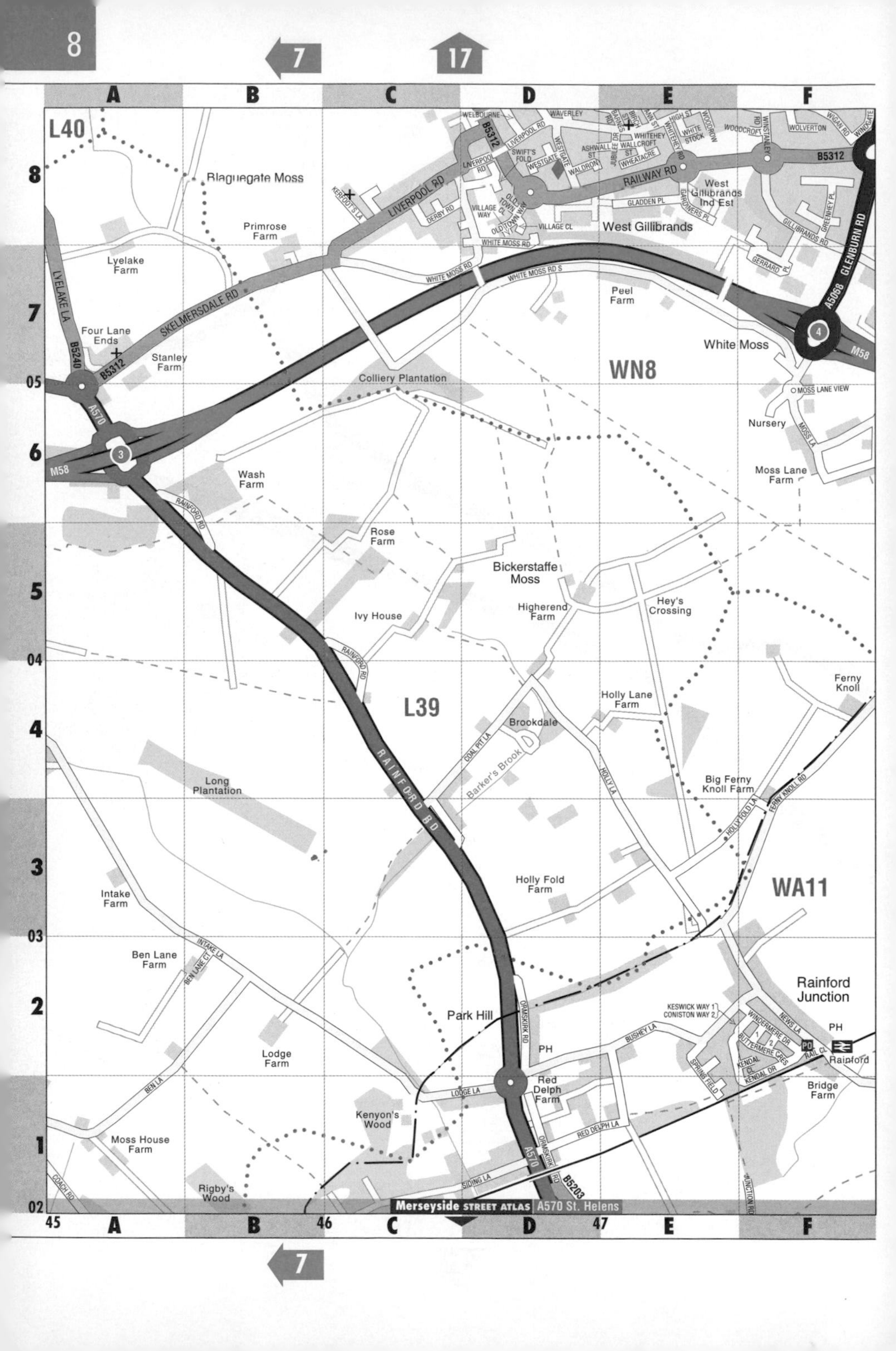
7
17
A
B
C
D
E
F
L40
Blaguegate Moss
Primrose Farm
Lyelake Farm
LYELAKE LA
SKELMERSDALE RD
LIVERPOOL RD
WHITE MOSS RD
WHITE MOSS RD S
RAILWAY RD
B5312
West Gillibrands Ind Est
West Gillibrands
GLENBURN RD
A5068
Peel Farm
White Moss
M58
WN8
Four Lane Ends
Stanley Farm
B5240
Colliery Plantation
MOSS LANE VIEW
Nursery
MOSS LA
Moss Lane Farm
A570
M58
Wash Farm
RAINFORD RD
Rose Farm
Bickerstaffe Moss
Higherend Farm
Hey's Crossing
Ivy House
L39
Holly Lane Farm
Ferny Knoll
Brookdale
COAL PIT LA
Barker's Brook
HOLLY LA
Long Plantation
RAINFORD RD
Big Ferny Knoll Farm
HOLLY FOLD LA
FERNY KNOLL RD
Holly Fold Farm
WA11
Intake Farm
INTAKE LA
BEN LANE CT
Ben Lane Farm
Park Hill
ORMSKIRK RD
Rainford Junction
KESWICK WAY 1
CONISTON WAY 2
PH
BUSHEY LA
NEWS LA
WINDERMERE DR
BUTTERMERE CRES
KENDAL CL
KENDAL DR
SPRING FIELD
RAIL CL
Rainford
Bridge Farm
Lodge Farm
LODGE LA
Red Delph Farm
BEN LA
Kenyon's Wood
RED DELPH LA
Moss House Farm
COACH RD
Rigby's Wood
SIDING LA
B5203
JUNCTION RD
Merseyside STREET ATLAS
A570 St. Helens
45
46
47
8
7
6
5
4
3
2
1
05
04
03
02

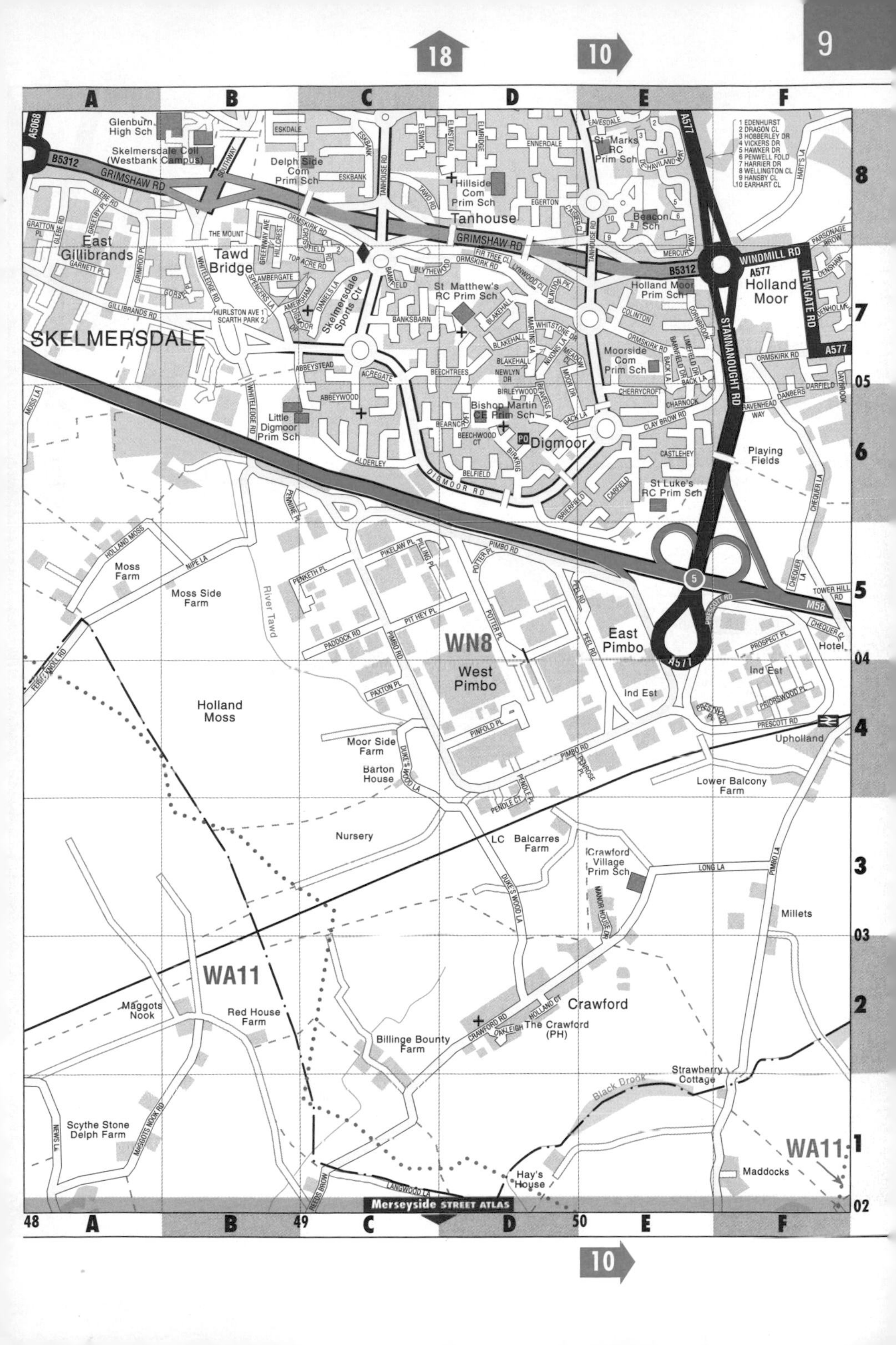
18
10
A
B
C
D
E
F
8
7
05
6
5
04
4
3
03
2
1
02
48
49
50
1 EDENHURST
2 DRAGON CL
3 HOBBERLEY DR
4 VICKERS DR
5 HAWKER DR
6 PENWELL FOLD
7 HARRIER DR
8 WELLINGTON CL
9 HANSBY CL
10 EARHART CL
Glenburn High Sch
Skelmersdale Coll (Westbank Campus)
Delph Side Com Prim Sch
Hillside Com Prim Sch
St Marks RC Prim Sch
Tanhouse
Beacon Sch
East Gillibrands
Tawd Bridge
SKELMERSDALE
Skelmersdale Sports Ctr
St Matthew's RC Prim Sch
Holland Moor Prim Sch
Holland Moor
Moorside Com Prim Sch
Little Digmoor Prim Sch
Bishop Martin CE Prim Sch
Digmoor
St Luke's RC Prim Sch
Playing Fields
GRIMSHAW RD
B5312
A5068
A577
WINDMILL RD
NEWGATE RD
STANNANOUGHT RD
ORMSKIRK RD
DIGMOOR RD
HURLSTON AVE 1
SCARTH PARK 2
Moss Farm
Moss Side Farm
River Tawd
WN8
West Pimbo
East Pimbo
Ind Est
Hotel
Upholland
PIMBO RD
M58
A577
PRESCOTT RD
Holland Moss
Moor Side Farm
Barton House
Lower Balcony Farm
Nursery
LC
Balcarres Farm
Crawford Village Prim Sch
LONG LA
PIMBO LA
Millets
DUKE'S WOOD LA
WA11
Maggots Nook
Red House Farm
Billinge Bounty Farm
Crawford
The Crawford (PH)
CRAWFORD RD
Strawberry Cottage
Black Brook
Scythe Stone Delph Farm
MAGGOTS NOOK RD
Hay's House
Maddocks
WA11
LANGWOOD LA
REEDS BROW

9
19

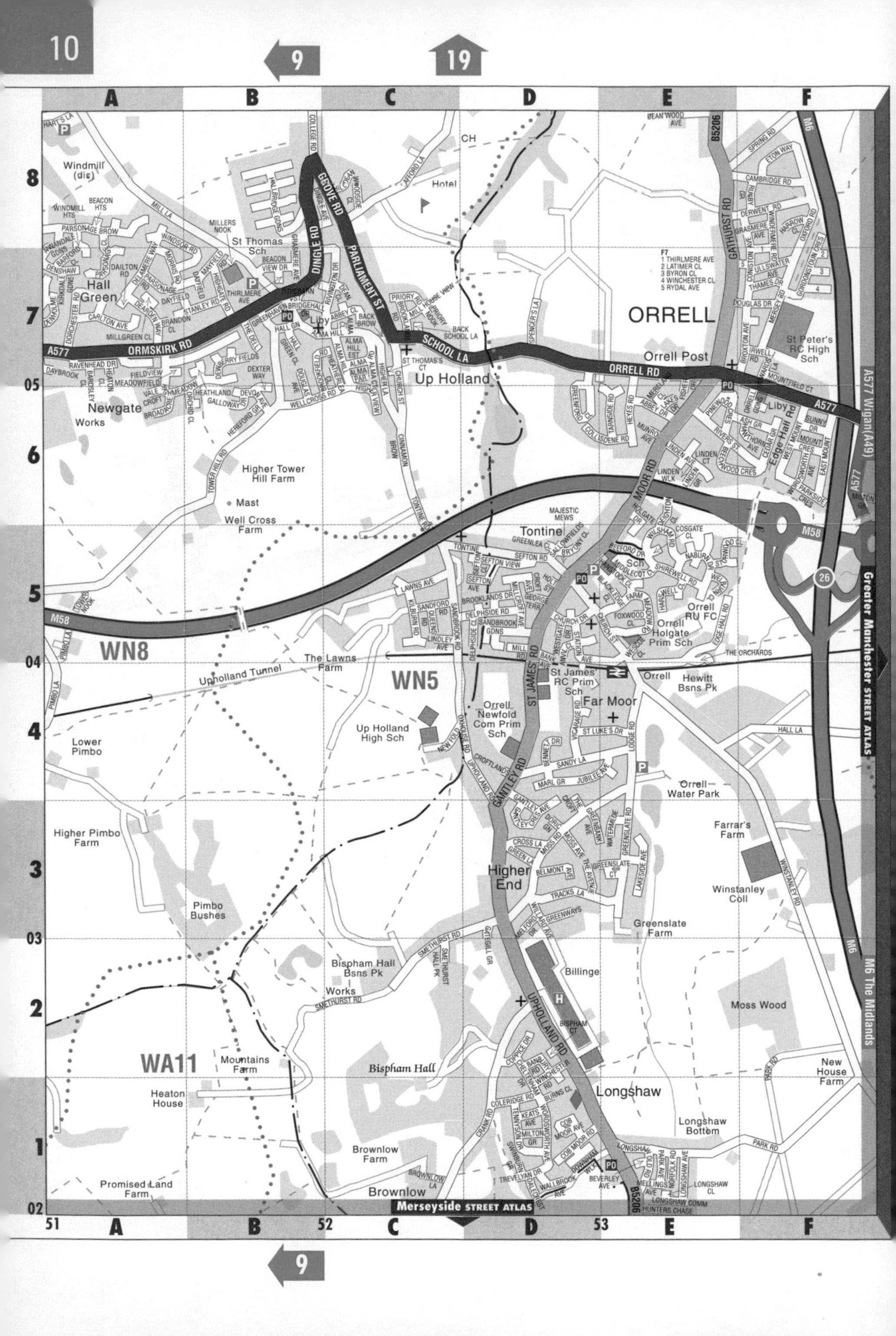
A
B
C
D
E
F
8
7
6
5
4
3
2
1
05
04
03
02
51
52
53
Windmill (dis)
Hall Green
St Thomas Sch
Newgate
Works
Higher Tower Hill Farm
Mast
Well Cross Farm
Up Holland
Hotel
CH
ORRELL
Orrell Post
St Peter's RC High Sch
Tontine
WN8
WN5
WA11
Upholland Tunnel
The Lawns Farm
Lower Pimbo
Up Holland High Sch
Orrell Newfold Com Prim Sch
St James' RC Prim Sch
Far Moor
Orrell
Hewitt Bsns Pk
Orrell RU FC
Orrell Holgate Prim Sch
Orrell Water Park
Farrar's Farm
Higher Pimbo Farm
Pimbo Bushes
Higher End
Winstanley Coll
Greenslate Farm
Billinge
Bispham Hall Bsns Pk
Works
Moss Wood
Mountains Farm
Heaton House
Bispham Hall
Longshaw
Longshaw Bottom
New House Farm
Brownlow Farm
Brownlow
Promised Land Farm
A577 ORMSKIRK RD
ORRELL RD
SCHOOL LA
PARLIAMENT ST
GROVE RD
DINGLE RD
GATHURST RD
MOOR RD
ST JAMES' RD
GANTLEY RD
UPHOLLAND RD
M58
M6
B5206
A577 Wigan (A49)
M6 The Midlands
Greater Manchester STREET ATLAS
Merseyside STREET ATLAS
F7
1 THIRLMERE AVE
2 LATIMER CL
3 BYRON CL
4 WINCHESTER CL
5 RYDAL AVE

9

20
12
A
B
C
D
E
F
8
7
09
6
5
08
4
3
07
2
1
06
27
28
29
2
12
Cloven-le-Dale
LC
Woodvale Airfield
Fisherman's Path
LC
Formby Hills
FRESHFIELD CVN PK
Nature Reserve
P
Clarence House Sch
LITTLE BREWERY LA
BREWERY LA
KENTON CL
OLD LA
PARADISE LA
ST ANNE'S CL
ST ANNE'S RD
YORK CL
WEST LA
STANLEY RD
PATH
ST ANNE'S
FISHERMANS CL
ARGARMEOLS RD
RIMMER'S AVE
MERSEY AVE
MASSAM'S LA
CANTERBURY CL
MONTAGU MEWS 1
LAWSWOOD 2
VICTORIA BLDGS 3
CH
STANLAWE RD
GREGSON'S AVE
CUMMINS AVE
MAYFIELD CT
RED BARNES
QUEENS AVE
ARGARMEOLS GR
HURSTWOOD
WRIGLEYS LA
WRIGLEYS CL
MONTAGU RD
THE BIRCHES
GOLF RD
Freshfield
TIMMS LA
TIMMS CL
CRICKET PATH
GREEN LA
THE PADDOCK
SHIREBURN RD
BADGERS RAKE
TOWER END
FAIRWAYS CT
VICTORIA RD
VICTORIA WAY
LC
COLLEGE PATH
GRANGE LA
GORES LA
DEANS CT
BORROWDALE
L37
Freshfield
HAZELBANK GDNS
PIERCEFIELD RD
FIRS CRES
FIRS CL
FIRS LINK
SQUIRREL GN
BIRCH GN
ST PETER'S AVE
DERBY CT
OLD TOWN CT
PO
FRESHFIELD CT
OLD TOWN LA
BYRON CL
GRABURN RD
WILLOW GR
GORSE WAY
PROCTOR RD
LARCH WAY
COLLEGE CL
HOLMWOOD DR
LENTON AVE
VICARAGE RD
VICARAGE CL
BREDON CT
RYMERS GN
LODGE LA
MANOR CT
OAKFIELD DR
VAUGHAN CL
ST GEORGE'S RD
OLD MILL LA
FORMBY GDNS
ST PETER'S CL
NORCOTE LODGE
FORMBY
DUNES DR
HARINGTON RD
LAFKHILL LA
BARKFIELD LA
THE EVERGREENS
HOLMFIELD PK
COLLEGE AVE
FRESHFIELD RD
Long La
ALDERSON CRES
Sandfield Farm
BLUNDELL AVE
WICKS CRES
WICKS GREEN CL
WARREN GN
BEECH DR
HOLMWOOD GDNS
BARKFIELD AVE
Formby High Sch
LONSDALE RD
CLIFDEN CT
DAVENHAM RD
INCE CRES
HOLMWOOD CL
COPPICE LEYS
Holy Trinity CE Prim Sch
PAGE CT
THE GALLERY
HARINGTON GN
HARINGTON CL
WICKS LA
ROSEMARY LA
FURNESS AVE
HALSALL LA
SCHOOL AVE
SCHOOL LA
SUNNINGDALE GDNS
ROSEMARY CT
THE CLOISTERS
CHAPEL ALLEY
CHAPEL LA
WICKS LA
Woodlands Prim Sch
BUTTERMERE CL
ENNERDALE CL
WICKS GDNS
GRISEDALE CL
LENDEL CL
HEYWOOD CL
ORMS WAY
ST MICHAELS CL
St Jerome's RC Prim Sch
DELPH LA
GREENLOON'S DR
WOODLANDS RD
HESKETH LODGE
BROWS LA
SUMNER RD
CROPTON RD
THREE TUNS LA
ELSON LA
NEWBY CT
SPRUCE WAY
FOXHILL CL
GRASMERE RD
TARN RD
ENNERDALE RD
GRANTON CL
DEWHURST DR
EDENHURST CL
HAZLEHURST CL
GREENLOON'S
DERWENT AVE
WOODLANDS CL
ESKDALE CL
RYDAL AVE
ESKDALE DR
MARSH BROW
BROWS CL
DUKES WAY
KIRKLAKE BANK
ASHDALE CL
SPRINGFIELD
CONISTON RD
MERE RD
LANGDALE AVE
LANGDALE CL
HILLARY CT
ASHURST CT
DUKE ST
PHILLIP'S CL
MEADOWCROFT
ELMDALE
KIRKLAKE RD
FORMBY BRIDGE
Formby
Liby
CONIFER CT
CHURCH WAY
CHURCH GN
ST LUKE'S DR
BROOKS WAY
WARD AVE
CHINDIT CL
SEFTON RD
FORMBY ST
KINGS CL
KINGS RD
PHILLIP'S LA
TYRERS
DICKINSON RD
NORBURN CRES
BUSHBY'S PK
BROOKS RD
QUEENS CROFT
MEOLS CL
RAVENSCROFT
WALKER CL
GLENDALE CL
DICKINSON CL
BIRKEY LA
Formby Point
BUSHBY'S LA
QUEEN'S RD
Eccles Crossing
RAVEN MEOLS LA
LIME TREE WAY
TRAP HILL
PINEWOOD CL
SEALAND CL
FOSTER RD
SEALAND AVE
ANDREWS LA
PARK AVE
NURSERY DR
HAREBELL CL
THE RAVENS
Shorrocks Hill
LIFEBOAT RD
MAPLE
St Luke's Sch
ELSON RD
ST ANDREWS YURT
BUCKINGHAM GR
KENSINGTON RD
SANDRINGHAM RD
WINDSOR RD
PARK WAY
CASTLE DR
Bill's La
ASHCROFT RD
FORMBY POINT CVN PK
ST LUKE'S CHURCH RD
BEECHWOOD DR
ELM DR
PINEWOOD AVE
JUBILEE RD
GEORGIAN PL
CARR'S CRES
CRESCENT AVE
ROSTRON CRES
HAMPTON RD
BALMORAL DR
EDINBURGH RD
LANCASTER RD
KENT RD
ASPEN GR
ASH GR
CEDAR DR
SYCAMORE GR
CHESTNUT WAY
FUNCHAL AVE
CARR'S CRES W
CAMBRIDGE RD
HADSTOCK AVE
MILFORD CL
MAYFIELD AVE
HEYDON CL
STAPLETON RD
ECCLES RD
ANDREWS CL
OSBORNE RD
MARINA RD
HOGGS HILL LA
ALTCAR LA
SANDHURST CL
MELDRETH CL
BURWELL AVE
BARTON HEYS RD
KEW RD
SUTTON RD
BELVEDERE DR
Sewage Works
ALEXANDRA RD
ALBERT RD
ELSWORTH CL
TADLOW CL
ORWELL CL
PARK RD

11
21

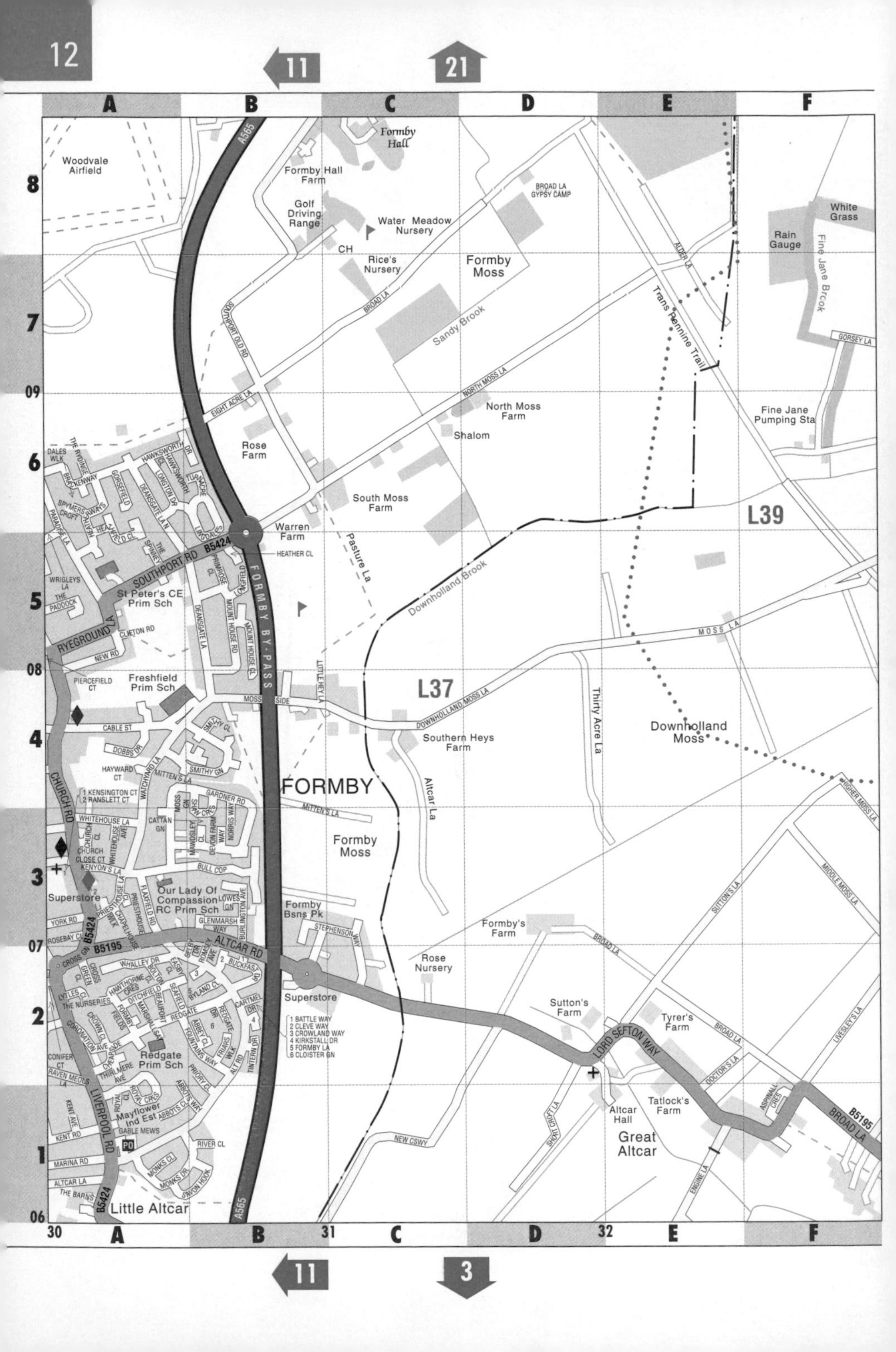
Woodvale Airfield
Formby Hall
Formby Hall Farm
Golf Driving Range
Water Meadow Nursery
CH
Rice's Nursery
BROAD LA GYPSY CAMP
Formby Moss
White Grass
Rain Gauge
Fine Jane Brook
Sandy Brook
Trans Pennine Trail
GORSEY LA
NORTH MOSS LA
North Moss Farm
Shalom
Fine Jane Pumping Sta
EIGHT ACRE LA
SOUTHPORT OLD RD
Rose Farm
South Moss Farm
Warren Farm
HEATHER CL
Pasture La
L39
Downholland Brook
FORMBY BY-PASS
SOUTHPORT RD
B5424
St Peter's CE Prim Sch
RYEGROUND LA
CLIFTON RD
NEW RD
MOSS LA
L37
DOWNHOLLAND MOSS LA
Freshfield Prim Sch
MOSS SIDE
LITTLE HEY LA
Thirty Acre La
Downholland Moss
Southern Heys Farm
CABLE ST
DOBBS DR
HAYWARD CT
CHURCH RD
FORMBY
Altcar La
HIGHER MOSS LA
MITTEN'S LA
1 KENSINGTON CT
2 RANSLETT CT
GARDNER RD
WHITEHOUSE LA
Formby Moss
CHURCH CLOSE CT
KENYON'S LA
BULL COP
MIDDLE MOSS LA
Superstore
Our Lady Of Compassion RC Prim Sch
Formby Bsns Pk
STEPHENSON WAY
SUTTON'S LA
Formby's Farm
BROAD LA
YORK RD
ROSEBAY CL
B5195
ALTCAR RD
Rose Nursery
Superstore
Sutton's Farm
LORD SEFTON WAY
Tyrer's Farm
LIVESLEY'S LA
1 BATTLE WAY
2 CLEVE WAY
3 CROWLAND WAY
4 KIRKSTALL DR
5 FORMBY LA
6 CLOISTER GN
DOCTOR'S LA
Redgate Prim Sch
LIVERPOOL RD
Altcar Hall
Tatlock's Farm
Great Altcar
Mayflower Ind Est
GABLE MEWS
NEW CSWY
SHORT CROFT LA
ENGINE LA
KENT RD
MARINA RD
RIVER CL
ALTCAR LA
THE BARNS
Little Altcar
A565
A
B
C
D
E
F
8
7
09
6
5
08
4
3
07
2
1
06
30
31
32

11
3

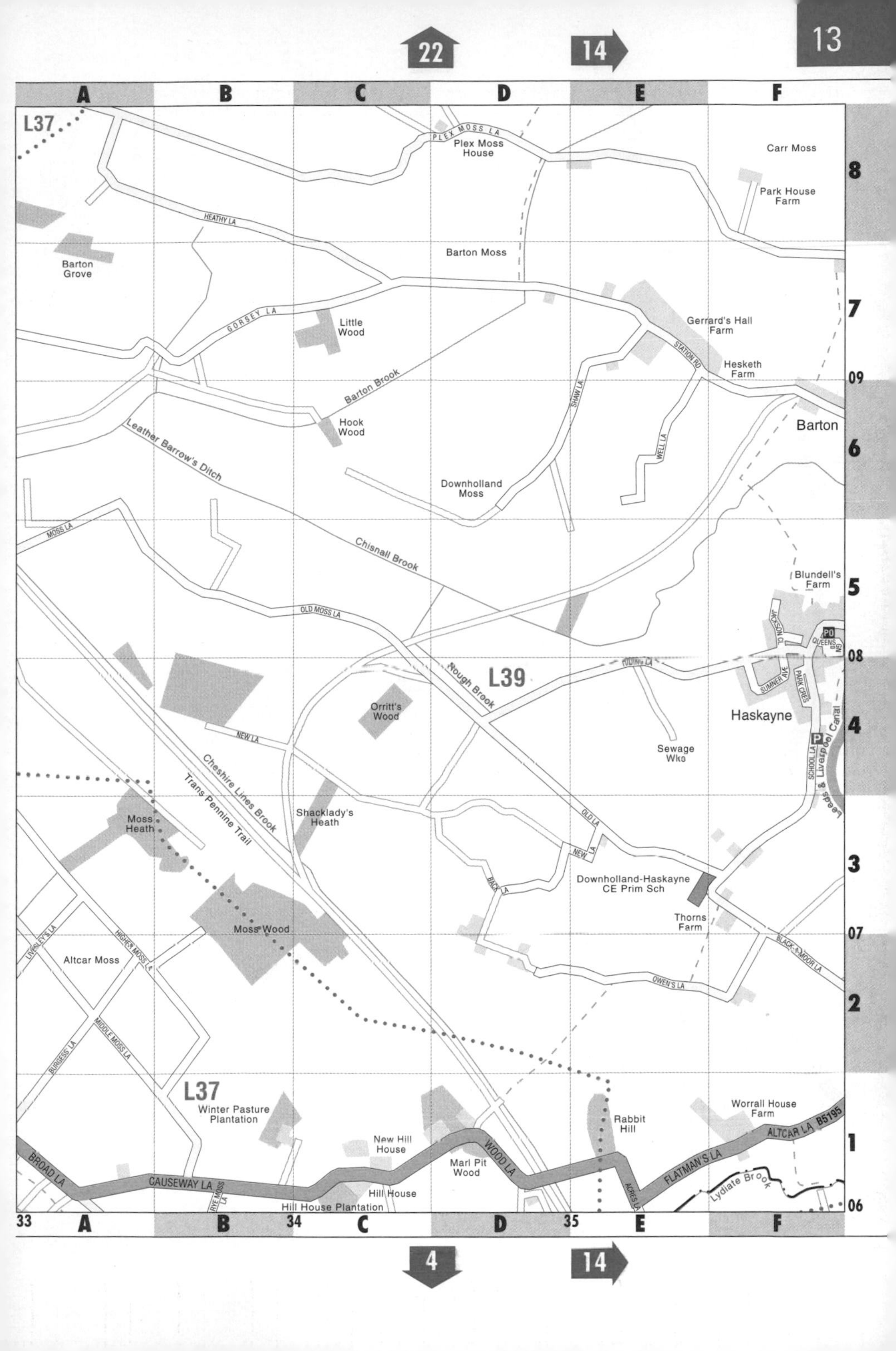
22
14
A
B
C
D
E
F
L37
Plex Moss La
Plex Moss House
Carr Moss
Park House Farm
Heathy La
Barton Grove
Barton Moss
Gorsey La
Little Wood
Gerrard's Hall Farm
Station Rd
Hesketh Farm
Barton Brook
Shaw La
Hook Wood
Barton
Leather Barrow's Ditch
Well La
Downholland Moss
Moss La
Chisnall Brook
Blundell's Farm
Old Moss La
Jackson Cl
PO
Queens
Nough Brook
L39
Sumner Ave
Park Cres
Orritt's Wood
Haskayne
New La
School La
Leeds & Liverpool Canal
Sewage Wks
Cheshire Lines Brook
Trans Pennine Trail
Shacklady's Heath
Moss Heath
Old La
New La
Back La
Downholland-Haskayne CE Prim Sch
Thorns Farm
Moss Wood
Black-a-Moor La
Altcar Moss
Livesley's La
Higher Moss La
Owen's La
Middle Moss La
Burgess La
L37
Winter Pasture Plantation
Rabbit Hill
Worrall House Farm
New Hill House
Wood La
Altcar La
B5195
Broad La
Causeway La
Marl Pit Wood
Flatman's La
Rye Moss La
Hill House
Acres La
Lydiate Brook
Hill House Plantation
8
7
09
6
5
08
4
3
07
2
1
06
33
34
35
4
14

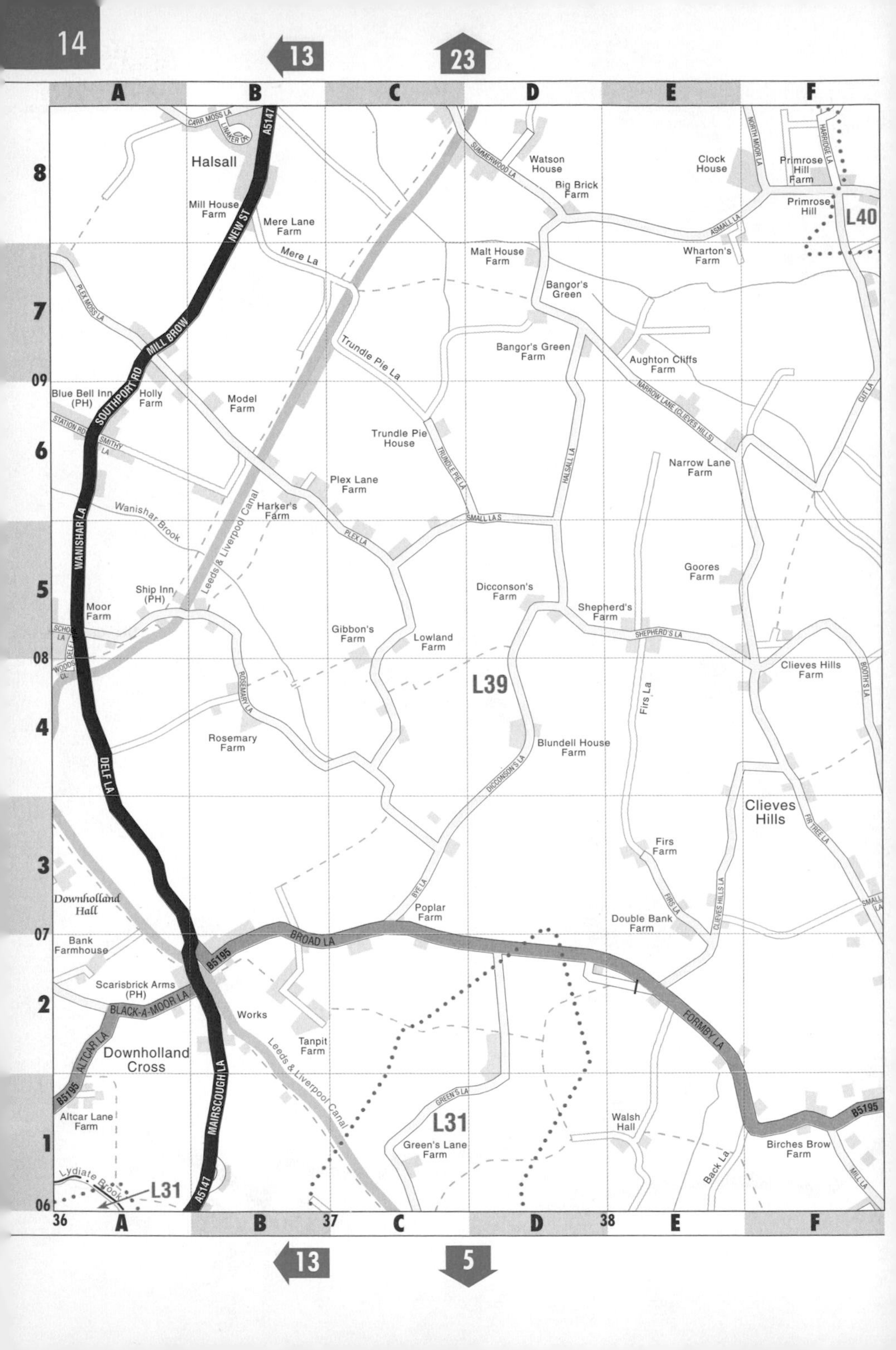

13
23
A
B
C
D
E
F
8
7
09
6
5
08
4
3
07
2
1
06
36
37
38
Halsall
CARR MOSS LA
LINAKER DR
A5147
NEW ST
MILL BROW
SOUTHPORT RD
WANISHAR LA
DELF LA
MAIRSCOUGH LA
Mill House Farm
Mere Lane Farm
Mere La
PLEX MOSS LA
Blue Bell Inn (PH)
Holly Farm
Model Farm
STATION RD
SMITHY LA
Wanishar Brook
Leeds & Liverpool Canal
Harker's Farm
Plex Lane Farm
PLEX LA
Trundle Pie La
Trundle Pie House
TRUNDLE PIE LA
SMALL LA S
SUMMERWOOD LA
Watson House
Big Brick Farm
Malt House Farm
Bangor's Green
Bangor's Green Farm
HALSALL LA
Clock House
NORTH MOOR LA
HARRIDGE LA
Primrose Hill Farm
Primrose Hill
L40
ASMALL LA
Wharton's Farm
Aughton Cliffs Farm
NARROW LANE (CLIEVES HILLS)
CUT LA
Narrow Lane Farm
Goores Farm
Dicconson's Farm
Shepherd's Farm
SHEPHERD'S LA
Ship Inn (PH)
Moor Farm
SCHOOL LA
DELF CL
WOODS CL
Gibbon's Farm
Lowland Farm
L39
Clieves Hills Farm
BOOTH'S LA
ROSEMARY LA
Rosemary Farm
Firs La
Blundell House Farm
DICCONSON'S LA
Clieves Hills
FIR TREE LA
Firs Farm
FIRS LA
CLIEVES HILLS LA
SMALL LA
Downholland Hall
Bank Farmhouse
RYE LA
Poplar Farm
BROAD LA
B5195
Double Bank Farm
FORMBY LA
Scarisbrick Arms (PH)
BLACK-A-MOOR LA
Works
ALTCAR LA
Downholland Cross
Tanpit Farm
Leeds & Liverpool Canal
Altcar Lane Farm
GREEN'S LA
L31
Green's Lane Farm
Walsh Hall
Back La
Birches Brow Farm
MILL LA
Lydiate Brook
L31
5

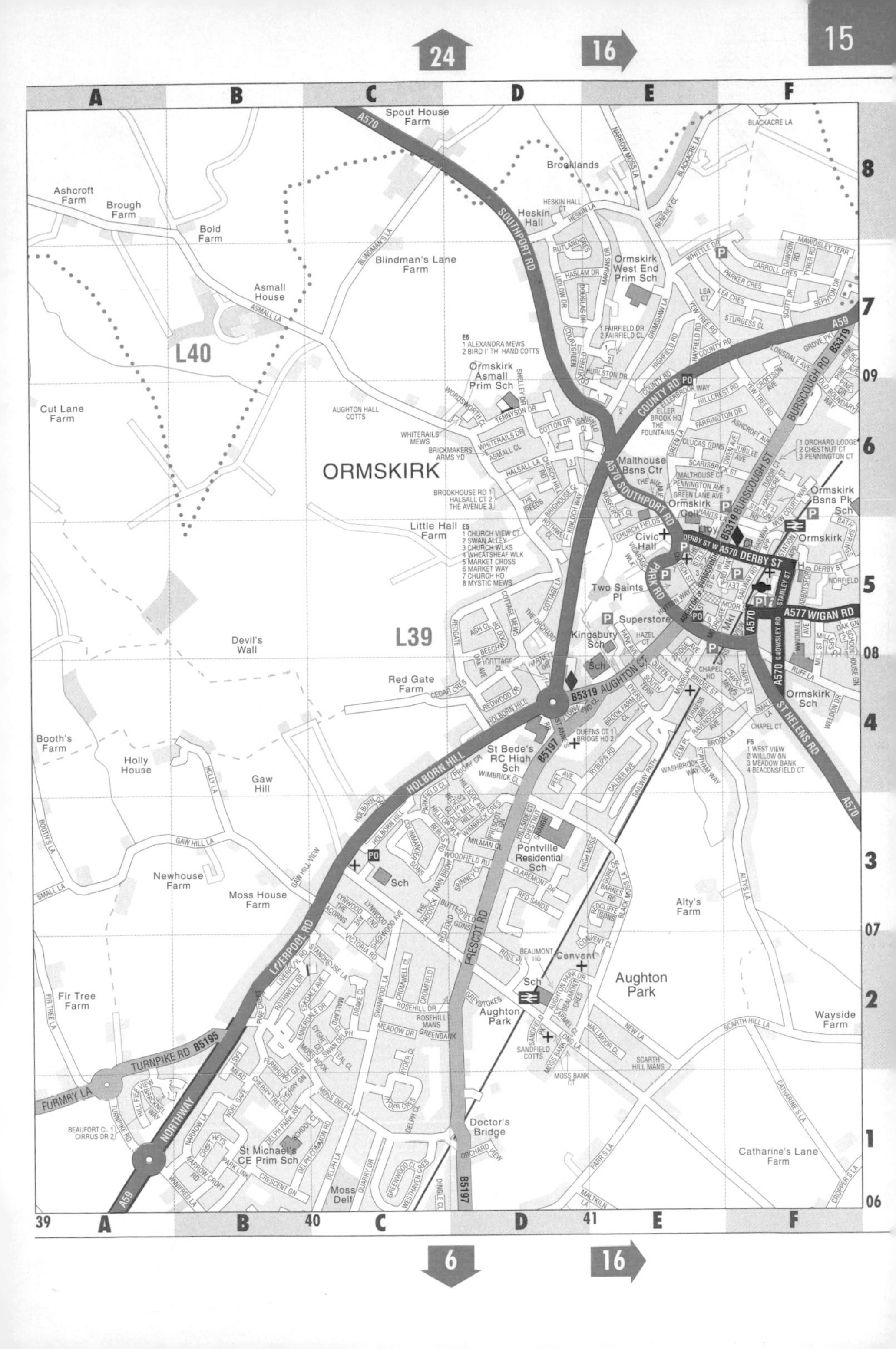
24
16
A
B
C
D
E
F
Spout House Farm
Brooklands
Ashcroft Farm
Brough Farm
Bold Farm
Heskin Hall
Blindman's Lane Farm
Ormskirk West End Prim Sch
Asmall House
L40
1 ALEXANDRA MEWS
2 BIRD I' TH' HAND COTTS
Ormskirk Asmall Prim Sch
Cut Lane Farm
AUGHTON HALL COTTS
WHITERAILS MEWS
BRICKMAKERS ARMS YD
ORMSKIRK
Malthouse Bsns Ctr
1 ORCHARD LODGE
2 CHESTNUT CT
3 PENNINGTON CT
Ormskirk Bsns Pk Sch
BROOKHOUSE RD 1
HALSALL CT 2
THE AVENUE 3
Ormskirk Coll
Little Hall Farm
1 CHURCH VIEW CT
2 SWAN ALLEY
3 CHURCH WLKS
4 WHEATSHEAF WLK
5 MARKET CROSS
6 MARKET WAY
7 CHURCH HO
8 MYSTIC MEWS
Civic Hall
Ormskirk
A570 DERBY ST
Two Saints Pl
Superstore
A577 WIGAN RD
Devil's Wall
L39
Kingsbury Sch
Sch
Red Gate Farm
B5319 AUGHTON ST
Ormskirk Sch
ST HELENS RD
Booth's Farm
Holly House
Gaw Hill
St Bede's RC High Sch
QUEENS CT 1
BRIDGE HO 2
1 WEST VIEW
2 WILLOW GN
3 MEADOW BANK
4 BEACONSFIELD CT
HOLBORN HILL
Pontville Residential Sch
Newhouse Farm
Moss House Farm
Sch
Alty's Farm
LIVERPOOL RD
PRESCOT RD
Convent
Aughton Park
Sch
Aughton Park
Fir Tree Farm
Wayside Farm
TURNPIKE RD B5195
FURMBY LA
NORTHWAY
SANDFIELD COTTS
SCARTH HILL MANS
BEAUFORT CL 1
CIRRUS DR 2
Doctor's Bridge
St Michael's CE Prim Sch
Catharine's Lane Farm
Moss Delf
B5197
A59
A570
8
7
09
6
5
08
4
3
07
2
1
06
39
40
41
6
16

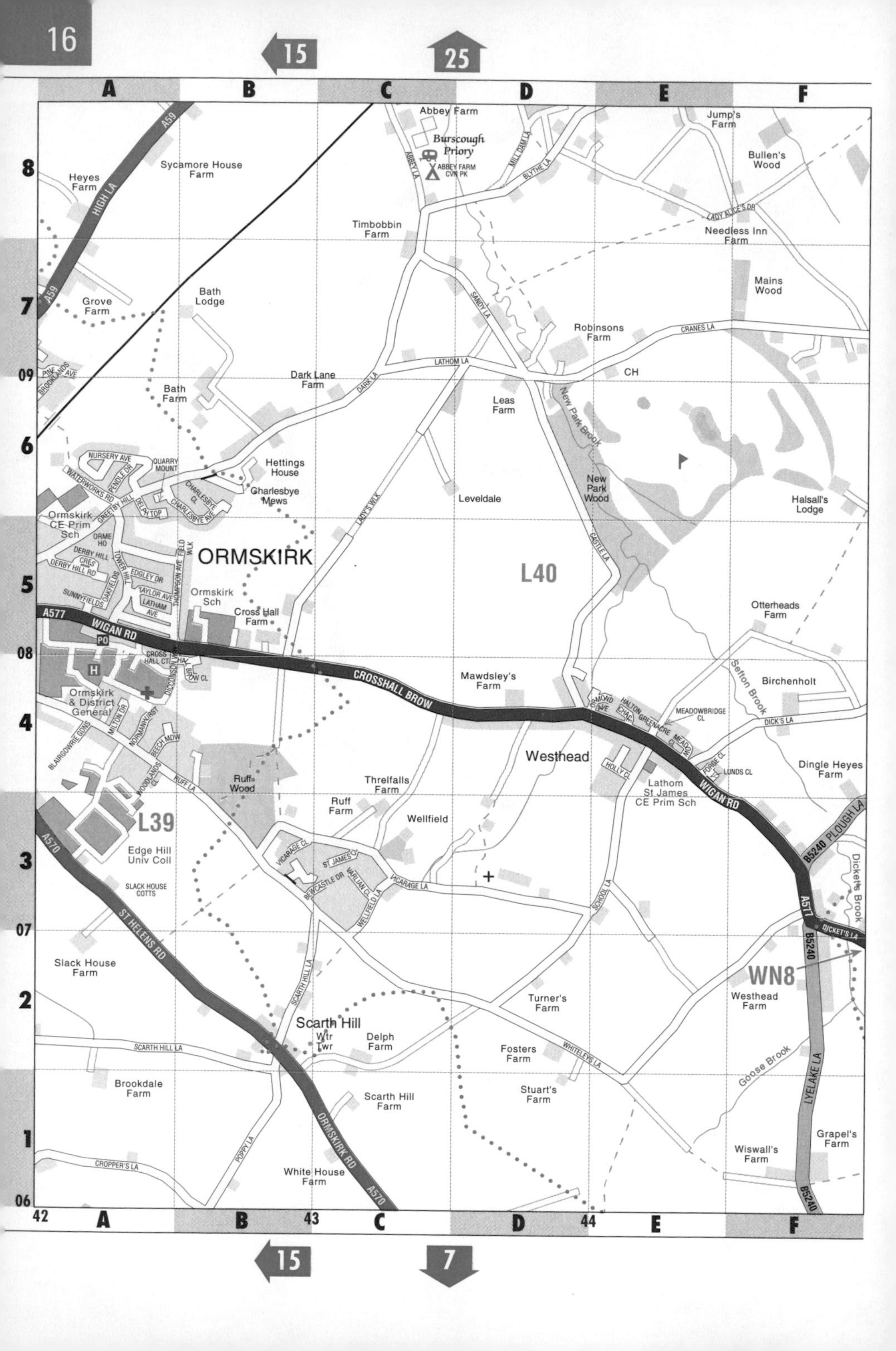
15
25
A
B
C
D
E
F
Abbey Farm
Burscough Priory
ABBEY FARM CVN PK
Jump's Farm
Bullen's Wood
Heyes Farm
Sycamore House Farm
HIGH LA
A59
Timbobbin Farm
Needless Inn Farm
LADY ALICE'S DR
Grove Farm
Bath Lodge
Mains Wood
Robinsons Farm
CRANES LA
SANDY LA
LATHOM LA
Dark Lane Farm
DARK LA
CH
Bath Farm
Leas Farm
New Park Brook
NURSERY AVE
QUARRY MOUNT
Hettings House
Charlesbye Mews
New Park Wood
Leveldale
Halsall's Lodge
Ormskirk CE Prim Sch
ORMSKIRK
L40
LADY'S WLK
CASTLE LA
Ormskirk Sch
Cross Hall Farm
Otterheads Farm
A577
WIGAN RD
PO
H
CROSSHALL BROW
Mawdsley's Farm
Birchenholt
Sefton Brook
Ormskirk & District General
MEADOWBRIDGE CL
DICK'S LA
Westhead
Ruff Wood
Threlfalls Farm
Ruff Farm
Lathom St James CE Prim Sch
Dingle Heyes Farm
L39
Wellfield
PLOUGH LA
B5240
Edge Hill Univ Coll
SLACK HOUSE COTTS
VICARAGE LA
SCHOOL LA
Dickets Brook
DICKET'S LA
ST HELENS RD
A570
Slack House Farm
WN8
Westhead Farm
Turner's Farm
SCARTH HILL LA
Scarth Hill
Wtr Twr
Delph Farm
Fosters Farm
WHITELEYS LA
Goose Brook
Brookdale Farm
Stuart's Farm
Scarth Hill Farm
LYELAKE LA
ORMSKIRK RD
Grapel's Farm
Wiswall's Farm
CROPPER'S LA
POPPY LA
White House Farm
42
43
44
8
7
09
6
5
08
4
3
07
2
1
06
15
7

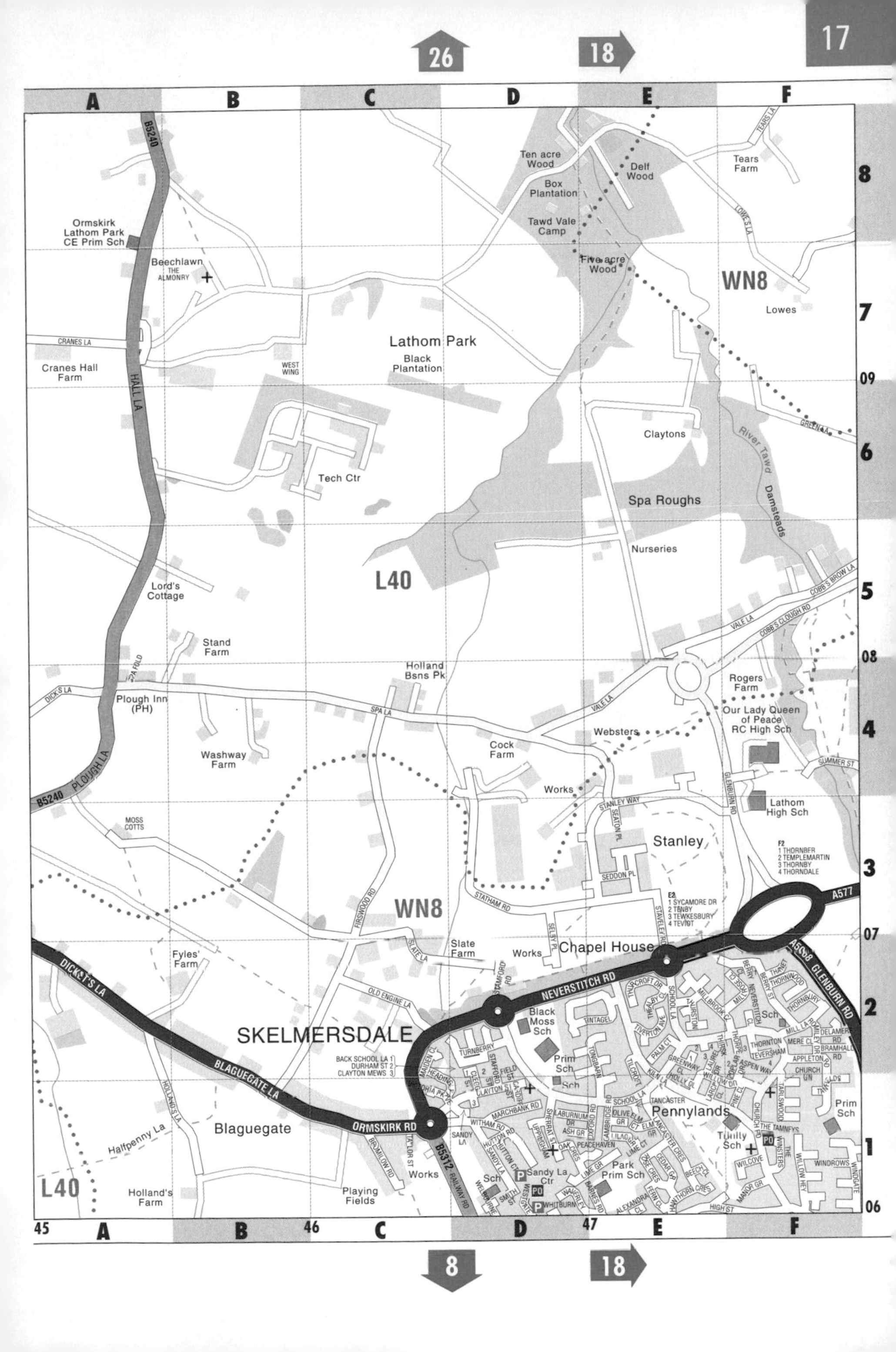
26
18
Ten acre Wood
Delf Wood
Tears Farm
Box Plantation
Tawd Vale Camp
Five acre Wood
Ormskirk Lathom Park CE Prim Sch
Beechlawn
THE ALMONRY
WN8
Lowes
CRANES LA
Cranes Hall Farm
Lathom Park
Black Plantation
WEST WING
HALL LA
B5240
Claytons
River Tawd
Tech Ctr
Spa Roughs
Damsteads
Nurseries
L40
Lord's Cottage
VALE LA
COBB'S BROW LA
COBB'S CLOUGH RD
Stand Farm
Holland Bsns Pk
Rogers Farm
DICK'S LA
Plough Inn (PH)
SPA LA
Our Lady Queen of Peace RC High Sch
Websters
Cock Farm
Washway Farm
SUMMER ST
PLOUGH LA
Works
GLENBURN RD
STANLEY WAY
SEATON PL
Lathom High Sch
MOSS COTTS
Stanley
F2
1 THORNBER
2 TEMPLEMARTIN
3 THORNBY
4 THORNDALE
SEDDON PL
E2
1 SYCAMORE DR
2 TENBY
3 TEWKESBURY
4 TEVIOT
STATHAM RD
WN8
A577
FIRSWOOD RD
SELBY PL
STAVELEY RD
Slate Farm
Works
Chapel House
Fyles' Farm
DICKET'S LA
SLATE LA
STAMFORD RD
NEVERSTITCH RD
A5068
OLD ENGINE LA
Black Moss Sch
SKELMERSDALE
TINTAGEL
BACK SCHOOL LA 1
DURHAM ST 2
CLAYTON MEWS 3
TURNBERRY
Prim Sch
Sch
BLAGUEGATE LA
MARCHBANK RD
SCHOOL LA
Pennylands
Trinity Sch
Blaguegate
ORMSKIRK RD
WITHAM RD
LABURNUM DR
ASH GR
PEACEHAVEN
Halfpenny La
B5312
SANDY LA
Works
Sch
Sandy La Ctr
Park Prim Sch
WINDROWS
WINDGATE
L40
Holland's Farm
Playing Fields
RAILWAY RD
WHITBURN
HIGH ST
8
7
09
6
5
08
4
3
07
2
1
06
A
B
C
D
E
F
45
46
47
8
18

17
27

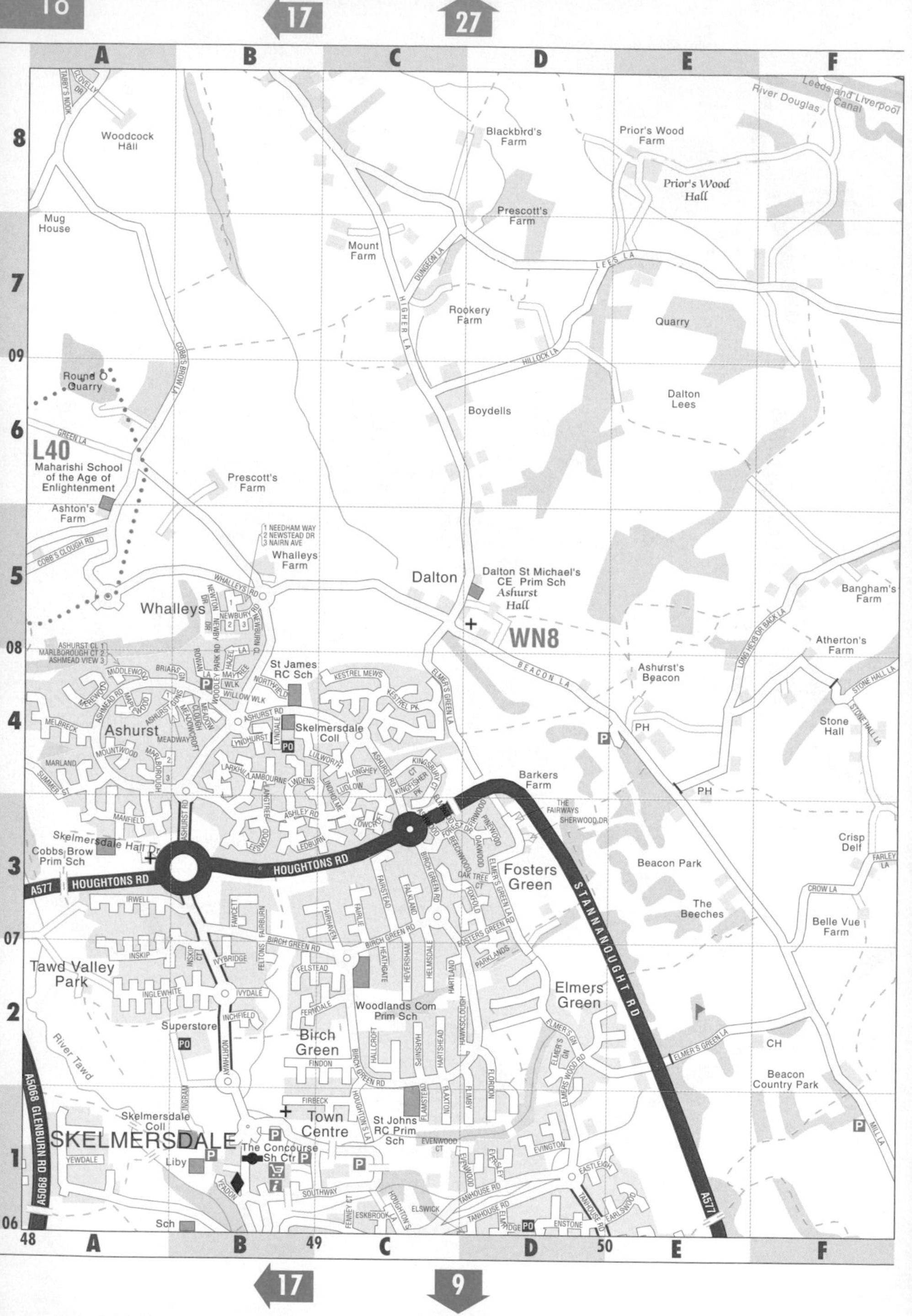
A
B
C
D
E
F
8
7
09
6
5
08
4
3
07
2
1
06
48
49
50
Woodcock Hall
Blackbird's Farm
Prior's Wood Farm
River Douglas
Leeds and Liverpool Canal
Prior's Wood Hall
Mug House
Prescott's Farm
Mount Farm
Rookery Farm
Quarry
LEES LA
HIGHER LA
DUNGEON LA
HILLOCK LA
COBB'S BROW LA
Round O Quarry
Boydells
Dalton Lees
GREEN LA
L40
Maharishi School of the Age of Enlightenment
Prescott's Farm
Ashton's Farm
COBB'S CLOUGH RD
1 NEEDHAM WAY
2 NEWSTEAD DR
3 NAIRN AVE
Whalleys Farm
Dalton
Dalton St Michael's CE Prim Sch
Ashurst Hall
Whalleys
WHALLEYS RD
WN8
BEACON LA
Bangham's Farm
Atherton's Farm
LONG HEYS OR BACK LA
ASHURST CL 1
MARLBOROUGH CT 2
ASHMEAD VIEW 3
St James RC Sch
KESTREL MEWS
KESTREL PK
Ashurst's Beacon
STONE HALL LA
Stone Hall
Ashurst
ASHURST RD
Skelmersdale Coll
PO
PH
Barkers Farm
THE FAIRWAYS
SHERWOOD DR
ELMER'S GREEN LA
Skelmersdale Hall Dr
Cobbs Brow Prim Sch
HOUGHTONS RD
A577
Fosters Green
Beacon Park
Crisp Delf
FARLEY LA
CROW LA
STANNANOUGHT RD
The Beeches
Belle Vue Farm
BIRCH GREEN RD
Tawd Valley Park
Elmers Green
Woodlands Com Prim Sch
Superstore
River Tawd
Birch Green
CH
Beacon Country Park
A5068 GLENBURN RD
Skelmersdale Coll
SKELMERSDALE
Town Centre
St Johns RC Prim Sch
The Concourse Sh Ctr
Liby
YEWDALE
SOUTHWAY
TANHOUSE RD
Sch
MILL LA

17
9

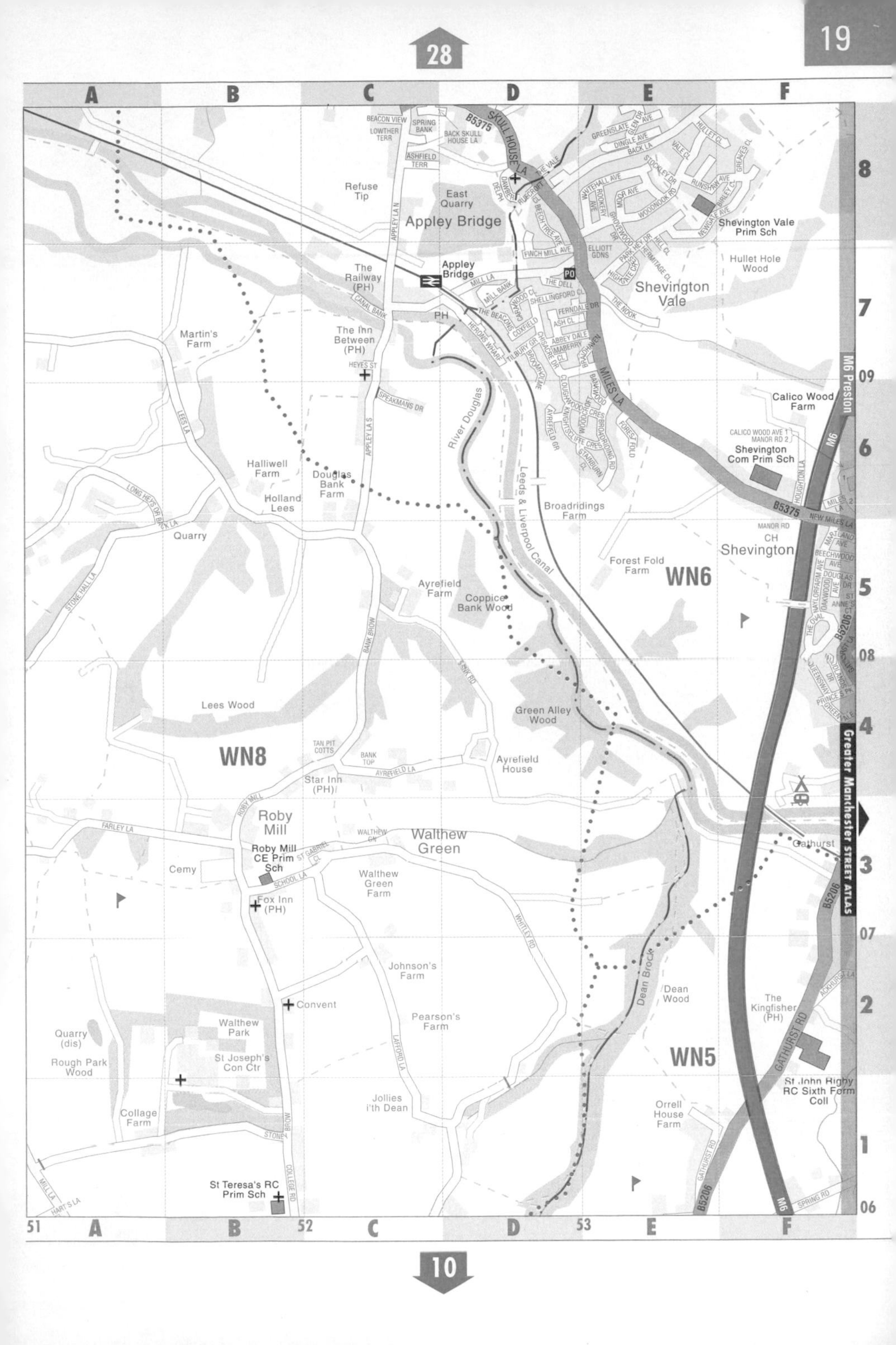

28
Refuse Tip
East Quarry
Appley Bridge
The Railway (PH)
Appley Bridge
PH
Martin's Farm
The Inn Between (PH)
Shevington Vale Prim Sch
Hullet Hole Wood
Shevington Vale
Calico Wood Farm
Shevington Com Prim Sch
River Douglas
Leeds & Liverpool Canal
Halliwell Farm
Douglas Bank Farm
Holland Lees
Quarry
Broadridings Farm
Shevington
Forest Fold Farm
WN6
Ayrefield Farm
Coppice Bank Wood
Lees Wood
Green Alley Wood
WN8
Ayrefield House
Star Inn (PH)
Roby Mill
Walthew Green
Roby Mill CE Prim Sch
Cemy
Walthew Green Farm
Fox Inn (PH)
Gathurst
Johnson's Farm
Convent
Dean Wood
Dean Brook
Pearson's Farm
The Kingfisher (PH)
Quarry (dis)
Walthew Park
Rough Park Wood
St Joseph's Con Ctr
WN5
St John Rigby RC Sixth Form Coll
Collage Farm
Jollies i'th Dean
Orrell House Farm
St Teresa's RC Prim Sch
B5375
B5206
M6
M6 Preston
Greater Manchester STREET ATLAS
10

A
B
C
D
E
F
8
7
13
6
5
12
4
3
11
2
1
10
27
28
29
Ainsdale-on-Sea
SHORE RD
PROMENADE
Southport
Holiday Village
Dunes
PR8
Ainsdale Sands
Ainsdale
Hills
Ainsdale Sand Dunes
National Nature Reserve
L37
Dunes
Long
Slack

11

Library
ving a
's event
ursday
July
am-1pm

Kirkham Library
is having a
children's event
on Thursday
21st July
from 11am-1pm

Next Door

St M's

Willows

Wesham St J

Wesham C of E

Weeton St M's

Weeton Camp

Wrea Green.

Library
ving a
's event
ursday
July
am-1pm

Kirkham Library
is having a
children's event
on Thursday
21st July
from 11am-1pm

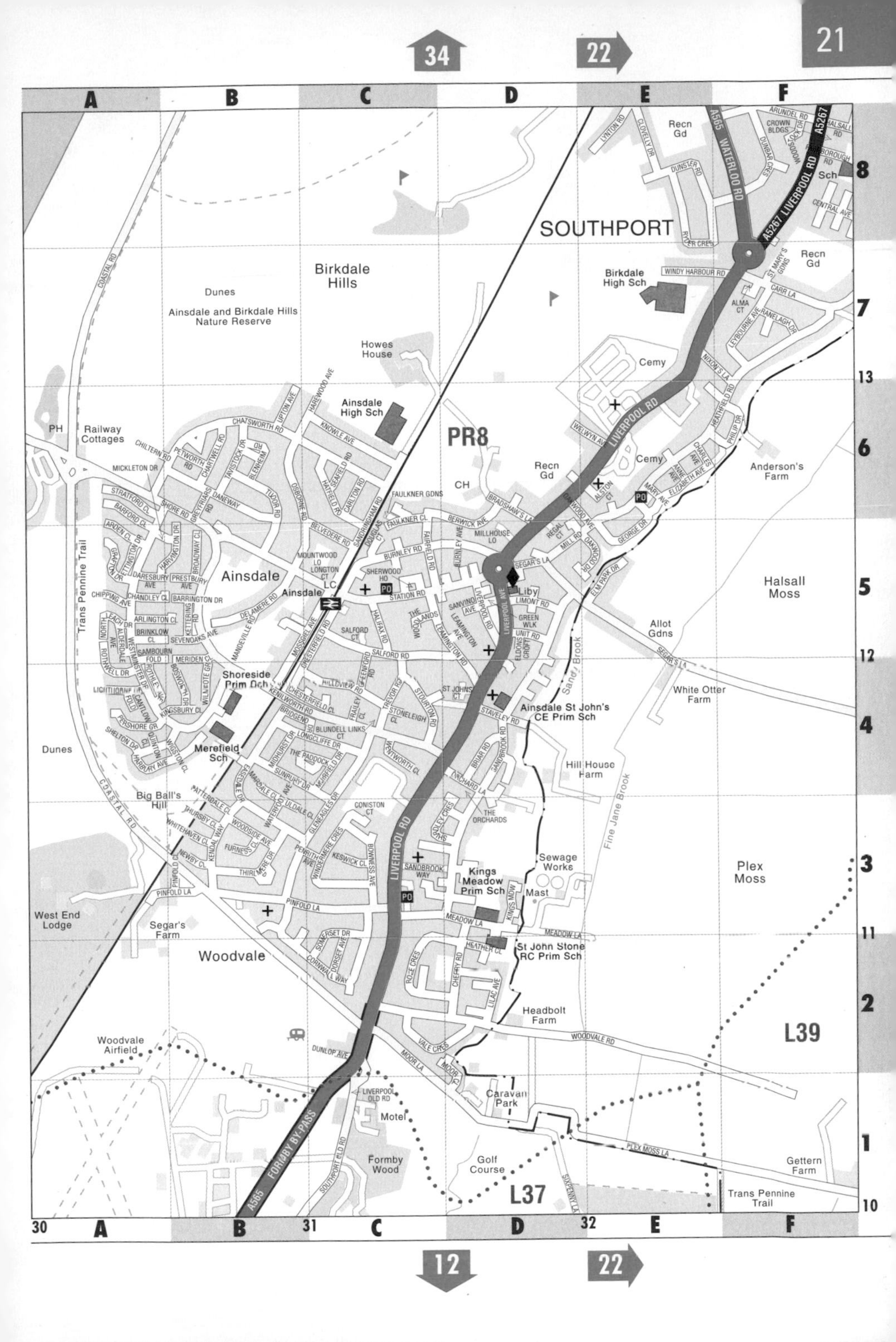
34
22
SOUTHPORT
Birkdale Hills
Dunes
Ainsdale and Birkdale Hills Nature Reserve
Howes House
Ainsdale High Sch
Birkdale High Sch
PR8
Railway Cottages
PH
Ainsdale
Shoreside Prim Sch
Merefield Sch
Big Ball's Hill
Dunes
Trans Pennine Trail
COASTAL RD
West End Lodge
Segar's Farm
Woodvale
Woodvale Airfield
Motel
Formby Wood
Golf Course
L37
Caravan Park
Headbolt Farm
St John Stone RC Prim Sch
Kings Meadow Prim Sch
Sewage Works
Mast
Hill House Farm
Ainsdale St John's CE Prim Sch
White Otter Farm
Allot Gdns
Halsall Moss
Anderson's Farm
Cemy
Recn Gd
Plex Moss
L39
Gettern Farm
Trans Pennine Trail
LIVERPOOL RD
WATERLOO RD
FORMBY BY-PASS
WOODVALE RD
PLEX MOSS LA
12
22

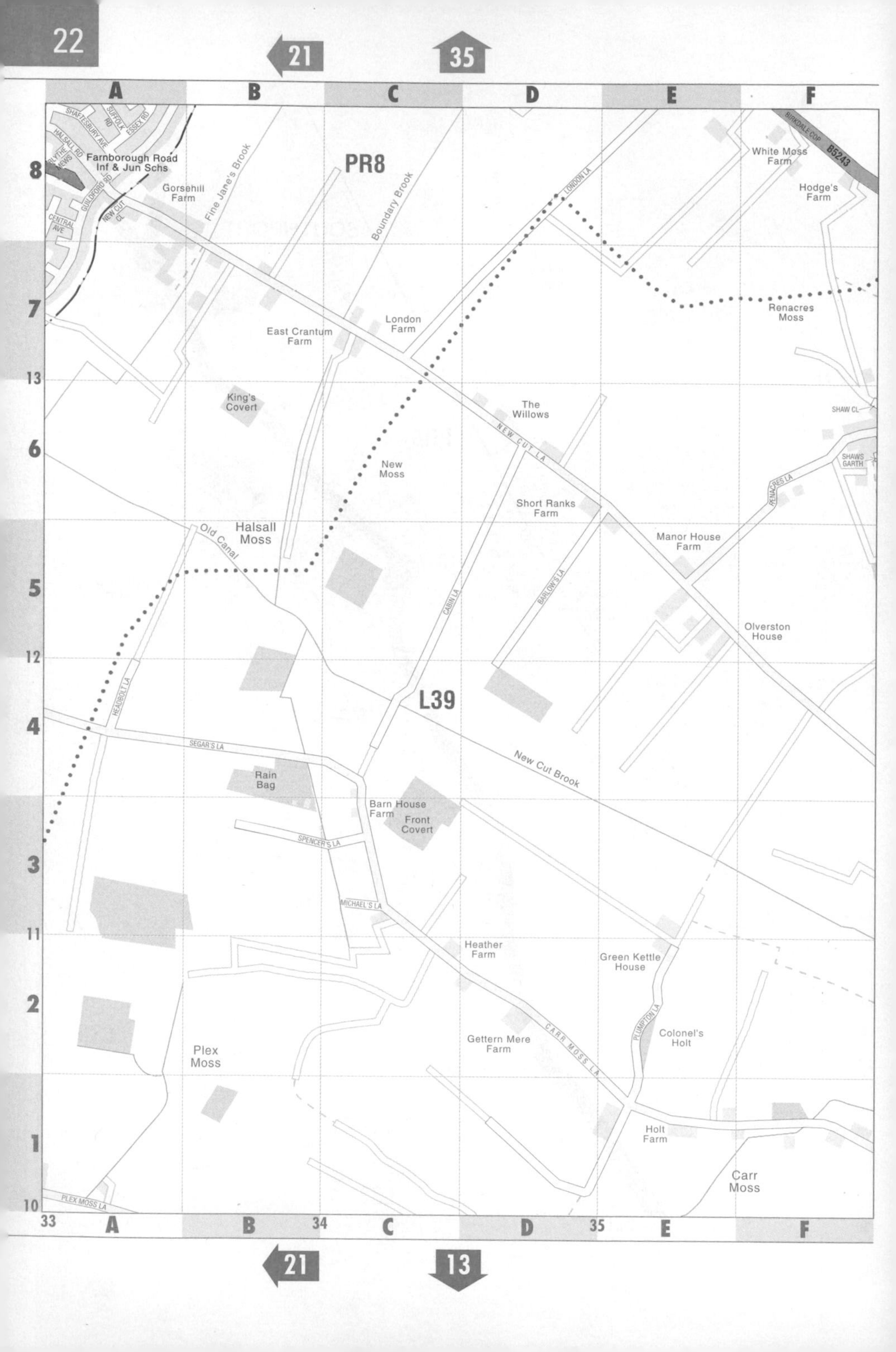
21
35
A
B
C
D
E
F
8
7
13
6
5
12
4
3
11
2
1
10
SHAFTESBURY AVE
SUFFOLK RD
ESSEX RD
HALSALL RD
BLYTHE MEWS
GUILDFORD RD
NEW CUT CL
CENTRAL AVE
Farnborough Road
Inf & Jun Schs
Gorsehill
Farm
Fine Jane's Brook
PR8
Boundary Brook
LONDON LA
BIRKDALE COP
B5243
White Moss
Farm
Hodge's
Farm
Renacres
Moss
East Crantum
Farm
London
Farm
King's
Covert
The
Willows
SHAW CL
NEW CUT LA
New
Moss
SHAWS
GARTH
RENACRES LA
Short Ranks
Farm
Old Canal
Halsall
Moss
Manor House
Farm
BARLOW'S LA
CABIN LA
Olverston
House
L39
HEADBOLT LA
SEGAR'S LA
New Cut Brook
Rain
Bag
Barn House
Farm
Front
Covert
SPENCER'S LA
MICHAEL'S LA
Heather
Farm
Green Kettle
House
CARR MOSS LA
PLUMPTON LA
Colonel's
Holt
Gettern Mere
Farm
Plex
Moss
Holt
Farm
Carr
Moss
PLEX MOSS LA
33
34
35
21
13

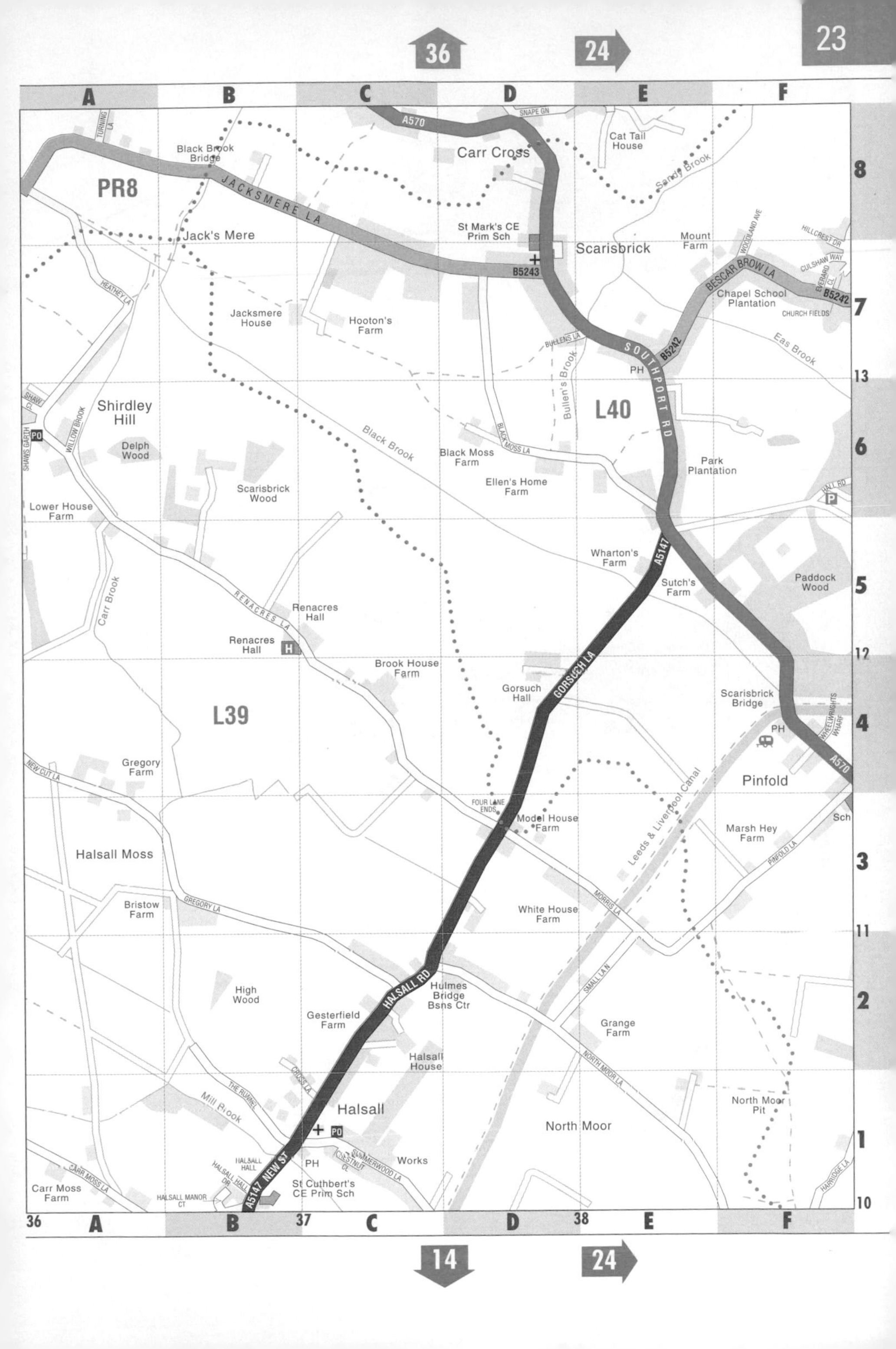
36
24
A
B
C
D
E
F
8
7
13
6
5
12
4
3
11
2
1
10
PR8
L40
L39
A570
B5243
B5242
A5147
Black Brook Bridge
JACKSMERE LA
Carr Cross
Cat Tail House
Sandy Brook
St Mark's CE Prim Sch
Scarisbrick
Mount Farm
Jack's Mere
HEATHEY LA
TURNING LA
SNAPE GN
WOODLAND AVE
HILLCREST DR
CULSHAW WAY
BESCAR BROW LA
EVERARD CL
Chapel School Plantation
CHURCH FIELDS
Eas Brook
Jacksmere House
Hooton's Farm
BULLENS LA
Bullen's Brook
SOUTHPORT RD
PH
Shirdley Hill
SHAW CL
SHAWS GARTH
PO
WILLOW BROOK
Delph Wood
Black Brook
Black Moss Farm
BLACK MOSS LA
Park Plantation
Ellen's Home Farm
Scarisbrick Wood
Lower House Farm
Wharton's Farm
Sutch's Farm
Paddock Wood
Carr Brook
RENACRES LA
Renacres Hall
H
Brook House Farm
GORSUCH LA
Gorsuch Hall
Scarisbrick Bridge
WHEELWRIGHTS WHARF
Gregory Farm
NEW CUT LA
Pinfold
FOUR LANE ENDS
Model House Farm
Leeds & Liverpool Canal
Marsh Hey Farm
Sch
PINFOLD LA
Halsall Moss
Bristow Farm
GREGORY LA
White House Farm
MORRIS LA
SMALL LA N
HALSALL RD
Hulmes Bridge Bsns Ctr
High Wood
Gesterfield Farm
Grange Farm
Halsall House
NORTH MOOR LA
CROSS LA
THE RUNNEL
Mill Brook
Halsall
North Moor
North Moor Pit
SUMMERWOOD LA
CHESTNUT CL
Works
HALSALL HALL
HALSALL HALL DR
NEW ST
St Cuthbert's CE Prim Sch
Carr Moss Farm
CARR MOSS LA
HALSALL MANOR CT
HARRIDGE LA
36
37
38
14
24

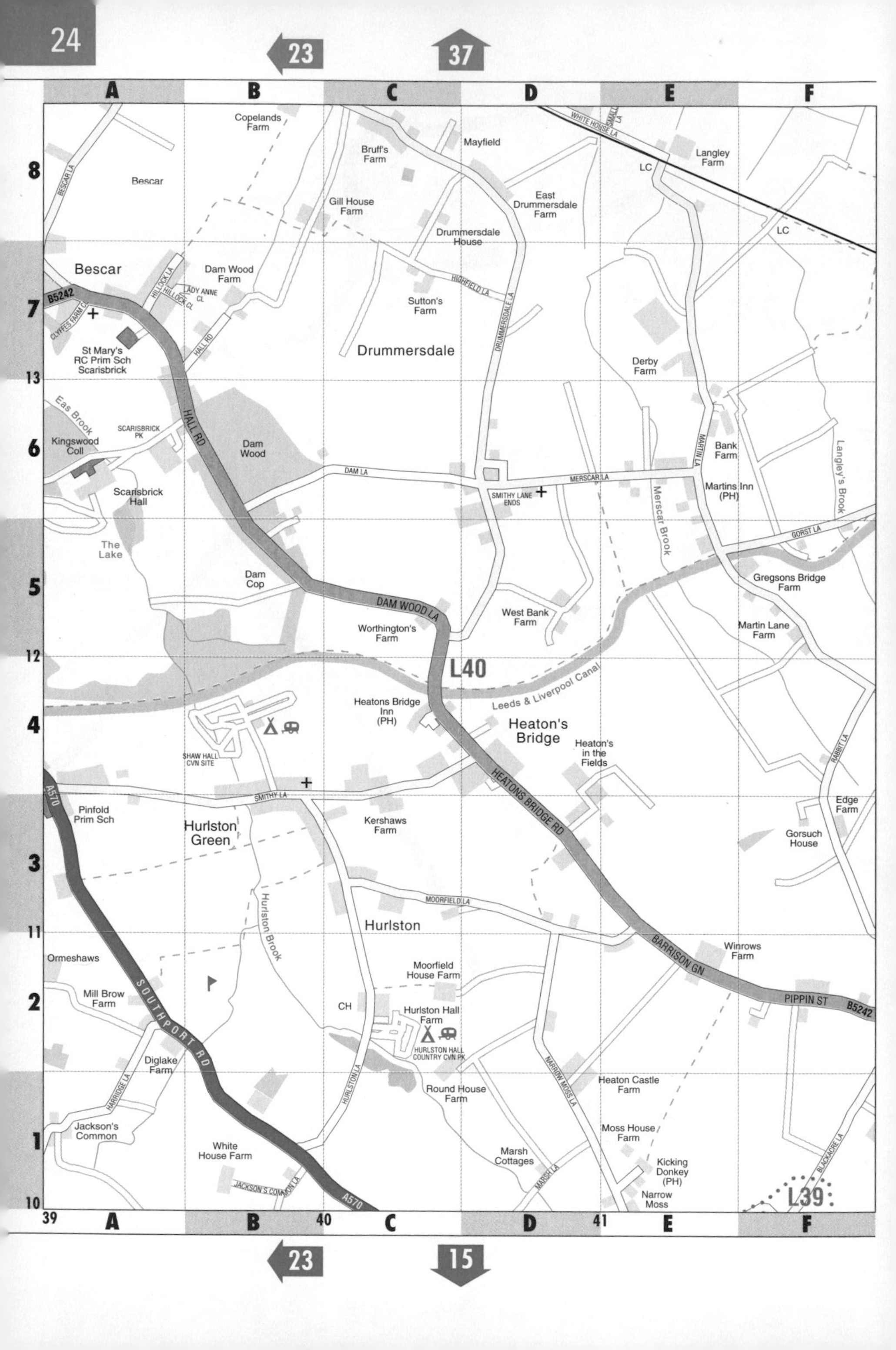
23
37
A
B
C
D
E
F
Copelands Farm
Bruff's Farm
Mayfield
Langley Farm
Bescar
Gill House Farm
East Drummersdale Farm
Drummersdale House
Bescar
Dam Wood Farm
Sutton's Farm
Drummersdale
St Mary's RC Prim Sch Scarisbrick
Derby Farm
Eas Brook
Kingswood Coll
Dam Wood
Bank Farm
Scarisbrick Hall
Martins Inn (PH)
Mercsar Brook
Langley's Brook
The Lake
Dam Cop
Gregsons Bridge Farm
West Bank Farm
Worthington's Farm
Martin Lane Farm
L40
Leeds & Liverpool Canal
Heatons Bridge Inn (PH)
Heaton's Bridge
Heaton's in the Fields
Pinfold Prim Sch
Hurlston Green
Kershaws Farm
Edge Farm
Gorsuch House
Hurlston Brook
Hurlston
Winrows Farm
Ormeshaws
Moorfield House Farm
Mill Brow Farm
CH
Hurlston Hall Farm
Diglake Farm
Round House Farm
Heaton Castle Farm
Jackson's Common
Moss House Farm
White House Farm
Marsh Cottages
Kicking Donkey (PH)
Narrow Moss
L39
HALL RD
DAM WOOD LA
HEATONS BRIDGE RD
BARRISON GN
PIPPIN ST
B5242
SOUTHPORT RD
A570
DAM LA
MERSCAR LA
GORST LA
MOORFIELD LA
SMITHY LA
HURLSTON LA
NARROW MOSS LA
MARSH LA
BLACKACRE LA
RABBIT LA
MARTIN LA
DRUMMERSDALE LA
HIGHFIELD LA
WHITE HOUSE LA
SMALL LA
BESCAR LA
HILLOCK LA
HILLOCK CL
LADY ANNE CL
HALL RD
CLYFFES FARM CL
SCARISBRICK PK
SMITHY LANE ENDS
SHAW HALL CVN SITE
HURLSTON HALL COUNTRY CVN PK
HARRIDGE LA
JACKSON'S COMMON LA
LC
LC
8
7
13
6
5
12
4
3
11
2
1
10
39
40
41
23
15

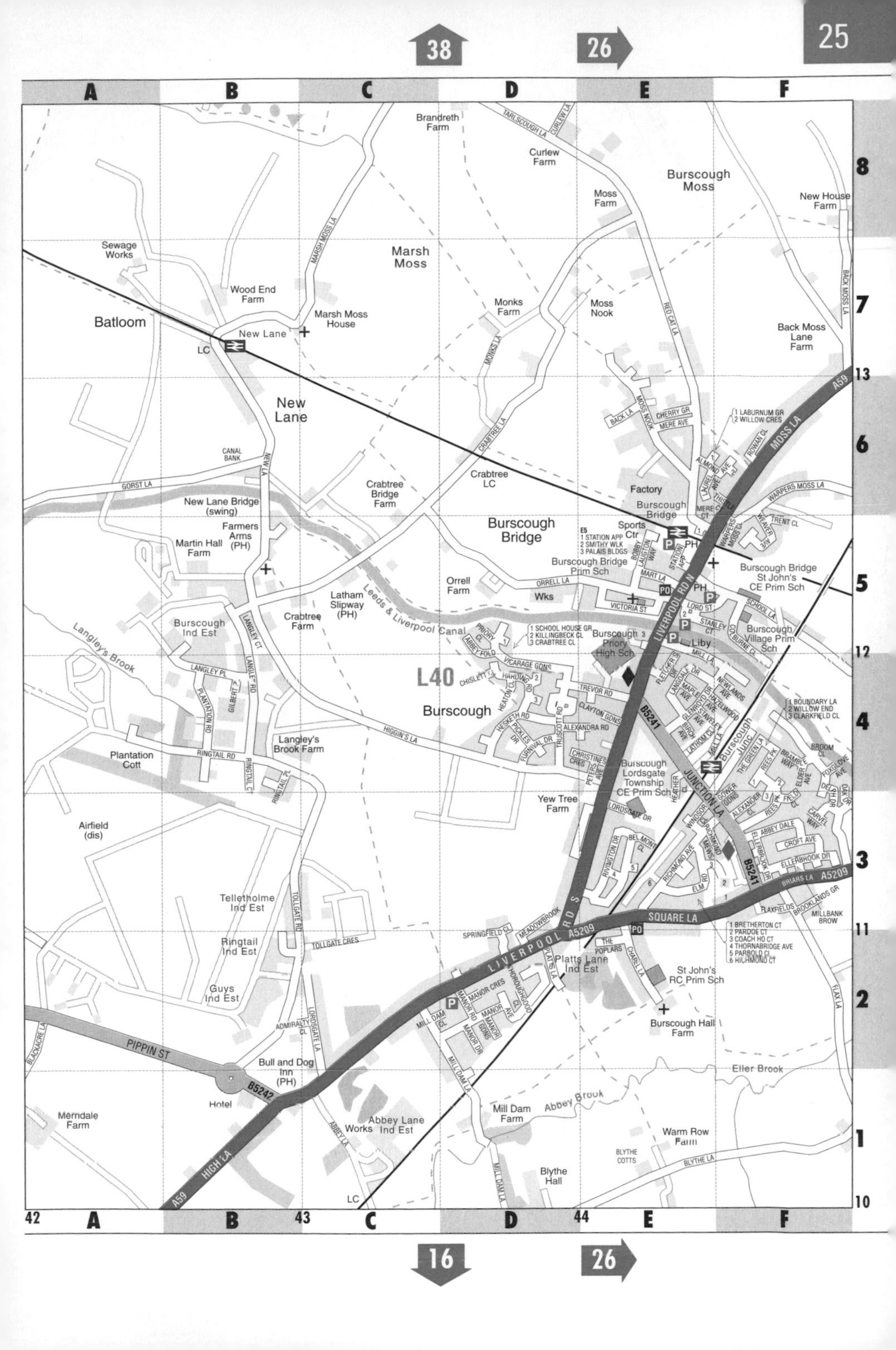
38
26
Brandreth Farm
Curlew Farm
Burscough Moss
Moss Farm
New House Farm
Sewage Works
Marsh Moss
Wood End Farm
Batloom
Marsh Moss House
New Lane
Monks Farm
Moss Nook
Back Moss Lane Farm
New Lane
Crabtree LC
Crabtree Bridge Farm
Factory
Burscough Bridge
New Lane Bridge (swing)
Farmers Arms (PH)
Martin Hall Farm
Burscough Bridge
Sports Ctr
Burscough Bridge Prim Sch
Burscough Bridge St John's CE Prim Sch
Orrell Farm
Latham Slipway (PH)
Crabtree Farm
Leeds & Liverpool Canal
Burscough Ind Est
Langley's Brook
Burscough Priory High Sch
Burscough Village Prim Sch
L40
Burscough
Plantation Cott
Langley's Brook Farm
Burscough Lordsgate Township CE Prim Sch
Yew Tree Farm
Airfield (dis)
Telletholme Ind Est
Ringtail Ind Est
Guys Ind Est
Platts Lane Ind Est
St John's RC Prim Sch
Burscough Hall Farm
Bull and Dog Inn (PH)
Hotel
Eller Brook
Merridale Farm
Mill Dam Farm
Abbey Brook
Abbey Lane Ind Est
Works
Warm Row Farm
Blythe Hall
BLYTHE COTTS
LIVERPOOL RD N
LIVERPOOL RD S
MOSS LA
SQUARE LA
JUNCTION LA
PIPPIN ST
HIGH LA
1 LABURNUM GR
2 WILLOW CRES
1 STATION APP
2 SMITHY WLK
3 PALAIS BLDGS
1 SCHOOL HOUSE GR
2 KILLINGBECK CL
3 CRABTREE CL
1 BOUNDARY LA
2 WILLOW END
3 CLARKFIELD CL
1 BRETHERTON CT
2 PARDOE CT
3 COACH HO CT
4 THORNABRIDGE AVE
5 PARBOLD CL
6 RICHMOND CT
16
26

25
39

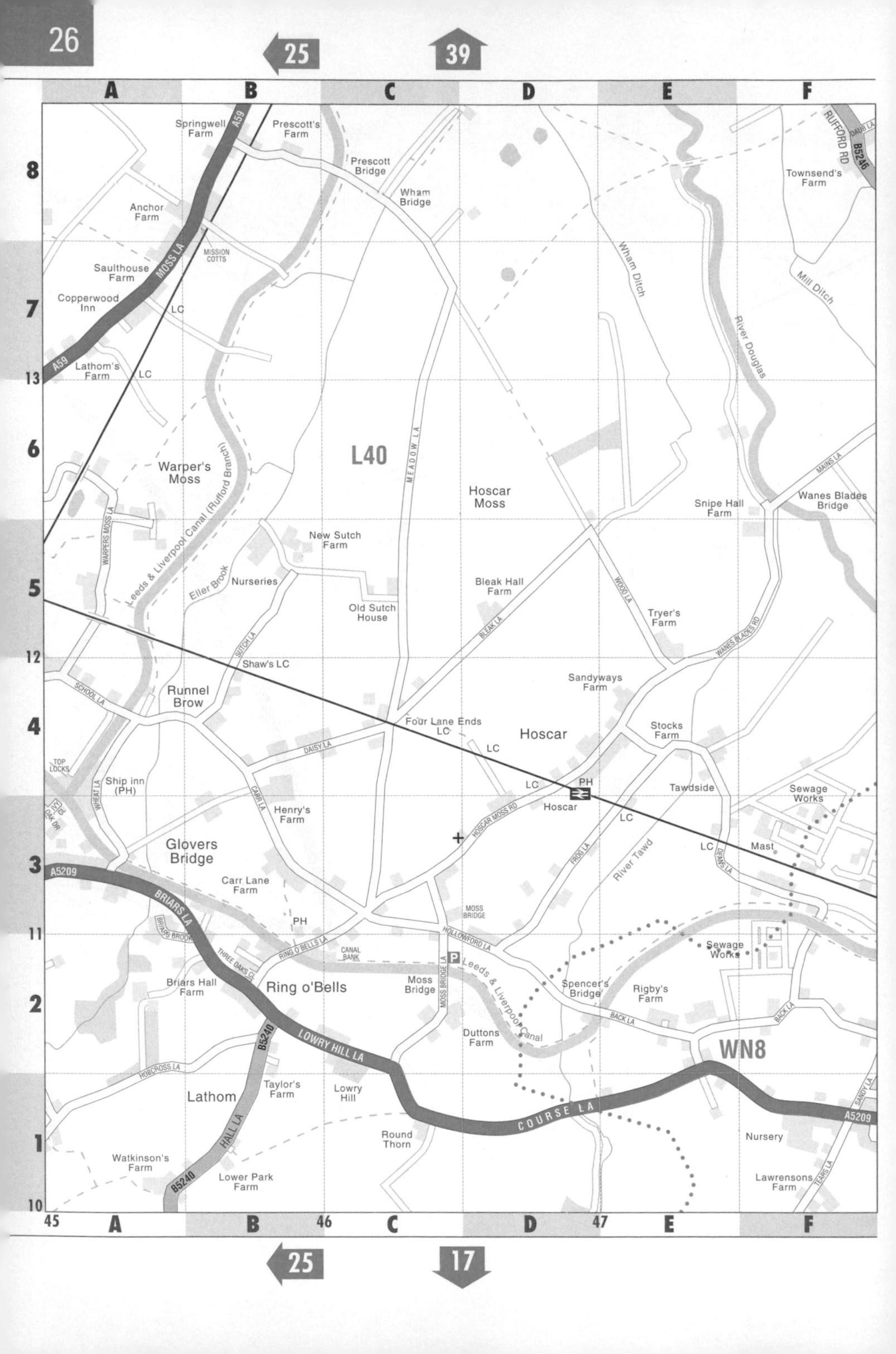
Springwell Farm
Prescott's Farm
Prescott Bridge
Wham Bridge
Anchor Farm
MISSION COTTS
Saulthouse Farm
Copperwood Inn
Lathom's Farm
Warper's Moss
L40
Hoscar Moss
New Sutch Farm
Nurseries
Eller Brook
Leeds & Liverpool Canal (Rufford Branch)
Old Sutch House
Bleak Hall Farm
Tryer's Farm
Snipe Hall Farm
Wanes Blades Bridge
Townsend's Farm
Wham Ditch
Mill Ditch
River Douglas
RUFFORD RD
B5246
MEADOW LA
WARPERS MOSS LA
MOSS LA
A59
BLEAK LA
WOOD LA
WANES BLADES RD
MAINS LA
Shaw's LC
SUTCH LA
SCHOOL LA
Runnel Brow
Four Lane Ends LC
Sandyways Farm
Hoscar
Stocks Farm
DAISY LA
TOP LOCKS
Ship inn (PH)
WHEAT LA
CARR LA
Henry's Farm
HOSCAR MOSS RD
PH
LC
Tawdside
Sewage Works
Glovers Bridge
Carr Lane Farm
FROG LA
River Tawd
DEANS LA
Mast
A5209
BRIARS LA
BRIARS BROOK
PH
MOSS BRIDGE
HOLLOWFORD LA
RING O'BELLS LA
CANAL BANK
THREE OAKS CL
Briars Hall Farm
Ring o'Bells
Moss Bridge
MOSS BRIDGE LA
Leeds & Liverpool Canal
Spencer's Bridge
Rigby's Farm
BACK LA
WN8
Duttons Farm
LOWRY HILL LA
B5240
HOBCROSS LA
Lathom
Taylor's Farm
Lowry Hill
COURSE LA
Round Thorn
Nursery
SANDY LA
HALL LA
Watkinson's Farm
Lower Park Farm
Lawrensons Farm
TEAS LA
A B C D E F
1 2 3 4 5 6 7 8
10 11 12 13
45 46 47

25
17

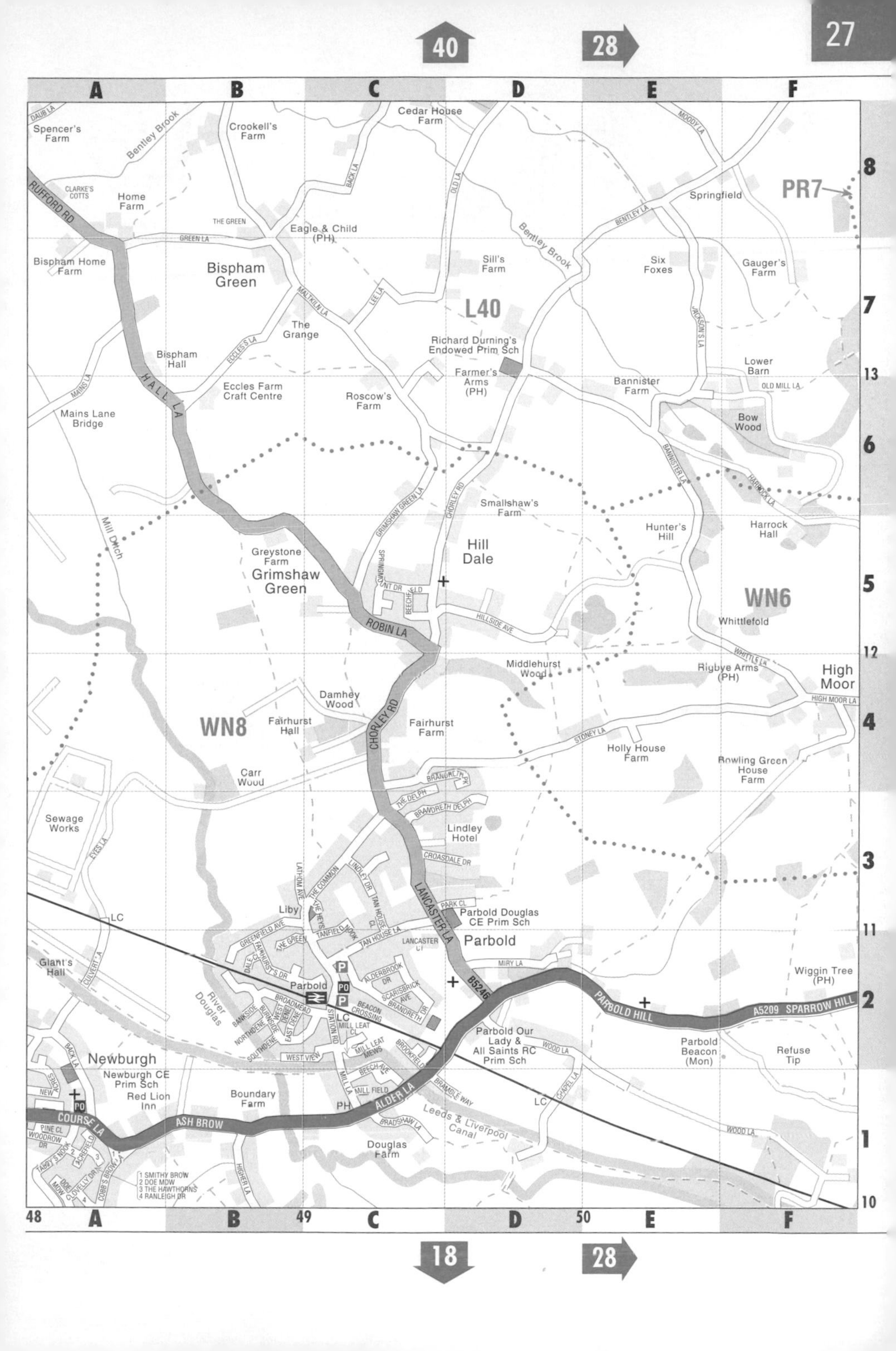
40
28
A
B
C
D
E
F
Spencer's Farm
Crookell's Farm
Cedar House Farm
Bentley Brook
Home Farm
CLARKE'S COTTS
RUFFORD RD
THE GREEN
GREEN LA
Eagle & Child (PH)
Bispham Home Farm
Bispham Green
Springfield
PR7
BENTLEY LA
Bentley Brook
Sill's Farm
Six Foxes
Gauger's Farm
L40
The Grange
Richard Durning's Endowed Prim Sch
Farmer's Arms (PH)
Bispham Hall
Eccles Farm Craft Centre
Roscow's Farm
Bannister Farm
Lower Barn
OLD MILL LA
Bow Wood
Mains Lane Bridge
HALL LA
Smallshaw's Farm
Hunter's Hill
Harrock Hall
Mill Ditch
Hill Dale
Greystone Farm
Grimshaw Green
WN6
Whittlefold
ROBIN LA
HILLSIDE AVE
Middlehurst Wood
Rigbye Arms (PH)
High Moor
HIGH MOOR LA
Damhey Wood
WN8
Fairhurst Hall
Fairhurst Farm
CHORLEY RD
STONEY LA
Holly House Farm
Bowling Green House Farm
Carr Wood
Sewage Works
Lindley Hotel
Liby
Parbold Douglas CE Prim Sch
Parbold
Giant's Hall
Parbold
River Douglas
PARBOLD HILL
A5209 SPARROW HILL
Wiggin Tree (PH)
Parbold Our Lady & All Saints RC Prim Sch
Parbold Beacon (Mon)
Refuse Tip
Newburgh
Newburgh CE Prim Sch
Red Lion Inn
Boundary Farm
COURSE LA
ASH BROW
ALDER LA
Leeds & Liverpool Canal
Douglas Farm
WOOD LA
1 SMITHY BROW
2 DOE MDW
3 THE HAWTHORNS
4 RANLEIGH DR
48
49
50
18
28
8
7
13
6
5
12
4
3
11
2
1
10

27
41

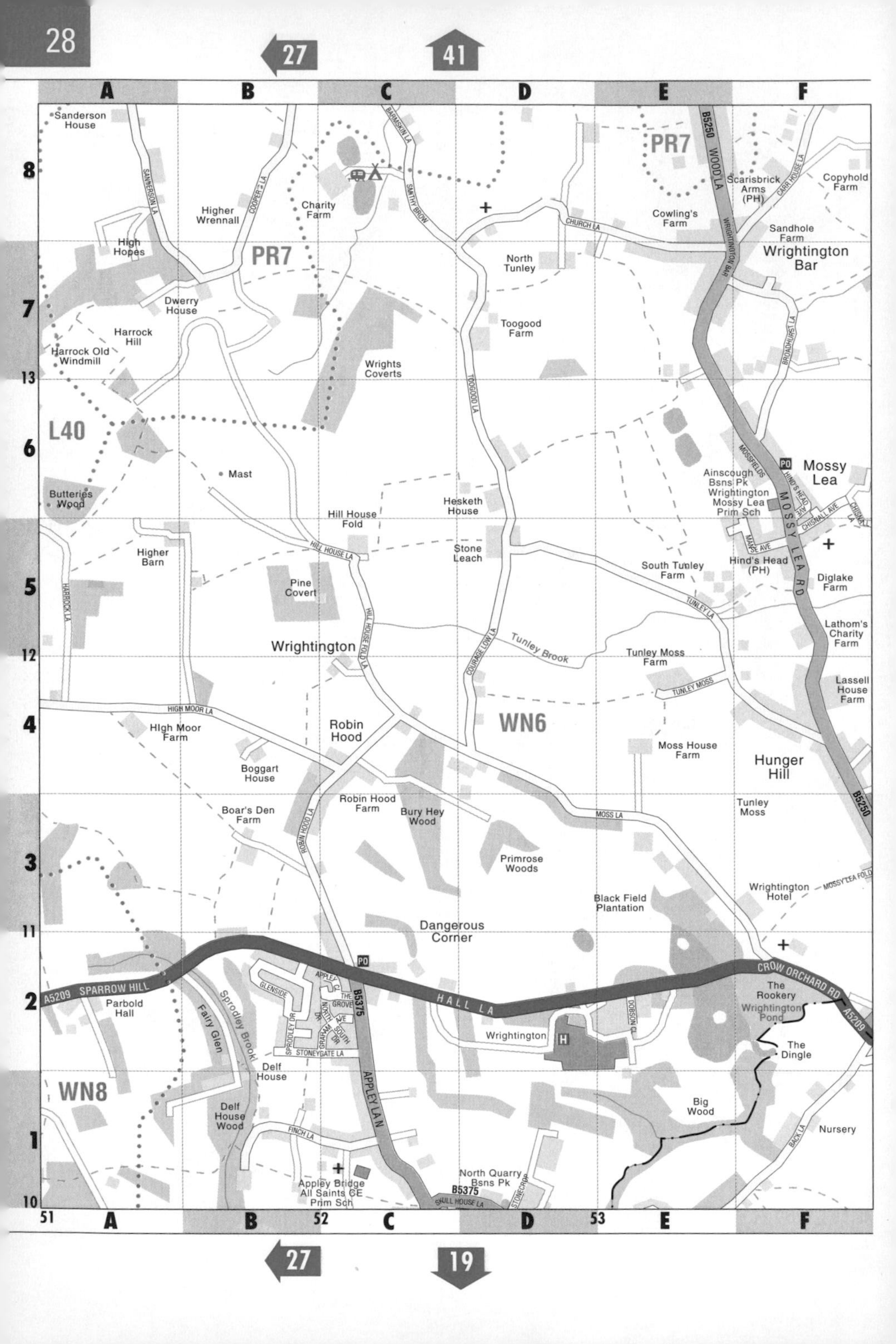
Sanderson House
SANDERSON LA
COOPER LA
Higher Wrennall
High Hopes
Charity Farm
BARNSKIN LA
SMITHY BROW
PR7
Dwerry House
Harrock Hill
Harrock Old Windmill
Wrights Coverts
L40
Mast
Butteries Wood
Higher Barn
HARROCK LA
Hill House Fold
HILL HOUSE LA
Pine Covert
Wrightington
HILL HOUSE FOLD LA
HIGH MOOR LA
High Moor Farm
Boggart House
Robin Hood
Robin Hood Farm
Boar's Den Farm
ROBIN HOOD LA
Bury Hey Wood
Primrose Woods
Dangerous Corner
A5209 SPARROW HILL
Parbold Hall
Fairy Glen
Sprodley Brook
GLENSIDE
APPLEY CL
THE GROVE
NORTH DR
GRAHAM DR
SOUTH AVE
SPRODLEY DR
STONEYGATE LA
B5375
APPLEY LA N
Delf House
Delf House Wood
WN8
FINCH LA
Appley Bridge All Saints CE Prim Sch
North Quarry Bsns Pk
STONECROP
SHULL HOUSE LA
HALL LA
Wrightington
DOBSON CL
Big Wood
CHURCH LA
North Tunley
Toogood Farm
TOOGOOD LA
Hesketh House
Stone Leach
COURAGE LOW LA
Tunley Brook
WN6
MOSS LA
Black Field Plantation
B5250 WOOD LA
WRIGHTINGTON BAR
Cowling's Farm
Scarisbrick Arms (PH)
CARR HOUSE LA
Copyhold Farm
Sandhole Farm
Wrightington Bar
BROADHURST LA
Ainscough Bsns Pk
Wrightington Mossy Lea Prim Sch
MOSSFIELDS
HIND'S HEAD AVE
CHISNALL AVE
CHISNALL LA
MAPLE AVE
Mossy Lea
MOSSY LEA RD
Hind's Head (PH)
Diglake Farm
South Tunley Farm
TUNLEY LA
Lathom's Charity Farm
Tunley Moss Farm
TUNLEY MOSS
Lassell House Farm
Moss House Farm
Hunger Hill
Tunley Moss
B5250
Wrightington Hotel
MOSSY LEA FOLD
CROW ORCHARD RD
A5209
The Rookery
Wrightington Pond
The Dingle
BACK LA
Nursery
A B C D E F
8 7 6 5 4 3 2 1
13 12 11 10
51 52 53

27
19

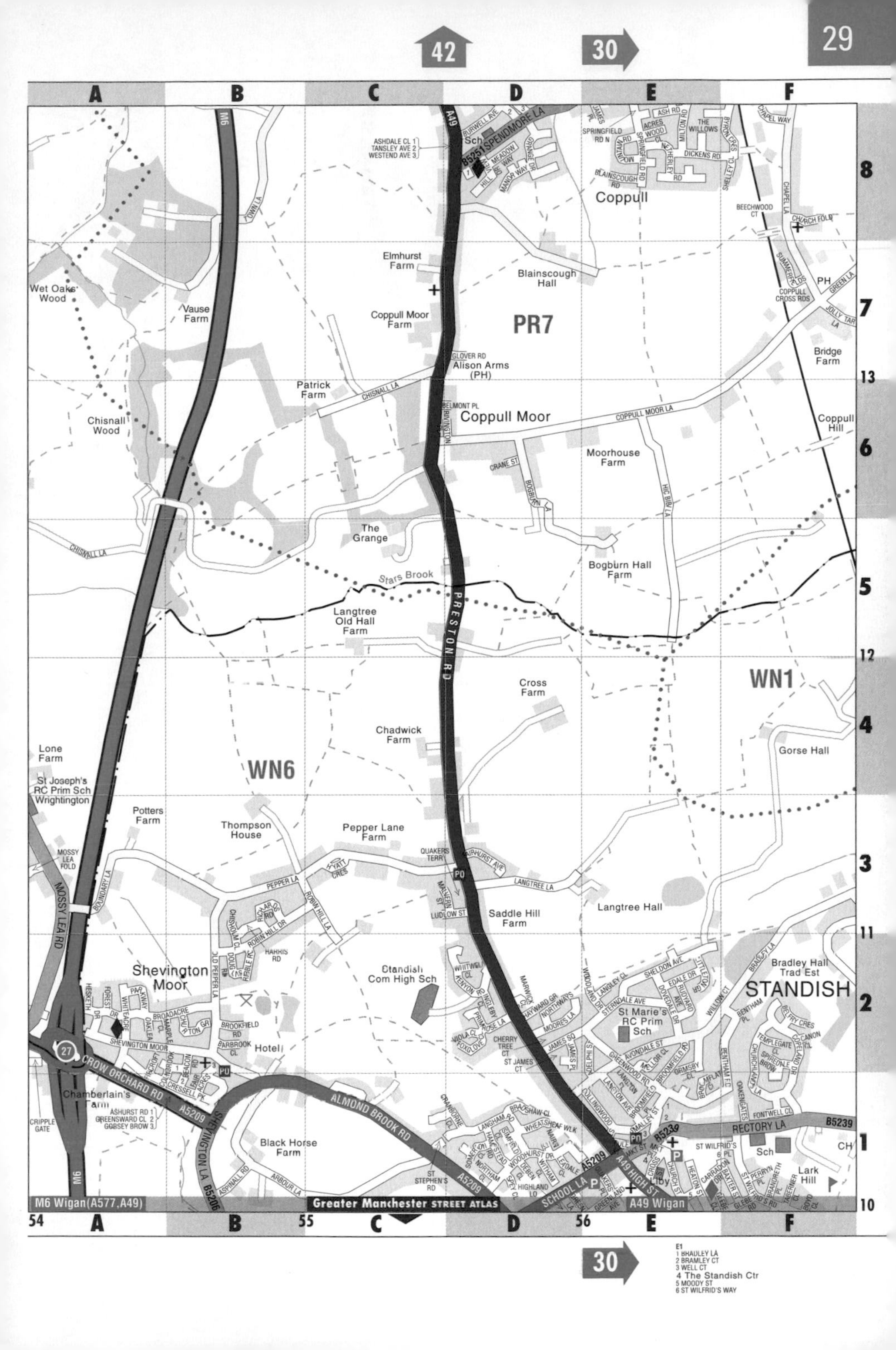
42
30
Coppull
PR7
Coppull Moor
WN6
WN1
STANDISH
Shevington Moor
Elmhurst Farm
Blainscough Hall
Coppull Moor Farm
Alison Arms (PH)
Patrick Farm
Wet Oaks Wood
Vause Farm
Chisnall Wood
Moorhouse Farm
Bridge Farm
Coppull Hill
The Grange
Bogburn Hall Farm
Stars Brook
Langtree Old Hall Farm
PRESTON RD
Cross Farm
Chadwick Farm
Gorse Hall
Lone Farm
St Joseph's RC Prim Sch Wrightington
Potters Farm
Thompson House
Pepper Lane Farm
Saddle Hill Farm
Langtree Hall
Standish Com High Sch
Bradley Hall Trad Est
St Marie's RC Prim Sch
Hotel
Chamberlain's Farm
Black Horse Farm
Lark Hill
CROW ORCHARD RD
ALMOND BROOK RD
RECTORY LA
COPPULL MOOR LA
CHISNALL LA
LANGTREE LA
PEPPER LA
MOSSY LEA RD
SPENDMORE LA
ASHDALE CL 1
TANSLEY AVE 2
WESTEND AVE 3
ASHURST RD 1
GREENSWARD CL 2
GOBSEY BROW 3
M6 Wigan(A577,A49)
Greater Manchester STREET ATLAS
A49 Wigan
54
55
56
30
E1
1 BRADLEY LA
2 BRAMLEY CT
3 WELL CT
4 The Standish Ctr
5 MOODY ST
6 ST WILFRID'S WAY

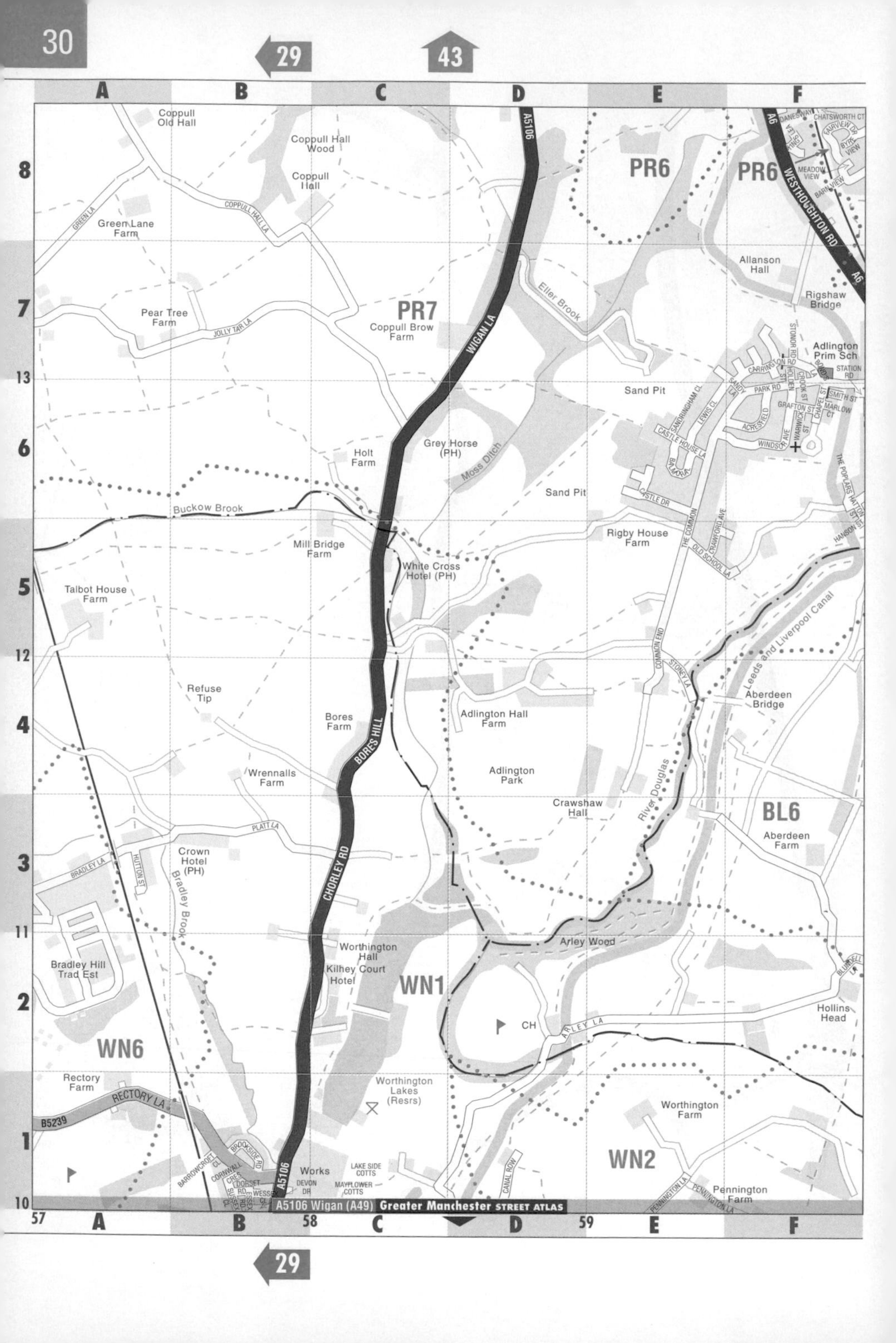
30
29
43
A
B
C
D
E
F
8
7
13
6
5
12
4
3
11
2
1
10
57
58
59
Coppull Old Hall
Coppull Hall Wood
Coppull Hall
COPPULL HALL LA
GREEN LA
Green Lane Farm
Pear Tree Farm
JOLLY TAR LA
PR7
Coppull Brow Farm
A5106
WIGAN LA
PR6
PR6
A6
DANESWAY
CHATSWORTH CT
FAIRVIEW DR
BYRE VIEW
MEADOW VIEW
BARN VIEW
WESTHOUGHTON RD
Allanson Hall
Rigshaw Bridge
Eller Brook
STONOR RD
Adlington Prim Sch
STATION RD
CARRINGTON RD
Sand Pit
SANDRINGHAM CL
LEWIS CL
SANDY LA
PARK RD
HOLDEN ST
CROOK ST
CHAPEL ST
SMITH ST
GRAFTON ST
MARLOW CT
ACRESFIELD
CASTLE HOUSE LA
WINDSOR AVE
WARWICK ST
BALMORAL
THE POPLARS
HATTON ST
HANSON ST
Holt Farm
Grey Horse (PH)
Moss Ditch
Sand Pit
CASTLE DR
THE COMMON
CRAWFORD AVE
OLD SCHOOL LA
Buckow Brook
Mill Bridge Farm
White Cross Hotel (PH)
Rigby House Farm
Talbot House Farm
Leeds and Liverpool Canal
COMMON END
STONEY LA
Refuse Tip
Bores Farm
BORES HILL
Adlington Hall Farm
Aberdeen Bridge
Wrennalls Farm
Adlington Park
River Douglas
Crawshaw Hall
BL6
Aberdeen Farm
PLATT LA
BRADLEY LA
HUTTON ST
Crown Hotel (PH)
Bradley Brook
CHORLEY RD
Arley Wood
Bradley Hill Trad Est
Worthington Hall
Kilhey Court Hotel
WN1
BLUEBELL LA
Hollins Head
CH
ARLEY LA
WN6
Rectory Farm
RECTORY LA
B5239
Worthington Lakes (Resrs)
Worthington Farm
BROOKSIDE RD
BARROWCROFT CL
CORNWALL CRES
DORSET RD
SUSSEX CL
WESSEX CL
DEVON DR
Works
LAKE SIDE COTTS
MAYFLOWER COTTS
CANAL ROW
WN2
PENNINGTON LA
Pennington Farm
A5106 Wigan (A49) Greater Manchester STREET ATLAS
29

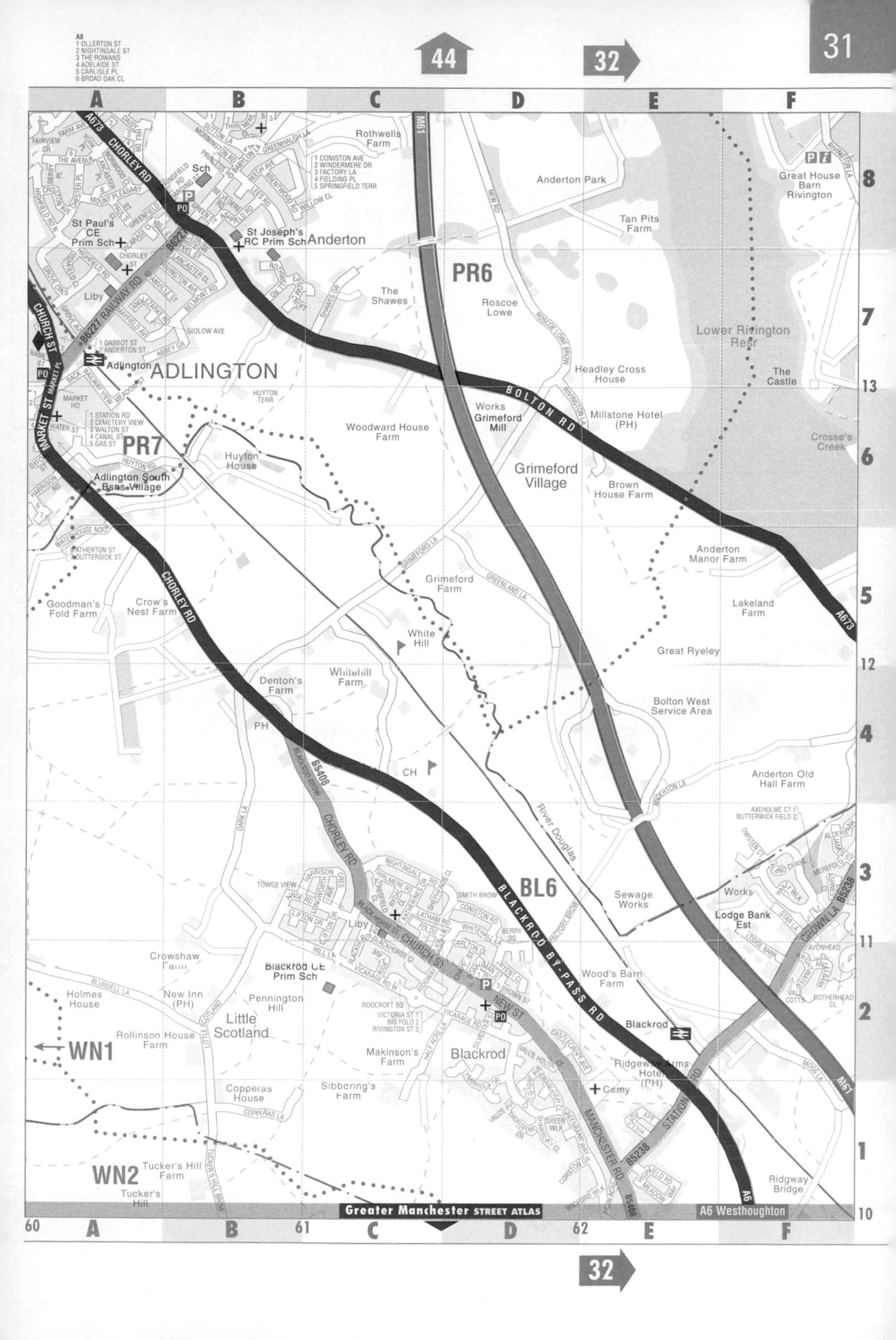
A8
1 OLLERTON ST
2 NIGHTINGALE ST
3 THE ROWANS
4 ADELAIDE ST
5 CARLISLE PL
6 BROAD OAK CL
44
32
A
B
C
D
E
F
8
7
13
6
5
12
4
3
11
2
1
10
60
61
62
A673
CHORLEY RD
Rothwells Farm
M61
1 CONISTON AVE
2 WINDERMERE DR
3 FACTORY LA
4 FIELDING PL
5 SPRINGFIELD TERR
Anderton Park
Great House Barn Rivington
Sch
St Paul's CE Prim Sch
St Joseph's RC Prim Sch
Anderton
Tan Pits Farm
PR6
Liby
B6227 RAILWAY RD
The Shawes
Roscoe Lowe
CHURCH ST
Lower Rivington Resr
1 GABBOT ST
2 ANDERTON ST
Adlington
ADLINGTON
Headley Cross House
The Castle
BOLTON RD
1 STATION RD
2 CEMETERY VIEW
3 WALTON ST
4 CANAL ST
5 GAS ST
Woodward House Farm
Works
Grimeford Mill
Millstone Hotel (PH)
Crosse's Creek
PR7
Huyton House
Grimeford Village
Brown House Farm
Adlington South Bsns Village
Anderton Manor Farm
Grimeford Farm
Goodman's Fold Farm
Crow's Nest Farm
CHORLEY RD
White Hill
Lakeland Farm
Great Ryeley
Whitehill Farm
Denton's Farm
Bolton West Service Area
PH
CH
Anderton Old Hall Farm
B5408
River Douglas
AXEHOLME CT 1
BUTTERWICK FIELD 2
BL6
Sewage Works
Works
Lodge Bank Est
BLACKROD BY-PASS RD
Liby
Crowshaw Farm
Blackrod CE Prim Sch
Wood's Barn Farm
Holmes House
New Inn (PH)
Pennington Hill
VICTORIA ST 1
BIG FOLD 2
RIVINGTON ST 3
Little Scotland
Rollinson House Farm
Blackrod
WN1
Makinson's Farm
Ridgeway Arms Hotel (PH)
Cemy
Copperas House
Sibbering's Farm
MANCHESTER RD
STATION RD
B5238
WN2
Tucker's Hill Farm
Tucker's Hill
Ridgway Bridge
A6
M61
Greater Manchester STREET ATLAS
A6 Westhoughton
CROWN LA B5238

32

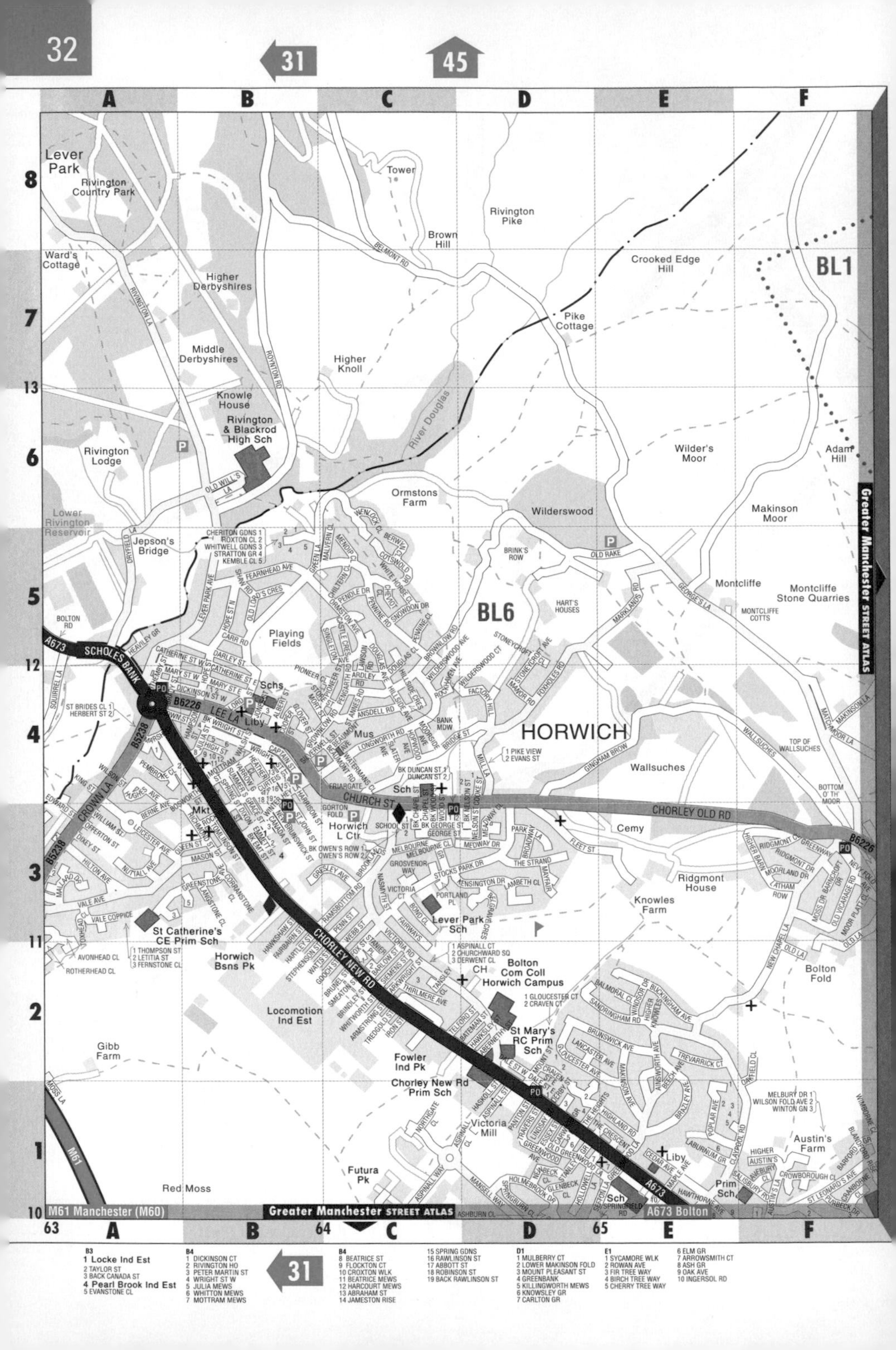

31
45
Lever Park
Rivington Country Park
Ward's Cottage
Higher Derbyshires
Middle Derbyshires
Knowle House
Rivington & Blackrod High Sch
Rivington Lodge
Lower Rivington Reservoir
Jepson's Bridge
Tower
Brown Hill
Rivington Pike
Crooked Edge Hill
BL1
Pike Cottage
Higher Knoll
River Douglas
Wilder's Moor
Adam Hill
Ormstons Farm
Wilderswood
Makinson Moor
Montcliffe
Montcliffe Stone Quarries
BL6
Playing Fields
HORWICH
Wallsuches
Schs
Liby
Mus
Mkt
Sch
Horwich L Ctr
Cemy
Ridgmont House
Knowles Farm
Lever Park Sch
St Catherine's CE Prim Sch
Horwich Bsns Pk
Bolton Com Coll Horwich Campus
Bolton Fold
Locomotion Ind Est
St Mary's RC Prim Sch
Gibb Farm
Fowler Ind Pk
Chorley New Rd Prim Sch
Victoria Mill
Austin's Farm
Futura Pk
Red Moss
Prim Sch
A673 SCHOLES BANK
B6226 LEE LA
CHURCH ST
CHORLEY OLD RD
CHORLEY NEW RD
B5238 CROWN LA
M61
M61 Manchester (M60)
Greater Manchester STREET ATLAS
A673 Bolton
Greater Manchester STREET ATLAS
A B C D E F
8 7 6 5 4 3 2 1 10
63 64 65
13 12 11
B3
1 Locke Ind Est
2 TAYLOR ST
3 BACK CANADA ST
4 Pearl Brook Ind Est
5 EVANSTONE CL
B4
1 DICKINSON CT
2 RIVINGTON HO
3 PETER MARTIN ST
4 WRIGHT ST W
5 JULIA MEWS
6 WHITTON MEWS
7 MOTTRAM MEWS
31
B4
8 BEATRICE ST
9 FLOCKTON CT
10 CROXTON WLK
11 BEATRICE MEWS
12 HARCOURT MEWS
13 ABRAHAM ST
14 JAMESTON RISE
15 SPRING GDNS
16 RAWLINSON ST
17 ABBOTT ST
18 ROBINSON ST
19 BACK RAWLINSON ST
D1
1 MULBERRY CT
2 LOWER MAKINSON FOLD
3 MOUNT PLEASANT ST
4 GREENBANK
5 KILLINGWORTH MEWS
6 KNOWSLEY GR
7 CARLTON GR
E1
1 SYCAMORE WLK
2 ROWAN AVE
3 FIR TREE WAY
4 BIRCH TREE WAY
5 CHERRY TREE WAY
6 ELM GR
7 ARROWSMITH CT
8 ASH GR
9 OAK AVE
10 INGERSOL RD

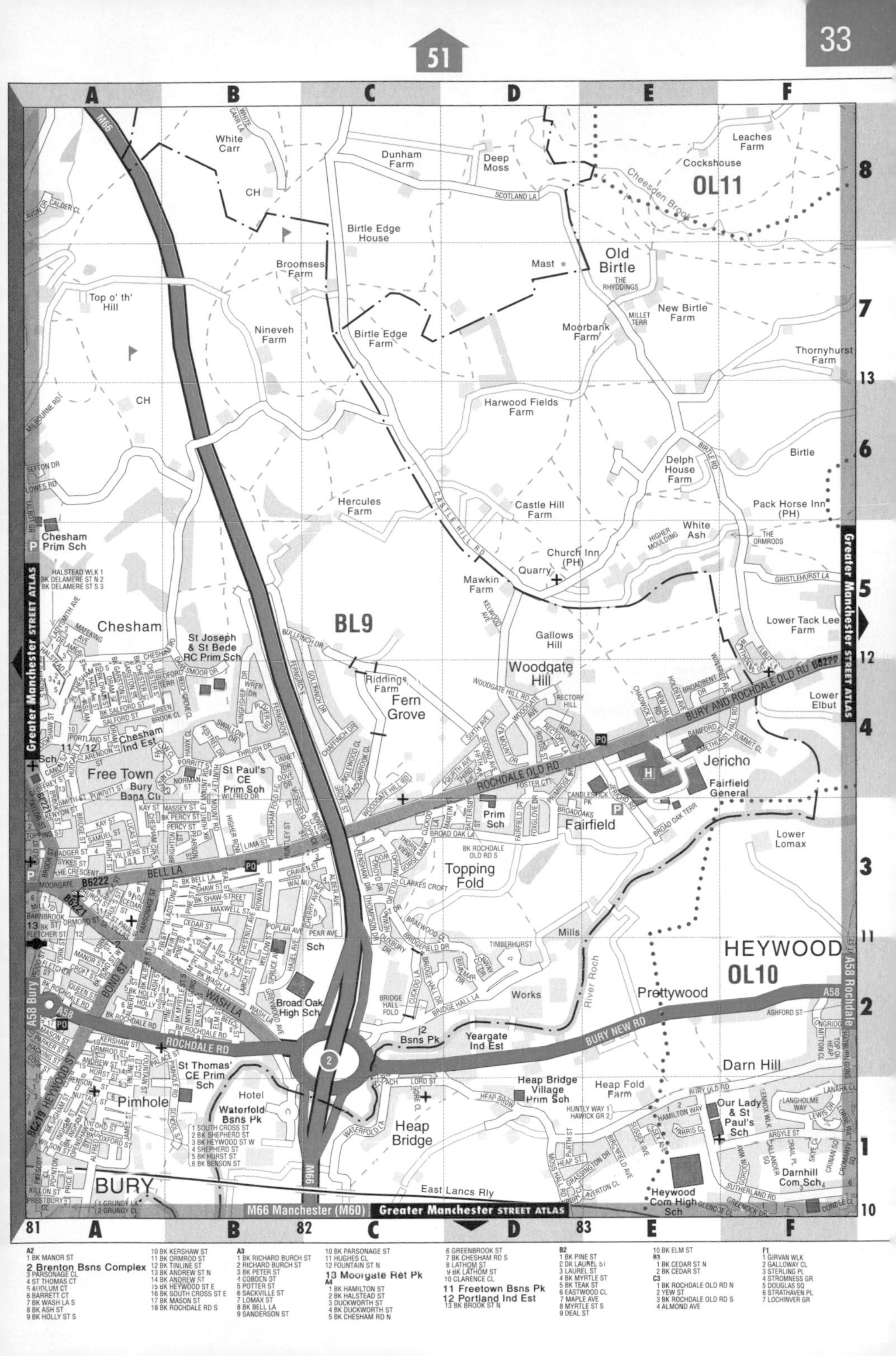
33
51
A
B
C
D
E
F
8
7
13
6
5
12
4
3
11
2
1
10
81
82
83
White Carr
CH
Dunham Farm
Deep Moss
Leaches Farm
Cockshouse
OL11
Cheesden Brook
SCOTLAND LA
Birtle Edge House
Broomses Farm
Mast
Old Birtle
THE RHYDDINGS
Top o' th' Hill
Nineveh Farm
Birtle Edge Farm
Moorbank Farm
MILLET TERR
New Birtle Farm
Thornyhurst Farm
Harwood Fields Farm
Birtle
BIRTLE RD
Delph House Farm
Hercules Farm
Castle Hill Farm
CASTLE HILL RD
Pack Horse Inn (PH)
White Ash
HIGHER MOULDING
THE ORMRODS
Church Inn (PH)
Quarry
Mawkin Farm
GRISTLEHURST LA
Chesham Prim Sch
Chesham
BL9
Gallows Hill
Lower Tack Lee Farm
St Joseph & St Bede RC Prim Sch
Riddings Farm
Fern Grove
Woodgate Hill
WOODGATE HILL RD
RECTORY HILL
BURY AND ROCHDALE OLD RD
B6222
Lower Elbut
Chesham Ind Est
Free Town
Bury Bsns Ctr
St Paul's CE Prim Sch
ROCHDALE OLD RD
Jericho
Fairfield General
Prim Sch
Fairfield
BROAD OAK LA
BROAD OAK TERR
Lower Lomax
BELL LA
MOORGATE
B6221
Topping Fold
CLARKES CROFT
Sch
Mills
TIMBERHURST
HEYWOOD
OL10
River Roch
Broad Oak High Sch
Works
Prettywood
A58
A58 Bury
A58 Rochdale
BRIDGE HALL FOLD
BRIDGE HALL LA
WASH LA
ROCHDALE RD
j2 Bsns Pk
Yeargate Ind Est
BURY NEW RD
ASHFORD ST
St Thomas' CE Prim Sch
Darn Hill
Pimhole
Hotel
Waterfold Bsns Pk
Heap Bridge Village Prim Sch
Heap Fold Farm
Heap Bridge
Our Lady & St Paul's Sch
B6219 HEYWOOD ST
BURY
M66
East Lancs Rly
Heywood Com High Sch
Darnhill Com Sch
M66 Manchester (M60)
Greater Manchester STREET ATLAS
A2
1 BK MANOR ST
2 Brenton Bsns Complex
3 PARSONAGE CL
4 ST THOMAS CT
5 AUDLUM CT
6 BARRETT CT
7 BK WASH LA S
8 BK ASH ST
9 BK HOLLY ST S
10 BK KERSHAW ST
11 BK ORMROD ST
12 BK TINLINE ST
13 BK ANDREW ST N
14 BK ANDREW ST
15 BK HEYWOOD ST E
16 BK SOUTH CROSS ST E
17 BK MASON ST
18 BK ROCHDALE RD S
A3
1 BK RICHARD BURCH ST
2 RICHARD BURCH ST
3 BK PETER ST
4 COBDEN ST
5 POTTER ST
6 SACKVILLE ST
7 LOMAX ST
8 BK BELL LA
9 SANDERSON ST
10 BK PARSONAGE ST
11 HUGHES CL
12 FOUNTAIN ST N
13 Moorgate Ret Pk
A4
1 BK HAMILTON ST
2 BK HALSTEAD ST
3 DUCKWORTH ST
4 BK DUCKWORTH ST
5 BK CHESHAM RD N
6 GREENBROOK ST
7 BK CHESHAM RD S
8 LATHOM ST
9 BK LATHOM ST
10 CLARENCE CL
11 Freetown Bsns Pk
12 Portland Ind Est
13 BK BROOK ST N
B2
1 BK PINE ST
2 BK LAUREL ST
3 LAUREL ST
4 BK MYRTLE ST
5 BK TEAK ST
6 EASTWOOD CL
7 MAPLE AVE
8 MYRTLE ST S
9 DEAL ST
10 BK ELM ST
B3
1 BK CEDAR ST N
2 BK CEDAR ST
C3
1 BK ROCHDALE OLD RD N
2 YEW ST
3 BK ROCHDALE OLD RD S
4 ALMOND AVE
F1
1 GIRVAN WLK
2 GALLOWAY CL
3 STERLING PL
4 STROMNESS GR
5 DOUGLAS SQ
6 STRATHAVEN PL
7 LOCHINVER GR

A
B
C
D
E
F
8
7
17
6
5
16
4
3
15
2
1
14
30
31
32
Princes Park
Southport Zoo
Pleasureland
P&R
L Ctr
VICTORIA WAY
MARINE DR
ESPLANADE
Victoria Park
PRIORY MEWS 1
THE HOLLIES 2
THE OAKS 3
THE PINES 4
THE ELMS 5
THE WILLOWS 6
DONNINGTON LODGE 7
TUDOR MANS 8
SUNCOURT 9
ST WYBURN CT 1
KINGSWOOD HO 2
WESTCLIFFE CT 3
Sunnymede Sch
ROTTEN ROW
BEACH RD
BEACHMEWS
Queens Jubilee Nature Trail
Victoria Park Miniature Rly
Birkdale Sands
PR8
KINGSWOOD PK
SHERWOOD LODGE
BLANDFORD CL
WARREN CT
WESTCLIFFE RD
PALATINE RD
LULWORTH LODGE
LULWORTH RD
A565
B5208
CLAIRVILLE
GLOUCESTER RD
CAMBERLEY CL
PALACE RD
ASCOT CL
WELD RD
SAXON RD
SAXON LODGE
SAXENHOLME
PRINCE CHARLES GDNS
HAYLEMERE CT
GROVEWOOD
CARNEGHIE CT 1
WELD PAR 2
HOMECHASE HO 3
VICTORIA CT 4
WELDALE 5
CARNOUSTIE CL 6
Dunes
OXFORD RD
WINDSOR CT
OXFORD GDNS
LANCASTER HO
SILVERDALE
WESTBOURNE RD
WESTBOURNE GDNS
THE HEYS
LISMORE PK
CANTERBURY CL
Birkdale
REGENT MEWS
REGENT RD
NELSON CT
GROSVENOR CT
GROSVENOR RD
LANCASTER RD
GRANVILLE RD
SELWORTHY RD
REGENCY GDNS
TRAFALGAR CT
TREESDALE CL
OXFORD CT
BELGRAVE RD
WALMER CT
ACRE GR
CROSBY RD
AINDOW CT
WORTHING CL
BROADLANDS
BELGRAVE PL
SULBY CL
SANDRINGHAM RD
GAINSBOROUGH RD
CHURCHFIELDS
CRICKET PATH
GROSVENOR GDNS
GROSVENOR PL
LC
CRESCENT RD
COASTAL RD
Trans Pennine Trail
WATERLOO RD
TRAFALGAR RD
HARROD DR
CONYERS AVE
DOVER RD
BURLINGTON RD
CAVENDISH RD
STANLEY AVE
BREEZE RD
SHERRINGHAM RD
BLUNDELL AVE
BLUNDELL DR
HARTLEY RD
HARTLEY CRES
GREENBANK DR
CROMER RD
DUNKIRK RD
Birkdale
BLUNDELL CRES
RICHMOND RD
KIRKSTALL RD
CLIVE RD
CLIVE LODGE
Dunes
The Royal Birkdale
Greenbank High Sch
GRINSTEAD CL
ST JOHN'S RD
CH
HASTINGS RD
Hillside
HILLSIDE RD
KIRKLEES RD
CARDIGAN RD
CARNARVON RD
Hillside
Liby
LYNTON DR
DUNBAR RD
SANDON RD
LIVERPOOL RD
A5267
Birkdale Hills
CH
LYNTON RD
PO
HAZELWOOD
LANGDALE GDNS
ASHTON RD
NORFOLK GR
NORFOLK RD
THE BRIARS

21

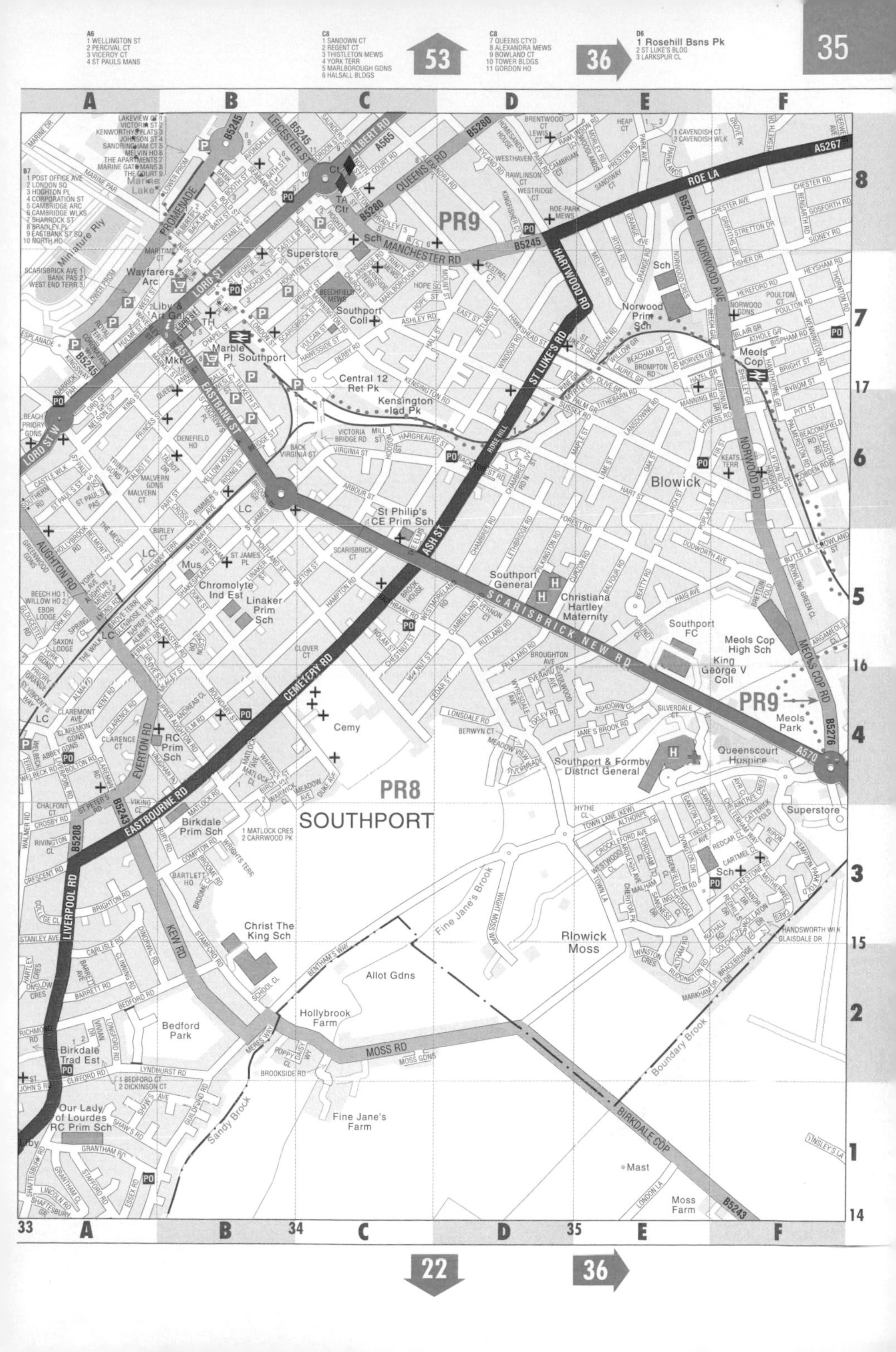

35
A6
1 WELLINGTON ST
2 PERCIVAL CT
3 VICEROY CT
4 ST PAULS MANS
C8
1 SANDOWN CT
2 REGENT CT
3 THISTLETON MEWS
4 YORK TERR
5 MARLBOROUGH GDNS
6 HALSALL BLDGS
53
C8
7 QUEENS CTYD
8 ALEXANDRA MEWS
9 BOWLAND CT
10 TOWER BLDGS
11 GORDON HO
36
D6
1 Rosehill Bsns Pk
2 ST LUKE'S BLDG
3 LARKSPUR CL
A
B
C
D
E
F
8
7
17
6
5
16
4
3
15
2
1
14
33
34
35
B7
1 POST OFFICE AVE
2 LONDON SQ
3 HOGHTON PL
4 CORPORATION ST
5 CAMBRIDGE ARC
6 CAMBRIDGE WLKS
7 SHARROCK ST
8 BRADLEY PL
9 EASTBANK ST SQ
10 NORTH HO
LAKEVIEW CT 1
VICTORIA ST 2
KENWORTHYS FLATS 3
JOHNSON ST 4
SANDRINGHAM CT 5
MELVIN HO 6
THE APARTMENTS 7
MARINE GATE MANS 8
THE COURT 9
SCARISBRICK AVE 1
BANK PAS 2
WEST END TERR 3
1 CAVENDISH CT
2 CAVENDISH WLK
PR9
PR8
SOUTHPORT
Marine Lake
Miniature Rly
Wayfarers Arc
Liby & Art Gal
Marble Pl
Southport
Superstore
Sch
TA Ctr
Southport Coll
Central 12 Ret Pk
Kensington Ind Pk
Norwood Prim Sch
Meols Cop
Blowick
St Philip's CE Prim Sch
Southport General
Christiana Hartley Maternity
Southport FC
Meols Cop High Sch
King George V Coll
Meols Park
Queenscourt Hospice
Southport & Formby District General
Chromolyte Ind Est
Linaker Prim Sch
Mus
RC Prim Sch
Cemy
Birkdale Prim Sch
1 MATLOCK CRES
2 CARRWOOD PK
Christ The King Sch
Allot Gdns
Hollybrook Farm
Bedford Park
Birkdale Trad Est
Our Lady of Lourdes RC Prim Sch
1 BEDFORD CT
2 DICKINSON CT
Fine Jane's Farm
Fine Jane's Brook
Blowick Moss
Boundary Brook
Sandy Brook
Mast
Moss Farm
Superstore
LORD ST
PROMENADE
LORD ST W
EASTBANK ST
MANCHESTER RD
QUEENS RD
ROE LA
HARTWOOD RD
ST LUKE'S RD
ASH ST
SCARISBRICK NEW RD
CEMETERY RD
EASTBOURNE RD
LIVERPOOL RD
AUGHTON RD
EVERTON RD
KEW RD
MOSS RD
BIRKDALE COP
NORWOOD AVE
NORWOOD RD
MEOLS COP RD
A5267
A565
A570
B5245
B5280
B5276
B5243
B5208
22
36

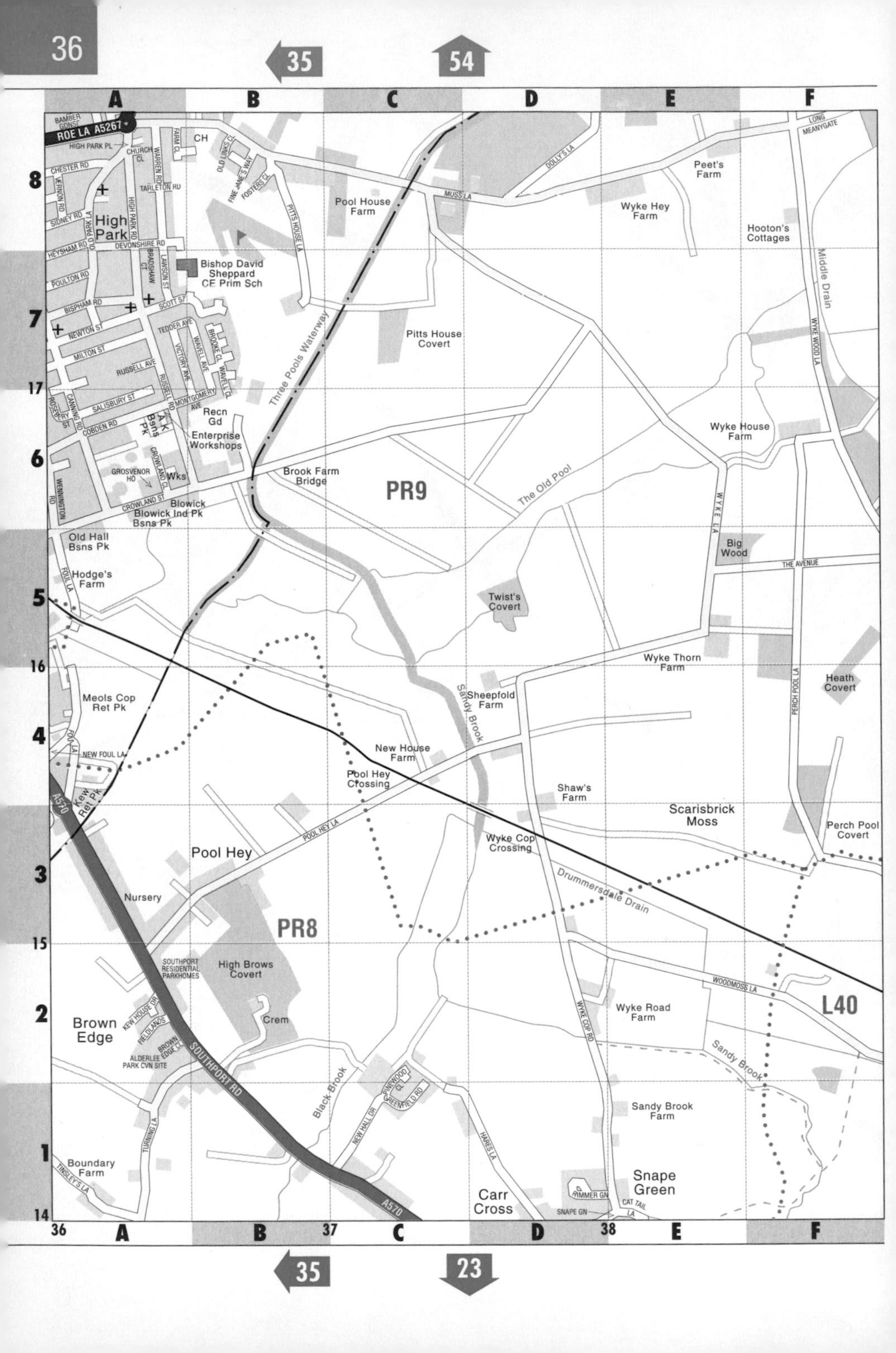

35
54
A
B
C
D
E
F
8
7
17
6
5
16
4
3
15
2
1
14
36
37
38
ROE LA A5267
BAMBER GDNS
HIGH PARK PL
CHESTER RD
VERNON RD
SIDNEY RD
High Park
HEYSHAM RD
POULTON RD
BISPHAM RD
NEWTON ST
MILTON ST
RUSSELL AVE
SALISBURY ST
CANNING RD
ROSEBERY ST
COBDEN RD
GROSVENOR HO
WENNINGTON RD
CROWLAND ST
CROWLAND CL
Wks
Blowick
Blowick Ind Pk
Bsns Pk
Old Hall Bsns Pk
Hodge's Farm
FOUL LA
Meols Cop Ret Pk
NEW FOUL LA
Kew Ret Pk
A570
CHURCH CL
HIGH PARK RD
OLD PARK LA
DEVONSHIRE RD
WARREN RD
FARM CL
TARLETON RD
BRADSHAW CT
LAWSON ST
SCOTT ST
Bishop David Sheppard CE Prim Sch
TEDDER AVE
VICTORY AVE
WAVELL AVE
BROOKE CL
WAVELL CL
RUSSELL RD
MONTGOMERY AVE
A K Bsns Pk
Recn Gd
Enterprise Workshops
CH
OLD LINKS CL
FINE JANE'S WAY
FOSTERS CL
PITTS HOUSE LA
Pool House Farm
Three Pools Waterway
Pitts House Covert
Brook Farm Bridge
PR9
MUSS LA
DOLLY'S LA
Peet's Farm
Wyke Hey Farm
Hooton's Cottages
LONG MEANYGATE
Middle Drain
WYKE WOOD LA
Wyke House Farm
The Old Pool
WYKE LA
Big Wood
THE AVENUE
Twist's Covert
Wyke Thorn Farm
Heath Covert
PERCH POOL LA
Sheepfold Farm
Sandy Brook
New House Farm
Pool Hey Crossing
Shaw's Farm
Scarisbrick Moss
Perch Pool Covert
Wyke Cop Crossing
Drummersdale Drain
POOL HEY LA
Pool Hey
Nursery
PR8
SOUTHPORT RESIDENTIAL PARKHOMES
High Brows Covert
Crem
Brown Edge
KEW HOUSE DR
FIELDLANDS
BROWN EDGE CL
ALDERLEE PARK CVN SITE
SOUTHPORT RD
TURNING LA
Black Brook
NEW HALL DR
PINEWOOD CL
GREENFIELD RD
HARES LA
WYKE COP RD
WOODMOSS LA
L40
Wyke Road Farm
Sandy Brook
Sandy Brook Farm
Snape Green
SNAPE GN
SKIMMER GN
CAT TAIL LA
Carr Cross
Boundary Farm
TINSLEY'S LA
A570
35
23

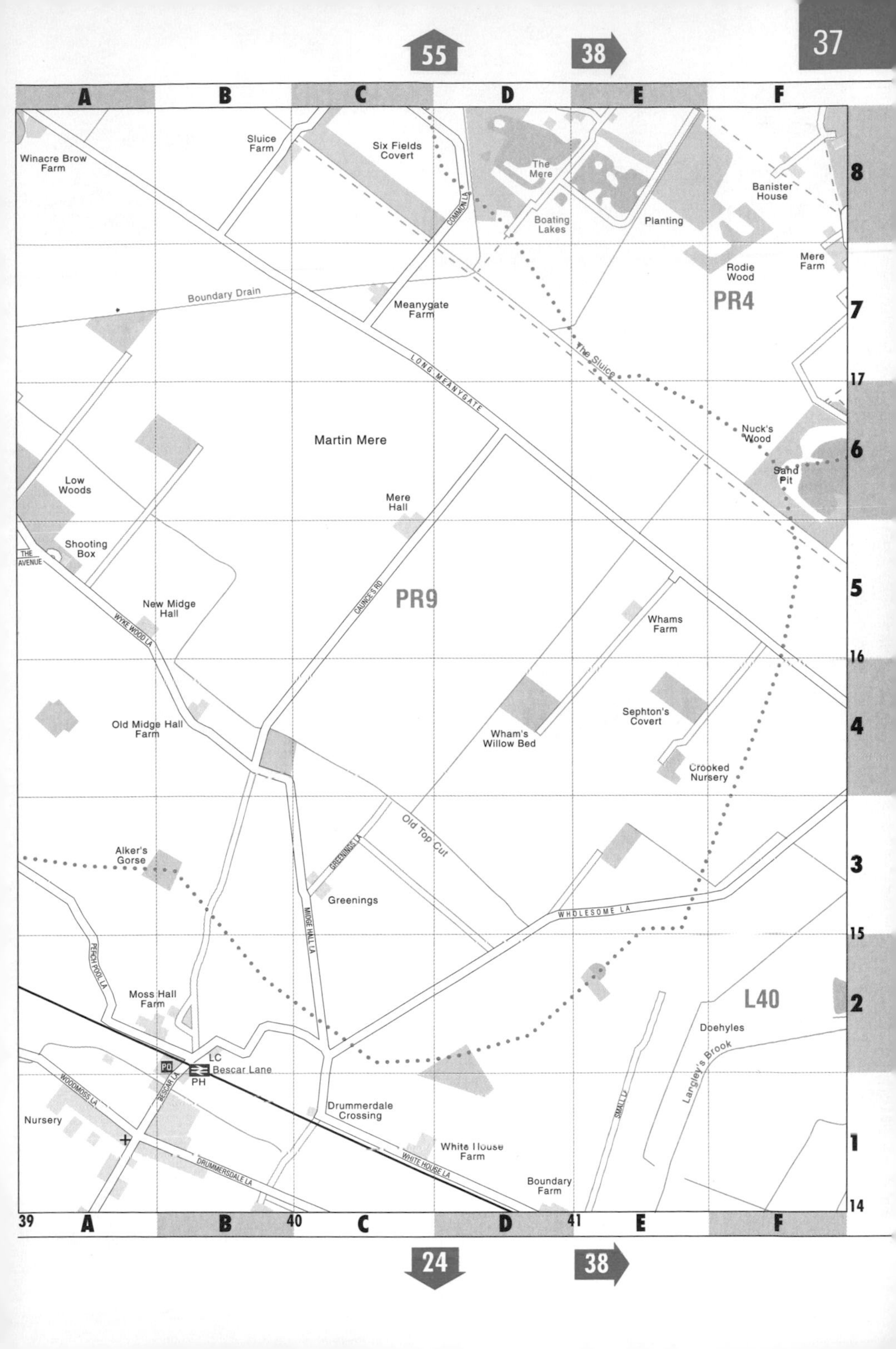
55
38
A
B
C
D
E
F
Winacre Brow Farm
Sluice Farm
Six Fields Covert
The Mere
Boating Lakes
Planting
Banister House
Mere Farm
Rodie Wood
PR4
COMMON LA
Boundary Drain
Meanygate Farm
The Sluice
LONG MEANYGATE
Nuck's Wood
Sand Pit
Martin Mere
Low Woods
Mere Hall
Shooting Box
THE AVENUE
New Midge Hall
WYKE WOOD LA
CAUNCE'S RD
PR9
Whams Farm
Old Midge Hall Farm
Sephton's Covert
Wham's Willow Bed
Crooked Nursery
Old Top Cut
Alker's Gorse
GREENINGS LA
Greenings
MIDGE HALL LA
WHOLESOME LA
PEACH POOL LA
Moss Hall Farm
L40
Doehyles
LC
Bescar Lane
PH
PO
BESCAR LA
WOODMOSS LA
Largley's Brook
SMALL LA
Drummerdale Crossing
Nursery
DRUMMERSDALE LA
White House Farm
WHITE HOUSE LA
Boundary Farm
8
7
17
6
5
16
4
3
15
2
1
14
39
40
41
24

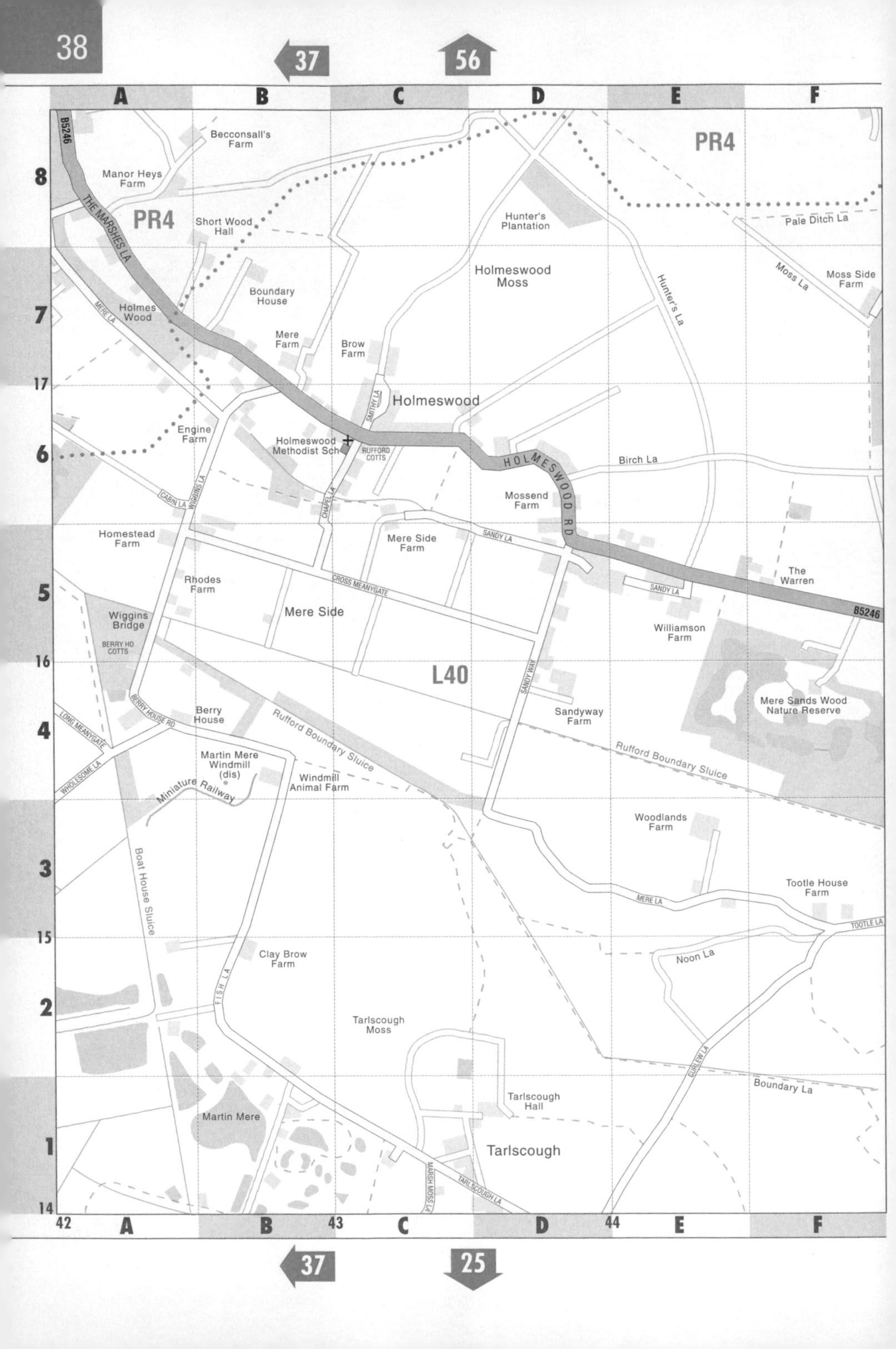
37
56
A B C D E F
8
7
17
6
5
16
4
3
15
2
1
14
42
43
44
B5246
THE MARSHES LA
Becconsall's Farm
Manor Heys Farm
PR4
Short Wood Hall
Hunter's Plantation
Pale Ditch La
Moss La
Moss Side Farm
Holmeswood Moss
Hunter's La
Boundary House
Holmes Wood
MERE LA
Mere Farm
Brow Farm
SMITHY LA
Holmeswood
Engine Farm
Holmeswood Methodist Sch
RUFFORD COTTS
HOLMESWOOD RD
Birch La
CABIN LA
WIGGINS LA
CHAPEL LA
Mossend Farm
Homestead Farm
Mere Side Farm
SANDY LA
Rhodes Farm
CROSS MEANYGATE
The Warren
Mere Side
Wiggins Bridge
BERRY HO COTTS
Williamson Farm
L40
SANDY WAY
Mere Sands Wood Nature Reserve
BERRY HOUSE RD
Berry House
Sandyway Farm
LONG MEANYGATE
Rufford Boundary Sluice
Martin Mere Windmill (dis)
WHOLESOME LA
Windmill Animal Farm
Miniature Railway
Woodlands Farm
Boat House Sluice
Tootle House Farm
MERE LA
TOOTLE LA
Noon La
Clay Brow Farm
FISH LA
Tarlscough Moss
GURLEW LA
Boundary La
Tarlscough Hall
Martin Mere
Tarlscough
MARSH MOSS LA
TARLSCOUGH LA
25

57
40

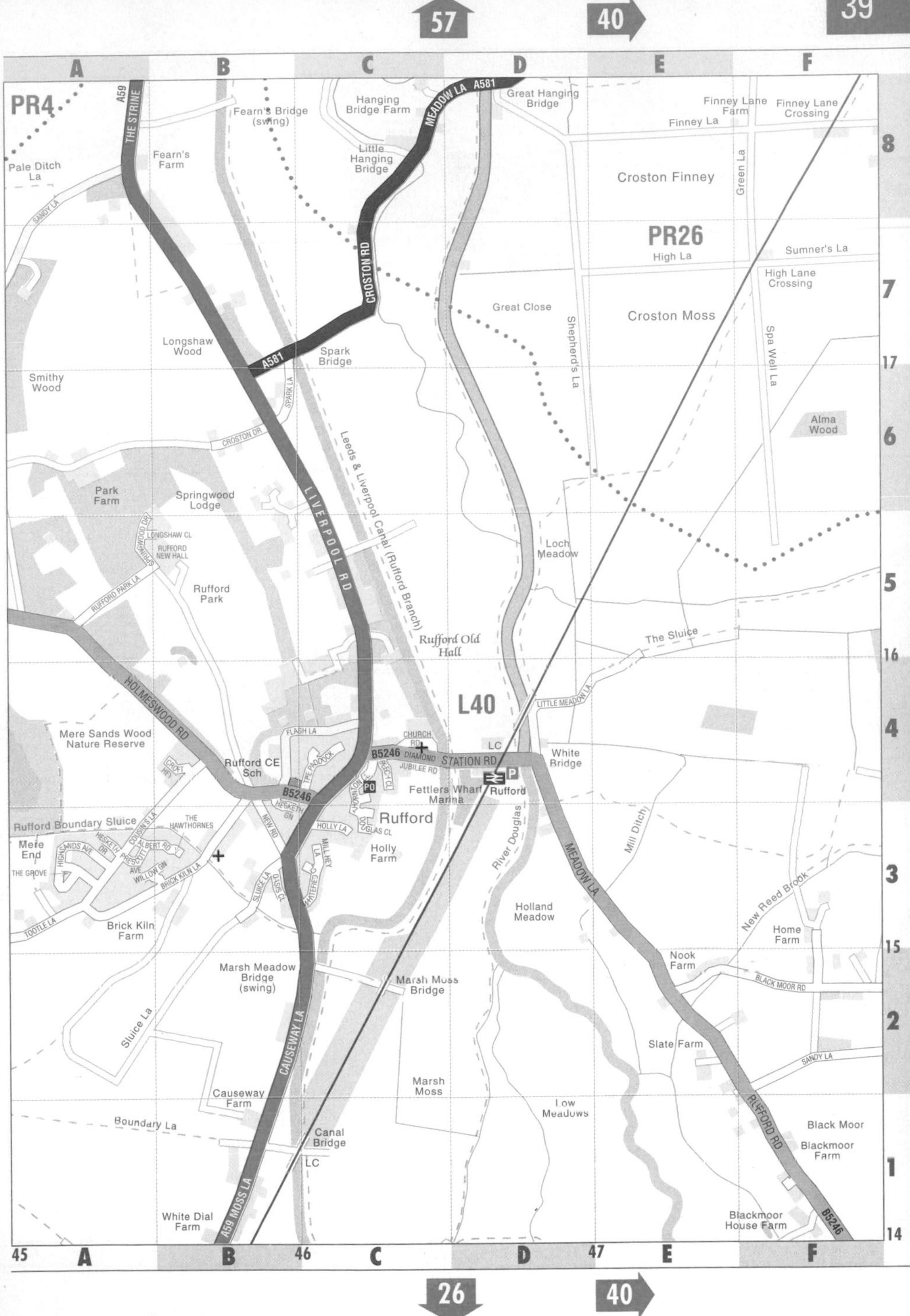
PR4
PR26
L40
Pale Ditch La
Fearn's Farm
Fearn's Bridge (swing)
Hanging Bridge Farm
Little Hanging Bridge
Great Hanging Bridge
Finney Lane Farm
Finney Lane Crossing
Finney La
Croston Finney
Green La
High La
Sumner's La
High Lane Crossing
Croston Moss
Great Close
Shepherd's La
Spa Well La
Alma Wood
Longshaw Wood
Smithy Wood
Spark Bridge
Leeds & Liverpool Canal (Rufford Branch)
Park Farm
Springwood Lodge
Rufford Park
Loch Meadow
The Sluice
Rufford Old Hall
Mere Sands Wood Nature Reserve
Rufford CE Sch
White Bridge
Fettlers Wharf Marina
Rufford
Rufford Boundary Sluice
Mere End
Holly Farm
River Douglas
Mill Ditch
New Reed Brook
Holland Meadow
Brick Kiln Farm
Home Farm
Nook Farm
Marsh Meadow Bridge (swing)
Marsh Moss Bridge
Sluice La
Slate Farm
Marsh Moss
Causeway Farm
Low Meadows
Black Moor
Boundary La
Canal Bridge
Blackmoor Farm
White Dial Farm
Blackmoor House Farm
THE STRINE
A59
MEADOW LA
A581
CROSTON RD
LIVERPOOL RD
HOLMESWOOD RD
B5246
STATION RD
CAUSEWAY LA
A59 MOSS LA
RUFFORD RD
MEADOW LA
BLACK MOOR RD
SANDY LA
LC
A B C D E F
8 7 6 5 4 3 2 1
17 16 15 14
45 46 47

26
40

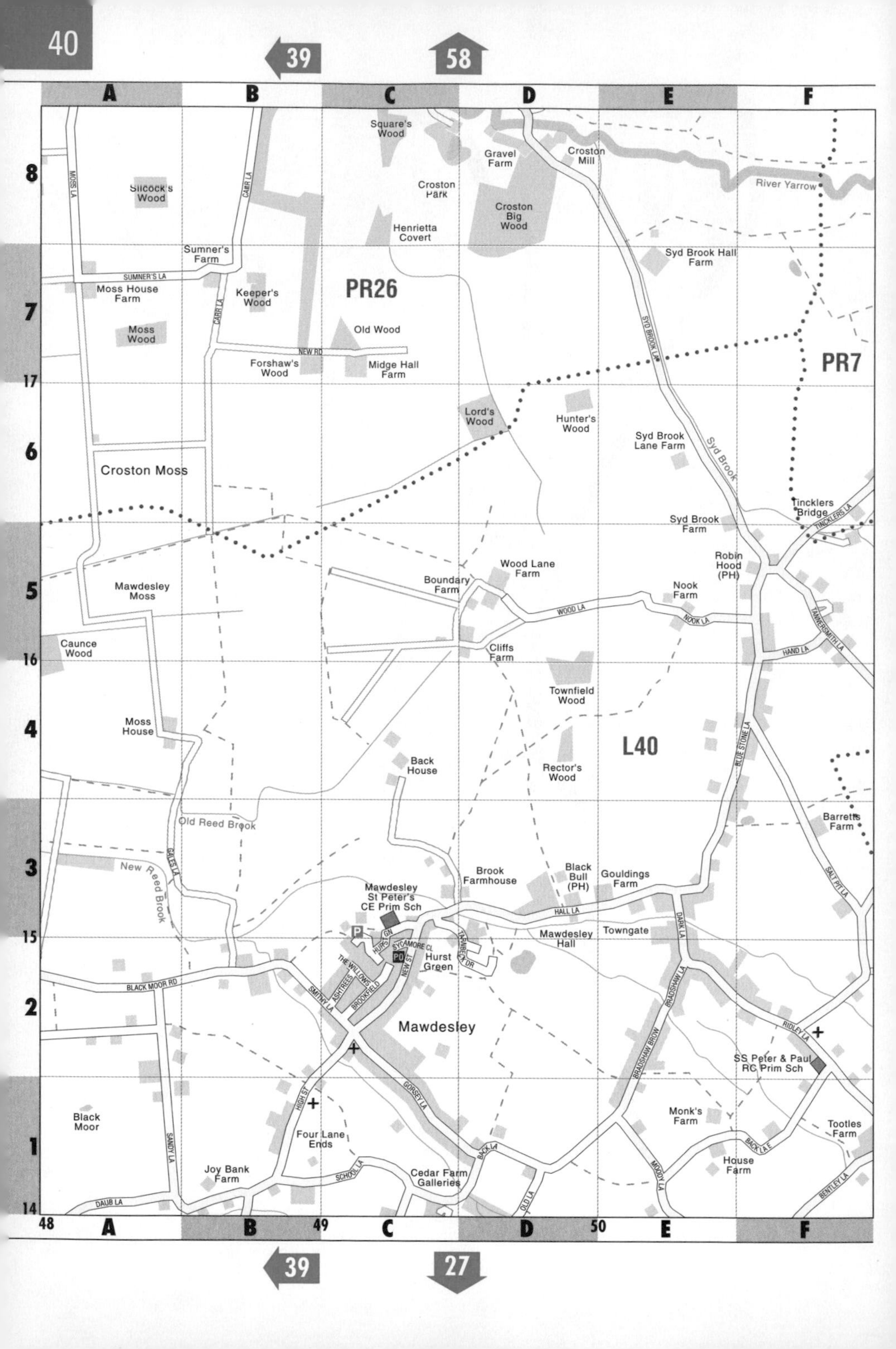
39
58
A
B
C
D
E
F
8
7
17
6
5
16
4
3
15
2
1
14
48
49
50
Square's Wood
Gravel Farm
Croston Mill
River Yarrow
Silcock's Wood
Croston Park
Croston Big Wood
Henrietta Covert
Sumner's Farm
Syd Brook Hall Farm
Moss House Farm
Keeper's Wood
PR26
Moss Wood
Old Wood
Forshaw's Wood
Midge Hall Farm
PR7
Lord's Wood
Hunter's Wood
Syd Brook Lane Farm
Syd Brook
Croston Moss
Tincklers Bridge
Syd Brook Farm
Robin Hood (PH)
Wood Lane Farm
Boundary Farm
Mawdesley Moss
Nook Farm
Caunce Wood
Cliffs Farm
Townfield Wood
Moss House
L40
Back House
Rector's Wood
Old Reed Brook
Barretts Farm
New Reed Brook
Brook Farmhouse
Black Bull (PH)
Gouldings Farm
Mawdesley St Peter's CE Prim Sch
Mawdesley Hall
Towngate
Hurst Green
Mawdesley
SS Peter & Paul RC Prim Sch
Black Moor
Four Lane Ends
Monk's Farm
Tootles Farm
House Farm
Joy Bank Farm
Cedar Farm Galleries
MOSS LA
CARR LA
SUMNER'S LA
NEW RD
SYD BROOK LA
TINCKLERS LA
WOOD LA
NOOK LA
HAND LA
TANNERSMITH LA
BLUE STONE LA
GALES LA
HALL LA
DARK LA
SALT PIT LA
HURST GN
SYCAMORE CL
TARNBECK DR
NEW ST
THE WILLOWS
ASHTREES
BROOKFIELD
SMITHY LA
BLACK MOOR RD
BRADSHAW LA
BRADSHAW BROW
RIDLEY LA
HIGH ST
GORSEY LA
BACK LA
BACK LA E
MOODY LA
SANDY LA
SCHOOL LA
DAUB LA
OLD LA
BENTLEY LA
P
PO
39
27

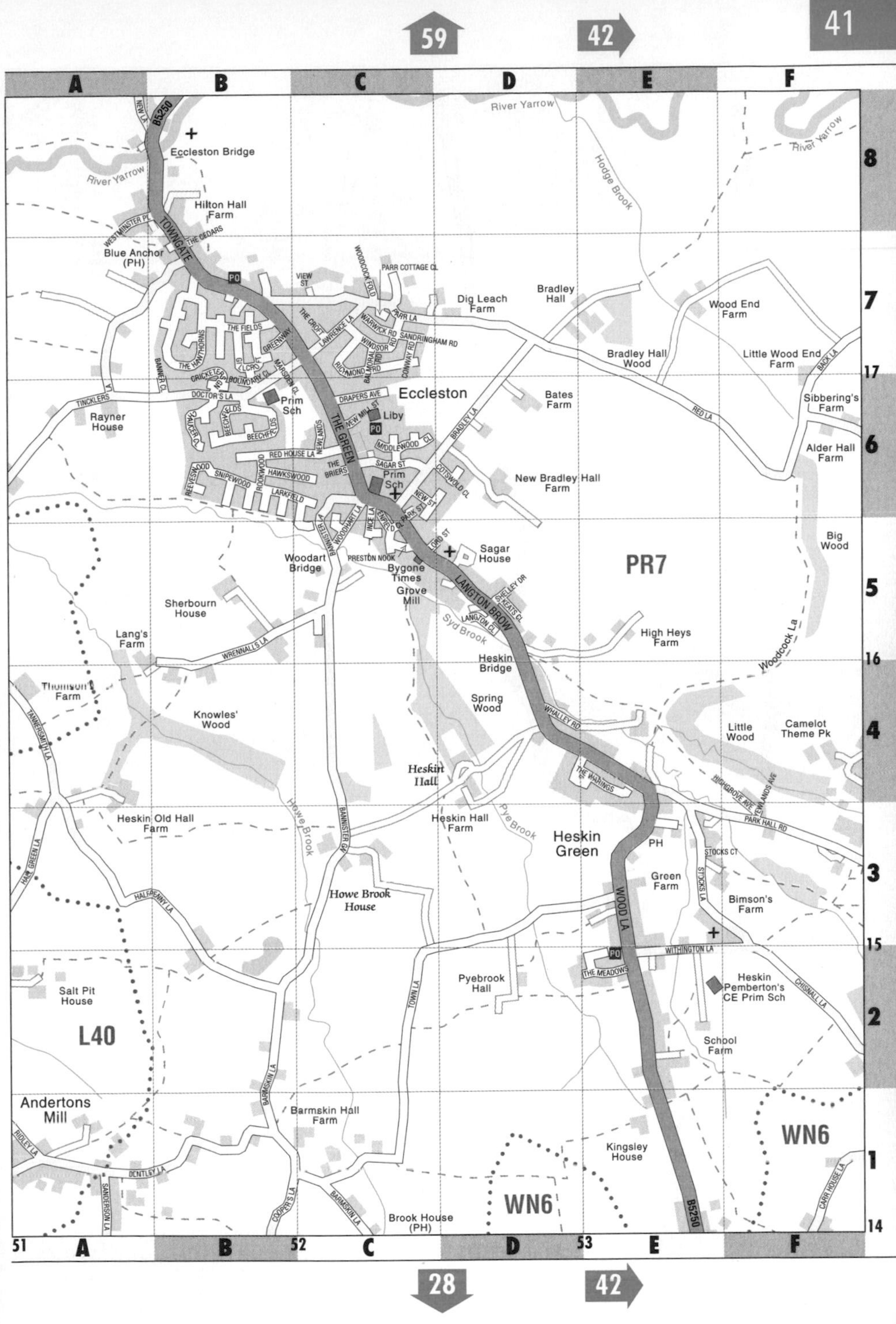
59
42
A
B
C
D
E
F
River Yarrow
Eccleston Bridge
Hodge Brook
Hilton Hall Farm
TOWNGATE
B5250
NEW LA
WESTMINSTER PL
THE CEDARS
Blue Anchor (PH)
PO
VIEW ST
WOODCOCK FOLD
PARR COTTAGE CL
Dig Leach Farm
Bradley Hall
Wood End Farm
THE FIELDS
THE CROFT
LAWRENCE LA
WARWICK RD
PARR LA
SANDRINGHAM RD
WINDSOR RD
BALMORAL RD
CONWAY RD
RICHMOND RD
GREENWAY
THE HAWTHORNS
BANNER CL
CRICKETERS
BOUNDARY CL
MARSDEN CL
Bradley Hall Wood
Little Wood End Farm
BACK LA
DRAPERS AVE
Eccleston
Bates Farm
TINCKLERS LA
DOCTOR'S LA
Prim Sch
Liby
NEW MILL ST
THE GREEN
BRADLEY LA
RED LA
Sibbering's Farm
Rayner House
BEECHFIELDS
CHAUCER
MIDDLEWOOD CL
RED HOUSE LA
NEWLANDS
Alder Hall Farm
REEVESWOOD
SNIPEWOOD
ROOKWOOD
HAWKSWOOD
THE BRIERS
SAGAR ST
COTSWOLD CL
New Bradley Hall Farm
LARKFIELD
NEW ST
PARK ST
BANNISTER LA
WOODHART LA
INCE LA
LORD ST
Sagar House
Big Wood
PRESTON NOOK
Woodart Bridge
Bygone Times
PR7
Grove Mill
LANGTON BROW
SHELLEY DR
KEATS CL
Sherbourn House
LANGTON CL
Syd Brook
Lang's Farm
WRENNALLS LA
High Heys Farm
Woodcock La
Heskin Bridge
Thomson's Farm
Spring Wood
Knowles' Wood
WHALLEY RD
TANNERSMITH LA
Little Wood
Camelot Theme Pk
Heskin Hall
THE WATHINGS
HIGHGROVE AVE
YEWLANDS AVE
Heskin Old Hall Farm
Howe Brook
BANNISTER GN
Heskin Hall Farm
Pye Brook
Heskin Green
PARK HALL RD
HALL GREEN LA
PH
STOCKS CT
Green Farm
WOOD LA
STOCKS LA
HALFPENNY LA
Howe Brook House
Bimson's Farm
WITHINGTON LA
Salt Pit House
Pyebrook Hall
TOWN LA
THE MEADOWS
Heskin Pemberton's CE Prim Sch
CHISNALL LA
L40
School Farm
BARMSKIN LA
Andertons Mill
Barmskin Hall Farm
WN6
RIDLEY LA
DENTLEY LA
Kingsley House
SANDERSON LA
COOPER'S LA
BARMSKIN LA
WN6
CARR HOUSE LA
Brook House (PH)
8
17
7
6
5
16
4
3
15
2
1
14
51
52
53
28
42

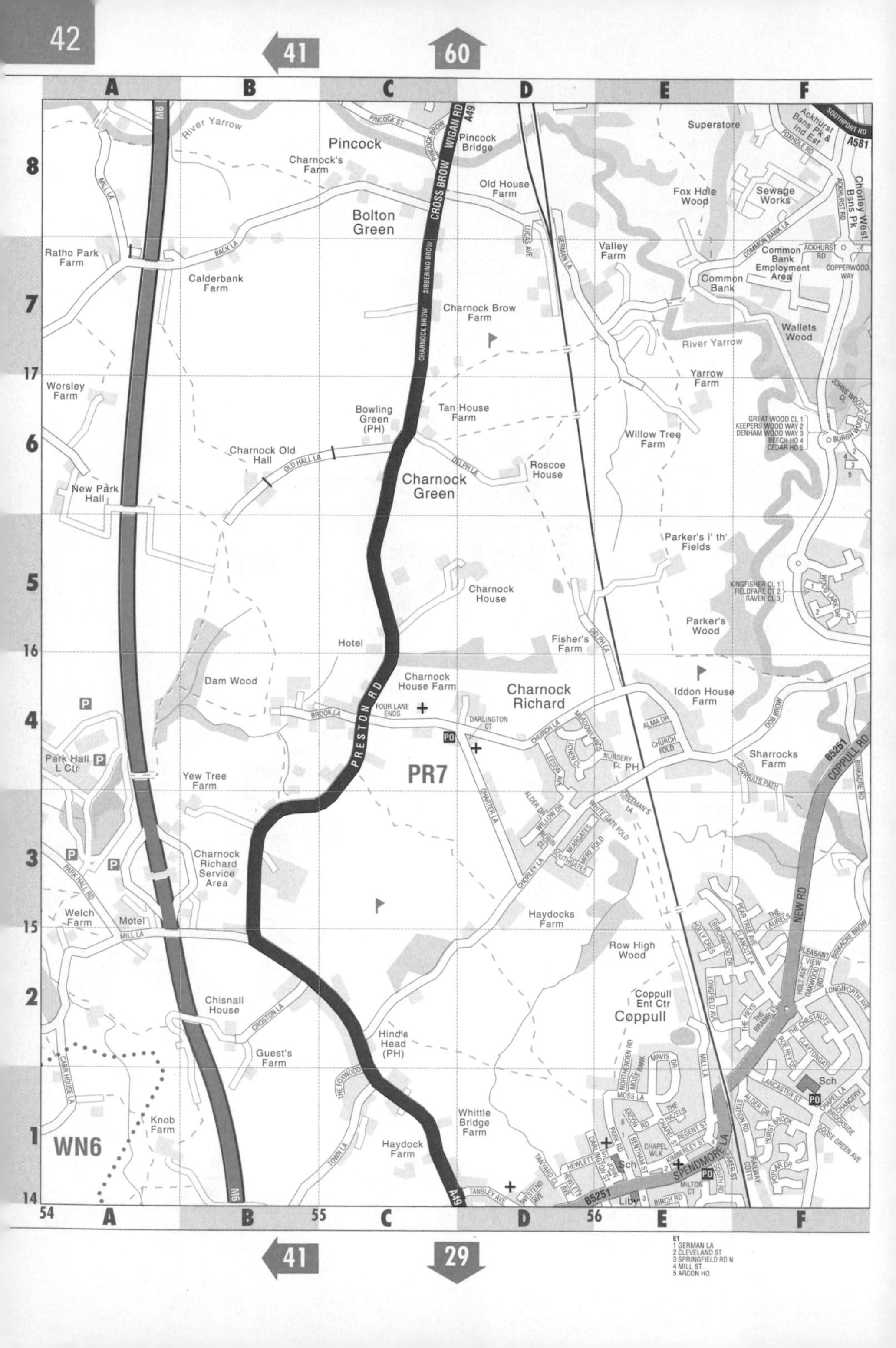
41
60
Pincock
Pincock Bridge
Charnock's Farm
River Yarrow
Old House Farm
Bolton Green
Superstore
Fox Hole Wood
Sewage Works
Ackhurst Bsns Pk & Ind Est
Chorley West Bsns Pk
A581
Ratho Park Farm
Calderbank Farm
Valley Farm
Common Bank
Common Bank Employment Area
Charnock Brow Farm
Wallets Wood
River Yarrow
Worsley Farm
Yarrow Farm
Bowling Green (PH)
Tan House Farm
Willow Tree Farm
Charnock Old Hall
Roscoe House
Charnock Green
New Park Hall
Parker's i' th' Fields
Charnock House
Parker's Wood
Hotel
Fisher's Farm
Dam Wood
Charnock House Farm
Charnock Richard
Iddon House Farm
Park Hall L Ctr
Yew Tree Farm
PR7
Sharrocks Farm
Charnock Richard Service Area
Welch Farm
Motel
Haydocks Farm
Row High Wood
Chisnall House
Coppull Ent Ctr
Coppull
Hind's Head (PH)
Guest's Farm
Knob Farm
Whittle Bridge Farm
Haydock Farm
WN6
Sch
Liby
M6
A49
B5251
41
29
E1
1 GERMAN LA
2 CLEVELAND ST
3 SPRINGFIELD RD N
4 MILL ST
5 ARCON HO

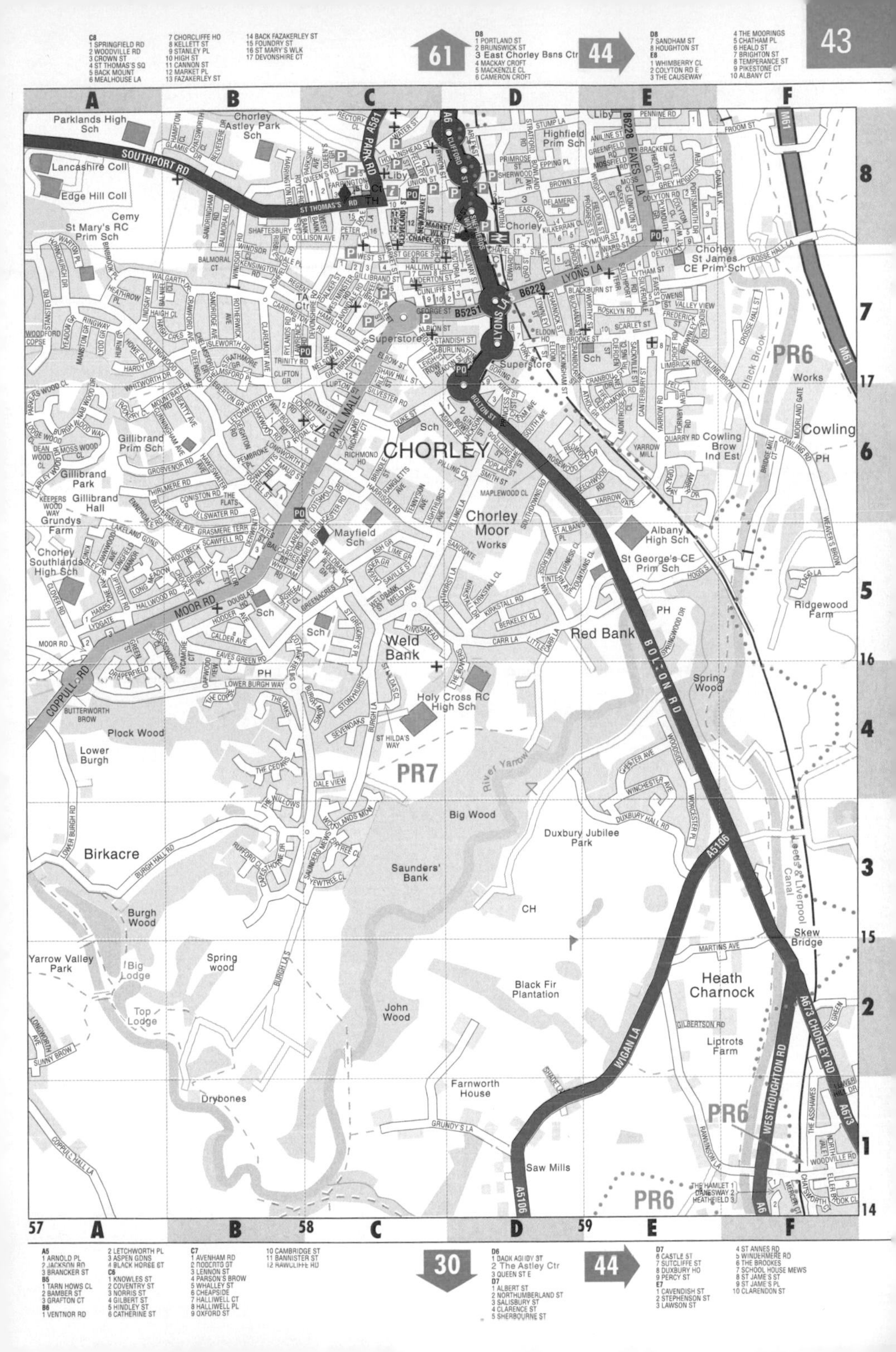

43
C8
1 SPRINGFIELD RD
2 WOODVILLE RD
3 CROWN ST
4 ST THOMAS'S SQ
5 BACK MOUNT
6 MEALHOUSE LA
7 CHORCLIFFE HO
8 KELLETT ST
9 STANLEY PL
10 HIGH ST
11 CANNON ST
12 MARKET PL
13 FAZAKERLEY ST
14 BACK FAZAKERLEY ST
15 FOUNDRY ST
16 ST MARY'S WLK
17 DEVONSHIRE CT
61
D8
1 PORTLAND ST
2 BRUNSWICK ST
3 East Chorley Bsns Ctr
4 MACKAY CROFT
5 MACKENZLE CL
6 CAMERON CROFT
44
D8
7 SANDHAM ST
8 HOUGHTON ST
E8
1 WHIMBERRY CL
2 COLYTON RD E
3 THE CAUSEWAY
4 THE MOORINGS
5 CHATHAM PL
6 HEALD ST
7 BRIGHTON ST
8 TEMPERANCE ST
9 PIKESTONE CT
10 ALBANY CT
Parklands High Sch
Chorley Astley Park Sch
Lancashire Coll
Edge Hill Coll
SOUTHPORT RD
Cemy
St Mary's RC Prim Sch
Highfield Prim Sch
Chorley
Chorley St James CE Prim Sch
LYONS LA
B6228
B5251
A6
A581
PARK RD
Superstore
PALL MALL
CHORLEY
Gillibrand Prim Sch
Gillibrand Park
Gillibrand Hall
Grundys Farm
Chorley Southlands High Sch
Mayfield Sch
Chorley Moor
Works
Albany High Sch
St George's CE Prim Sch
Cowling Brow Ind Est
Cowling
PR6
Black Brook
Ridgewood Farm
Red Bank
MOOR RD
Weld Bank
Holy Cross RC High Sch
Spring Wood
BOLTON RD
Plock Wood
Lower Burgh
PR7
River Yarrow
Big Wood
Duxbury Jubilee Park
Birkacre
Saunders' Bank
A5106
Leeds & Liverpool Canal
Burgh Wood
Skew Bridge
Yarrow Valley Park
Big Lodge
Spring wood
Black Fir Plantation
Heath Charnock
Top Lodge
John Wood
WIGAN LA
WESTHOUGHTON RD
A673 CHORLEY RD
Liptrots Farm
Farnworth House
Drybones
GRUNDY'S LA
Saw Mills
PR6
57
58
59
A
B
C
D
E
F
8
7
6
5
4
3
2
1
17
16
15
14
A5
1 ARNOLD PL
2 JACKSON RD
3 BRANCKER ST
B5
1 TARN HOWS CL
2 BAMBER ST
3 GRAFTON CT
B6
1 VENTNOR RD
2 LETCHWORTH PL
3 ASPEN GDNS
4 BLACK HORSE ST
C6
1 KNOWLES ST
2 COVENTRY ST
3 NORRIS ST
4 GILBERT ST
5 HINDLEY ST
6 CATHERINE ST
C7
1 AVENHAM RD
2 ROBERTS ST
3 LENNON ST
4 PARSON'S BROW
5 WHALLEY ST
6 CHEAPSIDE
7 HALLIWELL CT
8 HALLIWELL PL
9 OXFORD ST
10 CAMBRIDGE ST
11 BANNISTER ST
12 RAWCLIFFE RD
30
D6
1 BACK ASHBY ST
2 The Astley Ctr
3 QUEEN ST E
D7
1 ALBERT ST
2 NORTHUMBERLAND ST
3 SALISBURY ST
4 CLARENCE ST
5 SHERBOURNE ST
44
D7
6 CASTLE ST
7 SUTCLIFFE ST
8 DUXBURY HO
9 PERCY ST
E7
1 CAVENDISH ST
2 STEPHENSON ST
3 LAWSON ST
4 ST ANNES RD
5 WINDERMERE RD
6 THE BROOKES
7 SCHOOL HOUSE MEWS
8 ST JAME'S ST
9 ST JAME'S PL
10 CLARENDON ST

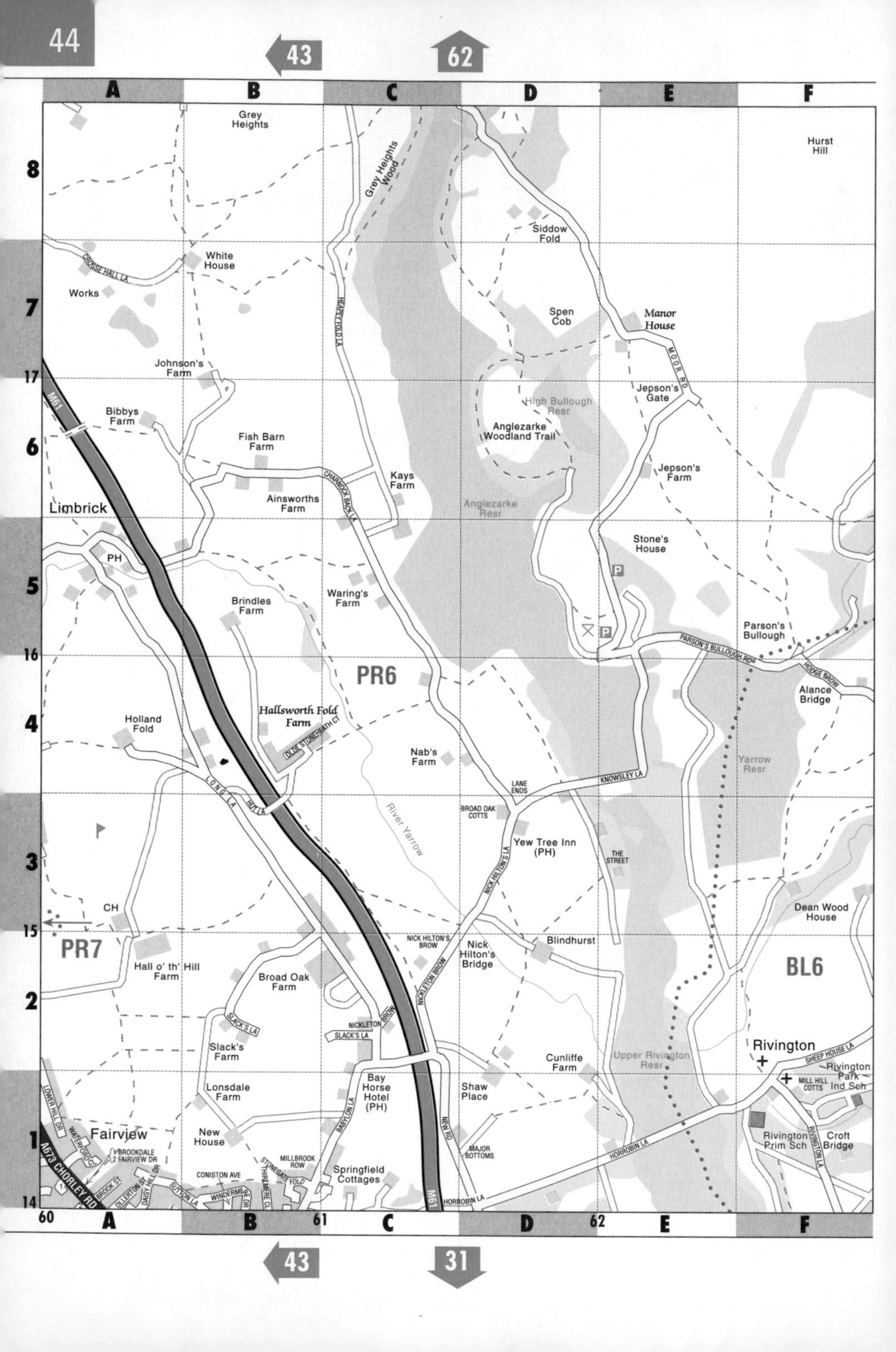

44
43
62
A
B
C
D
E
F
8
7
17
6
5
16
4
3
15
2
1
14
60
61
62
Grey Heights
Hurst Hill
Grey Heights Wood
Siddow Fold
White House
CROSSE HALL LA
Works
HEAPEY FOLD LA
Spen Cob
Manor House
MOOR RD
Johnson's Farm
M61
High Bullough Resr
Jepson's Gate
Bibbys Farm
Anglezarke Woodland Trail
Fish Barn Farm
Kays Farm
Jepson's Farm
CHARNOCK BACK LA
Limbrick
Ainsworths Farm
Anglezarke Resr
Stone's House
PH
Brindles Farm
Waring's Farm
Parson's Bullough
PARSON'S BULLOUGH RD
HODGE BROW
PR6
Alance Bridge
Hallsworth Fold Farm
Holland Fold
OLDE STONEHEATH CT
Nab's Farm
Yarrow Resr
LONG LA
HUT LA
LANE ENDS
KNOWSLEY LA
River Yarrow
BROAD OAK COTTS
Yew Tree Inn (PH)
NICK HILTON'S LA
THE STREET
CH
Dean Wood House
PR7
NICK HILTON'S BROW
Nick Hilton's Bridge
Blindhurst
Hall o' th' Hill Farm
Broad Oak Farm
NICKLETON BROW
BL6
SLACK'S LA
NICKLETON
Slack's Farm
Rivington
SHEEP HOUSE LA
Cunliffe Farm
Upper Rivington Resr
Rivington Park Ind Sch
MILL HILL COTTS
Lonsdale Farm
Bay Horse Hotel (PH)
Shaw Place
BABYLON LA
LOWER HILL DR
NEW RD
Fairview
New House
WATERFORD CL
1 BROOKDALE
2 FAIRVIEW DR
A673 CHORLEY RD
MILLBROOK ROW
MAJOR BOTTOMS
HORROBIN LA
Rivington Prim Sch
Croft Bridge
RIVINGTON LA
BROOK ST
OLLERTON ST
DAISY HILL DR
CONISTON AVE
STONEGATE FOLD
THIRLMERE CL
Springfield Cottages
SUTTON LA
WINDERMERE DR
31

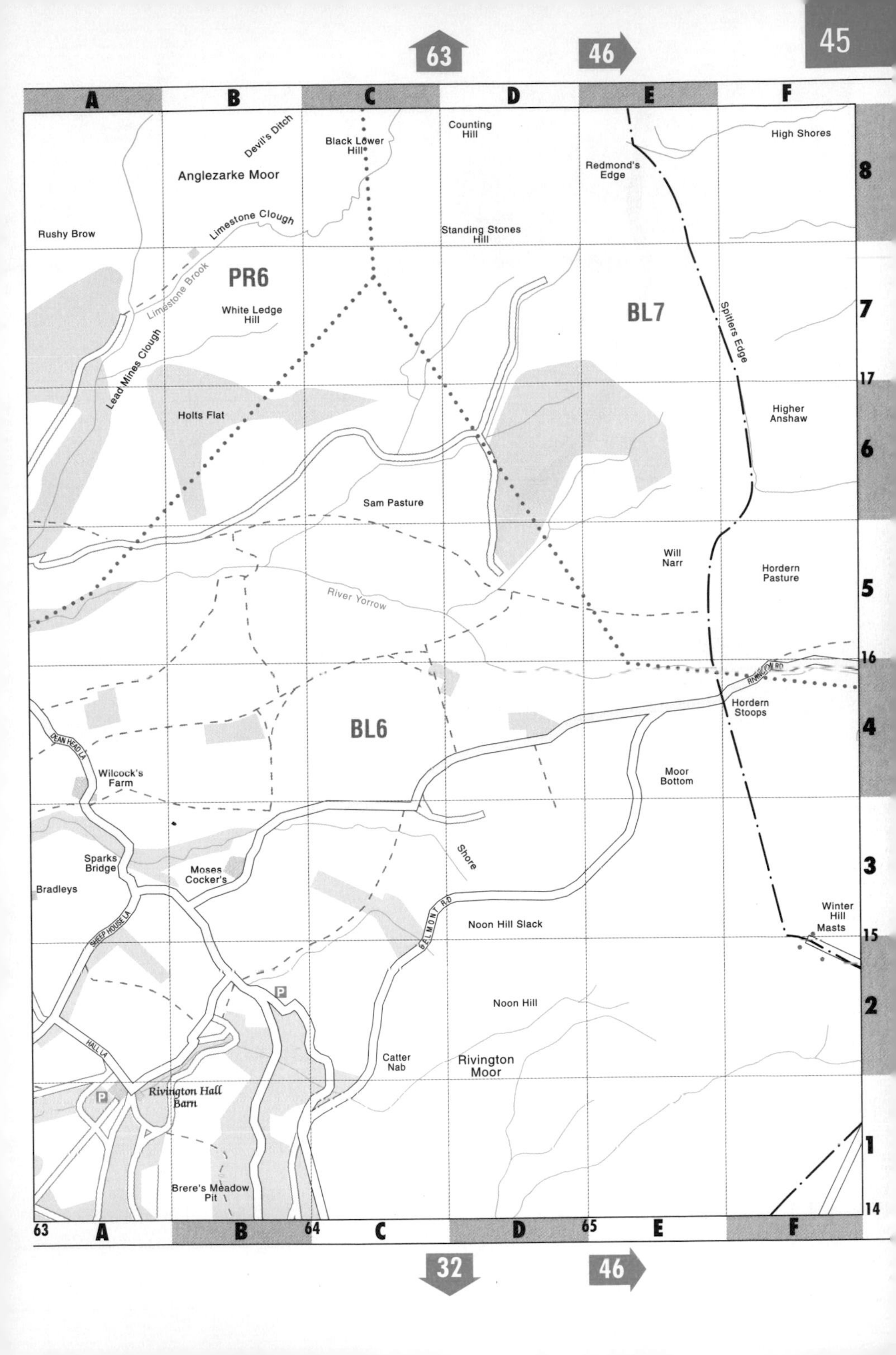
63
46
A
B
C
D
E
F
Devil's Ditch
Black Lower Hill
Counting Hill
High Shores
Anglezarke Moor
Redmond's Edge
8
Rushy Brow
Limestone Clough
Standing Stones Hill
PR6
Limestone Brook
White Ledge Hill
BL7
Spitlers Edge
7
Lead Mines Clough
17
Holts Flat
Higher Anshaw
6
Sam Pasture
Will Narr
Hordern Pasture
5
River Yorrow
16
RIVINGTON RD
Hordern Stoops
BL6
4
DEAN HEAD LA
Wilcock's Farm
Moor Bottom
Shore
Sparks Bridge
3
Moses Cocker's
Bradleys
BELMONT RD
Winter Hill Masts
Noon Hill Slack
SHEEP HOUSE LA
15
Noon Hill
2
HALL LA
Catter Nab
Rivington Moor
Rivington Hall Barn
1
Brere's Meadow Pit
14
63
A
B
64
C
D
65
E
F
32
46

45
64

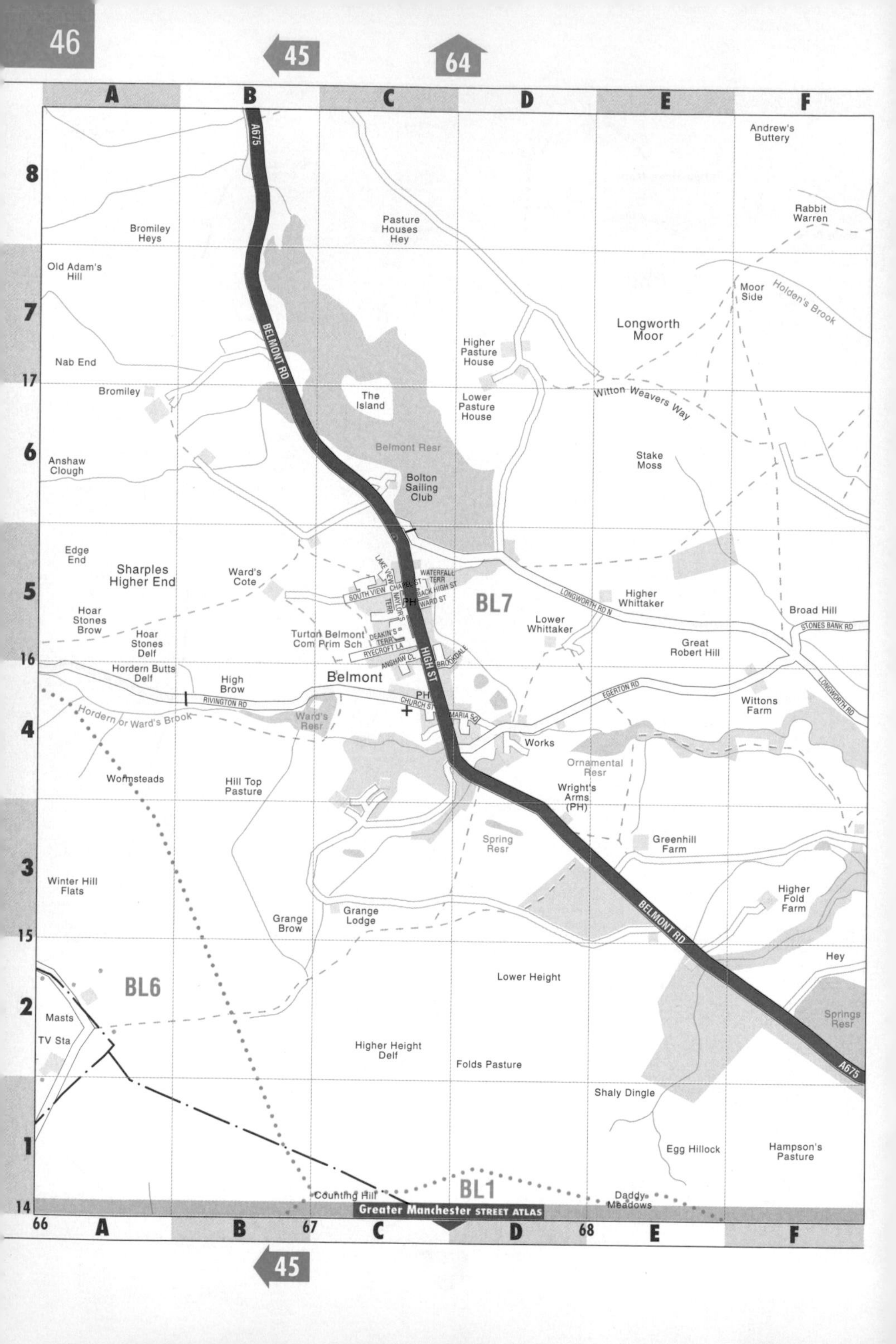
A
B
C
D
E
F
A675
Andrew's Buttery
Bromiley Heys
Pasture Houses Hey
Rabbit Warren
Old Adam's Hill
Moor Side
Holden's Brook
Longworth Moor
BELMONT RD
Higher Pasture House
Nab End
Bromiley
The Island
Lower Pasture House
Witton Weavers Way
Belmont Resr
Anshaw Clough
Bolton Sailing Club
Stake Moss
Edge End
Sharples Higher End
Ward's Cote
LAKE VIEW
WATERFALL TERR
CHAPEL ST
BACK HIGH ST
SOUTH VIEW
NAYLOR'S TERR
WARD ST
PH
BL7
LONGWORTH RD N
Higher Whittaker
Broad Hill
Hoar Stones Brow
Hoar Stones Delf
Turton Belmont Com Prim Sch
DEAKIN'S TERR
Lower Whittaker
STONES BANK RD
RYECROFT LA
HIGH ST
Great Robert Hill
ANSHAW CL
BROOKDALE
Hordern Butts Delf
High Brow
Belmont
EGERTON RD
LONGWORTH RD
RIVINGTON RD
CHURCH ST
MARIA SQ
Wittons Farm
Hordern or Ward's Brook
Ward's Resr
Works
Wormsteads
Hill Top Pasture
Ornamental Resr
Wright's Arms (PH)
Spring Resr
Greenhill Farm
Winter Hill Flats
Higher Fold Farm
Grange Brow
Grange Lodge
Hey
BL6
Lower Height
Masts
TV Sta
Springs Resr
Higher Height Delf
Folds Pasture
Shaly Dingle
Egg Hillock
Hampson's Pasture
Counting Hill
BL1
Daddy Meadows
8
7
17
6
5
16
4
3
15
2
1
14
66
67
68

45

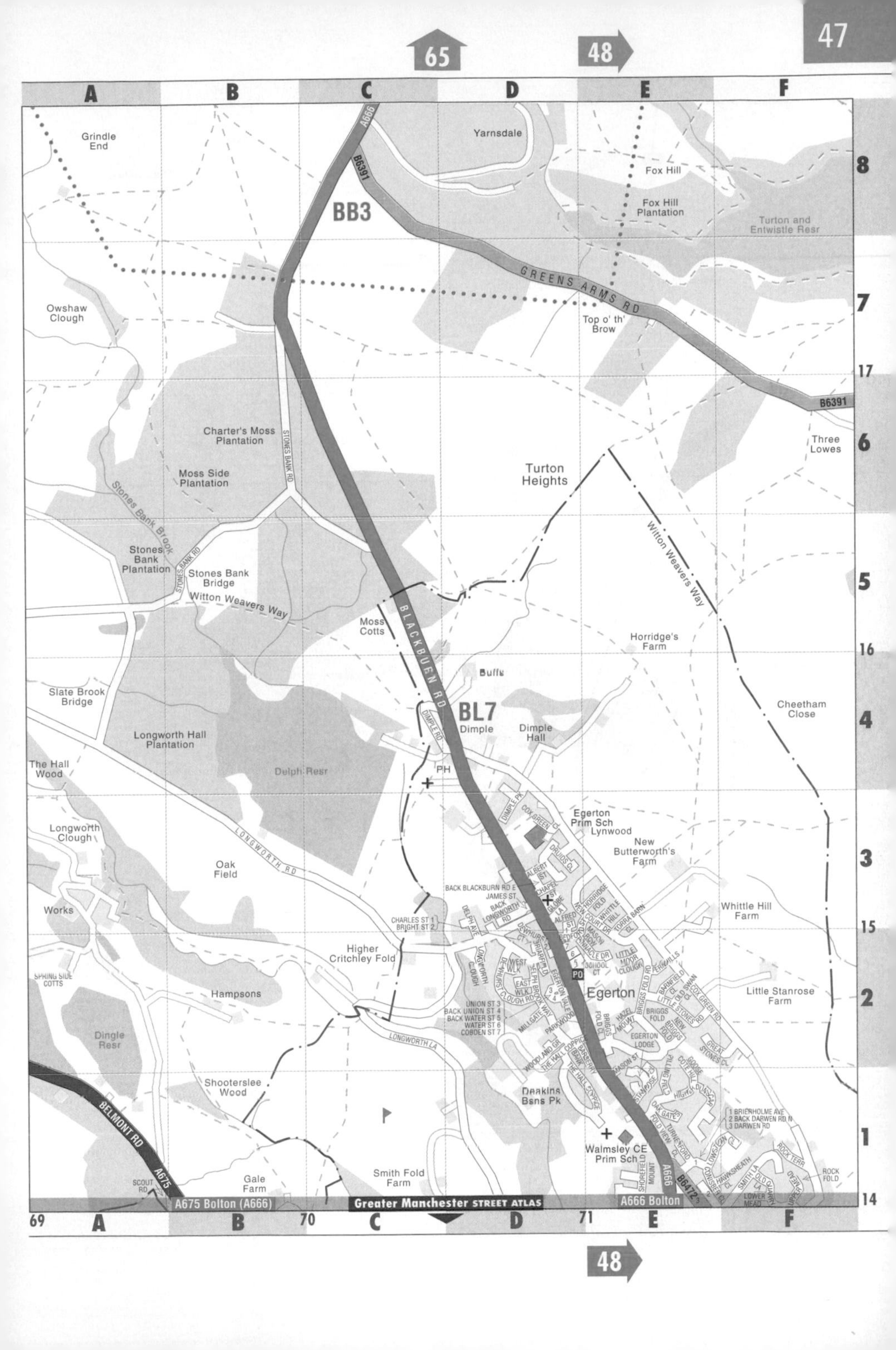
65
48
A
B
C
D
E
F
8
7
17
6
5
16
4
3
15
2
1
14
Grindle End
Yarnsdale
Fox Hill
Fox Hill Plantation
Turton and Entwistle Resr
BB3
A666
B6391
GREENS ARMS RD
Top o' th' Brow
Owshaw Clough
Charter's Moss Plantation
Moss Side Plantation
STONES BANK RD
Three Lowes
Turton Heights
Stones Bank Brook
Stones Bank Plantation
Stones Bank Bridge
Witton Weavers Way
Moss Cotts
BLACKBURN RD
Horridge's Farm
Buffs
Slate Brook Bridge
BL7
Dimple
Dimple Hall
DIMPLE RD
Cheetham Close
Longworth Hall Plantation
The Hall Wood
Delph Resr
PH
Egerton Prim Sch
Lynwood
New Butterworth's Farm
Longworth Clough
Oak Field
LONGWORTH RD
Works
Whittle Hill Farm
CHARLES ST 1
BRIGHT ST 2
Higher Critchley Fold
SPRING SIDE COTTS
Hampsons
Egerton
Little Stanrose Farm
UNION ST 3
BACK UNION ST 4
BACK WATER ST 5
WATER ST 6
COBDEN ST 7
LONGWORTH LA
Dingle Resr
Shooterslee Wood
Deakins Bsns Pk
BELMONT RD
A675
Walmsley CE Prim Sch
1 BRIERHOLME AVE
2 BACK DARWEN RD N
3 DARWEN RD
Gale Farm
Smith Fold Farm
SCOUT RD
ROCK TERR
ROCK FOLD
B6472
A675 Bolton (A666)
Greater Manchester STREET ATLAS
A666 Bolton
69
70
71

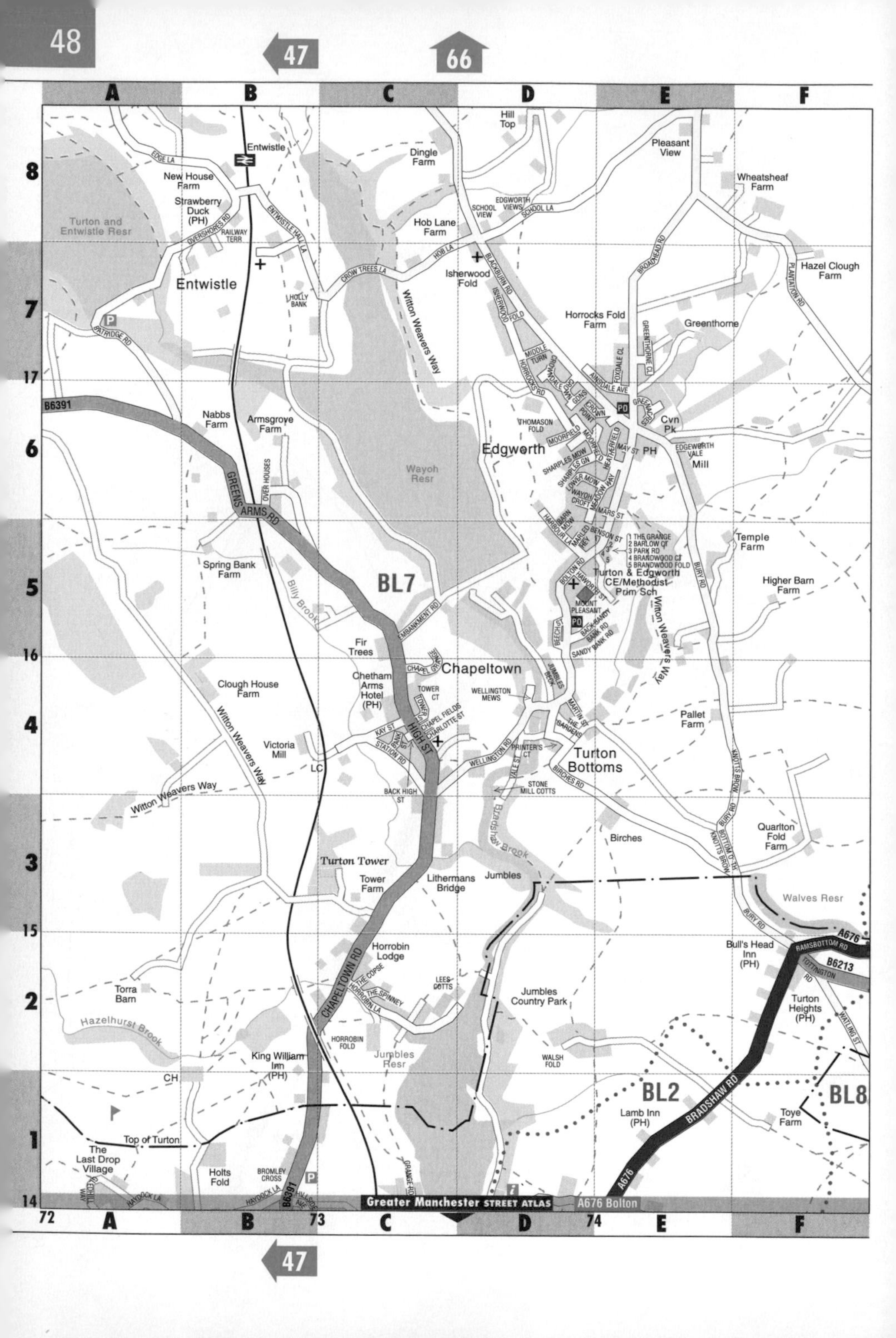

47
66
A
B
C
D
E
F
8
7
17
6
5
16
4
3
15
2
1
14
72
73
74
Hill Top
Entwistle
Dingle Farm
Pleasant View
EDGE LA
New House Farm
Wheatsheaf Farm
Strawberry Duck (PH)
Turton and Entwistle Resr
OVERSHORES RD
RAILWAY TERR
ENTWISTLE HALL LA
SCHOOL VIEW
EDGWORTH VIEWS
SCHOOL LA
Hob Lane Farm
HOB LA
BROADHEAD RD
PLANTATION RD
Hazel Clough Farm
Entwistle
HOLLY BANK
CROW TREES LA
Isherwood Fold
BLACKBURN RD
ISHERWOOD FOLD
Witton Weavers Way
Horrocks Fold Farm
Greenthorne
GREENTHORNE CL
FOXDALE CL
P
BATRIDGE RD
MIDDLE TURN
CROWNDALE
HORROCKS RD
AINSDALE AVE
GREENACRES
PO
Cvn Pk
B6391
Nabbs Farm
Armsgrove Farm
THOMASON FOLD
MOORFIELD
Edgworth
MAY ST
PH
EDGEWORTH VALE
Mill
SHARPLES MDW
SHARPLES GN
HEATHERFIELD
Wayoh Resr
OVER HOUSES
GREENS ARMS RD
LOWER MDW
WAYOH CROFT
MEADOW WAY
MARS ST
BARN MDW
HARBOUR LA
MARLED HEY
BENSON ST
1 THE GRANGE
2 BARLOW CT
3 PARK RD
4 BRANDWOOD CT
5 BRANDWOOD FOLD
Temple Farm
Spring Bank Farm
BOLTON RD
HAWORTH ST
Turton & Edgworth CE/Methodist Prim Sch
BURY RD
Higher Barn Farm
BL7
Billy Brook
EMBANKMENT RD
MOUNT PLEASANT
BACK SANDY BANK RD
SANDY BANK RD
BEECH ST
Fir Trees
Chapeltown
Clough House Farm
Chetham Arms Hotel (PH)
TOWER CT
WELLINGTON MEWS
JUMBLES BECK
Pallet Farm
Witton Weavers Way
Victoria Mill
KAY ST
HIGH ST
CHAPEL FIELDS
CHARLOTTE ST
STATION RD
MARTIN ST
THE GARDENS
Turton Bottoms
PRINTER'S CT
WELLINGTON RD
VALE ST
LC
Witton Weavers Way
BACK HIGH ST
STONE MILL COTTS
BIRCHES RD
KNOTTS BROW
Bradshaw Brook
Birches
Qarlton Fold Farm
Turton Tower
Tower Farm
Lithermans Bridge
Jumbles
Walves Resr
BURY RD
A676
RAMSBOTTOM RD
Horrobin Lodge
Bull's Head Inn (PH)
B6213
TOTTINGTON RD
CHAPELTOWN RD
THE COPSE
THE SPINNEY
HORROBIN LA
LEES COTTS
Torra Barn
Jumbles Country Park
Turton Heights (PH)
WATLING ST
Hazelhurst Brook
HORROBIN FOLD
Jumbles Resr
King William Inn (PH)
WALSH FOLD
CH
BL2
BRADSHAW RD
BL8
Lamb Inn (PH)
Toye Farm
Top of Turton
The Last Drop Village
Holts Fold
BROMLEY CROSS
HAYDOCK LA
GRANGE RD
Greater Manchester STREET ATLAS
A676 Bolton

47

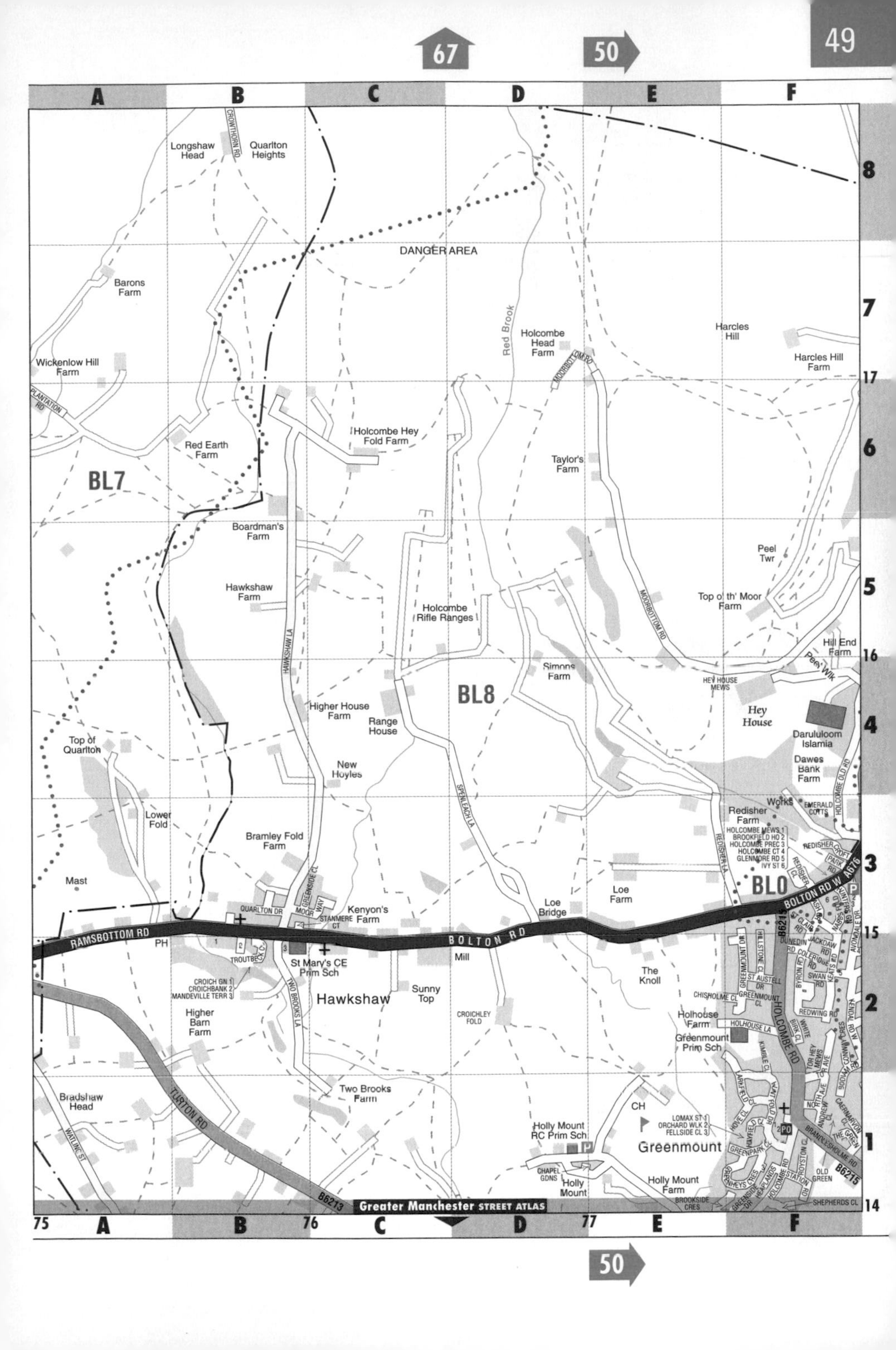

67
50
A
B
C
D
E
F
8
7
17
6
5
16
4
3
15
2
1
14
75
76
77
Longshaw Head
Quarlton Heights
CROWTHORN RD
DANGER AREA
Barons Farm
Wickenlow Hill Farm
PLANTATION RD
Red Earth Farm
BL7
Holcombe Hey Fold Farm
Red Brook
Holcombe Head Farm
MOORBOTTOM RD
Harcles Hill
Harcles Hill Farm
Taylor's Farm
Boardman's Farm
Hawkshaw Farm
Holcombe Rifle Ranges
Peel Twr
Top o' th' Moor Farm
Hill End Farm
Peel Wlk
HEY HOUSE MEWS
Simons Farm
BL8
Hey House
Darululoom Islamia
Higher House Farm
Range House
Top of Quarlton
New Hoyles
Dawes Bank Farm
HOLCOMBE OLD RD
Lower Fold
Works
EMERALD COTTS
Redisher Farm
Bramley Fold Farm
HOLCOMBE MEWS 1
BROOKFIELD HO 2
HOLCOMBE PREC 3
HOLCOMBE CT 4
GLENMORE RD 5
IVY ST 6
REDISHER CROFT
REDISHER LA
Mast
Loe Farm
BL0
Kenyon's Farm
QUARLTON DR
GREENSIDE CL
MOOR WAY
STANMERE CT
Loe Bridge
BOLTON RD W A676
RAMSBOTTOM RD
PH
BOLTON RD
TROUTBECK CL
St Mary's CE Prim Sch
Mill
The Knoll
GREENMOUNT DR
HILLSTONE CL
ST AUSTELL DR
GREENMOUNT CL
CHISHOLME CL
CROICH GN 1
CROICHBANK 2
MANDEVILLE TERR 3
TWO BROOKS LA
HAWKSHAW LA
SPENLEACH LA
Hawkshaw
Sunny Top
Higher Barn Farm
CROICHLEY FOLD
Holhouse Farm
HOLHOUSE LA
Greenmount Prim Sch
HOLCOMBE RD
B6215
Bradshaw Head
Two Brooks Farm
CH
TURTON RD
WATLING ST
Holly Mount RC Prim Sch
LOMAX ST 1
ORCHARD WLK 2
FELLSIDE CL 3
Greenmount
CHAPEL GDNS
Holly Mount
Holly Mount Farm
BROOKSIDE CRES
B6213
SHEPHERDS CL
OLD GREEN

50

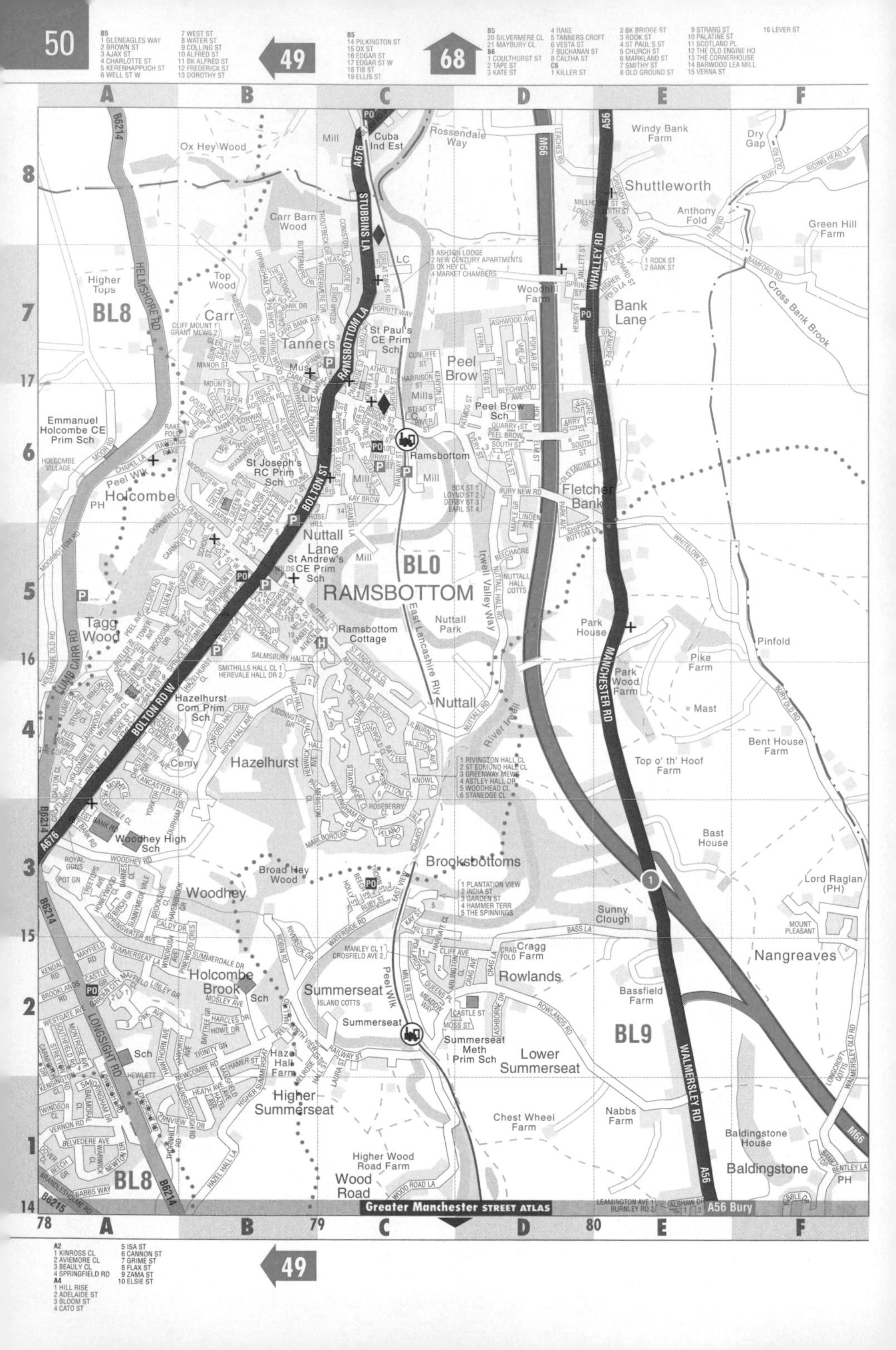

50
B5
1 GLENEAGLES WAY
2 BROWN ST
3 AJAX ST
4 CHARLOTTE ST
5 KERENHAPPUCH ST
6 WELL ST W
7 WEST ST
8 WATER ST
9 COLLING ST
10 ALFRED ST
11 BK ALFRED ST
12 FREDERICK ST
13 DOROTHY ST
49
B5
14 PILKINGTON ST
15 OX ST
16 EDGAR ST
17 EDGAR ST W
18 TIB ST
19 ELLIS ST
68
B5
20 SILVERMERE CL
21 MAYBURY CL
B6
1 COULTHURST ST
2 TAPE ST
3 KATE ST
4 RAKE
5 TANNERS CROFT
6 VESTA ST
7 BUCHANAN ST
8 CALTHA ST
C6
1 KILLER ST
2 BK BRIDGE ST
3 ROOK ST
4 ST PAUL'S ST
5 CHURCH ST
6 MARKLAND ST
7 SMITHY ST
8 OLD GROUND ST
9 STRANG ST
10 PALATINE ST
11 SCOTLAND PL
12 THE OLD ENGINE HO
13 THE CORNERHOUSE
14 BARWOOD LEA MILL
15 VERNA ST
16 LEVER ST
A
B
C
D
E
F
8
7
17
6
5
16
4
3
15
2
1
14
Ox Hey Wood
Mill
Cuba Ind Est
Rossendale Way
Windy Bank Farm
Dry Gap
Shuttleworth
Anthony Fold
Green Hill Farm
Carr Barn Wood
STUBBINS LA
Higher Tops
Top Wood
BL8
Carr
Tanners
St Paul's CE Prim Sch
Peel Brow
Woodhill Farm
Bank Lane
Cross Bank Brook
1 ASHTON LODGE
2 NEW CENTURY APARTMENTS
3 OX HEY CL
4 MARKET CHAMBERS
1 ROCK ST
2 BANK ST
Emmanuel Holcombe CE Prim Sch
Mus
Liby
Mills
Peel Brow Sch
Ramsbottom
St Joseph's RC Prim Sch
Holcombe
Fletcher Bank
HELMSHORE RD
RAMSBOTTOM LA
BOLTON ST
WHALLEY RD
M66
A56
A676
B6214
Nuttall Lane
St Andrew's CE Prim Sch
BL0
RAMSBOTTOM
Irwell Valley Way
East Lancashire Rly
Tagg Wood
Ramsbottom Cottage
Nuttall Park
Park House
Pinfold
Pike Farm
Park Wood Farm
Mast
Nuttall
Hazelhurst Com Prim Sch
River Irwell
BOLTON RD W
MANCHESTER RD
Hazelhurst
Cemy
Bent House Farm
Top o' th' Hoof Farm
1 RIVINGTON HALL CL
2 ST EDMUND HALL CL
3 GREENWAY MEWS
4 ASTLEY HALL DR
5 WOODHEAD CL
6 STANEDGE CL
Woodhey High Sch
Bast House
Brooksbottoms
Broad Hey Wood
Woodhey
Lord Raglan (PH)
1 PLANTATION VIEW
2 INDIA ST
3 GARDEN ST
4 HAMMER TERR
5 THE SPINNINGS
Sunny Clough
Cragg Farm
Nangreaves
Holcombe Brook
Sch
Summerseat
Rowlands
Bassfield Farm
MANLEY CL 1
CROSFIELD AVE 2
LONGSIGHT RD
Summerseat Meth Prim Sch
Lower Summerseat
BL9
Hazel Hall Farm
Higher Summerseat
WALMERSLEY RD
Chest Wheel Farm
Nabbs Farm
Baldingstone House
Higher Wood Road Farm
Wood Road
Baldingstone
BL8
Greater Manchester STREET ATLAS
A56 Bury
LEAMINGTON AVE 1
BURNLEY RD 2
78
79
80
A2
1 KINROSS CL
2 AVIEMORE CL
3 BEAULY CL
4 SPRINGFIELD RD
5 ISA ST
6 CANNON ST
7 GRIME ST
8 FLAX ST
9 ZAMA ST
10 ELSIE ST
A4
1 HILL RISE
2 ADELAIDE ST
3 BLOOM ST
4 CATO ST
49

69

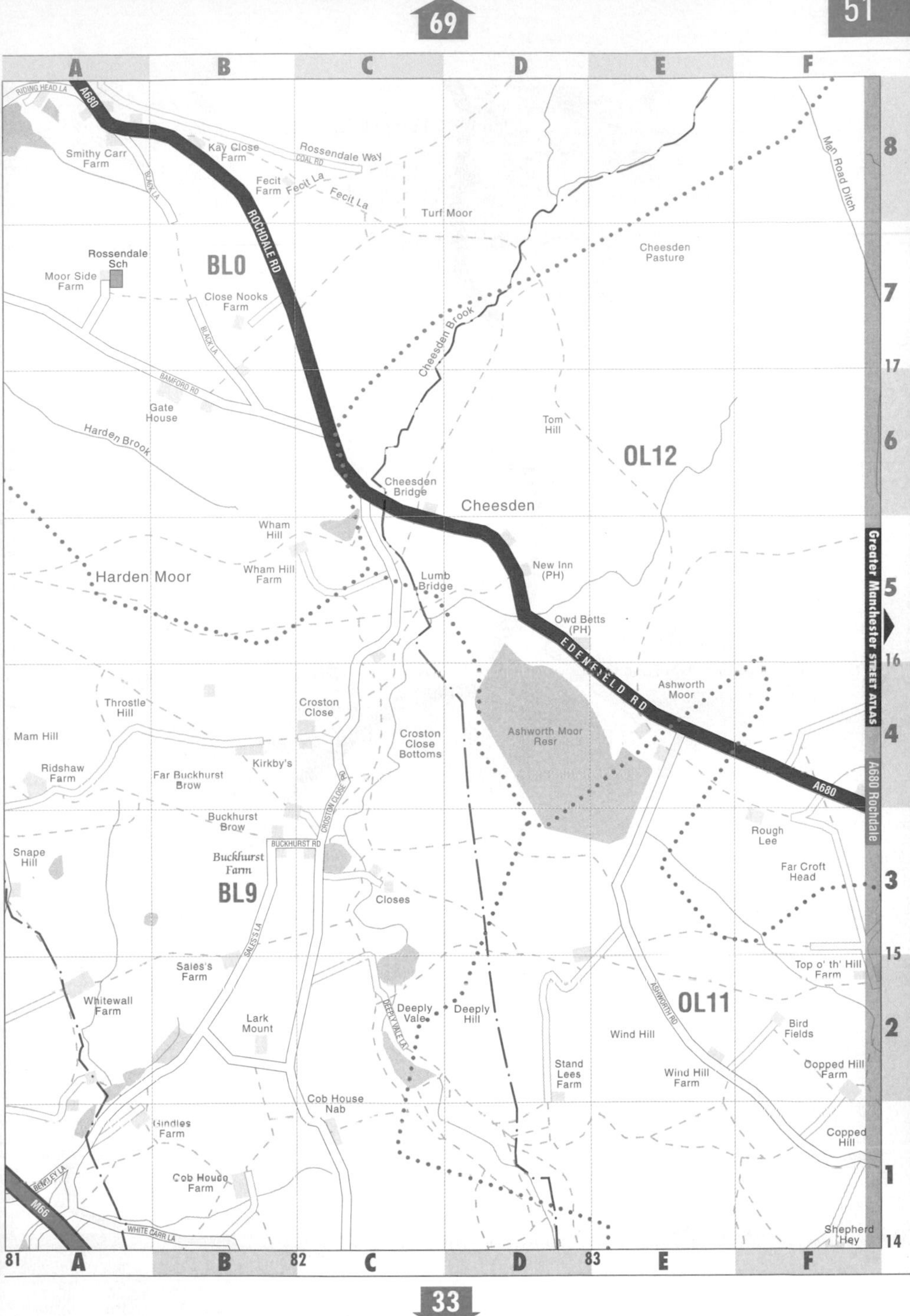
A
B
C
D
E
F
8
7
17
6
5
16
4
3
15
2
1
14
81
82
83
RIDING HEAD LA
A680
Smithy Carr Farm
BLACK LA
Kay Close Farm
Rossendale Way
COAL RD
Fecit Farm
Fecit La
Turf Moor
Man Road Ditch
ROCHDALE RD
Rossendale Sch
Moor Side Farm
BL0
Close Nooks Farm
Cheesden Pasture
Cheesden Brook
BAMFORD RD
Gate House
Harden Brook
Tom Hill
OL12
Cheesden Bridge
Cheesden
Wham Hill
Harden Moor
Wham Hill Farm
Lumb Bridge
New Inn (PH)
Owd Betts (PH)
EDENFIELD RD
Ashworth Moor
Throstle Hill
Croston Close
Mam Hill
Croston Close Bottoms
Ashworth Moor Resr
Ridshaw Farm
Far Buckhurst Brow
Kirkby's
CROSTON CLOSE RD
Buckhurst Brow
BUCKHURST RD
Rough Lee
Snape Hill
Buckhurst Farm
BL9
Far Croft Head
Closes
SALES'S LA
Sales's Farm
Top o' th' Hill Farm
Whitewall Farm
ASHWORTH RD
OL11
Deeply Vale
Deeply Hill
DEEPLY VALE LA
Lark Mount
Wind Hill
Bird Fields
Stand Lees Farm
Wind Hill Farm
Copped Hill Farm
Cob House Nab
Gindles Farm
Copped Hill
Cob House Farm
BENTLEY LA
M66
WHITE CARR LA
Shepherd Hey
Greater Manchester STREET ATLAS
A680 Rochdale

33

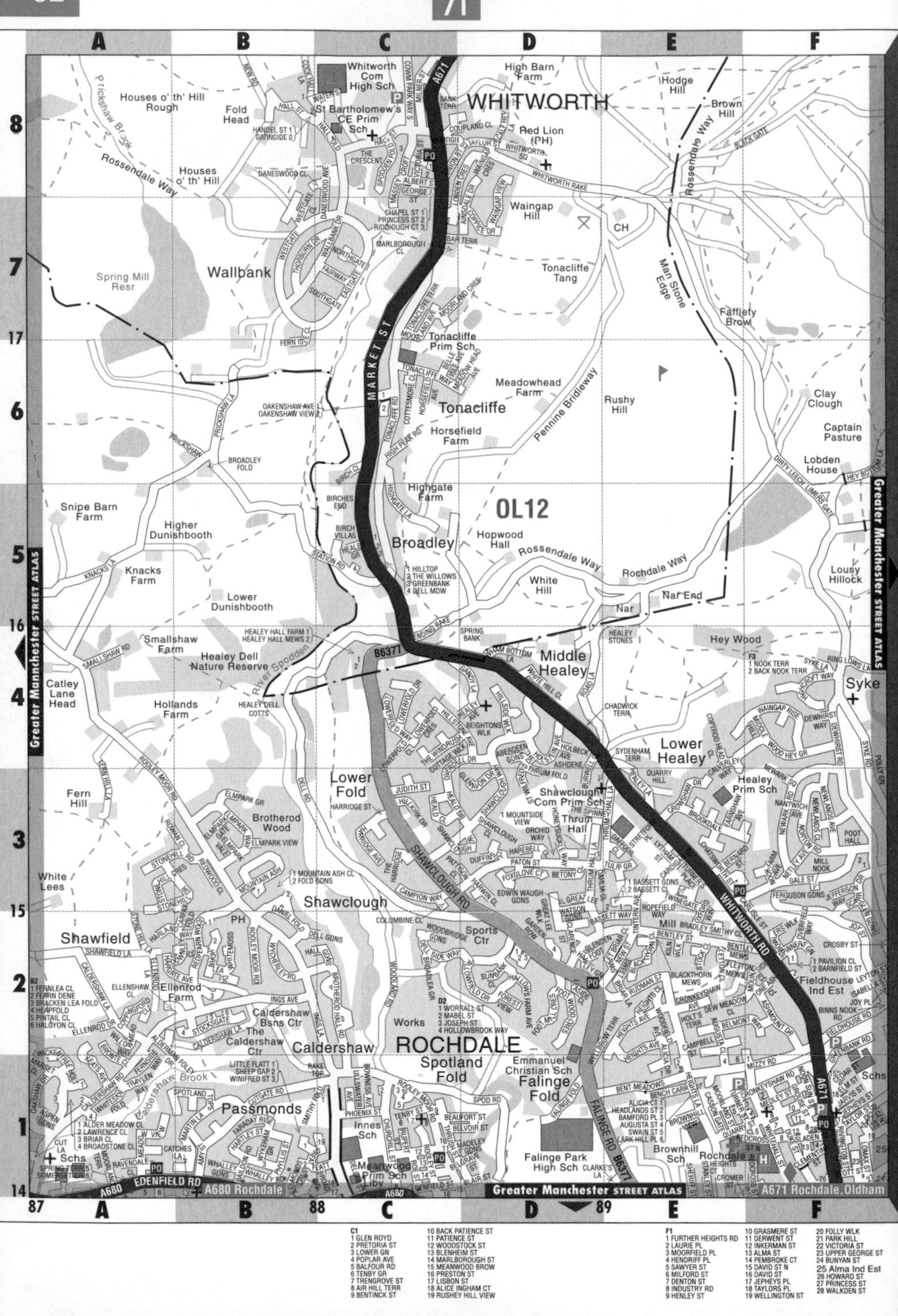

C1
1 GLEN ROYD
2 PRETORIA ST
3 LOWER GN
4 POPLAR AVE
5 BALFOUR RD
6 TENBY GR
7 TRENGROVE ST
8 AIR HILL TERR
9 BENTINCK ST
10 BACK PATIENCE ST
11 PATIENCE ST
12 WOODSTOCK ST
13 BLENHEIM ST
14 MARLBOROUGH ST
15 MEANWOOD BROW
16 PRESTON ST
17 LISBON ST
18 ALICE INGHAM CT
19 RUSHEY HILL VIEW

F1
1 FURTHER HEIGHTS RD
2 LAURIE PL
3 MOORFIELD PL
4 HENDRIFF PL
5 SAWYER ST
6 MILFORD ST
7 DENTON ST
8 INDUSTRY RD
9 HENLEY ST
10 GRASMERE ST
11 DERWENT ST
12 INKERMAN ST
13 ALMA ST
14 PEMBROKE CT
15 DAVID ST N
16 DAVID ST
17 JEPHEYS PL
18 TAYLORS PL
19 WELLINGTON ST
20 FOLLY WLK
21 PARK HILL
22 VICTORIA ST
23 UPPER GEORGE ST
24 BUNYAN ST
25 Alma Ind Est
26 HOWARD ST
27 PRINCESS ST
28 WALKDEN ST

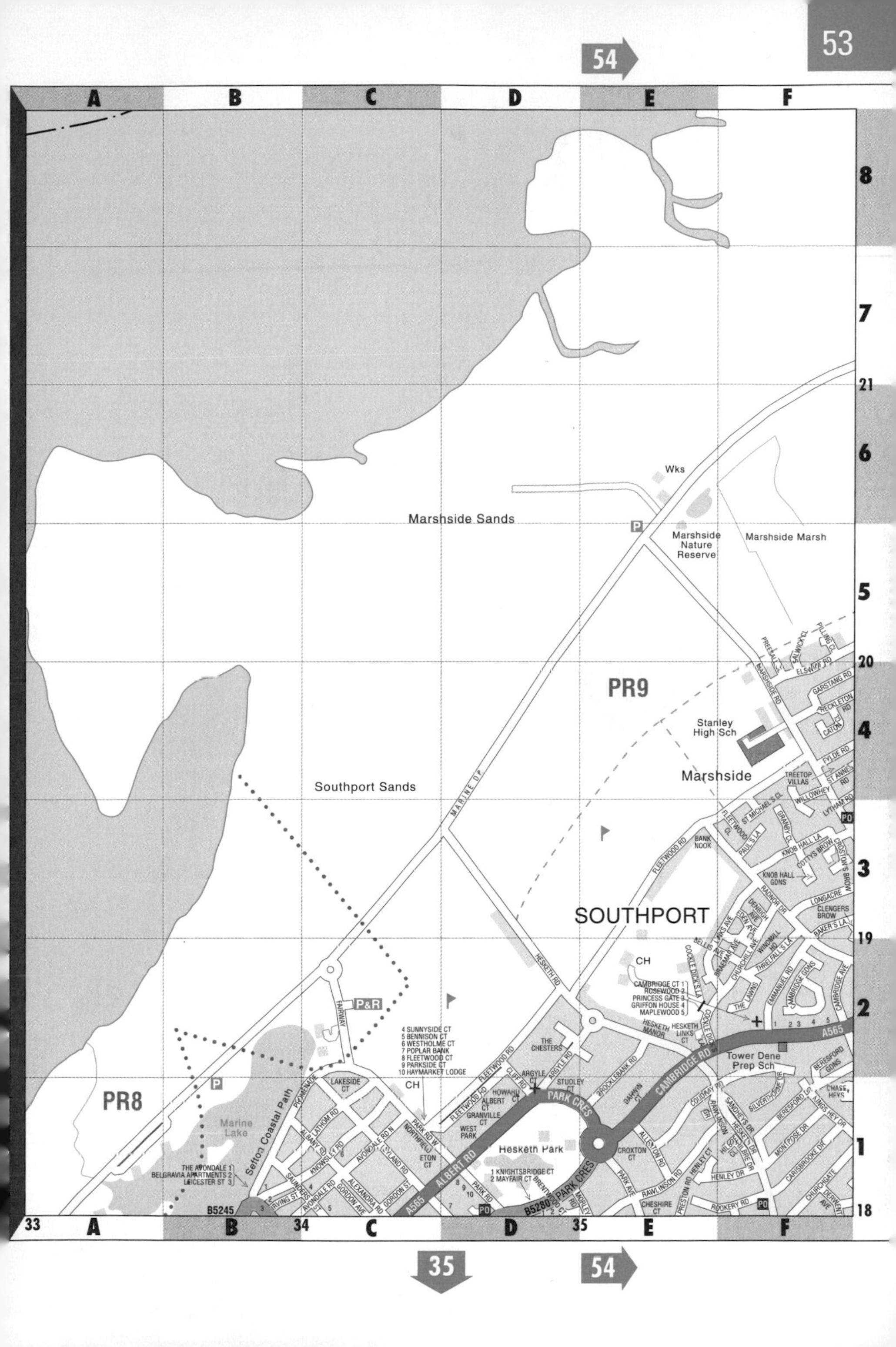

54
A
B
C
D
E
F
8
7
21
6
5
20
4
3
19
2
1
18
33
34
35
35
54
Wks
Marshside Sands
Marshside Nature Reserve
Marshside Marsh
PR9
Stanley High Sch
Marshside
Southport Sands
MARINE DR
SOUTHPORT
HESKETH RD
FLEETWOOD RD
CH
CAMBRIDGE CT 1
ROSEWOOD 2
PRINCESS GATE 3
GRIFFON HOUSE 4
MAPLEWOOD 5
Tower Dene Prep Sch
CAMBRIDGE RD
A565
PARK CRES
Hesketh Park
ALBERT RD
P&R
FAIRWAY
PR8
Marine Lake
Sefton Coastal Path
4 SUNNYSIDE CT
5 BENNISON CT
6 WESTHOLME CT
7 POPLAR BANK
8 FLEETWOOD CT
9 PARKSIDE CT
10 HAYMARKET LODGE
THE AVONDALE 1
BELGRAVIA APARTMENTS 2
LEICESTER ST 3
1 KNIGHTSBRIDGE CT
2 MAYFAIR CT
B5245
B5280
THE CHESTERS
LAKESIDE CT
ETON CT
WEST PARK
CROXTON CT
CHESHIRE CT
HESKETH MANOR
HESKETH LINKS CT
BANK NOOK
TREETOP VILLAS
KNOB HALL GDNS
CLENGERS BROW

53

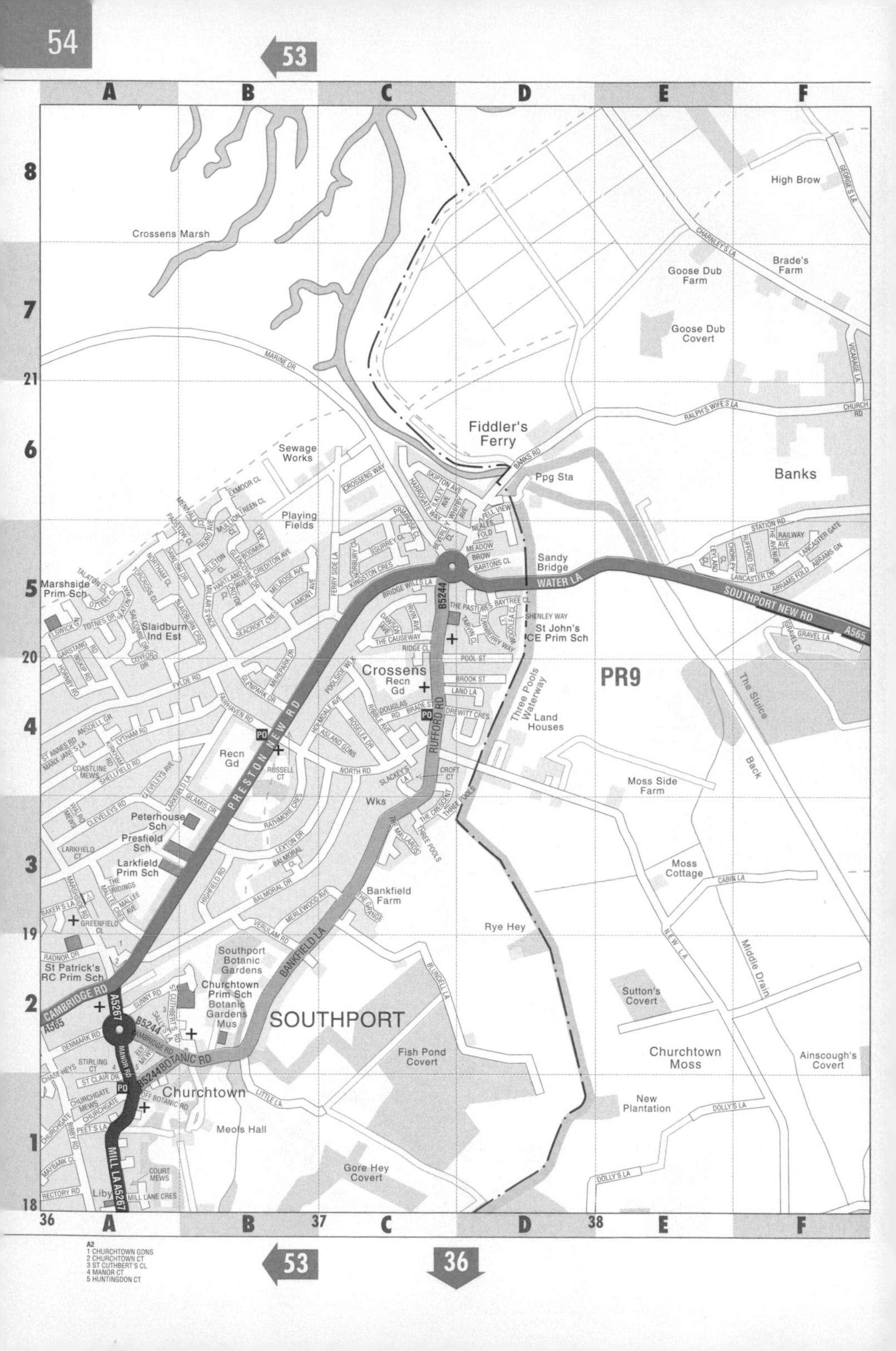
Crossens Marsh
High Brow
Brade's Farm
Goose Dub Farm
Goose Dub Covert
Fiddler's Ferry
Sewage Works
Ppg Sta
Banks
Playing Fields
Sandy Bridge
WATER LA
SOUTHPORT NEW RD
A565
Marshside Prim Sch
Slaidburn Ind Est
St John's CE Prim Sch
Crossens
Recn Gd
PR9
The Sluice
Three Pools Waterway
Land Houses
Recn Gd
PRESTON NEW RD
RUFFORD RD
B5244
Moss Side Farm
Back
Wks
Peterhouse Sch
Presfield Sch
Larkfield Prim Sch
Moss Cottage
Bankfield Farm
Rye Hey
Middle Drain
Southport Botanic Gardens
Churchtown Prim Sch
Botanic Gardens Mus
St Patrick's RC Prim Sch
CAMBRIDGE RD
SOUTHPORT
Sutton's Covert
Fish Pond Covert
Churchtown Moss
Ainscough's Covert
Churchtown
New Plantation
Meols Hall
Gore Hey Covert
MILL LA A5267
Liby
A2
1 CHURCHTOWN GDNS
2 CHURCHTOWN CT
3 ST CUTHBERT'S CL
4 MANOR CT
5 HUNTINGDON CT

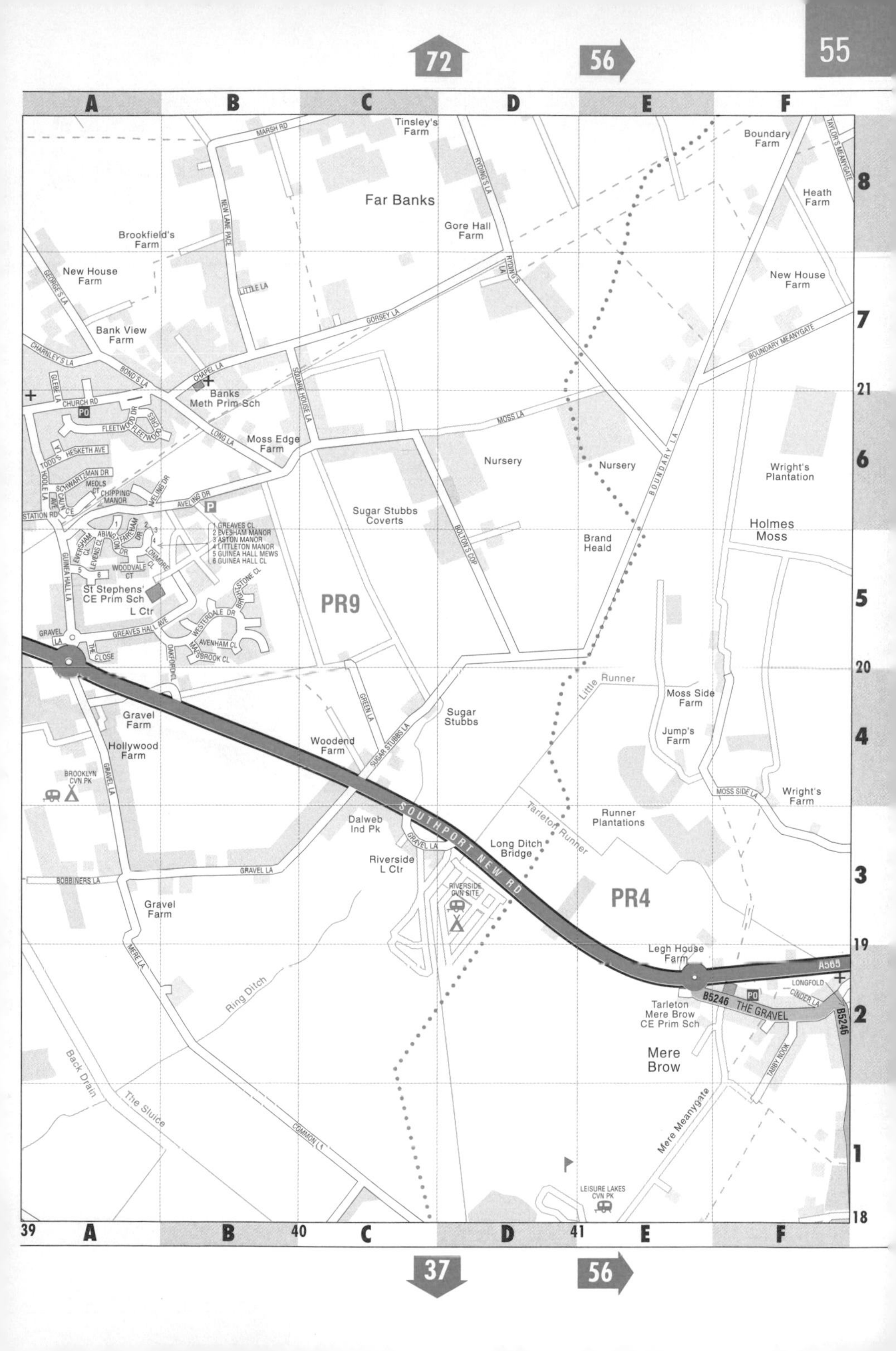
72
56
A
B
C
D
E
F
Tinsley's Farm
MARSH RD
Boundary Farm
TAYLOR'S MEANYGATE
Far Banks
Heath Farm
Brookfield's Farm
Gore Hall Farm
RYDING'S LA
NEW LANE PACE
New House Farm
GEORGE'S LA
LITTLE LA
New House Farm
Bank View Farm
GORSEY LA
BOUNDARY MEANYGATE
CHARLEY'S LA
CHAPEL LA
SQUARE HOUSE LA
BOND'S LA
GLEBE LA
Banks Meth Prim Sch
CHURCH RD
PO
MOSS LA
FLEETWOOD DR
FLEETWOOD CRES
LONG LA
Moss Edge Farm
HESKETH AVE
TODD'S LA
BOUNDARY LA
Nursery
Nursery
Wright's Plantation
SCHWARTZMAN DR
MEOLS CT
CHIPPING MANOR
AVELING DR
HOOLE LA
CALVIN AVE
STATION RD
P
Sugar Stubbs Coverts
Holmes Moss
1 GREAVES CL
2 EVESHAM MANOR
3 ASTON MANOR
4 LITTLETON MANOR
5 GUINEA HALL MEWS
6 GUINEA HALL CL
Brand Heald
BOLTON'S COP
EVESHAM CL
ABINGTON DR
FAREHAM DR
LONMORE CL
WOODVALE CT
GUINEA HALL LA
BRIGHTSTONE CL
St Stephens' CE Prim Sch
L Ctr
PR9
WESTERDALE DR
GRAVEL LA
GREAVES HALL AVE
AVENHAM CL
THE CLOSE
MAESBROOK CL
OAKFORD CL
Little Runner
Moss Side Farm
Gravel Farm
Sugar Stubbs
GREEN LA
Jump's Farm
Hollywood Farm
Woodend Farm
SUGAR STUBBS LA
BROOKLYN CVN PK
GRAVEL LA
MOSS SIDE LA
Wright's Farm
SOUTHPORT NEW RD
Dalweb Ind Pk
Tarleton Runner
Runner Plantations
GRAVEL LA
Long Ditch Bridge
Riverside L Ctr
BOBBINERS LA
GRAVEL LA
RIVERSIDE CVN SITE
PR4
Gravel Farm
MERE LA
Legh House Farm
A565
LONGFOLD
PO
CINDER LA
B5246
THE GRAVEL
B5246
Ring Ditch
Tarleton Mere Brow CE Prim Sch
Mere Brow
TABBY NOOK
Back Drain
The Sluice
Mere Meanygate
COMMON LA
LEISURE LAKES CVN PK
8
7
21
6
5
20
4
3
19
2
1
18
39
40
41
37
56

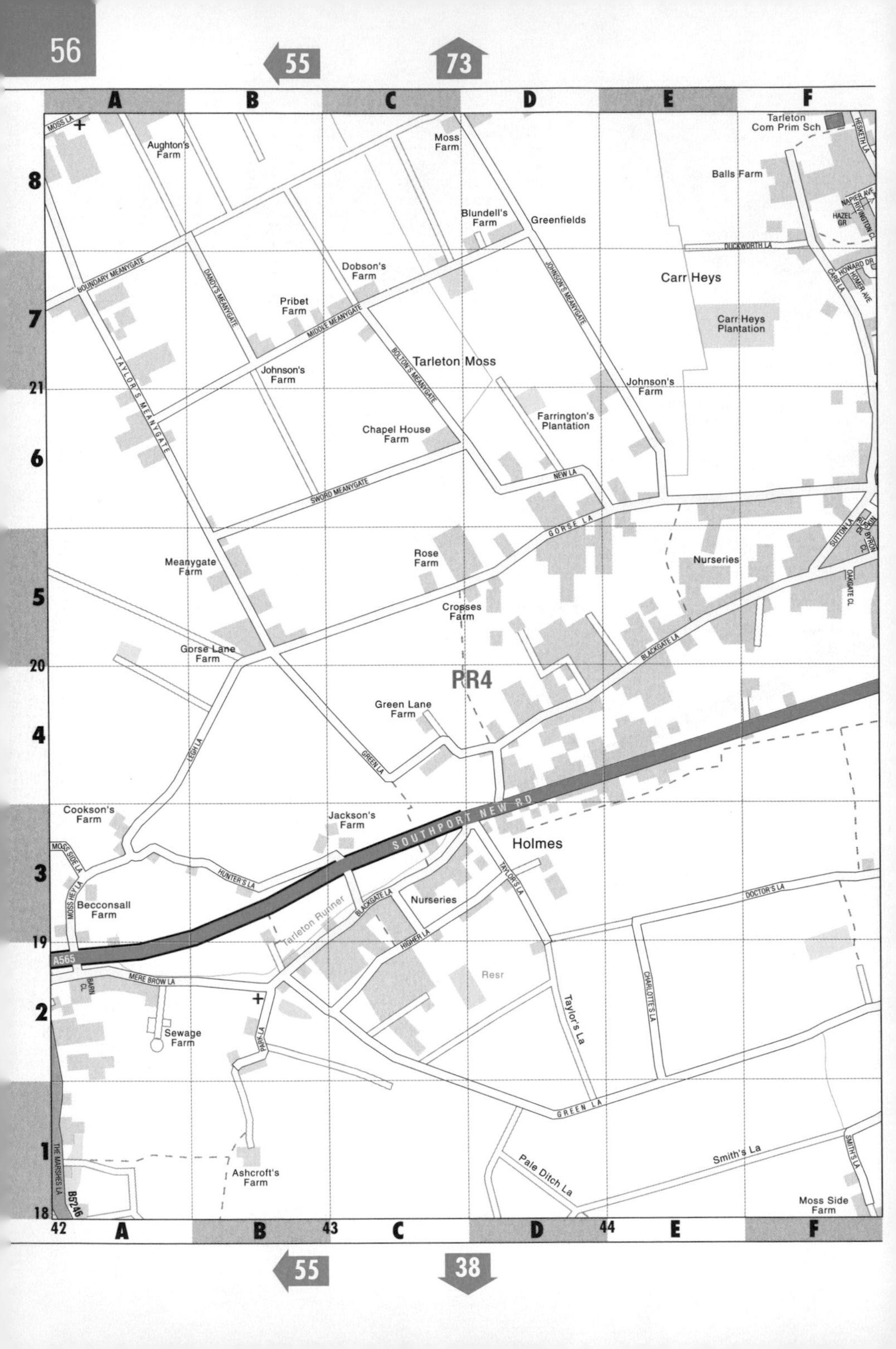
55
73
Aughton's Farm
Moss Farm
Tarleton Com Prim Sch
Balls Farm
Blundell's Farm
Greenfields
Dobson's Farm
Pribet Farm
Carr Heys
Carr Heys Plantation
Johnson's Farm
Tarleton Moss
Johnson's Farm
Farrington's Plantation
Chapel House Farm
Rose Farm
Nurseries
Meanygate Farm
Crosses Farm
Gorse Lane Farm
PR4
Green Lane Farm
Cookson's Farm
Jackson's Farm
Holmes
Becconsall Farm
Nurseries
Tarleton Runner
Resr
Sewage Farm
Taylor's La
Pale Ditch La
Smith's La
Ashcroft's Farm
Moss Side Farm
SOUTHPORT NEW RD
A565
B5246
MOSS LA
BOUNDARY MEANYGATE
DANDY'S MEANYGATE
MIDDLE MEANYGATE
TAYLOR'S MEANYGATE
BOLTON'S MEANYGATE
JOHNSON'S MEANYGATE
SWORD MEANYGATE
NEW LA
GORSE LA
BLACKGATE LA
GREEN LA
LEGH LA
HUNTER'S LA
MOSS SIDE LA
MOSS HEY LA
MERE BROW LA
BARN CL
PARK LA
HIGHER LA
TAYLOR'S LA
DOCTOR'S LA
CHARLOTTE'S LA
SMITH'S LA
THE MARSHES LA
DUCKWORTH LA
HESKETH LA
NAPIER AVE
RIVINGTON CL
HAZEL GR
HOWARD DR
HOMER AVE
CARR LA
SUTTON LA
BYRON CL
OAKGATE CL
A B C D E F
8 7 21 6 5 20 4 3 19 2 1 18
42 43 44
55
38

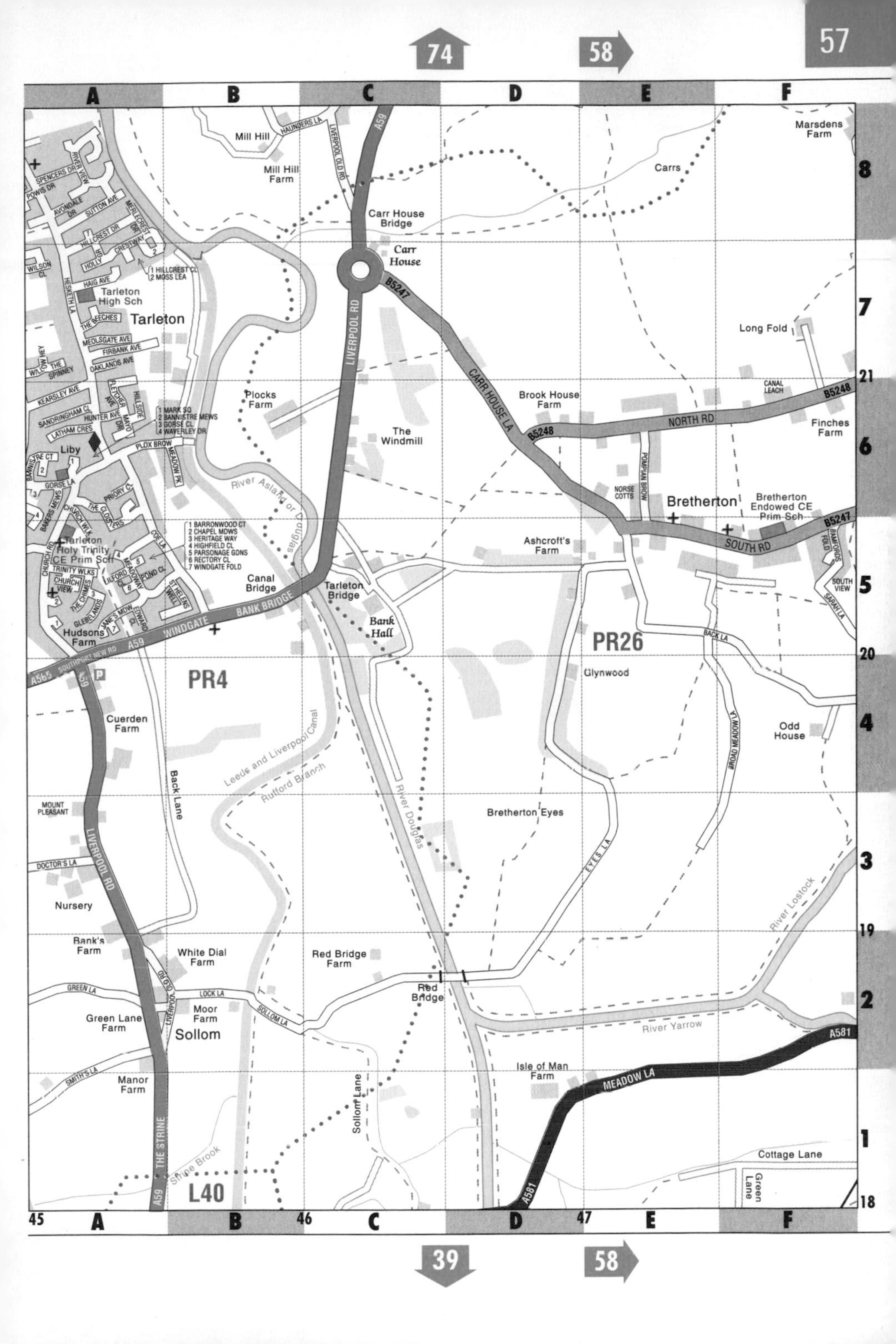
57
74
58
39
58
A
B
C
D
E
F
45
46
47
18
19
20
21
8
7
6
5
4
3
2
1
Mill Hill
HAUNDERS LA
LIVERPOOL OLD RD
A59
Mill Hill Farm
Marsdens Farm
Carrs
Carr House Bridge
Carr House
B5247
SPENCERS DR
RIVER VIEW
POWIS DR
AVONDALE DR
SUTTON AVE
MERLECREST DR
HILLCREST DR
CRESTWAY
HOLLY GR
WILSON CL
HESKETH LA
HAIG AVE
1 HILLCREST CL
2 MOSS LEA
Tarleton High Sch
Tarleton
THE BEECHES
MEOLSGATE AVE
FIRBANK AVE
OAKLANDS AVE
WILLOW WAY
THE SPINNEY
LIVERPOOL RD
CARR HOUSE LA
Long Fold
Plocks Farm
Brook House Farm
CANAL LEACH
B5248
NORTH RD
KEARSLEY AVE
SANDRINGHAM CL
HUNTER AVE
FLETCHER AVE
MAYO DR
HILLSIDE
LATHAM CRES
1 MARK SQ
2 BANNISTRE MEWS
3 GORSE CL
4 WAVERLEY DR
The Windmill
Finches Farm
Liby
PLOX BROW
MEADOW PK
GORSE LA
PRIORY CL
BAKERS MEWS
CHURCH WLK
THE CLOSE
River Asland or Douglas
NORSE COTTS
POMPIAN BROW
Bretherton
Bretherton Endowed CE Prim Sch
B5247
1 BARRONWOOD CT
2 CHAPEL MDWS
3 HERITAGE WAY
4 HIGHFIELD CL
5 PARSONAGE GDNS
6 RECTORY CL
7 WINDGATE FOLD
Tarleton Holy Trinity CE Prim Sch
Ashcroft's Farm
SOUTH RD
BAMFORDS FOLD
CHURCH RD
TRINITY WLKS
CHURCH VIEW
THE CHIMES
GLEBELANDS
LILFORD CL
MEADOWAY
POND CL
COE LA
ST HELENS WELL
Canal Bridge
Tarleton Bridge
SOUTH VIEW
SARAH LA
BANK BRIDGE
WINDGATE
JANE'S MDW
EDWARD CL
Hudsons Farm
Bank Hall
PR26
BACK LA
SOUTHPORT NEW RD
A565
A59
P
PR4
Glynwood
Cuerden Farm
Leeds and Liverpool Canal
Rufford Branch
Back Lane
BROAD MEADOW LA
Odd House
MOUNT PLEASANT
LIVERPOOL RD
River Douglas
Bretherton Eyes
EYES LA
DOCTOR'S LA
Nursery
River Lostock
Bank's Farm
White Dial Farm
Red Bridge Farm
GREEN LA
OLD RD
LIVERPOOL
LOCK LA
Red Bridge
Green Lane Farm
Moor Farm
SOLLOM LA
Sollom
River Yarrow
A581
Isle of Man Farm
MEADOW LA
SMITH'S LA
Manor Farm
Sollom Lane
THE STRINE
Strine Brook
Cottage Lane
Green Lane
L40
A581

57
75

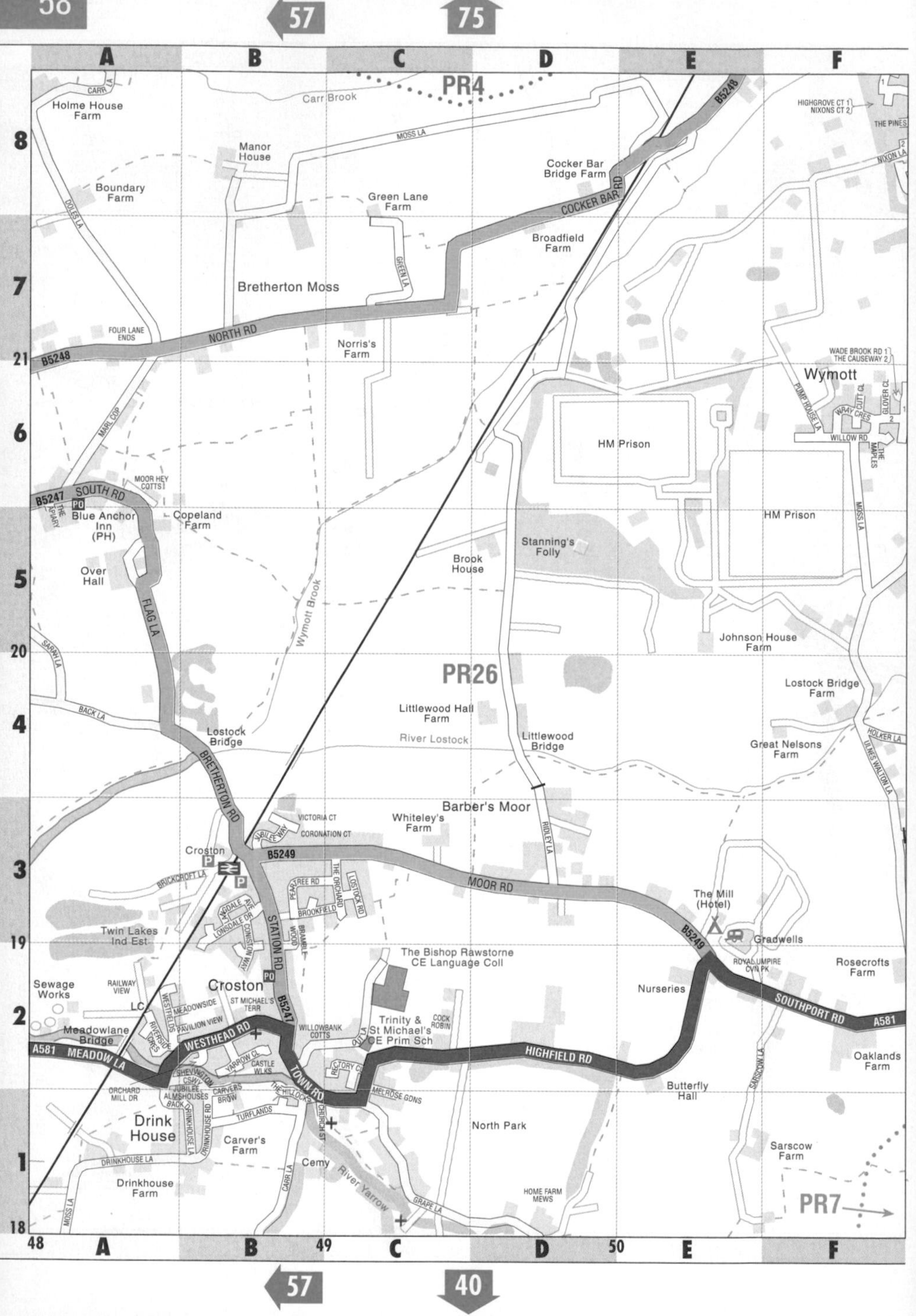
A
B
C
D
E
F
PR4
Carr Brook
CARR LA
Holme House
Farm
MOSS LA
HIGHGROVE CT 1
NIXONS CT 2
THE PINES
NIXON LA
8
Manor
House
Cocker Bar
Bridge Farm
B5248
Boundary
Farm
DOLES LA
Green Lane
Farm
COCKER BAR RD
Broadfield
Farm
GREEN LA
7
Bretherton Moss
FOUR LANE
ENDS
NORTH RD
Norris's
Farm
21
B5248
WADE BROOK RD 1
THE CAUSEWAY 2
Wymott
PUMP HOUSE LA
WRAY CRES
CUTT CL
GLOVER CL
WILLOW RD
THE MAPLES
MARL COP
6
HM Prison
MOOR HEY
COTTS
B5247
SOUTH RD
THE APIARY
PO
Blue Anchor
Inn
(PH)
Copeland
Farm
HM Prison
MOSS LA
Stanning's
Folly
Brook
House
Over
Hall
5
FLAG LA
Wymott Brook
Johnson House
Farm
20
SARAH LA
PR26
Lostock Bridge
Farm
BACK LA
Littlewood Hall
Farm
4
Lostock
Bridge
River Lostock
Littlewood
Bridge
HOLKER LA
Great Nelsons
Farm
ULNES WALTON LA
BRETHERTON RD
Barber's Moor
VICTORIA CT
JUBILEE WAY
CORONATION CT
Whiteley's
Farm
RIDLEY LA
Croston
P
B5249
3
BRICKCROFT LA
P
PEAR TREE RD
THE ORCHARD
LOSTOCK RD
MOOR RD
The Mill
(Hotel)
LANGDALE AVE
LONSDALE DR
BROOKFIELD
STATION RD
BRAMBLE WOOD
CONISTON WAY
Twin Lakes
Ind Est
B5249
Gradwells
19
The Bishop Rawstorne
CE Language Coll
ROYAL UMPIRE
CVN PK
Rosecrofts
Farm
Sewage
Works
RAILWAY
VIEW
Croston
PO
Nurseries
MEADOWSIDE
ST MICHAEL'S
TERR
LC
WESTFIELDS
B5247
SOUTHPORT RD
A581
2
PAVILION VIEW
Trinity &
St Michael's
CE Prim Sch
COCK
ROBIN
Meadowlane
Bridge
RIVERSIDE CRES
WESTHEAD RD
WILLOWBANK
COTTS
OUT LA
A581
MEADOW LA
YARROW CL
CASTLE
WLKS
HIGHFIELD RD
Oaklands
Farm
SHEVINGTON
CSWY
RECTORY CL
TOWN RD
ORCHARD
MILL DR
JUBILEE
ALMSHOUSES
CARVERS
BROW
THE HILLOCKS
MELROSE GDNS
Butterfly
Hall
BACK DRINKHOUSE RD
SARSCOW LA
TURFLANDS
CHURCH ST
Drink
House
DRINKHOUSE LA
Carver's
Farm
North Park
1
Cemy
Sarscow
Farm
DRINKHOUSE LA
Drinkhouse
Farm
River Yarrow
HOME FARM
MEWS
MOSS LA
CARR LA
GRAPE LA
PR7
18
48
A
B
49
C
D
50
E
F

57
40

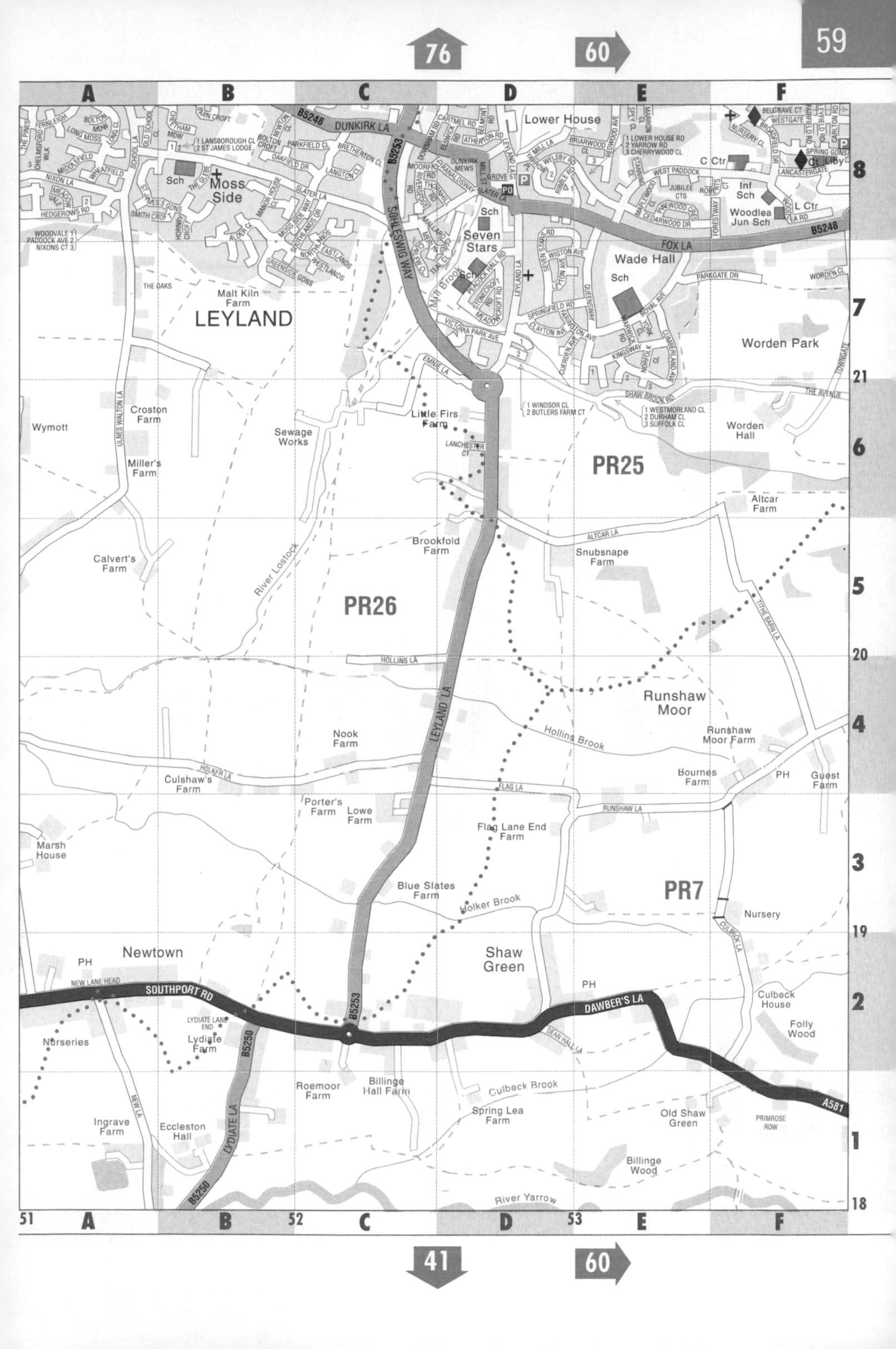
59
76
60
41
60
A
B
C
D
E
F
1
2
3
4
5
6
7
8
18
19
20
21
51
52
53
LEYLAND
Moss Side
Seven Stars
Lower House
Wade Hall
Worden Park
Worden Hall
Wymott
Croston Farm
Miller's Farm
Calvert's Farm
Malt Kiln Farm
THE OAKS
Sewage Works
Little Firs Farm
Brookfold Farm
Snubsnape Farm
Altcar Farm
PR25
PR26
PR7
River Lostock
HOLLINS LA
Runshaw Moor
Runshaw Moor Farm
Hollins Brook
Nook Farm
HOLKER LA
Culshaw's Farm
FLAG LA
RUNSHAW LA
Bournes Farm
PH
Guest Farm
Porter's Farm
Lowe Farm
Flag Lane End Farm
Marsh House
Blue Slates Farm
Holker Brook
Nursery
CULBECK LA
Newtown
Shaw Green
Culbeck House
Folly Wood
NEW LANE HEAD
SOUTHPORT RD
DAWBER'S LA
DEAN HALL LA
LYDIATE LANE END
Lydiate Farm
Nurseries
B5250
B5253
A581
Roemoor Farm
Billinge Hall Farm
Culbeck Brook
Spring Lea Farm
Old Shaw Green
PRIMROSE ROW
Ingrave Farm
Eccleston Hall
NEW LA
LYDIATE LA
Billinge Wood
River Yarrow
ULNES WALTON LA
LEYLAND LA
SCHLESWIG WAY
B5248
DUNKIRK LA
FOX LA
ALTCAR LA
TITHE BARN LA
SHAW BROOK RD
THE AVENUE
TOWNGATE
WORDEN CL
PARKGATE DR
EMNIE LA
LANCHESTER CT
VICTORIA PARK AVE
SPRINGFIELD RD
CLAYTON AVE
KINGSWAY
QUEENSWAY
ROYAL AVE
CUMBERLAND AVE
1 WINDSOR CL
2 BUTLERS FARM CT
1 WESTMORLAND CL
2 DURHAM CL
3 SUFFOLK CL
1 LOWER HOUSE RD
2 YARROW RD
3 CHERRYWOOD CL
1 LANSBOROUGH CL
2 ST JAMES LODGE
WOODVALE 1
PADDOCK AVE 2
NIXONS CT 3
Sch
C Ctr
Inf Sch
Woodlea Jun Sch
L Ctr
Ct Liby
PO
P
Mill Brook
LONG MOSS
NIXON LA
HEDGEROWS RD
MIDDLEFIELD
WHEATFIELD
SCHOOL LA
SMITH CROFT
THE GLEBE
OAKFIELD DR
PARKFIELD CL
BRETHERTON CL
LANGTON CL
SLATER LA
MOSS SIDE WAY
GREENSIDE GDNS
WESTLANDS
EASTLANDS
NORTHLANDS
SOUTHLANDS
CARTMEL RD
ATHERTON RD
DUNKIRK MEWS
GROVE ST
MILL ST
WEST PADDOCK
JUBILEE CTS
CEDARWOOD DR
PINEWOOD CRES
MAPLEWOOD
FORESTWAY
BELGRAVE CT
WESTGATE
NURSERY CL
SPRING GDNS
LANCASTERGATE
BRIARWOOD CL
MILL LA
WELSBY RD
RIBBLE RD
REDWOOD AVE
STONECROFT RD
MEADOWCROFT RD
PEACOCK HALL RD
TEAL CL
MALLARD CL
THORNHILL
RIVERSEDGE
MOORFIELD
GRANALDSWAY
DOWNHAM RD
WIGTON AVE
LEYTON AVE
SEVEN STARS RD
WARWICK RD
YORK CL
NORFOLK CL
CLERDEN AVE
FARINGTON AVE
BOLTON CROFT
NEWTON CL
BARN CROFT
CHETHAM MDW
BOLTON MDW
FERNLEIGH
CHELMSFORD WLK
THE PINES
ALDER CL
MANOR HOUSE CL
HORNBY CROFT
ST JAMES'S GDNS

A8
1 SOUTH VIEW TERR
2 EDWARD ST
3 BROAD ST
4 LIEGE RD
5 VICTORIA TERR
6 DEIGHTON AVE
7 SANDY PL
8 BROAD SQ

59
77

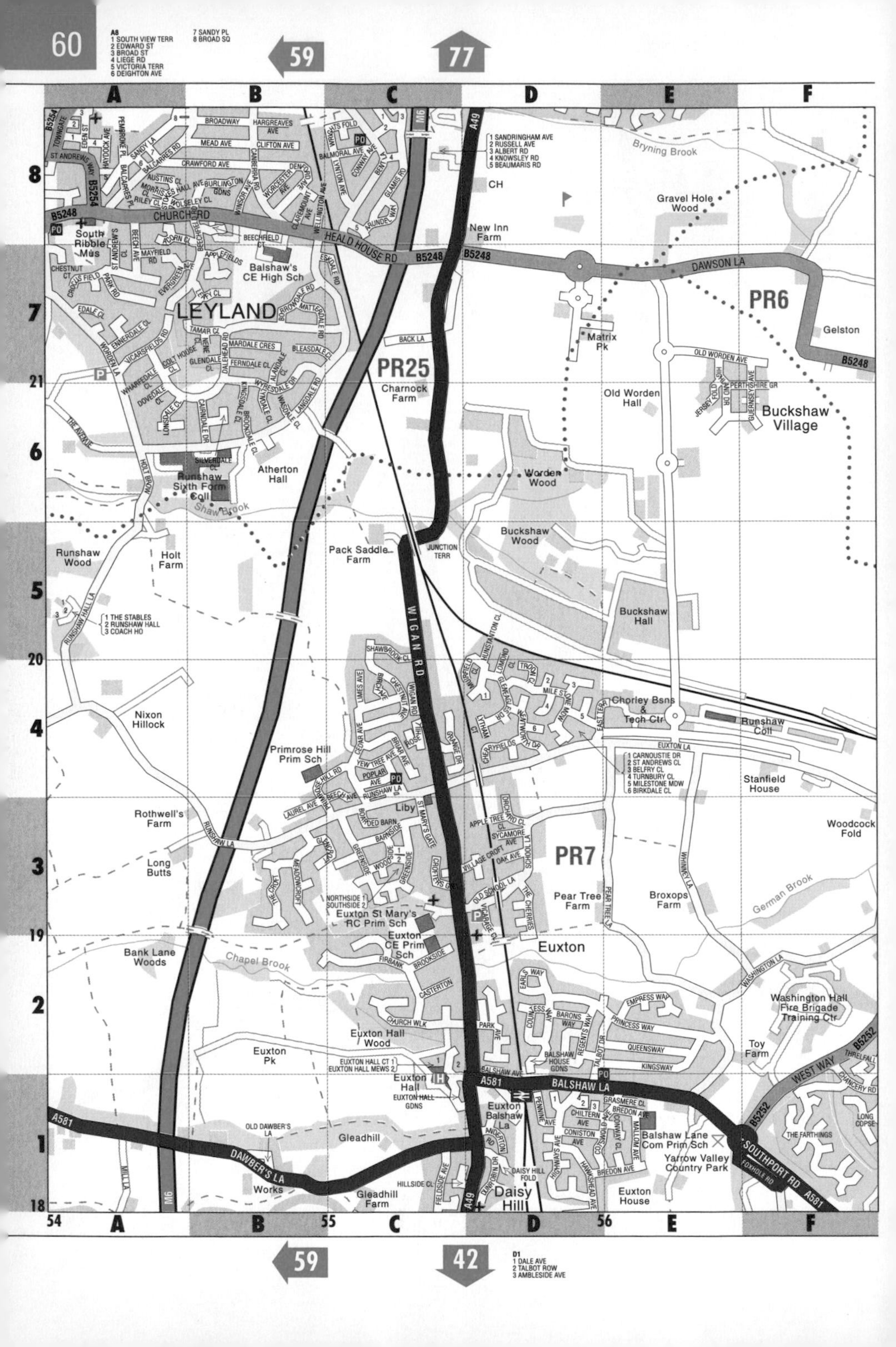

59
42

D1
1 DALE AVE
2 TALBOT ROW
3 AMBLESIDE AVE

78
62

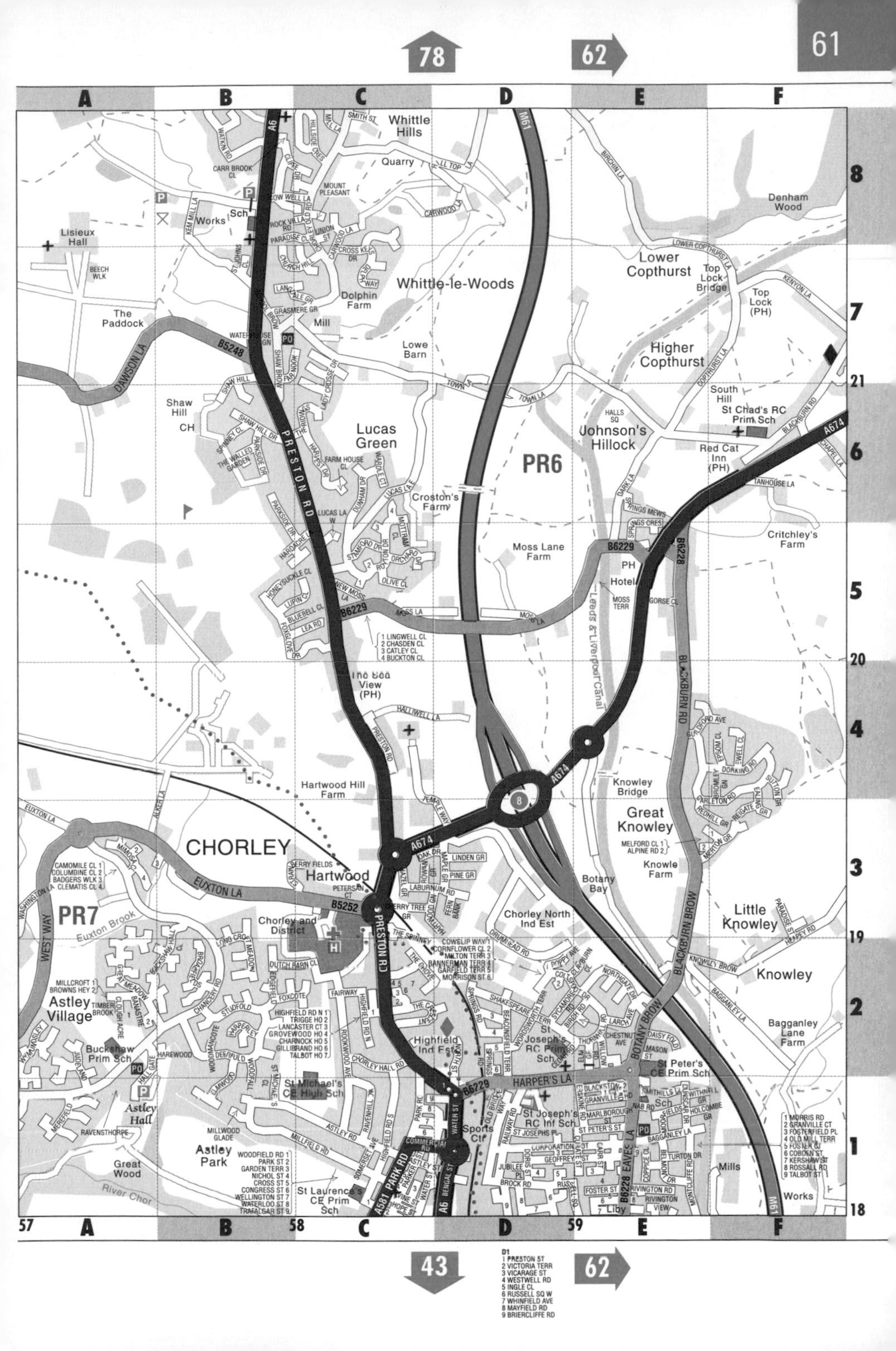
A
B
C
D
E
F
8
7
6
5
4
3
2
1
21
20
19
18
57
58
59
Whittle Hills
Quarry
Mount Pleasant
Lisieux Hall
Works
Sch
Beech Wlk
Whittle-le-Woods
Dolphin Farm
Mill
The Paddock
Lowe Barn
Lower Copthurst
Top Lock Bridge
Top Lock (PH)
Higher Copthurst
Denham Wood
South Hill
St Chad's RC Prim Sch
Johnson's Hillock
Red Cat Inn (PH)
Shaw Hill
CH
Lucas Green
PR6
Croston's Farm
Moss Lane Farm
Critchley's Farm
PH
Hotel
Leeds & Liverpool Canal
Preston Rd
1 LINGWELL CL
2 CHASDEN CL
3 CATLEY CL
4 BUCKTON CL
The Sea View (PH)
Hartwood Hill Farm
Knowley Bridge
Great Knowley
MELFORD CL 1
ALPINE RD 2
Knowle Farm
Botany Bay
CHORLEY
Hartwood
CAMOMILE CL 1
COLUMBINE CL 2
BADGERS WLK 3
CLEMATIS CL 4
PR7
Euxton Brook
Euxton La
Chorley and District
H
Chorley North Ind Est
Little Knowley
Knowley
Bagganley Lane Farm
COWSLIP WAY 1
CORNFLOWER CL 2
MILTON TERR 3
BANNERMAN TERR 4
GARFIELD TERR 5
MORRISON ST 6
MILLCROFT 1
BROWNS HEY 2
Astley Village
HIGHFIELD RD N 1
TRIGGE HO 2
LANCASTER CT 3
GROVEWOOD HO 4
CHARNOCK HO 5
GILLIBRAND HO 6
TALBOT HO 7
Highfield Ind Est
St Joseph's RC Prim Sch
St Peter's CE Prim Sch
Buckshaw Prim Sch
PO
St Michael's CE High Sch
Astley Hall
St Joseph's RC Inf Sch
Sports Ctr
Millwood Glade
Astley Park
WOODFIELD RD 1
PARK ST 2
GARDEN TERR 3
NICHOL ST 4
CROSS ST 5
CONGRESS ST 6
WELLINGTON ST 7
WATERLOO ST 8
TRAFALGAR ST 9
St Laurence's CE Prim Sch
Great Wood
River Chor
Ravensthorpe
1 MORRIS RD
2 GRANVILLE CT
3 FOSTERFIELD PL
4 OLD MILL TERR
5 FOSTER CT
6 COBDEN ST
7 KERSHAW ST
8 ROSSALL RD
9 TALBOT ST
Mills
Works
Liby
A6
A674
A581
B5248
B5252
B6229
B6228
M61
8
D1
1 PRESTON ST
2 VICTORIA TERR
3 VICARAGE ST
4 WESTWELL RD
5 INGLE CL
6 RUSSELL SQ W
7 WHINFIELD AVE
8 MAYFIELD RD
9 BRIERCLIFFE RD

43
62

61
79

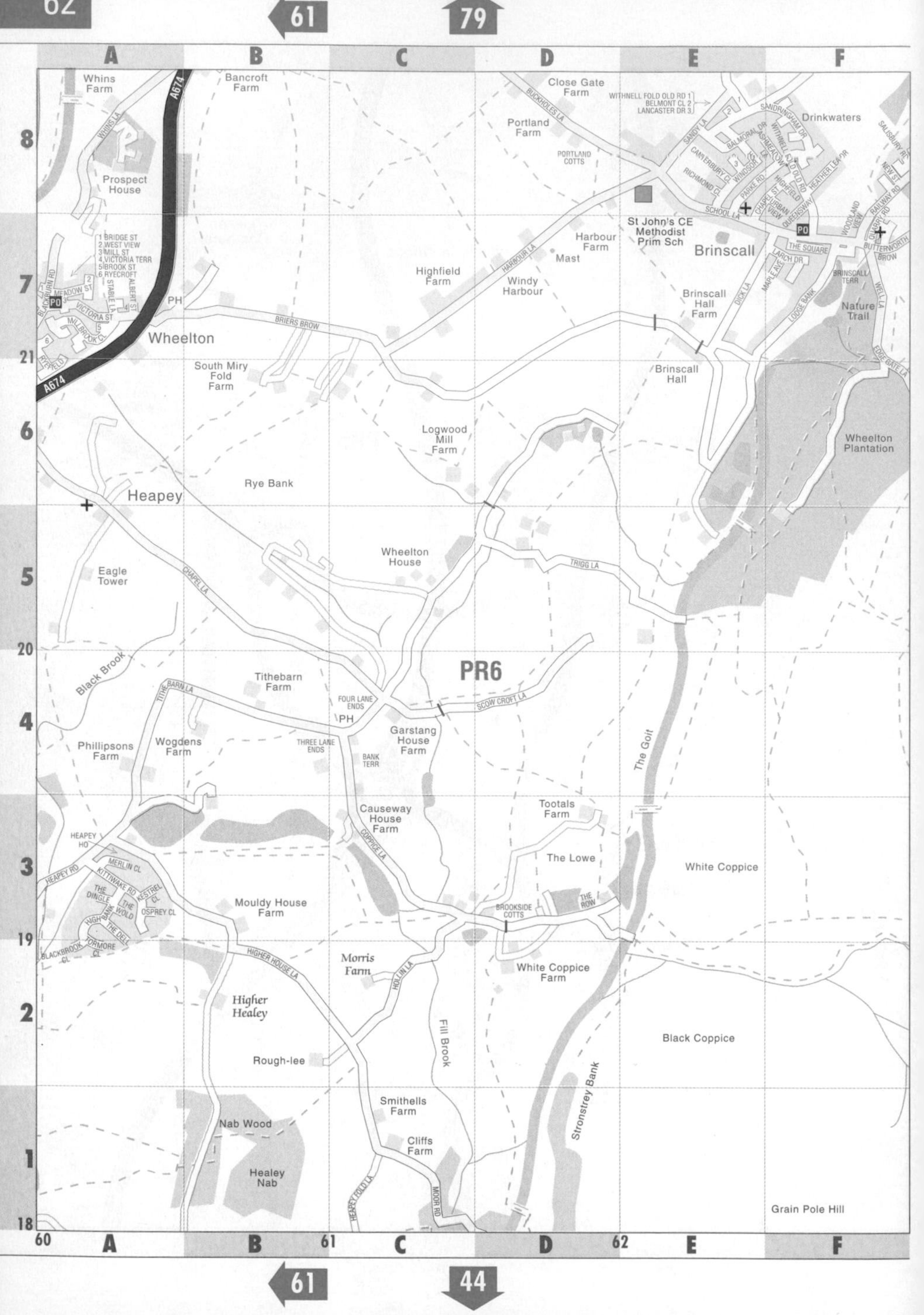
A
B
C
D
E
F
Whins Farm
Bancroft Farm
Close Gate Farm
Portland Farm
Drinkwaters
Prospect House
PORTLAND COTTS
WITHNELL FOLD OLD RD 1
BELMONT CL 2
LANCASTER DR 3
1 BRIDGE ST
2 WEST VIEW
3 MILL ST
4 VICTORIA TERR
5 BROOK ST
6 RYECROFT
St John's CE Methodist Prim Sch
Harbour Farm
Mast
Brinscall
Highfield Farm
Windy Harbour
Brinscall Hall Farm
Nature Trail
PH
Wheelton
South Miry Fold Farm
Brinscall Hall
A674
Logwood Mill Farm
Wheelton Plantation
Rye Bank
Heapey
Wheelton House
TRIGG LA
Eagle Tower
CHAPEL LA
PR6
Black Brook
Tithebarn Farm
FOUR LANE ENDS
SCOW CROFT LA
PH
Garstang House Farm
Phillipsons Farm
Wogdens Farm
THREE LANE ENDS
BANK TERR
The Goit
Causeway House Farm
Tootals Farm
HEAPEY HO
The Lowe
White Coppice
MERLIN CL
Mouldy House Farm
BROOKSIDE COTTS
THE ROW
HIGHER HOUSE LA
Morris Farm
White Coppice Farm
Higher Healey
Fill Brook
Black Coppice
Rough-lee
Stronstrey Bank
Smithells Farm
Nab Wood
Cliffs Farm
Healey Nab
MOOR RD
HEAPEY FOLD LA
Grain Pole Hill
8
7
21
6
5
20
4
3
19
2
1
18
60
61
62

61
44

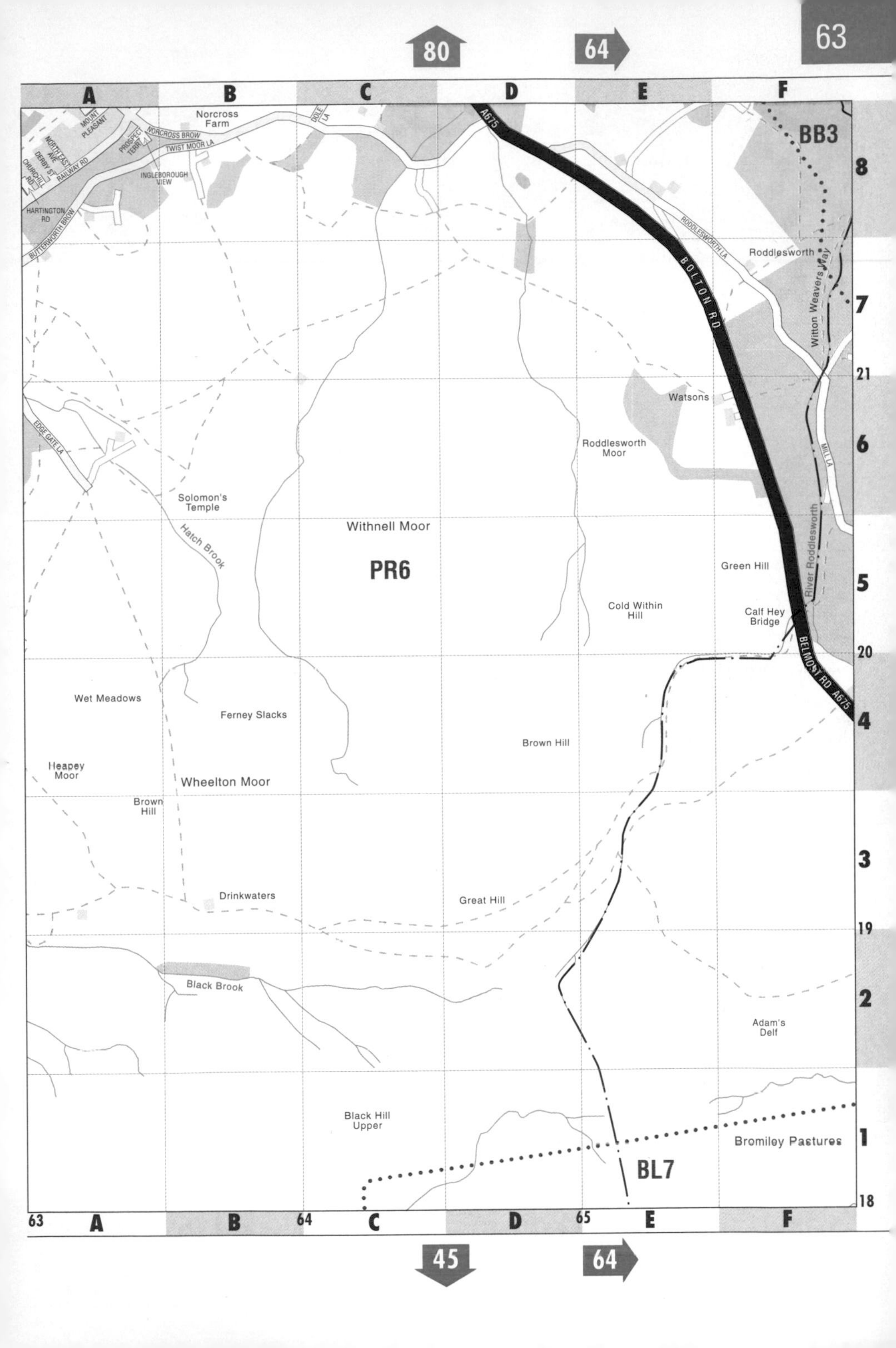
80
64
A B C D E F
Norcross Farm
MOUNT PLEASANT
NORCROSS BROW
TWIST MOOR LA
DOLE LA
PROSPECT TERR
INGLEBOROUGH VIEW
NORTH EAST AVE
DERBY ST
RAILWAY RD
CHURCHILL RD
HARTINGTON RD
BUTTERWORTH BROW
A675
BB3
RODDLESWORTH LA
BOLTON RD
Roddlesworth
Witton Weavers Way
Watsons
MILL LA
EDGE GATE LA
Roddlesworth Moor
Solomon's Temple
Hatch Brook
Withnell Moor
PR6
River Roddlesworth
Green Hill
Cold Within Hill
Calf Hey Bridge
BELMONT RD A675
Wet Meadows
Ferney Slacks
Brown Hill
Heapey Moor
Wheelton Moor
Brown Hill
Drinkwaters
Great Hill
Black Brook
Adam's Delf
Black Hill Upper
Bromiley Pastures
BL7
8 7 21 6 5 20 4 3 19 2 1 18
63 64 65
45
64

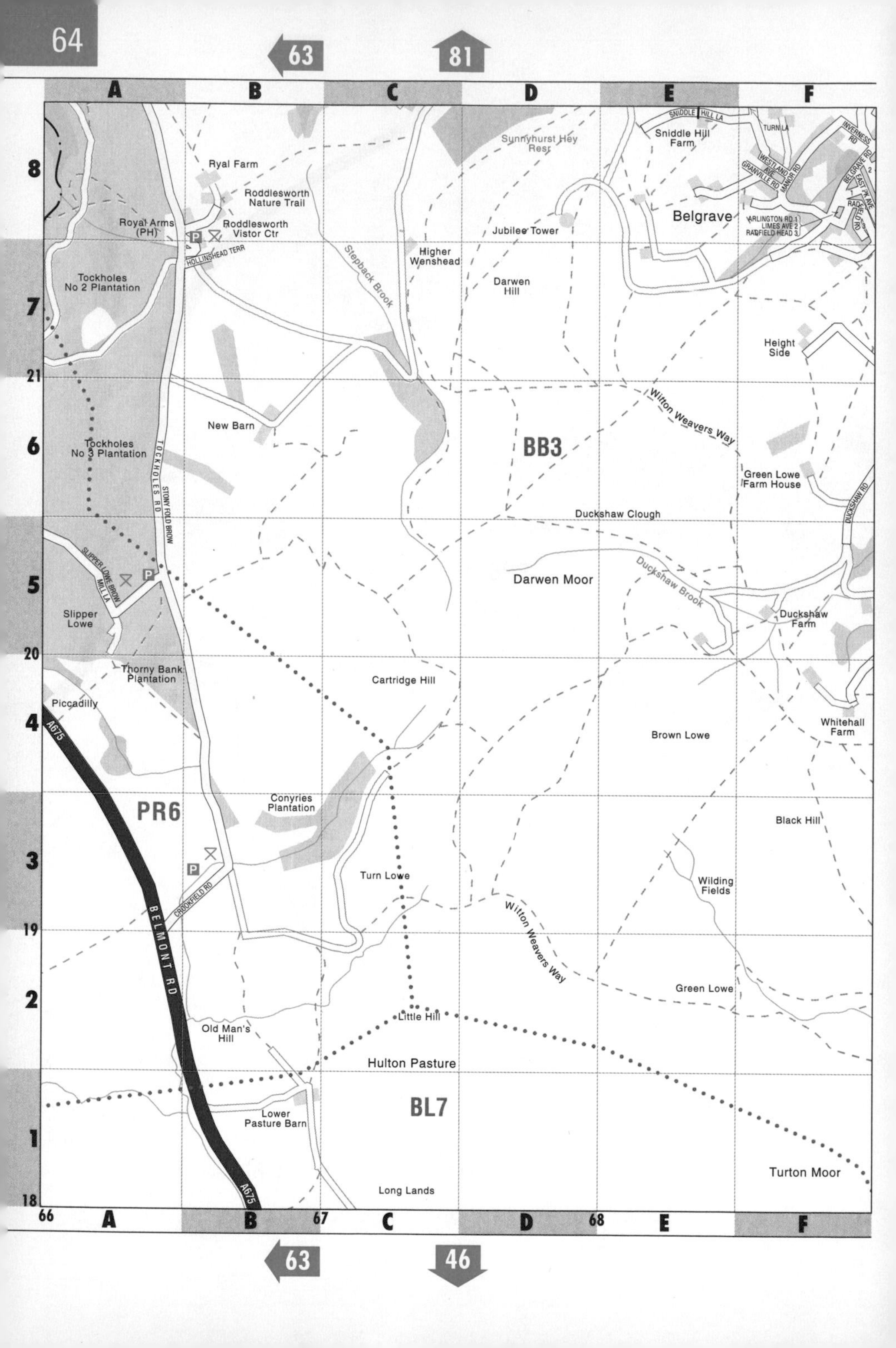
63
81
A
B
C
D
E
F
8
7
21
6
5
20
4
3
19
2
1
18
66
67
68
Ryal Farm
Roddlesworth
Nature Trail
Royal Arms
(PH)
Roddlesworth
Vistor Ctr
HOLLINSHEAD TERR
Tockholes
No 2 Plantation
Sunnyhurst Hey
Resr
Jubilee Tower
Higher
Wenshead
Stepback Brook
Darwen
Hill
SNIDDLE HILL LA
Sniddle Hill
Farm
TURN LA
INVERNESS
RD
WESTLAND
AVE
GRANVILLE RD
MANOR RD
BELGRAVE RD
EAST PK AVE
RADFIELD RD
Belgrave
ARLINGTON RD 1
LIMES AVE 2
RADFIELD HEAD 3
Height
Side
New Barn
Tockholes
No 3 Plantation
TOCKHOLES RD
STONY FOLD BROW
BB3
Witton Weavers Way
Green Lowe
Farm House
DUCKSHAW RD
Duckshaw Clough
SLIPPER LOWE BROW
MILL LA
Darwen Moor
Duckshaw Brook
Slipper
Lowe
Duckshaw
Farm
Thorny Bank
Plantation
Cartridge Hill
Piccadilly
A675
Brown Lowe
Whitehall
Farm
PR6
Conyries
Plantation
Black Hill
CROOKFIELD RD
BELMONT RD
Turn Lowe
Wilding
Fields
Witton Weavers Way
Green Lowe
Old Man's
Hill
Little Hill
Hulton Pasture
BL7
Lower
Pasture Barn
Turton Moor
Long Lands
A675
63
46

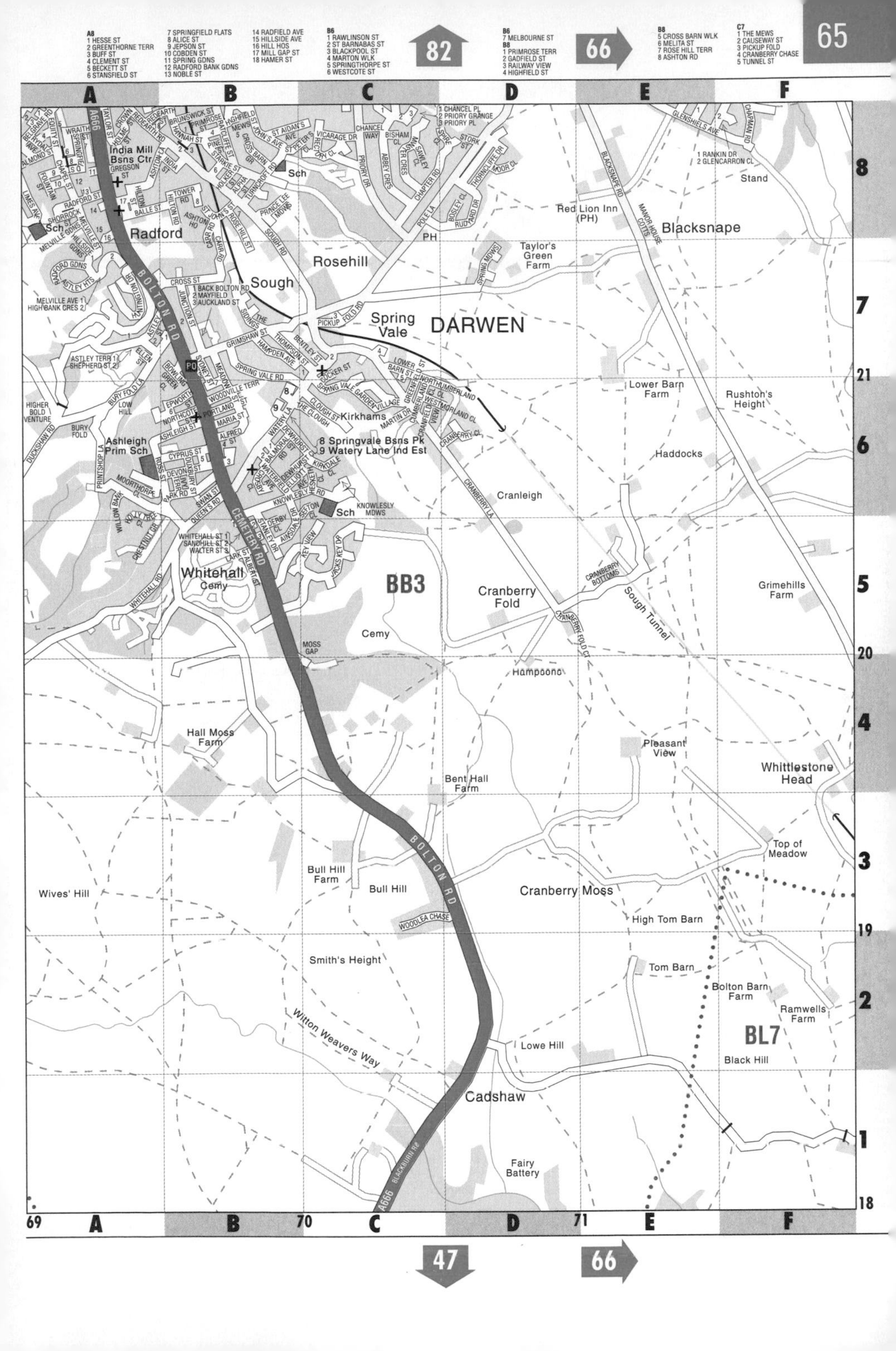
65
A8
1 HESSE ST
2 GREENTHORNE TERR
3 BUFF ST
4 CLEMENT ST
5 BECKETT ST
6 STANSFIELD ST
7 SPRINGFIELD FLATS
8 ALICE ST
9 JEPSON ST
10 COBDEN ST
11 SPRING GDNS
12 RADFORD BANK GDNS
13 NOBLE ST
14 RADFIELD AVE
15 HILLSIDE AVE
16 HILL HOS
17 MILL GAP ST
18 HAMER ST
B6
1 RAWLINSON ST
2 ST BARNABAS ST
3 BLACKPOOL ST
4 MARTON WLK
5 SPRINGTHORPE ST
6 WESTCOTE ST
82
B6
7 MELBOURNE ST
B8
1 PRIMROSE TERR
2 GADFIELD ST
3 RAILWAY VIEW
4 HIGHFIELD ST
66
B8
5 CROSS BARN WLK
6 MELITA ST
7 ROSE HILL TERR
8 ASHTON RD
C7
1 THE MEWS
2 CAUSEWAY ST
3 PICKUP FOLD
4 CRANBERRY CHASE
5 TUNNEL ST
A
B
C
D
E
F
A666
India Mill
Bsns Ctr
Radford
Sch
Rosehill
Sough
Spring
Vale
DARWEN
Red Lion Inn
(PH)
Blacksnape
Taylor's
Green
Farm
Stand
1 RANKIN DR
2 GLENCARRON CL
1 CHANCEL PL
2 PRIORY GRANGE
3 PRIORY PL
BOLTON RD
1 BACK BOLTON RD
2 MAYFIELD
3 AUCKLAND ST
MELVILLE AVE 1
HIGH BANK CRES 2
ASTLEY TERR 1
SHEPHERD ST 2
HIGHER
BOLD
VENTURE
BURY
FOLD
Ashleigh
Prim Sch
Kirkhams
8 Springvale Bsns Pk
9 Watery Lane Ind Est
Lower Barn
Farm
Rushton's
Height
Haddocks
Cranleigh
KNOWLESLY
MDWS
WHITEHALL ST 1
SANDHILL ST 2
WALTER ST 3
Whitehall
Cemy
CEMETERY RD
BB3
Cranberry
Fold
Sough Tunnel
Grimehills
Farm
MOSS
GAP
Hampoono
Hall Moss
Farm
Pleasant
View
Bent Hall
Farm
Whittlestone
Head
Top of
Meadow
Bull Hill
Farm
Bull Hill
Cranberry Moss
Wives' Hill
High Tom Barn
WOODLEA CHASE
Smith's Height
Tom Barn
Bolton Barn
Farm
Ramwells
Farm
Witton Weavers Way
BL7
Lowe Hill
Black Hill
Cadshaw
Fairy
Battery
BLACKBURN RD
8
7
21
6
5
20
4
3
19
2
1
18
69
70
71
47
66

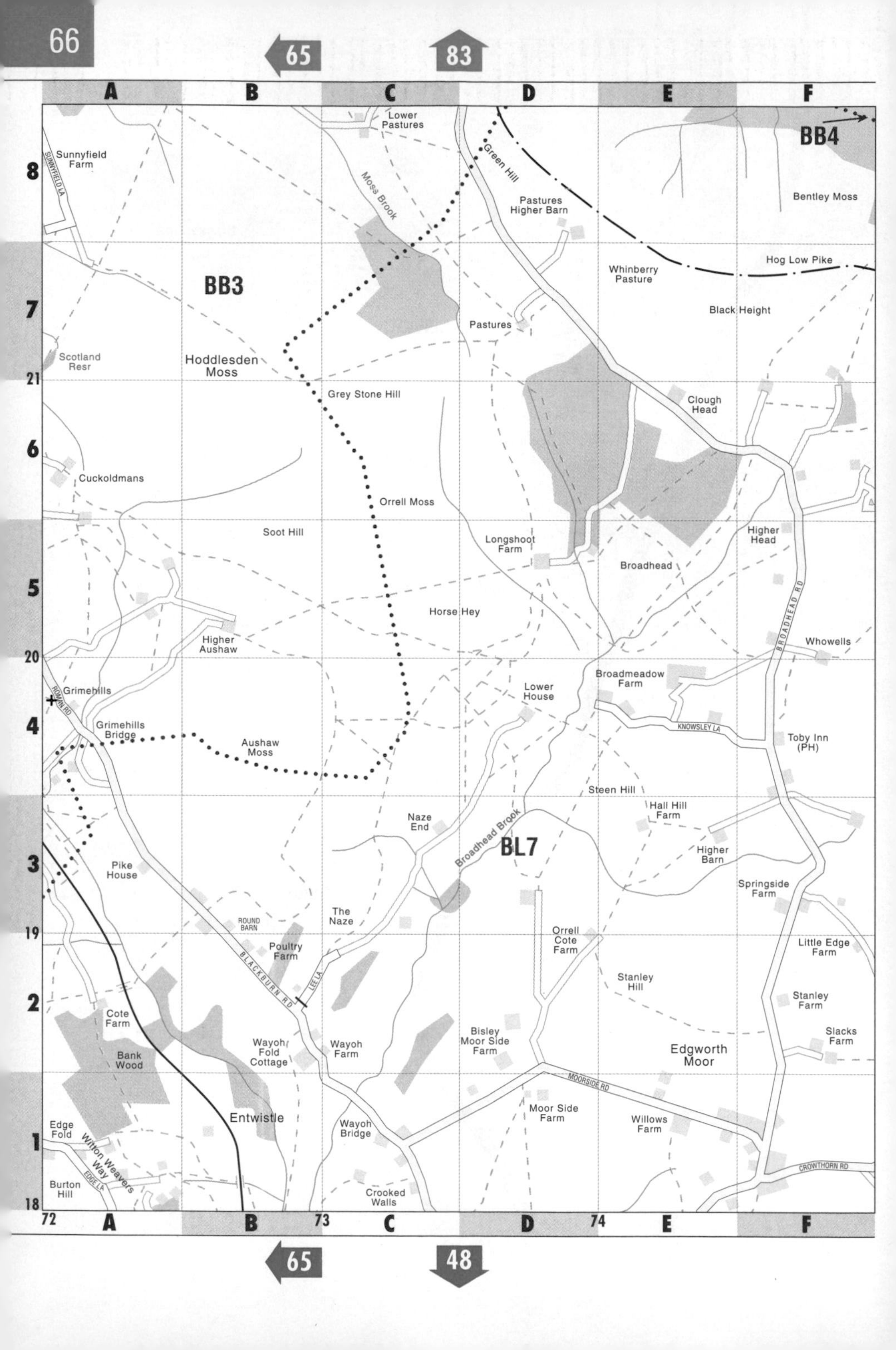
65
83
A
B
C
D
E
F
8
7
21
6
5
20
4
3
19
2
1
18
72
73
74
Lower Pastures
Sunnyfield Farm
SUNNYFIELD LA
Moss Brook
Green Hill
BB4
Pastures Higher Barn
Bentley Moss
BB3
Whinberry Pasture
Hog Low Pike
Black Height
Pastures
Scotland Resr
Hoddlesden Moss
Grey Stone Hill
Clough Head
Cuckoldmans
Orrell Moss
Soot Hill
Longshoot Farm
Higher Head
Broadhead
BROADHEAD RD
Horse Hey
Higher Aushaw
Whowells
Grimehills
ROMAN RD
Broadmeadow Farm
Lower House
Grimehills Bridge
KNOWSLEY LA
Aushaw Moss
Toby Inn (PH)
Steen Hill
Hall Hill Farm
Naze End
Broadhead Brook
BL7
Higher Barn
Pike House
Springside Farm
The Naze
ROUND BARN
Orrell Cote Farm
Poultry Farm
BLACKBURN RD
LEE LA
Little Edge Farm
Stanley Hill
Stanley Farm
Cote Farm
Bank Wood
Wayoh Fold Cottage
Wayoh Farm
Bisley Moor Side Farm
Slacks Farm
Edgworth Moor
MOORSIDE RD
Entwistle
Moor Side Farm
Willows Farm
Edge Fold
Witton Weavers Way
Wayoh Bridge
EDGE LA
CROWTHORN RD
Burton Hill
Crooked Walls
65
48

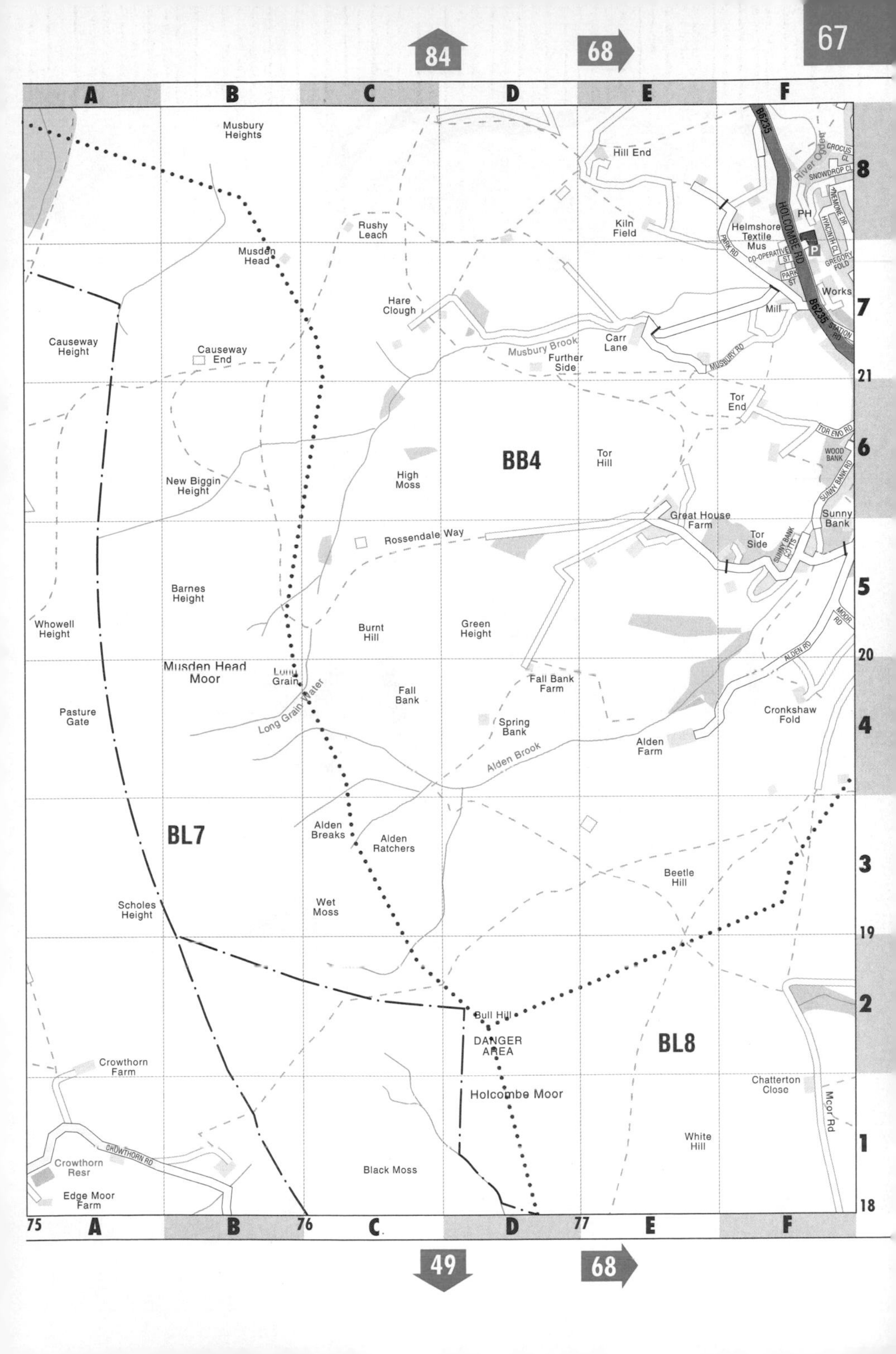
67
84
68
49
68
A
B
C
D
E
F
8
7
6
5
4
3
2
1
21
20
19
18
75
76
77
Musbury Heights
Hill End
Rushy Leach
Musden Head
Kiln Field
Helmshore Textile Mus
PH
P
HOLCOMBE RD
B6235
River Ogden
CROCUS CL
SNOWDROP CL
ANEMONE DR
HYACINTH CL
GREGORY FOLD
CO-OPERATIVE ST
PARK RD
PARK ST
Works
Mill
STATION RD
Hare Clough
Causeway Height
Causeway End
Musbury Brook
Carr Lane
Further Side
MUSBURY RD
Tor End
TOR END RD
WOOD BANK
SUNNY BANK RD
Sunny Bank
BB4
Tor Hill
High Moss
New Biggin Height
Great House Farm
Tor Side
SUNNY BANK COTTS
Rossendale Way
Barnes Height
Whowell Height
Burnt Hill
Green Height
MOOR RD
ALDEN RD
Musden Head Moor
Long Grain
Long Grain Water
Fall Bank
Fall Bank Farm
Pasture Gate
Spring Bank
Alden Farm
Cronkshaw Fold
Alden Brook
BL7
Alden Breaks
Alden Ratchers
Beetle Hill
Scholes Height
Wet Moss
Bull Hill
DANGER AREA
BL8
Crowthorn Farm
Holcombe Moor
Chatterton Close
Moor Rd
White Hill
CROWTHORN RD
Crowthorn Resr
Black Moss
Edge Moor Farm

67
85

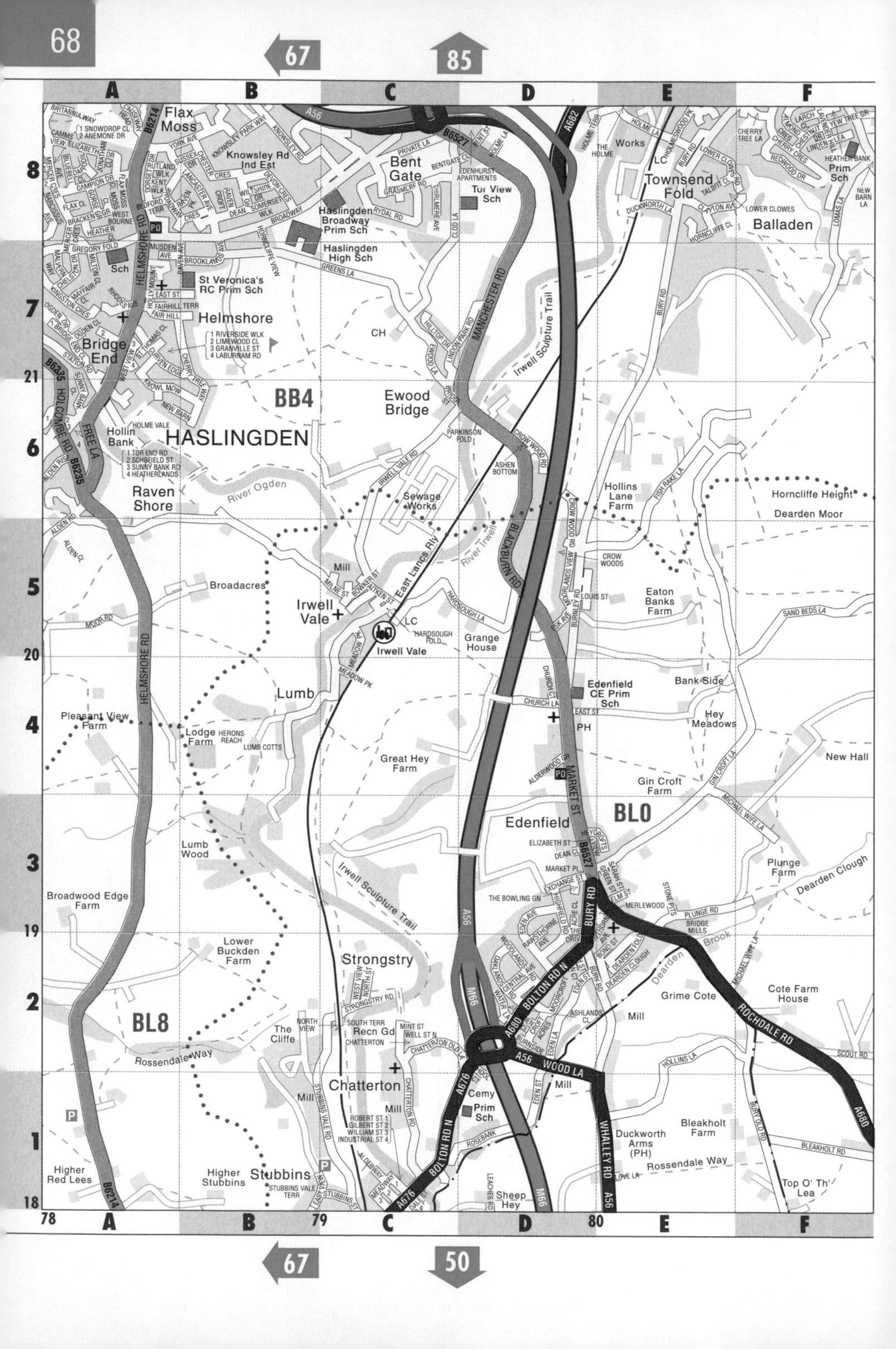
Flax Moss
Knowsley Rd Ind Est
Bent Gate
Tor View Sch
Haslingden Broadway Prim Sch
Haslingden High Sch
St Veronica's RC Prim Sch
Helmshore
Bridge End
Townsend Fold
Balladen
Heather-Bank Prim Sch
HASLINGDEN
BB4
Ewood Bridge
Hollin Bank
Raven Shore
River Ogden
Sewage Works
Irwell Sculpture Trail
Hollins Lane Farm
Horncliffe Height
Dearden Moor
Broadacres
Irwell Vale
Irwell Vale
Grange House
Eaton Banks Farm
Crow Woods
Lumb
Pleasant View Farm
Lodge Farm
Edenfield CE Prim Sch
Bank Side
Hey Meadows
New Hall
Great Hey Farm
Gin Croft Farm
Edenfield
BL0
Lumb Wood
Plunge Farm
Dearden Clough
Broadwood Edge Farm
Lower Buckden Farm
Strongstry
BL8
The Cliffe
Recn Gd
Chatterton
Grime Cote
Cote Farm House
Rossendale Way
Mill
Cemy
Prim Sch
Bleakholt Farm
Duckworth Arms (PH)
Higher Red Lees
Higher Stubbins
Stubbins
Sheep Hey
Top O' Th' Lea
HELMSHORE RD
MANCHESTER RD
BLACKBURN RD
BURY RD
MARKET ST
ROCHDALE RD
BOLTON RD N
WHALLEY RD
WOOD LA
A56
A680
A676
M66
B6527
B6214
B6235
A B C D E F
78 79 80
1 2 3 4 5 6 7 8
18 19 20 21

67
50

E8
1 THE CLOISTERS
2 JOE CONNOLLY WAY
3 SCHOFIELD ST
4 BALTIC FLATS
5 BALTIC BLDGS

E8
6 BALTIC RD
7 VICTORIA PAR
8 BURNLEY ROAD E
9 HOLT ST
10 IRWELL HO

F8
1 IVY ST
2 GEORGE'S ROW
3 PILLING ST
4 SPRING GARDENS ST
5 MARKET ST
6 TENTERFIELD ST
7 YARE ST
8 THORNFIELD AVE
9 WOOD LEA BANK
10 INDUSTRIAL COTTS
11 IVY COTTS

86
70

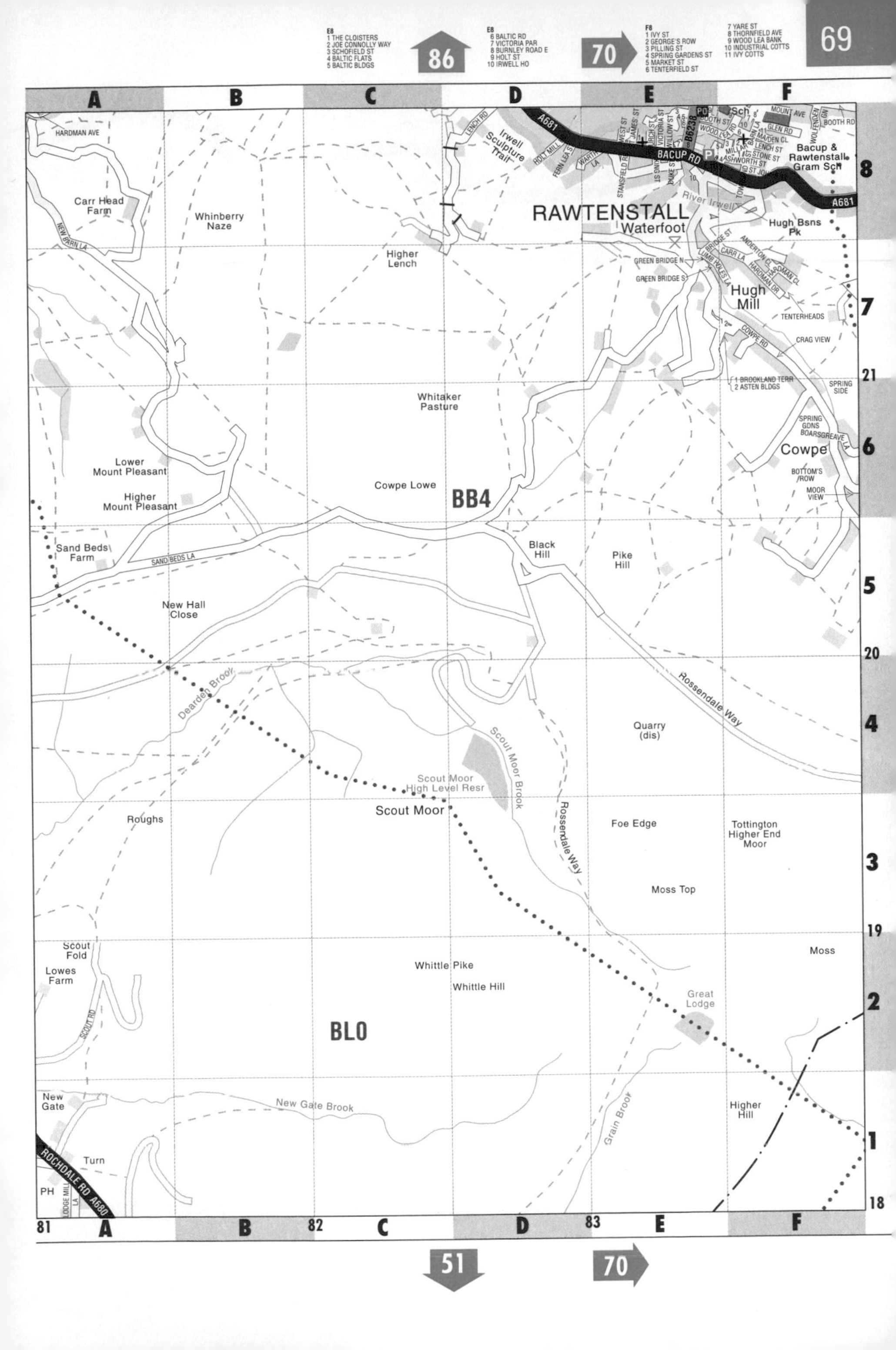

51
70

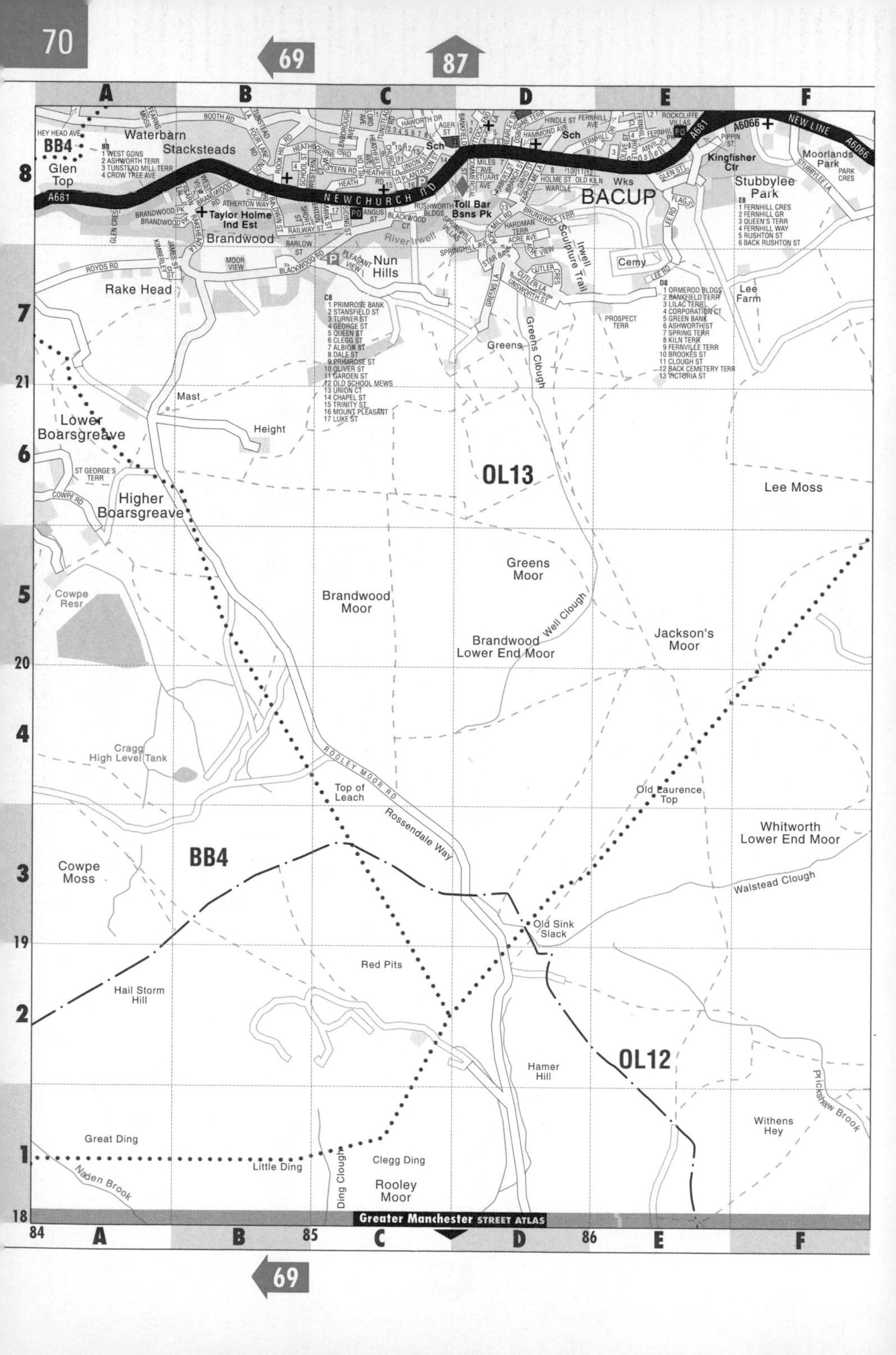
69
87
A
B
C
D
E
F
8
7
6
5
4
3
2
1
21
20
19
18
84
85
86
BB4
Glen Top
Waterbarn
Stacksteads
HEY HEAD AVE
BOOTH RD
A681
NEWCHURCH RD
Taylor Holme Ind Est
Brandwood
Nun Hills
Rake Head
ROYDS RD
River Irwell
Toll Bar Bsns Pk
Sch
BACUP
Wks
Kingfisher Ctr
A6066
NEW LINE
Moorlands Park
Stubbylee Park
STUBBYLEE LA
Cemy
Irwell Sculpture Trail
Greens
Greens Clough
Lee Farm
PROSPECT TERR
B8
1 WEST GDNS
2 ASHWORTH TERR
3 TUNSTEAD MILL TERR
4 CROW TREE AVE
C8
1 PRIMROSE BANK
2 STANSFIELD ST
3 TURNER ST
4 GEORGE ST
5 QUEEN ST
6 CLEGG ST
7 ALBION ST
8 DALE ST
9 PRIMROSE ST
10 OLIVER ST
11 GARDEN ST
12 OLD SCHOOL MEWS
13 UNION CT
14 CHAPEL ST
15 TRINITY ST
16 MOUNT PLEASANT
17 LUKE ST
D8
1 ORMEROD BLDGS
2 BANKFIELD TERR
3 LILAC TERR
4 CORPORATION CT
5 GREEN BANK
6 ASHWORTH ST
7 SPRING TERR
8 KILN TERR
9 FERNVILLE TERR
10 BROOKES ST
11 CLOUGH ST
12 BACK CEMETERY TERR
13 VICTORIA ST
E8
1 FERNHILL CRES
2 FERNHILL GR
3 QUEEN'S TERR
4 FERNHILL WAY
5 RUSHTON ST
6 BACK RUSHTON ST
Mast
Lower Boarsgreave
Height
ST GEORGE'S TERR
COWPE RD
Higher Boarsgreave
OL13
Lee Moss
Greens Moor
Brandwood Moor
Cowpe Resr
Well Clough
Brandwood Lower End Moor
Jackson's Moor
Cragg High Level Tank
ROOLEY MOOR RD
Top of Leach
Rossendale Way
Old Laurence Top
Whitworth Lower End Moor
BB4
Cowpe Moss
Walstead Clough
Old Sink Slack
Red Pits
Hail Storm Hill
OL12
Hamer Hill
Prickshaw Brook
Withens Hey
Great Ding
Little Ding
Clegg Ding
Ding Clough
Rooley Moor
Naden Brook
Greater Manchester STREET ATLAS

88

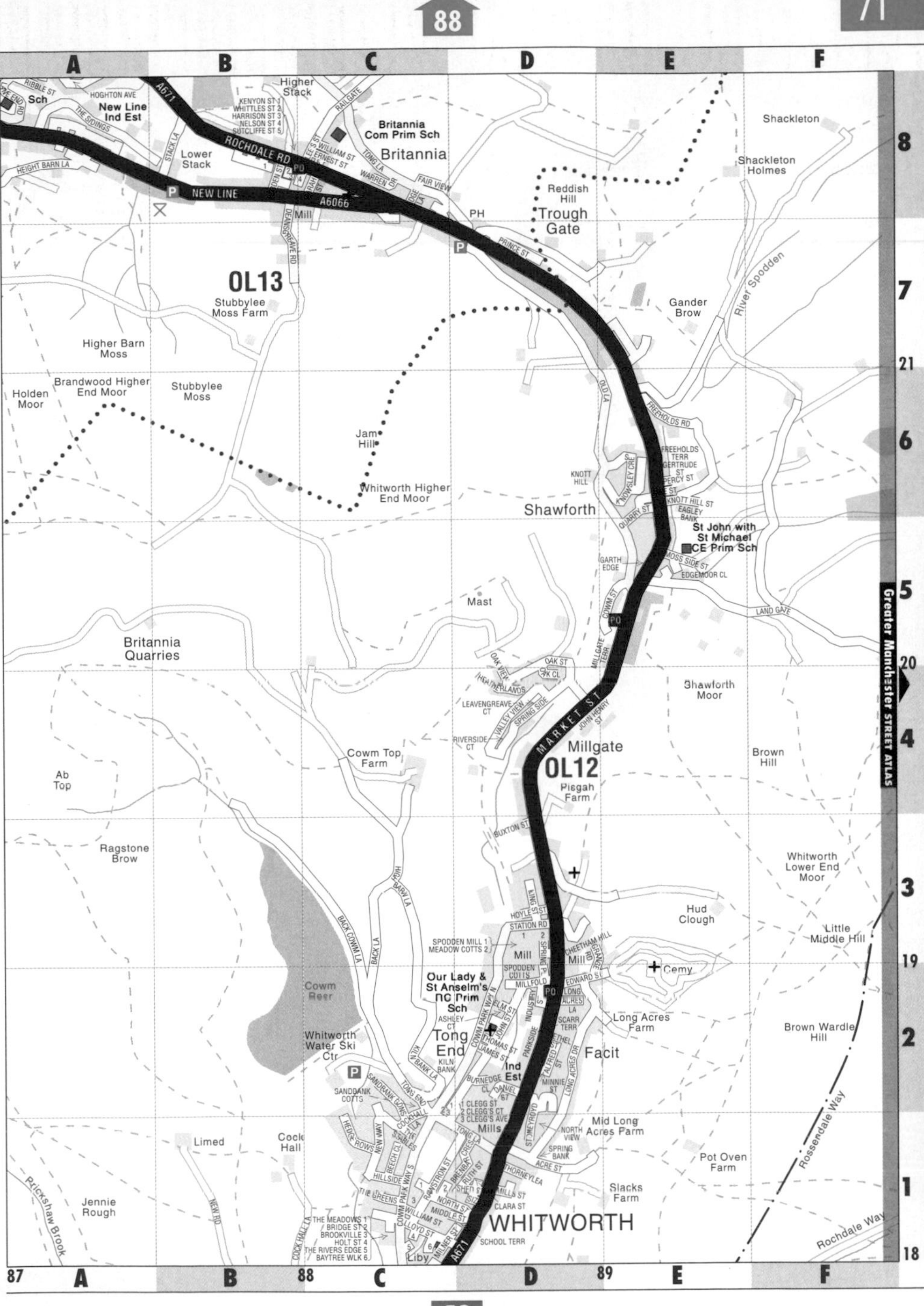
A
B
C
D
E
F
8
7
21
6
5
20
4
3
19
2
1
18
87
88
89
Sch
HOGHTON AVE
New Line
Ind Est
RIBBLE ST
THE SIDINGS
HEIGHT BARN LA
A671
KENYON ST 1
WHITTLES ST 2
HARRISON ST 3
NELSON ST 4
SUTCLIFFE ST 5
Higher
Stack
RAILGATE
Britannia
Com Prim Sch
Britannia
Lower
Stack
STACK LA
ROCHDALE RD
WILLIAM ST
ERNEST ST
TONG LA
WARREN DR
FAIR VIEW
NEW LINE
A6066
Mill
PH
DEANSGREAVE RD
PRINCE ST
Reddish
Hill
Trough
Gate
Shackleton
Shackleton
Holmes
OL13
Stubbylee
Moss Farm
Gander
Brow
River Spodden
Higher Barn
Moss
Holden
Moor
Brandwood Higher
End Moor
Stubbylee
Moss
OLD LA
FREEHOLDS RD
FREEHOLDS TERR
GERTRUDE ST
PERCY ST
Jam
Hill
KNOTT
HILL
KNOWSLEY CRES
KNOTT HILL ST
EAGLEY
BANK
Whitworth Higher
End Moor
Shawforth
QUARRY ST
St John with
St Michael
CE Prim Sch
GARTH
EDGE
MOSS SIDE ST
EDGEMOOR CL
Mast
COWM ST
LAND GATE
Britannia
Quarries
OAK ST
OAK VIEW
MILLGATE TERR
Greater Manchester STREET ATLAS
Shawforth
Moor
LEAVENGREAVE CT
SPRING SIDE
VALLEY VIEW
MARKET ST
JOHN HENRY ST
RIVERSIDE CT
Millgate
Cowm Top
Farm
OL12
Brown
Hill
Ab
Top
Pisgah
Farm
BUXTON ST
Ragstone
Brow
Whitworth
Lower End
Moor
KING ST
HOYLE ST
STATION RD
Hud
Clough
BACK COWM LA
BACK LA
HIGH BARN LA
SPODDEN MILL 1
MEADOW COTTS 2
Mill
Mill
CHEETHAM HILL
Little
Middle Hill
SPODDEN COTTS
MILLFOLD
EDWARD ST
Cemy
Cowm
Resr
Our Lady &
St Anselm's
RC Prim
Sch
ASHLEY CT
ELM ST
JOHN ST
COWM PARK WAY N
PARKSIDE
LONG ACRES LA
SCARR TERR
Long Acres
Farm
Brown Wardle
Hill
Whitworth
Water Ski
Ctr
Tong
End
THOMAS ST
JAMES ST
ETHEL ST
ALFRED ST
Facit
KILN BANK LA
KILN BANK
BURNEDGE CL
Ind
Est
MINNIE ST
LONG ACRES DR
SANDRANK GDNS
SANDBANK COTTS
TONG END
COCKHALL LA
1 CLEGG ST
2 CLEGG'S CT
3 CLEGG'S AVE
Mills
STONEYROYD
NORTH VIEW
Mid Long
Acres Farm
Limed
Cock
Hall
HEDGE ROWS
NEW WAY
BEECH CL
HILLSIDE
TONG LA
SPRING BANK
ACRE ST
Pot Oven
Farm
Rossendale Way
Prickshaw Brook
Jennie
Rough
NEW RD
THE GREENS
COWM PARK WAY S
RANSTRON ST
RUTH ST
THORNEYLEA
NORTH ST
SHED ST
MILLS ST
CLARA ST
Slacks
Farm
COCK HALL LA
THE MEADOWS 1
BRIDGE ST 2
BROOKVILLE 3
HOLT ST 4
THE RIVERS EDGE 5
BAYTREE WLK 6
WILLIAM ST
MIDDLE ST
LLOYD ST
MILNER ST
WHITWORTH
SCHOOL TERR
Rochdale Way
Liby
A671
PO
P

52

92

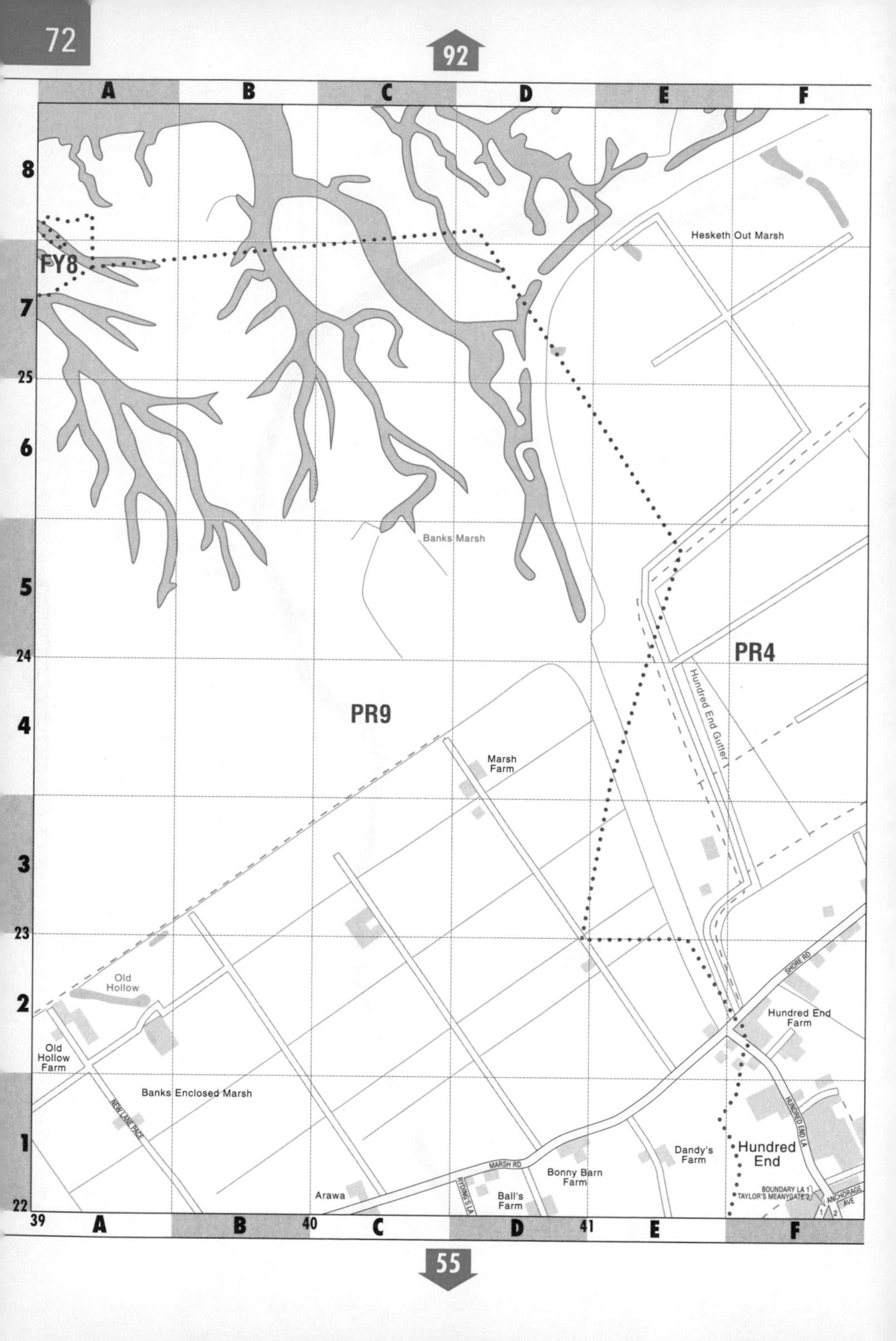
A
B
C
D
E
F
8
7
25
6
5
24
4
3
23
2
1
22
39
40
41
FY8
Hesketh Out Marsh
Banks Marsh
PR4
PR9
Hundred End Gutter
Marsh Farm
Old Hollow
Old Hollow Farm
Banks Enclosed Marsh
NEW LANE PACE
SHORE RD
Hundred End Farm
HUNDRED END LA
Dandy's Farm
Hundred End
MARSH RD
RYDING'S LA
Bonny Barn Farm
Ball's Farm
Arawa
BOUNDARY LA 1
TAYLOR'S MEANYGATE 2
ANCHORAGE AVE

55

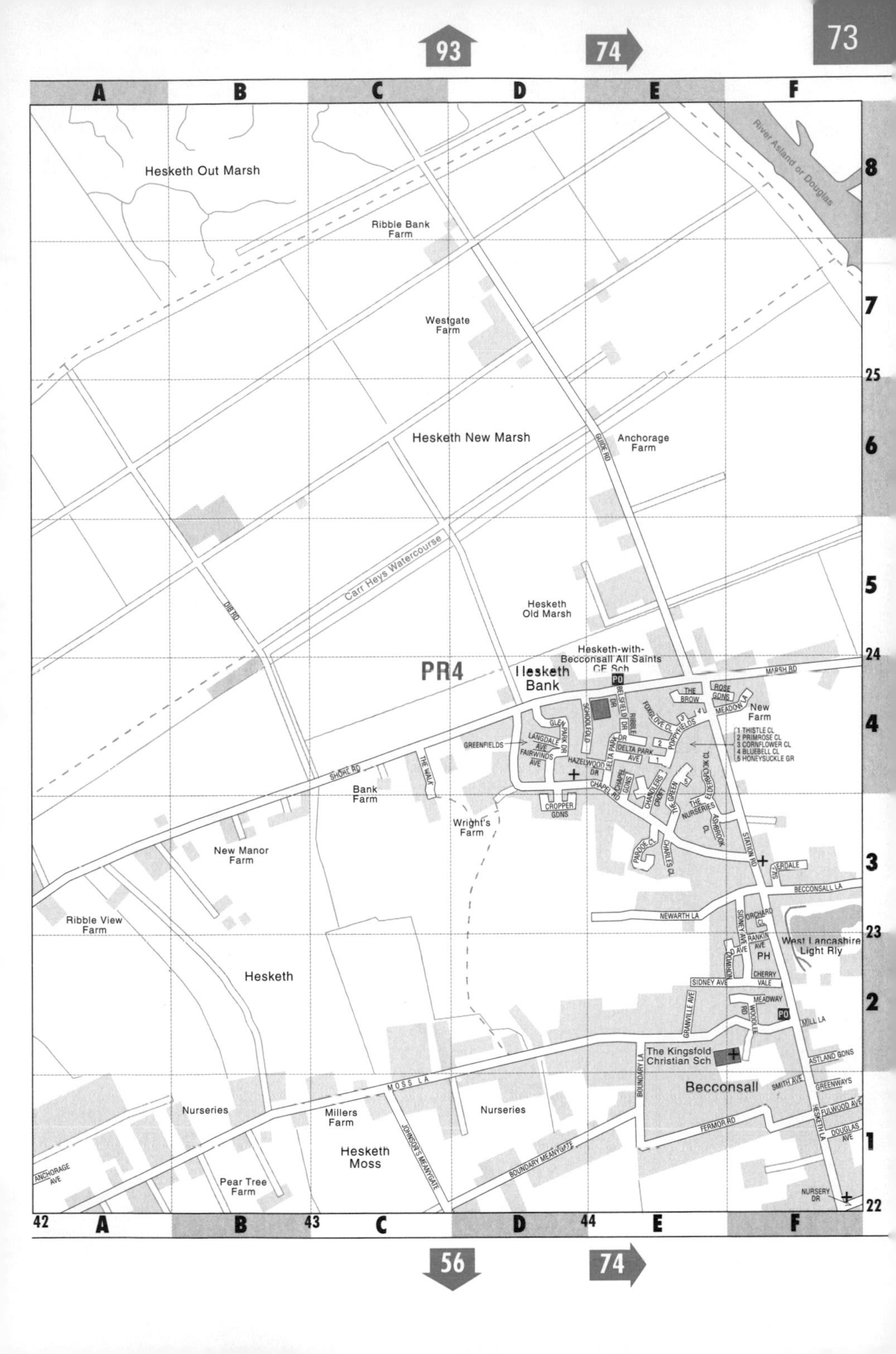
93
74
Hesketh Out Marsh
River Asland or Douglas
Ribble Bank Farm
Westgate Farm
Hesketh New Marsh
Anchorage Farm
GUIDE RD
Carr Heys Watercourse
DIB RD
Hesketh Old Marsh
Hesketh-with-Becconsall All Saints CE Sch
PR4
Hesketh Bank
MARSH RD
New Farm
1 THISTLE CL
2 PRIMROSE CL
3 CORNFLOWER CL
4 BLUEBELL CL
5 HONEYSUCKLE GR
GREENFIELDS
SHORE RD
THE WALK
Bank Farm
Wright's Farm
CROPPER GDNS
STATION RD
New Manor Farm
BECCONSALL LA
NEWARTH LA
Ribble View Farm
West Lancashire Light Rly
SIDNEY AVE
CHERRY VALE
Hesketh
MEADWAY
MILL LA
The Kingsfold Christian Sch
ASTLAND GDNS
Becconsall
MOSS LA
Nurseries
Millers Farm
Hesketh Moss
FERMOR RD
BOUNDARY MEANYGATE
JOHNSON'S MEANYGATE
Pear Tree Farm
ANCHORAGE AVE
NURSERY DR
56
74

73
94

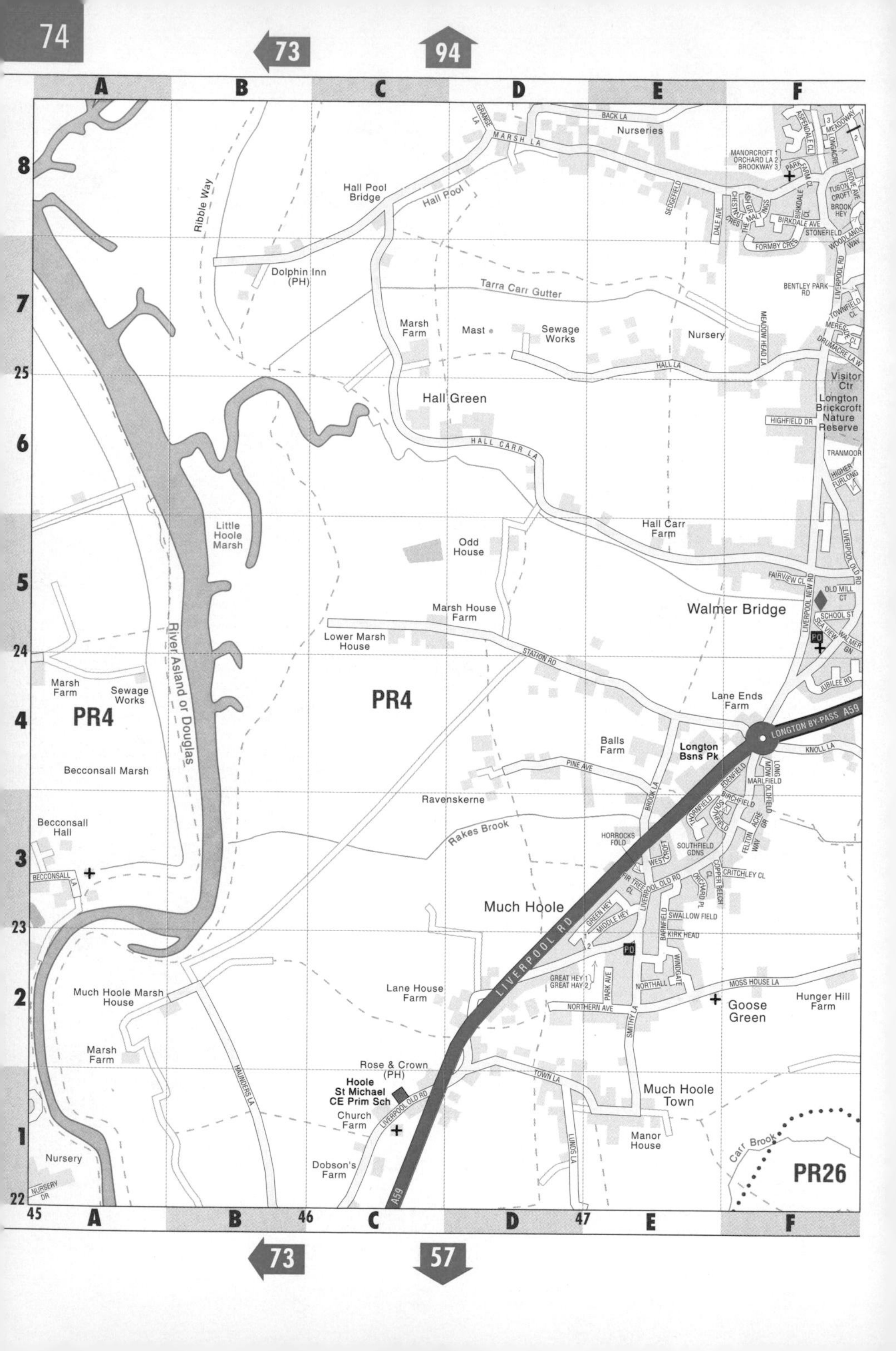
A
B
C
D
E
F
8
7
25
6
5
24
4
3
23
2
1
22
45
46
47
Nurseries
Back La
Marsh La
Grange La
Hall Pool Bridge
Hall Pool
Ribble Way
Dolphin Inn (PH)
Tarra Carr Gutter
Marsh Farm
Mast
Sewage Works
Nursery
Hall La
Hall Green
Hall Carr La
Little Hoole Marsh
Odd House
Hall Carr Farm
Walmer Bridge
Marsh House Farm
Lower Marsh House
Station Rd
Marsh Farm
Sewage Works
PR4
PR4
River Asland or Douglas
Lane Ends Farm
Longton By-Pass A59
Balls Farm
Longton Bsns Pk
Pine Ave
Becconsall Marsh
Ravenskerne
Becconsall Hall
Becconsall La
Rakes Brook
Horrocks Fold
Much Hoole
Liverpool Rd
Much Hoole Marsh House
Lane House Farm
Goose Green
Hunger Hill Farm
Moss House La
Northern Ave
Marsh Farm
Rose & Crown (PH)
Hoole St Michael CE Prim Sch
Church Farm
Liverpool Old Rd
Town La
Much Hoole Town
Manor House
Dobson's Farm
Nursery
Nursery Dr
Haunders La
Lunds La
Smithy La
Carr Brook
PR26
A59
Visitor Ctr
Longton Brickcroft Nature Reserve
Highfield Dr
Tranmoor
Higher Furlong
Liverpool Old Rd
Liverpool New Rd
Fairview Cl
Old Mill Ct
School St
Sea View
Walmer Gn
Jubilee Rd
Knoll La
Long Mdw
Marlfield
Oldfield
Edenfield
Birchfield
Hornfield
Southfield Gdns
Felton Way
Acre Gr
Critchley Cl
Copper Beech Cl
Orchard Pl
Westcroft
Fir Tree Cl
Brook La
Green Hey
Middle Hey
Barnfield
Swallow Field
Kirk Head
Windgate
Northall
Park Ave
Great Hey 1
Great Hay 2
Manorcroft 1
Orchard La 2
Brookway 3
Aspendale Cl
Meadoway
Longacre
Park Farm Cl
Grove Ave
Tuson Croft
Brook Hey
Sedgefield
Dale Ave
Chestnut Cres
Ash Gr
The Maltings
Birkdale Cl
Birkdale Ave
Stonefield
Woodlands Way
Formby Cres
Liverpool Rd
Bentley Park Rd
Townfield Cl
Meresyde Cl
Drumacre La W
Meadow Head La
PO
PO

73
57

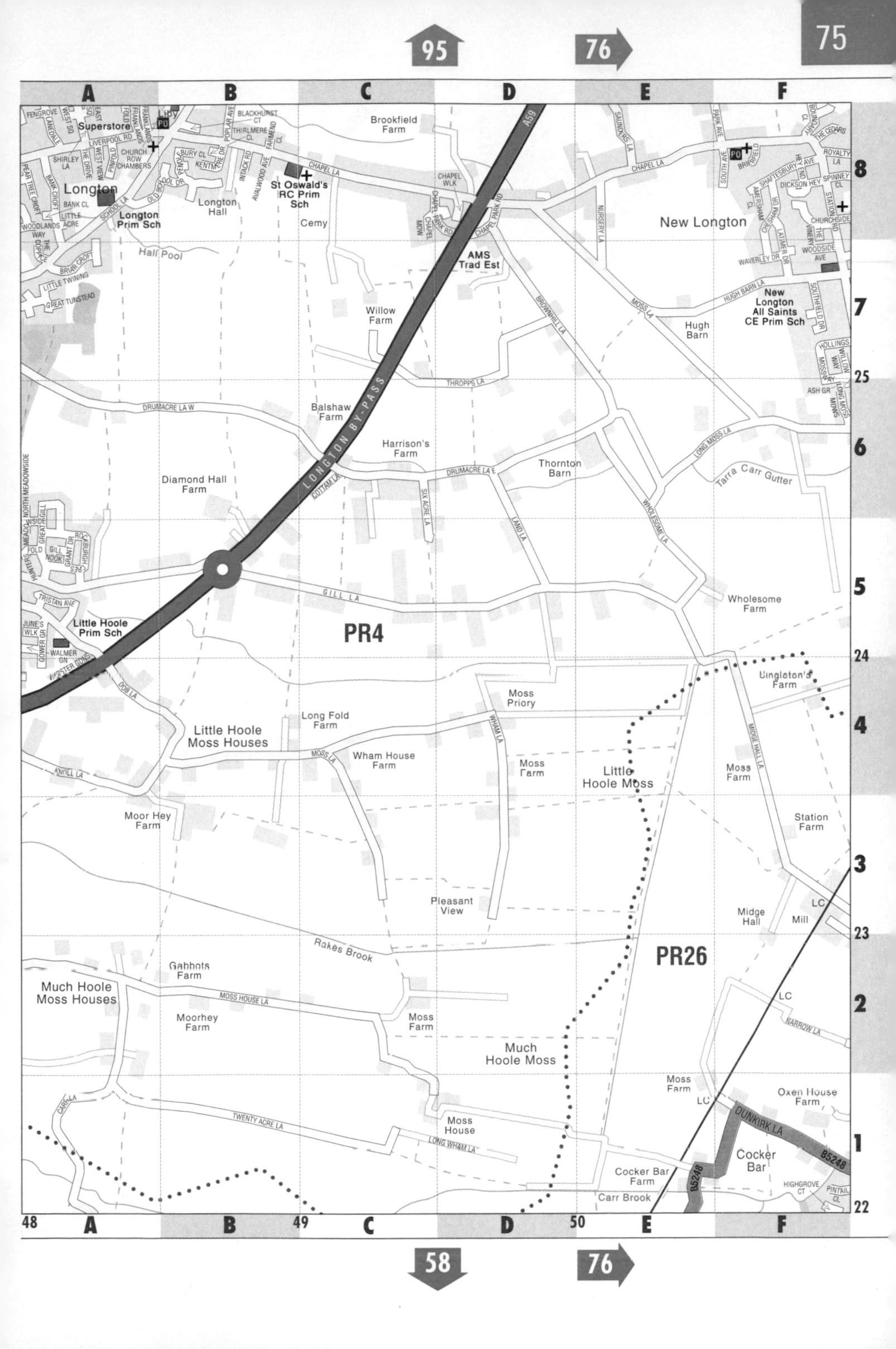

95
76
A
B
C
D
E
F
Superstore
Longton
Longton Prim Sch
St Oswald's RC Prim Sch
Longton Hall
Cemy
Hall Pool
Brookfield Farm
AMS Trad Est
Willow Farm
New Longton
Hugh Barn
New Longton All Saints CE Prim Sch
Balshaw Farm
Harrison's Farm
LONGTON BY-PASS
A59
Thornton Barn
Tarra Carr Gutter
Diamond Hall Farm
Little Hoole Prim Sch
GILL LA
PR4
Wholesome Farm
Moss Priory
Long Fold Farm
Little Hoole Moss Houses
Wham House Farm
Moss Farm
Little Hoole Moss
Moor Hey Farm
Station Farm
Pleasant View
Midge Hall
Mill
Rakes Brook
PR26
Gabbots Farm
Much Hoole Moss Houses
Moorhey Farm
Much Hoole Moss
Moss House
Cocker Bar Farm
Carr Brook
Oxen House Farm
Cocker Bar
B5248
DUNKIRK LA
8
7
6
5
4
3
2
1
25
24
23
22
48
49
50
58
76

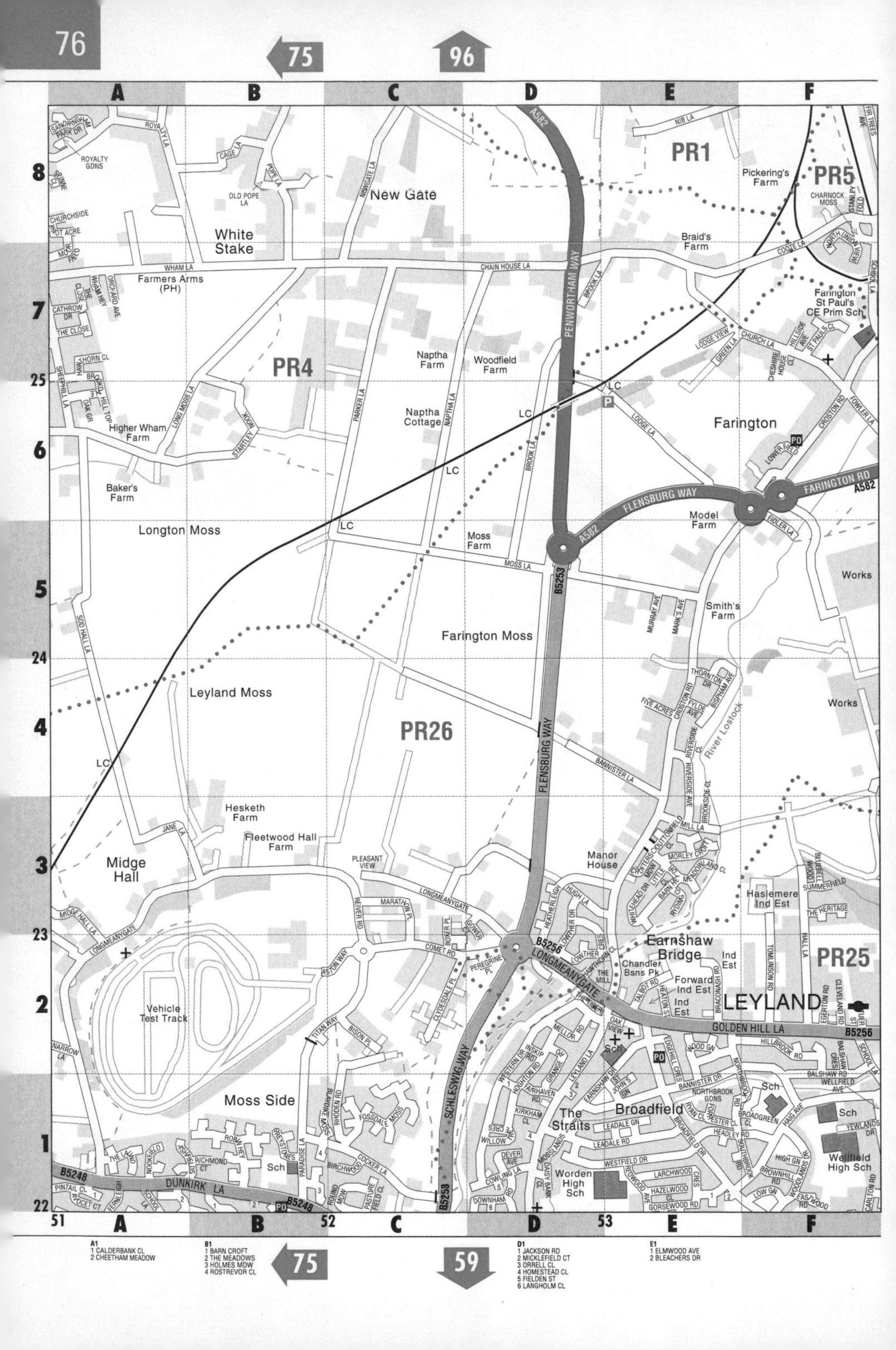

76
75
96
A
B
C
D
E
F
PR1
PR5
PR4
PR26
PR25
New Gate
White Stake
Farmers Arms (PH)
WHAM LA
CHAIN HOUSE LA
PENWORTHAM WAY
A582
Pickering's Farm
Braid's Farm
CHARNOCK MOSS
COOTE LA
Farington St Paul's CE Prim Sch
CHURCH LA
LODGE VIEW
GREEN LA
Naptha Farm
Woodfield Farm
Naptha Cottage
LC
LODGE LA
Farington
Higher Wham Farm
Baker's Farm
Longton Moss
FLENSBURG WAY
FARINGTON RD
Model Farm
FIDLER LA
Moss Farm
MOSS LA
B5253
Works
Smith's Farm
Farington Moss
Leyland Moss
River Lostock
FIVE ACRES
BANNISTER LA
Hesketh Farm
Fleetwood Hall Farm
PLEASANT VIEW
Midge Hall
Manor House
Haslemere Ind Est
LONGMEANYGATE
MARATHON PL
COMET RD
ASTON WAY
B5256
Earnshaw Bridge
Chandler Bsns Pk
Forward Ind Est
Ind Est
LEYLAND
GOLDEN HILL LA
Vehicle Test Track
SCHLESWIG WAY
Sch
Moss Side
The Straits
Broadfield
Worden High Sch
Wellfield High Sch
B5248
DUNKIRK LA
PO
51
52
53
A1
1 CALDERBANK CL
2 CHEETHAM MEADOW
B1
1 BARN CROFT
2 THE MEADOWS
3 HOLMES MDW
4 ROSTREVOR CL
59
D1
1 JACKSON RD
2 MICKLEFIELD CT
3 ORRELL CL
4 HOMESTEAD CL
5 FIELDEN ST
6 LANGHOLM CL
E1
1 ELMWOOD AVE
2 BLEACHERS DR

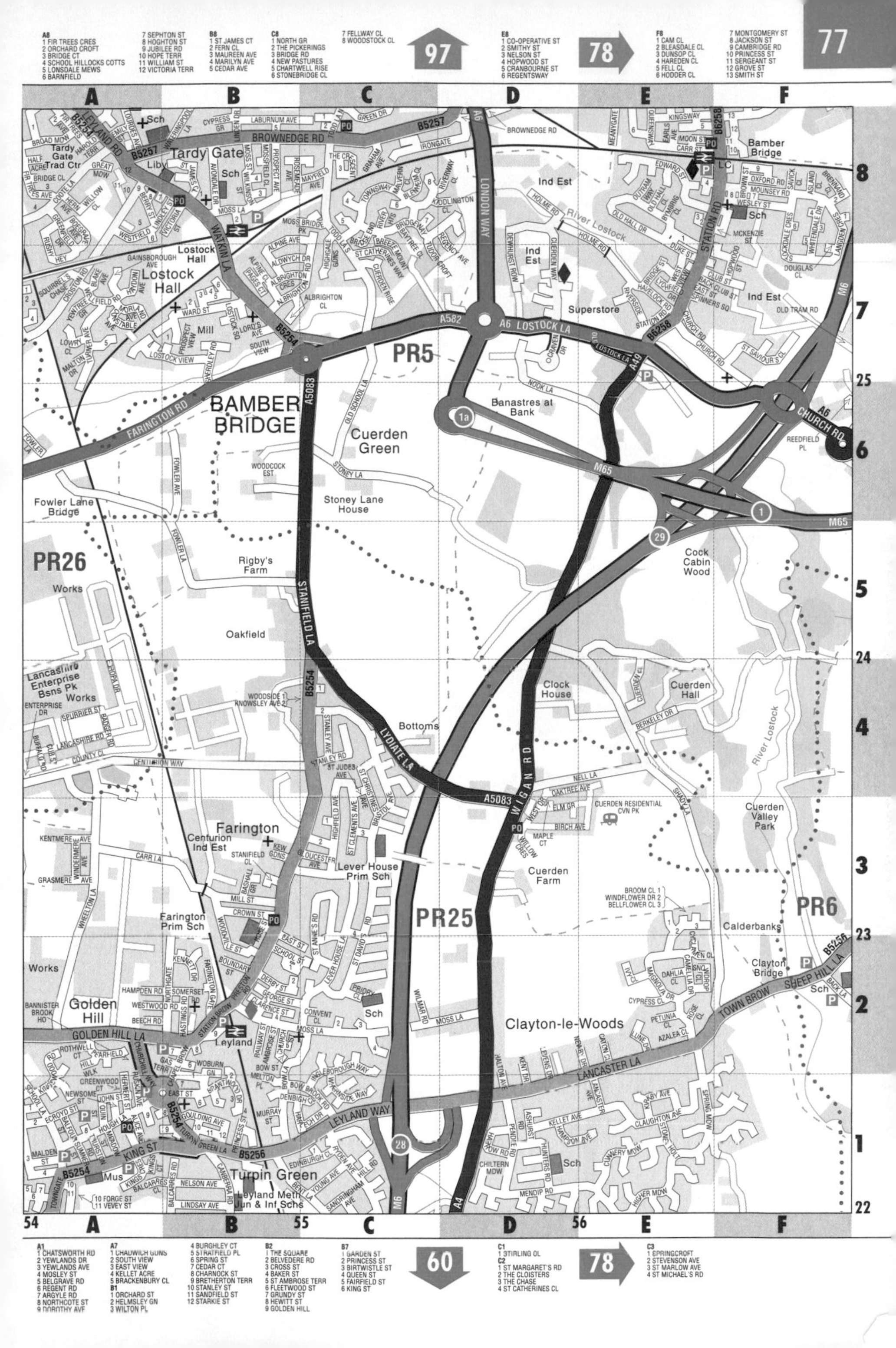
77
A8
1 FIR TREES CRES
2 ORCHARD CROFT
3 BRIDGE CT
4 SCHOOL HILLOCKS COTTS
5 LONSDALE MEWS
6 BARNFIELD
7 SEPHTON ST
8 HOGHTON ST
9 JUBILEE RD
10 HOPE TERR
11 WILLIAM ST
12 VICTORIA TERR
B8
1 ST JAMES CT
2 FERN CL
3 MAUREEN AVE
4 MARILYN AVE
5 CEDAR AVE
C8
1 NORTH GR
2 THE PICKERINGS
3 BRIDGE RD
4 NEW PASTURES
5 CHARTWELL RISE
6 STONEBRIDGE CL
7 FELLWAY CL
8 WOODSTOCK CL
97
E8
1 CO-OPERATIVE ST
2 SMITHY ST
3 NELSON ST
4 HOPWOOD ST
5 CRANBOURNE ST
6 REGENTSWAY
78
F8
1 CAM CL
2 BLEASDALE CL
3 DUNSOP CL
4 HAREDEN CL
5 FELL CL
6 HODDER CL
7 MONTGOMERY ST
8 JACKSON ST
9 CAMBRIDGE RD
10 PRINCESS ST
11 SERGEANT ST
12 GROVE ST
13 SMITH ST
Tardy Gate
Lostock Hall
BAMBER BRIDGE
Bamber Bridge
PR5
Cuerden Green
Stoney Lane House
Fowler Lane Bridge
PR26
Rigby's Farm
Oakfield
Lancashire Enterprise Bsns Pk
Bottoms
Clock House
Cuerden Hall
Cock Cabin Wood
Banastres at Bank
Superstore
Farington
Centurion Ind Est
Lever House Prim Sch
PR25
Cuerden Farm
Cuerden Valley Park
PR6
Calderbanks
Clayton Bridge
Clayton-le-Woods
Golden Hill
Leyland
Turpin Green
Leyland Meth Jun & Inf Schs
BROWNEDGE RD
LONDON WAY
A6 LOSTOCK LA
FARINGTON RD
STANIFIELD LA
LYDIATE LA
WIGAN RD
LANCASTER LA
LEYLAND WAY
GOLDEN HILL LA
TOWN BROW
SHEEP HILL LA
CHURCH RD
M65
M6
54
55
56
A1
1 CHATSWORTH RD
2 YEWLANDS DR
3 YEWLANDS AVE
4 MOSLEY ST
5 BELGRAVE RD
6 REGENT RD
7 ARGYLE RD
8 NORTHCOTE ST
9 DOROTHY AVE
A7
1 CHADWICH GDNS
2 SOUTH VIEW
3 EAST VIEW
4 KELLET ACRE
5 BRACKENBURY CL
B1
1 ORCHARD ST
2 HELMSLEY GN
3 WILTON PL
4 BURGHLEY CT
5 STRATFIELD PL
6 SPRING ST
7 CEDAR CT
8 CHARNOCK ST
9 BRETHERTON TERR
10 STANLEY ST
11 SANDFIELD ST
12 STARKIE ST
B2
1 THE SQUARE
2 BELVEDERE RD
3 CROSS ST
4 BAKER ST
5 ST AMBROSE TERR
6 FLEETWOOD ST
7 GRUNDY ST
8 HEWITT ST
9 GOLDEN HILL
B7
1 GARDEN ST
2 PRINCESS ST
3 BIRTWISTLE ST
4 QUEEN ST
5 FAIRFIELD ST
6 KING ST
60
C1
1 STIRLING CL
C2
1 ST MARGARET'S RD
2 THE CLOISTERS
3 THE CHASE
4 ST CATHERINES CL
78
C3
1 SPRINGCROFT
2 STEVENSON AVE
3 ST MARLOW AVE
4 ST MICHAEL'S RD

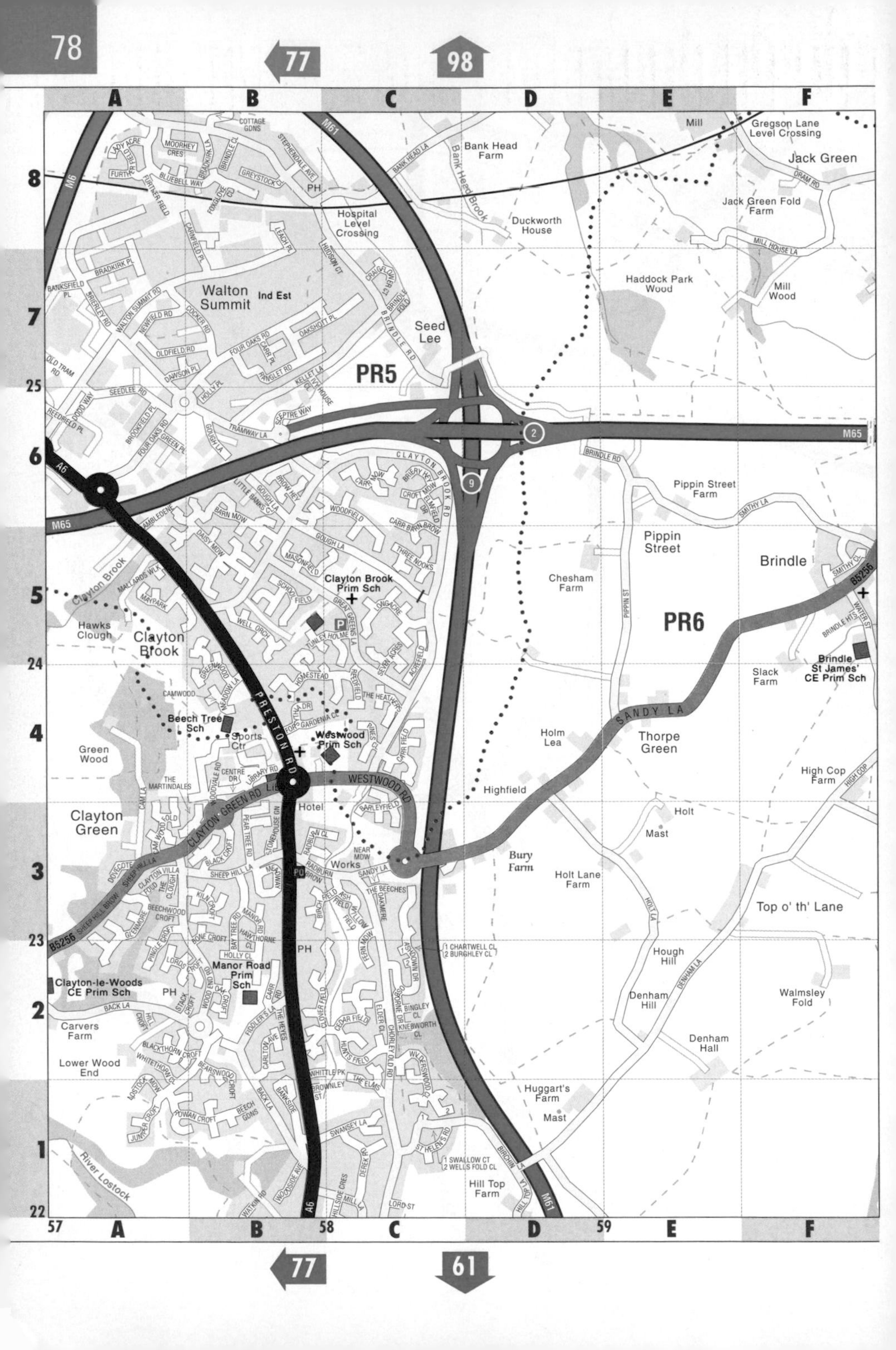
77
98
A
B
C
D
E
F
8
7
25
6
5
24
4
3
23
2
1
22
57
58
59
Walton Summit
Ind Est
Seed Lee
PR5
PR6
Bank Head Farm
Bank Head Brook
Hospital Level Crossing
Duckworth House
Mill
Gregson Lane Level Crossing
Jack Green
Jack Green Fold Farm
Haddock Park Wood
Mill Wood
M61
M6
M65
A6
B5256
Pippin Street Farm
Pippin Street
Brindle
Chesham Farm
Clayton Brook Prim Sch
Clayton Brook
Hawks Clough
Brindle St James' CE Prim Sch
Slack Farm
Beech Tree Sch
Sports Ctr
Westwood Prim Sch
Green Wood
Holm Lea
Thorpe Green
High Cop Farm
Highfield
Clayton Green
Hotel
Works
Holt
Mast
Bury Farm
Holt Lane Farm
Top o' th' Lane
Hough Hill
Denham Hill
Walmsley Fold
Denham Hall
Clayton-le-Woods CE Prim Sch
Manor Road Prim Sch
PH
Carvers Farm
Lower Wood End
Huggart's Farm
Hill Top Farm
River Lostock
PRESTON RD
CLAYTON GREEN RD
WESTWOOD RD
SANDY LA
CLAYTON BROOK RD
GOUGH LA
TRAMWAY LA
BRINDLE RD
SMITHY LA
PIPPIN ST
HOLT LA
DENHAM LA
BACK LA
SHEEP HILL LA
MILL HOUSE LA
ORAM RD
1 CHARTWELL CL
2 BURGHLEY CL
1 SWALLOW CT
2 WELLS FOLD CL
77
61

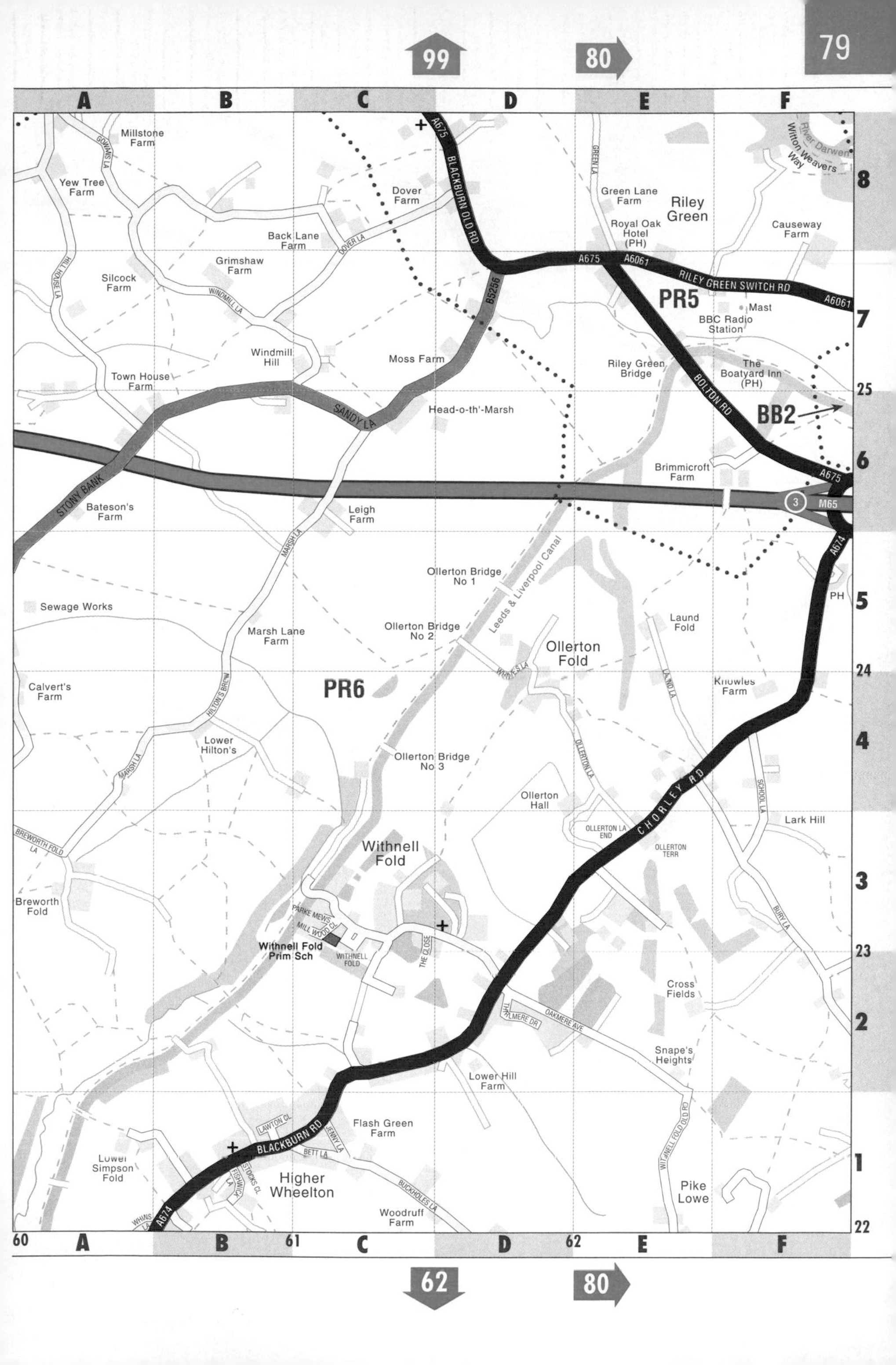
99
80
A
B
C
D
E
F
Millstone Farm
Yew Tree Farm
Dover Farm
Green Lane Farm
Riley Green
Royal Oak Hotel (PH)
Causeway Farm
Back Lane Farm
Grimshaw Farm
Silcock Farm
River Darwen
Witton Weavers Way
BLACKBURN OLD RD
A675
A6061
RILEY GREEN SWITCH RD
PR5
Mast
BBC Radio Station
B5256
Windmill Hill
Moss Farm
Riley Green Bridge
The Boatyard Inn (PH)
Town House Farm
SANDY LA
Head-o-th'-Marsh
BOLTON RD
BB2
STONY BANK
Brimmicroft Farm
Bateson's Farm
Leigh Farm
M65
A674
Ollerton Bridge No 1
Sewage Works
Leeds & Liverpool Canal
PH
Laund Fold
Marsh Lane Farm
Ollerton Bridge No 2
Ollerton Fold
Calvert's Farm
PR6
Knowles Farm
HILTON'S BROW
Lower Hilton's
Ollerton Bridge No 3
MARSH LA
OLLERTON LA
SCHOOL LA
Ollerton Hall
Lark Hill
BREWORTH FOLD LA
OLLERTON LA END
CHORLEY RD
OLLERTON TERR
Withnell Fold
Breworth Fold
PARKE MEWS
MILL WOOD CL
Withnell Fold Prim Sch
WITHNELL FOLD
THE CLOSE
BURY LA
Cross Fields
OAKMERE AVE
Snape's Heights
Lower Hill Farm
Flash Green Farm
LAWTON CL
JENNY LA
BLACKBURN RD
BETT LA
Lower Simpson Fold
Higher Wheelton
STOCKS CL
FISHWICK LA
BUCKHOLES LA
WITHNELL FOLD OLD RD
Pike Lowe
Woodruff Farm
WHINS LA
GREEN LA
DOVER LA
WINDMILL LA
HILL HOUSE LA
GOWANS LA
MARSH LA
LAUND LA
8
7
25
6
5
24
4
3
23
2
1
22
60
61
62
62
80

79
100

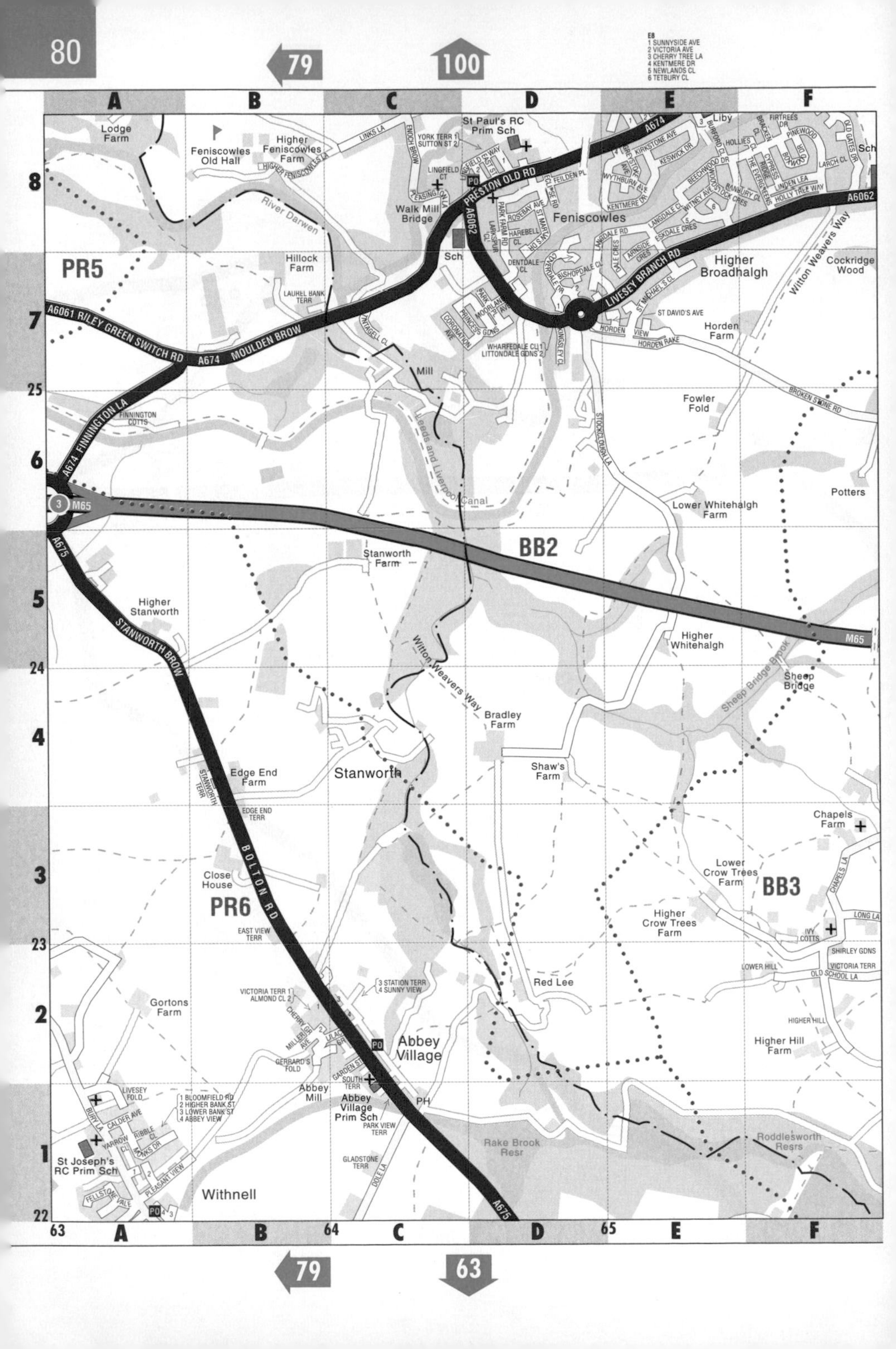
E8
1 SUNNYSIDE AVE
2 VICTORIA AVE
3 CHERRY TREE LA
4 KENTMERE DR
5 NEWLANDS CL
6 TETBURY CL
Lodge Farm
Feniscowles Old Hall
Higher Feniscowles Farm
St Paul's RC Prim Sch
YORK TERR 1
SUTTON ST 2
Walk Mill Bridge
PRESTON OLD RD
Feniscowles
A6062
A674
LIVESEY BRANCH RD
Higher Broadhalgh
Cockridge Wood
Witton Weavers Way
River Darwen
Hillock Farm
LAUREL BANK TERR
PR5
A6061 RILEY GREEN SWITCH RD
MOULDEN BROW
WHARFEDALE CL 1
LITTONDALE GDNS 2
Horden Farm
HORDEN RAKE
ST DAVID'S AVE
Mill
FINNINGTON LA
FINNINGTON COTTS
Fowler Fold
BROKEN STONE RD
Leeds and Liverpool Canal
STOCKCLOUGH LA
Potters
M65
Lower Whitehalgh Farm
BB2
A675
Stanworth Farm
Higher Stanworth
STANWORTH BROW
Higher Whitehalgh
Sheep Bridge Brook
Sheep Bridge
Bradley Farm
Shaw's Farm
Edge End Farm
Stanworth
STANWORTH TERR
EDGE END TERR
Chapels Farm
Lower Crow Trees Farm
BB3
Close House
PR6
BOLTON RD
Higher Crow Trees Farm
EAST VIEW TERR
LONG LA
IVY COTTS
SHIRLEY GDNS
LOWER HILL
VICTORIA TERR
OLD SCHOOL LA
Red Lee
VICTORIA TERR 1
ALMOND CL 2
3 STATION TERR
4 SUNNY VIEW
Gortons Farm
Abbey Village
HIGHER HILL
Higher Hill Farm
GERRARD'S FOLD
GARDEN ST
SOUTH TERR
Abbey Mill
Abbey Village Prim Sch
PH
LIVESEY FOLD
1 BLOOMFIELD RD
2 HIGHER BANK ST
3 LOWER BANK ST
4 ABBEY VIEW
BURY LA
CALDER AVE
YARROW CL
RIBBLE CL
PARK VIEW TERR
Rake Brook Resr
Roddlesworth Resrs
St Joseph's RC Prim Sch
PLEASANT VIEW
GLADSTONE TERR
DOLE LA
Withnell
FELLSTONE VALE
PO
A B C D E F
8 7 6 5 4 3 2 1
25 24 23 22
63 64 65

79
63

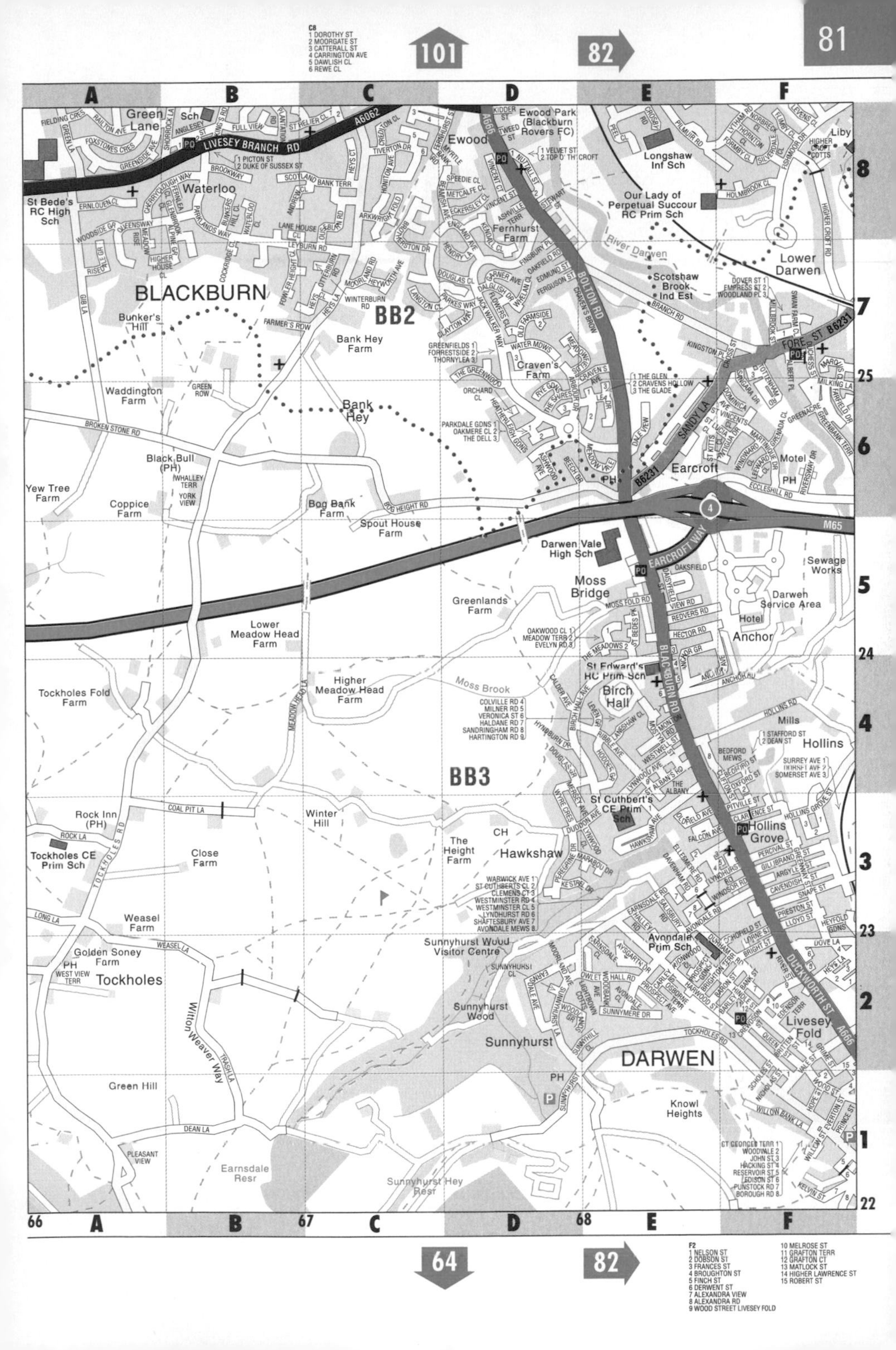
81
101
82
C8
1 DOROTHY ST
2 MOORGATE ST
3 CATTERALL ST
4 CARRINGTON AVE
5 DAWLISH CL
6 REWE CL
A
B
C
D
E
F
Green Lane
Sch
LIVESEY BRANCH RD
A6062
1 PICTON ST
2 DUKE OF SUSSEX ST
Waterloo
St Bede's RC High Sch
Ewood
Ewood Park (Blackburn Rovers FC)
1 VELVET ST
2 TOP O' TH' CROFT
Longshaw Inf Sch
Our Lady of Perpetual Succour RC Prim Sch
Lower Darwen
Liby
HIGHER CROFT COTTS
Fernhurst Farm
River Darwen
Scotshaw Brook Ind Est
1 DOVER ST
2 EMPRESS ST
3 WOODLAND PL
BLACKBURN
BB2
Bunker's Hill
Bank Hey Farm
GREENFIELDS 1
FORRESTSIDE 2
THORNYLEA 3
Craven's Farm
1 THE GLEN
2 CRAVENS HOLLOW
3 THE GLADE
BOLTON RD
A666
B6231
FORE ST
Waddington Farm
GREEN ROW
Bank Hey
PARKDALE GDNS 1
OAKMERE CL 2
THE DELL 3
BROKEN STONE RD
Black Bull (PH)
WHALLEY TERR
YORK VIEW
Yew Tree Farm
Coppice Farm
Bog Bank Farm
BOG HEIGHT RD
Spout House Farm
Earcroft
Motel
PH
ECCLESHILL RD
M65
Darwen Vale High Sch
EARCROFT WAY
Sewage Works
Moss Bridge
Darwen Service Area
Hotel
Anchor
Greenlands Farm
Lower Meadow Head Farm
OAKWOOD CL 1
MEADOW TERR 2
EVELYN RD 3
St Edward's RC Prim Sch
Birch Hall
BLACKBURN RD
Moss Brook
Tockholes Fold Farm
Higher Meadow Head Farm
MEADOW HEAD LA
COLVILLE RD 4
MILNER RD 5
VERONICA ST 6
HALDANE RD 7
SANDRINGHAM RD 8
HARTINGTON RD 9
Mills
Hollins
1 STAFFORD ST
2 DEAN ST
BEDFORD MEWS
SURREY AVE 1
DORSET AVE 2
SOMERSET AVE 3
BB3
COAL PIT LA
Rock Inn (PH)
Winter Hill
St Cuthbert's CE Prim Sch
THE ALBANY
Hollins Grove
ROCK LA
Tockholes CE Prim Sch
TOCKHOLES RD
Close Farm
The Height Farm
CH
Hawkshaw
WARWICK AVE 1
ST CUTHBERTS CL 2
CLEMENS CT 3
WESTMINSTER RD 4
WESTMINSTER CL 5
LYNDHURST RD 6
SHAFTESBURY AVE 7
AVONDALE MEWS 8
LONG LA
Weasel Farm
WEASEL LA
Golden Soney Farm
PH
WEST VIEW TERR
Tockholes
Sunnyhurst Wood Visitor Centre
Avondale Prim Sch
DUCKWORTH ST
Witton Weaver Way
Sunnyhurst Wood
Sunnyhurst
DARWEN
Livesey Fold
Green Hill
PH
TOCKHOLES RD
Knowl Heights
WILLOW BANK LA
DEAN LA
PLEASANT VIEW
Earnsdale Resr
Sunnyhurst Hey Resr
ST GEORGES TERR 1
WOODVALE 2
JOHN ST 3
HACKING ST 4
RESERVOIR ST 5
EDISON ST 6
PUNSTOCK RD 7
BOROUGH RD 8
8
7
25
6
5
24
4
3
23
2
1
22
66
67
68
64
82
F2
1 NELSON ST
2 DOBSON ST
3 FRANCES ST
4 BROUGHTON ST
5 FINCH ST
6 DERWENT ST
7 ALEXANDRA VIEW
8 ALEXANDRA RD
9 WOOD STREET LIVESEY FOLD
10 MELROSE ST
11 GRAFTON TERR
12 GRAFTON CT
13 MATLOCK ST
14 HIGHER LAWRENCE ST
15 ROBERT ST

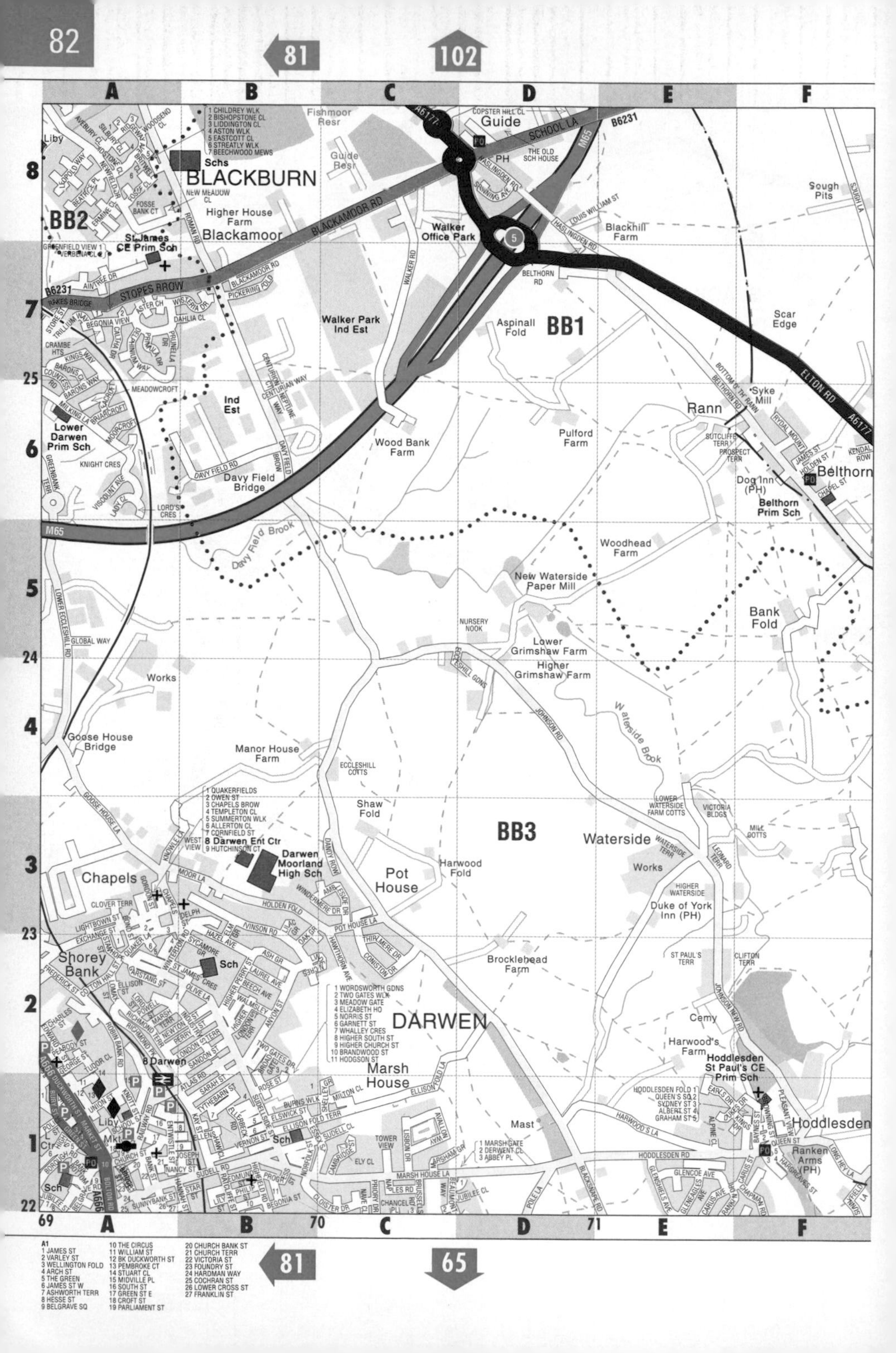
81
102
A
B
C
D
E
F
1 CHILDREY WLK
2 BISHOPSTONE CL
3 LIDDINGTON CL
4 ASTON WLK
5 EASTCOTT CL
6 STREATLY WLK
7 BEECHWOOD MEWS
Fishmoor Resr
Guide Resr
COPSTER HILL CL
Guide
SCHOOL LA
B6231
A6177
M65
PO
PH
THE OLD SCH HOUSE
HASLINGDEN RD
Liby
Schs
BLACKBURN
NEW MEADOW CL
FOSSE BANK CT
BB2
Higher House Farm
Blackamoor
BLACKAMOOR RD
ROMAN RD
Walker Office Park
LOUIS WILLIAM ST
Blackhill Farm
Sough Pits
St James CE Prim Sch
GREENFIELD VIEW 1
VERBENA CL 2
AINTREE DR
BLACKAMOOR RD
PICKERING FOLD
STOPES BROW
B6231
RAKES BRIDGE
WISTERIA DR
DAHLIA CL
BEGONIA VIEW
TRILLIUM WAY
WALKER RD
BELTHORN RD
Walker Park Ind Est
Aspinall Fold
BB1
Scar Edge
CRAMBE HTS
KINGS WAY
BARONS CL
BARONS WAY
COUNTESS RD
MEADOWCROFT
MILKING LA
BRIARCROFT
MOORCROFT
Lower Darwen Prim Sch
CENTURION WAY
NEPTUNE WAY
Ind Est
Syke Mill
Rann
BOTTOM O' TH' RANN
BELTHORN RD
ELTON RD
A6177
RYDAL MOUNT
SUTCLIFFE TERR
PROSPECT TERR
JAMES ST
HOLDEN ST
KENDAL ROW
Pulford Farm
Wood Bank Farm
KNIGHT CRES
DAVY FIELD RD
DAVY FIELD BROW
Davy Field Bridge
VISCOUNT AVE
LADY CL
LORD'S CRES
GREENBANK TERR
Dog Inn (PH)
Belthorn
CHAPEL ST
Belthorn Prim Sch
M65
Davy Field Brook
Woodhead Farm
New Waterside Paper Mill
LOWER ECCLESHILL RD
Bank Fold
NURSERY NOOK
GLOBAL WAY
Lower Grimshaw Farm
Higher Grimshaw Farm
ECCLESHILL GDNS
Works
JOHNSON RD
Waterside Brook
Goose House Bridge
Manor House Farm
ECCLESHILL COTTS
GOOSE HOUSE LA
1 QUAKERFIELDS
2 OWEN ST
3 CHAPELS BROW
4 TEMPLETON CL
5 SUMMERTON WLK
6 ALLERTON CL
7 CORNFIELD ST
8 Darwen Ent Ctr
9 HUTCHINSON CT
Shaw Fold
LOWER WATERSIDE FARM COTTS
VICTORIA BLDGS
MILL COTTS
BB3
Waterside
WATERSIDE TERR
LEONARD TERR
KNOWL LA
WEST VIEW
Darwen Moorland High Sch
Chapels
MOOR LA
Pot House
Harwood Fold
DANDY ROW
Works
HIGHER WATERSIDE
Duke of York Inn (PH)
CLOVER TERR
DELPH
HOLDEN FOLD
WINDERMERE DR
POT HOUSE LA
THIRLMERE DR
CONISTON DR
LIGHTBOWN ST
EXCHANGE ST
HAZEL AVE
SYCAMORE GR
ASH GR
HAWTHORN AVE
Shorey Bank
Sch
LAUREL AVE
BEECH AVE
ST JAMES CRES
OLIVE LA
Brocklehead Farm
ST PAUL'S TERR
CLIFTON TERR
FREDERICK ST
COTTON HALL ST
1 WORDSWORTH GDNS
2 TWO GATES WLK
3 MEADOW GATE
4 ELIZABETH HO
5 NORRIS ST
6 GARNETT ST
7 WHALLEY CRES
8 HIGHER SOUTH ST
9 HIGHER CHURCH ST
10 BRANDWOOD ST
11 HODGSON ST
DARWEN
JOHNSON NEW RD
Cemy
Harwood's Farm
Hoddlesden St Paul's CE Prim Sch
ROBIN BANK RD
RICHMOND TERR
8 Darwen
TWO GATES DR
Marsh House
ELLISON FOLD LA
MILTON CL
BURNS WLK
ELSWICK ST
ELLISON FOLD TERR
HODDLESDEN FOLD 1
QUEEN'S SQ 2
SYDNEY ST 3
ALBERT ST 4
GRAHAM ST 5
HARWOOD'S LA
PLEASANT VIEW
Hoddlesden
Liby
Mkt
Ctr
Sch
A666
BOLTON RD
DUCKWORTH ST
MARKET ST
Sch
TOWER VIEW
ELY CL
AVALON WAY
LISBON DR
Mast
1 MARSH GATE
2 DERWENT CL
3 ABBEY PL
HODDLESDEN RD
GLENCOE AVE
Ranken Arms (PH)
QUEEN ST
HARGREAVES ST
LONG HEY LA
MARSH HOUSE LA
JUBILEE CL
POLE LA
BLACKSNAPE RD
GLENSHIELS AVE
GLENEAGLES AVE
CARUS AVE
CHAPMAN RD
SUNNYBANK ST
BEGONIA ST
CLOISTER DR
CHANCEL PL
69
70
71
22
23
24
25
1
2
3
4
5
6
7
8
A1
1 JAMES ST
2 VARLEY ST
3 WELLINGTON FOLD
4 ARCH ST
5 THE GREEN
6 JAMES ST W
7 ASHWORTH TERR
8 HESSE ST
9 BELGRAVE SQ
10 THE CIRCUS
11 WILLIAM ST
12 BK DUCKWORTH ST
13 PEMBROKE CT
14 STUART CL
15 MIDVILLE PL
16 SOUTH ST
17 GREEN ST E
18 CROFT ST
19 PARLIAMENT ST
20 CHURCH BANK ST
21 CHURCH TERR
22 VICTORIA ST
23 FOUNDRY ST
24 HARDMAN WAY
25 COCHRAN ST
26 LOWER CROSS ST
27 FRANKLIN ST
81
65

103
84

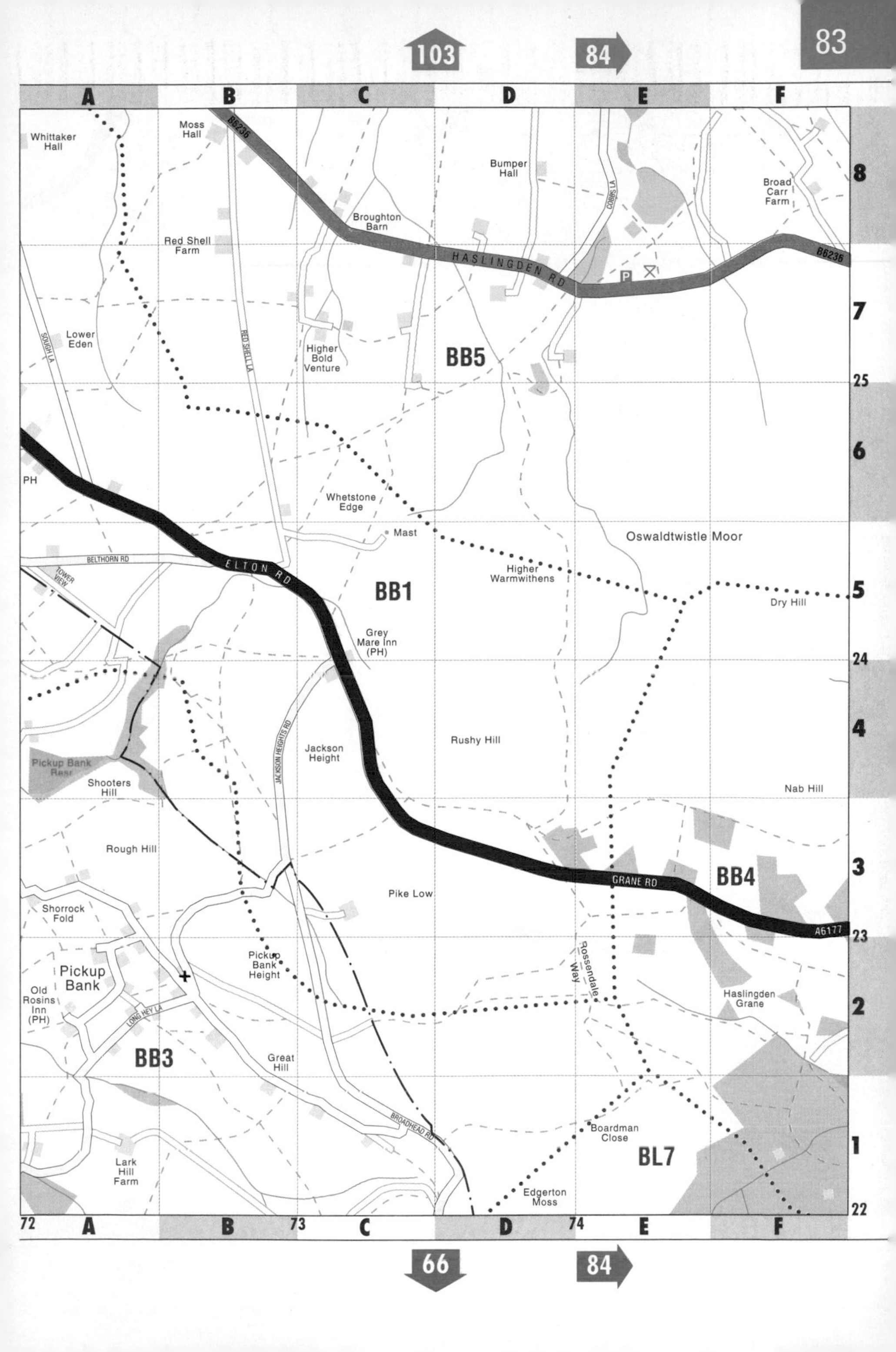
A
B
C
D
E
F
Whittaker Hall
Moss Hall
B6236
Bumper Hall
Broad Carr Farm
8
Broughton Barn
COBBS LA
Red Shell Farm
HASLINGDEN RD
B6236
P
7
SOUGH LA
Lower Eden
RED SHELL LA
Higher Bold Venture
BB5
25
6
PH
Whetstone Edge
Mast
Oswaldtwistle Moor
BELTHORN RD
ELTON RD
TOWER VIEW
Higher Warmwithens
BB1
5
Dry Hill
Grey Mare Inn (PH)
24
JACKSON HEIGHTS RD
Jackson Height
Rushy Hill
4
Pickup Bank Resr
Shooters Hill
Nab Hill
Rough Hill
3
GRANE RD
BB4
Shorrock Fold
Pike Low
A6177
23
Pickup Bank Height
Rossendale Way
Pickup Bank
Old Rosins Inn (PH)
LONG HEY LA
Haslingden Grane
2
BB3
Great Hill
BROADHEAD RD
Boardman Close
1
Lark Hill Farm
BL7
Edgerton Moss
22
72
73
74
A
B
C
D
E
F

66
84

83 104

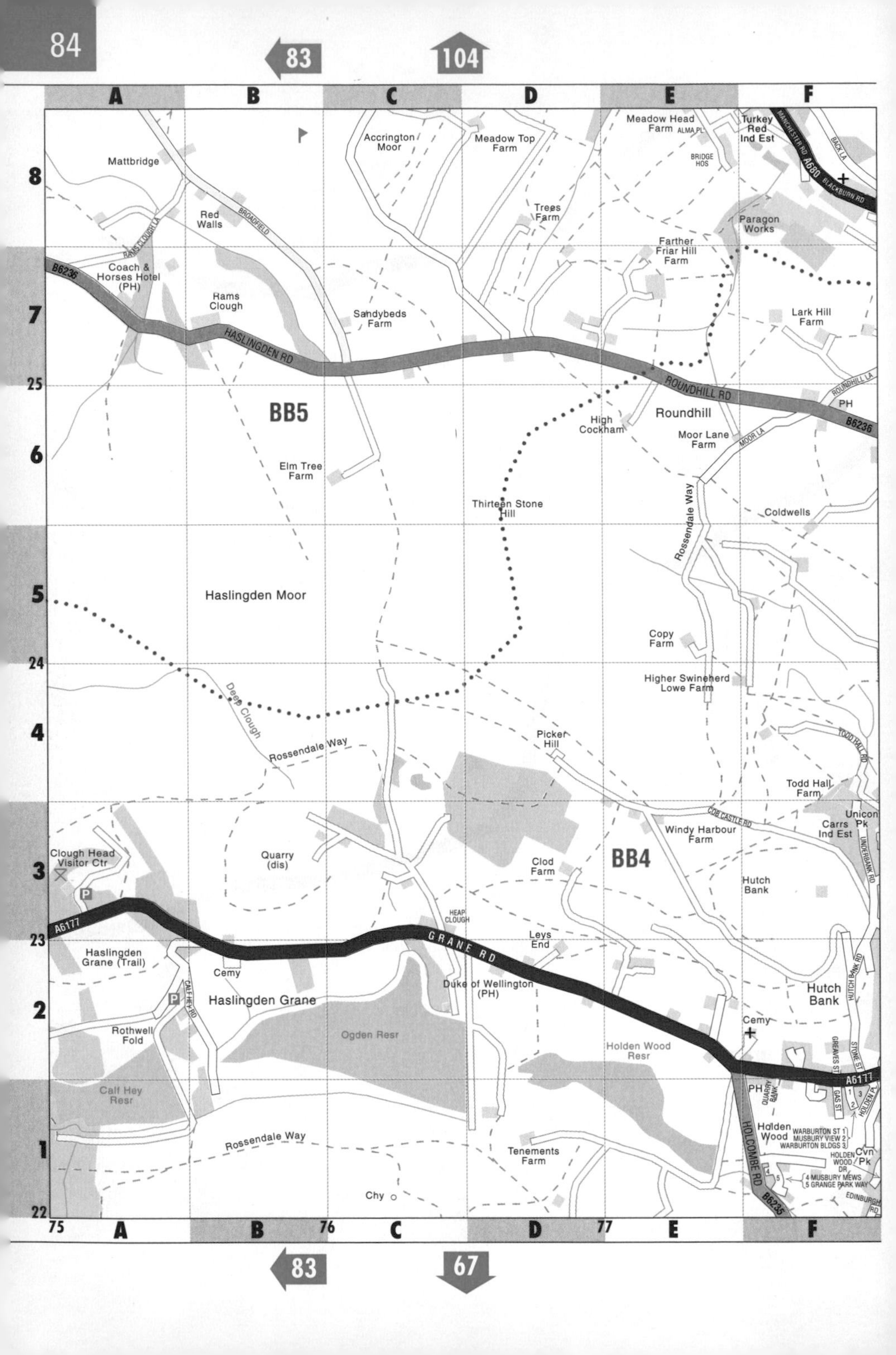

Mattbridge
Red Walls
BROADFIELD
RAMS CLOUGH LA
Coach & Horses Hotel (PH)
B6236
Hams Clough
HASLINGDEN RD
Accrington Moor
Meadow Top Farm
Sandybeds Farm
Trees Farm
Meadow Head Farm
ALMA PL
BRIDGE HOS
Turkey Red Ind Est
MANCHESTER RD
A680
BLACKBURN RD
BACK LA
Paragon Works
Farther Friar Hill Farm
Lark Hill Farm
ROUNDHILL RD
ROUNDHILL LA
PH
Roundhill
High Cockham
Moor Lane Farm
MOOR LA
BB5
Elm Tree Farm
Thirteen Stone Hill
Rossendale Way
Coldwells
Haslingden Moor
Copy Farm
Higher Swineherd Lowe Farm
Deep Clough
Rossendale Way
Picker Hill
TODD HALL RD
Todd Hall Farm
COB CASTLE RD
Windy Harbour Farm
Unicon Pk
Carrs Ind Est
UNDERBANK RD
Clough Head Visitor Ctr
Quarry (dis)
Clod Farm
BB4
Hutch Bank
A6177
HEAP CLOUGH
GRANE RD
Leys End
Haslingden Grane (Trail)
Cemy
CALF HEY RD
Haslingden Grane
Duke of Wellington (PH)
HUTCH BANK RD
Hutch Bank
Cemy
Rothwell Fold
Ogden Resr
Holden Wood Resr
GREAVES ST
STONE ST
A6177
PH
QUARRY BANK
GAS ST
HOLDEN PL
Calf Hey Resr
HOLCOMBE RD
Holden Wood
WARBURTON ST 1
MUSBURY VIEW 2
WARBURTON BLDGS 3
Rossendale Way
Tenements Farm
HOLDEN WOOD DR
Cvn Pk
4 MUSBURY MEWS
5 GRANGE PARK WAY
Chy
B6235
EDINBURGH RD

83 67

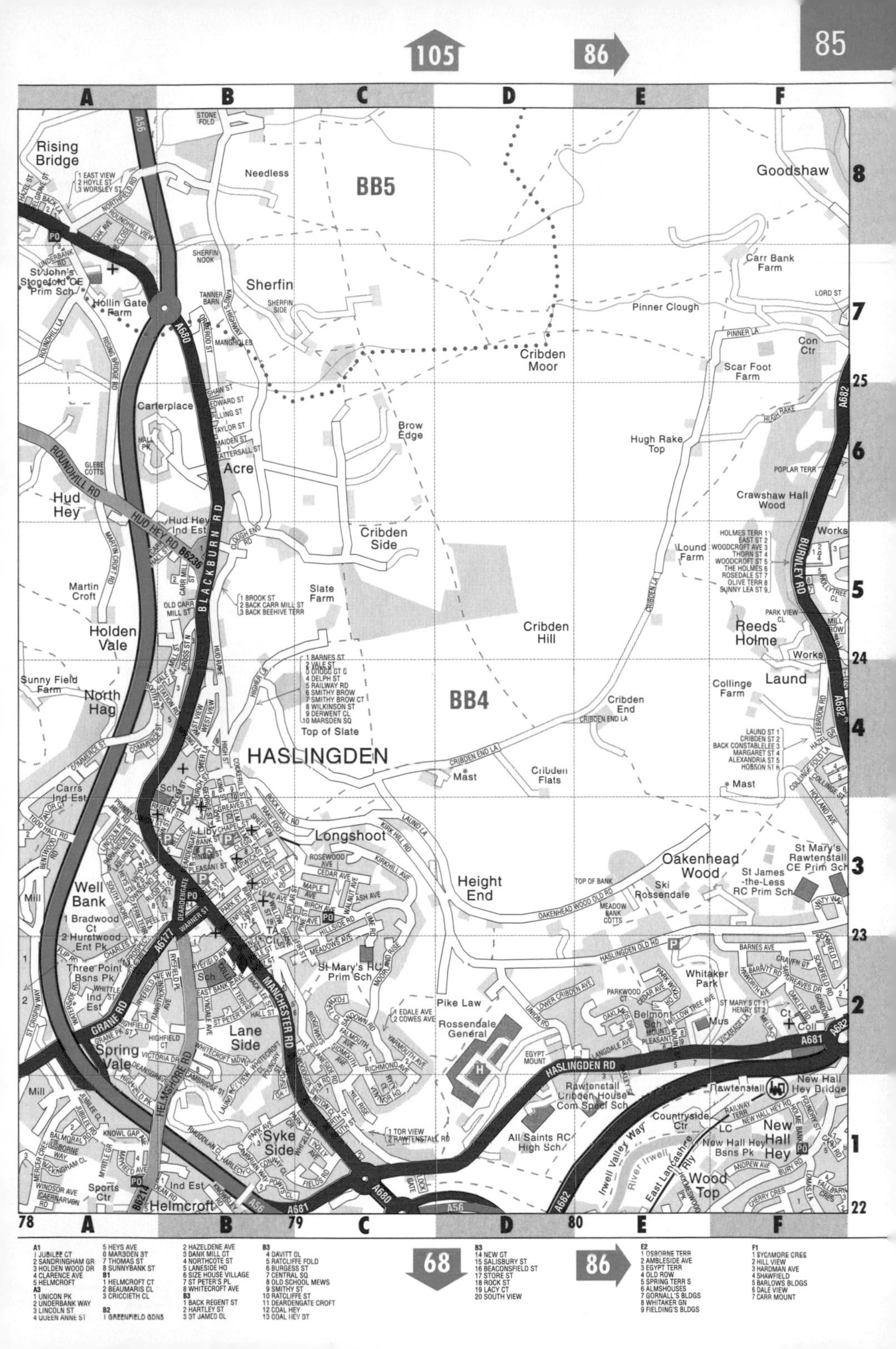
85
105
86
Rising Bridge
Needless
BB5
Goodshaw
Sherfin
Carr Bank Farm
Pinner Clough
Cribden Moor
Con Ctr
Scar Foot Farm
Carterplace
Brow Edge
Hugh Rake Top
Acre
Hud Hey
Hud Hey Ind Est
Crawshaw Hall Wood
Cribden Side
Lound Farm
Martin Croft
Slate Farm
Holden Vale
Cribden Hill
Reeds Holme
Laund
Sunny Field Farm
North Hag
Collinge Farm
BB4
Cribden End
Top of Slate
HASLINGDEN
Cribden Flats
Mast
Carrs Ind Est
Longshoot
Oakenhead Wood
St Mary's Rawtenstall CE Prim Sch
St James -the-Less RC Prim Sch
Ski Rossendale
Height End
Well Bank
Three Point Bsns Pk
St Mary's RC Prim Sch
Whitaker Park
Pike Law
Rossendale General
Lane Side
Spring Vale
Rawtenstall Cribden House Com Spec Sch
Countryside Ctr
New Hall Hey Bridge
New Hall Hey
All Saints RC High Sch
Syke Side
Sports Ctr
Helmcroft
Wood Top
Irwell Valley Way
River Irwell
East Lancashire Rly
BLACKBURN RD
MANCHESTER RD
BURNLEY RD
HASLINGDEN RD
GRANE RD
HUD HEY RD
ROUNDHILL RD
CRIBDEN END LA
OAKENHEAD WOOD OLD RD
HASLINGDEN OLD RD
A56
A680
A681
A682
A6177
B6236
B6214
78
79
80
8
7
25
6
5
24
4
3
23
2
1
22
A1
1 JUBILEE CT
2 SANDRINGHAM GR
3 HOLDEN WOOD DR
4 CLARENCE AVE
5 HELMCROFT
A3
1 UNICON PK
2 UNDERBANK WAY
3 LINCOLN ST
4 QUEEN ANNE ST
5 HEYS AVE
6 MARSDEN ST
7 THOMAS ST
8 SUNNYBANK ST
B1
1 HELMCROFT CT
2 BEAUMARIS CL
3 CRICCIETH CL
B2
1 GREENFIELD GDNS
2 HAZELDENE AVE
3 BANK MILL CT
4 NORTHCOTE ST
5 LANESIDE HO
6 SIZE HOUSE VILLAGE
7 ST PETER'S PL
8 WHITECROFT AVE
B3
1 BACK REGENT ST
2 HARTLEY ST
3 ST JAMES CL
B3
4 DAVITT CL
5 RATCLIFFE FOLD
6 BURGESS ST
7 CENTRAL SQ
8 OLD SCHOOL MEWS
9 SMITHY ST
10 RATCLIFFE ST
11 DEARDENGATE CROFT
12 COAL HEY
13 COAL HEY ST
68
B3
14 NEW CT
15 SALISBURY ST
16 BEACONSFIELD ST
17 STORE ST
18 ROCK ST
19 LACY CT
20 SOUTH VIEW
86
E2
1 OSBORNE TERR
2 AMBLESIDE AVE
3 EGYPT TERR
4 OLD ROW
5 SPRING TERR S
6 ALMSHOUSES
7 GORNALL'S BLDGS
8 WHITAKER GN
9 FIELDING'S BLDGS
F1
1 SYCAMORE CRES
2 HILL VIEW
3 HARDMAN AVE
4 SHAWFIELD
5 BARLOWS BLDGS
6 DALE VIEW
7 CARR MOUNT

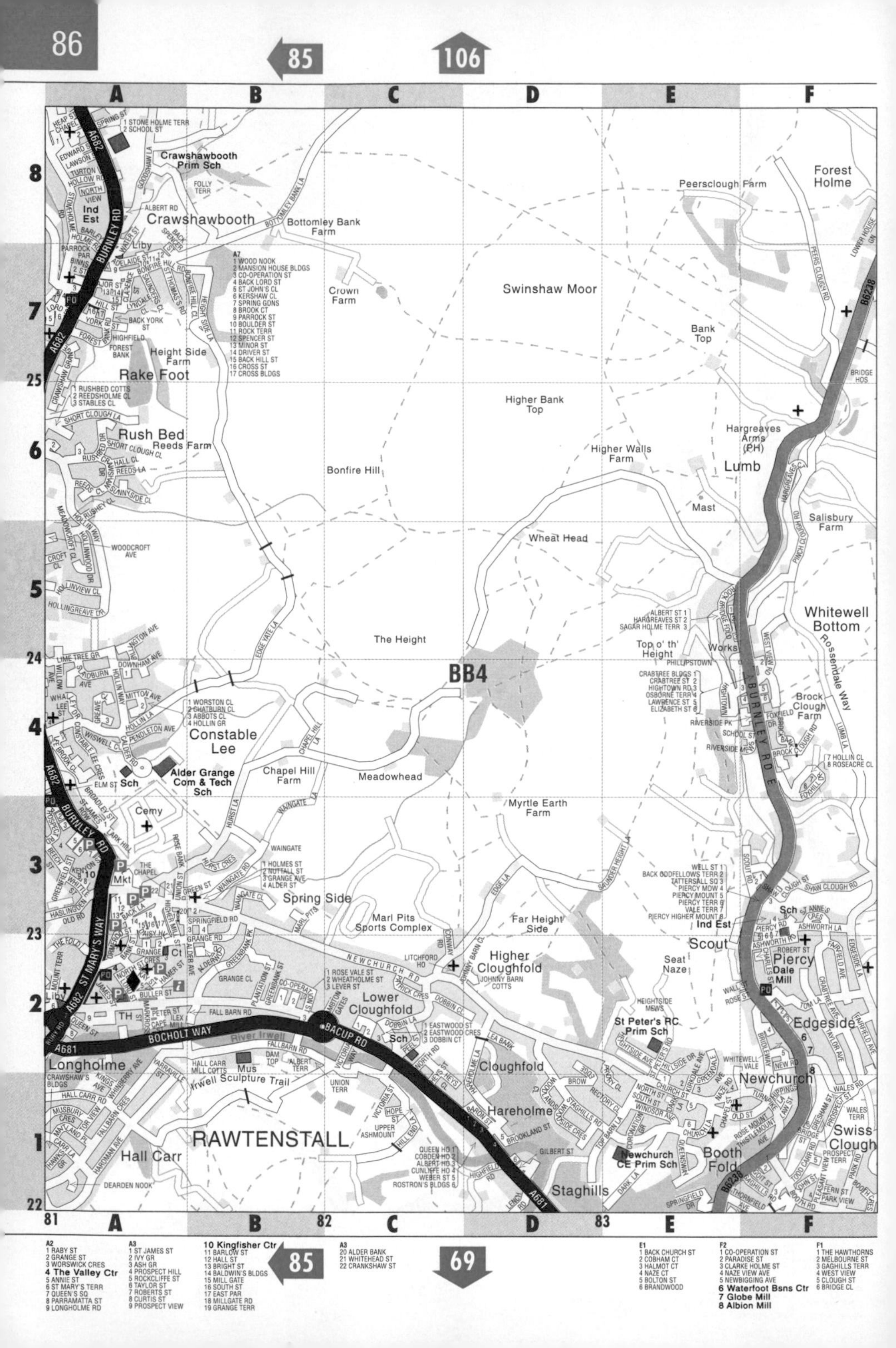
85
106
A
B
C
D
E
F
8
7
25
6
5
24
4
3
23
2
1
22
81
82
83
1 STONE HOLME TERR
2 SCHOOL ST
Crawshawbooth Prim Sch
Crawshawbooth
Ind Est
BURNLEY RD
A682
FOLLY TERR
ALBERT RD
BOTTOMLEY BANK LA
Bottomley Bank Farm
Liby
A7
1 WOOD NOOK
2 MANSION HOUSE BLDGS
3 CO-OPERATION ST
4 BACK LORD ST
5 ST JOHN'S CL
6 KERSHAW CL
7 SPRING GDNS
8 BROOK CT
9 PARROCK ST
10 BOULDER ST
11 ROCK TERR
12 SPENCER ST
13 MINOR ST
14 DRIVER ST
15 BACK HILL ST
16 CROSS ST
17 CROSS BLDGS
Crown Farm
Swinshaw Moor
Peersclough Farm
Forest Holme
Bank Top
B6238
BRIDGE HOS
Height Side Farm
Rake Foot
1 RUSHBED COTTS
2 REEDSHOLME CL
3 STABLES CL
Rush Bed
Reeds Farm
Higher Bank Top
Hargreaves Arms (PH)
Lumb
Higher Walls Farm
Bonfire Hill
Mast
Salisbury Farm
Wheat Head
WOODCROFT AVE
HOLLINGREAVE DR
Whitewell Bottom
Rossendale Way
ALBERT ST 1
HARGREAVES ST 2
SAGAR HOLME TERR 3
The Height
Top o' th' Height
Works
PHILLIPSTOWN
CRABTREE BLDGS 1
CRABTREE ST 2
HIGHTOWN RD 3
OSBORNE TERR 4
LAWRENCE ST 5
ELIZABETH ST 6
BURNLEY RD E
BB4
Brock Clough Farm
1 WORSTON CL
2 CHATBURN CL
3 ABBOTS CL
4 HOLLIN GR
Constable Lee
RIVERSIDE PK
SCHOOL ST
RIVERSIDE MEWS
7 HOLLIN CL
8 ROSEACRE CL
Alder Grange Com & Tech Sch
Sch
Chapel Hill Farm
Meadowhead
Cemy
Myrtle Earth Farm
WAINGATE
1 HOLMES ST
2 TUTTALL ST
3 GRANGE AVE
4 ALDER ST
WELL ST 1
BACK GOODFELLOWS TERR 2
TATTERSALL SQ 3
PIERCY MDW 4
PIERCY MOUNT 5
PIERCY TERR 6
VALE TERR 7
PIERCY HIGHER MOUNT 8
Mkt
Spring Side
Marl Pits Sports Complex
Far Height Side
Ind Est
Scout
Piercy
Dale Mill
NEWCHURCH RD
LITCHFORD HO
Higher Cloughfold
JOHNNY BARN COTTS
Seat Naze
ST MARY'S WAY
1 ROSE VALE ST
2 WHEATHOLME ST
3 LEVER ST
Lower Cloughfold
HEIGHTSIDE MEWS
St Peter's RC Prim Sch
Edgeside
TH
FALL BARN RD
BOCHOLT WAY
River Irwell
BACUP RD
1 EASTWOOD ST
2 EASTWOOD CRES
3 DOBBIN CT
A681
Longholme
Mus
Irwell Sculpture Trail
Cloughfold
Newchurch
UNION TERR
Hareholme
UPPER ASHMOUNT
RAWTENSTALL
Hall Carr
QUEEN HO 1
COBDEN HO 2
ALBERT HO 3
CUNLIFFE HO 4
WEBER ST 5
ROSTRON'S BLDGS 6
Newchurch CE Prim Sch
Booth Fold
Swiss Clough
DEARDEN NOOK
Staghills
A2
1 RABY ST
2 GRANGE ST
3 WORSWICK CRES
4 The Valley Ctr
5 ANNIE ST
6 ST MARY'S TERR
7 QUEEN'S SQ
8 PARRAMATTA ST
9 LONGHOLME RD
A3
1 ST JAMES ST
2 IVY GR
3 ASH GR
4 PROSPECT HILL
5 ROCKCLIFFE ST
6 TAYLOR ST
7 ROBERTS ST
8 CURTIS ST
9 PROSPECT VIEW
10 Kingfisher Ctr
11 BARLOW ST
12 HALL ST
13 BRIGHT ST
14 BALDWIN'S BLDGS
15 MILL GATE
16 SOUTH ST
17 EAST PAR
18 MILLGATE RD
19 GRANGE TERR
85
A3
20 ALDER BANK
21 WHITEHEAD ST
22 CRANKSHAW ST
69
E1
1 BACK CHURCH ST
2 COBHAM CT
3 HALMOT CT
4 NAZE CT
5 BOLTON ST
6 BRANDWOOD
F2
1 CO-OPERATION ST
2 PARADISE ST
3 CLARKE HOLME ST
4 NAZE VIEW AVE
5 NEWBIGGING AVE
6 Waterfoot Bsns Ctr
7 Globe Mill
8 Albion Mill
F1
1 THE HAWTHORNS
2 MELBOURNE ST
3 GAGHILLS TERR
4 WEST VIEW
5 CLOUGH ST
6 BRIDGE CL

107
88

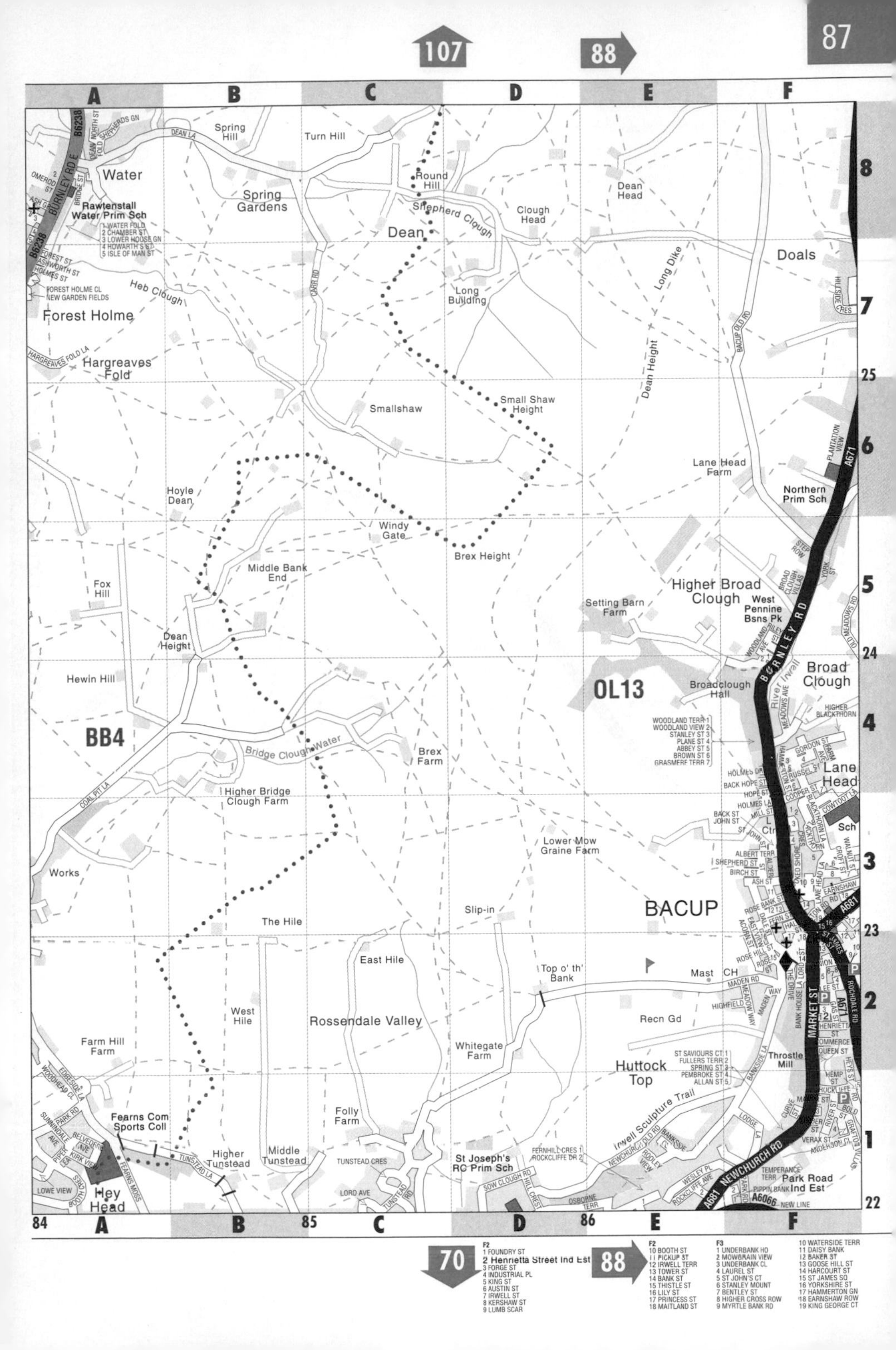

70
88

F2
1 FOUNDRY ST
2 Henrietta Street Ind Est
3 FORGE ST
4 INDUSTRIAL PL
5 KING ST
6 AUSTIN ST
7 IRWELL ST
8 KERSHAW ST
9 LUMB SCAR

F2
10 BOOTH ST
11 PICKUP ST
12 IRWELL TERR
13 TOWER ST
14 BANK ST
15 THISTLE ST
16 LILY ST
17 PRINCESS ST
18 MAITLAND ST

F3
1 UNDERBANK HO
2 MOWGRAIN VIEW
3 UNDERBANK CL
4 LAUREL ST
5 ST JOHN'S CT
6 STANLEY MOUNT
7 BENTLEY ST
8 HIGHER CROSS ROW
9 MYRTLE BANK RD
10 WATERSIDE TERR
11 DAISY BANK
12 BAKER ST
13 GOOSE HILL ST
14 HARCOURT ST
15 ST JAMES SQ
16 YORKSHIRE ST
17 HAMMERTON GN
18 EARNSHAW ROW
19 KING GEORGE CT

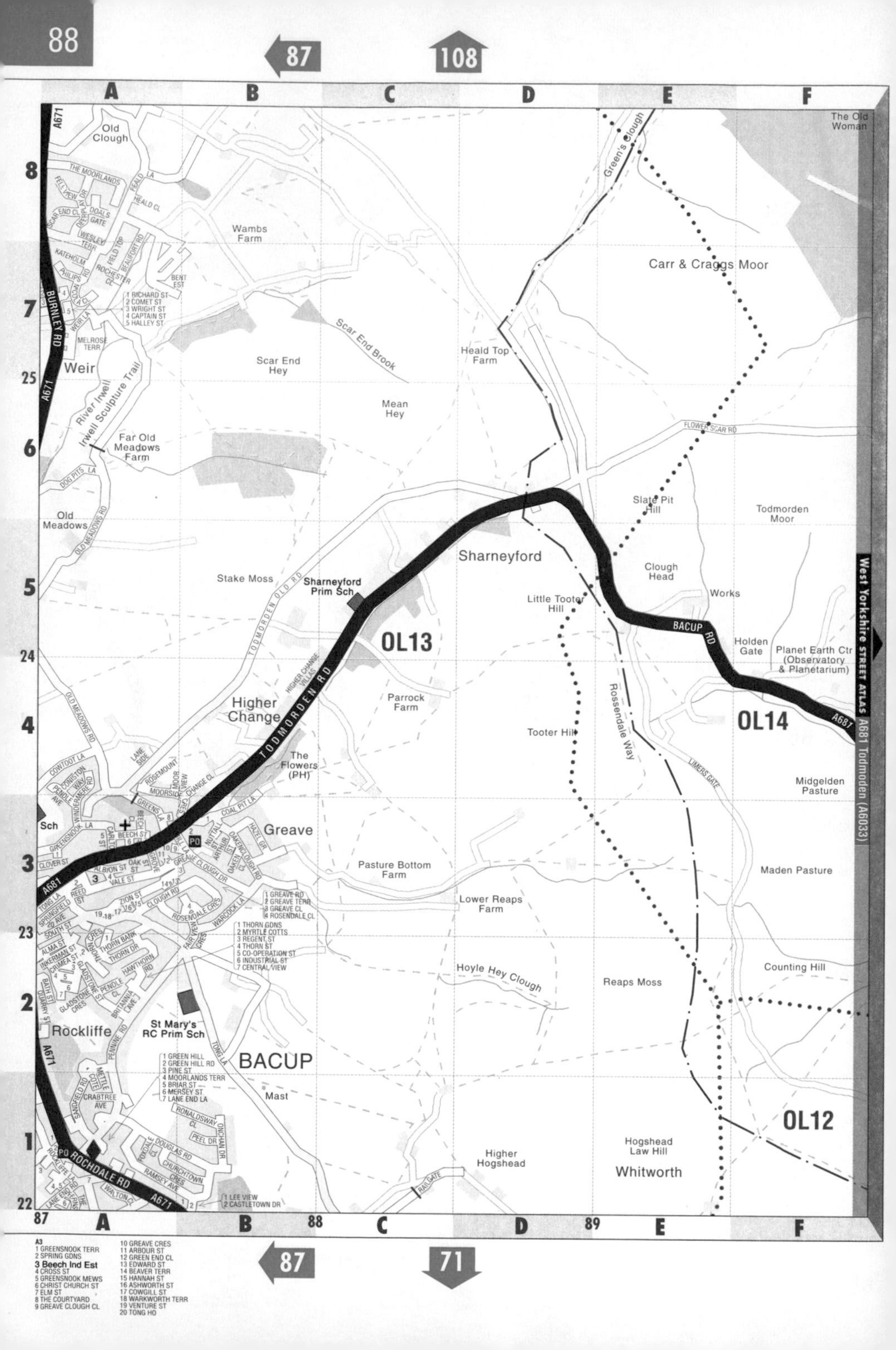
88
87
108
A
B
C
D
E
F
Old Clough
THE MOORLANDS
FEALD LA
HEALD CL
Wambs Farm
Carr & Craggs Moor
The Old Woman
Green's Clough
1 RICHARD ST
2 COMET ST
3 WRIGHT ST
4 CAPTAIN ST
5 HALLEY ST
BURNLEY RD
A671
Weir
Scar End Brook
Scar End Hey
Heald Top Farm
Mean Hey
River Irwell
Irwell Sculpture Trail
Far Old Meadows Farm
FLOWER SCAR RD
DOG PITS LA
Old Meadows
OLD MEADOWS RD
Slate Pit Hill
Todmorden Moor
Sharneyford
Stake Moss
Sharneyford Prim Sch
TODMORDEN OLD RD
Clough Head
Little Tooter Hill
Works
BACUP RD
OL13
Holden Gate
Planet Earth Ctr (Observatory & Planetarium)
Rossendale Way
Parrock Farm
HIGHER CHANGE VILLAS
Higher Change
TODMORDEN RD
Tooter Hill
OL14
A681
West Yorkshire STREET ATLAS A681 Todmorden (A6033)
The Flowers (PH)
LIMERS GATE
Midgelden Pasture
Sch
Greave
COAL PIT LA
Pasture Bottom Farm
Maden Pasture
1 GREAVE RD
2 GREAVE TERR
3 GREAVE CL
4 ROSENDALE CL
Lower Reaps Farm
1 THORN GDNS
2 MYRTLE COTTS
3 REGENT ST
4 THORN ST
5 CO-OPERATION ST
6 INDUSTRIAL ST
7 CENTRAL VIEW
Hoyle Hey Clough
Reaps Moss
Counting Hill
Rockliffe
St Mary's RC Prim Sch
BACUP
1 GREEN HILL
2 GREEN HILL RD
3 PINE ST
4 MOORLANDS TERR
5 BRIAR ST
6 MERSEY ST
7 LANE END LA
Mast
OL12
Higher Hogshead
Hogshead Law Hill
Whitworth
ROCHDALE RD
1 LEE VIEW
2 CASTLETOWN DR
RAILGATE
87
88
89
A3
1 GREENSNOOK TERR
2 SPRING GDNS
3 Beech Ind Est
4 CROSS ST
5 GREENSNOOK MEWS
6 CHRIST CHURCH ST
7 ELM ST
8 THE COURTYARD
9 GREAVE CLOUGH CL
10 GREAVE CRES
11 ARBOUR ST
12 GREEN END CL
13 EDWARD ST
14 BEAVER TERR
15 HANNAH ST
16 ASHWORTH ST
17 COWGILL ST
18 WARKWORTH TERR
19 VENTURE ST
20 TONG HO
87
71

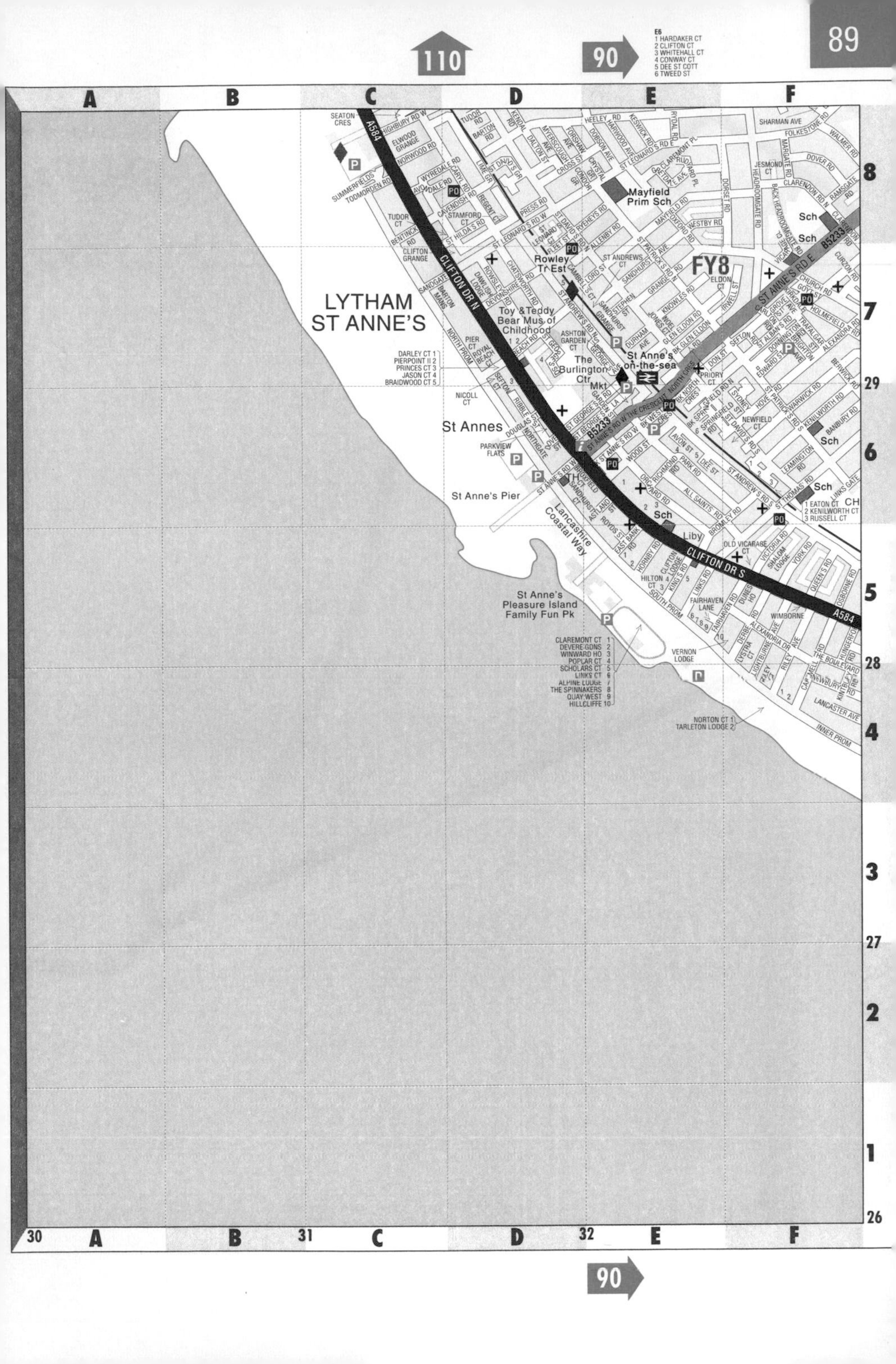
110
90
E6
1 HARDAKER CT
2 CLIFTON CT
3 WHITEHALL CT
4 CONWAY CT
5 DEE ST COTT
6 TWEED ST
A
B
C
D
E
F
8
7
29
6
5
28
4
3
27
2
1
26
30
31
32
LYTHAM
ST ANNE'S
FY8
St Annes
A584
B5233
CLIFTON DR N
CLIFTON DR S
ST ANNE'S RD E
SEATON CRES
SUMMERFIELDS
TODMORDEN RD
TUDOR CT
BENTINCK RD
CLIFTON GRANGE
SANDGATE
BARTON MANS
NORTH PROM
PIER CT
ROYAL BEACH CT
Mayfield Prim Sch
Rowley Tr Est
Toy & Teddy Bear Mus of Childhood
ASHTON GARDEN CT
The Burlington Ctr
Mkt
St Anne's on-the-sea
DARLEY CT 1
PIERPOINT II 2
PRINCES CT 3
JASON CT 4
BRAIDWOOD CT 5
NICOLL CT
PARKVIEW FLATS
St Anne's Pier
TH
Lancashire Coastal Way
St Anne's Pleasure Island Family Fun Pk
Sch
Liby
OLD VICARAGE CT
PRIORY CT
NEWFIELD CT
ELDON CT
JESMOND CT
SHARMAN AVE
FOLKESTONE RD
WALMER RD
DOVER RD
CLARENDON RD N
RAMSGATE RD
CHURCH RD
HOLMEFIELD RD
ALEXANDRA RD
BERWICK RD
WARWICK RD
KENILWORTH RD
BANBURY RD
LEAMINGTON RD
ST THOMAS RD
LINKS GATE
1 EATON CT
2 KENILWORTH CT
3 RUSSELL CT
CH
VICTORIA RD
YORK RD
QUEEN'S RD
OSBORNE RD
WIMBORNE
HUNGERFORD RD
THE BOULEVARD
NEWBURY RD
LANCASTER AVE
INNER PROM
SOUTH PROM
FAIRHAVEN LANE
VERNON LODGE
CLAREMONT CT 1
DEVERE GDNS 2
WINWARD HO 3
POPLAR CT 4
SCHOLARS CT 5
LINKS CT 6
ALPINE LODGE 7
THE SPINNAKERS 8
QUAY WEST 9
HILLCLIFFE 10
NORTON CT 1
TARLETON LODGE 2
HILTON CT
CLIFTON LODGE
KING'S RD
LINKS RD
HORNBY RD
ALL SAINTS' RD
BROMLEY RD
ST ANDREW'S RD S
ST DAVID'S RD S
PO
P
Sch
90

89
111

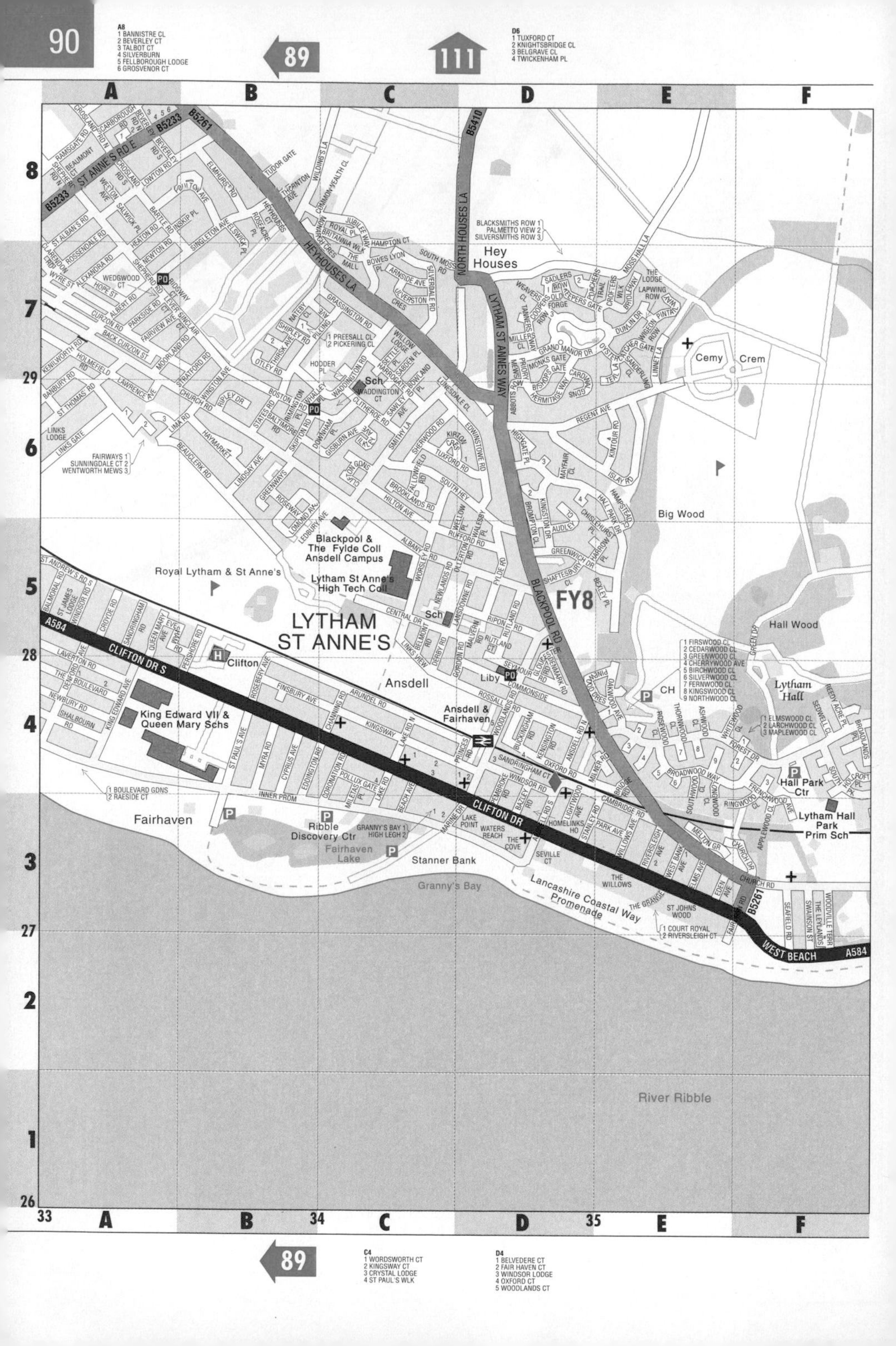

89

C4
1 WORDSWORTH CT
2 KINGSWAY CT
3 CRYSTAL LODGE
4 ST PAUL'S WLK

D4
1 BELVEDERE CT
2 FAIR HAVEN CT
3 WINDSOR LODGE
4 OXFORD CT
5 WOODLANDS CT

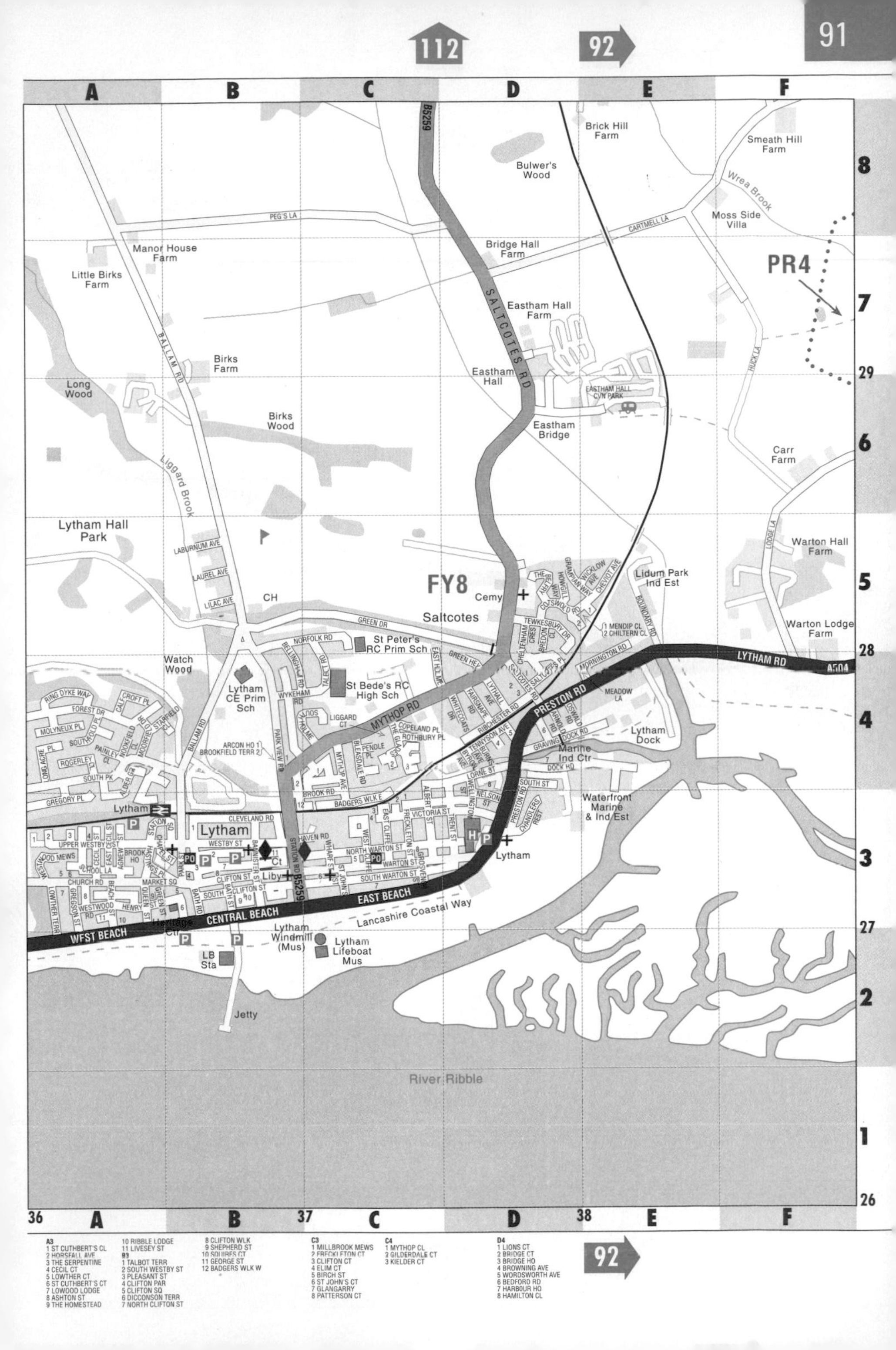

91
112
92
A
B
C
D
E
F
8
7
29
6
5
28
4
3
27
2
1
26
36
37
38
B5259
Brick Hill Farm
Smeath Hill Farm
Bulwer's Wood
Wrea Brook
PEG'S LA
CARTMELL LA
Moss Side Villa
Manor House Farm
Bridge Hall Farm
Little Birks Farm
PR4
SALTCOTES RD
Eastham Hall Farm
BALLAM RD
Birks Farm
Eastham Hall
EASTHAM HALL CVN PARK
HUCK LA
Long Wood
Birks Wood
Eastham Bridge
Liggard Brook
Carr Farm
Lytham Hall Park
LABURNUM AVE
LAUREL AVE
LILAC AVE
CH
FY8
Cemy
Saltcotes
GREEN DR
LODGE LA
Warton Hall Farm
Lidum Park Ind Est
Warton Lodge Farm
BOUNDARY RD
1 MENDIP CL
2 CHILTERN CL
NORFOLK RD
St Peter's RC Prim Sch
Watch Wood
Lytham CE Prim Sch
St Bede's RC High Sch
MYTHOP RD
LYTHAM RD
A584
PRESTON RD
MORNINGTON RD
MEADOW LA
DOCK RD
Lytham Dock
Marine Ind Ctr
Waterfront Marine & Ind Est
RING DYKE WAY
FOREST DR
MOLYNEUX PL
LONG ACRE
ROGERLEY CL
SOUTH PK
GREGORY PL
ARCON HO 1
BROOKFIELD TERR 2
Lytham
CLEVELAND RD
BADGERS WLK E
VICTORIA ST
Lytham
UPPER WESTBY ST
WESTBY ST
CHURCH RD
CLIFTON ST
NORTH WARTON ST
SOUTH WARTON ST
STATION RD
PO
Ct
Liby
H
P
Lytham
EAST BEACH
CENTRAL BEACH
WEST BEACH
Lancashire Coastal Way
Heritage Ctr
Lytham Windmill (Mus)
Lytham Lifeboat Mus
LB Sta
Jetty
River Ribble
A3
1 ST CUTHBERT'S CL
2 HORSFALL AVE
3 THE SERPENTINE
4 CECIL CT
5 LOWTHER CT
6 ST CUTHBERT'S CT
7 LOWOOD LODGE
8 ASHTON ST
9 THE HOMESTEAD
10 RIBBLE LODGE
11 LIVESEY ST
B3
1 TALBOT TERR
2 SOUTH WESTBY ST
3 PLEASANT ST
4 CLIFTON PAR
5 CLIFTON SQ
6 DICCONSON TERR
7 NORTH CLIFTON ST
8 CLIFTON WLK
9 SHEPHERD ST
10 SQUIRES CT
11 GEORGE ST
12 BADGERS WLK W
C3
1 MILLBROOK MEWS
2 FRECKLETON CT
3 CLIFTON CT
4 ELIM CT
5 BIRCH ST
6 ST JOHN'S CT
7 GLANGARRY
8 PATTERSON CT
C4
1 MYTHOP CL
2 GILDERDALE CT
3 KIELDER CT
D4
1 LIONS CT
2 BRIDGE CT
3 BRIDGE HO
4 BROWNING AVE
5 WORDSWORTH AVE
6 BEDFORD RD
7 HARBOUR HO
8 HAMILTON CL
92

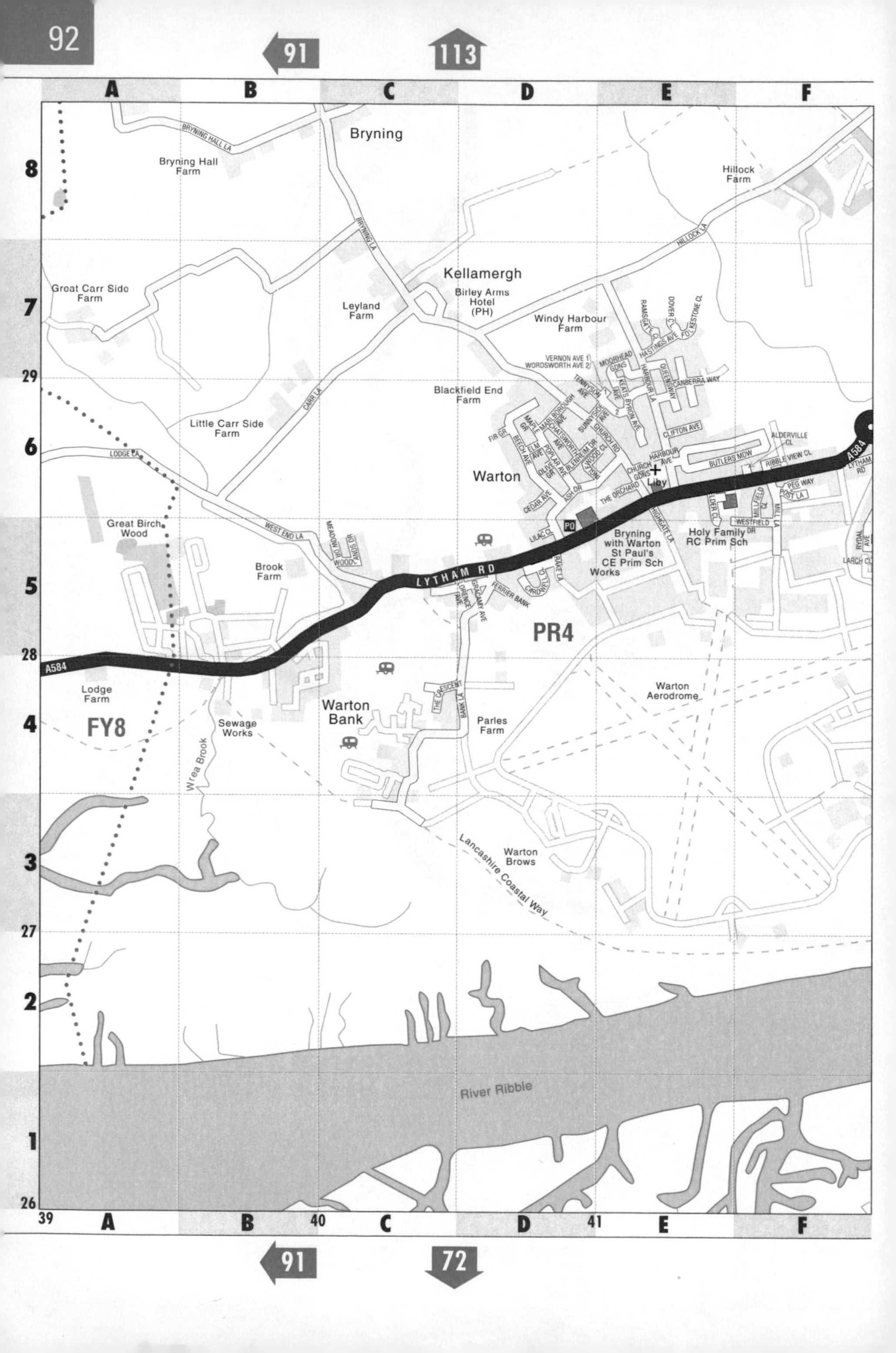
91
113
A
B
C
D
E
F
8
7
29
6
5
28
4
3
27
2
1
26
39
40
41
Bryning
BRYNING HALL LA
Bryning Hall Farm
Hillock Farm
BRYNING LA
HILLOCK LA
Kellamergh
Birley Arms Hotel (PH)
Great Carr Side Farm
Leyland Farm
Windy Harbour Farm
RAMSGATE CL
DOVER CL
FOLKESTONE CL
HASTINGS AVE
VERNON AVE 1
WORDSWORTH AVE 2
MOORHEAD GDNS
HARBOUR LA
QUEENSWAY
CANBERRA WAY
TENNYSON AVE
KEATS AVE
BYRON AVE
CARR LA
Blackfield End Farm
Little Carr Side Farm
MAPLE GR
MARLBOROUGH AVE
CHATSWORTH AVE
SUNNYSIDE AVE
CHURCH RD
CLIFTON AVE
ALDERVILLE CL
FIR GR
BEECH AVE
ELM AVE
POPLAR AVE
OLIVE GR
BLENHEIM DR
LYNWOOD CL
HARBOUR AVE
BUTLERS MDW
RIBBLE VIEW CL
A584
LYTHAM RD
LODGE LA
Warton
CHURCH GDNS
Liby
THE ORCHARD
CEDAR AVE
ASH DR
PEG WAY
POST LA
MILLFIELD CL
MILL LA
ELDER CL
Great Birch Wood
WEST END LA
MEADOW DR
LANDS DR
WOOD
PO
LILAC CL
HIGHGATE LA
WESTFIELD DR
Bryning with Warton St Paul's CE Prim Sch
Holy Family RC Prim Sch
RYDAL AVE
LARCH CL
Brook Farm
LYTHAM RD
FLORENCE AVE
GRACAMY AVE
FERRIER BANK
CROMWELL
RAKE LA
Works
PR4
Lodge Farm
FY8
THE CRESCENT
BANK LA
Warton Bank
Parles Farm
Warton Aerodrome
Sewage Works
Wrea Brook
Lancashire Coastal Way
Warton Brows
River Ribble

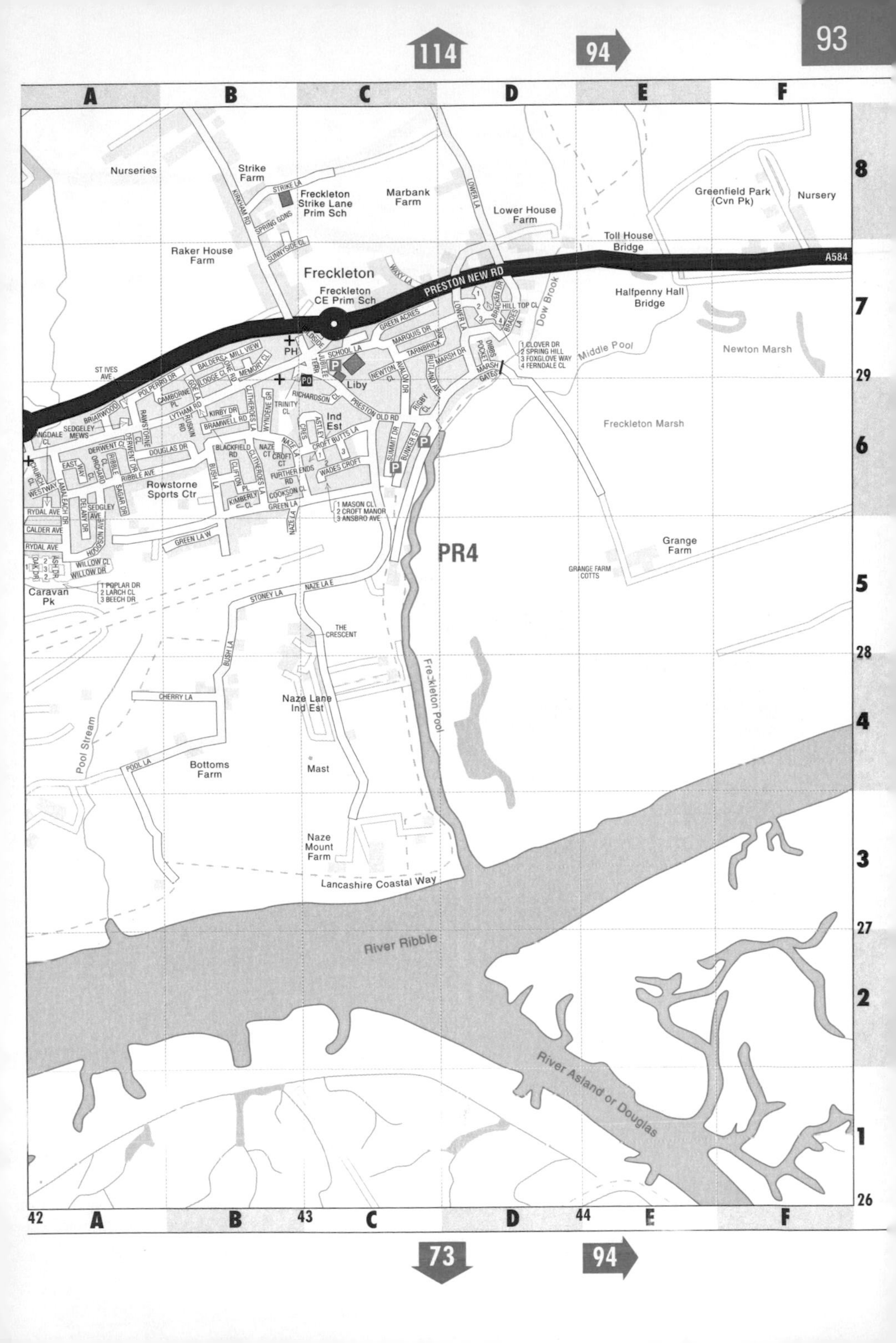
114
94
Nurseries
Strike Farm
Freckleton Strike Lane Prim Sch
Marbank Farm
Lower House Farm
Greenfield Park (Cvn Pk)
Nursery
Raker House Farm
Toll House Bridge
A584
Freckleton
Freckleton CE Prim Sch
PRESTON NEW RD
Halfpenny Hall Bridge
Dow Brook
Middle Pool
Newton Marsh
PH
Liby
Ind Est
Freckleton Marsh
Rowstorne Sports Ctr
PR4
Grange Farm
GRANGE FARM COTTS
Caravan Pk
1 POPLAR DR
2 LARCH CL
3 BEECH DR
1 CLOVER DR
2 SPRING HILL
3 FOXGLOVE WAY
4 FERNDALE CL
1 MASON CL
2 CROFT MANOR
3 ANSBRO AVE
THE CRESCENT
Naze Lane Ind Est
Freckleton Pool
Pool Stream
Bottoms Farm
Mast
Naze Mount Farm
Lancashire Coastal Way
River Ribble
River Asland or Douglas
42
43
44
29
28
27
26
73
94

93
115

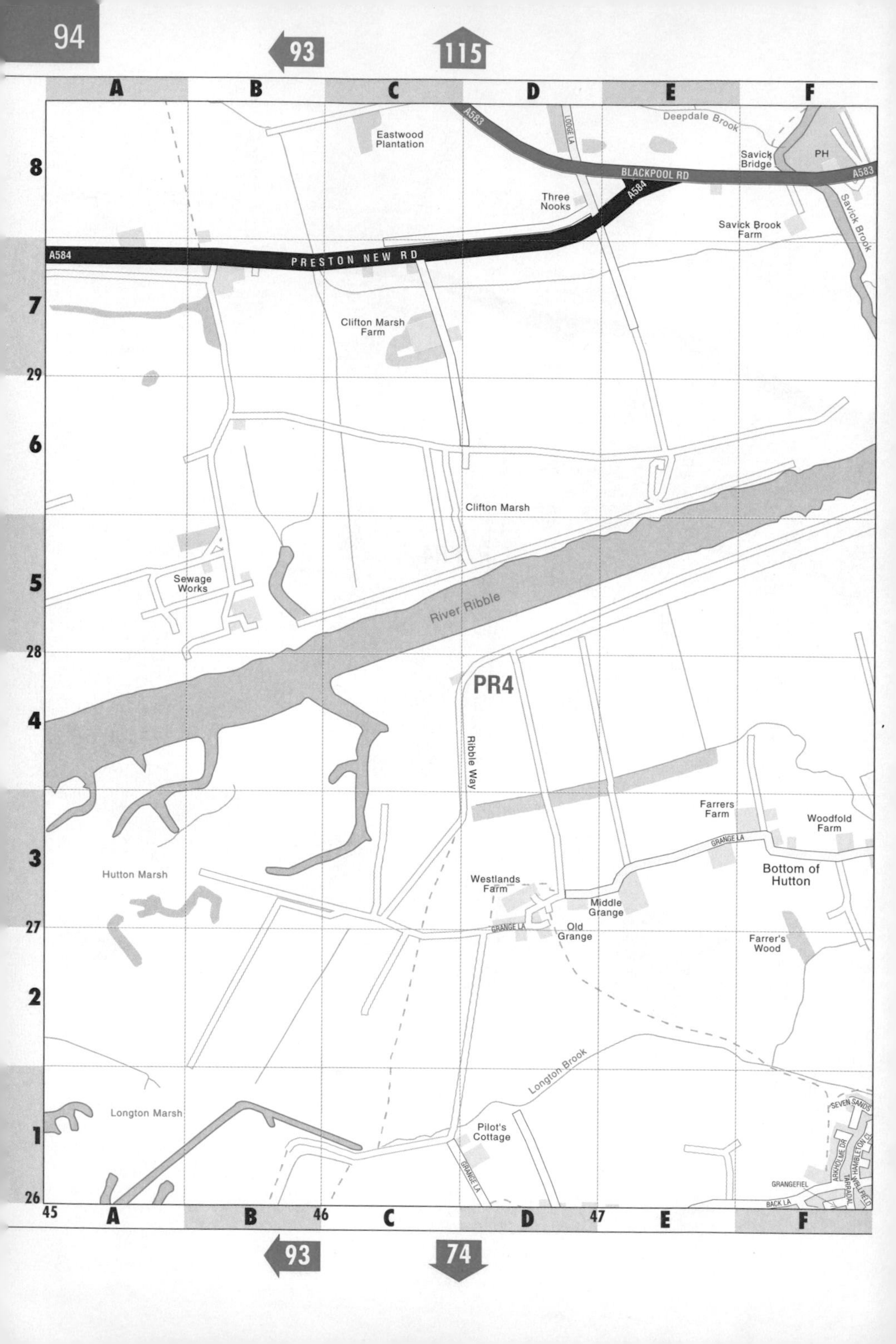
A
B
C
D
E
F
8
7
29
6
5
28
4
3
27
2
1
26
45
46
47
Deepdale Brook
Eastwood Plantation
A583
LODGE LA
Savick Bridge
PH
BLACKPOOL RD
A583
A584
Three Nooks
Savick Brook Farm
Savick Brook
A584
PRESTON NEW RD
Clifton Marsh Farm
Clifton Marsh
Sewage Works
River Ribble
PR4
Ribble Way
Farrers Farm
Woodfold Farm
GRANGE LA
Bottom of Hutton
Hutton Marsh
Westlands Farm
Middle Grange
GRANGE LA
Old Grange
Farrer's Wood
Longton Brook
Longton Marsh
Pilot's Cottage
GRANGE LA
SEVEN SANDS
ARKHOLME DR
HAMBLETON CL
TARRADAL
GRANGEFIEL
BACK LA

93
74

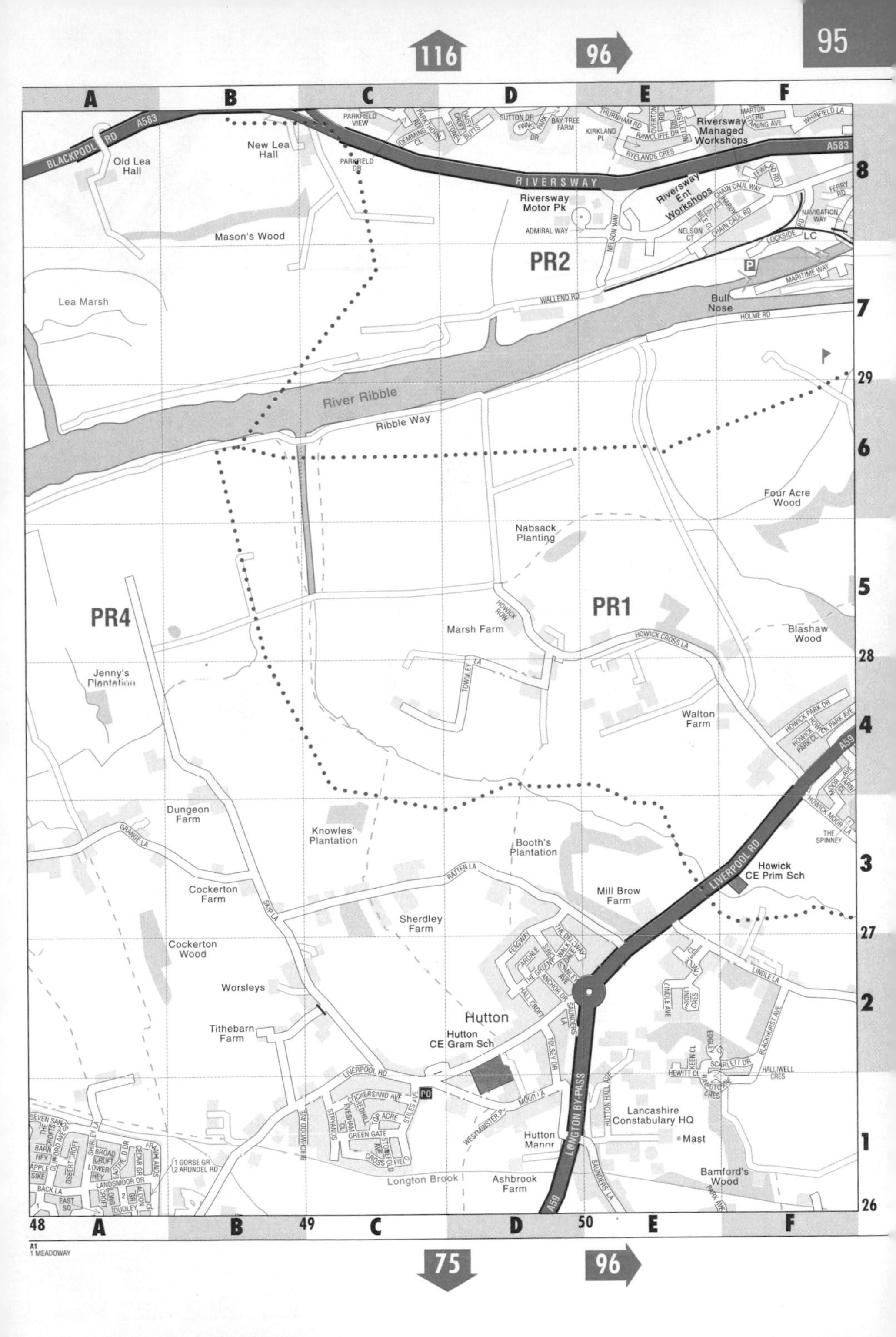
116
96
A
B
C
D
E
F
BLACKPOOL RD
A583
Old Lea Hall
New Lea Hall
PARKFIELD VIEW
PARKFIELD DR
SUTTON DR
BAY TREE FARM
KIRKLAND PL
RYELANDS CRES
Riversway Managed Workshops
WHINFIELD LA
RIVERSWAY
Riversway Motor Pk
ADMIRAL WAY
NELSON WAY
Riversway Ent Workshops
NELSON CT
CHAIN CAUL RD
LOCKSIDE
NAVIGATION WAY
FERRY RD
LC
MARITIME WAY
Mason's Wood
PR2
Lea Marsh
WALLEND RD
Bull Nose
HOLME RD
River Ribble
Ribble Way
Four Acre Wood
Nabsack Planting
PR4
PR1
HOWICK ROW
Marsh Farm
HOWICK CROSS LA
Blashaw Wood
Jenny's Plantation
TOWNLEY LA
Walton Farm
HOWICK PARK DR
HOWICK PARK AVE
A59
HOWICK MOOR LA
THE SPINNEY
Dungeon Farm
GRANGE LA
Knowles' Plantation
Booth's Plantation
RATTEN LA
Howick CE Prim Sch
LIVERPOOL RD
Cockerton Farm
SKIP LA
Sherdley Farm
Mill Brow Farm
Cockerton Wood
Worsleys
LINDLE LA
LINDLE AVE
BLACKHURST AVE
Hutton
Tithebarn Farm
Hutton CE Gram Sch
SAUNDERS LA
TOLSEY DR
HALL CROFT
ANCHOR DR
HEWITT CL
SCARLETT DR
HALLIWELL CRES
LIVERPOOL RD
PO
COCKERSAND AVE
STILES AVE
MOOR LA
WESTMINSTER PL
HUTTON HALL AVE
Lancashire Constabulary HQ
Mast
LONGTON BY-PASS
Hutton Manor
BIRCHWOOD AVE
GREEN GATE
SHIRLEY LA
1 GORSE GR
2 ARUNDEL RD
LANDSMOOR DR
BACK LA
Longton Brook
Ashbrook Farm
SAUNDERS LA
Bamford's Wood
PARK AVE
8
7
29
6
5
28
4
3
27
2
1
26
48
49
50
A1
1 MEADOWAY
75
96

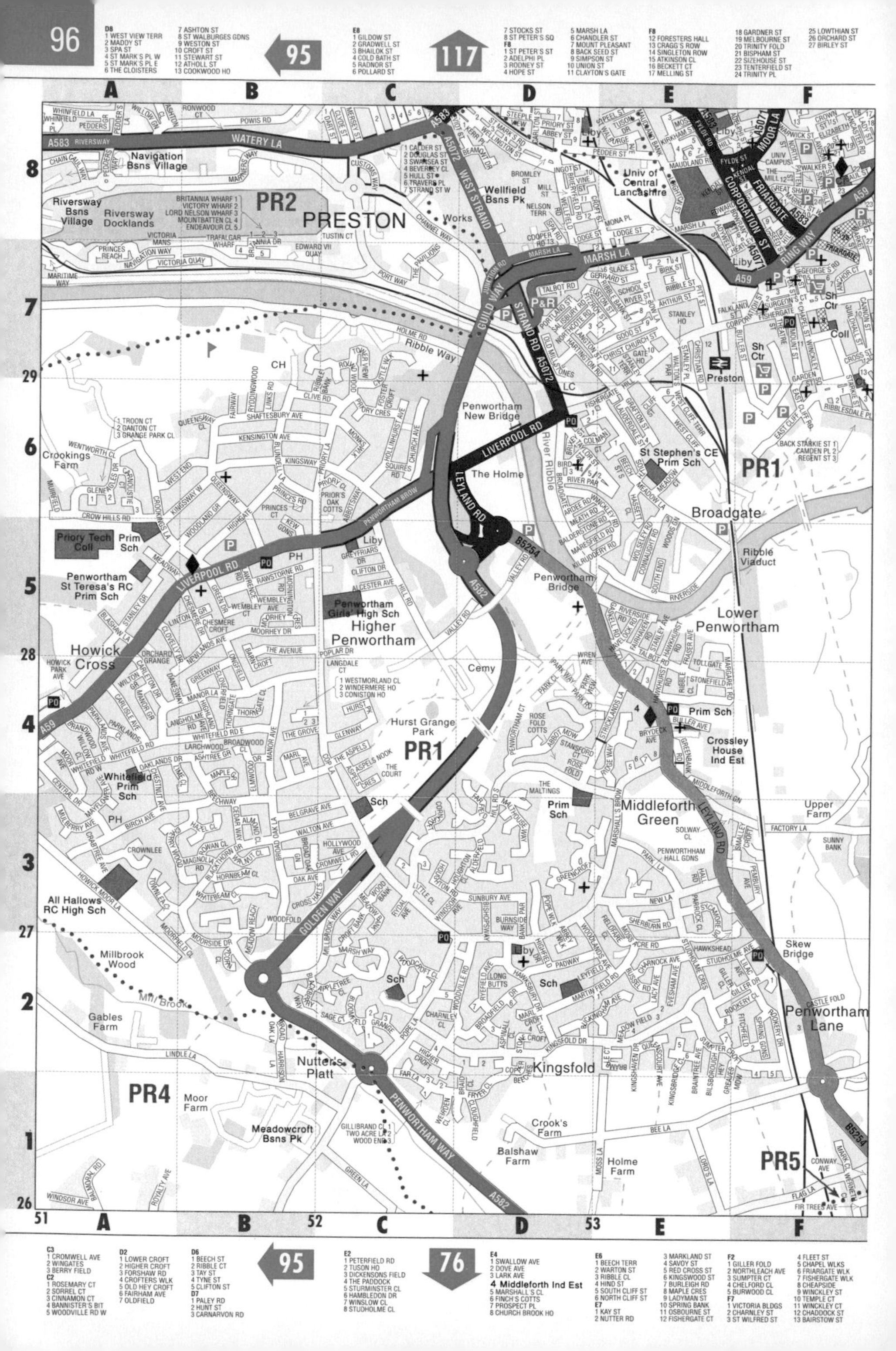
D8
1 WEST VIEW TERR
2 MADDY ST
3 SPA ST
4 ST MARK'S PL W
5 ST MARK'S PL E
6 THE CLOISTERS
7 ASHTON ST
8 ST WALBURGES GDNS
9 WESTON ST
10 CROFT ST
11 STEWART ST
12 ATHOLL ST
13 COOKWOOD HO
95
E8
1 GILDOW ST
2 GRADWELL ST
3 BHAILOK ST
4 COLD BATH ST
5 RADNOR ST
6 POLLARD ST
117
7 STOCKS ST
8 ST PETER'S SQ
F8
1 ST PETER'S ST
2 ADELPHI PL
3 RODNEY ST
4 HOPE ST
5 MARSH LA
6 CHANDLER ST
7 MOUNT PLEASANT
8 BACK SEED ST
9 SIMPSON ST
10 UNION ST
11 CLAYTON'S GATE
F8
12 FORESTERS HALL
13 CRAGG'S ROW
14 SINGLETON ROW
15 ATKINSON CL
16 BECKETT CT
17 MELLING ST
18 GARDNER ST
19 MELBOURNE ST
20 TRINITY FOLD
21 BISPHAM ST
22 SIZEHOUSE ST
23 TENTERFIELD ST
24 TRINITY PL
25 LOWTHIAN ST
26 ORCHARD ST
27 BIRLEY ST
PR2
PRESTON
Navigation Bsns Village
Riversway Bsns Village
Riversway Docklands
WATERY LA
WEST STRAND
Wellfield Bsns Pk
Univ of Central Lancashire
MARSH LA
RING WAY
CORPORATION ST
FRIARGATE
MOOR LA
STRAND RD
GUILD WAY
Ribble Way
Penwortham New Bridge
LIVERPOOL RD
LEYLAND RD
The Holme
River Ribble
St Stephen's CE Prim Sch
PR1
Broadgate
Preston
Ribble Viaduct
Crookings Farm
Priory Tech Coll
Prim Sch
Penwortham St Teresa's RC Prim Sch
Penwortham Girls' High Sch
Higher Penwortham
Penwortham Bridge
Lower Penwortham
Howick Cross
Cemy
Hurst Grange Park
Crossley House Ind Est
Whitefield Prim Sch
Middleforth Green
Upper Farm
All Hallows RC High Sch
GOLDEN WAY
Millbrook Wood
Mill Brook
Gables Farm
Skew Bridge
Penwortham Lane
Kingsfold
Nutter's Platt
PR4
Moor Farm
Meadowcroft Bsns Pk
PENWORTHAM WAY
Crook's Farm
Balshaw Farm
Holme Farm
PR5
A582
B5254
51
52
53
C3
1 CROMWELL AVE
2 WINGATES
3 BERRY FIELD
C2
1 ROSEMARY CT
2 SORREL CT
3 CINNAMON CT
4 BANNISTER'S BIT
5 WOODVILLE RD W
D2
1 LOWER CROFT
2 HIGHER CROFT
3 FORSHAW RD
4 CROFTERS WLK
5 OLD HEY CROFT
6 FAIRHAM AVE
7 OLDFIELD
D6
1 BEECH ST
2 RIBBLE CT
3 TAY ST
4 TYNE ST
5 CLIFTON ST
D7
1 PALEY RD
2 HUNT ST
3 CARNARVON RD
95
E2
1 PETERFIELD RD
2 TUSON HO
3 DICKENSONS FIELD
4 THE PADDOCK
5 STURMINSTER CL
6 HAMBLEDON DR
7 WINSLOW CL
8 STUDHOLME CL
76
E4
1 SWALLOW AVE
2 DOVE AVE
3 LARK AVE
4 Middleforth Ind Est
5 MARSHALL'S CL
6 FINCH'S COTTS
7 PROSPECT PL
8 CHURCH BROOK HO
E6
1 BEECH TERR
2 WARTON ST
3 RIBBLE CL
4 HIND ST
5 SOUTH CLIFF ST
6 NORTH CLIFF ST
E7
1 KAY ST
2 NUTTER RD
3 MARKLAND ST
4 SAVOY ST
5 RED CROSS ST
6 KINGSWOOD ST
7 BURLEIGH RD
8 MAPLE CRES
9 LADYMAN ST
10 SPRING BANK
11 OSBOURNE ST
12 FISHERGATE CT
F2
1 GILLER FOLD
2 NORTHLEACH AVE
3 SUMPTER CT
4 CHELFORD CL
5 BURWOOD CL
F7
1 VICTORIA BLDGS
2 CHARNLEY ST
3 ST WILFRED ST
4 FLEET ST
5 CHAPEL WLKS
6 FRIARGATE WLK
7 FISHERGATE WLK
8 CHEAPSIDE
9 WINCKLEY ST
10 TEMPLE CT
11 WINCKLEY CT
12 CHADDOCK ST
13 BAIRSTOW ST

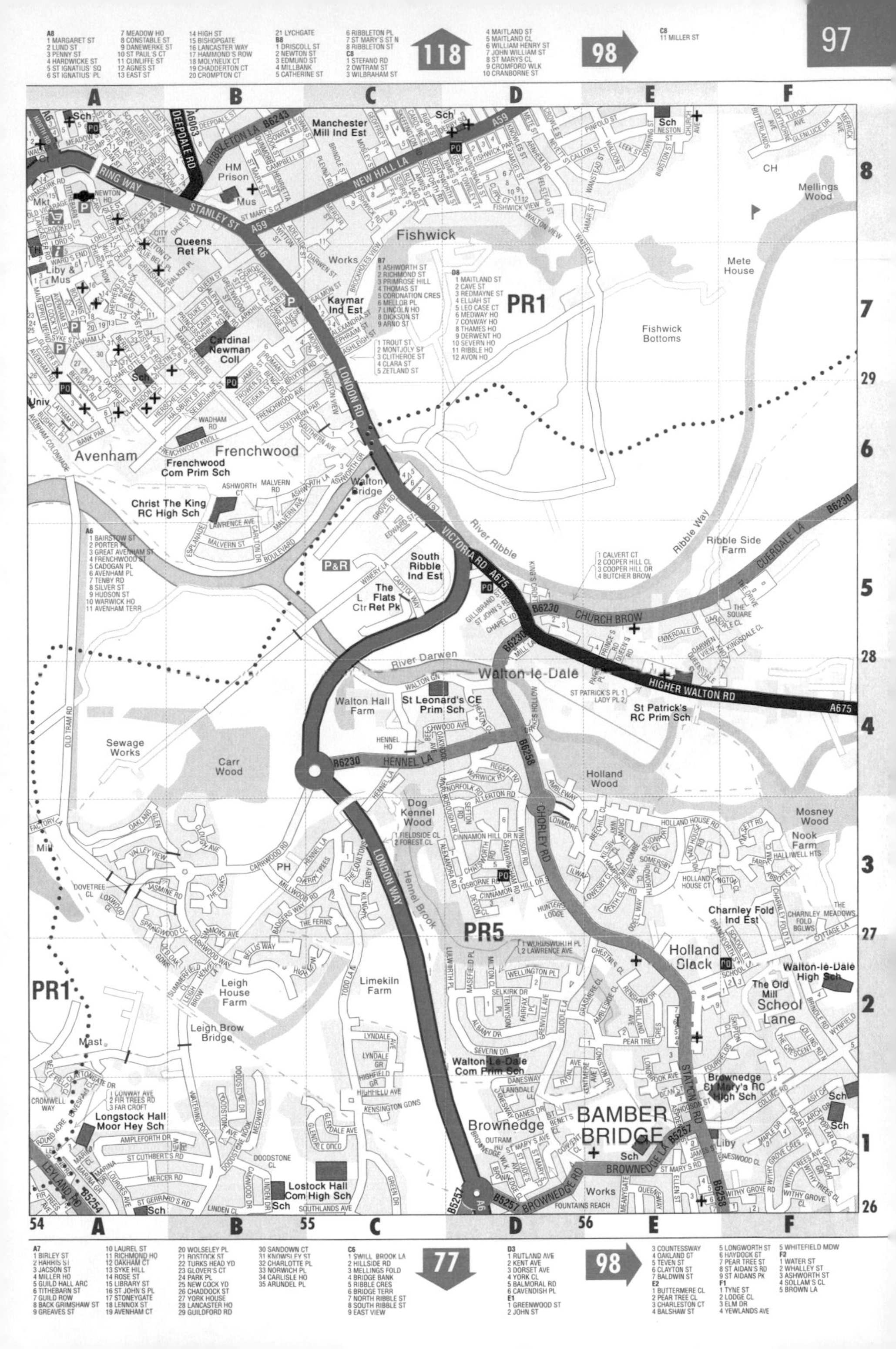
A8
1 MARGARET ST
2 LUND ST
3 PENNY ST
4 HARDWICKE ST
5 ST IGNATIUS' SQ
6 ST IGNATIUS' PL
7 MEADOW HO
8 CONSTABLE ST
9 DANEWERKE ST
10 ST PAUL'S CT
11 CUNLIFFE ST
12 AGNES ST
13 EAST ST
14 HIGH ST
15 BISHOPGATE
16 LANCASTER WAY
17 HAMMOND'S ROW
18 MOLYNEUX CT
19 CHADDERTON CT
20 CROMPTON CT
21 LYCHGATE
B8
1 DRISCOLL ST
2 NEWTON ST
3 EDMUND ST
4 MILLBANK
5 CATHERINE ST
6 RIBBLETON PL
7 ST MARY'S ST N
8 RIBBLETON ST
C8
1 STEFANO RD
2 OWTRAM ST
3 WILBRAHAM ST
118
4 MAITLAND ST
5 MAITLAND CL
6 WILLIAM HENRY ST
7 JOHN WILLIAM ST
8 ST MARYS CL
9 CROMFORD WLK
10 CRANBORNE ST
98
C8
11 MILLER ST
Manchester Mill Ind Est
HM Prison
Mus
Queens Ret Pk
Cardinal Newman Coll
Fishwick
Works
Kaymar Ind Est
PR1
Fishwick Bottoms
Mete House
Mellings Wood
Avenham
Frenchwood
Frenchwood Com Prim Sch
Christ The King RC High Sch
Walton Bridge
South Ribble Ind Est
The Flats Ret Pk
River Ribble
Ribble Way
Ribble Side Farm
River Darwen
Walton-le-Dale
St Leonard's CE Prim Sch
Walton Hall Farm
St Patrick's RC Prim Sch
Sewage Works
Carr Wood
Holland Wood
Dog Kennel Wood
Mosney Wood
Nook Farm
PR5
Charnley Fold Ind Est
Holland Slack
Walton-le-Dale High Sch
The Old Mill
School Lane
PR1
Leigh House Farm
Limekiln Farm
Leigh Brow Bridge
Walton-Le-Dale Com Prim Sch
Brownedge St Mary's RC High Sch
Longstock Hall Moor Hey Sch
Brownedge
BAMBER BRIDGE
Lostock Hall Com High Sch
Works
54
55
56
A7
1 BIRLEY ST
2 HARRIS ST
3 JACSON ST
4 MILLER HO
5 GUILD HALL ARC
6 TITHEBARN ST
7 GUILD ROW
8 BACK GRIMSHAW ST
9 GREAVES ST
10 LAUREL ST
11 RICHMOND HO
12 OAKHAM CT
13 SYKE HILL
14 ROSE ST
15 LIBRARY ST
16 ST JOHN'S PL
17 STONEYGATE
18 LENNOX ST
19 AVENHAM CT
20 WOLSELEY PL
21 BOSTOCK ST
22 TURKS HEAD YD
23 GLOVER'S CT
24 PARK PL
25 NEW COCK YD
26 CHADDOCK ST
27 YORK HOUSE
28 LANCASTER HO
29 GUILDFORD RD
30 SANDOWN CT
31 KNOWSLEY ST
32 CHARLOTTE PL
33 NORWICH PL
34 CARLISLE HO
35 ARUNDEL PL
C6
1 SWILL BROOK LA
2 HILLSIDE RD
3 MELLINGS FOLD
4 BRIDGE BANK
5 RIBBLE CRES
6 BRIDGE TERR
7 NORTH RIBBLE ST
8 SOUTH RIBBLE ST
9 EAST VIEW
77
D3
1 RUTLAND AVE
2 KENT AVE
3 DORSET AVE
4 YORK CL
5 BALMORAL RD
6 CAVENDISH PL
E1
1 GREENWOOD ST
2 JOHN ST
98
3 COUNTESSWAY
4 OAKLAND CT
5 TEVEN ST
6 CLAYTON ST
7 BALDWIN ST
E2
1 BUTTERMERE CL
2 PEAR TREE CL
3 CHARLESTON CT
4 BALSHAW ST
5 LONGWORTH ST
6 HAYDOCK ST
7 PEAR TREE ST
8 ST AIDAN'S RD
9 ST AIDANS PK
F1
1 TYNE ST
2 LODGE CL
3 ELM DR
4 YEWLANDS AVE
5 WHITEFIELD MDW
F2
1 WATER ST
2 WHALLEY ST
3 ASHWORTH ST
4 SOLLAM'S CL
5 BROWN LA

97
119

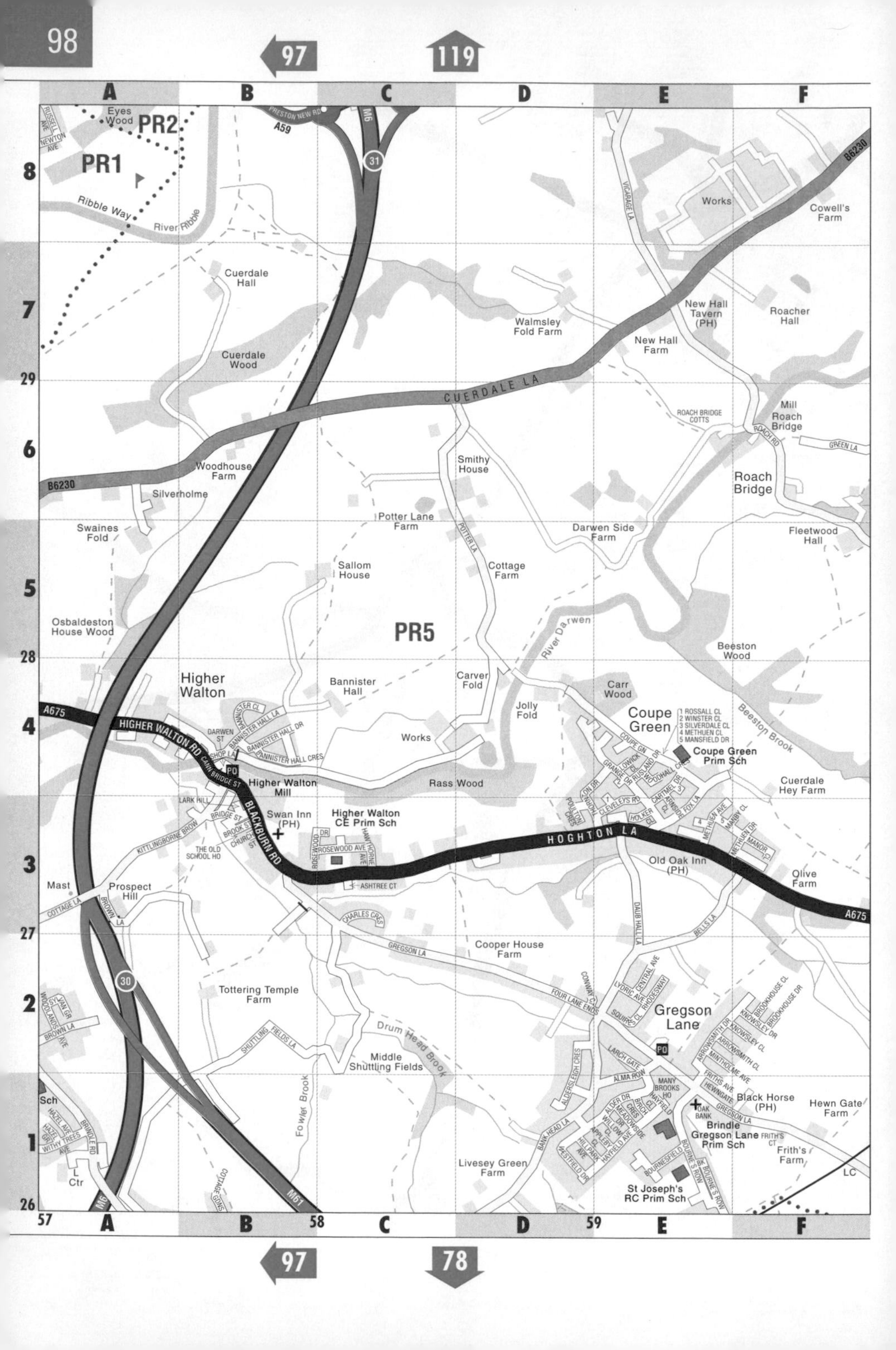
A
B
C
D
E
F
8
7
29
6
5
28
4
3
27
2
1
26
57
58
59
Eyes Wood
PR2
PR1
Ribble Way
River Ribble
PRESTON NEW RD
A59
M6
31
B6230
Works
Cowell's Farm
VICARAGE LA
Cuerdale Hall
New Hall Tavern (PH)
Roacher Hall
Walmsley Fold Farm
New Hall Farm
Cuerdale Wood
CUERDALE LA
ROACH BRIDGE COTTS
Mill
Roach Bridge
ROACH RD
GREEN LA
Woodhouse Farm
Smithy House
Roach Bridge
B6230
Silverholme
Swaines Fold
Potter Lane Farm
POTTER LA
Darwen Side Farm
Fleetwood Hall
Sallom House
Cottage Farm
PR5
River Darwen
Osbaldeston House Wood
Beeston Wood
Higher Walton
Bannister Hall
Carver Fold
Carr Wood
Jolly Fold
Coupe Green
1 ROSSALL CL
2 WINSTER CL
3 SILVERDALE CL
4 METHUEN CL
5 MANSFIELD DR
Beeston Brook
A675
HIGHER WALTON RD
BANNISTER CL
BANNISTER HALL LA
BANNISTER HALL DR
BANNISTER HALL CRES
DARWEN ST
SHOP LA
CANN BRIDGE ST
Works
COUPE GN
Coupe Green Prim Sch
PO
Higher Walton Mill
Rass Wood
Cuerdale Hey Farm
LARK HILL
BRIDGE ST
BROOK ST
CHURCH ST
BLACKBURN RD
Swan Inn (PH)
Higher Walton CE Prim Sch
KITTLINGBORNE BROW
THE OLD SCHOOL HO
ROSEWOOD DR
ROSEWOOD AVE
HAWTHORNE AVE
GRANGE DR
OWICK CL
RUSLAND DR
WOODHALL CRES
CARTMEL DR
CLEVELEYS RD
HOLKER CL
ARNSIDE CL
FOX LA
METHUEN AVE
MANBY CL
METHUEN DR
MANOR CL
HOGHTON LA
Old Oak Inn (PH)
Olive Farm
Mast
Prospect Hill
COTTAGE LA
BROWN LA
ASHTREE CT
CHARLES CRES
DAUB HALL LA
BELLS LA
A675
GREGSON LA
Cooper House Farm
30
Tottering Temple Farm
CONWAY CL
LYDRIC AVE
CENTRAL AVE
RHODESWAY
FOUR LANE ENDS
SQUIRES CL
Gregson Lane
BROOKHOUSE CL
BROOKHOUSE DR
KNOWSLEY DR
KNOWSLEY CL
ARROWSMITH DR
ARROWSMITH CL
MINTHOLME AVE
WOODLANDS AVE
BROWN LA
SHUTTLING FIELDS LA
Drum Head Brook
Middle Shuttling Fields
PO
LARCH GATE
ALMA ROW
MANY BROOKS HO
ALDERSLEIGH CRES
FRITHS AVE
HEWNGATE
Black Horse (PH)
Hewn Gate Farm
Sch
HAZEL AVE
WITHY TREES AVE
BRINDLE RD
Fowler Brook
ALDER DR
BIRCH CRES
HAYFIELD
MEADOWSIDE
WILLOW DR
HAYFIELD AVE
APPLEBY CL
HILL PARK AVE
WESTFIELD DR
BANK HEAD LA
OAK BANK
Brindle Gregson Lane Prim Sch
GREGSON LA
FRITH'S CT
Frith's Farm
BOURNESFIELD
BOURNE'S ROW
BK BOURNE'S ROW
Livesey Green Farm
LC
L Ctr
COTTAGE GDNS
St Joseph's RC Prim Sch
M6
M61

97
78

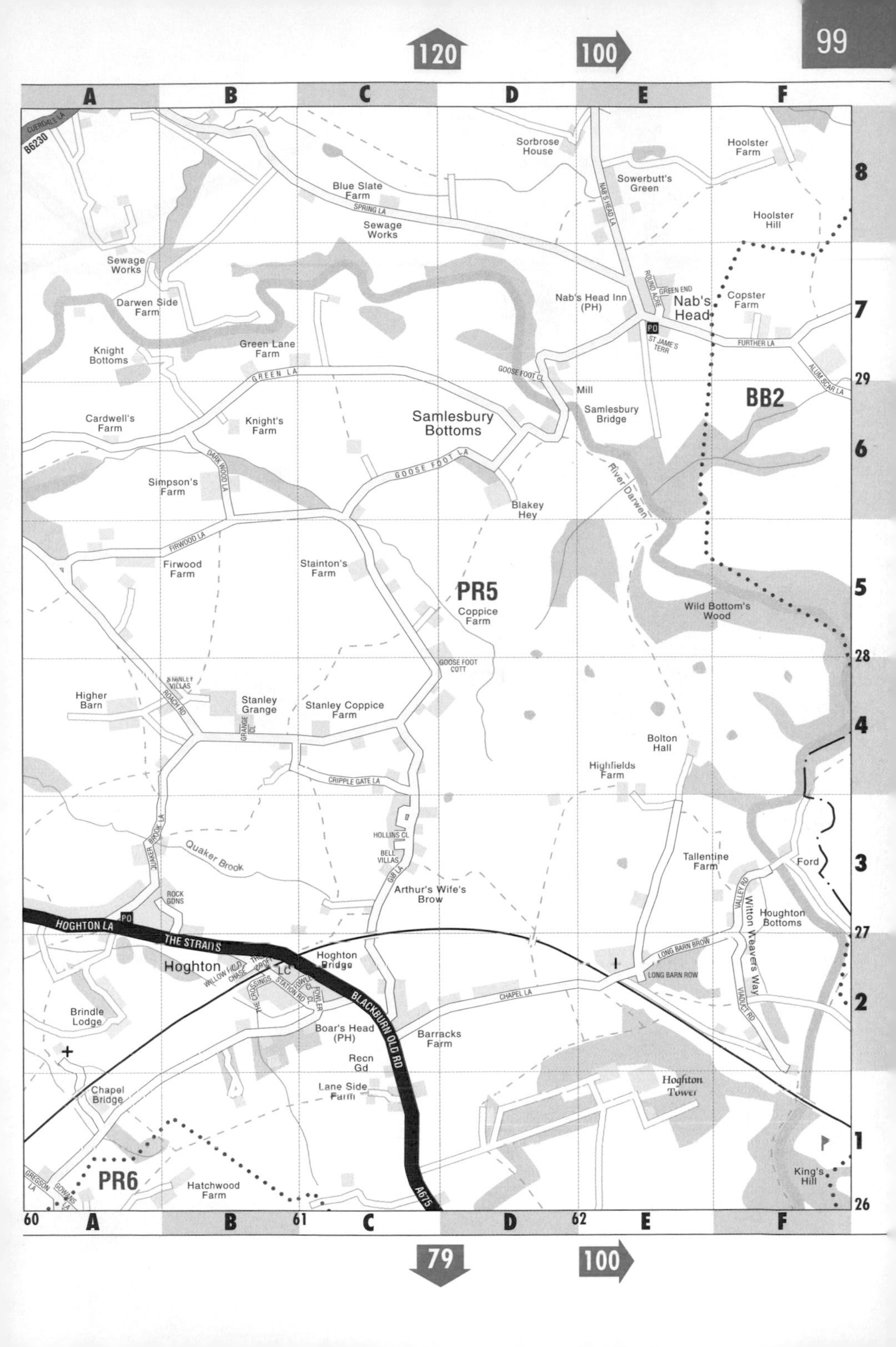

120
100
A
B
C
D
E
F
CUERDALE LA
B6230
Sorbrose House
Hoolster Farm
Blue Slate Farm
SPRING LA
Sowerbutt's Green
NAB'S HEAD LA
8
Sewage Works
Hoolster Hill
Sewage Works
ROUND ACRE
GREEN END
Darwen Side Farm
Nab's Head Inn (PH)
Nab's Head
Copster Farm
7
PO
ST JAMES'S TERR
FURTHER LA
Knight Bottoms
Green Lane Farm
GOOSE FOOT CL
ALUM SCAR LA
29
GREEN LA
Mill
BB2
Cardwell's Farm
Knight's Farm
Samlesbury Bottoms
Samlesbury Bridge
6
DARK WOOD LA
GOOSE FOOT LA
River Darwen
Simpson's Farm
Blakey Hey
FIRWOOD LA
Firwood Farm
Stainton's Farm
PR5
5
Coppice Farm
Wild Bottom's Wood
GOOSE FOOT COTT
28
STANLEY VILLAS
Higher Barn
ROACH RD
Stanley Grange
Stanley Coppice Farm
GRANGE CL
4
Bolton Hall
Highfields Farm
CRIPPLE GATE LA
HOLLINS CL
QUAKER BROOK LA
Quaker Brook
BELL VILLAS
Tallentine Farm
Ford
3
GIB LA
Arthur's Wife's Brow
VALLEY RD
ROCK GDNS
Witton Weavers Way
Houghton Bottoms
HOGHTON LA
PO
THE STRAITS
27
Hoghton Bridge
LONG BARN BROW
Hoghton
LC
LONG BARN ROW
WILLOW
CHASE
THE CROSSINGS
STATION RD
FOWLER CL
FOWLER
CHAPEL LA
VIADUCT RD
2
BLACKBURN OLD RD
Brindle Lodge
Boar's Head (PH)
Barracks Farm
Recn Gd
Hoghton Tower
Chapel Bridge
Lane Side Farm
1
King's Hill
GREGSON LA
GOWANS LA
PR6
Hatchwood Farm
A675
26
60
A
B
61
C
D
62
E
F
79
100

99
121

Stanley House
Bolton Fold
Hacking House
Lodge Wood
Ravenswing Farm
Woodfold Park Farm
Arley Brook
Arley Farm
Jeffery Wood
Woodfold Hall
Billinge Scarr
Lower Bencock Farm
White House Pond
Middle Shorrock Hey Farm
Westholme Sch
Stock's Farm
Wallbanks House
Old Woodfold Farm
Lower Shorrock Hey Farm
Pall Mall
Billinge Side
Alum House Wood
Clog and Billycock (PH)
Billinge Hill
River Darwen
Lee Farm
BB2
Close Farm
Witton Weavers Way
Billinge Nook
Butler's Delf
Woodcock Hill
Witton Country Park
Maiden House Farm
PR5
Visitors Ctr
Lower Fold
Crem
Cemy
Hunter's Hill
Pleasington Nature Reserve
Stonefield Cotts
Pleasington Old Hall
Trout Brook Farm
Higher Park Farm
Billinge View
Throstle Nest Brow
PH
Butler's Bridge
Cherry Tree
Brownlands Farm
Tongue Hill
Playing Fields
Pleasington
St Francis CE Prim Sch
Brownlow Terr
CH
Leeds and Liverpool Canal
A677
Preston New Rd
A6119
Yew Tree Dr
Further La
Alum Scar La
Meins Rd
Woodgates Rd
Billinge End Rd
Killiard La
Under Billinge La
Carr La
Scarr La
Heathfield Pk
Long La
Woodcock Hill Rd
Sandy La
Old Hall La
Priory Cl
Regents Cl
Bowden Ave
Victoria Rd
Rose Hill Rd
Tower Rd
Hillcrest Rd
A674
Preston Old Rd
Geddes St
Cherry Lea
Green La
Livesey Hall Cl
The Crescent
Wilton Ct 1
Country Mews 2
Lever Cl 3
Eden Pk 4
Cherry Tree Terr 1
Hunters Lodge 2
Gladstone Terr 3
Melfort Cl 4
Torridon Cl 5
A B C D E F
8 7 6 5 4 3 2 1
29 28 27 26
63 64 65

99
80

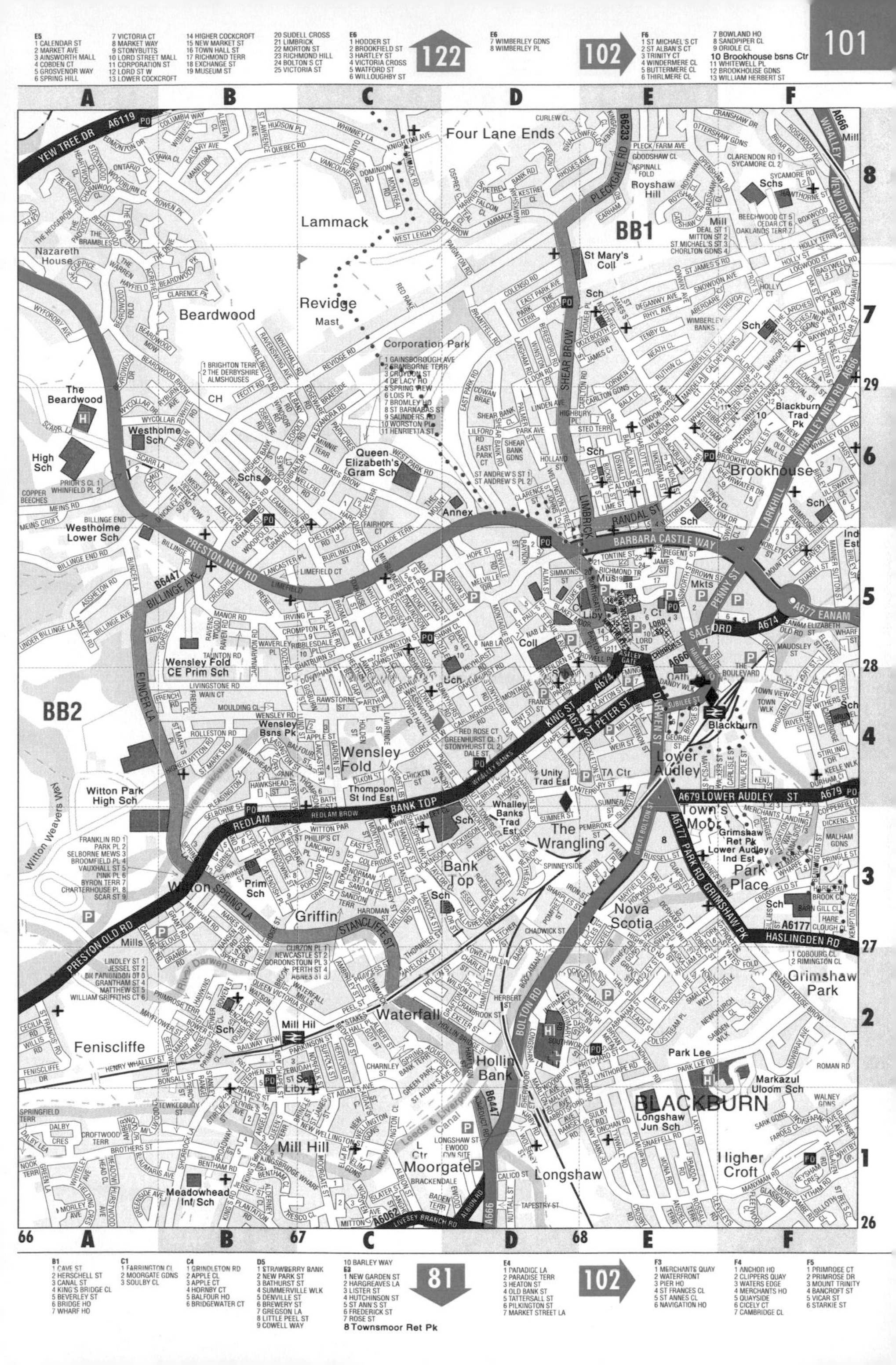

101
E5
1 CALENDAR ST
2 MARKET AVE
3 AINSWORTH MALL
4 COBDEN CT
5 GROSVENOR WAY
6 SPRING HILL
7 VICTORIA CT
8 MARKET WAY
9 STONYBUTTS
10 LORD STREET MALL
11 CORPORATION ST
12 LORD ST W
13 LOWER COCKCROFT
14 HIGHER COCKCROFT
15 NEW MARKET ST
16 TOWN HALL ST
17 RICHMOND TERR
18 EXCHANGE ST
19 MUSEUM ST
20 SUDELL CROSS
21 LIMBRICK
22 MORTON ST
23 RICHMOND HILL
24 BOLTON'S CT
25 VICTORIA ST
E6
1 HODDER ST
2 BROOKFIELD ST
3 HARTLEY ST
4 VICTORIA CROSS
5 WATFORD ST
6 WILLOUGHBY ST
122
E6
7 WIMBERLEY GDNS
8 WIMBERLEY PL
102
F6
1 ST MICHAEL'S CT
2 ST ALBAN'S CT
3 TRINITY CT
4 WINDERMERE CL
5 BUTTERMERE CL
6 THIRLMERE CL
7 BOWLAND HO
8 SANDPIPER CL
9 ORIOLE CL
10 Brookhouse bsns Ctr
11 WHITEWELL PL
12 BROOKHOUSE GDNS
13 WILLIAM HERBERT ST
A
B
C
D
E
F
8
7
29
6
5
28
4
3
27
2
1
26
66
67
68
Four Lane Ends
Lammack
Revidge
Mast
Beardwood
Nazareth House
Corporation Park
The Beardwood
Westholme Sch
High Sch
Queen Elizabeth's Gram Sch
Annex
Westholme Lower Sch
Royshaw Hill
BB1
St Mary's Coll
Brookhouse
Blackburn Trad Pk
BB2
Wensley Fold CE Prim Sch
Wensley Bsns Pk
Wensley Fold
Thompson St Ind Est
Witton Park High Sch
Whalley Banks Trad Est
The Wrangling
Unity Trad Est
Coll
Mus
Liby
Mkts
Blackburn
Lower Audley
Town's Moor
Grimshaw Ret Pk
Lower Audley Ind Est
Park Place
Bank Top
Griffin
Witton
Prim Sch
Nova Scotia
Grimshaw Park
Mills
Waterfall
Mill Hil
Feniscliffe
Hollin Bank
Park Lee
Markazul Uloom Sch
BLACKBURN
Longshaw Jun Sch
Mill Hill
Moorgate
Longshaw
Higher Croft
Meadowhead Inf Sch
PRESTON NEW RD
PRESTON OLD RD
BARBARA CASTLE WAY
LOWER AUDLEY ST
HASLINGDEN RD
WHALLEY NEW RD
REDLAM
BANK TOP
BOLTON RD
DARWEN ST
EANAM
YEW TREE DR
Leeds & Liverpool Canal
River Blakewater
River Darwen
Witton Weavers Way
B1
1 CAVE ST
2 HERSCHELL ST
3 CANAL ST
4 KING'S BRIDGE CL
5 BEVERLEY ST
6 BRIDGE HO
7 WHARF HO
C1
1 FARRINGTON CL
2 MOORGATE GDNS
3 SOULBY CL
C4
1 GRINDLETON RD
2 APPLE CL
3 APPLE CT
4 HORNBY CT
5 BALFOUR HO
6 BRIDGEWATER CT
D5
1 STRAWBERRY BANK
2 NEW PARK ST
3 BATHURST ST
4 SUMMERVILLE WLK
5 DENVILLE ST
6 BREWERY ST
7 GREGSON LA
8 LITTLE PEEL ST
9 COWELL WAY
10 BARLEY WAY
E3
1 NEW GARDEN ST
2 HARGREAVES LA
3 LISTER ST
4 HUTCHINSON ST
5 ST ANN'S ST
6 FREDERICK ST
7 ROSE ST
8 Townsmoor Ret Pk
81
E4
1 PARADISE LA
2 PARADISE TERR
3 HEATON ST
4 OLD BANK ST
5 TATTERSALL ST
6 PILKINGTON ST
7 MARKET STREET LA
102
F3
1 MERCHANTS QUAY
2 WATERFRONT
3 PIER HO
4 ST FRANCES CL
5 ST ANNES CL
6 NAVIGATION HO
F4
1 ANCHOR HO
2 CLIPPERS QUAY
3 WATERS EDGE
4 MERCHANTS HO
5 QUAYSIDE
6 CICELY CT
7 CAMBRIDGE CL
F5
1 PRIMROSE CT
2 PRIMROSE DR
3 MOUNT TRINITY
4 BANCROFT ST
5 VICAR ST
6 STARKIE ST

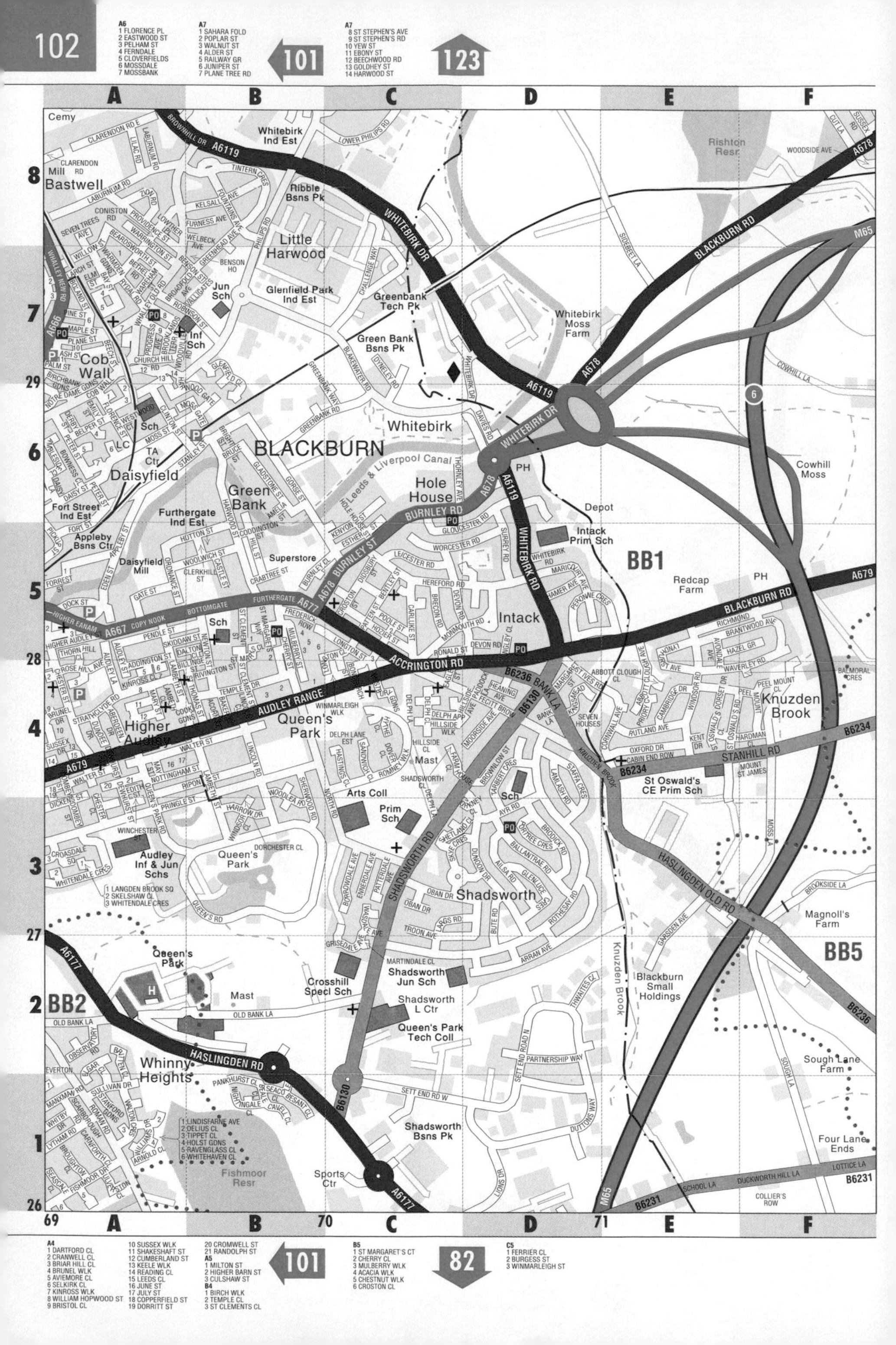
102
A6
1 FLORENCE PL
2 EASTWOOD ST
3 PELHAM ST
4 FERNDALE
5 CLOVERFIELDS
6 MOSSDALE
7 MOSSBANK
A7
1 SAHARA FOLD
2 POPLAR ST
3 WALNUT ST
4 ALDER ST
5 RAILWAY GR
6 JUNIPER ST
7 PLANE TREE RD
101
123
A7
8 ST STEPHEN'S AVE
9 ST STEPHEN'S RD
10 YEW ST
11 EBONY ST
12 BEECHWOOD RD
13 GOLDHEY ST
14 HARWOOD ST
A
B
C
D
E
F
8
7
29
6
5
28
4
3
27
2
1
26
69
70
71
Cemy
Bastwell
Whitebirk Ind Est
Ribble Bsns Pk
Little Harwood
Glenfield Park Ind Est
Greenbank Tech Pk
Green Bank Bsns Pk
Rishton Resr
Whitebirk Moss Farm
Cob Wall
Daisyfield
BLACKBURN
Whitebirk
Leeds & Liverpool Canal
Hole House
Green Bank
Furthergate Ind Est
Fort Street Ind Est
Appleby Bsns Ctr
Daisyfield Mill
Superstore
Cowhill Moss
Depot
Intack Prim Sch
BB1
Redcap Farm
Intack
Knuzden Brook
Higher Audley
Queen's Park
Mast
Arts Coll
Prim Sch
St Oswald's CE Prim Sch
Audley Inf & Jun Schs
Shadsworth
Magnoll's Farm
BB5
BB2
Queen's Park
Crosshill Specl Sch
Shadsworth Jun Sch
Shadsworth L Ctr
Queen's Park Tech Coll
Blackburn Small Holdings
Knuzden Brook
Whinny Heights
Shadsworth Bsns Pk
Sough Lane Farm
Four Lane Ends
Fishmoor Resr
Sports Ctr
Collier's Row
A6119
A678
M65
A679
A677
A667
A666
A6177
B6130
B6236
B6234
B6231
WHITEBIRK DR
BLACKBURN RD
BURNLEY RD
BURNLEY ST
ACCRINGTON RD
AUDLEY RANGE
BANK LA
STANHILL RD
HASLINGDEN OLD RD
HASLINGDEN RD
SHADSWORTH RD
SETT END RD W
PARTNERSHIP WAY
OLD BANK LA
SCHOOL LA
DUCKWORTH HILL LA
LOTTICE LA
1 LANGDEN BROOK SQ
2 SKELSHAW CL
3 WHITENDALE CRES
1 LINDISFARNE AVE
2 DELIUS CL
3 TIPPET CL
4 HOLST GDNS
5 RAVENGLASS CL
6 WHITEHAVEN CL
A4
1 DARTFORD CL
2 CRANWELL CL
3 BRIAR HILL CL
4 BRUNEL WLK
5 AVIEMORE CL
6 SELKIRK CL
7 KINROSS WLK
8 WILLIAM HOPWOOD ST
9 BRISTOL CL
10 SUSSEX WLK
11 SHAKESHAFT ST
12 CUMBERLAND ST
13 KEELE WLK
14 READING CL
15 LEEDS CL
16 JUNE ST
17 JULY ST
18 COPPERFIELD ST
19 DORRITT ST
20 CROMWELL ST
21 RANDOLPH ST
A5
1 MILTON ST
2 HIGHER BARN ST
3 CULSHAW ST
B4
1 BIRCH WLK
2 TEMPLE CL
3 ST CLEMENTS CL
101
82
B5
1 ST MARGARET'S CT
2 CHERRY CL
3 MULBERRY WLK
4 ACACIA WLK
5 CHESTNUT WLK
6 CROSTON CL
C5
1 FERRIER CL
2 BURGESS ST
3 WINMARLEIGH ST

124
104

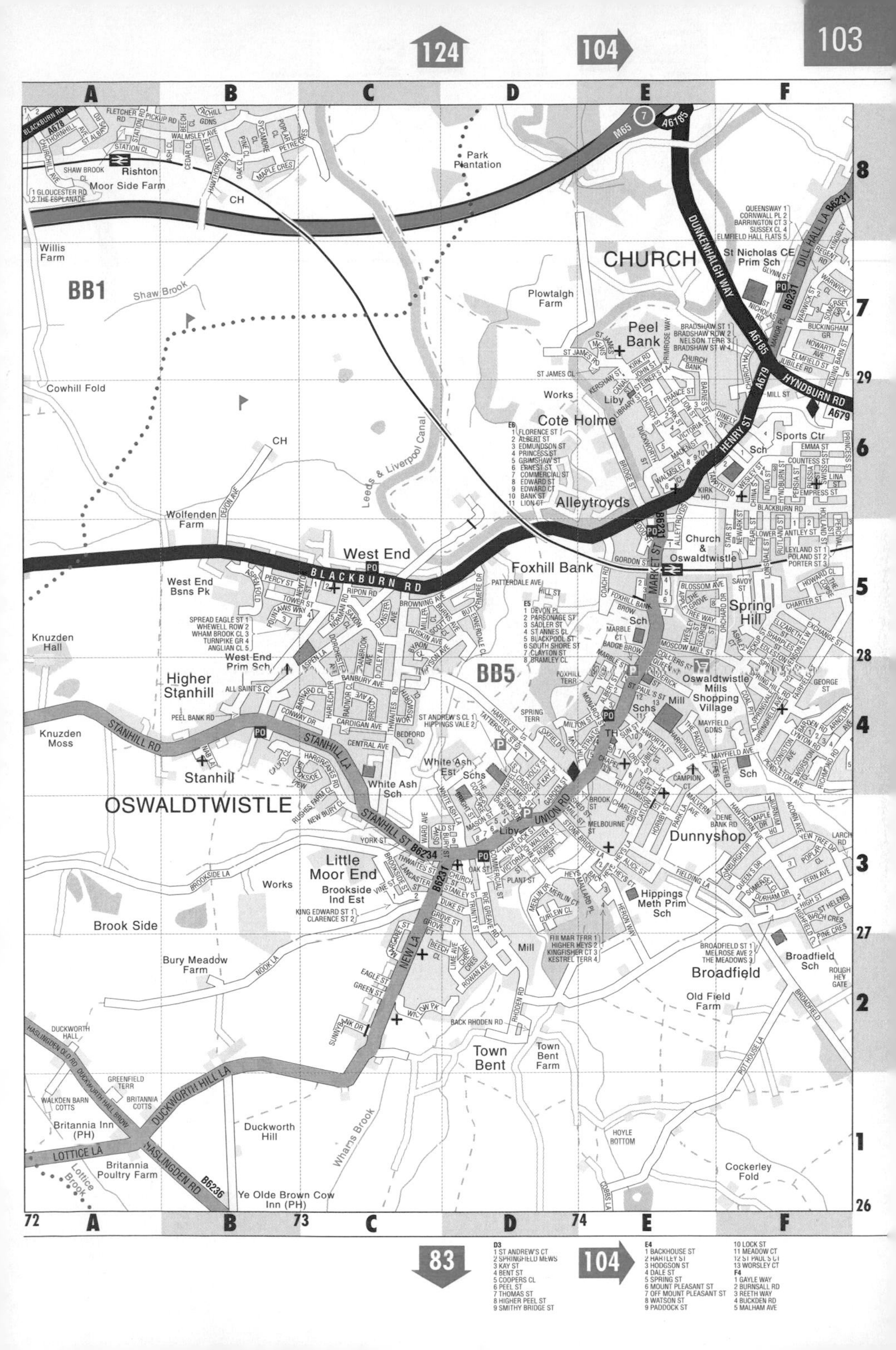

83
104

A7
1 LINCOLN CT
2 LINDSEY HO
3 BANBURY CL
4 WORCESTER AVE
5 EVESHAM CL
6 MALVERN CL
7 STRATFORD WAY
C5
1 CHRIST CHURCH SQ
2 CHRIST CHURCH ST
3 NUTTALL ST MEWS
4 PRIESTLEY NOOK
5 EDMUND ST
C5
6 NAPIER ST
7 WELLINGTON CT
8 SPRING GDNS
9 HARGREAVES ST
10 CHAPEL ST
11 ST LEGER CT
C5
12 MIDLAND ST
13 QUARRY ST
C6
1 MANOR BROOK
2 ARNOLD ST
3 BRADSHAW ST E
4 HOOD ST
5 RAILWAY VIEW
6 KENYON ST
7 MASON ST
8 BURNLEY RD
9 WATER ST
10 BACK WATER ST
11 INFANT ST
12 QUEEN ST
13 TASKER ST
14 BRIDGE ST
15 DUTTON ST

103
125

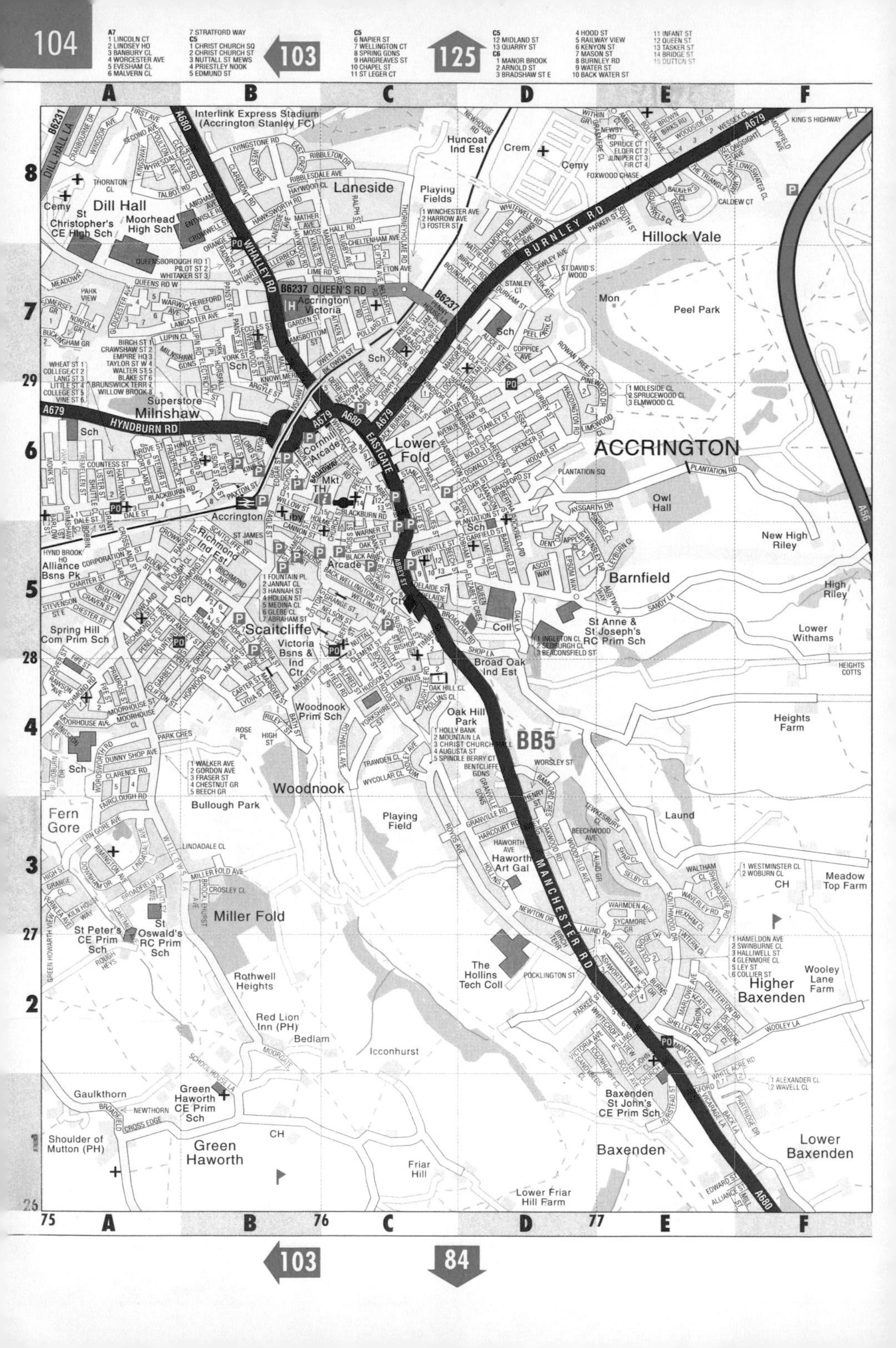

103
84

126
106

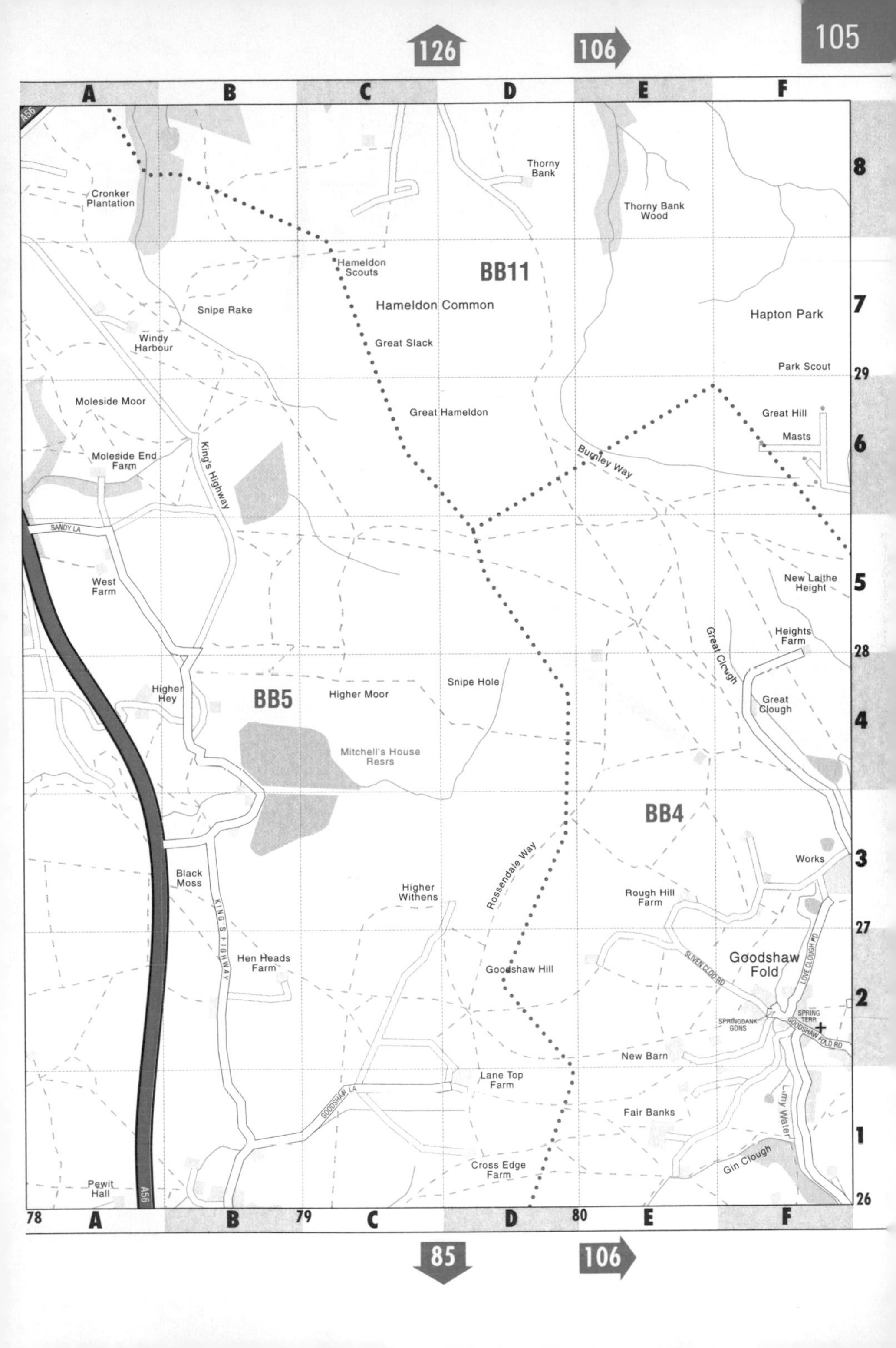

85
106

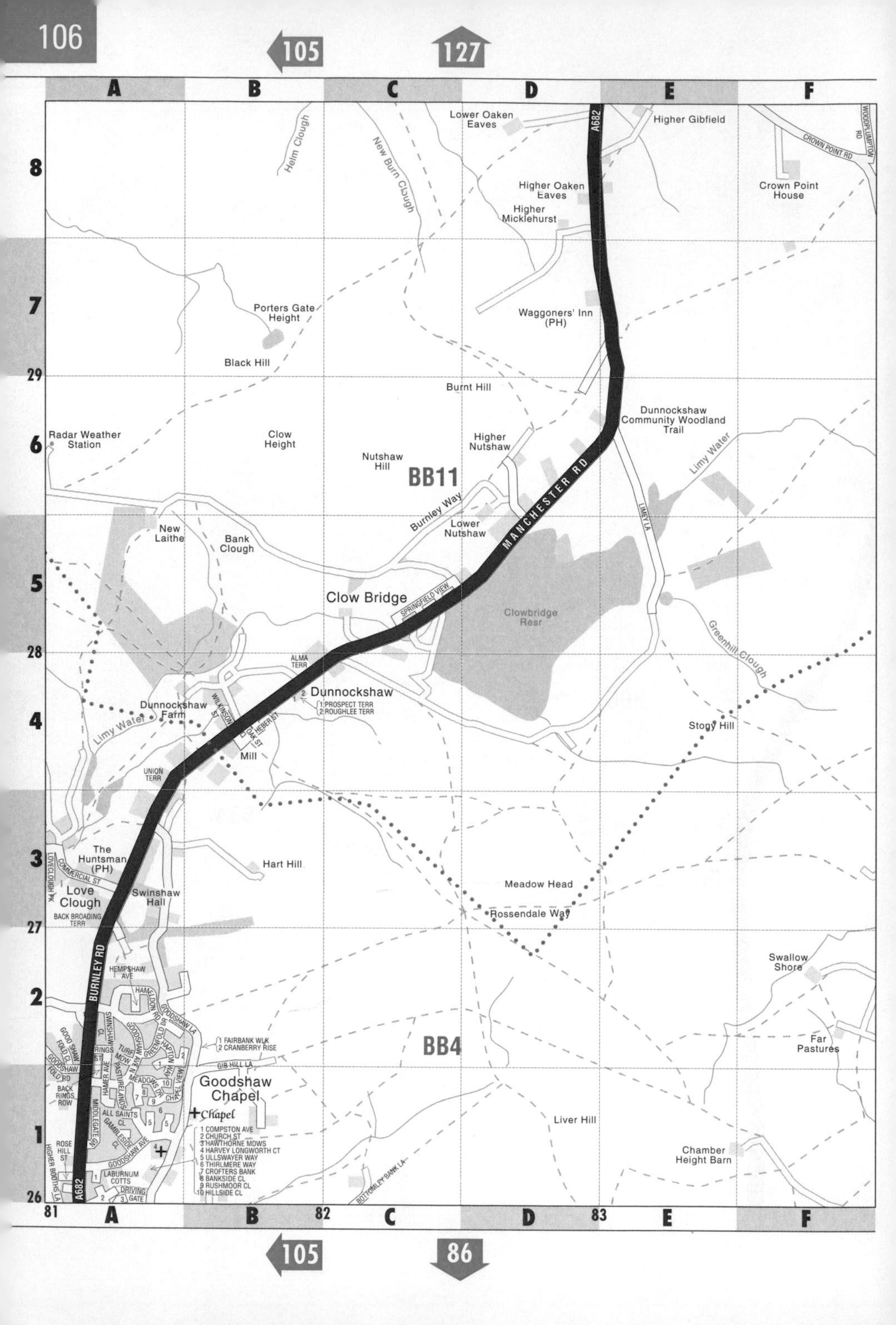
105
127
A
B
C
D
E
F
8
7
29
6
5
28
4
3
27
2
1
26
81
82
83
Lower Oaken Eaves
Higher Gibfield
A682
CROWN POINT RD
WOODPLUMPTON RD
Helm Clough
New Burn Clough
Higher Oaken Eaves
Higher Micklehurst
Crown Point House
Porters Gate Height
Waggoners' Inn (PH)
Black Hill
Burnt Hill
Dunnockshaw Community Woodland Trail
Radar Weather Station
Clow Height
Nutshaw Hill
BB11
Higher Nutshaw
MANCHESTER RD
Limy Water
Burnley Way
Lower Nutshaw
LIMEY LA
New Laithe
Bank Clough
Clow Bridge
SPRINGFIELD VIEW
Clowbridge Resr
Greenhill Clough
ALMA TERR
Dunnockshaw
1 PROSPECT TERR
2 ROUGHLEE TERR
Dunnockshaw Farm
WILKINSON ST
HEBER ST
OAK ST
Mill
Stony Hill
Limy Water
UNION TERR
The Huntsman (PH)
Hart Hill
LOVECLOUGH PK
COMMERCIAL ST
Love Clough
Swinshaw Hall
Meadow Head
Rossendale Way
BACK BROADING TERR
Swallow Shore
BURNLEY RD
HEMPSHAW AVE
HAMELDON RD
GOODSHAW LA
1 FAIRBANK WLK
2 CRANBERRY RISE
BB4
Far Pastures
GIB HILL LA
Goodshaw Chapel
Chapel
1 COMPSTON AVE
2 CHURCH ST
3 HAWTHORNE MDWS
4 HARVEY LONGWORTH CT
5 ULLSWAYER WAY
6 THIRLMERE WAY
7 CROFTERS BANK
8 BANKSIDE CL
9 RUSHMOOR CL
10 HILLSIDE CL
Liver Hill
Chamber Height Barn
BOTTOMLEY BANK LA
GOODSHAW FOLD CL
GOODSHAW FOLD RD
BACK RINGS ROW
RINGS ST
HAMER AVE
MIDDLEGATE GN
ALL SAINTS CL
GAMBLESIDE CL
GOODSHAW AVE
ROSE HILL ST
HIGHER BOOTHS LA
LABURNUM COTTS
DRIVING GATE
A682
105
86

128
108

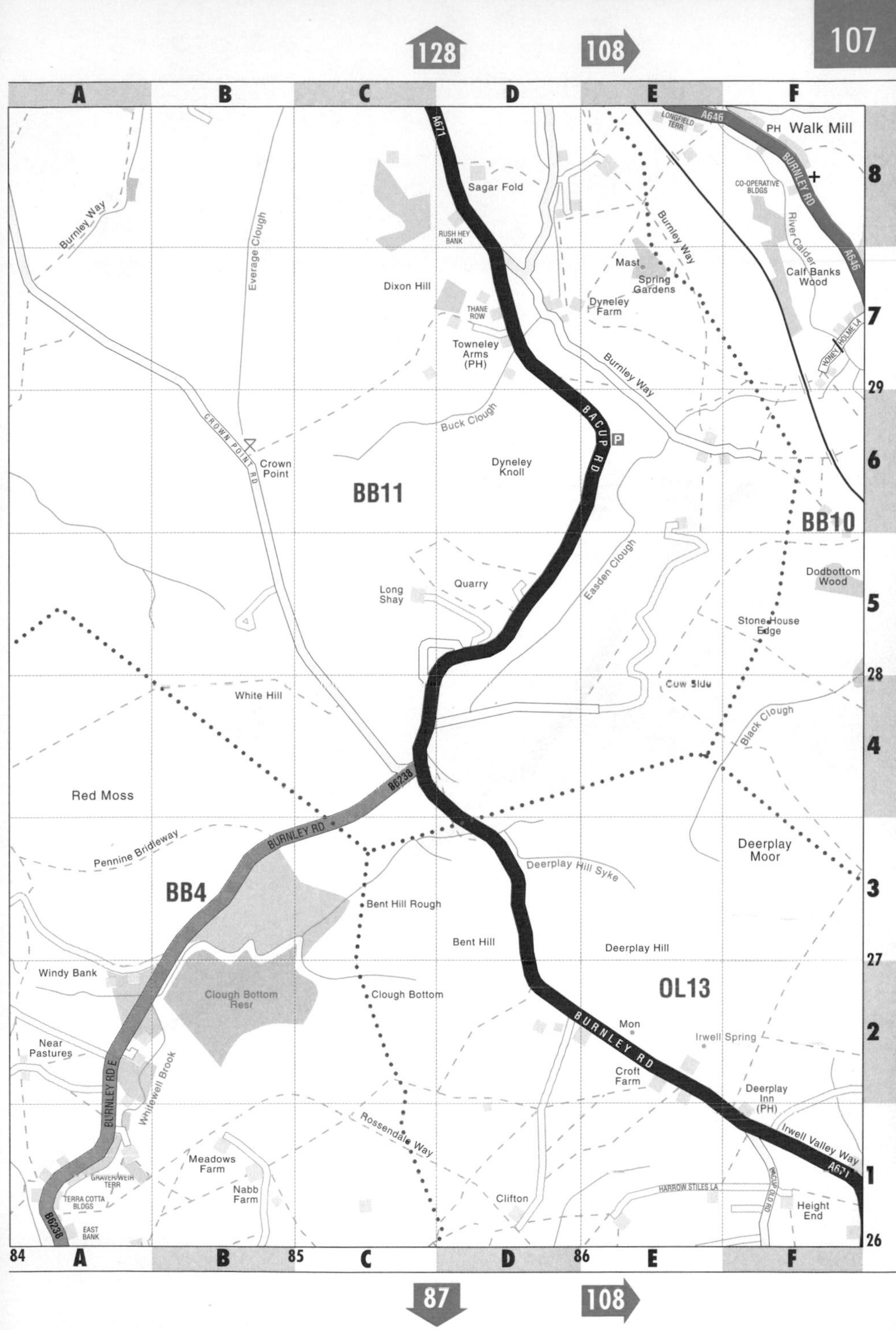

87
108

107
129

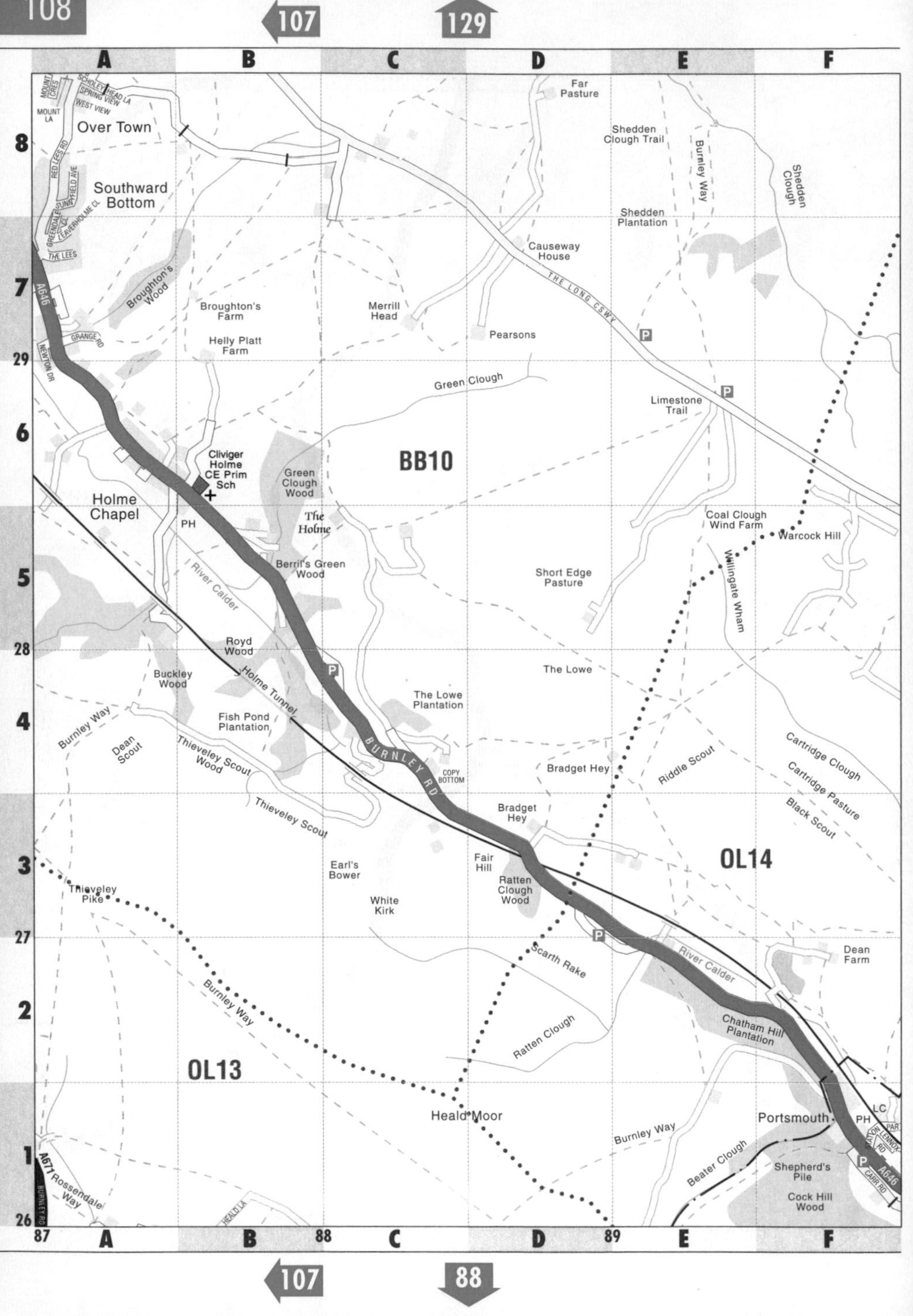

107
88

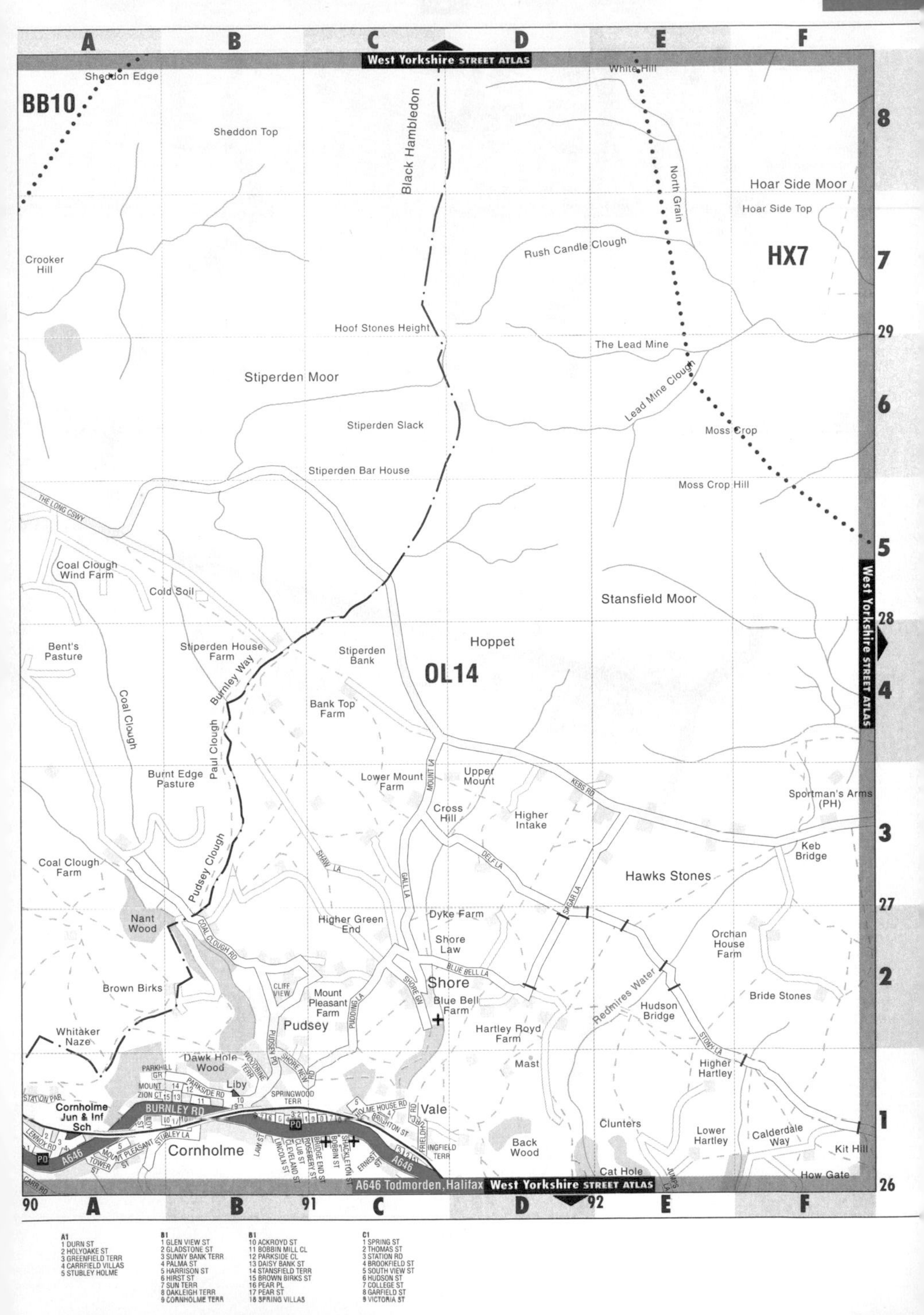

A1
1 DURN ST
2 HOLYOAKE ST
3 GREENFIELD TERR
4 CARRFIELD VILLAS
5 STUBLEY HOLME

B1
1 GLEN VIEW ST
2 GLADSTONE ST
3 SUNNY BANK TERR
4 PALMA ST
5 HARRISON ST
6 HIRST ST
7 SUN TERR
8 OAKLEIGH TERR
9 CORNHOLME TERR

B1
10 ACKROYD ST
11 BOBBIN MILL CL
12 PARKSIDE CL
13 DAISY BANK ST
14 STANSFIELD TERR
15 BROWN BIRKS ST
16 PEAR PL
17 PEAR ST
18 SPRING VILLAS

C1
1 SPRING ST
2 THOMAS ST
3 STATION RD
4 BROOKFIELD ST
5 SOUTH VIEW ST
6 HUDSON ST
7 COLLEGE ST
8 GARFIELD ST
9 VICTORIA ST

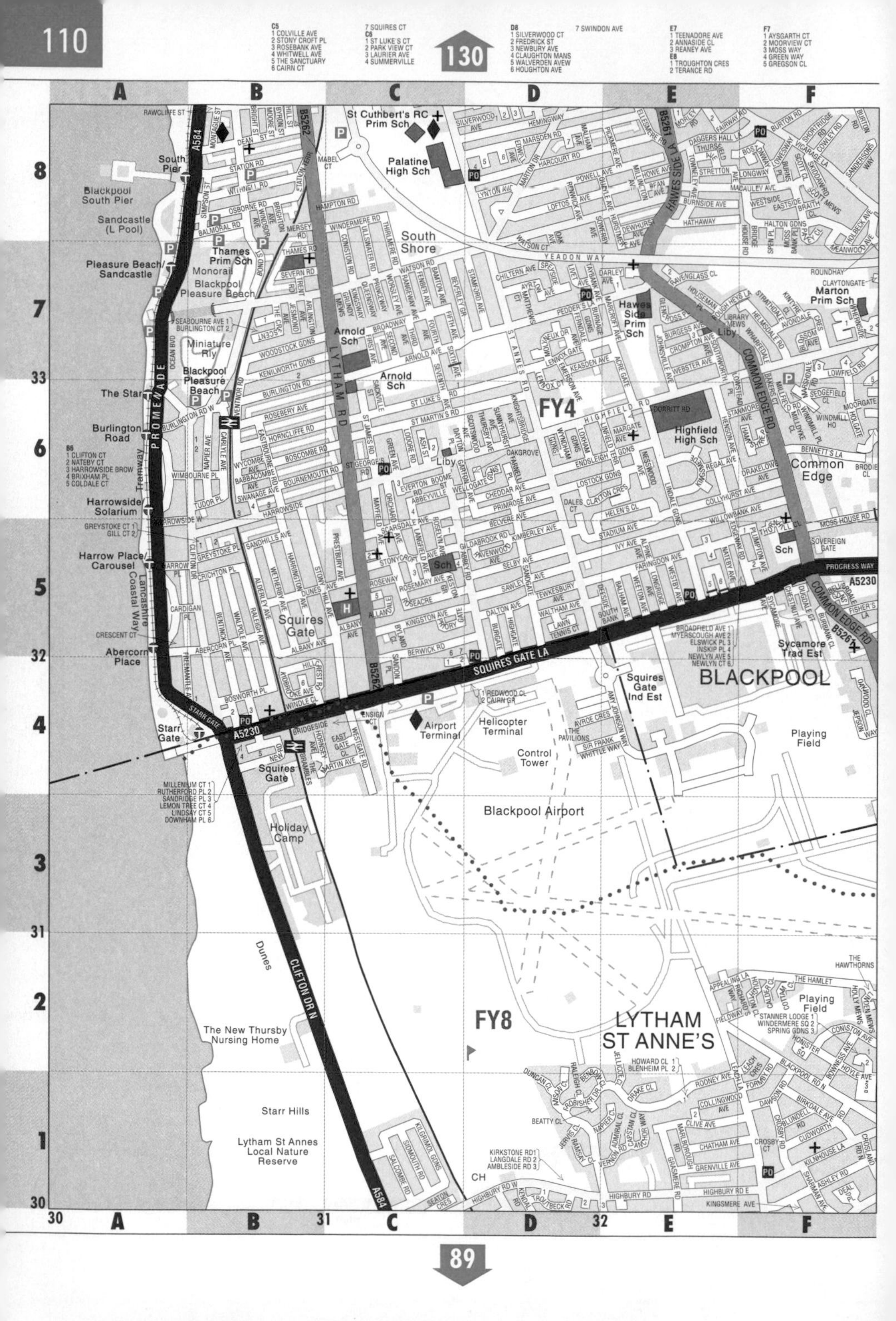
C5
1 COLVILLE AVE
2 STONY CROFT PL
3 ROSEBANK AVE
4 WHITWELL AVE
5 THE SANCTUARY
6 CAIRN CT
7 SQUIRES CT
C6
1 ST LUKE'S CT
2 PARK VIEW CT
3 LAURIER AVE
4 SUMMERVILLE
130
D8
1 SILVERWOOD CT
2 FREDRICK ST
3 NEWBURY AVE
4 CLAUGHTON MANS
5 WALVERDEN AVEW
6 HOUGHTON AVE
7 SWINDON AVE
E7
1 TEENADORE AVE
2 ANNASIDE CL
3 REANEY AVE
E8
1 TROUGHTON CRES
2 TERANCE RD
F7
1 AYSGARTH CT
2 MOORVIEW CT
3 MOSS WAY
4 GREEN WAY
5 GREGSON CL
A
B
C
D
E
F
8
7
33
6
5
32
4
3
31
2
1
30
South Pier
Blackpool South Pier
Sandcastle (L Pool)
Pleasure Beach/ Sandcastle
Thames Prim Sch
Monorail
Blackpool Pleasure Beach
Miniature Rly
Blackpool Pleasure Beach
The Star
Burlington Road
Harrowside/ Solarium
Harrow Place Carousel
Lancashire Coastal Way
Tramway
Abercorn Place
Starr Gate
PROMENADE
B6
1 CLIFTON CT
2 NATEBY CT
3 HARROWSIDE BROW
4 BRIXHAM PL
5 COLDALE CT
SEABOURNE AVE 1
BURLINGTON CT 2
GREYSTOKE CT 1
GILL CT 2
CRESCENT CT
St Cuthbert's RC Prim Sch
Palatine High Sch
South Shore
Arnold Sch
Arnold Sch
LYTHAM RD
B5262
A584
A5230
Squires Gate
Squires Gate
SQUIRES GATE LA
STARR GATE
MILLENIUM CT 1
RUTHERFORD PL 2
SANDRIDGE PL 3
LEMON TREE CT 4
LINDSAY CT 5
DOWNHAM PL 6
Holiday Camp
Airport Terminal
Helicopter Terminal
Control Tower
Blackpool Airport
1 REDWOOD CL
2 CAIRN GR
FY4
YEADON WAY
Hawes Side Prim Sch
Liby
Liby
Highfield High Sch
Marton Prim Sch
Common Edge
COMMON EDGE RD
HAWES SIDE LA
B5261
PROGRESS WAY
Sch
Sch
Sycamore Trad Est
BLACKPOOL
Squires Gate Ind Est
BROADFIELD AVE 1
MYERSCOUGH AVE 2
ELSWICK PL 3
INSKIP PL 4
NEWLYN AVE 5
NEWLYN CT 6
Playing Field
Dunes
CLIFTON DR N
The New Thursby Nursing Home
Starr Hills
Lytham St Annes Local Nature Reserve
FY8
LYTHAM ST ANNE'S
HOWARD CL 1
BLENHEIM PL 2
STANNER LODGE 1
WINDERMERE SQ 2
SPRING GDNS 3
Playing Field
THE HAWTHORNS
KIRKSTONE RD 1
LANGDALE RD 2
AMBLESIDE RD 3
BEATTY CL
CH
HIGHBURY RD
HIGHBURY RD E
KINGSMERE AVE
30
31
32

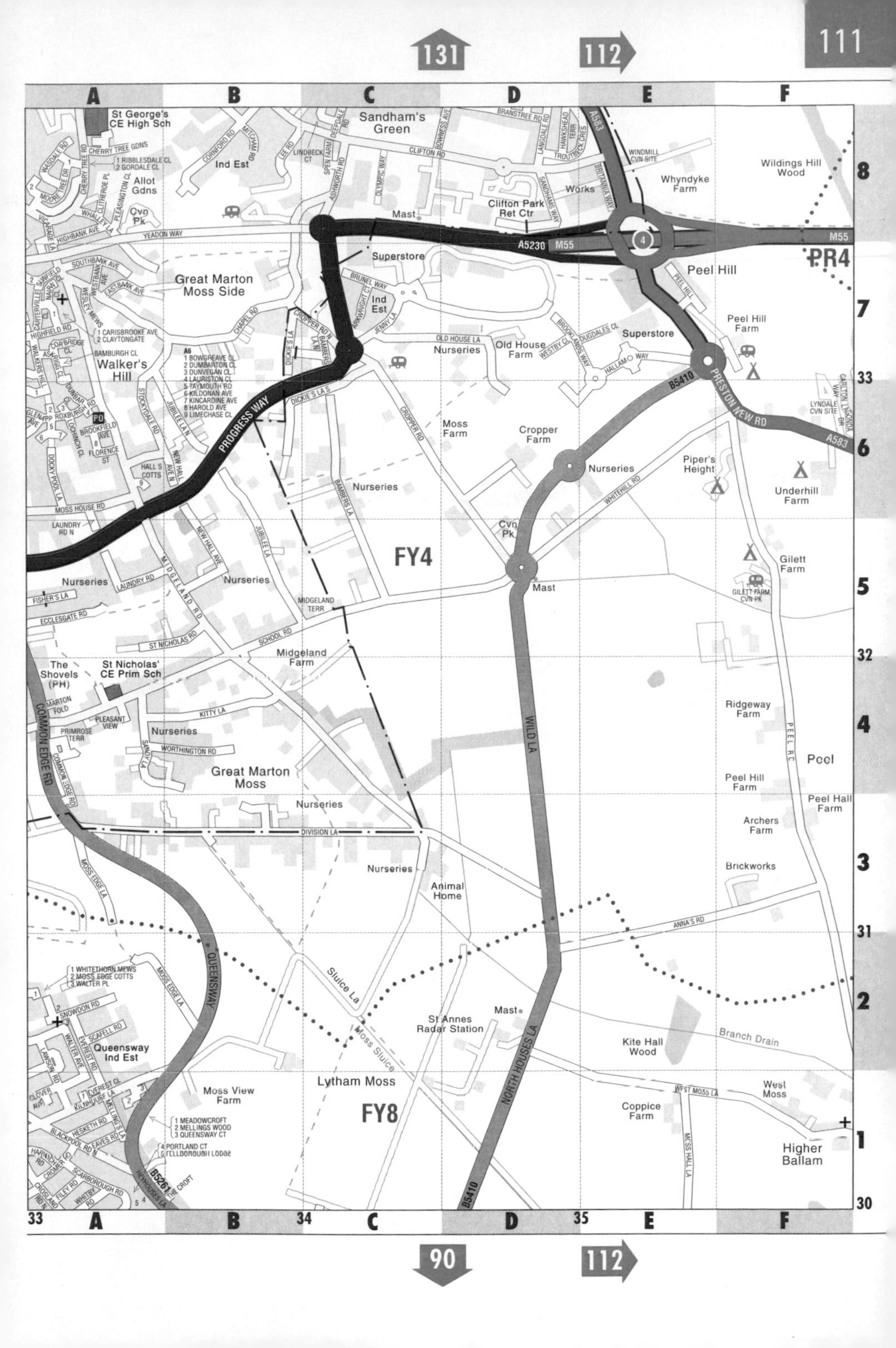
131
112
St George's CE High Sch
Sandham's Green
Ind Est
Allot Gdns
Cvn Pk
Clifton Park Ret Ctr
Works
Whyndyke Farm
Wildings Hill Wood
Mast
Superstore
Great Marton Moss Side
Ind Est
Peel Hill
PR4
Walker's Hill
Nurseries
Old House Farm
Superstore
Peel Hill Farm
Moss Farm
Cropper Farm
Piper's Height
Underhill Farm
Nurseries
Nurseries
FY4
Cvn Pk
Gilett Farm
Nurseries
Nurseries
Mast
Midgeland Farm
The Shovels (PH)
St Nicholas' CE Prim Sch
Ridgeway Farm
Nurseries
Great Marton Moss
Pool
Peel Hill Farm
Peel Hall Farm
Archers Farm
Nurseries
Brickworks
Nurseries
Animal Home
Sluice La
Moss Sluice
St Annes Radar Station
Mast
Branch Drain
Kite Hall Wood
Queensway Ind Est
Lytham Moss
FY8
Moss View Farm
Coppice Farm
West Moss
Higher Ballam
M55
A5230
A583
B5410
B5261
PROGRESS WAY
PRESTON NEW RD
WILD LA
NORTH HOUSES LA
COMMON EDGE RD
QUEENSWAY
DIVISION LA
CLIFTON RD
YEADON WAY
CROPPER RD
WHITEHILL RD
SCHOOL RD
MIDGELAND RD
PEEL RD
ANNA'S RD
WEST MOSS LA
MOSS HALL LA
MOSS EDGE LA
1 RIBBLESDALE CL
2 GORDALE CL
1 CARISBROOKE AVE
2 CLAYTONGATE
1 BOWGREAVE CL
2 DUMBARTON CL
3 DUNVEGAN CL
4 LAURISTON CL
5 TAYMOUTH RD
6 KILDONAN AVE
7 KINCARDINE AVE
8 HAROLD AVE
9 LIMECHASE CL
1 WHITETHORN MEWS
2 MOSS EDGE COTTS
3 WALTER PL
1 MEADOWCROFT
2 MELLINGS WOOD
3 QUEENSWAY CT
4 PORTLAND CT
A B C D E F
8 7 6 5 4 3 2 1
33 34 35
33 32 31 30
90
112

111
132

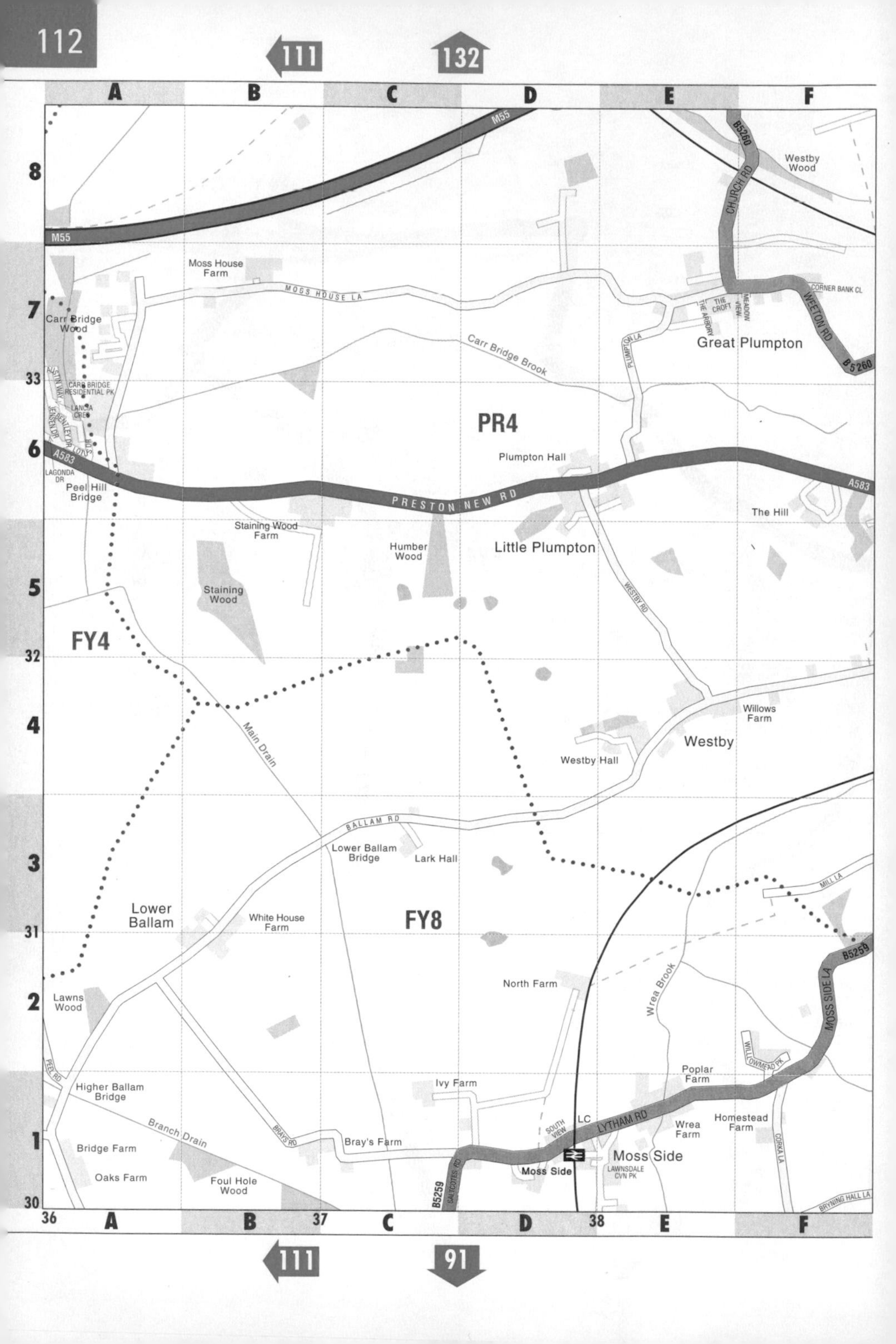

111
91

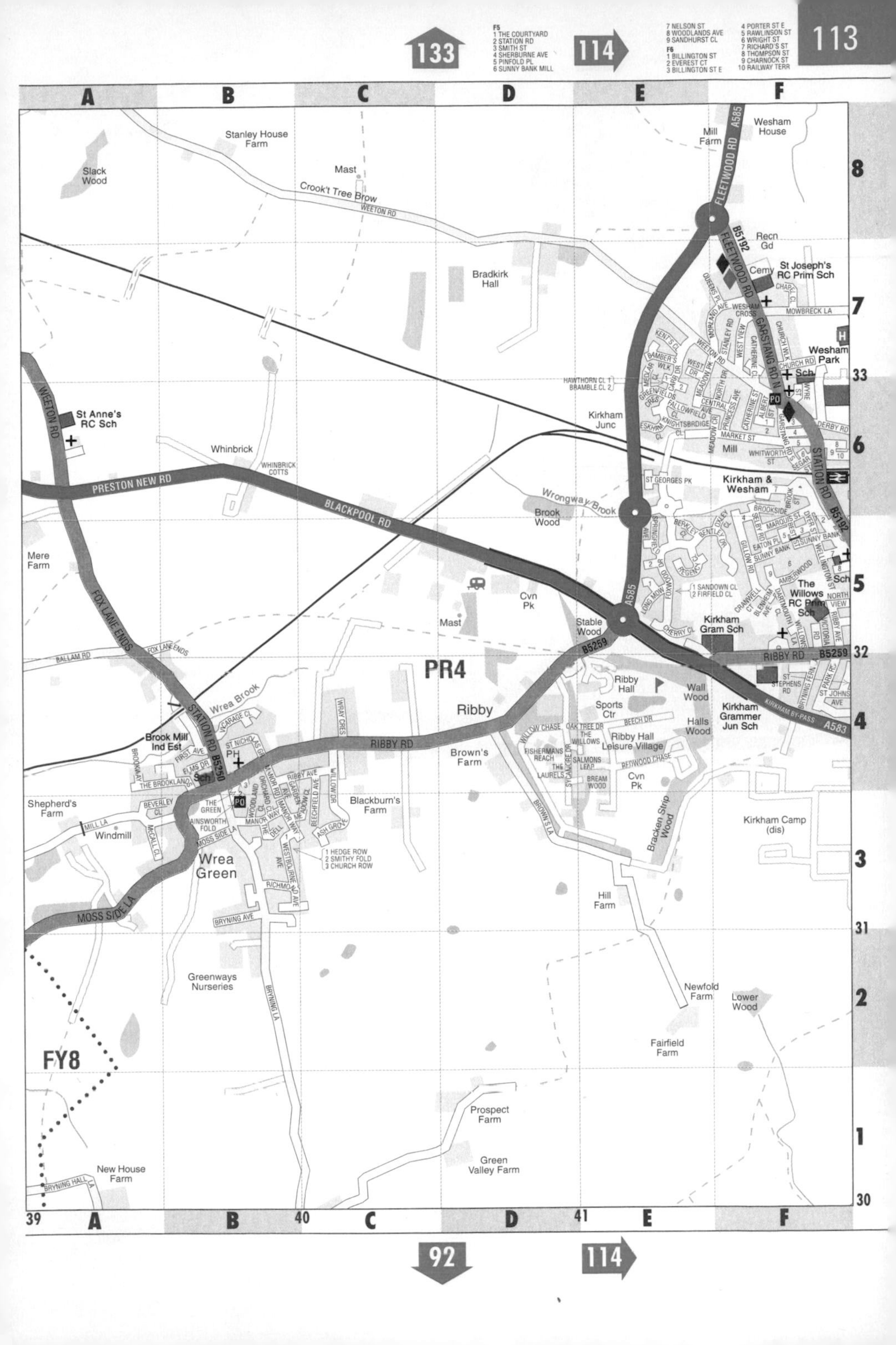
133
114
F5
1 THE COURTYARD
2 STATION RD
3 SMITH ST
4 SHERBURNE AVE
5 PINFOLD PL
6 SUNNY BANK MILL
7 NELSON ST
8 WOODLANDS AVE
9 SANDHURST CL
F6
1 BILLINGTON ST
2 EVEREST CT
3 BILLINGTON ST E
4 PORTER ST E
5 RAWLINSON ST
6 WRIGHT ST
7 RICHARD'S ST
8 THOMPSON ST
9 CHARNOCK ST
10 RAILWAY TERR
A
B
C
D
E
F
8
7
33
6
5
32
4
3
31
2
1
30
39
40
41
Stanley House Farm
Slack Wood
Mast
Crook't Tree Brow
WEETON RD
Mill Farm
Wesham House
FLEETWOOD RD
A585
B5192
Recn Gd
Cemy
St Joseph's RC Prim Sch
Bradkirk Hall
MOWBRECK LA
Wesham Park
Sch
HAWTHORN CL 1
BRAMBLE CL 2
Kirkham Junc
St Anne's RC Sch
Whinbrick
WHINBRICK COTTS
PRESTON NEW RD
BLACKPOOL RD
Wrongway Brook
Brook Wood
Kirkham & Wesham
STATION RD
MARKET ST
Mill
WHITWORTH ST
DERBY RD
ST GEORGES PK
Mere Farm
FOX LANE ENDS
Cvn Pk
Mast
Stable Wood
1 SANDOWN CL
2 FIRFIELD CL
The Willows RC Prim Sch
Kirkham Gram Sch
BALLAM RD
B5259
RIBBY RD
PR4
Ribby
Ribby Hall
Wall Wood
Sports Ctr
Kirkham Grammer Jun Sch
KIRKHAM BY-PASS
A583
Wrea Brook
Brook Mill Ind Est
STATION RD
B5250
PH
Sch
Ribby Hall Leisure Village
Halls Wood
Brown's Farm
Cvn Pk
Shepherd's Farm
MILL LA
Windmill
Blackburn's Farm
1 HEDGE ROW
2 SMITHY FOLD
3 CHURCH ROW
Bracken Strip Wood
Kirkham Camp (dis)
Wrea Green
MOSS SIDE LA
Hill Farm
BRYNING AVE
Greenways Nurseries
BRYNING LA
Newfold Farm
Lower Wood
FY8
Fairfield Farm
Prospect Farm
Green Valley Farm
New House Farm
BRYNING HALL LA

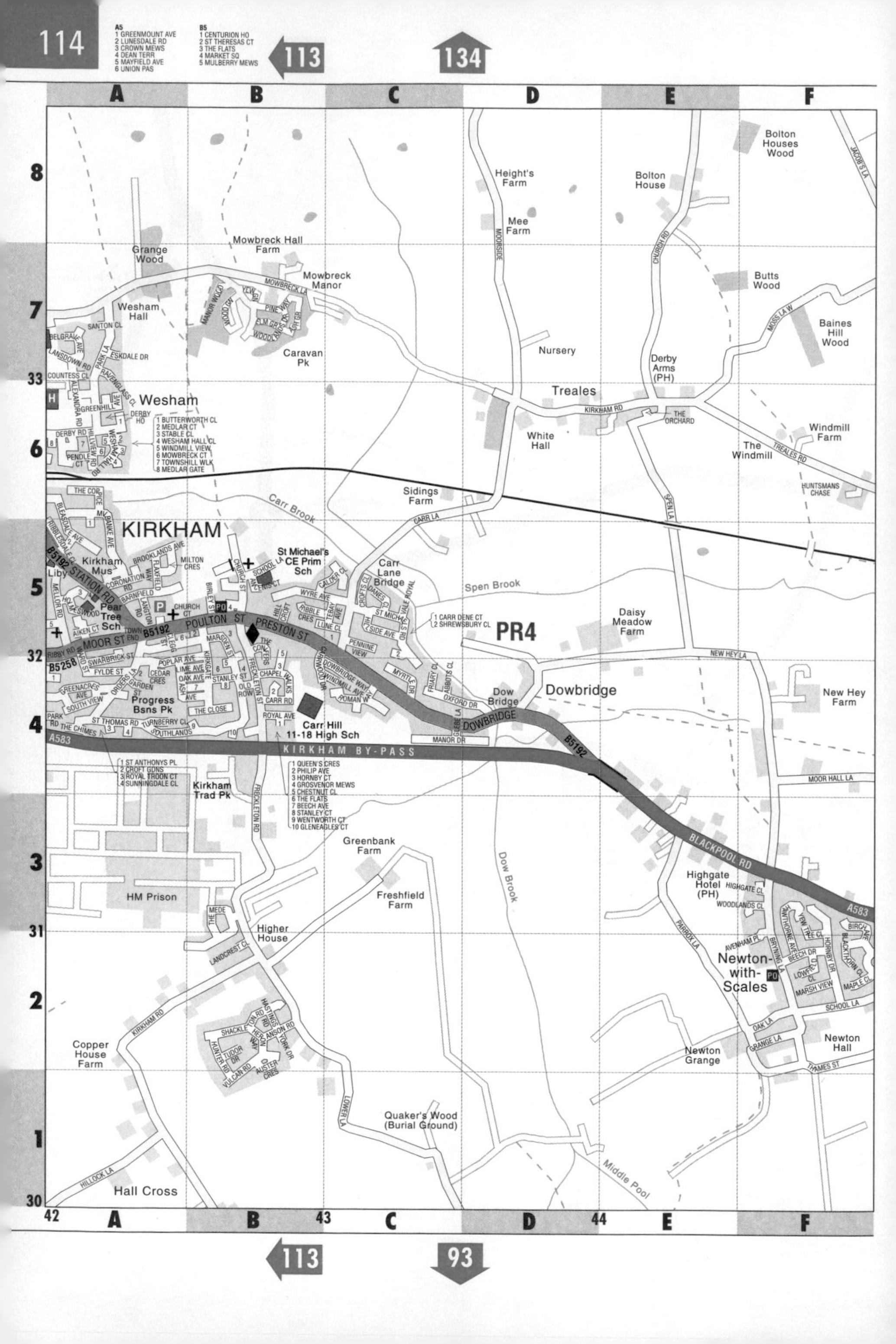
A5
1 GREENMOUNT AVE
2 LUNESDALE RD
3 CROWN MEWS
4 DEAN TERR
5 MAYFIELD AVE
6 UNION PAS
B5
1 CENTURION HO
2 ST THERESAS CT
3 THE FLATS
4 MARKET SQ
5 MULBERRY MEWS
113
134
93
KIRKHAM
Wesham
Treales
Dowbridge
Newton-with-Scales
PR4
Grange Wood
Mowbreck Hall Farm
Mowbreck Manor
Wesham Hall
Caravan Pk
Height's Farm
Mee Farm
Bolton House
Bolton Houses Wood
Butts Wood
Baines Hill Wood
Nursery
Derby Arms (PH)
White Hall
The Windmill
Windmill Farm
Sidings Farm
Carr Brook
Spen Brook
St Michael's CE Prim Sch
Carr Lane Bridge
Kirkham Mus
Liby
Pear Tree Sch
Daisy Meadow Farm
Dow Bridge
New Hey Farm
Progress Bsns Pk
Carr Hill 11-18 High Sch
Kirkham Trad Pk
HM Prison
Greenbank Farm
Freshfield Farm
Higher House
Highgate Hotel (PH)
Dow Brook
Copper House Farm
Newton Grange
Newton Hall
Quaker's Wood (Burial Ground)
Hall Cross
Middle Pool
1 BUTTERWORTH CL
2 MEDLAR CT
3 STABLE CL
4 WESHAM HALL CL
5 WINDMILL VIEW
6 MOWBRECK CT
7 TOWNSHILL WLK
8 MEDLAR GATE
1 CARR DENE CT
2 SHREWSBURY CL
1 ST ANTHONYS PL
2 CROFT GDNS
3 ROYAL TROON CT
4 SUNNINGDALE CL
1 QUEEN'S CRES
2 PHILIP AVE
3 HORNBY CT
4 GROSVENOR MEWS
5 CHESTNUT CL
6 THE FLATS
7 BEECH AVE
8 STANLEY CT
9 WENTWORTH CT
10 GLENEAGLES CT
KIRKHAM BY-PASS
BLACKPOOL RD
POULTON ST
PRESTON ST
MOOR ST
STATION RD
DOWBRIDGE
KIRKHAM RD
MOWBRECK LA
CARR LA
NEW HEY LA
MOOR HALL LA
SPEN LA
CHURCH RD
MOORSIDE
TREALES RD
MOSS LA W
JACOB'S LA
FRECKLETON RD
LOWER LA
HILLOCK LA
SCHOOL LA
THAMES ST
MANOR DR
B5192
B5258
A583

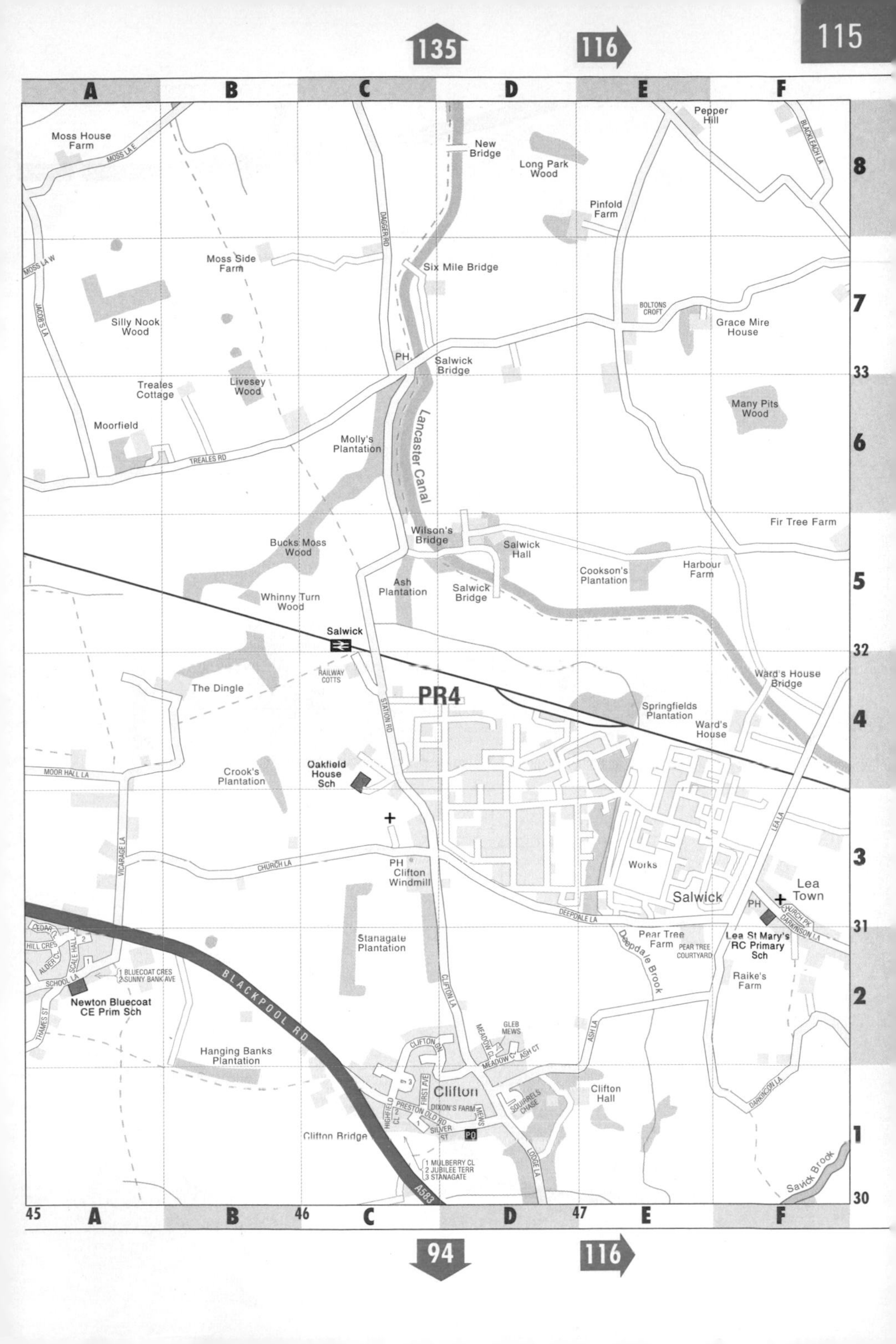
135
116
A
B
C
D
E
F
8
7
6
5
4
3
2
1
33
32
31
30
45
46
47
Moss House Farm
MOSS LA E
New Bridge
Long Park Wood
Pepper Hill
BLACKLEACH LA
Pinfold Farm
DAGGER RD
MOSS LA W
Moss Side Farm
Six Mile Bridge
JACOB'S LA
Silly Nook Wood
BOLTONS CROFT
Grace Mire House
PH
Salwick Bridge
Treales Cottage
Livesey Wood
Many Pits Wood
Moorfield
Lancaster Canal
TREALES RD
Molly's Plantation
Fir Tree Farm
Wilson's Bridge
Salwick Hall
Bucks Moss Wood
Cookson's Plantation
Harbour Farm
Ash Plantation
Salwick Bridge
Whinny Turn Wood
Salwick
RAILWAY COTTS
Ward's House Bridge
The Dingle
PR4
STATION RD
Springfields Plantation
Ward's House
MOOR HALL LA
Crook's Plantation
Oakfield House Sch
LEA LA
VICARAGE LA
CHURCH LA
PH
Clifton Windmill
Works
Lea Town
Salwick
PH
DEEPDALE LA
CHURCH PK
DARKINSON LA
CEDAR
HILL CRES
Stanagate Plantation
Pear Tree Farm
PEAR TREE COURTYARD
Lea St Mary's RC Primary Sch
Deepdale Brook
SCALE HALL
ALDER CL
SCHOOL LA
1 BLUECOAT CRES
2 SUNNY BANK AVE
BLACKPOOL RD
CLIFTON LA
Raike's Farm
Newton Bluecoat CE Prim Sch
THAMES ST
ASH LA
GLEB MEWS
MEADOW CL
Hanging Banks Plantation
CLIFTON DR
MEADOW CT
ASH CT
Clifton
FIRST AVE
Clifton Hall
HIGHFIELD CL
PRESTON OLD RD
DIXON'S FARM MEWS
SQUIRRELS CHASE
DARKINSON LA
SILVER ST
PO
Clifton Bridge
LODGE LA
1 MULBERRY CL
2 JUBILEE TERR
3 STANAGATE
A583
Savick Brook
94
116

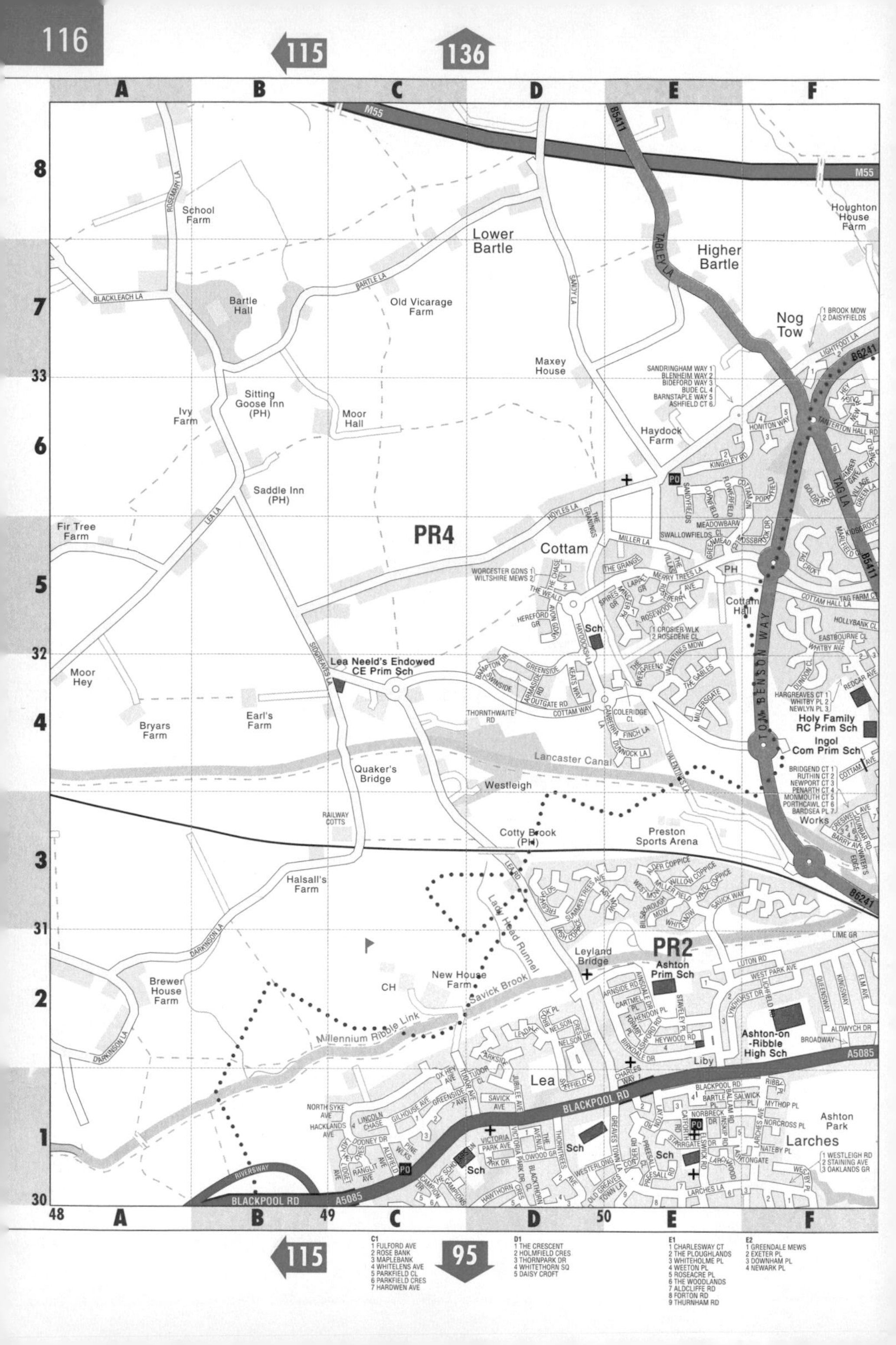
116
115
136
A
B
C
D
E
F
8
7
33
6
5
32
4
3
31
2
1
30
48
49
50
M55
B5411
School Farm
Lower Bartle
Higher Bartle
Houghton House Farm
TABLEY LA
BLACKLEACH LA
BARTLE LA
Bartle Hall
Old Vicarage Farm
SANDY LA
Nog Tow
1 BROOK MDW
2 DAISYFIELDS
LIGHTFOOT LA
B6241
Maxey House
SANDRINGHAM WAY 1
BLENHEIM WAY 2
BIDEFORD WAY 3
BUDE CL 4
BARNSTAPLE WAY 5
ASHFIELD CT 6
Sitting Goose Inn (PH)
Ivy Farm
Moor Hall
Haydock Farm
HONITON WAY
TANTERTON HALL RD
KINGSLEY RD
TAG LA
Saddle Inn (PH)
LEA LA
HOYLES LA
THE GRANINGS
SANDYFIELDS
COPPICE
FLOWERFIELD
COTTAM GN
POPPYFIELD
MEADOWBARN CL
SWALLOWFIELDS
GREENMEAD CL
MOSSBROOK DR
Fir Tree Farm
PR4
Cottam
MILLER LA
THE GRANGE
MERRY TREES LA
PH
WORCESTER GDNS 1
WILTSHIRE MEWS 2
THE CHASE
THE WEALD
LAPWING GR
ROSEBERRY AVE
SPIRES GR
MINSTER PK
ROSEWOOD
COTTAM HALL LA
TAG FARM CT
Cottam Hall
HOLLYBANK CL
HEREFORD GR
AVON GDNS
Sch
HAYDOCK LA
1 CROSIER WLK
2 ROSEDENE CL
EASTBOURNE CL
WHITBY AVE
32
Moor Hey
Lea Neeld's Endowed CE Prim Sch
SIDGREAVES LA
BAMPTON DR
SWINSIDE
GREENSIDE
ARMASIDE RD
KEATS WAY
THE EVERGREENS
VALENTINES MDW
THE GABLES
MILLERSGATE
DUNOON CL
REDCAR AVE
HARGREAVES CT 1
WHITBY PL 2
NEWLYN PL 3
Holy Family RC Prim Sch
Ingol Com Prim Sch
TOM BENSON WAY
Bryars Farm
Earl's Farm
OUTGATE RD
COTTAM WAY
THORNTHWAITE RD
COLERIDGE CL
CAMBERRA LA
FINCH LA
DUNNOCK LA
Lancaster Canal
Quaker's Bridge
Westleigh
VALENTINES LA
BRIDGEND CT 1
RUTHIN CT 2
NEWPORT CT 3
PENARTH CT 4
MONMOUTH CT 5
PORTHCAWL CT 6
BARDSEA PL 7
COTTAM AVE
Works
RAILWAY COTTS
Cotty Brook (PH)
Preston Sports Arena
CRESWELL AVE
DUNBAR RD
BARRY AVE
Halsall's Farm
LEA RD
Lady Head Runnel
SUMMER TREES AVE
ASH MDW
ALDER COPPICE
WILLOW COPPICE
HAZEL COPPICE
MILLER FIELD
WEST MDW
BILSBOROUGH MDW
WHITE MDW
SAVICK WAY
ASH COPPICE
DARKINSON LA
PR2
Leyland Bridge
Ashton Prim Sch
LIME GR
LUTON RD
WEST PARK AVE
KINGSWAY
ELM AVE
QUEENSWAY
Brewer House Farm
New House Farm
CH
Savick Brook
Millennium Ribble Link
ARNSIDE RD
AINSDALE DR
CARTMEL PL
HENDON PL
STAVELEY PL
LYNDHURST DR
LICHFIELD RD
Ashton-on-Ribble High Sch
ALDWYCH DR
BROADWAY
A5085
HEYWOOD RD
BIRKDALE DR
NELSON CRES
NELSON DR
DARKINSON LA
Lea
Liby
CHARLES WAY
OX HEY AVE
TUDOR AVE
TUDOR CL
JUBILEE AVE
SAVICK AVE
BLACKPOOL RD
BARTLE RD
BALLAM RD
SALWICK PL
MYTHOP PL
Ashton Park
NORTH SYKE AVE
HACKLANDS AVE
LINCOLN CHASE
GILHOUSE AVE
GREENSIDE
VICTORIA PARK AVE
Larches
NORBRECK DR
CATFORTH RD
NORCROSS PL
NATEBY PL
LARCHES AVE
PO
Sch
WESTERLONG
GREAVES TOWN LA
PREESALL RD
LARCHWOOD
ASHTONGATE
1 WESTLEIGH RD
2 STAINING AVE
3 OAKLANDS GR
RIVERSWAY
BLACKPOOL RD
A5085
CAMPION DR
THE CAMPIONS
HAWTHORN CRES
BLACKTHORN CL
LARCHES LA
OLD GREAVES TOWN LA
A
B
C
D
E
F
C1
1 FULFORD AVE
2 ROSE BANK
3 MAPLEBANK
4 WHITELENS AVE
5 PARKFIELD CL
6 PARKFIELD CRES
7 HARDWEN AVE
D1
1 THE CRESCENT
2 HOLMFIELD CRES
3 THORNPARK DR
4 WHITETHORN SQ
5 DAISY CROFT
E1
1 CHARLESWAY CT
2 THE PLOUGHLANDS
3 WHITEHOLME PL
4 WEETON PL
5 ROSEACRE PL
6 THE WOODLANDS
7 ALDCLIFFE RD
8 FORTON RD
9 THURNHAM RD
E2
1 GREENDALE MEWS
2 EXETER PL
3 DOWNHAM PL
4 NEWARK PL
115
95

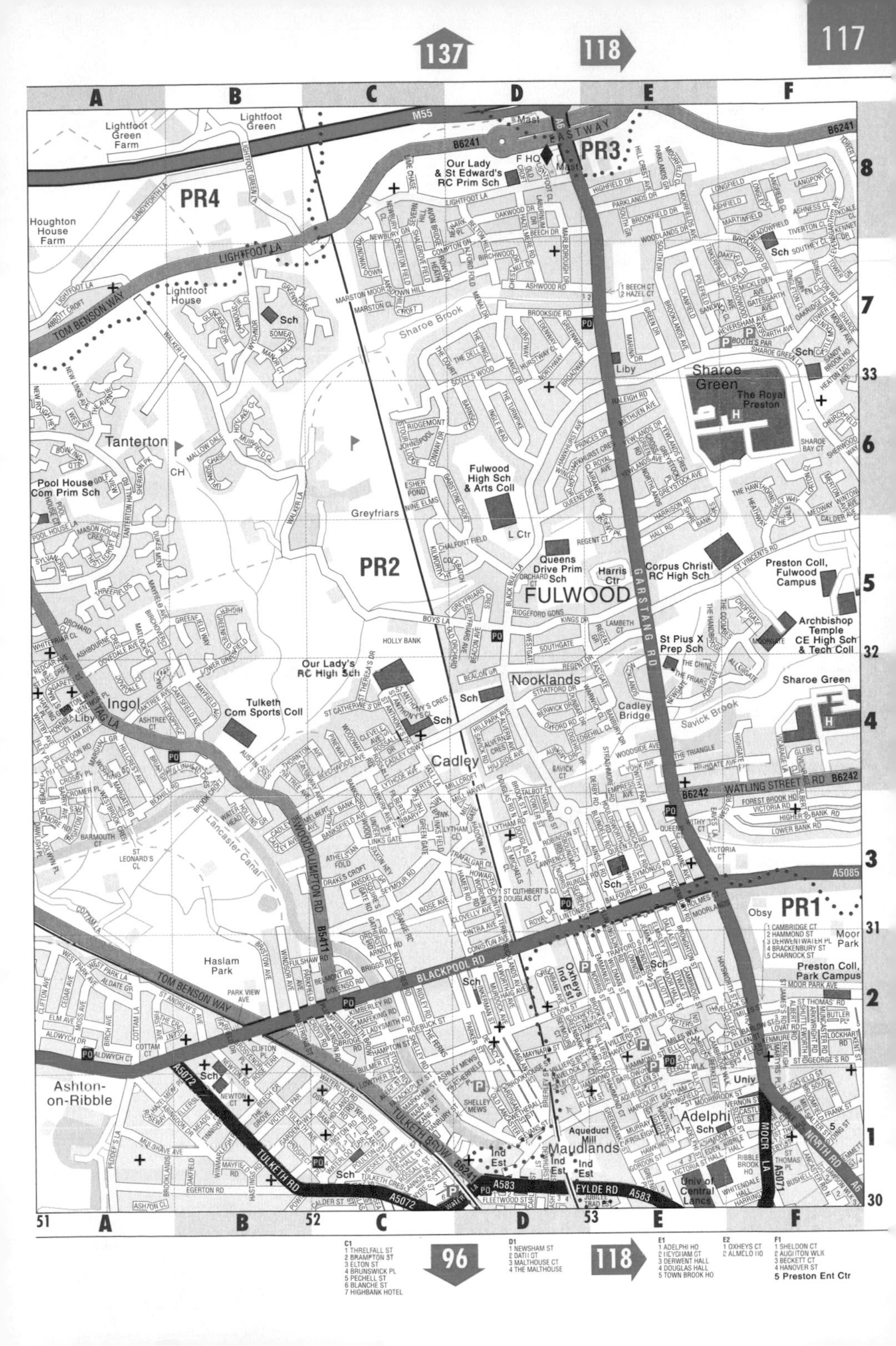
117
137
118
A
B
C
D
E
F
8
7
33
6
5
32
4
3
31
2
1
30
51
52
53
Lightfoot Green Farm
Lightfoot Green
M55
B6241
EASTWAY
PR3
PR4
PR2
PR1
Houghton House Farm
LIGHTFOOT LA
TOM BENSON WAY
Lightfoot House
Sch
Our Lady & St Edward's RC Prim Sch
F HQ
Mast
Sharoe Brook
Liby
Sharoe Green
The Royal Preston
H
Tanterton
CH
Pool House Com Prim Sch
Fulwood High Sch & Arts Coll
L Ctr
Greyfriars
Queens Drive Prim Sch
Harris Ctr
Corpus Christi RC High Sch
Preston Coll, Fulwood Campus
FULWOOD
GARSTANG RD
Archbishop Temple CE High Sch & Tech Coll
St Pius X Prep Sch
HOLLY BANK
Our Lady's RC High Sch
Nooklands
Sharoe Green
Savick Brook
Cadley Bridge
Ingol
Tulketh Com Sports Coll
Cadley
WATLING STREET RD
B6242
Lancaster Canal
WOODPLUMPTON RD
B5411
BLACKPOOL RD
A5085
Obsy
Moor Park
1 CAMBRIDGE CT
2 HAMMOND ST
3 DERWENTWATER PL
4 BRACKENBURY ST
5 CHARNOCK ST
Preston Coll, Park Campus
MOOR PARK AVE
Haslam Park
PARK VIEW AVE
Oxheys Ind Est
Ashton-on-Ribble
A5072
TULKETH RD
TULKETH BROW
Shelley Mews
Aqueduct Mill
Maudlands
Ind Est
Univ
Adelphi
MOOR LA
A5071
NORTH RD
A6
Univ of Central Lancs
FYLDE RD
A583
B6241
96
118
C1
1 THRELFALL ST
2 BRAMPTON ST
3 ELTON ST
4 BRUNSWICK PL
5 PECHELL ST
6 BLANCHE ST
7 HIGHBANK HOTEL
D1
1 NEWSHAM ST
2 DATII CT
3 MALTHOUSE CT
4 THE MALTHOUSE
E1
1 ADELPHI HO
2 HEYSHAM CT
3 DERWENT HALL
4 DOUGLAS HALL
5 TOWN BROOK HO
E2
1 OXHEYS CT
2 ALMELO HO
F1
1 SHELDON CT
2 AUGHTON WLK
3 BECKETT CT
4 HANOVER ST
5 Preston Ent Ctr

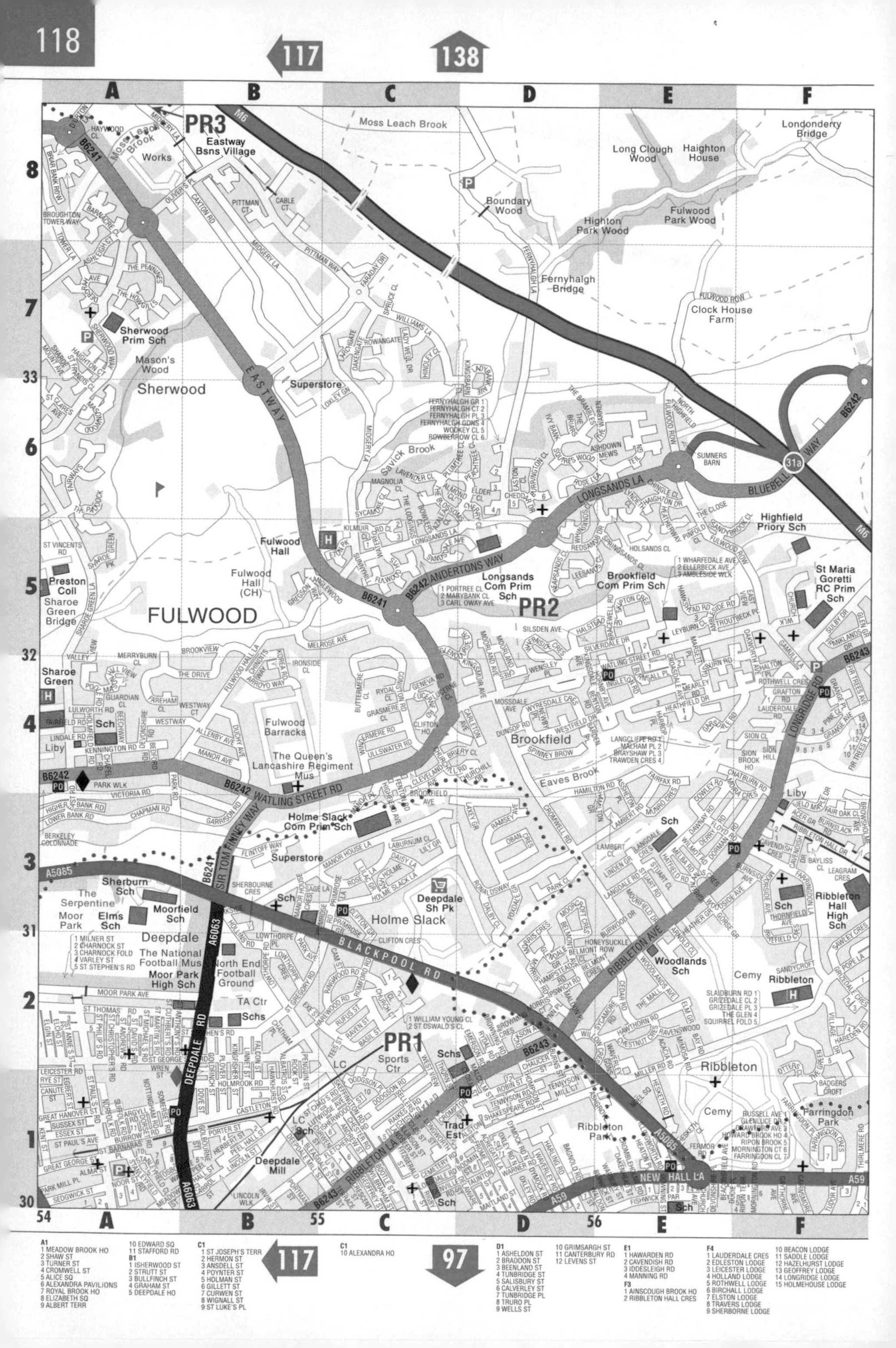

A1
1 MEADOW BROOK HO
2 SHAW ST
3 TURNER ST
4 CROMWELL ST
5 ALICE SQ
6 ALEXANDRA PAVILIONS
7 ROYAL BROOK HO
8 ELIZABETH SQ
9 ALBERT TERR
10 EDWARD SQ
11 STAFFORD RD

B1
1 ISHERWOOD ST
2 STRUTT ST
3 BULLFINCH ST
4 GRAHAM ST
5 DEEPDALE HO

C1
1 ST JOSEPH'S TERR
2 HERMON ST
3 ANSDELL ST
4 POYNTER ST
5 HOLMAN ST
6 GILLETT ST
7 CURWEN ST
8 WIGNALL ST
9 ST LUKE'S PL

C1
10 ALEXANDRA HO

D1
1 ASHELDON ST
2 BRADDON ST
3 BEENLAND ST
4 TUNBRIDGE ST
5 SALISBURY ST
6 CALVERLEY ST
7 TUNBRIDGE PL
8 TRURO PL
9 WELLS ST
10 GRIMSARGH ST
11 CANTERBURY RD
12 LEVENS ST

E1
1 HAWARDEN RD
2 CAVENDISH RD
3 IDDESLEIGH RD
4 MANNING RD

F3
1 AINSCOUGH BROOK HO
2 RIBBLETON HALL CRES

F4
1 LAUDERDALE CRES
2 EDLESTON LODGE
3 LEICESTER LODGE
4 HOLLAND LODGE
5 ROTHWELL LODGE
6 BIRCHALL LODGE
7 ELSTON LODGE
8 TRAVERS LODGE
9 SHERBORNE LODGE
10 BEACON LODGE
11 SADDLE LODGE
12 HAZELHURST LODGE
13 GEOFFREY LODGE
14 LONGRIDGE LODGE
15 HOLMEHOUSE LODGE

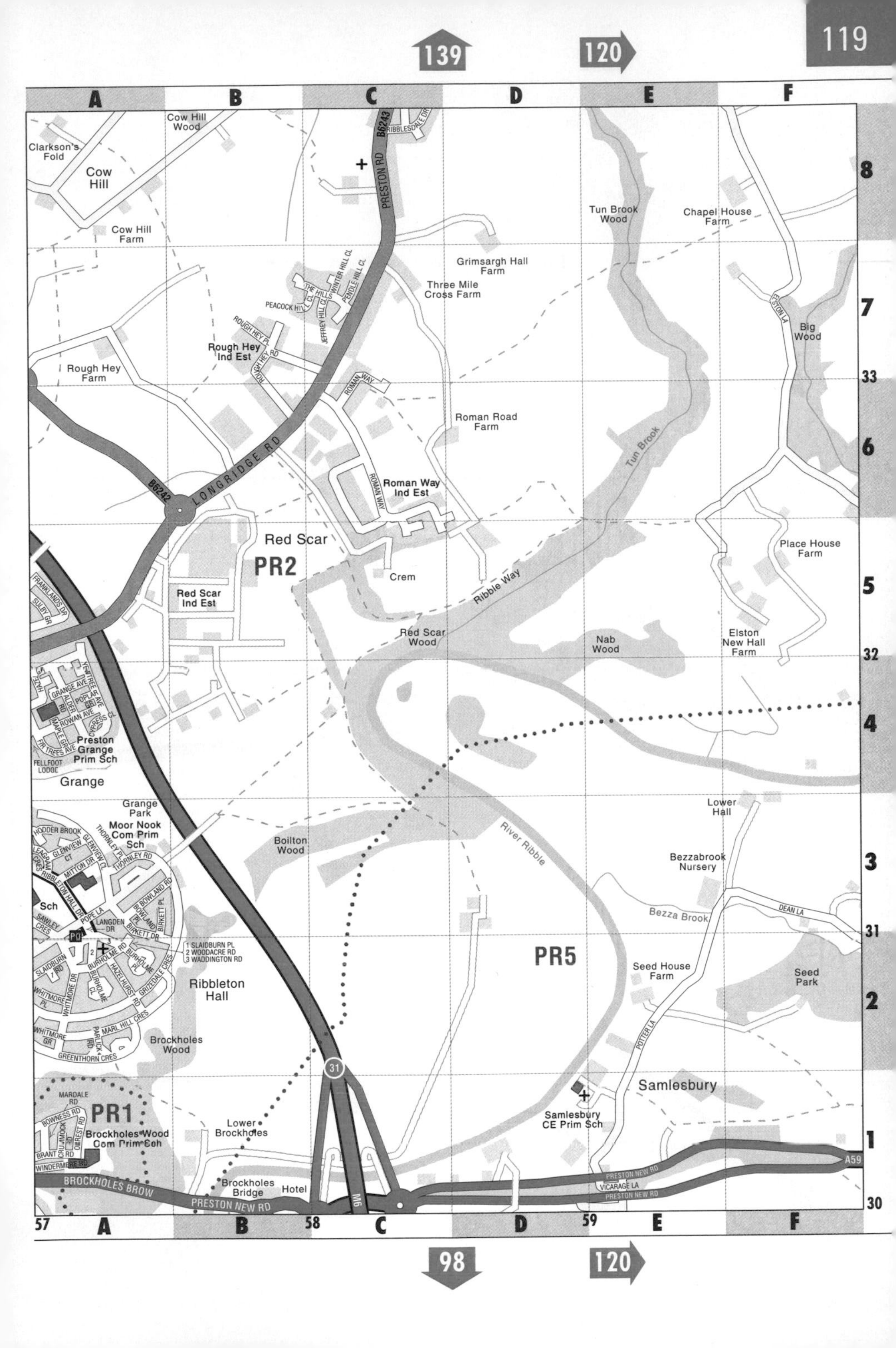
119
139
120
98
120
A
B
C
D
E
F
8
7
33
6
5
32
4
3
31
2
1
30
57
58
59
Clarkson's Fold
Cow Hill
Cow Hill Wood
Cow Hill Farm
PRESTON RD
B6243
RIBBLESDALE DR
Tun Brook Wood
Chapel House Farm
Grimsargh Hall Farm
Three Mile Cross Farm
THE HILLS
WINTER HILL CL
PENDLE HILL CL
PEACOCK HILL CL
JEFFREY HILL CL
ROUGH HEY PL
ROUGH HEY RD
Rough Hey Ind Est
Rough Hey Farm
ELSTON LA
Big Wood
ROMAN WAY
Roman Road Farm
Tun Brook
LONGRIDGE RD
B6242
Roman Way Ind Est
Red Scar
PR2
Crem
Place House Farm
Red Scar Ind Est
Ribble Way
Red Scar Wood
Nab Wood
Elston New Hall Farm
FRANKLANDS DR
SULBY GR
GRANGE AVE
ALDER RD
POPLAR AVE
ROWAN AVE
CYPRESS CL
MAPLE GR
FIR TREES AVE
Preston Grange Prim Sch
FELLFOOT LODGE
Grange
Grange Park
Moor Nook Com Prim Sch
HODDER BROOK
GLENVIEW CT
THORNLEY RD
MITTON DR
RIBBLETON HALL DR
Boilton Wood
River Ribble
Lower Hall
Bezzabrook Nursery
Sch
POPE LA
LANGDEN DR
BOWLAND RD
BIRKETT DR
BIRKETT PL
SAWLEY CRES
Bezza Brook
DEAN LA
1 SLAIDBURN PL
2 WOODACRE RD
3 WADDINGTON RD
SLAIDBURN PL
BURHOLME RD
BURHOLME PL
BURHOLME CL
HAZELHURST RD
GRIZEDALE CRES
PR5
Ribbleton Hall
Seed House Farm
Seed Park
WHITMORE DR
WHITMORE PL
WHITMORE GR
MARL HILL CRES
PARLICK RD
GREENTHORN CRES
Brockholes Wood
POTTER LA
31
Samlesbury
MARDALE RD
BOWNESS RD
CRUMMOCK RD
FOREST RD
PR1
Brockholes Wood Com Prim Sch
BRANT RD
WINDERMERE RD
Lower Brockholes
Samlesbury CE Prim Sch
A59
BROCKHOLES BROW
Brockholes Bridge
Hotel
PRESTON NEW RD
M6
VICARAGE LA

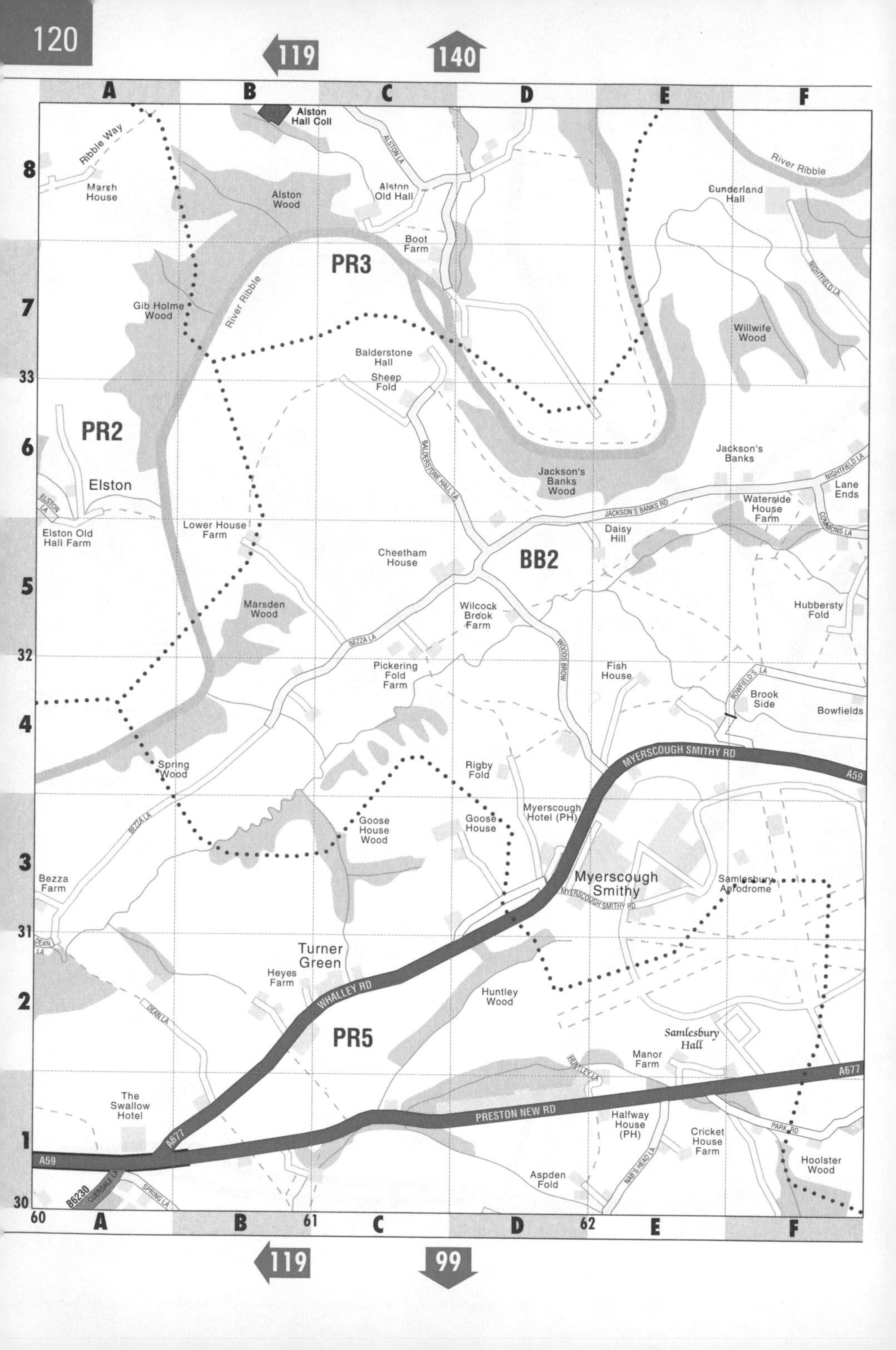
119
140
Alston Hall Coll
Ribble Way
Marsh House
Alston Wood
Alston Old Hall
ALSTON LA
River Ribble
Sunderland Hall
Boot Farm
PR3
Gib Holme Wood
River Ribble
NIGHTFIELD LA
Willwife Wood
Balderstone Hall
Sheep Fold
PR2
Elston
ELSTON LA
Elston Old Hall Farm
BALDERSTONE HALL LA
Jackson's Banks Wood
Jackson's Banks
NIGHTFIELD LA
Lane Ends
JACKSON'S BANKS RD
Waterside House Farm
COMMONS LA
Lower House Farm
Daisy Hill
Cheetham House
BB2
Marsden Wood
Wilcock Brook Farm
Hubbersty Fold
BEZZA LA
WOODS BROW
Pickering Fold Farm
Fish House
BOWFIELD'S LA
Brook Side
Bowfields
Spring Wood
Rigby Fold
MYERSCOUGH SMITHY RD
A59
BEZZA LA
Goose House Wood
Goose House
Myerscough Hotel (PH)
Bezza Farm
Myerscough Smithy
MYERSCOUGH SMITHY RD
Samlesbury Aerodrome
DEAN LA
Turner Green
Heyes Farm
WHALLEY RD
Huntley Wood
DEAN LA
PR5
Samlesbury Hall
Manor Farm
HUNTLEY LA
A677
The Swallow Hotel
PRESTON NEW RD
Halfway House (PH)
Cricket House Farm
PARK RD
A677
A59
NAB'S HEAD LA
Hoolster Wood
Aspden Fold
B6230
CUERDALE LA
SPRING LA
A B C D E F
8 7 33 6 5 32 4 3 31 2 1 30
60 61 62
119
99

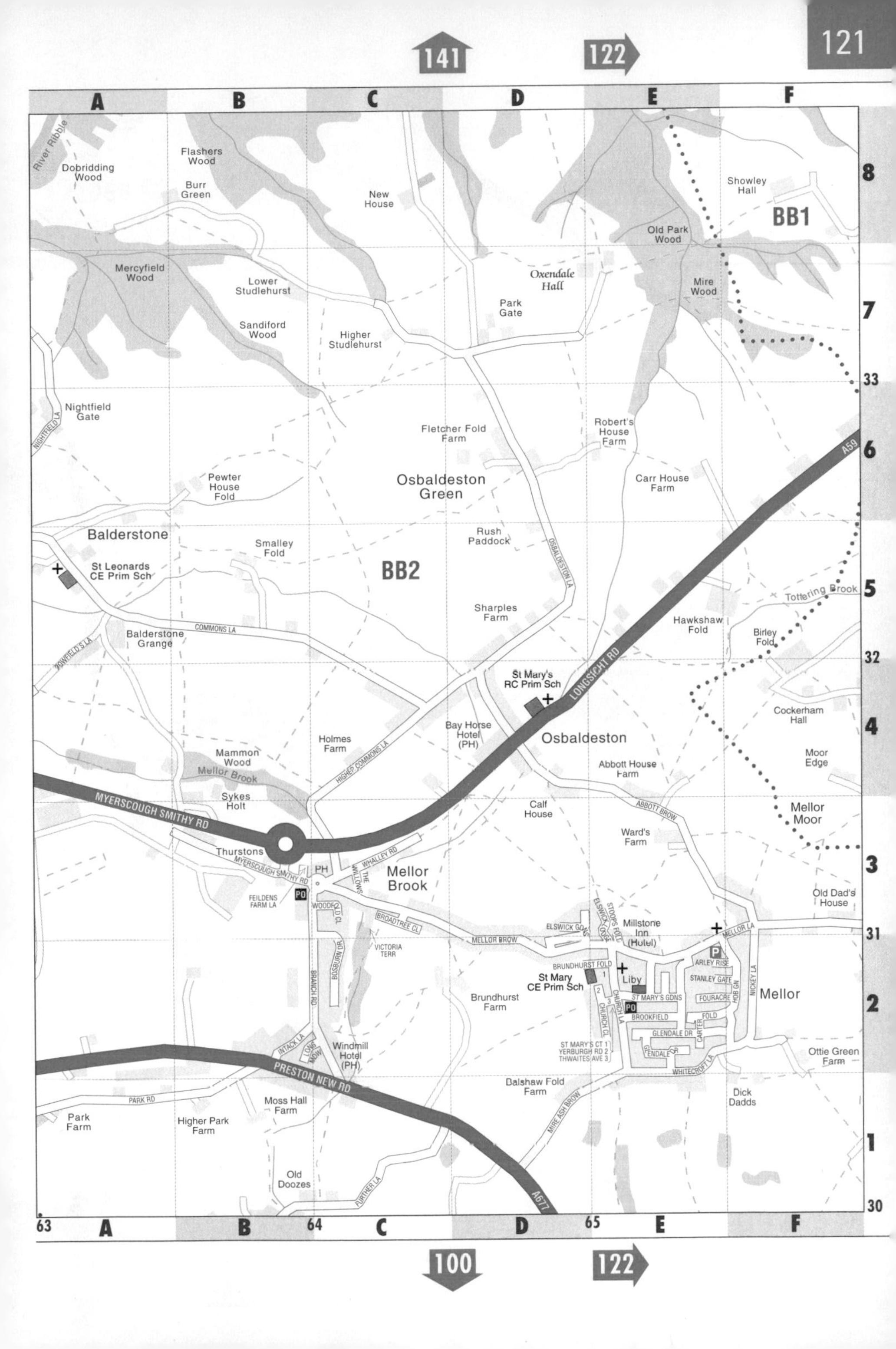
141
122
A
B
C
D
E
F
8
7
33
6
5
32
4
3
31
2
1
30
63
64
65
River Ribble
Dobridding Wood
Flashers Wood
Burr Green
New House
Showley Hall
BB1
Old Park Wood
Mercyfield Wood
Lower Studlehurst
Oxendale Hall
Park Gate
Mire Wood
Sandiford Wood
Higher Studlehurst
Nightfield Gate
NIGHTFIELD LA
Fletcher Fold Farm
Robert's House Farm
A59
Osbaldeston Green
Carr House Farm
Pewter House Fold
Balderstone
Smalley Fold
Rush Paddock
St Leonards CE Prim Sch
BB2
OSBALDESTON LA
Tottering Brook
Sharples Farm
Hawkshaw Fold
Birley Fold
Balderstone Grange
COMMONS LA
ROWFIELD'S LA
LONGSIGHT RD
St Mary's RC Prim Sch
Cockerham Hall
Bay Horse Hotel (PH)
Holmes Farm
Osbaldeston
Moor Edge
Mammon Wood
HIGHER COMMONS LA
Abbott House Farm
Mellor Brook
Sykes Holt
Calf House
ABBOTT BROW
Mellor Moor
MYERSCOUGH SMITHY RD
Ward's Farm
Thurstons
WHALLEY RD
MYERSCOUGH SMITHY RD
PH
THE WILLOWS
Mellor Brook
PO
FEILDENS FARM LA
WOODF
OLD CL
BROADTREE CL
ELSWICK GDNS
ELSWICK
STOOPS FOLD
Millstone Inn (Hotel)
Old Dad's House
MELLOR LA
MELLOR BROW
VICTORIA TERR
BOSBURN DR
BRUNDHURST FOLD
P
ARLEY RISE
St Mary CE Prim Sch
Liby
STANLEY GATE
NICKEY LA
BRANCH RD
ST MARY'S GDNS
HOB GN
FOURACRE
Mellor
Brundhurst Farm
CHURCH CL
CHURCH LA
PO
BROOKFIELD
FOLD
CARTER
GLENDALE DR
GLENDALE DR
ST MARY'S CT 1
YERBURGH RD 2
THWAITES AVE 3
Windmill Hotel (PH)
INTACK LA
LONG ROW
WHITECROFT LA
Ottie Green Farm
PRESTON NEW RD
Balshaw Fold Farm
PARK RD
Moss Hall Farm
Dick Dadds
Park Farm
Higher Park Farm
MIRE ASH BROW
Old Doozes
FURTHER LA
A677
100
122

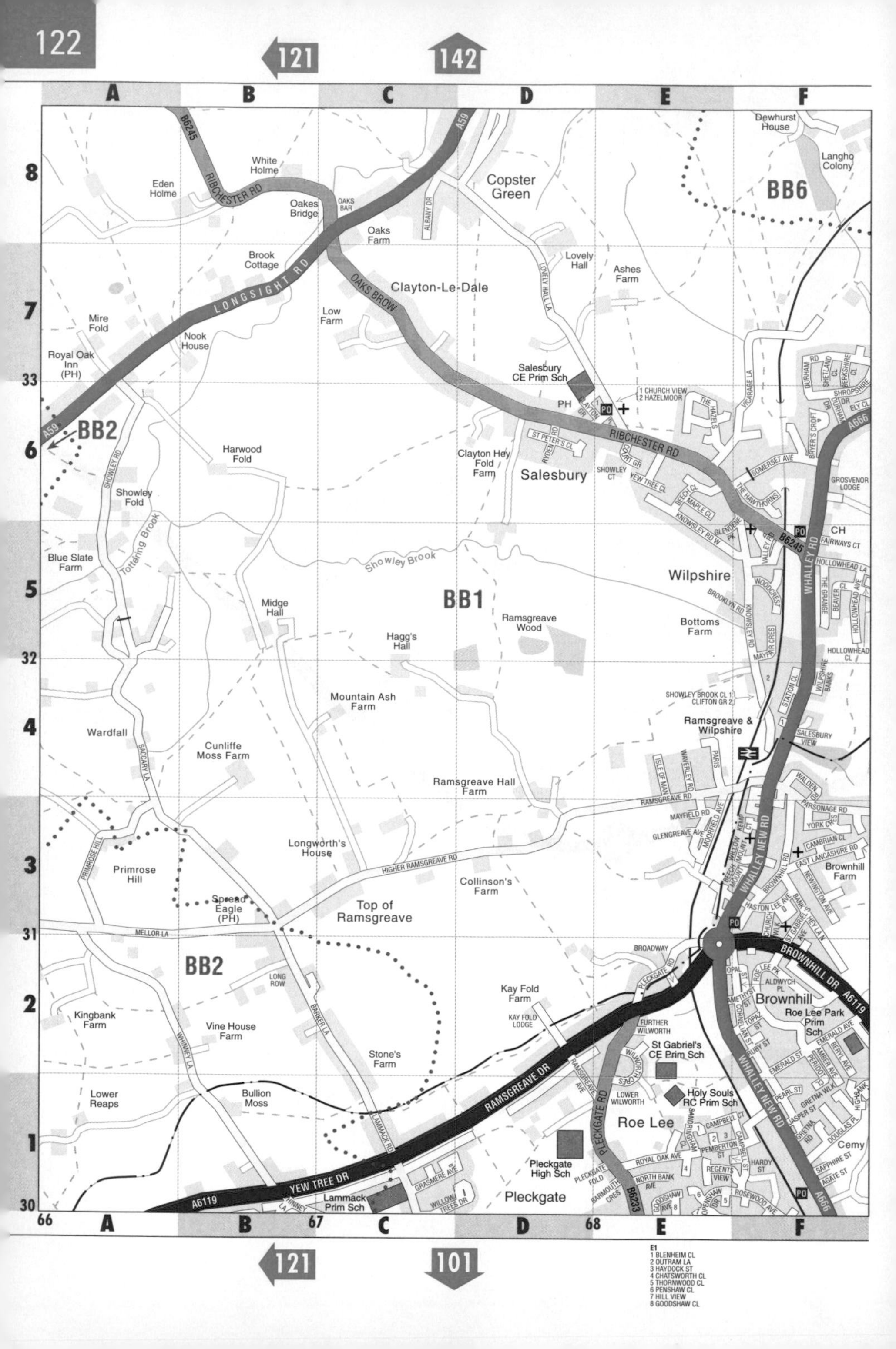

122
121
142
A
B
C
D
E
F
8
7
33
6
5
32
4
3
31
2
1
30
66
67
68
White Holme
Eden Holme
RIBCHESTER RD
B6245
A59
Oakes Bridge
OAKS BAR
Oaks Farm
ALBANY DR
Copster Green
Dewhurst House
Langho Colony
BB6
Brook Cottage
LONGSIGHT RD
OAKS BROW
Clayton-Le-Dale
Lovely Hall
LOVELY HALL LA
Ashes Farm
Mire Fold
Low Farm
Nook House
Royal Oak Inn (PH)
Salesbury CE Prim Sch
PH
1 CHURCH VIEW
2 HAZELMOOR
THE HAZELS
VICARAGE LA
DURHAM RD
SHETLAND CL
BERKSHIRE CL
SHROPSHIRE DR
DURHAM DR
ELY CL
A666
BB2
Harwood Fold
ST PETER'S CL
RYDEN RD
Clayton Hey Fold Farm
Salesbury
COURT GR
SHOWLEY CT
YEW TREE CL
BEECH CL
MAPLE CL
KNOWSLEY RD W
GLENDENE PK
SOMERSET AVE
BRYER'S CROFT
THE HAWTHORNS
GROSVENOR LODGE
SHOWLEY RD
Showley Fold
Tottering Brook
Blue Slate Farm
Showley Brook
B6245
WHALLEY RD
CH
FAIRWAYS CT
HOLLOWHEAD LA
Wilpshire
BB1
Midge Hall
Ramsgreave Wood
BROOKLYN RD
WOODCREST
VALLEY
THE GRANGE
BEAVER CL
HOLLOWHEAD AVE
KNOWSLEY RD
Bottoms Farm
Hagg's Hall
MAYFAIR CRES
HOLLOWHEAD CL
Mountain Ash Farm
STATION CL
WILPSHIRE BANKS
SHOWLEY BROOK CL 1
CLIFTON GR 2
Ramsgreave & Wilpshire
Wardfall
SACCARY LA
Cunliffe Moss Farm
SALESBURY VIEW
PARIS
WAVERLEY RD
ISLE OF MAN
Ramsgreave Hall Farm
RAMSGREAVE RD
MAYFIELD RD
MOORFIELD AVE
WALDEN GR
PARSONAGE RD
YORK CRES
GLENGREAVE AVE
KEMP CT
WILLOW MOUNT
BEECH MOUNT
WHALLEY NEW RD
CAMBRIAN CL
EAST LANCASHIRE RD
BROWNHILL RD
NEWINGTON AVE
Brownhill Farm
PRIMROSE HILL
Primrose Hill
Longworth's House
HIGHER RAMSGREAVE RD
Collinson's Farm
HASTON LEE AVE
Spread Eagle (PH)
Top of Ramsgreave
CHURCH WLK
ST GABRIEL'S AVE
HEY LA N
MELLOR LA
BROADWAY
BROWNHILL DR
A6119
BB2
LONG ROW
PLECKGATE RD
ROE LEE PK
ALDWYCH PL
Kay Fold Farm
AMETHYST ST
Brownhill
Kingbank Farm
KAY FOLD LODGE
FURTHER WILWORTH
TOPAZ ST
CORNELIAN ST
Roe Lee Park Prim Sch
EMERALD AVE
Vine House Farm
BANKER LA
WHINNEY LA
St Gabriel's CE Prim Sch
RUBY ST
EMERALD ST
BERYL AVE
AMBER AVE
PERIDOT CL
Stone's Farm
WILWORTH CRES
Lower Reaps
Bullion Moss
RAMSGREAVE DR
RAMSGREAVE AVE
LOWER WILWORTH
Holy Souls RC Prim Sch
PEARL ST
GRETNA WLK
HIGHBANK
SANDRINGHAM CL
JASPER ST
GRETNA RD
DOUGLAS PL
LAMMACK RD
Roe Lee
CAMPBELL CT
Cemy
PLECKGATE RD
PEMBERTON ST
CAMPBELL ST
HARDY ST
SAPPHIRE ST
AGATE ST
Pleckgate High Sch
ROYAL OAK AVE
YEW TREE DR
GRASMERE AVE
PLECKGATE FOLD
NORTH BANK AVE
REGENTS VIEW
A6119
Lammack Prim Sch
WILLOW TREES DR
Pleckgate
BARMOUTH CRES
B6233
GOODSHAW AVE
OPENSHAW DR
ROSEWOOD AVE
A666
WHINNEY LA
121
101
E1
1 BLENHEIM CL
2 OUTRAM LA
3 HAYDOCK ST
4 CHATSWORTH CL
5 THORNWOOD CL
6 PENSHAW CL
7 HILL VIEW
8 GOODSHAW CL

143
124

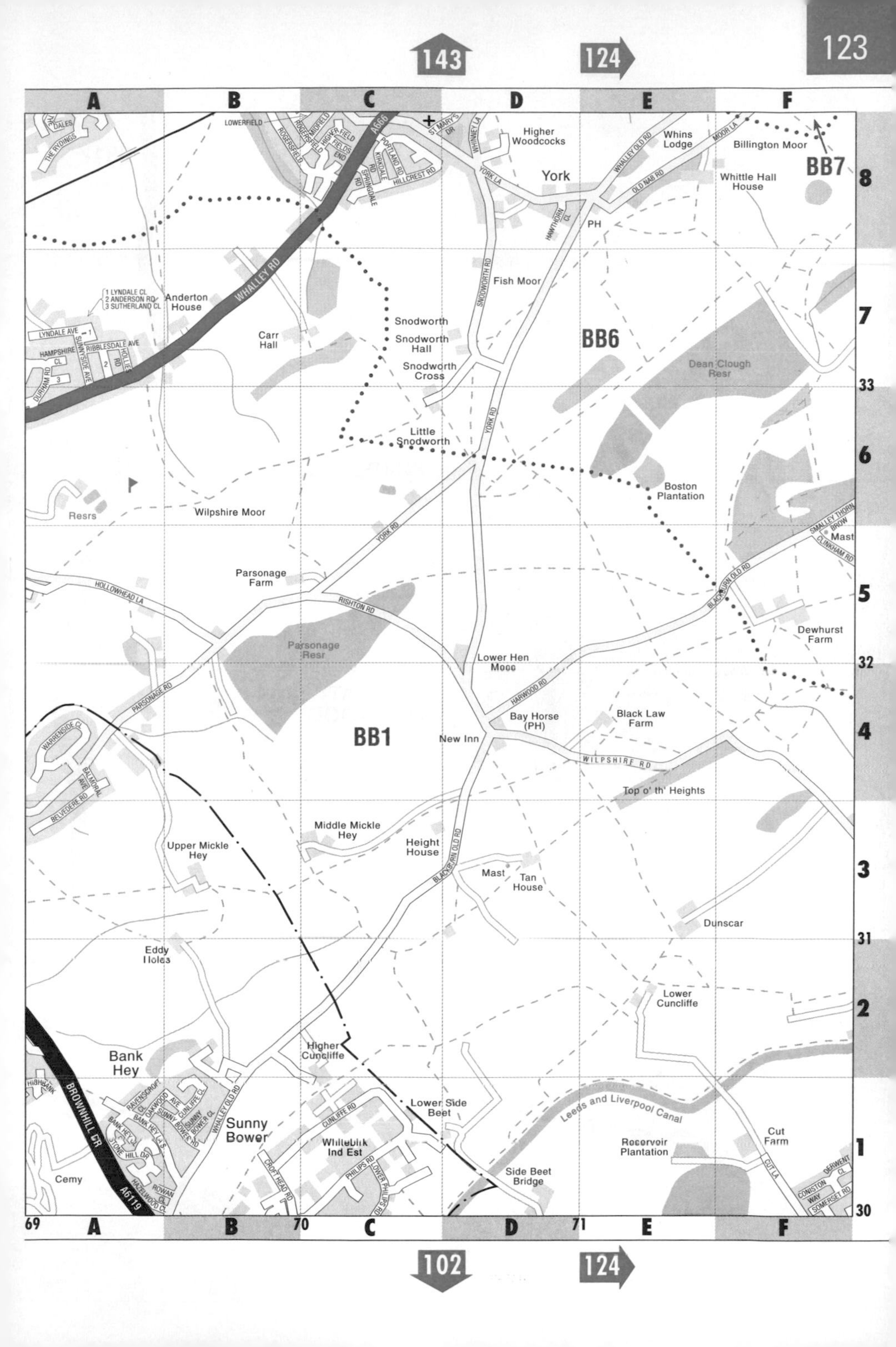

102
124

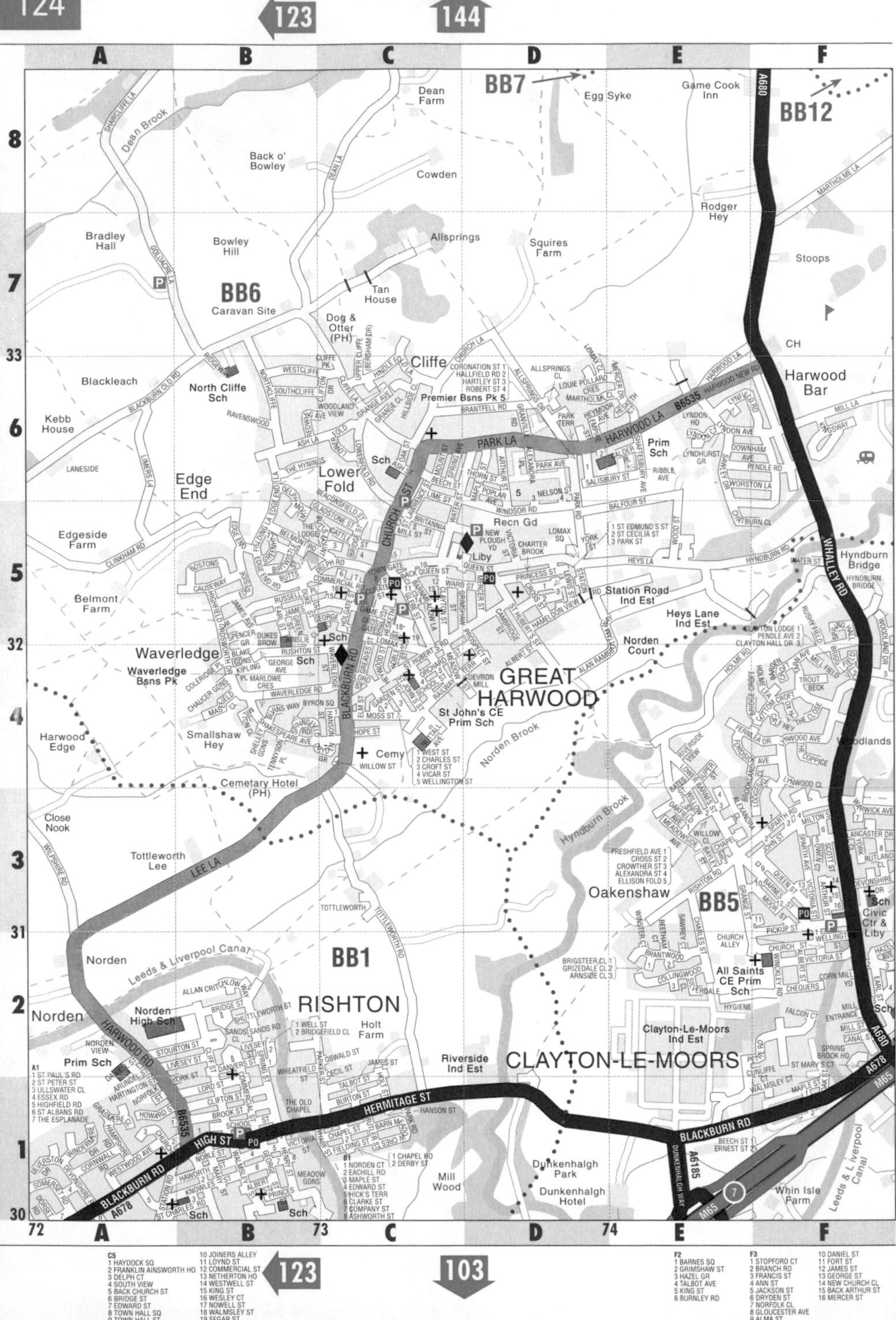
123
144
A
B
C
D
E
F
BB7
Egg Syke
Game Cook Inn
BB12
Dean Farm
Dean Brook
Back o' Bowley
Cowden
Rodger Hey
Bradley Hall
Bowley Hill
Allsprings
Squires Farm
Stoops
BB6
Caravan Site
Tan House
Dog & Otter (PH)
Cliffe
CH
Harwood Bar
Blackleach
North Cliffe Sch
Premier Bsns Pk 5
Kebb House
Edge End
Lower Fold
Sch
Prim Sch
Edgeside Farm
Recn Gd
Liby
Hyndburn Bridge
Belmont Farm
Station Road Ind Est
Heys Lane Ind Est
Norden Court
Waverledge
Waverledge Bsns Pk
GREAT HARWOOD
St John's CE Prim Sch
Harwood Edge
Smallshaw Hey
Cemy
Norden Brook
Woodlands
Cemetary Hotel (PH)
Close Nook
Hyndburn Brook
Tottleworth Lee
Oakenshaw
BB5
Civic Ctr & Liby
Norden
Leeds & Liverpool Canal
BB1
All Saints CE Prim Sch
RISHTON
Norden High Sch
Holt Farm
Clayton-Le-Moors Ind Est
Riverside Ind Est
CLAYTON-LE-MOORS
The Old Chapel
Dunkenhalgh Park
Dunkenhalgh Hotel
Mill Wood
Whin Isle Farm
LEE LA
HARWOOD RD
BLACKBURN RD
HIGH ST
HERMITAGE ST
PARK LA
HARWOOD LA
WHALLEY RD
CHURCH ST
A680
A678
A6185
B6535
B6535
M65
72
73
74
8
7
33
6
5
32
4
3
31
2
1
30
A1
1 ST PAUL'S RD
2 ST PETER ST
3 ULLSWATER CL
4 ESSEX RD
5 HIGHFIELD RD
6 ST ALBANS RD
7 THE ESPLANADE
B1
1 NORDEN CT
2 EACHILL RD
3 MAPLE ST
4 EDWARD ST
5 HICK'S TERR
6 CLARKE ST
7 COMPANY ST
8 ASHWORTH ST
1 WEST ST
2 CHARLES ST
3 CROFT ST
4 VICAR ST
5 WELLINGTON ST
1 CORONATION ST
2 HALLFIELD RD
3 HARTLEY ST
4 ROBERT ST
1 ST EDMUND'S ST
2 ST CECILIA ST
3 PARK ST
1 CLAYTON LODGE
2 PENDLE AVE
3 CLAYTON HALL DR
1 FRESHFIELD AVE
2 CROSS ST
3 CROWTHER ST
4 ALEXANDRA ST
5 ELLISON FOLD
1 BRIGSTEER CL
2 GRIZEDALE CL
3 ARNSIDE CL
1 BEECH ST
2 ERNEST ST
1 WELL ST
2 BRIDGEFIELD CL
1 CHAPEL HO
2 DERBY ST
C5
1 HAYDOCK SQ
2 FRANKLIN AINSWORTH HO
3 DELPH CT
4 SOUTH VIEW
5 BACK CHURCH ST
6 BRIDGE ST
7 EDWARD ST
8 TOWN HALL SQ
9 TOWN HALL ST
10 JOINERS ALLEY
11 LOYND ST
12 COMMERCIAL ST
13 NETHERTON HO
14 WESTWELL ST
15 KING ST
16 WESLEY CT
17 NOWELL ST
18 WALMSLEY ST
19 SEGAR ST
123
103
F2
1 BARNES SQ
2 GRIMSHAW ST
3 HAZEL GR
4 TALBOT AVE
5 KING ST
6 BURNLEY RD
F3
1 STOPFORD CT
2 BRANCH RD
3 FRANCIS ST
4 ANN ST
5 JACKSON ST
6 DRYDEN ST
7 NORFOLK CL
8 GLOUCESTER AVE
9 ALMA ST
10 DANIEL ST
11 FORT ST
12 JAMES ST
13 GEORGE ST
14 NEW CHURCH CL
15 BACK ARTHUR ST
16 MERCER ST

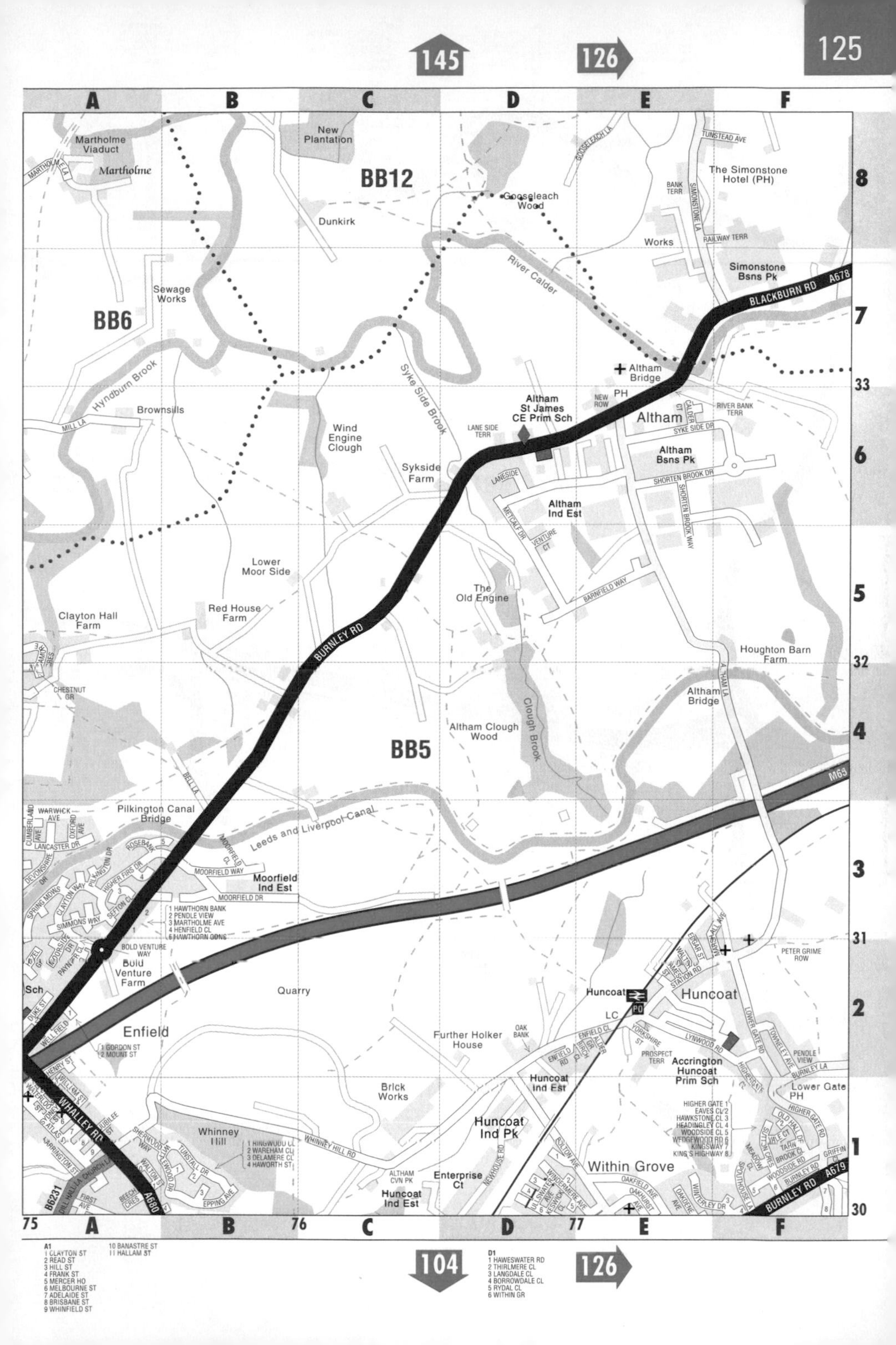
125
145
126
A
B
C
D
E
F
Martholme Viaduct
Martholme
MARTHOLME LA
New Plantation
BB12
Gooseleach Wood
GOOSELEACH LA
TUNSTEAD AVE
The Simonstone Hotel (PH)
BANK TERR
SIMONSTONE LA
Dunkirk
Works
RAILWAY TERR
Simonstone Bsns Pk
River Calder
Sewage Works
BB6
BLACKBURN RD
A678
Altham Bridge
Hyndburn Brook
Syke Side Brook
NEW ROW
PH
Altham St James CE Prim Sch
Altham
CALDER CT
RIVER BANK TERR
Brownsills
MILL LA
Wind Engine Clough
LANE SIDE TERR
SYKE SIDE DR
Altham Bsns Pk
Sykside Farm
LANESIDE
SHORTEN BROOK DR
Altham Ind Est
METCALF DR
VENTURE CT
SHORTEN BROOK WAY
Lower Moor Side
The Old Engine
BARNFIELD WAY
Clayton Hall Farm
Red House Farm
BURNLEY RD
Houghton Barn Farm
CHESTNUT GR
ALTHAM LA
Altham Bridge
Altham Clough Wood
Clough Brook
BB5
BELL LA
M65
WARWICK AVE
CUMBERLAND AVE
OXFORD AVE
LANCASTER DR
Pilkington Canal Bridge
Leeds and Liverpool Canal
ROSEBANK
DEVONSHIRE DR
PILKINGTON DR
HIGHER FIRS DR
MOORFIELD CL
MOORFIELD WAY
Moorfield Ind Est
MOORFIELD DR
SPRING MDWS
CLAYTON WAY
SEFTON CL
SIMMONS WAY
1 HAWTHORN BANK
2 PENDLE VIEW
3 MARTHOLME AVE
4 HENFIELD CL
5 HAWTHORN GDNS
BOLD VENTURE WAY
Bold Venture Farm
PAYNE ST
Sch
Quarry
PETER GRIME ROW
EDGAR ST
STATION RD
Huncoat
PO
LC
DUKE ST
WELLFIELD
Enfield
1 GORDON ST
2 MOUNT ST
Further Holker House
OAK BANK
ENFIELD CL
ENFIELD RD
YORKSHIRE ST
LYNWOOD RD
LOWER GATE RD
TOWNELEY AVE
PENDLE VIEW
BURNLEY LA
PROSPECT TERR
Accrington Huncoat Prim Sch
Lower Gate PH
HENRY ST
WHALLEY RD
Brick Works
Huncoat Ind Est
HIGHER GATE 1
EAVES CL 2
HAWKSTONE CL 3
HEADINGLEY CL 4
WOODSIDE CL 5
WEDGEWOOD RD 6
KINGSWAY 7
KING S HIGHWAY 8
HIGHER GATE RD
JUBILEE ST
Whinney Hill
1 HINGWOOD CL
2 WAREHAM CL
3 DELAMERE CL
4 HAWORTH ST
WHINNEY HILL RD
Huncoat Ind Pk
NEWHOUSE RD
Within Grove
WOODSIDE RD
BURNLEY RD
A679
LARRINGTON ST
TUNSTALL DR
WALTON ST
ALTHAM CVN PK
Enterprise Ct
WINDERMERE AVE
OAKFIELD AVE
OAKHURST AVE
WINTERLEY DR
SPOUTHOUSE LA
B6231
FIRST AVE
BEECH CRES
EPPING AVE
A680
Huncoat Ind Est
ULLSWATER AVE
KESWICK CL
8
7
6
5
4
3
2
1
33
32
31
30
75
76
77
104
126
A1
1 CLAYTON ST
2 READ ST
3 HILL ST
4 FRANK ST
5 MERCER HO
6 MELBOURNE ST
7 ADELAIDE ST
8 BRISBANE ST
9 WHINFIELD ST
10 BANASTRE ST
11 HALLAM ST
D1
1 HAWESWATER RD
2 THIRLMERE CL
3 LANGDALE CL
4 BORROWDALE CL
5 RYDAL CL
6 WITHIN GR

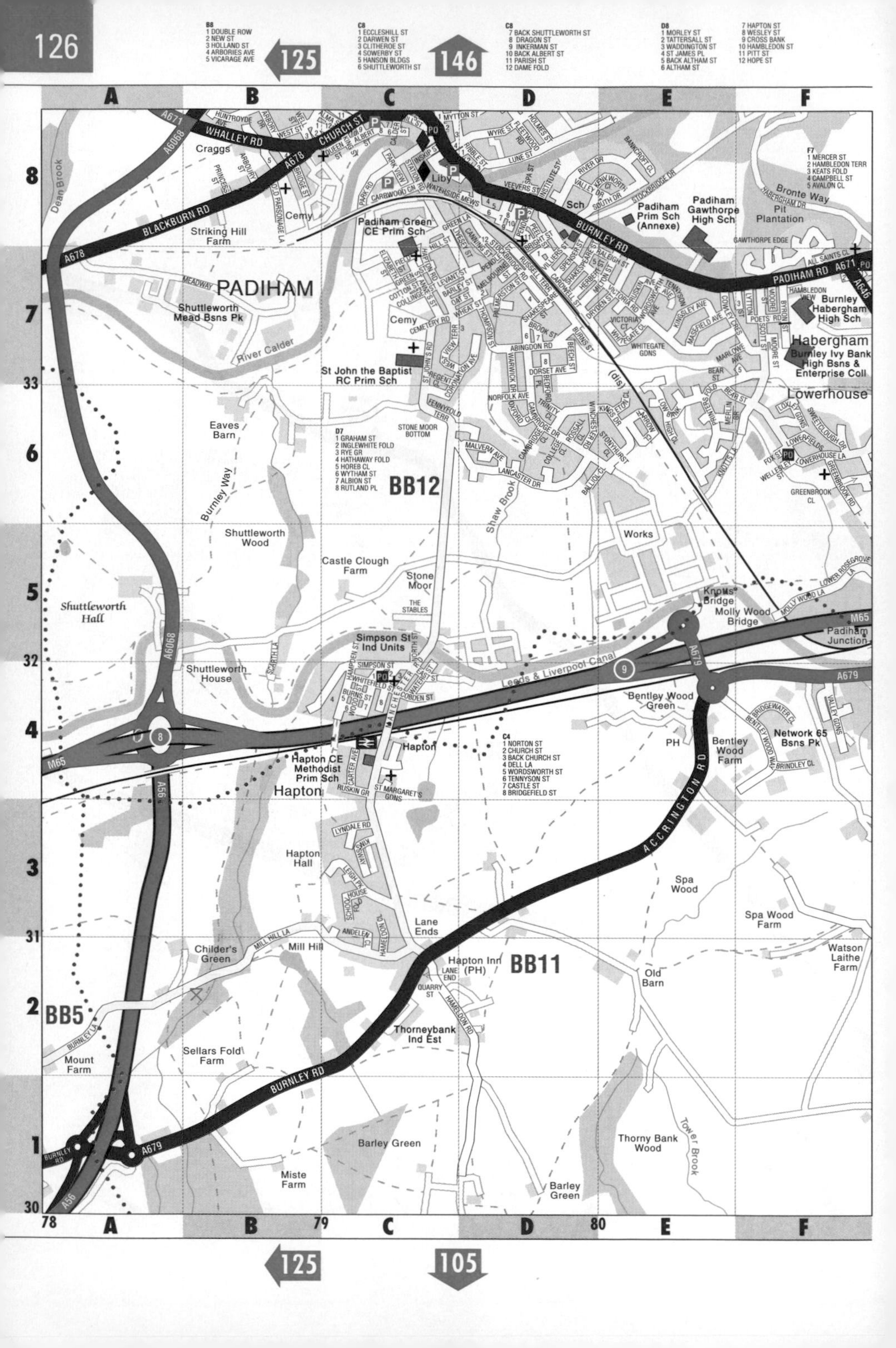
B8
1 DOUBLE ROW
2 NEW ST
3 HOLLAND ST
4 ARBORIES AVE
5 VICARAGE AVE
125
C8
1 ECCLESHILL ST
2 DARWEN ST
3 CLITHEROE ST
4 SOWERBY ST
5 HANSON BLDGS
6 SHUTTLEWORTH ST
146
C8
7 BACK SHUTTLEWORTH ST
8 DRAGON ST
9 INKERMAN ST
10 BACK ALBERT ST
11 PARISH ST
12 DAME FOLD
D8
1 MORLEY ST
2 TATTERSALL ST
3 WADDINGTON ST
4 ST JAMES PL
5 BACK ALTHAM ST
6 ALTHAM ST
7 HAPTON ST
8 WESLEY ST
9 CROSS BANK
10 HAMBLEDON ST
11 PITT ST
12 HOPE ST
F7
1 MERCER ST
2 HAMBLEDON TERR
3 KEATS FOLD
4 CAMPBELL ST
5 AVALON CL
D7
1 GRAHAM ST
2 INGLEWHITE FOLD
3 RYE GR
4 HATHAWAY FOLD
5 HOREB CL
6 WYTHAM ST
7 ALBION ST
8 RUTLAND PL
C4
1 NORTON ST
2 CHURCH ST
3 BACK CHURCH ST
4 DELL LA
5 WORDSWORTH ST
6 TENNYSON ST
7 CASTLE ST
8 BRIDGEFIELD ST
WHALLEY RD
CHURCH ST
BLACKBURN RD
BURNLEY RD
PADIHAM RD
ACCRINGTON RD
Craggs
Striking Hill Farm
PADIHAM
Shuttleworth Mead Bsns Pk
River Calder
Padiham Green CE Prim Sch
St John the Baptist RC Prim Sch
Padiham Prim Sch (Annexe)
Padiham Gawthorpe High Sch
Pit Plantation
Bronte Way
Burnley Habergham High Sch
Habergham
Burnley Ivy Bank High Bsns & Enterprise Coll
Lowerhouse
Eaves Barn
Dean Brook
Burnley Way
STONE MOOR BOTTOM
BB12
Shaw Brook
Shuttleworth Wood
Castle Clough Farm
Stone Moor
THE STABLES
Works
Knotts Bridge
Molly Wood Bridge
Padiham Junction
Shuttleworth Hall
Simpson St Ind Units
Shuttleworth House
Leeds & Liverpool Canal
Bentley Wood Green
Hapton
Hapton CE Methodist Prim Sch
Bentley Wood Farm
Network 65 Bsns Pk
Hapton Hall
Spa Wood
Spa Wood Farm
Lane Ends
Childer's Green
Mill Hill
Hapton Inn (PH)
BB11
Old Barn
Watson Laithe Farm
BB5
Thorneybank Ind Est
Sellars Fold Farm
Mount Farm
Barley Green
Thorny Bank Wood
Tower Brook
Miste Farm
M65
A56
A679
A6068
A678
A671
105

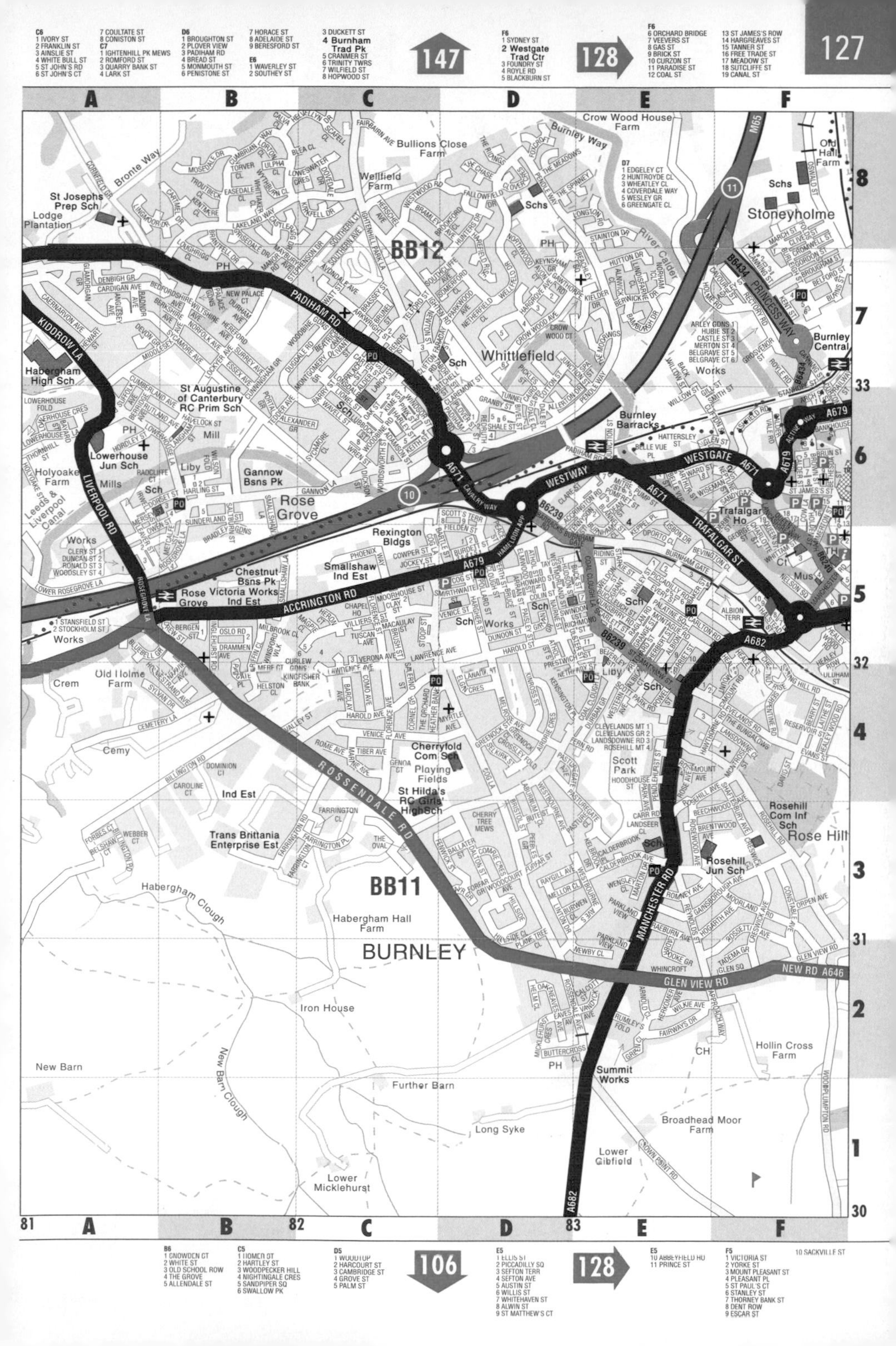

127
C6
1 IVORY ST
2 FRANKLIN ST
3 AINSLIE ST
4 WHITE BULL ST
5 ST JOHN'S RD
6 ST JOHN'S CT
7 COULTATE ST
8 CONISTON ST
C7
1 IGHTENHILL PK MEWS
2 ROMFORD ST
3 QUARRY BANK ST
4 LARK ST
D6
1 BROUGHTON ST
2 PLOVER VIEW
3 PADIHAM RD
4 BREAD ST
5 MONMOUTH ST
6 PENISTONE ST
7 HORACE ST
8 ADELAIDE ST
9 BERESFORD ST
E6
1 WAVERLEY ST
2 SOUTHEY ST
3 DUCKETT ST
4 Burnham Trad Pk
5 CRANMER ST
6 TRINITY TWRS
7 WILFIELD ST
8 HOPWOOD ST
147
F6
1 SYDNEY ST
2 Westgate Trad Ctr
3 FOUNDRY ST
4 ROYLE RD
5 BLACKBURN ST
128
F6
6 ORCHARD BRIDGE
7 VEEVERS ST
8 GAS ST
9 BRICK ST
10 CURZON ST
11 PARADISE ST
12 COAL ST
13 ST JAMES'S ROW
14 HARGREAVES ST
15 TANNER ST
16 FREE TRADE ST
17 MEADOW ST
18 SUTCLIFFE ST
19 CANAL ST
A B C D E F
8 7 33 6 5 32 4 3 31 2 1 30
81 82 83
Crow Wood House Farm
Burnley Way
M65
Bullions Close Farm
Wellfield Farm
Old Hall Farm
Schs
Stoneyholme
St Josephs Prep Sch
Lodge Plantation
Bronte Way
BB12
D7
1 EDGELEY CT
2 HUNTROYDE CL
3 WHEATLEY CL
4 COVERDALE WAY
5 WESLEY GR
6 GREENGATE CL
River Calder
PADIHAM RD
KIDDROW LA
Habergham High Sch
Whittlefield
PRINCESS WAY
B6434
Burnley Central
St Augustine of Canterbury RC Prim Sch
Lowerhouse Jun Sch
Holyoake Farm
Mills
Leeds & Liverpool Canal
Mill
Gannow Bsns Pk
Rose Grove
Burnley Barracks
WESTWAY
WESTGATE
A671
A679
A682
B6239
Works
Rexington Bldgs
Smallshaw Ind Est
Chestnut Bsns Pk
Victoria Works Ind Est
Rose Grove
ACCRINGTON RD
LIVERPOOL RD
TRAFALGAR ST
Trafalgar Ho
Mus
Old Holme Farm
Crem
Cemy
Cherryfold Com Sch
Playing Fields
St Hilda's RC Girls' High Sch
Scott Park
Ind Est
Trans Brittania Enterprise Est
ROSSENDALE RD
Rosehill Com Inf Sch
Rose Hill
Rosehill Jun Sch
MANCHESTER RD
Habergham Clough
Habergham Hall Farm
BB11
BURNLEY
GLEN VIEW RD
NEW RD A646
Iron House
New Barn Clough
New Barn
Further Barn
Summit Works
Hollin Cross Farm
Broadhead Moor Farm
Long Syke
Lower Gibfield
Lower Micklehurst
WOODPLUMPTON RD
B6
1 SNOWDEN CT
2 WHITE ST
3 OLD SCHOOL ROW
4 THE GROVE
5 ALLENDALE ST
C5
1 HOMER ST
2 HARTLEY ST
3 WOODPECKER HILL
4 NIGHTINGALE CRES
5 SANDPIPER SQ
6 SWALLOW PK
D5
1 WOODTOP
2 HARCOURT ST
3 CAMBRIDGE ST
4 GROVE ST
5 PALM ST
106
E5
1 ELLIS ST
2 PICCADILLY SQ
3 SEFTON TERR
4 SEFTON AVE
5 AUSTIN ST
6 WILLIS ST
7 WHITEHAVEN ST
8 ALWIN ST
9 ST MATTHEW'S CT
128
E5
10 ABBEYFIELD HO
11 PRINCE ST
F5
1 VICTORIA ST
2 YORKE ST
3 MOUNT PLEASANT ST
4 PLEASANT PL
5 ST PAUL'S CT
6 STANLEY ST
7 THORNEY BANK ST
8 DENT ROW
9 ESCAR ST
10 SACKVILLE ST

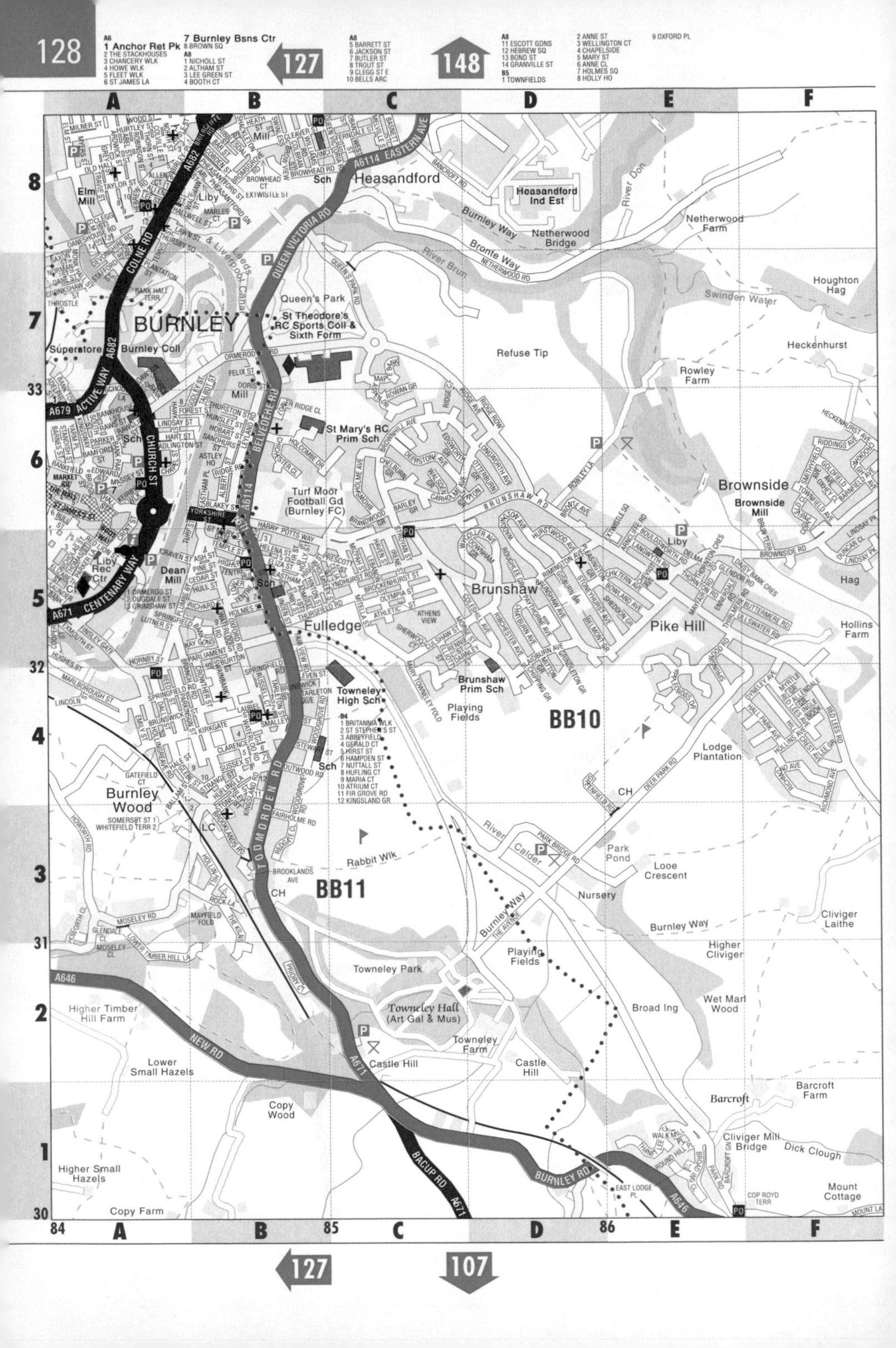
A6
1 Anchor Ret Pk
2 THE STACKHOUSES
3 CHANCERY WLK
4 HOWE WLK
5 FLEET WLK
6 ST JAMES LA
7 Burnley Bsns Ctr
8 BROWN SQ
A8
1 NICHOLL ST
2 ALTHAM ST
3 LEE GREEN ST
4 BOOTH CT
127
148
A8
5 BARRETT ST
6 JACKSON ST
7 BUTLER ST
8 TROUT ST
9 CLEGG ST E
10 BELLS ARC
A8
11 ESCOTT GDNS
12 HEBREW SQ
13 BOND ST
14 GRANVILLE ST
B5
1 TOWNFIELDS
2 ANNE ST
3 WELLINGTON CT
4 CHAPELSIDE
5 MARY ST
6 ANNE CL
7 HOLMES SQ
8 HOLLY HO
9 OXFORD PL
A
B
C
D
E
F
8
7
33
6
5
32
4
3
31
2
1
30
84
85
86
Heasandford
Heasandford Ind Est
Burnley Way
Netherwood Bridge
Netherwood Farm
Bronte Way
River Brun
River Don
Swinden Water
Houghton Hag
Heckenhurst
Refuse Tip
Rowley Farm
Queen's Park
St Theodore's RC Sports Coll & Sixth Form
BURNLEY
Superstore
Burnley Coll
Elm Mill
Liby
Mill
St Mary's RC Prim Sch
Turf Moor Football Gd (Burnley FC)
Brownside
Brownside Mill
Brunshaw
Pike Hill
Hag
Hollins Farm
Dean Mill
Liby Rec Ctr
Fulledge
Towneley High Sch
Brunshaw Prim Sch
Playing Fields
BB10
Lodge Plantation
Burnley Wood
B4
1 BRITANNIA WLK
2 ST STEPHEN'S ST
3 ABBEYFIELD
4 GERALD CT
5 HIRST ST
6 HAMPDEN ST
7 NUTTALL ST
8 HUFLING CT
9 MARIA CT
10 ATRIUM CT
11 FIR GROVE RD
12 KINGSLAND GR
1 ORMEROD ST
2 DUGDALE ST
3 GRIMSHAW ST
SOMERSET ST 1
WHITEFIELD TERR 2
Rabbit Wlk
River Calder
Park Pond
Looe Crescent
Nursery
BB11
Burnley Way
Cliviger Laithe
Higher Cliviger
Towneley Park
Towneley Hall (Art Gal & Mus)
Towneley Farm
Castle Hill
Broad Ing
Wet Marl Wood
Higher Timber Hill Farm
Lower Small Hazels
Copy Wood
Barcroft
Barcroft Farm
Cliviger Mill Bridge
Dick Clough
Higher Small Hazels
Copy Farm
Mount Cottage
A682
A679 ACTIVE WAY
A671 CENTENARY WAY
CHURCH ST
COLNE RD
A6114 EASTERN AVE
QUEEN VICTORIA RD
BELVEDERE RD
TODMORDEN RD
A646
NEW RD
BACUP RD
A671
BURNLEY RD
DEER PARK RD
BRUNSHAW RD
Leeds & Liverpool Canal

127
107

149

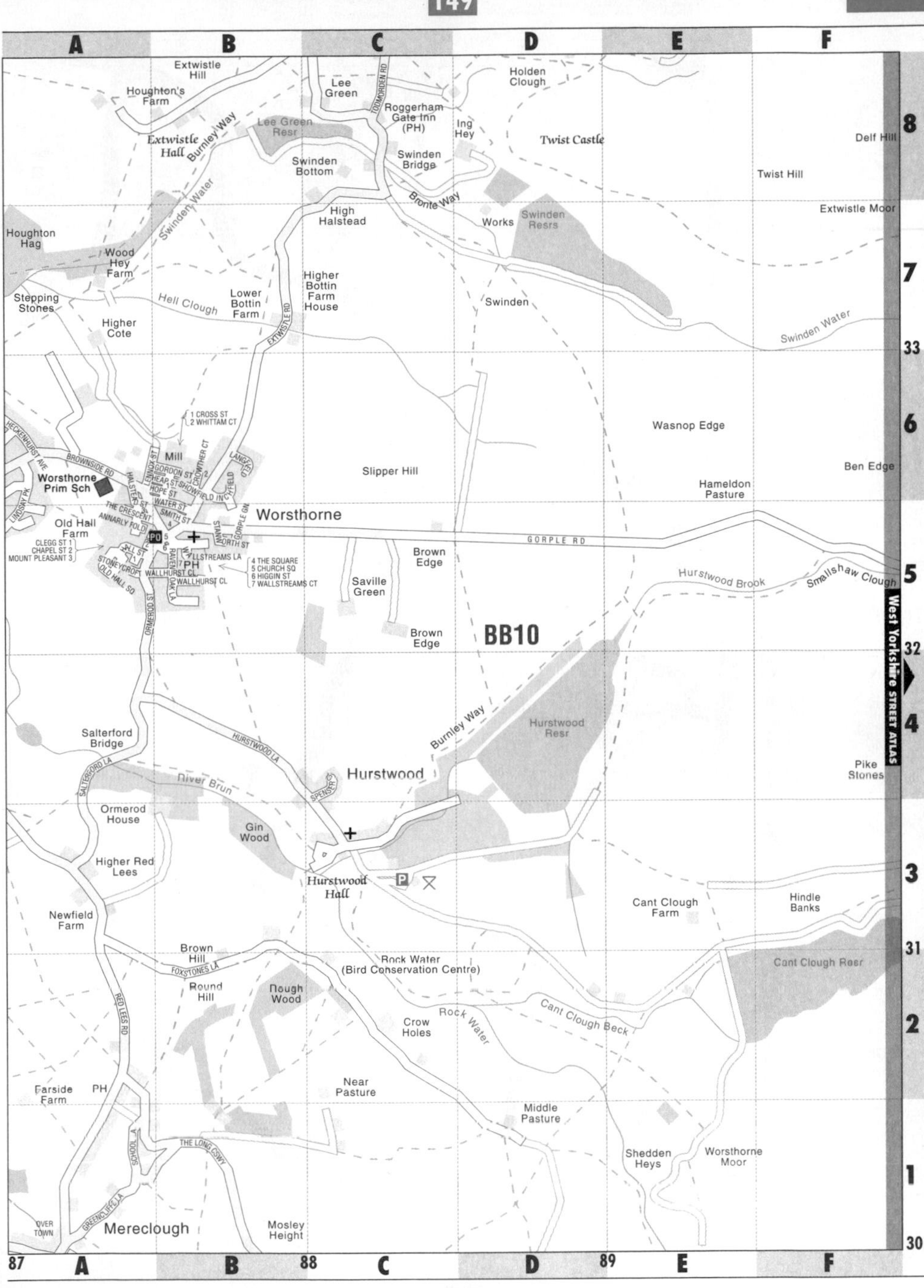
A
B
C
D
E
F
8
7
33
6
5
32
4
3
31
2
1
30
87
88
89
Extwistle Hill
Houghton's Farm
Lee Green
TODMORDEN RD
Roggerham Gate Inn (PH)
Holden Clough
Ing Hey
Lee Green Resr
Extwistle Hall
Burnley Way
Twist Castle
Delf Hill
Swinden Bottom
Swinden Bridge
Twist Hill
Swinden Water
Bronte Way
High Halstead
Works
Swinden Resrs
Extwistle Moor
Houghton Hag
Wood Hey Farm
Higher Bottin Farm House
Stepping Stones
Hell Clough
Lower Bottin Farm
Swinden
Higher Cote
EXTWISTLE RD
Swinden Water
1 CROSS ST
2 WHITTAM CT
Wasnop Edge
HECKENHURST AVE
BROWNSIDE RD
Mill
Slipper Hill
Ben Edge
Worsthorne Prim Sch
Hameldon Pasture
Old Hall Farm
Worsthorne
CLEGG ST 1
CHAPEL ST 2
MOUNT PLEASANT 3
GORPLE RD
Brown Edge
PH
4 THE SQUARE
5 CHURCH SQ
6 HIGGIN ST
7 WALLSTREAMS CT
Saville Green
Hurstwood Brook
Smallshaw Clough
Brown Edge
BB10
West Yorkshire STREET ATLAS
Hurstwood Resr
Salterford Bridge
Burnley Way
HURSTWOOD LA
Pike Stones
Hurstwood
River Brun
Ormerod House
Gin Wood
Higher Red Lees
Hurstwood Hall
Cant Clough Farm
Hindle Banks
Newfield Farm
Brown Hill
FOXSTONES LA
Rock Water (Bird Conservation Centre)
Cant Clough Resr
Round Hill
Rough Wood
RED LEES RD
Crow Holes
Rock Water
Cant Clough Beck
Near Pasture
Farside Farm
PH
Middle Pasture
THE LONG CSWY
SCHOOL LA
Shedden Heys
Worsthorne Moor
GREENCLIFFE LA
OVER TOWN
Mereclough
Mosley Height

108

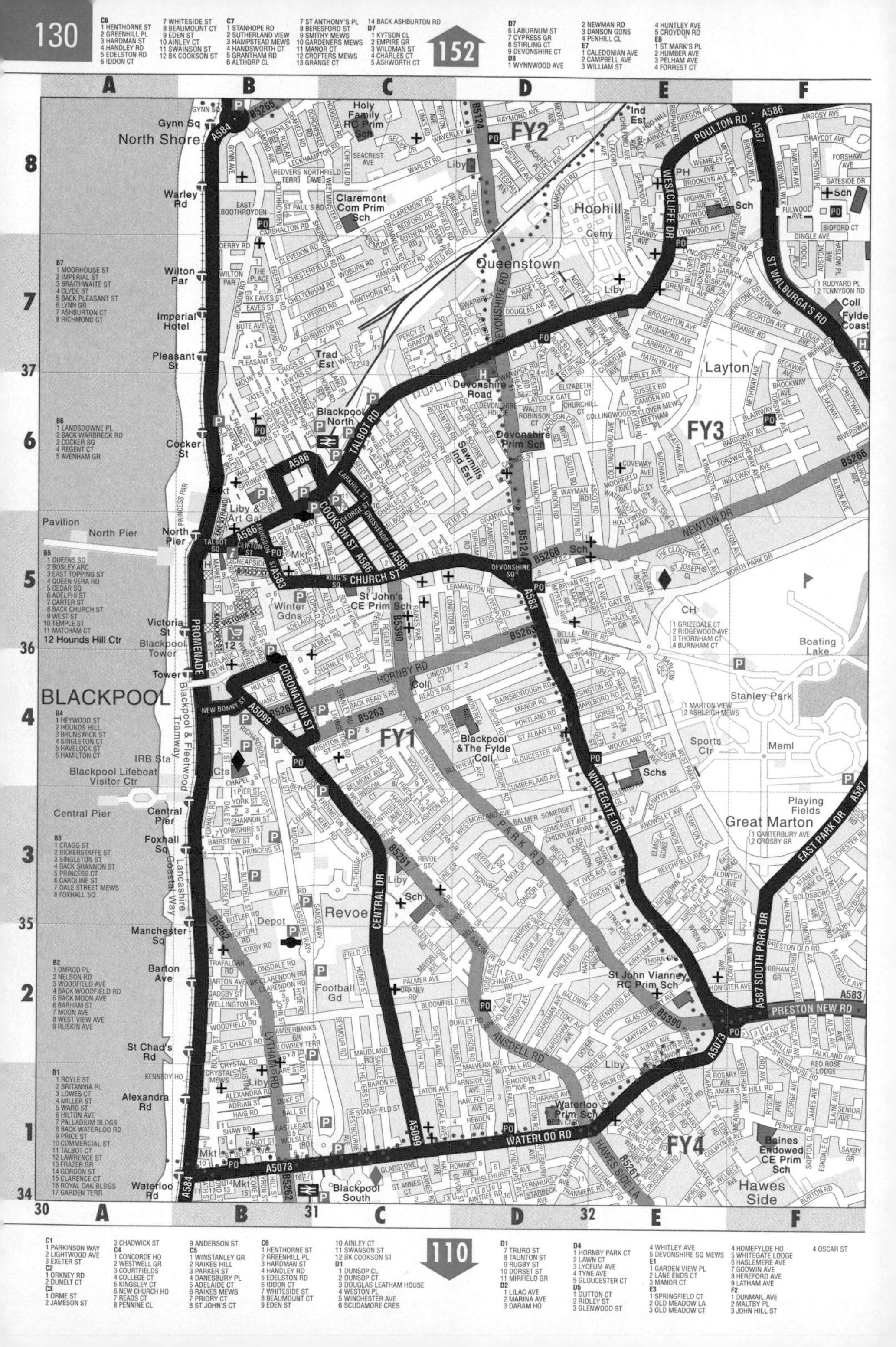
C6
1 HENTHORNE ST
2 GREENHILL PL
3 HARDMAN ST
4 HANDLEY RD
5 EDELSTON RD
6 IDDON CT
7 WHITESIDE ST
8 BEAUMOUNT CT
9 EDEN ST
10 AINLEY CT
11 SWAINSON ST
12 BK COOKSON ST
C7
1 STANHOPE RD
2 SUTHERLAND VIEW
3 HAMPSTEAD MEWS
4 HANDSWORTH CT
5 GRANTHAM RD
6 ALTHORP CL
7 ST ANTHONY'S PL
8 BERESFORD ST
9 SMITHY MEWS
10 GARDENERS MEWS
11 MANOR CT
12 CROFTERS MEWS
13 GRANGE CT
14 BACK ASHBURTON RD
D7
1 KYTSON CL
2 EMPIRE GR
3 WILDMAN ST
4 CHARLES CT
5 ASHWORTH CT
152
D7
6 LABURNUM ST
7 CYPRESS GR
8 STIRLING CT
9 DEVONSHIRE CT
D8
1 WYNNWOOD AVE
2 NEWMAN RD
3 DANSON GDNS
4 PENHILL CL
E7
1 CALEDONIAN AVE
2 CAMPBELL AVE
3 WILLIAM ST
4 HUNTLEY AVE
5 CROYDON RD
E8
1 ST MARK'S PL
2 HUMBER AVE
3 PELHAM AVE
4 FORREST CT
North Shore
Queenstown
Layton
BLACKPOOL
Revoe
Great Marton
Stanley Park
Hawes Side
FY1
FY2
FY3
FY4
PROMENADE
WATERLOO RD
WHITEGATE DR
CENTRAL DR
PARK RD
Blackpool North
Blackpool South
Blackpool Tower
North Pier
Central Pier
110
C1
1 PARKINSON WAY
2 LIGHTWOOD AVE
3 EXETER ST
C2
1 ORKNEY RD
2 DUNELT CT
C3
1 ORME ST
2 JAMESON ST
3 CHADWICK ST
C4
1 CONCORDE HO
2 WESTWELL GR
3 COURTFIELDS
4 COLLEGE CT
5 KINGSLEY CT
6 NEW CHURCH HO
7 READS CT
8 PENNINE CL
9 ANDERSON ST
C5
1 WINSTANLEY GR
2 RAIKES HILL
3 PARKER ST
4 DANESBURY PL
5 ADELAIDE CT
6 RAIKES MEWS
7 PRIORY CT
8 ST JOHN'S CT
C6
1 HENTHORNE ST
2 GREENHILL PL
3 HARDMAN ST
4 HANDLEY RD
5 EDELSTON RD
6 IDDON CT
7 WHITESIDE ST
8 BEAUMOUNT CT
9 EDEN ST
10 AINLEY CT
11 SWAINSON ST
12 BK COOKSON ST
D1
1 DUNSOP CL
2 DUNSOP CT
3 DOUGLAS LEATHAM HOUSE
4 WESTON PL
5 WINCHESTER AVE
6 SCUDAMORE CRES
D1
7 TRURO ST
8 TAUNTON ST
9 RUGBY ST
10 DORSET ST
11 MIRFIELD GR
D2
1 LILAC AVE
2 MARINA AVE
3 DARAM HO
D4
1 HORNBY PARK CT
2 LAWN CT
3 LYCEUM AVE
4 TYNE AVE
5 GLOUCESTER CT
D5
1 DUTTON CT
2 RIDLEY ST
3 GLENWOOD ST
4 WHITLEY AVE
5 DEVONSHIRE SQ MEWS
E1
1 GARDEN VIEW PL
2 LANE ENDS CT
3 MANOR CT
E3
1 SPRINGFIELD CT
2 OLD MEADOW LA
3 OLD MEADOW CT
4 HOMEFYLDE HO
5 WHITEGATE LODGE
6 HASLEMERE AVE
7 GODWIN AVE
8 HEREFORD AVE
9 LATHAM AVE
F2
1 DUNMAIL AVE
2 MALTBY PL
3 JOHN HILL ST
4 OSCAR ST

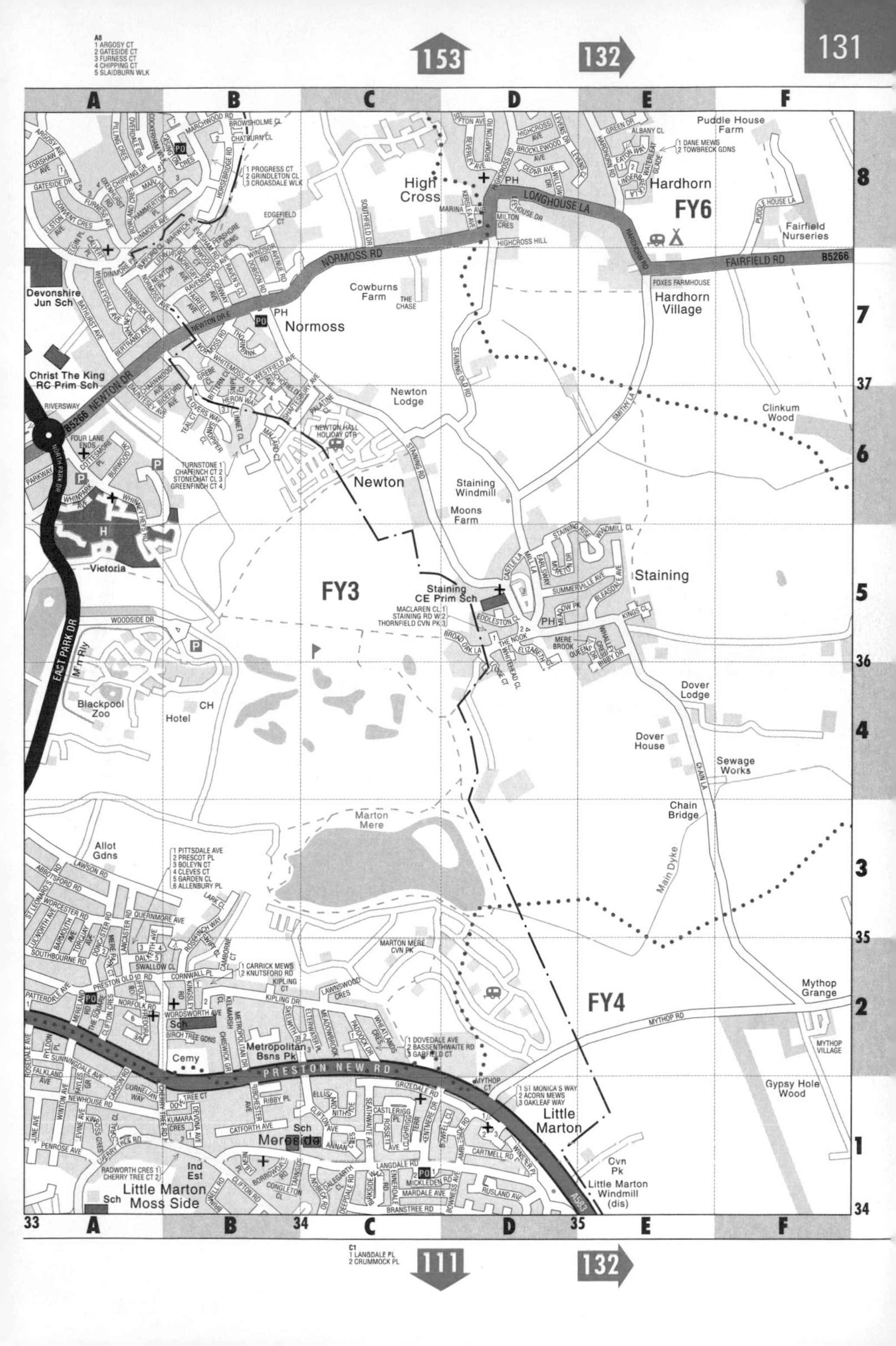
A8
1 ARGOSY CT
2 GATESIDE CT
3 FURNESS CT
4 CHIPPING CT
5 SLAIDBURN WLK
153
132
High Cross
Hardhorn
FY6
Puddle House Farm
Fairfield Nurseries
Devonshire Jun Sch
Cowburns Farm
Normoss
Hardhorn Village
Christ The King RC Prim Sch
Newton Lodge
Clinkum Wood
Newton
Staining Windmill
Moons Farm
Victoria
Staining
FY3
Staining CE Prim Sch
Blackpool Zoo
Hotel
Dover Lodge
Dover House
Sewage Works
Chain Bridge
Marton Mere
Allot Gdns
Main Dyke
MARTON MERE CVN PK
Mythop Grange
FY4
Metropolitan Bsns Pk
Cemy
PRESTON NEW RD
Gypsy Hole Wood
Little Marton
Mereside
Ind Est
Little Marton Moss Side
Cvn Pk
Little Marton Windmill (dis)
C1
1 LANGDALE PL
2 CRUMMOCK PL
111
132

131
154

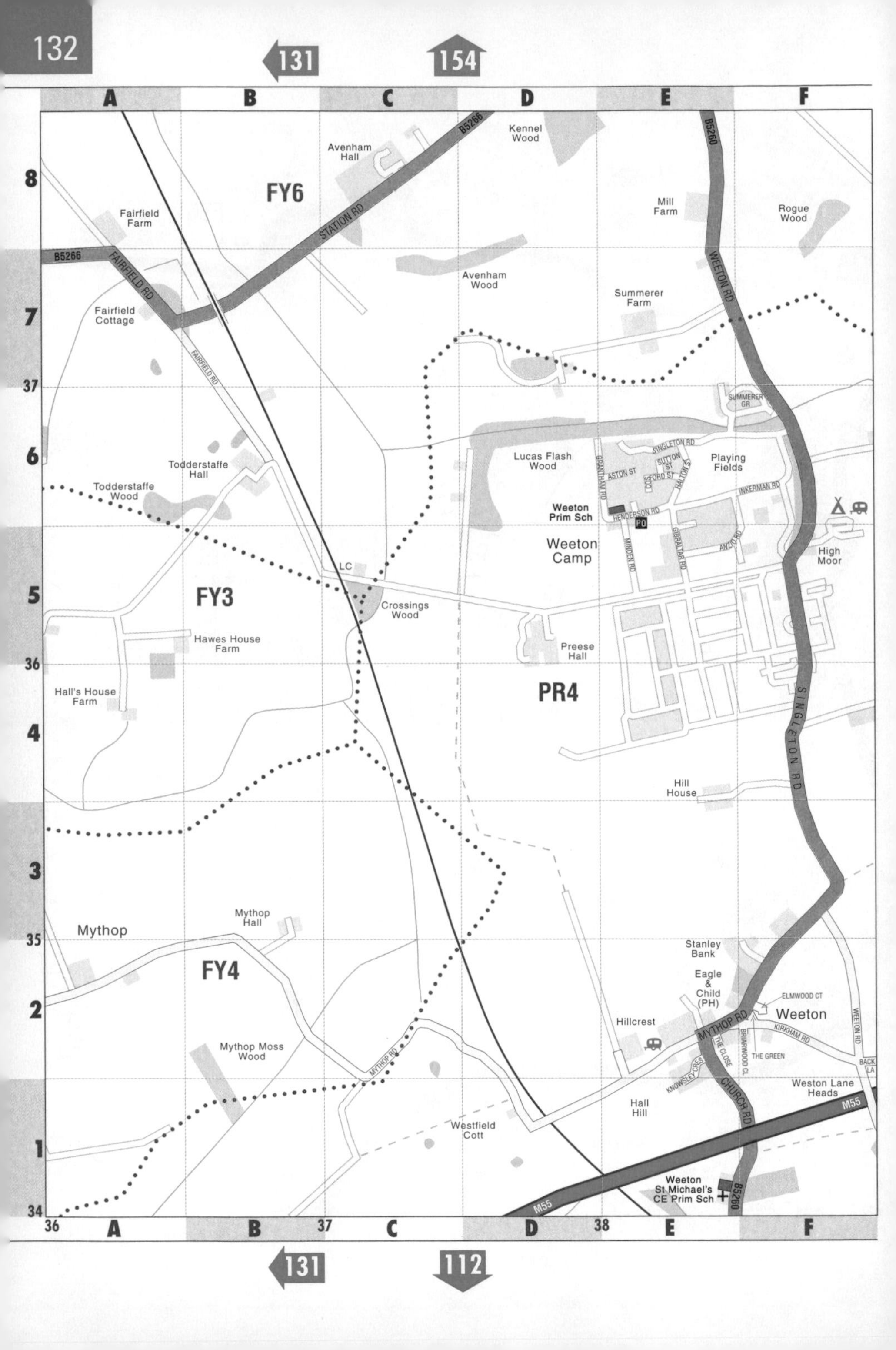

131
112

155
134

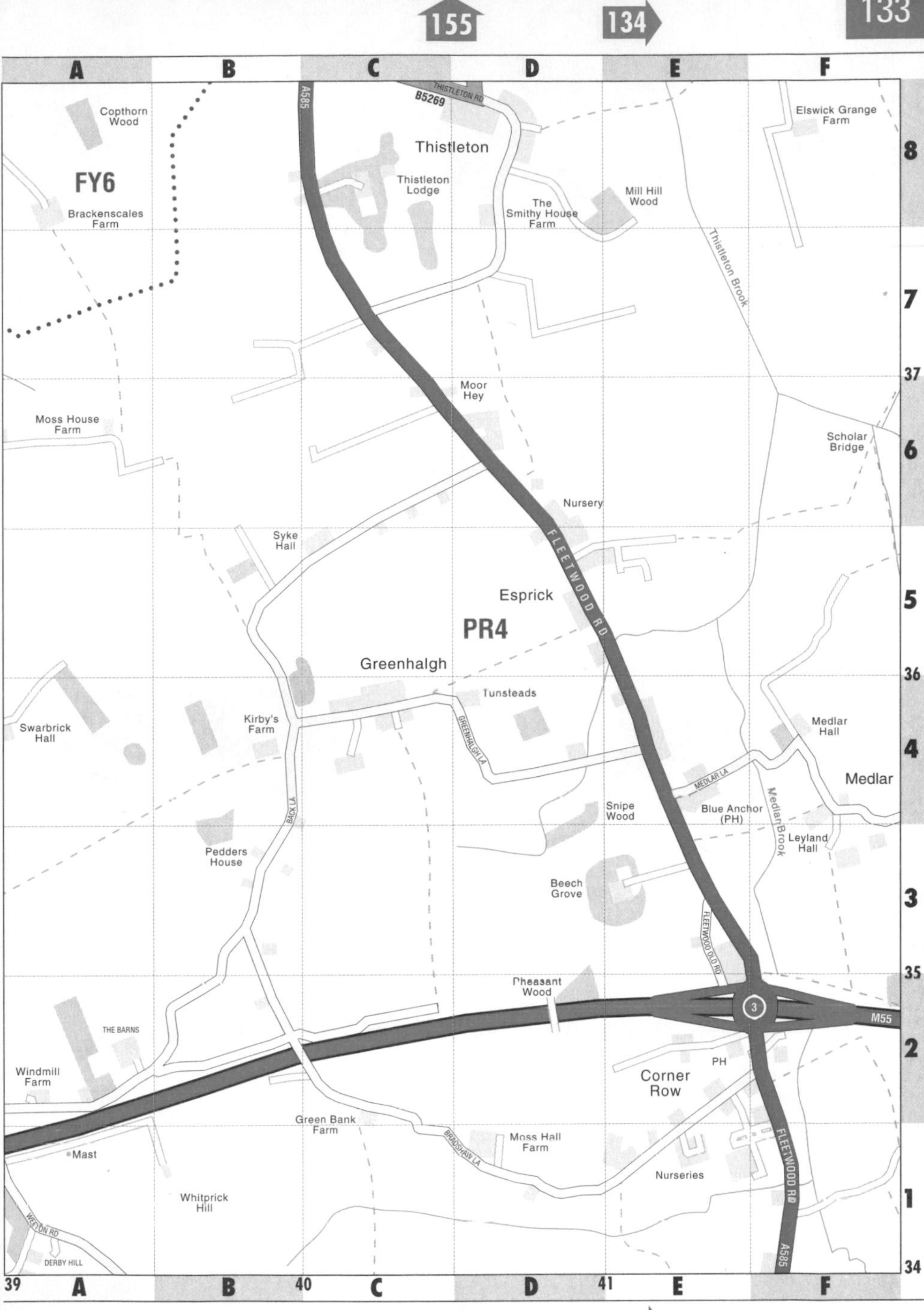

113
134

133
156

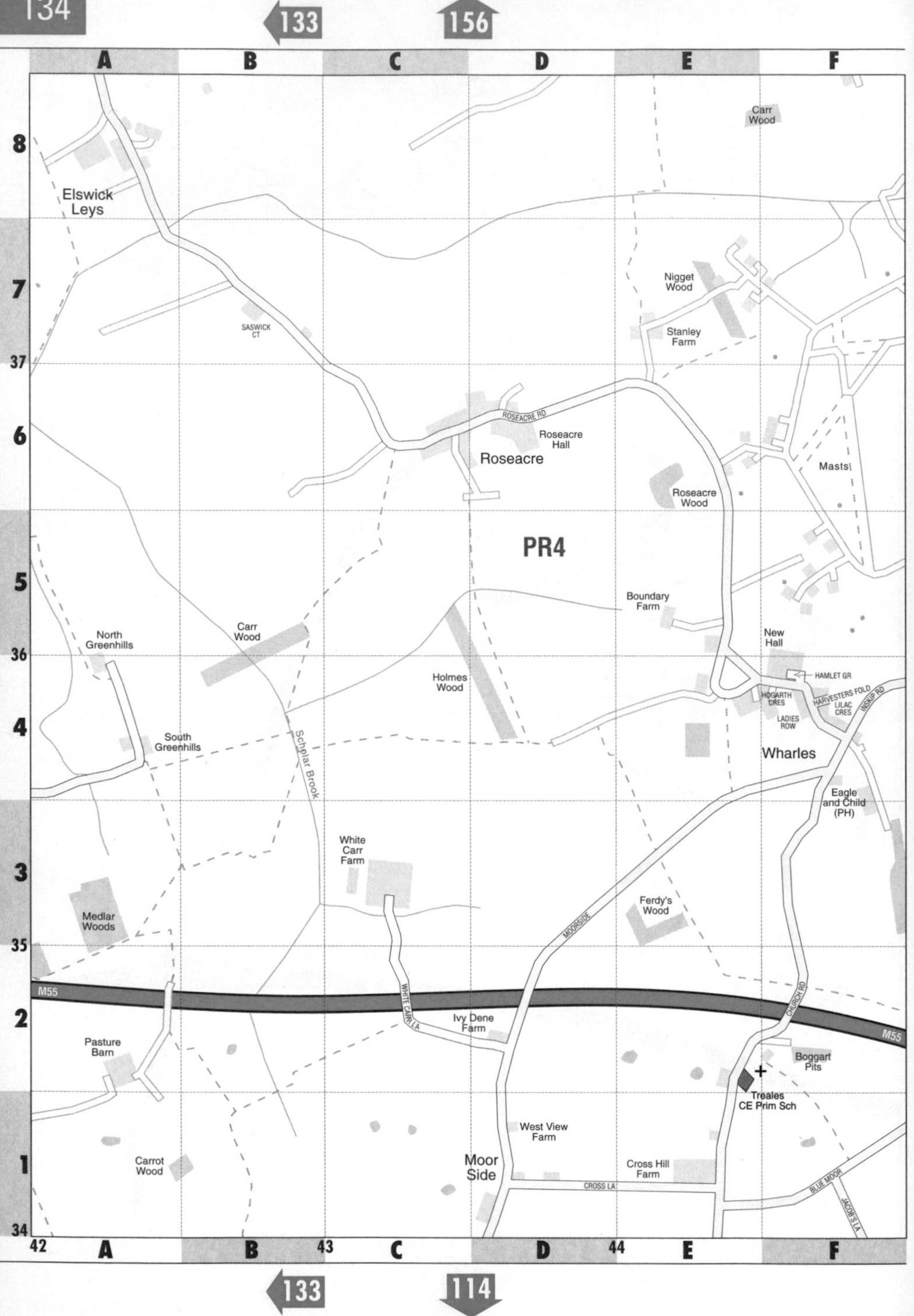

133
114

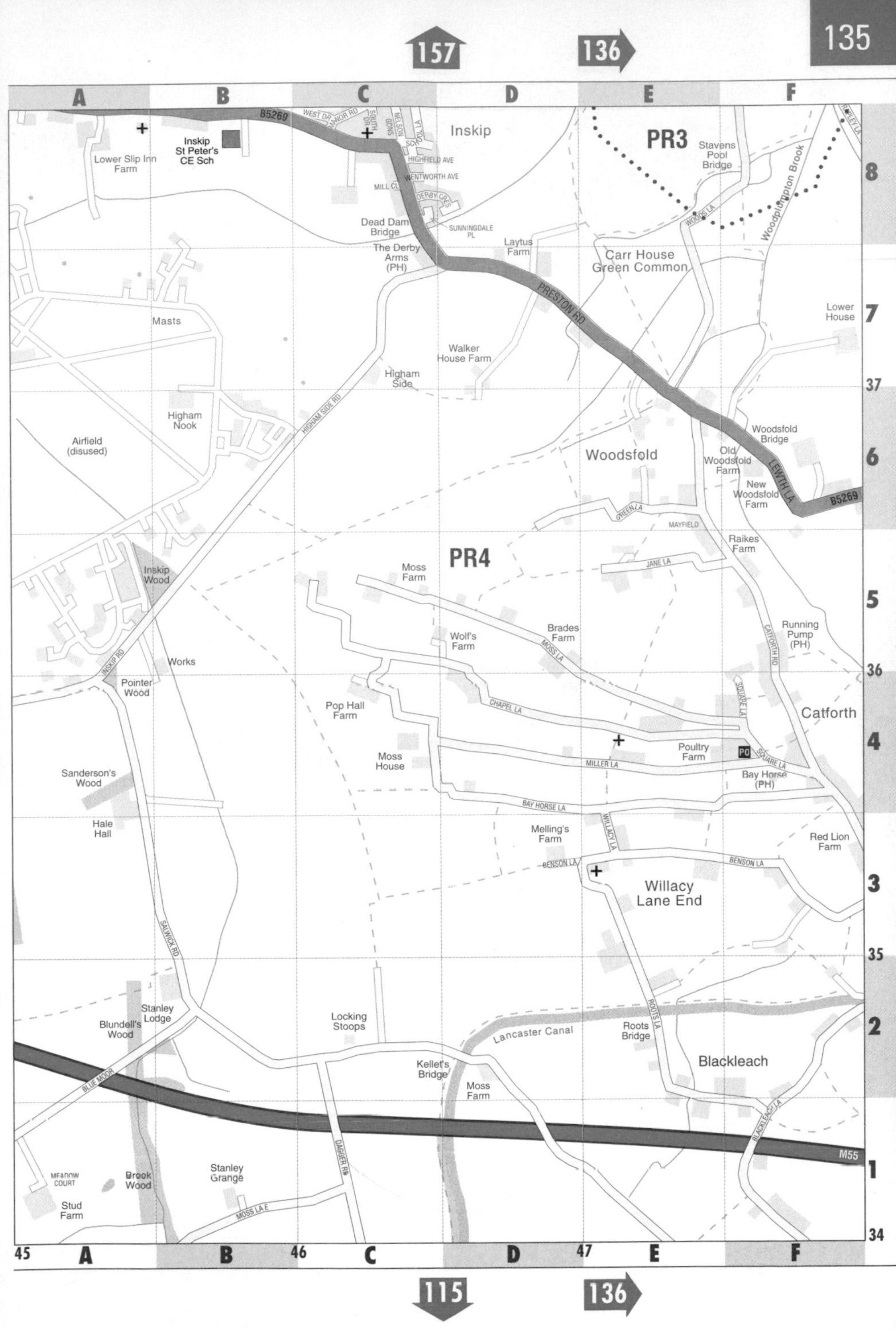
A
B
C
D
E
F
B5269
WEST DR
MANOR RD
SOUTH DR
GONS
NELSON
SCHOOL LA
Inskip
PR3
Stavens
Pool
Bridge
Lower Slip Inn
Farm
Inskip
St Peter's
CE Sch
HIGHFIELD AVE
WENTWORTH AVE
MILL CL
DERBY CRES
SUNNINGDALE PL
WOODS LA
Woodplumpton Brook
8
Dead Dam
Bridge
The Derby
Arms
(PH)
Laytus
Farm
Carr House
Green Common
PRESTON RD
Masts
Lower
House
7
Walker
House Farm
Higham
Side
37
Higham
Nook
HIGHAM SIDE RD
Airfield
(disused)
Woodsfold
Woodsfold
Bridge
Old
Woodsfold
Farm
New
Woodsfold
Farm
LEWTH LA
6
B5269
GREEN LA
MAYFIELD
Raikes
Farm
PR4
Moss
Farm
JANE LA
Inskip
Wood
5
Brades
Farm
Wolf's
Farm
MOSS LA
Running
Pump
(PH)
CATFORTH RD
Works
INSKIP RD
36
Pointer
Wood
SQUARE LA
Catforth
Pop Hall
Farm
CHAPEL LA
Poultry
Farm
PO
SQUARE LA
4
Moss
House
MILLER LA
Bay Horse
(PH)
Sanderson's
Wood
BAY HORSE LA
Hale
Hall
Melling's
Farm
WILLACY LA
Red Lion
Farm
BENSON LA
BENSON LA
3
Willacy
Lane End
SALWICK RD
35
Stanley
Lodge
Blundell's
Wood
Locking
Stoops
Lancaster Canal
Roots
Bridge
ROOTS LA
2
Blackleach
BLUE MOOR
Kellet's
Bridge
Moss
Farm
BLACKLEACH LA
DAGGER RD
M55
1
MEADOW
COURT
Brook
Wood
Stanley
Grange
Stud
Farm
MOSS LA E
34
45
A
B
46
C
D
47
E
F

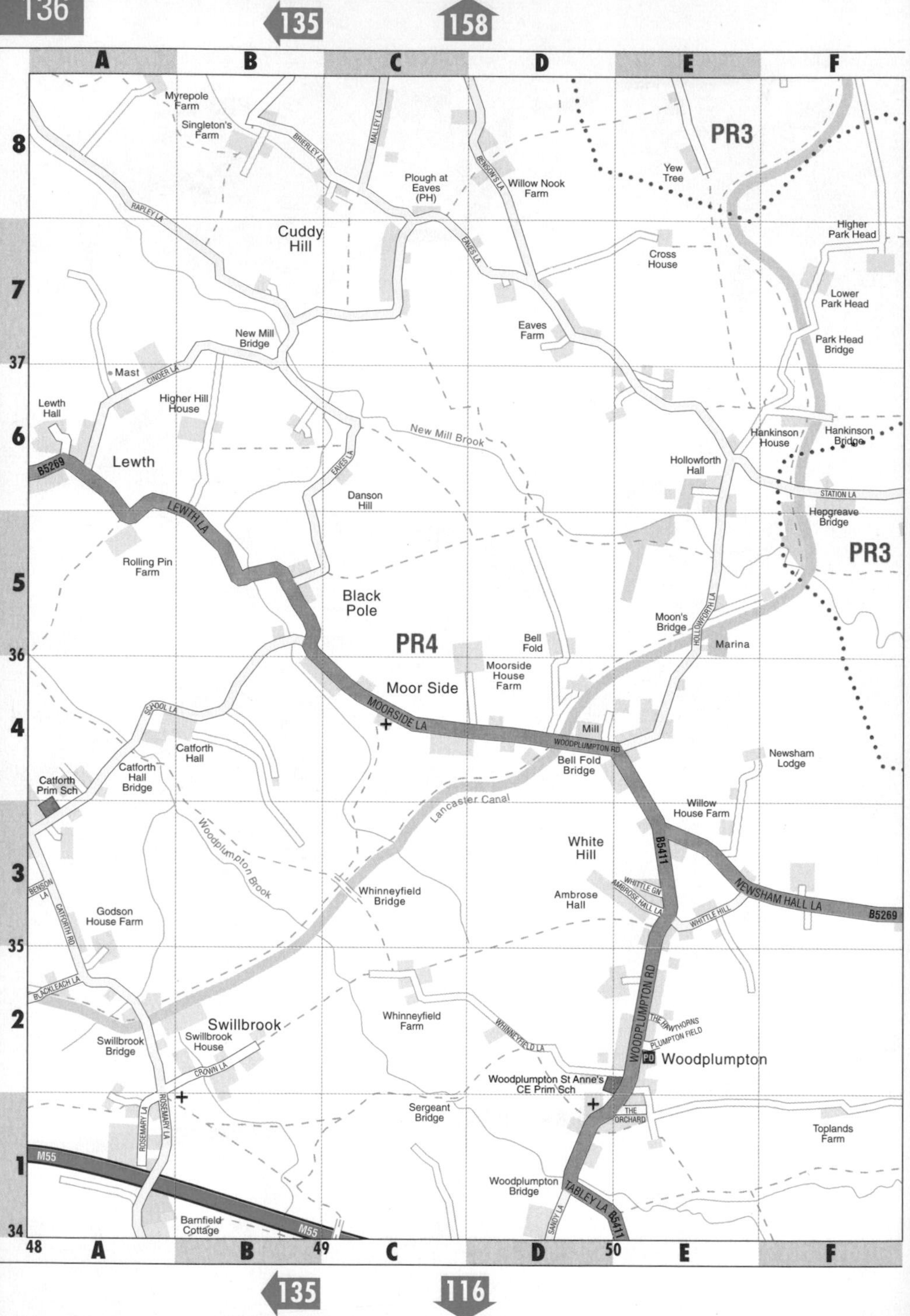
135
158
A
B
C
D
E
F
8
7
37
6
5
36
4
3
35
2
1
34
48
49
50
Myrepole Farm
Singleton's Farm
BRIERLEY LA
MALLEY LA
BENSON'S LA
Willow Nook Farm
Plough at Eaves (PH)
PR3
Yew Tree
RAPLEY LA
Cuddy Hill
EAVES LA
Cross House
Higher Park Head
Lower Park Head
New Mill Bridge
Eaves Farm
Park Head Bridge
Mast
CINDER LA
Lewth Hall
Higher Hill House
New Mill Brook
Hankinson House
Hankinson Bridge
Lewth
B5269
EAVES LA
Danson Hill
Hollowforth Hall
STATION LA
LEWTH LA
Hepgreave Bridge
PR3
Rolling Pin Farm
Black Pole
HOLLOWFORTH LA
Moon's Bridge
PR4
Bell Fold
Marina
Moorside House Farm
Moor Side
SCHOOL LA
MOORSIDE LA
Mill
WOODPLUMPTON RD
Catforth Hall
Newsham Lodge
Catforth Hall Bridge
Bell Fold Bridge
Catforth Prim Sch
Lancaster Canal
Willow House Farm
Woodplumpton Brook
White Hill
B5411
BENSON LA
WHITTLE GN
Ambrose Hall
AMBROSE HALL LA
Whinneyfield Bridge
NEWSHAM HALL LA
Godson House Farm
CATFORTH RD
WHITTLE HILL
B5269
WOODPLUMPTON RD
BLACKLEACH LA
THE HAWTHORNS
PLUMPTON FIELD
Swillbrook
Whinneyfield Farm
Swillbrook Bridge
Swillbrook House
WHINNEYFIELD LA
Woodplumpton
CROWN LA
Woodplumpton St Anne's CE Prim Sch
ROSEMARY LA
Sergeant Bridge
THE ORCHARD
Toplands Farm
M55
Woodplumpton Bridge
TABLEY LA
B5411
SANDY LA
Barnfield Cottage
M55
135
116

159
138

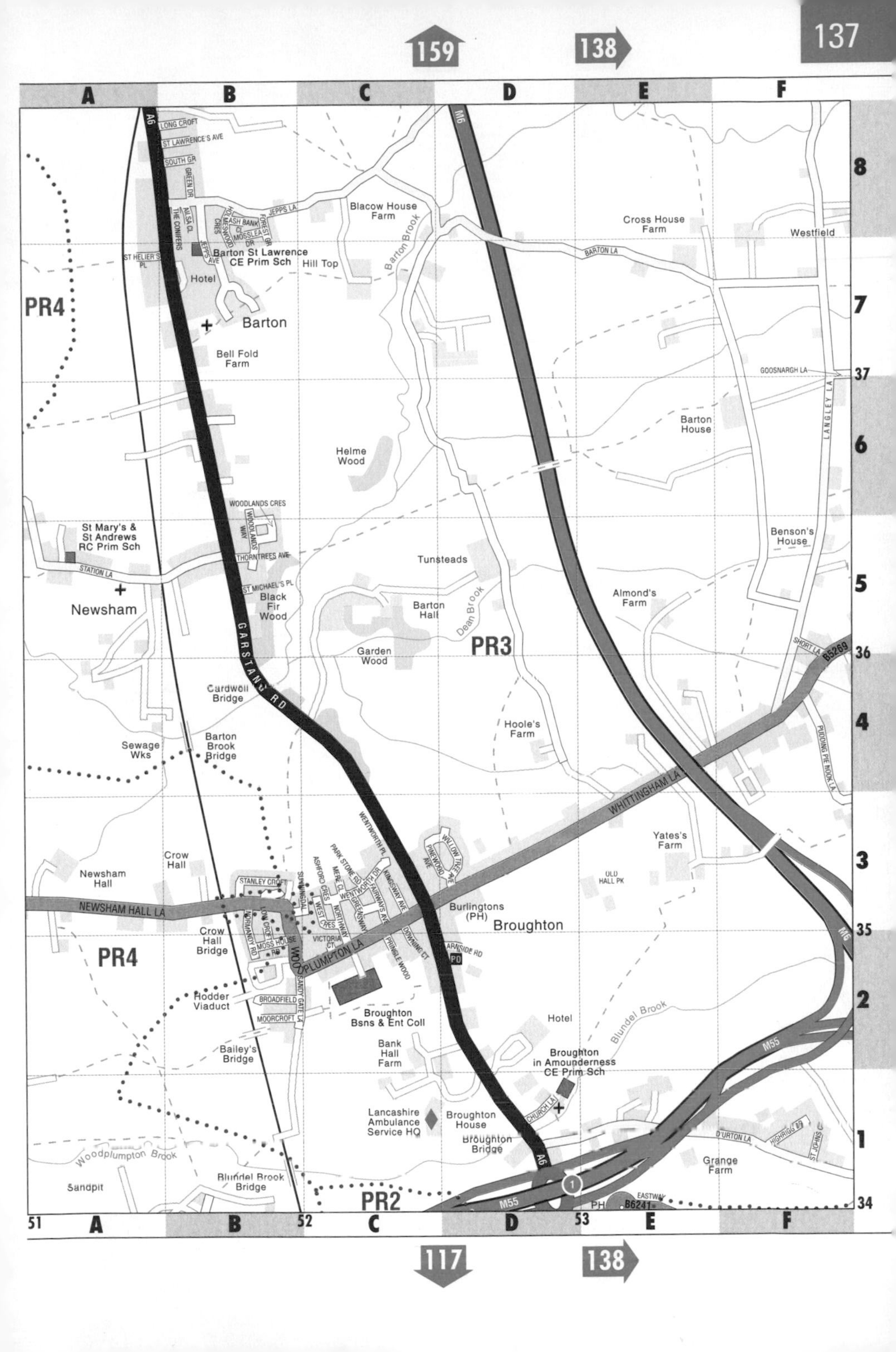

117
138

137
160

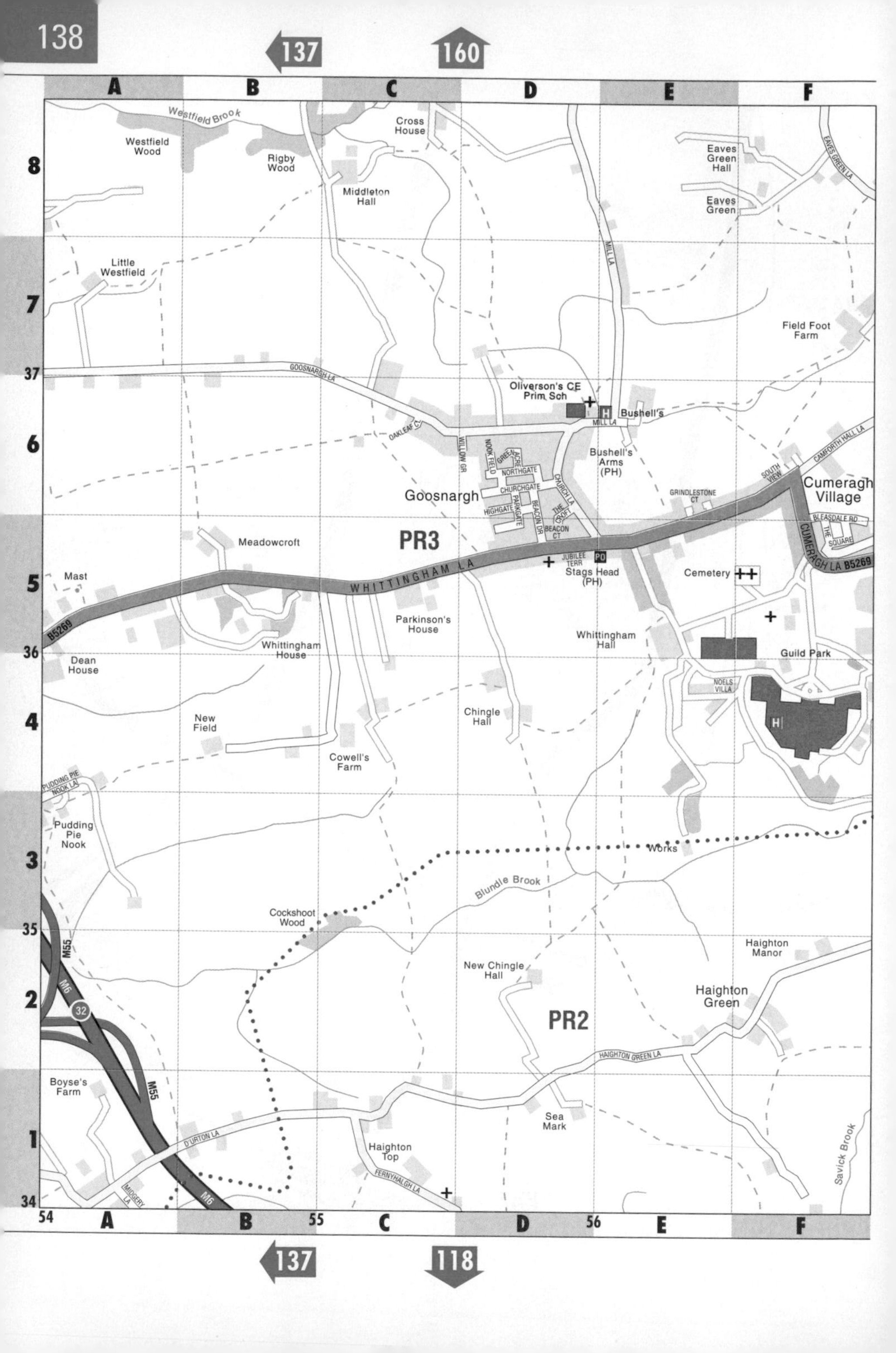

137
118

161
140

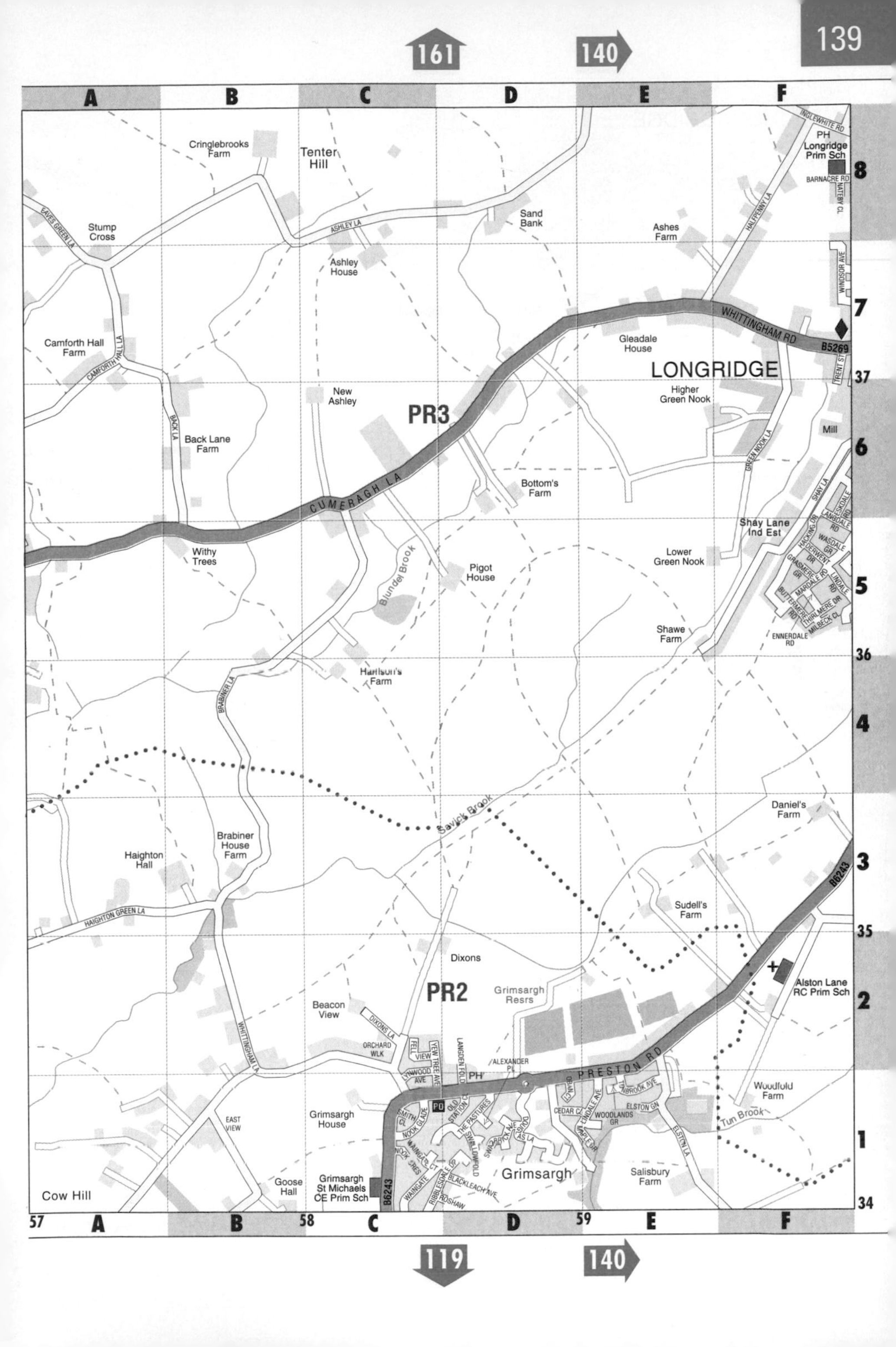

119
140

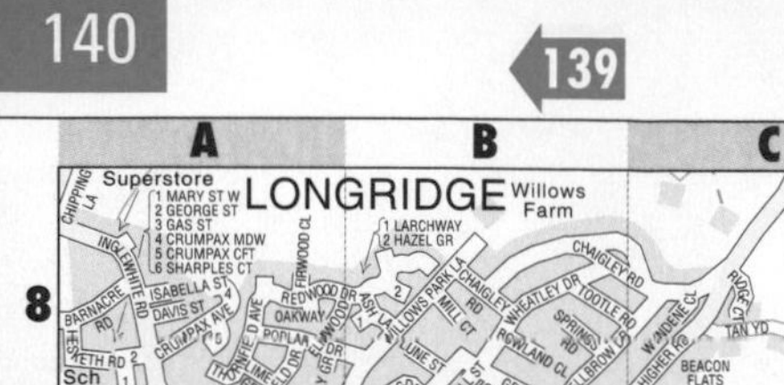

139
162

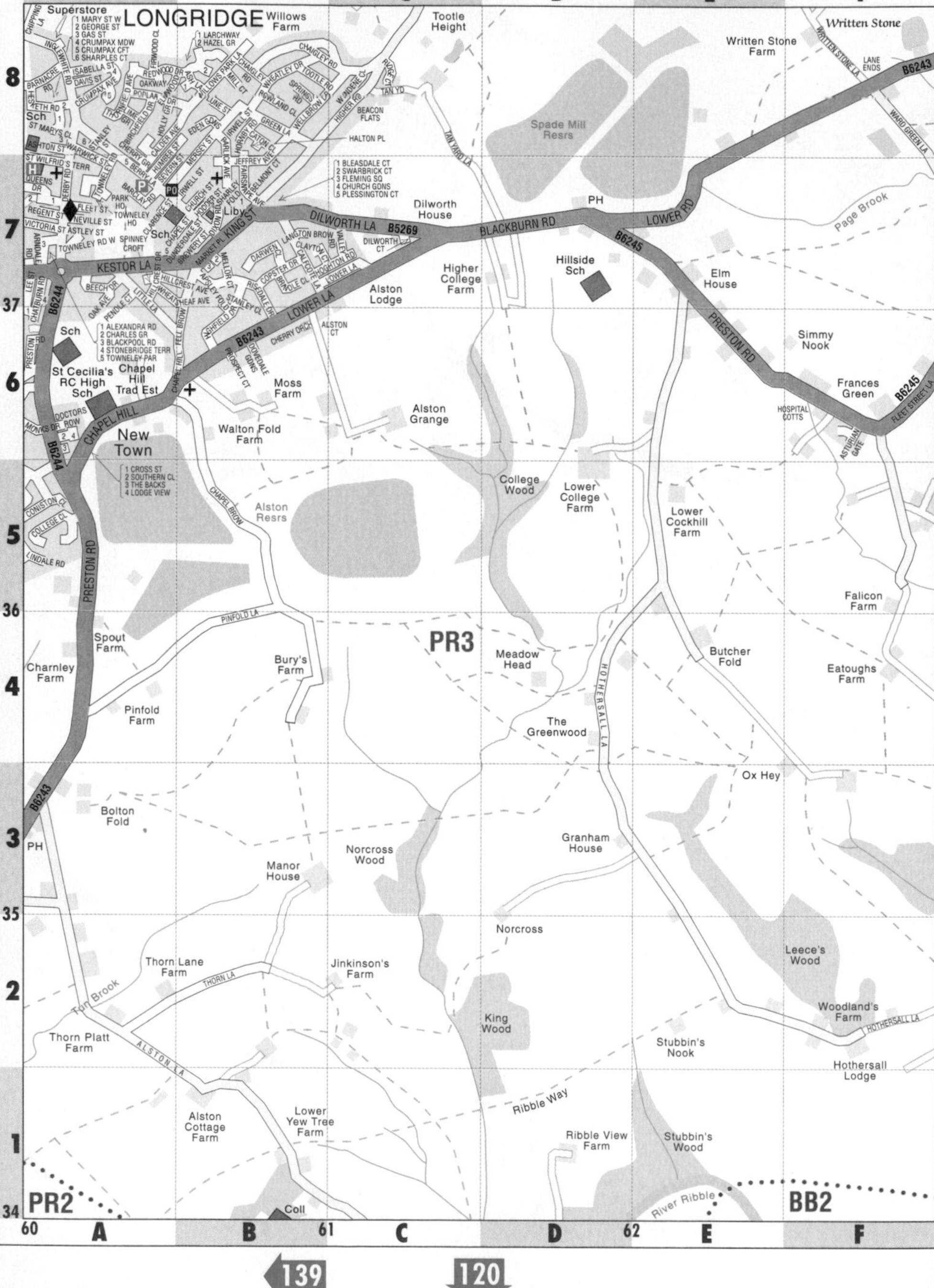

A
B
C
D
E
F
8
7
37
6
5
36
4
3
35
2
1
34
60
61
62
LONGRIDGE
Superstore
1 MARY ST W
2 GEORGE ST
3 GAS ST
4 CRUMPAX MDW
5 CRUMPAX CFT
6 SHARPLES CT
1 LARCHWAY
2 HAZEL GR
Willows Farm
Tootle Height
Written Stone
Written Stone Farm
WRITTEN STONE LA
LANE ENDS
B6243
WARD GREEN LA
Spade Mill Resrs
BEACON FLATS
HALTON PL
TAN YD
TAN YARD LA
1 BLEASDALE CT
2 SWARBRICK CT
3 FLEMING SQ
4 CHURCH GDNS
5 PLESSINGTON CT
Dilworth House
PH
DILWORTH LA
B5269
BLACKBURN RD
LOWER RD
Page Brook
B6245
KING ST
KESTOR LA
DILWORTH CT
Higher College Farm
Hillside Sch
Elm House
Alston Lodge
LOWER LA
B6243
PRESTON RD
Simmy Nook
Frances Green
B6245
FLEET STREET LA
HOSPITAL COTTS
ASTURIAN GATE
1 ALEXANDRA RD
2 CHARLES GR
3 BLACKPOOL RD
4 STONEBRIDGE TERR
5 TOWNELEY PAR
Sch
St Cecilia's RC High Sch
Chapel Hill Trad Est
CHAPEL HILL
DOCTORS ROW
MONKS DR
B6244
New Town
1 CROSS ST
2 SOUTHERN CL
3 THE BACKS
4 LODGE VIEW
Moss Farm
Alston Grange
Walton Fold Farm
CHAPEL BROW
Alston Resrs
College Wood
Lower College Farm
Lower Cockhill Farm
CONISTON CL
COLLEGE CL
LINDALE RD
PRESTON RD
Falicon Farm
PINFOLD LA
PR3
Meadow Head
Spout Farm
Charnley Farm
Bury's Farm
Butcher Fold
Eatoughs Farm
HOTHERSALL LA
Pinfold Farm
The Greenwood
Ox Hey
B6243
Bolton Fold
PH
Granham House
Norcross Wood
Manor House
Norcross
Thorn Lane Farm
THORN LA
Jinkinson's Farm
Leece's Wood
Tun Brook
Woodland's Farm
HOTHERSALL LA
Thorn Platt Farm
ALSTON LA
King Wood
Stubbin's Nook
Hothersall Lodge
Ribble Way
Alston Cottage Farm
Lower Yew Tree Farm
Ribble View Farm
Stubbin's Wood
PR2
River Ribble
BB2
Coll

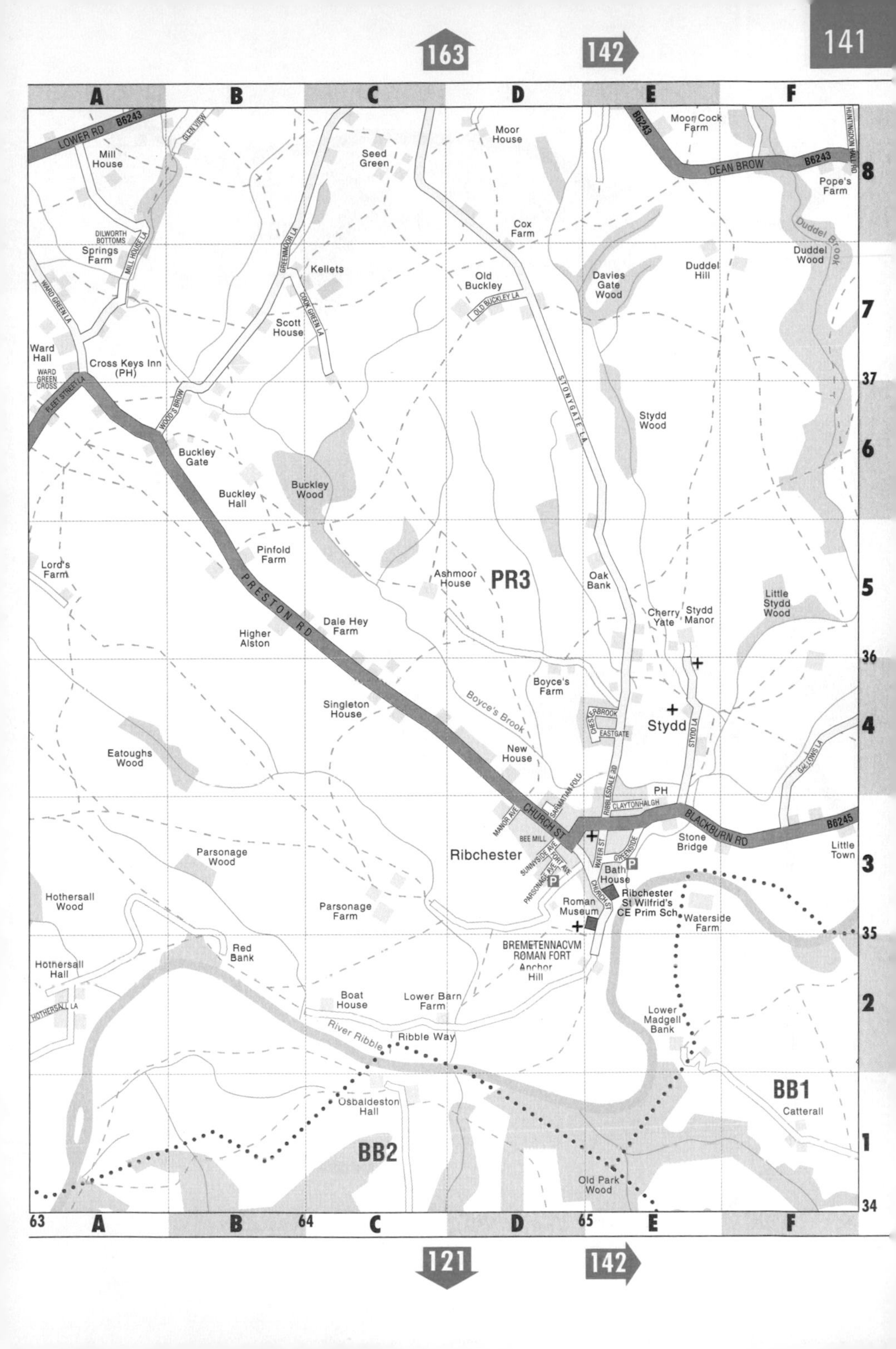
163
142
A
B
C
D
E
F
LOWER RD
B6243
GLEN VIEW
Mill House
Seed Green
Moor House
Moor Cock Farm
HUNTINGDON HALL RD
DEAN BROW
B6243
Pope's Farm
8
DILWORTH BOTTOMS
MILL HOUSE LA
Springs Farm
GREENMOOR LA
Kellets
Cox Farm
Duddel Brook
Duddel Wood
Duddel Hill
Davies Gate Wood
Old Buckley
OLD BUCKLEY LA
WARD GREEN LA
COOK GREEN LA
Scott House
7
Ward Hall
Cross Keys Inn (PH)
WARD GREEN CROSS
FLEET STREET LA
STONYGATE LA
37
WOOD'S BROW
Stydd Wood
6
Buckley Gate
Buckley Wood
Buckley Hall
Pinfold Farm
Lord's Farm
Ashmoor House
PR3
Oak Bank
5
PRESTON RD
Little Stydd Wood
Cherry Yate
Stydd Manor
Dale Hey Farm
Higher Alston
36
Boyce's Farm
Singleton House
Boyce's Brook
CHESTERBROOK
EASTGATE
Stydd
STYDD LA
4
Eatoughs Wood
New House
GALLOWS LA
SARMATIAN FOLD
RIBBLESDALE RD
PH
CLAYTONHALGH
MANOR AVE
CHURCH ST
BLACKBURN RD
B6245
BEE MILL
WATER ST
GREENSIDE
Stone Bridge
Little Town
Parsonage Wood
Ribchester
SUNNYSIDE AVE
FORT AVE
P
Bath House
3
PARSONAGE AVE
CHURCH ST
Ribchester St Wilfrid's CE Prim Sch
Hothersall Wood
Parsonage Farm
Roman Museum
Waterside Farm
35
BREMETENNACVM ROMAN FORT
Red Bank
Anchor Hill
Hothersall Hall
Boat House
Lower Barn Farm
2
Lower Madgell Bank
HOTHERSALL LA
River Ribble
Ribble Way
BB1
Osbaldeston Hall
Catterall
BB2
1
Old Park Wood
34
63
A
B
64
C
D
65
E
F
121
142

141
164

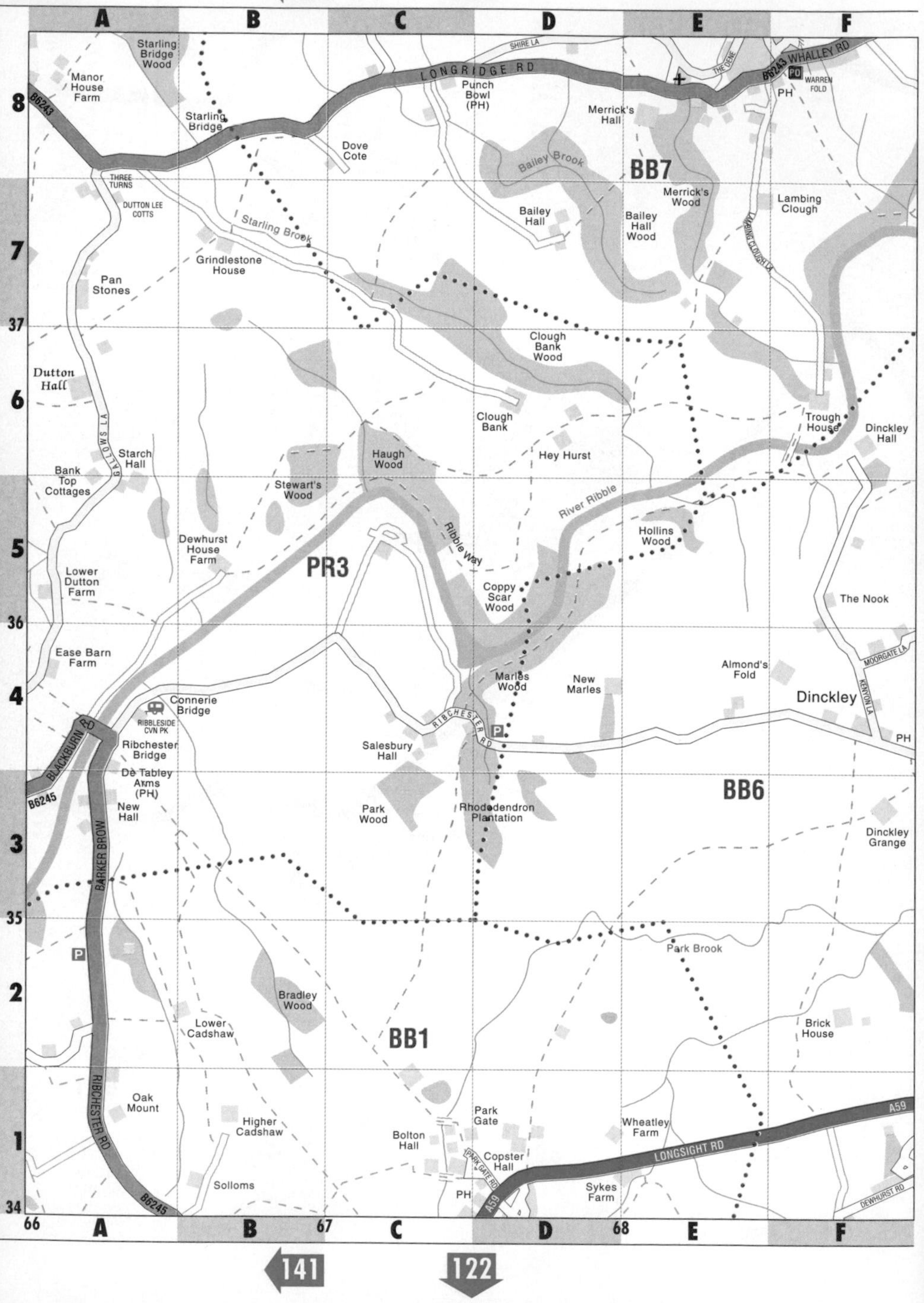

A
B
C
D
E
F
8
7
37
6
5
36
4
3
35
2
1
34
66
67
68
Starling Bridge Wood
Manor House Farm
B6243
Starling Bridge
LONGRIDGE RD
SHIRE LA
Punch Bowl (PH)
Dove Cote
THE DENE
B6243 WHALLEY RD
PO
WARREN FOLD
PH
Merrick's Hall
Bailey Brook
BB7
Merrick's Wood
Lambing Clough
THREE TURNS
DUTTON LEE COTTS
Starling Brook
Bailey Hall
Bailey Hall Wood
LAMBING CLOUGH LA
Grindlestone House
Pan Stones
Clough Bank Wood
Dutton Hall
GALLOWS LA
Clough Bank
Trough House
Dinckley Hall
Starch Hall
Haugh Wood
Hey Hurst
Bank Top Cottages
Stewart's Wood
River Ribble
Ribble Way
Hollins Wood
Dewhurst House Farm
PR3
Lower Dutton Farm
Coppy Scar Wood
The Nook
Ease Barn Farm
Marles Wood
New Marles
Almond's Fold
MOORGATE LA
KENYON LA
Connerie Bridge
Dinckley
BLACKBURN RD
RIBBLESIDE CVN PK
RIBCHESTER RD
P
Ribchester Bridge
Salesbury Hall
PH
De Tabley Arms (PH)
B6245
BB6
New Hall
Park Wood
Rhododendron Plantation
BARKER BROW
Dinckley Grange
P
Park Brook
Bradley Wood
Lower Cadshaw
BB1
Brick House
RIBCHESTER RD
Oak Mount
Park Gate
Higher Cadshaw
Bolton Hall
Wheatley Farm
A59
Copster Hall
LONGSIGHT RD
PARK GATE RD
Solloms
Sykes Farm
DEWHURST RD
PH
A59
B6245

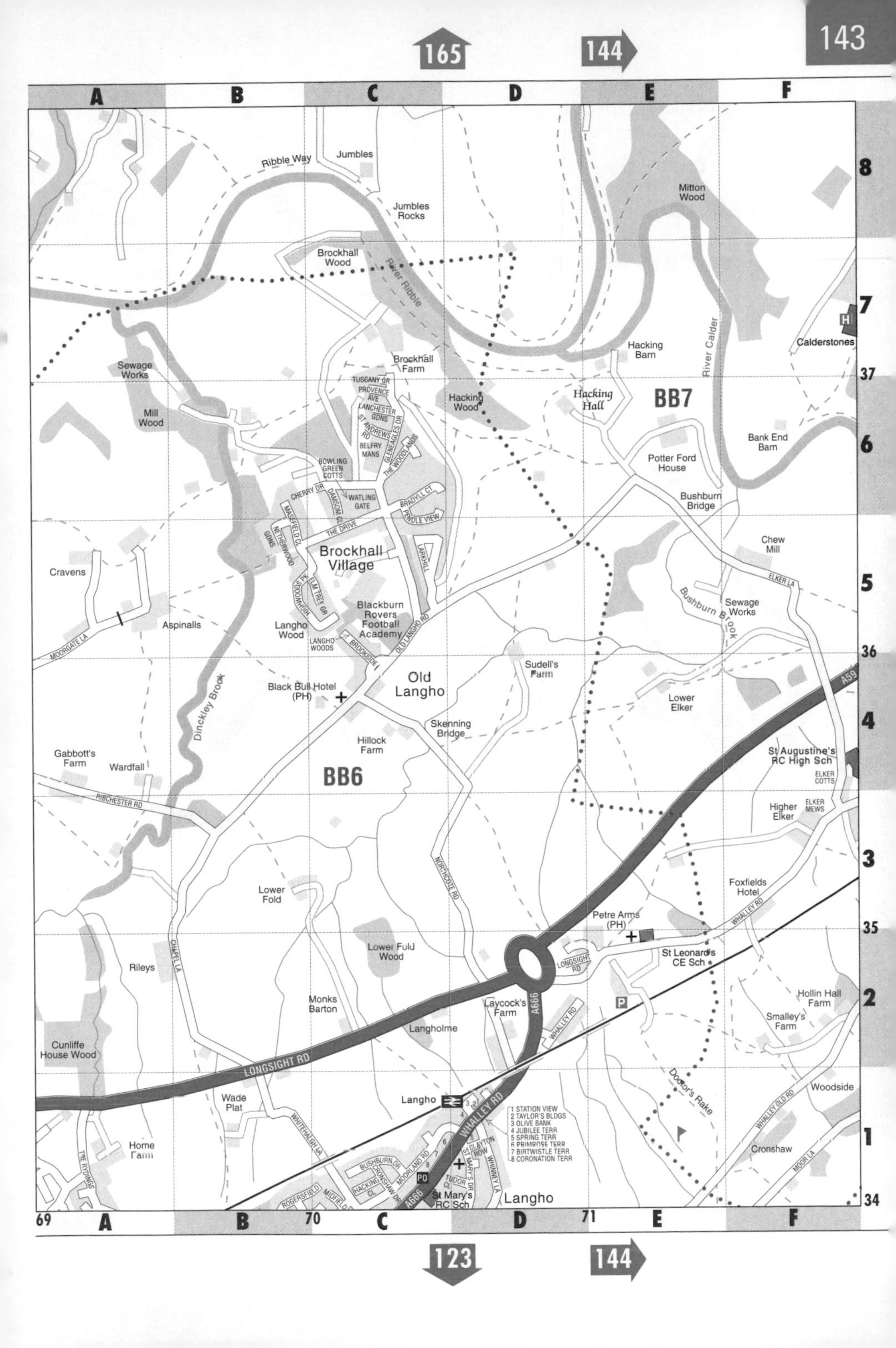
165
144
Ribble Way
Jumbles
Jumbles Rocks
Mitton Wood
Brockhall Wood
River Ribble
Sewage Works
Mill Wood
Brockhall Farm
Hacking Wood
Hacking Barn
Hacking Hall
BB7
River Calder
Calderstones
Bank End Barn
Potter Ford House
Bushburn Bridge
Brockhall Village
Cravens
Aspinalls
Chew Mill
Elker La
Sewage Works
Bushburn Brook
Blackburn Rovers Football Academy
Langho Wood
Old Langho
Black Bull Hotel (PH)
Sudell's Farm
Lower Elker
Skenning Bridge
Hillock Farm
Dinckley Brook
Gabbott's Farm
Wardfall
BB6
Ribchester Rd
Moorgate La
St Augustine's RC High Sch
Elker Cotts
Higher Elker
Elker Mews
A59
Foxfields Hotel
Whalley Rd
Lower Fold
Northcote Rd
Petre Arms (PH)
St Leonard's CE Sch
Longsight Rd
Lower Fold Wood
Rileys
Chapel La
Monks Barton
Laycock's Farm
A666
Hollin Hall Farm
Smalley's Farm
Langholme
Cunliffe House Wood
Longsight Rd
Doctor's Rake
Wade Plat
Langho
Woodside
Whalley Old Rd
Home Farm
Whitehalgh La
Whalley Rd
Cronshaw
Moor La
1 Station View
2 Taylor's Bldgs
3 Olive Bank
4 Jubilee Terr
5 Spring Terr
6 Primrose Terr
7 Birtwistle Terr
8 Coronation Terr
The Rydings
Bushburn Dr
Moorland Rd
Hacking Cl
Rogersfield
Midfield
St Mary's RC Sch
Tudor Cl
Whinney La
Langho
123
144

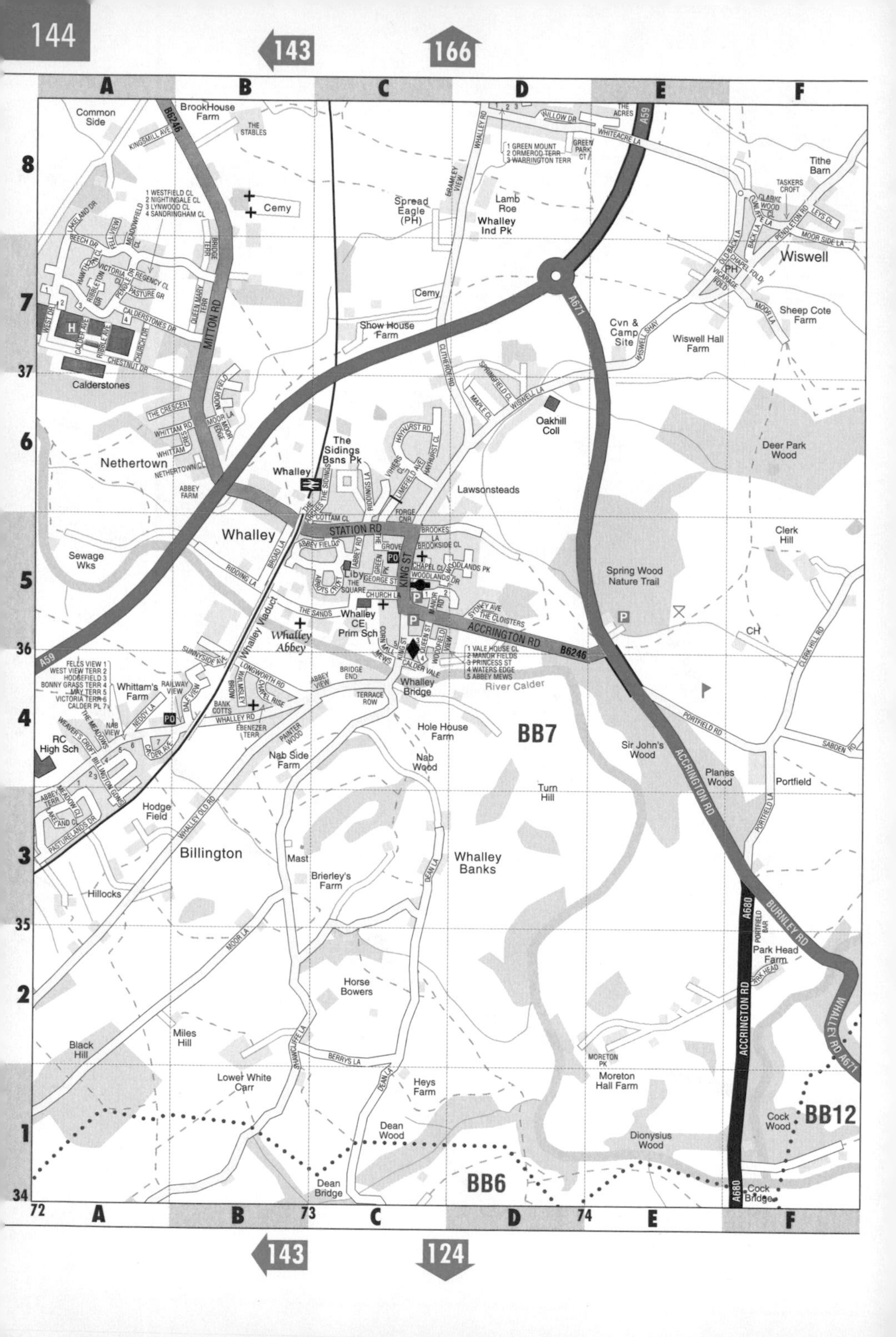
143
166
A
B
C
D
E
F
8
7
37
6
5
36
4
3
35
2
1
34
72
73
74
124
Common Side
BrookHouse Farm
THE STABLES
KINGSMILL AVE
B6246
Cemy
Spread Eagle (PH)
Lamb Roe
Whalley Ind Pk
WHALLEY RD
1 GREEN MOUNT
2 ORMEROD TERR
3 WARRINGTON TERR
WILLOW DR
THE ACRES
WHITEACRE LA
GREEN PARK CT
A59
Tithe Barn
TASKERS CROFT
Wiswell
PH
1 WESTFIELD CL
2 NIGHTINGALE CL
3 LYNWOOD CL
4 SANDRINGHAM CL
LAKELAND DR
BEECH DR
FELL VIEW
MEADOWFIELD CL
HAWTHORN CL
VICTORIA DR
REGENCY CL
PENDLE DR
PASTURE GR
CALDERSTONES DR
QUEEN MARY TERR
BRIDGE TERR
MITTON RD
WEST DR
H
CALDER AVE
RIBBLE AVE
CHURCH DR
CHESTNUT DR
Calderstones
Cemy
Show House Farm
A671
Cvn & Camp Site
Wiswell Hall Farm
Sheep Cote Farm
MOOR LA
WISWELL SHAY
SPRINGFIELD CL
MAPLE CL
WISWELL LA
CLITHEROE RD
Oakhill Coll
MOORFIELD
THE CRESCENT
WHITTAM RD
MOOR LA
MOOR EDGE
MANOR EDGE
WHITTAM CRES
Nethertown
NETHERTOWN CL
ABBEY FARM
The Sidings Bsns Pk
HAYHURST RD
HAYHURST CL
LIMEFIELD AVE
VIHIERS CL
RIDDINGS LA
Whalley
Deer Park Wood
Lawsonsteads
FORGE CNR
COTTAM CL
STATION RD
BROOKES LA
BROOKSIDE CL
Whalley
Clerk Hill
Sewage Wks
ABBEY FIELDS
ABBEY RD
THE GROVE
GREEN PK
PO
KING ST
CHAPEL CL
WOODLANDS DR
WOODLANDS PK
Liby
GEORGE ST
THE SQUARE
ABBOTS CROFT
RIDDING LA
BROAD LA
CHURCH LA
P
MANOR RD
Spring Wood Nature Trail
SYDNEY AVE
THE CLOISTERS
THE SANDS
Whalley CE Prim Sch
ACCRINGTON RD
P
CH
Whalley Viaduct
Whalley Abbey
QUEEN ST
WOODFIELD VIEW
CLERK HILL RD
1 VALE HOUSE CL
2 MANOR FIELDS
3 PRINCESS ST
4 WATERS EDGE
5 ABBEY MEWS
B6246
SUNNYSIDE AVE
CORN MILL MEWS
FELLS VIEW 1
WEST VIEW TERR 2
HODGEFIELD 3
BONNY GRASS TERR 4
MAY TERR 5
VICTORIA TERR 6
CALDER PL 7
Whittam's Farm
LONGWORTH RD
RAILWAY VIEW
DALE VIEW
ABBEY VIEW
BRIDGE END
CALDER VALE
Whalley Bridge
River Calder
CHAPEL RISE
WALMSLEY BROW
BANK COTTS
NEDDY LA
NAB VIEW
PO
WHALLEY RD
EBENEZER TERR
TERRACE ROW
PORTFIELD RD
THE MEADOWS
WEAVER'S CROFT
RC High Sch
BILLINGTON GDNS
CALDER AVE
PAINTER WOOD
Hole House Farm
BB7
Sir John's Wood
SABDEN RD
Nab Side Farm
Nab Wood
Planes Wood
Portfield
ABBEY TERR
MEADOW CL
PASTURELANDS DR
Hodge Field
WHALLEY OLD RD
Turn Hill
ACCRINGTON RD
PORTFIELD LA
Billington
Mast
Whalley Banks
DEAN LA
Brierley's Farm
Hillocks
A680
PORTFIELD BAR
BURNLEY RD
MOOR LA
Park Head Farm
PARK HEAD
Horse Bowers
ACCRINGTON RD
WHALLEY RD A671
Black Hill
Miles Hill
MORETON PK
SHAWCLIFFE LA
BERRYS LA
Lower White Carr
DEAN LA
Heys Farm
Moreton Hall Farm
Cock Wood
BB12
Dean Wood
Dionysius Wood
Dean Bridge
BB6
A680
Cock Bridge

143
124

167
146

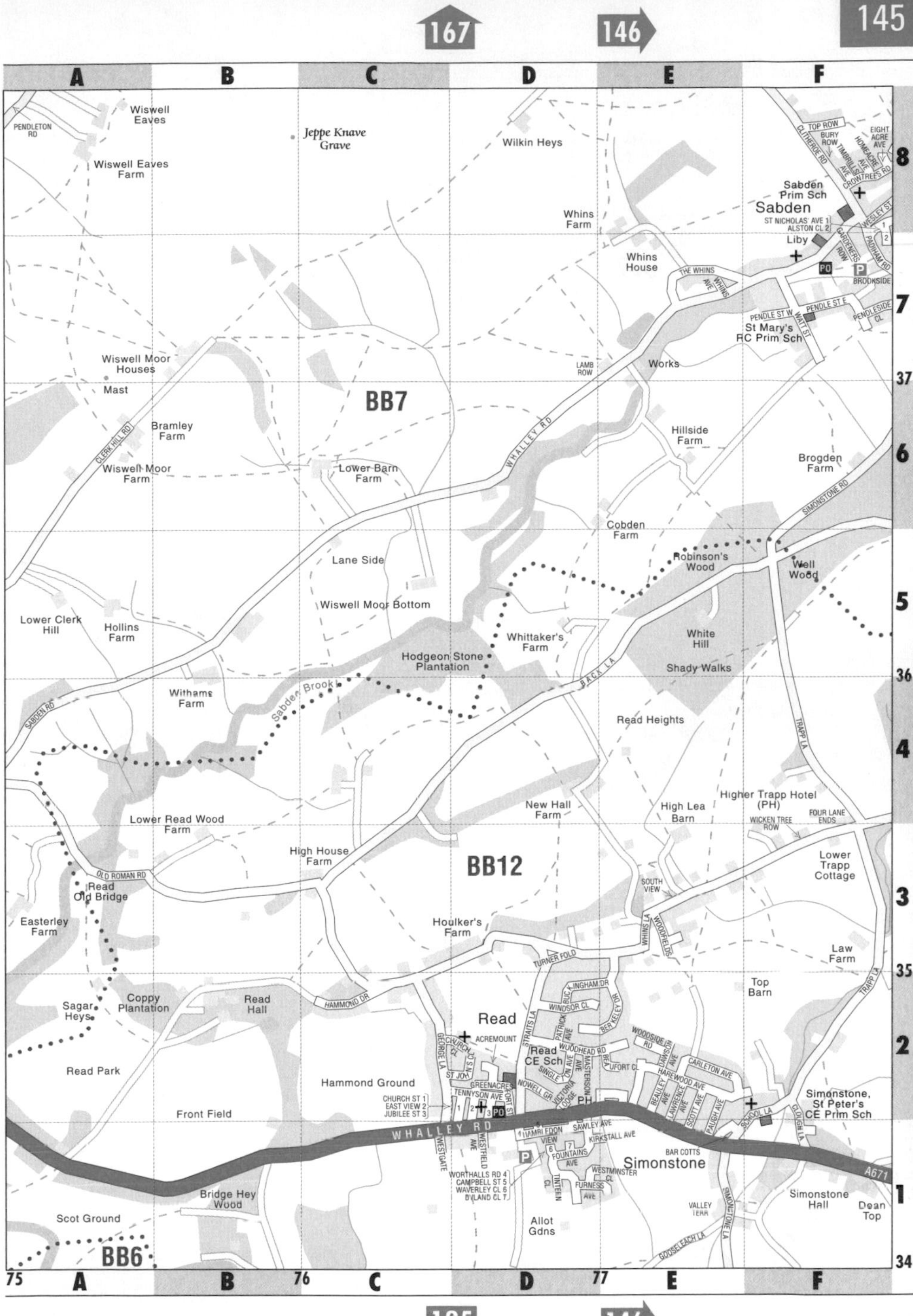

125
146

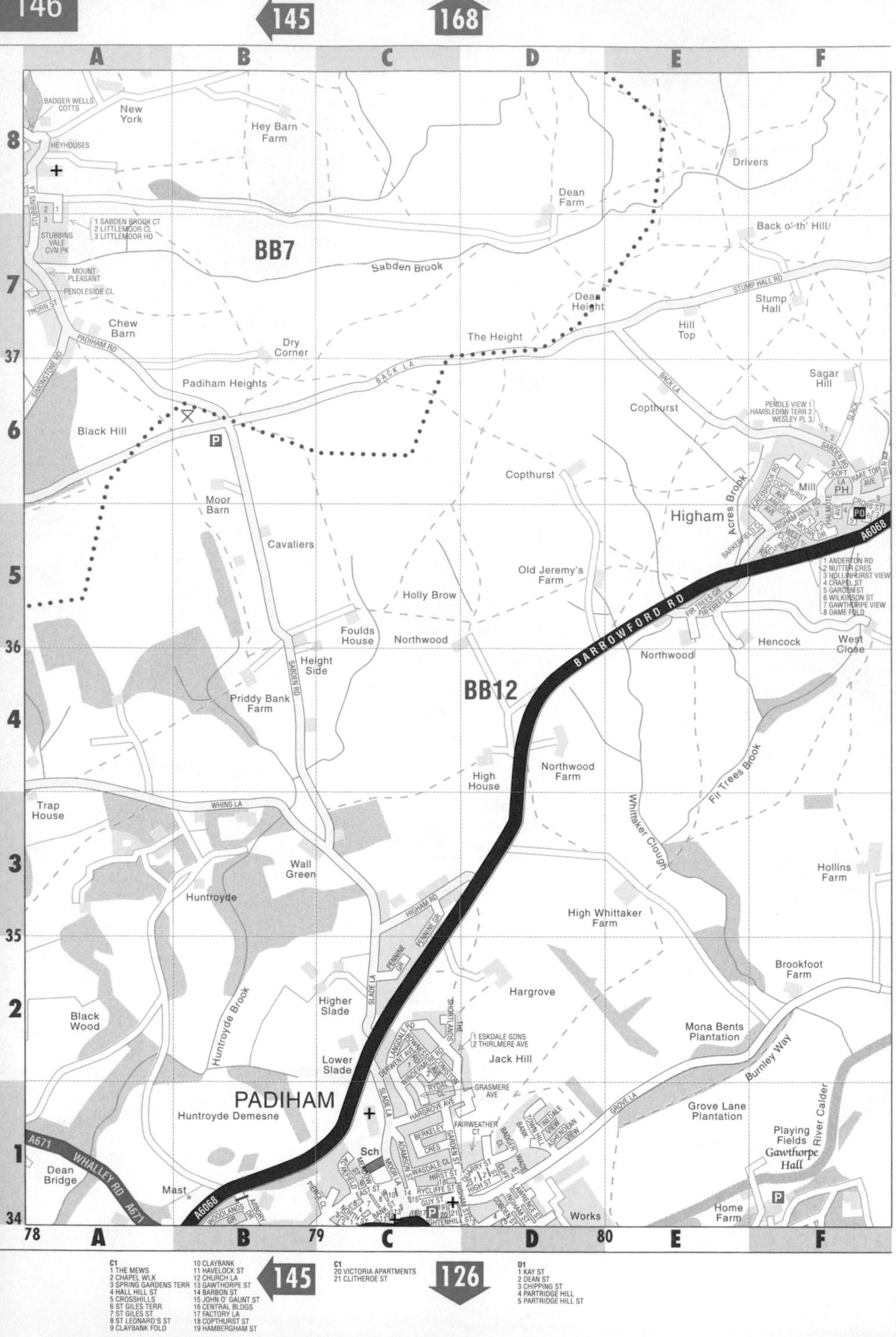
145
168
BB7
BB12
PADIHAM
Higham
BADGER WELLS COTTS
New York
Hey Barn Farm
HEYHOUSES
STUBBINS LA
1 SABDEN BROOK CT
2 LITTLEMOOR CL
3 LITTLEMOOR HO
STUBBINS VALE CVN PK
MOUNT PLEASANT
PENDLESIDE CL
THORN ST
Sabden Brook
Dean Farm
Drivers
Back o' th' Hill
STUMP HALL RD
Stump Hall
Hill Top
Dean Height
The Height
Chew Barn
Dry Corner
PADIHAM RD
SIMONSTONE RD
Padiham Heights
BACK LA
Black Hill
Copthurst
Sagar Hill
PENDLE VIEW 1
HAMBLEDON TERR 2
WESLEY PL 3
SABDEN RD
SLACK
Mill
PH
PO
Acres Brook
Moor Barn
Cavaliers
Old Jeremy's Farm
Holly Brow
BARROWFORD RD
FIR TREES GR
FIR TREES LA
A6068
1 ANDERTON RD
2 NUTTER CRES
3 HOLLINHURST VIEW
4 CHAPEL ST
5 GARDEN ST
6 WILKINSON ST
7 GAWTHORPE VIEW
8 DAME FOLD
Foulds House
Northwood
Hencock
West Close
Height Side
SABDEN RD
Priddy Bank Farm
Northwood Farm
High House
Fir Trees Brook
Whittaker Clough
Trap House
WHINS LA
Wall Green
Huntroyde
Hollins Farm
HIGHAM RD
PENNINE GR
High Whittaker Farm
Brookfoot Farm
SLADE LA
Higher Slade
Hargrove
Huntroyde Brook
Black Wood
THE SHORTLANDS
1 ESKDALE GDNS
2 THIRLMERE AVE
Jack Hill
Mona Bents Plantation
Burnley Way
Lower Slade
GRASMERE AVE
GROVE LA
Grove Lane Plantation
River Calder
Huntroyde Demesne
FAIRWEATHER CT
Playing Fields
Gawthorpe Hall
A671
WHALLEY RD
Dean Bridge
Sch
Mast
Works
Home Farm
P
A
B
C
D
E
F
1
2
3
4
5
6
7
8
34
35
36
37
78
79
80
C1
1 THE MEWS
2 CHAPEL WLK
3 SPRING GARDENS TERR
4 HALL HILL ST
5 CROSSHILLS
6 ST GILES TERR
7 ST GILES ST
8 ST LEONARD'S ST
9 CLAYBANK FOLD
10 CLAYBANK
11 HAVELOCK ST
12 CHURCH LA
13 GAWTHORPE ST
14 BARBON ST
15 JOHN O' GAUNT ST
16 CENTRAL BLDGS
17 FACTORY LA
18 COPTHURST ST
19 HAMBERGHAM ST
145
C1
20 VICTORIA APARTMENTS
21 CLITHEROE ST
126
D1
1 KAY ST
2 DEAN ST
3 CHIPPING ST
4 PARTRIDGE HILL
5 PARTRIDGE HILL ST

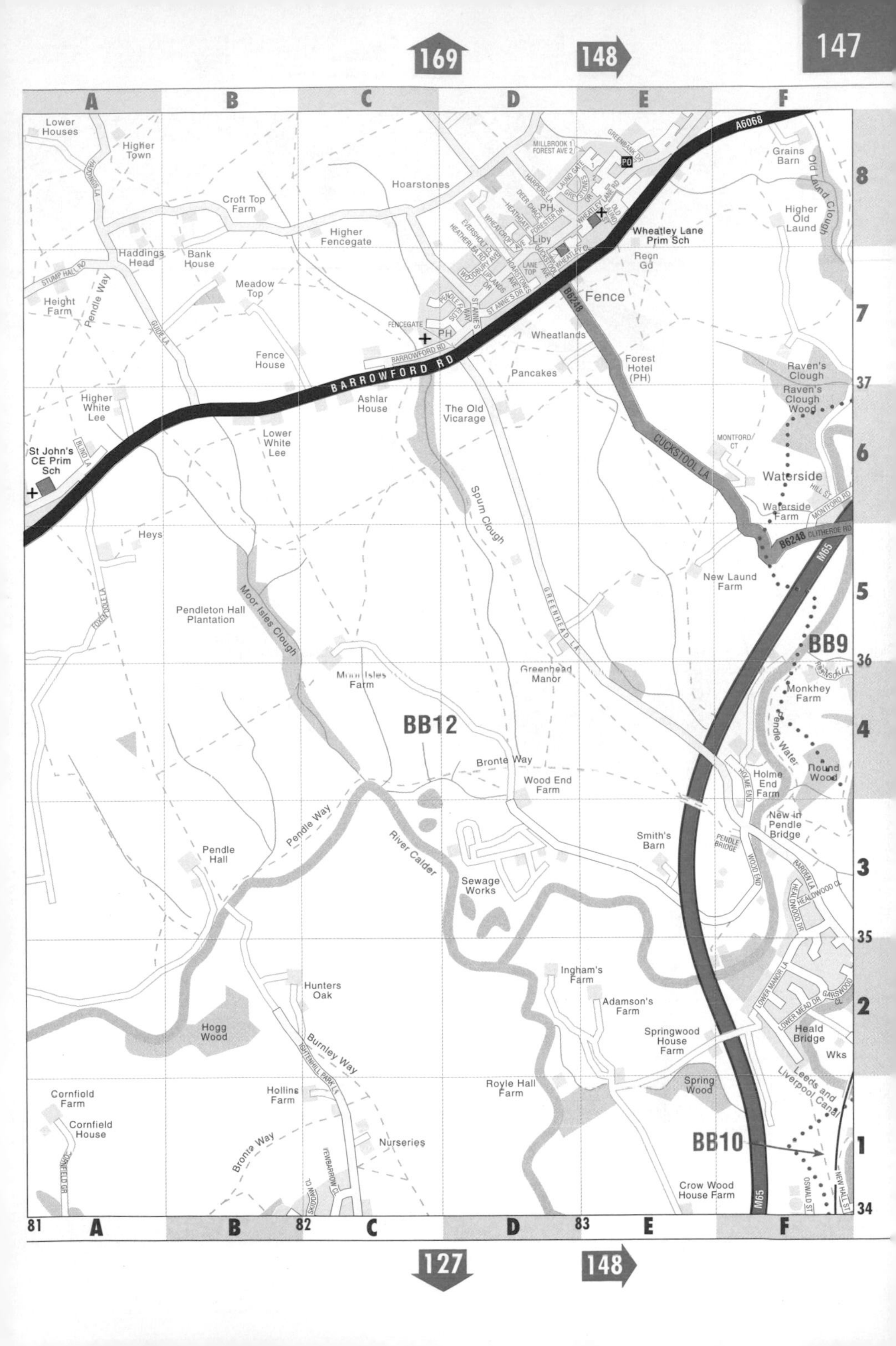
169
148
A
B
C
D
E
F
Lower Houses
Higher Town
Hoarstones
Croft Top Farm
Higher Fencegate
Haddings Head
Bank House
Meadow Top
Height Farm
Pendle Way
Fence House
Higher White Lee
St John's CE Prim Sch
Heys
Ashlar House
Lower White Lee
BARROWFORD RD
The Old Vicarage
Spurn Clough
Moor Isles Clough
Pendleton Hall Plantation
Moor Isles Farm
BB12
Bronte Way
Wood End Farm
Greenhead Manor
GREENHEAD LA
Pendle Hall
Pendle Way
River Calder
Sewage Works
Smith's Barn
Hunters Oak
Hogg Wood
Burnley Way
Ingham's Farm
Adamson's Farm
Springwood House Farm
Royle Hall Farm
Spring Wood
Hollins Farm
Cornfield Farm
Cornfield House
Bronte Way
Nurseries
Crow Wood House Farm
BB10
M65
Leeds and Liverpool Canal
Heald Bridge
Wks
New in Pendle Bridge
Holme End Farm
Pendle Water
Monkhey Farm
BB9
New Laund Farm
Waterside
Waterside Farm
B6248 CLITHEROE RD
CUCKSTOOL LA
Forest Hotel (PH)
Pancakes
Wheatlands
Fence
Wheatley Lane Prim Sch
Recn Gd
Higher Old Laund
Grains Barn
Old Laund Clough
A6068
Raven's Clough
Raven's Clough Wood
Round Wood
Liby
PH
8
7
6
5
4
3
2
1
37
36
35
34
81
82
83
127
148

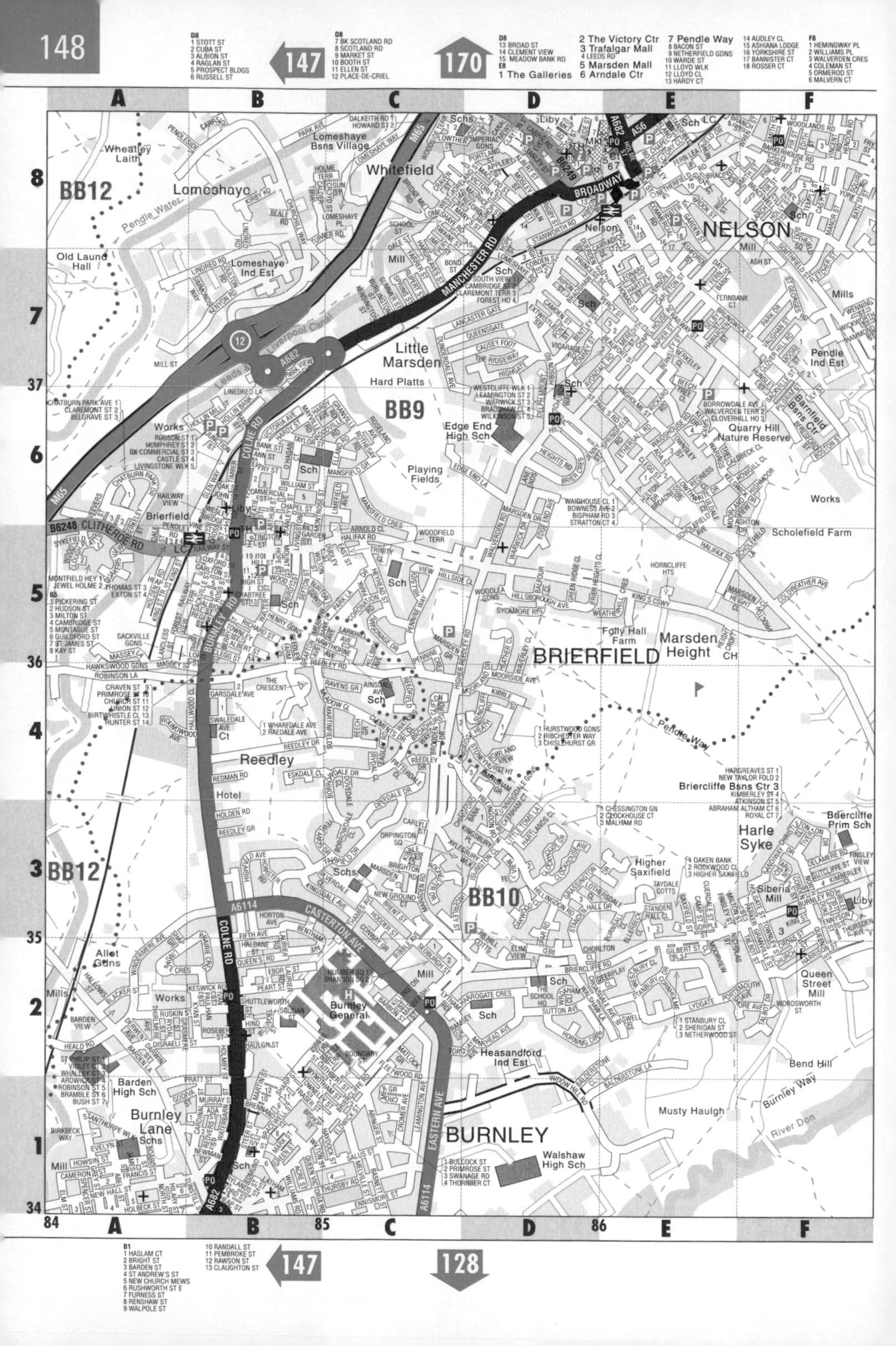
148
D8
1 STOTT ST
2 CUBA ST
3 ALBION ST
4 RAGLAN ST
5 PROSPECT BLDGS
6 RUSSELL ST
D8
7 BK SCOTLAND RD
8 SCOTLAND RD
9 MARKET ST
10 BOOTH ST
11 ELLEN ST
12 PLACE-DE-CRIEL
147
170
D8
13 BROAD ST
14 CLEMENT VIEW
15 MEADOW BANK RD
E8
1 The Galleries
2 The Victory Ctr
3 Trafalgar Mall
4 LEEDS RD
5 Marsden Mall
6 Arndale Ctr
7 Pendle Way
8 BACON ST
9 NETHERFIELD GDNS
10 WARDE ST
11 LLOYD WLK
12 LLOYD CL
13 HARDY CT
14 AUDLEY CL
15 ASHIANA LODGE
16 YORKSHIRE ST
17 BANNISTER CT
18 ROSSER CT
F8
1 HEMINGWAY PL
2 WILLIAMS PL
3 WALVERDEN CRES
4 COLEMAN ST
5 ORMEROD ST
6 MALVERN CT
A
B
C
D
E
F
8
7
37
6
5
36
4
3
35
2
1
34
84
85
86
Wheatley Laith
BB12
Lomeshaye
Pendle Water
Old Laund Hall
Lomeshaye Bsns Village
Whitefield
Lomeshaye Ind Est
NELSON
Nelson
BROADWAY
MANCHESTER RD
Little Marsden
Hard Platts
BB9
Edge End High Sch
Playing Fields
Quarry Hill Nature Reserve
Barnfield Bsns Ctr
Pendle Ind Est
Works
Scholefield Farm
Brierfield
CLITHEROE RD
B6248
M65
A682
COLNE RD
BURNLEY RD
BRIERFIELD
Marsden Height
Folly Hall Farm
Pendle Way
Reedley
Hotel
BB10
Higher Saxifield
Harle Syke
Briercliffe Prim Sch
Siberia Mill
Queen Street Mill
Briercliffe Bsns Ctr
CASTERTON AVE
A6114
Allot Gdns
Burnley General
Heasandford Ind Est
Barden High Sch
Burnley Lane Schs
BURNLEY
EASTERN AVE
Walshaw High Sch
Musty Haugh
Bend Hill
Burnley Way
River Don
B1
1 HASLAM CT
2 BRIGHT ST
3 BARDEN ST
4 ST ANDREW'S ST
5 NEW CHURCH MEWS
6 RUSHWORTH ST E
7 FURNESS ST
8 RENSHAW ST
9 WALPOLE ST
10 RANDALL ST
11 PEMBROKE ST
12 RAWSON ST
13 CLAUGHTON ST
147
128

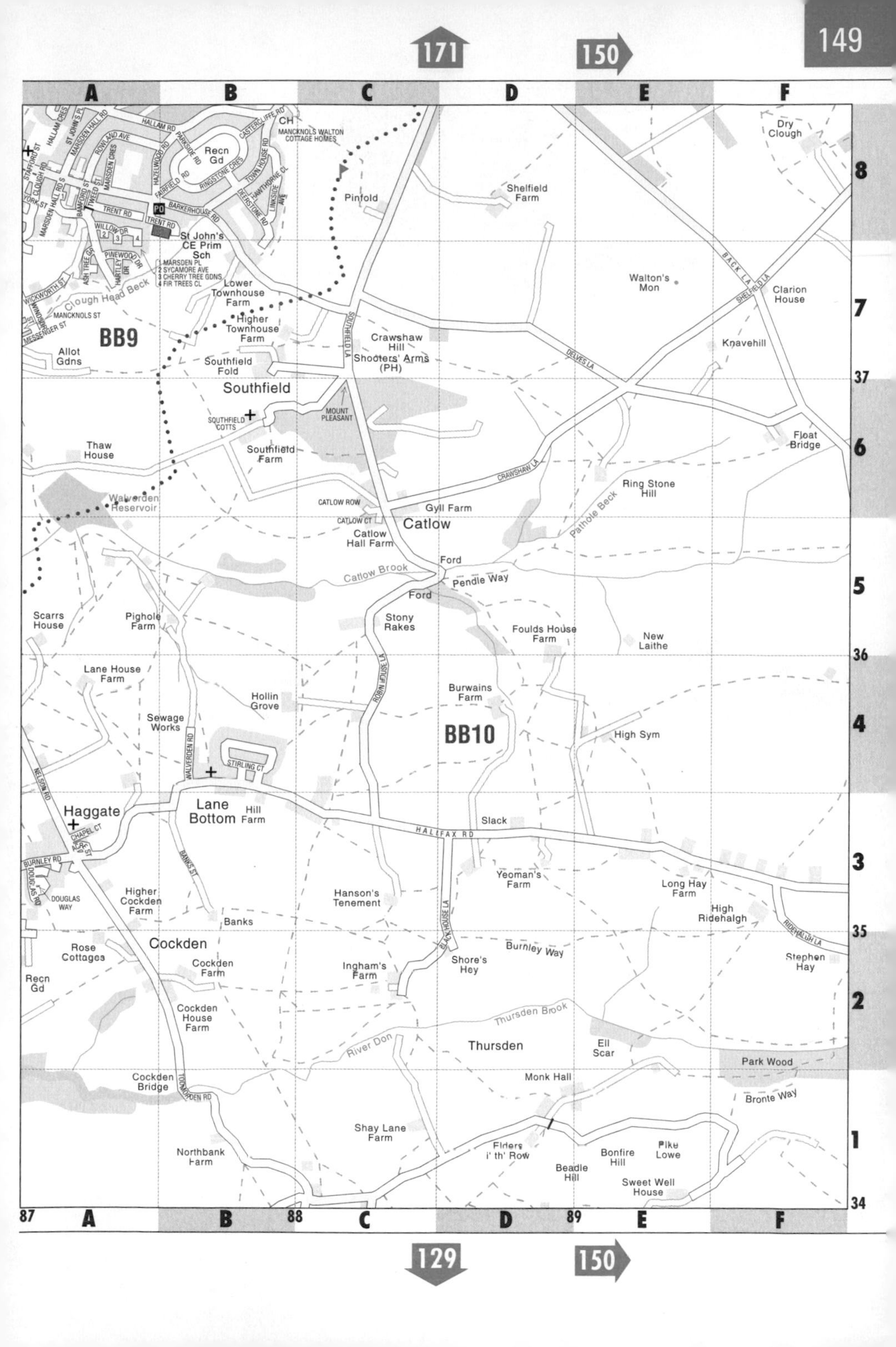
171
150
A
B
C
D
E
F
8
7
37
6
5
36
4
3
35
2
1
34
87
88
89
BB9
BB10
Recn Gd
CH
MANCKNOLS WALTON COTTAGE HOMES
Pinfold
Shelfield Farm
Dry Clough
St John's CE Prim Sch
Lower Townhouse Farm
Higher Townhouse Farm
Southfield Fold
Southfield
Walton's Mon
Clarion House
Knavehill
Crawshaw Hill
Shooters' Arms (PH)
MOUNT PLEASANT
SOUTHFIELD COTTS
Thaw House
Southfield Farm
Float Bridge
Ring Stone Hill
Pathole Beck
Walverden Reservoir
CATLOW ROW
CATLOW CT
Gyll Farm
Catlow
Catlow Hall Farm
Ford
Catlow Brook
Pendle Way
Scarrs House
Pighole Farm
Stony Rakes
Foulds House Farm
New Laithe
Lane House Farm
Hollin Grove
Burwains Farm
Sewage Works
High Sym
STIRLING CT
Haggate
Lane Bottom
Hill Farm
Slack
HALIFAX RD
Yeoman's Farm
Long Hay Farm
Higher Cockden Farm
Hanson's Tenement
High Ridehalgh
Banks
Cockden
Rose Cottages
Cockden Farm
Ingham's Farm
Shore's Hey
Burnley Way
Stephen Hay
Recn Gd
Cockden House Farm
Thursden Brook
River Don
Thursden
Ell Scar
Park Wood
Cockden Bridge
Monk Hall
Bronte Way
Shay Lane Farm
Northbank Farm
Elders i' th' Row
Beadle Hill
Bonfire Hill
Pike Lowe
Sweet Well House
Clough Head Beck
MANCKNOLS ST
MESSENGER ST
WICKWORTH ST
Allot Gdns
HALLAM RD
BARKERHOUSE RD
TRENT RD
CRAWSHAW LA
DELVES LA
BACK LA
SHELFIELD LA
SOUTHFIELD LA
ROBIN HOUSE LA
WALVERDEN RD
NELSON RD
BURNLEY RD
CHAPEL CT
DOUGLAS WAY
BANKS ST
BLACK HOUSE LA
TODMORDEN RD
RIDEHALGH LA
1 MARSDEN PL
2 SYCAMORE AVE
3 CHERRY TREE GDNS
4 FIR TREES CL
129
150

149
172

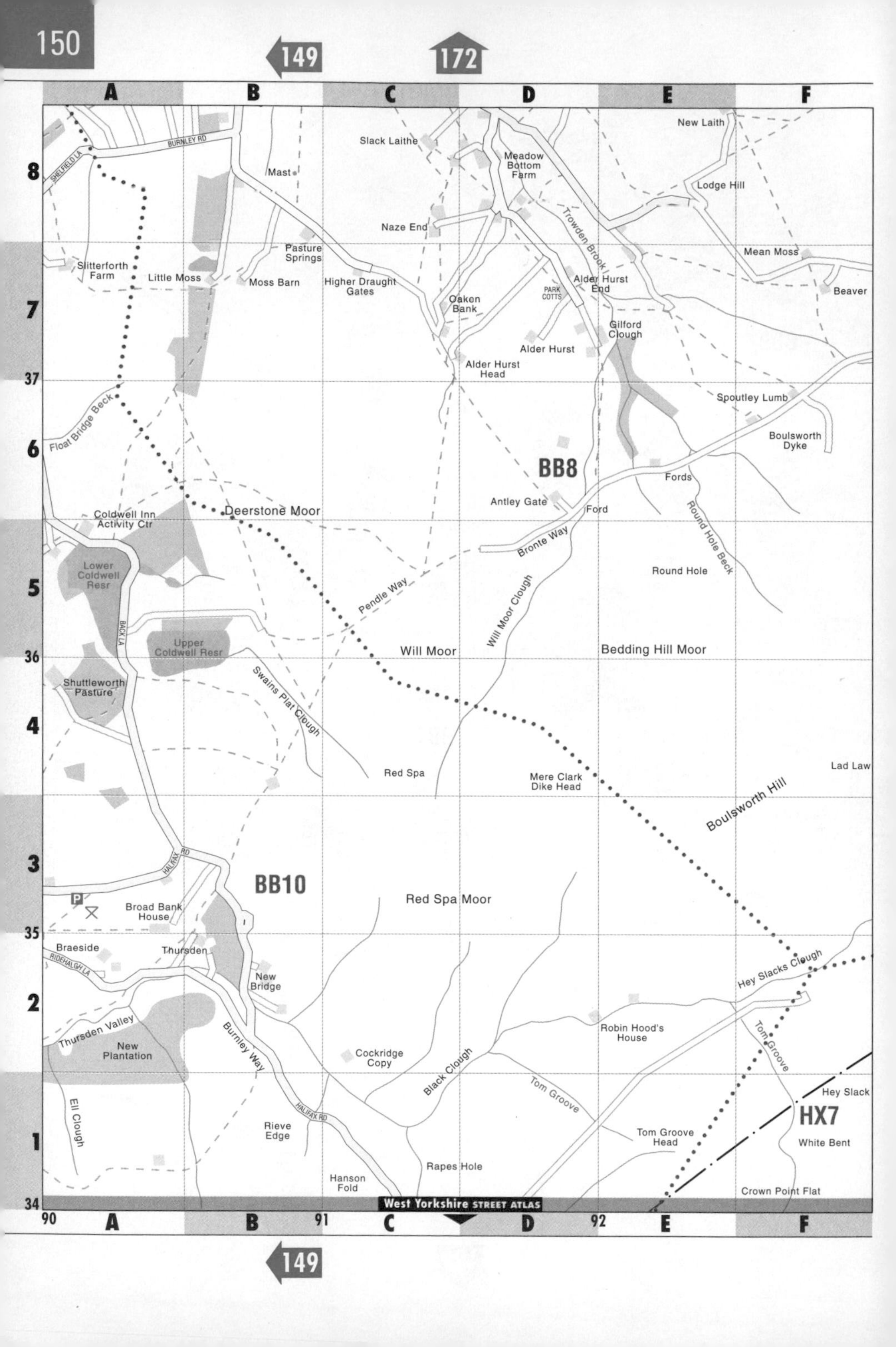
A
B
C
D
E
F
8
7
37
6
5
36
4
3
35
2
1
34
90
91
92
BURNLEY RD
SHELFIELD LA
Slack Laithe
Mast
Meadow Bottom Farm
New Laith
Lodge Hill
Naze End
Trowden Brook
Pasture Springs
Mean Moss
Slitterforth Farm
Little Moss
Moss Barn
Higher Draught Gates
Alder Hurst End
PARK COTTS
Beaver
Oaken Bank
Gilford Clough
Alder Hurst
Alder Hurst Head
Spoutley Lumb
Float Bridge Beck
Boulsworth Dyke
BB8
Fords
Antley Gate
Ford
Deerstone Moor
Coldwell Inn Activity Ctr
Round Hole Beck
Bronte Way
Round Hole
Lower Coldwell Resr
Pendle Way
Will Moor Clough
BACK LA
Upper Coldwell Resr
Will Moor
Bedding Hill Moor
Shuttleworth Pasture
Swains Plat Clough
Red Spa
Mere Clark Dike Head
Lad Law
Boulsworth Hill
HALIFAX RD
BB10
Broad Bank House
Red Spa Moor
Braeside
Thursden
RIDEHALGH LA
New Bridge
Hey Slacks Clough
Robin Hood's House
Thursden Valley
New Plantation
Burnley Way
Cockridge Copy
Tom Groove
Black Clough
Tom Groove
Hey Slack
HALIFAX RD
HX7
Ell Clough
Rieve Edge
Tom Groove Head
White Bent
Rapes Hole
Hanson Fold
Crown Point Flat

173

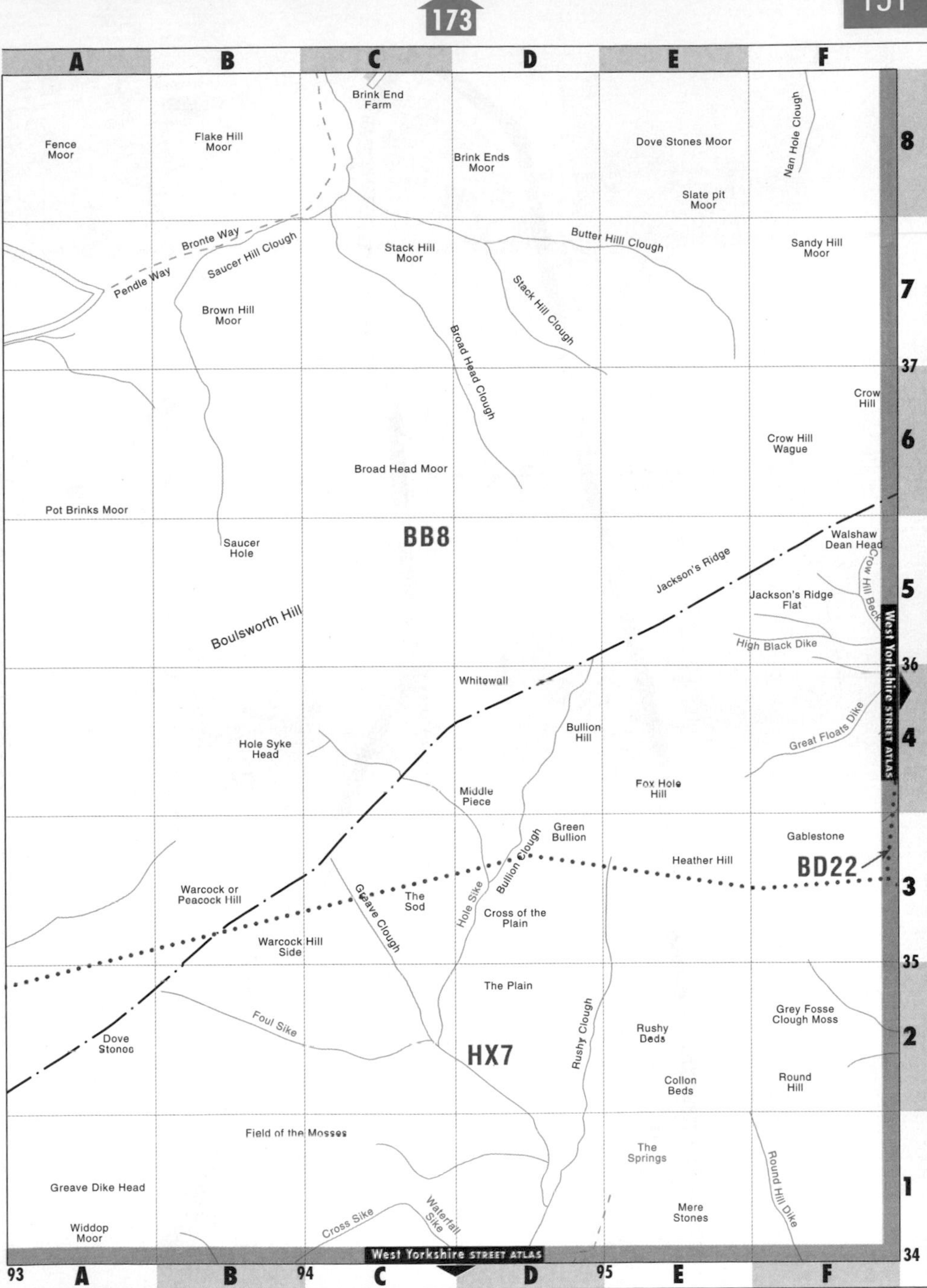
A
B
C
D
E
F
Brink End Farm
Fence Moor
Flake Hill Moor
Brink Ends Moor
Dove Stones Moor
Nan Hole Clough
Slate pit Moor
8
Bronte Way
Saucer Hill Clough
Pendle Way
Stack Hill Moor
Butter Hilll Clough
Sandy Hill Moor
Stack Hill Clough
Brown Hill Moor
Broad Head Clough
7
37
Crow Hill
Crow Hill Wague
6
Broad Head Moor
Pot Brinks Moor
BB8
Saucer Hole
Walshaw Dean Head
Jackson's Ridge
Crow Hill Beck
Jackson's Ridge Flat
5
Boulsworth Hill
High Black Dike
36
Whitewall
West Yorkshire STREET ATLAS
Bullion Hill
Great Floats Dike
Hole Syke Head
4
Fox Hole Hill
Middle Piece
Green Bullion
Gablestone
Bullion Clough
Heather Hill
BD22
Warcock or Peacock Hill
Greave Clough
The Sod
Hole Sike
3
Cross of the Plain
Warcock Hill Side
35
The Plain
Grey Fosse Clough Moss
Foul Sike
Rushy Clough
Rushy Deds
Dove Stones
HX7
2
Collon Beds
Round Hill
Field of the Mosses
The Springs
Greave Dike Head
Round Hill Dike
1
Waterfall Sike
Mere Stones
Cross Sike
Widdop Moor
West Yorkshire STREET ATLAS
34
93
94
95

175

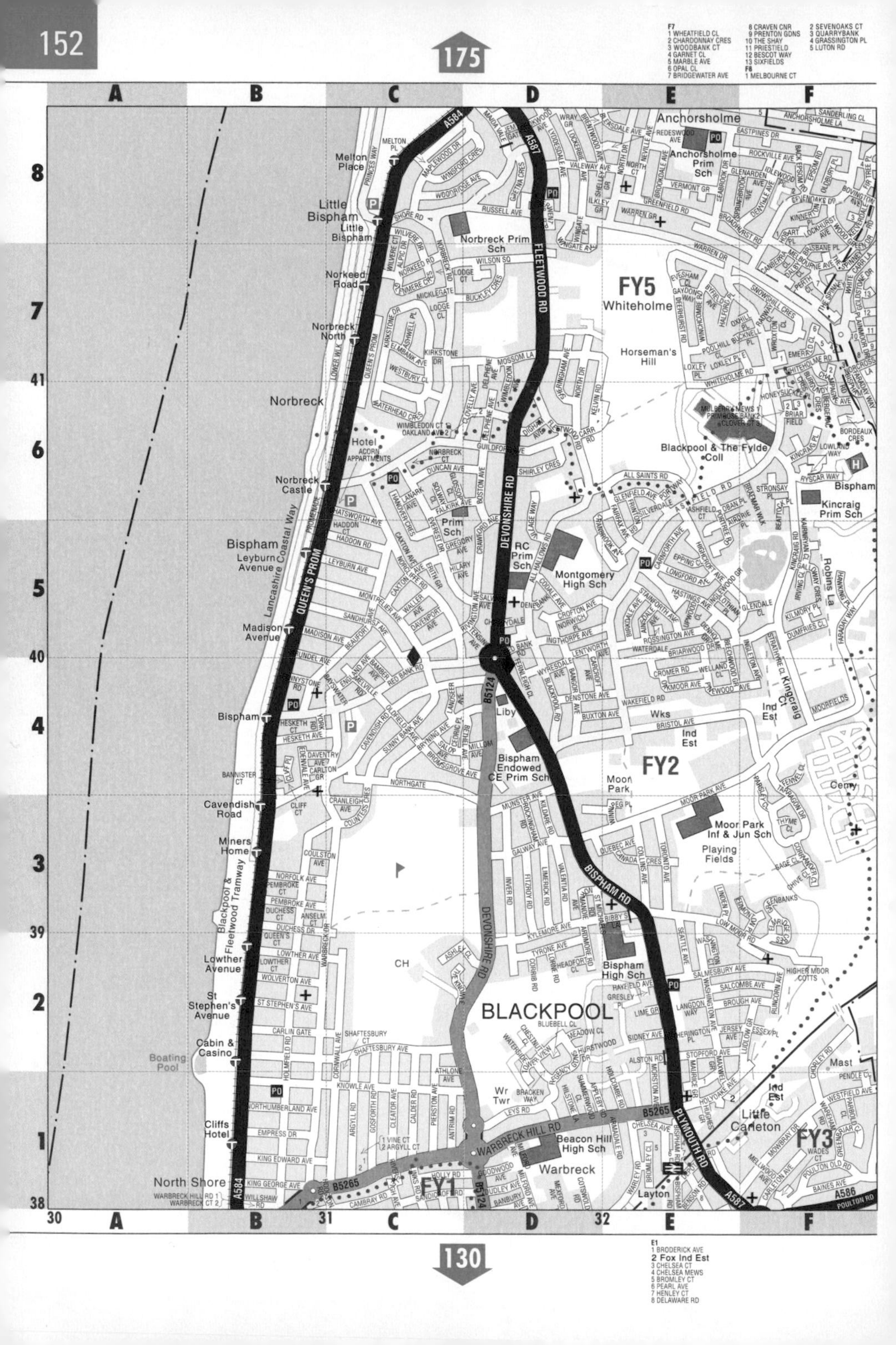
F7
1 WHEATFIELD CL
2 CHARDONNAY CRES
3 WOODBANK CT
4 GARNET CL
5 MARBLE AVE
6 OPAL CL
7 BRIDGEWATER AVE
8 CRAVEN CNR
9 PRENTON GDNS
10 THE SHAY
11 PRIESTIELD
12 BESCOT WAY
13 SIXFIELDS
F8
1 MELBOURNE CT
2 SEVENOAKS CT
3 QUARRYBANK
4 GRASSINGTON PL
5 LUTON RD
A
B
C
D
E
F
8
7
41
6
5
40
4
3
39
2
1
38
30
31
32
Anchorsholme
Anchorsholme Prim Sch
Melton Place
Little Bispham
Norbreck Prim Sch
FY5
Whiteholme
Norkeed Road
Norbreck North
Horseman's Hill
Norbreck
Hotel
Blackpool & The Fylde Coll
Norbreck Castle
Bispham
Kincraig Prim Sch
Prim Sch
RC Prim Sch
Bispham
Leyburn Avenue
Montgomery High Sch
Lancashire Coastal Way
Robins La
Madison Avenue
QUEEN'S PROM
FLEETWOOD RD
DEVONSHIRE RD
A584
A587
B5124
Liby
Kincraig Ct
Ind Est
Wks
Ind Est
Bispham Endowed CE Prim Sch
FY2
Moor Park
Cemy
Cavendish Road
Moor Park Inf & Jun Sch
Miners Home
Playing Fields
BISPHAM RD
Blackpool & Fleetwood Tramway
Lowther Avenue
CH
Bispham High Sch
St Stephen's Avenue
BLACKPOOL
Cabin & Casino
Boating Pool
Mast
Wr Twr
Ind Est
Cliffs Hotel
WARBRECK HILL RD
B5265
Beacon Hill High Sch
Little Carleton
FY3
PLYMOUTH RD
Warbreck
North Shore
FY1
Layton
A586
POULTON RD
E1
1 BRODERICK AVE
2 Fox Ind Est
3 CHELSEA CT
4 CHELSEA MEWS
5 BROMLEY CT
6 PEARL AVE
7 HENLEY CT
8 DELAWARE RD

130

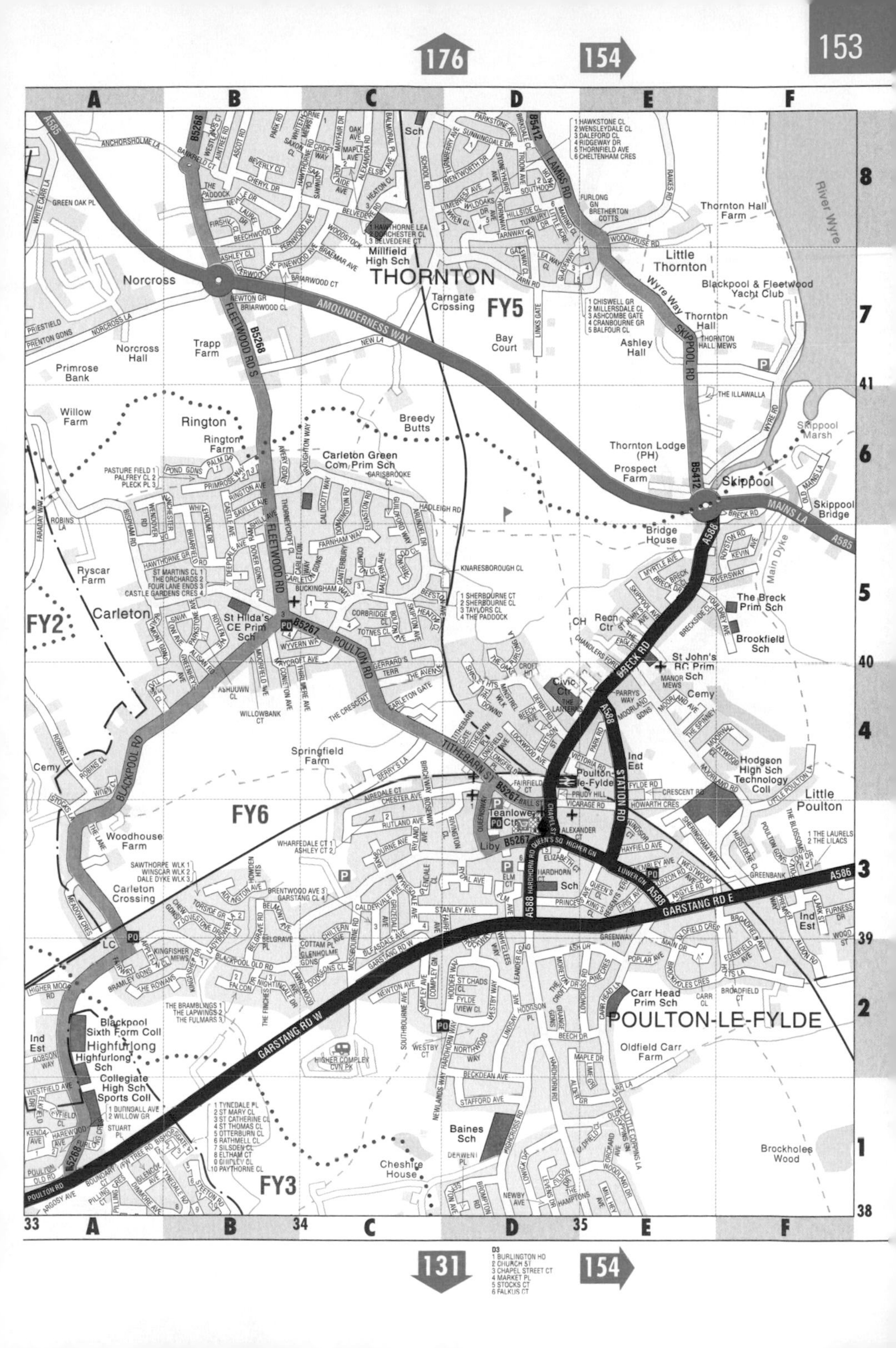
176
154
A
B
C
D
E
F
8
7
41
6
5
40
4
3
39
2
1
38
33
34
35
THORNTON
FY5
Norcross
Trapp Farm
Norcross Hall
Primrose Bank
Willow Farm
Rington
Rington Farm
Breedy Butts
Carleton Green Com Prim Sch
Millfield High Sch
Tarngate Crossing
Bay Court
Little Thornton
Thornton Hall Farm
Blackpool & Fleetwood Yacht Club
Thornton Hall
Ashley Hall
River Wyre
Skippool Marsh
Thornton Lodge (PH)
Prospect Farm
Skippool
Skippool Bridge
Bridge House
Ryscar Farm
Carleton
FY2
St Hilda's CE Prim Sch
Recn Ctr
Civic Ctr
The Breck Prim Sch
Brookfield Sch
St John's RC Prim Sch
Cemy
Springfield Farm
Ind Est
Hodgson High Sch Technology Coll
Little Poulton
FY6
Woodhouse Farm
Carleton Crossing
Teanlowe Ctr
Liby
Sch
Carr Head Prim Sch
POULTON-LE-FYLDE
Oldfield Carr Farm
Blackpool Sixth Form Coll
Highfurlong
Highfurlong Sch
Collegiate High Sch Sports Coll
Higher Complex Cvn Pk
Baines Sch
Cheshire House
FY3
Brockholes Wood
AMOUNDERNESS WAY
FLEETWOOD RD S
FLEETWOOD RD
BLACKPOOL RD
POULTON RD
TITHEBARN ST
BRECK RD
STATION RD
SKIPPOOL RD
GARSTANG RD E
GARSTANG RD W
MAINS LA
Wyre Way
A585
A586
A588
B5268
B5267
B5412
1 HAWKSTONE CL
2 WENSLEYDALE CL
3 DALEFORD CL
4 RIDGEWAY DR
5 THORNFIELD AVE
6 CHELTENHAM CRES
1 CHISWELL GR
2 MILLERSDALE CL
3 ASHCOMBE GATE
4 CRANBOURNE GR
5 BALFOUR CL
1 HAWTHORNE LEA
2 DORCHESTER CL
3 BELVEDERE CT
1 SHERBOURNE CT
2 SHERBOURNE CL
3 TAYLORS CL
4 THE PADDOCK
1 THE LAURELS
2 THE LILACS
1 TYNEDALE PL
2 ST MARY CL
3 ST CATHERINE CL
4 ST THOMAS CL
5 OTTERBURN CL
6 RATHMELL CL
7 SILSDEN CL
8 ELTHAM CT
9 GHIRLEY CL
10 PAYTHORNE CL
1 BURNSALL AVE
2 WILLOW GR
131
154
D3
1 BURLINGTON HO
2 CHURCH ST
3 CHAPEL STREET CT
4 MARKET PL
5 STOCKS CT
6 FALKUS CT

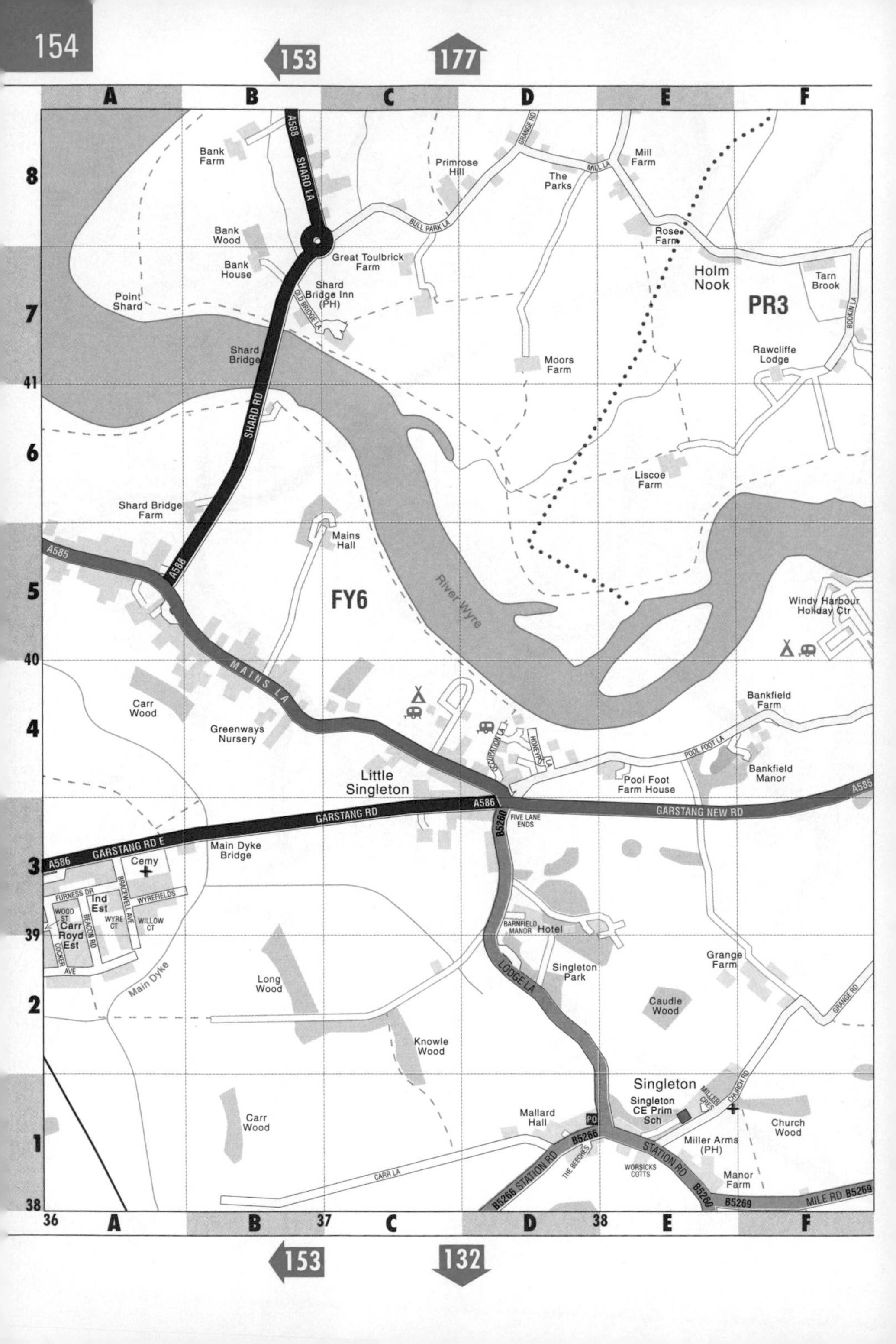
153
177
A
B
C
D
E
F
8
7
41
6
5
40
4
3
39
2
1
38
36
37
38
132
Bank Farm
A588
SHARD LA
Primrose Hill
GRANGE RD
The Parks
MILL LA
Mill Farm
Bank Wood
BULL PARK LA
Rose Farm
Bank House
Great Toulbrick Farm
Holm Nook
Tarn Brook
Point Shard
Shard Bridge Inn (PH)
OLD BRIDGE LA
PR3
BOOKIN LA
Shard Bridge
Moors Farm
Rawcliffe Lodge
SHARD RD
Liscoe Farm
Shard Bridge Farm
Mains Hall
A585
River Wyre
FY6
Windy Harbour Holiday Ctr
MAINS LA
Carr Wood
Bankfield Farm
Greenways Nursery
OCCUPATION LA
HONEYPOT LA
POOL FOOT LA
Bankfield Manor
Little Singleton
Pool Foot Farm House
A586
GARSTANG RD
FIVE LANE ENDS
GARSTANG NEW RD
B5260
GARSTANG RD E
Main Dyke Bridge
Cemy
FURNESS DR
Ind Est
BRACEWELL AVE
WYREFIELDS
WOOD ST
Carr Royd Est
BEACON RD
WYRE CT
WILLOW CT
BARNFIELD MANOR
Hotel
COCKER AVE
Grange Farm
Main Dyke
Long Wood
LODGE LA
Singleton Park
GRANGE RD
Caudle Wood
Knowle Wood
Singleton
MILLER CRES
CHURCH RD
Singleton CE Prim Sch
Carr Wood
Mallard Hall
PO
Church Wood
B5266
Miller Arms (PH)
CARR LA
THE BEECHES
STATION RD
WORSICKS COTTS
Manor Farm
B5266 STATION RD
B5269
MILE RD B5269

153
132

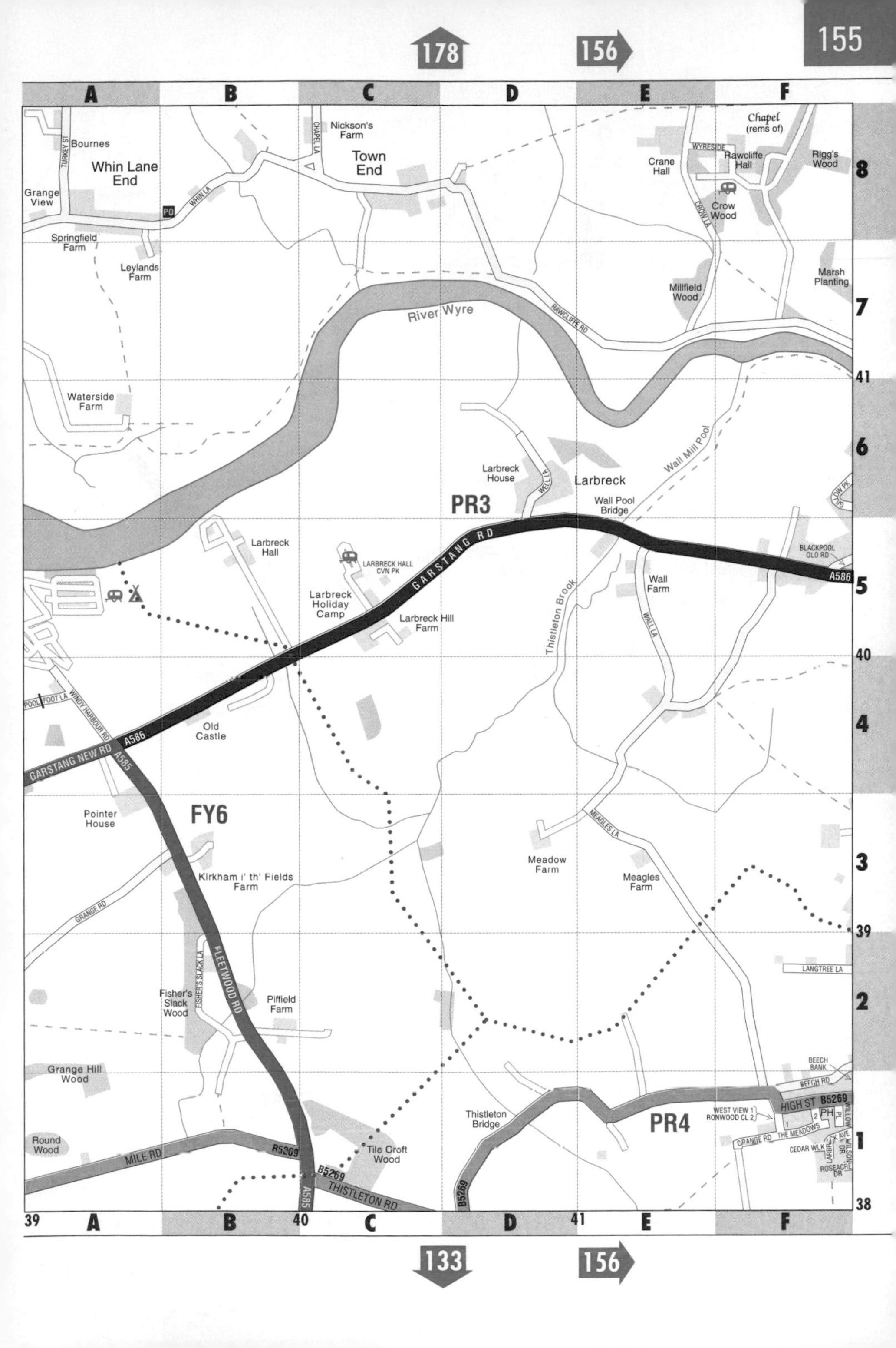
178
156
A
B
C
D
E
F
Bournes
Whin Lane End
Grange View
Springfield Farm
Leylands Farm
Nickson's Farm
Town End
Crane Hall
Rawcliffe Hall
Chapel (rems of)
Rigg's Wood
Crow Wood
Millfield Wood
Marsh Planting
River Wyre
RAWCLIFFE RD
Waterside Farm
Larbreck House
Larbreck
Wall Mill Pool
Wall Pool Bridge
PR3
GARSTANG RD
Larbreck Hall
LARBRECK HALL CVN PK
Larbreck Holiday Camp
Larbreck Hill Farm
Thistleton Brook
Wall Farm
BLACKPOOL OLD RD
A586
Old Castle
GARSTANG NEW RD
A585
FY6
Pointer House
Kirkham i' th' Fields Farm
Meadow Farm
Meagles Farm
MEAGLES LA
LANGTREE LA
FLEETWOOD RD
Fisher's Slack Wood
Piffield Farm
Grange Hill Wood
Round Wood
MILE RD
B5269
THISTLETON RD
Tile Croft Wood
Thistleton Bridge
PR4
HIGH ST
BEECH BANK
BEECH RD
WEST VIEW 1
RONWOOD CL 2
GRANGE RD
THE MEADOWS
CEDAR WLK
ROSEACRE DR
8
7
41
6
5
40
4
3
39
2
1
38
39
40
41

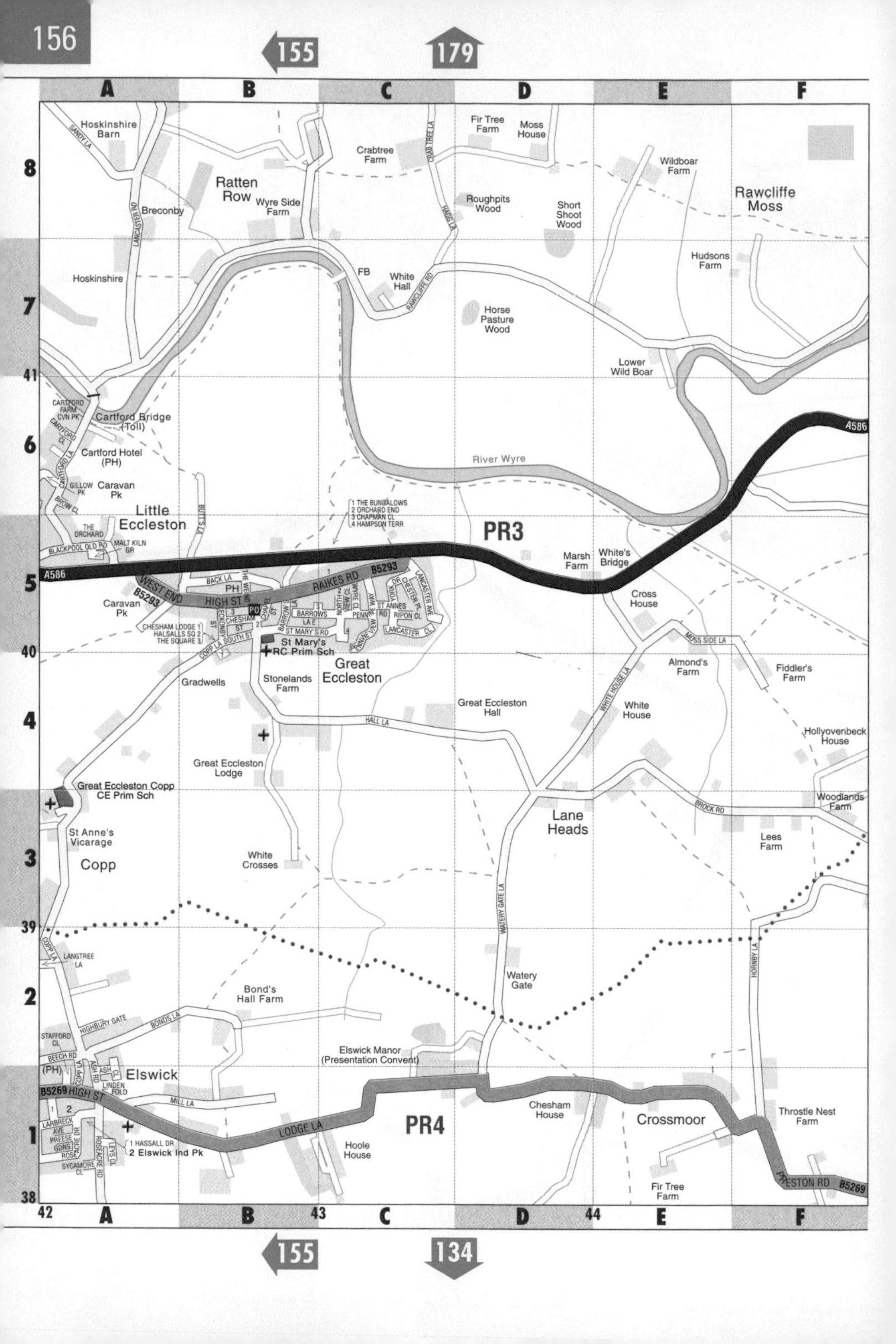
155
179
A
B
C
D
E
F
8
7
6
5
4
3
2
1
41
40
39
38
42
43
44
Hoskinshire Barn
SANDY LA
Ratten Row
Breconby
LANCASTER RD
Wyre Side Farm
Crabtree Farm
CRAB TREE LA
Fir Tree Farm
Moss House
Wildboar Farm
Rawcliffe Moss
Roughpits Wood
HAGG LA
Short Shoot Wood
Hudsons Farm
Hoskinshire
FB
White Hall
RAWCLIFFE RD
Horse Pasture Wood
Lower Wild Boar
CARTFORD FARM CVN PK
Cartford Bridge (Toll)
CARTFORD CL
Cartford Hotel (PH)
CARTFORD LA
GILLOW PK
Caravan Pk
BROW CL
Little Eccleston
BUTTS LA
THE ORCHARD
BLACKPOOL OLD RD
MALT KILN GR
River Wyre
A586
1 THE BUNGALOWS
2 ORCHARD END
3 CHAPMAN CL
4 HAMPSON TERR
PR3
Marsh Farm
White's Bridge
WEST END
B5293
BACK LA
PH
THE WEND
HIGH ST
RAIKES RD
LANCASTER AVE
CHESTER PL
Caravan Pk
CHESHAM LODGE 1
HALSALLS SQ 2
THE SQUARE 3
ECKONBY ST
CHESHAM ST
SOUTH ST
COPP LA
PO
CHAPEL ST
BARROWS LA
BARROWS LA E
ST MARY'S RD
WYRE CL
VIEW CL
NORTH ST
PENNINE VIEW
WAY
PENN RD
ST ANNES RD
RIPON CL
LANCASTER CL
Cross House
MOSS SIDE LA
St Mary's RC Prim Sch
Great Eccleston
Gradwells
Stonelands Farm
Almond's Farm
Fiddler's Farm
WHITE HOUSE LA
White House
Great Eccleston Hall
HALL LA
Hollyovenbeck House
Great Eccleston Lodge
Great Eccleston Copp CE Prim Sch
Lane Heads
BROCK RD
Woodlands Farm
St Anne's Vicarage
Copp
White Crosses
Lees Farm
WATERY GATE LA
COPP LA
LANGTREE LA
HORNBY LA
Watery Gate
Bond's Hall Farm
HIGHBURY GATE
BONDS LA
STAFFORD CL
BEECH RD
(PH)
COPP LA
ASH RD
ASH CL
Elsworth
Elswick
Elswick Manor (Presentation Convent)
LINDEN FOLD
B5269 HIGH ST
MILL LA
LARBRECK AVE
PREESE GDNS
ROSEACRE DR
ROSEACRE RD
LEYS CL
SYCAMORE CL
1 HASSALL DR
2 Elswick Ind Pk
LODGE LA
PR4
Chesham House
Crossmoor
Throstle Nest Farm
Hoole House
Fir Tree Farm
PRESTON RD
B5269
155
134

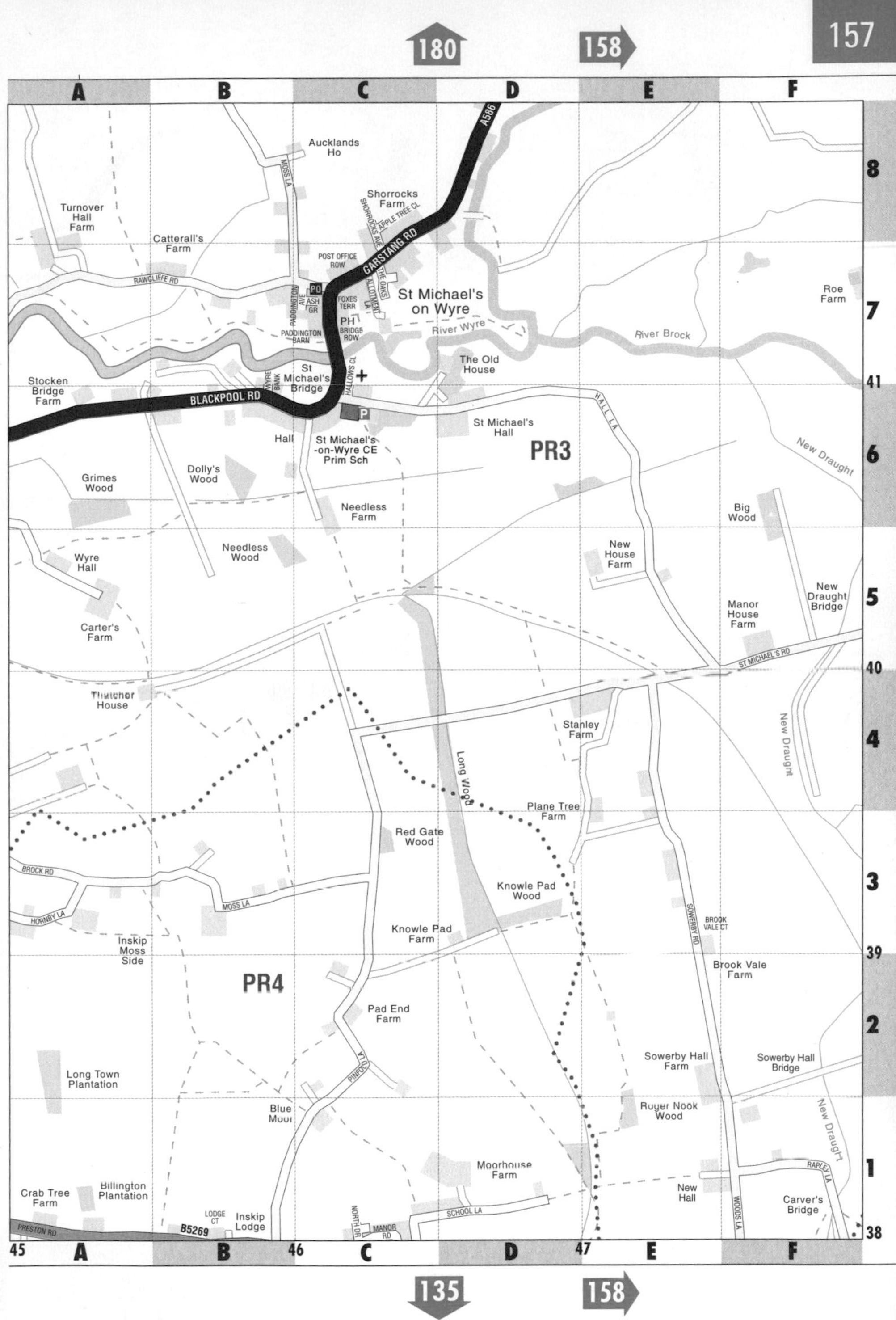
A
B
C
D
E
F
8
7
6
5
4
3
2
1
41
40
39
38
45
46
47
A586
Aucklands Ho
MOSS LA
Shorrocks Farm
SHORROCKS AVE
APPLE TREE CL
GARSTANG RD
Turnover Hall Farm
Catterall's Farm
POST OFFICE ROW
RAWCLIFFE RD
PO
PADDINGTON AVE
ASH GR
FOXES TERR
ALLOTMENT LA
THE OAKS
St Michael's on Wyre
Roe Farm
PH
BRIDGE ROW
PADDINGTON BARN
River Wyre
River Brock
The Old House
Stocken Bridge Farm
WYRE BANK
St Michael's Bridge
HALLOWS CL
BLACKPOOL RD
P
HALL LA
St Michael's Hall
Hall
St Michael's -on-Wyre CE Prim Sch
PR3
New Draught
Grimes Wood
Dolly's Wood
Needless Farm
Big Wood
Wyre Hall
Needless Wood
New House Farm
New Draught Bridge
Manor House Farm
Carter's Farm
ST MICHAEL'S RD
Thatcher House
New Draught
Stanley Farm
Long Wood
Plane Tree Farm
Red Gate Wood
BROCK RD
Knowle Pad Wood
MOSS LA
HORNBY LA
SOWERBY RD
BROOK VALE CT
Knowle Pad Farm
Inskip Moss Side
Brook Vale Farm
PR4
Pad End Farm
Sowerby Hall Farm
Sowerby Hall Bridge
PINFOLD LA
Long Town Plantation
Blue Moor
Roger Nook Wood
New Draught
Moorhouse Farm
RAPLEY LA
Crab Tree Farm
Billington Plantation
New Hall
Carver's Bridge
LODGE CT
Inskip Lodge
NORTH DR
MANOR RD
SCHOOL LA
WOODS LA
PRESTON RD
B5269

157
181

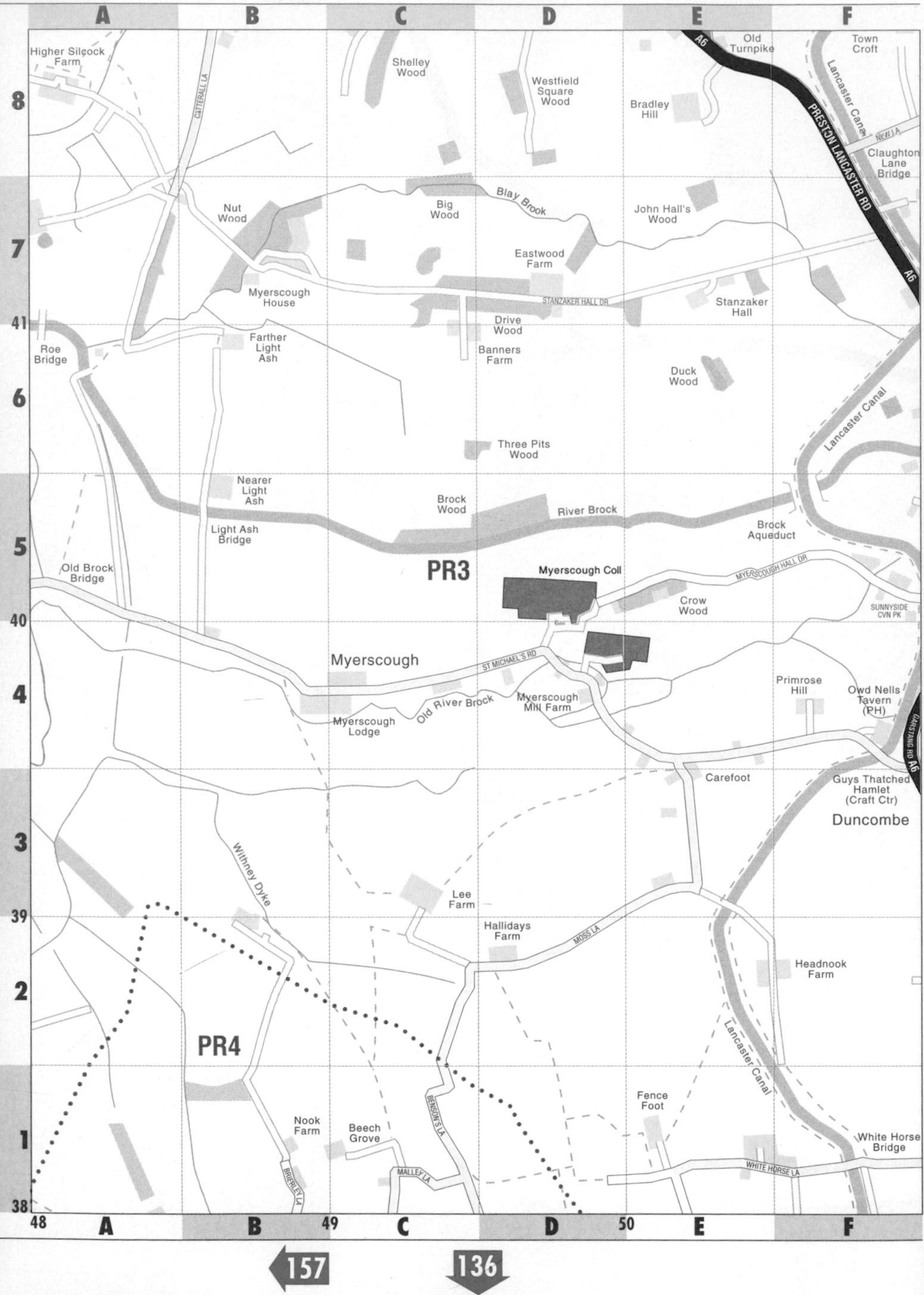
A
B
C
D
E
F
8
7
41
6
5
40
4
3
39
2
1
38
48
49
50
Higher Silcock Farm
Catterall La
Shelley Wood
Westfield Square Wood
Old Turnpike
Town Croft
Bradley Hill
Lancaster Canal
Preston Lancaster Rd
A6
Claughton Lane Bridge
Nut Wood
Big Wood
Blay Brook
John Hall's Wood
Eastwood Farm
Myerscough House
Stanzaker Hall Dr
Stanzaker Hall
Drive Wood
Roe Bridge
Farther Light Ash
Banners Farm
Duck Wood
Three Pits Wood
Nearer Light Ash
Brock Wood
River Brock
Light Ash Bridge
Brock Aqueduct
Old Brock Bridge
PR3
Myerscough Coll
Myerscough Hall Dr
Crow Wood
Sunnyside Cvn Pk
Myerscough
St Michael's Rd
Primrose Hill
Owd Nells Tavern (PH)
Old River Brock
Myerscough Mill Farm
Myerscough Lodge
Garstang Rd
Carefoot
Guys Thatched Hamlet (Craft Ctr)
Duncombe
Withney Dyke
Lee Farm
Hallidays Farm
Moss La
Headnook Farm
PR4
Fence Foot
Nook Farm
Beech Grove
Benson's La
Brierley La
Malley La
White Horse La
White Horse Bridge

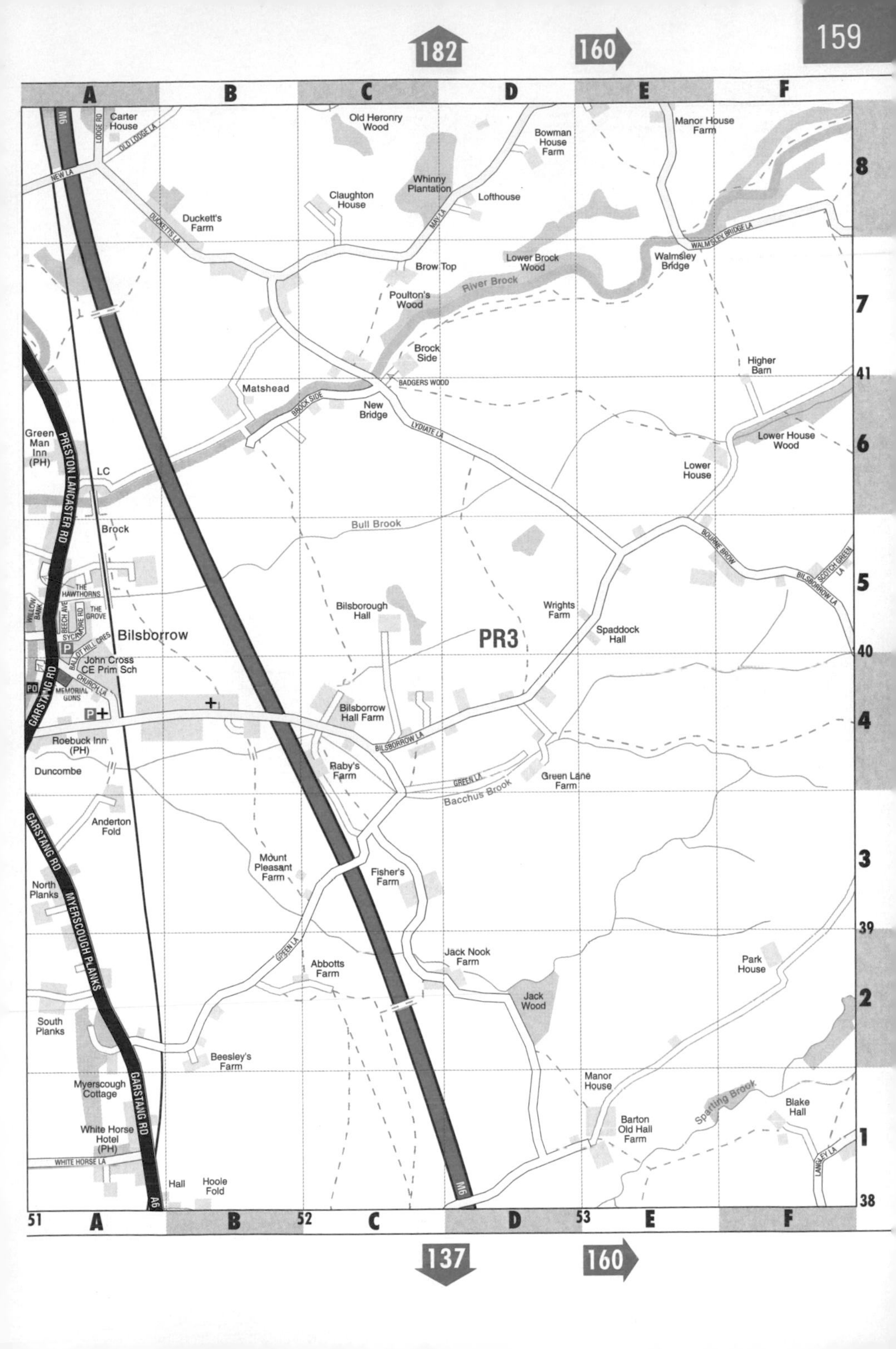
182
160
A
B
C
D
E
F
Carter House
Old Heronry Wood
Bowman House Farm
Manor House Farm
Whinny Plantation
Claughton House
Lofthouse
Duckett's Farm
Brow Top
Lower Brock Wood
Walmsley Bridge
River Brock
Poulton's Wood
Brock Side
Higher Barn
Matshead
BADGERS WOOD
New Bridge
BROCK SIDE
LYDIATE LA
Green Man Inn (PH)
PRESTON LANCASTER RD
Lower House Wood
Lower House
LC
Brock
Bull Brook
BOURNE BROW
BILSBORROW LA
SCOTCH GREEN LA
Bilsborough Hall
Wrights Farm
Spaddock Hall
PR3
Bilsborrow
John Cross CE Prim Sch
MEMORIAL GDNS
CHURCH LA
Bilsborrow Hall Farm
Roebuck Inn (PH)
Duncombe
Raby's Farm
GREEN LA
Green Lane Farm
Bacchus Brook
Anderton Fold
GARSTANG RD
Mount Pleasant Farm
Fisher's Farm
North Planks
MYERSCOUGH PLANKS
Abbotts Farm
Jack Nook Farm
Park House
Jack Wood
South Planks
Beesley's Farm
Myerscough Cottage
Manor House
Sparling Brook
Blake Hall
White Horse Hotel (PH)
Barton Old Hall Farm
WHITE HORSE LA
Hall
Hoole Fold
LANGLEY LA
M6
A6
NEW LA
OLD LODGE LA
LODGE LA
DUCKETTS LA
MAY LA
WALMSLEY BRIDGE LA
WILLOW BANK
THE HAWTHORNS
BEECH AVE
SYCAMORE RD
THE GROVE
BALLOT HILL CRES
8
7
41
6
5
40
4
3
39
2
1
38
51
52
53
137
160

159
183

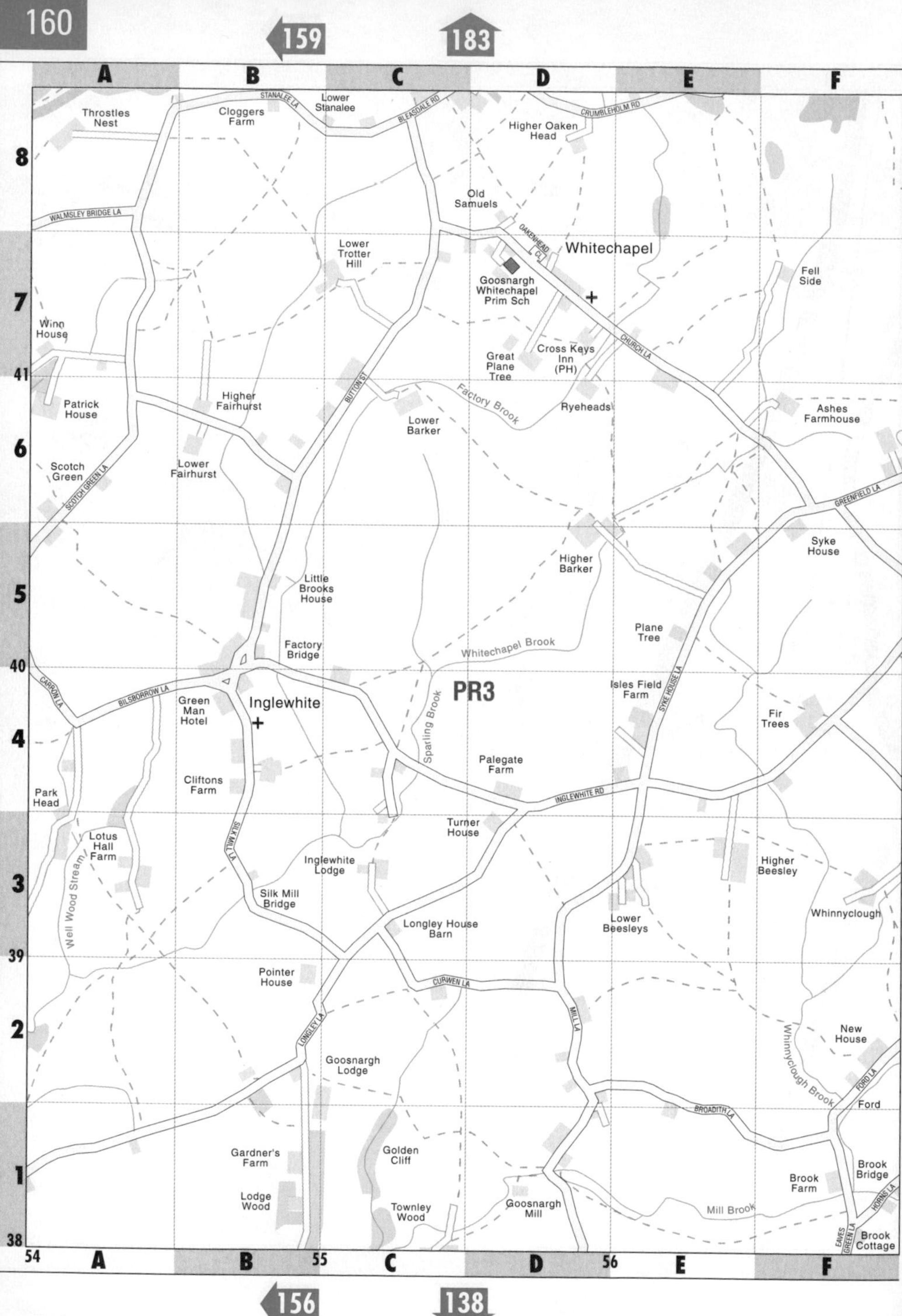

156
138

184
162

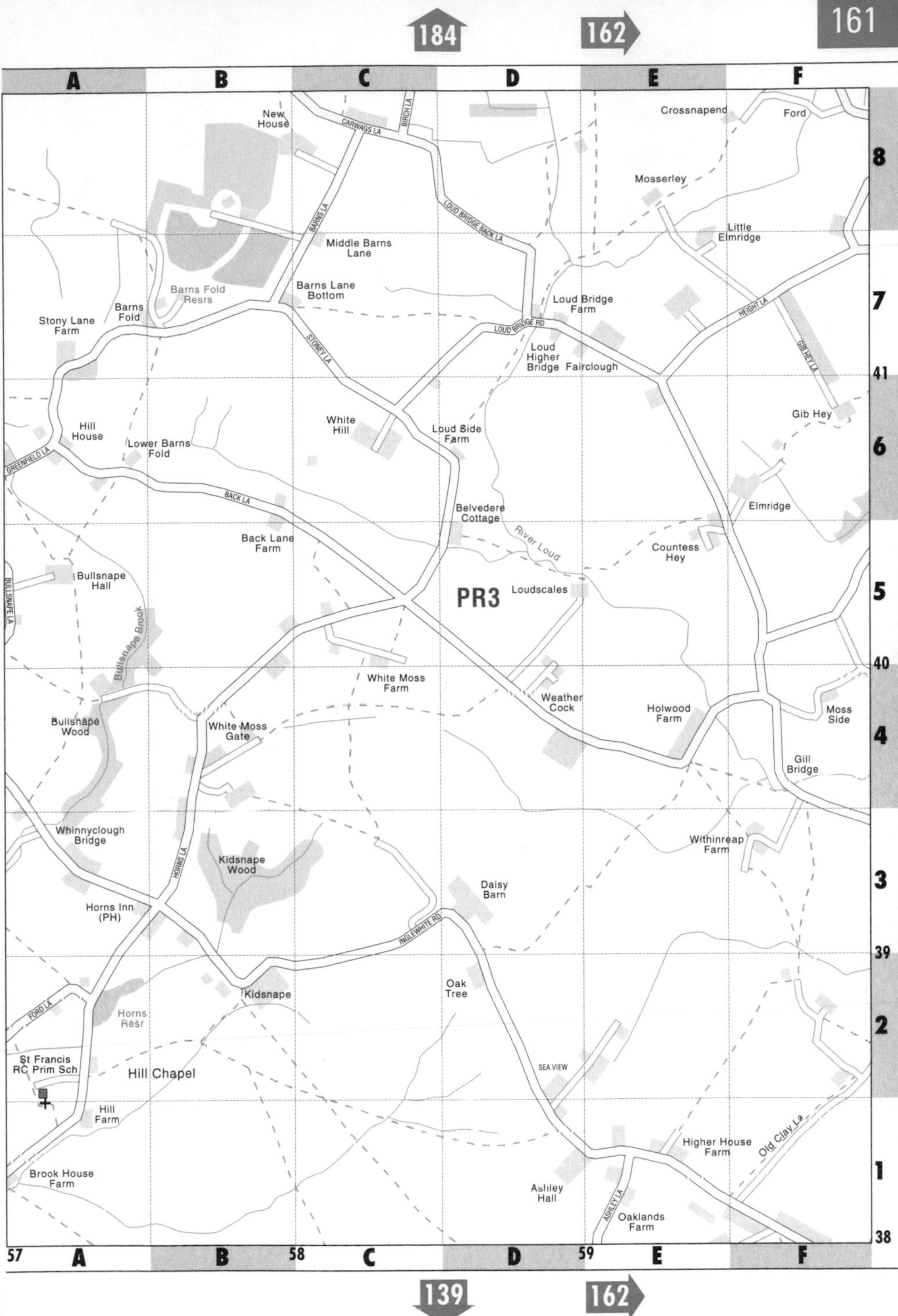

139
162

161
185

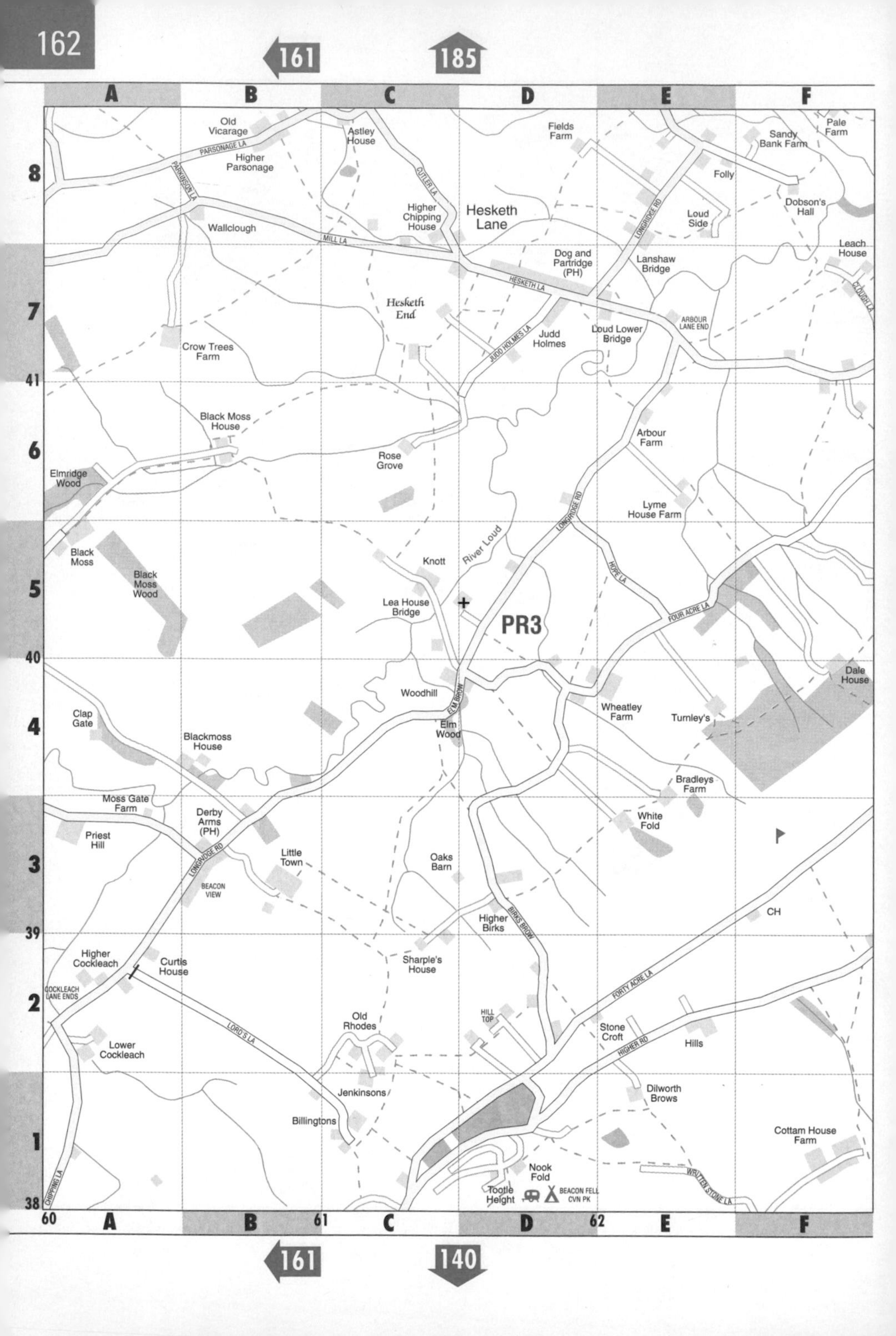

161
140

186
164

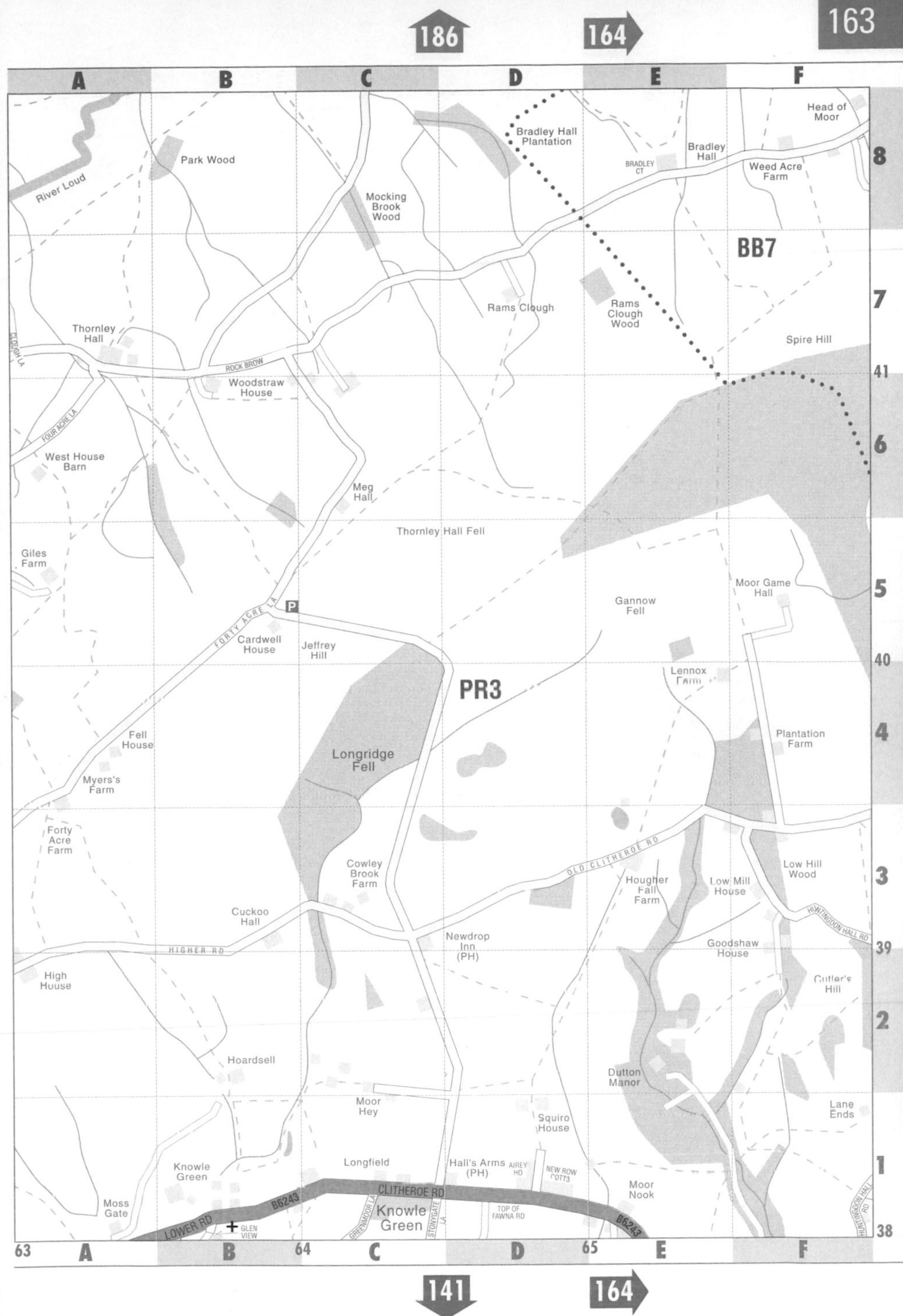

141
164

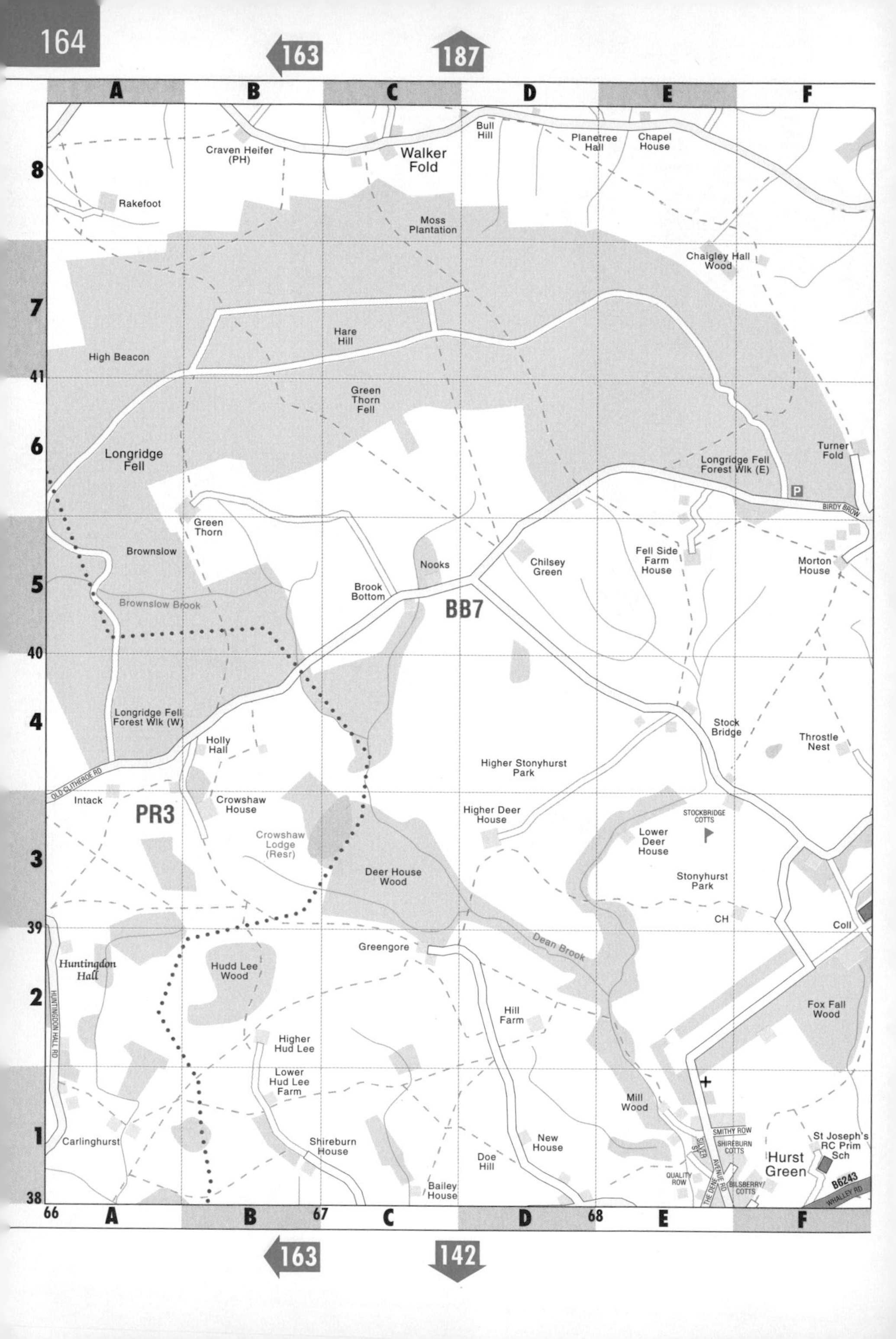
163
187
A
B
C
D
E
F
8
7
41
6
5
40
4
3
39
2
1
38
66
67
68
Craven Heifer (PH)
Walker Fold
Bull Hill
Planetree Hall
Chapel House
Rakefoot
Moss Plantation
Chaigley Hall Wood
Hare Hill
High Beacon
Green Thorn Fell
Longridge Fell
Turner Fold
Longridge Fell Forest Wlk (E)
P
BIRDY BROW
Green Thorn
Brownslow
Nooks
Chilsey Green
Fell Side Farm House
Morton House
Brook Bottom
Brownslow Brook
BB7
Longridge Fell Forest Wlk (W)
Holly Hall
Stock Bridge
Throstle Nest
Higher Stonyhurst Park
OLD CLITHEROE RD
Intack
PR3
Crowshaw House
Higher Deer House
STOCKBRIDGE COTTS
Lower Deer House
Crowshaw Lodge (Resr)
Deer House Wood
Stonyhurst Park
CH
Coll
Greengore
Dean Brook
Huntingdon Hall
Hudd Lee Wood
Fox Fall Wood
HUNTINGDON HALL RD
Hill Farm
Higher Hud Lee
Lower Hud Lee Farm
Mill Wood
SMITHY ROW
SILVER ST
SHIREBURN COTTS
St Joseph's RC Prim Sch
Carlinghurst
Shireburn House
New House
Doe Hill
Hurst Green
QUALITY ROW
THE DENE
AVENUE RD
BILSBERRY COTTS
B6243
WHALLEY RD
Bailey House
163
142

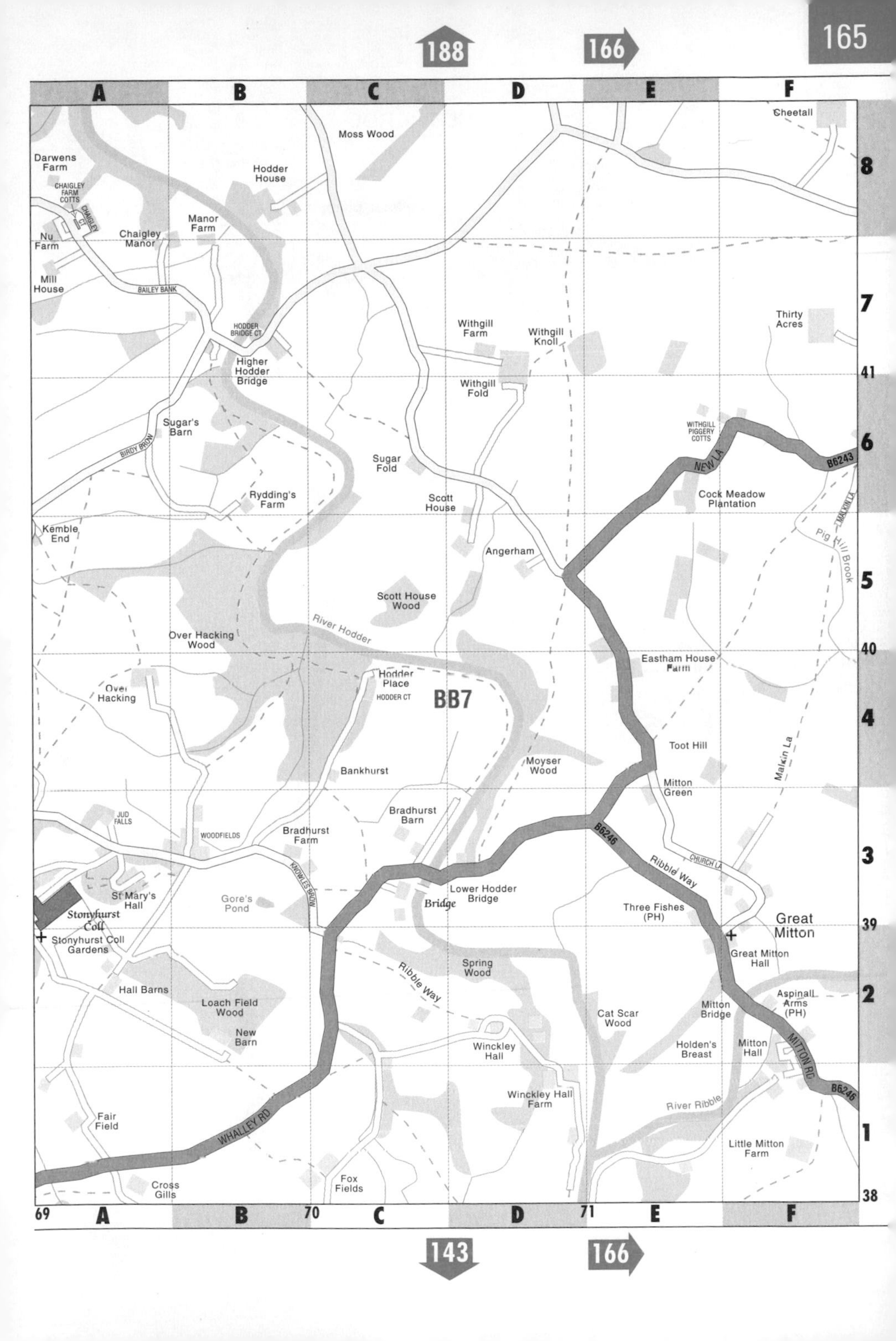
188
166
Cheetall
Moss Wood
Darwens Farm
Hodder House
CHAIGLEY FARM COTTS
CHAIGLEY CT
Manor Farm
Nu Farm
Chaigley Manor
Mill House
BAILEY BANK
HODDER BRIDGE CT
Withgill Farm
Withgill Knoll
Thirty Acres
Higher Hodder Bridge
Withgill Fold
Sugar's Barn
BIRDY BROW
WITHGILL PIGGERY COTTS
NEW LA
B6243
Sugar Fold
Rydding's Farm
Scott House
Cock Meadow Plantation
MALKIN LA
Kemble End
Angerham
Pig Hill Brook
Scott House Wood
River Hodder
Over Hacking Wood
Eastham House Farm
Over Hacking
Hodder Place
HODDER CT
BB7
Toot Hill
Bankhurst
Moyser Wood
Mitton Green
Malkin La
JUD FALLS
Bradhurst Barn
WOODFIELDS
Bradhurst Farm
B6246
KNOWLES BROW
Ribble Way
CHURCH LA
St Mary's Hall
Gore's Pond
Lower Hodder Bridge
Bridge
Three Fishes (PH)
Stonyhurst Coll
Great Mitton
Stonyhurst Coll Gardens
Great Mitton Hall
Spring Wood
Ribble Way
Hall Barns
Loach Field Wood
Aspinall Arms (PH)
Cat Scar Wood
Mitton Bridge
New Barn
Winckley Hall
Holden's Breast
Mitton Hall
MITTON RD
B6246
Winckley Hall Farm
River Ribble
Fair Field
WHALLEY RD
Little Mitton Farm
Fox Fields
Cross Gills
A
B
C
D
E
F
8
7
41
6
5
40
4
3
39
2
1
38
69
70
71
143
166

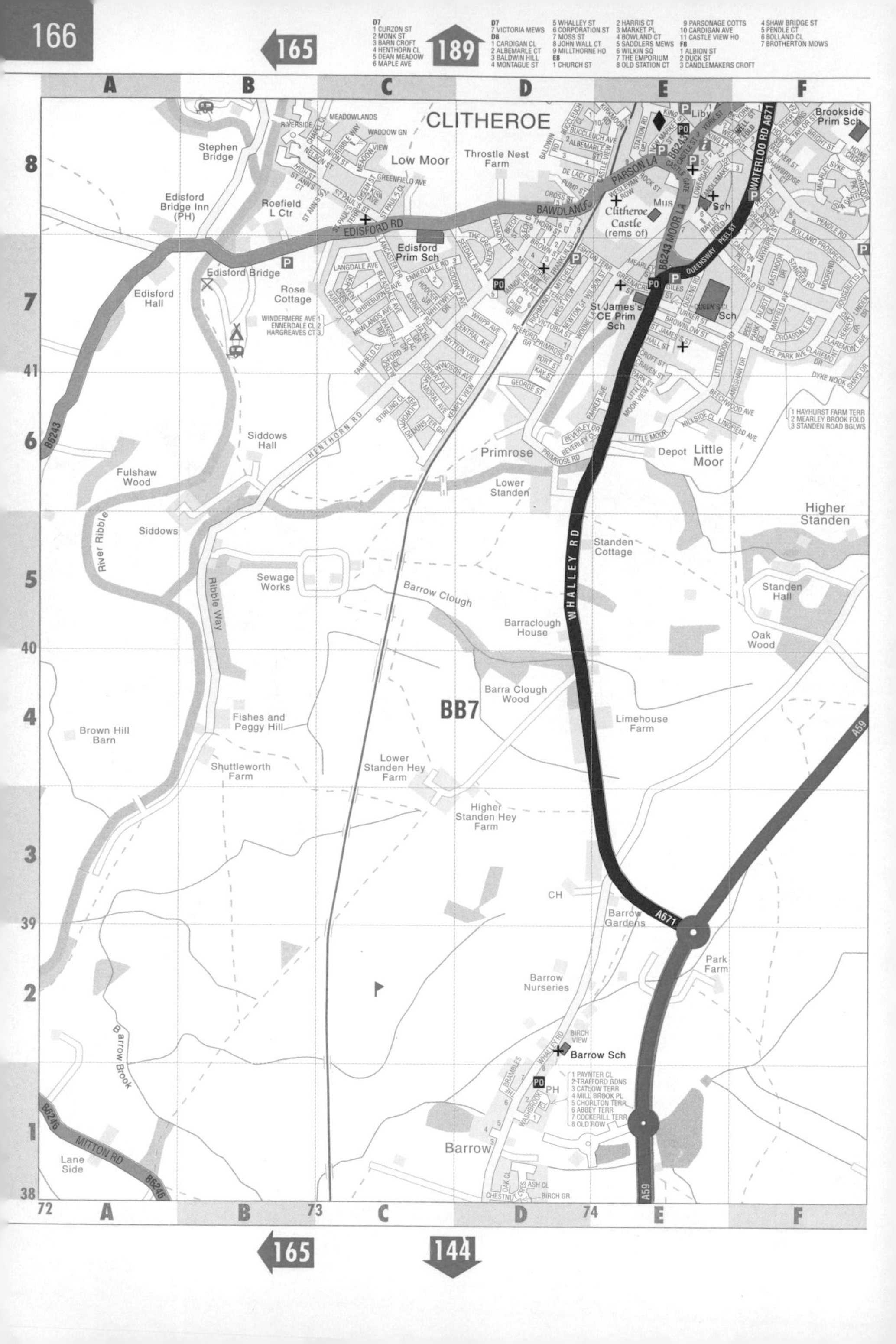
165
189
D7
1 CURZON ST
2 MONK ST
3 BARN CROFT
4 HENTHORN CL
5 DEAN MEADOW
6 MAPLE AVE
D7
7 VICTORIA MEWS
D8
1 CARDIGAN CL
2 ALBEMARLE CT
3 BALDWIN HILL
4 MONTAGUE ST
5 WHALLEY ST
6 CORPORATION ST
7 MOSS ST
8 JOHN WALL CT
9 MILLTHORNE HO
E8
1 CHURCH ST
2 HARRIS CT
3 MARKET PL
4 BOWLAND CT
5 SADDLERS MEWS
6 WILKIN SQ
7 THE EMPORIUM
8 OLD STATION CT
9 PARSONAGE COTTS
10 CARDIGAN AVE
11 CASTLE VIEW HO
F8
1 ALBION ST
2 DUCK ST
3 CANDLEMAKERS CROFT
4 SHAW BRIDGE ST
5 PENDLE CT
6 BOLLAND CL
7 BROTHERTON MDWS
CLITHEROE
Stephen Bridge
Low Moor
Throstle Nest Farm
Edisford Bridge Inn (PH)
Roefield L Ctr
EDISFORD RD
BAWDLANDS
PARSON LA
Clitheroe Castle (rems of)
Mus
Liby
Brookside Prim Sch
Edisford Prim Sch
Edisford Bridge
Edisford Hall
Rose Cottage
WINDERMERE AVE 1
ENNERDALE CL 2
HARGREAVES CT 3
St James's CE Prim Sch
Sch
WATERLOO RD A671
B6243
MOOR LA
QUEENSWAY
PEEL ST
HENTHORN RD
Siddows Hall
Fulshaw Wood
Primrose
Depot
Little Moor
Lower Standen
Higher Standen
1 HAYHURST FARM TERR
2 MEARLEY BROOK FOLD
3 STANDEN ROAD BGLWS
Siddows
River Ribble
Ribble Way
Sewage Works
Barrow Clough
Standen Cottage
Standen Hall
WHALLEY RD
Barraclough House
Oak Wood
Barra Clough Wood
BB7
Fishes and Peggy Hill
Brown Hill Barn
Limehouse Farm
Shuttleworth Farm
Lower Standen Hey Farm
Higher Standen Hey Farm
CH
Barrow Gardens
A671
A59
Park Farm
Barrow Nurseries
Barrow Brook
Barrow Sch
1 PAYNTER CL
2 TRAFFORD GDNS
3 CATLOW TERR
4 MILL BROOK PL
5 CHORLTON TERR
6 ABBEY TERR
7 COCKERILL TERR
8 OLD ROW
PH
Barrow
B6246
MITTON RD
Lane Side
B6243
A B C D E F
8 7 6 5 4 3 2 1
41 40 39 38
72 73 74
165
144

190 168

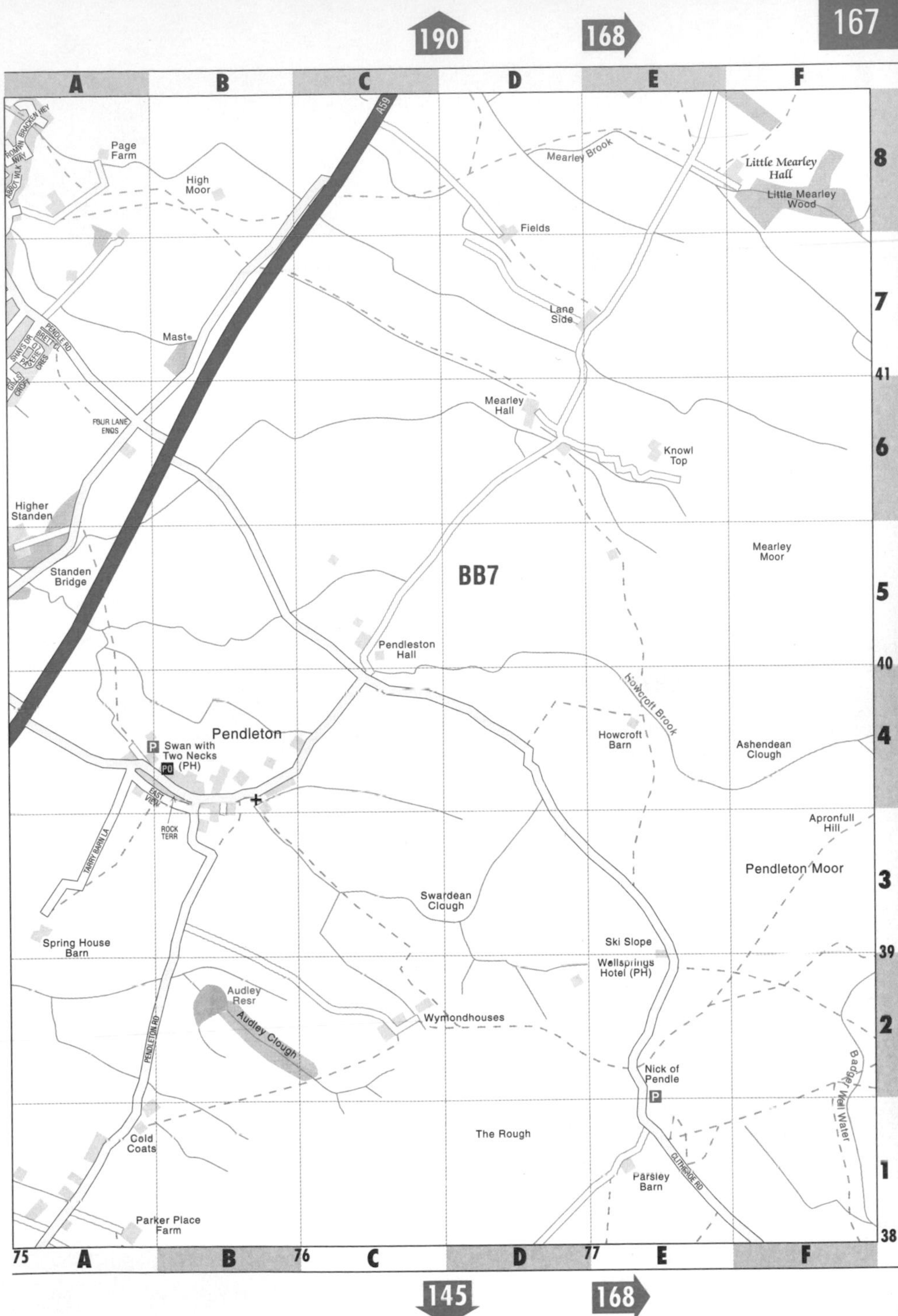

145 168

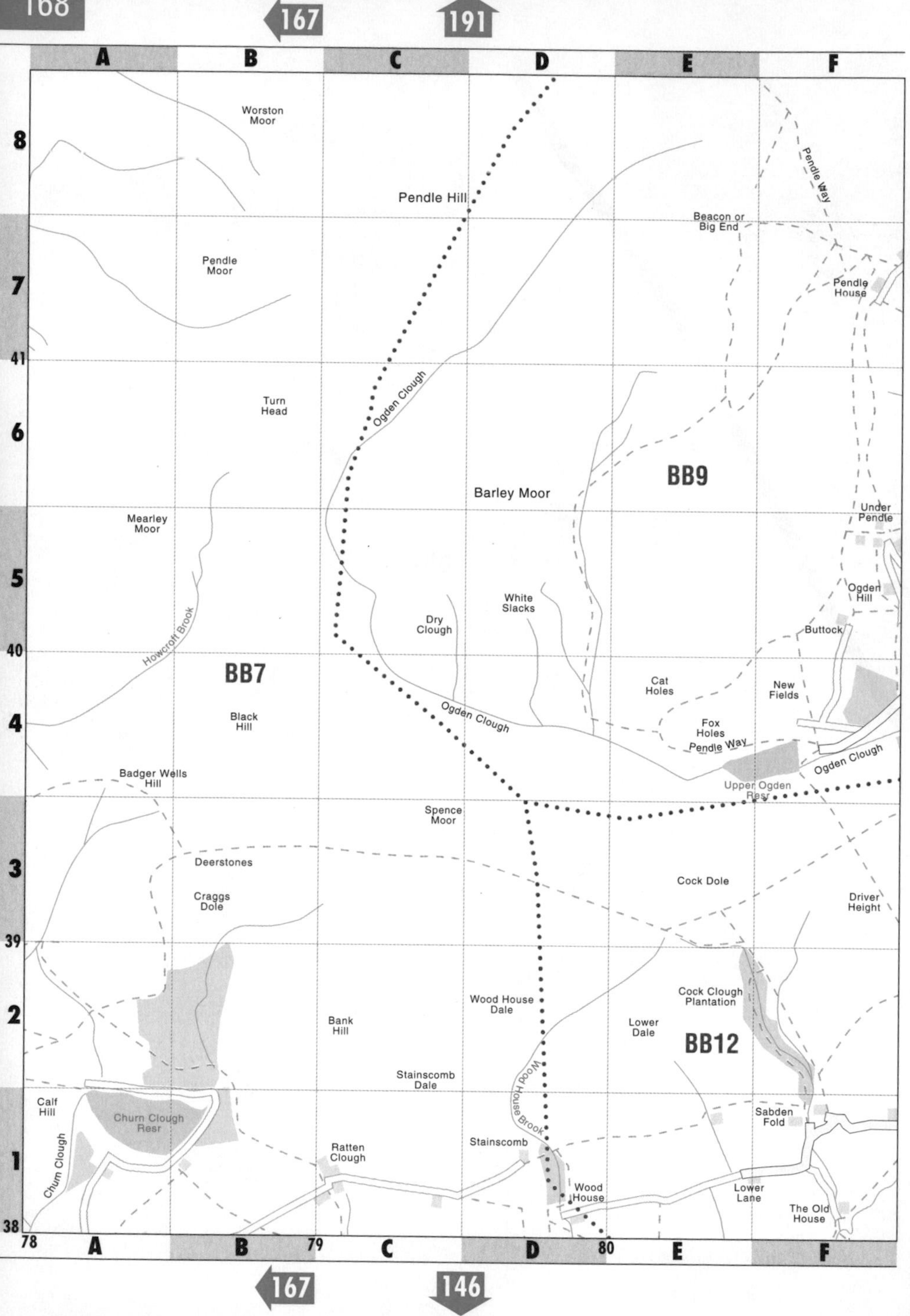
167
191
A
B
C
D
E
F
8
7
41
6
5
40
4
3
39
2
1
38
78
79
80
Worston Moor
Pendle Hill
Pendle Way
Beacon or Big End
Pendle Moor
Pendle House
Turn Head
Ogden Clough
BB9
Barley Moor
Mearley Moor
Under Pendle
Ogden Hill
White Slacks
Dry Clough
Buttock
Howcroft Brook
BB7
Cat Holes
New Fields
Black Hill
Fox Holes
Pendle Way
Badger Wells Hill
Upper Ogden Resr
Spence Moor
Deerstones
Craggs Dole
Cock Dole
Driver Height
Wood House Dale
Cock Clough Plantation
Bank Hill
Lower Dale
BB12
Stainscomb Dale
Wood House Brook
Calf Hill
Churn Clough Resr
Sabden Fold
Churn Clough
Ratten Clough
Stainscomb
Wood House
Lower Lane
The Old House
167
146

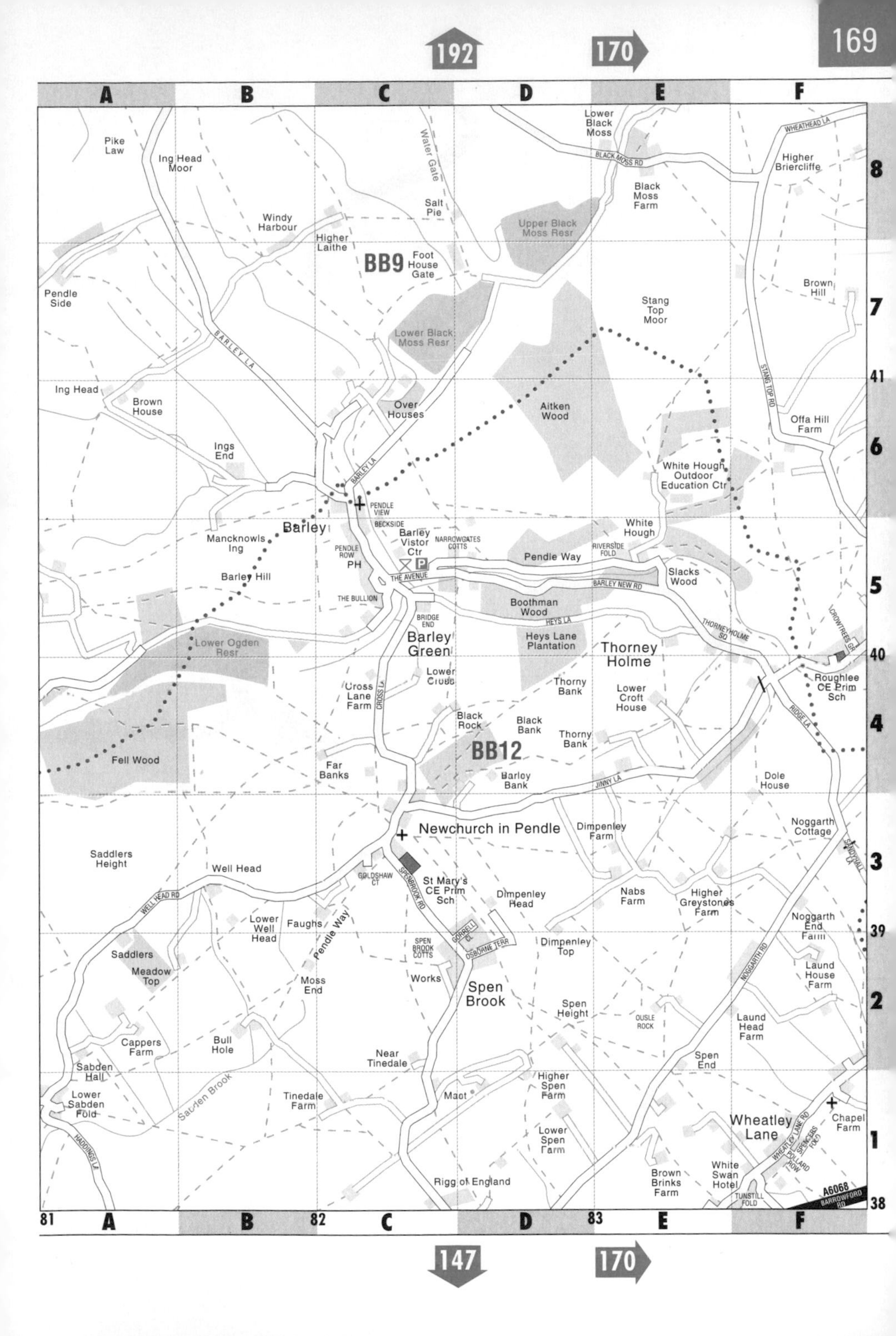
192
170
Pike Law
Ing Head Moor
Lower Black Moss
Black Moss Rd
Wheathead La
Higher Briercliffe
Water Gate
Black Moss Farm
Salt Pie
Windy Harbour
Upper Black Moss Resr
Higher Laithe
BB9
Foot House Gate
Pendle Side
Brown Hill
Stang Top Moor
Barley La
Lower Black Moss Resr
Ing Head
Brown House
Aitken Wood
Stang Top Rd
Offa Hill Farm
Over Houses
Ings End
White Hough Outdoor Education Ctr
Pendle View
Beckside
White Hough
Barley
Mancknowls Ing
Barley Vistor Ctr
Narrowgates Cotts
Riverside Fold
Pendle Row
PH
Pendle Way
Slacks Wood
Barley Hill
The Avenue
Barley New Rd
The Bullion
Boothman Wood
Bridge End
Heys La
Crowtrees Gr
Thorneyholme Sq
Lower Ogden Resr
Barley Green
Heys Lane Plantation
Thorney Holme
Lower Cross
Roughlee CE Prim Sch
Cross Lane Farm
Cross La
Thorny Bank
Lower Croft House
Ridge La
Black Rock
Black Bank
Thorny Bank
BB12
Fell Wood
Far Banks
Barley Bank
Jinny La
Dole House
Noggarth Cottage
Newchurch in Pendle
Dimpenley Farm
Saddlers Height
Well Head
Goldshaw Ct
St Mary's CE Prim Sch
Spenbrook Rd
Nabs Farm
Higher Greystones Farm
Well Head Rd
Dimpenley Head
Noggarth End Farm
Lower Well Head
Faughs
Gorrell Cl
Spen Brook Cotts
Osborne Terr
Dimpenley Top
Saddlers Meadow Top
Laund House Farm
Moss End
Works
Spen Brook
Noggarth Rd
Spen Height
Ousle Rock
Laund Head Farm
Cappers Farm
Bull Hole
Near Tinedale
Spen End
Sabden Hall
Sabden Brook
Higher Spen Farm
Lower Sabden Fold
Tinedale Farm
Moor
Chapel Farm
Wheatley Lane
Lower Spen Farm
Haddings La
Wheatley Lane Rd
Spencers Fold
Pollard Row
Rigg of England
Brown Brinks Farm
White Swan Hotel
Tunstill Fold
A6068
Barrowford Rd
A
B
C
D
E
F
1
2
3
4
5
6
7
8
81
82
83
38
39
40
41
147
170

170

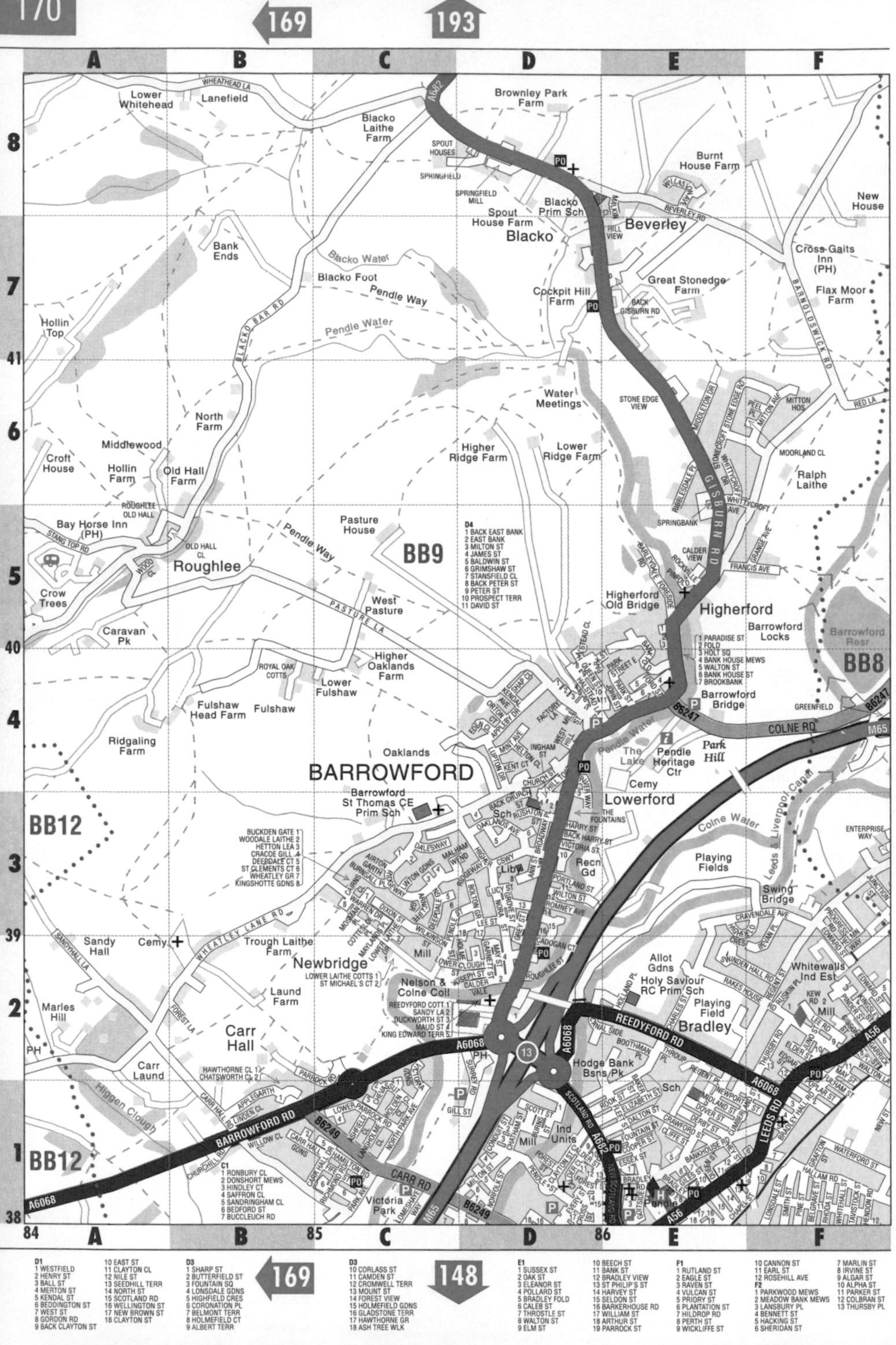
169
193
A
B
C
D
E
F
8
7
41
6
5
40
4
3
39
2
1
38
84
85
86
Lower Whitehead
Lanefield
WHEATHEAD LA
A682
Brownley Park Farm
Blacko Laithe Farm
SPOUT HOUSES
SPRINGFIELD
SPRINGFIELD MILL
Burnt House Farm
Spout House Farm
Blacko Prim Sch
Blacko
Beverley
BEVERLEY RD
HILL VIEW
MALKIN CL
VILLAS
New House
Bank Ends
Blacko Water
Blacko Foot
Pendle Way
Cross Gaits Inn (PH)
Great Stonedge Farm
Cockpit Hill Farm
BACK GISBURN RD
Flax Moor Farm
BARNOLDSWICK RD
Hollin Top
Pendle Water
BLACKO BAR RD
Water Meetings
STONE EDGE VIEW
MIDDLETON DR
STONE EDGE RD
PEEL ST
MITTON AVE
MITTON HOS
RED LA
North Farm
Middlewood
Higher Ridge Farm
Lower Ridge Farm
MOORLAND CL
Croft House
Hollin Farm
Old Hall Farm
STONECROFT
WHITTYCROFT DR
WHITTYCROFT AVE
RIBBLESDALE PL
Ralph Laithe
GISBURN RD
ROUGHLEE OLD HALL
Bay Horse Inn (PH)
STANG TOP RD
Pasture House
SPRINGBANK
GRANGE AVE
OLD HALL CL
Pendle Way
BB9
CALDER VIEW
ROCKVILLE
PINFOLD
FRANCIS AVE
WOOD CL
Roughlee
D4
1 BACK EAST BANK
2 EAST BANK
3 MILTON ST
4 JAMES ST
5 BALDWIN ST
6 GRIMSHAW ST
7 STANSFIELD CL
8 BACK PETER ST
9 PETER ST
10 PROSPECT TERR
11 DAVID ST
BARLEYDALE
FORESIDE
Crow Trees
West Pasture
PASTURE LA
Higherford Old Bridge
Higherford
Barrowford Locks
Barrowford Resr
Caravan Pk
1 PARADISE ST
2 FOLD
3 HOLT SQ
4 BANK HOUSE MEWS
5 WALTON ST
6 BANK HOUSE ST
7 BROOKBANK
BB8
ROYAL OAK COTTS
Higher Oaklands Farm
PARK STREET E
Lower Fulshaw
Barrowford Bridge
B6247
GREENFIELD
Fulshaw Head Farm
Fulshaw
KENDAL AVE
ORTON CT
APPLEBY DR
FACTORY LA
COLNE RD
M65
Ridgaling Farm
MNT AVE
HELTON CL
INGHAM ST
WEST HILL
Pendle Water
Pendle Heritage Ctr
Park Hill
Oaklands
LUPTON DR
KENT CT
The Lake
BARROWFORD
CHURCH ST
Cemy
Barrowford St Thomas CE Prim Sch
BACK CHURCH ST
Sch
RUSHTON ST
Lowerford
THE FOUNTAINS
BB12
Leeds & Liverpool Canal
BUCKDEN GATE 1
WOODALE LAITHE 2
HETTON LEA 3
CRACOE GILL 4
DEERDALE CT 5
ST CLEMENTS CT 6
WHEATLEY GR 7
KINGSHOTTE GDNS 8
DALESWAY
OAKLANDS AVE
HARRY ST
BACK HARRY ST
VICTORIA ST
Colne Water
ENTERPRISE WAY
AIRTON GARTH
MALHAM WEND
Recn Gd
Playing Fields
RIDGEWAY
CSWY
Liby
PORTLAND ST
WILTON ST
BOLTON GR
LUCY ST
ROMNEY AVE
Swing Bridge
JUNCTION ST
WHEATLEY LANE RD
DIXON ST
WILKINSON ST
DEEPDALE CT
LEE ST
CRAVENDALE AVE
HIGHFIELD CRES
SEVAN PL
PROGRESS RD
HELMN RD
EDWARD ST
WAY
SANDYHALL LA
Sandy Hall
Cemy
Trough Laithe Farm
Newbridge
Mill
CADOGAN CT
ROUGHLEE ST
LOWER CLOUGH ST
JOSEPH ST
Allot Gdns
Holy Saviour RC Prim Sch
SWINDEN HALL RD
Whitewalls Ind Est
Laund Farm
LOWER LAITHE COTTS 1
ST MICHAEL'S CT 2
Nelson & Colne Coll
CALDER VALE
RAKES HOUSE
REGENT ST
HOLLAND PL
Playing Field
Marles Hill
FOREST LA
REEDYFORD COTT 1
SANDY LA 2
DUCKWORTH ST 3
MAUD ST 4
KING EDWARD TERR 5
KEW RD
Mill
Carr Hall
A6068
CANAL SIDE
REEDYFORD RD
BOOTHMAN PL
THROUP PL
Bradley
PH
13
Hodge Bank Bsns Pk
A6068
A56
Carr Laund
HAWTHORNE CL 1
CHATSWORTH CL 2
PARROCK RD
SURREY RD
REGENT PL
Sch
NEWPORT ST
MIDLAND ST
CUMBERLAND ST
LEEDS RD
Higgen Clough
APPLEGARTH
LINDEN CL
LOWER PARROCK RD
GILL ST
SCOTT ST
ELIZABETH ST
DOVER ST
DERBY ST
BRADLEY HALL RD
BARROWFORD RD
B6249
CARR HALL RD
WILLOW CL
NORTH PARK AVE
CHATHAM ST
BURNS ST
DALTON ST
FOUNTAIN ST
COOPER ST
CRAWFORD ST
CLIFFE ST
Mill
Ind Units
SCOTLAND RD
A682
ESSEX ST
BANKHOUSE RD
WATERFORD ST
GRAFTON ST
HALLAM RD
BB12
CHURCHILL RD
C1
1 RONBURY CL
2 DONSHORT MEWS
3 HINDLEY CT
4 SAFFRON CL
5 SANDRINGHAM CL
6 BEDFORD ST
7 BUCCLEUCH RD
HAMILTON RD
FIFE ST
RICHMOND RD
PARK AVE
CARR RD
Victoria Park
LOMESHAYE WAY
M65
B6249
NORFOLK ST
FOREST ST
PENDLE ST
CLAYTON ST
EVERY ST
CROSS ST
GOITSIDE
Pendle
CHAPEL ST
LONSDALE ST
SMITH ST
PINE ST
BELGRAVE ST
RHODA ST
WHITEHALL ST
TAVISTOCK ST
HENDON RD
A6068
D1
1 WESTFIELD
2 HENRY ST
3 BALL ST
4 MERTON ST
5 KENDAL ST
6 BEDDINGTON ST
7 WEST ST
8 GORDON RD
9 BACK CLAYTON ST
10 EAST ST
11 CLAYTON CL
12 NILE ST
13 SEEDHILL TERR
14 NORTH ST
15 SCOTLAND RD
16 WELLINGTON ST
17 NEW BROWN ST
18 CLAYTON ST
D3
1 SHARP ST
2 BUTTERFIELD ST
3 FOUNTAIN SQ
4 LONSDALE GDNS
5 HIGHFIELD CRES
6 CORONATION PL
7 BELMONT TERR
8 HOLMEFIELD CT
9 ALBERT TERR
169
D3
10 CORLASS ST
11 CAMDEN ST
12 CROMWELL TERR
13 MOUNT ST
14 FOREST VIEW
15 HOLMEFIELD GDNS
16 GLADSTONE TERR
17 HAWTHORNE GR
18 ASH TREE WLK
148
E1
1 SUSSEX ST
2 OAK ST
3 ELEANOR ST
4 POLLARD ST
5 BRADLEY FOLD
6 CALEB ST
7 THROSTLE ST
8 WALTON ST
9 ELM ST
10 BEECH ST
11 BANK ST
12 BRADLEY VIEW
13 ST PHILIP'S ST
14 HARVEY ST
15 SELDON ST
16 BARKERHOUSE RD
17 WILLIAM ST
18 ARTHUR ST
19 PARROCK ST
F1
1 RUTLAND ST
2 EAGLE ST
3 RAVEN ST
4 VULCAN ST
5 PRIORY ST
6 PLANTATION ST
7 HILDROP RD
8 PERTH ST
9 WICKLIFFE ST
10 CANNON ST
11 EARL ST
12 ROSEHILL AVE
F2
1 PARKWOOD MEWS
2 MEADOW BANK MEWS
3 LANSBURY PL
4 BENNETT ST
5 HACKING ST
6 SHERIDAN ST
7 MARLIN ST
8 IRVINE ST
9 ALGAR ST
10 ALPHA ST
11 PARKER ST
12 COLBRAN ST
13 THURSBY PL

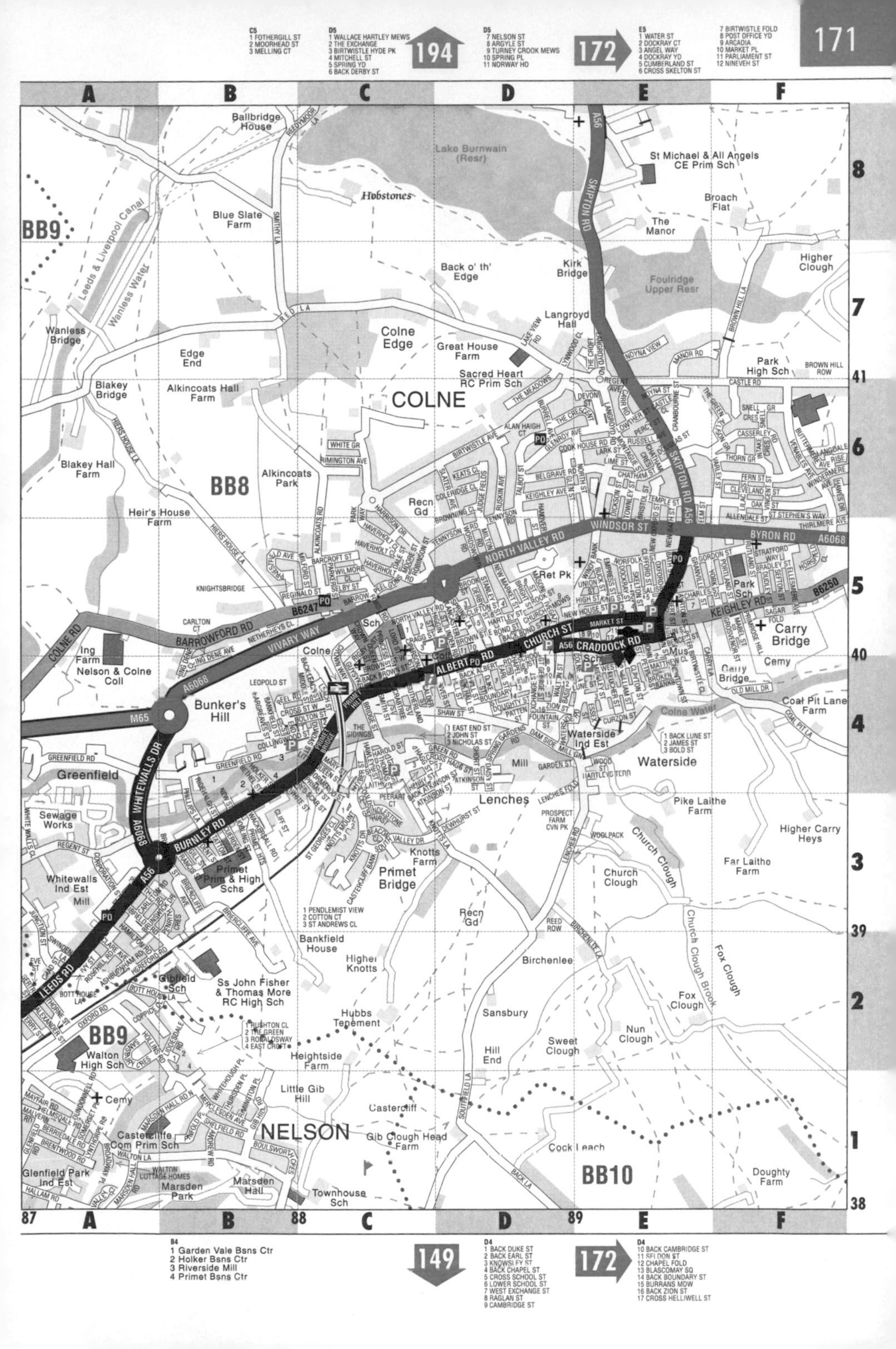

171
C5
1 FOTHERGILL ST
2 MOORHEAD ST
3 MELLING CT
D5
1 WALLACE HARTLEY MEWS
2 THE EXCHANGE
3 BIRTWISTLE HYDE PK
4 MITCHELL ST
5 SPRING YD
6 BACK DERBY ST
194
D5
7 NELSON ST
8 ARGYLE ST
9 TURNEY CROOK MEWS
10 SPRING PL
11 NORWAY HO
172
E5
1 WATER ST
2 DOCKRAY CT
3 ANGEL WAY
4 DOCKRAY YD
5 CUMBERLAND ST
6 CROSS SKELTON ST
7 BIRTWISTLE FOLD
8 POST OFFICE YD
9 ARCADIA
10 MARKET PL
11 PARLIAMENT ST
12 NINEVEH ST
A
B
C
D
E
F
8
7
6
5
4
3
2
1
41
40
39
38
87
88
89
Ballbridge House
Lake Burnwain (Resr)
Hobstones
St Michael & All Angels CE Prim Sch
Broach Flat
The Manor
Blue Slate Farm
BB9
Leeds & Liverpool Canal
Wanless Water
Back o' th' Edge
Kirk Bridge
Foulridge Upper Resr
Higher Clough
Langroyd Hall
Wanless Bridge
Edge End
Colne Edge
Great House Farm
Park High Sch
Sacred Heart RC Prim Sch
Blakey Bridge
Alkincoats Hall Farm
COLNE
Blakey Hall Farm
BB8
Alkincoats Park
Recn Gd
Heir's House Farm
SKIPTON RD
A56
WINDSOR ST
BYRON RD
A6068
NORTH VALLEY RD
Ret Pk
Park Sch
KEIGHLEY RD
B6250
Carry Bridge
BARROWFORD RD
B6247
VIVARY WAY
COLNE RD
Ing Farm
Nelson & Colne Coll
Colne
ALBERT RD
CHURCH ST
CRADDOCK RD
Mus
Cemy
Carry Bridge
Coal Pit Lane Farm
Bunker's Hill
M65
Colne Water
Waterside Ind Est
Waterside
Greenfield
Mill
Lenches
Pike Laithe Farm
Sewage Works
WHITEWALLS DR
BURNLEY RD
Knotts Farm
Higher Carry Heys
Whitewalls Ind Est
Mill
Primet Prim & High Schs
Primet Bridge
Church Clough
Far Laithe Farm
Recn Gd
Bankfield House
Higher Knotts
Birchenlee
Fox Clough
LEEDS RD
Gibfield Sch
Ss John Fisher & Thomas More RC High Sch
Sansbury
Fox Clough
Hubbs Tenement
Nun Clough
BB9
Walton High Sch
Heightside Farm
Hill End
Sweet Clough
Cemy
Little Gib Hill
Castercliff
NELSON
Castercliffe Com Prim Sch
Gib Clough Head Farm
Cock Leach
Glenfield Park Ind Est
BB10
Doughty Farm
Marsden Park
Marsden Hall
Townhouse Sch
B4
1 Garden Vale Bsns Ctr
2 Holker Bsns Ctr
3 Riverside Mill
4 Primet Bsns Ctr
149
D4
1 BACK DUKE ST
2 BACK EARL ST
3 KNOWSLEY ST
4 BACK CHAPEL ST
5 CROSS SCHOOL ST
6 LOWER SCHOOL ST
7 WEST EXCHANGE ST
8 RAGLAN ST
9 CAMBRIDGE ST
172
D4
10 BACK CAMBRIDGE ST
11 SELDON ST
12 CHAPEL FOLD
13 BLASCOMAY SQ
14 BACK BOUNDARY ST
15 BURRANS MDW
16 BACK ZION ST
17 CROSS HELLIWELL ST

171
195

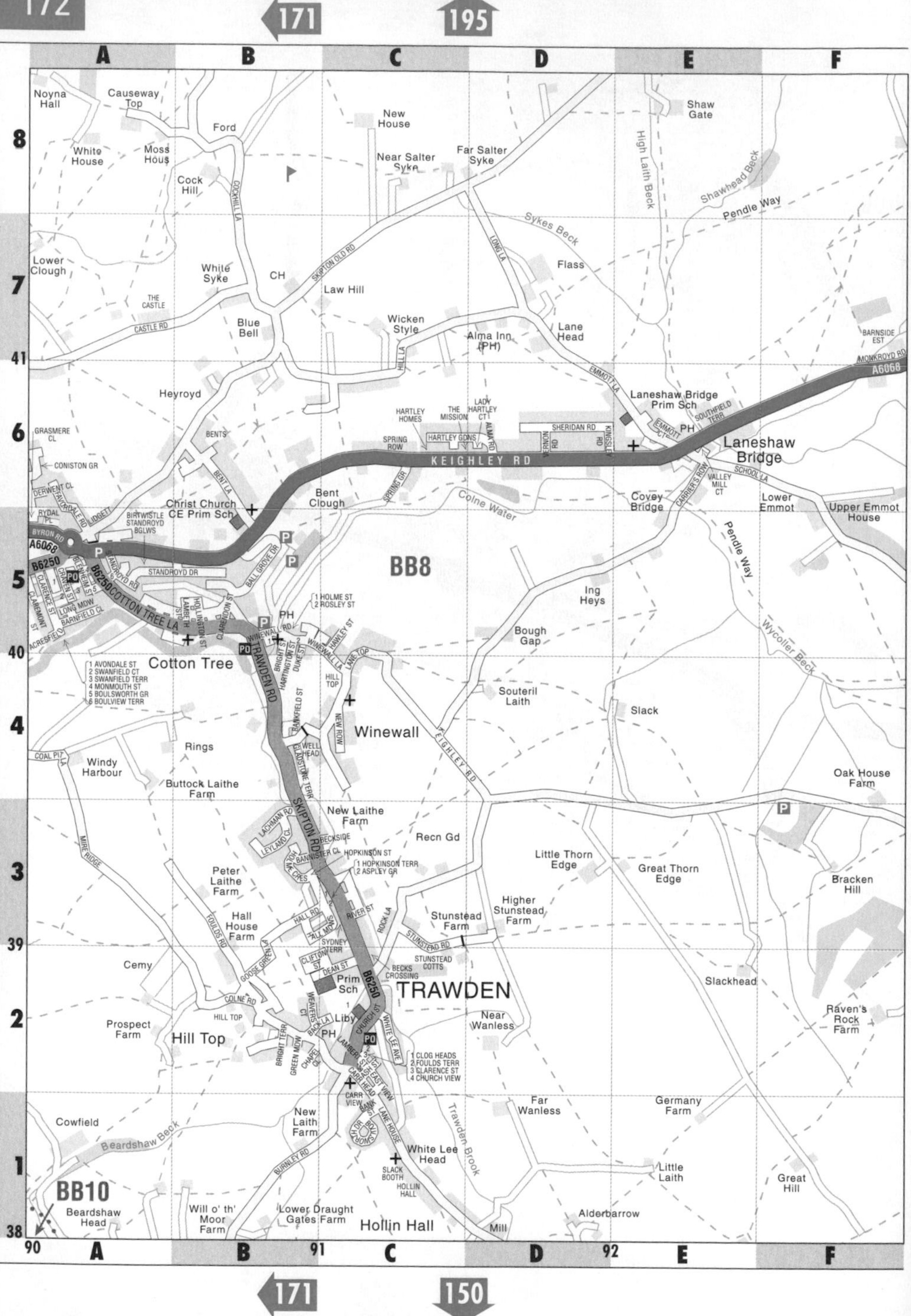

171
150

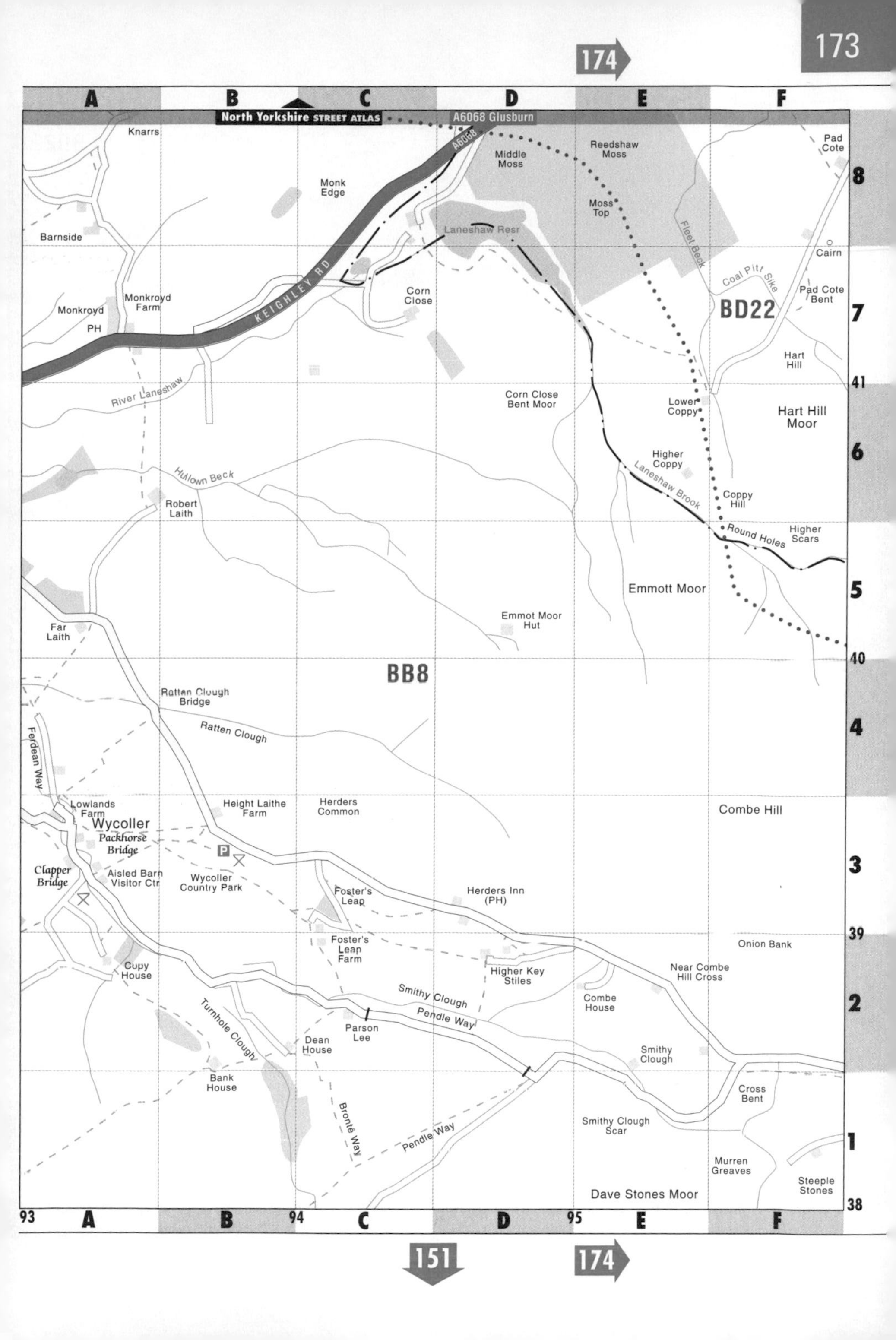
174
North Yorkshire STREET ATLAS
A6068 Glusburn
A B C D E F
Knarrs
Monk Edge
Middle Moss
Reedshaw Moss
Pad Cote
Moss Top
Barnside
Laneshaw Resr
Fleet Beck
Cairn
Coal Pitt Sike
Pad Cote Bent
Monkroyd Farm
Monkroyd
PH
KEIGHLEY RD
A6068
Corn Close
BD22
Hart Hill
River Laneshaw
Corn Close Bent Moor
Lower Coppy
Hart Hill Moor
Higher Coppy
Laneshaw Brook
Hullown Beck
Robert Laith
Coppy Hill
Round Holes
Higher Scars
Emmott Moor
Emmot Moor Hut
Far Laith
BB8
Ratten Clough Bridge
Ratten Clough
Ferdean Way
Lowlands Farm
Height Laithe Farm
Herders Common
Combe Hill
Wycoller
Packhorse Bridge
Clapper Bridge
Aisled Barn Visitor Ctr
Wycoller Country Park
P
Herders Inn (PH)
Foster's Leap
Foster's Leap Farm
Onion Bank
Copy House
Higher Key Stiles
Near Combe Hill Cross
Combe House
Smithy Clough
Pendle Way
Turnhole Clough
Parson Lee
Dean House
Smithy Clough
Bank House
Cross Bent
Brontë Way
Pendle Way
Smithy Clough Scar
Murren Greaves
Steeple Stones
Dave Stones Moor
8 7 41 6 5 40 4 3 39 2 1 38
93 94 95
151
174

173

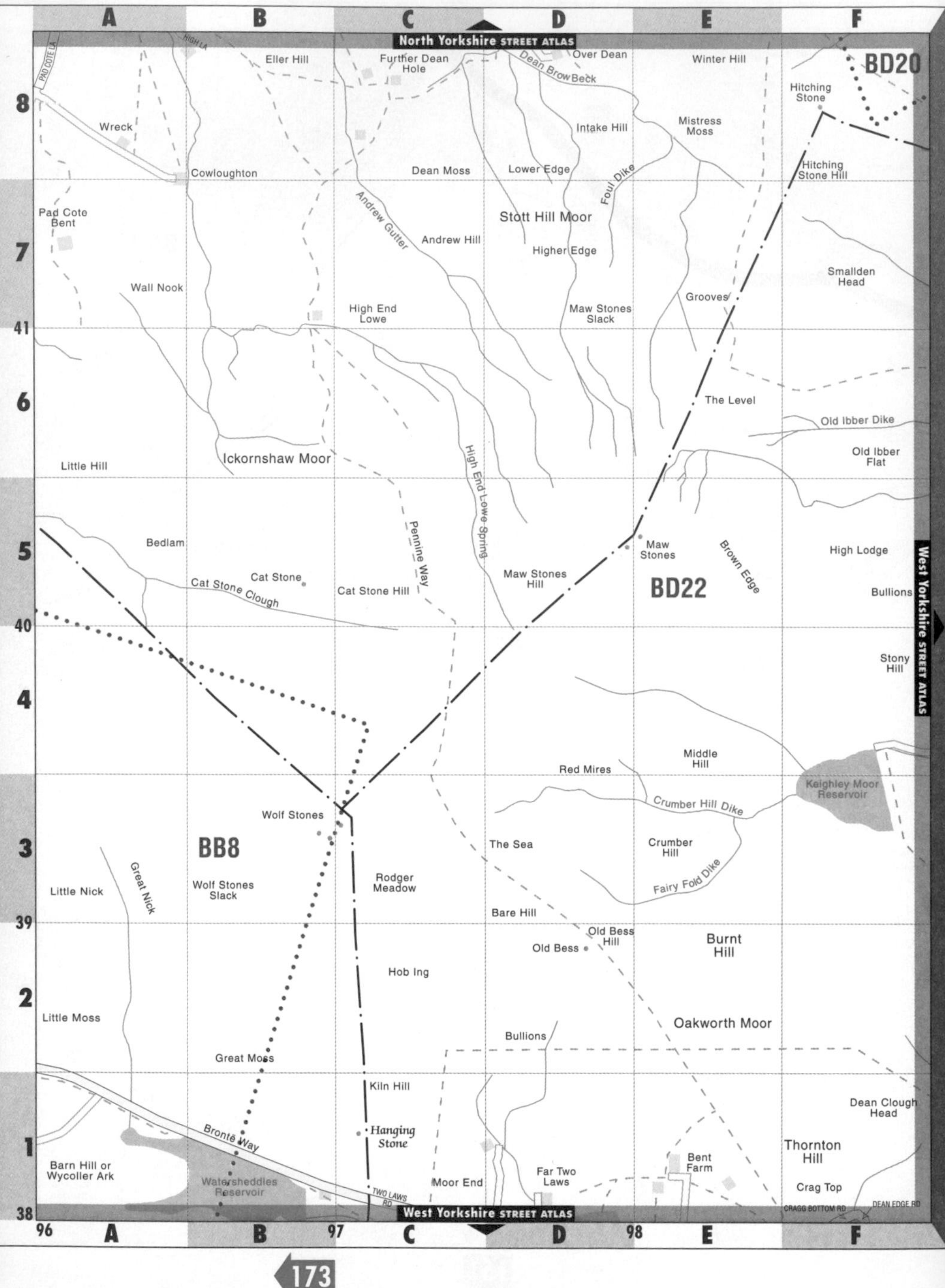

A
B
C
D
E
F
North Yorkshire STREET ATLAS
West Yorkshire STREET ATLAS
8
7
41
6
5
40
4
3
39
2
1
38
96
97
98
BD20
BD22
BB8
PAD COTE LA
HIGH LA
Eller Hill
Further Dean Hole
Over Dean
Dean Brow Beck
Winter Hill
Hitching Stone
Mistress Moss
Intake Hill
Wreck
Cowloughton
Dean Moss
Lower Edge
Hitching Stone Hill
Foul Dike
Pad Cote Bent
Stott Hill Moor
Andrew Gutter
Andrew Hill
Higher Edge
Smallden Head
Wall Nook
Grooves
High End Lowe
Maw Stones Slack
The Level
Old Ibber Dike
Old Ibber Flat
Little Hill
Ickornshaw Moor
High End Lowe Spring
Pennine Way
Bedlam
Maw Stones
Brown Edge
High Lodge
Cat Stone
Cat Stone Clough
Cat Stone Hill
Maw Stones Hill
Bullions
Stony Hill
Middle Hill
Red Mires
Keighley Moor Reservoir
Crumber Hill Dike
Wolf Stones
The Sea
Crumber Hill
Great Nick
Little Nick
Wolf Stones Slack
Rodger Meadow
Fairy Fold Dike
Bare Hill
Old Bess Hill
Old Bess
Burnt Hill
Hob Ing
Little Moss
Oakworth Moor
Bullions
Great Moss
Kiln Hill
Dean Clough Head
Bronte Way
Hanging Stone
Thornton Hill
Barn Hill or Wycoller Ark
Bent Farm
Far Two Laws
Moor End
Watersheddles Reservoir
TWO LAWS RD
Crag Top
CRAGG BOTTOM RD
DEAN EDGE RD

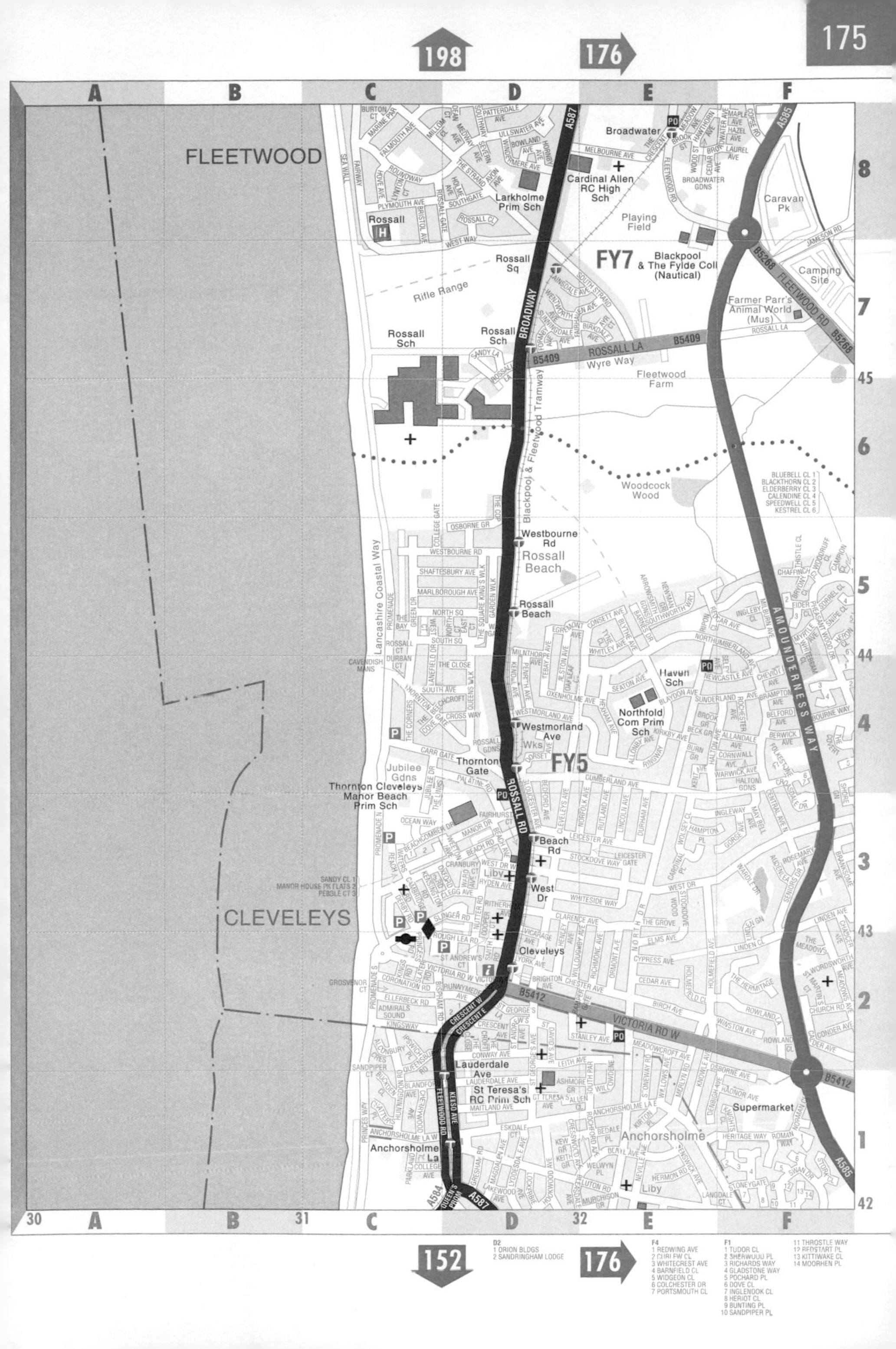
198
176
A
B
C
D
E
F
FLEETWOOD
CLEVELEYS
FY7
FY5
8
7
6
5
4
3
2
1
45
44
43
42
30
31
32
Broadwater
Cardinal Allen RC High Sch
Larkholme Prim Sch
Rossall
Playing Field
Caravan Pk
Rossall Sq
Blackpool & The Fylde Coll (Nautical)
Camping Site
Rifle Range
Farmer Parr's Animal World (Mus)
Rossall Sch
ROSSALL LA
B5409
Wyre Way
Fleetwood Farm
BROADWAY
A587
A585
B5268
FLEETWOOD RD
Blackpool & Fleetwood Tramway
Woodcock Wood
BLUEBELL CL 1
BLACKTHORN CL 2
ELDERBERRY CL 3
CALENDINE CL 4
SPEEDWELL CL 5
KESTREL CL 6
Westbourne Rd
Rossall Beach
Lancashire Coastal Way
AMOUNDERNESS WAY
Haven Sch
Northfold Com Prim Sch
Westmorland Ave
Wks
Thornton Gate
Jubilee Gdns
Thornton Cleveleys Manor Beach Prim Sch
ROSSALL RD
Beach Rd
West Dr
Liby
Cleveleys
SANDY CL 1
MANOR HOUSE PK FLATS 2
PEBBLE CT 3
B5412
VICTORIA RD W
Lauderdale Ave
St Teresa's RC Prim Sch
Supermarket
Anchorsholme
Anchorsholme La
A584
152
176
D2
1 ORION BLDGS
2 SANDRINGHAM LODGE
F4
1 REDWING AVE
2 CURLEW CL
3 WHITECREST AVE
4 BARNFIELD CL
5 WIDGEON CL
6 COLCHESTER DR
7 PORTSMOUTH CL
F1
1 TUDOR CL
2 SHERWOOD PL
3 RICHARDS WAY
4 GLADSTONE WAY
5 POCHARD PL
6 DOVE CL
7 INGLENOOK CL
8 HERIOT CL
9 BUNTING PL
10 SANDPIPER PL
11 THROSTLE WAY
12 REDSTART PL
13 KITTIWAKE CL
14 MOORHEN PL

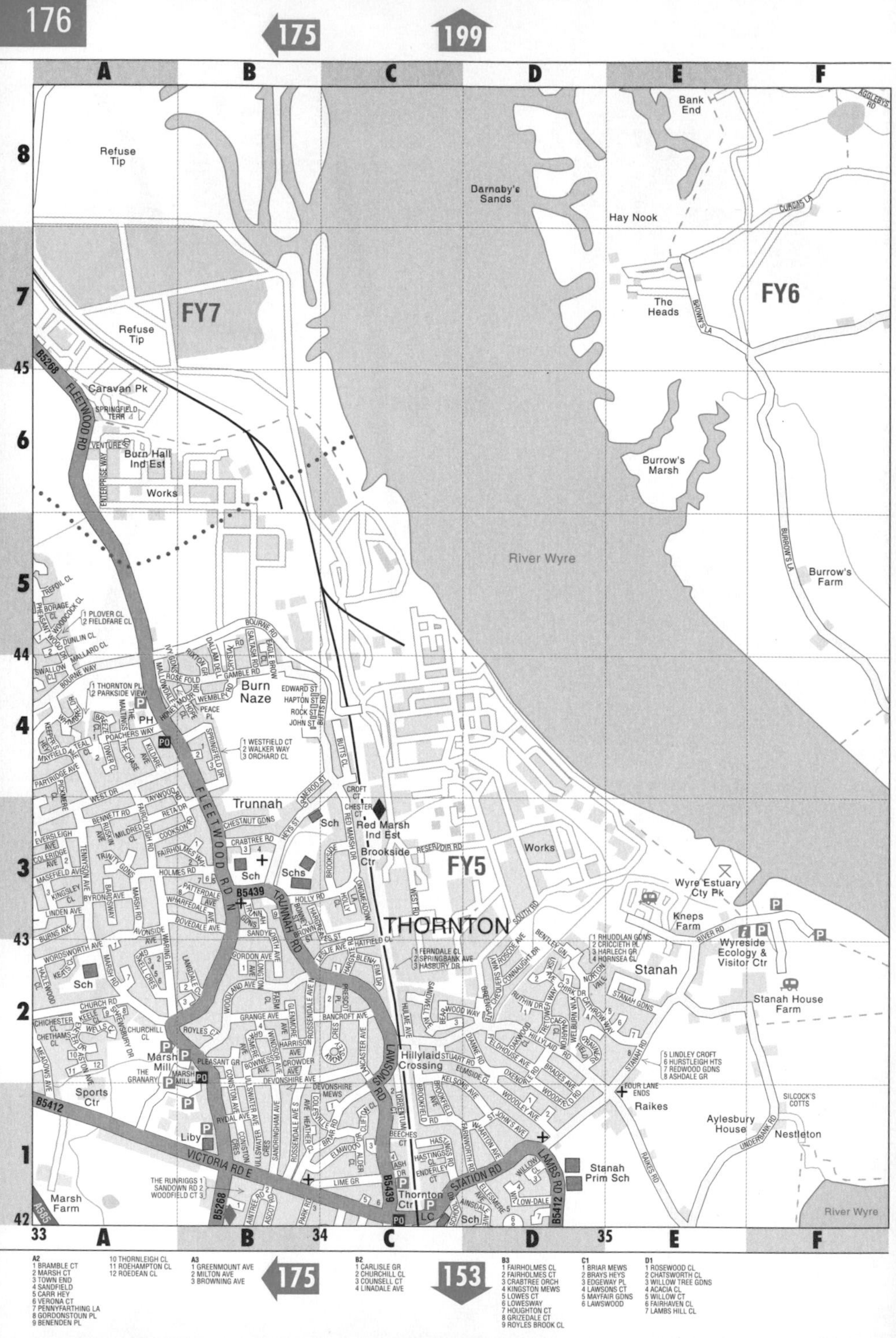

A2
1 BRAMBLE CT
2 MARSH CT
3 TOWN END
4 SANDFIELD
5 CARR HEY
6 VERONA CT
7 PENNYFARTHING LA
8 GORDONSTOUN PL
9 BENENDEN PL
10 THORNLEIGH CL
11 ROEHAMPTON CL
12 ROEDEAN CL

A3
1 GREENMOUNT AVE
2 MILTON AVE
3 BROWNING AVE

175

B2
1 CARLISLE GR
2 CHURCHILL CL
3 COUNSELL CT
4 LINADALE AVE

153

B3
1 FAIRHOLMES CL
2 FAIRHOLMES CT
3 CRABTREE ORCH
4 KINGSTON MEWS
5 LOWES CT
6 LOWESWAY
7 HOUGHTON CT
8 GRIZEDALE CT
9 ROYLES BROOK CL

C1
1 BRIAR MEWS
2 BRAYS HEYS
3 EDGEWAY PL
4 LAWSONS CT
5 MAYFAIR GDNS
6 LAWSWOOD

D1
1 ROSEWOOD CL
2 CHATSWORTH CL
3 WILLOW TREE GDNS
4 ACACIA CL
5 WILLOW CT
6 FAIRHAVEN CL
7 LAMBS HILL CL

200
178

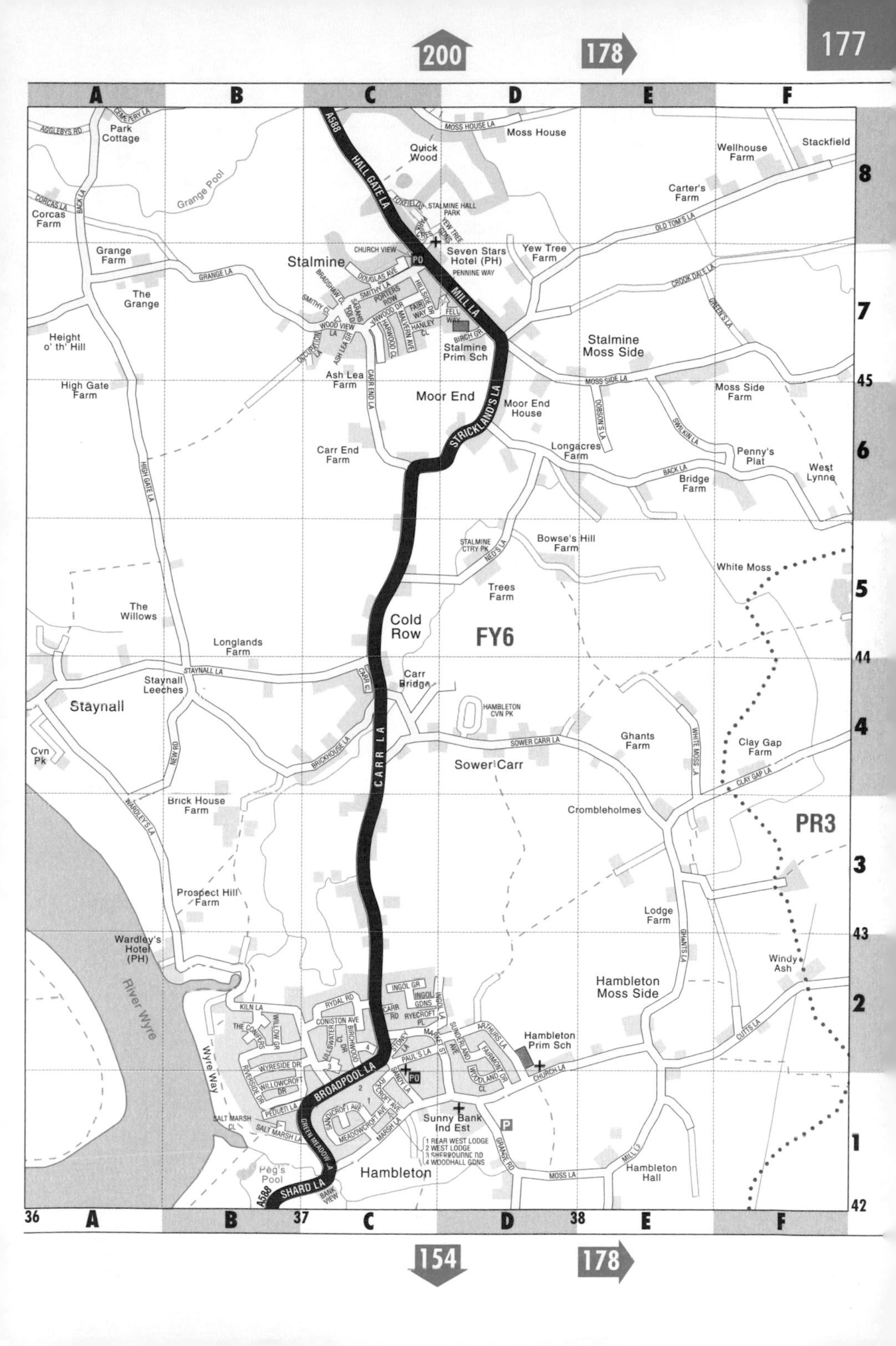

154
178

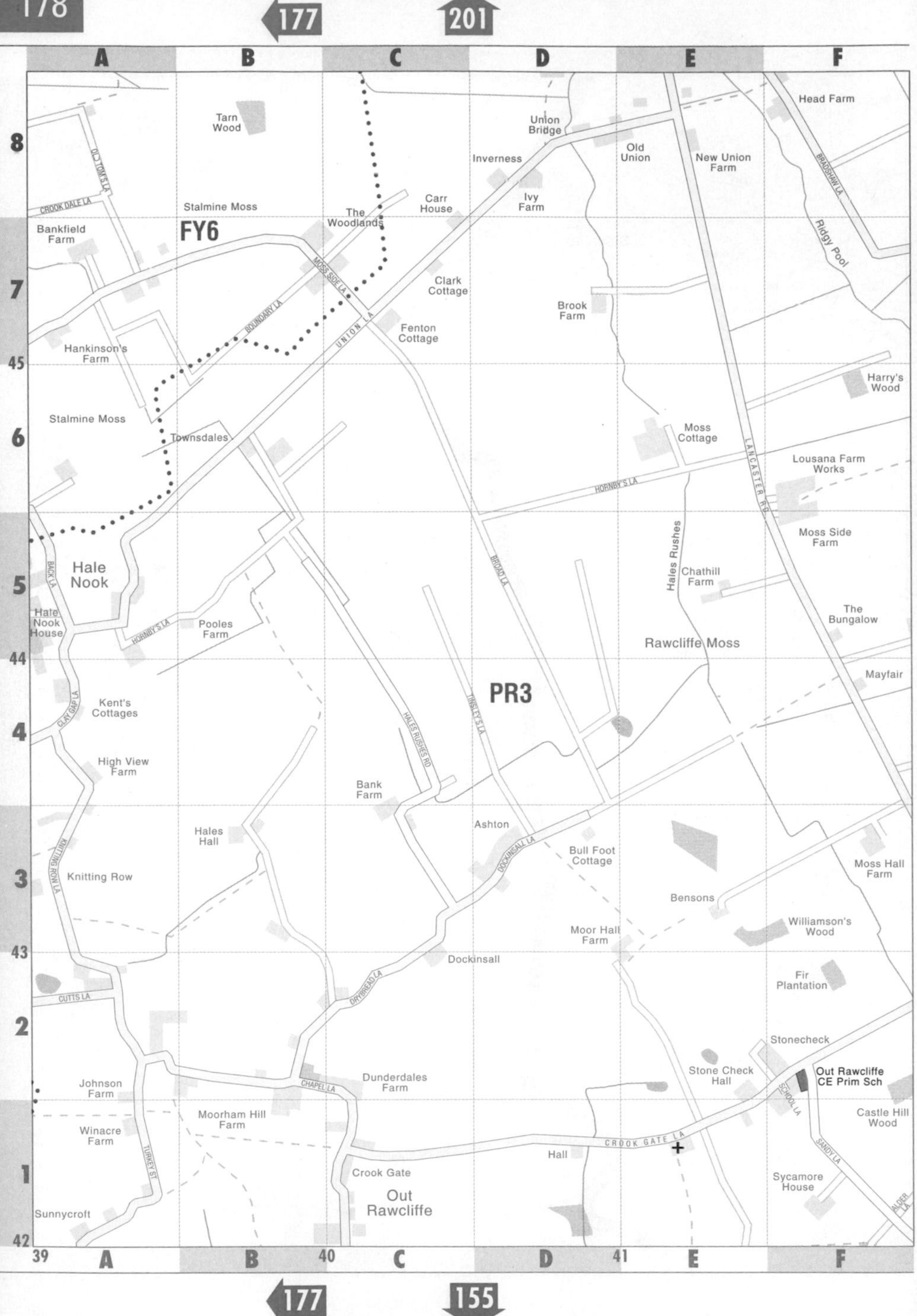
177
201
A
B
C
D
E
F
8
7
6
5
4
3
2
1
45
44
43
42
39
40
41
Tarn Wood
Union Bridge
Head Farm
OLD TOWN'S LA
Inverness
Old Union
New Union Farm
BRADSHAW LA
CROOK DALE LA
Stalmine Moss
The Woodlands
Carr House
Ivy Farm
Bankfield Farm
FY6
Ridgy Pool
MOSS SIDE LA
Clark Cottage
Brook Farm
BOUNDARY LA
UNION LA
Fenton Cottage
Hankinson's Farm
Harry's Wood
Stalmine Moss
Moss Cottage
Townsdales
Lousana Farm Works
LANCASTER RD
HORNBY'S LA
Moss Side Farm
Hales Rushes
Hale Nook
BACK LA
BRIDAD LA
Chathill Farm
Hale Nook House
HORNBY'S LA
Pooles Farm
The Bungalow
Rawcliffe Moss
Mayfair
Kent's Cottages
CLAY GAP LA
PR3
HALES RUSHES RD
TINSLEY'S LA
High View Farm
Bank Farm
Hales Hall
Ashton
DOCKINSALL LA
Bull Foot Cottage
Moss Hall Farm
KNITTING ROW LA
Knitting Row
Bensons
Williamson's Wood
Moor Hall Farm
Dockinsall
DRYBREAD LA
Fir Plantation
CUTTS LA
Stonecheck
Johnson Farm
CHAPEL LA
Dunderdales Farm
Stone Check Hall
Out Rawcliffe CE Prim Sch
SCHOOL LA
Castle Hill Wood
Moorham Hill Farm
Winacre Farm
TURKEY ST
CROOK GATE LA
Hall
SANDY LA
Crook Gate
Out Rawcliffe
Sycamore House
ALDER LA
Sunnycroft
177
155

202
180

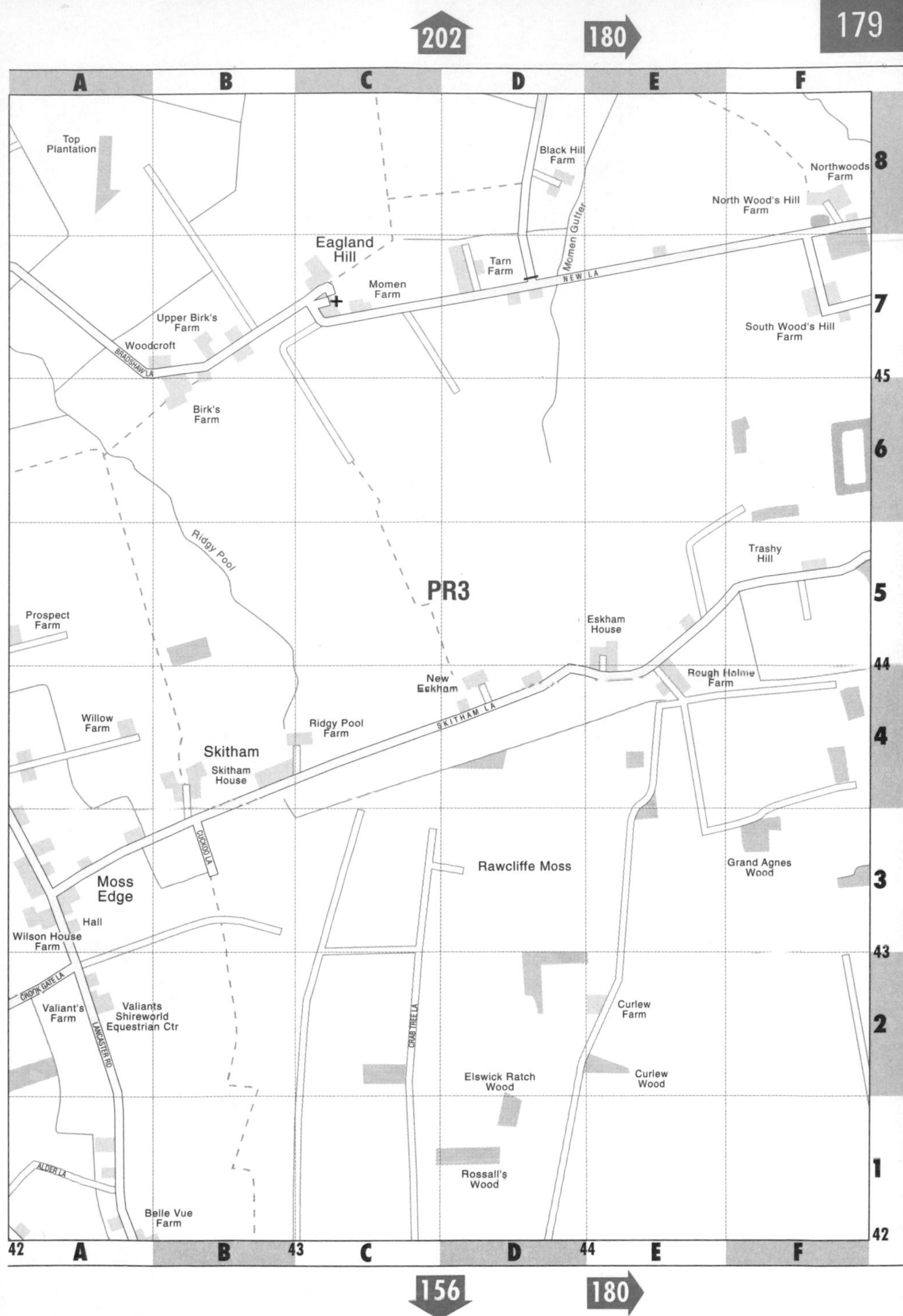

156
180

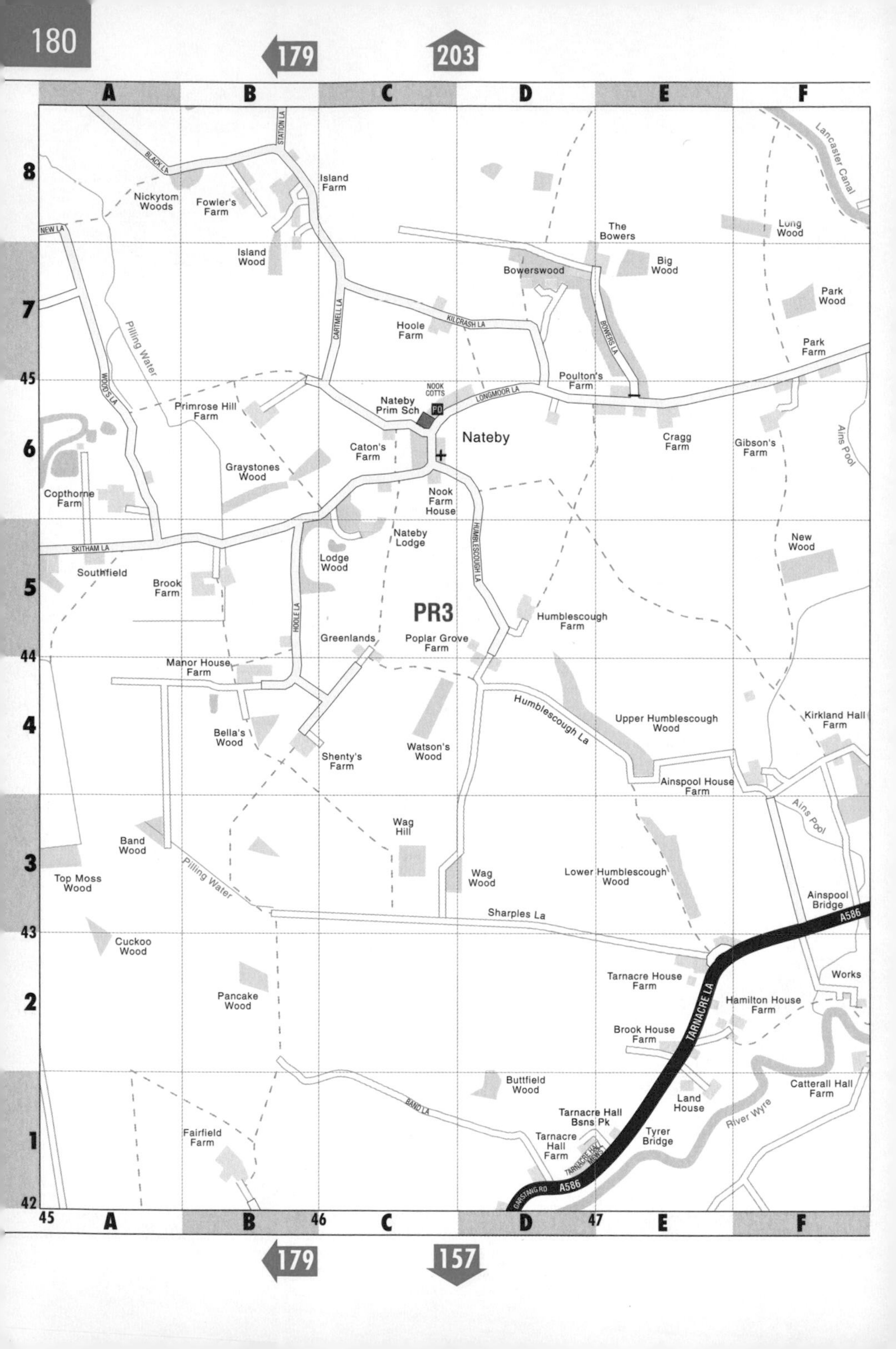
180
179
203
A
B
C
D
E
F
8
7
6
5
4
3
2
1
45
44
43
42
46
47
BLACK LA
STATION LA
Island Farm
Nickytom Woods
Fowler's Farm
NEW LA
Island Wood
The Bowers
Long Wood
Lancaster Canal
Bowerswood
Big Wood
Park Wood
CARTMELL LA
KILCRASH LA
Hoole Farm
BOWERS LA
Park Farm
Pilling Water
WOOD'S LA
NOOK COTTS
Poulton's Farm
LONGMOOR LA
Nateby Prim Sch
PO
Primrose Hill Farm
Nateby
Cragg Farm
Gibson's Farm
Ains Pool
Caton's Farm
Graystones Wood
Nook Farm House
Copthorne Farm
HUMBLESCOUGH LA
Nateby Lodge
New Wood
SKITHAM LA
Southfield
Lodge Wood
Brook Farm
PR3
HOOLE LA
Humblescough Farm
Greenlands
Poplar Grove Farm
Manor House Farm
Humblescough La
Upper Humblescough Wood
Kirkland Hall Farm
Bella's Wood
Watson's Wood
Shenty's Farm
Ainspool House Farm
Ains Pool
Wag Hill
Band Wood
Pilling Water
Top Moss Wood
Wag Wood
Lower Humblescough Wood
Ainspool Bridge
Sharples La
A586
Cuckoo Wood
Tarnacre House Farm
Works
TARNACRE LA
Hamilton House Farm
Pancake Wood
Brook House Farm
Buttfield Wood
Catterall Hall Farm
BAND LA
Land House
River Wyre
Tarnacre Hall Bsns Pk
Tyrer Bridge
Fairfield Farm
Tarnacre Hall Farm
TARNACRE HALL MEWS
GARSTANG RD
A586
179
157

204
182

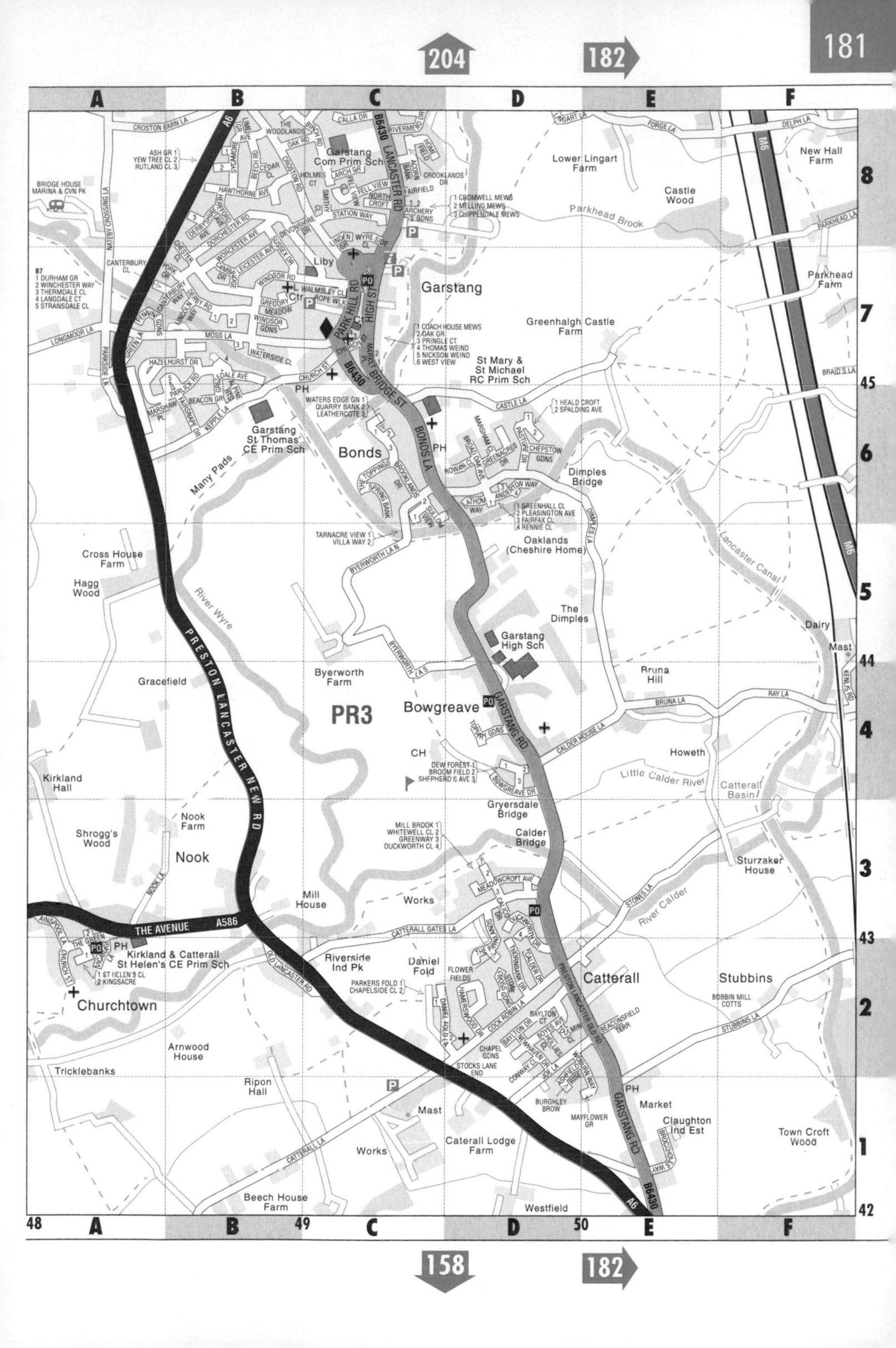

158
182

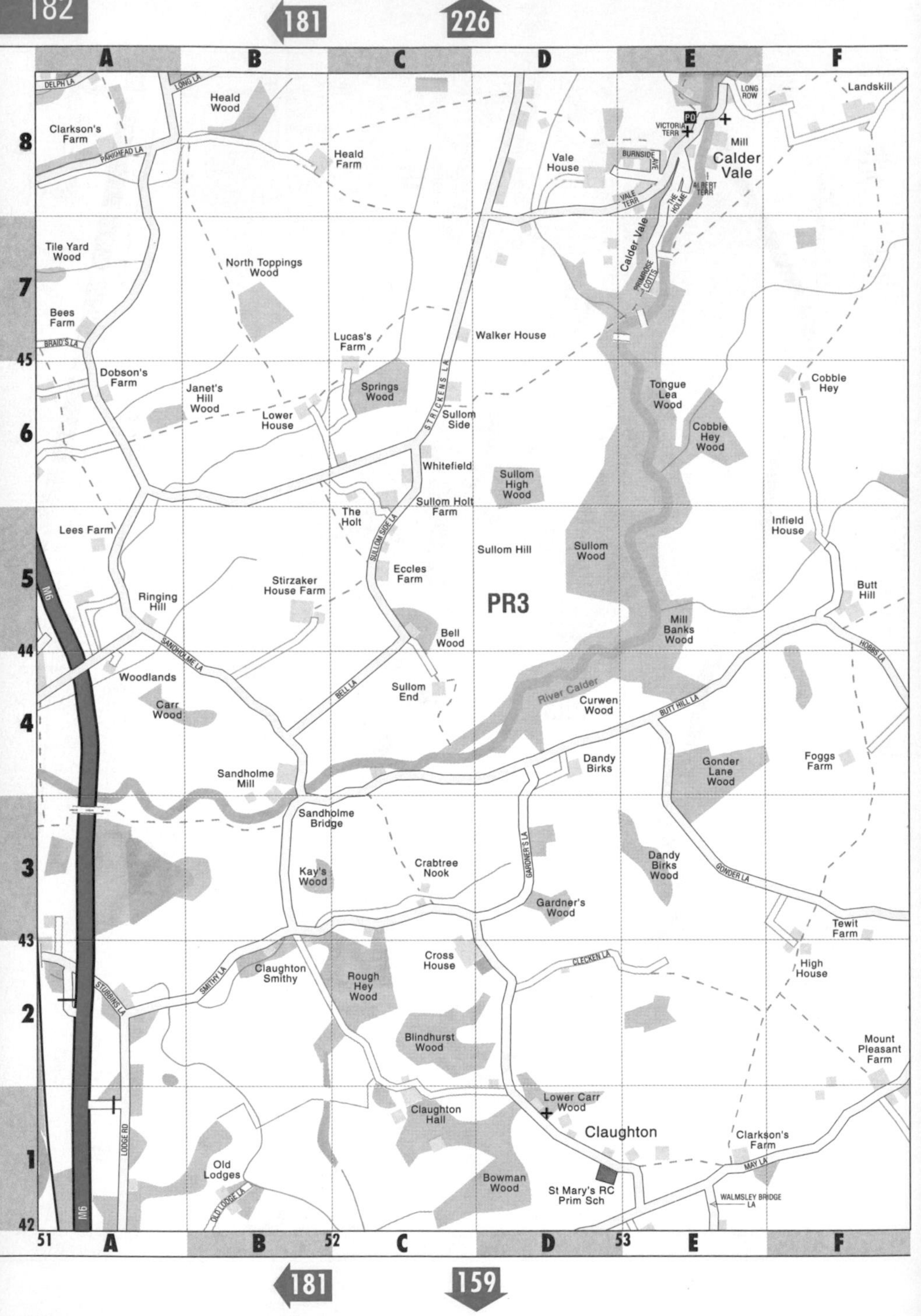

181
226
A
B
C
D
E
F
8
7
45
6
5
44
4
3
43
2
1
42
51
52
53
DELPH LA
LONG LA
Heald Wood
Clarkson's Farm
PARKHEAD LA
Heald Farm
Vale House
BURNSIDE
AVE
VICTORIA TERR
PO
LONG ROW
Landskill
Mill
Calder Vale
VALE TERR
THE HOLME
ALBERT TERR
Tile Yard Wood
North Toppings Wood
Calder Vale
PRIMROSE COTTS
Bees Farm
BRAID'S LA
Lucas's Farm
Walker House
Dobson's Farm
Janet's Hill Wood
Springs Wood
STRICKENS LA
Tongue Lea Wood
Cobble Hey
Lower House
Sullom Side
Cobble Hey Wood
Whitefield
Sullom High Wood
Sullom Holt Farm
The Holt
Lees Farm
SULLOM SIDE LA
Sullom Hill
Sullom Wood
Infield House
Eccles Farm
Ringing Hill
Stirzaker House Farm
PR3
Butt Hill
M6
Bell Wood
Mill Banks Wood
SANDHOLME LA
HOBBS LA
Woodlands
BELL LA
Sullom End
River Calder
Curwen Wood
BUTT HILL LA
Carr Wood
Dandy Birks
Gonder Lane Wood
Foggs Farm
Sandholme Mill
Sandholme Bridge
GARDNER'S LA
Kay's Wood
Crabtree Nook
Dandy Birks Wood
GONDER LA
Gardner's Wood
Tewit Farm
Cross House
CLECKEN LA
High House
STUBBINS LA
SMITHY LA
Claughton Smithy
Rough Hey Wood
Blindhurst Wood
Mount Pleasant Farm
Lower Carr Wood
Claughton Hall
Claughton
LODGE RD
Clarkson's Farm
MAY LA
Old Lodges
Bowman Wood
St Mary's RC Prim Sch
WALMSLEY BRIDGE LA
OLD LODGE LA
A
B
C
D
E
F
181
159

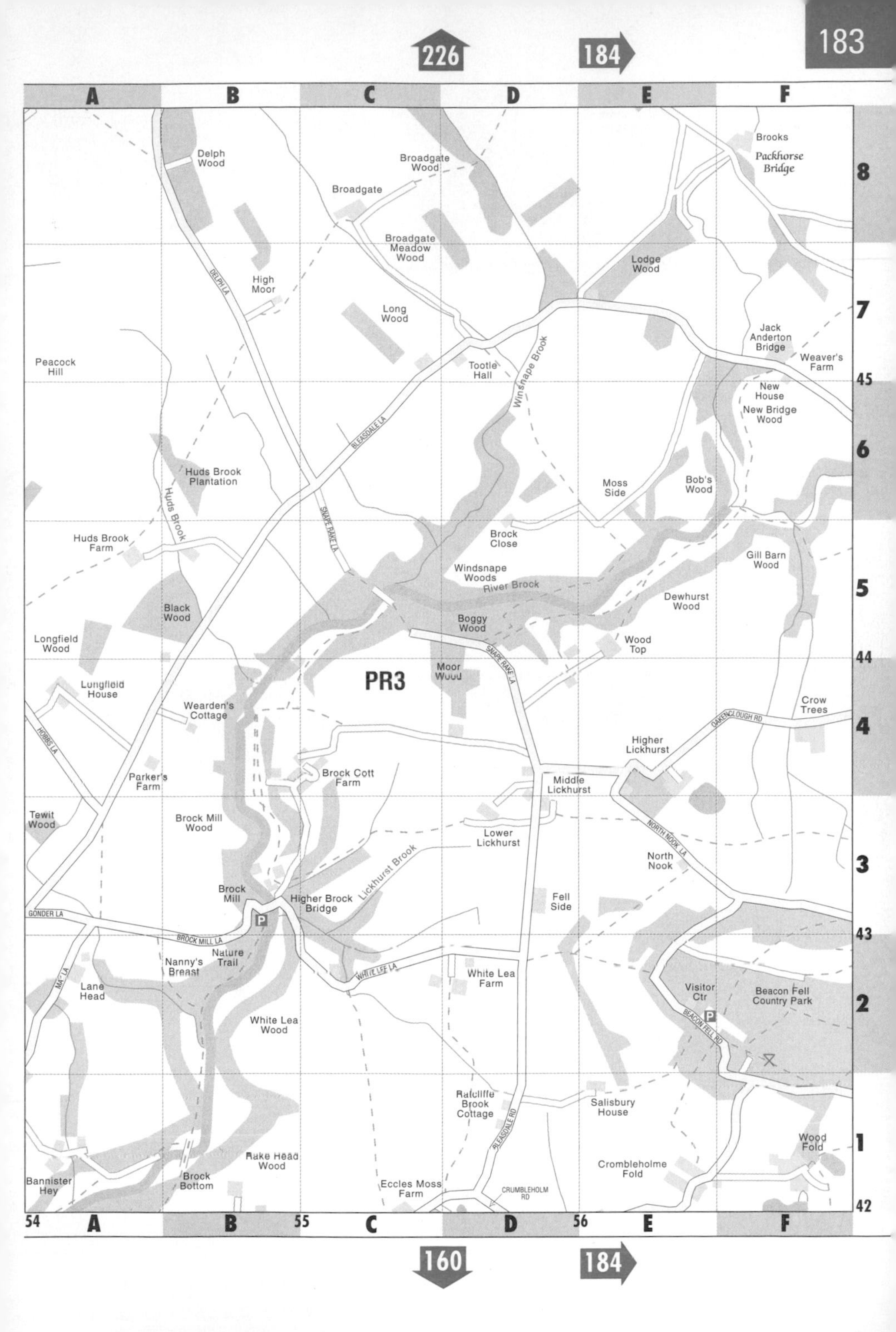
226
184
A
B
C
D
E
F
8
7
6
5
4
3
2
1
45
44
43
42
54
55
56
Delph Wood
Broadgate Wood
Broadgate
Brooks
Packhorse Bridge
Broadgate Meadow Wood
Lodge Wood
High Moor
DELPH LA
Long Wood
Jack Anderton Bridge
Weaver's Farm
Peacock Hill
Tootle Hall
Winsnape Brook
New House
New Bridge Wood
BLEASDALE LA
Huds Brook Plantation
Huds Brook
Moss Side
Bob's Wood
SNAPE RAKE LA
Brock Close
Huds Brook Farm
Windsnape Woods
River Brock
Gill Barn Wood
Black Wood
Dewhurst Wood
Boggy Wood
Longfield Wood
Wood Top
Moor Wood
PR3
Longfield House
Wearden's Cottage
Crow Trees
OAKENCLOUGH RD
HOBBS LA
Higher Lickhurst
Parker's Farm
Brock Cott Farm
Middle Lickhurst
Tewit Wood
Brock Mill Wood
Lower Lickhurst
NORTH NOOK LA
North Nook
Lickhurst Brook
Brock Mill
Higher Brock Bridge
Fell Side
GONDER LA
BROCK MILL LA
Nanny's Breast
Nature Trail
WHITE LEE LA
White Lea Farm
MAC LA
Lane Head
Visitor Ctr
Beacon Fell Country Park
BEACON FELL RD
White Lea Wood
Ratcliffe Brook Cottage
Salisbury House
BLEASDALE RD
Wood Fold
Rake Head Wood
Crombleholme Fold
Bannister Hey
Brock Bottom
Eccles Moss Farm
CRUMBLEHOLM RD
160
184

183
227

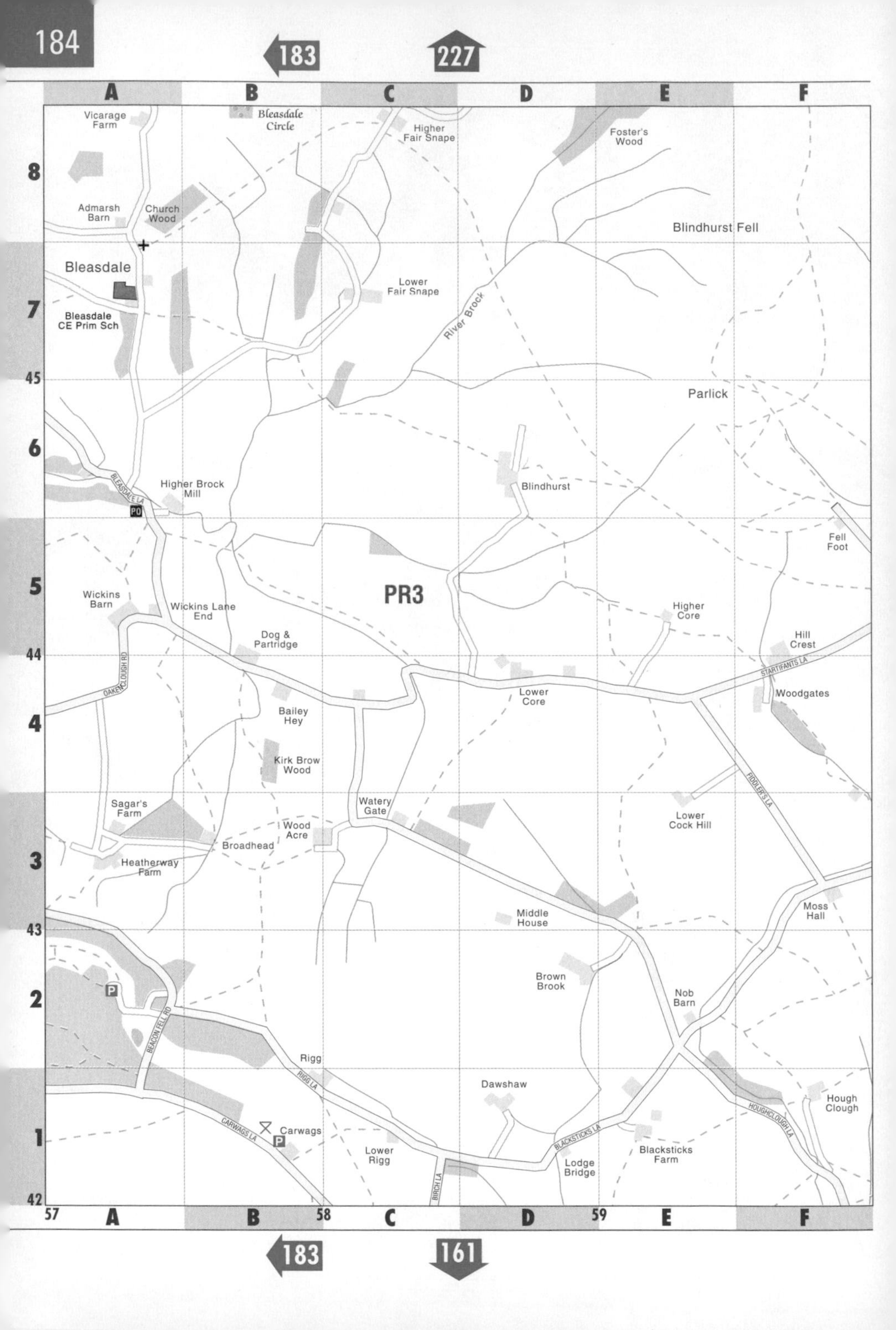

183
161

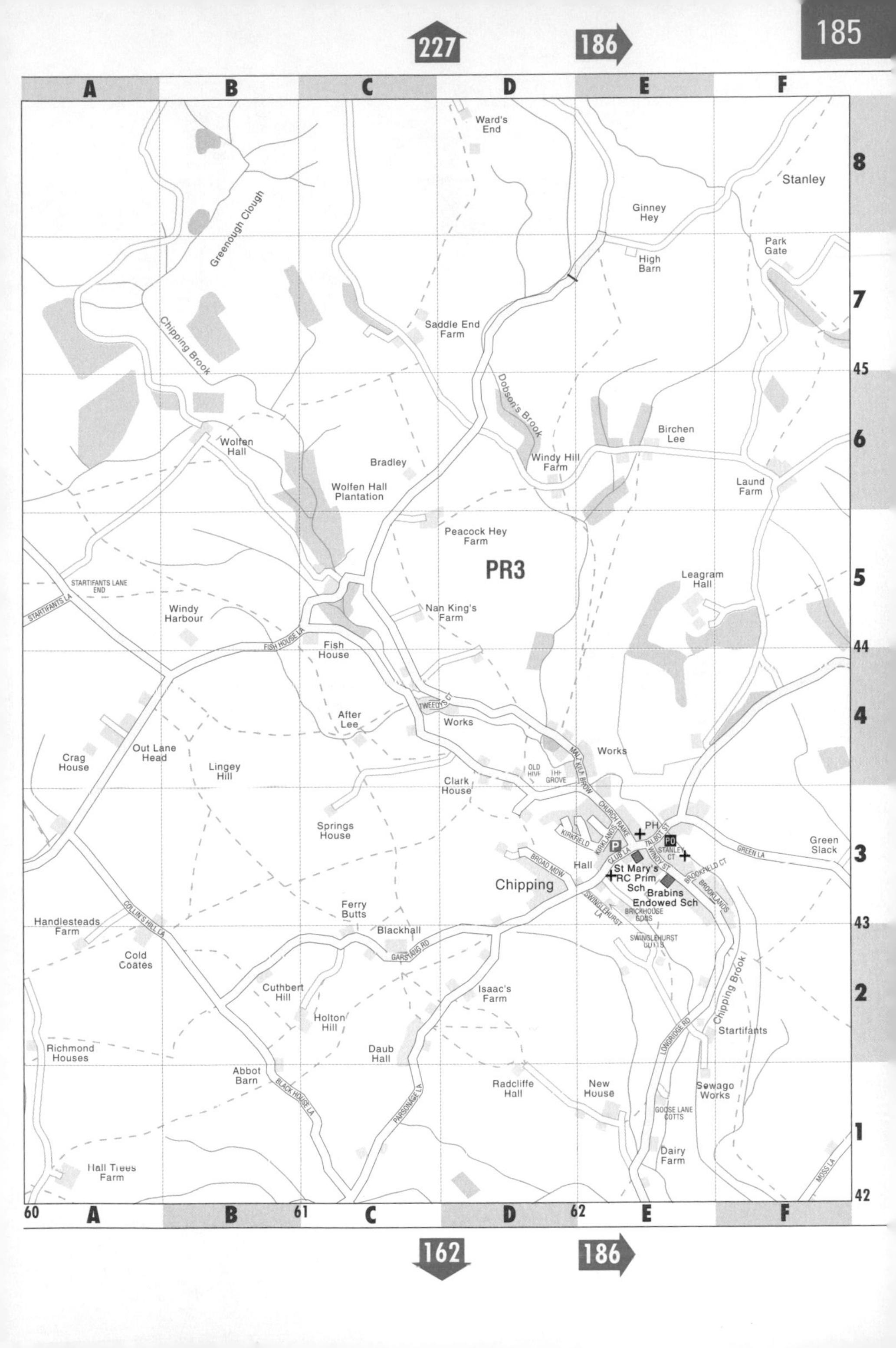
227
186
Ward's End
Stanley
Greenough Clough
Ginney Hey
High Barn
Park Gate
Chipping Brook
Saddle End Farm
Dobson's Brook
Birchen Lee
Wolfen Hall
Bradley
Windy Hill Farm
Laund Farm
Wolfen Hall Plantation
Peacock Hey Farm
PR3
Leagram Hall
STARTIFANTS LANE END
STARTIFANTS LA
Windy Harbour
Nan King's Farm
FISH HOUSE LA
Fish House
TWEEDYS CT
After Lee
Works
Works
MALT KILN BROW
Crag House
Out Lane Head
Lingey Hill
OLD HIVE
THE GROVE
Clark House
CHURCH RAIKE
Springs House
KIRKFIELD
KIRKLANDS
PH
TALBOT ST
PO
STANLEY CT
WINDY ST
CLUB LA
GREEN LA
Green Slack
BROAD MDW
Hall
St Mary's RC Prim Sch
BROOKFIELD CT
Chipping
Brabins Endowed Sch
BROOKLANDS
SWINGLEHURST LA
BRICKHOUSE GDNS
COLLIN'S HILL LA
Ferry Butts
Handlesteads Farm
Blackhall
SWINGLEHURST COTTS
GARSTANG RD
Cold Coates
Cuthbert Hill
Isaac's Farm
Holton Hill
LONGRIDGE RD
Startifants
Richmond Houses
Daub Hall
Abbot Barn
BLACK HOUSE LA
PARSONAGE LA
Radcliffe Hall
New House
Sewage Works
GOOSE LANE COTTS
Dairy Farm
Hall Trees Farm
MOSS LA
A
B
C
D
E
F
8
7
6
5
4
3
2
1
45
44
43
42
60
61
62
162
186

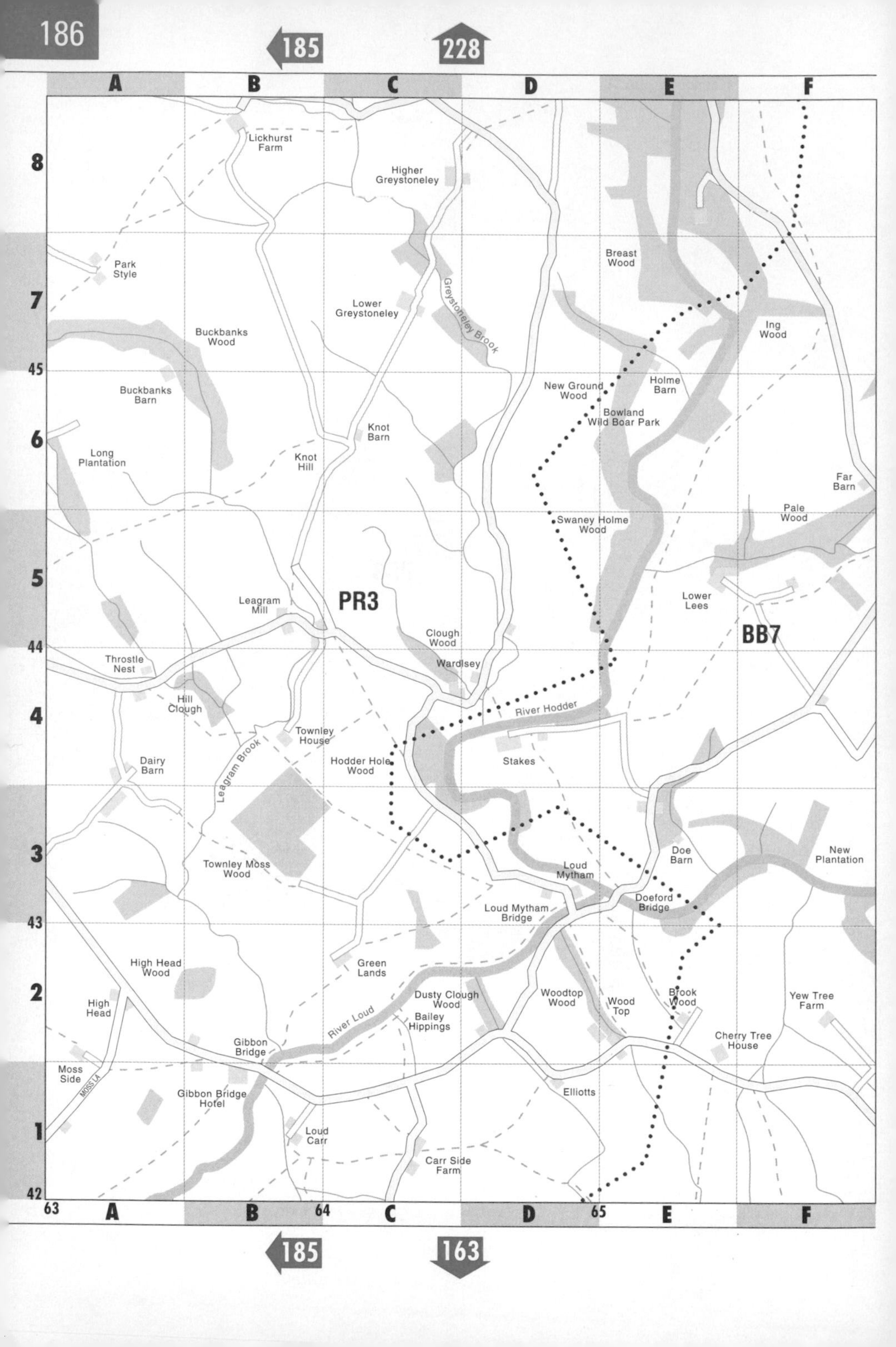
185
228
A
B
C
D
E
F
8
7
45
6
5
44
4
3
43
2
1
42
63
64
65
Lickhurst Farm
Higher Greystoneley
Park Style
Breast Wood
Lower Greystoneley
Greystoneley Brook
Buckbanks Wood
Ing Wood
Buckbanks Barn
New Ground Wood
Holme Barn
Bowland Wild Boar Park
Knot Barn
Long Plantation
Knot Hill
Far Barn
Pale Wood
Swaney Holme Wood
PR3
Leagram Mill
Lower Lees
BB7
Clough Wood
Throstle Nest
Wardlsey
Hill Clough
River Hodder
Townley House
Leagram Brook
Dairy Barn
Hodder Hole Wood
Stakes
Doe Barn
New Plantation
Townley Moss Wood
Loud Mytham
Doeford Bridge
Loud Mytham Bridge
High Head Wood
Green Lands
Dusty Clough Wood
Woodtop Wood
Wood Top
Brook Wood
Yew Tree Farm
High Head
River Loud
Bailey Hippings
Gibbon Bridge
Cherry Tree House
Moss Side
MOSS LA
Gibbon Bridge Hotel
Elliotts
Loud Carr
Carr Side Farm
185
163

228
188

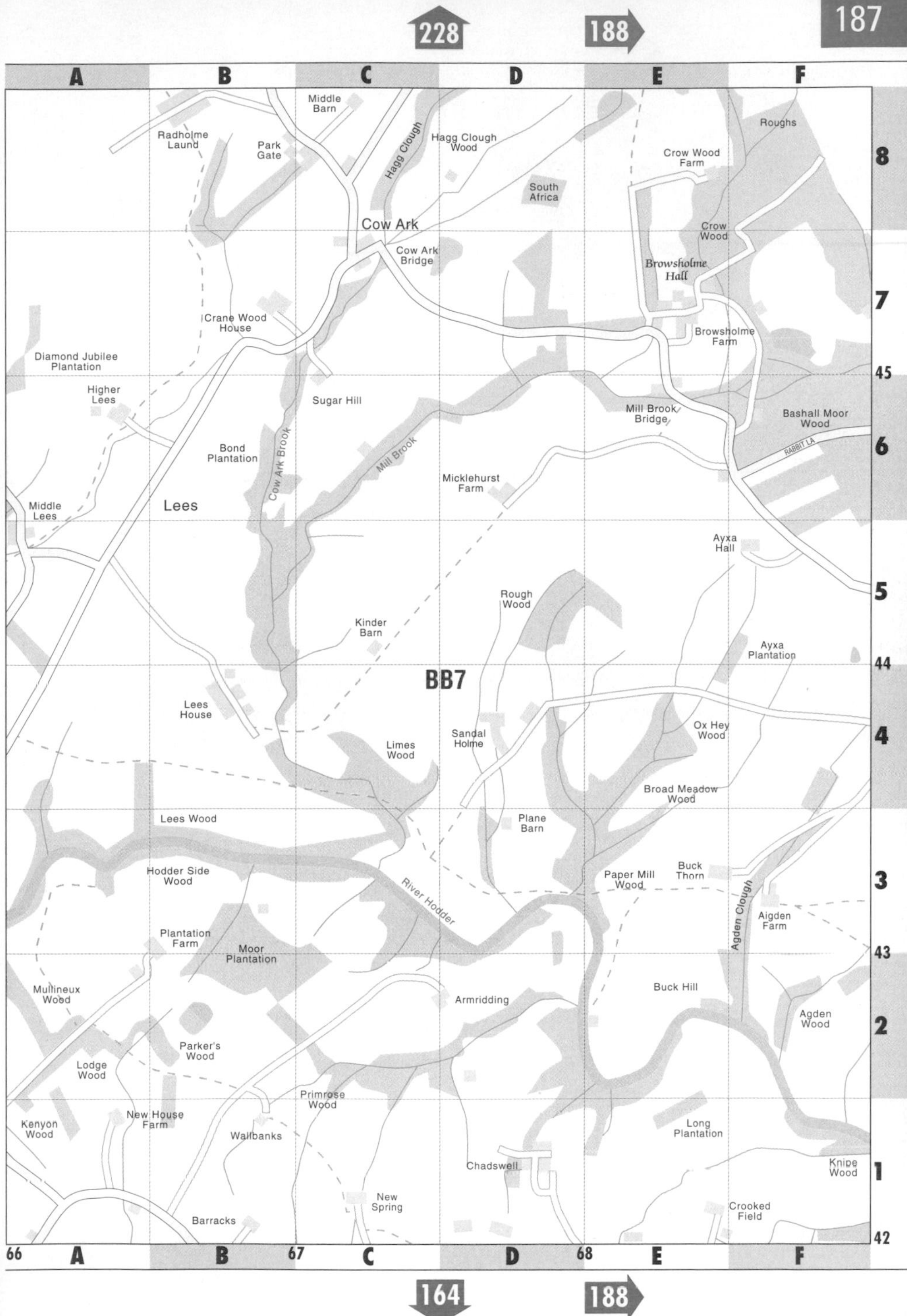

164
188

187

229

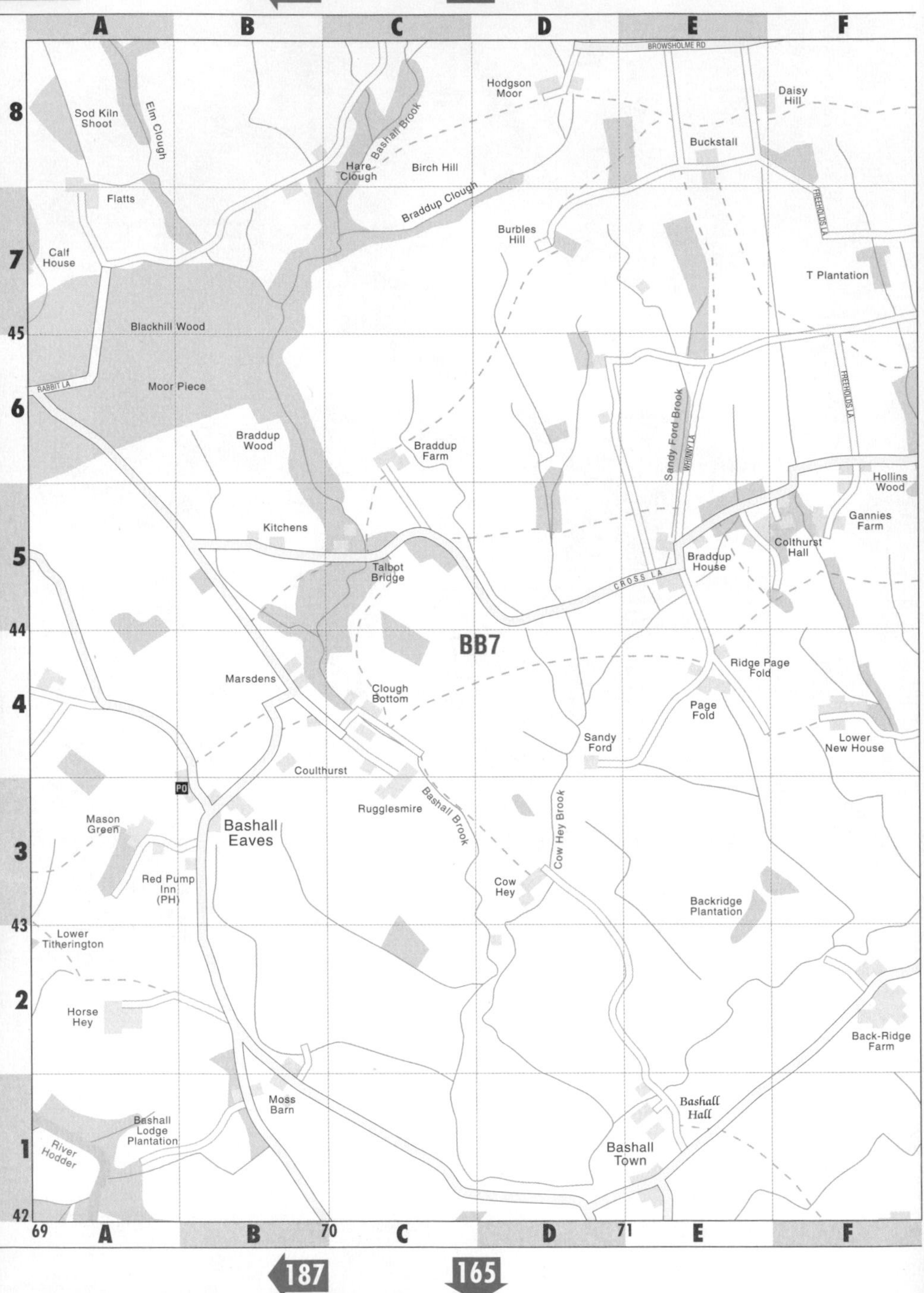

187
165

190

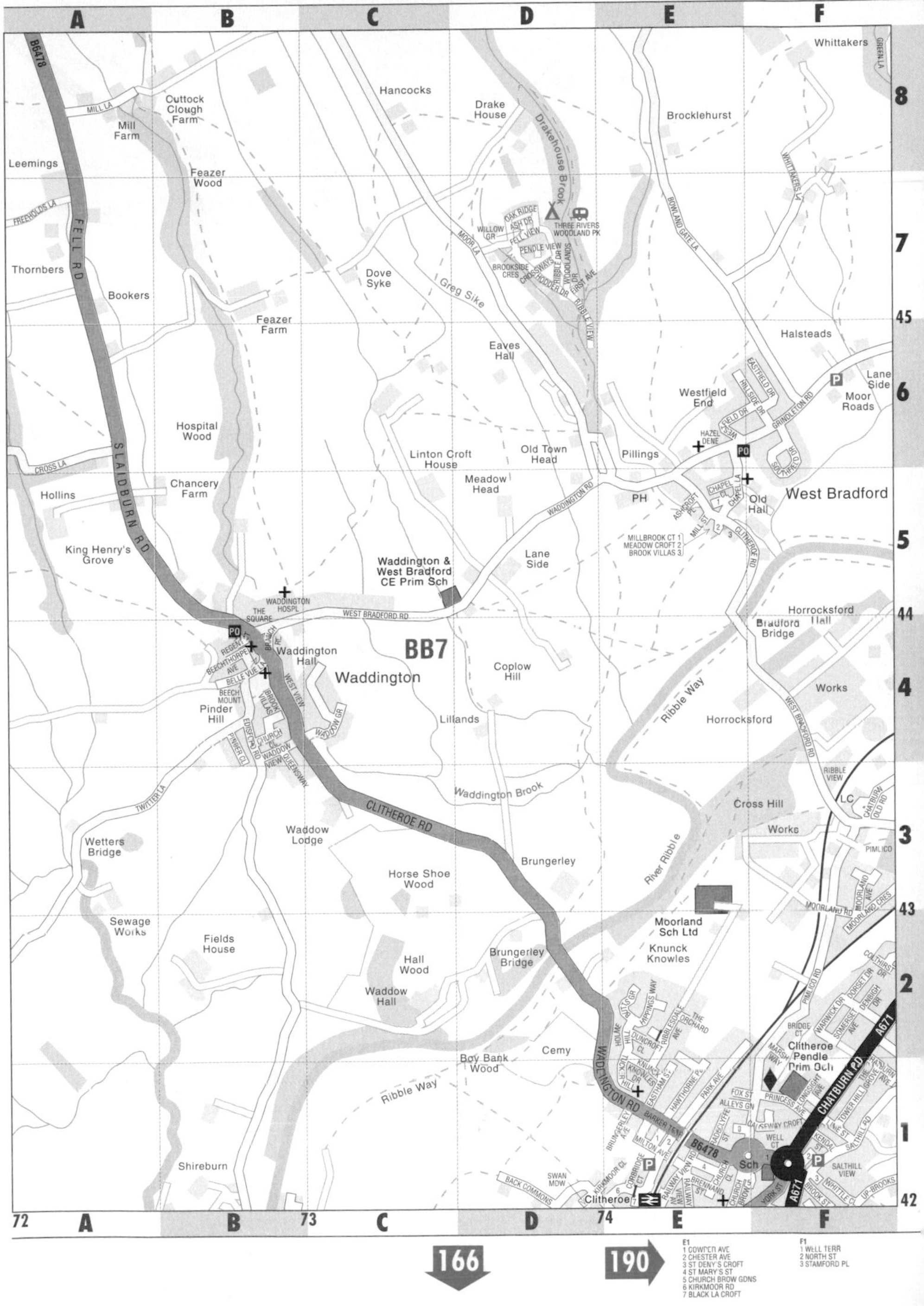

A B C D E F

166

190

E1
1 COWPER AVE
2 CHESTER AVE
3 ST DENY'S CROFT
4 ST MARY'S ST
5 CHURCH BROW GDNS
6 KIRKMOOR RD
7 BLACK LA CROFT

F1
1 WELL TERR
2 NORTH ST
3 STAMFORD PL

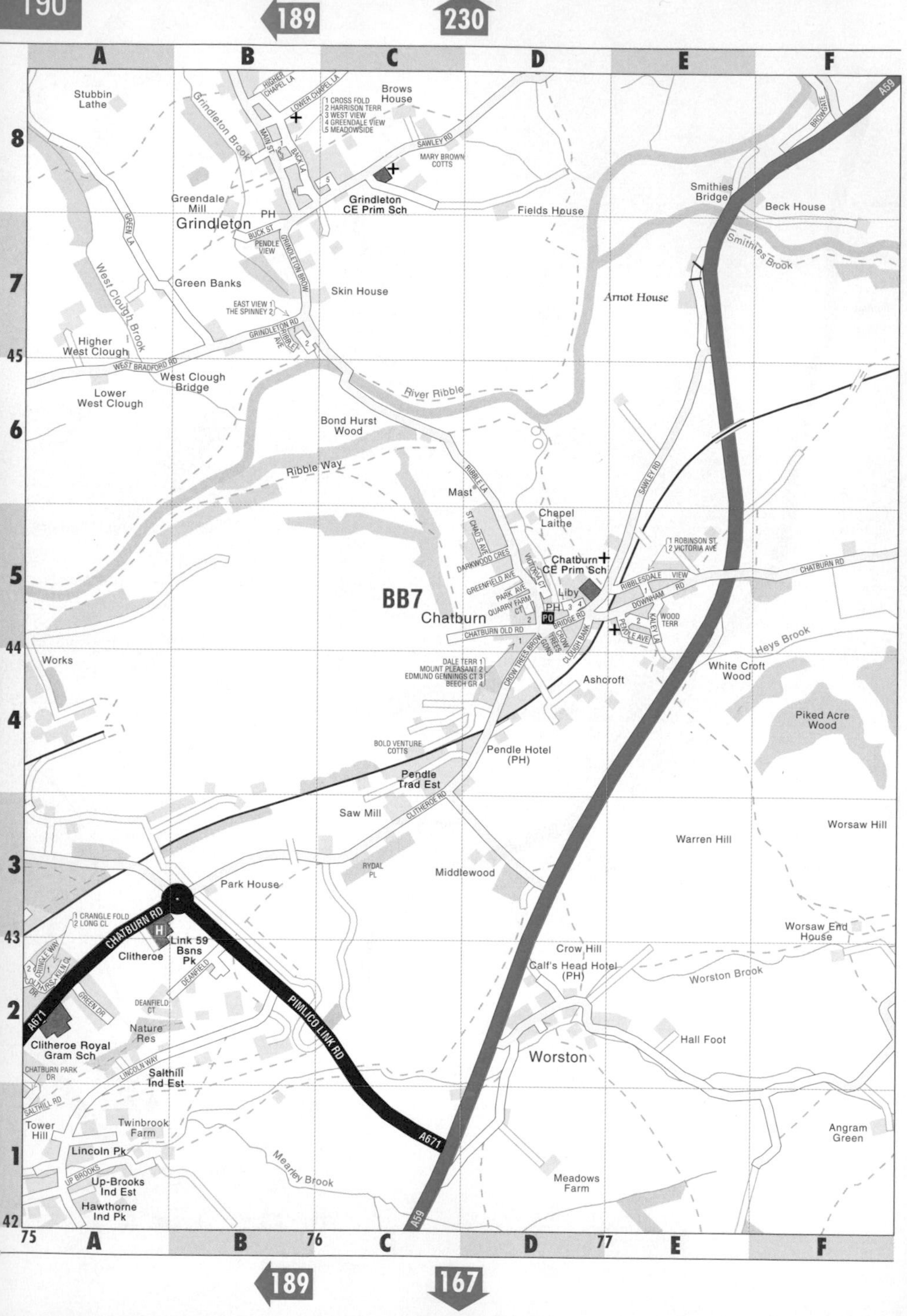

189
230
167
A
B
C
D
E
F
8
7
6
5
4
3
2
1
45
44
43
42
75
76
77
Stubbin Lathe
Brows House
HIGHER CHAPEL LA
LOWER CHAPEL LA
1 CROSS FOLD
2 HARRISON TERR
3 WEST VIEW
4 GREENDALE VIEW
5 MEADOWSIDE
Grindleton Brook
MAIN ST
BUCK LA
SAWLEY RD
MARY BROWN COTTS
BROWGATE
A59
Greendale Mill
PH
Grindleton
Grindleton CE Prim Sch
Fields House
Smithies Bridge
Beck House
Smithies Brook
BUCK ST
PENDLE VIEW
GRINDLETON BROW
GREEN LA
West Clough Brook
Green Banks
Skin House
Arnot House
EAST VIEW 1
THE SPINNEY 2
GRINDLETON RD
RIBBLE AVE
Higher West Clough
WEST BRADFORD RD
West Clough Bridge
Lower West Clough
River Ribble
Bond Hurst Wood
Ribble Way
RIBBLE LA
Mast
SAWLEY RD
Chapel Laithe
ST CHAD'S AVE
DARKWOOD CRES
VICTORIA CT
Chatburn CE Prim Sch
1 ROBINSON ST
2 VICTORIA AVE
RIBBLESDALE VIEW
CHATBURN RD
GREENFIELD AVE
PARK AVE
QUARRY FARM CT
Liby
PH
DOWNHAM RD
BB7
Chatburn
PO
BRIDGE RD
WOOD TERR
KALEY LA
PENDLE AVE
CHATBURN OLD RD
CROW TREES BROW
CROW TREES GDNS
CLOUGH BANK
Heys Brook
Works
DALE TERR 1
MOUNT PLEASANT 2
EDMUND GENNINGS CT 3
BEECH GR 4
Ashcroft
White Croft Wood
Piked Acre Wood
BOLD VENTURE COTTS
Pendle Hotel (PH)
Pendle Trad Est
Saw Mill
CLITHEROE RD
Worsaw Hill
Warren Hill
RYDAL PL
Middlewood
Park House
1 CRANGLE FOLD
2 LONG CL
CHATBURN RD
H
Link 59 Bsns Pk
Clitheroe
Worsaw End House
Crow Hill
Calf's Head Hotel (PH)
Worston Brook
DEANFIELD
DEANFIELD CT
PIMLICO LINK RD
GREEN DR
A671
Nature Res
Hall Foot
Clitheroe Royal Gram Sch
Worston
CHATBURN PARK DR
LINCOLN WAY
Salthill Ind Est
SALTHILL RD
Tower Hill
Twinbrook Farm
A671
Angram Green
Lincoln Pk
UP BROOKS
Mearley Brook
Up-Brooks Ind Est
Meadows Farm
Hawthorne Ind Pk
A59

230
192

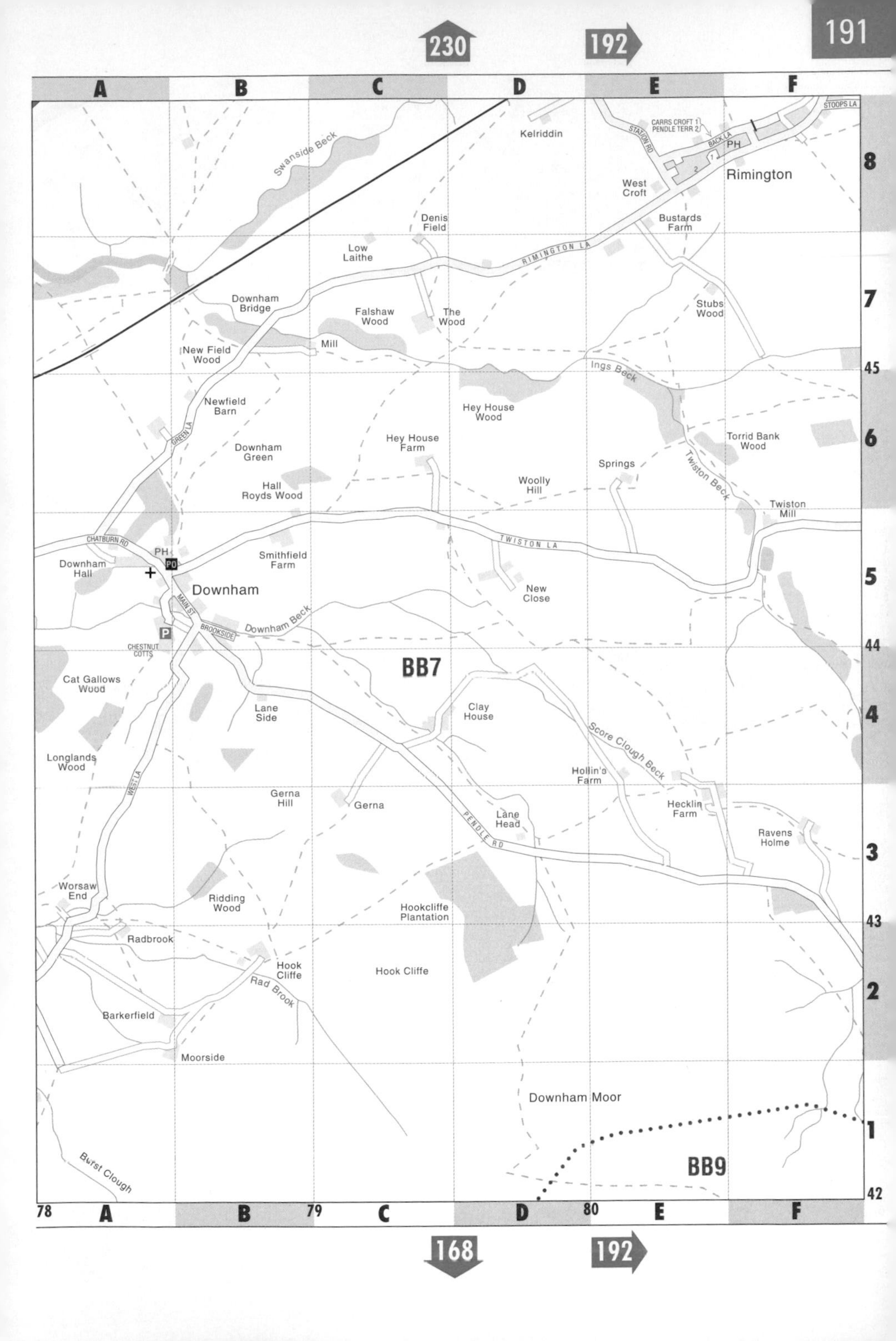

168
192

191
231

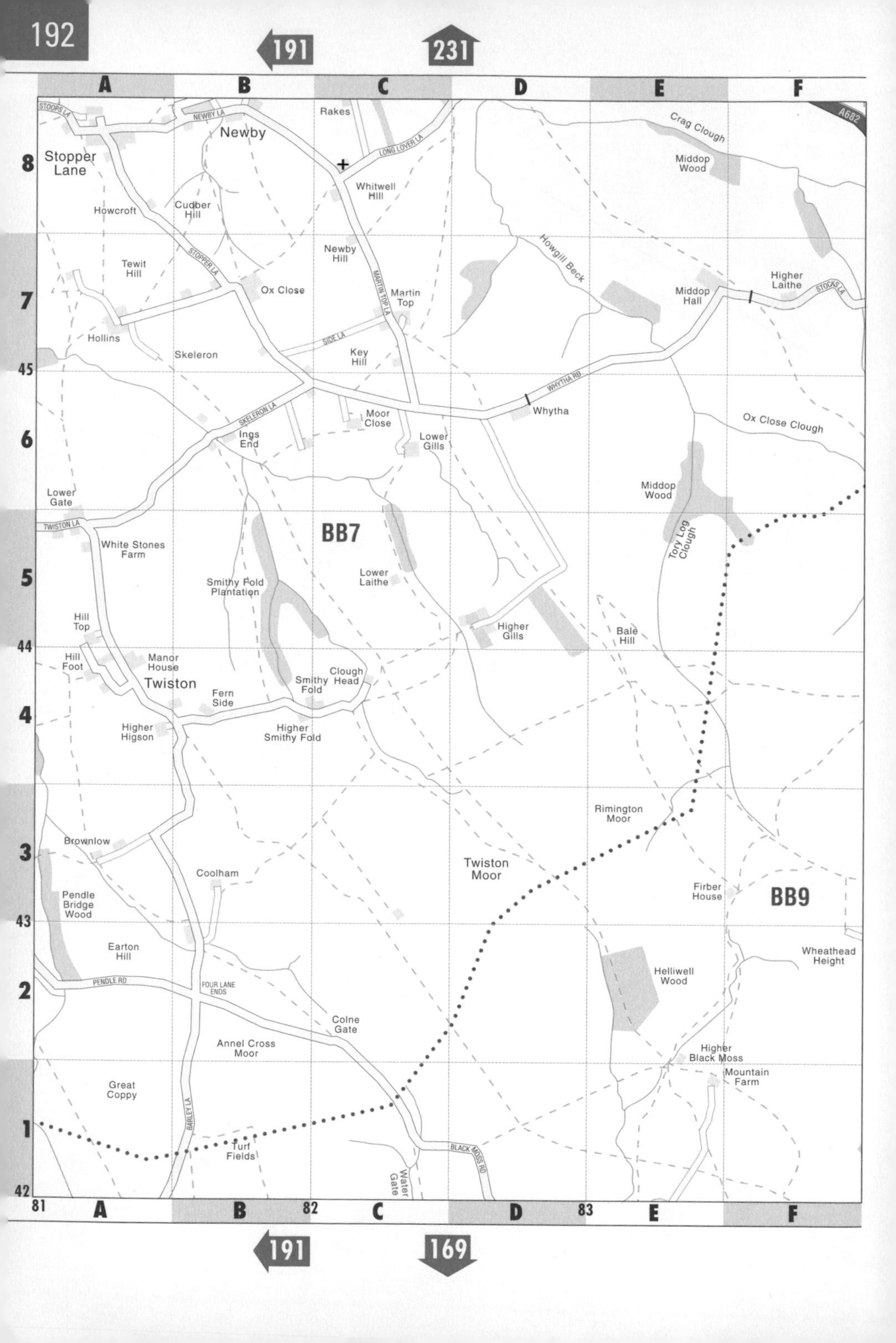

191
169

231
194

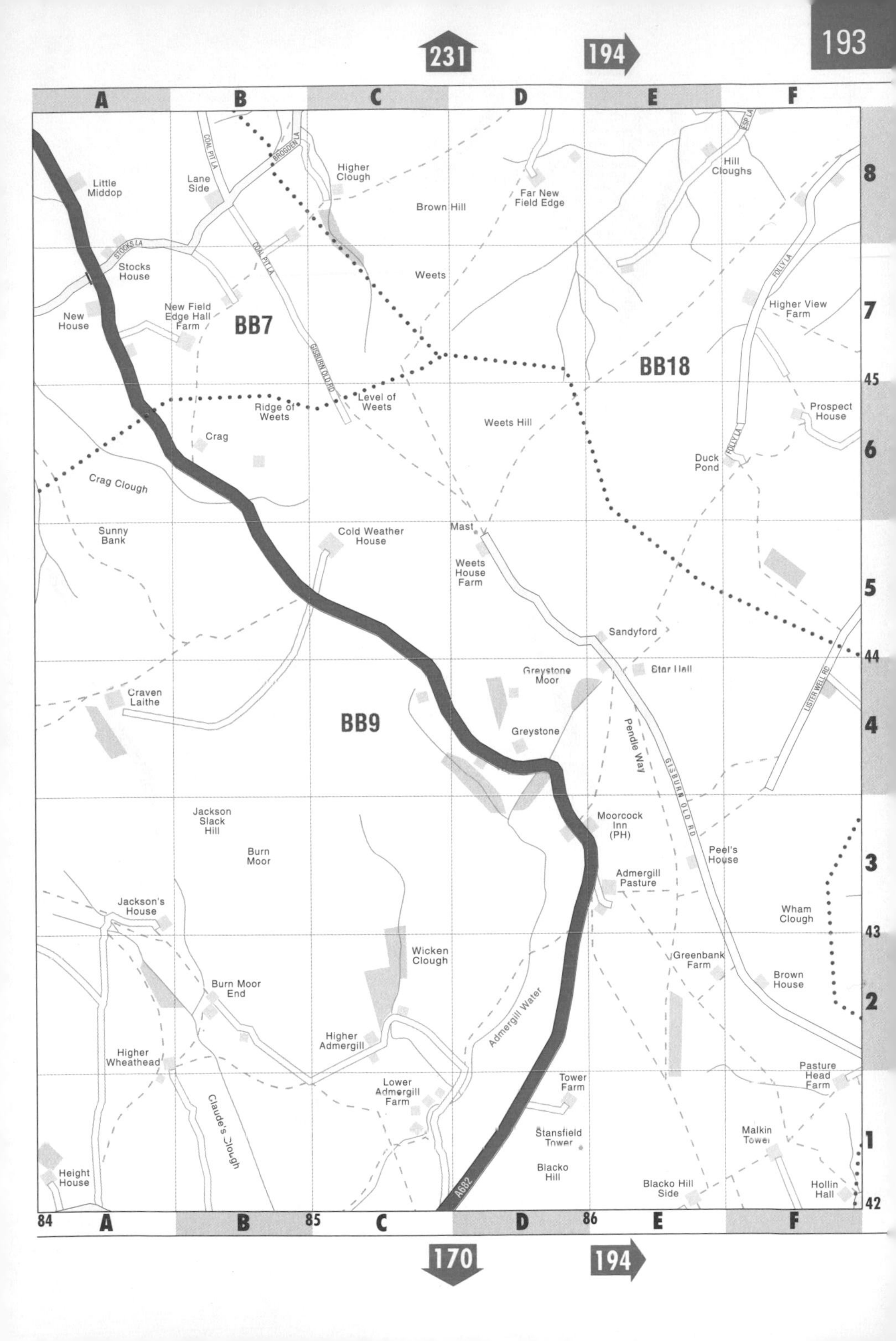

170
194

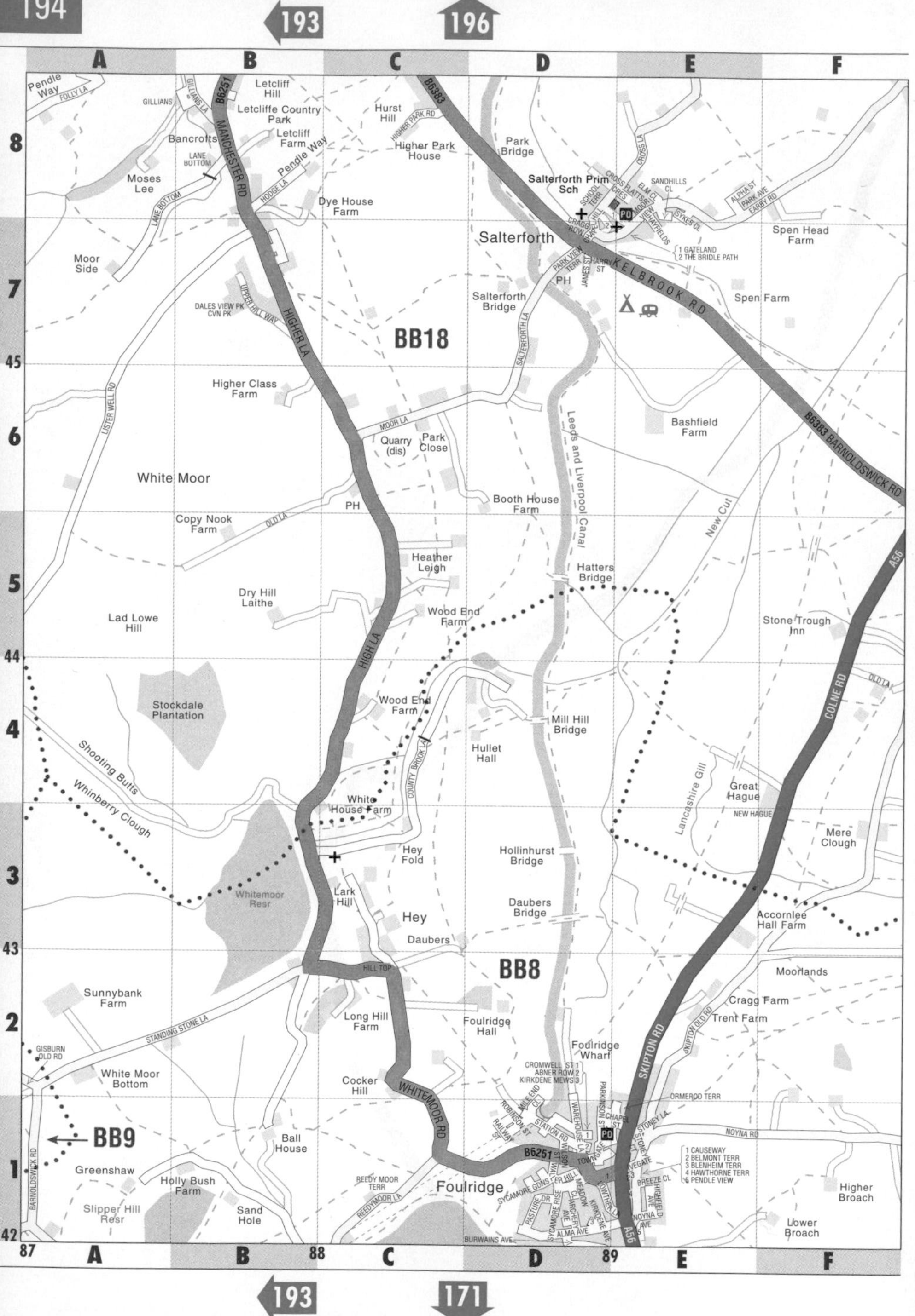
193
196
Pendle Way
FOLLY LA
GILLIANS
Letcliff Hill
Letcliffe Country Park
Hurst Hill
Bancrofts
Letcliff Farm
Higher Park House
Park Bridge
Moses Lee
Dye House Farm
Salterforth Prim Sch
Salterforth
Spen Head Farm
Moor Side
1 GATELAND
2 THE BRIDLE PATH
KELBROOK RD
Salterforth Bridge
Spen Farm
DALES VIEW PK CVN PK
BB18
HIGHER LA
Higher Class Farm
Bashfield Farm
MOOR LA
Quarry (dis)
Park Close
Leeds and Liverpool Canal
B6383 BARNOLDSWICK RD
White Moor
Booth House Farm
Copy Nook Farm
OLD LA
New Cut
Heather Leigh
Hatters Bridge
Dry Hill Laithe
Lad Lowe Hill
Wood End Farm
Stone Trough Inn
HIGH LA
Stockdale Plantation
Wood End Farm
Mill Hill Bridge
COLNE RD
Hullet Hall
Shooting Butts
Whinberry Clough
White House Farm
Great Hague
Lancashire Gill
NEW HAGUE
Mere Clough
Hey Fold
Hollinhurst Bridge
Lark Hill
Whitemoor Resr
Hey
Daubers Bridge
Accornlee Hall Farm
Daubers
BB8
HILL TOP
Moorlands
Sunnybank Farm
Cragg Farm
STANDING STONE LA
Long Hill Farm
Foulridge Hall
Trent Farm
SKIPTON RD
Foulridge Wharf
White Moor Bottom
Cocker Hill
WHITEMOOR RD
CROMWELL ST 1
ABNER ROW 2
KIRKDENE MEWS 3
ORMEROD TERR
NOYNA RD
BB9
Ball House
1 CAUSEWAY
2 BELMONT TERR
3 BLENHEIM TERR
4 HAWTHORNE TERR
5 PENDLE VIEW
Greenshaw
Holly Bush Farm
REEDY MOOR TERR
Foulridge
Higher Broach
Slipper Hill Resr
Sand Hole
Lower Broach
BURWAINS AVE
A56
87
88
89
42
43
44
45
A
B
C
D
E
F
193
171

197

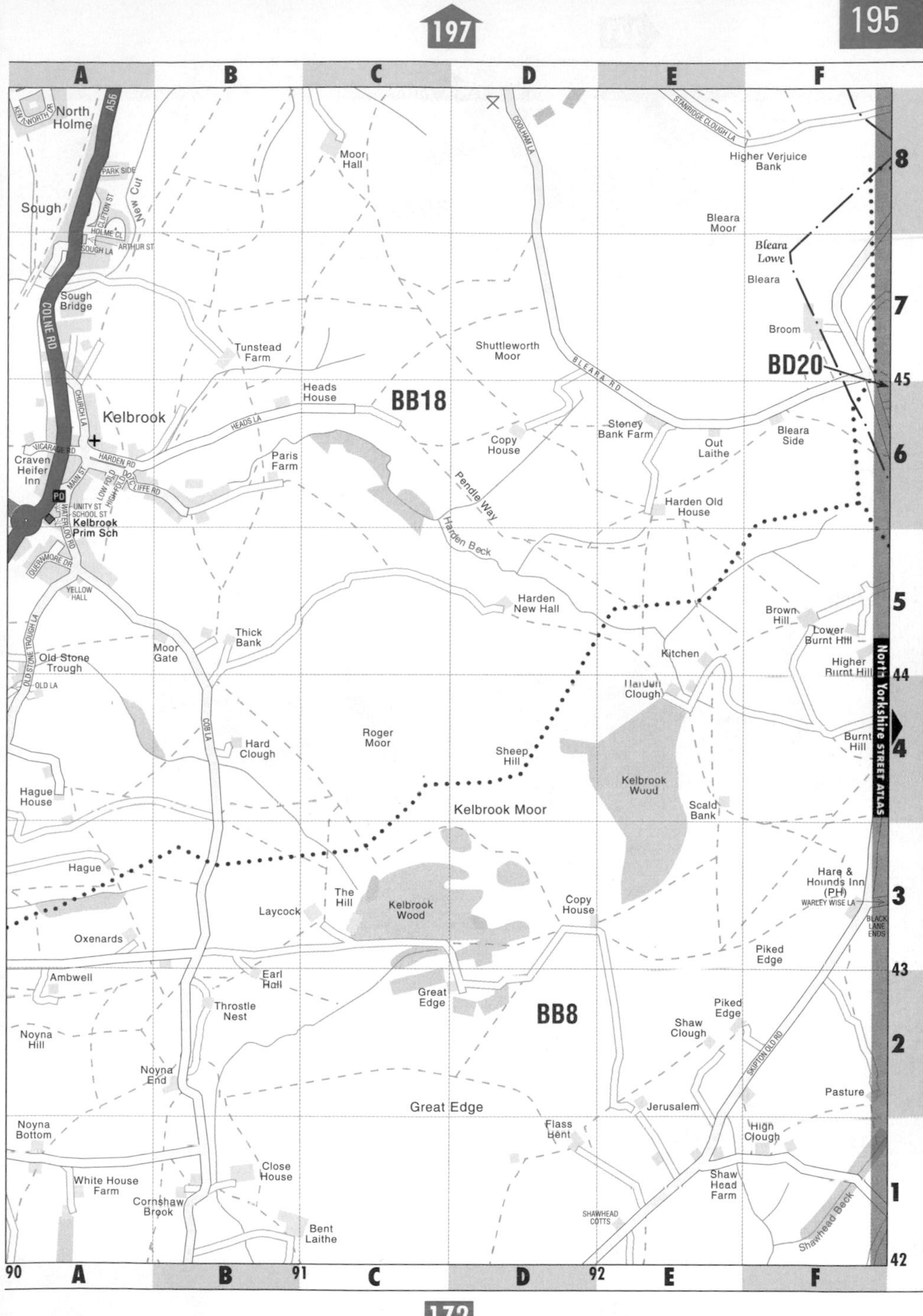

A
B
C
D
E
F
North Holme
KENILWORTH DR
A56
PARK SIDE
New Cut
Sough
CLIFTON ST
HOLME CL
SOUGH LA
ARTHUR ST
Sough Bridge
COLNE RD
Moor Hall
COOLHAM LA
STANRIDGE CLOUGH LA
Higher Verjuice Bank
Bleara Moor
Bleara Lowe
Bleara
Broom
BD20
Tunstead Farm
Shuttleworth Moor
BLEARA RD
Heads House
BB18
CHURCH LA
Kelbrook
HEADS LA
Stoney Bank Farm
Out Laithe
Bleara Side
Copy House
VICARAGE RD
HARDEN RD
Paris Farm
Craven Heifer Inn
MAIN ST
LOW FOLD
HIGH FOLD
DOTCLIFFE RD
Pendle Way
PO
UNITY ST
SCHOOL ST
WATERLOO RD
Kelbrook Prim Sch
Harden Old House
Harden Beck
QUERNMORE DR
YELLOW HALL
Harden New Hall
Brown Hill
Lower Burnt Hill
OLD STONE TROUGH LA
Moor Gate
Thick Bank
Old Stone Trough
Kitchen
Higher Burnt Hill
OLD LA
Harden Clough
North Yorkshire STREET ATLAS
COB LA
Hard Clough
Roger Moor
Sheep Hill
Burnt Hill
Kelbrook Wood
Hague House
Scald Bank
Kelbrook Moor
Hague
Hare & Hounds Inn (PH)
WARLEY WISE LA
The Hill
Laycock
Kelbrook Wood
Copy House
BLACK LANE ENDS
Oxenards
Piked Edge
Ambwell
Earl Hall
Great Edge
Throstle Nest
BB8
Piked Edge
Noyna Hill
Shaw Clough
SKIPTON OLD RD
Noyna End
Pasture
Great Edge
Jerusalem
Noyna Bottom
Flass Bent
High Clough
Close House
White House Farm
Shaw Head Farm
Cornshaw Brook
SHAWHEAD COTTS
Shawhead Beck
Bent Laithe
8
7
45
6
5
44
4
3
43
2
1
42
90
91
92

172

231

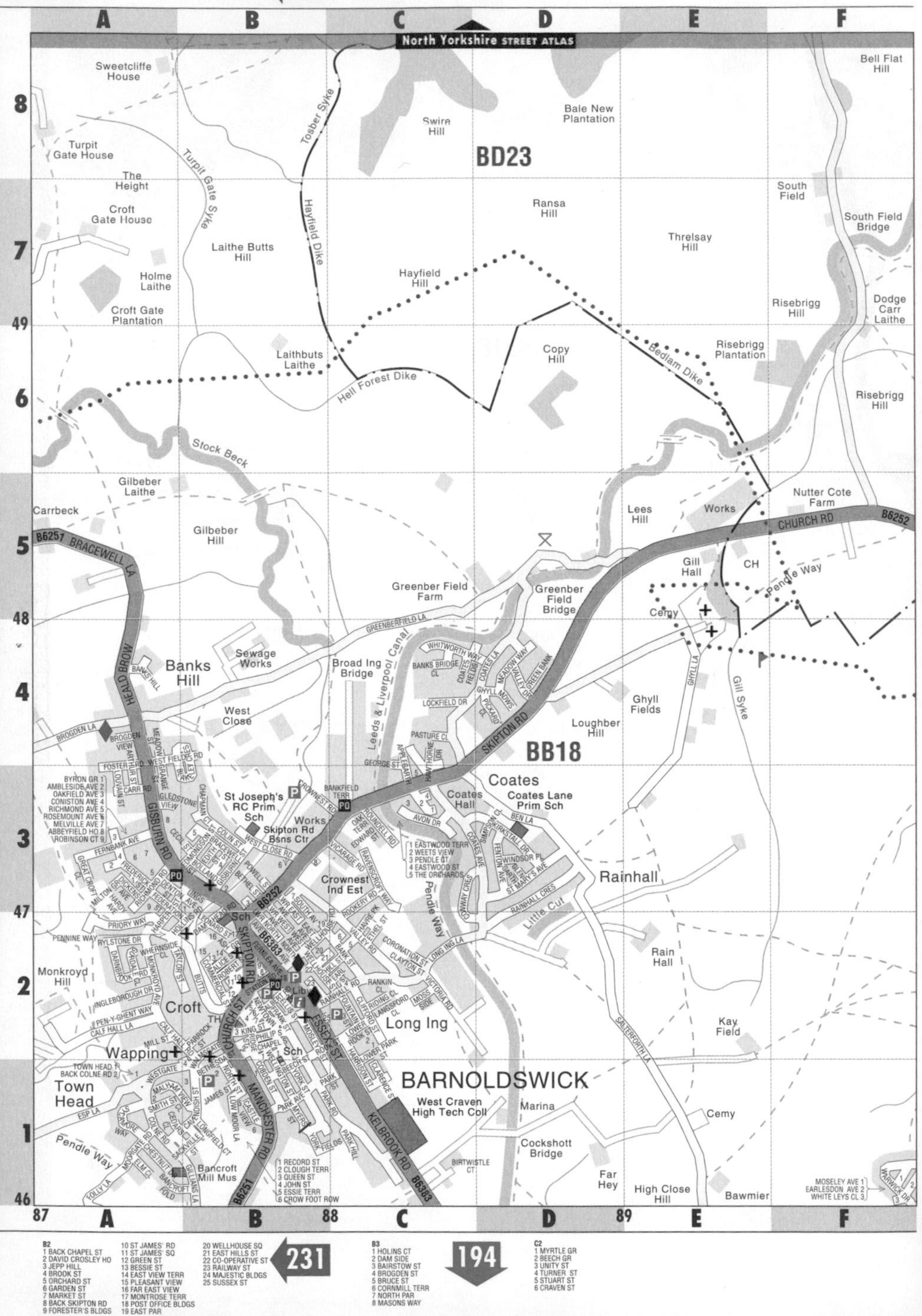

B2
1 BACK CHAPEL ST
2 DAVID CROSLEY HO
3 JEPP HILL
4 BROOK ST
5 ORCHARD ST
6 GARDEN ST
7 MARKET ST
8 BACK SKIPTON RD
9 FORESTER'S BLDGS
10 ST JAMES' RD
11 ST JAMES' SQ
12 GREEN ST
13 BESSIE ST
14 EAST VIEW TERR
15 PLEASANT VIEW
16 FAR EAST VIEW
17 MONTROSE TERR
18 POST OFFICE BLDGS
19 EAST PAR
20 WELLHOUSE SQ
21 EAST HILLS ST
22 CO-OPERATIVE ST
23 RAILWAY ST
24 MAJESTIC BLDGS
25 SUSSEX ST

231

B3
1 HOLINS CT
2 DAM SIDE
3 BAIRSTOW ST
4 BROGDEN ST
5 BRUCE ST
6 CORNMILL TERR
7 NORTH PAR
8 MASONS WAY

194

C2
1 MYRTLE GR
2 BEECH GR
3 UNITY ST
4 TURNER ST
5 STUART ST
6 CRAVEN ST

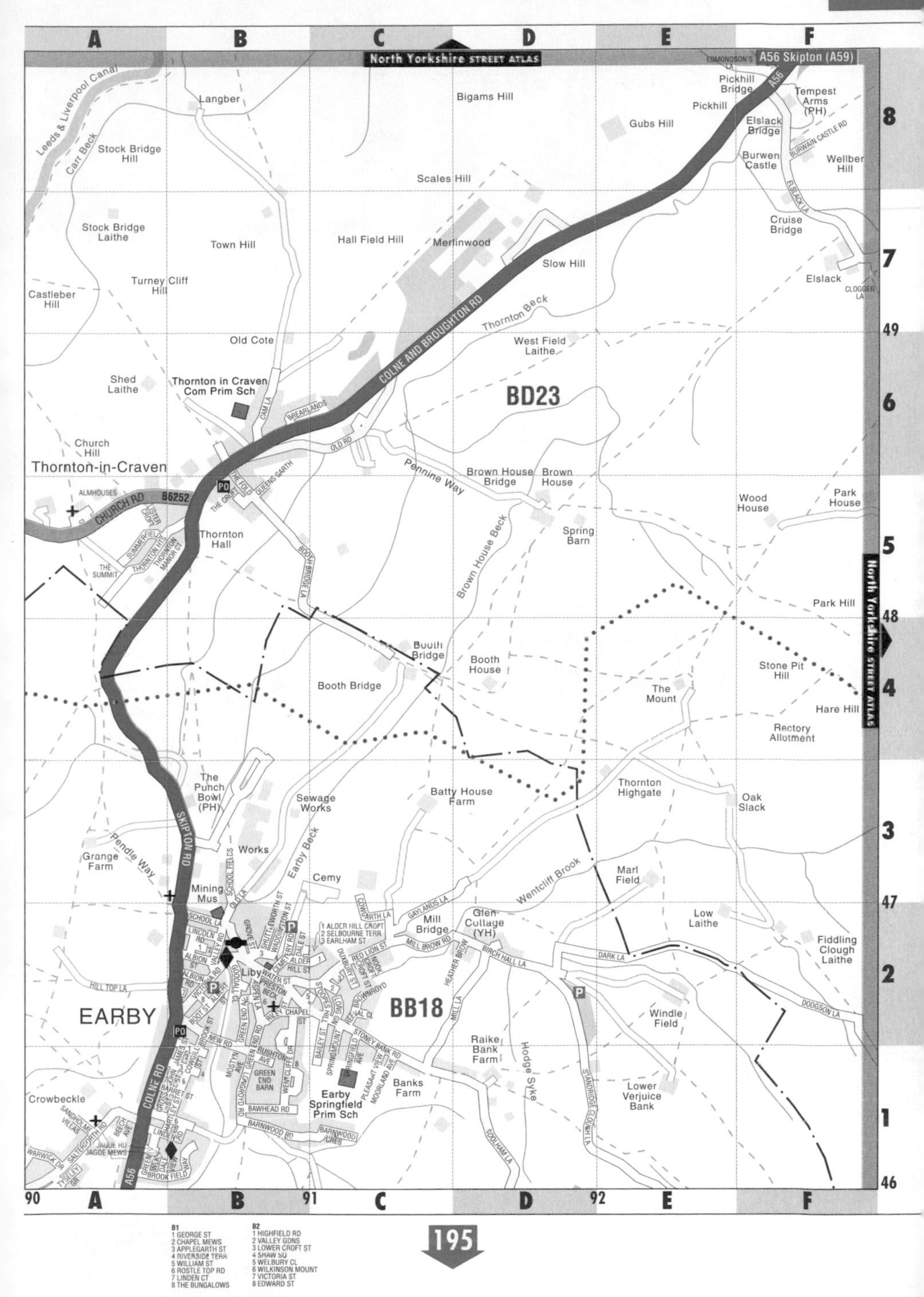
North Yorkshire STREET ATLAS
A56 Skipton (A59)
A
B
C
D
E
F
8
7
49
6
5
48
4
3
47
2
1
46
90
91
92
Leeds & Liverpool Canal
Carr Beck
Langber
Bigams Hill
Pickhill Bridge
Pickhill
Tempest Arms (PH)
Gubs Hill
Elslack Bridge
BURWAIN CASTLE RD
Stock Bridge Hill
Burwen Castle
Wellber Hill
Scales Hill
ELSLACK LA
Stock Bridge Laithe
Town Hill
Hall Field Hill
Merlinwood
Cruise Bridge
Slow Hill
Elslack
CLOGGER LA
Turney Cliff Hill
Castleber Hill
COLNE AND BROUGHTON RD
Thornton Beck
Old Cote
West Field Laithe
Shed Laithe
Thornton in Craven Com Prim Sch
BD23
CAM LA
BREARLANDS
OLD RD
Church Hill
Thornton-in-Craven
Pennine Way
Brown House Bridge
Brown House
ALMHOUSES
CHURCH RD
B6252
PO
THE FOLD
QUEENS GARTH
THE CROFT
Wood House
Park House
Spring Barn
Thornton Hall
SUMMERFIELD
THORNTON HTS
THORNTON MANOR CT
THE SUMMIT
BOOTH BRIDGE LA
Brown House Beck
Park Hill
Booth Bridge
Booth House
Stone Pit Hill
Booth Bridge
The Mount
Hare Hill
Rectory Allotment
The Punch Bowl (PH)
Sewage Works
Batty House Farm
Thornton Highgate
Oak Slack
SKIPTON RD
Earby Beck
Works
Grange Farm
Pendle Way
SCHOOL FIELDS
Cemy
Wentcliff Brook
Marl Field
Mining Mus
OLD LA
GROVE ST
SHUTTLEWORTH ST
WADDINGTON ST
P
1 ALDER HILL CROFT
2 SELBOURNE TERR
3 EARLHAM ST
GAYLANDS LA
Mill Bridge
Glen Cottage (YH)
Low Laithe
Fiddling Clough Laithe
SCHOOL LA
LINCOLN RD
VALLEY RD
MILL BROW RD
DARK LA
ALBION ST
RED LION ST
BIRCH HALL LA
HILL TOP LA
Liby
WATER ST
BROWNROYD
HEATHER BROW
EARBY
BB18
MILL LA
Windle Field
DODGSON LA
PO
NEW RD
CHAPEL ST
RUSHTON AVE
STONEY BANK RD
Raike Bank Farm
Hodge Syke
GREEN END BARN
Banks Farm
Earby Springfield Prim Sch
Lower Verjuice Bank
STANDRIDGE CLOUGH LA
Crowbeckle
COLNE RD
BAWHEAD RD
BARNWOOD RD
BARNWOOD CRES
SOOLHAM LA
JAGOE MEWS
WARWICK DR
A56
195
B1
1 GEORGE ST
2 CHAPEL MEWS
3 APPLEGARTH ST
4 RIVERSIDE TERR
5 WILLIAM ST
6 ROSTLE TOP RD
7 LINDEN CT
8 THE BUNGALOWS
B2
1 HIGHFIELD RD
2 VALLEY GDNS
3 LOWER CROFT ST
4 SHAW SQ
5 WELBURY CL
6 WILKINSON MOUNT
7 VICTORIA ST
8 EDWARD ST

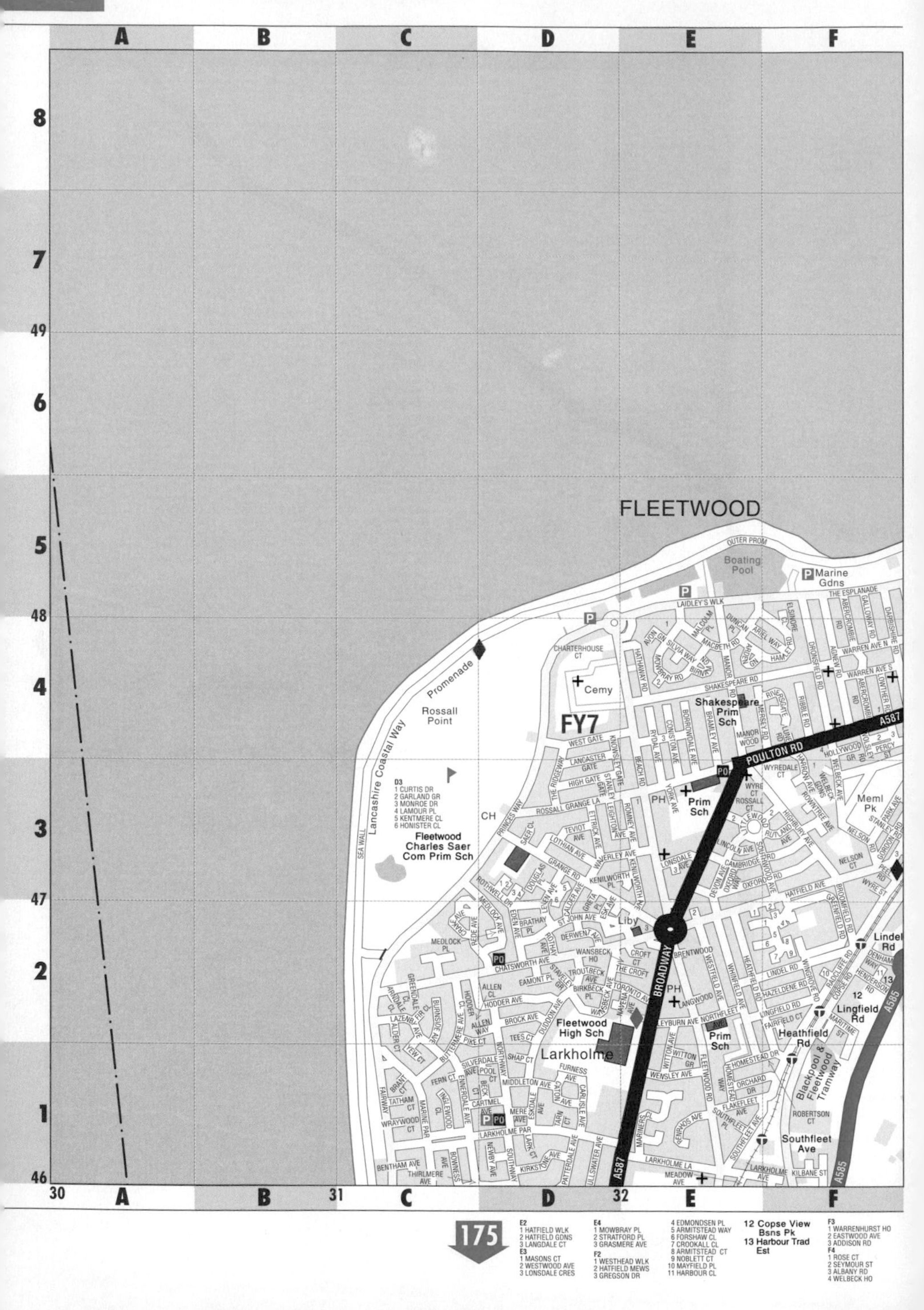

175

E2
1 HATFIELD WLK
2 HATFIELD GDNS
3 LANGDALE CT
E3
1 MASONS CT
2 WESTWOOD AVE
3 LONSDALE CRES

E4
1 MOWBRAY PL
2 STRATFORD PL
3 GRASMERE AVE
F2
1 WESTHEAD WLK
2 HATFIELD MEWS
3 GREGSON DR
4 EDMONDSEN PL
5 ARMITSTEAD WAY
6 FORSHAW CL
7 CROOKALL CL
8 ARMITSTEAD CT
9 NOBLETT CT
10 MAYFIELD PL
11 HARBOUR CL
12 Copse View Bsns Pk
13 Harbour Trad Est

F3
1 WARRENHURST HO
2 EASTWOOD AVE
3 ADDISON RD
F4
1 ROSE CT
2 SEYMOUR ST
3 ALBANY RD
4 WELBECK HO

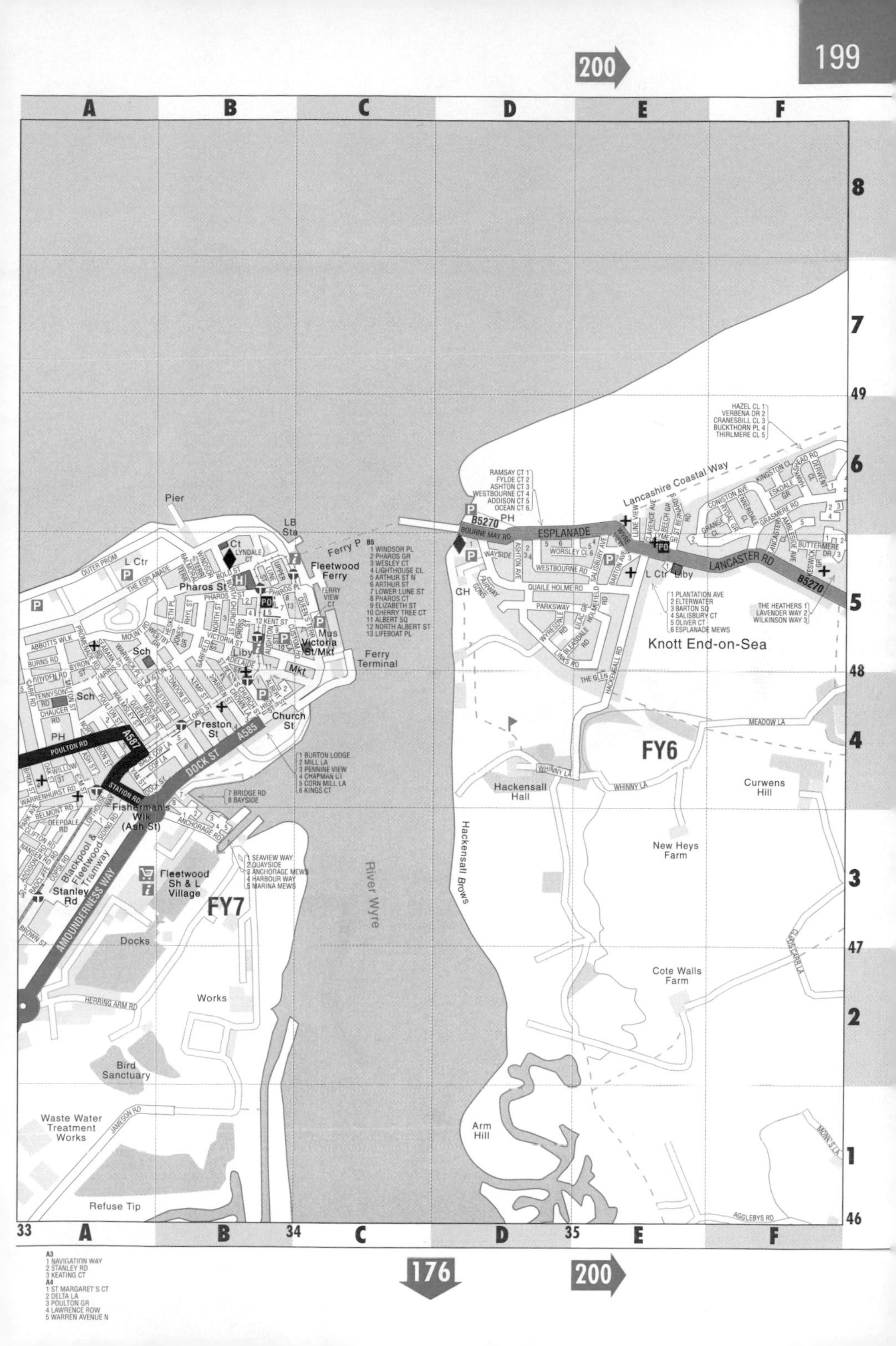

199
200
176
A
B
C
D
E
F
8
7
6
5
4
3
2
1
49
48
47
46
33
34
35
Pier
L Ctr
LB Sta
Ferry P
Fleetwood Ferry
Pharos St
Liby
Mus
Victoria St/Mkt
Mkt
Ferry Terminal
Sch
PH
Preston St
Church St
Fisherman's Wlk (Ash St)
Fleetwood Sh & L Village
FY7
Docks
Works
Bird Sanctuary
Waste Water Treatment Works
Refuse Tip
Stanley Rd
Blackpool & Fleetwood Tramway
River Wyre
Hackensall Brows
Arm Hill
Hackensall Hall
FY6
Curwens Hill
New Heys Farm
Cote Walls Farm
Knott End-on-Sea
Lancashire Coastal Way
ESPLANADE
LANCASTER RD
B5270
A587
A585
DOCK ST
POULTON RD
STATION RD
AMOUNDERNESS WAY
HERRING ARM RD
JAMESON RD
BROWN ST
WHINNY LA
MEADOW LA
AGGLEBYS RD
MONKS LA
GH
L Ctr
Liby
B5
1 WINDSOR PL
2 PHAROS GR
3 WESLEY CT
4 LIGHTHOUSE CL
5 ARTHUR ST N
6 ARTHUR ST
7 LOWER LUNE ST
8 PHAROS CT
9 ELIZABETH ST
10 CHERRY TREE CT
11 ALBERT SQ
12 NORTH ALBERT ST
13 LIFEBOAT PL
1 BURTON LODGE
2 MILL LA
3 PENNINE VIEW
4 CHAPMAN CT
5 CORN MILL LA
6 KINGS CT
7 BRIDGE RD
8 BAYSIDE
1 SEAVIEW WAY
2 QUAYSIDE
3 ANCHORAGE MEWS
4 HARBOUR WAY
5 MARINA MEWS
RAMSAY CT 1
FYLDE CT 2
ASHTON CT 3
WESTBOURNE CT 4
ADDISON CT 5
OCEAN CT 6
HAZEL CL 1
VERBENA DR 2
CRANESBILL CL 3
BUCKTHORN PL 4
THIRLMERE CL 5
1 PLANTATION AVE
2 ELTERWATER
3 BARTON SQ
4 SALISBURY CT
5 OLIVER CT
6 ESPLANADE MEWS
THE HEATHERS 1
LAVENDER WAY 2
WILKINSON WAY 3
A3
1 NAVIGATION WAY
2 STANLEY RD
3 KEATING CT
A4
1 ST MARGARET'S CT
2 DELTA LA
3 POULTON GR
4 LAWRENCE ROW
5 WARREN AVENUE N

199

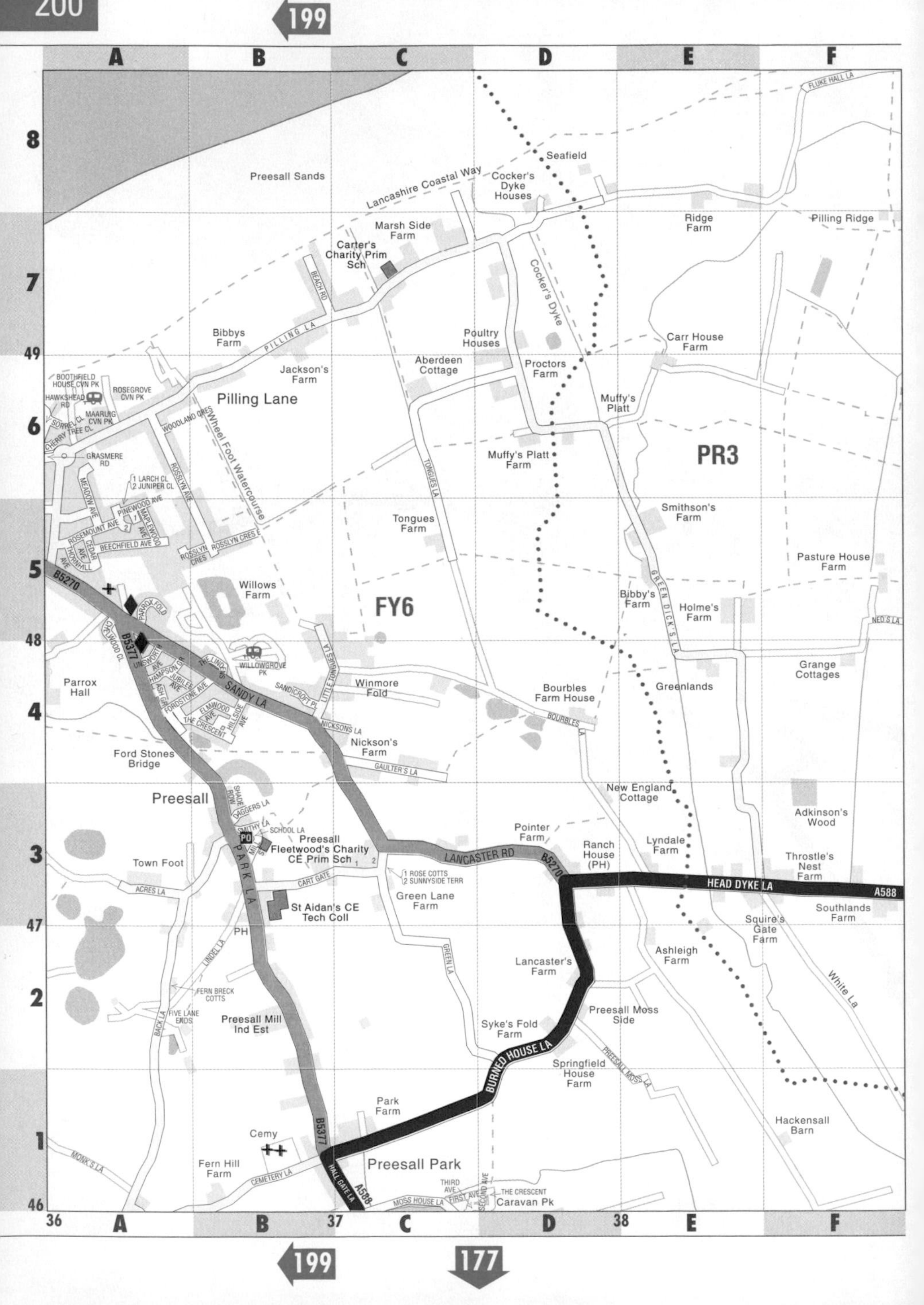

A
B
C
D
E
F
8
7
49
6
5
48
4
3
47
2
1
46
36
37
38
Preesall Sands
Lancashire Coastal Way
Seafield
Cocker's Dyke Houses
Marsh Side Farm
Carter's Charity Prim Sch
Ridge Farm
Pilling Ridge
FLUKE HALL LA
BEACH RD
Cocker's Dyke
Bibbys Farm
PILLING LA
Poultry Houses
Aberdeen Cottage
Proctors Farm
Carr House Farm
Jackson's Farm
Pilling Lane
BOOTHFIELD HOUSE CVN PK
HAWKSHEAD RD
ROSEGROVE CVN PK
MAARUIG CVN PK
SORREL CL
CHERRY TREE CL
GRASMERE RD
WOODLAND GRES
Wheel Foot Watercourse
ROSSLYN AVE
Muffy's Platt
Muffy's Platt Farm
PR3
1 LARCH CL
2 JUNIPER CL
PINEWOOD AVE
MEADOW AVE
MAPLEWOOD AVE
ROSEMOUNT AVE
BEECHFIELD AVE
CEDAR AVE
THORNHILL AVE
ROSSLYN CRES
TONGUES LA
Tongues Farm
Smithson's Farm
Pasture House Farm
B5270
Willows Farm
FY6
PARROX FOLD
Bibby's Farm
Holme's Farm
GREEN DICK'S LA
NED'S LA
B5377
CHEWOOD CL
UNSWORTH AVE
HAMPSON GR
JUBILEE AVE
ASH GR
FORDSTONE AVE
THE LINDENS
SANDY LA
WILLOWGROVE PK
SANDICROFT PL
LITTLE TONGUES LA
Winmore Fold
Parrox Hall
ELMWOOD AVE
HILLSIDE AVE
THE CRESCENT
Grange Cottages
Bourbles Farm House
Greenlands
BOURBLES LA
NICKSONS LA
Nickson's Farm
Ford Stones Bridge
GAULTER'S LA
New England Cottage
Preesall
SHADE ROW
DAGGERS LA
SMITHY LA
SCHOOL LA
Adkinson's Wood
PO
Preesall Fleetwood's Charity CE Prim Sch
Pointer Farm
Ranch House (PH)
Lyndale Farm
Throstle's Nest Farm
Town Foot
PARK LA
LANCASTER RD
1 ROSE COTTS
2 SUNNYSIDE TERR
HEAD DYKE LA
A588
ACRES LA
CART GATE
Green Lane Farm
St Aidan's CE Tech Coll
Southlands Farm
Squire's Gate Farm
PH
Ashleigh Farm
LINDEL LA
GREEN LA
Lancaster's Farm
White La
FERN BRECK COTTS
FIVE LANE ENDS
Preesall Moss Side
BACK LA
Preesall Mill Ind Est
Syke's Fold Farm
BURNED HOUSE LA
Springfield House Farm
PREESALL MOSS LA
Park Farm
Hackensall Barn
Cemy
MONK'S LA
Fern Hill Farm
Preesall Park
CEMETERY LA
HALL GATE LA
THIRD AVE
SECOND AVE
THE CRESCENT
MOSS HOUSE LA
FIRST AVE
Caravan Pk

199
177

202

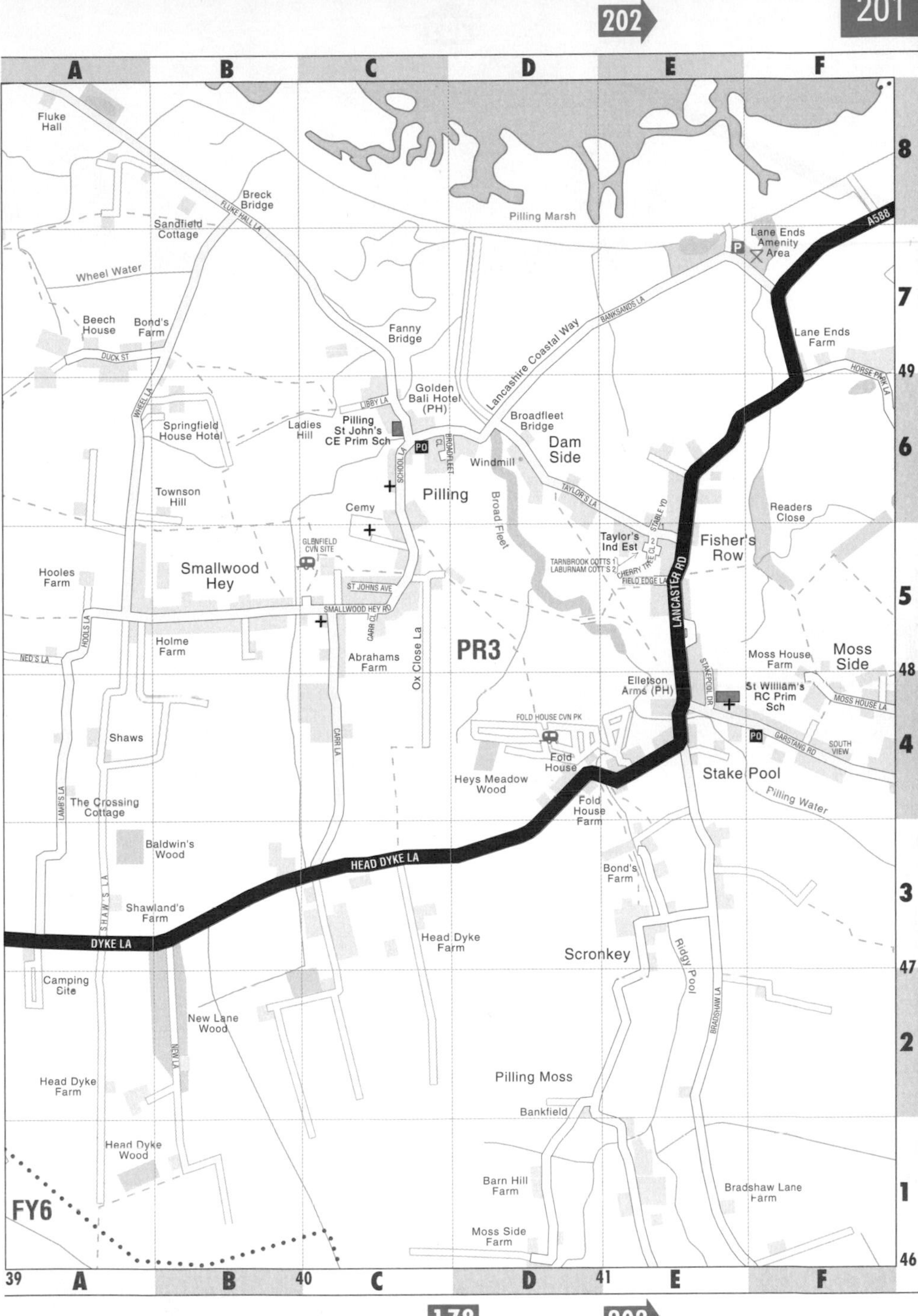
Fluke Hall
Breck Bridge
Sandfield Cottage
FLUKE HALL LA
Pilling Marsh
Lane Ends Amenity Area
A588
Wheel Water
Beech House
Bond's Farm
DUCK ST
Fanny Bridge
BANKSANDS LA
Lancashire Coastal Way
Lane Ends Farm
HORSE PARK LA
WHEEL LA
Springfield House Hotel
LIBBY LA
Golden Ball Hotel (PH)
Ladies Hill
Pilling St John's CE Prim Sch
Broadfleet Bridge
Dam Side
BROADFLEET
CL
SCHOOL LA
Windmill
Townson Hill
Pilling
TAYLOR'S LA
Broad Fleet
Cemy
STABLE YD
Readers Close
GLENFIELD CVN SITE
Taylor's Ind Est
Fisher's Row
CHERRY TREE CL
TARNBROOK COTTS 1
LABURNAM COTT'S 2
FIELD EDGE LA
Hooles Farm
Smallwood Hey
ST JOHNS AVE
SMALLWOOD HEY RD
LANCASTER RD
HOOLS LA
NED'S LA
Holme Farm
CARR CL
Ox Close La
PR3
Abrahams Farm
Moss House Farm
Moss Side
STAKEPOOL DR
Elletson Arms (PH)
St William's RC Prim Sch
MOSS HOUSE LA
FOLD HOUSE CVN PK
Shaws
CARR LA
GARSTANG RD
SOUTH VIEW
Fold House
Stake Pool
Heys Meadow Wood
Pilling Water
LAMB'S LA
The Crossing Cottage
Fold House Farm
Baldwin's Wood
HEAD DYKE LA
Bond's Farm
SHAW'S LA
Shawland's Farm
DYKE LA
Head Dyke Farm
Scronkey
Ridgy Pool
Camping Site
BRADSHAW LA
New Lane Wood
NEW LA
Head Dyke Farm
Pilling Moss
Bankfield
Head Dyke Wood
Barn Hill Farm
Bradshaw Lane Farm
FY6
Moss Side Farm
A B C D E F
8 7 49 6 5 48 4 3 47 2 1 46
39 40 41

178
202

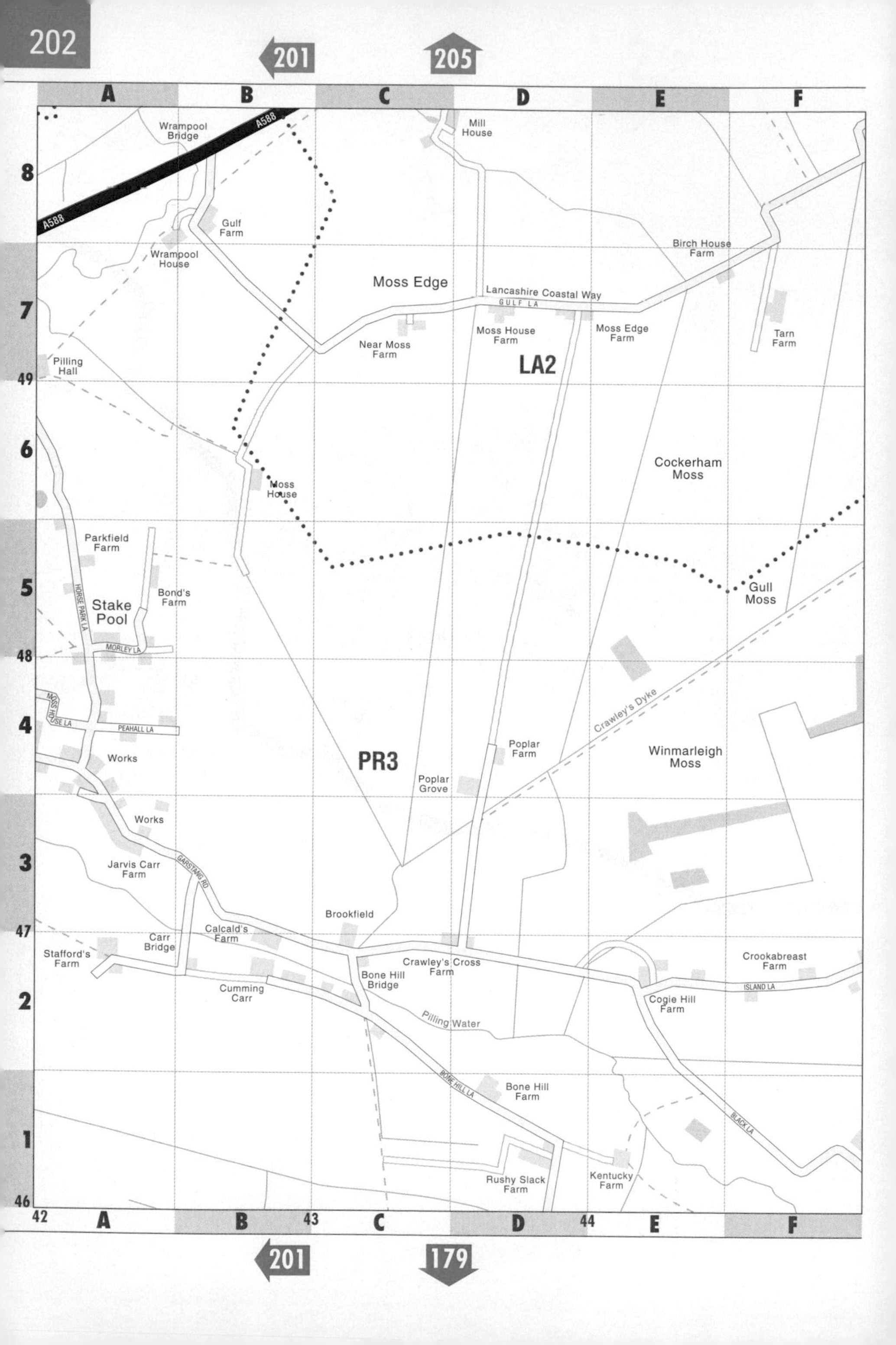
201
205
A
B
C
D
E
F
Wrampool Bridge
A588
Mill House
8
Gulf Farm
Wrampool House
Birch House Farm
Moss Edge
Lancashire Coastal Way
GULF LA
7
Moss House Farm
Moss Edge Farm
Near Moss Farm
Tarn Farm
Pilling Hall
LA2
49
6
Cockerham Moss
Moss House
Parkfield Farm
5
Gull Moss
Bond's Farm
Stake Pool
HORSE PARK LA
MORLEY LA
48
MOSS HOUSE LA
PEAHALL LA
Crawley's Dyke
4
Poplar Farm
Winmarleigh Moss
Works
PR3
Poplar Grove
Works
3
Jarvis Carr Farm
GARSTANG RD
Brookfield
47
Calcald's Farm
Carr Bridge
Stafford's Farm
Crawley's Cross Farm
Crookabreast Farm
Bone Hill Bridge
ISLAND LA
Cumming Carr
Cogie Hill Farm
2
Pilling Water
BONE HILL LA
Bone Hill Farm
BLACK LA
1
Rushy Slack Farm
Kentucky Farm
46
42
43
44
201
179

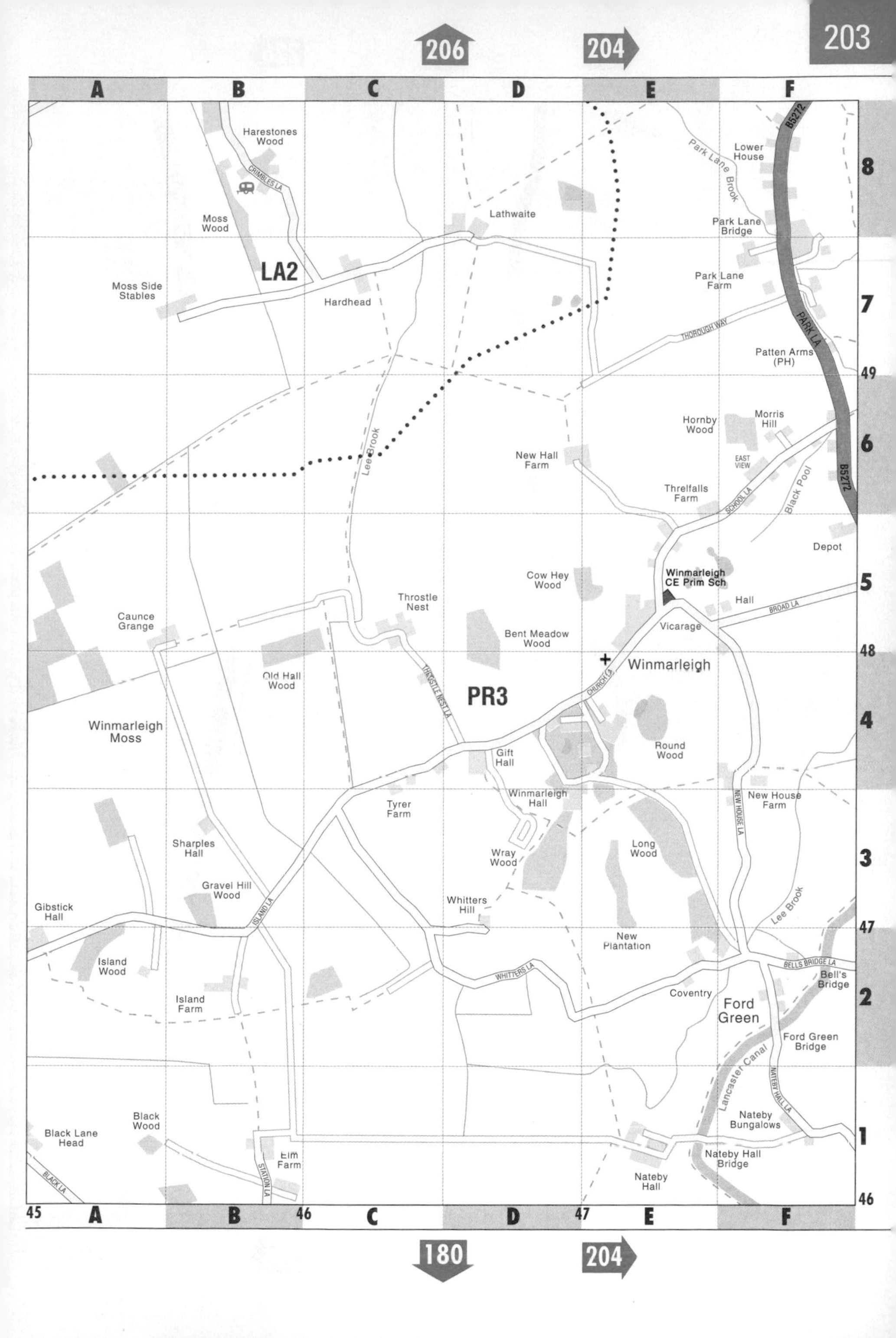
206
204
A
B
C
D
E
F
Harestones Wood
CRIMBLES LA
Moss Wood
LA2
Moss Side Stables
Hardhead
Lathwaite
Park Lane Brook
Lower House
Park Lane Bridge
Park Lane Farm
B5272
PARK LA
THOROUGH WAY
Patten Arms (PH)
Hornby Wood
Morris Hill
EAST VIEW
Lee Brook
New Hall Farm
Threlfalls Farm
SCHOOL LA
Black Pool
Depot
Cow Hey Wood
Winmarleigh CE Prim Sch
Hall
BROAD LA
Throstle Nest
Caunce Grange
Bent Meadow Wood
Vicarage
Winmarleigh
Old Hall Wood
THROSTLE NEST LA
PR3
CHURCH LA
Winmarleigh Moss
Round Wood
Gift Hall
Winmarleigh Hall
New House Farm
NEW HOUSE LA
Tyrer Farm
Sharples Hall
Wray Wood
Long Wood
Gravel Hill Wood
Gibstick Hall
Whitters Hill
ISLAND LA
Lee Brook
New Plantation
Island Wood
WHITTERS LA
BELLS BRIDGE LA
Bell's Bridge
Island Farm
Coventry
Ford Green
Ford Green Bridge
Lancaster Canal
NATEBY HALL LA
Black Wood
Black Lane Head
Nateby Bungalows
Elm Farm
STATION LA
Nateby Hall Bridge
BLACK LA
Nateby Hall
8
7
49
6
5
48
4
3
47
2
1
46
45
46
47
180
204

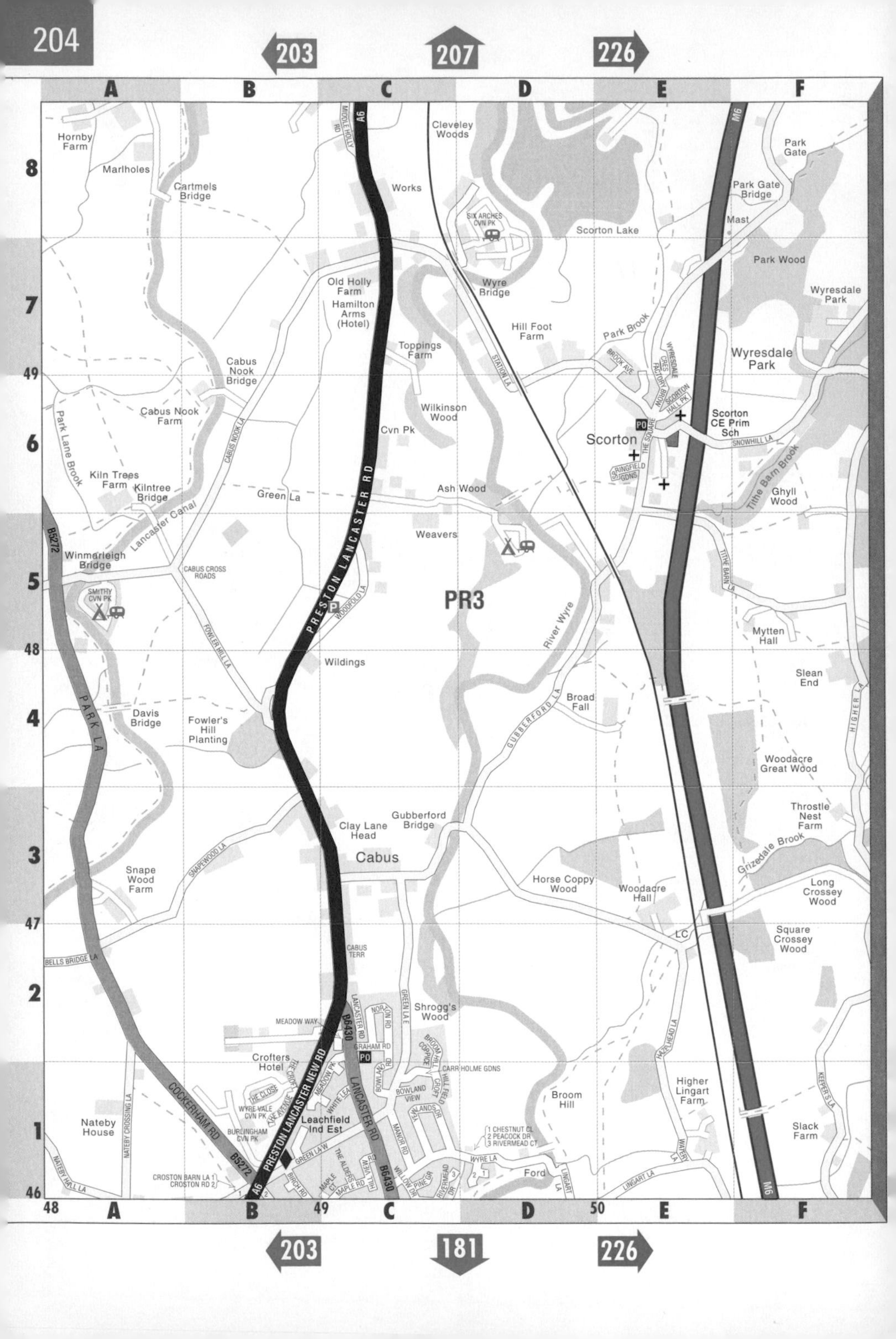
203
207
226
A
B
C
D
E
F
8
7
49
6
5
48
4
3
47
2
1
46
48
49
50
Hornby Farm
Marlholes
Cartmels Bridge
Cleveley Woods
Works
Six Arches Cvn Pk
Scorton Lake
Park Gate
Park Gate Bridge
Mast
Park Wood
Wyresdale Park
Old Holly Farm
Hamilton Arms (Hotel)
Wyre Bridge
Hill Foot Farm
Park Brook
Toppings Farm
Cabus Nook Bridge
Cabus Nook Farm
Wilkinson Wood
Cvn Pk
Scorton
Scorton CE Prim Sch
Park Lane Brook
Kiln Trees Farm
Kiltree Bridge
Green La
Ash Wood
Tithe Barn Brook
Ghyll Wood
Lancaster Canal
Weavers
Winmarleigh Bridge
Cabus Cross Roads
Smithy Cvn Pk
PR3
River Wyre
Mytten Hall
Wildings
Slean End
Broad Fall
Davis Bridge
Fowler's Hill Planting
Woodacre Great Wood
Throstle Nest Farm
Clay Lane Head
Gubberford Bridge
Cabus
Grizedale Brook
Snape Wood Farm
Horse Coppy Wood
Woodacre Hall
Long Crossey Wood
LC
Square Crossey Wood
Shrogg's Wood
Meadow Way
Crofters Hotel
Broom Hill
Higher Lingart Farm
Nateby House
Leachfield Ind Est
Slack Farm
Ford
1 Chestnut Cl
2 Peacock Dr
3 Rivermead Ct
Croston Barn La 1
Croston Rd 2
A6
M6
B5272
B6430
Preston Lancaster Rd
Preston Lancaster New Rd
Lancaster Rd
Park La
Cockerham Rd
Station La
Gubberford La
Snapewood La
Fowler Hill La
Cabus Nook La
Woodfold La
Middle Holly Rd
Brook Ave
Wyresdale Cres
Factory Brow
Scorton Hall Pk
The Square
Snowhill La
Springfield Gdns
Tithe Barn La
Higher La
Bells Bridge La
Cabus Terr
Green Lane
Graham Rd
Bowland Rd
Broom Hill Coppice
Hill Field Croft
Carr Holme Gdns
Bowland View
Meadow Pk
The Close
The Croft
The Avenue
Wyre Vale Cvn Pk
Burlingham Cvn Pk
White Lea
Green La W
The Alders
Maple Ct
Maple Rd
Birch Rd
Manor Rd
Willow Dr
Pine Gr
Rivermead Dr
Wyre La
Lingart La
Hazelhead La
Watery La
Keeper's La
Nateby Crossing La
Nateby Hall La
Norton Rd
Lancaster Rd
203
181
226

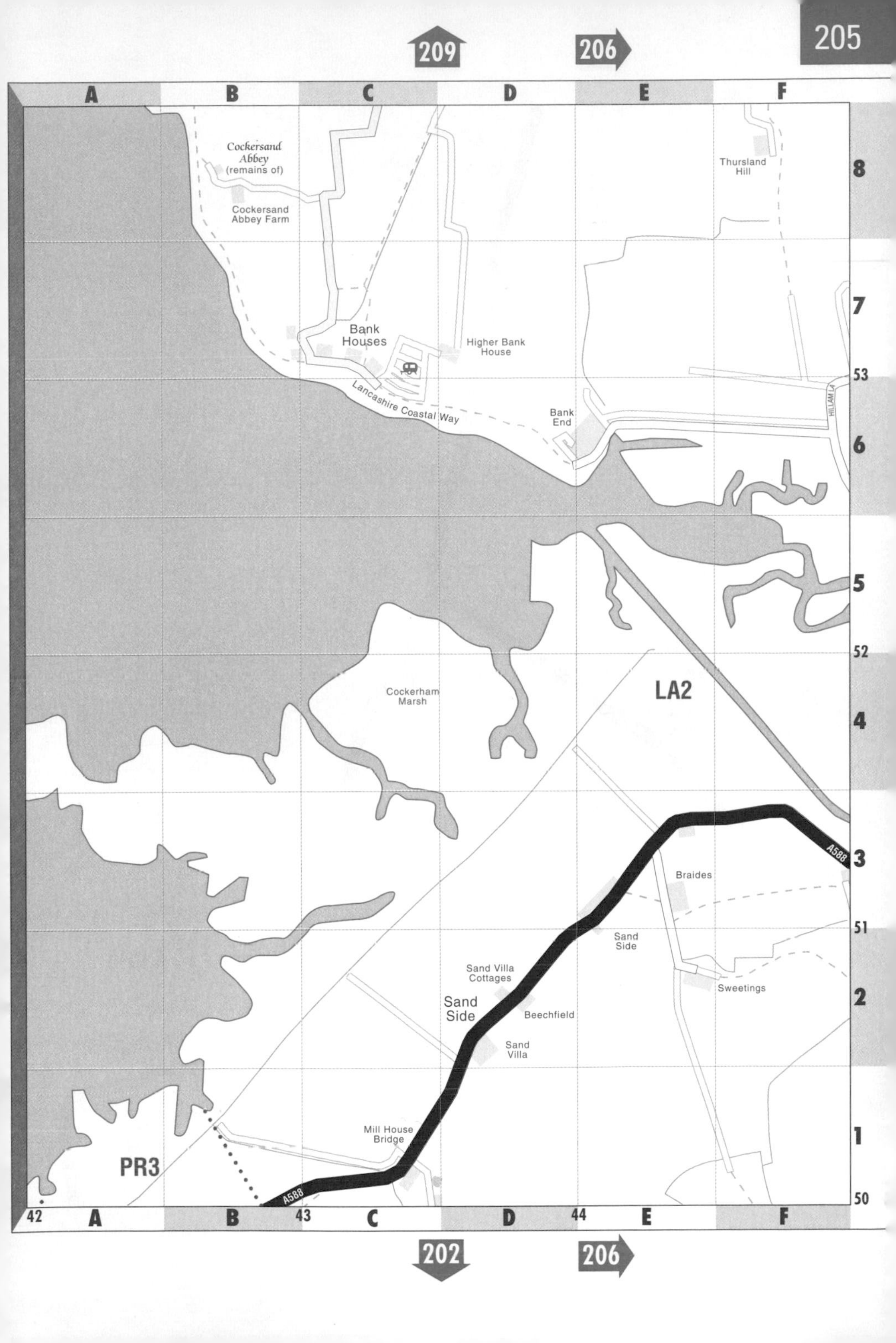
209
206
A
B
C
D
E
F
Cockersand Abbey (remains of)
Cockersand Abbey Farm
Thursland Hill
8
7
Bank Houses
Higher Bank House
53
Lancashire Coastal Way
Bank End
HILLAM LA
6
5
52
Cockerham Marsh
LA2
4
A588
3
Braides
51
Sand Side
Sand Villa Cottages
Sand Side
Beechfield
Sweetings
2
Sand Villa
Mill House Bridge
1
PR3
A588
50
42
43
44
202
206

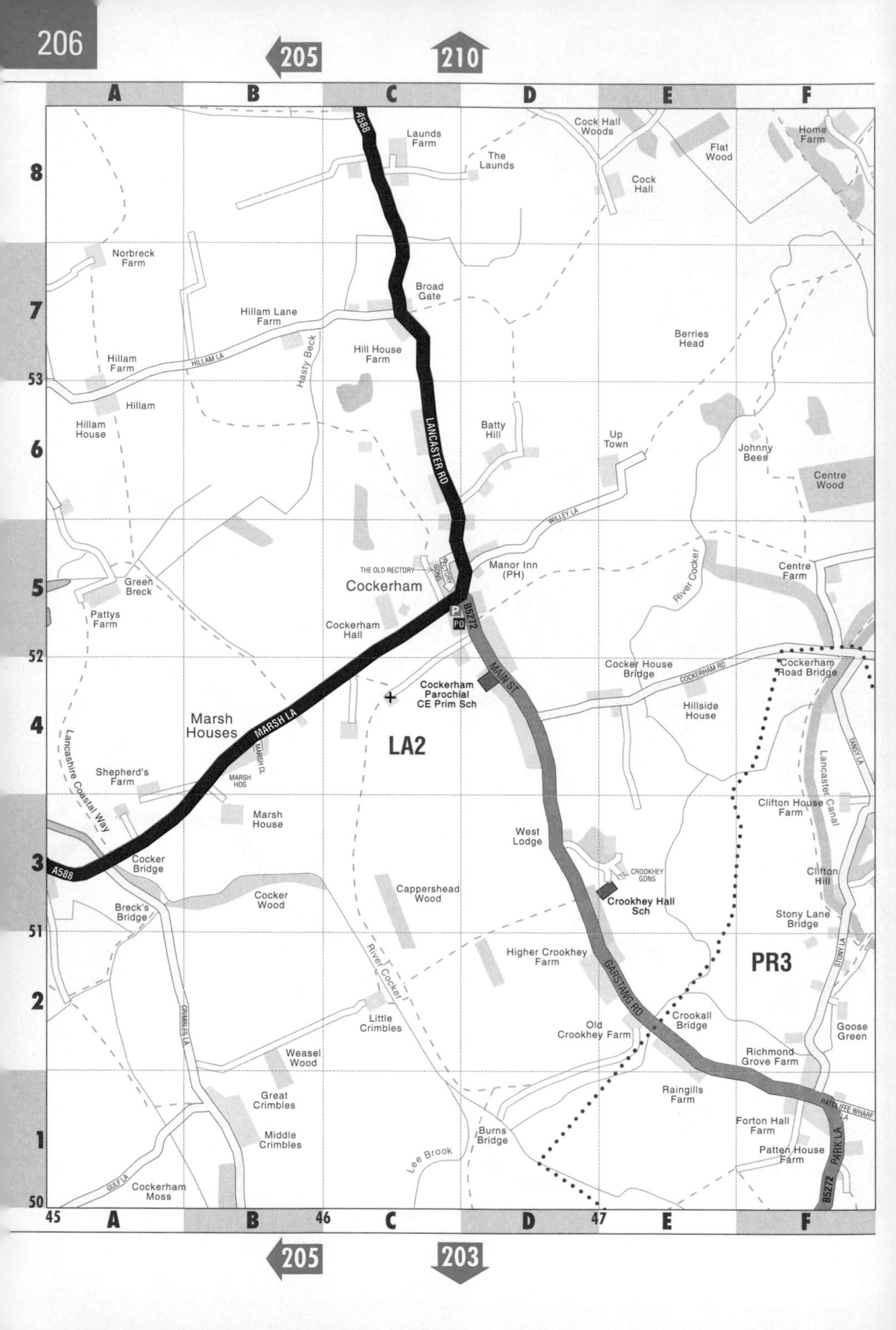
205
210
A588
Launds Farm
The Launds
Cock Hall Woods
Flat Wood
Home Farm
Cock Hall
Norbreck Farm
Broad Gate
Hillam Lane Farm
Hill House Farm
Berries Head
Hillam Farm
HILLAM LA
Hasty Beck
Hillam
Hillam House
LANCASTER RD
Batty Hill
Up Town
Johnny Bees
Centre Wood
WILLEY LA
River Cocker
THE OLD RECTORY
Manor Inn (PH)
Centre Farm
Green Breck
Cockerham
Pattys Farm
Cockerham Hall
B5272
Cocker House Bridge
COCKERHAM RD
Cockerham Road Bridge
MAIN ST
Cockerham Parochial CE Prim Sch
Hillside House
Marsh Houses
MARSH LA
LA2
Lancashire Coastal Way
MARSH CL
MARSH HDS
Shepherd's Farm
TANSY LA
Lancaster Canal
Clifton House Farm
Marsh House
West Lodge
Cocker Bridge
CROOKHEY GDNS
Clifton Hill
A588
Cappershead Wood
Cocker Wood
Crookhey Hall Sch
Breck's Bridge
Stony Lane Bridge
River Cocker
Higher Crookhey Farm
PR3
GARSTANG RD
STONY LA
CRIMBLES LA
Crookall Bridge
Little Crimbles
Old Crookhey Farm
Goose Green
Weasel Wood
Richmond Grove Farm
Great Crimbles
Raingills Farm
RATCLIFFE WHARF LA
Forton Hall Farm
Middle Crimbles
Burns Bridge
Lee Brook
Patten House Farm
PARK LA
GULF LA
Cockerham Moss
B5272
A B C D E F
8 7 53 6 5 52 4 3 51 2 1 50
45 46 47
203

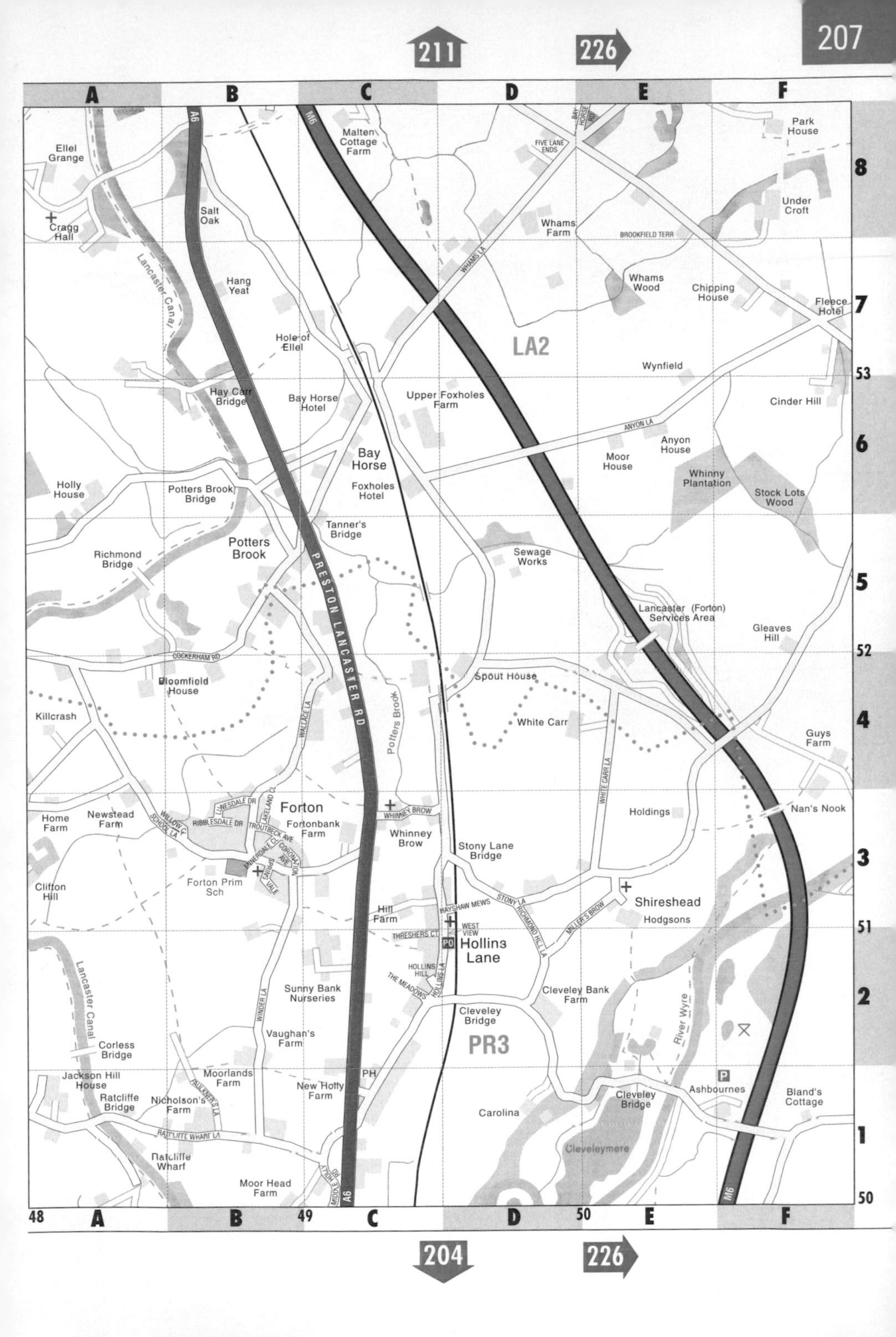
211
226
A
B
C
D
E
F
Ellel Grange
Cragg Hall
Salt Oak
Malten Cottage Farm
FIVE LANE ENDS
BAY HORSE RD
Park House
Under Croft
Whams Farm
BROOKFIELD TERR
WHAMS LA
Lancaster Canal
Hang Yeat
Whams Wood
Chipping House
Fleece Hotel
Hole of Ellel
LA2
Wynfield
Hay Carr Bridge
Bay Horse Hotel
Upper Foxholes Farm
Cinder Hill
ANYON LA
Anyon House
Moor House
Bay Horse
Whinny Plantation
Holly House
Potters Brook Bridge
Foxholes Hotel
Stock Lots Wood
Tanner's Bridge
Potters Brook
Richmond Bridge
Sewage Works
PRESTON LANCASTER RD
Lancaster (Forton) Services Area
Gleaves Hill
COCKERHAM RD
Bloomfield House
Spout House
Killcrash
WALLACE LA
Potters Brook
White Carr
Guys Farm
WHITE CARR LA
Forton
WHINNEY BROW
Holdings
Nan's Nook
Home Farm
Newstead Farm
LUNESDALE DR
RIBBLESDALE DR
LAKELAND CL
TROUTBECK AVE
WILLOW CL
SCHOOL LA
Fortonbank Farm
Whinney Brow
Stony Lane Bridge
ENNERDALE CL
CORONATION AVE
SPRING VALE
Clifton Hill
Forton Prim Sch
STONY LA
Shireshead
MILLER'S BROW
HAYSHAW MEWS
Hill Farm
Hodgsons
THRESHERS CT
WEST VIEW
PO
Hollins Lane
RICHMOND HILL LA
HOLLINS HILL
HOLLINS LA
THE MEADOWS
Sunny Bank Nurseries
Cleveley Bank Farm
WINDER LA
Cleveley Bridge
Lancaster Canal
Vaughan's Farm
PR3
River Wyre
Corless Bridge
Jackson Hill House
Moorlands Farm
PH
New Holly Farm
P
Ashbournes
Ratcliffe Bridge
Nicholson's Farm
FAULKNER'S LA
Cleveley Bridge
Bland's Cottage
Carolina
RATCLIFFE WHARF LA
Cleveleymere
Ratcliffe Wharf
Moor Head Farm
MIDDLE HOLLY RD
A6
M6
8
7
53
6
5
52
4
3
51
2
1
50
48
49
50
204
226

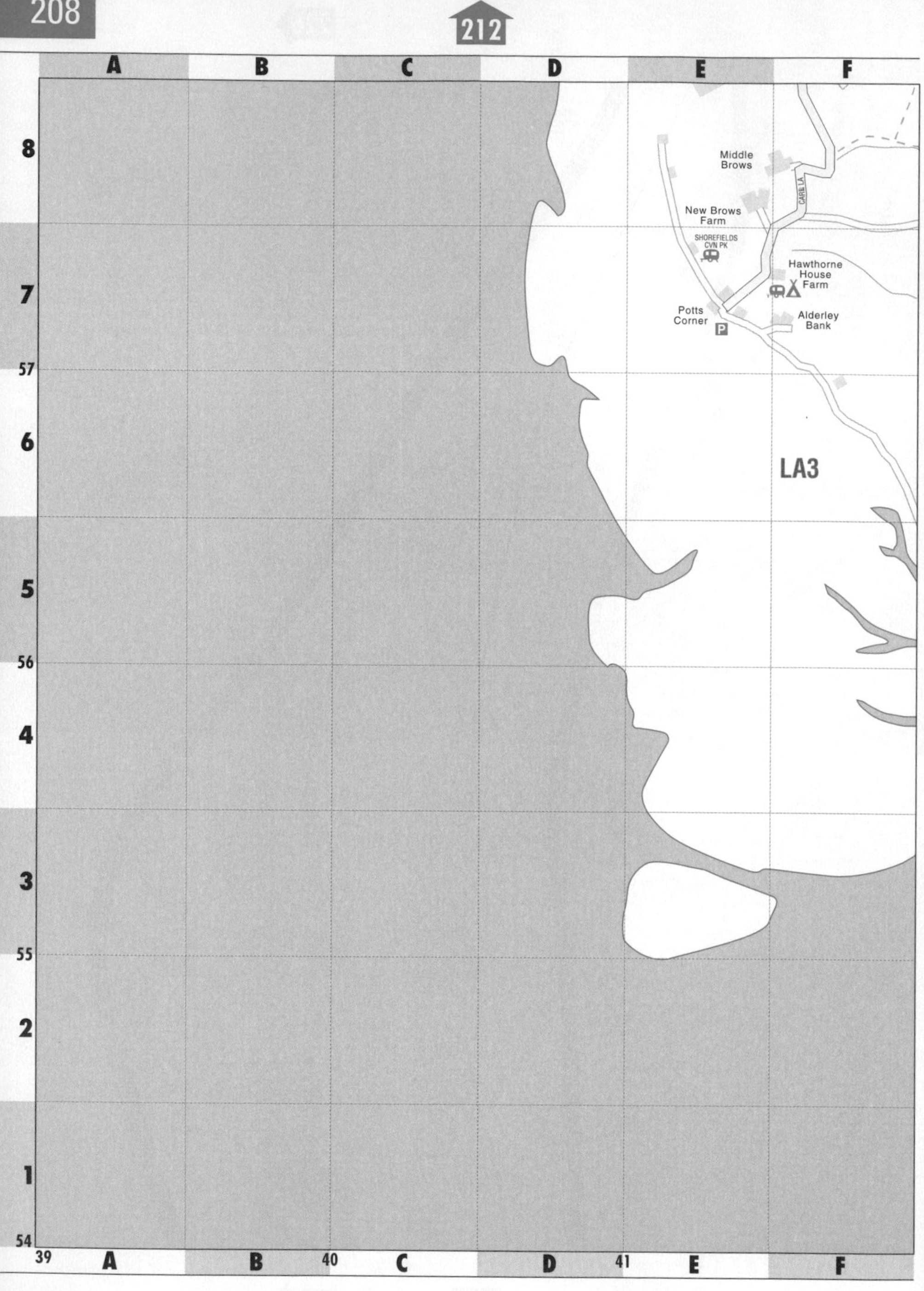
212
A
B
C
D
E
F
8
7
57
6
5
56
4
3
55
2
1
54
39
40
41
Middle Brows
CARE LA
New Brows Farm
SHOREFIELDS CVN PK
Hawthorne House Farm
Potts Corner
P
Alderley Bank
LA3

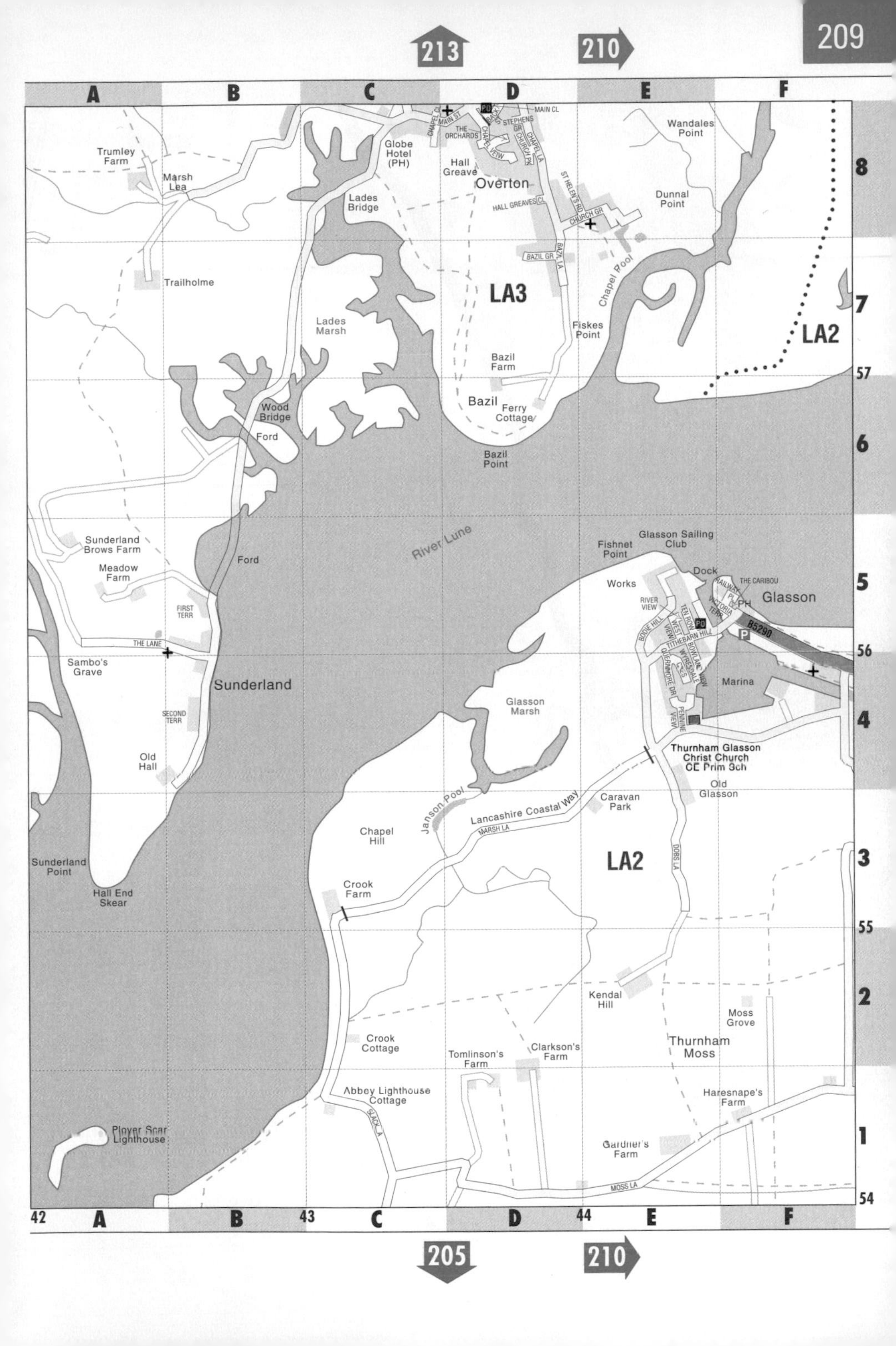
213
210
A
B
C
D
E
F
Trumley Farm
Marsh Lea
Globe Hotel (PH)
Hall Greave
Overton
Lades Bridge
Wandales Point
Dunnal Point
Trailholme
LA3
Chapel Pool
Lades Marsh
Fiskes Point
LA2
Bazil Farm
Bazil
Ferry Cottage
Wood Bridge
Ford
Bazil Point
River Lune
Glasson Sailing Club
Fishnet Point
Sunderland Brows Farm
Meadow Farm
Ford
Dock
Works
THE CARIBOU
Glasson
PH
RIVER VIEW
B5290
FIRST TERR
THE LANE
Sambo's Grave
Sunderland
Glasson Marsh
Marina
SECOND TERR
Old Hall
Thurnham Glasson Christ Church CE Prim Sch
Old Glasson
Janson Pool
Caravan Park
Lancashire Coastal Way
MARSH LA
Chapel Hill
LA2
DOBS LA
Sunderland Point
Hall End Skear
Crook Farm
Kendal Hill
Moss Grove
Crook Cottage
Thurnham Moss
Clarkson's Farm
Tomlinson's Farm
Abbey Lighthouse Cottage
Haresnape's Farm
SLACK LA
Plover Scar Lighthouse
Gardner's Farm
MOSS LA
MAIN ST
CHAPEL CL
THE ORCHARDS
CHAPEL VEIW
ST STEPHENS GR
CHURCH PK
CHAPEL LA
MAIN CL
ST HELEN'S RD
HALL GREAVES CL
CHURCH GR
BAZIL GR
BAZIL LA
BODIE HILL
TEN ROW
WEST VIEW
TITHEBARN HILL
BOWLAND VIEW
WYRESDALE
QUERNMORE DR
PENNINE VIEW
VICTORIA TERR
RAILWAY PL
8
7
57
6
5
56
4
3
55
2
1
54
42
43
44
205
210

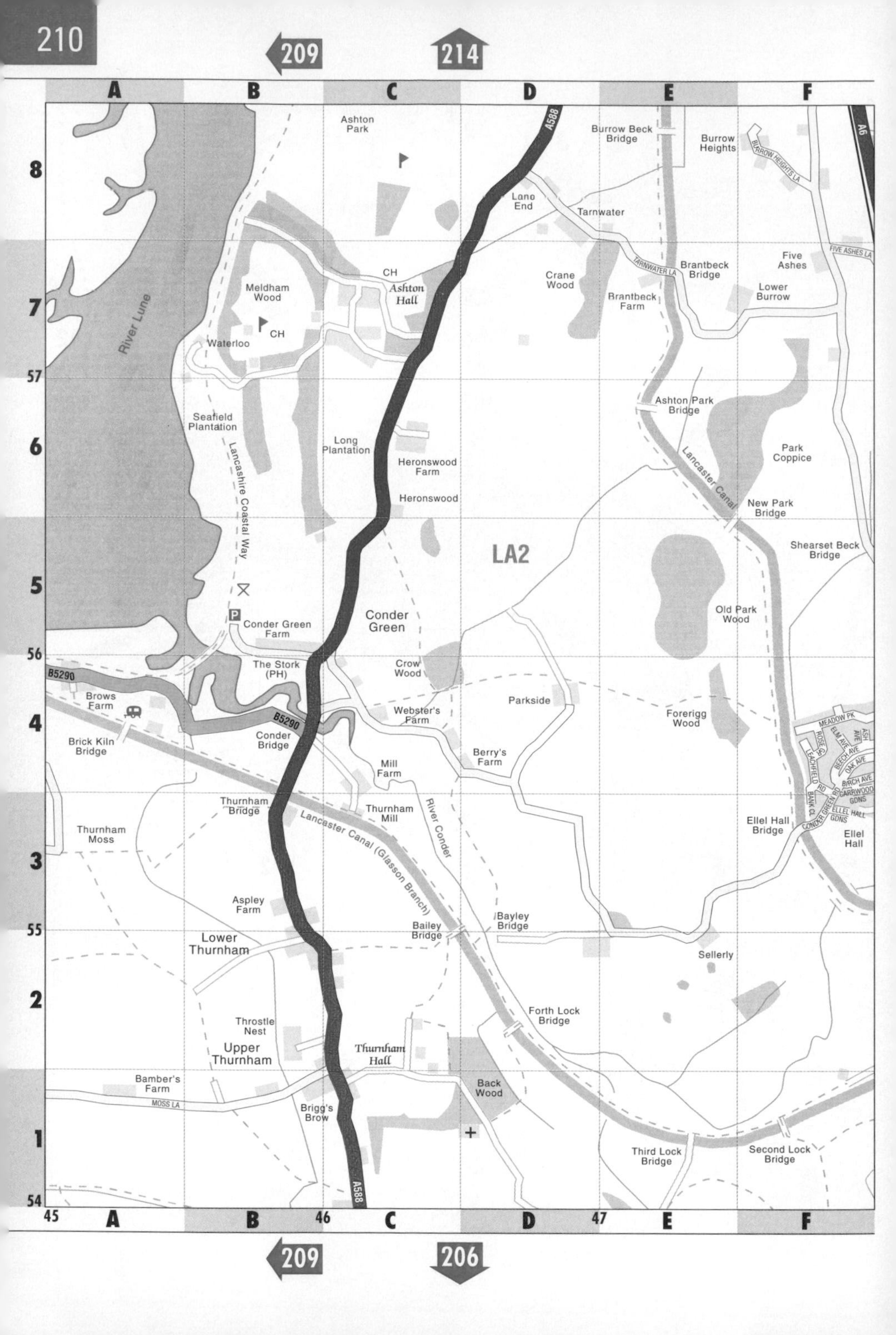
209
214
A B C D E F
8 7 6 5 4 3 2 1
57 56 55 54
45 46 47
River Lune
Ashton Park
Burrow Beck Bridge
Burrow Heights
BURROW HEIGHTS LA
A6
A588
Lane End
Tarnwater
TARNWATER LA
CH
Ashton Hall
Meldham Wood
CH
Waterloo
Crane Wood
Brantbeck Bridge
Brantbeck Farm
Five Ashes
FIVE ASHES LA
Lower Burrow
Seafield Plantation
Long Plantation
Lancashire Coastal Way
Heronswood Farm
Heronswood
Ashton Park Bridge
Lancaster Canal
Park Coppice
New Park Bridge
Shearset Beck Bridge
LA2
Old Park Wood
Conder Green
Conder Green Farm
The Stork (PH)
Crow Wood
B5290
Brows Farm
Brick Kiln Bridge
Conder Bridge
Webster's Farm
Parkside
Forerigg Wood
Berry's Farm
Mill Farm
MEADOW PK
ROSE GR
ELM AVE
ASH AVE
BEECH AVE
OAK AVE
LEACHFIELD RD
BIRCH AVE
CARRWOOD GDNS
BANK CL
CONDER GREEN RD
ELLEL HALL GDNS
Thurnham Bridge
Thurnham Mill
River Conder
Thurnham Moss
Lancaster Canal (Glasson Branch)
Ellel Hall Bridge
Ellel Hall
Aspley Farm
Bailey Bridge
Bayley Bridge
Lower Thurnham
Sellerly
Throstle Nest
Forth Lock Bridge
Upper Thurnham
Thurnham Hall
Bamber's Farm
MOSS LA
Back Wood
Brigg's Brow
Third Lock Bridge
Second Lock Bridge
209
206

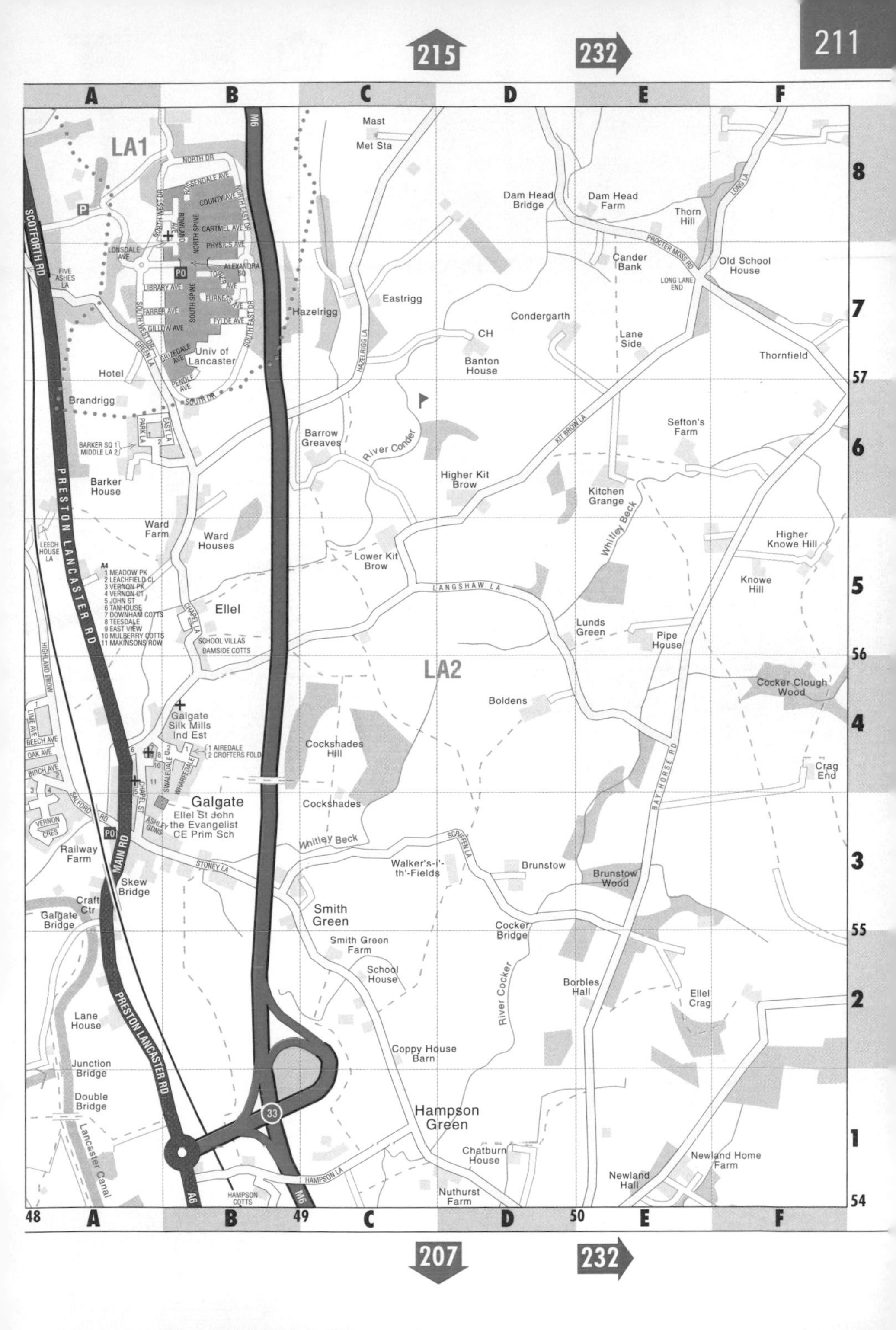
215
232
A
B
C
D
E
F
8
7
57
6
5
56
4
3
55
2
1
54
48
49
50
LA1
LA2
M6
Mast
Met Sta
NORTH DR
ROSSENDALE AVE
COUNTY AVE
NORTH WEST DR
BOWLAND AVE
NORTH SPINE
NORTH EAST DR
CARTMEL AVE
PHYSICS AVE
LONSDALE AVE
ALEXANDRA SQ
TOWER AVE
FURNESS AVE
LIBRARY AVE
SOUTH SPINE
FARRER AVE
FYLDE AVE
GILLOW AVE
SOUTH WEST DR
SOUTH EAST DR
GREEN LA
GRIZEDALE AVE
PENDLE AVE
SOUTH DR
Univ of Lancaster
SCOTFORTH RD
FIVE ASHES LA
Hotel
Brandrigg
PARK LA
EAST LA
BARKER SQ 1
MIDDLE LA 2
Barker House
Ward Farm
Ward Houses
LEECH HOUSE LA
A4
1 MEADOW PK
2 LEACHFIELD CL
3 VERNON PK
4 VERNON CT
5 JOHN ST
6 TANHOUSE
7 DOWNHAM COTTS
8 TEESDALE
9 EAST VIEW
10 MULBERRY COTTS
11 MAKINSONS ROW
PRESTON LANCASTER RD
Ellel
CHAPEL LA
SCHOOL VILLAS
DAMSIDE COTTS
HIGHLAND BROW
LIME AVE
BEECH AVE
OAK AVE
BIRCH AVE
SALFORD RD
VERNON CRES
Galgate Silk Mills Ind Est
1 AIREDALE
2 CROFTERS FOLD
SWALEDALE
WHARFEDALE
CHAPEL ST
Galgate
Ellel St John the Evangelist CE Prim Sch
ASHLEY GDNS
Railway Farm
MAIN RD
Skew Bridge
STONEY LA
Craft Ctr
Galgate Bridge
Lane House
Junction Bridge
Double Bridge
Lancaster Canal
A6
HAMPSON COTTS
HAMPSON LA
Hazelrigg
HAZELRIGG LA
Eastrigg
Barrow Greaves
River Conder
Lower Kit Brow
LANGSHAW LA
Cockshades Hill
Cockshades
Whitley Beck
Walker's-i'-th'-Fields
Smith Green
Smith Green Farm
School House
Coppy House Barn
Hampson Green
Chatburn House
Nuthurst Farm
Dam Head Bridge
Dam Head Farm
Thorn Hill
LONG LA
PROCTER MOSS RD
Cander Bank
Old School House
LONG LANE END
Condergarth
CH
Banton House
Lane Side
Thornfield
KIT BROW LA
Higher Kit Brow
Sefton's Farm
Kitchen Grange
Whitley Beck
Higher Knowe Hill
Knowe Hill
Lunds Green
Pipe House
Boldens
Cocker Clough Wood
Crag End
BAY HORSE RD
SCRIPPEN LA
Brunstow
Brunstow Wood
Cocker Bridge
River Cocker
Borbles Hall
Ellel Crag
Newland Home Farm
Newland Hall
33
207
232

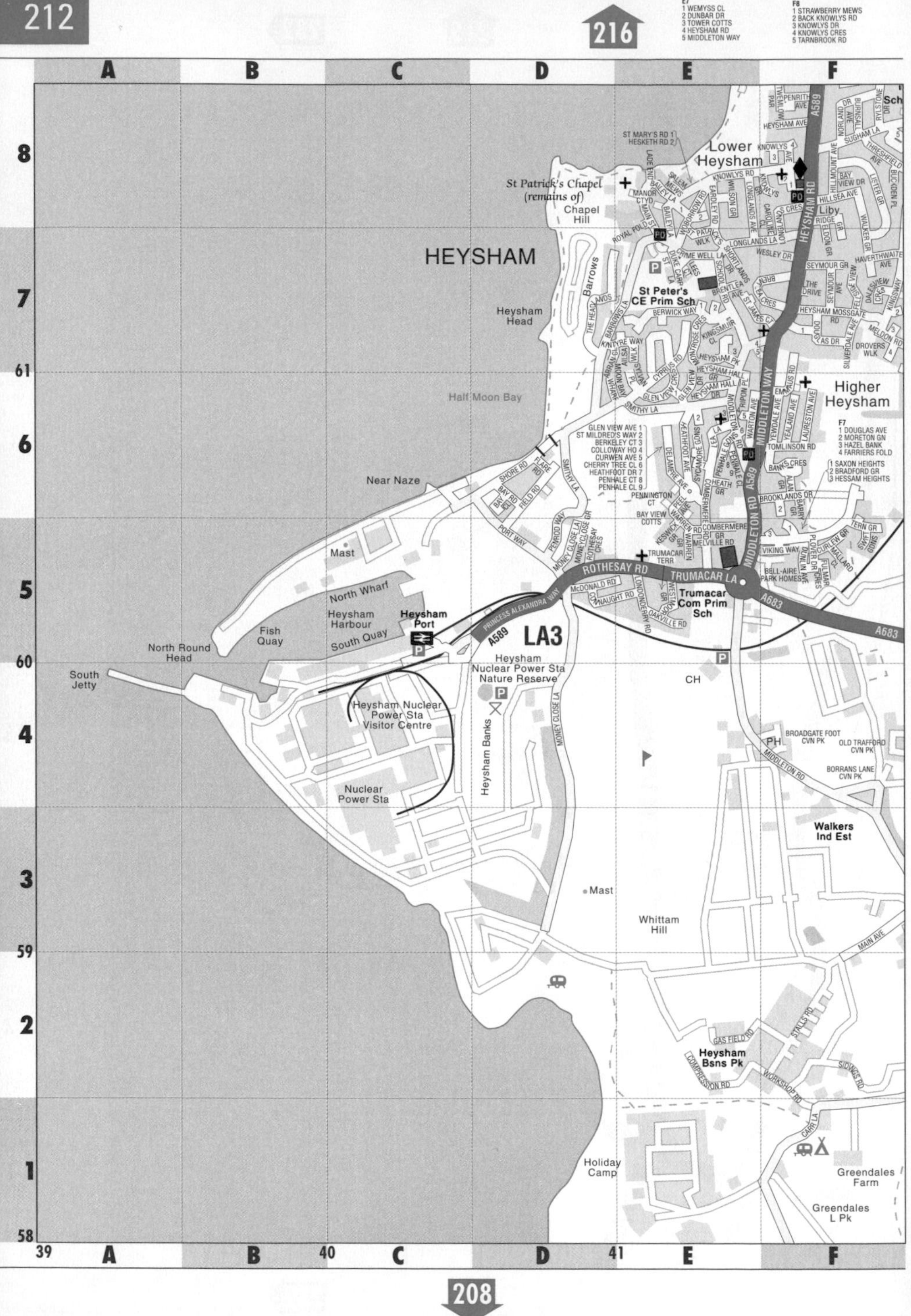

216
E7
1 WEMYSS CL
2 DUNBAR DR
3 TOWER COTTS
4 HEYSHAM RD
5 MIDDLETON WAY
F8
1 STRAWBERRY MEWS
2 BACK KNOWLYS RD
3 KNOWLYS DR
4 KNOWLYS CRES
5 TARNBROOK RD
A
B
C
D
E
F
8
7
61
6
5
60
4
3
59
2
1
58
39
40
41
Lower Heysham
St Patrick's Chapel (remains of)
Chapel Hill
HEYSHAM
Barrows
St Peter's CE Prim Sch
Heysham Head
Half Moon Bay
Higher Heysham
Liby
F7
1 DOUGLAS AVE
2 MORETON GN
3 HAZEL BANK
4 FARRIERS FOLD
1 SAXON HEIGHTS
2 BRADFORD GR
3 HESSAM HEIGHTS
GLEN VIEW AVE 1
ST MILDRED'S WAY 2
BERKELEY CT 3
COLLOWAY HO 4
CURWEN AVE 5
CHERRY TREE CL 6
HEATHFOOT DR 7
PENHALE CT 8
PENHALE CL 9
ST MARY'S RD 1
HESKETH RD 2
HEYSHAM RD
MIDDLETON WAY
MIDDLETON RD
A589
A683
ROTHESAY RD
TRUMACAR LA
PRINCESS ALEXANDRA WAY
Near Naze
Mast
North Wharf
Heysham Harbour
Heysham Port
Fish Quay
South Quay
North Round Head
South Jetty
LA3
Trumacar Com Prim Sch
Heysham Nuclear Power Sta Nature Reserve
Heysham Nuclear Power Sta Visitor Centre
Nuclear Power Sta
Heysham Banks
MONEY CLOSE LA
CH
PH
BROADGATE FOOT CVN PK
OLD TRAFFORD CVN PK
BORRANS LANE CVN PK
Walkers Ind Est
Mast
Whittam Hill
MAIN AVE
GAS FIELD RD
Heysham Bsns Pk
COMPRESSION RD
WORKSHOP RD
STALLS RD
SIDINGS RD
CARR LA
Holiday Camp
Greendales Farm
Greendales L Pk
BELL-AIRE PARK HOMES

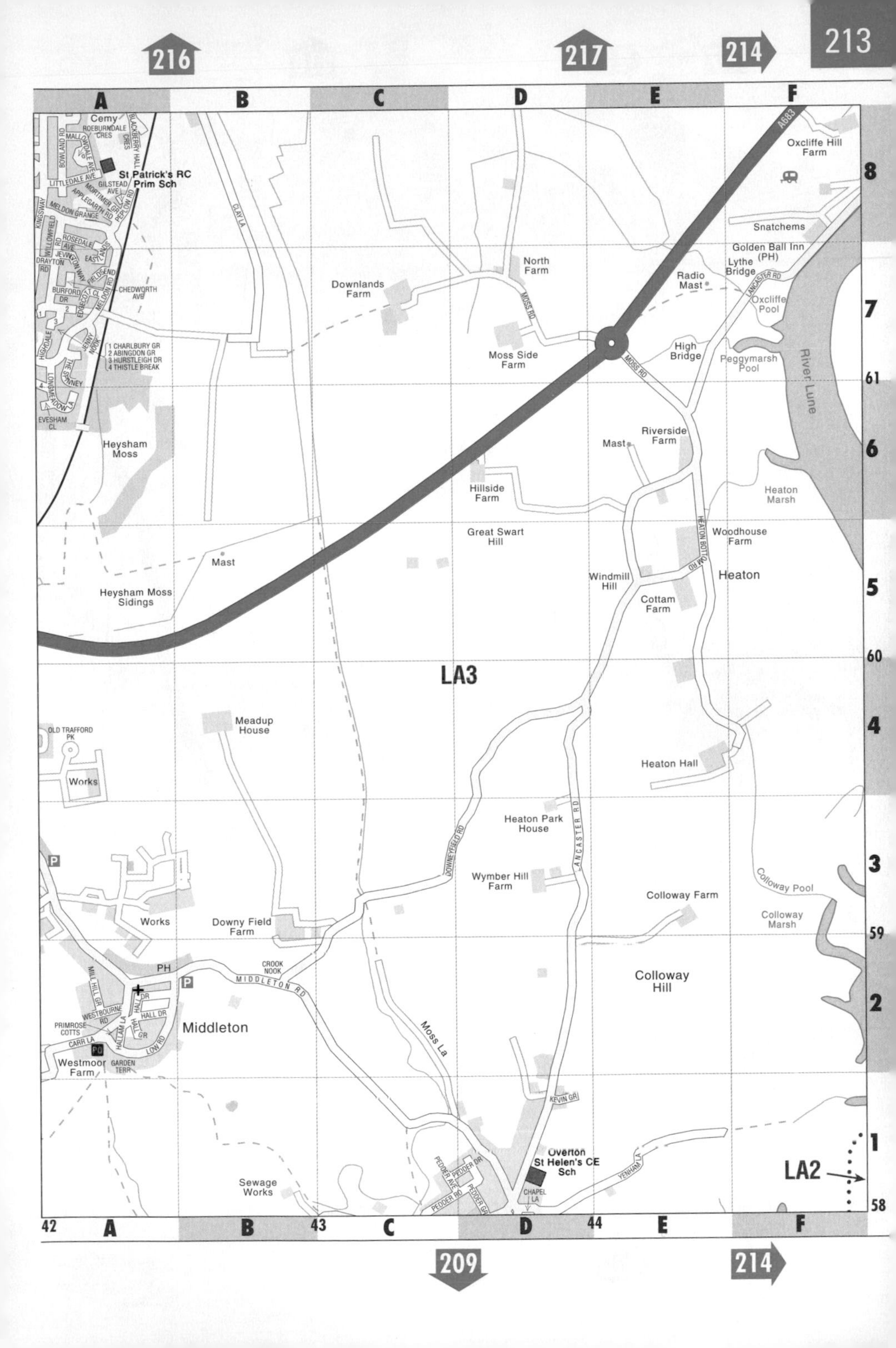
213
216
217
214
209
214
A
B
C
D
E
F
8
7
61
6
5
60
4
3
59
2
1
58
42
43
44
A683
Cemy
ROEBURNDALE CRES
BLACKBERRY HALL
BOWLAND RD
MALLOWDALE AVE
St Patrick's RC Prim Sch
LITTLEDALE AVE
GILSTEAD AVE
MORTIMER GR
PEPLOW RD
KINGSWAY
APPLEGARTH RD
MELDON GRANGE
WILLOWFIELD
ROSEDALE AVE
DRAYTON
JEVINGTON WAY
EASTLANDS
FIELDSEND
MELDON RD
BURFORD DR
EDGECOTT CL
CHEDWORTH AVE
HIGHDALE
JENNY NOOK
1 CHARLBURY GR
2 ABINGDON GR
3 HURSTLEIGH DR
4 THISTLE BREAK
THE SPINNEY
LONGMEADOW LA
EVESHAM CL
CLAY LA
Heysham Moss
Mast
Heysham Moss Sidings
Downlands Farm
North Farm
MOSS RD
Moss Side Farm
Oxcliffe Hill Farm
Snatchems
Golden Ball Inn (PH)
Lythe Bridge
Radio Mast
LANCASTER RD
Oxcliffe Pool
High Bridge
Peggymarsh Pool
River Lune
MOSS RD
Riverside Farm
Mast
Hillside Farm
Heaton Marsh
Great Swart Hill
HEATON BOTTOM RD
Woodhouse Farm
Windmill Hill
Heaton
Cottam Farm
LA3
Meadup House
OLD TRAFFORD PK
Works
Heaton Hall
Heaton Park House
DOWNEYFIELD RD
LANCASTER RD
Wymber Hill Farm
Colloway Pool
Colloway Farm
Colloway Marsh
P
Works
Downy Field Farm
CROOK NOOK
MIDDLETON RD
PH
P
Colloway Hill
MILL HILL GR
WESTBOURNE RD
HALL DR
HALL GR
PRIMROSE COTTS
HALLAM LA
LOW RD
Middleton
CARR LA
PO
Westmoor Farm
GARDEN TERR
Moss La
KEVIN GR
Sewage Works
PEDDER DR
PEDDER AVE
PEDDER RD
PEDDER GR
Overton St Helen's CE Sch
CHAPEL LA
YENHAM LA
LA2

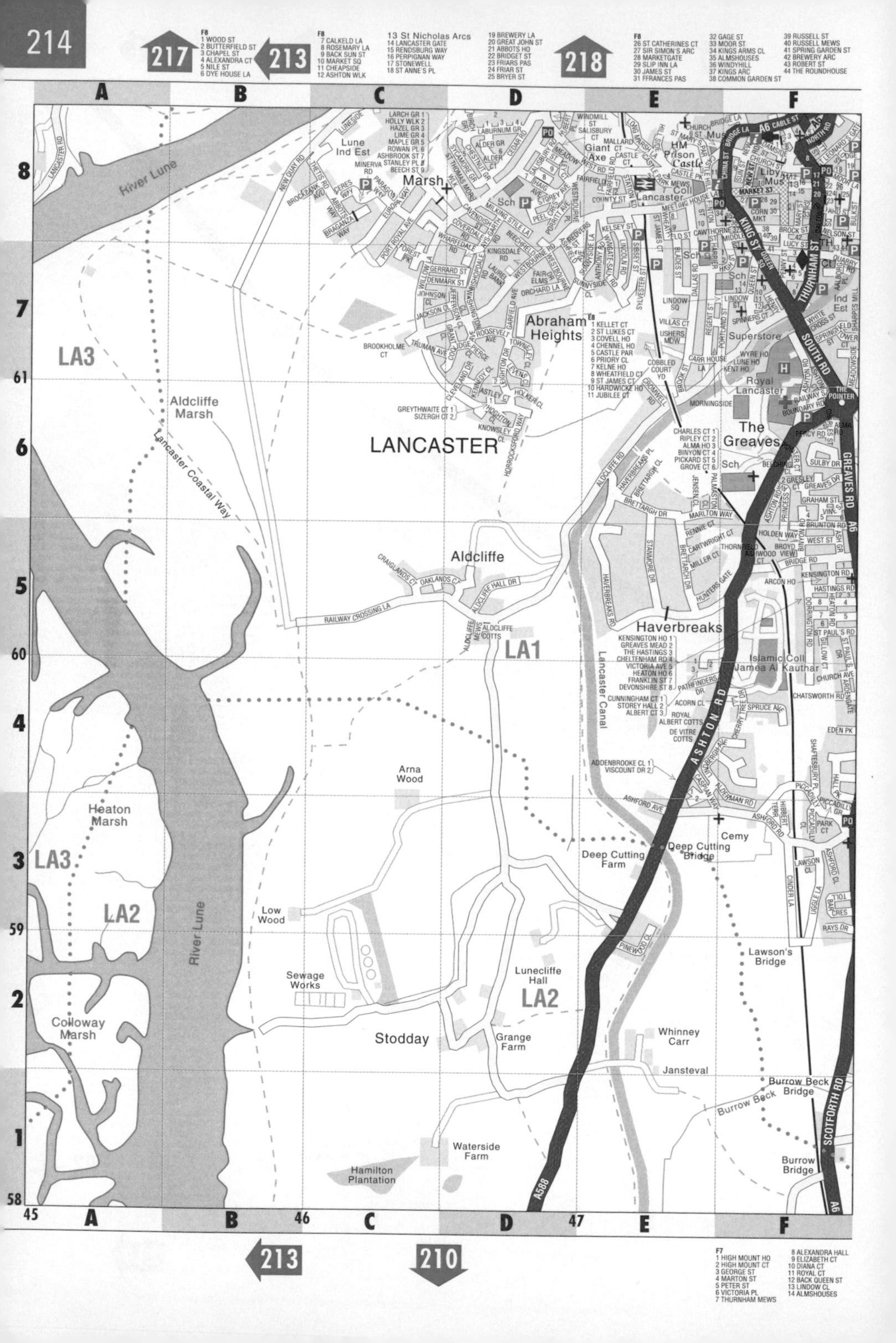
217
213
218
F8
1 WOOD ST
2 BUTTERFIELD ST
3 CHAPEL ST
4 ALEXANDRA CT
5 NILE ST
6 DYE HOUSE LA
F8
7 CALKELD LA
8 ROSEMARY LA
9 BACK SUN ST
10 MARKET SQ
11 CHEAPSIDE
12 ASHTON WLK
13 St Nicholas Arcs
14 LANCASTER GATE
15 RENDSBURG WAY
16 PERPIGNAN WAY
17 STONEWELL
18 ST ANNE'S PL
19 BREWERY LA
20 GREAT JOHN ST
21 ABBOTS HO
22 BRIDGET ST
23 FRIARS PAS
24 FRIAR ST
25 BRYER ST
F8
26 ST CATHERINES CT
27 SIR SIMON'S ARC
28 MARKETGATE
29 SLIP INN LA
30 JAMES ST
31 FFRANCES PAS
32 GAGE ST
33 MOOR ST
34 KINGS ARMS CL
35 ALMSHOUSES
36 WINDYHILL
37 KINGS ARC
38 COMMON GARDEN ST
39 RUSSELL ST
40 RUSSELL MEWS
41 SPRING GARDEN ST
42 BREWERY ARC
43 ROBERT ST
44 THE ROUNDHOUSE
A
B
C
D
E
F
8
7
61
6
5
60
4
3
59
2
1
58
45
46
47
River Lune
LA3
Aldcliffe Marsh
Lancaster Coastal Way
Lune Ind Est
Marsh
LARCH GR 1
HOLLY WLK 2
HAZEL GR 3
LIME GR 4
MAPLE GR 5
ROWAN PL 6
ASHBROOK ST 7
STANLEY PL 8
BEECH ST 9
Giant Axe
HM Prison
Castle
Lancaster
Abraham Heights
E8
1 KELLET CT
2 ST LUKES CT
3 COVELL HO
4 CHENNEL HO
5 CASTLE PAR
6 PRIORY CL
7 KELNE HO
8 WHEATFIELD CT
9 ST JAMES CT
10 HARDWICKE HO
11 JUBILEE CT
BROOKHOLME CT
GREYTHWAITE CT 1
SIZERGH CT 2
LANCASTER
Superstore
Royal Lancaster
The Pointer
The Greaves
CHARLES CT 1
RIPLEY CT 2
ALMA HO 3
BINYON CT 4
PICKARD ST 5
GROVE CT 6
Aldcliffe
RAILWAY CROSSING LA
LA1
Haverbreaks
KENSINGTON HO 1
GREAVES MEAD 2
THE HASTINGS 3
CHELTENHAM RD 4
VICTORIA AVE 5
HEATON HO 6
FRANKLIN ST 7
DEVONSHIRE ST 8
CUNNINGHAM CT 1
STOREY HALL 2
ALBERT CT 3
Islamic Coll Jamea Al Kauthar
Lancaster Canal
ASHTON RD
ADDENBROOKE CL 1
VISCOUNT DR 2
Arna Wood
Heaton Marsh
LA3
LA2
Deep Cutting Farm
Deep Cutting Bridge
Cemy
Low Wood
Sewage Works
Lunecliffe Hall
LA2
River Lune
Colloway Marsh
Stodday
Grange Farm
Whinney Carr
Jansteval
Lawson's Bridge
Burrow Beck Bridge
Burrow Beck
Waterside Farm
Hamilton Plantation
Burrow Bridge
A588
SCOTFORTH RD
GREAVES RD
SOUTH RD
A6
213
210
F7
1 HIGH MOUNT HO
2 HIGH MOUNT CT
3 GEORGE ST
4 MARTON ST
5 PETER ST
6 VICTORIA PL
7 THURNHAM MEWS
8 ALEXANDRA HALL
9 ELIZABETH CT
10 DIANA CT
11 ROYAL CT
12 BACK QUEEN ST
13 LINDOW CL
14 ALMSHOUSES

215
A8
1 DE VITRE ST
2 SHAW ST
3 GARNET ST
4 SIDNEY TERR
5 SEYMOUR ST
6 PRIORY WLK
7 BATH MILL SQ
218
A8
8 WHITBARROW SQ
9 HAYLOT SQ
10 CROSSDALE SQ
11 MELBOURNE RD
12 GREENFIELD ST
13 NORWOOD CT
14 MOOR GATE
15 DAVIDSON ST
16 ST PETERS MEWS
17 MILL HO MEWS
18 GREENFIELD HO
19 MILL HO
20 GLEBE CT
21 CITY HEIGHTS CL
A7
1 SWAN YD
2 GREENFIELD CT
3 ARGYLE ST
4 ELGIN ST
5 DUNKELD ST
6 PRIMROSE CT
7 BRADSHAW ST
8 VINCENT ST
A6
1 BOWERHAM TERR
2 CUMBERLAND VIEW
3 HANMER PL
219
232
Lancaster Christ Church CE Prim Sch
Cemy
Lancaster Moor
Freehold
Moorlands
Lancaster Royal Gram Sch (Annexe)
Butterfly House
Ashton Meml
Williamson Park
Recess Plantation
The Gables Poultry Farm
LA1
Golgotha
The Lancaster & Lakeland
St Martin's Coll
Bowerham Com Prim Sch
Oatlands
Well House
Lancaster L Pk
Bowerham
Filter House
Newlands
West View Farm
Westbourne Heights
Langthwaite House
Langthwaite
Mast
Moorside Prim Sch
Recn Gd
The Grange
LA2
Conderdell
Middle Langthwaite
Lower Langthwaite
Conder Mill Farm
Langthwaite Resr
Lee End
Scotforth
Kirklands Poultry Farm
River Conder
Scotforth Heights
Mount Vernon
Blea Tarn Resr
Sunnymede Farm
Conder Side
Hazelrigg Wood
Blea Tarn Farm
Bailrigg
Bailrigg Farm
QUERNMORE RD
NEWLANDS RD
LANGTHWAITE RD
LITTLE FELL RD
LITTLE FELL LA
WYRESDALE RD
BLEA TARN RD
SCOTFORTH RD
M6
A6
48
49
50
58
59
60
61
A5
1 GORDON TERR
2 BRUNTON HO
3 GREAVES CT
4 CHILTERN CT
A3
1 SCOTFORTH CT
2 INGLETON HO
3 GRESSINGHAM HO
4 MELLING HO
5 LENTWORTH HO
6 SANDFIELD HO
7 BECK VIEW
8 ABBEYSTEAD HO
9 WINDMILL CT
10 TUNSTALL HO
11 LECK HO
211
232

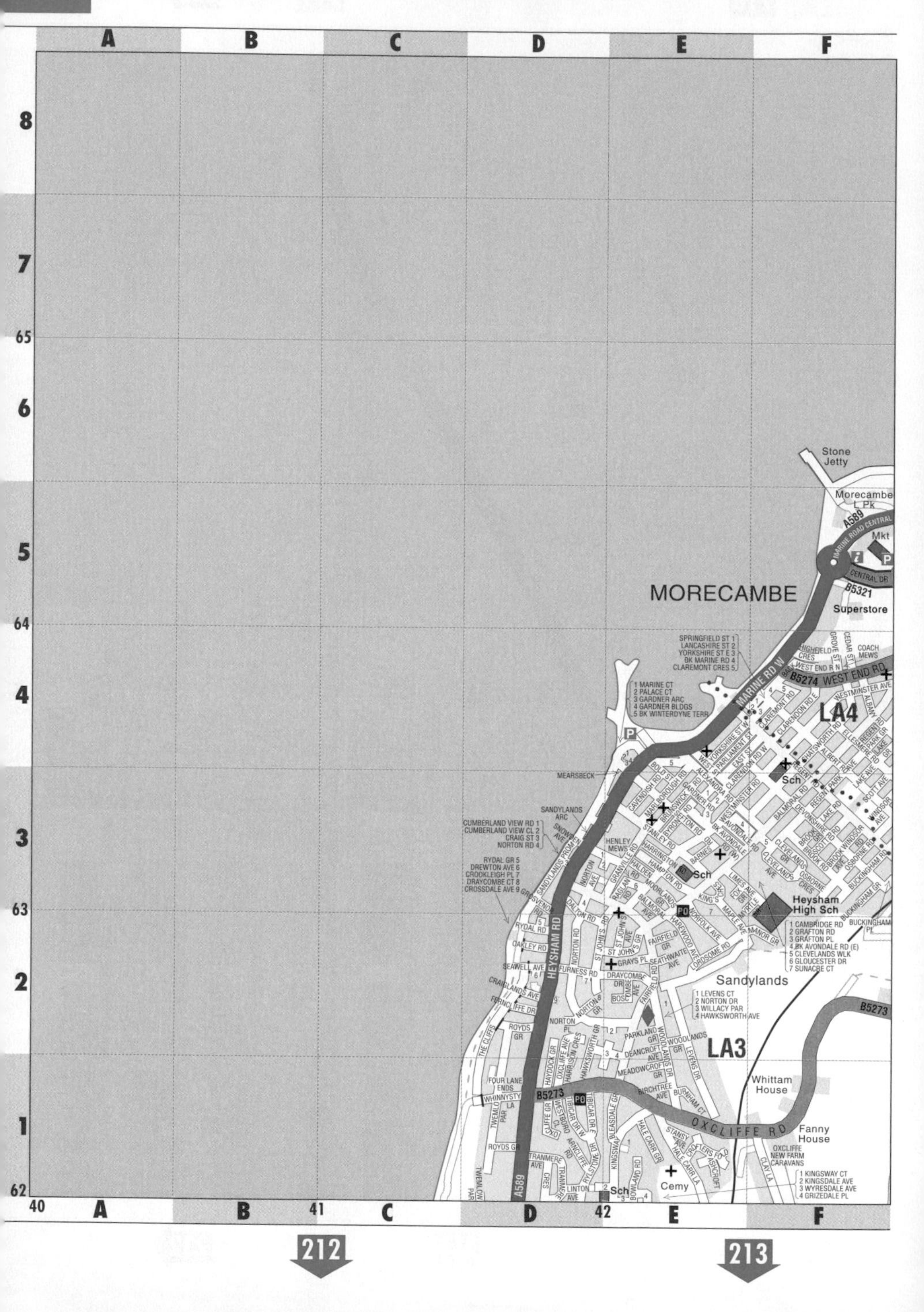
A
B
C
D
E
F
8
7
65
6
5
64
4
3
63
2
1
62
40
41
42
Stone Jetty
Morecambe L Pk
A589
MARINE ROAD CENTRAL
Mkt
P
CENTRAL DR
B5321
MORECAMBE
Superstore
SPRINGFIELD ST 1
LANCASHIRE ST 2
YORKSHIRE ST E 3
BK MARINE RD 4
CLAREMONT CRES 5
HIGHFIELD CRES
GROVE ST
CEDAR ST
COACH MEWS
WEST END RD N
B5274 WEST END RD
WESTMINSTER AVE
1 MARINE CT
2 PALACE CT
3 GARDNER ARC
4 GARDNER BLDGS
5 BK WINTERDYNE TERR
MARINE RD W
LA4
MEARSBECK
SANDYLANDS ARC
CUMBERLAND VIEW RD 1
CUMBERLAND VIEW CL 2
CRAIG ST 3
NORTON RD 4
RYDAL GR 5
DREWTON AVE 6
CROOKLEIGH PL 7
DRAYCOMBE CT 8
CROSSDALE AVE 9
SANDYLANDS PROM
HENLEY MEWS
Sch
Heysham High Sch
1 CAMBRIDGE RD
2 GRAFTON RD
3 GRAFTON PL
4 BK AVONDALE RD (E)
5 CLEVELANDS WLK
6 GLOUCESTER DR
7 SUNACRE CT
BUCKINGHAM PL
Sandylands
1 LEVENS CT
2 NORTON DR
3 WILLACY PAR
4 HAWKSWORTH AVE
B5273
HEYSHAM RD
LA3
Whittam House
Fanny House
OXCLIFFE RD
OXCLIFFE NEW FARM CARAVANS
1 KINGSWAY CT
2 KINGSDALE AVE
3 WYRESDALE AVE
4 GRIZEDALE PL
Cemy
FOUR LANE ENDS
WHINNYSTY LA
THE CLIFFS
ROYDS GR
A589

212
213

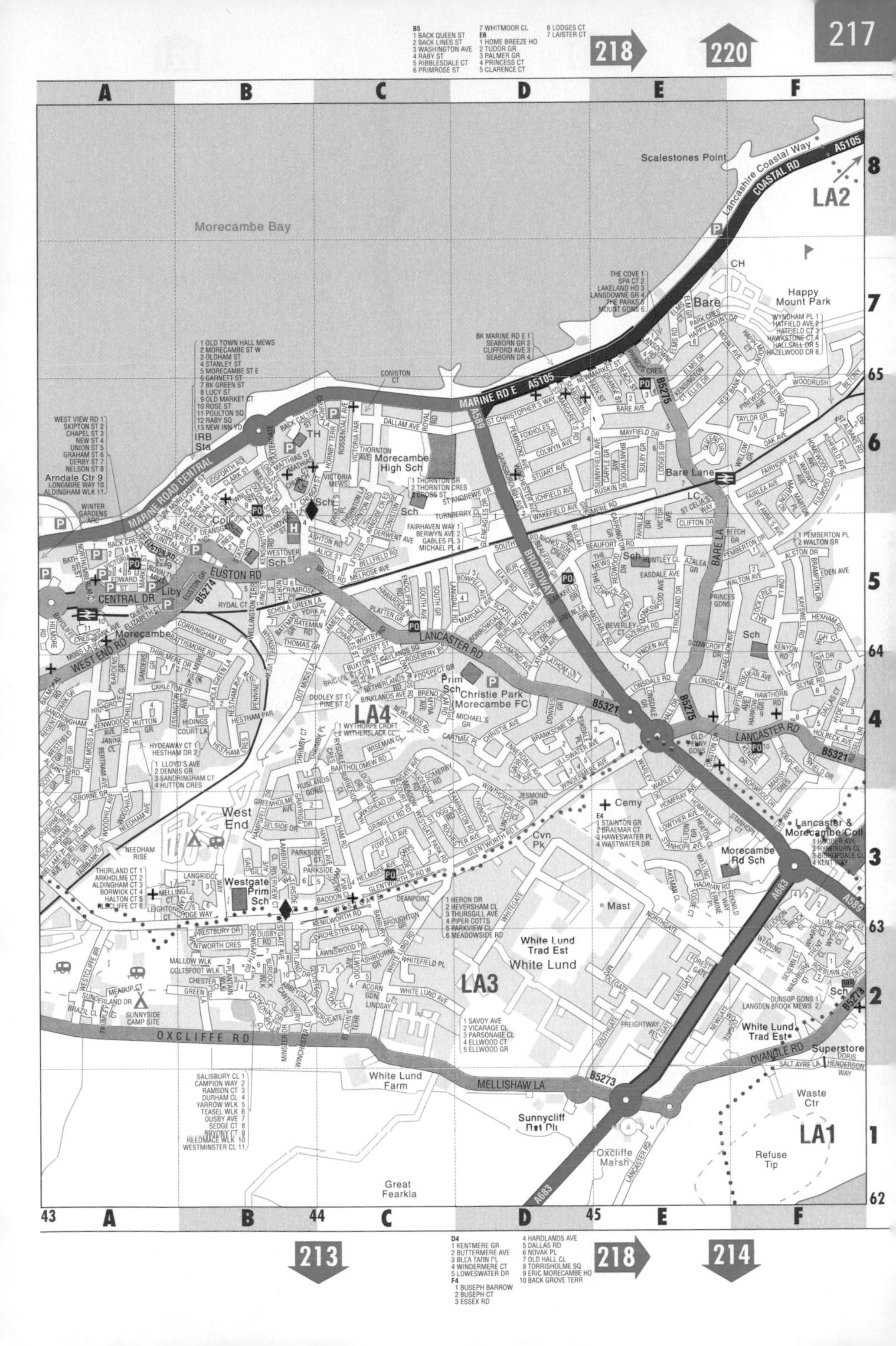

B5
1 BACK QUEEN ST
2 BACK LINES ST
3 WASHINGTON AVE
4 RABY ST
5 RIBBLESDALE CT
6 PRIMROSE ST
7 WHITMOOR CL
E6
1 HOME BREEZE HO
2 TUDOR GR
3 PALMER GR
4 PRINCESS CT
5 CLARENCE CT
6 LODGES CT
7 LAISTER CT
218
220
A
B
C
D
E
F
Scalestones Point
Lancashire Coastal Way
COASTAL RD
A5105
LA2
Morecambe Bay
CH
Happy Mount Park
Bare
THE COVE 1
SPA CT 2
LAKELAND HO 3
LANSDOWNE GR 4
THE PARKS 5
MOUNT GDNS 6
WYNDHAM PL 1
HATFIELD AVE 2
HATFIELD CT 3
HAWKSTONE CT 4
HALLSALL DR 5
HAZELWOOD CR 6
BK MARINE RD E 1
SEABORN GR 2
CLIFFORD AVE 3
SEABORN DR 4
1 OLD TOWN HALL MEWS
2 MORECAMBE ST W
3 OLDHAM ST
4 STANLEY ST
5 MORECAMBE ST E
6 GARNETT ST
7 BK GREEN ST
8 LUCY ST
9 OLD MARKET CT
10 ROSE ST
11 POULTON SQ
12 RABY SQ
13 NEW INN YD
CONISTON CT
MARINE RD E
A5105
A589
B5275
WOODRUSH
WEST VIEW RD 1
SKIPTON ST 2
CHAPEL ST 3
NEW ST 4
UNION ST 5
GRAHAM ST 6
DERBY ST 7
NELSON ST 8
Arndale Ctr 9
LONGMIRE WAY 10
ALDINGHAM WLK 11
IRB Sta
TH
MARINE ROAD CENTRAL
Morecambe High Sch
1 THORNTON GR
2 THORNTON CRES
3 CROSS ST
Bare Lane
LC
WINTER GARDENS ARC
Coll
Sch
FAIRHAVEN WAY 1
BERWYN AVE 2
GABLES PL 3
MICHAEL PL 4
1 PEMBERTON PL
2 WALTON GR
EUSTON RD
B5274
CENTRAL DR
Liby
BROADWAY
BARE LA
Morecambe
WEST END RD
LANCASTER RD
Christie Park (Morecambe FC)
Prim Sch
LA4
B5321
DUDLEY ST 1
PINE ST 2
1 WYTHORPE CROFT
2 WITHERSLACK CL
HYDEAWAY CT 1
HESTHAM DR 2
1 LLOYD'S AVE
2 DENNIS GR
3 SANDRINGHAM CT
4 HUTTON CRES
West End
NEEDHAM RISE
THURLAND CT 1
ARKHOLME CT 2
ALDINGHAM CT 3
BORWICK CT 4
HALTON CT 5
ALDCLIFFE CT 6
Westgate Prim Sch
Cemy
E4
1 STAINTON GR
2 BRAEMAR CT
3 HAWESWATER PL
4 WASTWATER DR
Cvn Pk
Lancaster & Morecambe Coll
1 HODDER AVE
2 HYNDBURN CL
3 RIBBLESDALE CL
4 KENT WAY
Morecambe Rd Sch
1 HERON DR
2 HEVERSHAM CL
3 THURSGILL AVE
4 PIPER COTTS
5 PARKVIEW CL
6 MEADOWSIDE RD
Mast
White Lund Trad Est
White Lund
A683
A589
LA3
SUNNYSIDE CAMP SITE
OXCLIFFE RD
1 SAVOY AVE
2 VICARAGE CL
3 PARSONAGE CL
4 ELLWOOD CT
5 ELLWOOD GR
White Lund Trad Est
Superstore
OVANGLE RD
SALT AYRE LA
DUNSOP GDNS 1
LANGDEN BROOK MEWS 2
SALISBURY CL 1
CAMPION WAY 2
RAMSON CT 3
DURHAM CL 4
YARROW WLK 5
TEASEL WLK 6
OUSBY AVE 7
SEDGE CT 8
BRYONY CT 9
REEDMACE WLK 10
WESTMINSTER CL 11
White Lund Farm
MELLISHAW LA
B5273
Sunnycliff Bsns Pk
Waste Ctr
LA1
Refuse Tip
Oxcliffe Marsh
Great Fearkla
8
7
65
6
5
64
4
3
63
2
1
62
43
44
45
D4
1 KENTMERE GR
2 BUTTERMERE AVE
3 BLEA TARN PL
4 WINDERMERE CT
5 LOWESWATER DR
F4
1 BUSEPH BARROW
2 BUSEPH CT
3 ESSEX RD
4 HARDLANDS AVE
5 DALLAS RD
6 NOVAK PL
7 OLD HALL CL
8 TORRISHOLME SQ
9 ERIC MORECAMBE HO
10 BACK GROVE TERR
213
218
214

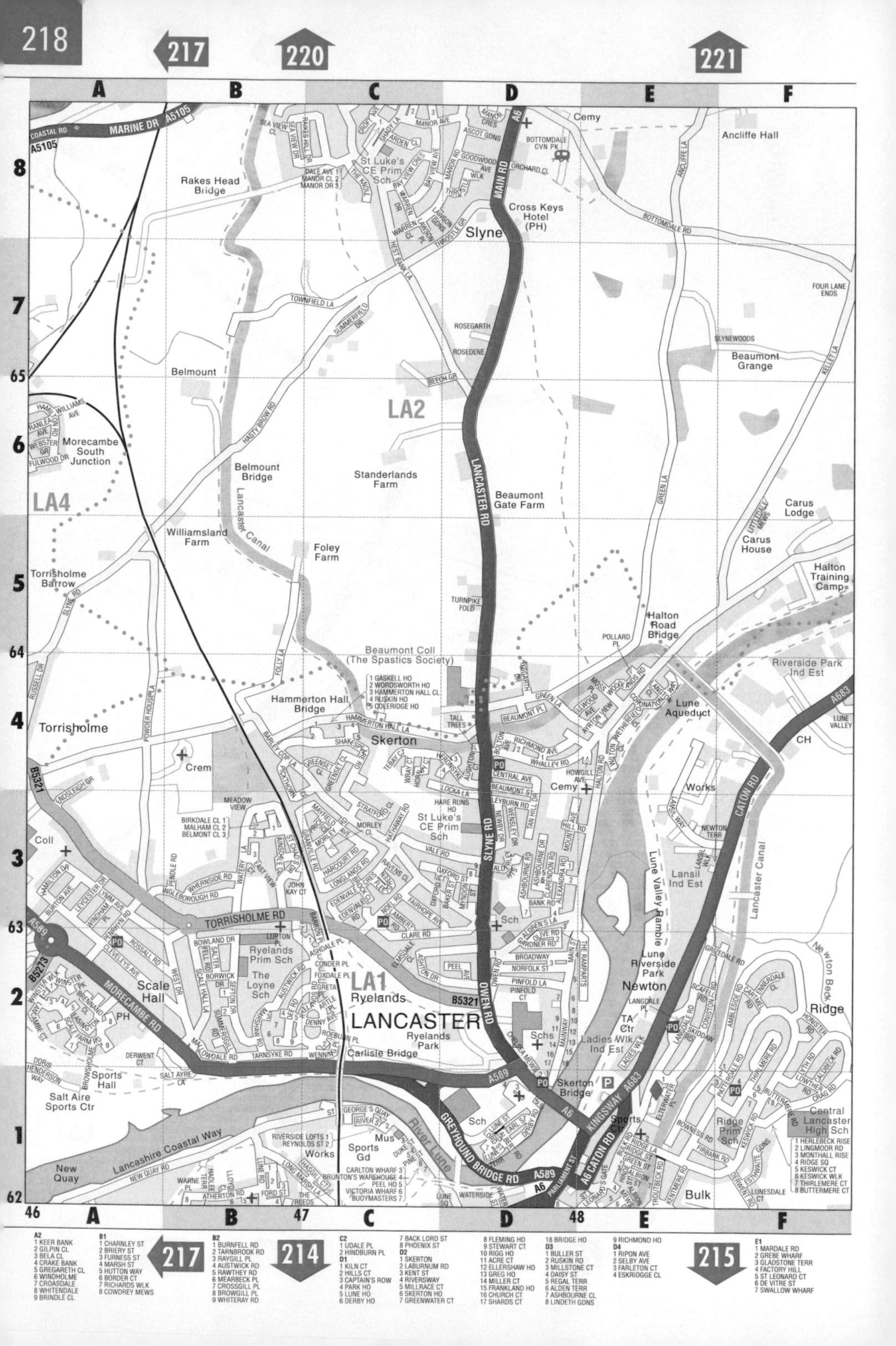

218
217
220
221
A
B
C
D
E
F
8
7
6
5
4
3
2
1
65
64
63
62
46
47
48
MARINE DR
A5105
COASTAL RD
Rakes Head
Bridge
St Luke's
CE Prim
Sch
DALE AVE 1
MANOR CL 2
MANOR DR 3
MANOR AVE
ASCOT GDNS
MAIN RD
A6
Cemy
BOTTOMDALE
CVN PK
ORCHARD CL
Ancliffe Hall
ANCLIFFE LA
Cross Keys
Hotel
(PH)
Slyne
BOTTOMDALE RD
HEST BANK LA
THROSTLE GR
TOWNFIELD LA
SUMMERFIELD DR
FOUR LANE
ENDS
ROSEGARTH
ROSEDENE
SLYNEWOODS
Beaumont
Grange
KELLET LA
BEECH GR
Belmount
LA2
Morecambe
South
Junction
HASTY BROW RD
Belmount
Bridge
Standerlands
Farm
LANCASTER RD
Beaumont
Gate Farm
GREEN LA
Carus
Lodge
Carus
House
LA4
Lancaster Canal
Williamsland
Farm
Foley
Farm
Halton
Training
Camp
Torrisholme
Barrow
SLYNE RD
TURNPIKE
FOLD
Halton
Road
Bridge
POLLARD
PL
Beaumont Coll
(The Spastics Society)
1 GASKELL HO
2 WORDSWORTH HO
3 HAMMERTON HALL CL
4 RUSKIN HO
5 COLERIDGE HO
Riverside Park
Ind Est
Hammerton Hall
Bridge
Lune
Aqueduct
A683
LUNE
VALLEY
Torrisholme
Skerton
CH
RUSSELL DR
POWDER HOUSE LA
Crem
B5321
ENDSLEIGH GR
Works
CATON RD
MEADOW
VIEW
BIRKDALE CL 1
MALHAM CL 2
BELMONT CL 3
St Luke's
CE Prim
Sch
Cemy
SLYNE RD
Coll
NEWTON
TERR
Lune Valley Ramble
Lansil
Ind Est
Lancaster Canal
TORRISHOLME RD
A589
WHERNSIDE RD
INGLEBOROUGH RD
Sch
Ryelands
Prim Sch
The
Loyne
Sch
Scale
Hall
MORECAMBE RD
LA1
Ryelands
LANCASTER
Ryelands
Park
Carlisle Bridge
B5321
OWEN RD
Lune
Riverside
Park
Newton
Newton Beck
Ridge
TA
Ctr
Ladies Wlk
Ind Est
Schs
PH
B5273
Sports
Hall
Salt Aire
Sports Ctr
SALT AYRE LA
Skerton
Bridge
KINGSWAY
A6
Sports
Ctr
Central
Lancaster
High Sch
1 HERLEBECK RISE
2 LINGMOOR RD
3 MONTHALL RISE
4 RIDGE SQ
5 KESWICK CT
6 KESWICK WLK
7 THIRLEMERE CT
8 BUTTERMERE CT
Ridge
Prim
Sch
Lancashire Coastal Way
River Lune
GREYHOUND BRIDGE RD
A589
A6 CATON RD
RIVERSIDE LOFTS 1
REYNOLDS ST 2
Works
Mus
Sports
Gd
Sch
New
Quay
NEW QUAY RD
CARLTON WHARF 3
BRUNTON'S WAREHOUSE 4
PEEL HO 5
VICTORIA WHARF 6
BUOYMASTERS 7
Bulk
LUNESDALE
CT
A2
1 KEER BANK
2 GILPIN CL
3 BELA CL
4 CRAKE BANK
5 GREGARETH CL
6 WINDHOLME
7 CROASDALE
8 WHITENDALE
9 BRINDLE CL
B1
1 CHARNLEY ST
2 BRIERY ST
3 FURNESS ST
4 MARSH ST
5 HUTTON WAY
6 BORDER CT
7 RICHARDS WLK
8 COWDREY MEWS
217
B2
1 BURNFELL RD
2 TARNBROOK RD
3 RAYGILL PL
4 AUSTWICK RD
5 RAWTHEY RD
6 MEARBECK PL
7 CROSSGILL PL
8 BROWGILL PL
9 WHITERAY RD
214
C2
1 UDALE PL
2 HINDBURN PL
D1
1 KILN CT
2 HILLS CT
3 CAPTAIN'S ROW
4 PARK HO
5 LUNE HO
6 DERBY HO
7 BACK LORD ST
8 PHOENIX ST
D2
1 SKERTON
2 LABURNUM RD
3 KENT ST
4 RIVERSWAY
5 MILLRACE CT
6 SKERTON HO
7 GREENWATER CT
8 FLEMING HO
9 STEWART CT
10 RIGG HO
11 ACRE CT
12 ELLERSHAW HO
13 GREG HO
14 MILLER CT
15 FRANKLAND HO
16 CHURCH CT
17 SHARDS CT
18 BRIDGE HO
D3
1 BULLER ST
2 RUSKIN RD
3 MILLSTONE CT
4 DAISY ST
5 REGAL TERR
6 ALDEN TERR
7 ASHBOURNE CL
8 LINDETH GDNS
9 RICHMOND HO
D4
1 RIPON AVE
2 SELBY AVE
3 FARLETON CT
4 ESKRIDGGE CL
215
E1
1 MARDALE RD
2 GREBE WHARF
3 GLADSTONE TERR
4 FACTORY HILL
5 ST LEONARD CT
6 DE VITRE ST
7 SWALLOW WHARF

221
237
237
A
B
C
D
E
F
Cote Farm
LA5
M6
KELLET LA
SCARGILL RD
LAVERICK RD
Lane End
Arrow Barn
KIRKBY LONSDALE RD
GREEN LA
Arrow Lane Farm
ARROW LA
OAK DR
POINTER GR
HARROWDALE PK
Halton Green
Cote Beck
St Wilfrid's CE Prim Sch
BEECH RD
SYKELANDS GR
SYKELANDS AVE
PENNY STONE RD
LUNESDALE VIEW
HAYLOT DR
SCHOOLHOUSE LA
FOUNDRY LA
MEADOWFIELD CL 1
HOUGHTON CT 2
WALTHAM CT 3
MEADOWFIELD
FELL AVE
LOW RD
THRUSHGILL
LYTHE DR
Haverbreaks Farm
ROWAN BANK
ST WILFRID'S PK
NEW ST
PO
HIGH RD
Halton
CLOUGHA AVE
THE GARDENS
FOUNDRY LA
FORGEWOOD CL
Dale Wood
RECTORY PADDOCK
PINE CL
QUARRY RD
WISP HILL GR
FORGEWOOD DR
Town End Mill
Halton Mills
CHURCH ST
CHURCH BROW
RIVERSIDE CL
PH
STATION RD
MILL LA
River Lune
1 VICTORIA PL
2 THE OLD SCHOOL
LUNE VIEW CVN PK
Bulk Bridge
Lune Valley Ramble
P
Denny Beck Farm
DENNY BECK LA
LA2
CROOK O'LUNE CVN PK
A683
Hotel
34
DENNY BANK
Hotel
CATON RD
Cottam's Farm
New Parkside Farm
Long Bank Wood
Denny Beck
Old Hall Farm
Moss Syke Wood
Old Parkside Farm
Davies's Farm
Moor Side
GRIMESHAW LA
Ridge Wood
Ridge Farm
LA1
Old Parkside Fell
Quernmore Park Hall
Newton Beck
RIDGE LA
Knots Wood
HM Prison
Ridge Lea
MOOR LA
FAR MOOR LA
Stanley Farm
Stanley Farm Fell
QUERNMORE RD
H
M6
8
7
65
6
5
64
4
3
63
2
1
62
49
50
51
215
237
232

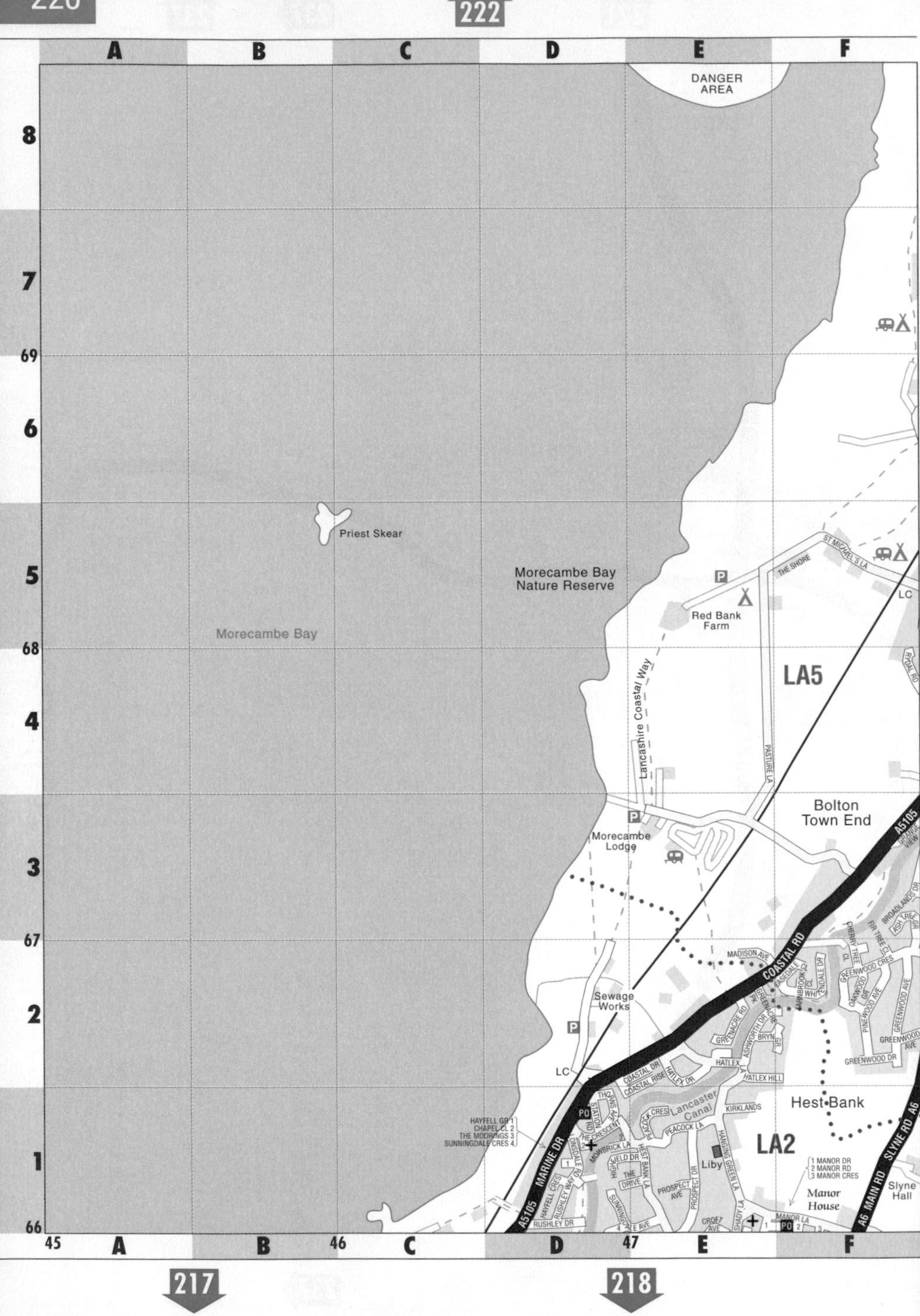
222
A
B
C
D
E
F
DANGER AREA
8
7
69
6
Priest Skear
5
Morecambe Bay Nature Reserve
Morecambe Bay
68
4
3
67
2
1
66
THE SHORE
ST MICHAEL'S LA
LC
Red Bank Farm
LA5
Lancashire Coastal Way
PASTURE LA
RYDAL RD
Bolton Town End
A5105
GRANGE VIEW
Morecambe Lodge
BROADLANDS DR
ASH TREE GR
FIR TREE CL
CHERRY TREE CL
MADISON AVE
COASTAL RD
EASEDALE
GREENWOOD CRES
OAKWOOD GR
PINEWOOD AVE
GREENWOOD AVE
GREENWOOD AVE
GREENWOOD DR
Sewage Works
GREENACRE RD
ASHWORTH DR
BRYN GR
HATLEX
HATLEX HILL
LC
COASTAL DR
COASTAL RISE
HATLEX DR
Lancaster Canal
KIRKLANDS
Hest Bank
PEACOCK CRES
PEACOCK LA
STATION RD
THE CRESCENT
HAYFELL GR 1
CHAPEL CL 2
THE MOORINGS 3
SUNNINGDALE CRES 4
MARINE DR
MOWBRICK LA
HIGHFIELD DR
HEST BANK LA
THE DRIVE
Liby
LA2
1 MANOR DR
2 MANOR RD
3 MANOR CRES
SLYNE RD
A6
HANGING GREEN LA
PROSPECT AVE
PROSPECT DR
Manor House
Slyne Hall
A6 MAIN RD
A5105
HAYFELL CRES
RUSHLEY WAY
LONSDALE RD
SUNNINGDALE AVE
RUSHLEY DR
CROFT AVE
SHADY LA
MANOR LA
45
46
47
217
218

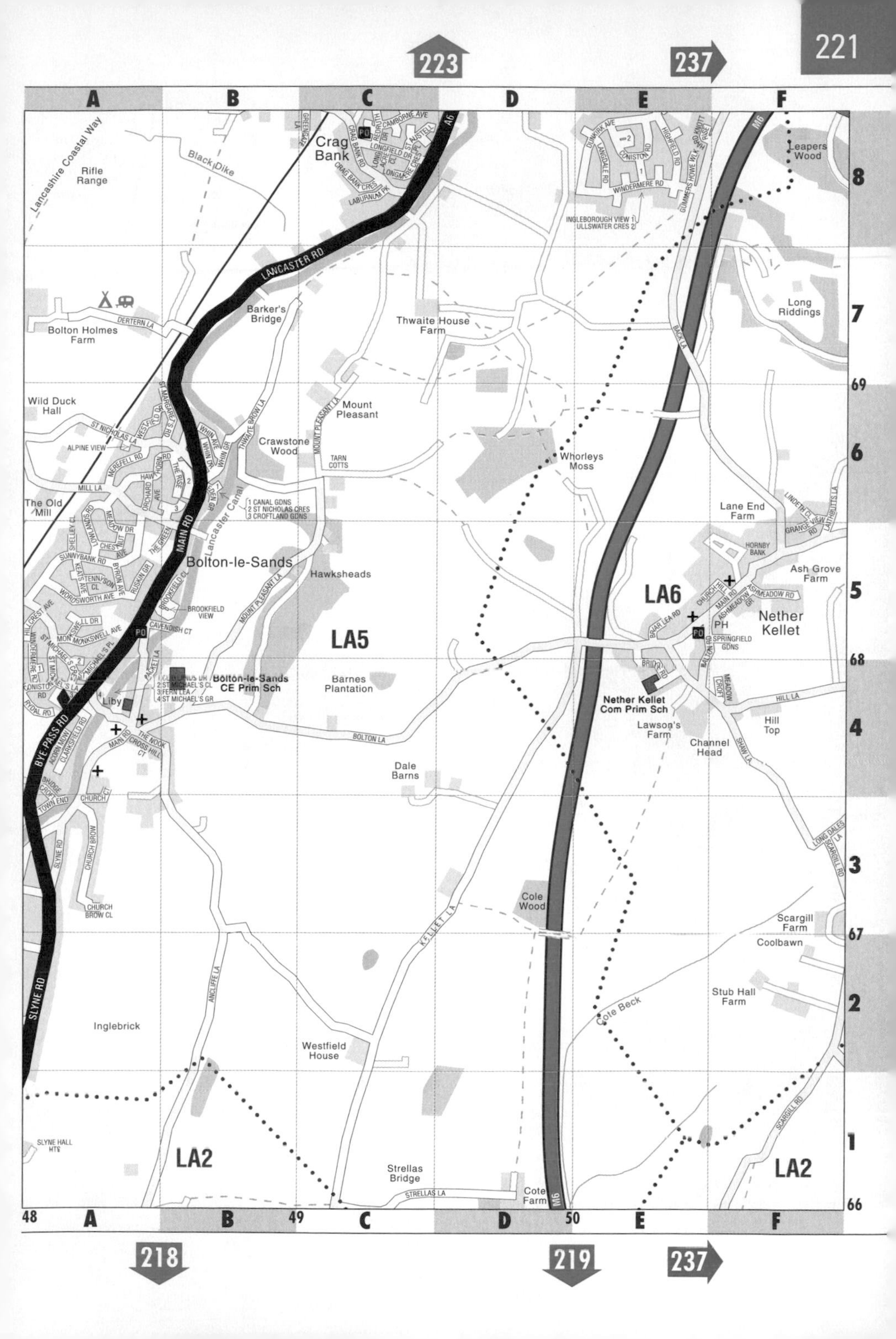
223
237
Crag Bank
Rifle Range
Lancashire Coastal Way
Black Dike
LANCASTER RD
Barker's Bridge
Thwaite House Farm
Bolton Holmes Farm
DERTERN LA
Wild Duck Hall
Mount Pleasant
Crawstone Wood
Whorleys Moss
The Old Mill
Lancaster Canal
Bolton-le-Sands
Hawksheads
Lane End Farm
Ash Grove Farm
LA6
Nether Kellet
LA5
Barnes Plantation
Bolton-le-Sands CE Prim Sch
Nether Kellet Com Prim Sch
Lawson's Farm
Channel Head
Hill Top
BOLTON LA
Dale Barns
Long Riddings
Leapers Wood
Cole Wood
Scargill Farm
Coolbawn
Stub Hall Farm
Cote Beck
Inglebrick
Westfield House
LA2
Strellas Bridge
Cote Farm
SLYNE HALL HTS
MAIN RD
KELLET LA
ANCLIFFE LA
STRELLAS LA
SCARGILL RD
SLYNE RD
BYE-PASS RD
M6
A6
218
219
237

224

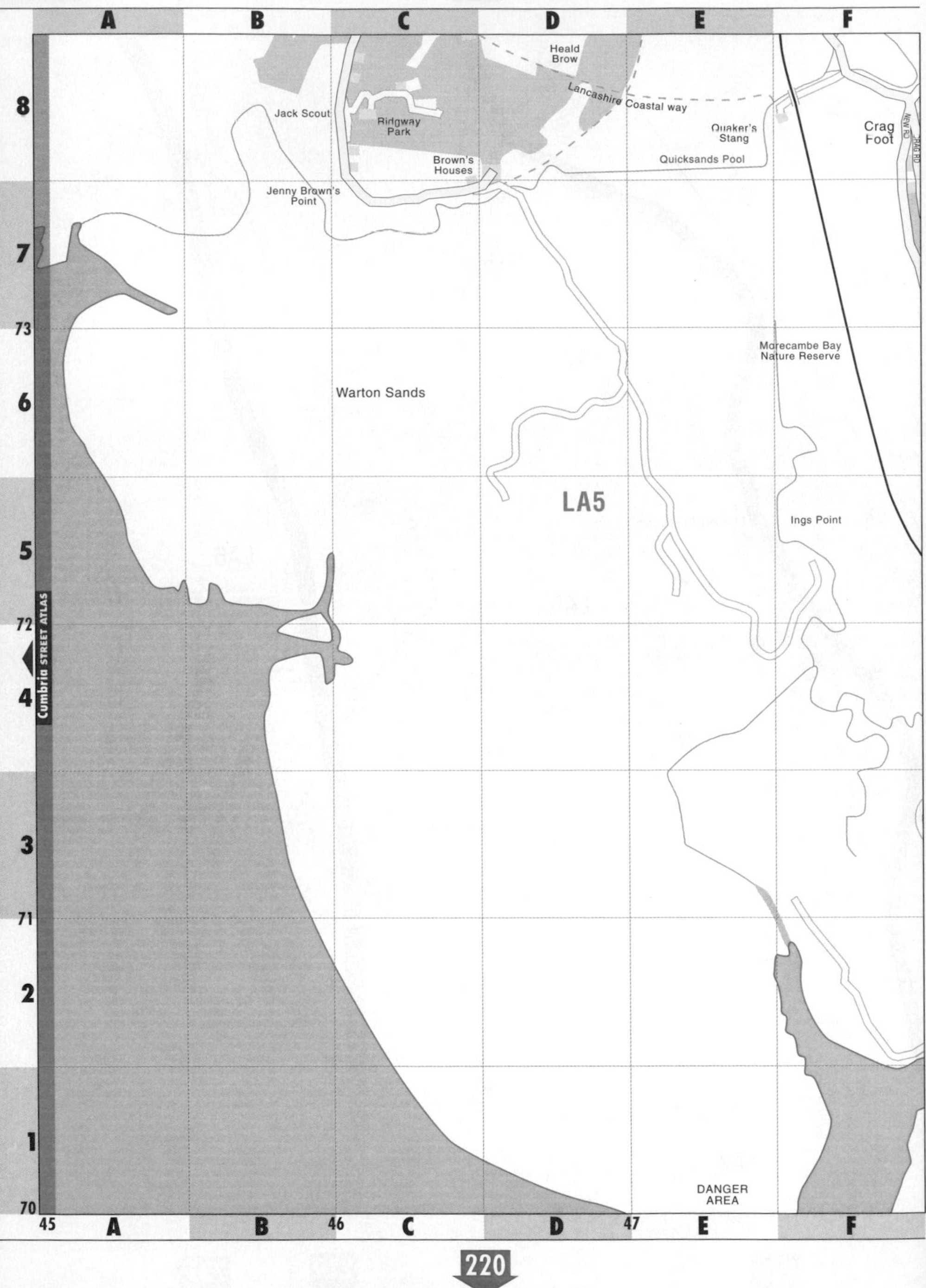
A
B
C
D
E
F
8
7
73
6
5
72
4
3
71
2
1
70
45
46
47
Heald Brow
Lancashire Coastal way
Jack Scout
Ridgway Park
Brown's Houses
Quaker's Stang
Quicksands Pool
Crag Foot
NEW RD
CRAG RD
Jenny Brown's Point
Morecambe Bay Nature Reserve
Warton Sands
LA5
Ings Point
Cumbria STREET ATLAS
DANGER AREA
220

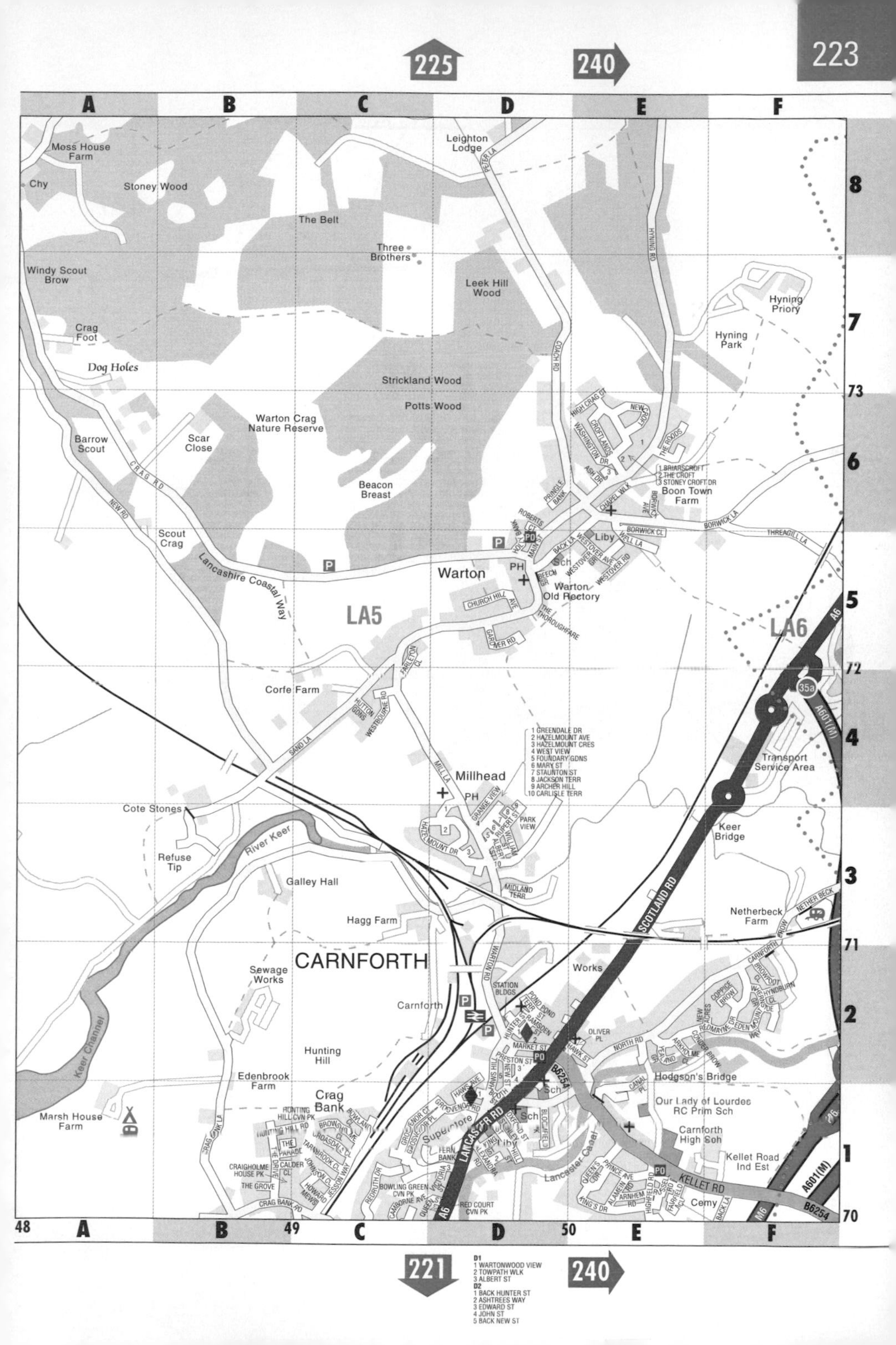

225
240
Moss House Farm
Chy
Stoney Wood
The Belt
Three Brothers
Windy Scout Brow
Leek Hill Wood
Crag Foot
Dog Holes
Hyning Priory
Hyning Park
Strickland Wood
Potts Wood
Warton Crag Nature Reserve
Barrow Scout
Scar Close
Beacon Breast
Boon Town Farm
Scout Crag
Warton
Warton Old Rectory
LA5
LA6
Lancashire Coastal Way
Corfe Farm
Millhead
Transport Service Area
Cote Stones
Refuse Tip
Keer Bridge
River Keer
Galley Hall
Hagg Farm
Netherbeck Farm
CARNFORTH
Works
Sewage Works
Carnforth
Hunting Hill
Edenbrook Farm
Crag Bank
Hodgson's Bridge
Our Lady of Lourdes RC Prim Sch
Marsh House Farm
Carnforth High Sch
Kellet Road Ind Est
Lancaster Canal
Cemy
Keer Channel
1 BRIARSCROFT
2 THE CROFT
3 STONEY CROFT DR
1 GREENDALE DR
2 HAZELMOUNT AVE
3 HAZELMOUNT CRES
4 WEST VIEW
5 FOUNDARY GDNS
6 MARY ST
7 STAUNTON ST
8 JACKSON TERR
9 ARCHER HILL
10 CARLISLE TERR
48
49
50
221
240
D1
1 WARTONWOOD VIEW
2 TOWPATH WLK
3 ALBERT ST
D2
1 BACK HUNTER ST
2 ASHTREES WAY
3 EDWARD ST
4 JOHN ST
5 BACK NEW ST

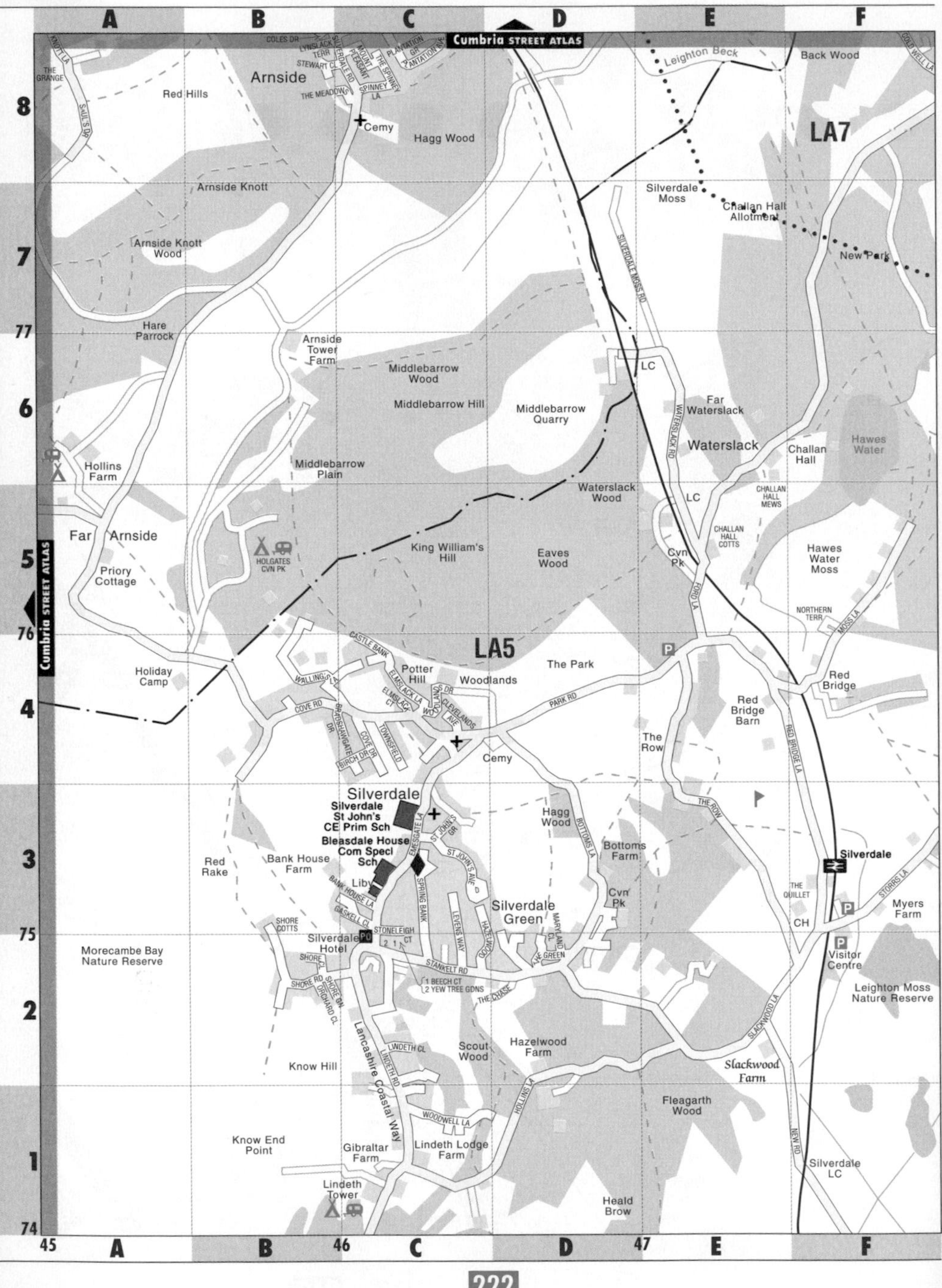

A
B
C
D
E
F
Cumbria STREET ATLAS
8
7
77
6
5
76
4
3
75
2
1
74
45
46
47
COLES DR
LYNSLACK TERR
SILVERDALE RD
STEWART CL
MOUNT PLEASANT
THE SPINNEY
PLANTATION GR
PLANTATION AVE
THE MEADOWS
SPINNEY LA
KNOTT LA
THE GRANGE
SLIL'S DR
Arnside
Red Hills
Cemy
Hagg Wood
Leighton Beck
Back Wood
LA7
Arnside Knott
Silverdale Moss
Challan Hall Allotment
Arnside Knott Wood
New Park
SILVERDALE MOSS RD
Hare Parrock
Arnside Tower Farm
Middlebarrow Wood
LC
Middlebarrow Hill
Middlebarrow Quarry
Far Waterslack
WATERSLACK RD
Waterslack
Challan Hall
Hawes Water
Hollins Farm
Middlebarrow Plain
Waterslack Wood
LC
CHALLAN HALL MEWS
CHALLAN HALL COTTS
Far
Arnside
HOLGATES CVN PK
King William's Hill
Eaves Wood
Cvn Pk
Hawes Water Moss
Priory Cottage
FORD LA
NORTHERN TERR
MOSS LA
CASTLE BANK
LA5
The Park
P
Holiday Camp
Potter Hill
Woodlands
Red Bridge
WALLINGS LA
ELMSLACK LA
ELMSLACK CT
WOODLANDS DR
CLEVELANDS AVE
PARK RD
Red Bridge Barn
COVE RD
BRADSHAWGATE DR
COVE DR
TOWNSFIELD
BIRCH DR
The Row
RED BRIDGE LA
Cemy
Silverdale
Silverdale St John's CE Prim Sch
Bleasdale House Com Specl Sch
EMESGATE LA
ST JOHN'S GR
Hagg Wood
BOTTOMS LA
THE ROW
Red Rake
Bank House Farm
Bottoms Farm
Silverdale
Liby
ST JOHN'S AVE
BANK HOUSE LA
SPRING BANK
THE QUILLET
STORRS LA
GASKELL CL
Silverdale Green
Cvn Pk
Myers Farm
SHORE COTTS
LEVENS WAY
HAZELWOOD
MARYLAND CL
CH
P
P
STONELEIGH CT
Morecambe Bay Nature Reserve
Silverdale Hotel
PO
2 1
THE GREEN
Visitor Centre
SHORE CL
STANKELT RD
SHORE RD
SHORE GN
ORCHARD CL
1 BEECH CT
2 YEW TREE GDNS
Leighton Moss Nature Reserve
THE CHASE
SLACKWOOD LA
Lancashire Coastal Way
LINDETH CL
Scout Wood
Hazelwood Farm
Slackwood Farm
Know Hill
LINDETH RD
HOLLINS LA
Fleagarth Wood
WOODWELL LA
Know End Point
Gibraltar Farm
Lindeth Lodge Farm
NEW RD
Silverdale LC
Lindeth Tower
Heald Brow

222

240

Cumbria STREET ATLAS
A6 Kendal
A B C D E F
8 7 6 5 4 3 2 1
77 76 75 74
48 49 50
LA7
LA5
Leighton House
Leighton Beck Bridge
COLD WELL LA
BEETHAM CVN PK
SILVER RIDGE CVN PK
FELL END CVN PK
Oasis Wildlife Ctr
Hale Moss
BRACKENTHWAITE RD
Leighton Beck
Brackenthwaite Farm
Gait Barrows Nature Reserve
Hall More Farm
HALL MORE CVN PK
Main Drain
East Coppice
Thrang End Wood
Thrang End Farm
Hazel Grove
Thrang Moss
White Moss
THRANG BROW LA
Thrang Coppice
West Coppice
Birch Cottage
Yealand Hall Allotment
Moss La
Trough Plantation
Yealand Storrs
Yealand Hall
SILVERDALE RD
The Trough
Brow Foot Farm
EIGHT ACRE LA
NINETEEN ACRE LA
STORRS LA
HILL TOP CL
Yealand Redmayne
Round Top
Storrs Moss
MEADOWS CL
THE MEADOWS
PO
WELL LA
Cringlebarrow Wood
Storrs Farm
FOOTERAN LA
Leighton Moss Nature Reserve
Yealand CE Prim Sch
FLAT LA
ROSE ACRE LA
Old Hall Farm
KYLBARROW LA
New Inn (PH)
Dykes Farm
Grisedale Farm
Deepdale Wood
The Pool
Yealand Manor
DYKES LA
Leighton Hall Home Farm
Dykes House
YEALAND RD
Yealand Conyers
Grisedale Wood
Leighton Hall
Leighton Park
PETER LA
Hermitage Wood
HYNING RD
SNAPE LA
A6

223
240

207
204
232

Scale: 1⅓ inches to 1 mile

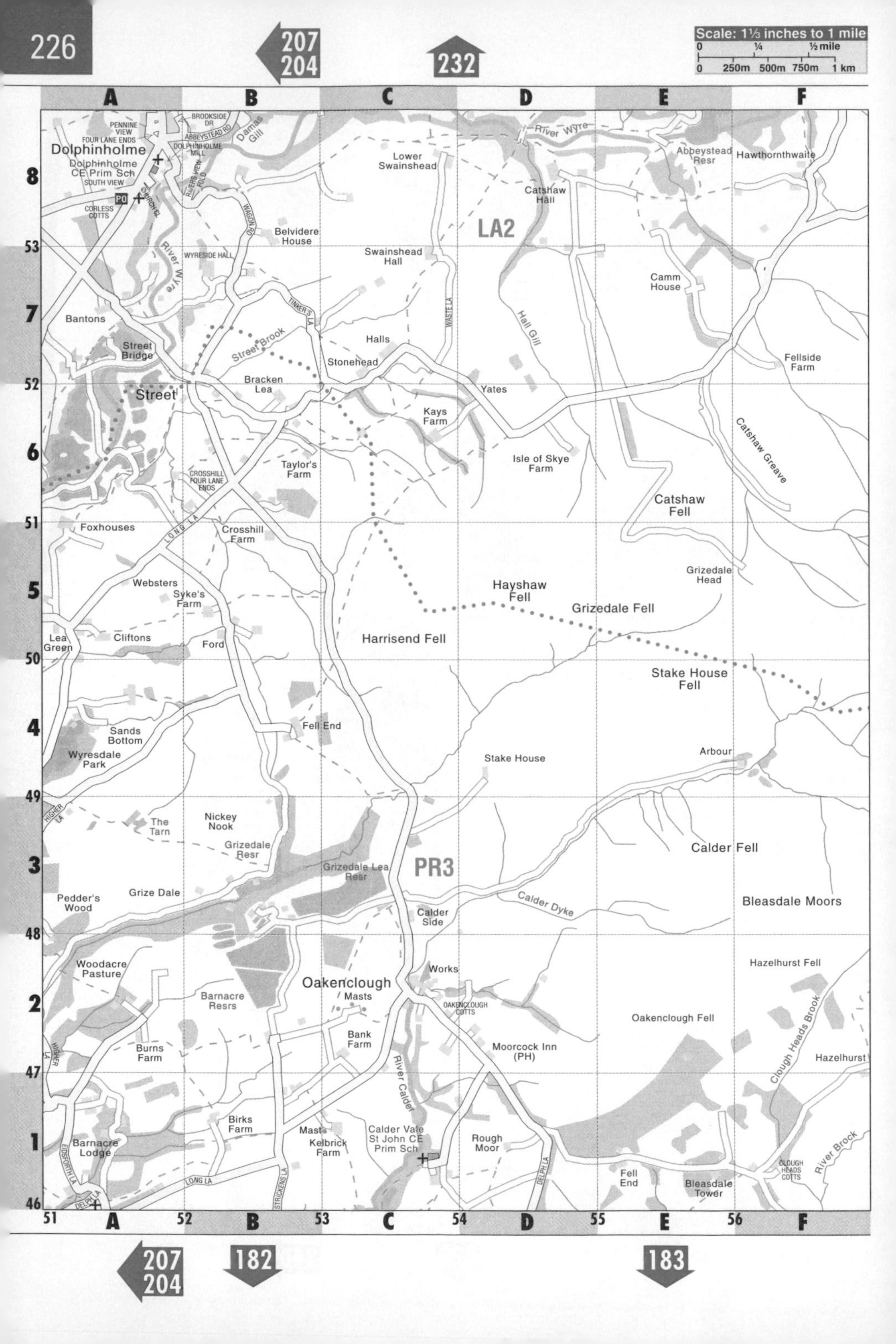

207
204
182
183

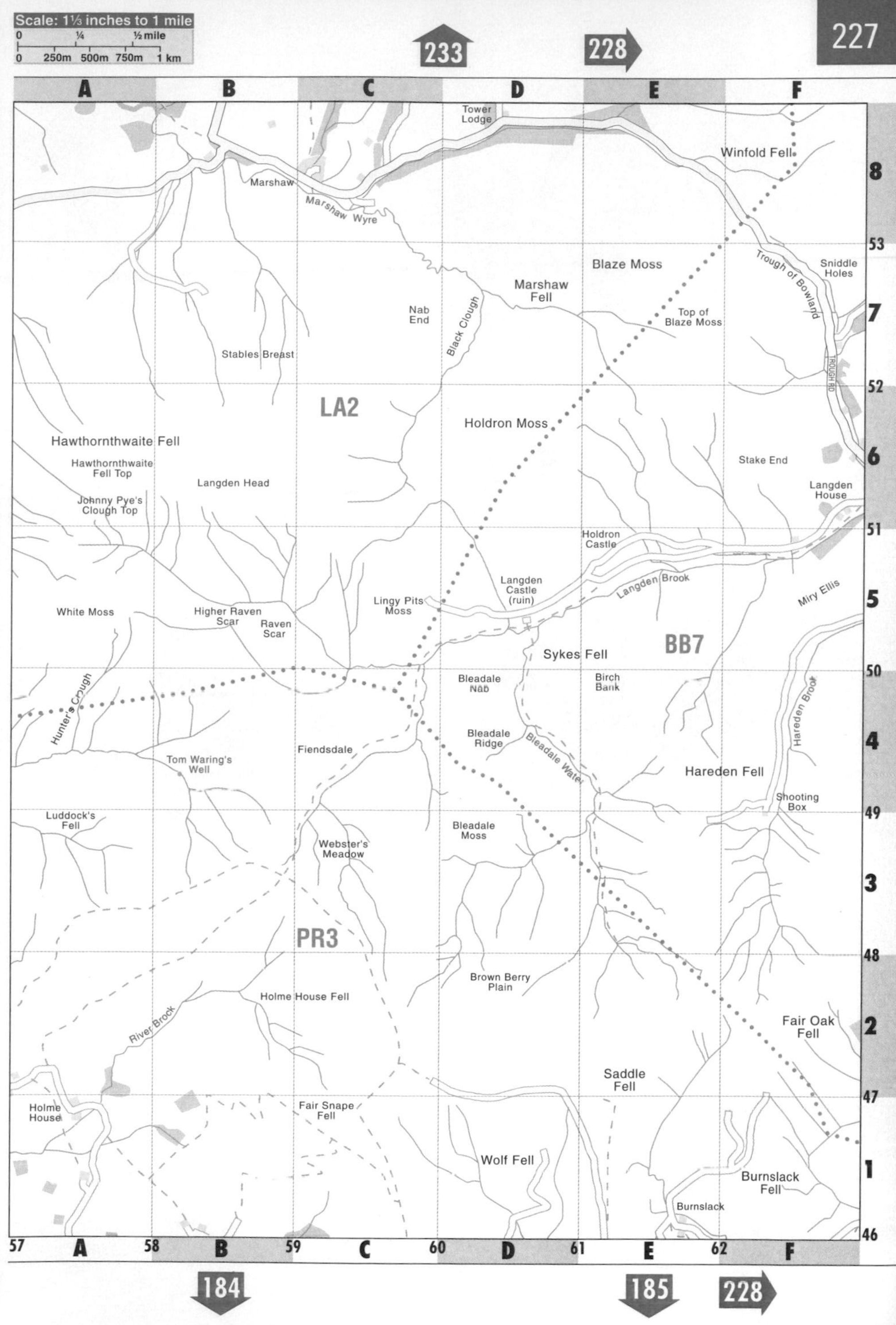

Scale: 1⅓ inches to 1 mile
0 ¼ ½ mile
0 250m 500m 750m 1 km
233
228
A B C D E F
Tower Lodge
Winfold Fell
Marshaw
Marshaw Wyre
8
53
Blaze Moss
Snidde Holes
Trough of Bowland
Marshaw Fell
Nab End
Black Clough
Top of Blaze Moss
7
Stables Breast
TROUGH RD
52
LA2
Holdron Moss
Hawthornthwaite Fell
Hawthornthwaite Fell Top
Stake End
6
Langden Head
Langden House
Johnny Pye's Clough Top
51
Holdron Castle
Langden Castle (ruin)
Langden Brook
Miry Ellis
Lingy Pits Moss
5
White Moss
Higher Raven Scar
Raven Scar
Sykes Fell
BB7
50
Bleadale Nab
Birch Bank
Hunter's Clough
Hareden Brook
Bleadale Ridge
4
Fiendsdale
Bleadale Water
Tom Waring's Well
Hareden Fell
Shooting Box
49
Luddock's Fell
Bleadale Moss
Webster's Meadow
3
PR3
48
Brown Berry Plain
Holme House Fell
Fair Oak Fell
2
River Brock
Saddle Fell
47
Holme House
Fair Snape Fell
Wolf Fell
1
Burnslack Fell
Burnslack
46
57 58 59 60 61 62
184
185
228

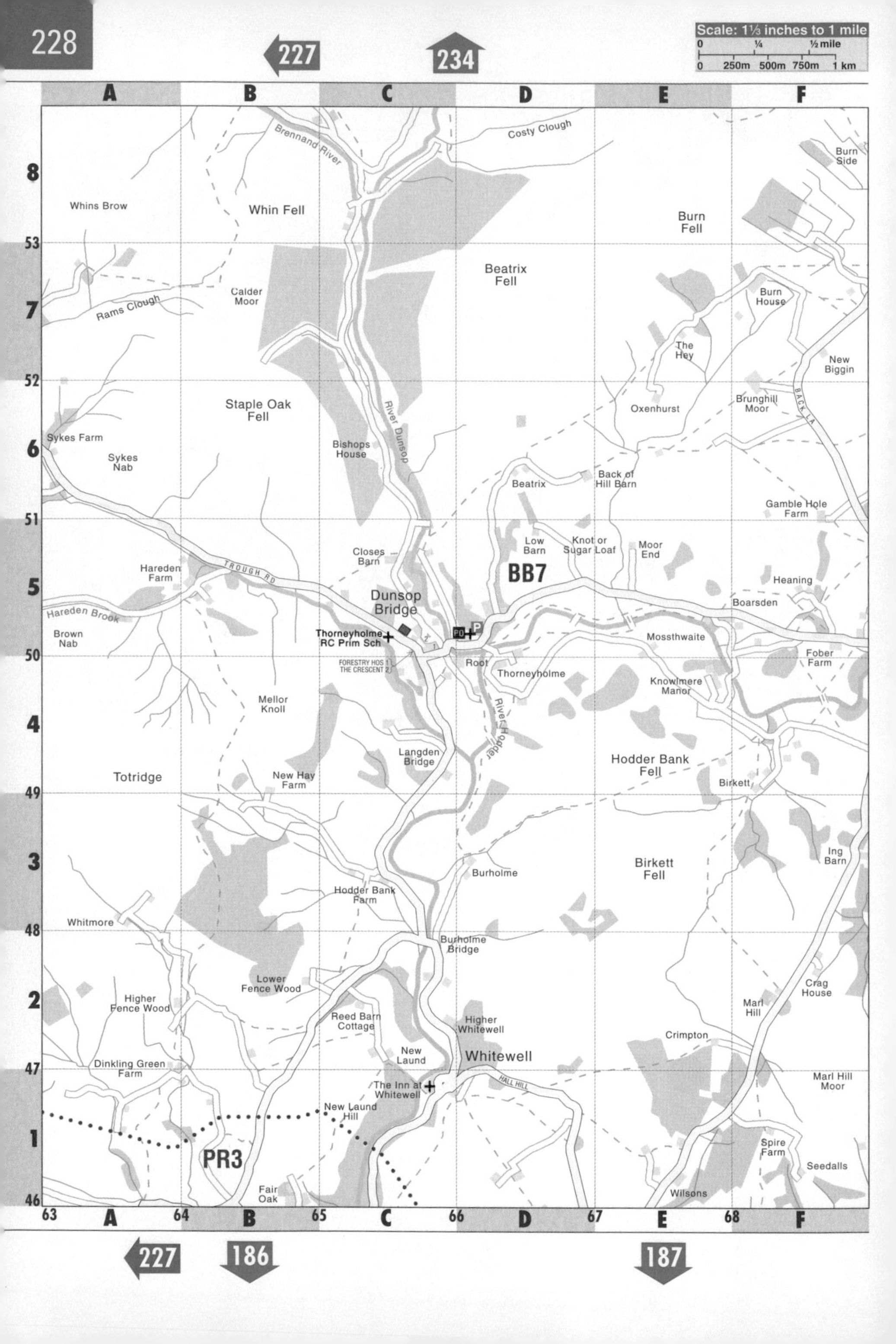
227
234
Scale: 1⅓ inches to 1 mile
0 ¼ ½ mile
0 250m 500m 750m 1 km
A B C D E F
8 53 7 52 6 51 5 50 4 49 3 48 2 47 1 46
63 64 65 66 67 68
Brennand River
Costy Clough
Burn Side
Whins Brow
Whin Fell
Burn Fell
Beatrix Fell
Calder Moor
Rams Clough
Burn House
The Hey
New Biggin
Staple Oak Fell
Oxenhurst
Brunghill Moor
BACK LA
River Dunsop
Sykes Farm
Sykes Nab
Bishops House
Beatrix
Back of Hill Barn
Gamble Hole Farm
Low Barn
Knot or Sugar Loaf
Moor End
Closes Barn
Hareden Farm
TROUGH RD
BB7
Heaning
Dunsop Bridge
Boarsden
Hareden Brook
Brown Nab
Thorneyholme RC Prim Sch
Mossthwaite
Fober Farm
FORESTRY HOS 1
THE CRESCENT 2
Root
Thorneyholme
Knowlmere Manor
Mellor Knoll
River Hodder
Langden Bridge
Hodder Bank Fell
Totridge
New Hay Farm
Birkett
Ing Barn
Birkett Fell
Burholme
Hodder Bank Farm
Whitmore
Burholme Bridge
Lower Fence Wood
Crag House
Higher Fence Wood
Marl Hill
Reed Barn Cottage
Higher Whitewell
Crimpton
New Laund
Whitewell
Dinkling Green Farm
The Inn at Whitewell
HALL HILL
Marl Hill Moor
New Laund Hill
Spire Farm
PR3
Seedalls
Fair Oak
Wilsons
227
186
187

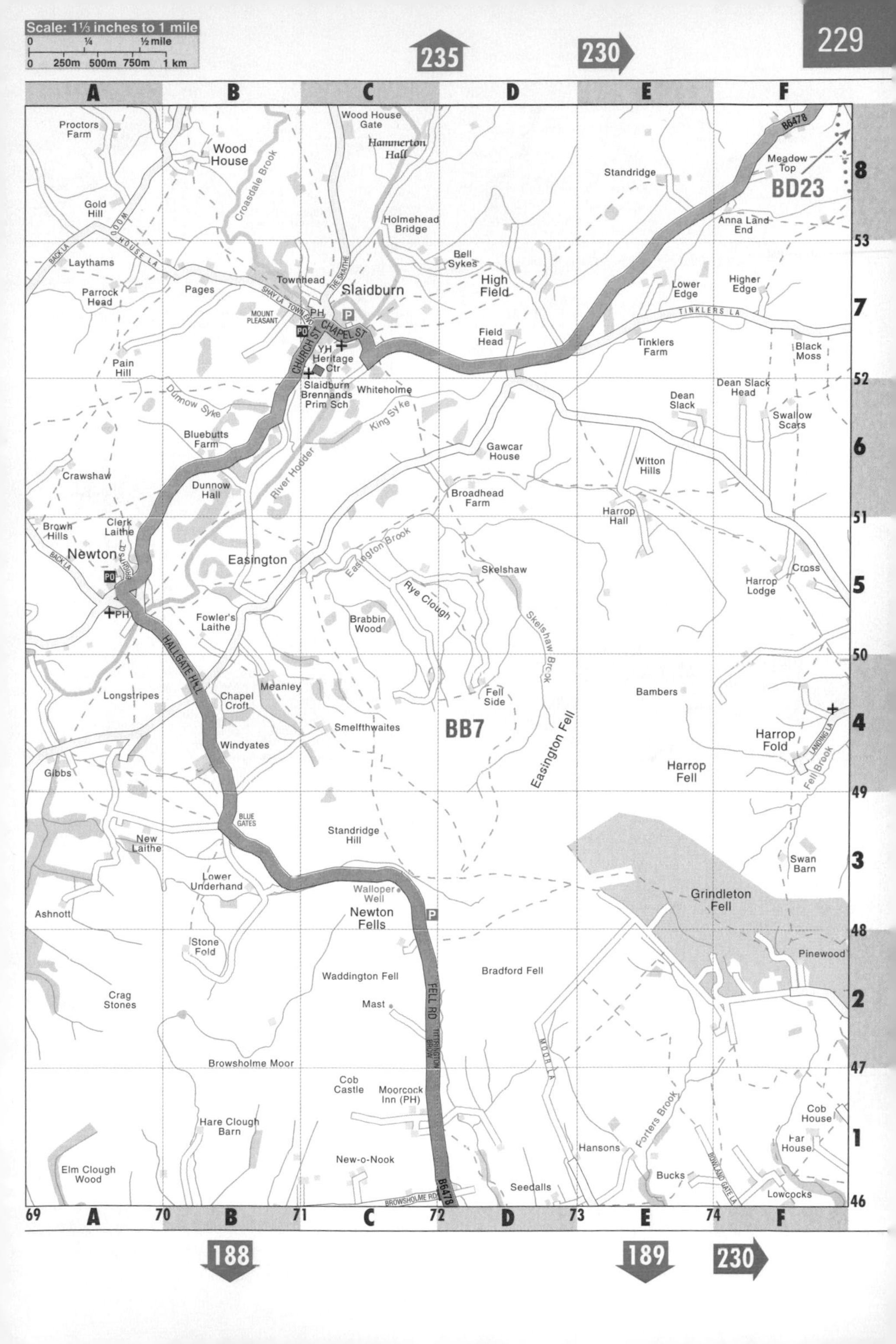

Scale: 1⅓ inches to 1 mile
0 ¼ ½ mile
0 250m 500m 750m 1 km
235
230
A B C D E F
Proctors Farm
Wood House
Wood House Gate
Hammerton Hall
Croasdale Brook
Standridge
Meadow Top
BD23
Gold Hill
Holmehead Bridge
Anna Land End
Laythams
Bell Sykes
Townhead
Slaidburn
High Field
Lower Edge
Higher Edge
Parrock Head
Pages
Mount Pleasant
Church St
Chapel St
Tinklers La
Field Head
Tinklers Farm
Black Moss
Heritage Ctr
Pain Hill
Slaidburn Brennands Prim Sch
Whiteholme
Dean Slack
Dean Slack Head
Swallow Scars
Dunnow Syke
King Syke
Bluebutts Farm
Gawcar House
Witton Hills
Crawshaw
Dunnow Hall
River Hodder
Broadhead Farm
Harrop Hall
Brown Hills
Clerk Laithe
Newton
Easington
Easington Brook
Skelshaw
Cross
Harrop Lodge
Rye Clough
Fowler's Laithe
Brabbin Wood
Skelshaw Brook
Hallgate Hill
Meanley
Bambers
Longstripes
Chapel Croft
Fell Side
Smelfthwaites
BB7
Easington Fell
Harrop Fold
Windyates
Harrop Fell
Gibbs
Fell Brook
Blue Gates
Standridge Hill
New Laithe
Swan Barn
Lower Underhand
Walloper Well
Grindleton Fell
Ashnott
Newton Fells
Stone Fold
Pinewood
Bradford Fell
Waddington Fell
Fell Rd
Crag Stones
Mast
Moor La
Browsholme Moor
Cob Castle
Moorcock Inn (PH)
Cob House
Hare Clough Barn
Porters Brook
Hansons
Far House
Elm Clough Wood
New-o-Nook
Bucks
Bowland Gate La
Seedalls
Lowcocks
Browsholme Rd
B6478
69 70 71 72 73 74
46 47 48 49 50 51 52 53
1 2 3 4 5 6 7 8
188
189
230

229
236

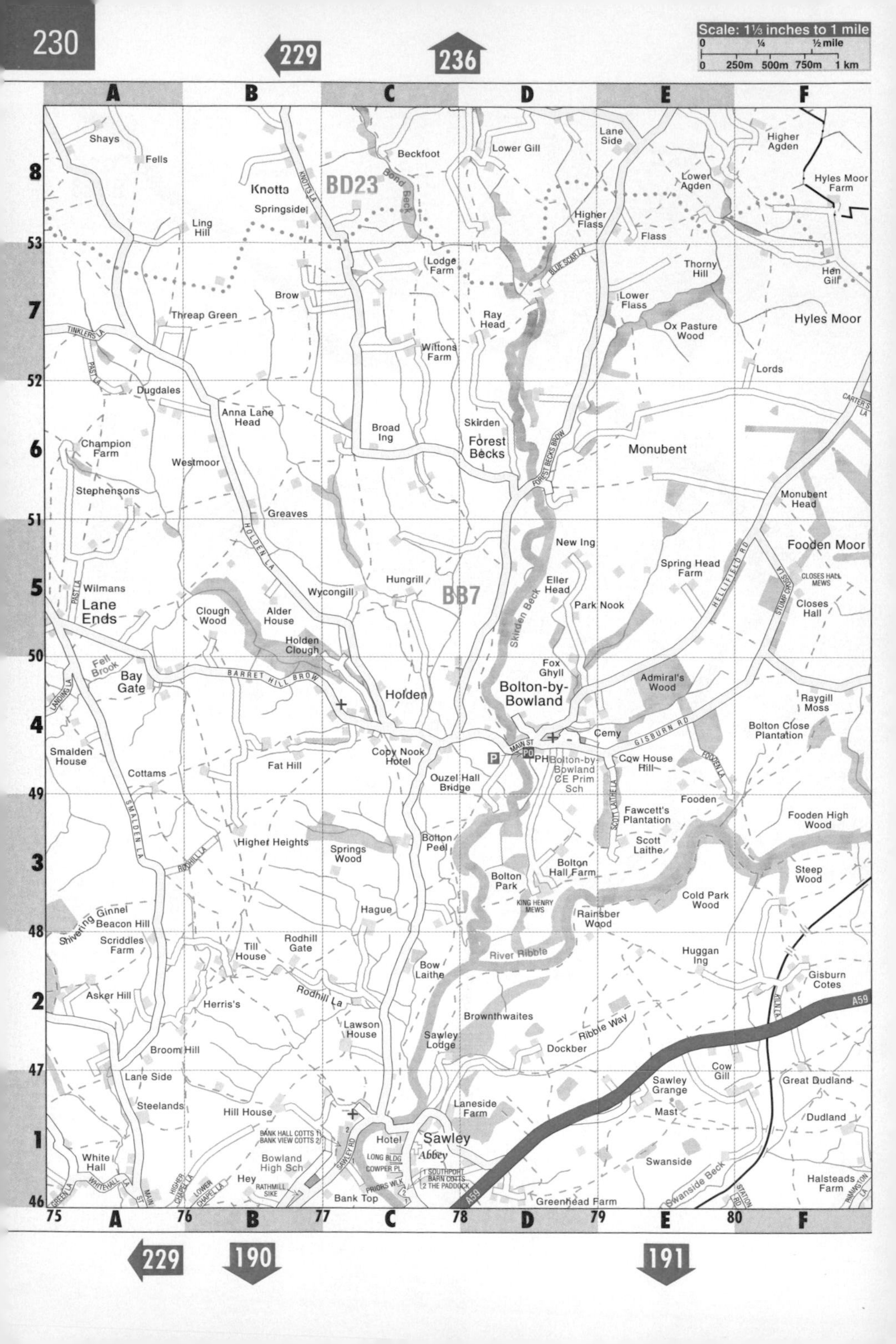

229
190
191

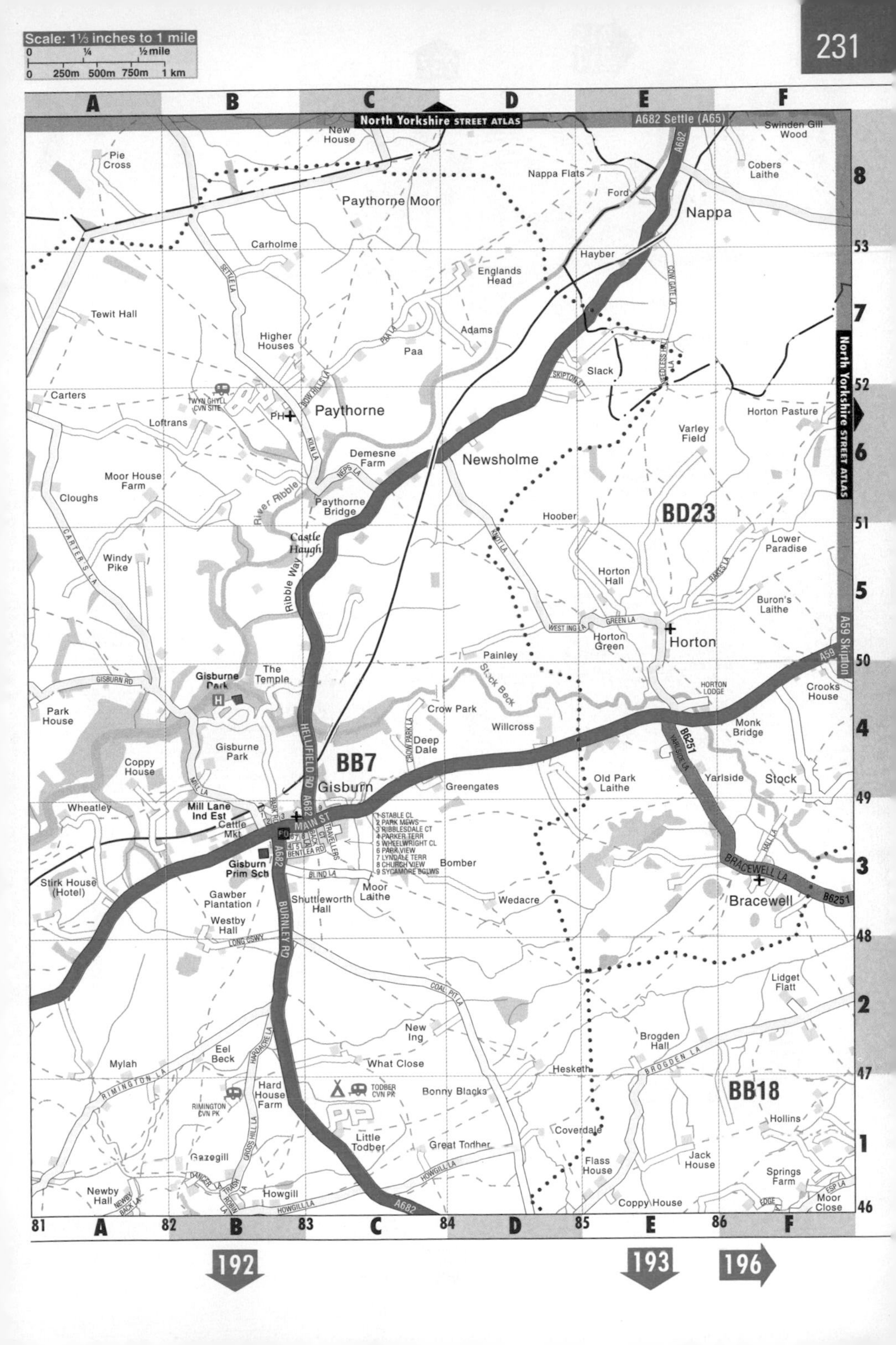
Scale: 1⅓ inches to 1 mile
North Yorkshire STREET ATLAS
A682 Settle (A65)
A59 Skipton
New House
Pie Cross
Paythorne Moor
Nappa Flats
Ford
Nappa
Swinden Gill Wood
Cobers Laithe
Carholme
Hayber
Englands Head
Tewit Hall
Higher Houses
Adams
Paa
Slack
Carters
TWYN GHYLL CVN SITE
Paythorne
Loftrans
Demesne Farm
Newsholme
Horton Pasture
Varley Field
Moor House Farm
Cloughs
River Ribble
Paythorne Bridge
Hoober
BD23
Castle Haugh
Windy Pike
Ribble Way
Horton Hall
Lower Paradise
Buron's Laithe
Horton Green
Horton
Painley
Gisburne Park
The Temple
Stock Beck
HORTON LODGE
Crooks House
Park House
Crow Park
Willcross
Monk Bridge
Deep Dale
Gisburne Park
Coppy House
BB7
Gisburn
Greengates
Old Park Laithe
Yarlside
Stock
Wheatley
Mill Lane Ind Est
Cattle Mkt
1 STABLE CL
2 PARK MEWS
3 RIBBLESDALE CT
4 PARKER TERR
5 WHEELWRIGHT CL
6 PARK VIEW
7 LYNDALE TERR
8 CHURCH VIEW
9 SYCAMORE BGLWS
Bomber
Gisburn Prim Sch
Stirk House (Hotel)
Gawber Plantation
Shuttleworth Hall
Moor Laithe
Wedacre
Bracewell
Westby Hall
Lidget Flatt
New Ing
Brogden Hall
Eel Beck
Mylah
What Close
Hesketh
Hard House Farm
TODBER CVN PK
Bonny Blacks
BB18
RIMINGTON CVN PK
Hollins
Little Todber
Great Todber
Coverdale
Gazegill
Flass House
Jack House
Springs Farm
Newby Hall
Howgill
Coppy House
Moor Close
A682
A59
B6251
SETTLE LA
COW GATE LA
NEEDLESS HALL LA
SKIPTON ST
PAA LA
BOW HILLS LA
KILN LA
NEPS LA
CARTER'S LA
KNOT LA
RAKES LA
WEST ING LA
GREEN LA
GISBURN RD
HELLIFIELD RD
CROW PARK LA
YARLSIDE LA
MILL LA
PARK RD
MAIN ST
BACK LA
TRAVELLERS CT
BENTLEA RD
BLIND LA
BRACEWELL LA
HALL LA
BURNLEY RD
LONG CSWY
COAL PIT LA
HARDACRE LA
RIMINGTON LA
BROGDEN LA
CROSS HILL LA
DANCER LA
TRASH LA
ROBIN LA
NEWBY BACK LA
HOWGILL LA
EDGE
ESP LA

192 193 196

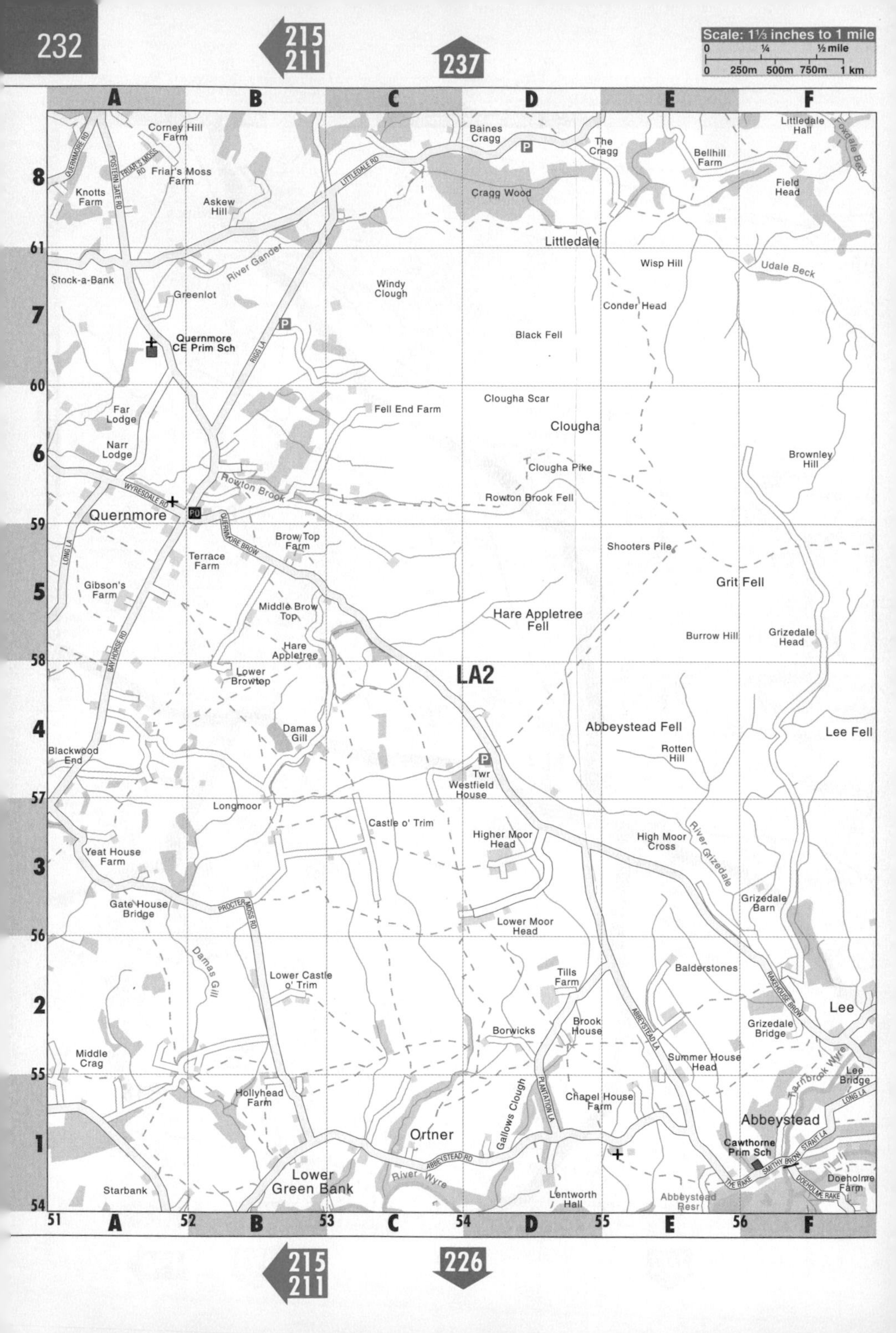

215
211
237
Scale: 1⅓ inches to 1 mile
0 ¼ ½ mile
0 250m 500m 750m 1 km
A B C D E F
Corney Hill Farm
Baines Cragg
The Cragg
Littledale Hall
Bellhill Farm
Foxdale Beck
QUERNMORE RD
POSTERN GATE RD
FRIAR'S MOSS RD
Friar's Moss Farm
LITTLEDALE RD
Cragg Wood
Field Head
Knotts Farm
Askew Hill
Littledale
River Gander
Wisp Hill
Udale Beck
Stock-a-Bank
Windy Clough
Greenlot
Conder Head
Quernmore CE Prim Sch
RIGGS LA
Black Fell
Clougha Scar
Far Lodge
Fell End Farm
Clougha
Narr Lodge
Brownley Hill
Clougha Pike
WYRESDALE RD
Rowton Brook
Rowton Brook Fell
Quernmore
PO
QUERNMORE BROW
Brow Top Farm
Shooters Pile
LONG LA
Terrace Farm
Grit Fell
Gibson's Farm
Middle Brow Top
Hare Appletree Fell
Burrow Hill
Grizedale Head
Hare Appletree
BAY HORSE RD
LA2
Lower Browtop
Damas Gill
Abbeystead Fell
Lee Fell
Blackwood End
Rotten Hill
Twr
Westfield House
Longmoor
Castle o' Trim
Higher Moor Head
High Moor Cross
River Grizedale
Yeat House Farm
PROCTER MOSS RD
Grizedale Barn
Gate House Bridge
Lower Moor Head
Damas Gill
Tills Farm
Balderstones
Lower Castle o' Trim
RAKEHOUSE BROW
Lee
Brook House
ABBEYSTEAD LA
Grizedale Bridge
Borwicks
Middle Crag
Summer House Head
Tarnbrook Wyre
Lee Bridge
Hollyhead Farm
Gallows Clough
PLANTATION LA
Chapel House Farm
LONG LA
Abbeystead
Ortner
Cawthorne Prim Sch
STRAIT LA
ABBEYSTEAD RD
SMITHY BROW
THE RAKE
River Wyre
DOEHOLME RAKE
Doeholme Farm
Lower Green Bank
Starbank
Lentworth Hall
Abbeystead Resr
8
61
7
60
6
59
5
58
4
57
3
56
2
55
1
54
51 52 53 54 55 56
215
211
226

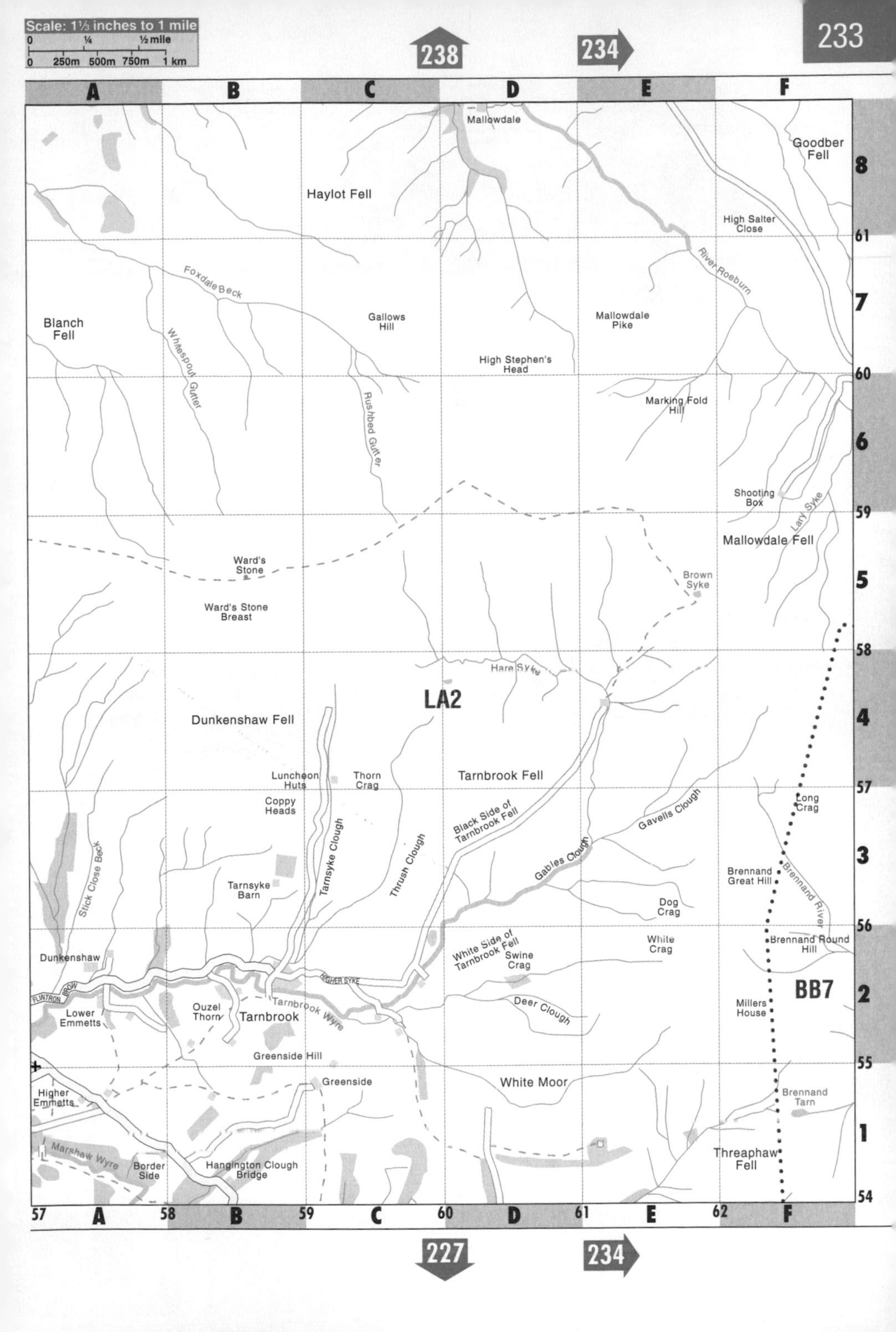
Scale: 1⅓ inches to 1 mile
0
¼
½ mile
0
250m
500m
750m
1 km
238
234
A
B
C
D
E
F
Mallowdale
Goodber Fell
Haylot Fell
High Salter Close
River Roeburn
Foxdale Beck
Blanch Fell
Whitespout Gutter
Gallows Hill
Mallowdale Pike
High Stephen's Head
Rushbed Gutter
Marking Fold Hill
Shooting Box
Lary Syke
Mallowdale Fell
Ward's Stone
Brown Syke
Ward's Stone Breast
Hare Syke
LA2
Dunkenshaw Fell
Luncheon Huts
Thorn Crag
Tarnbrook Fell
Coppy Heads
Long Crag
Black Side of Tarnbrook Fell
Gavells Clough
Tarnsyke Clough
Thrush Clough
Stick Close Beck
Gables Clough
Brennand Great Hill
Brennand River
Tarnsyke Barn
Dog Crag
White Crag
Brennand Round Hill
White Side of Tarnbrook Fell
Swine Crag
Dunkenshaw
HIGHER SYKE
FLINTRON BROW
BB7
Ouzel Thorn
Tarnbrook
Tarnbrook Wyre
Deer Clough
Millers House
Lower Emmetts
Greenside Hill
Greenside
White Moor
Higher Emmetts
Brennand Tarn
Marshaw Wyre
Border Side
Hangington Clough Bridge
Threaphaw Fell
8
61
7
60
6
59
5
58
4
57
3
56
2
55
1
54
57
58
59
60
61
62
227
234

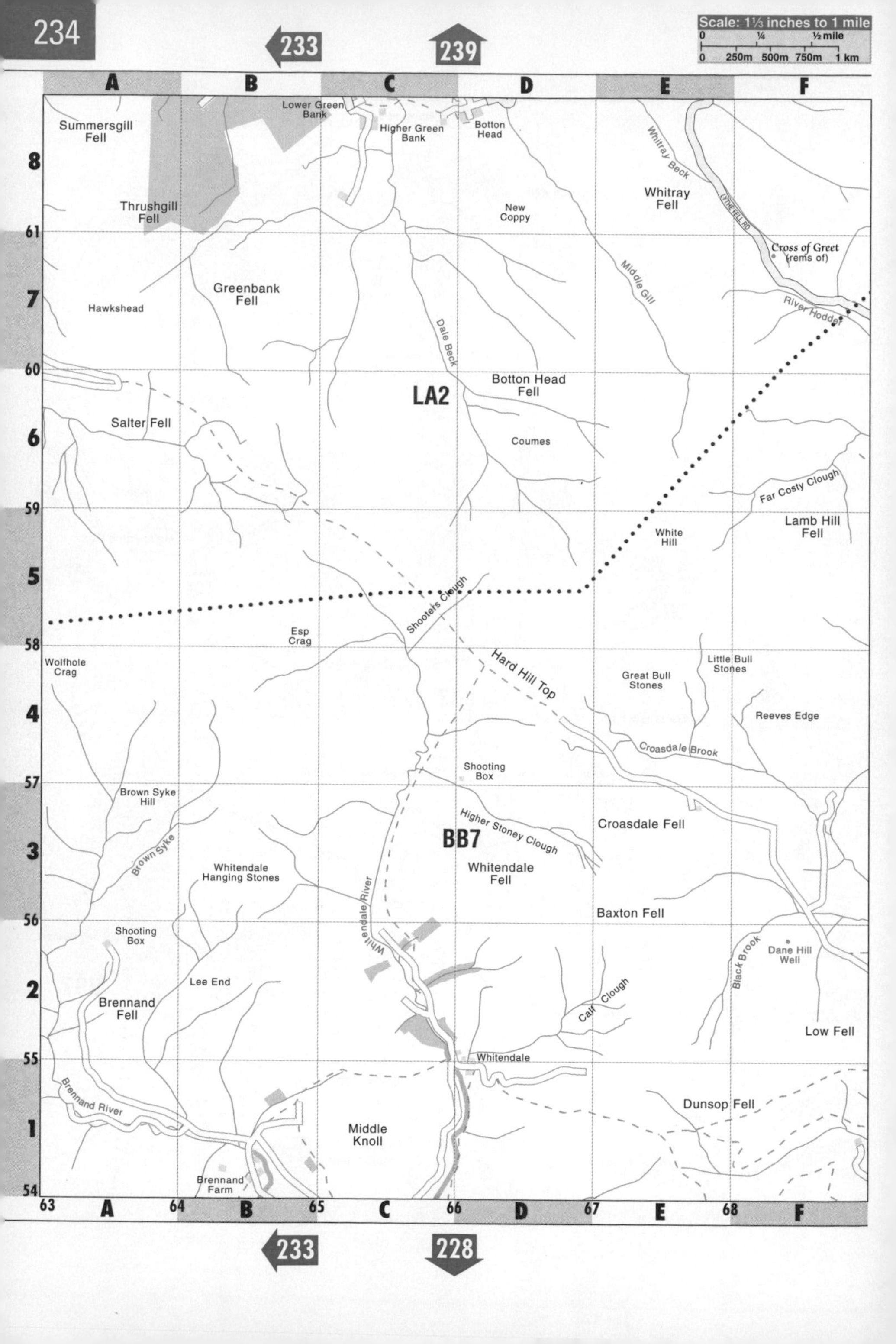
233
239
Scale: 1⅓ inches to 1 mile
0 ¼ ½ mile
0 250m 500m 750m 1 km
A B C D E F
8 61 7 60 6 59 5 58 4 57 3 56 2 55 1 54
63 64 65 66 67 68
Summersgill Fell
Lower Green Bank
Higher Green Bank
Botton Head
Whitray Beck
Whitray Fell
Thrushgill Fell
New Coppy
(THE FELL RD)
Cross of Greet (rems of)
Greenbank Fell
Middle Gill
Hawkshead
River Hodder
Dale Beck
Botton Head Fell
LA2
Salter Fell
Coumes
Far Costy Clough
Lamb Hill Fell
White Hill
Shooters Clough
Esp Crag
Wolfhole Crag
Hard Hill Top
Little Bull Stones
Great Bull Stones
Reeves Edge
Croasdale Brook
Shooting Box
Brown Syke Hill
Higher Stoney Clough
Croasdale Fell
BB7
Brown Syke
Whitendale Hanging Stones
Whitendale Fell
Whitendale River
Baxton Fell
Shooting Box
Dane Hill Well
Black Brook
Lee End
Brennand Fell
Calf Clough
Low Fell
Whitendale
Brennand River
Dunsop Fell
Middle Knoll
Brennand Farm
233
228

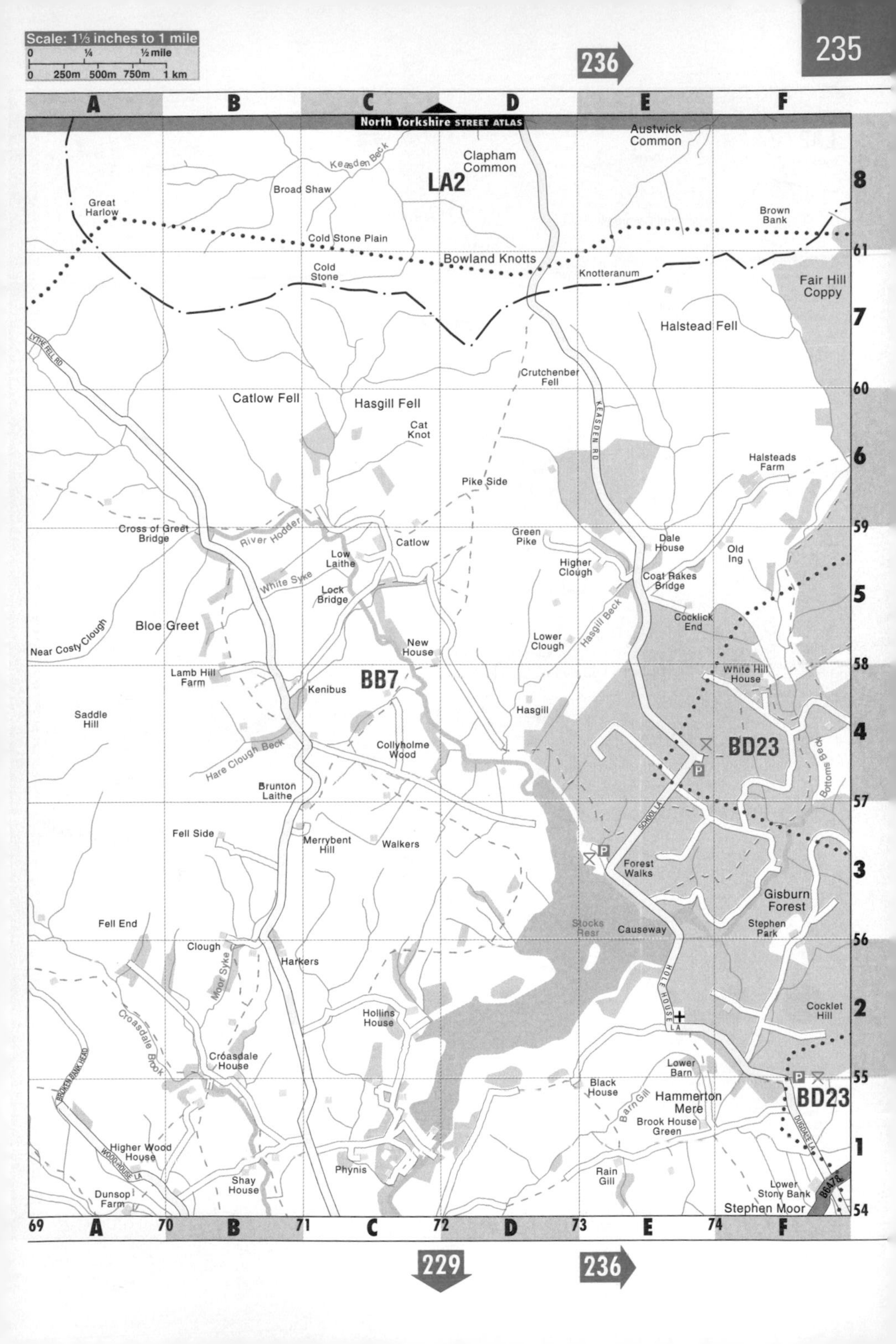
Scale: 1⅓ inches to 1 mile
0 ¼ ½ mile
0 250m 500m 750m 1 km
236
North Yorkshire STREET ATLAS
Austwick Common
Clapham Common
Keasden Beck
LA2
Broad Shaw
Great Harlow
Brown Bank
Cold Stone Plain
Bowland Knotts
Cold Stone
Knotteranum
Fair Hill Coppy
Halstead Fell
LYTHE FELL RD
Crutchenber Fell
KEASDEN RD
Catlow Fell
Hasgill Fell
Cat Knot
Halsteads Farm
Pike Side
Cross of Greet Bridge
River Hodder
Green Pike
Catlow
Low Laithe
Dale House
Old Ing
Higher Clough
Coat Rakes Bridge
White Syke
Lock Bridge
Cocklick End
Bloe Greet
Near Costy Clough
Lower Clough
Hasgill Beck
New House
Lamb Hill Farm
BB7
Kenibus
White Hill House
Saddle Hill
Hasgill
BD23
Collyholme Wood
Hare Clough Beck
Bottoms Beck
Brunton Laithe
SCHOOL LA
Fell Side
Merrybent Hill
Walkers
Forest Walks
Gisburn Forest
Fell End
Stocks Resr
Causeway
Stephen Park
Clough
Harkers
Moor Syke
HOLE HOUSE LA
Croasdale Brook
Hollins House
Cocklet Hill
BROKEN BANK HEAD
Croasdale House
Lower Barn
Black House
Barn Gill
Hammerton Mere
Brook House Green
BD23
DUGDALE LA
Higher Wood House
WOOD HOUSE LA
Phynis
Rain Gill
Shay House
Dunsop Farm
Lower Stony Bank
Stephen Moor
B6478
A B C D E F
8 61 7 60 6 59 5 58 4 57 3 56 2 55 1 54
69 70 71 72 73 74
229
236

235

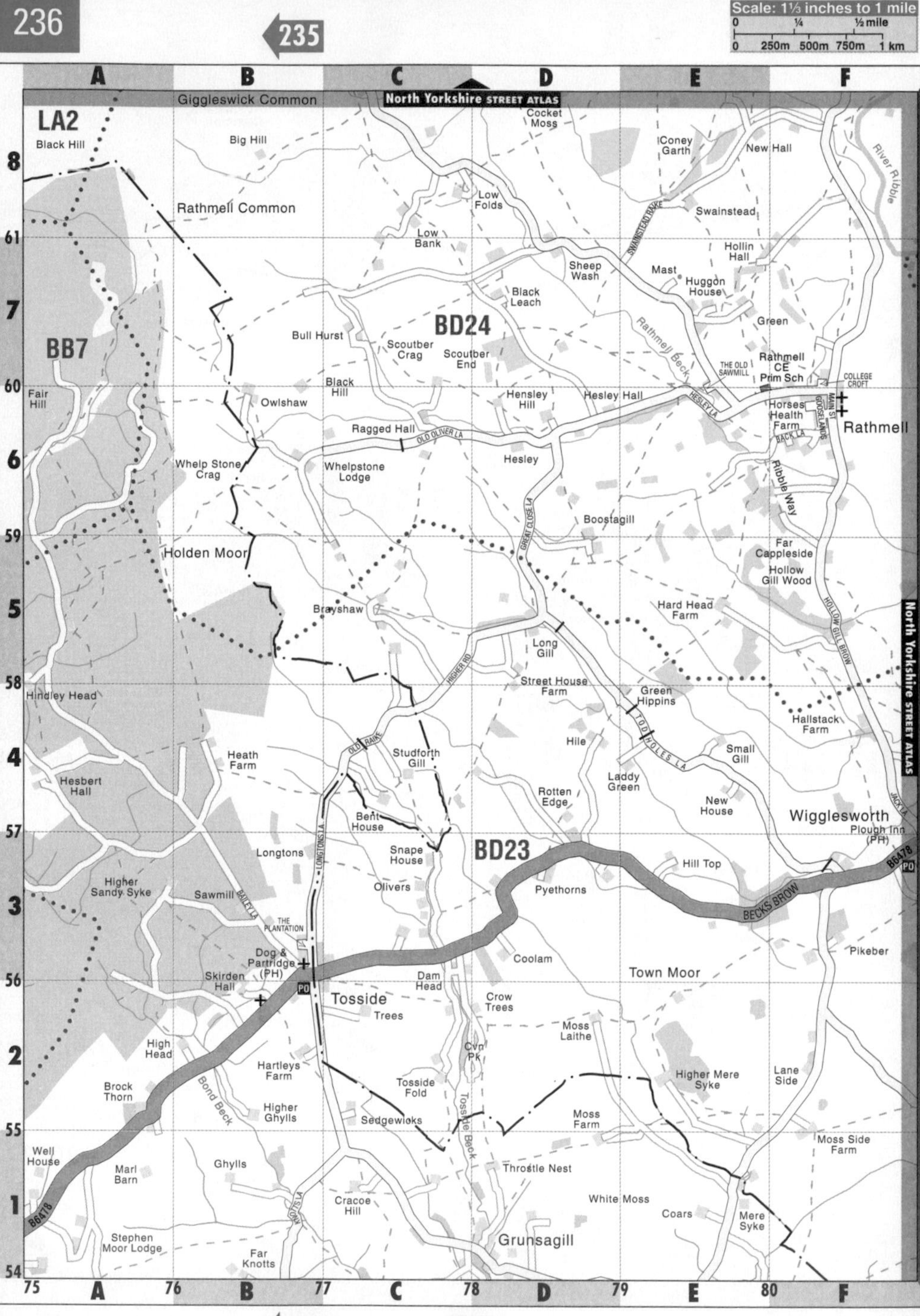
Scale: 1⅓ inches to 1 mile
North Yorkshire STREET ATLAS
Giggleswick Common
LA2
Black Hill
Big Hill
Cocket Moss
Coney Garth
New Hall
River Ribble
Low Folds
Rathmell Common
Swainstead
Low Bank
Hollin Hall
Sheep Wash
Mast
Huggon House
Black Leach
BB7
BD24
Green
Bull Hurst
Scoutber Crag
Scoutber End
Rathmell Beck
Rathmell CE Prim Sch
THE OLD SAWMILL
COLLEGE CROFT
Fair Hill
Black Hill
Owlshaw
Hensley Hill
Hesley Hall
Horses Health Farm
Rathmell
Ragged Hall
OLD OLIVER LA
Whelp Stone Crag
Whelpstone Lodge
Hesley
Ribble Way
Boostagill
Holden Moor
GREAT CLOSE LA
Far Cappleside
Hollow Gill Wood
Brayshaw
Hard Head Farm
HOLLOW GILL BROW
Long Gill
Hindley Head
HIGHER RD
Street House Farm
Green Hippins
Hallstack Farm
Heath Farm
OLD RAIKE
Studforth Gill
Hile
TODHOLES LA
Small Gill
Hesbert Hall
Laddy Green
Rotten Edge
New House
Wigglesworth
Plough Inn (PH)
Bent House
Longtons
Snape House
BD23
Hill Top
B6478
Higher Sandy Syke
Sawmill
Olivers
Pyethorns
BECKS BROW
THE PLANTATION
Dog & Partridge (PH)
Coolam
Pikeber
Skirden Hall
Dam Head
Town Moor
Tosside
Crow Trees
Trees
Moss Laithe
High Head
Cvn Pk
Hartleys Farm
Higher Mere Syke
Lane Side
Brock Thorn
Tosside Fold
Bond Beck
Higher Ghylls
Sedgewicks
Tosside Beck
Moss Farm
Moss Side Farm
Well House
Marl Barn
Ghylls
Throstle Nest
White Moss
Cracoe Hill
KNOTTS LA
Coars
Mere Syke
Stephen Moor Lodge
Grunsagill
Far Knotts
LONGTONS LA
BAILEY LA

235
230

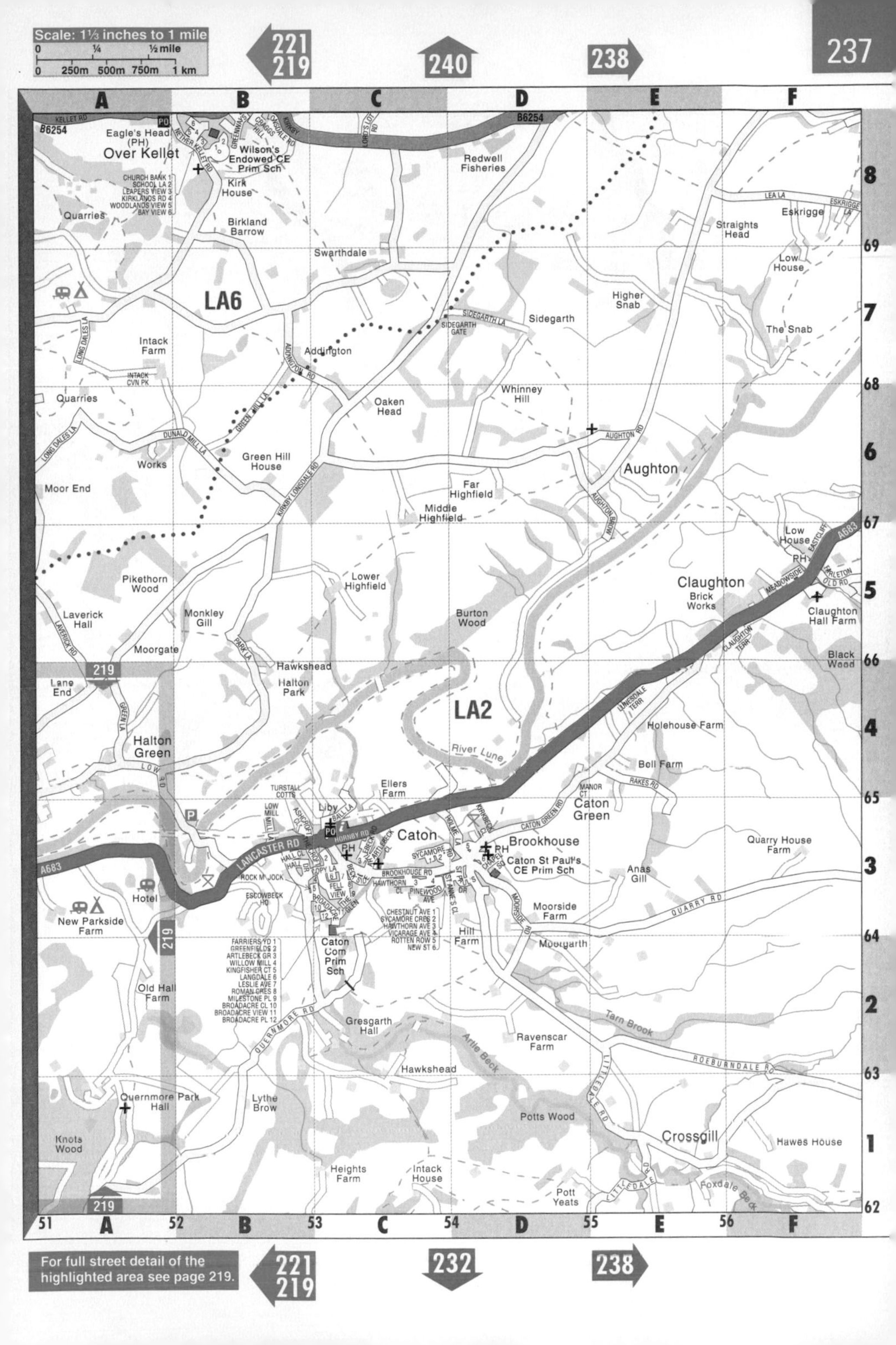
Scale: 1⅓ inches to 1 mile
0 ¼ ½ mile
0 250m 500m 750m 1 km
221
219
240
238
A
B
C
D
E
F
B6254
KELLET RD
Eagle's Head (PH)
Over Kellet
NETHER KELLET RD
GREENWAYS
CRAGGS HILL
LONSDALE RD
KIRKBY
LORD'S LOT RD
Wilson's Endowed CE Prim Sch
Kirk House
CHURCH BANK 1
SCHOOL LA 2
LEAPERS VIEW 3
KIRKLANDS RD 4
WOODLANDS VIEW 5
BAY VIEW 6
Redwell Fisheries
Quarries
Birkland Barrow
Swarthdale
LEA LA
ESKRIGGE LA
Eskrigge
Straights Head
Low House
LA6
Higher Snab
SIDEGARTH LA
SIDEGARTH GATE
Sidegarth
The Snab
Intack Farm
LONG DALES LA
INTACK CVN PK
Addington
ADDINGTON RD
Oaken Head
Whinney Hill
Quarries
GREEN HILL LA
DUNALD MILL LA
AUGHTON RD
Works
Green Hill House
KIRKBY LONSDALE RD
Aughton
Moor End
Far Highfield
Middle Highfield
AUGHTON BROW
Low House
EASTCLIFF
A683
PH
FARLETON OLD RD
MEADOWSIDE
Claughton
Brick Works
Claughton Hall Farm
Pikethorn Wood
Lower Highfield
Laverick Hall
LAVERICK RD
Monkley Gill
Burton Wood
CLAUGHTON TERR
Black Wood
Moorgate
PARK LA
Hawkshead
Halton Park
219
Lane End
GREEN LA
LA2
LUNESDALE TERR
Holehouse Farm
Halton Green
LOW RD
River Lune
Boll Farm
RAKES RD
TURSTALL COTTS
Ellers Farm
MANOR CT
Caton Green
CATON GREEN RD
LOW MILL
ASHCROFT
Liby
BALLA
PO
HORNBY RD
Caton
HOLME LA
KIRKBECK CL
Brookhouse
Quarry House Farm
LANCASTER RD
PH
SYCAMORE RD
Caton St Paul's CE Prim Sch
A683
HALL CL
HALL DR
COPY LA
FELL VIEW
THE CROFT
BECK SIDE
HARTLEBECK CL
BROOKHOUSE RD
HAWTHORN CL
PINEWOOD AVE
ST PAUL'S DR
ST ANNE'S CL
CHAPEL LA
Anas Gill
ROCK M. JOCK
ESCOWBECK HO
BROADACRE
THE GLEN
Hotel
Moorside Farm
MOORSIDE RD
QUARRY RD
New Parkside Farm
CHESTNUT AVE 1
SYCAMORE CRES 2
HAWTHORN AVE 3
VICARAGE AVE 4
ROTTEN ROW 5
NEW ST 6
Hill Farm
Moorgarth
Caton Com Prim Sch
FARRIERS YD 1
GREENFIELDS 2
ARTLEBECK GR 3
WILLOW MILL 4
KINGFISHER CT 5
LANGDALE 6
LESLIE AVE 7
ROMAN CRES 8
MILESTONE PL 9
BROADACRE CL 10
BROADACRE VIEW 11
BROADACRE PL 12
Old Hall Farm
Tarn Brook
QUERNMORE RD
Gresgarth Hall
Artle Beck
Ravenscar Farm
ROEBURNDALE RD
Hawkshead
LITTLEDALE RD
Quernmore Park Hall
Lythe Brow
Potts Wood
Crossgill
Hawes House
Knots Wood
Heights Farm
Intack House
LITTLEDALE RD
Foxdale Beck
Pott Yeats
219
8
69
7
68
6
67
5
66
4
65
3
64
2
63
1
62
51
52
53
54
55
56
For full street detail of the highlighted area see page 219.
221
219
232
238

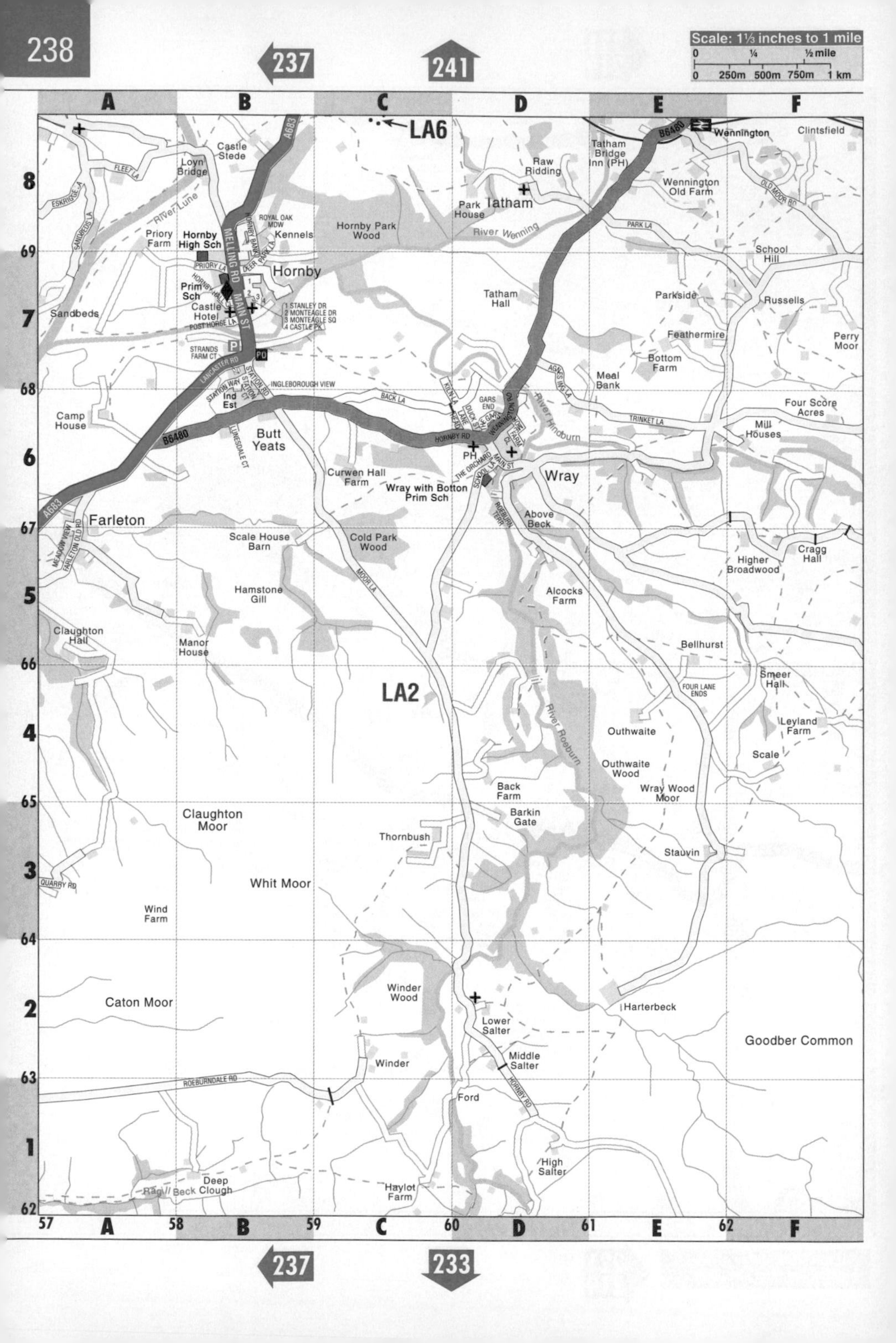
237
241
Scale: 1⅓ inches to 1 mile
LA6
Castle Stede
Loyn Bridge
Tatham
Raw Ridding
Tatham Bridge Inn (PH)
Wennington
Clintsfield
Wennington Old Farm
Park House
Hornby Park Wood
River Wenning
Priory Farm
Hornby High Sch
Kennels
Hornby
Prim Sch
Castle Hotel
Sandbeds
River Lune
1 STANLEY DR
2 MONTEAGLE DR
3 MONTEAGLE SQ
4 CASTLE PK
Tatham Hall
Parkside
Russells
School Hill
Feathermire
Perry Moor
Bottom Farm
Meal Bank
Four Score Acres
Mill Houses
Ind Est
Camp House
Butt Yeats
INGLEBOROUGH VIEW
River Hindburn
Wray
Curwen Hall Farm
Wray with Botton Prim Sch
Farleton
Above Beck
Scale House Barn
Cold Park Wood
Higher Broadwood
Cragg Hall
Hamstone Gill
Alcocks Farm
Claughton Hall
Manor House
Bellhurst
Smeer Hall
LA2
FOUR LANE ENDS
Leyland Farm
River Roeburn
Outhwaite
Scale
Outhwaite Wood
Back Farm
Wray Wood Moor
Claughton Moor
Barkin Gate
Thornbush
Stauvin
Whit Moor
Wind Farm
Caton Moor
Winder Wood
Harterbeck
Lower Salter
Goodber Common
Middle Salter
Winder
Ford
High Salter
Deep Clough
Rag Beck
Haylot Farm
B6480
A683
MELLING RD
MAIN ST
HORNBY RD
MOOR LA
ROEBURNDALE RD
QUARRY RD
PARK LA
TRINKET LA
BACK LA
OLD MOOR RD
FLEET LA
ESKRIGGE LA
SANDBEDS LA
FARLETON OLD RD
MEADOW VIEW
A B C D E F
57 58 59 60 61 62
62 63 64 65 66 67 68 69
1 2 3 4 5 6 7 8

237
233

Scale: 1⅓ inches to 1 mile
0 ¼ ½ mile
0 250m 500m 750m 1 km

B8
1 CHEAPSIDE
2 BANK COTT
3 CROWTREES
4 BAYNES COTTS
5 GREENFOOT
6 GREEN HEAD COTTS
7 THE TERRACE
8 VICTORIA BLDGS

D8
1 PINEWOOD COTTS
2 ASHFIELD COTTS
3 TWEED STREET CT
4 TWEED ST
5 SUNNYSIDE
6 MILL GDNS
7 COLLINGWOOD TERR
8 GRASMERE CL
9 GRASMERE DR
10 BANKS RISE
11 LAKEBER CL
12 BANKS WAY
13 LAKEBER DR
14 INGLEBOROUGH VIEW
15 GOODENBER CRES
16 BUTTERBERGH
17 HIGHCROFT
18 POLICE YARD
19 JUBILEE BLDGS

242

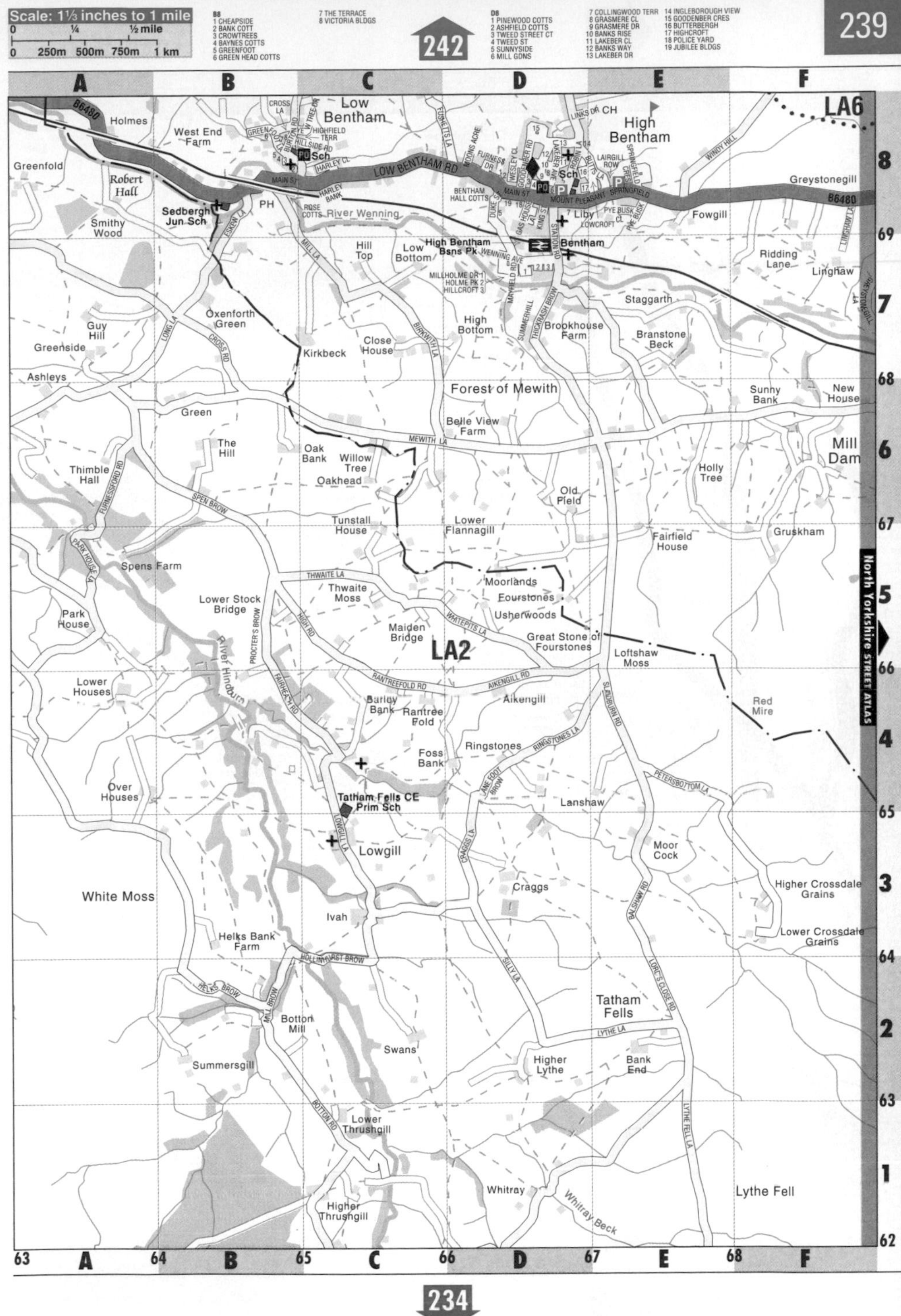

234

225
223

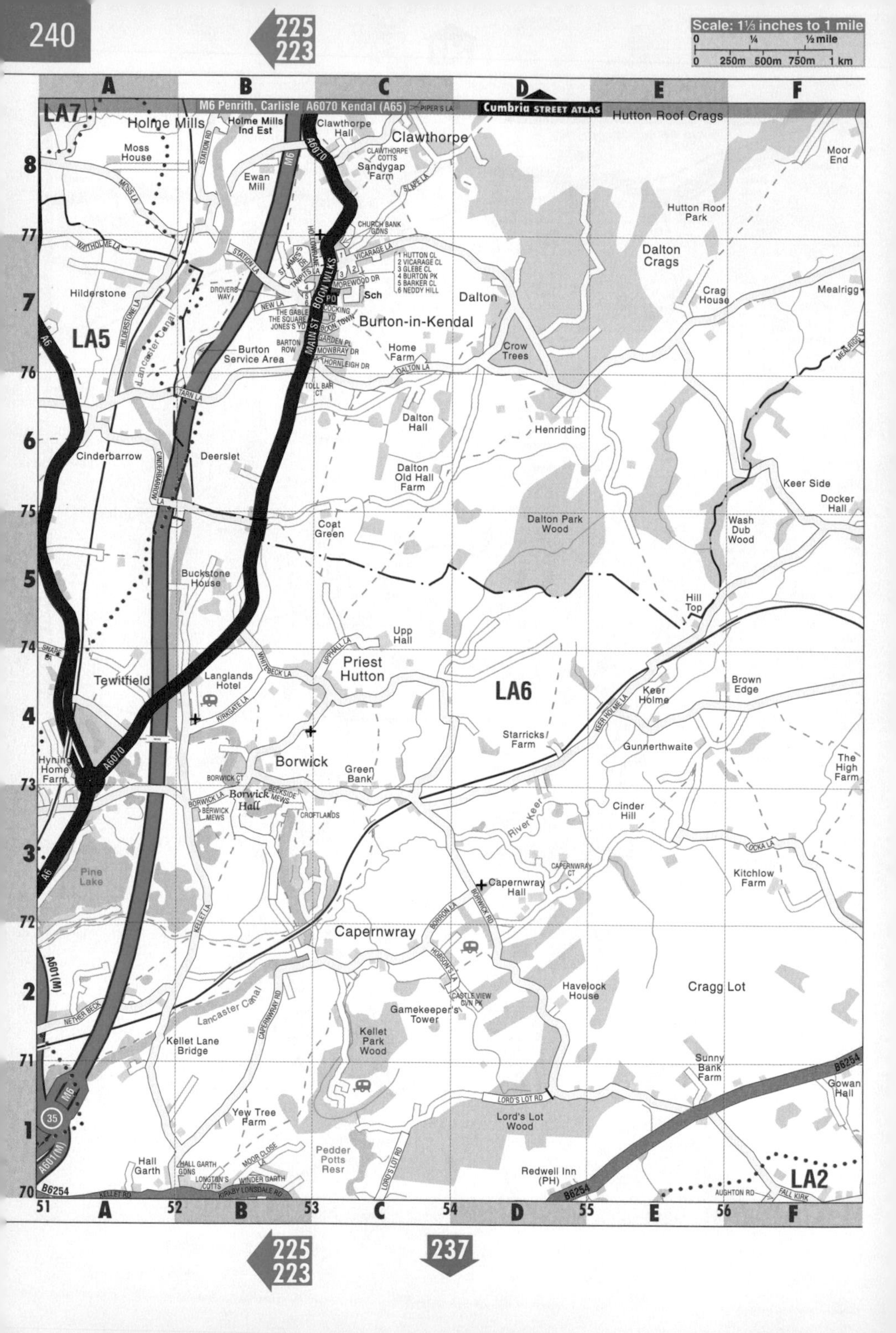

225
223
237

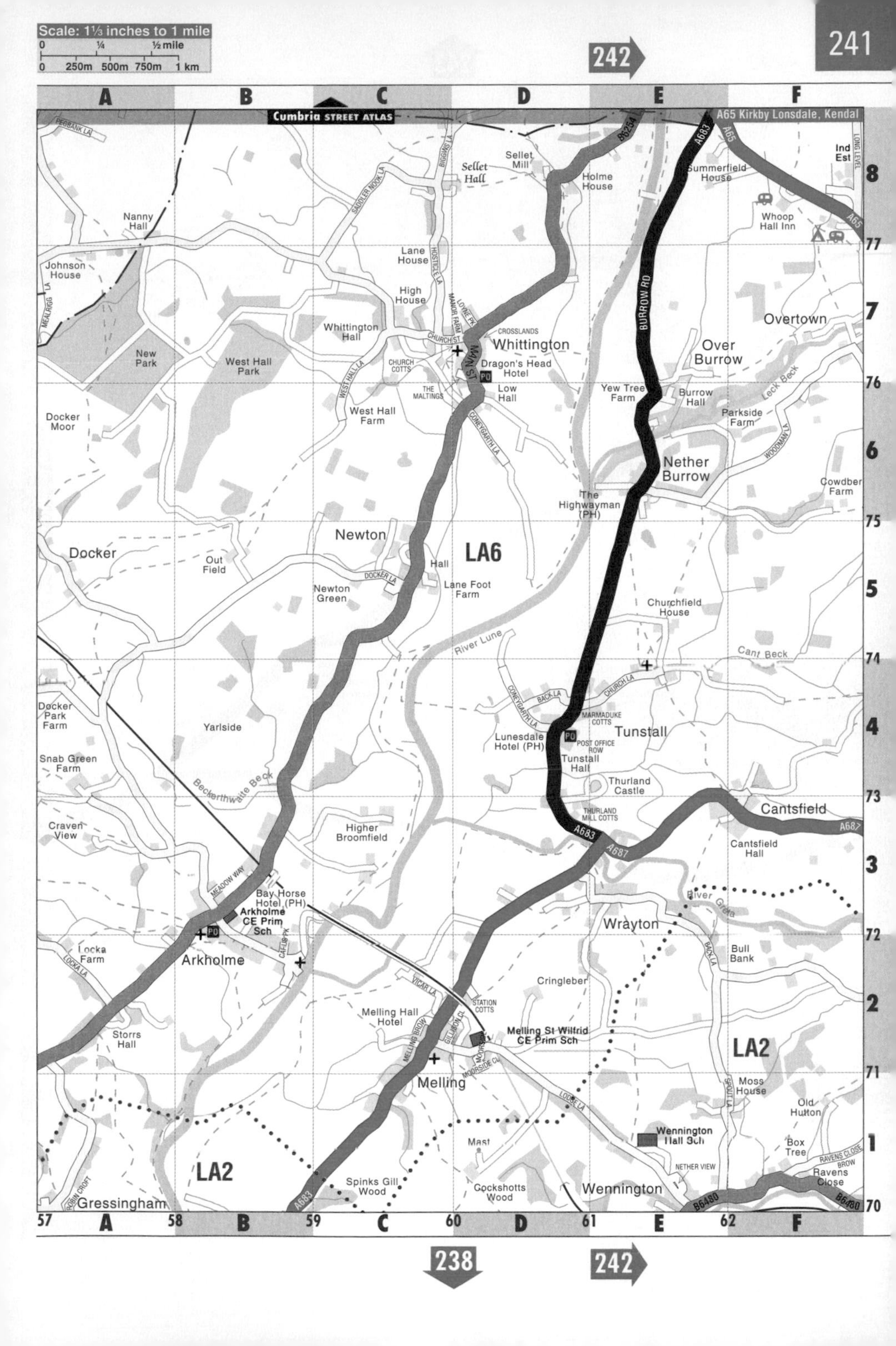

Scale: 1⅓ inches to 1 mile
0 ¼ ½ mile
0 250m 500m 750m 1 km
242
Cumbria STREET ATLAS
A65 Kirkby Lonsdale, Kendal
Sellet Hall
Sellet Mill
Holme House
Summerfield House
Ind Est
Nanny Hall
Whoop Hall Inn
Johnson House
Lane House
High House
Whittington Hall
Whittington
Dragon's Head Hotel
Over Burrow
Overtown
New Park
West Hall Park
Low Hall
Yew Tree Farm
Burrow Hall
Parkside Farm
Docker Moor
West Hall Farm
Nether Burrow
Cowdber Farm
The Highwayman (PH)
Newton
Docker
Out Field
Hall
LA6
Lane Foot Farm
Newton Green
Churchfield House
River Lune
Cant Beck
Docker Park Farm
Yarlside
Lunesdale Hotel (PH)
Tunstall
Tunstall Hall
Snab Green Farm
Thurland Castle
Beckerthwaite Beck
Cantsfield
Craven View
Higher Broomfield
Cantsfield Hall
Bay Horse Hotel (PH)
Arkholme CE Prim Sch
River Greta
Wrayton
Locka Farm
Arkholme
Bull Bank
Cringleber
Melling Hall Hotel
Melling St Wilfrid CE Prim Sch
Storrs Hall
LA2
Melling
Moss House
Old Hutton
Wennington Hall Sch
Mast
Box Tree
Ravens Close
LA2
Spinks Gill Wood
Gockshotts Wood
Wennington
Gressingham
A683
A65
A687
B6254
B6480
BURROW RD
MAIN ST
CHURCH ST
238
242

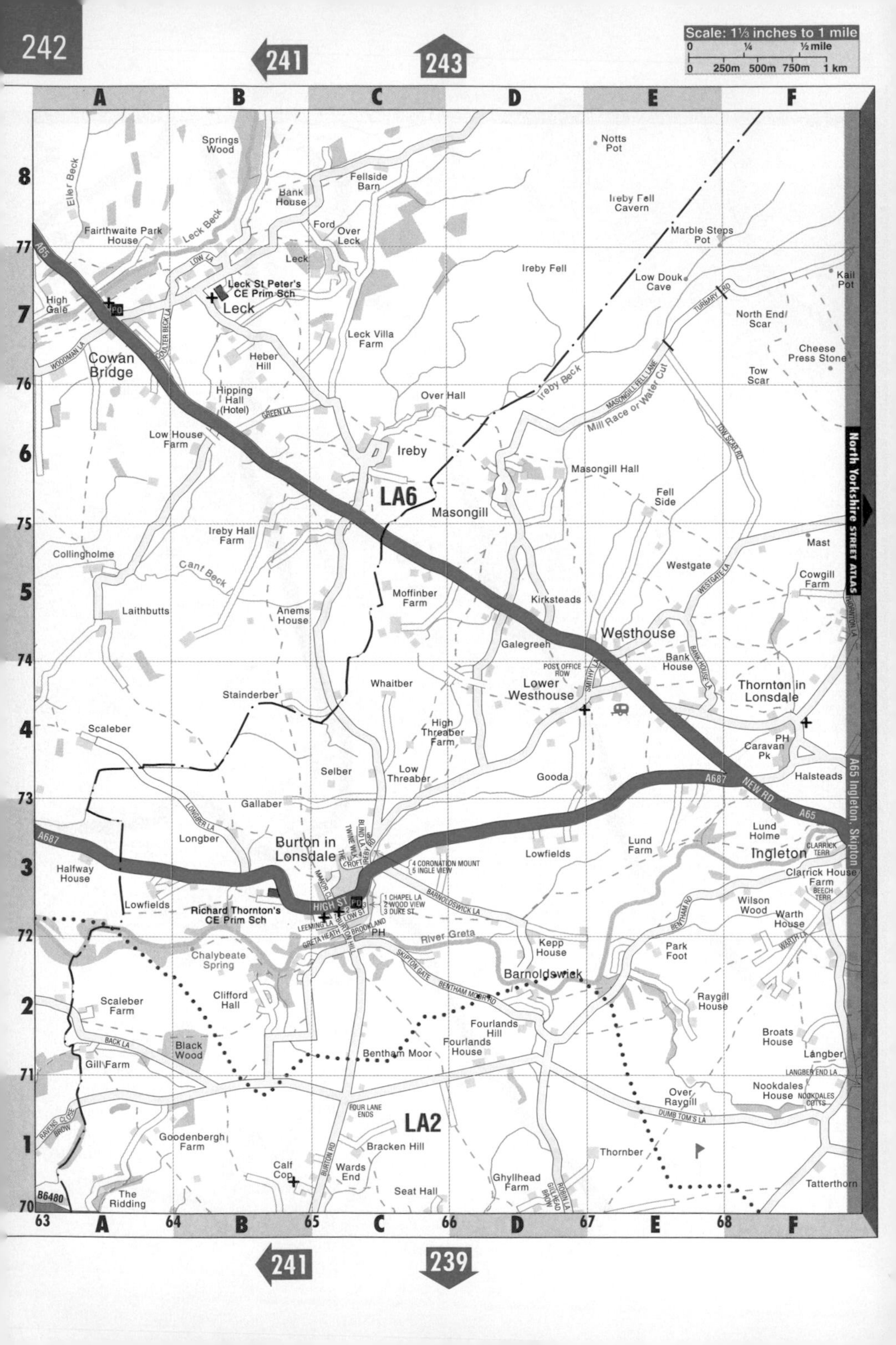

242
241
243
Scale: 1⅓ inches to 1 mile
0
¼
½ mile
0
250m
500m
750m
1 km
A
B
C
D
E
F
Springs Wood
Notts Pot
Fellside Barn
Bank House
Ireby Fell Cavern
Eller Beck
Fairthwaite Park House
Leck Beck
Ford
Over Leck
Marble Steps Pot
Leck
Ireby Fell
Kail Pot
Low Douk Cave
High Gale
Leck St Peter's CE Prim Sch
Leck
North End Scar
Leck Villa Farm
Cheese Press Stone
Cowan Bridge
Heber Hill
Tow Scar
Ireby Beck
Hipping Hall (Hotel)
Over Hall
Mill Race or Water Cut
Low House Farm
Ireby
Masongill Hall
LA6
Masongill
Fell Side
Ireby Hall Farm
Mast
Collingholme
Cant Beck
Westgate
Cowgill Farm
Moffinber Farm
Kirksteads
Laithbutts
Anems House
North Yorkshire STREET ATLAS
Westhouse
Galegreen
Bank House
Post Office Row
Whaitber
Lower Westhouse
Thornton in Lonsdale
Stainderber
High Threaber Farm
Scaleber
PH
Caravan Pk
Selber
Low Threaber
Gooda
Halsteads
Gallaber
A687
New Rd
A65
Longber
Burton in Lonsdale
Lund Farm
Lund Holme
A65 Ingleton, Skipton
Halfway House
Lowfields
Ingleton
4 Coronation Mount
5 Ingle View
Clarrick House Farm
Lowfields
Richard Thornton's CE Prim Sch
High St
1 Chapel La
2 Wood View
3 Duke St
Barnoldswick La
Wilson Wood
Warth House
PH
River Greta
Kepp House
Park Foot
Chalybeate Spring
Barnoldswick
Clifford Hall
Raygill House
Scaleber Farm
Fourlands Hill
Broats House
Back La
Black Wood
Bentham Moor
Fourlands House
Langber
Gill Farm
Langber End La
Over Raygill
Nookdales House
Four Lane Ends
Dumb Tom's La
LA2
Goodenbergh Farm
Bracken Hill
Thornber
Calf Cop
Wards End
Ghyllhead Farm
Tatterthorn
Seat Hall
The Ridding
B6480
Burton Rd
Skipton Gate
Bentham Moor Rd
63
64
65
66
67
68
70
71
72
73
74
75
76
77
1
2
3
4
5
6
7
8
239

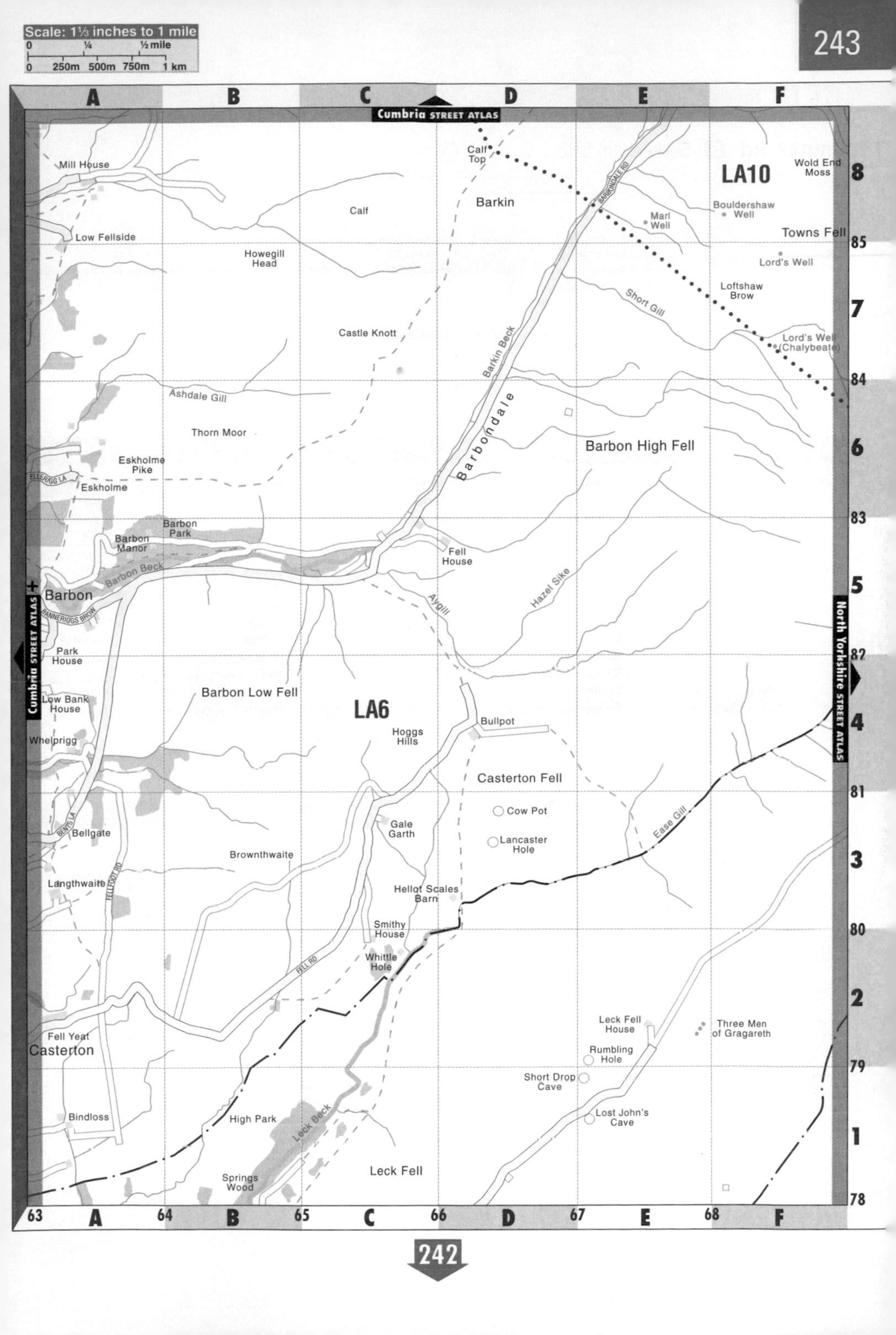

Scale: 1⅓ inches to 1 mile
0
¼
½ mile
0
250m
500m
750m
1 km
Cumbria STREET ATLAS
North Yorkshire STREET ATLAS
242
LA10
LA6
Mill House
Low Fellside
Calf Top
Barkin
Calf
Howegill Head
Castle Knott
Barkin Beck
Barbondale
BARBONDALE RD
Marl Well
Bouldershaw Well
Wold End Moss
Towns Fell
Lord's Well
Loftshaw Brow
Short Gill
Lord's Well (Chalybeate)
Ashdale Gill
Thorn Moor
Eskholme Pike
Eskholme
ELLERIGG LA
Barbon High Fell
Barbon Park
Barbon Manor
Barbon Beck
Barbon
BANNERIGGS BROW
Fell House
Aygill
Hazel Sike
Park House
Barbon Low Fell
Low Bank House
Whelprigg
Hoggs Hills
Bullpot
Casterton Fell
Cow Pot
Lancaster Hole
Ease Gill
Gale Garth
BENTS LA
Bellgate
Brownthwaite
FELLFOOT RD
Langthwaite
Hellot Scales Barn
Smithy House
Whittle Hole
FELL RD
Fell Yeat
Casterton
Leck Fell House
Three Men of Gragareth
Rumbling Hole
Short Drop Cave
Lost John's Cave
Bindloss
High Park
Leck Beck
Springs Wood
Leck Fell
A
B
C
D
E
F
63
64
65
66
67
68
78
1
79
2
80
3
81
4
82
5
83
6
84
7
85
8

Index

Church Rd **6** Beckenham BR2.......... **53** C6

Place name	Location number	Locality, town or village	Postcode district	Page and grid square
May be abbreviated on the map	Present when a number indicates the place's position in a crowded area of mapping	Shown when more than one place has the same name	District for the indexed place	Page number and grid reference for the standard mapping

Public and commercial buildings are highlighted in **magenta**. **Places of interest** are highlighted in blue with a star*

Abbreviations used in the index

Abbreviation	Meaning
Acad	Academy
App	Approach
Arc	Arcade
Ave	Avenue
Bglw	Bungalow
Bldg	Building
Bsns, Bus	Business
Bvd	Boulevard
Cath	Cathedral
Cir	Circus
Cl	Close
Cnr	Corner
Coll	College
Com	Community
Comm	Common
Cott	Cottage
Cres	Crescent
Cswy	Causeway
Ct	Court
Ctr	Centre
Ctry	Country
Cty	County
Dr	Drive
Dro	Drove
Ed	Education
Emb	Embankment
Est	Estate
Ex	Exhibition
Gd	Ground
Gdn	Garden
Gn	Green
Gr	Grove
H	Hall
Ho	House
Hospl	Hospital
HQ	Headquarters
Hts	Heights
Ind	Industrial
Inst	Institute
Int	International
Intc	Interchange
Junc	Junction
L	Leisure
La	Lane
Liby	Library
Mdw	Meadow
Meml	Memorial
Mkt	Market
Mus	Museum
Orch	Orchard
Pal	Palace
Par	Parade
Pas	Passage
Pk	Park
Pl	Place
Prec	Precinct
Prom	Promenade
Rd	Road
Recn	Recreation
Ret	Retail
Sh	Shopping
Sq	Square
St	Street
Sta	Station
Terr	Terrace
TH	Town Hall
Univ	University
Wk, Wlk	Walk
Wr	Water
Yd	Yard

Index of localities, towns and villages

A

Abbeystead ... 232 F1
Abbey Village ... 80 C2
Abraham Heights ... 214 D7
Accrington ... 104 E6
Acre ... 85 B6
Adelphi ... 117 E1
Adlington ... 31 B7
Ainsdale ... 21 B5
Ainsdale-on-Sea ... 20 F6
Alleytroyds ... 103 D6
Altham ... 125 E6
Anchor ... 81 F5
Anchorsholme ... 175 E1
Anderton ... 31 C8
Andertons Mill ... 41 A1
Ansdell ... 90 C4
Appley Bridge ... 19 C8
Arkholme ... 241 B2
Ashton-on-Ribble ... 117 A1
Ashurst ... 18 A4
Astley Village ... 61 A2
Aughton Lancaster ... 237 E6
Aughton Maghull ... 6 A7
Aughton Park ... 15 E2
Avenham ... 97 A6

B

Bacup ... 70 E8
Bailrigg ... 215 A1
Balderstone ... 121 A5
Baldingstone ... 50 F1
Balladen ... 68 F8
Bamber Bridge ... 97 E1
Bank Fold ... 82 F5
Bank Hey ... 123 A2
Bank Houses ... 205 C7
Bank Lane ... 50 E7
Banks ... 54 F6
Banks Hill ... 196 A4
Bank Top ... 101 D3
Barber's Moor ... 58 D3
Barbon ... 243 A5
Bare ... 217 E7
Barley ... 169 B5
Barley Green ... 169 C5
Barnfield ... 104 E5
Barnoldswick Ingleton ... 242 D2
Barnoldswick Nelson ... 196 C1
Barrow ... 166 D1
Barrowford ... 170 C4
Barrow Nook ... 7 F2
Barton Preston ... 137 B7
Barton Southport ... 13 F6
Bashall Eaves ... 188 A3
Bastwell ... 102 A8
Baxenden ... 104 E1
Bay Horse ... 207 C6
Beardwood ... 101 B7
Becconsall ... 73 E1
Belgrave ... 64 E8
Belmont ... 46 C4
Belthorn ... 82 F6
Bent Gate ... 68 C8
Bescar ... 24 A7
Beverley ... 170 E7
Bickerstaffe ... 7 F5
Billington ... 144 B3
Bilsborrow ... 159 A5
Birch Green ... 18 B2
Birch Hall ... 81 E4
Birkacre ... 43 A3
Birkdale ... 34 F2
Bispham ... 152 B5
Bispham Green ... 27 B7
Blackamoor ... 82 B8
Blackburn ... 101 E1
Blackleach ... 135 E2
Blacko ... 170 D7
Black Pole ... 136 C5
Blackpool ... 130 A4
Blackrod ... 31 D2
Blacksnape ... 65 E8
Blaguegate ... 17 B1
Bleasdale ... 184 A7
Blowick ... 35 E6
Bolton-by-Bowland ... 230 D4
Bolton Green ... 42 C8
Bolton-le-Sands ... 221 B5
Bolton Town End ... 220 F3
Bonds ... 181 C6
Booth Fold ... 86 E1
Borwick ... 240 B4
Bottom of Hutton ... 94 F3
Bowerham ... 215 B6
Bowgreave ... 181 D4
Bowker's Green ... 6 D5
Bracewell ... 231 F3
Bradley ... 170 E2
Brandwood ... 70 B8
Bretherton ... 57 E6
Bridge End ... 68 A7
Brierfield ... 148 D5
Brindle ... 78 F5
Brinscall ... 62 E7
Britannia ... 71 C8
Broad Clough ... 87 F4
Broadfield Leyland ... 76 E1
Broadfield Oswaldtwistle ... 103 F2
Broadgate ... 96 E6
Broadly ... 52 C4
Brockhall Village ... 143 C5
Brookfield ... 118 D4
Brookhouse Blackburn ... 101 F6
Brookhouse Lancaster ... 237 D3
Brooksbottoms ... 50 C3
Broughton ... 137 D3
Brownedge ... 97 D1
Brown Edge ... 36 A2
Brownhill ... 122 F2
Brownlow ... 10 C1
Brownside ... 128 F6
Brunshaw ... 128 D5
Bryning ... 92 C8
Buckshaw Village ... 60 F6
Bulk ... 218 E1
Bunker's Hill ... 171 B4
Burnley ... 128 A7
Burnley Lane ... 148 A1
Burnley Wood ... 128 A4
Burn Naze ... 176 B4
Burscough ... 25 D4
Burscough Bridge ... 25 D5
Burton-in-Kendal ... 240 C7
Burton in Lonsdale ... 242 C3
Bury ... 33 A1
Butt Yeats ... 238 B6

C

Cabus ... 204 C3
Cadley ... 117 C4
Cadshaw ... 65 D1
Caldershaw ... 52 B2
Calder Vale ... 182 E8
Cantsfield ... 241 F3
Capernwray ... 240 C2
Carleton ... 153 A5
Carnforth ... 223 C2
Carr ... 50 B7
Carr Cross ... 23 D8
Carr Hall ... 170 B2
Carry Bridge ... 171 F5
Casterton ... 243 A2
Catforth ... 135 F4
Catlow ... 149 C5
Caton ... 237 C3
Caton Green ... 237 D3
Catterall ... 181 E2
Chapel House ... 17 E2
Chapels ... 82 A3
Chapeltown ... 48 C4
Charnock Green ... 42 C6
Charnock Richard ... 42 D4
Chatburn ... 190 D5
Chatterton ... 68 C1
Cheesden ... 51 D6
Cherry Tree ... 100 E1
Chesham ... 33 A5
Chipping ... 185 D3

Chorley 43 C6
Chorley Moor 43 D6
Church 103 E7
Churchtown Garstang 181 A2
Church Town Southport 54 A1
Claughton Catterall 182 D1
Claughton Lancaster 237 E5
Clawthorpe 240 C8
Clayton Brook 78 A5
Clayton Green 78 A3
Clayton-Le-Dale 122 C7
Clayton-le-Moors 124 D2
Clayton-le-Woods 77 D2
Cleveleys 175 C3
Cliffe 124 C6
Clifton 115 D1
Clitheroe 166 D8
Cloughfold 86 D2
Clow Bridge 106 C5
Coates 196 D3
Cob Wall 102 A7
Cockden 149 B2
Cocker Bar 75 F1
Cockerham 206 C5
Cold Row 177 C5
Colne 171 C6
Colne Edge 171 C7
Common Edge 110 F6
Conder Green 210 C5
Constable Lee 86 B4
Copp 156 A3
Coppull 42 E2
Coppull Moor 29 D6
Copster Green 122 D8
Corner Row 133 E2
Cornholme 109 B1
Cote Holme 103 D6
Cottam 116 D5
Cotton Tree 172 B4
Coupe Green 98 E4
Cowan Bridge 242 A7
Cow Ark 187 C8
Cowling 43 F6
Cowpe 69 F6
Crag Bank 221 C8
Cranberry Fold 65 D5
Crawford 9 D2
Crawshawbooth 86 A8
Croft 196 B2
Crossens 54 C4
Crossgill 237 E1
Croston 58 B2
Cuddy Hill 136 B7
Cuerden Green 77 C6
Cumeragh Village 138 F6

D

Daisyfield 102 A6
Daisy Hill 60 D1
Dalton Burton-in-Kendal 240 D7
Dalton Skelmersdale 18 C5
Dam Side 201 D6
Dangerous Corner 28 C2
Darn Hill 33 F2
Darwen 81 E1
Dean 87 C8
Deepdale 118 A2
Digmoor 9 D6
Dill Hall 104 A8
Doals 87 F7
Docker 241 A4
Dolphinholme 226 A8
Dowbridge 114 D4
Downham 191 B5
Downholland Cross 14 A2
Drink House 58 A1
Drummersdale 24 C7
Duncombe 158 F3
Dunnockshaw 106 B4
Dunnyshop 103 E3
Dunsop Bridge 228 C5

E

Eagland Hill 179 C8
Earby 197 A2
Earcroft 81 E6
Earnshaw Bridge 76 E2
Easington 229 B5
East Gillibrands 9 A8
East Pimbo 9 E5
Eccleston 41 C7
Edenfield 68 D3
Edge End 124 B6
Edgeside 86 F2
Edgworth 48 D6
Egerton 47 E2
Ellel 211 B5
Elmers Green 18 D2
Elston 120 A6
Elswick 156 A1
Elswick Leys 134 A8
Enfield 125 A2
Entwistle 48 B7
Esprick 133 D5
Euxton 60 D3
Ewood 81 D8
Ewood Bridge 68 C6

F

Facit 71 D2
Fairfield 33 D3
Fairhaven 90 A3
Fairview 44 A1
Falinge Fold 52 D1
Far Arnside 224 A5
Far Banks 55 C8
Farington Bamber Bridge 76 F6
Farington Leyland 77 B3
Farleton 238 A6
Far Moor 10 D4
Farringdon Park 118 F1
Fence 147 E7
Feniscliffe 101 A2
Feniscowles 80 D8
Fern Gore 104 A3
Fern Grove 33 C4
Fiddler's Ferry 54 D6
Fisher's Row 201 E5
Fishwick 97 C8
Flax Moss 68 A8
Fleetwood 198 E5
Fletcher Bank 50 D6
Ford Green 203 F2
Forest Becks 230 D6
Forest Holme 87 A7
Formby 11 E4
Forton 207 B3
Foulridge 194 D1
Four Lane Ends 101 D8
Foxhill Bank 103 D5
Freckleton 93 C7
Freehold 215 B8
Free Town 33 A4
Frenchwood 97 B6
Freshfield 11 E5
Fulledge 128 B5
Fulwood 117 D5
Fulwood Row 118 E6

G

Galgate 211 B3
Garstang 181 C7
Gisburn 231 C4
Glasson 209 F5
Glen Top 70 A8
Glovers Bridge 26 A3
Golden Hill 77 A2
Golgotha 215 B6
Goodshaw 85 F8
Goodshaw Chapel 106 B1
Goodshaw Fold 105 F2
Goose Green 74 F2
Goosnargh 138 C6
Granville Park 6 B8
Great Altcar 12 E1
Great Eccleston 156 C4
Great Harwood 124 D4
Great Knowley 61 E3
Great Marton 130 F3
Great Marton Moss 111 B4
Great Marton Moss Side 111 B7
Great Mitton 165 F3
Great Plumpton 112 E7
Greave 88 B3
Green Bank 102 B6
Greenfield 171 A4
Greenhalgh 133 C5
Green Haworth 104 B1
Green Lane 81 A8
Greenmount 49 E1
Gregson Lane 98 E2
Griffin 101 C3
Grimeford Village 31 D6
Grimsargh 139 D1
Grimshaw Green 27 B5
Grimshaw Park 101 F2
Grindleton 190 B7
Guide 82 D8

H

Habergham 126 F7
Haggate 149 A3
Hale Nook 178 A5
Hall Carr 86 A1
Hall Cross 114 A1
Hall Green Preston 74 C8
Hall Green Skelmersdale 10 A7
Halsall 23 C1
Halton 219 D7
Halton Green 219 F7
Hambleton 177 C1
Hambleton Moss Side 177 E2
Hammerton Mere 235 E1
Hampson Green 211 C1
Hapton 126 B4
Hardhorn 131 E8
Hardhorn Village 131 E7
Hareholme 86 D1
Harle Syke 148 F3
Harrop Fold 229 F4
Hartwood 61 C3
Harwood Bar 124 F6
Haskayne 13 F4
Haslingden 85 B4
Haverbreaks 214 E5
Hawes Side 130 F1
Hawkshaw Blackburn 81 D3
Hawkshaw Ramsbottom 49 C2
Hazelhurst 50 B4
Heap Bridge 33 C1
Heapey 62 A6
Heasandford 128 C8
Heath Charnock 43 E2
Heaton 213 E5
Heaton's Bridge 24 D4
Height End 85 D3
Helmcroft 85 B1
Helmshore 68 B7
Hesketh Bank 73 D4
Hesketh Lane 162 D8
Hesketh Moss 73 C1
Heskin Green 41 D3
Hest Bank 220 F1
Hey Head 87 A1
Hey Houses 90 D7
Heysham 212 D7
Heywood 33 F2
Higham 146 E5
High Bentham 239 E8
High Cross 131 C8
Higher Audley 102 A4
Higher Bartle 116 E7
Higher Baxenden 104 F2
Higher Boarsgreave 70 A6
Higher Broad Clough 87 F5
Higher Broadhalgh 80 E7
Higher Change 88 B4
Higher Cloughfold 86 D2
Higher Copthurst 61 E7
Higher Croft 101 F1
Higher End 10 D3
Higherford 170 E5
Higher Heysham 212 F6
Higher Penwortham 96 C5
Higher Standen 166 F6
Higher Stanhill 103 B4
Higher Summerseat 50 B1
Higher Walton 98 B4
Higher Wheelton 79 B1
Highfurlong 153 A2
High Moor 27 F4
High Park 36 A8
Hightown 2 F3
Hill Dale 27 D5
Hillock Vale 104 E8
Hillside 34 F1
Hill Top 172 B2
Hoddlesden 82 F1
Hoghton 99 B2
Holcombe 50 A6
Holcombe Brook 50 B2
Holden 230 C4
Holden Vale 85 A5
Hole House 102 C6
Holland Slack 97 E2
Hollin Bank 101 D2
Hollin Hall 172 C1
Hollins 81 F4
Hollins Grove 81 F3
Hollins Lane 207 D2
Holme Chapel 108 A6
Holme Mills 240 A8
Holmes 56 D3
Holme Slack 118 C3
Holmeswood 38 C6
Holm Nook 154 E7
Holt Green 6 A7
Hoohill 130 D8
Hornby 238 B7
Horton 231 E5
Horwich 32 D4
Hoscar 26 D4
Howick Cross 96 A5
Hud Hey 85 A6
Hugh Mill 69 F7
Huncoat 125 E2
Hundred End 72 F1
Hunger Hill 28 F4
Hurlston 24 C3
Hurlston Green 24 B3
Hurst Green 164 F1
Hurstwood 129 C4
Hutch Bank 84 F2
Huttock Top 86 E2
Hutton 95 D2

I

Ince Blundell 3 E4
Ingleton 242 F3
Inglewhite 160 B4
Ingol 117 A4
Inskip 135 D8
Intack 102 D5
Ireby 242 C6
Irwell Vale 68 B5

J

Jack Green 78 F8
Jericho 33 F4
Johnson's Hillock 61 E6

K

Kelbrook 195 A6
Kellamergh 92 C7
Kingsfold 96 D2
Kirkby 1 A3
Kirkham 114 A5
Knott End-on-Sea 199 E5
Knowle Green 163 C1
Knowley 61 F2
Knuzden Brook 102 F4

L

Lady Green 3 D4
Lammack 101 C8
Lancaster 214 C6
Lane Bottom 149 B3
Lane Ends 230 A5
Lane Head 87 F4
Lane Heads 156 D3
Laneshaw Bridge 172 E6
Laneside 104 C8
Lane Side 85 B2
Langho 143 D1
Larches 116 F1
Larkholme 198 D1
Laund 85 F4
Layton 130 E7
Lea 116 D1
Lea Town 115 F3
Leck 242 B7
Lee 232 F2
Lees 187 B6
Lenches 171 D3
Lewth 136 A6
Leyland 76 F2
Lightfoot Green 117 B8
Limbrick 44 A6
Little Altcar 12 A1
Little Bispham 152 C8
Little Carleton 152 F1
Little Eccleston 156 A6
Little Harwood 102 B8
Little Hoole Moss Houses 75 B4
Little Knowley 61 F3
Little Marsden 148 C7
Little Marton 131 D1
Little Marton Moss Side 131 A1
Little Moor End 103 C3
Little Plumpton 112 D5
Little Poulton 153 F4
Little Scotland 31 B2
Little Singleton 154 C4
Little Thornton 153 E7
Livesey Fold 81 F2
Lomeshaye 148 B8
Longholme 86 A2
Long Ing 196 C2
Longridge 140 A8
Longshaw Blackburn 101 D1
Longshaw Skelmersdale 10 E1
Longshoot 85 C3
Longton 75 A8
Lostock Hall 77 A7
Love Clough 106 A3
Low Bentham 239 C8
Lower Audley 101 E4
Lower Ballam 112 A3
Lower Bartle 116 D8
Lower Baxenden 104 F1
Lower Boarsgreave 70 A6
Lower Cloughfold 86 C2
Lower Copthurst 61 E7
Lower Darwen 81 F7
Lower Fold Accrington 104 C6
Lower Fold Great Harwood 124 C6
Lower Fold Rochdale 52 C3
Lowerford 170 E3
Lower Green Bank 232 B1
Lower Healey 52 E4
Lower Heysham 212 E8
Lowerhouse 126 F6
Lower House 59 D8
Lower Penwortham 96 E5
Lower Summerseat 50 D2
Lower Thurnham 210 B2
Lower Westhouse 242 D4
Lowgill 239 C3
Low Moor 166 C8
Lucas Green 61 C6
Lumb Haslingden 68 B4
Lumb Rawtenstall 86 F6
Lydiate 5 D4
Lytham 91 B3
Lytham St Anne's 90 B5

M

Maghull 5 B1
Marsden Height 148 E5
Marsh 214 C8
Marsh House Blackburn 82 C2
Marsh Houses Lancaster 206 B4
Marshside 53 E4
Masongill 242 D6
Maudlands 117 D1
Mawdesley 40 C2
Medlar 133 F4
Melling 241 C1
Mellor 121 F2
Mellor Brook 121 C3
Mere Brow 55 E2
Mereclough 129 A1
Mereside 131 B1
Middleforth Green 96 E3
Middle Healey 52 D4
Middleton 213 B2
Midge Hall 76 A3
Mill Dam 239 F6
Miller Fold 104 B3
Millgate 71 D4
Millhead 223 D4
Mill Hill 101 B1
Milnshaw 104 A7
Moor End 177 C6
Moorgate 101 C1
Moorlands 215 B7
Moor Side Kirkham 134 D1
Moor Side Preston 136 C4
Morecambe 216 E5
Moss Bridge 81 E5
Moss Edge Fisher's Row 202 C7
Moss Edge Hambleton 179 A3
Moss Side Blackpool 112 E1
Moss Side Fisher's Row 201 F5
Moss Side Leyland 76 B1
Moss Side Maghull 6 A1
Mossy Lea 28 F6
Much Hoole 74 D3
Much Hoole Moss Houses 75 A2
Much Hoole Town 74 E1
Myerscough 158 C4
Myerscough Smithy 120 D3
Mythop 132 A3

N

Nab's Head 99 E7
Nangreaves 50 F2
Nappa 231 E8
Nateby 180 D6
Nelson 148 E8
Nether Burrow 241 E6
Nether Kellet 221 F5
Newbridge 170 C2
Newburgh 27 A2
Newby 192 B8
Newchurch 86 F1
Newchurch in Pendle 169 C3
Newgate 10 A6
New Gate 76 C8
New Hall Hey 85 F1
Newlands 215 C5
New Lane 25 B6
New Longton 75 E8
Newsham 137 A5
Newsholme 231 D6
Newton Blackpool 131 C6
Newton Kirkby Lonsdale 241 C5
Newton Lancaster 218 E2
Newton Slaidburn 229 A5
Newton-with-Scales 114 F2
Newtown Leyland 59 A2
New Town Longridge 140 A6
Nog Tow 116 F7
Nook 181 B3
Nooklands 117 D4
Norbreck 152 B6
Norcross 153 A7
Norden 124 A2
Normoss 131 B7
North End 3 B6
North Hag 85 A4
North Holme 195 A8
North Shore 130 A8
Northwood 1 A3
Nova Scotia 101 E3
Nun Hills 70 C7
Nuttall 50 C4
Nuttall Lane 50 B5
Nutter's Platt 96 B2

O

Oakenclough 226 C2
Oakenhead Wood 85 E3
Oakenshaw 124 E3
Old Birtle 33 E7
Ogho 143 C4
Ollerton Fold 79 D5
Ormskirk 15 C6
Orrell 10 E7
Orrell Post 10 E7
Ortner 232 C1
Osbaldeston 121 D4
Osbaldestone Green 121 C6
Oswaldtwistle 103 B3
Out Rawcliffe 178 C1
Over Burrow 241 E7
Over Kellet 237 A8
Overton 209 D8
Overtown Kirkby Lonsdale 241 F7
Over Town Burnley 108 A8

P

Padiham 126 B7
Parbold 27 D2
Park Place 101 F3
Passmonds 52 B1
Paythorne 231 C6
Peel 111 F4
Peel Bank 103 E7
Peel Brow 50 C7
Peel Hill 111 E7
Pendleton 167 B4
Pennylands 17 E1
Penwortham 96 C5
Penwortham Lane 96 F2
Pickup Bank 83 A2
Piercy 86 F2
Pike Hill 128 E5
Pilling 201 C6
Pilling Lane 200 B6
Pimhole 33 A1
Pincock 42 C8
Pinfold 23 F4
Pippin Street 78 E5
Pleasington 100 C1
Pleckgate 122 D1
Pool Hey 36 B3
Portsmouth 108 F1
Pot House 82 C3
Potters Brook 207 B5
Poulton-le-Fylde 153 E2
Preesall 200 A3
Preesall Park 200 C1
Preston 96 C8
Prettywood 33 E2
Priest Hutton 240 C4
Primet Bridge 171 C3
Primrose 166 D6
Pudsey 109 B2

Q

Queen's Park 102 B4
Queenstown 130 D7
Quernmore 232 A6

R

Radford 65 A8
Rainford Junction 8 F2
Rainhill 196 D3
Rake Foot 86 A7
Rake Head 70 A7
Ramsbottom 50 C5
Rann 82 E6
Rathmell 236 F6
Ratten Row 156 B8
Raven Shore 68 A6
Rawtenstall 86 B1
Read 145 D2
Red Bank 43 E5
Red Scar 119 B5
Reedley 148 B4
Reeds Holme 85 F5
Revidge 101 C7
Revoe 130 C3
Ribbleton 118 E2
Ribby 113 D4
Ribchester 141 D3
Ridge 218 F2
Riley Green 79 E8
Rimington 191 F8
Ring o'Bells 26 B2
Rishton 124 C2
Rising Bridge 85 A8
Rivington 44 F2
Roach Bridge 98 F6
Robin Hood 28 C4
Roby Mill 19 B3
Rochdale 52 C2
Rockcliffe 88 A2
Roe Lee 122 E1
Roseacre 134 D6
Rose Grove 127 B6
Rosehill 65 C7
Rose Hill 127 F3
Rossall Beach 175 D5
Roughlee 170 B5
Rowlands 50 D2
Royal Oak 6 F4
Rufford 39 C3
Runshaw Moor 59 E4
Rush Bed 86 A6
Ryelands 218 C2

S

Sabden 145 F8
St Annes 89 D6
St Michael's on Wyre 157 C7
Salesbury 122 D6
Saltcotes 91 D5
Salterforth 194 D7
Salwick 115 E3
Samlesbury 119 E1
Samlesbury Bottoms 99 D6
Sandham's Green 111 C8
Sand Side 205 D2
Sandylands 216 B2
Sawley 230 C1
Scaitcliffe 104 B5
Scale Hall 218 A2
Scarisbrick 23 E7
Scarth Hill 16 C2
School Lane 97 F2
Scorton 204 E6
Scotforth 215 A3
Scout 86 E2
Scronkey 201 E3
Seven Stars 59 D8
Shadsworth 102 D3
Sharneyford 88 D5
Sharoe Green 117 E7
Shawclough 52 C3
Shawfield 52 A2
Shawforth 71 D6
Shaw Green 59 D2
Sherfin 85 B7
Sherwood 118 A6
Shevington 19 F5
Shevington Moor 29 A2
Shevington Vale 19 E7
Shirdley Hill 23 A6
Shireshead 207 E3
Shore 109 C2
Shorey Bank 82 A2
Shuttleworth 50 E8
Silverdale 224 C3
Simonstone 145 E1
Singleton 154 E1
Skelmersdale 18 A1
Skerton 218 C4
Skippool 153 F3
Skitham 179 B4
Slaidburn 229 C7
Slyne 218 D8
Smallwood Hey 201 B5
Smith Green 210 C3
Snape Green 36 E1
Sollom 57 B2
Sough 195 A8
Sough 65 B7
Southfield 149 B6
Southport 35 C3
South Shore 110 C8
Southward Bottom 108 A8
Sower Carr 177 D4
Spen Brook 169 D2
Spotland Fold 52 C1
Spring Hill 103 F5
Spring Side 86 B3
Spring Vale Darwen 65 C7
Spring Vale Haslingden 85 A2
Squires Gate 110 B5
Stacksteads 70 B8
Staghills 86 D1
Staining 131 E5
Stake Pool 201 E4
Stake Pool 202 A5
Stalmine 177 C7
Stalmine Moss Side 177 E7
Stanah 176 E2
Standish 29 F2
Stanhill 103 B4
Stanley 17 E3
Stanley Gate 7 E7
Stanworth 80 C4
Staynall 177 A4
Stodday 214 C2
Stoneyholme 127 F8
Stopper Lane 192 A8
Street 226 A6
Strongstry 68 C2
Stubbins 68 B1
Stydd 141 E4
Summerseat 50 C2
Sunderland 209 B4
Sunny Bower 123 B1
Swillbrook 136 B2
Swiss Clough 86 F1
Syke 52 F4
Syke Side 85 B1

T

Tagg Wood 50 A5
Tanhouse 9 D8
Tanners 50 B7
Tanterton 117 A6
Tardy Gate 77 B8
Tarleton 57 A7
Tarleton Moss 56 C7
Tarlscough 38 D1
Tarnbrook 233 B2
Tatham 238 D8
Tawd Bridge 9 B7
Tawd Valley Park 18 A2
Tewitfield 240 A4
The Greaves 214 F6
The Straits 76 D1
The Wrangling 101 D3
Thistleton 133 C8
Thorney Holme 169 E5
Thornton 176 C3
Thornton-in-Craven 197 A6
Thornton in Lonsdale 242 F4
Thorpe Green 78 E4
Tockholes 81 A2
Tonacliffe 52 C6
Tong End 71 C2
Tontine 10 D5
Top of Ramsgreave 122 C3
Top o' th' Lane 78 F3
Topping Fold 33 D3
Torrisholme 218 A4
Tosside 236 C2
Town Bent 103 D2
Town End 155 C8
Town Green 6 D7
Town Head 196 A1
Townsend Fold 68 E8
Town's Moor 101 E3
Trawden 172 C2
Treales 114 D6
Trough Gate 71 D8
Trunnah 176 B3
Tunstall 241 E4
Turner Green 120 C2
Turpin Green 77 B1
Turton Bottoms 48 D4
Twiston 192 A4

U

Up Holland 10 C7
Upper Thurnham 210 B2

V

Vale 109 C1

W

Waddington 189 C4
Wade Hall 59 E7
Walker Fold 164 C8
Walker's Hill 111 A7
Walk Mill 107 F8
Wallbank 52 B7
Walmer Bridge 74 F5
Walton-le-Dale 97 D4
Walton Summit 78 B8
Wapping 196 A2
Warbreck 152 D1
Warton Carnforth 223 D5
Warton Freckleton 92 D6
Warton Bank 92 C4
Water 87 A8
Waterbarn 70 A8
Waterfall 101 C2
Waterfoot 69 E8
Waterloo 81 B8
Waterside Colne 171 E4
Waterside Darwen 82 E3
Waterslack 224 E6
Waverledge 124 A4
Weeton 132 F2
Weeton Camp 132 D5
Weir 88 A7
Weld Bank 43 C5
Well Bank 85 A3
Wennington 241 E1
Wensley Fold 101 C4
Wesham 114 A6
West Bradford 189 F5
Westby 112 E4
West End Morecombe 217 B3
West End Oswaldtwistle 103 C5
West Gillibrands 8 E8
Westhead 16 D4
Westhouse 242 E5
West Pimbo 9 D4
Whalley 144 B5
Whalley Banks 144 D3
Whalleys 18 A5
Wharles 134 F4
Wheatley Lane 169 F1
Wheelton 62 A7
Whin Lane End 155 A8
Whinny Heights 102 A2
Whitebirk 102 C6
Whitechapel 160 D7
Whitefield 148 C8
Whitehall 65 B5
Whiteholme 152 E7
White Lund 217 E2
White Stake 76 B8
Whitewell 228 D2
Whitewell Bottom 86 F5
Whittington 241 D7
Whittlefield 127 D7
Whittle-le-Woods 61 C7
Whittlestone Head 65 F4
Whitworth 71 D1
Wigglesworth 236 F4
Willacy Lane End 135 E3
Wilpshire 122 E5
Winewall 172 C4
Winmarleigh 203 E4
Wiswell 144 F7
Within Grove 125 E1
Withnell 80 B1
Withnell Fold 79 C3
Witton 101 B3
Woodgate Hill 33 D4
Woodhey 50 B3
Woodnook 104 B4
Woodplumpton 136 E2
Wood Road 50 C1
Woodsfold 135 E6
Wood Top 85 E1
Woodvale 21 B2
Worsthorne 129 B5
Worston 190 D2
Wray 238 D6
Wrayton 241 E3
Wrea Green 113 B3
Wrightington 28 B5
Wrightington Bar 28 F7
Wycoller 173 A3
Wymott 58 F6

Y

Yealand Conyers 225 F1
Yealand Redmayne 225 E4
Yealand Storrs 225 C5
York 123 D8

A

A K Bsns Pk PR9 36 A6
Aalborg Pl LA1 214 F7
Abbey Cl Formby L37 12 B2
Skelmersdale WN8 10 C7
Abbey Cres BB3 65 C8
Abbey Dale
Appley Bridge WN6 19 D7
Burscough L40 25 F3
Abbey Dr WN5 10 E6
Abbey Farm BB7 144 B6
Abbey Farm Cvn Pk L40 16 C8
Abbey Fields BB7 144 C5
Abbey Fold L40 25 D5
Abbey Gdns PR8 35 A4
Abbey Gr PR6 31 B7
Abbey La L40 25 C1
Abbey Lane Ind Est L40 25 C1
Abbey Mews BB7 144 C5
Abbey Pl BB3 82 C1
Abbey Rd Blackpool FY4 110 D5
Whalley BB7 144 C5
Abbey St Accrington BB5 104 C6
Accrington,Scaitcliffe BB5 104 C5
Bacup OL13 87 F4
Preston PR2 96 D8
Abbey Terr Barrow BB7 166 D1
Billington BB7 144 A3
Abbey View Whalley BB7 144 C4
Withnell PR6 80 A1
Abbey Village Prim Sch
PR6 80 C1
Abbey Wlk PR1 96 D3
Abbeydale LA3 217 B2
Abbeyfield 3 BB11 128 B4
Abbeyfield Cl LA1 215 A3
Abbeyfield Ho
Barnoldswick BB18 196 A3
10 Burnley BB11 127 E5
Abbeystead WN8 9 C7
Abbeystead Dr LA1 215 A3
Abbeystead Ho 8 LA1 215 A3
Abbeystead La LA2 232 E2
Abbeystead Rd LA2 232 C1
Abbeyville FY4 110 C6
Abbeywood WN8 9 C6
Abbot Mdw PR1 96 D4
Abbot Wlk BB7 167 A8
Abbots Cl Formby L37 12 A1
Kirkham PR4 114 C4
Rawtenstall BB4 86 A4
Abbots Croft BB7 144 C5
Abbots Ho 21 LA1 214 F8
Abbots Row FY8 90 D6
Abbots Way Formby L37 12 B1
Lancaster LA1 214 C8
Abbotsford L39 15 F5
Abbotsford Ave BB2 101 D1
Abbotsford Rd FY3 131 A3
Abbotsway PR1 96 C6
Abbott Brow BB2 121 E3
Abbott Clough Ave BB1 102 E4
Abbott Clough Cl BB1 102 E4
Abbott Croft PR2 117 A7
Abbott St 17 BL6 32 B4
Abbotts Cl PR5 97 F3
Abbotts Wlk FY7 199 A5
Abel St BB10 128 A8
Abercorn Pl FY4 110 B5
Abercrombie Rd FY7 198 F4
Aberdare Cl BB1 101 E7
Aberdeen Dr BB1 102 A4
Aberdeen Gdns OL12 52 D4
Aberdeen Rd LA1 215 A7
Abernethy St BL6 32 D2
Abingdon Dr PR2 117 B1
Abingdon Gr LA3 213 A7
Abingdon Rd BB12 126 D7
Abingdon St FY1 130 B5
Abinger St BB10 148 C1
Abington Dr PR9 55 A5
Abner Row BB8 194 D1
Abraham Altham Ct
BB10 148 F3
Abraham St
Accrington BB5 104 B5
Blackburn BB2 101 E2
13 Horwich BL6 32 B4
Abrams Fold PR9 54 F5
Abrams Gn PR9 54 F5
Acacia Cl 4 FY5 176 D1
Acacia Rd PR2 118 E2
Acacia Wlk 4 BB1 102 B5
Accrington & Rossendale
Coll BB5 104 D5
Accrington & Rossendale
Coll Rawtenstall Campus
BB4 85 F2
Accrington Huncoat Prim
Sch BB5 125 F2
Accrington Rd
Blackburn BB1 102 C4
Burnley BB11 127 C5
Hapton BB11 126 E3
Whalley BB6,BB7 144 E4
Accrington Sta BB5 104 B6
Accrington Victoria Hospl
BB5 104 B7
Acer Gr PR2 118 F3
Ackhurst Bsns Pk & Ind Est
PR7 42 F8
Ackhurst La WN5 19 F2
Ackhurst Rd PR7 42 F8
Ackroyd St 10 OL14 109 B1
Acorn Appartments
FY2 152 C6
Acorn Ave BB5 103 F3
Acorn Bank PR3 181 C8
Acorn Bsns Ctr L33 1 B1
Acorn Cl Kingsfold PR1 96 B2
Lancaster LA1 214 F4
Leyland PR25 60 A8
Acorn Gdn LA3 217 C2
Acorn Mdw LA5 221 A4
Acorn Mews FY4 131 D1
Acorn St Bacup OL13 87 F2
Blackburn BB1 102 B4
Acorn Venture Urban Farm*
L33 1 D4
Acornfield Rd L33 1 D2
Acorns The L39 15 C3
Acre Ave OL13 70 D8
Acre Cl BL0 68 D3
Acre Ct 11 LA1 218 D2
Acre Gate FY4 110 E7
Acre Gr Much Hoole PR4 74 F3
Southport PR8 34 F3
Acre Mill Rd OL13 70 D8
Acre Moss La LA4 217 A4
Acre St Brierfield BB10 149 A3
Burnley BB10 148 B1
Whitworth OL12 71 D1
Acre View OL13 70 D7
Acrefield Blackburn BB2 101 A7
Clayton Brook PR5 78 C5
Newburgh WN8 27 A1
Padiham BB12 146 C1
Acregate WN8 9 C7
Acregate La PR1 118 D1
Acremount BB12 145 D2
Acres La Great Altcar L37 3 E8
Maghull L31,L39 4 E7
Preesall FY6 200 A3
Acres The BB6 144 E8
Acresbrook Rd BB12 146 F6
Acresfield Adlington PR7 30 F6
Colne BB8 172 A5
Acresfield Cl BL6 31 C3
Acreswood Cl PR7 29 E8
Active Way BB11 128 A6
Acton Rd FY4 130 E1
Ada St Blackburn BB2 101 C5
Burnley BB10 148 B1
Nelson BB9 148 E6
Ramsbottom BL0 50 B5
Adamson St
Burnley BB12 127 C6
Padiham BB12 146 C1
Addenbrooke Cl LA1 214 E4
Addington Rd LA2,LA6 237 B7
Addington St BB1 102 A4
Addison Cres FY3 130 D6
Addison Ct FY6 199 D5
Addison Rd FY7 199 A3
Addison St
Accrington BB5 104 C7
Blackburn BB2 101 C5
Addle St LA1 215 A4
Adelaide Ave FY5 153 C8
Adelaide Ct 5 FY1 130 C5
Adelaide La BB5 104 C5
Adelaide St
Accrington BB5 104 C5
Adlington PR6 31 A8
Blackpool FY1 130 B5
8 Burnley BB11 127 D6
7 Clayton-le-M BB5 125 A1
Fleetwood FY7 199 B5
Preston PR1 97 B8
2 Ramsbottom BL0 50 A4
Rawtenstall BB4 86 A7
Adelaide St W FY1 130 B4
Adelaide Terr BB2 101 C5
Adelphi Ho 1 PR1 117 E1
Adelphi Pl 2 PR1 96 F8
Adelphi St
6 Blackpool FY1 130 B5
Burnley BB11 128 A7
Lancaster LA1 215 A6
Preston PR1 117 E1
Standish WN6 29 E2
Adlington Ave FY6 153 B3
Adlington Prim Sch PR7 30 F7
Adlington South Bsns Village
PR6 31 A7
Adlington St BB11 128 A6
Adlington Sta PR6 31 A7
Admiral Cl FY8 110 E1
Admiral St BB10 128 B5
Admiral Way PR2 95 D7
Admirals Sound FY5 175 C2
Admiralty Cl L40 25 C2
Adrian St FY1 130 B1
Adstone Ave FY3 130 F7
Agate St BB1 122 F1
Ager St OL13 70 C8
Agglebys Rd FY6 176 F8
Agnes Ing La LA2 238 D7
Agnes St Blackburn BB2 101 C3
12 Preston PR1 97 A8
Agnew Rd FY7 198 F4
Agnew St FY8 91 A3
Aiken Ct PR4 114 A5
Aikengill Rd LA2 239 D4
Ailsa Ave FY4 130 F2
Ailsa Cl PR3 137 B8
Ailsa Rd BB1 102 D3
Ailsa Wlk LA3 212 E7
Aindow Ct PR8 34 E3
Ainley Ct 10 FY1 130 C6
Ainscough Brook Ho 1
PR2 118 F3
Ainscough Bsns Pk WN6 28 F6
Ainsdale & Birkdale Hills
Nature Reserve* PR8 21 B7
Ainsdale Ave
Blackpool FY2 152 E5
Brierfield BB10 148 C5
Edgworth BL7 48 E6
Fleetwood FY7 175 D7
Thornton FY5 176 D1
Ainsdale Cl LA1 218 B3
Ainsdale Dr Darwen BB3 65 B5
Preston PR2 116 E2
Whitworth OL12 52 D7
Ainsdale High Sch PR8 21 C6
Ainsdale Sand Dunes
National Nature Reserve*
PR8 20 E3
Ainsdale St John's CE Prim
Sch PR8 21 D4
Ainsdale Sta PR8 21 C5
Ainse Rd BL6 31 B3
Ainslie Cl BB6 124 B5
Ainslie Rd PR2 117 E3
Ainslie St 3 BB12 127 C6
Ainspool La PR3 181 A3
Ainsworth Ave BL6 32 E2
Ainsworth Fold PR4 113 B3
Ainsworth Mall 3 BB1 101 E5
Ainsworth St BB1 101 E5
Aintree Cres PR8 35 F4
Aintree Dr BB3 82 A7
Aintree Rd Blackpool FY4 130 D1
Thornton FY5 153 B8
Air Hill Terr 8 OL12 52 C1
Airdrie Cres BB11 127 D4
Airdrie Pl FY2 152 E6
Aire Cl LA3 217 F3
Airedale LA2 211 B4
Airedale Ave FY3 130 E3
Airedale Ct FY6 153 C4
Airegate L31 5 B2
Airey Ho PR3 163 D1
Airey St BB5 104 D3
Airton Garth BB9 170 C3
Aisled Barn Visitor Ctr*
BB8 173 A3
Aitken Cl BL0 50 B5
Aitken St Accrington BB5 104 C7
Haslingden BL0 68 C5
Ajax St 3 BL0 50 B5
Akeman Cl LA3 217 E3
Alamein Rd LA5 223 E1
Alan Gr LA3 212 F6
Alan Haigh Ct BB8 171 D6
Alan Ramsbottam Way
BB6 124 E4
Alandale Cl PR25 60 B7
Alaska St BB2 101 E2
Albany Ave FY4 110 B5
Albany Cl FY6 131 E8
Albany Ct PR7 43 E8
Albany Dr
Bamber Bridge PR5 97 D2
Copster Green BB1 122 C8
Albany High Sch PR7 43 E5
Albany Rd Blackburn BB2 101 B6
3 Fleetwood FY7 198 F4
Lytham St Anne's FY8 90 C5
Morecambe LA4 216 F4
Southport PR9 53 C1
Albany The BB3 81 E4
Albatros St PR1 118 B1
Albemarle Ct 2 BB7 166 D8
Albemarle St BB7 166 D8
Albert Ct Lancaster LA1 214 E4
Southport PR9 53 D1
Albert Ho BB4 86 D1
Albert Pl Blackburn BB3 81 F7
Southport PR8 35 B8
Albert Rd
Barnoldswick BB18 196 B2
Blackpool FY1 130 C5
Colne BB8 171 D4
Formby L37 2 B8
Fulwood PR2 117 F3
Lancaster LA1 218 D1
Leyland PR25 60 C8
Lytham St Anne's FY8 90 A7
Morecambe LA4 216 F4
Preston PR1 117 F2
Rawtenstall BB4 86 A8
Rufford L40 39 A3
Southport PR9 53 D1
Albert Sq 11 FY7 199 B5
Albert St Accrington BB5 104 C5
Blackburn BB2 101 C2
Brierfield BB9 148 B5
Burnley BB11 128 B6
Bury BL9 33 A2
3 Carnforth LA5 223 D1
Carnforth,Millhead LA5 223 D3
1 Chorley PR7 43 D7
2 Church BB5 103 E6
Clayton-le-M BB5 124 F2
Darwen BB3 65 B5
Earby BB18 197 B2
Egerton BL7 47 D3
Fleetwood FY7 199 B4
Great Harwood BB6 124 D4
Hoddlesden BB3 82 F1
Horwich BL6 32 B4
Kirkham PR4 113 F6
Lytham St Anne's FY8 91 C3
Nelson BB9 148 D8
Oswaldtwistle BB5 103 E4
Padiham BB12 126 C8
Ramsbottom BL0 50 B6
Rishton BB1 124 B1
Wheelton PR6 62 A7
Albert St continued
Whitewell Bottom BB4 86 E5
Whitworth OL12 52 C8
Albert Terr Bacup OL13 87 F3
9 Barrowford BB9 170 D3
Calder Vale PR3 182 E8
9 Preston PR1 118 A1
Rawtenstall BB4 86 B2
Southport PR8 35 A5
Alberta Cl BB2 101 B8
Albion Ave FY3 130 F6
Albion Ct BB11 127 E4
Albion Mews LA1 218 E1
Albion Mill 8 BB4 86 F2
Albion Rd Blackburn BB2 101 D1
Earby BB18 197 B2
Albion St Accrington BB5 104 B6
Bacup OL13 88 A3
7 Bacup,Stacksteads OL13 70 C8
Blackburn BB2 101 C1
Brierfield BB9 148 B5
Burnley BB11 127 E5
Chorley PR7 43 C7
1 Clitheroe BB7 166 F8
Earby BB18 197 B2
Lancaster LA1 218 E1
3 Nelson BB9 148 D8
7 Padiham BB12 126 D7
Albion Terr BB11 127 F5
Albrighton Cl PR5 77 B7
Albrighton Cres PR5 77 B7
Albrighton Rd PR5 77 C7
Albyn Bank Rd PR1 97 B7
Albyn St E PR1 97 B7
Alcester Ave PR1 96 C5
Alconbury Cres FY5 175 C2
Aldate Gr PR2 117 A2
Aldcliffe Cotts LA1 214 D5
Aldcliffe Ct LA4 217 B3
Aldcliffe Hall Dr LA1 214 D5
Aldcliffe Mews LA1 214 D5
Aldcliffe Rd
Lancaster LA1 214 E6
7 Preston PR2 116 E1
Alden Cl BB4 68 A6
Alden Rd BB4,BL8 67 F5
Alden Rise BB4 68 A6
Alden Terr 6 LA1 218 D3
Alder Ave Bury BL9 33 C3
Rawtenstall BB4 86 B2
Alder Bank
Blackburn BB2 101 B4
20 Rawtenstall BB4 86 A3
Alder Cl Leyland PR26 59 B8
Newton-w-S PR4 115 A2
Thornton FY5 176 C1
Alder Coppice PR2 116 E3
Alder Ct Fleetwood FY7 198 C2
Lancaster LA1 214 D8
Alder Dr
Charnock Richard PR7 42 D3
Gregson Lane PR5 98 E1
Alder Gr Blackpool FY3 130 E7
Coppull PR7 42 F1
Huncoat BB5 125 E2
Lancaster LA1 214 D8
Lytham St Anne's FY8 91 A4
Poulton-le-F FY6 153 D1
Alder Grange Com & Tech
Sch BB4 86 A4
Alder Hill Croft BB18 197 C2
Alder Hill St BB18 197 B2
Alder La Formby L37,L39 12 E7
Moss Edge PR3 179 A1
Parbold WN8 27 C1
Alder Meadow Cl OL12 52 A1
Alder Rd PR2 119 A4
Alder St Bacup OL13 87 F3
4 Blackburn BB1 102 A7
Burnley BB12 127 C7
Rawtenstall BB4 86 B3
Alderbank BL6 31 F3
Alderbrook Dr WN8 27 C2
Alderdale Ave PR8 21 A5
Alderfield PR1 96 D3
Alderford Cl BB7 166 C7
Alderlee Park Cvn Site
PR8 36 A2
Alderley WN8 9 C6
Alderley Ave FY4 110 B5
Alderley Hts LA1 218 D3
Alderman Foley Dr OL12 52 A2
Alderman Rd LA1 214 F4
Alderney Cl BB2 101 B1
Alders The PR3 204 C1
Aldersleigh Cres PR5 98 D1
Alderson Cres L37 11 F4
Alderville Cl PR4 92 F6
Alderway BL0 68 C1
Alderwood BB4 86 B2
Alderwood Gr BL0 68 D4
Aldfield Ave PR2 116 C1
Aldingham Ct LA4 217 B3
Aldingham Wlk LA4 217 A5
Aldon Gr PR4 95 A1
Aldon Rd FY6 153 F2
Aldren's La LA1 218 D3
Aldwych Ave FY3 130 E3
Aldwych Ct PR2 117 A2
Aldwych Dr
Bamber Bridge PR5 77 B7
Preston PR2 117 A2
Aldwych Pl BB1 122 F2
Alert St PR2 117 C1
Alexander Cl
Accrington BB5 104 E1
Burscough L40 25 F3
Alexander Ct FY6 153 D3
Alexander Dr L31 5 D3
Alexander Gr BB12 127 B6
Alexander Pl PR2 139 D1
Alexander St BB9 171 A2
Alexander Wharf 4 L31 5 C1
Alexandra Cl
Clayton-le-M BB5 124 E3
Skelmersdale WN8 17 E1
Alexandra Ct 4 LA1 214 F8
Alexandra Hall 8 LA1 214 F7
Alexandra Ho 10 PR1 118 C1
Alexandra Mews
1 Ormskirk L39 15 E6
8 Southport PR9 35 C8
Alexandra Pavilions 6
PR1 118 A1
Alexandra Pl BB6 124 D6
Alexandra Rd
Bamber Bridge PR5 97 D3
Blackburn BB2 101 C6
Blackpool FY1 130 B1
Burscough L40 25 D4
Carnforth LA5 223 D1
8 Darwen BB3 81 F2
Formby L37 11 B1
Kirkham PR4 114 A6
Lancaster LA1 218 D3
Longridge PR3 140 A7
Lytham St Anne's FY8 90 A7
Morecambe LA3 216 E3
Southport PR9 35 D8
Thornton FY5 153 C8
Alexandra Sq LA1 211 B7
Alexandra St
Clayton-le-M BB5 124 E3
Preston PR1 97 C7
Alexandra View 7 BB3 81 F2
Alexandria Dr FY8 89 F5
Alexandria St BB4 85 F4
Alford Fold PR2 117 D7
Alfred St Blackpool FY1 130 C5
Bury BL9 33 A1
Darwen BB3 65 B6
Egerton BL7 47 D3
Lancaster LA1 215 A8
10 Ramsbottom BL0 50 B5
Whitworth OL12 71 D2
Algar St 9 BB9 170 F2
Alice Ave PR25 77 A1
Alice Ingham Ct 18 OL12 52 C1
Alice Sq 5 PR1 118 A1
Alice St Accrington BB5 104 D7
Barnoldswick BB18 196 B2
8 Darwen BB3 65 A8
Morecambe LA4 217 C5
Oswaldtwistle BB5 103 E3
Alicia Ct OL12 52 E1
Alicia Dr OL12 52 E1
Alisan Rd FY6 153 B5
Alker La PR7 61 B3
Alker St PR7 43 C7
Alkincoats Rd BB8 171 C5
All Hallows RC High Sch
PR1 96 A3
All Hallows Rd FY2 152 D5
All Saint's Cl BB5 103 B4
All Saints CE Prim Sch
Appley Bridge WN6 28 C1
Clayton-le-M BB5 124 F2
All Saints Cl
Padiham BB12 126 F7
Rawtenstall BB4 106 A1
All Saints RC High Sch
BB4 85 D1
All Saints Rd FY2 152 E6
All Saints' Rd FY8 89 E6
Allan Critchlow Way
BB1 124 B2
Allan St OL13 87 F1
Allandale FY4 110 C5
Allandale Ave FY5 175 F4
Allen Cl Cleveleys FY5 175 D1
Fleetwood FY7 198 D2
Allen Ct BB10 128 A8
Allen St BB10 128 A8
Allen Way FY7 198 D2
Allenbury Pl FY3 131 A2
Allenby Ave PR2 118 B4
Allenby Rd FY8 89 E8
Allendale Gr BB10 128 F4
Allendale St
5 Burnley BB12 127 B6
Colne BB8 171 F5
Allengate PR2 117 F4
Allerton Cl BB3 82 A2
Allerton Dr BB12 127 D6
Allerton Rd
Bamber Bridge PR5 97 D4
Southport PR9 53 E1
Alleys Gn BB7 189 E1
Alleytroyds BB5 103 E5
Alliance Bsns Pk BB5 104 A5
Alliance St BB5 104 F1
Allington Cl PR5 97 E3
Allison Gr BB8 171 F6
Allonby Ave FY5 175 E4
Allotment La PR3 157 C7
Allsprings Cl BB6 124 D6
Allsprings Dr BB6 124 D6
Alma Ave BB8 194 D1
Alma Cl WN8 10 C7
Alma Ct Skelmersdale WN8 10 C7
Southport PR8 21 F7
Alma Dr PR7 42 E4
Alma Hill WN8 10 C7

Alma Hill Est WN8 ....10 C7
Alma Ho LA1 ....214 F6
Alma Ind Est 25 OL12 .....52 F1
Alma Par WN8 ....10 C7
Alma Pl Accrington BB5 ....84 E8
Clitheroe BB7 ....166 D7
Alma Rd Lancaster LA1 ...214 F6
Laneshaw Bridge BB8 ....172 D6
Skelmersdale WN8 ....10 C7
Southport PR8 ....35 A4
Alma Row PR5 ....98 E1
Alma St Bacup OL13 ....88 A2
Blackburn BB2 ....101 D5
9 Clayton-le-M BB5 ......124 F3
Padiham BB12 ....126 C8
Preston PR1 ....118 A1
13 Rochdale OL12 ....52 F1
Alma Terr BB11 ....106 B4
Almelo Ho 1 PR1 ....117 E2
Almhouses BD23 ....197 A5
Almond Ave
Burscough Bridge L40 ......25 E6
4 Bury BL9 ....33 C3
Almond Brook Rd WN6 ...29 C1
Almond Cl
Abbey Village PR6 ....80 B2
Fulwood PR2 ....118 D6
Higher Penwortham PR1 ....96 B3
Almond Cres BB4 ....68 F8
Almond St BB3 ....65 A8
Almonry The L40 ....17 B7
Almshouse Bglws L39 ......6 A6
Almshouses Aughton L39 ...6 A7
14 Lancaster LA1 ....214 F7
35 Lancaster LA1 ....214 F8
6 Rawtenstall BB4 ....85 E2
Alnwick Cl BB12 ....127 E7
Alpha St Darwen BB3 ......65 B8
10 Nelson BB9 ....170 F2
Salterforth BB18 ....194 E8
Alpic Dr FY5 ....152 C7
Alpine Ave
Bamber Bridge PR5 ....77 B7
Blackpool FY4 ....110 E5
Alpine Cl
Bamber Bridge PR5 ....77 B7
Hoddlesden BB3 ....82 E1
Alpine Gr BB2 ....81 B8
Alpine Hts PR3 ....181 B6
Alpine Lodge FY8 ....89 E5
Alpine Rd PR6 ....61 E3
Alpine View LA5 ....221 A6
Alsop St PR1 ....117 F2
Alston Ave FY5 ....175 D4
Alston Cl BB7 ....145 F7
Alston Ct Longridge PR3 ..140 B6
Southport PR8 ....21 E6
Alston Dr LA4 ....217 F5
Alston Hall Coll PR3 ....120 B8
Alston La PR3 ....140 A2
Alston Lane RC Prim Sch
PR3 ....139 F2
Alston Rd FY2 ....152 E2
Alston St PR1 ....118 D1
Alt Rd Formby L37 ....12 B2
Hightown L38 ....3 A4
Altcar La Formby L37 ......11 F1
Haskayne L39 ....14 A2
Maghull L31 ....4 F5
Runshaw Moor PR25 ......59 E5
Altcar Rd L37 ....12 B2
Altham Bsns Pk BB5 ....125 E6
Altham Cvn Pk BB5 .....125 C1
Altham Ind Est BB5 .....125 D6
Altham La BB5 ....125 F4
Altham Rd
Morecambe LA4 ....217 C3
Southport PR8 ....35 E2
Altham St
2 Burnley BB10 ....128 A8
6 Padiham BB12 ....126 D8
Altham St James CE Prim
Sch BB5 ....125 D6
Altham Wlk LA4 ....217 C3
Althorp Cl 6 FY1 ....130 C7
Althorpe Dr PR8 ....35 E3
Altom St BB1 ....101 E6
Alton Cl L38 ....2 F2
Altys La L39 ....15 F3
Alum Scar La BB2 ....100 A6
Alvern Ave PR2 ....117 D4
Alvern Cres PR2 ....117 D4
Alvina La L33 ....1 A5
Alwin St 8 BB11 ....127 E5
Alwood Ave FY3 ....130 F6
Amber Ave BB1 ....122 F2
Amber Dr PR6 ....43 E6
Amberbanks Gr FY1 .....130 B2
Ambergate Fulwood PR2 ..116 F6
Skelmersdale WN8 ....9 B7
Amberley St BB2 ....101 C2
Amberwood PR4 ....113 F5
Amberwood Dr BB2 ......101 A1
Ambledene PR5 ....78 A5
Ambleside Ave
Barnoldswick BB18 ....196 A3
3 Euxton PR7 ....60 D1
Knott End-on-S FY6 ......199 F6
2 Rawtenstall BB4 ....85 E2
Ambleside Cl
Accrington,Hillock Vale
BB5 ....104 E8
Bamber Bridge PR5 ....97 E2
Blackburn BB1 ....102 A6
Ambleside Dr BB3 ....82 C3
Ambleside Rd
Blackpool FY4 ....131 D1
Fulwood PR2 ....118 E5
Lancaster LA1 ....218 F2
Lytham St Anne's FY8 ....110 E1
Maghull L31 ....5 D2
Ambleside Wlk PR2 .....118 E5
Ambleway PR5 ....97 C4
Ambrose Hall La PR4 ...136 E3
Ambrose St PR25 ....77 B2
Amelia St BB1 ....102 B6
Amersham WN8 ....9 C7
Amersham Cl PR4 ....75 F8
Amersham Gr BB10 .....148 D4
Amethyst St BB1 ....122 F2
Amounderness Way
Cleveleys FY5 ....175 F4
Fleetwood FY7 ....199 A3
Thornton FY5 ....153 C7
Ampleforth Dr PR5 ....97 A1
Ams Trad Est PR4 ....75 D7
Amy Johnson Way FY4 ..110 E4
Amy St OL12 ....52 B1
Ancenis Ct PR4 ....114 B5
Anchor Ave BB3 ....81 F4
Anchor Ct PR1 ....96 F7
Anchor Dr PR4 ....95 D2
Anchor Gr BB3 ....81 E5
Anchor Ho 1 BB1 ....101 F4
Anchor Rd BB3 ....81 F4
Anchor Ret Pk 1 BB11 ..128 A6
Anchor St PR9 ....35 B7
Anchor Way FY8 ....110 E1
Anchorage Ave PR4 ......72 F1
Anchorage Mews FY7 ...199 B3
Anchorage Rd FY7 ......199 B3
Anchorsholme La
Cleveleys FY5 ....152 F8
Thornton FY5 ....153 A8
Anchorsholme La E FY5 .175 E1
Anchorsholme La W
FY5 ....175 C1
Anchorsholme Prim Sch
FY5 ....152 E8
Ancliffe La LA2,LA5 .....221 B2
Andelen Cl BB11 ....126 C3
Anders Dr L33 ....1 A5
Anderson Cl Bacup OL13 ..87 F1
Lancaster LA1 ....215 B6
Anderson Rd BB1 ....123 A7
Anderson St 9 FY1 .....130 C4
Anderton Cl BB4 ....69 F7
Anderton La BL6 ....31 E4
Anderton Prim Sch PR6 ..31 B8
Anderton Rd Euxton PR7 ..60 D1
Higham BB12 ....146 F5
Anderton St Adlington PR7 .31 A7
Chorley PR7 ....43 C7
Anderton Way PR3 .....181 D6
Andertons Way PR2 ....118 D5
Andreas Cl PR8 ....35 B4
Andrew Ave BB4 ....85 F1
Andrew Cl Blackburn BB2 ..81 B8
Ramsbottom BL8 ....49 F1
Andrew Rd BB9 ....171 B1
Andrew St Bury BL9 ......33 A2
Preston PR1 ....118 C1
Andrews Cl L37 ....11 E1
Andrews La L37 ....11 E1
Andrews Yort L37 ....11 E1
Anemone Dr BB4 ....67 F8
Angel Way 3 BB8 ....171 E5
Angela St BB2 ....101 B1
Angelbank BL6 ....31 F2
Anger's Hill Rd FY4 .....130 F1
Angle St BB10 ....128 A8
Anglesey Ave BB12 .....127 A7
Anglesey St BB2 ....81 B8
Anglezarke Rd PR6 ....31 A7
Anglezarke Woodland Trail*
PR6 ....44 D6
Anglian Cl BB5 ....103 C5
Angus St OL13 ....70 C8
Aniline St PR6 ....43 E8
Ann St Barrowford BB9 ...170 D3
Brierfield BB9 ....148 B6
4 Clayton-le-M BB5 ......124 F3
Skelmersdale WN8 ....8 E8
Anna's Rd FY4 ....111 E3
Annan Cres FY4 ....131 C1
Annandale Gdns WN8 ....10 A7
Annarly Fold BB10 .....129 A5
Annaside Cl 2 FY4 .....110 E7
Anne Ave PR8 ....21 E6
Anne Cl 6 BB10 ....128 B5
Anne St 2 BB11 ....128 B5
Annesley Ave FY3 ....130 E8
Annie St Accrington BB5 ..104 C7
Ramsbottom BL0 ....50 A4
5 Rawtenstall BB4 ....86 A2
Annis St PR1 ....97 C8
Ansbro Ave PR4 ....93 C6
Ansdell & Fairhaven Sta
FY8 ....90 D4
Ansdell Gr Fulwood PR2 ..117 C3
Southport PR9 ....54 A4
Ansdell Prim Sch FY8 ....90 C5
Ansdell Rd Blackpool FY1 .130 D2
Horwich BL6 ....32 C4
Ansdell Rd N FY8 ....90 D4
Ansdell Rd S FY8 ....90 D3
Ansdell St 3 PR1 ....118 C1
Ansdell Terr BB2 ....101 E1
Anselm Ct FY2 ....152 B3
Anshaw Cl BL7 ....46 C5
Anson Cl FY8 ....110 D1
Anson Rd PR4 ....114 B2
Anstable Rd LA4 ....217 E5
Anthony Rd LA1 ....214 E7
Antigua Dr BB3 ....81 F6
Antrim Rd FY2 ....152 C1
Anvil Cl WN5 ....10 D5
Anvil St OL13 ....70 E8
Anyon La LA2 ....207 E6
Anyon St BB3 ....82 B2
Anzio Rd PR4 ....132 E5
Apartments The PR9 .....35 B8
Apiary The PR26 ....58 A6
Appealing La FY8 ......110 E2
Apple Cl 2 BB2 ....101 C4
Apple Ct 3 BB2 ....101 C4
Apple St BB2 ....101 C4
Apple Tree Cl Euxton PR7 ..60 D3
St Michael's on W PR3 ....157 C8
Apple Tree Way BB5 ....103 E5
Appleby Bsns Ctr BB1 ...102 A5
Appleby Cl
Accrington BB5 ....104 D5
Gregson Lane PR5 ....98 E1
Appleby Dr BB9 ....170 D4
Appleby Rd FY2 ....152 D1
Appleby St
Blackburn BB1 ....102 A5
Nelson BB9 ....148 D8
Preston PR1 ....117 F1
Applecross Dr BB10 ....128 E4
Applefields PR25 ....60 B7
Applegarth
Barnoldswick BB18 ......196 C3
Barrowford BB9 ....170 B1
Applegarth Rd LA3 .....213 A8
Applegarth St 3 BB18 ..197 B1
Applesike PR4 ....95 A1
Appleton Cl FY6 ....153 A2
Appleton Rd WN8 ....17 F2
Appletree Cl
Kingsfold PR1 ....96 C2
Lancaster LA1 ....215 A3
Appletree Dr LA1 ......215 A3
Applewood Cl FY8 ....90 F3
Appley Bridge Sta WN6 ..19 C7
Appley Cl WN6 ....28 C2
Appley La N WN6 ....28 C1
Appley La S WN6,WN8 ....19 C6
Approach Way BB11 .....127 F2
Apsley Brow L31 ....5 B1
Apsley Fold PR3 ....140 B6
Aquaduct Street Ind Est
PR1 ....117 D1
Aqueduct Mill PR1 ......117 D1
Aqueduct Rd BB2 ....101 D1
Aqueduct St PR1 ....117 E1
Arago St BB5 ....104 C7
Aragon Cl L31 ....5 E3
Arbories Ave 4 BB12 ...126 B8
Arbory Dr BB12 ....126 B8
Arbory The PR4 ....112 E7
Arbour Dr BB2 ....81 D6
Arbour La Kirkby L33 ......1 B2
Shevington Moor WN6 .....29 B1
Arbour Lane End PR3 ...162 E7
Arbour St 11 Bacup OL13 ..88 A3
Southport PR8 ....35 C6
Arboury St BB12 ....126 B8
Arcade BB5 ....104 C5
Arcadia 9 BB8 ....171 E5
Arcadia Ave L31 ....5 D3
Arch St Burnley BB11 ...127 F6
4 Darwen BB3 ....82 A1
Archbishop Temple CE High
Sch & tech Coll PR2 ...117 F5
Archer Hill LA5 ....223 D3
Archery Ave BB8 ....194 D1
Archery Gdns PR3 ......181 C8
Arches The BB7 ....144 B6
Arcon Ho 5 Coppull PR7 ..42 E1
Lancaster LA1 ....214 F5
Lytham St Anne's FY8 .....91 B4
Arcon Rd PR7 ....42 E1
Ardee Rd PR1 ....96 D6
Arden Cl Slyne LA2 ......218 C8
Southport PR8 ....21 A5
Arden Gn FY7 ....198 E4
Ardengate LA1 ....214 F4
Ardleigh Ave PR8 ....35 E3
Ardley Rd BL6 ....32 C4
Ardmore Rd FY2 ....152 D2
Ardwick St BB10 ....128 A8
Argameols Cl PR8 ....35 F5
Argarmeols Gr L37 ......11 E5
Argarmeols Rd L37 ......11 E6
Argosy Ave FY3 ....130 F8
Argosy Ct 1 FY3 ....131 A8
Argyle Ct PR9 ....53 D1
Argyle Rd 7 Leyland PR25 .77 A1
Poulton-le-F FY6 ....153 E3
Southport PR9 ....53 D2
Argyle St Accrington BB5 .104 B6
8 Colne BB8 ....171 D5
Darwen BB3 ....81 F3
Heywood OL10 ....33 F1
3 Lancaster LA1 ....215 A7
Argyll Ct FY2 ....152 C1
Argyll Rd Blackpool FY2 ..152 C1
Preston PR1 ....118 A1
Ariel Way FY7 ....198 E4
Arkholme Ave FY1 ......130 D2
Arkholme CE Prim Sch
LA6 ....241 B3
Arkholme Cl LA5 ....223 E2
Arkholme Ct LA4 ....217 B3
Arkholme Dr PR4 ....94 F1
Arkwright Ct FY4 ......111 C7
Arkwright Fold BB2 .....81 C8
Arkwright Rd PR1 ......117 F2
Arkwright St
Burnley BB12 ....127 C7
Horwich BL6 ....32 C2
Arley Gdns BB12 ....127 F7
Arley La WN1,WN2 ....30 D2
Arley Rise BB2 ....121 E2
Arley St PR6 ....43 D8
Arley Wood Dr PR7 ......43 A6
Arlington Ave FY4 .....110 B7
Arlington Cl
Ramsbottom BL9 ....50 C2
Southport PR8 ....21 A5
Arlington Rd BB3 ....64 F8
Armadale Rd FY2 ....152 E1
Armaside Rd PR4 ....116 D4
Armitstead Ct 8 FY7 ...198 F2
Armitstead Way 5 FY7 ..198 F2
Armstrong St Horwich BL6 .32 C2
Preston PR2 ....117 B2
Arncliffe Ave BB5 ......103 F4
Arncliffe Gr BB9 ....170 C3
Arncliffe Rd
Burnley BB10 ....128 E5
Morecambe LA3 ....216 D1
Arndale Cl FY7 ....198 C2
Arndale Ctr
Morecambe LA4 ....217 A5
6 Nelson BB9 ....148 E8
Arndale Rd PR3 ....140 A7
Arnhem Rd
Carnforth LA5 ....223 E1
Preston PR1 ....97 D8
Arnian Ct L39 ....6 C7
Arno St 9 PR1 ....97 B7
Arnold Ave FY4 ....110 C7
Arnold Cl Blackburn BB2 ..102 A1
Brierfield BB9 ....148 C5
Burnley BB11 ....127 E2
Fulwood PR2 ....118 E2
Arnold Pl 1 PR7 ....43 A5
Arnold Rd FY8 ....91 D4
Arnold Sch FY4 ....110 C7
Arnold St 2 BB5 ....104 C6
Arnott Rd Blackpool FY4 ..130 E1
Fulwood PR2 ....117 C2
Arnside Ave
Blackpool FY1 ....130 D1
Lytham St Anne's FY8 .....90 C7
Arnside Cl
Clayton-le-M BB5 ....124 E2
Coupe Green PR5 ....98 E4
Lancaster LA1 ....215 B3
Arnside Cres
Blackburn BB2 ....80 E8
Morecambe LA4 ....217 C6
Arnside Rd
Broughton PR3 ....137 D2
Preston PR2 ....116 E2
Southport PR9 ....35 C7
Arnside Terr PR9 ....35 C7
Arran Ave BB1 ....102 D2
Arran Cl LA3 ....212 E7
Arran St BB11 ....127 D5
Arrow La LA2 ....219 D7
Arrowsmith Cl PR5 ......98 E2
Arrowsmith Ct 7 BL6 ....32 E1
Arrowsmith Dr PR5 ......98 E2
Arrowsmith Gdns FY5 ...175 E5
Arroyo Way PR2 ....118 B4
Arthur St Bacup OL13 ....88 B3
Barnoldswick BB18 ......196 A3
Blackburn BB2 ....101 C4
Brierfield BB9 ....148 B6
Burnley BB11 ....127 E6
Clayton-le-M BB5 ....124 F3
Earby BB18 ....195 A7
6 Fleetwood FY7 ....199 B5
Great Harwood BB6 .....124 D6
18 Nelson BB9 ....170 E1
Preston PR1 ....96 E7
Arthur St N 5 FY7 .....199 B5
Arthur Way BB2 ....101 C4
Arthurs La FY6 ....177 D2
Artle Pl LA1 ....218 C2
Artlebeck Cl LA2 ....237 C3
Artlebeck Gr LA2 ....237 C3
Artlebeck Rd LA2 ....237 C3
Arundel Ave FY2 ....152 B5
Arundel Dr FY6 ....153 C5
Arundel Pl 35 PR1 ....97 A7
Arundel Rd Longton PR4 ..95 A1
Lytham St Anne's FY8 ....90 C4
Southport PR8 ....21 F8
Arundel St BB1 ....124 A2
Arundel Way PR25 ....60 C8
Ascot Cl Lancaster LA1 ..215 B4
Southport PR8 ....34 E5
Ascot Gdns LA2 ....218 D8
Ascot Rd Blackpool FY3 ..130 E6
Thornton FY5 ....153 B8
Ascot Way BB5 ....104 D5
Ash Ave Galgate LA2 .....210 F4
Haslingden BB4 ....85 C3
Kirkham PR4 ....114 A4
Ash Bank Cl PR3 ......137 B8
Ash Brow WN8 ....27 B1
Ash Cl Appley Bridge WN6 ..19 D7
Barrow BB7 ....166 D1
Elswick PR4 ....156 A1
Ormskirk L39 ....15 D5
Rishton BB1 ....103 B8
Ash Coppice PR2 ......116 D2
Ash Ct PR4 ....115 D2
Ash Dr Freckleton PR4 ....93 A5
Poulton-le-F FY6 ....153 E2
Thornton FY5 ....176 C1
Warton LA5 ....223 E6
Warton PR4 ....92 D6
Ash Dr *continued*
West Bradford BB7 ......189 D7
Ash Field PR6 ....78 C3
Ash Gr Bamber Bridge PR5 ..97 F1
Barnoldswick BB18 ......196 B2
Chorley PR7 ....43 C5
Darwen BB3 ....82 B2
Formby L37 ....11 C1
Garstang PR3 ....181 B8
8 Horwich BL6 ....32 E1
Kirkham PR4 ....114 B7
Lancaster LA1 ....214 F5
Longton PR4 ....74 F8
New Longton PR4 ....75 F6
Orrell WN5 ....10 F6
Preesall FY6 ....200 A4
Ramsbottom BL0 ....49 F3
3 Rawtenstall BB4 ....86 A3
Skelmersdale WN8 ....17 D1
St Michael's on W PR3 ...157 C7
Water BB4 ....87 A8
Wrea Green PR4 ....113 C3
Ash Holme PR1 ....118 C3
Ash La Clifton PR4 .....115 E2
Great Harwood BB6 .....124 B6
Longridge PR3 ....140 B8
Ash Lea Gr FY6 ....177 C7
Ash Mdw PR2 ....116 E3
Ash Rd Coppull PR7 ......29 E8
Elswick PR4 ....156 A1
Ash St Bacup OL13 ....87 F3
Blackburn BB1 ....102 A7
Blackpool FY4 ....110 C6
Burnley BB11 ....128 B5
Bury BL9 ....33 A2
Fleetwood FY7 ....199 A4
Great Harwood BB6 .....124 C6
Nelson BB9 ....148 F8
Oswaldtwistle BB5 ......103 D4
Southport PR8 ....35 C5
Trawden BB8 ....172 C2
Ash Tree Gr
Hest Bank LA5 ....220 F3
Nelson BB9 ....149 A7
Ash Tree Wlk 18 BB9 ...170 D3
Ashborne Dr BL9 ....50 D2
Ashbourne Cl 7 LA1 ....218 D3
Ashbourne Cres PR2 ....117 A5
Ashbourne Dr LA1 ......218 D3
Ashbourne Gr LA3 ......217 C2
Ashbourne Rd LA1 .....218 D3
Ashbrook Cl PR4 ....73 E3
Ashbrook St LA1 ....214 D8
Ashburn Cl BL6 ....32 D1
Ashburnham Rd BB8 ....171 A2
Ashburton Ct 7 FY1 ....130 B7
Ashburton Rd FY1 .....130 B7
Ashby St PR7 ....43 D6
Ashcombe Gate FY5 ....153 D7
Ashcroft LA3 ....216 E1
Ashcroft Ave L39 ....15 F6
Ashcroft Cl LA2 ....237 B3
Ashcroft Pl BB7 ....189 E5
Ashcroft Rd Formby L37 ...11 F1
Kirkby L33 ....1 C3
Ashdale Cl Coppull PR7 ...29 D8
Formby L37 ....11 C2
Ashdale Gr FY5 ....176 E2
Ashdale Pl LA1 ....218 C2
Ashdene OL12 ....52 D4
Ashdown Cl Carleton FY6 .153 B5
Southport PR8 ....35 E4
Ashdown Dr PR6 ....78 C2
Ashdown Mews PR2 ....118 E6
Asheldon St 1 PR1 .....118 D1
Ashen Bottom BB4 ....68 D6
Ashendean View BB12 ..146 D1
Ashfield PR2 ....117 F8
Ashfield Ave
Lancaster LA1 ....214 D7
Morecambe LA4 ....217 F6
Ashfield Cl BB9 ....170 C1
Ashfield Cotts 2 LA2 ...239 D8
Ashfield Ct Blackpool FY2 .152 E6
Fulwood PR2 ....116 F6
Ashfield Rd Adlington PR6 .31 B8
Blackpool FY2,FY5 ....152 E6
Burnley BB11 ....127 F6
Chorley PR7 ....43 B7
Ashfield Rise PR3 ......181 D2
Ashfield Terr WN6 ....19 C8
Ashfields PR26 ....76 B1
Ashford Ave LA1 ....214 E3
Ashford Cl LA1 ....214 F3
Ashford Cres PR3 ......137 C3
Ashford Rd
Lancaster LA1 ....214 F3
Preston PR2 ....116 E2
Ashford St Heywood OL10 ..33 F2
Nelson BB9 ....148 E7
Ashgrove PR1 ....118 E1
Ashiana Lodge 15 BB9 ..148 E8
Ashlands Cl BL0 ....68 D2
Ashleigh Ct PR2 ....118 A7
Ashleigh Mews FY3 .....130 E4
Ashleigh Prim Sch BB3 ..65 A6
Ashleigh St Darwen BB3 ..65 B6
Preston PR1 ....97 C7
Ashley Cl Blackpool FY2 ..152 D2
Thornton FY5 ....153 B7
Ashley Ct Accrington BB5 .103 F5
Poulton-le-F FY6 ....153 C3
Whitworth OL12 ....71 D2
Ashley Gdns LA2 ....211 A3
Ashley La PR3 ....139 C8
Ashley Mews PR2 ......117 C1
Ashley Rd
Lytham St Anne's FY8 ....110 F1

Ashley Rd continued
Skelmersdale WN8 18 B3
Southport PR9 35 C7
Ashley St BB12 127 F7
Ashmead Rd WN8 18 A4
Ashmead View WN8 18 A4
Ashmeadow Gr LA6 221 F5
Ashmeadow La PR6 62 F8
Ashmeadow Rd LA6 221 F5
Ashmoor St PR1 117 E1
Ashmore Gr FY5 175 D1
Ashmount Dr OL12 52 F2
Ashness Cl Fulwood PR2 117 F8
Horwich BL6 31 F3
Ashton Ave FY6 199 D5
Ashton Cl PR2 96 A8
Ashton Ct
Knott End-on-S FY6 199 D5
Lancaster LA1 214 F7
Ashton Dr Lancaster LA1 218 C2
Nelson BB9 148 F6
Ashton Garden Ct FY8 89 E7
Ashton Ho BB3 65 B8
Ashton La BB3 65 A8
Ashton Meml* LA1 215 B7
Ashton Prim Sch PR2 116 E2
Ashton Rd Blackpool FY1 130 C3
8 Darwen BB3 65 B8
Lancaster LA1,LA2 214 E4
Morecambe LA4 217 C5
Southport PR8 34 F1
Ashton St Longridge PR3 140 A8
8 Lytham St Anne's FY8 91 A3
7 Preston PR2 96 D8
Ashton Wlk 12 LA1 214 F8
Ashton-on-Ribble High Sch
PR2 116 F2
Ashtongate PR2 116 F1
Ashtree Ct Fulwood PR2 117 A4
Higher Walton PR5 98 C3
Ashtree Gr PR1 96 B4
Ashtrees L40 40 C2
Ashtrees Way 2 LA5 223 D2
Ashurst Cl WN8 18 A4
Ashurst Ct L37 11 E2
Ashurst Gdns WN8 18 B4
Ashurst Rd
Clayton-le-W PR25 77 D1
Shevington Moor WN6 29 B2
Skelmersdale WN8 18 B4
Ashville Terr BB2 81 D8
Ashwall St WN8 8 E8
Ashwell Pl FY5 152 C7
Ashwood WN8 18 C3
Ashwood Ave
Blackburn BB3 81 D6
Ramsbottom BL0 50 D7
Ashwood Cl FY8 90 E4
Ashwood Ct LA1 214 F5
Ashwood Rd PR2 117 D7
Ashworth Cl BB2 101 C5
Ashworth Ct
5 Blackpool FY3 130 D7
Preston PR1 97 B6
Ashworth Dr LA2 220 E2
Ashworth Gr PR1 97 C6
Ashworth Hospl L31 6 B2
Ashworth La
Newchurch BB4 86 F3
Preston PR1 97 C6
Ashworth Rd
Blackpool FY4 111 C8
Newchurch BB4 86 F2
Rochdale OL11 51 E2
Ashworth St
Accrington BB5 104 E2
16 Bacup OL13 88 A3
6 Bacup,Stacksteads OL13 70 D8
3 Bamber Bridge PR5 97 F2
Forest Holme BB4 87 A7
1 Preston PR1 97 B7
Rawtenstall BB4 69 F8
3 Rishton BB1 124 B1
Ashworth Terr
2 Bacup OL13 70 B8
7 Darwen BB3 82 A1
Askrigg Cl
Accrington BB5 104 E5
Blackpool FY4 111 A7
Asland Cl PR5 77 F8
Asland Gdns PR9 54 C4
Asmall Cl L39 15 D6
Asmall La
Haskayne L39,L40 14 E8
Ormskirk L39,L40 15 B7
Aspden St PR5 97 E1
Aspels Cres PR1 96 C4
Aspels Nook PR1 96 C4
Aspels The PR1 96 C4
Aspen Dr BB10 128 C7
Aspen Fold BB5 103 B5
Aspen Gdns
3 Chorley PR7 43 B6
Rochdale OL12 52 A1
Aspen Gr L37 11 C1
Aspen La Earby BB18 197 B2
Oswaldtwistle BB5 103 C4
Aspendale Cl PR4 74 F8
Aspinall Cl Horwich BL6 32 C1
Kingsfold PR1 96 D2
Aspinall Cres L37 12 F1
Aspinall Ct BL6 32 C2
Aspinall Fold BB1 101 E8
Aspinall Rd WN6 29 B1
Aspinall St BL6 32 D1
Aspinall Way BL6 32 C1
Aspley Gr BB8 172 C3
Asshawes The PR6 43 F1
Assheton Pl PR2 118 E4
Assheton Rd BB2 101 A5
Asten Bldgs BB4 69 F7
Aster Ch BB3 82 A7
Astland Gdns PR4 73 F2
Astland St FY8 89 E6
Astley Cres PR4 93 C6
Astley Ct LA1 214 D6
Astley Ctr The 2 PR7 43 D6
Astley Gate BB2 101 E5
Astley Hall* PR7 61 A1
Astley Hall Dr BL0 50 C4
Astley Ho BB11 128 B6
Astley Hts BB3 65 A7
Astley Rd PR7 61 C1
Astley St Chorley PR7 61 C1
Darwen BB3 65 A7
Longridge PR3 140 A7
Astley Terr BB3 65 A7
Aston Ave FY5 176 A2
Aston Manor PR9 55 A5
Aston St PR4 132 E6
Aston Way PR26 76 C2
Aston Wlk BB2 82 A8
Asturian Gate PR3 140 F6
Athelstan Fold PR2 117 C3
Athens View BB10 128 C5
Atherton Rd PR25 59 D8
Atherton St Adlington PR7 31 A6
Bacup OL13 70 C8
Atherton Way OL13 70 B8
Athletic St BB10 128 C5
Athlone Ave FY2 152 C2
Athol Gr PR6 43 E6
Athol St Nelson BB9 148 F8
Ramsbottom BL0 50 C7
Athol St N BB11 127 D5
Athol St S BB11 127 D5
Athole Gr PR9 35 F7
Atholl St 12 PR1 96 D8
Atkinson Art Gal PR8 35 B7
Atkinson Cl 15 PR1 96 F8
Atkinson Liby PR8 35 B7
Atkinson St
Brierfield BB10 148 F3
Colne BB8 171 C3
Colne BB8 171 D4
Atlas Rd BB3 82 B1
Atlas St BB5 125 A1
Atrium Ct 10 BB11 128 B4
Aubigny Dr PR2 117 D4
Auburn Gr FY1 130 D2
Auckland St BB3 65 B7
Audenlea FY5 175 F3
Audenshaw Rd LA4 217 C4
Audley Cl
Lytham St Anne's FY8 90 D5
14 Nelson BB9 148 E8
Audley Inf & Jun Schs
BB1 102 A3
Audley La BB1 102 A4
Audley Range BB1 102 B4
Audley St BB1 102 A5
Audlum Ct 5 BL9 33 A2
Aughton Brow LA2 237 E6
Aughton Christ Church CE
Prim Sch L39 15 C3
Aughton Ct LA1 218 D4
Aughton Hall Cotts L39 15 C6
Aughton Mews PR8 35 A5
Aughton Park Dr L39 15 D2
Aughton Park Sta L39 15 D2
Aughton Rd Aughton LA2 237 E6
Southport PR8 35 A5
Aughton St
Fleetwood FY7 199 B5
Ormskirk L39 15 E4
Aughton St Michael's CE
Prim Sch L39 15 B1
Aughton Town Green Sch
L39 6 C8
Aughton Wlk 2 PR1 117 F1
Augusta Cl OL12 52 E2
Augusta St
Accrington BB5 104 C4
Rochdale OL12 52 E1
Auster Cres PR4 114 B2
Austin Cres PR2 117 B4
Austin Gr FY1 130 B1
Austin St 6 Bacup OL13 87 F2
5 Burnley BB11 127 E5
Austin Way FY4 112 A7
Austin's La BL6 32 F1
Austins Cl PR25 60 A8
Austwick Rd 4 LA1 218 B2
Austwick Way BB5 104 E5
Avallon Way BB3 82 C1
Avalon Cl 5 BB12 126 F7
Avalon Dr PR4 93 C7
Avalwood Ave PR4 75 B8
Avebury Cl Blackburn BB2 82 A8
Horwich BL6 32 F1
Aveling Dr PR9 55 A6
Avelon Cl L31 5 B5
Avenham Cl PR9 55 B5
Avenham Colonnade
PR1 97 A6
Avenham Ct 19 PR1 97 A7
Avenham Gr 5 FY1 130 B6
Avenham La PR1 97 A7
Avenham Pl
Newton-w-S PR4 114 F2
6 Preston PR1 97 A6
Avenham Rd
1 Chorley PR7 43 C7
Preston PR1 97 A7
Avenham St PR1 97 A7
Avenham Terr 11 PR1 97 A6
Avenue Par BB5 104 D6
Avenue Rd
Hurst Green BB7 164 E1
Normoss FY3 131 B7
Avenue The Adlington PR6 31 A8
Banks PR9 54 F5
Barley BB12 169 C5
Burnley BB10,BB11 128 D3
Carleton FY6 153 C4
Churchtown PR3 181 A3
Fulwood PR2 117 A6
Garstang PR3 204 B1
Higher Penwortham PR1 96 B5
Leyland PR25 60 A6
Ormskirk L39 15 D6
Ormskirk L39 15 E6
Orrell WN5 10 D3
Preston PR2 116 D1
Southport PR8 36 F5
Avery Gdns FY6 153 B6
Aviemore Cl
5 Blackburn BB1 102 A4
2 Ramsbottom BL0 50 A2
Avocet Ct PR26 76 A1
Avon Ave FY7 175 D8
Avon Bridge PR2 117 C8
Avon Cl BB2 101 D3
Avon Ct BB12 127 D7
Avon Dr
Barnoldswick BB18 196 C3
Bury BL9 33 A8
Avon Gdns PR4 116 D5
Avon Gn FY7 198 E4
Avon Ho 12 PR1 97 D8
Avon Pl FY1 130 C8
Avon St FY8 89 E6
Avondale Ave
Blackburn BB1 102 E5
Burnley BB12 127 C7
Avondale Cl BB3 81 E2
Avondale Cres FY4 110 F7
Avondale Dr
Bamber Bridge PR5 77 B8
Ramsbottom BL0 49 F3
Tarleton PR4 57 A8
Avondale Mews BB3 81 E3
Avondale Prim Sch BB3 81 E2
Avondale Rd Chorley PR7 43 C7
Darwen BB3 81 E3
Lancaster LA1 215 A6
Lytham St Anne's FY8 89 C8
Morecambe LA3 216 E3
Nelson BB9 148 D7
Southport PR9 35 B8
Avondale Rd N PR9 53 C1
Avondale St Colne BB8 172 A5
Standish WN6 29 E2
Avondale The PR9 53 B1
Avonhead Cl BL6 31 F3
Avonside Ave FY5 176 A3
Avonwood Cl BB3 81 E2
Avroe Cres FY4 110 D4
Axeholme Ct BL6 31 F3
Aylesbury Ave FY4 130 D1
Aylesbury Ho L31 5 B4
Aylesbury Wlk BB10 148 D3
Ayr Cl PR8 35 F4
Ayr Ct FY7 175 E7
Ayr Gr BB11 127 D3
Ayr Rd BB1 102 D3
Ayr St LA1 215 B7
Ayrefield Gr WN6 19 D6
Ayrefield La WN8 19 C4
Ayrton Ave FY4 110 D7
Ayrton St BB8 171 E5
Ayrton View LA2 218 E4
Ays-Garth Rd LA1 214 D8
Aysgarth Ave PR2 117 F7
Aysgarth Ct 1 FY4 110 F7
Aysgarth Dr
Accrington BB5 104 D6
Darwen BB3 81 E2
Lancaster LA1 218 D4
Azalea Cl
Clayton-le-W PR25 77 E2
Fulwood PR2 118 C6
Azalea Gr LA4 217 E5
Azalea Rd BB2 101 B6

B

Babbacombe Ave FY4 110 B6
Babylon La PR6 31 B8
Back Albert Rd BB8 171 D4
Back Albert St Bury BL9 33 A2
10 Padiham BB12 126 C8
Back Alfred St 11 BL0 50 B5
Back Altham St 5
BB12 126 D8
Back Andrew St 14 BL9 33 A2
Back Andrew St N 13
BL9 33 A2
Back Arthur St 15 BB5 124 F3
Back Ash St 8 BL9 33 A2
Back Ashburton Rd 14
FY1 130 C7
Back Ashby St 1 PR7 43 D6
Back Atkinson St BB8 171 C4
Back Avondale Rd (E)
LA3 216 E3
Back Avondale Rd (W)
LA3 216 E3
Back Bath St PR8 35 B8
Back Bell La 8 Bury BL9 33 A3
Bury BL9 33 B3
Back Benson St BL9 33 A1
Back Blackburn Rd E
BL7 47 D3
Back Bolton Rd BB3 65 B7
Back Bond St BB8 171 D5
Back Bond St W BL9 33 A2
Back Boundary St 14
BB8 171 D4
Back Bourne's Row PR5 98 E1
Back Bridge St 2 BL0 50 C6
Back Broading Terr
BB4 106 A3
Back Brook St N 13 BL9 33 A4
Back Brow WN8 10 C7
Back Brown St BB8 171 C4
Back Burnley Rd BB5 104 C6
Back Calton St LA4 217 B6
Back Cambridge St 10
BB8 171 D4
Back Canada St 3 BL6 32 B3
Back Carr Mill St BB4 85 B5
Back Cedar St 2 BL9 33 B3
Back Cedar St N 1 BL9 33 B3
Back Cemetery Terr 12
OL13 70 D8
Back Chapel St
1 Barnoldswick BB18 196 B2
4 Colne BB8 171 D4
Horwich BL6 32 C3
Back Chesham Rd N 5
BL9 33 A4
Back Chesham Rd S 7
BL9 33 A4
Back Chester St BL9 33 A4
Back Church St
Barrowford BB9 170 D3
8 Blackpool FY1 130 B5
5 Great Harwood BB6 124 C5
3 Hapton BB12 126 C4
1 Newchurch BB4 86 E1
Back Clarendon Rd FY1 130 B2
Back Clayton St 9 BB9 170 D1
Back Club St PR5 77 E7
Back Colne Rd BB18 196 A1
Back Commons BB7 189 D1
Back Constablelee BB4 85 F4
Back Cookson St 12
FY1 130 C6
Back Cop La FY7 199 A4
Back Cowm La OL12 71 C3
Back Crescent St LA4 217 A5
Back Crown St BL6 32 A4
Back Curzon St FY8 90 A7
Back Darwen Rd N BL7 47 E1
Back Deal St BL9 33 B2
Back Delamere St N BL9 33 A5
Back Delamere St S BL9 33 A5
Back Derby St 6 BB8 171 D5
Back Drinkhouse La
PR26 58 B1
Back Duckworth St
4 Bury BL9 33 A4
12 Darwen BB3 82 A1
Back Duke St 1 BB8 171 D4
Back Duncan St BL6 32 C3
Back Earl St 2 BB8 171 D4
Back East Bank 1 BB9 170 D4
Back Eaves St FY1 130 B7
Back Elm St 10 BL9 33 B2
Back Emmett St BL6 32 B3
Back Epsom Rd FY5 152 F8
Back Fazakerley St 14
PR7 43 C8
Back Fir St BL9 33 B2
Back Fletcher St BL9 33 A2
Back Forest Rd PR8 35 D6
Back Garston St BL9 33 A4
Back George St BL6 32 C3
Back Gisburn Rd BB9 170 E7
Back Glen Eldon Rd FY8 89 E7
Back Green St LA4 217 B6
Back Grimshaw St 8
PR1 97 A7
Back Grove Terr 10 LA4 217 F4
Back Hall St BB8 171 D4
Back Halstead St 2 BL9 33 A4
Back Hamilton St 1 BL9 33 A4
Back Harry St BB9 170 D3
Back Haslam St BL9 33 A4
Back Headroomgate Rd
FY8 89 F8
Back Heys BB5 103 E3
Back Heywood St E 15
BL9 33 A2
Back Heywood St W BL9 33 A1
Back High St Belmont BL7 46 C5
Blackpool FY1 130 B6
Chapeltown BL7 48 C4
Back Hill St 15 BB4 86 A7
Back Holly St BL9 33 A2
Back Holly St S 9 BL9 33 A2
Back Hope St OL13 87 F4
Back Hunter St 1 LA5 223 D2
Back Huntley Mount Rd
BL9 33 B3
Back Hurst St BL9 33 A1
Back Ingham St BL9 33 A1
Back Ingham St E BL9 33 A1
Back Kershaw St 10 BL9 33 A2
Back Knowlys Rd 2
LA3 212 F8
Back La Accrington BB5 104 E1
Appley Bridge WN6 19 E8
Bolton Green PR7 42 B7
Bretherton PR26 57 E5
Burscough Bridge L40 25 E6
Carnforth LA5,LA6 221 E7
Clayton Green PR6 78 A2
Clayton Green PR6 78 B1
Back La continued
Cumeragh Village PR3 139 B6
Gisburn BB7 231 C3
Great Eccleston PR3 156 B5
Greenhalgh PR4 133 B4
Grindleton BB7 190 B8
Haskayne L39 13 D3
Higham BB12 146 E6
Leyland PR25 60 C7
Longridge PR3 161 B6
Longton PR4 74 E8
Maghull L39 5 E6
Mawdesley L40 40 D1
Nelson BB10 149 F7
Newburgh L40,WN8 26 E2
Newton BB7 228 F6
Preesall FY6 200 A2
Rathmell BD24 236 F6
Rawtenstall BB4 86 A3
Rimington BB7 191 E8
Royal Oak L39 7 B2
Sabden BB12,BB7 146 C6
Skelmersdale,Digmoor WN8 9 D6
Skelmersdale,Holland Moor
WN8 9 E7
Stalmine FY6 177 E6
Trawden BB8 172 B2
Tunstall LA6 241 D4
Warton LA5 223 D5
Whitworth OL12 71 C3
Wiswell BB7 144 F8
Wray LA2 238 C6
Wrayton LA6 241 E2
Back La E L40 40 F1
Back Lathom St 9 BL9 33 A4
Back Laurel St 2 BL9 33 B2
Back Leach St BB8 171 C4
Back Lee St BB4 85 B2
Back Lines St 2 LA4 217 B5
Back Longworth Rd BL7 47 D3
Back Lord St
Blackpool FY1 130 B6
7 Lancaster LA1 218 D1
4 Rawtenstall BB4 86 A7
Back Lune St BB8 171 E4
Back Manor St 1 BL9 33 A2
Back Marine Rd LA4 216 F4
Back Marine Rd E LA4 217 D6
Back Mason St 17 BL9 33 A2
Back Moon Ave 5 FY1 130 B2
Back Morecambe St
LA4 217 B6
Back Moss La L40 25 F7
Back Mount 5 PR7 43 C8
Back Myrtle St 4 BL9 33 B2
Back Myrtle St S BL9 33 B2
Back Nelson St 5 BL6 32 D3
Back New St 5 LA5 223 D2
Back Nook Terr 2 OL12 52 F3
Back North Cres FY8 89 E6
Back O The Town La L38 3 E3
Back Oddfellows Terr
BB4 86 F3
Back Oram St BL9 33 A4
Back Ormrod St 11 BL9 33 A2
Back Owen's Row BL6 32 C3
Back Oxford St BL9 33 A1
Back Parkinson St BB2 101 B2
Back Parsonage St 10
BL9 33 A3
Back Patience St 10
OL12 52 C1
Back Percy St BL9 33 B3
Back Peter St
8 Barrowford BB9 170 D4
3 Bury BL9 33 A3
Back Pine St 1 BL9 33 B2
Back Pleasant St 5
FY1 130 B7
Back Queen St
Great Harwood BB6 124 C5
12 Lancaster LA1 214 F7
1 Morecambe LA4 217 B5
Back Railway View PR7 31 A7
Back Rawlinson St 19
BL6 32 B4
Back Read's Rd FY1 130 C4
Back Regent St 1 BB4 85 B3
Back Rhoden Rd BB5 103 D2
Back Richard Burch St 1
BL9 33 A3
Back Rings Row BB4 106 A1
Back Rochdale Old Rd N 1
BL9 33 C3
Back Rochdale Old Rd S
Bury BL9 33 C3
Bury,Fairfield BL9 33 D3
Back Rochdale Rd BL9 33 B2
Back Rochdale Rd S 18
BL9 33 A2
Back Rushton St 6 OL13 70 E8
Back Salford St BL9 33 A4
Back Sandy Bank Rd BL7 48 D5
Back School La
Skelmersdale,Chapel House
WN8 17 D2
Skelmersdale,Up Holland
WN8 10 C7
Back Seed St 8 PR1 96 F8
Back Shannon St 4
FY1 130 B3
Back Shaw-Street BL9 33 B3
Back Shuttleworth St 7
BB12 126 C8

Back Skipton Rd 8 BB18 196 B2
Back Skull House La WN6 19 D8
Back South Cross St E 16 BL9 33 A2
Back Spencer St BB4 86 A7
Back Springfield Rd N FY8 89 E6
Back Square St BL0 50 C6
Back St LA3 209 D8
Back St Anne's Rd W FY8 89 E6
Back St John St OL13 87 F3
Back Stanley St BL0 50 B5
Back Starkie St PR1 96 F6
Back Sun St 9 LA1 214 F8
Back Teak St 5 BL9 33 B2
Back Tinline St 12 BL9 33 A2
Back Union St BL7 47 D2
Back Virginia St PR8 35 B6
Back Warbreck Rd 2 FY1 130 B6
Back Wash La BL9 33 B2
Back Wash La S 7 BL9 33 A2
Back Water St
10 Accrington BB5 104 C6
Egerton BL7 47 D2
Back Waterloo Rd 8 FY1 130 B1
Back Wellington St BB5 104 C5
Back West Cres FY8 89 E6
Back West End Rd N LA4 216 F4
Back Willow St BB12 127 E6
Back Winterdyne Terr LA3 216 E4
Back Wood St BL6 32 C3
Back Woodfield Rd 4 FY1 130 B2
Back Wright St BL6 32 B4
Back York St
Clitheroe BB7 166 F8
Rawtenstall BB4 86 A7
Back Zion St 16 BB8 171 D4
Backhouse St 1 BB5 103 E4
Backs The PR3 140 A6
Bacon St 8 BB9 148 E8
Bacup & Rawtenstall Gram Sch BB4 69 F8
Bacup Mus* OL13 87 F3
Bacup Old Rd OL13 87 F7
Bacup Rd
Rawtenstall BB4,OL13 69 E8
Rawtenstall,Lower Cloughfold BB4 86 C2
Sharneyford OL14 88 E5
Walk Mill BB11 107 E6
Bacup Thorn Prim Sch OL13 87 F3
Baddon Cl LA4 217 C3
Baden Terr BB2 101 D1
Badge Brow BB5 103 E5
Badger Cl BB12 146 D1
Badger Rd PR26 77 A4
Badger St BL9 33 A3
Badger Wells Cotts BB7 146 A8
Badgers Cl BB5 104 E8
Badgers Croft PR2 118 F1
Badgers Rake L37 11 C5
Badgers Way PR5 97 B3
Badgers Wlk PR7 61 A3
Badgers Wlk E FY8 91 C3
Badgers Wlk W 12 FY8 91 B3
Badgers Wood PR3 159 C7
Bagganley La Chorley PR6 61 E1
Great Knowley PR6 61 F2
Bagnold Rd PR1 118 D1
Bagot St FY1 130 B1
Baildon Rd OL12 52 B1
Bailey Bank BB7 165 A7
Bailey Ct FY3 130 E6
Bailey La Heysham LA3 212 E8
Tosside BD23 236 B3
Bailey St Burnley BB11 127 E5
Earby BB18 197 C2
Bailrigg Chase LA1 215 B1
Bailrigg La LA1 215 A1
Baines Ave FY3 152 F1
Baines Endowed CE Prim Sch FY4 130 F1
Baines Sch FY6 153 D1
Bairstow St
3 Barnoldswick BB18 196 B3
Blackpool FY1 130 B3
13 Preston PR1 96 F7
Baker St 12 Bacup OL13 87 F3
Blackburn BB1 102 B4
Burnley BB11 127 E5
Coppull PR7 42 E1
Lancaster LA1 218 D3
4 Leyland PR25 77 B2
Nelson BB9 170 E1
Ramsbottom BL0 50 B5
Baker's La PR9 53 F3
Bakers Ct FY4 110 F7
Bakers Mews PR4 57 A6
Bala Cl BB1 101 E6
Balaclava St BB1 101 E6
Balcarres Cl PR25 77 A1
Balcarres Pl PR25 60 A8
Balcarres Rd Chorley PR7 43 B5
Leyland PR25 60 A8
Preston PR2 117 C2
Leyland PR25 77 B1
Balderstone Cl BB10 148 D2
Balderstone Hall La BB2 120 C6
Balderstone La BB10 148 E2
Balderstone Rd
Freckleton PR4 93 B7
Preston PR1 96 D5
Baldwin Gr FY1 130 D2
Baldwin Hill 3 BB7 166 D8
Baldwin Rd BB7 166 D8
Baldwin St Bacup OL13 70 B8
7 Bamber Bridge PR5 97 E1
5 Barrowford BB9 170 D4
Blackburn BB2 101 C3
Baldwin's Bldgs 14 BB4 86 A3
Balfour Cl Brierfield BB9 148 D5
Thornton FY5 153 D7
Balfour Ho 5 BB2 101 C4
Balfour Rd Fulwood PR2 117 E3
5 Rochdale OL12 52 C1
Southport PR8 35 E5
Balfour St Blackburn BB2 101 C4
Great Harwood BB6 124 E5
Leyland PR25 77 A1
Balham Ave FY4 110 E5
Ball Grove Dr BB8 172 B5
Ball La LA2 237 C3
Ball St Blackpool FY1 130 B1
3 Nelson BB9 170 D1
Poulton-le-F FY6 153 D3
Ball's Pl PR8 35 B7
Ballam Rd
Lower Ballam FY8 112 C3
Lytham St Anne's FY8 91 B4
Preston PR2 116 E1
Ballam St BB11 128 A4
Ballantrae Rd BB1 102 D3
Ballater St BB11 127 D3
Balle St BB3 65 A8
Balliol Cl BB12 126 D6
Ballot Hill Cres PR3 159 A5
Balm St BL0 50 A4
Balmer Gr FY1 130 D3
Balmoral PR7 30 E6
Balmoral Ave
Blackburn BB1 123 A4
Clitheroe BB7 166 C6
Leyland PR25 60 C8
Morecambe LA3 216 E3
Balmoral Cl Horwich BL6 32 E2
Ramsbottom BL8 50 A1
Southport PR9 54 B3
Balmoral Cres BB1 102 F4
Balmoral Ct PR7 43 B8
Balmoral Dr Brinscall PR6 62 E8
Formby L37 11 E1
Southport PR9 54 B3
Balmoral Pl FY5 153 C8
Balmoral Rd
Accrington BB5 104 D7
5 Bamber Bridge PR5 97 D3
Blackpool FY4 110 B8
Chorley PR7 43 B8
Darwen BB3 65 B6
Eccleston PR7 41 C7
Haslingden BB4 85 A1
Lancaster LA1 215 A7
Lytham St Anne's FY8 90 A5
3 Maghull L31 5 C1
Morecambe LA3,LA4 216 F3
New Longton PR4 96 A1
Balmoral Terr FY7 199 B5
Balniel Cl PR7 43 A7
Balshaw Ave PR7 60 D2
Balshaw Cres PR25 76 F2
Balshaw House Gdns PR7 60 D2
Balshaw La PR7 60 D1
Balshaw Lane Com Prim Sch PR7 60 E1
Balshaw Rd Leyland PR25 76 F1
Lowgill LA2 239 E3
Balshaw St 4 PR5 97 E2
Balshaw's CE High Sch PR25 60 B7
Baltic Bldgs 5 BB4 69 E8
Baltic Flats 4 BB4 69 E8
Baltic Rd 6 BB4 69 E8
Baltimore Rd FY8 90 B6
Bamber Ave FY2 152 C4
Bamber Bridge Sta PR5 77 E8
Bamber Gdns PR9 36 A8
Bamber St 2 PR7 43 B5
Bamber's Wlk PR4 113 E7
Bambers La FY4 111 C6
Bambers La N FY4 111 C7
Bamburgh Cl FY4 111 A7
Bamburgh Dr BB12 127 E7
Bamford Cl BL9 33 E4
Bamford Cres BB5 104 D4
Bamford Pl OL12 52 E1
Bamford Rd BL0 51 B6
Bamford St Burnley BB11 128 A6
Nelson BB9 149 A8
Bamfords Fold PR26 57 F5
Bampton Dr PR4 116 D4
Bamton Ave FY4 110 C7
Banastre PR7 61 A2
Banastre Rd PR8 35 B5
Banastre St 10 BB5 125 A1
Banbury Ave
Blackpool FY2 152 D1
Oswaldtwistle BB5 103 C4
Banbury Cl
3 Accrington BB5 104 A7
Blackburn BB2 80 F8
Banbury Dr PR2 117 E4
Banbury Rd
Longshaw WN5 10 D2
Banbury Rd *continued*
Lytham St Anne's FY8 90 A6
Morecambe LA3 217 C3
Bancroft Ave FY5 176 C2
Bancroft Fold BB18 196 A1
Bancroft Mill Engine Steam Mus* BB18 196 B1
Bancroft Rd BB10 128 C8
Bancroft St 4 BB1 101 F5
Band La PR3 180 D1
Bangor Ave FY2 152 D4
Bangor St BB1 101 F7
Bank Ave WN5 10 D5
Bank Bottom BB3 82 A1
Bank Bridge PR4 57 B5
Bank Brow WN8 19 C5
Bank Cl Galgate LA2 210 F3
Preston PR1 75 A8
Bank Cott 2 LA2 239 B8
Bank Cotts BB7 144 B4
Bank Croft PR4 75 A8
Bank Fold BB9 170 E4
Bank Hall Cotts BB7 230 C1
Bank Hall Terr BB10 128 A7
Bank Head La PR5 98 D1
Bank Hey Cl BB1 123 A1
Bank Hey La N BB1 122 F3
Bank Hey La S BB1 123 A1
Bank Hey St FY1 130 B5
Bank House La
Bacup OL13 87 F2
Silverdale LA5 224 C3
Westhouse LA6 242 E4
Bank House St BB9 170 E4
Bank La Blackburn BB1 102 D4
Warton PR4 92 D4
Bank Mdw BL6 32 C4
Bank Mill St 3 BB4 85 B2
Bank Nook PR9 53 E3
Bank Par Burnley BB11 128 A6
Middleworth Green PR1 96 D3
Preston PR1 97 A6
Bank Pas PR8 35 A7
Bank Pl PR2 117 C1
Bank Rd Lancaster LA1 218 D3
Roby Mill WN8 19 D4
Bank Sq PR8 35 B8
Bank St Accrington BB5 104 C5
Adlington PR7 31 A7
14 Bacup OL13 87 F2
Bank Lane BL0 50 E7
Barnoldswick BB18 196 C2
Brierfield BB9 148 B6
Chapeltown BL7 48 C4
Chorley PR7 43 C8
10 Church BB5 103 E6
Darwen BB3 82 A1
Haslingden BB4 85 B3
11 Nelson BB9 170 E1
Padiham BB12 146 C1
Rawtenstall BB4 86 A2
Trawden BB8 172 C1
Bank Terr Heapey PR6 62 C4
Simonstone BB12 125 E8
Whitworth OL12 52 C8
Bank Top Baldingstone BL9 50 F1
Blackburn BB2 101 C4
Burnley BB11 128 A6
Roby Mill WN8 19 C4
Bank View FY6 177 C1
Bank View Cotts BB7 230 C1
Bankcroft Cl BB12 126 E8
Bankfield Burnley BB11 128 A6
Skelmersdale WN8 9 C7
Bankfield Ct FY5 153 B8
Bankfield Gr FY1 130 E3
Bankfield La PR9 54 B2
Bankfield St Bacup OL13 70 D8
Colne BB8 171 B4
Trawden BB8 172 B4
Bankfield Terr
2 Bacup OL13 70 D8
Barnoldswick BB18 196 C3
Bankhouse Mews BB9 170 E4
Bankhouse Rd BB9 170 E1
Bankhouse St
Burnley BB11 127 F6
Burnley BB11 128 A6
Banks Bridge Cl BB18 196 C4
Banks Cres LA3 212 F6
Banks Hill BB18 196 A4
Banks Meth Prim Sch PR9 55 B7
Banks Rd Fulwood PR2 117 C3
Southport PR9 54 D6
Banks Rise 10 LA2 239 D8
Banks St Blackpool FY1 130 B6
Lane Bottom BB10 149 B3
Banks Way 12 LA2 239 D8
Banksands La PR3 201 E7
Banksbarn WN8 9 C7
Banksfield Ave PR2 117 C3
Banksfield Pl PR5 78 A7
Bankside Blackburn BB2 101 E2
Clayton Green PR6 78 B1
Hightown L38 2 F3
Parbold WN8 27 B2
Bankside Cl Bacup OL13 87 E1
Goodshaw Chapel BB4 106 A1
Bankside La OL13 87 F2
Bankwood WN6 19 E6
Banner Cl PR7 41 B6
Banneriggs Brow LA6 243 A5
Bannerman Terr PR6 61 D2
Bannister Brook Ho PR25 77 A2
Bannister Cl
Higher Walton PR5 98 B4
Bannister Cl *continued*
Trawden BB8 172 B3
Bannister Ct
Blackpool FY2 152 B4
17 Nelson BB9 148 E8
Bannister Dr PR25 76 E1
Bannister Gn PR7 41 C3
Bannister Hall Cres PR5 98 B4
Bannister Hall Dr PR5 98 B4
Bannister Hall La PR5 98 B4
Bannister La
Eccleston PR7 41 C5
Hill Dale L40,WN6 27 E6
Leyland PR26 76 E4
Bannister St
11 Chorley PR7 43 C7
Lytham St Anne's FY8 91 B3
Bannister's Bit 4 PR1 96 C2
Bannistre Cl 1 FY8 90 A8
Bannistre Ct PR4 57 A6
Bannistre Mews PR4 57 A6
Bar Cotts BB12 145 E1
Bar St BB10 128 B8
Bar Terr OL12 52 C7
Barbara Castle Way BB1 101 E5
Barberry Bank BL7 47 E2
Barbon Pl LA1 218 C2
Barbon St Burnley BB10 148 C2
14 Padiham BB12 146 C1
Barbondale Rd LA6,LA10 243 E8
Barbrook Cl WN6 29 B2
Barclay Ave
Blackpool FY4 130 F2
Burnley BB11 127 C4
Barclay Rd PR3 140 A7
Barcroft Gn BB10 128 E1
Barcroft St BB8 171 C5
Barden Com Inf Sch BB10 148 A1
Barden Croft BB5 124 F4
Barden High Sch BB10 148 A2
Barden Jun Sch BB10 148 A1
Barden La BB10,BB12 148 A2
Barden Pl PR2 118 D4
Barden Rd BB5 103 F4
Barden St 3 BB10 148 B1
Barden View BB10 148 A2
Bardsea Pl PR2 116 F3
Bardsley Cl WN8 10 A7
Bardsway FY5 176 A3
Bardsway Ave FY3 130 F6
Bare Ave LA4 217 E6
Bare La LA4 217 E5
Bare Lane Sta LA4 217 E6
Barford Cl
Skelmersdale WN8 10 A7
Southport PR8 21 A6
Barford Gr BL6 32 F1
Bargee Cl BB1 101 F3
Barham St 6 FY1 130 B2
Barker Brow BB1,PR7 142 A3
Barker Cl LA6 240 B7
Barker La BB2 122 C2
Barker Sq LA2 211 A6
Barker Terr BB7 189 E1
Barkerfield Cl BB12 146 F5
Barkerhouse Rd BB10, BB9 149 B8
Barkfield Ave L37 11 E4
Barkfield La L37 11 D4
Barley Bank St BB3 81 F2
Barley Cl BB2 101 D5
Barley Cop La LA1 218 B4
Barley Gr BB10 128 C6
Barley Holme Rd BB4 86 A8
Barley La BB9 169 B7
Barley New Rd BB12 169 E5
Barley St BB12 126 C7
Barley Vistors Ctr* BB12 169 C5
Barley Way 10 BB2 101 D5
Barleydale Rd BB9 170 E5
Barleyfield PR5 78 C3
Barlow Cres FY3 130 E4
Barlow Ct BL7 48 E5
Barlow St Accrington BB5 104 A6
Bacup OL13 70 B7
Horwich BL6 32 C2
Preston PR1 117 E1
Preston PR1 117 F2
11 Rawtenstall BB4 86 A3
Barlow's La L39 22 D5
Barlows Bldgs 5 BB4 85 F1
Barmouth Ave FY3 131 A3
Barmouth Cres BB1 122 E1
Barmouth Ct PR2 117 A3
Barmskin La PR7 41 B2
Barn Acre BL6 31 E1
Barn Cl PR4 56 A2
Barn Croft
3 Clitheroe BB7 166 D7
Higher Penwortham PR1 96 B4
1 Leyland PR26 76 B1
Barn Gill Cl BB1 101 F3
Barn Hey PR4 95 A1
Barn Hey Dr PR26 76 E3
Barn Hey Rd L33 1 A2
Barn Mdw
Clayton Brook PR5 78 B6
Edgworth BL7 48 D5
Barn Meadow Cres BB1 124 C1
Barn View PR6 30 F8
Barnacre Cl
Fulwood PR2 118 A8
Lancaster LA1 215 B2
Barnacre Rd PR3 140 A8
Barnard Cl BB5 103 C4
Barnbrook St BL9 33 A3
Barncroft Dr BL6 32 F3
Barnes Ave BB4 85 F2
Barnes Cl BL0 50 A3
Barnes Dr Cleveleys FY5 175 E5
Maghull L31 5 C3
Barnes Rd
Morecambe LA3 216 E3
Ormskirk L39 15 E3
Skelmersdale WN8 17 E1
Barnes Sq 1 BB5 124 F2
Barnes St Accrington BB5 104 C6
Burnley BB11 128 A6
Church BB5 103 E6
Clayton-le-M BB5 124 F3
Haslingden BB4 85 B4
Barnfield
6 Bamber Bridge PR5 77 A8
Kirkham PR4 114 A5
Much Hoole PR4 74 E3
Barnfield Ave BB10 128 F6
Barnfield Bsns Ctr BB9 148 F6
Barnfield Cl
4 Cleveleys FY5 175 F4
Colne BB8 172 A5
Egerton BL7 47 E2
Barnfield Dr WN8 9 E7
Barnfield Manor FY6 154 D3
Barnfield St
Accrington BB5 104 D5
Rochdale OL12 52 F2
Barnfield Way BB5 125 E5
Barnmeadow La BB6 124 C5
Barnoldswick CE Prim Sch BB18 196 B2
Barnoldswick La LA6 242 D3
Barnoldswick Rd
Beverley BB8,BB9 170 F7
Kelbrook BB18 194 F6
Barns La PR3 161 C8
Barns The Formby L37 12 A1
Weeton PR4 133 A2
Barnsfold PR2 117 D6
Barnside Euxton PR7 60 C3
Whitworth OL12 52 B8
Barnside Est BB8 172 F7
Barnstaple Way PR4 116 F6
Barnwood Cres BB18 197 C1
Barnwood Rd BB18 197 B1
Baron Rd FY1 130 C1
Baron St Darwen BB3 81 F2
Rawtenstall BB4 86 D1
Barons Cl BB3 82 A7
Barons Way
Blackburn BB3 82 A6
Euxton PR7 60 D2
Barracks Rd BB11 127 D6
Barret Hill Brow BB7 230 B4
Barret St BB18 197 A1
Barrett Ave PR8 35 A2
Barrett Ct 6 BL9 33 A2
Barrett Rd PR8 35 A2
Barrett St 5 BB10 128 A8
Barrington Ct BB5 103 F7
Barrington Dr PR8 21 B5
Barrison Gn L40 24 E2
Barritt Rd BB4 85 F2
Barronwood Ct PR4 57 A5
Barrow Nook La L39 7 E2
Barrow Sch BB7 166 D2
Barrow's La PR3 156 B5
Barrowcroft Cl WN1 30 B1
Barrowford Rd
Barrowford BB9 170 B1
Colne BB8 171 B5
Fence BB12 147 C7
Barrowford Sch BB9 170 D3
Barrowford St Thomas Prim Sch BB9 170 C3
Barrows La LA3 212 E7
Barrows La E PR3 156 B5
Barry Ave PR2 117 A3
Barry Gr LA3 212 F6
Barry St BB12 127 C7
Bartholomew Rd LA4 217 C4
Bartle La PR4 116 C7
Bartle Pl PR2 116 E1
Bartle Rd FY8 90 A8
Bartle St BB11 127 D5
Bartlett Ho PR8 35 B3
Barton Ave Blackpool FY1 130 B2
Knott End-on-S FY6 199 E5
Barton Ct LA1 215 A4
Barton Gdns LA1 215 B5
Barton Heys Rd L37 11 D1
Barton La PR3 137 E7
Barton Mans FY8 89 C7
Barton Rd Lancaster LA1 215 A4
Lytham St Anne's FY8 89 D8
Barton Row LA6 240 B7
Barton Sq FY6 199 E5
Barton St BB2 101 E5
Barton St Lawrence CE Prim Sch PR3 137 B7
Barton Streety BB2 101 E5
Bartons Cl PR9 54 D5
Barwood Lea Mill 14 BL0 50 C6
Bashall Gr PR25 77 B3
Basil St Colne BB8 171 D4
Preston PR1 118 C2
Basnett St BB10 148 C1
Bass La BL9 50 D3
Bassenthwaite Rd FY3 131 C2
Basset Cl OL12 52 E3
Basset Gdns OL12 52 E3
Bassett Way OL12 52 E2
Bastwell Rd BB1 101 F7
Bateman Gr LA4 217 B5

Bateman Rd LA4 217 B5
Bateman St BL6 32 D2
Bates St BB5 124 E3
Bath Mill La LA1 215 A8
Bath Mill Sq 7 LA1 215 A8
Bath Rd FY8 91 B3
Bath Springs L39 15 F5
Bath St Accrington BB5 104 B4
Blackburn BB2 101 C4
Blackpool FY4 130 B1
Colne BB8 171 E5
Lancaster LA1 215 A8
Lytham St Anne's FY8 91 B3
Morecambe LA4 217 A5
Nelson BB9 148 F8
2 Preston PR2 117 D1
Southport PR8 35 B8
Bacup OL13 88 A2
Bath St N PR9 35 B8
Bathurst Ave FY3 131 A7
Bathurst St 3 BB2 101 D5
Batridge Rd BL7 48 A7
Battersby St BL9 33 D3
Battismore Rd LA4 217 B5
Battle Way L37 12 B2
Bawdlands BB7 166 D8
Bawhead Rd BB18 197 B1
Baxenden St John's CE Prim Sch BB5 104 E1
Baxter St WN6 29 F1
Baxtergate LA4 217 B6
Bay Cl LA3 212 D6
Bay Horse Dr LA1 215 B3
Bay Horse La PR4 135 D4
Bay Horse Rd LA2 211 E4
Bay Rd Fulwood PR2 118 E2
Heysham LA3 212 D6
Bay St BB1 102 A7
Bay The FY5 175 C5
Bay Tree Farm PR2 95 D8
Bay Tree Rd PR6 78 B3
Bay View LA6 237 B8
Bay View Ave LA2 218 C8
Bay View Cotts LA3 212 E6
Bay View Cres LA2 218 C8
Bay View Dr LA3 212 F8
Bayard St BB12 127 A6
Baycliffe Cres LA4 217 A5
Bayley Fold BB7 166 E8
Bayley St BB5 124 E3
Bayliss Cl PR2 118 F3
Baylton Ct PR3 181 D2
Baylton Dr PR3 181 D2
Baynes Cotts 4 LA2 239 B8
Baynes St BB3 82 F1
Bayside FY7 199 B4
Bayswater FY2 152 C4
Baytree Cl
Bamber Bridge PR5 77 C8
Southport PR9 54 D5
Baytree Gr BL0 50 B2
Baytree Wlk OL12 71 C1
Baywood St BB1 101 F7
Bazil Gr LA3 209 D7
Bazil La LA3 209 D7
Bazley Rd FY8 90 D3
Beach Ave Cleveleys FY5 175 D3
Lytham St Anne's FY8 90 C3
Beach Priory Gdns PR8 35 A6
Beach Rd Cleveleys FY5 175 D3
Fleetwood FY7 198 E3
Lytham St Anne's FY8 89 D7
Pilling Lane FY6 200 B7
Southport PR8 34 F6
Beach St
Lytham St Anne's FY8 91 A3
Morecambe LA4 217 E7
Beacham Rd PR8 35 E7
Beachcomber Dr FY5 175 C3
Beachley Rd PR2 117 A4
Beachley Sq BB12 127 D7
Beachmews PR8 34 F6
Beacon Ave PR2 117 D5
Beacon Cl BB8 171 C3
Beacon Crossing WN8 27 C2
Beacon Ct PR3 138 D5
Beacon Ctry Pk* WN8 18 F2
Beacon Dr PR3 138 D6
Beacon Fell Ctry Pk* PR3 183 F2
Beacon Fell Cvn Pk PR3 162 D1
Beacon Fell Rd PR3 183 E2
Beacon Flats PR3 140 C8
Beacon Gr Fulwood PR2 117 D4
Garstang PR3 181 B6
Beacon Hill High Sch FY2 152 D1
Beacon Hts WN8 10 A8
Beacon La L40,WN8 18 D4
Beacon Lodge 10 PR2 118 F4
Beacon Rd
Poulton-le-F FY6 154 A3
Shevington Moor WN6 29 B2
Beacon Sch WN8 9 E8
Beacon St PR7 43 D7
Beacon View
Appley Bridge WN6 19 C8
Longridge PR3 162 B3
Beacon View Dr WN8 10 B7
Beacons The WN6 19 D7
Beaconsfield Ave PR1 118 E1
Beaconsfield Ct 4 L39 15 F5
Beaconsfield Rd PR9 35 F6
Beaconsfield St
Accrington BB5 104 D5
Great Harwood BB6 124 C5
16 Haslingden BB4 85 B3
Beaconsfield Terr
Catterall PR3 181 E2
Chorley PR6 61 D2
Beale Cl BB1 102 B1
Beale Rd BB9 148 B8
Beamish Ave BB2 81 D8
Beamont Dr PR1 96 D8
Bean Ave FY4 110 E8
Bear St BB12 126 F6
Beardshaw Ave FY1 130 D2
Beardsworth St BB1 102 A7
Beardwood BB2 101 A8
Beardwood Brow BB2 101 B7
Beardwood Dr BB2 101 A7
Beardwood Fold BB2 101 A7
Beardwood High Sch BB2 101 A6
Beardwood Hospl The BB2 101 A6
Beardwood Mdw BB2 101 A7
Beardwood Pk BB2 101 B7
Bearncroft WN8 9 D6
Bearswood Croft PR6 78 B2
Bearwood Way FY5 176 C2
Beatie St BB9 148 B6
Beatrice Ave BB12 127 C7
Beatrice Mews 11 BL6 32 B4
Beatrice Pl BB2 82 A8
Beatrice St 8 BL6 32 B4
Beattock Pl FY2 152 F6
Beatty Ave PR7 43 B6
Beatty Cl FY8 110 D1
Beatty Rd PR8 35 E5
Beauclerk Rd FY8 90 B6
Beaufort L37 12 A2
Beaufort Ave FY2 152 C5
Beaufort Cl Ormskirk L39 15 A1
Simonstone BB12 145 E2
Beaufort Gr LA4 217 D5
Beaufort Rd
Morecambe LA4 217 E5
Weir OL13 88 A7
Beaufort St Nelson BB9 148 E7
Rochdale OL12 52 C1
Beauley Ave BB12 145 E2
Beauly Cl 3 BL0 50 A2
Beaumaris Ave BB2 101 A1
Beaumaris Cl 2 BB4 85 B1
Beaumaris Rd PR25 60 C8
Beaumont Ave BL6 32 C4
Beaumont Coll (The Spastics Society) LA1 218 D4
Beaumont Cres L39 15 D2
Beaumont Ct
8 Blackpool FY1 130 C6
Lytham St Anne's FY8 90 A8
Beaumont Gdns FY6 153 A5
Beaumont Ho L39 15 D2
Beaumont Pl LA1 218 D4
Beaumont Rd BL6 32 C4
Beaumont St LA1 218 D4
Beaumont Way BB3 82 C1
Beaver Cl BB1 122 F5
Beaver Terr 14 OL13 88 A3
Beavers La WN8 9 D6
Bebles Rd L39 15 C3
Becconsall La PR4 73 F3
Beck Ct FY7 198 D1
Beck Gr FY5 175 E4
Beck Side LA2 237 C3
Beck View 7 LA1 215 A3
Beckdean Ave FY6 153 D2
Beckenham Ct BB10 148 D3
Beckett Ct 18 PR1 96 F8
Beckett St 5 BB3 65 A8
Becks Brow BD23 236 F3
Becks Crossing BB8 172 C2
Beckside Barley BB12 169 C5
Trawden BB8 172 C3
Beckside Mews LA6 240 B3
Beckway Ave FY3 130 F7
Bedale Pl FY5 175 E1
Beddington St 6 BB9 170 D1
Bedford Ave FY5 175 D3
Bedford Cl BB5 103 C4
Bedford Ct PR8 35 A2
Bedford Mews BB3 81 F4
Bedford Pl Lancaster LA1 215 A4
Padiham BB12 126 D7
Bedford Rd
Blackpool FY1 130 C8
Fulwood PR2 118 A4
6 Lytham St Anne's FY8 91 D4
Southport PR8 35 A2
Bedford St
6 Barrowford BB9 170 C1
Blackburn BB2 101 C2
Darwen BB3 81 F4
Egerton BL7 47 D2
Bedford Terr Bury BL9 33 A4
Haslingden BB4 68 A8
Bedfordshire Ave BB12 127 B7
Bee La PR1 96 E1
Bee Mill PR3 141 D3
Beech Ave Adlington PR6 31 B8
Bilsborrow PR3 159 A5
Blackpool FY3 130 E5
Darwen BB3 82 B2
Earby BB18 197 A1
Euxton PR7 60 C4
Galgate LA2 210 F4
Horwich BL6 32 E1
Kirkham PR4 114 B4
Leyland PR25 60 A7
Parbold WN8 27 C2
Poulton-le-F FY6 153 D4
Warton PR4 92 D6
Beech Bank PR4 155 F1
Beech Cl Bacup OL13 88 A3
Clitheroe BB7 166 D8
Oswaldtwistle BB5 103 C2
Rishton BB1 103 B8
Rufford L40 39 C4
Skelmersdale WN8 17 E1
Whitworth OL12 71 C1
Wilpshire BB1 122 E6
Beech Cres BB5 125 A1
Beech Ct Fulwood PR2 117 E7
Silverdale LA5 224 C2
Beech Dr Formby L37 11 D4
Freckleton PR4 93 A5
Fulwood PR2 117 D8
Haslingden BB4 85 C2
Kirkham PR4 113 E4
Longridge PR3 140 A7
Newton-w-S PR4 114 F2
Poulton-le-F FY6 153 D2
Whalley BB7 144 A7
Beech Gdns PR6 78 B1
Beech Gr Accrington BB5 104 A4
2 Barnoldswick BB18 196 C2
Blackburn BB3 81 D6
Brierfield BB10 148 C4
Chatburn BB7 190 D5
Knott End-on-S FY6 199 E6
Morecambe LA4 217 E5
Preston PR2 117 B1
Ramsbottom BL8 50 A1
Slyne LA2 218 C6
Southport PR9 35 F7
Warton LA5 223 D5
Beech Grove Cl BL9 33 B4
Beech Ho Southport PR8 35 A5
Chorley PR7 42 F6
Beech Ind Est 3 OL13 88 A3
Beech Mdw L39 16 A4
Beech Mount
Blackburn BB1 122 F3
Waddington BB7 189 B4
Beech Rd Aughton L39 6 A6
Elswick PR4 155 F1
Garstang PR3 181 B8
Halton LA2 219 C7
Leyland PR25 77 A2
Beech St Accrington BB5 104 C5
Bacup OL13 88 A3
Barnoldswick BB18 196 B1
Blackburn BB1 102 A7
Bury BL9 33 B2
Clayton-le-M BB5 124 F1
Clitheroe BB7 166 D8
Edgworth BL7 48 D5
Great Harwood BB6 124 C6
Lancaster LA1 214 D8
10 Nelson BB9 170 E1
Padiham BB12 126 D7
1 Preston PR1 96 D6
Ramsbottom BL0 50 C3
Rawtenstall BB4 86 A3
Beech St S PR1 96 E6
Beech Terr Ingleton LA6 242 F3
1 Preston PR1 96 E6
Beech Tree Ave WN6 19 D8
Beech Tree Cl BB9 148 E7
Beech Tree Sch PR5 78 B4
Beech Wlk PR6 61 A7
Beechacre BL0 50 D5
Beecham St LA4 217 B6
Beechcroft Cleveleys FY5 175 C4
1 Maghull L31 5 D1
Beeches Ct FY5 176 C1
Beeches The
Clayton Green PR6 78 C3
Singleton FY6 154 D1
Tarleton PR4 57 A7
Beechfield Hill Dale WN8 27 C5
Lancaster LA1 214 D7
Maghull L31 5 E1
Beechfield Ave
Blackpool FY3 130 E3
Knott End-on-S FY6 200 A5
Wrea Green PR4 113 C4
Beechfield Ct PR25 60 B8
Beechfield Gdns PR8 34 F6
Beechfield Mews PR9 35 C7
Beechfield Rd PR25 60 B8
Beechfields PR7 41 B6
Beechill Cl PR5 97 E3
Beeching Cl LA1 214 F6
Beechthorpe Ave BB7 189 B4
Beechtrees WN8 9 D7
Beechway Fulwood PR2 118 A4
Higher Penwortham PR1 96 B3
Maghull L31 6 B2
Beechway Ave L31 6 B2
Beechwood WN8 18 C3
Beechwood Ave
Accrington BB5 104 D3
Bamber Bridge PR5 97 D4
Burnley BB11 127 F3
Clitheroe BB7 166 E6
Fulwood PR2 117 C4
Ramsbottom BL0 50 D6
Shevington WN6 19 F5
Beechwood Cres WN5 10 E6
Beechwood Croft PR6 78 A3
Beechwood Ct
Blackburn BB1 101 F7
Coppull PR7 29 F8
Maghull L31 5 F1
Skelmersdale WN8 9 D6
Beechwood Dr
Blackburn BB2 80 E8
Formby L37 11 C1
Ormskirk L39 15 D5
Thornton FY5 153 B8
Beechwood Gdns LA1 215 A2
Beechwood Gr FY2 152 E4
Beechwood Mews BB1 82 A8
Beechwood Rd
12 Blackburn BB1 102 A7
Chorley PR7 43 E6
Beeford Dr WN5 10 E5
Beenland St 3 PR1 118 D1
Beeston Ave FY6 153 C5
Beetham Ct BB5 124 E2
Beetham Cvn Pk LA5, LA7 225 C8
Beetham Pl FY3 130 E6
Begonia St BB3 82 B1
Begonia View BB3 82 A7
Beightons Wlk OL12 52 D4
Bela Cl 3 LA1 218 A2
Bela Gr FY1 130 D2
Belfield WN8 9 D6
Belfield Rd BB5 104 C4
Belford Ave FY5 175 F4
Belford St BB12 127 F7
Belfry Cl PR7 60 D4
Belfry Cres WN6 29 F2
Belfry Mans BB6 143 C6
Belfry The FY8 91 D5
Belgarth Rd BB5 104 C7
Belgrave Ave
Higher Penwortham PR1 96 B3
Kirkham PR4 114 A7
Belgrave Cl
Blackburn BB2 101 B3
3 Lytham St Anne's FY8 90 D6
Belgrave Cres BL6 32 D3
Belgrave Ct
Burnley BB12 127 F7
Leyland PR25 59 F8
Belgrave Pl
Poulton-le-F FY6 153 B2
Southport PR8 34 F3
Belgrave Rd
Blackpool FY4 130 E1
Colne BB8 171 D6
Darwen BB3 65 A8
5 Leyland PR25 77 A1
Poulton-le-F FY6 153 B3
Southport PR8 34 F3
Belgrave Sq 9 BB3 82 A1
Belgrave St
Brierfield BB9 148 A6
Burnley BB12 127 F7
Nelson BB9 170 F1
Rising Bridge BB5 85 A8
Rochdale OL12 52 D1
Belgravia Apartments PR9 53 B1
Bell La Bury BL9 33 A3
Claughton PR3 182 C4
Clayton-le-M BB5 125 B4
Bell St BB4 85 B3
Bell Villas PR5 99 C3
Bell's Cl L31 5 C4
Bell's La L31 5 B3
Bell-Aire Park Homes LA3 212 F5
Bellamy Ave LA4 217 A3
Belle Field Cl PR1 97 A1
Belle Isle Ave OL12 52 C6
Belle View Pl FY3 130 D5
Belle Vue Ave LA1 215 A5
Belle Vue Dr LA1 215 A5
Belle Vue La BB7 189 B4
Belle Vue Pl BB11 127 E6
Belle Vue St
Blackburn BB2 101 C5
Burnley BB11 127 E6
Bellfield Rd LA4 217 C5
Bellflower Cl PR25 77 E3
Bellingham Rd FY8 91 B4
Bellis Ave PR9 53 F2
Bellis Way PR5 97 B2
Bells Arc 10 BB10 128 A8
Bells Bridge La PR3 203 F2
Bells La PR5 98 E3
Belmont Ave
Blackpool FY1 130 C4
Fulwood PR2 118 D2
Orrell WN5 10 D3
Poulton-le-F FY6 153 B3
Belmont Cl Brinscall PR6 62 E8
Burscough L40 25 E3
Fulwood PR2 118 D2
Lancaster LA1 218 B3
Belmont Cres PR2 118 D2
Belmont Ct PR3 140 B7
Belmont Dr PR6 61 E1
Belmont Gr BB10 128 D5
Belmont Pl PR7 29 C6
Belmont Rd Adlington PR6 31 B7
Belmont BB3,BL7 64 A2
Fleetwood FY7 199 A3
Fulwood PR2 117 C2
Great Harwood BB6 124 B5
Horwich BL6 32 C7
Leyland PR25 59 D8
Lytham St Anne's FY8 90 C5
Rivington BL6 45 C3
Belmont Sch BB4 85 E2
Belmont St PR8 35 A5
Belmont Terr
7 Barrowford BB9 170 D3
Foulridge BB8 194 E1
Belmont Way OL12 52 E2
Belper St BB1 102 A6
Belsfield Dr PR4 73 E4
Belshaw Ct BB11 127 A3
Belthorn Prim Sch BB1 82 F6
Belthorn Rd BB1 82 E6
Belton Hill PR2 117 D8
Belvedere Ave
Ramsbottom BL8 50 A1
Rawtenstall BB4 87 A1
Belvedere Ct
1 Lytham St Anne's FY8 90 D4
Thornton FY5 153 C8
Belvedere Dr Chorley PR7 43 B8
Formby L37 11 F1
Belvedere Pk L39 6 C7
Belvedere Rd
Adlington PR6 31 B8
Blackburn BB1 123 A3
Burnley BB10 128 B6
2 Leyland PR25 77 B2
Southport PR8 21 C5
Thornton FY5 153 C8
Belverdale Gdns FY4 110 F5
Belvere Ave FY4 110 D6
Belvoir St OL12 52 C1
Ben La
Barnoldswick BB18 196 D3
Rainford Junction L39 8 A1
Ben Lane Ct L39 8 B2
Benbow Cl FY8 110 D2
Bence Rd PR1 97 B6
Bence St BB8 171 E5
Bench Carr OL12 52 E1
Benenden Pl 9 FY5 176 A2
Bengal St PR7 61 D1
Bengarth Rd PR9 35 F8
Benjamin Hargreaves CE Prim Sch BB5 104 D5
Bennett Ave FY1 130 C4
Bennett Dr WN5 10 D4
Bennett House Sch The PR6 61 E1
Bennett Rd FY5 176 A3
Bennett St 4 BB9 170 F2
Bennett's La FY4 110 F6
Bennington St BB1,BB2 101 F3
Bennison Ct PR9 53 C1
Benson Ave LA4 217 D4
Benson Ho BB1 102 C8
Benson La PR4 135 F3
Benson Rd FY3 152 E1
Benson St Blackburn BB1 102 B7
Bury BL9 33 A1
Edgworth BL7 48 E5
Benson's La PR4 158 C1
Bent Est OL13 88 A7
Bent Gap La BB2 101 C4
Bent La Colne BB8 172 B6
Leyland PR25 60 C8
Bent St Blackburn BB2 101 D4
Haslingden BB4 68 D8
4 Oswaldtwistle BB5 103 D3
Bentcliffe Gdns BB5 104 D4
Bentgate Cl BB4 68 D8
Bentham Ave
Burnley BB10 148 B3
Fleetwood FY7 198 C1
Bentham Cl BB2 101 B1
Bentham Hall Cotts LA2 239 D8
Bentham Moor Rd LA6 242 D2
Bentham Pl WN6 29 F2
Bentham Rd
Blackburn BB2 101 B1
Ingleton LA6 242 E3
Lancaster LA1 215 A2
Standish WN6 29 F2
Bentham St Coppull PR7 42 E1
Southport PR8 35 B5
Bentham Sta LA2 239 D7
Bentham's Way PR8 35 C2
Bentinck Ave FY4 110 B5
Bentinck Rd FY8 89 C8
Bentinck St 9 OL12 52 C1
Bentlea Rd BB7 231 B3
Bentley Dr Kirkham PR4 113 E5
Peel Hill FY4 112 A6
Bentley Gn FY5 176 D2
Bentley La
Andertons Mill L40,PR7 41 A1
Bispham Green L40 27 E8
Bury BL9 51 A1
Bentley Mews OL12 52 E2
Bentley Park Rd PR4 74 F7
Bentley St 7 Bacup OL13 87 F3
Blackburn BB1 102 C5
Darwen BB3 65 C7
Nelson BB9 148 D7
Rochdale OL12 52 E2
Bentley Wood Way BB11 126 F4
Bentmeadows OL12 52 E1
Benton Rd PR2 118 D4
Bents BB8 172 B6
Bents La LA6 243 A3
Bentwood Rd BB4 85 A3
Beresford Dr PR9 53 F1
Beresford Gdns PR9 53 F2
Beresford Rd BB1 101 D7
Beresford St
8 Blackpool FY1 130 C7
9 Burnley BB11 127 D6
Nelson BB9 148 F6
Bergen St BB11 127 B5
Bergerac Cres FY5 152 F6
Berkeley Cl Chorley PR7 43 D5
Nelson BB9 148 E7
Berkeley Colonnade PR2 118 A4
Berkeley Cres BB12 146 C1

Berkeley Ct LA3 212 E6
Berkeley Dr
Clayton-le-W PR5 77 E4
Simonstone BB12 145 E2
Berkeley St
Brierfield BB9 148 A5
Nelson BB9 148 E7
Preston PR1 117 E1
Berkley Cl PR4 113 E5
Berkshire Ave BB12 127 B7
Berkshire Cl BB1 122 F7
Bernard St OL12 52 E3
Berne Ave BL6 32 A3
Berridge Ave BB12 127 A6
Berriedale Rd BB9 171 A1
Berry Cl WN8 17 F2
Berry Field 3 PR1 96 C3
Berry Ho Cotts L40 38 A5
Berry House Rd L40 38 A4
Berry La PR3 140 A7
Berry Sq BL6 31 D3
Berry St
Bamber Bridge PR5 77 A8
Brierfield BB9 148 B5
Burnley BB11 127 F4
Preston PR1 97 A7
Skelmersdale WN8 17 F2
Berry's La FY6 153 C4
Berrys La BB7 144 C2
Bertha St BB5 104 D6
Bertram Ave LA4 217 A4
Bertrand Ave FY3 131 A7
Berwick Ave
Cleveleys FY5 175 F4
Southport PR8 21 D5
Berwick Dr Burnley BB12 127 E7
Fulwood PR2 117 D4
Berwick Rd
Blackpool FY4 110 C5
Lytham St Anne's FY8 89 F7
Preston PR1 97 A6
Berwick St PR1 118 E1
Berwick Way LA3 212 E7
Berwyn Ave LA4 217 D6
Berwyn Cl BL6 32 C5
Berwyn Ct PR8 35 D4
Beryl Ave Blackburn BB1 122 F2
Cleveleys FY5 175 E1
Besant Cl BB1 102 B1
Bescar Brow La L40 23 F7
Bescar La L40 37 B1
Bescar La Sta L40 37 B2
Bescot Way 12 FY5 152 F7
Bessie St 13 BB18 196 B2
Best St PR4 113 F5
Bethel Ave FY2 152 D4
Bethel Rd BB1 102 A7
Bethel St
Barnoldswick BB18 196 B3
Colne BB8 171 B4
Bethesda Cl BB2 101 D3
Bethesda Rd FY1 130 B4
Bethesda St
Barnoldswick BB18 196 B2
Burnley BB11 127 F6
Betony LA4 217 F6
Betony Cl OL12 52 D3
Bett La PR6 79 C1
Beulah Ave LA4 217 D5
Bevan Pl BB9 170 F2
Beverley Ave
Longshaw WN5 10 E1
Poulton-le-F FY6 131 D8
Beverley Cl
Clitheroe BB7 166 E6
Preston PR2 96 C8
Southport PR9 54 C5
Wrea Green PR4 113 A3
Beverley Ct
2 Lytham St Anne's FY8 90 A8
Morecambe LA4 217 E5
Beverley Dr BB7 166 D6
Beverley Gr FY4 110 C7
Beverley Rd BB9 170 E8
Beverley Rd N FY8 90 A8
Beverley Rd S FY8 90 A8
Beverley St
5 Blackburn BB2 101 B1
Burnley BB11 127 E5
Beverly Cl FY5 153 B8
Bevington Cl BB11 127 E5
Bewcastle Dr L40 16 C3
Bexhill Rd PR2 117 A4
Bexley Ave FY2 130 D8
Bexley Pl FY8 90 E5
Bezza La BB2,PR5 120 C5
Bhailok St 3 PR1 96 E8
Bibby Dr FY3 131 E5
Bibby Rd PR9 54 A1
Bibby's La FY2 152 E3
Bickerstaffe CE Sch L39 7 E5
Bickerstaffe St 2 FY1 130 B3
Bickerton Rd PR8 34 F4
Bicknell St BB1 101 E6
Bideford Ave FY3 131 A6
Bideford Way PR4 116 F6
Bidston St PR1 97 E8
Big Fold BL6 31 D2
Bigdale Dr L33 1 A3
Billinge Ave BB2 101 B5
Billinge Cl BB2 101 B5
Billinge End BB2 101 A6
Billinge End Rd
Blackburn BB2 100 F5
Pleasington BB2 100 B4
Billinge Hospl WN5 10 D2
Billinge Side BB2 100 F5
Billinge St BB1 102 B4
Billinge View BB2 100 F2
Billington Ave BB4 86 A5
Billington Gdns BB7 144 A4
Billington Rd BB11 127 B3
Billington St 1 PR4 113 F6
Billington St E 3 PR4 113 F6
Bilsberry Cotts BB7 164 F1
Bilsborough Hey PR1 96 E2
Bilsborough Mdw PR2 116 E3
Bilsborrow La
Bilsborrow PR3 159 C4
Inglewhite PR3 160 A4
Binbrook Pl PR7 43 A7
Bingley Ave FY3 130 F6
Bingley Cl PR6 78 C2
Binns Nook Rd OL12 52 F2
Binns St BB4 86 A7
Binyon Ct LA1 214 F6
Binyon Rd LA1 214 F5
Birbeck Rd L33 1 A3
Birbeck Wlk L33 1 A3
Birch Ave Burscough L40 25 E4
Clayton-le-W PR25 77 D3
Cleveleys FY5 175 E2
Euxton PR7 60 C4
Galgate LA2 211 A4
Haslingden BB4 85 C3
Higher Penwortham PR1 96 A3
Newton-w-S PR4 114 F3
Preston PR2 117 A2
Birch Cl Huncoat BB5 125 E2
Maghull L31 5 F1
Whitworth OL12 52 C6
Birch Cres
Gregson Lane PR5 98 E1
Oswaldtwistle BB5 103 F3
Birch Dr LA5 224 C4
Birch Field PR6 78 B3
Birch Gn L37 11 D4
Birch Gr Barrow BB7 166 D1
Lancaster LA1 214 D8
Ramsbottom BL0 50 A3
Stalmine FY6 177 D7
Birch Green Rd WN8 18 C3
Birch Hall Ave BB3 81 D4
Birch Hall La BB18 197 D2
Birch La PR3 184 C1
Birch Rd Chorley PR6 61 E2
Coppull PR7 42 E1
Garstang PR3 181 C8
Birch St Accrington BB5 104 B6
Bacup OL13 87 F3
Fleetwood FY7 199 A4
5 Lytham St Anne's FY8 91 C3
Skelmersdale WN8 8 E8
Southport PR8 35 B4
Birch Terr BB5 104 D2
Birch Tree Gdns FY3 131 B2
Birch Tree Way 4 BL6 32 E1
Birch View BB7 166 D1
Birch Villas OL12 52 C5
Birch Way FY6 153 C4
Birch Wlk 1 BB1 102 B4
Birchall Lodge 6 PR2 118 F4
Birchbank Gdns BB1 102 A7
Birchenlee La BB8 171 E2
Birches End OL12 52 C5
Birches Rd BL7 48 D4
Birches The L37 11 E5
Birchfield PR4 74 F4
Birchfield Ave BL9 33 E1
Birchfield Dr PR3 140 A8
Birchfield Way L31 5 B5
Birchill Rd L33 1 C2
Birchin La PR6 78 D1
Birchover Cl PR2 117 A5
Birchtree Ave LA3 216 E1
Birchway Ave FY3 130 E6
Birchwood PR26 76 C1
Birchwood Ave PR4 95 B1
Birchwood Cl FY8 90 E4
Birchwood Dr Coppull PR7 42 E2
Fulwood PR2 117 D7
Hambleton FY6 177 C2
Birchwood Way L33 1 A5
Bird i' th' Hand Cotts 2 L39 15 E6
Bird St Brierfield BB9 148 B5
Preston PR1 96 D6
Birdy Brow BB7 165 A6
Birk St PR1 96 E7
Birkacre Brow PR7 42 F2
Birkacre Rd PR7 42 F4
Birkbeck Pl FY7 198 D2
Birkbeck Way BB10 148 A1
Birkdale Ave
Blackpool FY2 152 E5
Fleetwood FY7 175 E7
Longton PR4 74 F8
Lytham St Anne's FY8 110 F1
Birkdale Cl Euxton PR7 60 D4
Lancaster LA1 218 B3
Longton PR4 74 F8
Thornton FY5 153 D8
Birkdale Cop PR8 35 E1
Birkdale Dr PR2 116 E2
Birkdale High Sch PR8 21 E7
Birkdale Prim Sch PR8 35 B3
Birkdale Sta PR8 34 F4
Birkdale Trad Est PR8 35 A2
Birkett Dr PR2 119 A3
Birkett Pl PR2 119 A3
Birkett Rd BB5 104 D7
Birkett's Pl LA4 217 C5
Birkey La L37 11 F2
Birklands Ave LA4 217 C4
Birkrig WN8 9 D6
Birks Brow PR3 162 D3
Birkside Way FY4 131 C1
Birkwith La LA2 239 C7
Birley Cl WN6 19 F8
Birley Ct PR8 35 B5
Birley Pl BB10 128 A8
Birley St Blackburn BB1 101 F5
Blackburn BB1 101 F6
Blackpool FY1 130 B5
Kirkham PR4 114 B5
1 Preston PR1 97 A7
Birleywood WN8 9 D6
Birnam Gn FY7 198 E4
Birtle Rd BL9 33 E6
Birtwistle Ave BB8 171 D6
Birtwistle Cl BB9 148 B5
Birtwistle Ct BB18 196 C1
Birtwistle Fold 7 BB8 171 E5
Birtwistle Hyde Pk 3 BB8 171 D5
Birtwistle St
Accrington BB5 104 C5
3 Bamber Bridge PR5 77 B7
Great Harwood BB6 124 B5
Birtwistle Standroyd Bglws BB8 172 A5
Birtwistle Terr BB6 143 C1
Bisham Cl BB3 65 C8
Bishop David Sheppard CE Prim Sch PR9 36 B7
Bishop Martin CE Prim Sch WN8 9 D6
Bishop Rawstorne CE Language Coll The PR26 58 C2
Bishop St Accrington BB5 104 C5
Burnley BB10 148 B1
Nelson BB9 148 D8
Bishopdale Cl
Blackburn BB2 80 D7
Morecambe LA3 217 F3
Bishopdale Rd LA1 214 D7
Bishopgate 15 PR1 97 A8
Bishops Gate FY8 90 D7
Bishopsgate
Blackpool FY3 153 B1
Lancaster LA1 215 A4
Bishopstone Cl BB2 82 A8
Bishopsway PR1 96 D3
Bison Pl PR26 76 C2
Bispham Ave PR26 76 E4
Bispham Ct WN5 10 D2
Bispham Endowed CE Jun Sch FY2 152 D4
Bispham Hall Bsns Pk WN5 10 C2
Bispham High Sch FY2 152 E2
Bispham Hospl FY2 152 F6
Bispham Rd
Blackpool FY2 152 D3
Blackpool,Warbreck FY3 130 E8
Carleton FY5,FY6 153 A6
Cleveleys FY5 175 C2
Cleveleys,Whiteholme FY5 152 F6
Nelson BB9 148 E6
Southport PR9 35 F7
Bispham St 21 PR1 96 F8
Bittern Cl FY3 131 B6
Bivel St BB12 127 D6
Bk Alfred St BL0 50 B5
Bk Commercial St BB9 148 B6
Bk Dawson St BL9 33 A4
Bk Owen St BB5 104 C7
Bk Scotland Rd 7 BB9 148 D8
Bk Shepherd St BL9 33 A1
Black Abbey St BB5 104 C5
Black Bull La PR2 117 D5
Black Croft PR6 78 B3
Black Horse St
Blackrod BL6 31 C3
4 Chorley PR7 43 B6
Black House La
Chipping PR3 185 B1
Lane Bottom BB10 149 D3
Black La Nateby PR3 180 A8
Ramsbottom BL0 51 B7
Black Lane Croft 7 BB7 189 E1
Black Lane Ends BB8 195 F3
Black Moor Rd L40 40 A2
Black Moss La
Ormskirk L39 15 E3
Scarisbrick L40 23 D6
Black Moss Rd BB9 169 E8
Black Moss Sch WN8 17 D2
Black-A-Moor La L39 14 A2
Blackacre La L39,L40 15 E8
Blackamoor Rd BB1 82 C8
Blackberry Hall Cres LA3 213 A8
Blackberry Way PR1 96 B2
Blackbrook CL PR6 62 A2
Blackburn Brow PR6 61 E3
Blackburn Cathedral* BB1 101 E4
Blackburn Coll BB2 101 D5
Blackburn Mus & Art Gall* BB1 101 E5
Blackburn Old Rd
Blackburn BB1 123 D3
Great Harwood BB1,BB6 123 F5
Hoghton PR5 99 C2
Blackburn Rd
Accrington BB5 104 C6
Blackburn BB1 102 E8
Church BB5 103 F6
Blackburn Rd *continued*
Clayton-le-M BB5 124 E1
Darwen BB3 81 E4
Edenfield BL0,BB4 68 D5
Egerton BL7 47 C4
Great Harwood BB6 124 C4
Great Knowley PR6 61 E4
Haslingden BB4,BB5 85 B5
Higher Walton PR5 98 B3
Higher Wheelton PR6 79 C1
Longridge PR3 140 D7
Oswaldtwistle BB5,BB1 103 C5
Padiham BB12 126 A8
Ribchester PR3 141 E3
Rishton BB1 124 A1
Wheelton PR6 61 F6
Whittlestone Head BB3,BL7 66 B2
Blackburn Royal Infmy BB2 101 D2
Blackburn St
Blackburn BB1 101 E6
5 Burnley BB11 127 F6
Chorley PR6 43 E7
Blackburn Sta BB1 101 F4
Blackburn Trad Pk BB1 101 F6
Blackcar La L29 4 A3
Blacker St BB10 148 A2
Blackfen Pl FY2 130 D8
Blackfield Rd PR4 93 B6
Blackgate La Holmes PR4 56 C3
Tarleton PR4 56 E5
Blackhorse Ave BL6 31 C2
Blackhorse Cl BL6 31 C3
Blackhurst Ave PR4 95 F2
Blackhurst Ct PR4 75 B8
Blackhurst Rd L31 5 C5
Blackleach Ave PR2 139 D1
Blackleach La PR4 135 F1
Blackledge Cl WN5 10 E5
Blackley Gr L33 1 A6
Blacko Bar Rd BB9 170 B7
Blacko Prim Sch BB9 170 D8
Blackpool & Fleetwood Tramway* FY2 152 B3
Blackpool & The Fylde Coll
Blackpool FY1 130 C4
Blackpool FY1 130 D4
Blackpool,Whiteholme FY2 152 E6
Blackpool & The Fylde Coll (Nautical) FY7 175 E7
Blackpool & The Fylde Coll Ansdell Campus FY8 90 C5
Blackpool Airport FY4 110 D3
Blackpool Central Pier* FY1 130 A3
Blackpool Lifeboat Visitor Ctr* FY1 130 A4
Blackpool North Pier* FY1 130 A5
Blackpool North Sta FY1 130 C6
Blackpool Old Rd
Little Eccleston PR3 156 A5
Poulton-le-F FY6 153 B2
Blackpool Pleasure Beach* FY4 110 B7
Blackpool Pleasure Beach Sta FY4 110 B6
Blackpool Rd
Blackpool FY2 152 D4
Carleton FY6 153 A4
Clifton PR4 94 E8
Longridge PR3 140 A7
Lytham St Anne's FY8 90 D5
Newton-w-S PR4 115 B2
Preston PR1,PR2 117 C2
Preston,Larches PR2 116 E1
St Michael's on W PR3 157 B6
Wrea Green PR4 113 C6
Blackpool Rd N FY8 110 F2
Blackpool Sixth Form Coll FY3 153 A2
Blackpool South Pier* FY4 110 A8
Blackpool South Sta FY4 130 B1
Blackpool St
5 Church BB5 103 E5
3 Darwen BB3 65 B6
Blackpool Twr* FY1 130 B5
Blackpool Zoo* FY3 131 A4
Blackrod Brow BL6 31 B4
Blackrod By-Pass Rd BL6 31 D2
Blackrod CE Prim Sch BL6 31 C2
Blackrod Sta BL6 31 E2
Blacksmiths Row FY8 90 D7
Blacksnape Rd BB3 82 D2
Blacksticks La PR3 184 D1
Blackstone Rd PR6 61 E1
Blackthorn Cl
Cleveleys FY5 175 F5
Newton-w-S PR4 114 F2
Preston PR2 116 D1
Rochdale OL12 52 E2
Blackthorn Cres OL13 87 F3
Blackthorn Croft PR6 78 A2
Blackthorn Dr PR1 96 B3
Blackthorn La OL13 87 F3
Blackthorn Mews OL12 52 E2
Blackwood Ct OL13 70 C8
Blackwood Pl LA1 215 B5
Blackwood Rd OL13 70 B7
Blades St LA1 214 E7
Blaguegate La WN8 17 B2
Blainscough Rd PR7 29 E8
Blair Gr PR9 35 F7
Blair St OL12 52 D1
Blairgowrie Gdns L39 16 A4
Blairway Ave FY3 130 F6
Blake Ave PR5 77 A7
Blake Gdns BB6 124 B4
Blake St BB5 104 B6
Blakehall WN8 9 D7
Blakeley Cres BB18 196 B3
Blakewater Rd BB1 102 C7
Blakey Moor BB2 101 D5
Blakey St BB11 128 B6
Blakiston St FY7 199 A4
Blanche St 6 PR2 117 C1
Blandford Ave FY5 175 C1
Blandford Cl PR8 34 F5
Blandford Rise BL6 32 F1
Blannel St BB11 127 E6
Blascomay Sq 10 BB8 171 D4
Blashaw La PR1 96 A5
Blaydike Moss PR26 76 B1
Blaydon Ave FY5 175 E4
Blaydon Pk WN8 9 D7
Blea Cl BB12 127 B8
Blea Tarn Pl 3 LA4 217 D4
Blea Tarn Rd LA2 215 C2
Bleachers Dr 2 PR25 76 E1
Bleak La L40 26 D5
Bleakholt Rd BL0 68 F1
Bleara Rd BB18 195 D7
Bleasdale Ave
Blackpool FY5 152 E8
Clitheroe BB7 166 C7
Kirkham PR4 114 A5
Poulton-le-F FY6 153 C2
Staining FY3 131 E5
Bleasdale CE Prim Sch PR3 184 A7
Bleasdale Cl
2 Bamber Bridge PR5 77 F8
Leyland PR25 60 B7
Ormskirk L39 6 D7
Bleasdale Ct PR3 140 B7
Bleasdale Gr LA3 216 E1
Bleasdale House Com Specl Sch LA5 224 C3
Bleasdale La PR3 183 C6
Bleasdale Rd
Cumeragh Village PR3 138 F6
Knott End-on-S FY6 199 D5
Lytham St Anne's FY8 91 C4
Whitechapel PR3 183 D1
Bleasdale St E PR1 118 C1
Blelock St PR1 97 A7
Blenheim Ave
Blackpool FY1 130 D4
Kirkham PR4 113 F5
Blenheim Cl
Bamber Bridge PR5 77 C8
1 Blackburn BB1 122 E1
Blenheim Dr
Thornton FY5 176 C2
Warton PR4 92 D6
Blenheim Pl FY8 110 E1
Blenheim Rd PR8 21 B6
Blenheim St Colne BB8 172 A5
13 Rochdale OL12 52 C1
Blenheim Terr BB8 194 E1
Blenheim Way PR4 116 E6
Blessed Sacrament RC Prim Sch PR2 118 F3
Blind La Burton in L LA6 242 C3
Gisburn BB7 231 C3
Higham BB12 147 A6
Blindman's La L39 15 C7
Bloom St 3 BL0 50 A4
Bloomfield Ct PR1 117 E2
Bloomfield Grange PR1 96 C2
Bloomfield Pk LA5 223 D1
Bloomfield Rd
Blackpool FY1 130 C2
Withnell PR6 80 A1
Bloomfield Road Football Gd (Blackpool FC) FY1 130 C2
Blossom Ave
Blackpool FY4 110 F7
Oswaldtwistle BB5 103 E5
Blossoms The
Fulwood PR2 118 C6
Poulton-le-F FY6 153 F3
Blowick Bsns Pk PR9 36 A6
Blowick Ind Pk PR9 36 A6
Blucher St BB8 171 E4
Blue Bell La OL14 109 D2
Blue Bell Pl PR1 97 A7
Blue Gates BB7 229 B3
Blue Moor PR4 135 A2
Blue Scar La BB7 230 D7
Blue Stone La L40 40 F4
Bluebell Ave BB4 68 A8
Bluebell Cl
Blackpool FY2 152 D2
Cleveleys FY5 175 F5
Hesketh Bank PR4 73 E4
Lucas Green PR6 61 C5
Bluebell Gr BB11 127 A5
Bluebell Way
Fulwood PR2 118 F6
Walton Summit PR5 78 A8
Bluebell Wood PR25 76 F3
Bluecoat Cres PR4 115 A2
Bluestone La L31 5 E1
Blundell Ave Formby L37 11 B4
Hightown L38 2 F3
Southport PR8 34 F2
Blundell Cres PR8 34 F2
Blundell Dr PR8 34 F2
Blundell Gr L38 2 F3
Blundell La Blackrod BL6 31 A2

Blundell La *continued*
Higher Penwortham PR1 ....96 B6
Southport PR9 ....54 C2
Blundell Links Ct PR8 ....21 C4
Blundell Rd Fulwood PR2 .117 E3
Hightown L38 ....2 F3
Lytham St Anne's FY8 .....110 F1
Blundell St FY1 ....130 B3
Blythe Ave FY5 ....175 E5
Blythe Cotts L40 ....25 E1
Blythe La L40 ....25 E1
Blythe Mews PR8 ....22 A8
Blythewood WN8 ....9 D7
Board St BB10 ....148 A1
Boarded Barn PR7 ....60 C3
Boardman Ave FY1 .....130 D2
Boardman St BL6 ....31 D2
Boarsgreave La BB4 ......69 F6
Bobbin Cl BB5 ....104 A5
Bobbin Mill Cl 11 OL14 ..109 B1
Bobbin Mill Cotts PR3 ...181 F2
Bobbin St OL14 ....109 C1
Bobbiners La PR9 ....55 A3
Bobby Langton Way L40 ..25 E5
Bocholt Way BB4 ....86 A2
Bodiam Rd BL8 ....49 F2
Bodie Hill LA2 ....209 E5
Bodkin La PR3 ....154 F7
Bodmin Ave PR9 ....54 B5
Bodmin St PR1 ....118 D1
Boegrave Ave PR5 ....77 A8
Bog Height Rd BB3 ......81 C6
Bogburn La PR7 ....29 D6
Boland St BB1 ....102 A7
Bold La L39 ....6 B7
Bold St Accrington BB5 ...104 D6
Bacup OL13 ....87 F1
Blackburn BB1 ....101 E6
Bury BL9 ....33 A3
Colne BB8 ....171 E4
Fleetwood FY7 ....199 B5
Morecambe LA3 ....216 E4
Preston PR1 ....117 D1
Southport PR9 ....35 B8
Bold Venture Cotts BB7 .190 C4
Bold Venture Way BB5 ..125 A3
Boleyn Ct FY3 ....131 A2
Boleyn The L31 ....5 E3
Bolland Cl 6 BB7 ....166 F8
Bolland Prospect BB7 ...166 F7
Bolland St BB18 ....196 B3
Bolton Ave
Accrington BB5 ....125 D1
Carleton FY6 ....153 C5
Lancaster LA1 ....218 D4
Bolton Cl L37 ....12 A2
Bolton Com Coll Horwich Campus BL6 ....32 D2
Bolton Croft PR26 ....59 B8
Bolton Gr BB9 ....170 D3
Bolton La LA5 ....221 C4
Bolton Mdw PR26 ....59 A8
Bolton Rd
Abbey Village PR6 ....80 B3
Adlington BL60,PR6 ....31 D6
Blackburn BB2 ....101 D2
Blackburn,Ewood BB2 ......81 E7
Chorley PR6 ....43 E4
Darwen BB3 ....65 B7
Darwen,Cadshaw BB3 ......65 C3
Edgworth BL7 ....48 D5
Hawkshaw BL8 ....49 D2
Riley Green PR5,PR6 ......79 E6
Southport PR8 ....35 A4
Bolton Rd N BL0 ....68 D2
Bolton Rd W BL0,BL8 .....50 A4
Bolton St Blackpool FY1 ..130 B2
Chorley PR7 ....43 C7
Colne BB8 ....171 C4
5 Newchurch BB4 ....86 E1
Ramsbottom BL0 ....50 B6
Bolton's Cop PR9 ....55 D5
Bolton's Ct 24 BB1 ....101 E5
Bolton's Meanygate PR4 .56 C7
Bolton-by-Bowland CE Prim Sch BB7 ....230 D4
Bolton-le-Sands CE Prim Sch LA5 ....221 B4
Boltons Croft PR4 ......115 E7
Boltons Ct PR1 ....97 A7
Bombay St BB2 ....101 C3
Bonchurch St BB1 ......102 C4
Bond Cl BL6 ....32 C3
Bond St Blackpool FY4 ...110 B7
18 Burnley BB10 ....128 A8
Bury BL9 ....33 A2
Colne BB8 ....171 D5
Darwen BB3 ....82 A2
Edenfield BL0 ....68 E2
Lancaster LA1 ....215 A8
Nelson BB9 ....148 D7
Bond's La Adlington PR7 ...30 F7
Banks PR9 ....55 A7
Bonds La Bonds PR3 .....181 C6
Elswick PR4 ....156 A2
Bone Croft PR6 ....78 B3
Bone Hill La PR3 ....202 D1
Bonfire Hill Cl BB4 ......86 B7
Bonfire Hill Rd BB4 ......86 A7
Bonney St FY5 ....176 B3
Bonny Grass Terr BB7 ..144 A4
Bonny St FY1 ....130 B4
Bonsall St BB2 ....101 B2
Boome St FY4 ....110 C6
Boon Town LA6 ....240 C7
Boon Wlks LA6 ....240 C7
Boot St BB18 ....197 B2
Boot Way BB11 ....128 A5
Booth Bridge La BD23 ...197 B5
Booth Cres BB4 ....87 A1
Booth Ct 4 BB10 ....128 A8
Booth Rd OL13 ....70 B8
Booth St Accrington BB5 ..104 C4
10 Bacup OL13 ....87 F2
Carnforth LA5 ....223 D1
Haslingden BB4 ....85 A4
10 Nelson BB9 ....148 D8
Rawtenstall BB4 ....69 E8
Southport PR8 ....35 B8
Booth's La L39 ....14 F4
Booth's Par PR2 ....117 F7
Boothfield House Cvn Pk FY6 ....200 A6
Boothley Rd FY1 ....130 D6
Boothman Pl BB9 ....170 E2
Boothman St BB2 ....101 D2
Boothroyden FY1 ....130 B8
Bootle St PR1 ....118 C1
Borage Cl FY5 ....176 A5
Bordeaux Cres FY5 ......152 F6
Border Ct 6 LA1 ....218 B1
Bores Hill WN1 ....30 C4
Borough Rd BB3 ....82 A1
Borrans Lane Cvn Pk LA3 ....212 F4
Borron La LA6 ....240 C3
Borrowdale L37 ....11 F5
Borrowdale Ave
Blackburn BB1 ....102 C3
Fleetwood FY7 ....198 E4
Nelson BB9 ....148 F7
Borrowdale Cl
4 Accrington BB5 ....125 D1
Brierfield BB10 ....148 C3
Borrowdale Dr BB10 ....148 C4
Borrowdale Gr LA4 .....217 D5
Borrowdale Rd
Blackpool FY4 ....131 B1
Lancaster LA1 ....215 A8
Leyland PR25 ....60 B7
Borwick Ave LA5 ....223 E6
Borwick Cl LA5 ....223 E6
Borwick Ct Borwick LA6 ..240 B4
Morecambe LA4 ....217 B3
Borwick Dr LA1 ....218 B2
Borwick La LA6 ....240 B3
Borwick Mews LA6 ....240 B3
Borwick Rd LA6 ....240 D3
Bosburn Dr BB2 ....121 C2
Boscombe Ave LA3 ......216 E2
Boscombe Rd FY4 ......110 B6
Bosley Arc 2 FY1 ....130 B5
Bosley Cl BB3 ....65 D8
Bostock St 21 PR1 ....97 A7
Boston Ave FY2 ....152 D6
Boston Rd Bacup OL13 ....87 F3
Lytham St Anne's FY8 ......90 D6
Boston St BB9 ....148 F6
Bostons BB6 ....124 B5
Bostonway FY4 ....110 F8
Bosworth Dr PR8 ....21 B4
Bosworth Pl FY4 ....110 B4
Bosworth St BL6 ....32 B4
Botanic Gardens Mus* PR9 ....54 B2
Botanic Rd PR9 ....54 B2
Botany Bay* PR6 ....61 E3
Botany Brow PR6 ....61 E2
Bott House La BB8,BB9 ..171 A2
Bottom o' th' Knotts Brow BL7 ....48 E3
Bottom O' Th' Moor BL6 ..32 F3
Bottom O' Th' Rann BB1 ....82 F6
Bottom's Row BB4 ....69 F6
Bottomdale Cvn Pk LA2 .218 D8
Bottomdale Rd LA2 ......218 E8
Bottomgate BB1 ....102 B5
Bottomley Bank La BB4 ...86 B8
Bottomley St BB9 ....148 E8
Bottoms La LA5 ....224 D3
Botton Rd LA2 ....239 C1
Boulder St 10 BB4 ....86 A7
Bouldsworth Rd BB10 ....128 E5
Boulevard PR1 ....97 B5
Boulevard Gdns FY8 ......90 A4
Boulevard The
Blackburn BB1 ....101 E4
Lytham St Anne's FY8 .....90 A4
Boulsworth Cres BB9 ....171 B1
Boulsworth Dr BB8 ......172 C1
Boulsworth Gr BB8 ......172 A5
Boulview Terr BB8 ....172 A5
Boundary Cl Eccleston PR7 .41 B6
New Longton PR4 ....75 F8
Boundary Ct FY3 ....153 A1
Boundary La
Becconsall PR4 ....73 E1
Burscough L40 ....25 F4
Hale Nook FR6,PR3 ....178 B7
Holmes PR4,PR9 ....55 E6
Kirkby L33 ....1 F2
Shevington Moor WN6 ......29 A3
Boundary Meanygate
Becconsall PR4 ....73 D1
Holmes PR4 ....55 F7
Boundary Prim Sch FY3 .130 F8
Boundary Rd
Accrington BB5 ....104 D7
Fulwood PR2 ....117 D3
Lancaster LA1 ....214 F6
Lytham St Anne's FY8 .....91 E5
Boundary St
Burnley BB10 ....148 C2
Colne BB8 ....171 D4
Leyland PR25 ....77 B2
Boundary St *continued*
Southport PR8 ....35 B4
Bourbles La FY6 ....200 D4
Bourne Brow PR3 ....159 E5
Bourne May Rd FY6 .....199 D5
Bourne Rd FY5 ....176 B5
Bourne Way FY5 ....176 A4
Bourne's Row PR5 ....98 E1
Bournemouth Rd FY4 ....110 B6
Bournesfield PR5 ....98 E1
Bovington Ave FY5 ......152 F8
Bow Brook Rd PR25 ......77 C1
Bow Hills La BB7 ....231 C6
Bow La Leyland PR25 .....77 B1
Preston PR1 ....96 E7
Bow St PR25 ....77 B2
Bowden Ave BB2 ....100 C1
Bowen St BB2 ....101 B2
Bower Cl BB2 ....101 B2
Bower St Blackburn BB2 ..101 B2
Bury BL9 ....33 C3
Bowerham Com Prim Sch LA1 ....215 A6
Bowerham La LA1 ....215 B3
Bowerham Rd LA1 ......215 A5
Bowerham Terr 1 LA1 ...215 A6
Bowers La PR3 ....180 E7
Bowers The PR7 ....43 D4
Bowes Lyon Pl FY8 ....90 C7
Bowfell Ave LA4 ....217 D5
Bowfell Cl FY4 ....131 D1
Bowfield's La BB2 ....120 F4
Bowgreave Cl 1 FY4 .....111 A6
Bowgreave Dr PR3 ......181 D4
Bowker St BL0 ....68 C5
Bowker's Green La L39 ....6 E4
Bowland Ave
Burnley BB10 ....128 E5
Chorley PR6 ....43 D8
Fleetwood FY7 ....175 D8
Lancaster LA1 ....211 B8
Bowland Cl
Carnforth LA5 ....223 C1
Longridge PR3 ....140 B8
Bowland Cres FY3 ......131 A8
Bowland Ct
4 Clitheroe BB7 ....166 E8
9 Southport PR9 ....35 C8
Bowland Dr LA1 ....218 B2
Bowland Gate La BB7 ...189 E7
Bowland High Sch BB7 ..230 B1
Bowland Ho 7 BB1 ......101 F6
Bowland Pl Fulwood PR2 .119 A3
Lytham St Anne's FY8 .....90 C6
Bowland Rd
Fulwood PR2 ....119 A3
Garstang PR3 ....204 C1
Heysham LA3 ....213 A8
Bowland View
Brierfield BB9 ....148 D4
Garstang PR3 ....204 C1
Glasson LA2 ....209 E4
Bowland Wild Boar Pk* BB7 ....186 E6
Bowlers Cl PR2 ....118 C5
Bowlers Wlk OL12 ....52 F2
Bowling Gn The BL0 .....68 D3
Bowling Green Cl
Darwen BB3 ....65 B7
Southport PR8 ....35 F5
Bowling Green Cotts BB6 ....143 C6
Bowling Green Cvn Pk LA5 ....223 C1
Bowlingfield PR2 ....117 A6
Bowness Ave
Blackpool FY4 ....131 D1
Fleetwood FY7 ....198 C1
Lytham St Anne's FY8 ....110 F2
Nelson BB9 ....148 E6
Rochdale OL12 ....52 C1
Southport PR8 ....21 C3
Thornton FY5 ....176 B2
Bowness Cl BB1 ....102 A6
Bowness Rd
Lancaster LA1 ....218 E1
Padiham BB12 ....146 C2
Preston PR1 ....119 A1
Bowood Ct FY3 ....131 B7
Bowran St PR1 ....96 F8
Box St BL0 ....50 D6
Boxer Pl PR26 ....76 C2
Boxwood Dr BB2 ....80 F8
Boxwood St BB1 ....101 F8
Boyd Cl WN6 ....29 F1
Boyes Ave PR3 ....181 D2
Boyle St BB1 ....101 F6
Boys La PR2 ....117 C5
Brabiner La PR2,PR3 ....139 B4
Brabins Endowed Sch PR3 ....185 E3
Bracebridge Dr PR8 ......35 F2
Bracewell Ave FY6 ......154 A3
Bracewell Cl BB9 ....148 E8
Bracewell La BD23 ......231 F3
Bracewell Rd PR2 ....118 E5
Bracewell St
Barnoldswick BB18 ....196 B3
Burnley BB10 ....148 B1
Nelson BB9 ....148 F8
Bracken Cl Blackburn BB2 ..80 F8
Chorley PR6 ....43 E8
Bracken Dr PR4 ....93 D7
Bracken Gr BB4 ....68 A8
Bracken Hey BB7 ....167 A8
Bracken Lea Fold 3 OL12 ....52 B2
Bracken Way FY2 ....152 D2
Brackenbury Cl 5 PR5 ....77 A7
Brackenbury Rd PR1, PR2 ....117 E3
Brackenbury St PR1 .....117 F2
Brackendale BB2 ....101 C1
Brackenthaite Rd LA5, LA7 ....225 B7
Brackenway L37 ....12 A6
Bracknel Way L39 ....15 A1
Braconash Rd PR25 ......76 E2
Bradda Rd BB2 ....101 E1
Braddon St 2 PR1 ......118 D1
Brade St PR9 ....54 C4
Brades Ave FY5 ....176 D2
Brades La PR4 ....93 D7
Bradford Gr LA3 ....212 F6
Bradford St BB5 ....104 D6
Bradkirk La PR5 ....78 B8
Bradkirk Pl PR5 ....78 A7
Bradley Ct BB7 ....163 E8
Bradley Fold 5 BB9 .....170 E1
Bradley Gdns BB12 ......127 B5
Bradley Hall Rd BB9 ....170 F1
Bradley Hall Trad Est WN6 ....29 F2
Bradley Hill Trad Est WN6 ....30 A2
Bradley La Eccleston PR7 ..41 D6
Standish WN6 ....29 F2
1 Standish WN6 ....29 E1
Bradley Pl 8 PR8 ....35 B7
Bradley Prim Sch BB9 ..170 E1
Bradley Rd BB9 ....170 E1
Bradley Rd E BB9 ....170 E1
Bradley Smithy Cl OL12 ..52 E2
Bradley St Colne BB8 ....171 F5
Southport PR9 ....35 C8
Bradley View 12 BB9 ....170 E1
Bradman Rd L33 ....1 D3
Bradshaw Brow L40 ....40 E2
Bradshaw Cl
Blackburn BB1 ....101 E8
Nelson BB9 ....148 E7
Stalmine FY6 ....177 C7
Standish WN6 ....29 D1
Bradshaw Ct PR9 ....36 A7
Bradshaw La
Corner Row PR4 ....133 D1
Eagland Hill PR3 ....179 A7
Mawdesley L40 ....40 E2
Parbold WN8 ....27 C1
Scronkey PR3 ....201 E2
Bradshaw Rd BL7 ....48 E1
Bradshaw Row BB5 ......103 F6
Bradshaw St Church BB5 .103 F6
7 Lancaster LA1 ....215 A7
Nelson BB9 ....148 D7
Bradshaw St E 3 BB5 ...104 C6
Bradshaw St W BB5 .....103 F6
Bradshaw's La PR8 ....21 D6
Bradshawgate Dr LA5 ...224 C4
Bradwood Ct BB4 ....85 A2
Brady St BL6 ....32 A4
Bradyll Ct BB6 ....143 C6
Braefield Cres PR2 ......118 F2
Braemar Ave
Southport PR9 ....53 F2
Thornton FY5 ....153 C7
Braemar Ct 2 LA4 ....217 E4
Braemar Dr BL9 ....33 D2
Braemar Wlk FY2 ....152 F6
Braeside BB2 ....101 C6
Braewood Cl BL9 ....33 C3
Braganza Way LA1 ......214 C8
Braid Cl PR1 ....96 D1
Braid's La PR3 ....182 A7
Braidhaven WN6 ....19 E7
Braidwood Ct FY8 ....89 D7
Braintree Ave PR1 ....96 E2
Braith Cl FY4 ....110 F8
Braithwaite St 3 FY1 ...130 B7
Bramble Cl PR4 ....113 E6
Bramble Ct Kingsfold PR1 ..96 E2
1 Thornton FY5 ....176 A2
Bramble St BB10 ....148 A1
Bramble Way
Burscough L40 ....25 F4
Parbold WN8 ....27 C1
Brambles The
Barrow BB7 ....166 D1
Blackburn BB2 ....101 A8
Blackpool FY8 ....110 B4
Coppull PR7 ....42 F2
Fulwood PR2 ....118 D6
Bramblewood PR26 ....58 B2
Bramblings The FY6 .....153 B2
Bramcote Cl L33 ....1 A4
Bramcote Rd L33 ....1 A4
Bramhall Rd WN8 ....17 F2
Bramley Ave
Burnley BB12 ....127 C8
Fleetwood FY7 ....198 E4
Bramley Cl 8 BB5 ......103 E5
Bramley Ct 7 WN6 ....29 E1
Bramley Gdns FY6 ......153 A2
Bramley View BB7 ....144 D8
Brampton Ave FY5 ......175 F4
Brampton Dr LA4 ....217 F5
Brampton St 2 PR2 .....117 C1
Bramwell Rd PR4 ....93 B6
Bramworth Ave BL0 ......50 B6
Branch Rd
Blackburn BB2,BB3 ....81 E7
Burnley BB11 ....128 B4
2 Clayton-le-M BB5 .....124 F3
Mellor Brook BB2 ....121 C2
Waddington BB7 ....189 B4
Branch St Bacup OL13 .....70 D8
Branch St *continued*
Nelson BB9 ....148 F8
Brancker St 3 PR7 ....43 A5
Brandiforth St PR5 ....97 F2
Brandlesholme Rd BL8 ...50 A1
Brandon Cl WN8 ....10 A7
Brandreth Delph WN8 ....27 C3
Brandreth Dr WN8 ....27 C2
Brandreth Pk WN8 ....27 D4
Brandreth Pl WN6 ....29 F1
Brandwood
Higher Penwortham PR1 ...96 A4
6 Newchurch BB4 ....86 E1
Brandwood Ct BL7 ....48 E5
Brandwood Fold BL7 .....48 E5
Brandwood Gr BB10 ....128 C6
Brandwood Pk OL13 ......70 B8
Brandwood Rd OL13 ......70 B8
Brandwood St BB3 ....82 B1
Brandy House Brow BB2 ....101 F2
Branksome Ave FY5 .....175 F3
Branksome Dr LA4 ......217 D4
Branston Rd FY4 ....130 E1
Branstree Rd FY4 ....131 C1
Brant Ct FY7 ....198 C1
Brant Rd PR1 ....119 A1
Brantfell Dr BB12 ....127 B8
Brantfell Rd
Blackburn BB1 ....101 D7
Great Harwood BB6 ......124 D6
Brantwood BB5 ....124 E2
Brantwood Ave
Blackburn BB1 ....102 F5
Morecambe LA4 ....217 E6
Brantwood Dr
Lancaster LA1 ....215 A2
Leyland PR25 ....77 B1
Brassey St BB12 ....127 C7
Brathay Pl FY7 ....198 D2
Bray St PR2 ....117 C1
Brays Heys 2 FY5 ....176 C1
Brays Rd FY8 ....112 B1
Brayshaw Pl PR2 ....118 E4
Brazil Cl LA3 ....217 A2
Brazley Ave BL6 ....32 E1
Bread St 4 BB12 ....127 D6
Bream Wood PR4 ....113 E4
Brearlands BD23 ....197 B6
Brearley St OL13 ....70 D8
Breck Cl FY6 ....153 E5
Breck Dr FY6 ....153 E5
Breck Prim Sch The FY6 ....153 F5
Breck Rd Blackpool FY3 ...130 E4
Poulton-le-F FY6 ....153 F6
Breckside Cl FY6 ....153 E5
Brecon Ave BB5 ....103 C4
Brecon Cl FY1 ....130 D3
Brecon Rd BB1 ....102 C5
Bredon Ave PR7 ....60 E1
Bredon Cl FY8 ....91 D5
Bredon Ct L37 ....11 E4
Breeze Cl Foulridge BB8 ..194 E1
Thornton FY5 ....176 A4
Breeze Mount PR5 ....77 C8
Breeze Rd PR8 ....34 E2
Brenbar Cres OL12 ....71 D1
Brendjean Rd LA4 ......217 C4
Brendon Wlk FY3 ....130 F8
Brennand Cl
Bamber Bridge PR5 ....77 F8
Lancaster LA1 ....218 A2
Brennand St
Burnley BB10 ....148 B1
Clitheroe BB7 ....189 E1
Brent St BB10 ....148 C3
Brentlea Ave LA3 ....212 E7
Brentlea Cres LA3 ......212 E7
Brenton Bsns Complex 2 BL9 ....33 A2
Brentwood FY7 ....198 E2
Brentwood Ave
Blackpool FY5 ....152 D8
Burnley BB11 ....127 E3
Poulton-le-F FY6 ....153 C3
Brentwood Cl L38 ....2 F2
Brentwood Ct PR9 ....53 D1
Brentwood Rd
Adlington PR6 ....31 B8
Nelson BB9 ....171 A1
Bretherton Cl PR26 ......59 C8
Bretherton Cotts FY5 ...153 E8
Bretherton Ct L40 ....25 F3
Bretherton Endowed CE Prim Sch PR26 ....57 F5
Bretherton Rd PR26 ......58 B4
Bretherton Terr 9 PR25 ..77 B1
Brett Cl BB7 ....167 A7
Brettarch Dr LA1 ....214 E5
Brettargh Cl LA1 ....214 E6
Brettargh Dr LA1 ....214 E6
Bretton Fold PR8 ....35 F5
Brewery Arc 42 LA1 .....214 F8
Brewery La Formby L37 ...11 F6
19 Lancaster LA1 ....214 F8
Brewery St
6 Blackburn BB2 ....101 D5
Longridge PR3 ....140 B7
Breworth Fold La PR6 ....79 A3
Briar Ave PR7 ....60 C4
Briar Bank Row PR2 ....118 A8
Briar Cl OL12 ....52 A1
Briar Croft PR4 ....75 A7
Briar Field FY2 ....152 F6

Briar Gr PR2 .117 A4
Briar Hill Cl 3 BB1 .102 A4
Briar Lea Rd LA6 .221 E5
Briar Mews 1 FY5 .176 C1
Briar Rd Blackburn BB1 .101 F8
Southport PR8 .21 D4
Thornton FY5 .176 C1
Briar St OL13 .88 A1
Briarcroft BB3 .82 A6
Briarfield BL7 .47 D2
Briarfield Rd FY6 .153 B5
Briars Brook L40 .26 A2
Briars Gn WN8 .18 B4
Briars La Maghull L31 .5 E1
Ring o'Bells L40 .26 A3
Briars The Fulwood PR2 .118 D6
Southport PR8 .34 F1
Briarscroft LA5 .223 E6
Briarwood PR4 .93 A6
Briarwood Cl
Leyland PR25 .59 E8
Weeton PR4 .132 F2
Briarwood Ct FY5 .153 B7
Briarwood Dr FY2 .152 E5
Briary Croft L38 .2 F3
Brick Kiln La L40 .39 B3
Brick St 9 Burnley BB11 .127 F6
Bury BL9 .33 A3
Brickcroft La PR26 .58 B3
Brickhouse Gdns PR3 .185 E3
Brickhouse La FY6 .177 C4
Brickmakers Arms Yd
L39 .15 D6
Bridge Ave L39 .15 E5
Bridge Bank 4 PR5 .97 C6
Bridge Cl
Bamber Bridge PR5 .77 A8
6 Newchurch BB4 .86 F1
Bridge Croft
Bolton-le-S LA5 .221 A4
Clayton-le-M BB5 .124 E4
Bridge Ct
3 Bamber Bridge PR5 .77 A8
Clitheroe BB7 .189 F2
2 Lytham St Anne's FY8 .91 D4
Bridge End
Bamber Bridge PR5 .77 C8
Barley BB12 .169 C5
Whalley BB7 .144 C4
Bridge End Cl BB4 .68 A7
Bridge End St OL14 .109 C1
Bridge Farm Dr L31 .5 F2
Bridge Gr PR8 .35 B6
Bridge Hall Dr BL9 .33 C2
Bridge Hall Fold BL9 .33 C2
Bridge Hall La BL9 .33 D2
Bridge Ho
6 Blackburn BB2 .101 B1
18 Lancaster LA1 .218 D2
3 Lytham St Anne's FY8 .91 D4
Ormskirk L39 .15 E4
Bridge Hos Accrington BB5 .84 E8
Whitewell Bottom BB4 .86 F7
Bridge House Marina & Cvn Pk PR3 .181 A8
Bridge House Rd FY4 .110 F8
Bridge La LA1 .214 F8
Bridge Mill Ct PR6 .43 F6
Bridge Mill Rd BB9 .148 C8
Bridge Mills BL0 .68 E3
Bridge Rd
3 Bamber Bridge PR5 .77 C8
Chatburn BB7 .190 D5
Fleetwood FY7 .199 B4
Lancaster LA1 .214 F5
Lytham St Anne's FY8 .90 E4
Morecambe LA4 .217 C5
Nether Kellet LA6 .221 E4
Preston PR2 .117 C2
Bridge Row PR3 .157 C7
Bridge St
14 Accrington BB5 .104 C6
Bamber Bridge PR5 .77 E7
Blackburn BB1 .101 E4
Brierfield BB9 .148 B5
Burnley BB11 .128 A6
Bury BL9 .33 A3
Church BB5 .103 E6
Colne BB8 .171 C4
Darwen BB3 .82 A1
Garstang PR3 .181 C6
6 Great Harwood BB6 .124 C5
Haslingden BB4 .68 C6
Higher Walton PR5 .98 B3
Horwich BL6 .32 C4
Newchurch BB4 .86 F1
Ormskirk L39 .15 E4
Padiham BB12 .126 B8
Ramsbottom BL0 .50 C6
Rawtenstall BB4 .69 E7
Rishton BB1 .124 B2
Southport PR8 .35 B6
Water BB4 .87 A8
Wheelton PR6 .62 A7
Whitworth OL12 .71 C1
Bridge Terr
6 Preston PR5 .97 C6
Whalley BB7 .144 B7
Bridge Wills La PR9 .54 C5
Bridgefield Cl BB1 .124 B2
Bridgefield Dr BL9 .33 C2
Bridgefield St 8 BB12 .126 C4
Bridgehall Dr WN8 .10 B7
Bridgemill Rd BB1 .101 F4
Bridgend Ct PR2 .116 F3
Bridgend Dr PR8 .21 B4
Bridgeside FY8 .110 B4
Bridget St 22 LA1 .214 F8
Bridgewater Ave 7 FY5 .152 F7
Bridgewater Cl BB11 .126 F4
Bridgewater Ct 6 BB2 .101 C4
Bridgeway PR5 .77 C8
Bridle Path The BB18 .194 D7
Bridleway
Lytham St Anne's FY8 .90 E7
Newchurch BB4 .86 F2
Brief St BB10 .128 A8
Brier Cres BB9 .148 D6
Brier Dr LA3 .212 E7
Brier Heights Cl BB9 .140 D5
Briercliffe Ave
Blackpool FY3 .130 F2
Colne BB8 .171 B3
Briercliffe Bsns Ctr
BB10 .148 F3
Briercliffe Prim Sch
BB10 .148 F3
Briercliffe Rd
Brierfield BB10 .148 D2
Burnley BB10 .148 C1
9 Chorley PR6 .61 D1
Briercliffe St BB8 .171 B3
Brierfield
New Longton PR4 .75 F8
Skelmersdale WN8 .9 D6
Brierfield Sta BB9 .148 B5
Brierholme Ave BL7 .47 E1
Brierley Ave FY3 .130 E7
Brierley La PR4 .136 B8
Brierley Rd PR5 .78 A7
Brierley St PR2 .117 D1
Briers Brow PR6 .62 B7
Briers The PR7 .41 C6
Briery Cl PR2 .118 C4
Briery Hey PR5 .78 C6
Briery St 2 LA1 .218 B1
Brieryfield Rd PR1 .96 D8
Brigg Field BB5 .124 F4
Briggs Fold BL7 .47 E2
Briggs Fold Cl BL7 .47 E2
Briggs Fold Rd BL7 .47 E2
Briggs Rd PR2 .117 C2
Brighouse Cl L39 .15 D6
Bright St Blackburn BB1 .102 B6
Blackpool FY4 .110 B8
2 Burnley BB10 .148 B1
Bury BL9 .33 A3
Clitheroe BB7 .166 F8
Colne BB8 .171 D5
Colne,Cotton Tree BB8 .172 B5
Darwen BB3 .81 F2
Egerton BL7 .47 D2
Oswaldtwistle BB5 .103 D3
Padiham BB12 .126 D8
13 Rawtenstall BB4 .86 A3
Southport PR9 .35 F7
Bright Terr BB8 .172 B2
Bright's Cl BB7 .229 A5
Brighton Ave
Blackpool FY4 .110 B8
Cleveleys FY5 .175 D2
Lytham St Anne's FY8 .89 F7
Brighton Cres PR2 .117 A3
Brighton Rd
Brierfield BB10 .148 C3
Southport PR8 .35 A3
Brighton St Bury BL9 .33 B3
7 Chorley PR6 .43 E8
Cornholme OL14 .109 C1
Brighton Terr
Blackburn BB2 .101 B6
Darwen BB3 .81 E2
Brightstone Cl PR9 .55 B5
Brightwater BL6 .31 F2
Brigsteer Cl BB5 .124 E2
Brindle Cl
9 Lancaster LA1 .218 A2
Longridge PR3 .140 B7
Walton Summit PR5 .78 B8
Brindle Fold PR5 .78 C7
Brindle Gregson Lane Prim Sch PR5 .98 E1
Brindle Hts PR6 .78 F5
Brindle Rd
Bamber Bridge PR5 .97 F2
Walton Summit PR5,PR6 .78 C7
Brindle St Blackburn BB2 .101 C1
Chorley PR7 .43 C6
Preston PR1 .97 C8
Brindle St James' CE Prim Sch PR6 .78 F5
Brindley Cl BB11 .126 F4
Brindley St BL6 .32 C2
Brink's Row BL6 .32 D5
Brinklow Cl PR8 .21 A5
Brinscall Terr PR6 .62 F7
Brinwell Rd FY4 .131 B1
Brisbane Pl FY5 .152 F7
Brisbane St 8 BB5 .125 A1
Bristol Ave Blackpool FY2 .152 E4
Fleetwood FY7 .175 C8
Leyland PR25 .77 C3
Bristol Cl 9 BB1 .102 A4
Bristol St Burnley BB11 .127 D3
Colne BB8 .171 E5
Morecambe LA4 .217 C4
Bristow Ave PR2 .117 B2
Britannia Ave OL13 .88 A2
Britannia Com Prim Sch
OL13 .71 C8
Britannia Cotts BB5 .103 A1
Britannia Dr PR2 .96 B7
Britannia Pl 2 FY1 .130 B1
Britannia St BB6 .124 C5
Britannia Way
Blackpool FY4 .111 E8
Haslingden BB4 .68 A8
Britannia Wharf PR2 .96 B8
Britannia Wlk
1 Burnley BB11 .128 B4
Lytham St Anne's FY8 .90 C8
British Commercial Vehicle Mus* PR25 .77 A1
British in India Mus*
BB8 .171 E5
British Lawnmower Mus*
PR8 .35 B5
Britton Cl BB2 .102 A2
Britten St BB3 .81 F2
Britwell Cl BB2 .82 A8
Brixey St PR1 .96 D6
Brixham Pl 4 FY4 .110 B6
Brixton Rd PR1 .97 B7
Broad Clough Villas
OL13 .87 F5
Broad Croft PR4 .95 A1
Broad Gate BB3 .82 B2
Broad Ing OL12 .52 C1
Broad Ing Cl BB10 .128 E1
Broad La Formby L37 .12 E2
Hale Nook PR3 .178 D5
Haskayne L39 .14 B2
Kirkby L32 .1 A1
Maghull L29 .4 C2
Whalley BB7 .144 B5
Winmarleigh PR3 .203 F5
Broad Lane Gypsy Camp
L37 .12 D8
Broad Mdw
Bamber Bridge PR5 .77 A8
Chipping PR3 .185 D3
Broad Meadow La PR26 .57 F4
Broad Oak Ave PR3 .181 D6
Broad Oak Cl PR6 .31 A8
Broad Oak Cotts PR6 .44 D3
Broad Oak Gn PR1 .96 B3
Broad Oak High Sch BL9 .33 B2
Broad Oak Ind Est BB5 .104 D4
Broad Oak La Bury BL9 .33 D3
Higher Penwortham PR1 .96 B3
Kingsfold PR4 .96 B2
Staining FY3 .131 D5
Broad Oak Rd BB5 .104 D5
Broad Oak Terr BL9 .33 E3
Broad Sq 8 PR25 .60 A8
Broad St 3 Leyland PR25 .60 A8
18 Nelson BB9 .148 D8
Broadacre Caton LA2 .237 C3
Shevington Moor WN6 .29 B2
Skelmersdale WN8 .10 A6
Broadacre Cl LA2 .237 C3
Broadacre Pl LA2 .237 C3
Broadacre View LA2 .237 C3
Broadbent Dr BL9 .33 E4
Broadfield Accrington BB5 .84 B8
Broughton PR3 .137 B2
Oswaldtwistle BB5 .103 F2
Broadfield Ave
Blackpool FY4 .110 F5
Poulton-le-F FY6 .153 F3
Broadfield Ct FY6 .153 F3
Broadfield Dr
Kingsfold PR1 .96 D2
Leyland PR25 .76 E1
Broadfield Rd BB5 .104 A3
Broadfield Sch BB5 .103 F3
Broadfield St BB5 .103 F3
Broadfields PR7 .61 B2
Broadfleet Cl PR3 .201 C6
Broadfold Ave BB1 .102 B7
Broadgate PR1 .96 D6
Broadgate Foot Cvn Pk
LA3 .212 F4
Broadgreen Cl PR25 .76 F1
Broadhead Rd BB3,BL7 .66 F5
Broadhurst La WN6 .28 F7
Broadhurst Rd FY5 .152 E8
Broadhurst Way BB9 .148 C4
Broadith La PR3 .160 E1
Broadlands PR8 .34 E3
Broadlands Dr LA5 .220 F3
Broadlands Pl FY8 .90 F4
Broadlands Sch BB1 .82 B8
Broadlea Gr OL12 .52 C2
Broadley Fold OL12 .52 B6
Broadley St BB4 .86 A3
Broadmead WN8 .27 B2
Broadness Dr BB9 .148 E6
Broadoak Rd L31 .5 E1
Broadoaks BL9 .33 D3
Broadpool La FY6 .177 C1
Broadriding Rd WN6 .19 E6
Broadstone Cl OL12 .52 A1
Broadstone Ct LA1 .215 C7
Broadtree Cl BB2 .121 C3
Broadwater Ave FY7 .175 F8
Broadwater Gdns FY7 .175 E8
Broadway Accrington BB5 .104 B6
Blackburn BB1 .122 E2
Blackpool FY4 .110 C7
Fleetwood FY7 .198 E2
Fulwood PR2 .117 D7
Haslingden BB4 .68 B8
Horwich BL6 .32 D3
Lancaster LA1 .218 D2
Leyland PR25 .60 B8
Morecambe LA4 .217 D5
Nelson BB9 .148 D8
Preston PR2 .116 F2
Broadway Cl PR8 .21 B5
Broadway Cres BB4 .68 A8
Broadway Pl
Barrowford BB9 .170 D3
Nelson BB9 .171 A1
Broadway St BB2 .101 B1
Broadwood Cl PR1 .96 B4
Broadwood Dr PR2 .117 F7
Broadwood Way FY8 .90 E4
Brock Ave FY7 .198 D2
Brock Bank BB4 .86 F4
Brock Cl LA1 .218 C3
Brock Clough Rd BB4 .86 F4
Brock Mill La PR3 .183 B2
Brock Rd Chorley PR6 .61 D1
Lane Heads PR3,PR4 .156 E3
Brock Side PR3 .159 C6
Brock St LA1 .214 F8
Brockbank Ave LA1 .214 C8
Brockenhurst St BB10 .128 C5
Brockholes Brow PR1, PR2 .119 A1
Brockholes Cres FY6 .153 E2
Brockholes View PR1 .97 C7
Brockholes Way PR3 .181 E1
Brockholes Wood Com Prim Sch PR1 .119 A1
Brocklebank Rd PR9 .53 E2
Brocklehurst Ave BB5 .104 B3
Brocklewood Ave FY6 .131 D8
Brockway FY6 .153 D2
Brockway Ave FY3 .130 F6
Broderick Ave 1 FY2 .152 E1
Brodick Rd BB1 .102 D3
Brodie Cl FY4 .110 F6
Brogden La BB18 .231 E2
Brogden St 4 BB18 .196 B3
Brogden View BB18 .196 A4
Broken Bank Head BB7 .235 A2
Broken Banks BB8 .171 E4
Broken Stone Rd BB3 .81 A6
Bromilow Rd WN8 .17 C1
Bromley Cl FY2 .152 E1
Bromley Cross BL7 .48 B1
Bromley Ct 5 FY2 .152 E1
Bromley Gn PR6 .61 F4
Bromley Ho BB2 .101 C5
Bromley Rd FY8 .89 F6
Bromley St
Blackburn BB2 .101 C5
Preston PR1 .96 D8
Brompton Ave L33 .1 A5
Brompton Cl FY8 .90 D5
Brompton Rd
Poulton-le-F FY6 .131 D8
Southport PR8 .35 E7
Bromsgrove Ave FY2 .152 C4
Bromsgrove Rd BB10 .128 B8
Bronte Ave BB10 .128 D6
Bronte Cl OL12 .52 A1
Brooden Dr BB9 .148 C4
Brook Ave Maghull L31 .5 E2
Morecambe LA3 .216 F3
Scorton PR3 .204 E7
Brook Croft PR2 .117 B4
Brook Ct 8 BB4 .86 A7
Brook Farm Cl L39 .15 E4
Brook Field Way BB18 .197 B1
Brook Gr Cleveleys FY5 .175 E4
Morecambe LA3 .216 F3
Brook Hey PR4 .74 F8
Brook Hey Dr L33 .1 A3
Brook Hey Wlk L33 .1 A3
Brook Ho
Lytham St Anne's FY8 .91 A3
Southport PR8 .35 C5
Brook La
Charnock Richard PR7 .42 C4
Farington PR26,PR4 .76 D6
Much Hoole PR4 .74 E3
Ormskirk L39 .15 E4
Brook Mdw PR4 .116 F7
Brook Mill Ind Est PR4 .113 B4
Brook Pl PR2 .116 D2
Brook Rd
Lytham St Anne's FY8 .91 C3
Morecambe LA3 .216 F3
Brook Side L31 .5 E1
Brook St Adlington PR6 .44 A1
4 Barnoldswick BB18 .196 B2
Blackburn BB2 .101 B2
Blackpool FY4 .130 E1
Bury BL9 .33 A3
Clitheroe BB7 .189 F1
Colne BB8 .171 D5
Earby BB18 .197 B2
Fleetwood FY7 .175 E8
Haslingden BB4 .85 B5
Higher Walton PR5 .98 B3
Kirkham PR4 .113 F6
Lancaster LA1 .214 E7
Nelson BB9 .148 E8
Oswaldtwistle BB5 .103 E4
Padiham BB12 .126 D7
Preston PR1 .117 E2
Rishton BB1 .124 B1
Southport PR9 .54 D4
Wheelton PR6 .62 A7
Brook St N PR2 .117 D3
Brook Vale Ct PR3 .157 E3
Brook Villas
Waddington BB7 .189 B4
West Bradford BB7 .189 E5
Brookbank BB9 .170 E4
Brookdale Adlington PR6 .44 A1
Belmont BL7 .46 C5
New Longton PR4 .76 A6
Rochdale OL12 .52 E3
Brookdale Ave FY5 .152 E8
Brookdale Cl PR25 .60 B6
Brooke Cl Accrington BB5 .104 E2
Southport PR9 .36 B7
Brooke St PR6 .43 E7
Brookes La BB7 .144 C5
Brookes St 10 OL13 .70 D8
Brookes The 6 PR6 .43 E7
Brookfield Croston PR26 .58 B3
Mawdesley L40 .40 C2
Mellor BB2 .121 E2
Parbold WN8 .27 C2
Brookfield Ave
Blackpool FY4 .111 A6
Fulwood PR2 .118 C4
Thornton FY5 .176 C1
Brookfield Cl LA5 .221 B5
Brookfield Com Prim Sch
PR2 .118 E5
Brookfield Ct PR3 .185 E3
Brookfield Dr PR2 .117 E8
Brookfield Ho BL0 .49 F3
Brookfield La L39 .6 A5
Brookfield Park Prim Sch
WN8 .17 D2
Brookfield Pl PR5 .78 A6
Brookfield Rd
Shevington Moor WN6 .29 B2
Skelmersdale WN8 .10 B7
Thornton FY5 .176 C1
Brookfield Sch FY6 .153 F5
Brookfield St
2 Blackburn BB1 .101 E6
4 Cornholme OL14 .109 C1
Preston PR1 .117 F1
Brookfield Terr
Hampson Green LA2 .207 E8
Lytham St Anne's FY8 .91 B4
Brookfield View LA5 .221 B5
Brookford Cl BB12 .127 D8
Brookholme Ct LA1 .214 C7
Brookhouse Bsns Ctr 10
BB1 .101 F6
Brookhouse Cl
Blackburn BB1 .101 F6
Gregson Lane PR5 .98 F2
Brookhouse Dr PR5 .98 F2
Brookhouse Gdns 12
BB1 .101 F6
Brookhouse La BB1 .101 F6
Brookhouse Prim Sch
BB1 .101 F7
Brookhouse Rd
Caton LA2 .237 C3
Ormskirk L39 .15 D6
Brookhouse St PR2 .117 D1
Brookland LA6 .242 C3
Brookland Cl BB5 .124 F4
Brookland St BB4 .86 D1
Brookland Terr BB4 .69 F7
Brooklands Chipping PR3 .185 F3
Horwich BL6 .32 C3
Ormskirk L39 .16 A6
Preston PR2 .117 A1
Brooklands Ave
Burnley BB11 .128 B3
Fulwood PR2 .117 E7
Haslingden BB4 .68 B7
Kirkham PR4 .114 A5
Brooklands Ct LA1 .215 A4
Brooklands Dr
Bonds PR3 .181 C6
Heysham LA3 .212 F6
Orrell WN5 .10 D5
Brooklands Gr L40 .25 F3
Brooklands Rd
Burnley BB11 .128 B3
Lytham St Anne's FY8 .90 C6
Ramsbottom BL0 .50 A2
Skelmersdale WN8 .10 C7
Brooklands Terr BB1 .102 A7
Brooklands The PR4 .113 B4
Brooklands Way FY4 .111 E7
Brooklyn Ave FY3 .130 E8
Brooklyn Cvn Pk PR9 .55 A4
Brooklyn Rd BB1 .122 F5
Brooks Rd L37 .11 D2
Brooks Way L37 .11 D2
Brooksbottom Cl BL0 .50 C4
Brookshaw St BL9 .33 A4
Brookside
Brockhall Village BB6 .143 C5
Coppull PR7 .42 F1
Downham BB7 .191 B5
Euxton PR7 .60 C2
Kirkham PR4 .113 F6
Sabden BB7 .145 F7
Thornton FY5 .176 C3
Brookside Cl Leyland PR26 .76 E3
Ramsbottom BL0 .50 A3
Whalley BB7 .144 C5
Brookside Cotts PR6 .62 D3
Brookside Cres
Ramsbottom BL8 .49 E1
West Bradford BB7 .189 D7
Brookside Ctr FY5 .176 C3
Brookside Dr LA2 .226 A8
Brookside Ind Est BB5 .103 C3
Brookside La BB5 .103 B3
Brookside Prim Sch
BB7 .166 F8
Brookside Rd
Fulwood PR2 .117 D7
Southport PR8 .35 C2
Standish WN1 .30 B1
Brookside St BB5 .103 C3
Brookside View BB5 .103 B4
Brookview PR2 .118 B5
Brookville OL12 .71 C1
Brookway Blackburn BB2 .81 B8

Brookway continued
Longton PR4 74 F8
Wrea Green PR4 113 A4
Broom Cl Burscough L40 25 F4
Clayton-le-W PR25 77 E3
Broom Field PR3 181 D4
Broom Hill Coppice PR3 204 C2
Broome Cl PR8 35 B3
Broome Rd PR8 35 B3
Broomfield Mill St PR1 117 F1
Broomfield Pl
Blackburn BB2 101 B3
Standish WN6 29 E1
Broomfield Rd
Fleetwood FY7 198 F2
Standish WN6 29 E2
Broomflat Cl WN6 29 E1
Broomholme WN6 19 D7
Brotherod Hall Rd OL12 52 C2
Brothers St BB2 101 A1
Brotherston Dr BB2 81 C8
Brotherton Mdws 7 BB7 166 F8
Brough Ave FY2 152 F2
Brougham St BB12 127 F7
Broughton Ave
Blackpool FY3 130 E7
Southport PR8 35 D4
Broughton Bsns & Ent Coll PR3 137 C2
Broughton Cl BB2 102 A1
Broughton Gr LA3 217 C3
Broughton in Amounderness CE Prim Sch PR3 137 D1
Broughton St
1 Burnley BB12 127 D6
4 Darwen BB3 81 F2
Preston PR1 117 E2
Broughton Tower Way PR2 118 A8
Broughton Way FY6 153 C6
Brow Cl PR3 156 A6
Brow Edge BB4 86 D1
Brow Hey PR5 78 B6
Brow The PR4 73 E4
Brow View BB10 128 B8
Browfoot Cl LA5 223 F2
Browgate BB7 190 F8
Browgill Pl 8 LA1 218 B2
Browhead Ct BB10 128 B8
Browhead Rd BB10 128 B8
Brown Birks Rd BB5 104 E8
Brown Birks St 15 OL14 109 B1
Brown Edge Cl PR8 36 A2
Brown Hill La BB8 171 F7
Brown Hill Row BB8 171 F7
Brown La
Bamber Bridge PR5 98 A2
Higher Walton PR5 98 A3
Brown Sq 8 BB11 128 A6
Brown St Accrington BB5 104 B5
Bacup OL13 87 F4
Bamber Bridge PR5 77 F8
Blackburn BB1 101 E5
Blackrod BL6 31 D2
Burnley BB11 127 F6
Chorley PR6 43 D8
Clitheroe BB7 166 D7
Fleetwood FY7 199 A3
2 Ramsbottom BL0 50 B5
Thornton FY5 176 B3
Brown St E BB8 171 D5
Brown St W BB8 171 C4
Brown's La Kirkham PR4 113 D3
Thornton FY6 176 E7
Brownedge Cl PR5 97 D1
Brownedge La PR5 97 E1
Brownedge Rd PR5 77 B8
Brownedge St Mary's RC High Sch PR5 97 E1
Brownedge Wlk PR5 97 D1
Brownhill Ave BB10 128 C6
Brownhill Dr BB1 123 A1
Brownhill La PR4 75 D7
Brownhill Rd
Blackburn BB1 122 F3
Leyland PR25 76 F1
Brownhill Sch OL12 52 E1
Brownhill View OL12 52 E1
Browning Ave
4 Lytham St Anne's FY8 91 D4
Oswaldtwistle BB5 103 C5
3 Thornton FY5 176 A3
Browning Cl BB8 171 D6
Browning Cres PR1 118 D2
Browning Rd PR1 118 D2
Browning St BB3 82 F1
Brownley St Chorley PR6 43 E7
Clayton Green PR6 78 B1
Brownlow La WN5 10 C1
Brownlow Rd BL6 32 C5
Brownlow St
Blackburn BB1 102 D4
Clitheroe BB7 166 E7
Brownlow Terr BB2 100 C1
Brownroyd BB18 197 C2
Browns Hey PR7 61 A2
Brownside Mill BB10 128 F6
Brownside Rd BB10 128 F5
Brows Cl L37 11 E3
Brows La L37 11 E3
Browsholme LA1 218 A2
Browsholme Ave
Burnley BB10 128 C6
Fulwood PR2 118 F3
Browsholme Cl
Carnforth LA5 223 C1
Browsholme Cl continued
Normoss FY3 131 B8
Browsholme Hall* BB7 187 E7
Browsholme Rd BB7 229 C1
Broxfield Ct FY8 89 D6
Broxton Ave WN5 10 F7
Broyd View LA1 214 F5
Bruce St
5 Barnoldswick BB18 196 B3
Blackburn BB1 102 B6
Burnley BB11 127 D5
Brun Gr FY1 130 E1
Brun St BB11 127 F6
Brun Terr BB10 128 F5
Bruna La PR3 181 E4
Brundhurst Fold BB2 121 E2
Brunel Dr BB1 102 A4
Brunel St Burnley BB12 127 C7
Horwich BL6 32 C2
Brunel Way FY4 111 C7
Brunel Wlk BB1 101 F4
Brungerley Ave BB7 189 E1
Brunshaw Ave BB10 128 D5
Brunshaw Prim Sch BB10 128 D4
Brunshaw Rd BB10 128 D6
Brunswick Ave BL6 32 E2
Brunswick Dr BB8 171 A3
Brunswick Pl 4 PR2 117 C1
Brunswick Rd LA3 216 E3
Brunswick St
Blackburn BB2 101 D4
3 Blackpool FY1 130 B4
Burnley BB11 128 A4
2 Chorley PR6 43 D8
Darwen BB3 65 B8
Nelson BB9 148 E7
Brunswick Terr
Accrington BB5 104 B6
Bacup OL13 70 D8
Brunton Ho 2 LA1 215 A5
Brunton Rd LA1 214 F6
Brunton's Warehouse LA1 218 C1
Brush St BB11 127 C5
Brussells Rd BB3 82 C1
Bryan Rd FY3 130 D5
Bryan St BB2 101 E2
Brydeck Ave PR1 96 E4
Bryer St 25 LA1 214 F8
Bryer's Croft BB1 122 F6
Bryn Gr LA2 220 E2
Bryning Ave
Blackpool FY2 152 C4
Wrea Green PR4 113 B3
Bryning Fern La PR4 113 F4
Bryning Hall La
Saltcotes,Moss Side FY8 112 F1
Warton PR4 92 B8
Wrea Green FY8,PR4 113 A1
Bryning La
Newton-w-S PR4 114 F2
Wrea Green PR4 113 B2
Bryning with Warton St Paul's CE Prim Sch PR4 92 D6
Bryony Cl Cleveleys FY5 175 F5
Orrell WN5 10 D5
Bryony Ct LA3 217 B2
Buccleuch Ave BB7 166 D8
Buccleuch Cl BB7 166 D8
Buccleuch Rd 7 BB9 170 C1
Buccleuch St BB11 127 E5
Buchanan St
Blackpool FY1 130 C6
Chorley PR6 43 D7
7 Ramsbottom BL0 50 B6
Buck St Burnley BB11 127 E5
Colne BB8 171 E5
Grindleton BB7 190 B7
Buckden Cl FY5 175 C1
Buckden Gate BB9 170 C3
Buckden Pl LA3 212 F8
Buckden Rd 4 BB5 103 F4
Buckfast Dr L37 12 B2
Buckholes La PR6 79 C1
Buckhurst Rd BL9 51 C3
Buckingham Ave
Horwich BL6 32 E2
Kingsfold PR1 96 E2
Buckingham Cl BB4 85 A1
Buckingham Dr BB12 145 D2
Buckingham Gr
Church BB5 103 F7
Formby L37 11 E1
Morecambe LA3 216 F3
Buckingham Pl LA3 216 F3
Buckingham Rd
Lytham St Anne's FY8 90 D4
6 Maghull L31 5 C1
Morecambe LA3,LA4 216 F3
Buckingham St PR6 43 D7
Buckingham Way FY6 153 C5
Bucklands Ave PR2 117 D2
Buckley Cres FY5 152 D7
Bucknell Pl FY5 152 F7
Buckshaw Hall Cl PR7 61 B2
Buckshaw Prim Sch PR7 61 A2
Buckthorn Pl FY6 199 F6
Buckton Cl PR6 61 C6
Bude Cl PR4 116 F6
Buff St 3 BB3 65 A8
Buffalo Rd PR26 77 A4
Bulcock St BB10 148 C1
Bulk Rd LA1 218 E1
Bulk St LA1 214 F8
Bull Cop L37 12 B3
Bull Park La FY6 154 C8
Bull St BB11 128 A6
Bullens La L40 23 E7
Buller Ave PR1 96 E4
Buller St
1 Lancaster LA1 218 D3
Rawtenstall BB4 86 A2
Bullfinch Dr BL9 33 B5
Bullfinch St 3 PR1 118 B1
Bullion The BB12 169 C5
Bullough Cl BB5 104 A5
Bullsnape La PR3 161 A5
Bulmer St PR2 117 C2
Buncer La BB2 101 A4
Bungalows The
Burnley BB11 127 F4
9 Earby BB18 197 B1
Great Eccleston PR3 156 C5
Bunker St PR4 93 C6
Bunkers Hill Cl BB2 81 B8
Bunting Pl 9 FY5 175 F1
Bunyan St 24 OL12 52 F1
Buoymaster LA1 218 C1
Burbank Cl FY4 110 F5
Burdett St BB11 127 D5
Burdock Wlk LA3 217 B2
Burford Cl Blackburn BB2 80 E8
Blackpool FY3 131 A7
Burford Dr LA3 213 A7
Burgate FY4 110 D5
Burgess Ave FY4 110 E7
Burgess Gdns L31 5 C2
Burgess St
2 Blackburn BB1 102 C5
6 Haslingden BB4 85 B3
Burgess' La L37 13 A2
Burgh Hall Rd PR7 43 A3
Burgh La PR7 43 C4
Burgh La S PR7 43 B2
Burgh Mdws PR7 43 C4
Burgh Wood Cl PR7 42 F6
Burgh Wood Way PR7 43 A6
Burghley Brow PR3 181 D1
Burghley Cl PR6 78 C2
Burghley Ct 4 PR25 77 B1
Burgundy Cres FY5 152 F7
Burholme Cl PR2 119 A2
Burholme Pl PR2 119 A2
Burholme Rd PR2 119 A2
Burleigh Rd 7 PR1 96 E7
Burleigh St BB12 127 F7
Burlingham Cvn Pk PR3 204 B1
Burlington Ave
Formby L37 12 B3
Morecambe LA4 217 D5
Burlington Ct FY4 110 B7
Burlington Ctr The FY8 89 E6
Burlington Gdns PR25 60 B8
Burlington Gr LA4 217 D5
Burlington Ho 1 FY6 153 D3
Burlington Rd
Blackpool FY4 110 B6
Southport PR8 34 F3
Burlington Rd W FY4 110 A6
Burlington St
Blackburn BB2 101 C5
Chorley PR7 43 D7
Nelson BB9 148 C7
Burn Gr FY5 175 E4
Burn Hall Ind Est FY7 176 A6
Burnage Gdns FY4 110 D7
Burned House La FY6 200 D2
Burnedge Cl OL12 71 D2
Burneside Cl LA4 217 C4
Burnfell Rd 1 LA1 218 B2
Burnham Cl BB11 127 E5
Burnham Ct
Blackpool FY3 130 E5
Morecambe LA3 216 E1
Burnham Gate BB11 127 E5
Burnham Trad Pk 4 BB11 127 E6
Burnley Ave PR8 21 D5
Burnley Barracks Sta BB12 127 E6
Burnley Bsns Ctr 7 BB11 128 A6
Burnley Central Sta BB12 127 F7
Burnley Cl BB1 102 B5
Burnley Coll BB11 128 A7
Burnley General Hospl BB10 148 C2
Burnley Habergham High Sch BB12 126 F7
Burnley Ivy Bank High Bsns & Enterprise Coll BB12 126 F7
Burnley La BB11,BB5 126 A2
Burnley Manchester Road Sta BB11 127 F5
Burnley Rd
Accrington,Hillock Vale BB5 104 D8
8 Accrington,Lower Fold BB5 104 C6
Baldingstone BL9 50 E1
Blackburn BB1 102 C6
Brierfield BB9,BB10 148 B5
Brierfield,Harle Syke BB10 148 F3
Burnley BB10,BB11 128 D1
Clayton-le-M BB5 125 C5
Colne BB8,BB9 171 B3
Edenfield BL0 68 D5
Gisburn BB7 231 B3
Hapton BB11,BB5 126 B1
Holme Chapel BB10,OL14 108 C4
Padiham BB12 126 D8
Rawtenstall BB4 85 F5
Rawtenstall,Goodshaw Fold BB4 106 A2
Burnley Rd continued
Southport PR8 21 C5
Trawden BB8 172 B1
Weir BB11,BB4 107 C3
Whalley BB6 144 F3
Burnley Rd E Water BB4 107 A2
Whitewell Bottom BB4 86 F4
Burnley St BB1 102 C5
Burns Ave
Lytham St Anne's FY8 91 D4
Oswaldtwistle BB5 103 D5
Thornton FY5 176 A3
Burns Cl WN5 10 D1
Burns Dr BB5 104 E2
Burns Pl FY4 110 F8
Burns Rd FY7 199 A5
Burns St Burnley BB12 127 F7
Hapton BB12 126 C4
Nelson BB9 170 D1
Padiham BB12 126 D7
Preston PR1 118 D2
Burns Way BB6 124 B4
Burns Wlk BB3 82 B1
Burnsall Ave
Blackpool FY3 153 A1
Heysham LA3 212 F8
Burnsall Cl BB10 148 E3
Burnsall Pl
Barrowford BB9 170 C3
Fulwood PR2 118 E4
Burnsall Rd 2 BB5 103 F4
Burnside Edenfield BL0 68 D2
Parbold WN8 27 B2
Burnside Ave
Blackpool FY4 110 E8
Calder Vale PR3 182 E8
Fleetwood FY7 198 C2
Fulwood PR2 118 F3
Burnside Way PR1 96 D3
Burnslack Rd PR2 118 F3
Burrans Mdw 15 BB8 171 D4
Burrell Ave BB8 171 D6
Burrington Cl PR2 118 D6
Burrow Heights La LA2 210 F8
Burrow Rd
Over Burrow LA6 241 E7
Preston PR1 118 A1
Burrow's La FY6 176 F5
Burscough Bridge Prim Sch L40 25 E5
Burscough Bridge St John's CE Prim Sch L40 25 F5
Burscough Bridge Sta L40 25 E5
Burscough Ind Est L40 25 B5
Burscough Junc Sta L40 25 F4
Burscough Lordsgate Township CE Prim Sch L40 25 E3
Burscough Priory High Sch L40 25 E5
Burscough Rd L39 15 F7
Burscough St L39 15 F6
Burscough Village Prim Sch L40 25 F5
Burton Ave LA1 218 A3
Burton Ct FY7 175 C8
Burton Gdns BB9 148 B5
Burton Hill LA6 242 C3
Burton Lodge FY7 199 B4
Burton Morewood CE Prim Sch LA6 240 C7
Burton Pk LA6 240 B7
Burton Rd Blackpool FY4 130 F1
Low Bentham LA2 239 B8
Burton St Burnley BB11 128 B5
Rishton BB1 124 C1
Burwain Castle Rd BD23 197 F8
Burwains Ave BB8 194 D1
Burwell Ave Coppull PR7 29 D8
Formby L37 11 D1
Burwell Cl Kirkby L33 1 A3
Rochdale OL12 52 D4
Burwen Cl BB11 127 D3
Burwood Cl 5 PR1 96 F2
Burwood Dr
Blackpool FY3 131 A6
Fulwood PR2 118 E3
Bury & Rochdale Old Rd BL9 33 F4
Bury Bsns Ctr BL9 33 A4
Bury Fold BB3 65 A6
Bury Fold La BB3 65 A6
Bury La PR6 79 F3
Bury New Rd
Heywood BL9,OL10 33 E2
Ramsbottom BL0 50 D6
Bury Old Rd Edenfield BL0 68 F1
Heywood BL9,OL10 33 E1
Nangreaves BL0,BL9 50 F4
Bury Rd Edenfield BL0 68 D3
Haslingden BB4 85 B3
Rawtenstall BB4 68 E7
Southport PR8 35 B3
Turton Bottoms BL7 48 E3
Bury Row BB7 145 F8
Bury St Darwen BB3 82 A1
Oswaldtwistle BB5 103 D3
Buseph Barrow 1 LA4 217 F4
Buseph Ct 2 LA4 217 F4
Buseph Dr LA4 217 F4
Bush La Freckleton PR4 93 B5
Freckleton PR4 93 B6
Bush St BB10 148 B1
Bushburn Dr BB6 143 C1
Bushby's La L37 11 C2
Bushby's Pk L37 11 D2
Bushell Pl PR1 97 A6
Bushell St PR1 117 F1
Bushell's Hosp PR3 138 E6
Bushey La WA11 8 E2
Bussel Rd PR1 96 E2
Butcher Brow PR5 97 E5
Butchers La L39 6 B3
Bute Ave FY1 130 B7
Bute Rd BB1 102 D3
Bute St BB11 127 D3
Butler Pl PR1 117 F2
Butler Rd FY1 130 B3
Butler St Blackpool FY1 130 C6
7 Burnley BB10 128 A8
Preston PR1 96 F7
Ramsbottom BL0 50 A5
Rishton BB1 124 C1
Butlers Farm Ct PR25 59 D7
Butlers Mdw PR4 92 E6
Butt Hill La PR3 182 E4
Butt's La PR3 156 B5
Butterbergh 16 LA2 239 D8
Buttercross Cl BB11 127 D2
Butterfield Gdns L39 15 D3
Butterfield St
2 Barrowford BB9 170 D3
2 Lancaster LA1 214 F8
Butterlands PR1 97 F8
Buttermere Ave
Chorley PR7 43 B6
Colne BB8 171 F6
Fleetwood FY7 198 C2
2 Morecambe LA4 217 D4
Buttermere Cl
1 Bamber Bridge PR5 97 E2
5 Blackburn BB1 101 F6
Formby L37 11 D3
Fulwood PR2 118 C4
Maghull L31 5 E1
Buttermere Cres WA11 8 F2
Buttermere Ct LA1 218 F1
Buttermere Dr
Knott End-on-S FY6 199 F5
Oswaldtwistle BB5 103 D5
Ramsbottom BL0 50 B7
Buttermere Rd
Burnley BB10 128 F5
Lancaster LA1 218 F1
Longridge PR3 139 F5
Butterwick Field BL6 31 F3
Butterworth Brow
Brinscall PR6 63 A7
Chorley PR7 43 A4
Butterworth Cl PR4 114 A6
Button St PR3 160 C6
Butts Barnoldswick BB18 196 B2
Great Harwood BB6 124 B5
Butts Cl FY5 176 C4
Butts Gr BB7 189 E2
Butts La
High Bentham LA2 239 E8
Southport PR8 35 F5
Butts Mount BB6 124 C5
Butts Rd FY5 176 C4
Buxton Ave FY2 152 D4
Buxton St Accrington BB5 104 A5
Morecambe LA4 217 C4
Whitworth OL12 71 D3
Bye La L39 14 C3
Bye Rd BL0 50 E8
Bye-Pass Rd LA5 221 A4
Byerworth La N PR3 181 C5
Byerworth La S PR3 181 C4
Byfield Ave FY5 152 E7
Bygone Times* PR7 41 C5
Byland Cl Blackpool FY4 110 C5
Formby L37 12 B2
Read BB12 145 D1
Bymbrig Cl PR5 77 E8
Byre View PR6 30 F8
Byrom St Blackburn BB2 101 D4
Southport PR9 35 F7
Byron Ave
Bolton-le-S LA5 221 A5
Lytham St Anne's FY8 91 D4
Thornton FY5 176 A3
Warton PR4 92 E6
Byron Cl Accrington BB5 104 E2
Formby L37 11 F4
3 Orrell WN5 10 F7
Oswaldtwistle BB5 103 C5
Tarleton PR4 56 F5
Byron Cres PR7 29 F8
Byron Gr BB18 196 A3
Byron Rd Colne BB8 171 F5
Maghull L31 5 D3
Morecambe LA3 216 E3
Ramsbottom BL8 49 F2
Byron Sq BB6 124 B4
Byron St Blackpool FY4 130 B1
Chorley PR6 43 D8
Fleetwood FY7 199 A5
Padiham BB12 126 F7
Byron Terr BB2 101 B3
Byton Wlk L33 1 A4

C

Cabin End Row BB1 102 E4
Cabin La Halsall L39 22 C5
Holmeswood L40 38 A6
Maghull L31 4 F4
Southport,Churchtown Moss PR9 54 F3

Cable Ct PR2 118 B8
Cable St Formby L37 12 A4
Lancaster LA1 214 F8
Southport PR8 35 B7
Cabus Cross Roads PR3 204 A5
Cabus Nook La PR3 204 B6
Cabus Terr PR3 204 C2
Cadby Ave FY3 130 F3
Cadley Ave PR2 117 B3
Cadley Cswy PR2 117 C4
Cadley Dr PR2 117 B3
Cadogan Pl 5 PR1 97 A6
Cadogan St BB9 170 D2
Cadshaw Cl BB1 101 E8
Cadwell Rd L31 5 B5
Caernarfon Cl FY5 176 D2
Caernarvon Ave BB12 127 A7
Caernarvon Cl BL8 49 F1
Caernarvon Rd BB4 85 A1
Cage La PR4 76 B8
Cairn Ct 6 FY4 110 C5
Cairn Gr FY4 110 C4
Cairndale Dr PR25 60 B6
Cairns Cl BB9 170 C3
Cairnsmore Ave PR1 118 F1
Cairo St BB12 127 D6
Caister Cl WN8 9 E8
Calcott St BB11 127 E2
Caldbeck Cl BB9 148 E6
Caldbeck Rd LA1 218 F1
Calder Ave Billington BB7 144 A4
Chorley PR7 43 B5
Cleveleys FY5 175 F2
Darwen BB3 81 D4
Fleetwood FY7 198 D3
Freckleton PR4 93 A5
Fulwood PR2 117 F6
Longridge PR3 140 A8
Ormskirk L39 15 E4
Whalley BB7 144 A7
Withnell PR6 80 A1
Calder Banks BB1 101 F7
Calder Cl Bury BL9 33 A8
Carnforth LA5 223 B1
Kirkby L33 1 A6
Kirkham PR4 114 C5
Lytham St Anne's FY8 110 F2
Nelson BB9 170 D1
Calder Ct BB5 125 E6
Calder Dr Catterall PR3 181 D2
Maghull L31 5 F2
Calder House La PR3 181 D4
Calder Pl Billington BB7 144 A4
Great Harwood BB6 124 E6
Calder Rd Blackpool FY2 152 C1
Rawtenstall BB4 86 A4
Calder St Blackburn BB1 101 F7
Burnley BB11 127 F6
Colne BB8 171 C4
Nelson BB9 170 D1
Padiham BB12 126 C8
Preston PR2 117 C1
Calder Terr BB9 148 B8
Calder Vale
Barrowford BB9 170 D2
Whalley BB7 144 C4
Calder Vale Rd BB12 127 F6
Calder Vale St John CE Prim Sch PR3 226 C1
Calder View BB9 170 E5
Calder View Sch BB12 127 F8
Calder Way LA3 217 F2
Calderbank Cl 1 PR26 76 A1
Calderbrook Ave BB11 127 E3
Calderbrook Pl BB11 127 E3
Caldershaw Bsns Ctr OL12 52 B2
Caldershaw Ctr The OL12 52 B2
Caldershaw La OL12 52 A2
Caldershaw Prim Sch OL12 52 A1
Caldershaw Rd OL11, OL12 52 A1
Calderstones Dr BB7 144 A7
Calderstones Hospl BB7 144 A7
Caldervale Ave FY6 153 C3
Caldew Ct BB5 104 E8
Caldicott Way FY6 153 C6
Caldy Dr BL8 50 A3
Caleb St 6 BB9 170 E1
Caledonian Ave 1 FY3 130 E7
Calendar St 1 BB1 101 E5
Calendine Cl FY5 175 F5
Calf Croft Pl FY8 91 A4
Calf Hall La BB18 196 A2
Calf Hall Rd BB18 196 A2
Calf Hey BB5 124 F4
Calf Hey La OL12 52 D8
Calf Hey Rd BB4 84 B2
Calfcote La PR3 140 B7
Calgary Ave BB2 101 B8
Calico Cl BB5 103 B4
Calico Dr PR3 181 D3
Calico St BB2 101 D1
Calico Wood Ave WN6 19 F6
Calkeld La 7 LA1 214 F8
Calla Dr PR3 181 C8
Callander Sq OL10 33 F1
Callender St BL0 50 B6
Callon St PR1 97 E8
Caltha Dr BB3 82 A7
Caltha St 8 BL0 50 B6
Calva Cl BB12 127 B8
Calverley St 6 PR1 118 D1
Calverley Way OL12 52 E4
Calvert Ct PR5 97 D5
Calvert Pl FY3 131 A7
Cam Cl 1 PR5 77 F8
Cam La Clayton Green PR6 78 A4
Thornton-in-C BD23 197 B6
Cam St PR1 118 C2
Cam Wood Fold PR6 78 A3
Cambell's Ct FY8 89 E7
Camberley Cl PR8 34 E5
Camborne Ave LA5 221 C8
Camborne Ct FY3 131 B2
Camborne Pl PR4 93 B6
Cambray Rd FY1 152 C1
Cambrian Cl BB1 122 F3
Cambrian Ct PR9 35 D8
Cambrian Way BB4 85 B1
Cambridge Arc 5 PR8 35 B7
Cambridge Ave
Lancaster LA1 215 B5
Southport PR9 53 F2
Cambridge Cl
7 Blackburn BB1 101 F4
Padiham BB12 126 D6
Preston PR1 117 E2
Cambridge Ct
Preston PR1 117 F2
Southport PR9 53 F2
Cambridge Dr
Blackburn BB1 102 E4
Garstang PR3 181 B7
Padiham BB12 126 D6
Cambridge Gdns PR9 53 F2
Cambridge Rd
9 Bamber Bridge PR5 77 F8
Blackpool FY1 130 D5
Cleveleys FY5 175 C3
Fleetwood FY7 198 E3
Formby L37 11 D1
Lytham St Anne's FY8 90 E3
Morecambe LA3 216 E3
Orrell WN5 10 F8
Skelmersdale WN8 17 E1
Southport PR9 53 E2
Cambridge St
Accrington BB5 104 D6
Blackburn BB1 101 F4
Brierfield BB9 148 B5
3 Burnley BB11 127 D5
10 Chorley PR7 43 C7
9 Colne BB8 171 D4
Darwen BB3 82 C1
Great Harwood BB6 124 D5
Haslingden BB4 85 B1
Nelson BB9 148 D7
Preston PR1 117 E2
Cambridge Wlk PR1 117 E2
Cambridge Wlks 6 PR8 35 B7
Camden Pl PR1 96 F6
Camden Rd FY3 130 E6
Camden St
11 Barrowford BB9 170 D3
Nelson BB9 148 D7
Camellia Dr PR25 77 E2
Camelot Theme Pk* PR7 41 F4
Cameron Ave FY3 130 E7
Cameron Croft 6 PR6 43 D8
Cameron St BB10 148 A1
Camforth Hall La PR3 139 A7
Camms View BB4 68 A8
Camomile Cl PR7 61 A3
Camp St BB10 148 E3
Campbell Ave 2 FY3 130 E7
Campbell St
Blackburn BB1 122 F1
4 Padiham BB12 126 F7
Preston PR1 97 B8
Read BB12 145 D1
Rochdale OL12 52 E2
Campion Cl FY5 175 F5
Campion Ct BB5 103 E4
Campion Dr
Haslingden BB4 68 A8
Preston PR2 116 C1
Campion Way
Morecambe LA3 217 B2
Rochdale OL12 52 C3
Campions The PR2 116 C1
Camwood PR5 78 B4
Camwood Dr PR5 97 B1
Canada Cres FY2 152 E3
Canada St BL6 32 B3
Canal Bank
Appley Bridge WN6 19 C7
Burscough Bridge L40 25 B6
Ring o'Bells L40 26 C2
Canal Bank Cotts L31 5 C7
Canal Bank Pygons Hill L31 5 C7
Canal Gdns LA5 221 B6
Canal Leach PR26 57 F6
Canal Mews BB9 148 D8
Canal Pl LA5 223 E1
Canal Row WN2 30 D1
Canal Side BB9 170 D2
Canal St Adlington PR7 31 A6
3 Blackburn BB2 101 B1
19 Burnley BB11 127 F6
Church BB5 103 E6
Clayton-le-M BB5 124 F2
Canal Wlk PR6 43 F8
Canalside BB1 101 F3
Canalside Craft Ctr* LA2 211 A3
Canberra Cl FY5 152 F7
Canberra La PR4 116 E4
Canberra Rd PR25 60 B8
Canberra Way PR4 92 E6
Candlemakers Croft 3 BB7 166 F8
Candlemakers Ct BB7 166 E8
Candlestick Pk BL9 33 D4
Cann Bridge St PR5 98 B4
Canning Rd PR9 36 A6
Canning St Burnley BB12 127 F7
Padiham BB12 126 D7
Cannock Ave FY3 130 E8
Cannock Gn L31 5 B1
Cannon Hill PR2 117 C1
Cannon St
Accrington BB5 104 B5
11 Chorley PR7 43 C8
10 Nelson BB9 170 F1
Preston PR1 96 F7
6 Ramsbottom BL0 50 A4
Canon Cl WN6 29 F2
Canon St BL9 33 A4
Canterbury Ave
Blackpool FY3 130 F3
Lancaster LA1 215 B5
Canterbury Cl
Brinscall PR6 62 E8
Carleton FY6 153 C5
Formby L37 11 F5
Garstang PR3 181 A7
Morecambe LA3 217 B2
Southport PR8 34 F4
Canterbury Rd 11 PR1 118 D1
Canterbury St
Blackburn BB2 101 E4
Chorley PR6 43 E6
Canterbury Way PR3 181 B7
Cantlow Fold PR8 21 A4
Cantsfield Ave PR2 117 B4
Canute St PR1 118 A1
Cape St BB4 86 A2
Capernwray Ct LA6 240 D3
Capernwray Rd LA6 240 B2
Capesthorne Dr PR7 43 B3
Capilano Pk L39 6 C8
Capitol Trad Est L33 1 C2
Capitol Way PR5 97 C5
Capstan Cl FY8 110 E1
Captain St Horwich BL6 32 B4
Weir OL13 88 A7
Captain's Row 3 LA1 218 D1
Carawood Cl WN6 19 D7
Carcroft Ave FY2 152 D4
Cardale PR4 95 D2
Cardiff St WN8 17 D1
Cardigan Ave
Burnley BB12 127 A7
10 Clitheroe BB7 166 E8
Oswaldtwistle BB5 103 C4
Cardigan Cl 1 BB7 166 D8
Cardigan Pl FY4 110 A5
Cardigan Rd PR8 34 F1
Cardigan St Preston PR2 117 D1
Rochdale OL12 52 E3
Cardinal Allen RC High Sch FY7 175 E8
Cardinal Gdns FY8 90 D6
Cardinal Newman Coll PR1 97 B7
Cardinal Pl FY5 175 E3
Cardinal St BB10 148 B1
Cardwell Cl PR4 92 D5
Cardwell Pl BB2 101 E5
Cardwell St BB12 126 D7
Carfax Fold OL12 52 B2
Carfax Rd L33 1 A4
Carfield WN8 9 E6
Carham Rd BB1 101 E8
Carholme Ave BB10 128 C6
Caribou The LA2 209 F5
Carisbrooke Ave FY4 111 A7
Carisbrooke Cl FY6 153 C6
Carisbrooke Dr PR9 53 F1
Carl Oway Ave PR2 118 C5
Carl's Way L33 1 A6
Carleton Ave
Blackpool FY3 152 F1
Fulwood PR2 118 D4
Simonstone BB12 145 E2
Carleton Dr PR1 96 A4
Carleton Gate FY6 153 C4
Carleton Gdns FY6 153 B5
Carleton Green Com Prim Sch FY6 153 C6
Carleton Rd Colne BB8 171 A3
Great Knowley PR6 61 F3
Carleton St
Morecambe LA4 217 A4
Nelson BB9 148 E7
Carleton Way FY6 153 B5
Carley St BB3 81 E2
Carlin Gate FY2 152 B2
Carlinghurst Rd BB2 101 D4
Carlisle Ave
Fleetwood FY7 198 D1
Higher Penwortham PR1 96 A4
Carlisle Gr 1 FY5 176 B2
Carlisle Ho 24 PR1 97 A7
Carlisle Pl PR6 31 A8
Carlisle Rd
Accrington BB5 104 D7
Southport PR8 35 A2
Carlisle St Blackburn BB1 101 F4
Preston PR1 97 A8
Rochdale OL12 52 E3
Carlisle Terr LA5 223 D3
Carlton Ave
Clayton Green PR6 78 B2
Skelmersdale WN8 10 A7
Carlton Cl BL6 31 D2
Carlton Ct BB8 171 B5
Carlton Dr PR1 97 B5
Carlton Gdns BB1 101 E6
Carlton Gr Blackpool FY2 152 B4
7 Horwich BL6 32 D1
Carlton Pl BB7 166 F7
Carlton Rd
Blackburn BB1 101 E6
Burnley BB11 127 E5
Leyland PR25 59 F8
Lytham St Anne's FY8 89 F7
Southport PR8 21 C6
Carlton St Bacup OL13 88 A3
Brierfield BB9 148 B5
Preston PR2 96 D8
Carlton Wharf LA1 218 C1
Carluke St BB1 102 C5
Carlyle Ave FY4 110 B6
Carlyle St BB10 148 C3
Carmel Cl L39 15 D2
Carnarvon Rd
Blackburn BB2 101 B5
3 Preston PR1 96 D7
Southport PR8 34 F1
Carneghie Ct PR8 34 F4
Carnfield Pl PR5 78 B8
Carnforth Ave FY2 152 E5
Carnforth Brow LA5 223 F2
Carnforth Christ Church CE Prim Sch LA5 223 D1
Carnforth Cl BB2 102 A1
Carnforth Dr BL8 50 A2
Carnforth High Sch LA5 223 E1
Carnforth Sta LA5 223 D2
Carnoustie Cl
Fulwood PR2 117 B7
Southport PR8 34 F4
Carnoustie Ct PR1 96 A6
Carnoustie Dr Euxton PR7 60 D4
Ramsbottom BL0 50 B5
Caroline Cl LA3 212 F8
Caroline Ct BB11 127 B4
Caroline St
6 Blackpool FY1 130 B3
Preston PR1 97 C8
Carr Bank Ave BL0 50 B7
Carr Bank Dr BL0 50 B7
Carr Bank Rd BL0 50 B7
Carr Barn Brow PR5 78 C6
Carr Bridge Residential Pk FY4 112 A6
Carr Brook Cl PR6 61 B8
Carr Cl Cold Row FY6 177 C4
Poulton-le-F FY6 153 E2
Smallwood Hey PR3 201 C5
Carr Dene Ct PR4 114 C5
Carr Dr PR4 113 E7
Carr End La FY6 177 C6
Carr Field PR5 78 C4
Carr Fold BL0 50 B7
Carr Gate FY5 175 C4
Carr Hall Dr BB9 170 C1
Carr Hall Gdns BB9 170 B1
Carr Hall Rd BB9 170 B1
Carr Hall St BB4 85 A5
Carr Head BB8 172 C2
Carr Head La FY6 153 E2
Carr Head Prim Sch FY6 153 E2
Carr Hey 5 FY5 176 A2
Carr Hill 11-18 High Sch PR4 114 B4
Carr Holme Gdns PR3 204 C1
Carr House La
Bretherton PR26 57 D6
Heskin Green WN6 41 F1
Ince Blundell L38 3 E4
Lancaster LA1 214 E7
Carr La Blackburn BB2 100 F6
Chorley PR7 43 D5
Cold Row FY6 177 C4
Croston PR5 40 B8
Heysham LA3 212 E7
Kirkham PR4 114 C6
Leyland PR25 77 A3
Maghull L31 4 F5
Middleton LA3 212 F1
Much Hoole PR4,PR5 75 A1
Rawtenstall,Hall Carr BB4 86 A1
Rawtenstall,Hugh Mill BB4 69 F7
Ring o'Bells L40 26 B3
Singleton FY6 154 C1
Smallwood Hey PR3 201 C4
Southport PR8 21 F7
Tarleton PR4 56 F7
Warton PR4 92 B6
Carr Mdw PR5 78 C6
Carr Mill St BB4 85 B5
Carr Moss La Halsall L39 22 D2
Haskayne L39 14 B8
Carr Mount 7 BB4 85 F1
Carr Pl PR5 78 B7
Carr Rd
Barnoldswick BB18 196 A3
Barrowford BB9 170 C1
Blackpool FY5 152 D6
Burnley BB11 127 E3
Clayton Green PR6 78 B2
Colne BB8 171 E6
Cornholme OL14 108 F1
Darwen BB3 65 B8
Fleetwood FY7 199 A4
Hambleton FY6 177 C2
Horwich BL6 32 B5
Kirkham PR4 114 B4
Rawtenstall BB4 85 F1
Water BB4 87 C7
Carr Royd Est FY6 154 A3
Carr Side La L29 4 A3
Carr St Bamber Bridge PR5 77 E8
Blackburn BB1 101 E6
Chorley PR6 61 E1
Preston PR1 97 B7
Ramsbottom BL0 50 B7
Carr View BB8 172 C1
Carr's Cres L37 11 E1
Carr's Cres W L37 11 D1
Carradice Cl BB9 148 D8
Carradon Dr WN6 29 E1
Carrfield Villas 4 OL14 109 A1
Carrick Mews FY3 131 B2
Carrier's Row BB8 172 E6
Carrington Ave BB2 81 C8
Carrington Gr LA4 217 E5
Carrington Rd
Adlington PR7 30 F7
Chorley PR7 43 C7
Carrol St PR1 118 B1
Carroll Cres L39 15 F7
Carron La PR3 160 A4
Carrs Croft BB7 191 E8
Carrs Ind Est BB4 85 A4
Carrs Wood BB2 100 F6
Carrside BB9 148 B8
Carrwood Dr PR4 114 B4
Carrwood Gn BB12 126 C8
Carrwood Hey BL0 50 A4
Carrwood Pk PR8 35 B4
Carrwood Rd PR5 97 B3
Carrwood Way PR5 97 B2
Carry La BB8 171 E4
Carshalton Rd FY1 130 B8
Carsluith Ave FY3 130 F3
Carson Rd FY4 131 A1
Cart Gate FY6 200 B3
Carter Ave BB11 126 C4
Carter Fold BB2 121 E2
Carter St Accrington BB5 104 B4
7 Blackpool FY1 130 B5
Burnley BB12 127 C7
Carter's Charity Prim Sch FY6 200 C7
Carter's La BB7 231 A5
Carterville Cl FY4 111 A7
Cartford Cl PR3 156 A6
Cartford Farm Cvn Pk PR4 156 A6
Cartford La PR3 156 A6
Cartmel Ave
Accrington BB5 104 A3
Fleetwood FY7 198 D1
Lancaster LA1 211 B8
Maghull L31 5 E2
Cartmel Cl PR8 35 F3
Cartmel Dr Burnley BB12 127 B8
Coupe Green PR5 98 E4
Formby L37 12 B2
Cartmel Pl
Morecambe LA4 217 D4
Preston PR2 116 E2
Cartmel Rd
Blackburn BB2 101 A3
Lancaster LA1 218 F2
Leyland PR25 59 D8
Cartmell La
Lytham St Anne's FY8 91 E8
Nateby PR3 180 C7
Cartmell Rd
Blackpool FY4 131 D1
Lytham St Anne's FY8 89 F5
Cartwright Ct LA1 214 E5
Carus Ave BB3 82 E1
Carus Pk LA6 241 B2
Carus St BB3 82 F1
Carvel Way L40 25 F3
Carvers Brow PR26 58 B1
Carwags La PR3 161 C8
Carwood Gr BL6 32 D1
Carwood La PR6 61 C8
Caryl Rd FY8 89 D8
Caryle Gr LA4 217 E6
Caspian Way LA1 214 E4
Casserley Rd BB8 171 F6
Casson Gate OL12 52 E1
Castercliff Bank BB8 171 C3
Castercliffe Com Prim Sch BB9 171 B1
Castercliffe Rd BB9 149 B8
Casterton PR7 60 C2
Casterton Ave BB10 148 C3
Casterton Prim Sch BB10 148 C3
Castle Ave FY6 153 B6
Castle Bank LA5 224 C4
Castle Cl BB8 171 E6
Castle Cres BL6 32 C5
Castle Ct LA1 214 E8
Castle Dr Adlington PR7 30 E6
Formby L37 11 F1
Castle Fold PR1 96 F2
Castle Gardens Cres FY6 153 B5
Castle Gate BB7 166 E8
Castle Gr BL0 50 A2
Castle Hill LA1 214 E8
Castle Hill Rd BL9 33 D5
Castle House La PR7 30 E6
Castle La Bonds PR3 181 D6
Staining FY3 131 D5
Westhead L40 16 E5
Castle Mount PR2 117 F7
Castle Par 5 LA1 214 E8
Castle Park Mews LA1 214 E8
Castle Pk Hornby LA2 238 B7
Lancaster LA1 214 E8

Castle Rd BB8 172 A7
Castle St Blackburn BB1 102 B5
Brierfield BB9 148 B6
Burnley BB12 127 F7
6 Chorley PR7 43 D7
Clitheroe BB7 166 E8
7 Hapton BB12 126 C4
Nelson BB9 148 F8
Preston PR1 117 F1
Ramsbottom BL9 50 D2
Southport PR9 35 B8
Castle The BB8 172 A7
Castle View
Barnoldswick BB18 196 B1
Clitheroe BB7 166 E8
Castle View Cvn Pk LA6 240 D2
Castle View Ho 11 BB7 166 E8
Castle Wlk
Higher Penwortham PR1 96 C7
Southport PR8 35 A6
Castle Wlks PR26 58 B2
Castlecroft Ave BL6 31 D2
Castlegate FY1 130 B1
Castlehey WN8 9 E6
Castlerigg Dr BB12 127 B8
Castlerigg Pl FY4 131 C1
Castleton Rd PR1 118 B1
Castletown Dr OL13 88 B1
Cat Tail La PR8 36 E1
Catches La OL11 52 B1
Catforth Ave FY4 131 B1
Catforth Prim Sch PR4 136 A4
Catforth Rd Catforth PR4 135 F5
Preston PR2 116 E1
Catharine's La L39 15 F1
Cathedral Dr LA3 217 B2
Cathedral RC Prim Sch The
LA1 215 A7
Catherine Cl PR4 113 F7
Catherine St
6 Chorley PR7 43 C6
Kirkham PR4 113 F6
5 Preston PR1 97 B8
Catherine St E BL6 32 B4
Catherine St W BL6 32 B5
Cathrow Dr PR4 76 A7
Cathrow Way FY5 176 D2
Catley Cl PR6 61 C5
Catlow Ct BB10 149 C5
Catlow Hall St BB5 103 E4
Catlow Row BB10 149 C6
Catlow Terr BB7 166 D1
Cato St 4 BL0 50 A4
Caton Ave FY7 198 D1
Caton Cl
Clayton-le-W PR25 77 E2
Longridge PR3 140 B8
Southport PR9 53 F4
Caton Com Prim Sch
LA2 237 C3
Caton Gr FY3 130 F7
Caton Green Rd LA2 237 D3
Caton Rd LA1 218 F4
Caton St Paul's CE Prim Sch
LA2 237 D3
Cattan Gn L37 12 B3
Catterall Cl FY1 130 D7
Catterall Gates La PR3 181 C3
Catterall La PR3 181 C1
Catterall St BB2 81 C8
Catterick Fold PR8 35 F3
Cattle St BB6 124 C5
Caunce Ave PR9 55 A6
Caunce St FY1,FY3 130 D6
Caunce's Rd PR9 37 C5
Causeway Foulridge BB8 194 D1
Great Harwood BB6 124 B5
Causeway Ave PR2 117 C4
Causeway Croft BB7 189 F1
Causeway Head BB4 68 A8
Causeway La
Haskayne L37 13 B1
Rufford L40 39 B2
Causeway St 2 BB3 65 C7
Causeway The
3 Chorley PR6 43 E8
Southport PR9 54 C5
Wymott PR26 58 F6
Causey Foot BB9 148 D7
Cavalry Way BB11 127 D6
Cave St 1 Blackburn BB2 101 B1
2 Preston PR1 97 D8
Cavell Cl BB1 102 B1
Cavendish Cres PR2 118 F3
Cavendish Ct
Bolton-le-S LA5 221 A5
Southport PR9 35 E8
Cavendish Dr PR2 118 F3
Cavendish Mans FY5 175 C4
Cavendish Pl
6 Bamber Bridge PR5 97 D3
Blackburn BB2 101 B3
Cavendish Rd
Blackpool FY2 152 C4
Lytham St Anne's FY8 89 D8
Morecambe LA3 216 E3
2 Preston PR1 118 E1
Southport PR8 34 F3
Cavendish St
Barnoldswick BB18 196 B1
1 Chorley PR6 43 E7
Darwen BB3 81 F3
Lancaster LA1 214 D8
Cavendish Wlk PR9 35 E8
Cavour St BB12 127 F7
Cawthorne Prim Sch
LA2 232 F1
Cawthorne St LA1 214 E8
Caxton Ave FY2 152 C5
Caxton Rd PR2 118 B8
Cecil Ct FY8 91 A3
Cecil St
Barnoldswick BB18 196 B3
Blackpool FY1 130 C7
4 Lytham St Anne's FY8 91 A3
Oswaldtwistle BB5 103 E4
Rishton BB1 124 C2
Cecilia Rd BB2 101 A2
Cecilia St PR1 118 D1
Cedar Ave
5 Bamber Bridge PR5 77 B8
Cleveleys FY5 175 E2
Euxton PR7 60 C4
Fleetwood FY7 175 E8
Haslingden BB4 85 C3
Horwich BL6 32 E1
Knott End-on-S FY6 200 A5
Poulton-le-F FY6 131 D8
Preston PR2 117 A2
Rawtenstall BB4 85 E2
Warton PR4 92 D6
Cedar Cl Garstang PR3 181 B8
Grimsargh PR2 139 D1
Newton-w-S PR4 115 A3
Rishton BB1 103 B8
Cedar Cres Kirkham PR4 114 A4
Ormskirk L39 15 D4
Ramsbottom BL0 50 C7
Cedar Ct Blackburn BB1 101 F7
7 Leyland PR25 77 B1
Cedar Dr L37 11 C1
Cedar Farm Galleries*
L40 40 C1
Cedar Field PR6 78 C2
Cedar Gr Longton PR4 95 A1
Orrell WN5 10 F6
Skelmersdale WN8 17 E1
Cedar Ho PR7 42 F6
Cedar Rd Chorley PR6 61 D2
Fulwood PR2 118 E2
Lancaster LA1 214 D8
Cedar Sq 5 FY1 130 B5
Cedar St Accrington BB5 104 D6
Blackburn BB1 101 F8
Burnley BB11 128 B5
Bury BL9 33 A3
Bury BL9 33 B3
Morecambe LA4 216 F4
Rochdale OL12 52 F1
Southport PR8 35 D4
Cedar Way PR1 96 B3
Cedar Wlk PR4 155 F1
Cedars Cl BB18 196 A1
Cedars Inf Sch BB1 101 F8
Cedars The Chorley PR7 43 B4
Eccleston PR7 41 B7
New Longton PR4 75 F8
Cedarwood Cl FY8 90 E4
Cedarwood Dr PR25 59 E8
Cedarwood Pl LA1 215 C7
Cedric Pl FY2 152 C4
Celia St BB10 128 C5
Cemetery La
Burnley BB11 127 A4
Preesall Park FY6 200 B1
Cemetery Rd Darwen BB3 65 B5
Earby BB18 197 B2
Padiham BB12 126 C7
Preston PR1 118 C1
Ramsbottom BL0 50 A4
Southport PR8 35 C4
Cemetery View PR7 31 A6
Centenary Way BB11 128 A5
Central 12 Ret Pk PR9 35 C7
Central Ave
Clitheroe BB7 166 D7
Edenfield BL0 68 D2
Gregson Lane PR5 98 E2
Kirkham PR4 113 F6
Lancaster LA1 218 D4
Oswaldtwistle BB5 103 C4
Southport PR8 21 F8
Central Ave N FY5 175 F3
Central Beach FY8 91 B3
Central Bldgs 16 BB12 146 C1
Central Dr Blackpool FY1 130 C3
Higher Penwortham PR1 96 A4
Lytham St Anne's FY8 90 C5
Morecambe LA4 217 A5
Central Lancaster High Sch
LA1 218 F1
Central Sq
7 Haslingden BB4 85 B3
Maghull L31 5 D2
Central St BL0 50 C6
Central View OL13 88 A2
Centre Dr PR6 78 B4
Centurian Way BB1 82 B6
Centurion Ct BB1 82 B7
Centurion Ho 1 PR4 114 B5
Centurion Ind Est PR25 77 B3
Centurion Way PR25,
PR26 77 A4
Ceres Way LA1 214 C8
Chad St BB8 171 A2
Chadderton Ct 19 PR1 97 A8
Chaddock St 26 PR1 97 A7
Chadfield Rd FY1 130 D2
Chadwich Gdns 1 PR5 77 A7
Chadwick St
Blackburn BB2 101 D3
3 Blackpool FY1 130 C3
Bury BL9 33 E4
Chadwick Terr OL12 52 D4
Chaffinch Cl FY5 175 F5
Chaffinch Ct FY3 131 B6
Chaffinch Dr BL9 33 C4
Chaigley Ct BB7 165 A8
Chaigley Farm Cotts
BB7 165 A8
Chaigley Rd PR3 140 B8
Chain Caul Rd PR2 95 F8
Chain Caul Way PR2 95 F8
Chain House La PR4 76 D7
Chain La FY3,FY4 131 E4
Chalfont Ct PR8 35 A3
Chalfont Field PR2 117 C5
Challan Hall Cotts LA5 224 E5
Challan Hall Mews LA5 224 E5
Challenge Way BB1 102 C7
Chamber St BB4 87 A8
Chambres Rd PR8 35 D5
Chambres Rd N PR8 35 D6
Champagne Ave FY5 152 F7
Chancel Pl BB3 65 C8
Chancel Way BB3 65 C8
Chancery Cl PR7 42 F1
Chancery Rd PR7 61 B2
Chancery Wlk 3 BB11 128 A6
Chandler Bsns Pk PR25 76 E2
Chandler St 6 PR1 96 F8
Chandlers Croft PR4 73 E4
Chandlers Ford FY6 153 E4
Chandlers Rest FY8 91 D3
Chandley Cl PR8 21 A5
Change Cl OL13 88 B4
Changford Gn L33 1 A3
Changford Rd L33 1 A3
Channel Way PR2 96 C8
Channing Rd FY8 90 C4
Chapel Alley L37 11 F3
Chapel Brow Leyland PR25 77 B2
Longridge PR3 140 B5
Chapel Cl Clitheroe BB7 166 B8
Hest Bank LA2 220 D1
Kirkham PR4 113 F7
Overton LA3 209 C8
Trawden BB8 172 B2
West Bradford BB7 189 E5
Whalley BB7 144 C5
Chapel Ct Brierfield BB10 149 A3
Ormskirk L39 15 F4
Chapel Fields BL7 48 C4
Chapel Fold
12 Colne BB8 171 D4
Wiswell BB7 144 F7
Chapel Gdns
Catterall PR3 181 D2
Hesketh Bank PR4 73 E4
Ramsbottom BL8 49 D1
Chapel Grange BL7 48 C4
Chapel Hill
Longridge PR3 140 A6
Salterforth BB18 194 D7
Chapel Hill La BB4 86 B4
Chapel Hill Trad Est
PR3 140 A6
Chapel Ho Burnley BB11 127 C5
4 Maghull L31 5 D1
Ormskirk L39 15 E4
Rishton BB1 124 C1
Chapel House Rd BB9 148 E7
Chapel La Banks PR9 55 B7
Burscough L40 25 E2
Burton in L LA6 242 C3
Catforth PR4 135 D4
Coppull PR7 42 F1
Formby L37 11 F3
Galgate LA2 211 B5
Hoghton PR5 99 D2
Holmeswood L40 38 B6
Langho BB6 143 B2
Longton PR4 75 C8
New Longton PR4 75 E8
Out Rawcliffe PR3 178 B2
Overton LA3 209 D8
Parbold WN8 27 D1
Ramsbottom BL8 50 A6
West Bradford BB7 189 E5
Whelton PR6 62 B5
Chapel Mdw PR4 75 C8
Chapel Mdws PR4 57 A5
Chapel Mews
2 Earby BB18 197 B1
Ormskirk L39 15 F4
Chapel Park Rd PR4 75 D8
Chapel Rd Blackpool FY4 111 B7
Fulwood PR2 118 A4
Hesketh Bank PR4 73 E4
Chapel Rise BB7 144 B4
Chapel Sq LA2 237 D3
Chapel St
10 Accrington BB5 104 C5
Adlington PR7 30 F6
14 Bacup OL13 70 C8
Barnoldswick BB18 196 B2
Belmont BL7 46 C5
Belthorn BB1 82 F6
Blackburn BB2 101 D4
Blackpool FY1 130 B4
Blackrod BL6 31 D2
Brierfield BB9 148 B6
Brinscall PR6 62 F8
Burnley BB11 128 A6
Chorley PR7 43 C8
Clayton-le-M BB5 124 E3
Colne BB8 171 D4
Coppull PR7 42 E1
Darwen BB3 65 A8
Earby BB18 197 B2
Egerton BL7 47 D3
Foulridge BB8 194 E1
Galgate LA2 211 A3
Great Eccleston PR3 156 B5
Chapel St *continued*
Haslingden BB4 85 B3
Higham BB12 146 F5
Horwich BL6 32 C3
3 Lancaster LA1 214 F8
Longridge PR3 140 B7
Lytham St Anne's FY8 91 A3
Morecambe LA4 217 A5
Nelson BB9 148 E8
Newchurch BB4 86 E1
Ormskirk L39 15 F4
Oswaldtwistle BB5 103 E4
Poulton-le-F FY6 153 D3
Preston PR1 96 F7
Rawtenstall BB4 86 A8
Rishton BB1 124 C1
Slaidburn BB7 229 C7
Southport PR8 35 B7
Whitworth OL12 52 C8
Worsthorne BB10 129 A5
Chapel Street Ct 3 FY6 153 D3
Chapel The BB4 86 A3
Chapel View
Goodshaw Chapel BB4 106 A1
Overton LA3 209 D8
Chapel Way PR7 29 F8
Chapel Wlk Coppull PR7 42 E1
Longton PR4 75 D8
2 Padiham BB12 146 C1
Warton LA5 223 E6
Chapel Wlks
Kirkham PR4 114 B4
5 Preston PR1 96 F7
Chapel Yd PR5 97 D5
Chapelhouse Wlk L37 12 A3
Chapels BB3 82 A3
Chapels Brow BB3 82 A3
Chapels La BB3 80 F3
Chapelside 4 BB10 128 B5
Chapelside Cl PR3 181 D2
Chapeltown Rd BL7 48 C2
Chapman Cl PR3 156 C5
Chapman Ct
Barnoldswick BB18 196 B3
Fleetwood FY7 199 B4
Chapman Rd
Fulwood PR2 118 A3
Hoddlesden BB3 82 F1
Chapter Rd BB3 65 C8
Chardonnay Cres 2
FY5 152 F7
Charlbury Gr LA3 213 A7
Charles Ave PR8 21 E6
Charles Cl PR4 73 E3
Charles Cres PR5 98 C3
Charles Ct
4 Blackpool FY3 130 D7
Lancaster LA1 214 F6
Charles Gr PR3 140 A7
Charles La BB4 85 A2
Charles St Blackburn BB2 101 D2
Blackpool FY1 130 C6
Clayton-le-M BB5 124 E2
Colne BB8 171 E5
Darwen BB3 82 A2
Egerton BL7 47 D2
Great Harwood BB6 124 C4
Lancaster LA1 214 F6
Morecambe LA4 217 C5
Nelson BB9 170 E2
Newchurch BB4 86 F2
Oswaldtwistle BB5 103 E3
Charles Way PR2 116 E1
Charlesbye Ave L39 16 B6
Charlesbye Cl L39 16 B6
Charleston Ct 3 PR5 97 E2
Charlesway Ct 1 PR2 116 F1
Charlesworth Cl L31 5 B5
Charley Wood Rd L33 1 C1
Charlotte Pl 32 PR1 97 A7
Charlotte St
Blackburn BB1 101 E6
Burnley BB11 127 F5
Chapeltown BL7 48 C4
Preston PR1 97 A7
4 Ramsbottom BL0 50 B5
Charlotte's La PR4 56 E2
Charnley Cl PR1 96 C2
Charnley Fold Bglws PR5 97 F3
Charnley Fold Ind Est
PR5 97 F3
Charnley Fold La PR5 97 F3
Charnley Rd FY1 130 C4
Charnley St
Blackburn BB2 101 C2
1 Lancaster LA1 218 B1
2 Preston PR1 96 F7
Charnley's La PR9 54 E7
Charnock WN8 9 E6
Charnock Ave PR1 96 E2
Charnock Back La PR6 44 C6
Charnock Brow PR7 42 C7
Charnock Fold PR1 118 A2
Charnock Ho PR7 61 C2
Charnock Moss PR5 76 F8
Charnock St Chorley PR6 43 D7
9 Kirkham PR4 113 F6
8 Leyland PR25 77 B1
Preston PR1 117 F2
Charnwood Ave FY3 131 A7
Charnwood Cl BB2 101 A8
Charter Brook BB6 124 D5
Charter La PR7 42 D3
Charter St BB5 104 A5
Charterhouse Ct FY7 198 D4
Charterhouse Pl BB2 101 B3
Chartwell Cl PR6 78 C2
Chartwell Rd PR8 21 B6
Chartwell Rise 5 PR5 77 C8
Chasden Cl PR6 61 C5
Chase Cl PR8 34 F4
Chase Heys PR9 54 A1
Chase The Burnley BB12 127 D8
Cottam PR4 116 D5
3 Leyland PR25 77 C2
Normoss FY3 131 C7
Silverdale LA5 224 D2
Thornton FY5 176 A4
Chatburn Ave
Burnley BB10 128 D5
Clitheroe BB7 189 F1
Chatburn CE Prim Sch
BB7 190 D5
Chatburn Cl
Great Harwood BB6 124 E5
Normoss FY3 131 B8
Rawtenstall BB4 86 A4
Chatburn Gdns OL10 33 F2
Chatburn Old Rd BB7 190 D5
Chatburn Park Ave BB9 148 A6
Chatburn Park Dr
Brierfield BB9 148 A6
Clitheroe BB7 190 A2
Chatburn Rd
Chatburn BB7 190 F5
Clitheroe BB7 190 A3
Fulwood PR2 118 F4
Longridge PR3 140 A7
Chatburn St BB2 101 C5
Chatham Ave FY8 110 E1
Chatham Cres BB8 171 E6
Chatham Pl
5 Chorley PR6 43 E8
Preston PR1 118 B2
Chatham St Colne BB8 171 E6
Nelson BB9 170 D1
Chatsworth Ave
Blackpool FY2 152 C6
Fleetwood FY7 198 D2
Warton PR4 92 D6
Chatsworth Cl
Barrowford BB9 170 B1
4 Blackburn BB1 122 E1
Chorley PR7 43 B8
2 Thornton FY5 176 D1
Chatsworth Ct PR6 43 F1
Chatsworth Rd
Bamber Bridge PR5 97 D3
Lancaster LA1 214 F4
1 Leyland PR25 77 A1
Lytham St Anne's FY8 89 D7
Morecambe LA4 216 F4
Southport PR8 21 B6
Chatsworth St
Preston PR1 97 D8
Rochdale OL12 52 E3
Chatteris Pl FY5 175 E1
Chatterton BL0 68 C2
Chatterton Dr BB5 104 E2
Chatterton Old La BL0 68 C2
Chatterton Rd BL0 68 C1
Chaucer Ave FY5 175 F2
Chaucer Cl PR7 41 B6
Chaucer Gdns BB6 124 B4
Chaucer Rd FY7 199 A4
Chaucer St PR1 118 D2
Cheam Ave PR7 43 D6
Cheapside Blackpool FY1 130 B5
6 Chorley PR7 43 C7
Formby L37 12 A2
11 Lancaster LA1 214 F8
1 Low Bentham LA2 239 B8
8 Preston PR1 96 F7
Cheddar Ave FY4 110 D6
Cheddar Dr PR2 118 D6
Chedworth Ave LA3 213 A7
Cheetham Hill OL12 71 D3
Cheetham Mdw PR26 59 B8
Cheetham St BB2 101 C5
Chelburn Gr BB10 128 C6
Chelford Ave FY3 130 E8
Chelford Cl 4 PR1 96 F2
Chelmsford Cl LA1 215 B5
Chelmsford Gr PR7 43 B7
Chelmsford Pl PR7 43 B7
Chelmsford Wlk PR26 59 A8
Chelsea Ave FY2 152 E1
Chelsea Ct 3 FY2 152 E1
Chelsea Mews
4 Blackpool FY2 152 E1
Lancaster LA1 218 D2
Chelston Dr BB4 68 A7
Cheltenham Ave BB5 104 C8
Cheltenham Cres
Lytham St Anne's FY8 91 D5
Thornton FY5 153 D8
Cheltenham Dr WN5 10 D2
Cheltenham Rd
Blackburn BB2 101 C5
Blackpool FY1 130 B7
Lancaster LA1 214 F5
Cheltenham Way PR8 35 F3
Chelwood Cl FY6 200 A5
Chennel Ho 4 LA1 214 E8
Chepstow Gdns PR3 181 D6
Chepstow Rd FY3 130 F8
Chequer Cl WN8 9 F5
Chequer La WN8 9 F6
Chequers BB5 124 F2
Chequers Ave LA1 215 B4
Chequers Way FY5 176 D2
Cheriton Field PR2 117 C7
Cheriton Gdns BL6 32 B5

Cheriton Pk PR8 35 E3
Cherries The PR7 60 D3
Cherry Ave BL9 33 C3
Cherry Cl
2 Blackburn BB1 102 B5
Fulwood PR2 118 D6
Kirkham PR4 113 E5
Cherry Cres
Oswaldtwistle BB5 103 D2
Rawtenstall BB4 68 F8
Cherry Dr BB6 143 C6
Cherry Gn L39 15 B1
Cherry Gr
Abbey Village PR6 80 B2
Burscough Bridge L40 25 E6
Longridge PR3 140 A7
Cherry La PR4 93 B4
Cherry Lea BB2 100 F2
Cherry Orch PR3 140 B6
Cherry Rd PR8 21 D2
Cherry St BB1 102 B5
Cherry Tree Cl
Fisher's Row PR3 201 E5
Hest Bank LA5 220 F2
Heysham LA3 212 E6
Knott End-on-S FY6 200 A6
Cherry Tree Ct
Blackpool FY4 131 B1
10 Fleetwood FY7 199 B5
Standish WN6 29 D2
Cherry Tree Dr LA1 214 F4
Cherry Tree Gdns
Blackpool FY4 111 A8
Nelson BB9 149 A8
Cherry Tree Gr PR6 61 C3
Cherry Tree La
3 Blackburn BB2 80 E8
Ormskirk L39 15 B1
Rawtenstall BB4 68 F8
Cherry Tree Mews
BB11 127 D3
Cherry Tree Rd FY4 131 A1
Cherry Tree Rd N FY4 131 A1
Cherry Tree Sta BB2 100 F1
Cherry Tree Terr BB2 100 F1
Cherry Tree Way
Haslingden BB4 68 B7
5 Horwich BL6 32 E1
Cherry Trees PR5 97 C3
Cherry Vale PR4 73 F2
Cherry View L33 1 A5
Cherry Wood PR1 96 A3
Cherryclough Way BB2 81 B8
Cherrycroft WN8 9 E6
Cherrydale FY2 152 D5
Cherryfields PR7 60 D4
Cherryfold Com Sch
BB11 127 D4
Cherrywood Ave
Cleveleys FY5 175 C1
Lytham St Anne's FY8 90 E4
Cherrywood Cl PR25 59 E8
Cheryl Dr FY5 153 B8
Chesham Cres BL9 33 A3
Chesham Dr PR4 75 F8
Chesham Fold Rd BL9 33 B4
Chesham Ind Est BL9 33 A4
Chesham Lodge PR3 156 B5
Chesham Prim Sch BL9 33 A5
Chesham Rd BL9 33 A5
Chesham St PR3 156 B5
Cheshire Ct
Ramsbottom BL0 50 D6
Southport PR9 53 E1
Cheshire House Cl PR26 76 F7
Chesmere Croft PR1 96 B5
Chesmere Dr PR1 96 B5
Chessington Gn BB10 148 D3
Chester Ave Chorley PR7 43 E4
Cleveleys FY5 175 E2
2 Clitheroe BB7 189 E1
Poulton-le-F FY6 153 C4
Southport PR9 35 F8
Chester Cl Blackburn BB1 102 A3
Garstang PR3 181 B7
Morecambe LA3 217 B2
Chester Cres BB4 68 B8
Chester Ct FY5 176 C3
Chester Dr BL0 50 A4
Chester Pl Adlington PR6 31 A8
Great Eccleston PR3 156 C5
Lancaster LA1 215 A5
Chester Rd
Blackpool FY3 130 D6
Preston PR1 118 C1
Southport PR9 35 F8
Chester St
Accrington BB5 104 A5
Blackburn BB1 102 A4
Bury BL9 33 A4
Chesterbrook PR3 141 E4
Chesterfield Cl PR8 21 C4
Chesterfield Rd
Blackpool FY1 130 C7
Southport PR8 21 C5
Chesters The PR9 53 D2
Chestnut Ave
Blackpool FY4 110 F5
Bolton-le-S LA5 221 A5
Bury BL9 33 B2
Caton LA2 237 C3
Chorley PR6 61 E2
Euxton PR7 60 C4
Higher Penwortham PR1 96 A4
Chestnut Bsns Pk BB12 127 B5
Chestnut Cl
Bamber Bridge PR5 97 E2
Blackpool FY2 152 D2
Garstang PR3 204 D1
Halsall L39 23 C1
Kirkham PR4 114 B5
Chestnut Cotts BB7 191 A5
Chestnut Cres
Barrow BB7 166 D1
Fulwood PR2 118 E2
Longton PR4 74 F8
Chestnut Ct Leyland PR25 60 A7
Ormskirk L39 15 F6
Chestnut Dr
Barnoldswick BB18 196 A1
Fulwood PR2 117 D7
Morecambe LA4 217 F6
Rawtenstall BB4 68 F8
Whalley BB7 144 A7
Chestnut Gdns
Blackburn BB1 101 F7
Thornton FY5 176 B3
Chestnut Gr
Accrington BB5 104 A4
Clayton-le-M BB5 125 A4
Darwen BB3 65 A5
Lancaster LA1 214 D8
Chestnut Grange L39 15 D3
Chestnut Rise BB11 127 F4
Chestnut St PR8 35 C5
Chestnut Way L37 11 C1
Chestnut Wlk 5 BB1 102 B5
Chestnuts The PR7 42 F2
Chethams Cl FY5 176 A2
Chevassut Cl BB9 170 C1
Cheviot Ave
Burnley BB10 128 E5
Cleveleys FY5 175 F4
Lytham St Anne's FY8 91 E5
Cheviot Cl Horwich BL6 32 C5
Ramsbottom BL0 50 C4
Cheviot St PR1 96 C8
Chew Gdns FY6 153 B3
Chichester Cl
Burnley BB10 128 B6
Thornton FY5 176 A2
Chicken St BB2 101 C4
Chiddlingford Ct FY1 130 D3
Childrey Wlk BB2 82 A8
Chilgrove Ave BL6 31 D1
Chiltern Ave
Blackpool FY4 110 D7
Burnley BB10 128 E5
Euxton PR7 60 D1
Poulton-le-F FY6 153 C3
Chiltern Cl Horwich BL6 32 C5
Lytham St Anne's FY8 91 D5
Ramsbottom BL0 50 C4
Chiltern Ct 4 LA1 215 A5
Chiltern Mdw PR25 77 D1
Chiltern Rd
Ramsbottom BL0 50 C4
Southport PR8 21 B6
Chilton Cl L31 5 D1
Chilton Ct 5 L31 5 D1
Chilton Mews 2 L31 5 D1
Chimes The Kirkham PR4 114 A4
Tarleton PR4 57 A5
China St Accrington BB5 103 F6
Lancaster LA1 214 F8
Chindit Cl L37 11 D2
Chindits Way PR2 118 B4
Chines The PR2 117 E4
Chingford Bank BB10 148 D3
Chingle Cl PR2 118 E6
Chippendale Mews PR3 181 C8
Chipping Ave PR8 21 A5
Chipping Ct 4 FY3 131 A8
Chipping Gr
Burnley BB10 128 D4
Normoss FY3 131 A8
Chipping La PR3 140 A8
Chipping Manor PR9 55 A6
Chipping St 3 BB12 146 D1
Chirk Dr FY5 176 D2
Chisacre Dr WN6 19 D7
Chisholm Cl WN6 29 B2
Chisholme Cl BL8 49 F2
Chislehurst Ave FY4 130 D1
Chislehurst Gr BB10 148 D4
Chislehurst Pl FY8 90 E5
Chislett Cl L40 25 D4
Chisnall Ave WN6 28 F6
Chisnall La Coppull PR7 29 C6
Heskin Green PR7 41 F2
Wrightington Bar WN6 29 A5
Chiswell Gr FY5 153 D8
Chiswick Gr FY3 131 B2
Chitheroe Rd PR3 163 C1
Chive Cl FY2 152 F3
Chorcliffe Ho 7 PR7 43 C8
Chorley & District Hospl
PR7 61 C2
Chorley All Saints CE Prim Sch PR7 43 B5
Chorley Astley Park Sch
PR7 43 B8
Chorley Bsns & Tech Ctr
PR7 60 E4
Chorley Cl PR9 54 F5
Chorley Hall Rd PR7 61 C2
Chorley Info Ctr PR7 43 C8
Chorley La PR7 42 D3
Chorley New Rd BL6 32 C2
Chorley New Road Prim Sch
BL6 32 D2
Chorley North Ind Est
PR6 61 D3
Chorley Old Rd
Clayton Green PR6 78 C2
Horwich BL6 32 E3
Whittle-le-W PR6 61 C8
Chorley Rd Adlington PR6 31 A8
Adlington,Blackrod BL6,PR7 31 B5
Bamber Bridge PR5 97 D3
Blackpool FY3 152 F2
Hill Dale L40,WN8 27 D6
Ollerton Fold BB2,PR6 79 E4
Parbold WN8 27 C4
Standish WN1 30 C3
Chorley Southlands High Sch
PR7 43 A5
Chorley St PR6 31 B8
Chorley St James CE Prim Sch PR6 43 E7
Chorley Sta PR6 43 D8
Chorley West Bsns Pk
PR7 42 F8
Chorlton Cl BB10 148 D2
Chorlton Gdns BB1 101 F7
Chorlton St BB1 101 F7
Chorlton Terr BB7 166 D1
Christ Church CE Prim Sch
BB8 172 B5
Christ Church Hall BB5 104 C4
Christ Church Sq 1
BB5 104 C5
Christ Church St
2 Accrington BB5 104 C5
6 Bacup OL13 88 A3
Preston PR1 96 E7
Christ The King RC High Sch
PR1 97 B6
Christ The King RC Prim Sch
Blackpool FY3 131 A7
Burnley BB11 127 E3
Christ The King Sch PR8 35 B2
Christian Rd PR1 96 E7
Christiana Hartley Maternity Hospl PR8 35 D5
Christie Ave LA4 217 D4
Christie Park (Morecambe FC) LA4 217 D4
Christines Cres L40 25 E4
Christleton Cl BB10 148 F3
Church & Oswaldtwistle Sta
BB5 103 E5
Church Alley BB5 124 F2
Church Ave
Accrington BB5 104 E2
Higher Penwortham PR1 96 C6
Lancaster LA1 214 F4
Preston PR1 97 E8
Church Bank Church BB5 103 E7
Over Kellet LA6 237 B8
Church Bank Gdns LA6 240 C7
Church Bank St 20 BB3 82 A1
Church Brook Ho 8 PR1 96 E4
Church Brow
Bolton-le-S LA5 221 A3
Clitheroe BB7 189 E1
Halton LA2 219 C6
Walton-le-D PR5 97 E5
Church Brow Cl LA5 221 A3
Church Brow Gdns 5
BB7 189 E1
Church Cl Clitheroe BB7 189 E1
Dolphinholme LA2 226 A8
Formby L37 12 A3
Freckleton PR4 93 A6
Mellor BB2 121 E2
Ramsbottom BL0 50 B5
Read BB12 145 D2
Southport PR9 36 A8
Waddington BB7 189 B4
Church Close Ct L37 12 A3
Church Cotts LA6 241 C7
Church Ct
Bolton-le-S LA5 221 A3
Edenfield BL0 68 D4
Kirkham PR4 114 A5
16 Lancaster LA1 218 D2
Preston PR1 118 C2
Church Dr
Lytham St Anne's FY8 90 F3
Orrell WN5 10 D5
Whalley BB7 144 A7
Church Fields Bescar L40 23 F7
Ormskirk L39 15 E5
Church Fold
Charnock Richard PR7 42 E4
Coppull PR7 29 F8
Church Gdns
Longridge PR3 140 B7
Warton PR4 92 E6
Church Gn Formby L37 11 C2
Skelmersdale WN8 17 F1
Church Gr LA3 209 E8
Church Hall BB5 103 F7
Church Hill
Nether Kellet LA6 221 F5
Whittle-le-W PR6 61 C7
Church Hill Ave LA5 223 D5
Church Hill Rd
Blackburn BB1 102 A7
Ormskirk L39 15 D6
Church Ho 7 L39 15 E5
Church House Mus PR3 137 D1
Church La
Accrington BB5 125 A1
Aughton L39 6 A7
Bilsborrow PR3 159 A4
Broughton PR3 137 D1
Charnock Richard PR7 42 D4
Edenfield BL0 68 D4
Farington PR4,PR26 76 F7
Church La *continued*
Goosnargh PR3 138 D6
Great Harwood BB6 124 C6
Great Mitton BB7 165 E3
Hambleton FY6 177 D1
Kelbrook BB18 195 A6
Maghull L31 5 A8
Mellor BB2 121 E2
Morecambe LA4 217 B6
Newchurch BB4 86 E1
Newton-w-S PR4 115 B3
12 Padiham BB12 146 C1
Tunstall LA6 241 E4
Whalley BB7 144 C5
Whitechapel PR3 160 E7
Winmarleigh PR3 203 F4
Wrightington Bar WN6 28 D8
Church Mdws BB8 171 D5
Church Pk Lea Town PR4 115 F3
Overton LA3 209 D8
Church Raike PR3 185 E3
Church Rd
Bamber Bridge PR5 77 E7
Bamber Bridge PR5 77 F6
Banks PR9 55 A6
Bickerstaffe L39 7 E6
Formby L37 12 A5
Kirkham PR4 113 F7
Leyland PR25 60 A8
Lytham FY8 90 F3
Lytham St Anne's FY8 90 B6
Rufford L40 39 C4
Shuttleworth BL0 50 E8
Singleton FY6 154 F1
Skelmersdale WN8 17 F1
Tarleton PR4 57 A5
Thornton FY5 176 A2
Thornton-in-C BD23 197 A5
Warton PR4 92 E6
Weeton PR4 132 F1
Wharles PR4 134 F2
Church Row Preston PR1 97 A7
Wrea Green PR4 113 B4
Church Row Chambers
PR4 75 A8
Church Sq BB10 129 B5
Church St
Accrington BB5 104 C5
Adlington PR7 31 A7
Bacup OL13 70 C8
Barnoldswick BB18 196 B2
Barrowford BB9 170 D4
Belmont BL7 46 C4
Blackburn BB1 101 E5
Blackpool FY1 130 C5
Blackrod BL6 31 C2
Brierfield BB9 148 B5
Brierfield,Harle Syke BB10 148 F2
Burnley BB11 128 A6
Bury BL9 33 A3
Chorley PR7 43 C7
Church BB5 103 E6
Churchtown PR3 181 A2
Clayton-le-M BB5 124 F2
1 Clitheroe BB7 166 E8
Colne BB8 171 D5
Croston PR26 58 B1
Darwen BB3 82 A1
Fleetwood FY7 199 B4
Garstang PR3 181 C7
Goodshaw Chapel BB4 106 A1
Great Harwood BB6 124 C5
Halton LA2 219 B6
2 Hapton BB12 126 C4
Haslingden BB4 85 B4
Higher Walton PR5 98 B3
Horwich BL6 32 C3
Kirkham PR4 114 B5
Lancaster LA1 214 E8
Lancaster LA1 214 F8
Leyland PR25 77 B2
Longridge PR3 140 B7
Morecambe LA4 217 B6
Newchurch BB4 86 E1
Ormskirk L39 15 E5
Orrell,Far Moor WN5 10 E5
Oswaldtwistle BB5 103 D3
Padiham BB12 126 C8
2 Poulton-le-F FY6 153 D3
Preston PR1 97 A7
5 Ramsbottom BL0 50 C6
Rawtenstall BB4 69 E8
Read BB12 145 D2
Rishton BB1 124 A1
Skelmersdale WN8 10 C7
Slaidburn BB7 229 C7
Southport PR9 35 C7
Standish WN6 29 E1
Trawden BB8 172 C2
Whittington LA6 241 C7
Whitworth OL12 52 C8
Ribchester PR3 141 D3
Church Terr 21 BB3 82 A1
Church View Aughton L39 6 A7
Gisburn BB7 231 B3
Salesbury BB1 122 E6
Stalmine FY6 177 C7
Tarleton PR4 57 A5
Trawden BB8 172 C2
Church View Ct 1 L39 15 E5
Church Way Formby L37 11 C2
Nelson BB9 148 D6
Church Wlk
Blackburn BB1 122 F3
Euxton PR7 60 C2
Fulwood PR2 118 F5
Kirkham PR4 113 F7
Tarleton PR4 57 A6
Church Wlks 3 L39 15 E5
Churchfield PR2 117 F6
Churchfields PR8 34 F3
Churchgate
Goosnargh PR3 138 D6
Southport PR9 53 F1
Churchgate Mews PR9 54 A1
Churchill Ave
Rishton BB1 103 A8
Southport PR9 53 F2
Churchill Cl 2 FY5 176 B2
Churchill Ct FY3 130 D6
Churchill Dr PR2 118 D4
Churchill Rd
Barrowford BB9 170 B1
Brinscall PR6 63 A8
Fulwood PR2 118 C4
Churchill St OL12 52 C1
Churchill Way
Leyland PR25 77 A2
Nelson BB9 148 B8
Churchlands La WN6 29 F1
Churchside PR4 75 F8
Churchtown Cres OL13 88 B1
Churchtown Ct 2 PR9 54 A2
Churchtown Gdns 1
PR9 54 A2
Churchtown Prim Sch
PR9 54 B2
Churchward Sq BL6 32 C2
Churton Gr WN6 29 B2
Cicely Ct 6 BB1 101 F4
Cicely La BB1 101 F5
Cicely St BB1 101 F4
Cinder La Lancaster LA1 214 F3
Lewth PR4 136 A6
Mere Brow PR4 55 F2
Cinderbarrow La LA5,
LA6 240 A6
Cinnamon Brow WN8 10 C6
Cinnamon Ct 3 PR1 96 C2
Cinnamon Hill Dr N PR5 97 D3
Cinnamon Hill Dr S PR5 97 D3
Cintra Ave PR2 117 D3
Cintra Terr PR2 117 D3
Circus The 10 BB3 82 A1
Cirrus Dr L39 15 A1
City Ct PR1 97 A8
City Heights Cl 21 LA1 215 A8
City Mus* LA1 214 F8
Clairane Ave PR2 117 E6
Clairville PR8 34 F5
Clancut La PR7 42 F2
Clanfield PR2 117 E7
Clara St Preston PR1 97 C7
Whitworth OL12 71 D1
Clare Ave BB8 171 A2
Clare Rd LA1 218 C2
Clare St Blackpool FY1 130 B1
Burnley BB11 127 D6
Claremont Ave
Chorley PR7 43 B7
Clitheroe BB7 166 F7
Southport PR8 35 A4
Claremont Com Prim Sch
FY1 130 C8
Claremont Cres LA4 216 F4
Claremont Ct
Blackpool FY1 130 C7
Lytham St Anne's FY8 89 E5
Claremont Dr
Clitheroe BB7 166 F7
Ormskirk L39 15 D3
Claremont Gdns PR8 35 A4
Claremont Pl FY8 89 E8
Claremont Rd
Accrington BB5 104 B8
Blackpool FY1 130 C8
Chorley PR7 43 B5
Morecambe LA4 216 F4
Southport PR8 35 A4
Claremont St
Brierfield BB9 148 A6
Burnley BB12 127 D6
Colne BB8 172 A5
Claremont Terr BB9 148 D7
Claremount Ave PR25 60 B8
Clarence Ave
Cleveleys FY5 175 D3
4 Haslingden BB4 85 A1
Knott End-on-S FY6 199 E5
Clarence Cl 10 BL9 33 A4
Clarence Ct
15 Blackpool FY4 130 B1
5 Morecambe LA4 217 E6
Southport PR8 35 A4
Clarence House Sch L37 11 F6
Clarence Pk BB2 101 B7
Clarence Rd
Accrington BB5 104 A4
Southport PR8 35 A4
Clarence St
Barnoldswick BB18 196 C1
Blackburn BB1 101 D6
Burnley BB11 128 B4
4 Chorley PR7 43 D7
Colne BB8 172 A5
Darwen BB3 81 F3
Lancaster LA1 215 A7
Leyland PR25 77 B2
Longridge PR3 140 A8
Morecambe LA4 217 B5
Oswaldtwistle BB5 103 C3
Rawtenstall BB4 86 A7
Rochdale OL12 52 D2
Trawden BB8 172 C2
Clarendon Gr L31 5 C5

Clarendon Rd
Blackburn BB1 101 F8
Blackpool FY1 130 B2
Lancaster LA1 218 D3
Lytham St Anne's FY8 90 A8
Clarendon Rd E
Blackburn BB1 102 A8
Morecambe LA4 216 F4
Clarendon Rd N FY8 89 F8
Clarendon Rd W LA3 216 E4
Clarendon St
Accrington BB5 104 D6
Bury BL9 33 A4
10 Chorley PR6 43 E7
Colne BB8 172 B5
Preston PR1 97 A6
Claret St BB5 104 A5
Clark St Morecambe LA4 217 B6
Poulton-le-F FY6 153 F3
Clarke Holme St 3 BB4 86 F2
Clarke St 6 BB1 124 B1
Clarke Wood Cl BB7 144 F8
Clarke's Cotts L40 27 A8
Clarke's La OL12 52 E1
Clarkes Croft BL9 33 C3
Clarkfield Cl L40 25 F3
Clarkfield Dr LA4 217 D5
Clarksfield Rd LA5 221 A4
Clarrick Terr LA6 242 F3
Claton-le-Wold CE Prim Sch PR6 77 F2
Claughton Ave PR25 77 E1
Claughton Dr LA1 215 A3
Claughton Ind Est PR3 181 E1
Claughton Mans 5 FY4 110 D8
Claughton St 13 BB10 148 B1
Claughton Terr LA2 237 F5
Clawthorpe Cotts LA6 240 C8
Clay Brow Rd WN8 9 E6
Clay Gap La FY6,PR3 177 F4
Clay La LA3 213 B8
Clay St BB11 127 C5
Claybank 10 BB12 146 C1
Claybank Fold 9 BB12 146 C1
Clayburn Cl PR6 61 E2
Claylands Dr LA5 221 A4
Claypool Prim Sch BL6 32 F1
Claypool Rd BL6 32 E1
Clayton Ave Leyland PR25 59 D7
Rawtenstall BB4 68 E8
Clayton Brook Prim Sch PR5 78 B5
Clayton Brook Rd PR5 78 C6
Clayton Cl 11 BB9 170 D1
Clayton Cres FY4 110 E6
Clayton Ct PR3 140 B7
Clayton Gdns L40 25 E4
Clayton Gr BB1 122 D6
Clayton Green Rd PR6 78 B3
Clayton Hall Dr BB5 124 F4
Clayton Lodge BB5 124 F4
Clayton Mews WN8 17 D1
Clayton Row BB6 143 D1
Clayton St
1 Accrington BB5 125 A1
6 Bamber Bridge PR5 97 E1
Barnoldswick BB18 196 C2
Blackburn BB2 101 E4
Colne BB8 171 E4
Great Harwood BB6 124 C5
18 Nelson BB9 170 D1
7 Oswaldtwistle BB5 103 E5
Skelmersdale WN8 17 D1
Clayton Street Ind Units BB9 170 D1
Clayton Villa Fold PR6 78 A3
Clayton Way
Blackburn BB2 81 D7
Clayton-le-M BB5 125 A3
Clayton's Gate 11 PR1 96 F8
Clayton-le-Moors Ind Est BB5 124 E2
Clayton-le-Woods CE Prim Sch PR6 78 A2
Clayton-le-Woods Manor Road Prim Sch PR6 78 B2
Claytongate
Blackpool FY4 111 A7
Coppull PR7 42 F2
Claytongate Dr PR1,PR5 97 A2
Claytonhalgh PR3 141 E3
Cleator Ave FY2 152 C1
Cleaver Cotts L38 3 A6
Cleaver St Blackburn BB1 101 F5
Burnley BB10 128 B8
Clecken La PR3 182 D2
Clegg Ave FY5 175 D3
Clegg St 6 Bacup OL13 70 C8
Brierfield BB9 148 B5
Burnley BB10 128 A8
Haslingden BB4 85 B3
Kirkham PR4 114 A5
Nelson BB9 148 E6
Skelmersdale WN8 17 D1
Whitworth OL12 71 C2
Worsthorne BB10 129 A5
Clegg St E 9 BB10 128 A8
Clegg's Ave OL12 71 C2
Clegg's Ct OL12 71 C2
Clematis Cl PR7 61 A3
Clematis St BB2 101 B6
Clemens Ct BB3 81 E3
Clement St
Accrington BB5 104 C5
4 Darwen BB3 65 A8
Clement View 14 BB9 148 D8
Clementina St OL12 52 F1
Clements Dr BB9 148 C4
Clengers Brow PR9 54 A3
Clent Ave L31 5 C3
Clent Gdns L31 5 C3
Clent Rd L31 5 C3
Clerk Hill Rd BB7 144 F5
Clerkhill St BB1 102 B5
Clery St BB12 127 A5
Cleve Way L37 12 B2
Clevedon Rd
Blackpool FY1 130 B7
Fulwood PR2 117 A4
Cleveland Ave PR2 118 C4
Cleveland Cl BL0 50 C3
Cleveland Dr LA1 214 D7
Cleveland Rd
Leyland PR25 76 F2
Lytham St Anne's FY8 91 B3
Cleveland St Chorley PR7 43 C8
Colne BB8 171 F6
2 Coppull PR7 42 E1
Cornholme OL14 109 B1
Clevelands Ave
Morecambe LA3 216 F3
Silverdale LA5 224 C4
Clevelands Gr
Burnley BB11 127 E4
Morecambe LA3 216 F3
Clevelands Mt BB11 127 E4
Clevelands Rd BB11 127 F4
Clevelands Wlk LA3 216 F3
Cleveleys Ave
Cleveleys FY5 175 D3
Fulwood PR2 117 C4
Lancaster LA1 218 A2
Southport PR9 54 A4
Cleveleys Rd
Accrington BB5 104 B8
Blackburn BB2 101 F1
Coupe Green PR5 98 E3
Southport PR9 54 A3
Cleves Ct FY3 131 A2
Cleves The L31 5 E3
Clieves Hills La L39 14 E3
Clifden Ct L37 11 F3
Cliff Ave BL9 50 C2
Cliff Ct FY2 152 B4
Cliff Mount BL0 50 B7
Cliff Pl FY2 152 B4
Cliff Rd PR9 53 D1
Cliff St Colne BB8 171 B3
Padiham BB12 146 D1
Preston PR1 96 E6
Rishton BB1 124 B2
Cliff View OL14 109 B2
Cliffe Ct PR1 97 D8
Cliffe Dr PR6 61 B8
Cliffe La BB6 124 C6
Cliffe Pk BB6 124 C6
Cliffe St BB9 170 E1
Clifford Ave Longton PR4 95 A1
Morecambe LA4 217 D6
Clifford Rd Blackpool FY1 130 C7
Southport PR8 35 A2
Clifford St
Barnoldswick BB18 196 C2
Chorley PR7 43 D8
Colne BB8 171 E5
Cliffs The LA3 216 D2
Clifton Ave
Accrington BB5 104 C7
Blackpool FY4 131 C1
Leyland PR25 60 B8
Preston PR2 117 A2
Warton PR4 92 E6
Clifton Cl FY5 176 C1
Clifton Cres
Blackpool FY3 131 A2
Preston PR1 118 C2
Clifton Ct
1 Blackpool FY4 110 B6
3 Lytham St Anne's,Lytham FY8 91 C3
2 Lytham St Anne's,St Annes FY8 89 E6
Clifton Dr Blackpool FY4 110 B5
Blackrod BL6 31 C3
Great Harwood BB6 124 C6
Higher Penwortham PR1 96 C5
Lytham St Anne's FY8 90 D3
Morecambe LA4 217 E5
Clifton Dr N FY8 110 B2
Clifton Dr S FY8 89 E5
Clifton Gdns FY8 90 C6
Clifton Gn PR4 115 D2
Clifton Gr Chorley PR7 43 B7
Preston PR1 118 C3
Wilpshire BB1 122 F4
Clifton Grange FY8 89 D7
Clifton Ho PR2 118 C4
Clifton Hospl FY8 90 B5
Clifton La PR4 115 D2
Clifton Lodge FY8 89 E5
Clifton Par 4 FY8 91 B3
Clifton Pk Ret Ctr FY4 111 D8
Clifton Pl Freckleton PR4 93 B6
Fulwood PR2 117 B2
Clifton Prim Sch FY8 90 C6
Clifton Rd Blackpool FY4 111 C8
Brierfield BB9 148 C4
Burnley BB12 127 C7
Fleetwood FY7 199 A3
Formby L37 12 A5
Southport PR8 35 F6
Clifton Sq 5 FY8 91 B3
Clifton St Accrington BB5 104 A4
Blackpool FY1 130 B5
Burnley BB12 127 F6
Colne BB8 171 D5
Clifton St *continued*
Darwen BB3 81 F4
Earby BB18 195 A8
Lytham St Anne's FY8 91 B3
5 Preston PR1 96 D6
Rishton BB1 124 B1
Trawden BB8 172 C2
Clifton Terr BB3 82 E2
Clifton Wlk 8 FY8 91 B3
Clinkham Rd BB6 124 A5
Clinning Rd PR8 35 A2
Clinton Ave FY1 130 C4
Clinton St BB1 102 A6
Clippers Quay 2 BB1 101 F4
Clitheroe Castle* BB7 166 E8
Clitheroe Castle Mus* BB7 166 E8
Clitheroe Hospl BB7 190 A3
Clitheroe Pendle Prim Sch BB7 189 F1
Clitheroe Pl FY4 111 A8
Clitheroe Rd
Brierfield BB9 148 A5
Chatburn BB7 190 C3
Lytham St Anne's FY8 90 C6
Sabden BB7 167 E1
Waddington BB7 189 C3
West Bradford BB7 189 F5
Whalley BB7 144 C7
Clitheroe Royal Gram Sch
Clitheroe BB7 189 F1
Clitheroe BB7 190 A2
Clitheroe St
3 Padiham BB12 126 C8
Preston PR1 97 C7
Clitheroe Sta BB7 189 E1
Clitheroes La PR4 93 B6
Clive Ave FY8 110 E1
Clive Lodge PR8 34 F2
Clive Rd
Higher Penwortham PR1 96 B6
Southport PR8 34 F2
Clive St BB12 127 F8
Cliviger Holme CE Prim Sch BB10 108 B6
Clockhouse Ave BB10 148 D3
Clockhouse Ct BB10 148 D3
Clockhouse Gr BB10 148 D3
Clod La BB4 68 C8
Clods Carr La FY6 199 F3
Clog Heads BB8 172 C2
Clogger La BD23 197 F7
Cloister Dr BB3 82 C1
Cloister Gn L37 12 B2
Cloisters LA3 217 C2
Cloisters The
Blackpool FY3 130 E5
Formby L37 11 F3
2 Leyland PR25 77 C2
6 Preston PR2 96 D8
1 Rawtenstall BB4 69 E8
Tarleton PR4 57 A6
Whalley BB7 144 D5
Clorain Cl L33 1 A3
Clorain Rd L33 1 A3
Close The Banks PR9 55 A5
Clayton-le-M BB5 124 F4
Cleveleys FY5 175 D2
Cleveleys,Rossall Beach FY5 175 D4
Fulwood PR2 118 E6
Garstang PR3 204 B1
Ince Blundell L38 3 E3
Kirkham PR4 114 B4
New Longton PR4 76 A7
Rising Bridge BB5 85 A8
Weeton PR4 132 E2
Withnell Fold PR6 79 C3
Closes Hall Mews BB7 230 F5
Clough Acre PR7 61 A2
Clough Ave PR5 97 B3
Clough Bank BB7 190 D5
Clough End Rd BB4 85 B5
Clough Head Visitor Ctr* BB4 84 A3
Clough Heads Cotts PR3 226 F1
Clough La
Hesketh Lane PR3 163 A7
Simonstone BB12 145 F1
Clough Rd Bacup OL13 88 A3
Nelson BB9 149 A8
Clough St 11 Bacup OL13 70 D8
Burnley BB11 127 D5
Darwen BB3 65 C6
5 Newchurch BB4 86 F1
Clough Terr BB18 196 B1
Clough The
Clayton Green PR6 78 A3
Darwen BB3 65 C6
Clougha Ave Halton LA2 219 D7
Lancaster LA1 215 B6
Cloughfield PR1 96 D1
Cloughfold Prim Sch BB4 86 C2
Cloughwood Cres WN6 19 D6
Clovelly Ave
Blackpool FY5 152 D6
Fulwood PR2 117 D3
Clovelly Dr
Higher Penwortham PR1 96 A5
Newburgh WN8 27 A1
Skelmersdale WN8 18 A8
Southport PR8 21 E8
Clover Ave FY8 111 A1
Clover Cres BB12 127 D8
Clover Ct Blackpool FY2 152 F6
Southport PR8 35 B5
Clover Dr PR4 93 D7
Clover Field PR6 78 B2
Clover Hill Rd BB9 148 F7
Clover Mews FY3 130 E6
Clover Rd PR7 43 A5
Clover St OL13 88 A3
Clover Terr BB3 82 A3
Cloverfield PR1 96 B4
Cloverfields 5 BB1 102 A6
Cloverhill Ho BB9 148 F7
Club La PR3 185 E3
Club St Bamber Bridge PR5 77 F7
Cornholme OL14 109 B1
Clucas Gdns L39 15 E6
Clyde St Blackburn BB2 101 B3
4 Blackpool FY1 130 B7
Preston PR2 96 C8
Clydesdale Pl PR26 76 C2
Clyffes Farm Cl L40 24 A7
Co-operation St
Bacup OL13 88 A2
1 Newchurch BB4 86 F2
Rawtenstall,Cloughfold BB4 86 B2
3 Rawtenstall,Crawshawbooth BB4 86 A7
Co-operative Bldgs BB10 107 F8
Co-operative St
1 Bamber Bridge PR5 77 E8
22 Barnoldswick BB18 196 B2
Haslingden BB4 67 F7
Coach Ho PR7 60 A5
Coach Ho Ct L40 25 E3
Coach House Mews PR3 181 C7
Coach Mews LA4 216 F4
Coach Rd Bickerstaffe L39 7 F1
Church BB5 103 E5
Warton LA5 223 D7
Coal Clough La BB11 127 E4
Coal Clough Rd OL14 109 B2
Coal Hey 12 BB4 85 B3
Coal Hey St 13 BB4 85 B3
Coal Pit La
Accrington BB5 103 F4
Bacup OL13 88 B3
Barnoldswick BB7 193 B7
Colne BB8 171 F4
Gisburn BB7 231 D2
Rawtenstall BB4 87 A4
Skelmersdale L39 8 D4
Tockholes BB3 81 B3
Coal Rd BL0 51 C8
Coal St 12 BB11 127 F6
Coastal Dr LA2 220 E2
Coastal Rd
Hest Bank LA2,LA5 220 F2
Morecambe LA4 217 F8
Southport,Birkdale PR8 34 C3
Southport,Woodvale PR8 21 A4
Coastal Rise LA2 220 E2
Coastline Mews PR9 54 A4
Coates Ave BB18 196 C3
Coates Fields BB18 196 C4
Coates La BB18 196 D4
Coates Lane Prim Sch BB18 196 D3
Cob Castle Rd BB4 84 E3
Cob La BB8,BB18 195 B4
Cob Moor Ave WN5 10 D1
Cob Moor Rd WN5 10 D1
Cob Wall BB1 102 A6
Cobb's Brow La WN8 18 B6
Cobb's Clough Rd L40 17 F5
Cobbled Court Yd LA1 214 E7
Cobbs Brow Prim Sch WN8 18 A3
Cobbs La BB5 83 E8
Cobden Ct 4 BB1 101 E5
Cobden Ho BB4 86 D1
Cobden Rd PR9 36 A6
Cobden St Bacup OL13 71 B8
Barnoldswick BB18 196 B1
Brierfield BB10 148 F3
Burnley BB10 128 B8
4 Bury BL9 33 A3
Chorley PR6 61 E1
10 Darwen BB3 65 A8
Egerton BL7 47 D2
Hapton BB12 126 C4
Nelson BB9 148 D7
Padiham BB12 146 D1
Cobham Ct 2 BB4 86 E1
Cobham Rd BB5 104 D5
Cobourg Cl BB2 101 F2
Cochran St 25 BB3 82 A1
Cock Hall La OL12 52 C8
Cock Robin PR26 58 C2
Cock Robin La PR3 181 D2
Cocker Ave FY6 154 A2
Cocker Bar Rd PR26 58 D8
Cocker La PR26 76 C1
Cocker Rd PR5 78 B7
Cocker Sq 3 FY1 130 B6
Cocker St Blackpool FY1 130 B6
Darwen BB3 65 C7
Cocker Trad Est FY1 130 C7
Cockerham Parochial CE Prim Sch LA2 206 D4
Cockerham Rd
Forton LA2,PR3 207 B4
Garstang PR3 204 B1
Cockerham Wlk FY3 131 A8
Cockerill St BB4 85 B4
Cockerill Terr BB7 166 D1
Cockersand Ave PR4 95 C1
Cockersand Dr LA1 215 A3
Cockhall La OL12 71 C1
Cockhill La BB8 172 B8
Cocking Yd LA6 240 C7
Cockle Dick's La PR9 53 E2
Cockleach Lane Ends PR3 162 A2
Cockridge Cl BB2 81 B7
Codale Ave FY2 152 D5
Coddington St BB1 102 B5
Coe La PR4 57 A5
Cog La BB11 127 D4
Cog St BB11 127 D5
Colbran St Burnley BB10 128 B8
12 Nelson BB9 170 F2
Colburne Cl L40 25 F5
Colchester Ave LA1 215 B5
Colchester Dr 6 FY5 175 F4
Colchester Rd
Blackpool FY3 130 F3
Southport PR8 35 F3
Cold Bath St 4 PR1 96 E8
Cold Well La LA7 224 F8
Coldale Ct 5 FY4 110 B6
Coldstream Pl BB2 101 E2
Coldweather Ave BB9 148 F5
Cole Cres L39 6 C8
Colebatch PR2 117 D5
Coleman St 4 BB9 148 F8
Colenso Rd
Blackburn BB1 101 D7
Fulwood PR2 117 C2
Coleridge Ave FY5 176 A3
Coleridge Cl Colne BB8 171 D6
Cottam PR4 116 E4
Coleridge Dr BB5 104 E2
Coleridge Ho LA2 218 C4
Coleridge Pl BB6 124 B4
Coleridge Rd
Blackpool FY1 130 D6
Longshaw WN5 10 D1
Ramsbottom BL8 49 F2
Coleridge St BB2 101 C3
Coles Dr LA5 224 B8
Coleshill Ave BB10 128 D5
Colesville Ave FY5 176 B1
Colin St
Barnoldswick BB18 196 B3
Burnley BB11 127 D5
Colinmander Gdns L39 15 C3
Colinton WN8 9 E7
Colldale Terr BB4 85 B2
College Ave
Cleveleys FY5 175 C1
Formby L37 11 E4
College Cl Formby L37 11 D4
Longridge PR3 140 A5
Padiham BB12 126 D6
Southport PR8 35 A3
College Croft BD24 236 F7
College Ct
Accrington BB5 104 A6
4 Blackpool FY1 130 C4
Preston PR1 117 F2
College Gate FY5 175 C5
College Path L37 11 D5
College Rd WN8 19 B1
College St
Accrington BB5 104 A6
7 Cornholme OL14 109 C1
Collegiate High Sch Sports Coll FY3 153 A1
Collier St BB5 104 E2
Collier's Row BB1 102 F1
Colliers St BB5 103 E5
Collin's Hill La PR3 185 A3
Colling St 9 BL0 50 B5
Collinge Fold La BB4 85 F4
Collinge St
Padiham BB12 126 C7
Rawtenstall BB4 85 F4
Collingham Pk LA1 215 A2
Collingwood BB5 124 E2
Collingwood Ave
Blackpool FY3 130 E6
Lytham St Anne's FY8 110 E1
Collingwood Pl FY3 130 E6
Collingwood Rd PR7 43 B7
Collingwood St
Colne BB8 171 C4
Standish WN6 29 E1
Collingwood Terr 7 LA2 239 D8
Collins Ave FY2 152 E3
Collins Dr BB5 104 E2
Collins Rd PR5 97 F1
Collins Rd N PR5 97 F2
Collinson St PR1 118 C1
Collisdene Rd WN5 10 E6
Collison Ave PR7 43 C8
Colloway Ho LA3 212 E6
Collyhurst Ave FY4 110 E6
Colman Ct PR1 96 D6
Colnbrook WN6 29 B1
Colne & Broughton Rd BD23 197 C6
Colne La BB8 171 E4
Colne Rd
Barnoldswick BB18 196 A1
Barrowford BB8,BB9 170 F4
Brierfield BB9 148 B6
Burnley BB10,BB11 128 A8
Burnley,Burnley Lane BB10 148 B3
Kelbrook BB18 195 A7
Trawden BB8 172 B2
Colne Sta BB8 171 C4

Colonnade The LA1 .....215 C7
Colt House Cl PR25 .....60 A7
Colthurst Dr BB7 .....190 A2
Coltsfoot Dr PR6 .....61 D2
Coltsfoot Wlk LA3 .....217 B2
Columbia Way BB2 .....101 B8
Columbine Cl Chorley PR7 .61 A3
Rochdale OL12 .....52 C3
Colville Ave 1 FY4 .....110 C5
Colville Rd BB3 .....81 E4
Colville St BB10 .....128 A8
Colwall Cl L33 .....1 A2
Colwall Rd L33 .....1 A2
Colwall Wlk L33 .....1 A2
Colwyn Ave
Blackpool FY4 .....130 E1
Morecambe LA4 .....217 D6
Colwyn Pl PR2 .....117 A3
Colyton Cl PR6 .....43 E8
Colyton Rd PR6 .....43 E8
Colyton Rd E 2 PR6 .....43 E8
Combermere Gr LA3 .....212 E5
Combermere Rd LA3 .....212 E6
Comer Gdns L31 .....5 C3
Comet Rd PR26 .....76 C2
Comet St OL13 .....88 A7
Commerce St Bacup OL13 .87 F2
Haslingden BB4 .....85 A4
Commercial Rd
Chorley PR7 .....61 C1
Great Harwood BB6 .....124 C5
Nelson BB9 .....148 E8
Commercial St
Bacup OL13 .....70 D8
Barnoldswick BB18 .....196 B2
10 Blackpool FY1 .....130 B1
Brierfield BB9 .....148 B6
7 Church BB5 .....103 E6
12 Great Harwood BB6 .....124 C5
Oswaldtwistle BB5 .....103 D3
Rawtenstall BB4 .....106 A3
Rishton BB1 .....124 B1
Common Bank Employment Area PR7 .....42 F8
Common Bank La PR7 .....42 F8
Common Edge Rd FY4 .....110 F6
Common End PR7 .....30 E5
Common Garden St 33 LA1 .....214 F8
Common La PR9 .....55 C1
Common The
Adlington PR7 .....30 E5
Parbold WN8 .....27 C3
Commons La BB2 .....121 B5
Commonside FY8 .....90 D4
Commonwealth Cl FY8 .....90 C8
Como Ave BB11 .....127 C4
Company St 7 BB1 .....124 B1
Compley Ave FY6 .....153 C2
Compley Gn FY6 .....153 C2
Compression Rd LA3 .....212 E2
Compston Ave BB4 .....106 A1
Compton Cl FY6 .....153 C5
Compton Gn PR2 .....117 D7
Compton Rd PR8 .....35 B3
Comrie Cres BB11 .....127 D3
Concorde Ho 1 FY1 .....130 C4
Concourse Sh Ctr The WN8 .....18 B1
Conder Ave FY5 .....175 F2
Conder Brow LA5 .....223 E2
Conder Green Rd LA2 .....210 F3
Conder Pl LA1 .....218 C2
Conder Rd PR2 .....116 E1
Condor Gr Blackpool FY1 .130 D3
Lytham St Anne's FY8 .....89 E8
Conduit St BB9 .....170 D1
Coneygarth La
Tunstall LA6 .....241 D4
Whittington LA6 .....241 D6
Congleton Cl FY4 .....131 B1
Congress St PR7 .....61 C1
Conifer Ct L37 .....11 F2
Conifers The Barton PR3 .137 B8
Hambleton FY6 .....177 B2
Kirkham PR4 .....114 B5
Maghull L31 .....5 C3
Conisber Cl BL7 .....47 E1
Coniston Ave
Accrington BB5 .....103 F4
Adlington PR6 .....31 B8
Barnoldswick BB18 .....196 A3
Carleton FY6 .....153 B4
Euxton PR7 .....60 D1
Fleetwood FY7 .....198 E4
Hambleton FY6 .....177 C2
Knott End-on-S FY6 .....199 F6
Lytham St Anne's FY8 .....110 F2
Orrell WN5 .....10 F7
Padiham BB12 .....146 C2
Preston PR2 .....117 D2
Thornton FY5 .....176 B1
Coniston Cl
Longridge PR3 .....140 A5
Ramsbottom BL0 .....50 C7
Coniston Cres FY5 .....176 B1
Coniston Ct
Morecambe LA4 .....217 C6
Southport PR8 .....21 C3
Coniston Dr
Bamber Bridge PR5 .....97 E2
Darwen BB3 .....82 C2
Coniston Gr BB8 .....172 A6
Coniston Ho PR1 .....96 B4
Coniston Rd
Blackburn BB1 .....102 A8
Blackpool FY4 .....110 C7
Blackrod BL6 .....31 D3
Bolton-le-S LA5 .....221 A4
Carnforth LA5 .....221 E8
Chorley PR7 .....43 B6
Formby L37 .....11 D2
Fulwood PR2 .....118 C4
Lancaster LA1 .....218 E2
Maghull L31 .....5 E2
Morecambe LA4 .....217 C6
Coniston St 8 BB12 .....127 C6
Coniston Way Bacup OL13 .88 A4
Croston PR26 .....58 B3
Rainford Junction WA11 .....8 F2
Rishton BB1 .....123 F1
Connaught Dr FY5 .....176 D2
Connaught Rd
Heysham LA3 .....212 D5
Lancaster LA1 .....215 B5
Preston PR1 .....96 E5
Consett Ave FY5 .....175 E5
Constable Ave
Bamber Bridge PR5 .....77 A7
Burnley BB11 .....127 F3
Constable Lee Cres BB4 .86 A4
Constable St 8 PR1 .....97 A8
Convent Cl
Bamber Bridge PR5 .....97 D1
Leyland PR25 .....77 C2
Ormskirk L39 .....15 E2
Convent Cres FY3 .....131 A8
Conway Ave
Bamber Bridge PR5 .....97 A1
Blackburn BB1 .....101 E7
Cleveleys FY5 .....175 D2
Clitheroe BB7 .....166 C6
Leyland PR25 .....60 C8
Normoss FY3 .....131 B7
Conway Cl Catterall PR3 .181 D2
Euxton PR7 .....60 E1
Haslingden BB4 .....85 B1
Ramsbottom BL0 .....50 B6
Conway Cres
Barnoldswick BB18 .....196 C3
Ramsbottom BL8 .....49 F2
Conway Ct
Gregson Lane PR5 .....98 D2
4 Lytham St Anne's FY8 .....89 E6
Conway Dr Bury BL9 .....33 D2
Fulwood PR2 .....117 C6
Oswaldtwistle BB5 .....103 B4
Conway Gr BB10 .....148 C3
Conway Ho 7 PR1 .....97 D8
Conway Rd Eccleston PR7 .41 C7
Rawtenstall BB4 .....86 C2
Conyers Ave PR8 .....34 F3
Cook Gdns BB1 .....102 B4
Cook Green La PR3 .....141 C7
Cook House Rd BB8 .....171 E6
Cook St BL9 .....33 A2
Cooke St BL6 .....32 D4
Cookson Cl PR4 .....93 B6
Cookson Rd FY5 .....176 B3
Cookson St FY1 .....130 C5
Cookwood Ho 13 PR1 .....96 D8
Coolham La BB18 .....197 D1
Coolidge Ave LA1 .....214 D7
Coombes The PR2 .....117 F5
Coop St FY1 .....130 B3
Cooper Ct FY5 .....175 D3
Cooper Hill Cl PR5 .....97 D5
Cooper Hill Dr PR5 .....97 D5
Cooper Rd PR1 .....96 D8
Cooper St Bacup OL13 .....87 F4
Burnley BB11 .....128 A5
Horwich BL6 .....32 B4
Nelson BB9 .....170 E1
Cooper's La PR7 .....28 B8
Cooper's Way FY1 .....130 D7
Cooperage The BB5 .....103 D3
Coopers Cl 5 BB5 .....103 D3
Coote La PR4,PR5 .....76 F7
Cop La Fleetwood FY7 .....199 A4
Higher Penwortham PR1 .....96 C4
Cop Lane CE Prim Sch PR1 .....96 C3
Cop Royd Terr BB10 .....128 F1
Cop The FY5 .....175 D6
Copeland Dr WN6 .....29 F1
Copeland Pl FY8 .....91 C4
Copp La PR3,PR4 .....156 A2
Copper Beech Cl PR4 .....74 E3
Copper Beeches
Blackburn BB2 .....101 A6
Kingsfold PR1 .....96 D2
Copperas La BL6 .....31 B1
Copperfield Cl BB10 .....128 F6
Copperfield St BB1 .....101 F3
Copperwood Way PR7 .....42 F7
Coppice Ave BB5 .....104 D7
Coppice Brow LA5 .....223 F2
Coppice Cl Chorley PR6 .....61 E1
Nelson BB9 .....171 A2
Coppice Dr
Longshaw WN5 .....10 D2
Whitworth OL12 .....52 D7
Coppice La PR6 .....62 C3
Coppice Leys L37 .....11 E3
Coppice Sch The PR5 .....97 F1
Coppice St BL9 .....33 C3
Coppice The
Blackburn BB2 .....101 A7
Clayton-le-M BB5 .....124 F4
Fulwood PR2 .....117 B4
Kirkham PR4 .....114 A6
Longton PR4 .....75 A7
Coppice The *continued*
Morecambe LA4 .....217 E5
Ramsbottom BL0 .....50 A4
Coppingford Cl OL12 .....52 A2
Coppins Gn FY6 .....153 E1
Coppull CE Prim Sch PR7 .....42 F1
Coppull Cross Rds PR7 .....29 F7
Coppull Ent Ctr PR7 .....42 E2
Coppull Hall La PR7 .....43 A1
Coppull Moor La PR7 .....29 E6
Coppull Prim Sch PR7 .....42 E1
Coppull Rd Chorley PR7 .....43 A4
Maghull L31 .....5 C4
Copse Rd FY7 .....198 F2
Copse The
Accrington BB5 .....103 F5
Chapeltown BL7 .....48 C2
Chorley PR7 .....43 B4
Copse View Bsns Pk 12 FY7 .....198 F2
Copster Dr PR3 .....140 B7
Copster Hill Cl BB1 .....82 D8
Copthurst Ave BB12 .....146 F6
Copthurst La PR6 .....61 F7
Copthurst St 18 BB12 .....146 C1
Coptrod Head Cl OL12 .....52 E4
Copy Bottom BB10 .....108 C4
Copy La LA2 .....237 C3
Copy Nook BB1 .....102 A5
Coral Cl FY4 .....131 A1
Corbridge Cl
Blackpool FY4 .....111 A7
Carleton FY6 .....153 C5
Corbridge Ct BB7 .....189 E1
Corcas La FY6 .....176 F8
Cork Rd LA1 .....215 B5
Cork St BL9 .....33 A2
Corka La FY8 .....112 F1
Corlass St 10 BB9 .....170 D3
Corless Cotts LA2 .....226 A8
Corn Mill La FY7 .....199 B4
Corn Mill Lo L31 .....5 C2
Corn Mill Mews BB7 .....144 C5
Corn Mill Yd BB5 .....124 F2
Corn Mkt LA1 .....214 F8
Cornbrook WN8 .....9 E7
Corncroft PR1 .....96 C3
Cornel Gr BB11 .....127 C4
Cornelian St BB1 .....122 F2
Cornelian Way FY3 .....131 A1
Corner Bank Cl PR4 .....112 F7
Cornerhouse The 13 BL0 .....50 C6
Corners The FY5 .....175 C4
Cornfield PR4 .....116 E6
Cornfield Cl PR4 .....73 E4
Cornfield Gr BB12 .....127 A8
Cornfield St BB3 .....82 B2
Cornflower Cl PR6 .....61 D2
Cornford Rd FY4 .....111 B8
Cornhill Arc BB5 .....104 B6
Cornholme BB10 .....148 E2
Cornholme Jun & Infs Sch OL14 .....109 A1
Cornholme Terr 9 OL14 .....109 B1
Cornmill Terr 6 BB18 .....196 B3
Cornthwaite Rd PR2 .....117 E3
Cornwall Ave
Blackburn BB1 .....102 E4
Blackpool FY2 .....152 C2
Cleveleys FY5 .....175 F4
Cornwall Cres WN1 .....30 B1
Cornwall Pl
Blackpool FY3 .....131 B2
Church BB5 .....103 F7
Cornwall Rd BB1 .....124 A1
Cornwall Way PR8 .....21 C2
Corona Ave L31 .....5 C5
Coronation Ave
Blackburn BB2 .....80 C7
Formby L37 .....12 A2
Forton PR3 .....207 B3
Padiham BB12 .....126 C7
Coronation Cres 5 PR1 .....97 B7
Coronation Ct PR26 .....58 B3
Coronation Gr BB4 .....86 E1
Coronation Mount LA6 .....242 C3
Coronation Pl 6 BB9 .....170 D3
Coronation Rd
Brierfield BB9 .....148 C5
Cleveleys FY5 .....175 C2
Kirkham PR4 .....114 A5
Lytham St Anne's FY8 .....90 C4
Maghull L31 .....5 D3
Coronation St
Barnoldswick BB18 .....196 C2
Blackpool FY1 .....130 B4
Great Harwood BB6 .....124 D6
Coronation Terr BB6 .....143 C1
Coronation Way LA1 .....218 E4
Coronation Wlk PR8 .....35 A7
Corporation Ct 4 OL13 .....70 D8
Corporation St
Accrington BB5 .....104 A5
11 Blackburn BB2 .....101 E5
Blackpool FY1 .....130 B5
Chorley PR6 .....61 D1
6 Clitheroe BB7 .....166 D8
Colne BB8 .....171 A3
Preston PR1 .....96 F8
4 Southport PR8 .....35 B7
Corpus Christi RC High Sch PR2 .....117 E5
Corranstone Cl BL6 .....32 B3
Corriander Cl FY2 .....152 F3
Corrib Rd FY2 .....152 D2
Corringham Rd LA4 .....217 B5
Corston Gr BL6 .....31 D1
Corwen Cl BB1 .....101 E7
Cosford St PR4 .....132 E6
Cosgate Cl WN5 .....10 E5
Cotswold Ave PR7 .....60 D1
Cotswold Cl Eccleston PR7 .41 D6
Ramsbottom BL0 .....50 C4
Cotswold Dr BL6 .....32 C5
Cotswold Rd
Blackpool FY2 .....152 D1
Chorley PR7 .....43 C6
Lytham St Anne's FY8 .....91 D5
Cottage Cl L39 .....15 D4
Cottage Fields PR7 .....43 B5
Cottage Gdns PR5 .....78 B8
Cottage La
Bamber Bridge PR5 .....97 F3
Ormskirk L39 .....15 D5
Cottage Mews L39 .....15 D5
Cottage Wlk OL12 .....52 C4
Cottam Ave PR2 .....117 A4
Cottam Cl
Lytham St Anne's FY8 .....110 F2
Whalley BB7 .....144 C5
Cottam Ct PR2 .....117 A2
Cottam Gn PR4 .....116 F6
Cottam Hall La PR2 .....116 F5
Cottam La PR2 .....117 A2
Cottam Pl FY6 .....153 C2
Cottam Prim Sch PR4 .....116 D5
Cottam St PR7 .....43 C6
Cottam Way PR4 .....116 D4
Cottesloe Pl BB9 .....170 C3
Cottesmore Cl OL12 .....52 C6
Cottesmore Pl FY3 .....131 A6
Cottom Croft BB5 .....124 F4
Cotton Ct Colne BB8 .....171 C3
Preston PR1 .....97 A8
Cotton Dr L39 .....15 D6
Cotton Hall St BB3 .....82 A2
Cotton St Accrington BB5 .104 B5
Burnley BB12 .....127 D7
Padiham BB12 .....126 C7
Cotton Tree La BB8 .....172 A5
Cottys Brow PR9 .....53 F3
Coudray Rd PR9 .....53 E1
Coulston Ave FY2 .....152 B3
Coulston Rd LA1 .....215 B6
Coultate St 7 BB12 .....127 C6
Coulter Beck La LA6 .....242 A7
Coulthurst St 1 BL0 .....50 B6
Coulton Rd BB9 .....148 B7
Counsell Ct 3 FY5 .....176 B2
Countess Cl PR4 .....114 A7
Countess Cres FY2 .....152 C3
Countess Rd BB3 .....82 A7
Countess St BB5 .....104 A6
Countess Way PR7 .....60 D2
Countessway 3 PR5 .....97 E1
Country Mews BB2 .....100 F7
County Ave LA1 .....211 B8
County Brook La BB8, BB18 .....194 C4
County Cl PR26 .....77 A4
County Rd Kirkby L32 .....1 A1
Ormskirk L39 .....15 E6
County St LA1 .....214 E8
Coupe Gn PR5 .....98 E4
Coupe Green Prim Sch PR5 .....98 E4
Coupland Cl OL12 .....52 C8
Courage Low La WN6 .....28 D5
Course La L40,WN8 .....26 D1
Court Gr BB1 .....122 E6
Court Hey L31 .....5 E1
Court Mews PR9 .....54 A1
Court Rd PR9 .....35 C8
Court Royal FY8 .....90 E3
Court The Fulwood PR2 .....117 C7
Higher Penwortham PR1 .....96 C4
Southport PR9 .....35 B8
Courtfield L39 .....15 D7
Courtfield Ave FY2 .....130 D8
Courtfields 3 FY1 .....130 C4
Courtgreen L39 .....15 D7
Courtyard The
8 Bacup OL13 .....88 A3
1 Kirkham PR4 .....113 F5
Courtyard Wks L33 .....1 C2
Cousin's La L40 .....39 A3
Cove Dr LA5 .....224 C4
Cove Rd LA5 .....224 B4
Cove The Cleveleys FY5 .....175 C4
Lytham St Anne's FY8 .....90 D3
Morecambe LA4 .....217 E7
Covell Ho 3 LA1 .....214 E8
Coventry St 2 PR7 .....43 C6
Coverdale Dr BB2 .....80 D7
Coverdale Rd LA1 .....214 D8
Coverdale Way 4 BB12 .127 D7
Covert The FY5 .....175 F4
Coveway Ave FY3 .....130 E6
Cow Gate La BD23 .....231 E7
Cow La BB11 .....127 F6
Cow Well La PR6 .....61 B8
Cowan Brae BB1 .....101 D6
Cowdrey Mews 8 LA1 .....218 B1
Cowell Way 9 BB2 .....101 D5
Cowes Ave BB4 .....85 C2
Cowgarth La BB18 .....197 C2
Cowgill St 17 Bacup OL13 .88 A3
Earby BB18 .....197 B1
Cowhill La BB1 .....102 F7
Cowley Cres BB12 .....126 E7
Cowley Rd Blackpool FY4 .110 F8
Fulwood PR2 .....118 E4
Cowling Brow PR6 .....43 E7
Cowling Brow Ind Est PR6 .....43 F6
Cowling La PR25 .....76 D1
Cowling Rd PR6 .....43 F6
Cowm Park Way N OL12 .71 D2
Cowm Park Way S OL12 .71 C1
Cowm St OL12 .....71 E5
Cowpe Rd BB4 .....69 F7
Cowper Ave 1 BB7 .....189 E1
Cowper Pl BB7 .....230 C1
Cowper St Blackburn BB1 .101 F7
Burnley BB11 .....127 C5
Cowslip Way PR6 .....61 D2
Cowtoot La OL13 .....88 A4
Cox Green Cl BL7 .....47 D3
Cox Green Rd BL7 .....47 E2
Coxfield WN6 .....19 D7
Coyford Dr PR9 .....54 A4
Crab Tree La PR3 .....179 C2
Crabtree Ave Bacup OL13 .88 A1
Higher Penwortham PR1 .....96 A3
Newchurch BB4 .....86 F2
Crabtree Bldgs BB4 .....86 F4
Crabtree Cl L40 .....25 D4
Crabtree La L40 .....25 D6
Crabtree Orch 3 FY5 .....176 B3
Crabtree Rd FY5 .....176 B3
Crabtree St
Blackburn BB1 .....102 B5
Brierfield BB9 .....148 B5
Colne BB8 .....171 C4
Whitewell Bottom BB4 .....86 F4
Cracoe Gill BB9 .....170 C3
Craddock Rd BB8 .....171 E5
Crag Ave BL9 .....50 D2
Crag Bank Cres LA5 .....221 C8
Crag Bank La LA5 .....223 B1
Crag Bank Rd
Carnforth LA5 .....223 B1
Crag Bank LA5 .....221 C8
Crag Fold BL9 .....50 D2
Crag La BL9 .....50 D2
Crag Rd Lancaster LA1 .....218 F1
Warton LA5 .....223 A6
Crag View BB4 .....69 F7
Cragg Bottom Rd BD22 .174 F1
Cragg Row BB18 .....194 D7
Cragg St
1 Blackpool FY1 .....130 B3
Colne BB8 .....171 C5
Cragg's Row 18 PR1 .....96 F8
Craggs Hill LA6 .....237 B8
Craggs La LA2 .....239 D3
Craig St LA3 .....216 D3
Craigflower Ct PR5 .....78 C7
Craigholme House Pk LA5 .....223 B1
Craiglands Ave LA3 .....216 D2
Craiglands Ct LA1 .....214 C5
Crail Pl OL10 .....33 F1
Crake Ave FY7 .....198 C2
Crake Bank 4 LA1 .....218 A2
Crambe Hts BB3 .....82 A7
Cranberry Bottoms BB3 .65 E5
Cranberry Chase 4 BB3 .65 C7
Cranberry Cl BB3 .....65 D6
Cranberry Fold Ct BB3 .65 D5
Cranberry La BB3 .....65 D6
Cranberry Rise BB4 .....106 A2
Cranborne Cl Horwich BL6 .32 F1
Standish WN6 .....29 D1
Cranborne St 10 PR1 .....97 C8
Cranborne Terr BB2 .....101 C6
Cranbourne Dr
Chorley PR6 .....43 E7
Church BB5 .....104 A8
Cranbourne Gr FY5 .....153 E7
Cranbourne St
5 Bamber Bridge PR5 .....77 E8
Chorley PR6 .....43 D7
Colne BB8 .....171 E6
Cranbrook Ave
Blackpool FY2 .....152 E5
Oswaldtwistle BB5 .....103 C4
Cranbrook St BB2 .....101 D2
Cranbury Ct FY5 .....175 D3
Crane St PR7 .....29 D6
Cranes La L40 .....16 E7
Cranesbill Cl FY6 .....199 F6
Cranfield View BB3 .....65 C6
Crangle Fold BB7 .....190 A2
Crank Rd WN5 .....10 D1
Crankshaw St 22 BB4 .....86 A3
Cranleigh Ave FY2 .....152 C3
Cranleigh Cl BL6 .....31 D1
Cranmer St 5 BB11 .....127 E6
Cranshaw Dr BB1 .....101 F8
Cranston Rd L33 .....1 C2
Cranwell Ave LA1 .....215 B5
Cranwell Cl 2 BB1 .....102 A4
Cranwell Ct PR4 .....113 F5
Craven Cl PR2 .....117 F7
Craven Cnr 8 FY5 .....152 F7
Craven Ct BL6 .....32 D2
Craven Dr PR5 .....77 D7
Craven St Accrington BB5 .104 A5
6 Barnoldswick BB18 .....196 C2
Brierfield BB9 .....148 B5
Burnley BB11 .....128 A5
Bury BL9 .....33 C3
Clitheroe BB7 .....166 E7
Colne BB8 .....172 A5
Nelson BB9 .....148 C8
Rawtenstall BB4 .....85 F2
Craven St E BL6 .....32 D2
Craven's Ave BB2 .....81 D6
Craven's Brow BB2 .....81 E7
Cravendale Ave BB9 .....170 F3

Cravens Hollow BB2 .....81 D6
Cravens Hollows BB2 ....81 E6
Crawford Ave
Adlington PR7 ....30 E5
Blackpool FY2 ....152 D5
Chorley PR7 ....43 B7
Leyland PR25 ....60 B8
Maghull L31 ....5 B3
Preston PR1 ....118 F1
Crawford Rd WN8 ....9 D2
Crawford St BB9 ....170 E1
Crawford Village Prim Sch
WN8 ....9 E3
Crawshaw Dr BB4 ....86 A6
Crawshaw Grange BB4 ...86 A7
Crawshaw La BB10 .....149 D6
Crawshaw St BB5 ....104 B6
Crawshaw's Bldgs BB4 ...86 A1
Crawshawbooth Prim Sch
BB4 ....86 A8
Crediton Ave PR9 ....54 B5
Crediton Cl BB2 ....81 C8
Crescent Ave
Cleveleys FY5 ....175 D2
Formby L37 ....11 E1
Crescent Ct FY4 ....110 A5
Crescent E FY5 ....175 D2
Crescent Gn L39 ....15 B1
Crescent Rd
Poulton-le-F FY6 ....153 E4
Southport PR8 ....34 F3
Crescent St PR1 ....118 C1
Crescent The
Bamber Bridge PR5 ....77 C8
Bamber Bridge,School Lane
PR5 ....97 F2
Blackburn BB2 ....100 E1
Blackpool FY4 ....110 B7
Brierfield BB10 ....148 B4
Bury BL9 ....33 A3
Carleton FY6 ....153 C4
Chorley PR7 ....61 C2
Clitheroe BB7 ....166 D7
Colne BB8 ....171 E6
Dunsop Bridge BB7 ....228 C5
Fleetwood FY7 ....175 E8
Freckleton PR4 ....93 C5
Hest Bank LA2 ....220 D1
Horwich BL6 ....32 E1
Lytham St Anne's FY8 ......89 E6
Preesall FY6 ....200 B4
Preesall Park FY6 ....200 D1
Preston,Ashton-on-R PR2 ..117 B2
1 Preston,Lea PR2 ......116 D1
Southport PR9 ....54 C3
Warton PR4 ....92 C4
Whalley BB7 ....144 A6
Whitworth OL12 ....52 C8
Worsthorne BB10 ....129 A5
Crescent W FY5 ....175 D2
Cressell Pk WN6 ....29 B1
Cresswood Ave FY5 .....175 D1
Crestway Blackpool FY3 ...130 F6
Tarleton PR4 ....57 A8
Creswell Ave PR2 ....116 F3
Creswick Ave BB11 ......127 F3
Creswick Cl BB11 ....127 F3
Crewdson St BB3 ....81 F2
Crewgarth Rd LA3 ....217 B2
Cribden End La BB4 .....85 D4
Cribden La BB4 ....85 E5
Cribden St BB4 ....85 F4
Criccieth Cl 3 BB4 ....85 B1
Criccieth Pl FY5 ....176 D2
Crichton Pl FY4 ....110 B5
Cricket Path Formby L37 ...11 F5
Southport PR8 ....34 F3
Cricketers Gn PR7 ....41 B6
Crimbles La LA2 ....206 B2
Crime Well La LA3 ......212 E7
Crimea St OL13 ....88 A2
Crinan Sq OL10 ....33 F1
Cringle Way BB7 ....190 A2
Cripple Gate WN6 ....29 A2
Cripple Gate La PR5 .....99 C4
Critchley Cl PR4 ....74 F3
Croasdale 7 LA1 ....218 A2
Croasdale Ave
Brierfield BB10 ....148 E2
Fulwood PR2 ....118 E4
Croasdale Cl LA5 ....223 C1
Croasdale Dr
Cleveleys FY5 ....175 F4
Clitheroe BB7 ....166 F7
Parbold WN8 ....27 C3
Croasdale Sq BB1 ......102 A3
Croasdale Wlk FY3 .....131 B8
Crockleford Ave PR8 .....35 E3
Crocus Cl BB4 ....67 F8
Crocus Field PR25 ....60 A7
Croft Acres BL0 ....68 D2
Croft Ave Burscough L40 ...25 F3
Orrell WN5 ....10 D5
Slyne LA2 ....218 C8
Croft Bank PR1 ....96 C3
Croft Butts La PR4 ....93 C6
Croft Cl BB4 ....86 A5
Croft Ct Fleetwood FY7 ...198 E2
Freckleton PR4 ....93 B6
Southport PR9 ....54 C4
Thornton FY5 ....176 C3
Croft Field L31 ....5 E1
Croft Gdns PR4 ....114 A4
Croft Head Rd BB1 ......123 B1
Croft Hey L40 ....39 B4
Croft Heys L39 ....15 B1
Croft Ho FY6 ....153 D4
Croft La BB12 ....146 F6
Croft Manor PR4 ....93 C6
Croft Mdw PR5 ....78 C6
Croft Rd PR6 ....43 E7
Croft St Bacup OL13 ......87 F3
Burnley BB11 ....128 A5
Bury BL9 ....33 A2
Clitheroe BB7 ....166 E7
18 Darwen BB3 ....82 A1
Earby BB18 ....197 C2
Great Harwood BB6 ....124 C4
Morecambe LA4 ....217 C5
10 Preston PR1 ....96 D8
Preston PR1 ....96 E8
Croft The Blackburn BB1 ..101 D7
Burton in L LA6 ....242 C3
Caton LA2 ....237 C3
Cleveleys FY5 ....175 D2
Colne BB8 ....171 E7
Eccleston PR7 ....41 C7
Euxton PR7 ....60 B3
Fleetwood FY7 ....198 E2
Garstang PR3 ....204 B1
Goosnargh PR3 ....138 D6
Great Plumpton PR4 ....112 E7
Hoghton PR5 ....99 B2
Lytham St Anne's FY8 .....111 B1
Maghull L31 ....5 B5
Orrell WN5 ....10 D3
Poulton-le-F FY6 ....153 D2
Thornton-in-C BD23 ......197 B5
Warton LA5 ....223 E6
Croft Way FY5 ....153 C8
Crofters Bank BB4 ......106 A1
Crofters Fold
Galgate LA2 ....211 B4
Morecambe LA3 ....216 E1
Crofters Gn Euxton PR7 ...60 C3
Preston PR1 ....117 E2
Crofters La L33 ....1 A5
Crofters Mdw PR26 ....76 E3
Crofters Mews 12 FY1 ...130 C7
Crofters Wlk
4 Kingsfold PR1 ....96 D2
Lytham St Anne's FY8 ......90 E7
Croftgate PR2 ....117 F5
Croftland Gdns LA5 .....221 B6
Croftlands Borwick LA6 ...240 B3
Orrell WN5 ....10 D4
Ramsbottom BL0 ....50 A3
Warton LA5 ....223 E6
Crofton Ave FY2 ....152 D5
Crofts Cl PR4 ....114 C5
Crofts The PR4 ....95 A1
Croftson Ave L39 ....15 F7
Croftwood Terr BB2 .....101 A1
Croich Gn BL8 ....49 B2
Croichbank BL8 ....49 B2
Croichley Fold BL8 ......49 D2
Cromarty Sq OL10 ....33 F1
Crombleholme Rd PR1 ....118 E1
Cromer Ave BB10 ....148 C1
Cromer Gr BB10 ....148 C1
Cromer Pl Blackburn BB1 ..101 E7
Fulwood PR2 ....117 A4
Cromer Rd Blackpool FY2 .152 E4
Lytham St Anne's FY8 .....111 A1
Southport PR8 ....34 E2
Cromer St OL12 ....52 E1
Cromfield L39 ....15 C2
Cromford Wlk 9 PR1 .....97 C8
Crompton Ave FY4 ....110 E7
Crompton Ct 20 PR1 .....97 A8
Crompton Pl BB2 ....101 C5
Crompton St PR1 ....118 C1
Cromwell Ave 1 PR1 .....96 C3
Cromwell Cl L39 ....15 C2
Cromwell Mews PR3 .....181 C8
Cromwell Rd
Blackpool FY1 ....130 C7
Fulwood PR2 ....118 D3
Higher Penwortham PR1 ....96 C3
Lancaster LA1 ....214 E6
Cromwell St
Accrington BB5 ....104 B8
20 Blackburn BB1 ....102 A4
Burnley BB12 ....127 F8
Foulridge BB8 ....194 D1
4 Preston PR1 ....118 A1
Cromwell Terr 12 BB9 ...170 D3
Cromwell Way PR1 ....97 A1
Cronkeyshaw Ave OL12 ....52 E2
Cronkeyshaw Rd OL12 ....52 F1
Cronkshaw St BB10 ......128 A7
Cronshaw Dr BB6 ....143 C1
Crook Dale La FY6 ......177 E7
Crook Gate La PR3 ......178 E1
Crook Nook LA3 ....213 B2
Crook O'Lune Cvn Pk
LA2 ....219 F5
Crook St Adlington PR7 ....30 F7
Chorley PR7 ....43 B5
Preston PR1 ....97 B8
Crookall Cl 7 FY7 ......198 F2
Crooked La PR1 ....97 A8
Crooked Shore OL13 ......87 F3
Crookfield Rd BL7 ....64 B3
Crookhalgh Ave BB10 ....128 F6
Crookhey Gdns LA2 ......206 E3
Crookhey Hall Sch LA2 ..206 E3
Crookings La PR1 ....96 A6
Crooklands Dr PR3 ......181 C8
Crookleigh Pl LA3 ......216 D2
Cropper Gdns PR4 ....73 D3
Cropper Rd FY4 ....111 C6
Cropper Rd N FY4 ....111 C7
Cropper's La L39 ....16 A1
Cropton Rd L37 ....11 F3
Crosby Cl BB3 ....65 B6
Crosby Ct FY8 ....110 F1
Crosby Gr FY3 ....130 F3
Crosby Pl PR2 ....117 A4
Crosby Rd Blackburn BB2 .101 E1
Lytham St Anne's FY8 .....110 F1
Southport PR8 ....35 A3
Crosby St OL12 ....52 F2
Crosfield Ave BL9 ....50 C2
Crosier Wlk PR4 ....116 E5
Crosland Rd L32 ....1 A1
Crosland Rd N FY8 ....90 A8
Crosland Rd S FY8 ....90 A8
Crosley Cl BB5 ....104 B3
Cross Bank 9 BB12 .....126 D8
Cross Barn Gr BB3 ....65 B8
Cross Barn La L38 ....3 E3
Cross Barn Wlk 5 BB3 ...65 B8
Cross Bldgs 17 BB4 ......86 A7
Cross Brow PR7 ....42 C8
Cross Edge BB5 ....104 A1
Cross Field PR4 ....95 C1
Cross Flatts Cres BB18 ..194 E8
Cross Fold BB7 ....190 B8
Cross Gates BB6 ....124 C5
Cross Gn L37 ....12 A2
Cross Green Cl L37 ......12 A2
Cross Green Rd PR2 .....117 E6
Cross Hagg St BB8 ......171 C4
Cross Hall Ct L39 ....16 A4
Cross Halls PR1 ....96 C3
Cross Helliwell St 17
BB8 ....171 D4
Cross Hill Ct LA5 ....221 A4
Cross Hill Four Lane Ends
PR3 ....226 B6
Cross Hill La BB7 ....231 B1
Cross Hos PR7 ....42 C8
Cross Keys Dr PR6 ....61 C7
Cross La
Barley Green BB12 ....169 C4
Halsall L39 ....23 C1
Low Bentham LA2 ....239 B8
Orrell WN5 ....10 D3
Ramsbottom BL8 ....50 A6
Salterforth BB18 ....194 E8
Treales PR4 ....134 D1
Waddington BB7 ....188 E5
Cross Meanygate L40 ....38 C5
Cross Rd LA2 ....239 B7
Cross School St 5 BB8 .171 D4
Cross Skelton St 6
BB8 ....171 E5
Cross St Accrington BB5 ..104 C5
4 Bacup OL13 ....88 A3
Blackburn BB3 ....81 F7
Blackpool FY1 ....130 B7
Brierfield BB9 ....148 B5
Brierfield,Harle Syke BB10 .148 F3
Chorley PR7 ....61 C1
Clayton-le-M BB5 ....124 E3
Clitheroe BB7 ....166 D8
Darwen BB3 ....65 B7
Earby BB18 ....197 A1
Fleetwood FY7 ....199 B5
Great Harwood BB6 ....124 D5
Higham BB12 ....146 F6
3 Leyland PR25 ....77 B2
Longridge PR3 ....140 A6
Lytham St Anne's FY8 ......89 D8
Morecambe LA4 ....217 C5
Nelson BB9 ....148 D8
Oswaldtwistle BB5 ....103 D4
Preston PR1 ....96 F7
Ramsbottom BL0 ....50 C6
16 Rawtenstall BB4 ....86 A7
Southport PR8 ....35 B6
Standish WN6 ....29 E1
Worsthorne BB10 ....129 B6
Cross St N BB4 ....85 B5
Cross St S BB4 ....85 B4
Cross St W BB8 ....171 B4
Cross Swords Cl PR7 .....43 A5
Cross The L38 ....3 E4
Cross Way FY5 ....175 D4
Crossdale Ave LA3 ......216 D2
Crossdale Sq 10 LA1 ....215 A8
Crosse Hall La PR6 ......43 F7
Crosse Hall St PR6 ......43 F7
Crossens Way PR9 ....54 C6
Crossfield Rd WN8 ....9 C8
Crossfield St BB2 ......101 F3
Crossgill Pl 7 LA1 .....218 B2
Crosshall Brow L40 ......16 C4
Crosshill Rd BB2 ....101 B5
Crosshill Specl Sch
BB1 ....102 C2
Crosshills 5 BB12 ......146 C1
Crossings The PR5 ....99 B2
Crossland Rd FY4 ....130 E1
Crossland St BB5 ....104 A5
Crosslands LA6 ....241 D7
Crossley Fold BB11 .....127 D4
Crossley House Ind Est
PR1 ....96 E4
Crossways BB7 ....189 D7
Croston Ave PR6 ....31 A8
Croston Barn La PR3 ....181 A8
Croston Cl 6 BB1 ....102 B5
Croston Close Rd BL9,
OL12 ....51 C4
Croston Dr L40 ....39 B6
Croston La PR7 ....42 B2
Croston Rd
Croston L40,PR26 ....39 C7
Farington PR26 ....76 F6
Garstang PR3 ....181 B8
Leyland PR26 ....76 E4
Croston St BB1 ....102 C5
Croston Sta PR26 ....58 B3
Croston's Brow PR9 ......53 F3
Crow Foot Row BB18 ....196 B1
Crow Hills Rd PR1 ....96 A6
Crow La Ramsbottom BL0 ..50 C6
Skelmersdale WN8 ....18 F3
Town End PR3 ....155 E8
Crow Orch Prim Sch
WN8 ....17 F2
Crow Orchard Rd WN6 ....29 A1
Crow Park La BB7 ....231 C4
Crow Tree Ave 4 OL13 ....70 B8
Crow Trees Brow BB7 ...190 D4
Crow Trees Gdns BB7 ...190 D5
Crow Trees La BL7 ....48 C7
Crow Wood Ave BB12 ....127 D7
Crow Wood Ct BB12 .....127 E7
Crow Wood Rd BB4 ....68 D6
Crow Woods BL0 ....68 D5
Crowborough Cl BL6 .....32 F1
Crowder Ave FY5 ....176 B2
Crowell Way PR5 ....97 E3
Crowland Cl PR9 ....36 A6
Crowland St PR9 ....36 A6
Crowland Way L37 ....12 B2
Crowle St PR1 ....97 D8
Crown Bldgs PR8 ....21 F8
Crown Cl L37 ....12 A2
Crown Gdns BL7 ....48 D6
Crown La Fleetwood FY7 ..199 B4
Horwich BL6 ....32 A4
Swillbrook PR4 ....136 B2
Crown Mews 3 PR4 ......114 A5
Crown Point BL7 ....48 D6
Crown Point Rd BB11 ....127 E1
Crown St Accrington BB5 .104 A5
3 Chorley PR7 ....43 C8
Darwen BB3 ....65 A8
Leyland PR25 ....77 B3
Preston PR1 ....96 F8
Crown Way BB8 ....171 C5
Crowndale BL7 ....48 D7
Crownest Ind Est BB18 ..196 C3
Crownest Rd BB18 ......196 C3
Crownlee PR1 ....96 A3
Crowshaw Dr OL12 ....52 E3
Crowther Ct BB10 ......129 B6
Crowther St
Burnley BB11 ....128 B4
Clayton-le-M BB5 ....124 E3
Crowthorn Rd BL7 ....67 A1
Crowtrees 3 LA2 ....239 B8
Crowtrees Gr BB9 ....169 F5
Crowtrees Rd BB7 ....145 F8
Croxteth Cl L31 ....5 E3
Croxton Ct PR9 ....53 E1
Croxton Wlk 10 BL6 .....32 B4
Croyde Cl PR9 ....54 B5
Croyde Rd FY8 ....90 A5
Croydon Rd 5 FY3 ......130 E7
Croydon St BB2 ....101 C5
Crummock Pl 2 FY4 .....131 C1
Crummock Rd PR1 ......119 A1
Crumpax Ave PR3 ....140 A8
Crumpax Cft PR3 ....140 A8
Crumpax Gdns PR3 ......140 A7
Crumpax Mdw PR3 ....140 A8
Crystal Gr FY8 ....89 E8
Crystal Lodge 3 FY8 .....90 C4
Crystal Mews FY1 ......130 B1
Crystal Rd Blackpool FY1 .130 B1
Thornton FY5 ....176 B5
Cub St PR26 ....77 A4
Cuba Ind Est BL0 ....50 C8
Cuba St 2 BB9 ....148 D8
Cuckoo Brow BB1 ....101 D8
Cuckoo La Bury BL9 ......33 C2
Bury BL9 ....33 C3
Skitham PR3 ....179 B3
Cuckstool La BB12 .....147 E6
Cudworth Rd FY8 ....110 F1
Cuerdale La PR5 ....98 D6
Cuerdale St BB10 ....148 E3
Cuerden Ave PR25 ....59 D7
Cuerden Church Sch PR5 .77 F8
Cuerden Cl PR5 ....77 F4
Cuerden Residential Cvn Pk
PR25 ....77 E3
Cuerden Rise PR5 ....77 C7
Cuerden St Chorley PR6 ...43 E7
Colne BB8 ....171 B3
Cuerden Valley Pk* PR5 ...77 F3
Cuerden Way PR5 ....77 D7
Culbeck La PR7 ....59 F2
Culshaw St
3 Blackburn BB1 ....102 A5
Burnley BB10 ....128 C5
Culshaw Way L40 ....23 F7
Culvert La WN8 ....27 A2
Cumberland Ave
Blackpool FY1 ....130 D4
Burnley BB12 ....127 A6
Clayton-le-M BB5 ....125 A3
Cleveleys FY5 ....175 E4
Leyland PR25 ....59 F7
Cumberland Cl BB3 ....65 C6
Cumberland Rd PR8 ....35 D5
Cumberland St
12 Blackburn BB1 ....102 A4
5 Colne BB8 ....171 E5
Nelson BB9 ....170 E1
Cumberland View 2
LA1 ....215 A6
Cumberland View Cl
LA3 ....216 D3
Cumberland View Rd
LA3 ....216 D3
Cumbrian Ave FY3 ....130 E7
Cumbrian Way BB12 .....127 B8
Cumeragh La PR3 ....139 C6
Cummins Ave L37 ....11 E5
Cumpstey St BB2 ....101 E3
Cunliffe Ave BL0 ....50 A4
Cunliffe Cl BB1 ....123 B1
Cunliffe Ct BB5 ....124 F2
Cunliffe Ho BB4 ....86 D1
Cunliffe La BB7 ....144 F8
Cunliffe Rd
Blackburn BB1 ....123 C1
Blackpool FY1 ....130 D2
Cunliffe St Chorley PR7 ...43 D7
11 Preston PR1 ....97 A8
Ramsbottom BL0 ....50 C7
Cunnery Mdw PR25 ....77 E1
Cunningham Ave PR7 .....43 A6
Cunningham Ct LA1 .....214 E5
Cunningham Gr BB12 ...127 B6
Cunscough La L31,L39 .....6 D3
Curate St Chorley PR6 ....61 E1
Great Harwood BB6 ....124 C5
Curlew Cl Blackburn BB1 .101 E8
2 Cleveleys FY5 ....175 F4
Leyland PR25 ....59 C7
Oswaldtwistle BB5 ....103 D3
Curlew Gdns BB11 ......127 C5
Curlew Gr LA3 ....212 F5
Curlew La L40 ....38 E2
Curteis St BL6 ....32 B4
Curtis Dr 1 FY7 ....198 D3
Curtis St 8 BB4 ....86 A3
Curve St OL13 ....87 F1
Curven Edge BB4 ....68 A7
Curwen Ave LA3 ....212 E6
Curwen La PR3 ....160 C2
Curwen St 7 PR1 ....118 C1
Curzon Pl BB2 ....101 C3
Curzon Rd
Lytham St Anne's FY8 ......90 A7
Poulton-le-F FY6 ....153 E3
Southport PR8 ....35 E5
Curzon St
10 Burnley BB11 ....127 F6
1 Clitheroe BB7 ....166 D7
Colne BB8 ....171 E4
Cusson Rd L33 ....1 B1
Custom House La FY7 ...199 C5
Customs Way PR2 ....96 C8
Cut La Haskayne L39,L40 ...14 F6
Rishton BB1 ....123 F1
Rochdale OL12 ....52 A1
Cutgate Rd OL12 ....52 B1
Cutler Cl BB2 ....101 C5
Cutler Cres OL13 ....70 D7
Cutler La Bacup OL13 .....70 D7
Hesketh Lane PR3 ....162 C8
Cutt Cl PR26 ....58 F6
Cutts La FY6 ....177 F2
Cyclamen Cl PR25 ....77 E2
Cygnet Cl L39 ....15 C2
Cygnet Ct L33 ....1 A2
Cypress Ave FY5 ....175 E2
Cypress Cl
Clayton-le-W PR25 ....77 E2
Fulwood PR2 ....119 A4
Cypress Gr
Bamber Bridge PR5 ....77 B8
7 Blackpool FY3 ....130 D7
Cypress Rd PR8 ....35 F6
Cypress Ridge BB2 ....80 F8
Cyprus Ave FY8 ....90 B4
Cyprus Rd LA3 ....212 E7
Cyprus St BB3 ....65 B6

D

D'urton La PR2,PR3 .....137 F1
Daffodil Cl Haslingden BB4 .68 A8
Rochdale OL12 ....52 E3
Dagger Rd PR4 ....115 C8
Daggers Hall La FY4 ....110 E8
Daggers La FY6 ....200 B3
Dahlia Cl Blackburn BB3 ...82 B7
Clayton-le-W PR25 ....77 E2
Rochdale OL12 ....52 D3
Dailton Rd WN8 ....10 A7
Daisy Bank 11 Bacup OL13 .87 F3
Lancaster LA1 ....215 D7
Daisy Bank Cl PR25 ......76 D1
Daisy Bank Cres BB10 ...128 E5
Daisy Bank St 18 OL14 ...109 B1
Daisy Croft PR2 ....95 D8
Daisy Fold PR6 ....61 E2
Daisy Hill BB4 ....86 A3
Daisy Hill Dr PR6 ....31 A8
Daisy Hill Fold PR7 ......60 D1
Daisy La Blackburn BB1 ...101 F6
Preston PR1 ....118 C3
Ring o'Bells L40 ....26 B4
Daisy Mdw PR5 ....78 B5
Daisy St Blackburn BB1 ...102 A6
Colne BB8 ....171 D4
4 Lancaster LA1 ....218 D3
Daisy Wy PR8 ....35 C2
Daisyfield Mill BB1 .....102 A5
Daisyfield Prim Sch
BB1 ....102 A6
Daisyfield St BB3 ....81 E5
Daisyfields PR4 ....116 F7
Dalby Cl Blackpool FY5 ...152 F7
Preston PR1 ....118 D3
Dalby Cres BB2 ....101 A1
Dalby Lea BB2 ....101 A1

Dale Ave 1 Euxton PR7 60 D1
Longton PR4 74 E8
Slyne LA2 218 C8
Dale Cl Burnley BB12 127 D6
Maghull L31 5 C2
Parbold WN8 27 B2
Dale Cres BB2 80 E7
Dale Dyke Wlk FY6 153 B3
Dale La L33 1 B4
Dale Mill BB4 86 F2
Dale St Accrington BB5 104 A6
Bacup OL13 87 F3
8 Bacup,Stacksteads OL13 70 C8
Blackburn BB2 101 D4
Blackpool FY1 130 B3
Brierfield BB9 148 A5
Burnley BB12 127 D6
Colne BB8 171 C5
Earby BB18 197 B2
Haslingden BB4 85 B3
Lancaster LA1 215 A7
Nelson BB9 148 C8
4 Oswaldtwistle BB5 103 E4
Preston PR1 97 B8
Ramsbottom BL0 68 C1
Dale St E BL6 32 D2
Dale St W BL6 32 D2
Dale Street Mews 7 FY1 130 B3
Dale Terr BB7 190 D5
Dale View Billington BB7 144 B4
Blackburn BB2 81 E6
Chorley PR7 43 C4
Earby BB18 197 A1
6 Rawtenstall BB4 85 F1
Dalecrest WN5 10 D1
Daleford Cl FY5 153 C8
Dalegarth Cl FY4 131 C1
Dalehead Rd PR25 60 B7
Dales Ct FY4 110 D6
Dales The BB6 123 A8
Dales View Pk Cvn Pk BB18 194 B7
Dales Wlk L37 12 A6
Dalesford BB4 85 B1
Dalesview Cres LA3 212 F7
Dalesway BB9 170 C3
Dalewood Ave FY4 130 E1
Dalglish Dr BB2 81 D7
Dalkeith Ave FY3 131 A2
Dalkeith Rd BB9 148 C8
Dall St BB11 128 A4
Dallam Ave LA4 217 C6
Dallam Dell FY5 176 B4
Dallas Ct LA4 217 F4
Dallas Rd Lancaster LA1 214 E7
5 Morecambe LA4 217 F4
Dallas St PR1 117 E2
Dalmore Rd PR2 117 A3
Dalton Ave FY4 110 D5
Dalton Cl Blackburn BB1 102 B5
Ramsbottom BL0 50 A4
Dalton La LA6 240 C7
Dalton Rd Lancaster LA1 215 A8
Morecambe LA3 216 D3
Dalton Sq LA1 214 F8
Dalton St Burnley BB11 127 D3
Lytham St Anne's FY8 89 D8
Nelson BB9 170 E1
Dalton St Michael's CE Prim Sch WN8 18 D5
Dalweb Ind Pk PR9 55 C3
Dam Head Rd BB18 196 B2
Dam La L40 24 C6
Dam Side
2 Barnoldswick BB18 196 B3
Colne BB8 171 D4
Dam Top BB4 86 B2
Dam Wood La L40 24 C5
Dame Fold Higham BB12 146 F6
12 Padiham BB12 126 C8
Damfield La L31 5 C1
Damside Cotts LA2 211 B5
Damside St LA1 214 F8
Damsom Cl BB6 143 C6
Danbers WN8 9 F6
Dancer La BB7 231 B1
Dandy Row BB3 82 C3
Dandy Wlk BB1 101 E4
Dandy's Meanygate PR4 56 A8
Dane Mews FY6 131 E8
Dane St BB10 128 A7
Danes Cl PR4 114 C5
Danes Dr PR5 97 D1
Danesbury Pl 4 FY1 130 C5
Daneshouse Rd BB10 128 A8
Danesmoor Dr BL9 33 B4
Danesway Adlington PR7 43 F1
Bamber Bridge PR5 97 D1
Higher Penwortham PR1 96 A4
Daneswood Ave OL12 52 C8
Daneswood Cl OL12 52 C8
Daneway PR8 21 B6
Danewerke St 9 PR1 97 A8
Daniel Fold OL12 52 B2
Daniel Fold La PR3 181 D2
Daniel St
10 Clayton-le-M BB5 124 F3
Whitworth OL12 71 D2
Daniell St BB1 124 A2
Daniels La WN8 9 C7
Danson Gdns 3 FY2 130 D8
Danvers St BB1 124 B2
Daram Ho 3 FY1 130 D2
Darbishire Rd FY7 198 F4
Daresbury Ave PR8 21 A5
Darfield WN8 9 F7
Dark La Blackrod BL6 31 B3
Earby BB18 197 E2
Johnson's Hillock PR6 61 E6
Maghull L31 5 E1
Mawdesley L40 40 E3
Newchurch BB4 86 E1
Ormskirk L40 16 C6
Dark Wood La PR5 99 B6
Darkinson La
Lea Town PR4 115 F1
Preston PR4 116 B2
Darkwood Cres BB7 190 D5
Darley Ave FY4 110 E7
Darley Ct FY8 89 D7
Darley St BL6 32 B5
Darlington Ct PR7 42 D4
Darlington St PR7 42 E1
Darmond Rd L33 1 A3
Darnbrook Rd BB18 196 A2
Darnhill Com Sch OL10 33 F1
Darnley St BB10 128 C5
Dart St PR2 96 C8
Dartford Cl 1 BB1 102 A4
Dartmouth Cl PR4 113 F5
Darululoom Islamia BL8 49 F4
Darwen Cl PR3 140 B7
Darwen Ent Ctr BB3 82 A2
Darwen L Ctr BB3 82 A1
Darwen Moorland High Sch BB3 82 B3
Darwen Rd BL7 47 E1
Darwen St Blackburn BB2 101 E4
Higher Walton PR5 98 B4
2 Padiham BB12 126 C8
Preston PR1 97 C7
Darwen St Barnabas CE Prim Sch BB3 65 C6
Darwen St Peter's CE Prim Sch BB3 65 B8
Darwen Sta BB3 82 A1
Darwen Vale High Sch BB3 81 E5
Darwen View PR5 97 E5
Darwin Ct PR9 53 E1
Darwin St BB10 148 A2
Daub Hall La PR5 98 E3
Daub La L40 40 A1
Dauntesey Ave FY3 131 A6
Davenham Rd
Darwen BB3 81 E3
Formby L37 11 F3
Davenport Ave FY2 152 C5
Daventry Ave FY2 152 B4
David Crosley Ho 2 BB18 196 B2
David St Bacup OL13 70 D8
11 Barrowford BB9 170 D4
Burnley BB11 127 F4
16 Rochdale OL12 52 F1
David St N 15 OL12 52 F1
Davidson St 15 LA1 215 A8
Davies Rd BB1 102 D6
Davis St PR3 140 A8
Davitt Cl 4 BB4 85 B3
Davy Field Brow BB1 82 B6
Davy Field Rd BB1 82 B6
Dawber Delph WN6 19 D8
Dawber's La PR7 59 E2
Dawlish Ave FY3 130 F8
Dawlish Cl BB2 81 C8
Dawlish Dr PR9 54 A5
Dawlish Lodge FY8 89 D7
Dawlish Pl PR2 117 A3
Dawnay Rd PR2 118 E3
Dawson Ave
Simonstone BB12 145 E2
Southport PR9 54 C5
Dawson Gdns L31 5 C2
Dawson La PR6,PR7,PR25 60 E7
Dawson Pl PR5 78 A7
Dawson Rd
Lytham St Anne's FY8 110 F1
Ormskirk L39 15 F7
Dawson Sq BB11 128 A7
Dawson St BL9 33 A4
Dawson Wlk PR1 117 F1
Day St BB9 148 E7
Daybrook WN8 9 F7
Dayfield WN8 10 B7
Dayton Pl FY4 110 C6
De Lacy Ho BB2 101 C5
De Lacy St Clitheroe BB7 166 D8
Preston PR2 117 D2
De Vitre Cotts LA1 214 E4
De Vitre St 7 LA1 218 E1
De-Haviland Way WN8 9 E8
Deakin's Terr BL7 46 C5
Deakins Bsns Pk BL7 47 D1
Deal Pl FY8 110 F1
Deal St Blackburn BB1 101 F7
9 Bury BL9 33 B2
Dean Brow PR3 141 F8
Dean Cl Edenfield BL0 68 D3
Skelmersdale WN8 10 C7
Dean Ct FY7 175 D8
Dean Edge Rd BD22 174 F1
Dean Fold BB4 87 A8
Dean Hall La PR7 59 D2
Dean Head La BL6 45 A4
Dean La
Billington BB6,BB7 144 C1
Samlesbury PR5 119 F3
Tockholes BB3 81 B1
Water BB4 87 B8
Dean Mdw 5 BB7 166 D7
Dean Mill BB11 128 A5
Dean Rd BB4 85 B1
Dean St
Bamber Bridge PR5 97 E1
Blackpool FY4 110 B8
Burnley BB11 127 E6
Darwen BB3 81 F4
2 Padiham BB12 146 D1
Trawden BB8 172 C2
Dean Terr 4 PR4 114 A5
Dean Wood Ave WN5 10 E8
Dean Wood Cl PR7 43 A6
Deancroft Ave LA3 216 E2
Deanfield BB7 190 B2
Deanfield Ct BB7 190 A2
Deanpoint LA3 217 C3
Deans Ct L37 11 F5
Deans La L40,WN8 26 E3
Deansgate Blackpool FY1 130 B5
Morecambe LA4 217 B5
Deansgate La L37 12 B5
Deansgate La N L37 12 A6
Deansgrave BB4 85 B1
Deansgreave Rd OL13 71 B7
Dearden Clough BL0 68 E2
Dearden Fold BL0 68 E2
Dearden Nook BB4 86 A1
Dearden Way WN8 10 A7
Deardengate BB4 85 B3
Deardengate Croft 11 BB4 85 B3
Deben Cl WN6 29 D1
Deborah Ave PR2 118 A7
Dee Rd LA1 218 B2
Dee St FY8 89 E6
Dee St Cott 5 FY8 89 E6
Deepdale Ave FY6 153 B5
Deepdale Ct BB9 170 C3
Deepdale Dr BB10 148 C4
Deepdale Gn BB9 170 C3
Deepdale Ho 5 PR1 118 B1
Deepdale Inf Sch PR1 118 B2
Deepdale Jun Sch PR1 118 B2
Deepdale La PR4 115 E3
Deepdale Mill PR1 118 B1
Deepdale Mill St PR1 118 B1
Deepdale Rd
Blackpool FY4 131 C1
Fleetwood FY7 199 A3
Preston PR1 118 B2
Deepdale Sh Pk PR1 118 C3
Deepdale St 8 PR1 97 B8
Deeply Vale La BL9 51 C2
Deer Chace BB12 147 D8
Deer Park La LA2 238 B7
Deer Park Rd BB10 128 E4
Deer Pk BB5 104 E8
Deerfold PR7 61 B2
Deerhurst Rd FY5 152 E7
Deerplay Cl BB10 148 E2
Deerplay Dr OL13 88 A8
Deerstone Ave BB10 128 C6
Deerstone Rd BB9 149 B8
Deeside FY4 110 E5
Deganwy Ave BB1 101 E7
Deighton Ave 6 PR25 60 A8
Deighton Cl WN5 10 E5
Deighton Rd PR7 43 B6
Delamere Ave LA3 212 E6
Delamere Cl
Accrington BB5 125 B1
Blackburn BB2 101 B2
Delamere Pl PR6 43 D8
Delamere Rd
Brierfield BB10 148 F3
Skelmersdale WN8 17 F2
Southport PR8 21 B5
Delamere St BL9 33 A5
Delamere Way WN8 10 A7
Delany Dr PR4 93 A6
Delaware Rd 8 FY3 152 E1
Delaware St PR1 118 D1
Delf La Haskayne L39 14 A4
Shore OL14 109 D3
Delfby Cres L32 1 A1
Delius Cl BB2 102 A1
Dell Gdns OL12 52 B2
Dell La 4 BB12 126 C4
Dell Mdw OL12 52 C5
Dell Rd OL12 52 B3
Dell Side Way OL12 52 C2
Dell The
Appley Bridge WN6 19 D7
Blackburn BB2 81 D6
Fulwood PR2 117 D7
Knowley PR6 62 A3
Skelmersdale WN8 10 B7
Wrea Green PR4 113 B3
Dellar St OL12 52 C1
Dellfield La L31 5 E1
Dellway The PR4 95 D2
Delma Rd BB10 128 E5
Delph App BB1 102 C4
Delph Ave BL7 47 D3
Delph Brook Way BL7 47 D2
Delph Cl Blackburn BB1 102 C4
Ormskirk L39 15 C1
Delph Common Rd L39 15 C1
Delph Ct 3 BB6 124 C5
Delph Dr L40 25 F4
Delph La Blackburn BB1 102 C3
Blackburn BB1 102 C4
Charnock Green PR7 42 D6
Coppull PR7 42 E5
Formby L37 11 C3
Garstang PR3 181 F8
Oakenclough PR3 183 B7
Ormskirk L39 15 C1
Delph Lane Est BB1 102 C4
Delph Mount
Great Harwood BB6 124 B6
Nelson BB9 148 D6
Delph Park Ave L39 15 B1
Delph Rd BB6 124 C5
Delph Side Com Prim Sch WN8 9 C8
Delph St Darwen BB3 82 B3
Haslingden BB4 85 B4
Delph The WN8 27 C3
Delph Top L39 16 A6
Delph Way PR6 61 C7
Delphene Ave FY5 152 D6
Delphinium Way BB3 82 A7
Delphside Cl WN5 10 D5
Delphside Rd WN5 10 D5
Delta La 2 FY7 199 A4
Delta Park Ave PR4 73 E4
Delta Park Dr PR4 73 E4
Deltic Way L33 1 B1
Delves La BB10 149 E7
Demming Cl PR2 95 C8
Denbigh Ave
Cleveleys FY5 175 E1
Southport PR9 53 F3
Denbigh Cl PR25 77 B1
Denbigh Dr BB7 189 F2
Denbigh Gr BB12 127 A7
Denby Cl PR5 97 C3
Dene Bank Rd BB5 103 E3
Dene The Blackburn BB2 101 B7
Hurst Green BB7 142 E8
Denebank FY2 152 D5
Denefield Ho PR8 35 B6
Deneway Ave FY3 130 F6
Denford Ave Leyland PR25 60 B8
Lytham St Anne's FY8 90 A4
Denham La PR6 78 E2
Denham Way FY7 198 F2
Denham Wood Way PR7 42 F6
Denholme WN8 9 F7
Denholme Gr FY2 152 E5
Denis St LA1 215 A8
Denmark Rd
Lytham St Anne's FY8 90 D4
Southport PR9 54 A2
Denmark St LA1 214 D7
Dennis Gr LA4 217 A4
Denny Ave LA1 218 C2
Denny Bank LA2 219 C5
Denny Beck La LA2 219 C5
Denshaw WN8 9 F7
Denstone Ave FY2 152 D4
Dent Dale BB5 104 D5
Dent Row 8 BB11 127 F5
Dent St BB8 171 B3
Denton St
Barnoldswick BB18 196 A3
7 Rochdale OL12 52 F1
Denville Ave FY5 152 F8
Denville Rd
Blackburn BB2 101 D5
Preston PR1 118 C1
Denville St 5 BB2 101 D5
Depot Rd Blackpool FY3 152 E1
Kirkby L33 1 D4
Derbe Rd FY8 89 F5
Derby Cl BB3 65 B5
Derby Cres PR4 135 C8
Derby Ct L37 11 E5
Derby Hill PR4 133 A1
Derby Hill Cres L39 16 A5
Derby Hill Rd L39 16 A5
Derby Ho Kirkham PR4 114 A6
6 Lancaster LA1 218 D1
Derby Pl PR6 31 A8
Derby Rd Blackpool FY1 130 B7
Cleveleys FY5 175 C3
Formby L37 11 E5
Fulwood PR2 117 E3
Garstang PR3 181 B7
Kirkham PR4 114 A6
Lancaster LA1 218 D1
Longridge PR3 140 A7
Lytham St Anne's FY8 90 C5
Poulton-le-F FY6 153 D4
Skelmersdale WN8 8 C8
Southport PR9 35 C7
Derby Sq PR1 97 D8
Derby St Accrington BB5 104 C6
Blackburn BB1 102 A6
Brinscall PR6 63 A8
Burnley BB11 127 F5
Clitheroe BB7 166 F8
Colne BB8 171 D5
Horwich BL6 32 D1
Leyland PR25 77 B2
Morecambe LA4 217 A5
Nelson BB9 170 E1
Ormskirk L39 15 F5
Preston PR1 97 A8
Ramsbottom BL0 50 D6
Rishton BB1 124 C1
Derby St W L39 15 E5
Derbyshire Almshouses The BB2 101 B6
Derbyshire Ave PR3 181 B8
Derek Rd PR6 78 C1
Derham St BB2 101 E3
Derry Rd PR2 118 E3
Dertern La LA5 221 A7
Derwent Ave
Burnley BB10 148 A2
Fleetwood FY7 198 D2
Formby L37 11 D2
Morecambe LA4 217 C5
Padiham BB12 146 C2
Southport PR9 53 F1
Derwent Cl Colne BB8 172 A6
Darwen BB3 82 C1
Freckleton PR4 93 A6
Haslingden BB4 85 B4
Horwich BL6 32 C2
Knott End-on-S FY6 199 F6
Maghull L31 5 F2
Rishton BB1 123 F1
Derwent Cres BB7 166 C7
Derwent Ct LA1 218 A2
Derwent Dr
Freckleton PR4 93 A6
Longridge PR3 139 F5
Derwent Hall 3 PR1 117 E1
Derwent Ho 9 PR1 97 D8
Derwent Pl
Blackpool FY5 152 D8
Poulton-le-F FY6 153 D1
Derwent Rd Chorley PR7 43 B5
Lancaster LA1 215 B8
Lytham St Anne's FY8 111 A1
Orrell WN5 10 F8
Derwent St
6 Darwen BB3 81 F2
11 Rochdale OL12 52 F1
Derwentwater Pl PR1 117 F2
Dever Ave PR25 76 D1
Devere Gdns FY8 89 E5
Devon Ave
Fleetwood FY7 198 E3
Oswaldtwistle BB5 103 B6
Skelmersdale WN8 10 B6
Devon Cl PR5 97 D3
Devon Cres BB4 68 B8
Devon Dr WN1 30 B1
Devon Farm Way L37 12 B3
Devon Gr BB12 127 A7
Devon Pl 1 Church BB5 103 E5
Lancaster LA1 215 A4
Devon Rd BB1 102 C5
Devon St Blackpool FY4 130 D1
Colne BB8 171 E6
Darwen BB3 65 B6
Devona Ave FY4 131 B1
Devonport Cl PR5 97 E3
Devonport Rd BB2 101 C5
Devonport Way PR6 43 E8
Devonshire Ave FY5 176 B2
Devonshire Ct
9 Blackpool FY3 130 D7
17 Chorley PR7 43 C8
Devonshire Dr
Clayton-le-M BB5 125 A3
Garstang PR3 181 B8
Devonshire Ho FY3 130 D6
Devonshire Jun Sch FY3 131 A7
Devonshire Mews FY5 176 B1
Devonshire Pl PR1 118 E1
Devonshire Prim Sch FY3 130 D6
Devonshire Rd
Blackpool FY2 152 D2
Burnley BB10 128 A8
Chorley PR7 43 C7
Fulwood PR2 118 A4
Lytham St Anne's FY8 89 D7
Morecambe LA3 216 F3
Rishton BB1 124 A1
Southport PR9 36 A8
Devonshire Road Hospl FY1 130 D7
Devonshire Sq FY3 130 D5
Devonshire Square Mews 5 FY3 130 D5
Devonshire St
Accrington BB5 104 B7
Lancaster LA1 214 F5
Devron Mill BB6 124 D4
Dew Forest PR3 181 D4
Dew Meadow Cl OL12 52 E2
Dewberry Fields WN8 10 B7
Dewhirst Rd OL12 52 F4
Dewhirst Way OL12 52 F4
Dewhurst Ave FY4 110 E8
Dewhurst Cl BB3 65 C6
Dewhurst Clough Rd BL7 47 D2
Dewhurst Ct BL7 47 D3
Dewhurst Ind Est PR2 117 D1
Dewhurst Rd BB6 142 F1
Dewhurst Row PR5 77 D7
Dewhurst St
Blackburn BB1 102 A4
Colne BB8 171 D3
Darwen BB3 65 B6
Preston PR2 117 D1
Dexter Way WN8 10 B6
Deycroft Ave L33 1 A4
Deycroft Wlk L33 1 A4
Deyes Ct L31 5 E1
Deyes End L31 5 E1
Deyes High Sch L31 5 D1
Deyes La Maghull L31 5 D1
Maghull,Moss Side L31 5 F1
Diamond Jubilee Rd L40 39 C4
Diana Ct 10 LA1 214 F7
Dianne Rd FY5 176 D2
Dib Rd PR4 73 B5
Dibbs Pocket PR4 93 D7
Dicconson Terr 6 FY8 91 B3
Dicconson Way L39 16 A5
Dicconson's La L39 14 D4
Dick La PR6 62 E7
Dick's La L40 16 F4
Dickens Ave BB18 196 A3
Dickens Rd PR7 29 E8
Dickens St BB1 102 A3
Dickensons Field 3 PR1 96 E2

Dicket's La WN8 ....17 A2
Dickie's La FY4 ....111 B7
Dickie's La S FY4 ....111 C6
Dickinson Cl
Blackburn BB2 ....101 C3
Formby L37 ....11 F2
Dickinson Ct
1 Horwich BL6 ....32 B4
Southport PR8 ....35 A2
Dickinson Rd L37 ....11 F2
Dickinson St BB2 ....101 D3
Dickinson St W BL6 ....32 B4
Dickson Ave PR1 ....118 D2
Dickson Hey PR4 ....75 F8
Dickson Rd FY1 ....130 B7
Dickson St Burnley BB12 .127 C6
Colne BB8 ....171 E6
8 Preston PR1 ....97 B7
Didsbury St BB1 ....102 C5
Digham Ave FY5 ....152 D6
Digmoor Dr WN8 ....9 C7
Digmoor Rd WN8 ....9 D6
Dill Hall La BB5 ....103 F7
Dilworth Bottoms PR3 ..141 A8
Dilworth Ct PR3 ....140 C7
Dilworth La PR3 ....140 C7
Dimmock St BB2 ....101 C2
Dimple Pk BL7 ....47 D3
Dimple Rd BL7 ....47 C4
Dimples La PR3 ....181 E5
Dinckley Gr FY1 ....130 D3
Dinckley Sq BB2 ....101 B6
Dinely St BB5 ....103 F6
Dingle Ave
Appley Bridge WN6 ....19 E8
Blackpool FY3 ....130 F8
Skelmersdale WN8 ....10 C8
Dingle Cl L39 ....15 C1
Dingle Rd WN8 ....10 B7
Dingle The Fulwood PR2 ..117 D7
Knowley PR6 ....62 A3
Dinmore Ave FY3 ....131 A8
Dinmore Pl FY3 ....131 A7
Dinorwic Rd PR8 ....35 A2
Dirty Leech OL12 ....52 F6
Disraeli St BB10 ....148 A2
Ditchfield L37 ....12 A2
Division La FY4 ....111 C3
Dixey St BL6 ....32 A3
Dixon Rd PR3 ....140 B7
Dixon St Barrowford BB9 .170 C3
Blackburn BB2 ....101 C4
Horwich BL6 ....32 B3
Dixon's Farm Mews
PR4 ....115 D1
Dixons La PR2 ....139 C2
Doals Gate OL13 ....88 A8
Dob Brow PR7 ....42 F4
Dob La PR4 ....75 A4
Dobbin Cl BB4 ....86 C2
Dobbin Ct BB4 ....86 C2
Dobbin La BB4 ....86 C2
Dobbs Dr L37 ....12 A4
Dobs La LA2 ....209 E3
Dobson Ave FY8 ....89 E8
Dobson Cl WN6 ....28 E2
Dobson Rd FY3 ....131 B7
Dobson St 2 BB3 ....81 F2
Dobson's La FY6 ....177 E6
Dock Rd FY8 ....91 D4
Dock St Blackburn BB1 ...102 A5
Fleetwood FY7 ....199 B4
Docker La LA6 ....241 C5
Docker Park Farm*
LA6 ....241 A4
Dockinsall La PR3 ....178 D3
Dockray Ct 2 BB8 ....171 E5
Dockray St BB8 ....171 E5
Dockray Yd 4 BB8 ....171 E5
Docky Pool La FY4 ....111 A6
Doctor's La Eccleston PR7 .41 B6
Great Altcar L37 ....12 E2
Sollom PR4 ....56 F3
Doctors Row PR3 ....140 A6
Dodd Way PR5 ....78 A6
Dodd's La L31 ....5 D2
Dodgeons Cl FY6 ....153 C2
Dodgson La BB18 ....197 F2
Dodgson Pl PR1 ....118 C1
Dodgson Rd PR1 ....118 C1
Dodney Dr PR2 ....116 C1
Dodworth Ave PR8 ....35 E5
Doe Mdw WN8 ....27 A1
Doeholme Rake LA2 ....232 F1
Dog Pits La OL13 ....88 A6
Dole La Abbey Village PR6 ..80 C1
Chorley PR7 ....43 C8
Doles La PR26 ....58 A7
Dolls House & Fleetwood Mus The* FY7 ....199 C5
Dolly's La PR9 ....36 D8
Dolphinholme CE Prim Sch
LA2 ....226 A8
Dolphinholme Mill LA2 .226 A8
Dombey St
Blackburn BB1 ....102 A3
Blackburn BB1 ....102 A4
Dominica Ave BB3 ....81 F6
Dominion Ct BB11 ....127 B4
Dominion Rd BB2 ....101 C8
Don St FY8 ....89 E7
Doncaster Rd FY3 ....131 A3
Donnington Lodge PR8 ...34 F6
Donnington Rd
Carleton FY6 ....153 C6
Lytham St Anne's FY8 ....89 F7
Donshort Mews 2 BB9 .170 C1
Doodstone Ave PR5 ....97 B1
Doodstone Cl PR5 ....97 B1
Doodstone Dr PR5 ....97 B1
Doodstone Nook PR5 ....97 B1
Dora St BL0 ....50 A4
Dorchester Ave BB5 ....103 C4
Dorchester Cl
Blackburn BB1 ....102 B3
Thornton FY5 ....153 C8
Dorchester Dr L33 ....1 A5
Dorchester Gdns LA3 ...217 C2
Dorchester Rd
Blackpool FY1 ....130 B8
Garstang PR3 ....181 B8
Skelmersdale WN8 ....10 A7
Doric Gn WN5 ....10 D3
Doris Henderson Way
LA1 ....217 F1
Doris St Burnley BB11 ....128 B7
Chorley PR6 ....61 D1
Dorking Rd PR6 ....61 F4
Dorman Rd PR2 ....118 E3
Dorothy Ave 9 PR25 ....77 A1
Dorothy St Blackburn BB2 ..81 C8
13 Ramsbottom BL0 ....50 B5
Dorrington Rd LA1 ....214 F5
Dorritt Rd FY4 ....110 E6
Dorritt St 19 BB1 ....102 A4
Dorset Ave
3 Bamber Bridge PR5 ....97 D3
Cleveleys FY5 ....175 D4
Darwen BB3 ....81 F3
Padiham BB12 ....126 D7
Southport PR8 ....21 C2
Dorset Dr Blackburn BB1 .102 E4
Clitheroe BB7 ....189 F2
Haslingden BB4 ....68 A8
Dorset Rd
Lytham St Anne's FY8 ....89 F8
Preston PR1 ....118 A1
Rishton BB1 ....124 A1
Standish WN1 ....30 B1
Dorset St
10 Blackpool FY4 ....130 D1
Burnley BB12 ....127 A6
Dotcliffe Rd BB18 ....195 A6
Double Row 1 BB12 ....126 B8
Doughty St BB8 ....171 D4
Douglas Ave
Becconsall PR4 ....73 F1
Blackpool FY3 ....130 D7
1 Heysham LA3 ....212 F7
Horwich BL6 ....32 C5
Skelmersdale WN8 ....10 B7
Stalmine FY6 ....177 C7
Douglas Cl
Bamber Bridge PR5 ....77 F7
Blackburn BB2 ....81 D7
Horwich BL6 ....32 C5
Rufford L40 ....39 C3
Douglas Ct Fulwood PR2 .117 D3
Southport PR8 ....21 C5
Douglas Dr Freckleton PR4 .93 B6
Heysham LA3 ....212 F7
Maghull L31 ....5 F2
Ormskirk L39 ....15 D7
Orrell WN5 ....10 F7
Shevington WN6 ....19 F5
Douglas Gr BB3 ....81 D4
Douglas Hall 4 PR1 ....117 E1
Douglas Ho PR7 ....43 D5
Douglas La PR2 ....139 D1
Douglas Leatham Ho 3
FY1 ....130 D1
Douglas Pl
Blackburn BB1 ....122 F1
Fleetwood FY7 ....198 D3
Douglas Rd Bacup OL13 ...88 A1
Brierfield BB10 ....149 A3
Fulwood PR2 ....117 D3
Shevington Moor WN6 ....29 B2
Southport PR9 ....54 C4
Douglas Rd N PR2 ....117 D3
Douglas Sq 5 OL10 ....33 F1
Douglas St Colne BB8 ....171 E6
Lytham St Anne's FY8 ....89 D6
Preston PR2 ....96 C8
Ramsbottom BL0 ....50 B6
Douglas Way BB10 ....149 A3
Doultons The PR5 ....97 C3
Dove Ave 2 PR1 ....96 E4
Dove Cl 6 FY5 ....175 F1
Dove Dr BL9 ....33 B4
Dove La BB3 ....81 F2
Dove St
Lytham St Anne's FY8 ....89 D6
Preston PR1 ....118 B1
Dove Tree Ct FY4 ....131 B1
Dovecote PR6 ....78 A3
Dovedale Ave
Blackpool FY3 ....131 C2
Fulwood PR2 ....117 A5
Maghull L31 ....5 C2
Thornton FY5 ....176 B3
Dovedale Cl
Brierfield BB10 ....148 C4
Fulwood PR2 ....117 A4
Leyland PR25 ....60 A6
Dovedale Dr
Burnley BB12 ....127 C8
Standish WN6 ....29 E2
Dovedale Gdns PR3 ....140 B6
Dover Cl Blackburn BB1 ..102 C4
Ramsbottom BL8 ....50 A1
Warton PR4 ....92 E7
Dover Ct FY1 ....130 D2
Dover Gdns FY6 ....153 B5
Dover La PR5,PR6 ....79 C8
Dover Rd Blackpool FY1 ..130 E2
Dover Rd *continued*
Lytham St Anne's FY8 ....89 F8
Southport PR8 ....34 F2
Dover St Accrington BB5 .104 A4
Blackburn BB3 ....81 F7
Nelson BB9 ....170 E1
Dovestone Dr FY6 ....153 B3
Dovetree Cl PR5 ....97 A3
Dowbridge PR4 ....114 C4
Dowbridge Way PR4 ....114 C5
Downes Gr LA4 ....217 D4
Downeyfield Rd LA3 ....213 C3
Downfield Cl BL0 ....50 B6
Downham Ave
Great Harwood BB6 ....124 F6
Rawtenstall BB4 ....86 A4
Downham Cotts 7 LA2 .211 A4
Downham Dr BB5 ....104 A3
Downham Gr BB10 ....128 D5
Downham Pl
Lytham St Anne's FY8 ....90 C6
3 Preston PR2 ....116 E2
Downham Rd
Chatburn BB7 ....190 E5
Leyland PR25 ....76 D1
Downham St BB2 ....101 C4
Downham Wlk WN5 ....10 D1
Downholland Moss La
L37 ....12 C4
Downholland-Haskayne CE Prim Sch L39 ....13 E3
Downing Ct PR3 ....137 C3
Downing St PR1 ....97 E8
Downley Cl OL12 ....52 B2
Downs The FY6 ....153 D4
Dowry St BB5 ....104 C6
Dragon Cl WN8 ....9 E8
Dragon St 8 BB12 ....126 C8
Drake Cl
Lytham St Anne's FY8 ....110 E1
Ormskirk L39 ....15 C2
Drakelowe Ave FY4 ....110 F6
Drakes Croft PR2 ....117 C3
Drakes Hollow PR5 ....97 D4
Drammen Ave BB11 ....127 B5
Draperfield PR7 ....43 A4
Drapers Ave PR7 ....41 C6
Draw Well Rd L33 ....1 D2
Draycombe Ct LA3 ....216 D2
Draycombe Dr LA3 ....216 E2
Draycot Ave FY3 ....130 F8
Drayton Rd LA3 ....213 A7
Drew St BB11 ....127 B5
Drewitt Cres PR9 ....54 D4
Drewton Ave LA3 ....216 D2
Drinkhouse La PR26 ....58 A1
Drinkhouse Rd PR26 ....58 B1
Driscoll St 1 PR1 ....97 B8
Drive The Bacup OL13 ....87 F2
Brockhall Village BB6 ....143 C5
Carnforth LA5 ....223 D1
Edenfield BL0 ....68 D3
Fulwood PR2 ....118 B4
Hest Bank LA2 ....220 E1
Heysham LA3 ....212 F7
Longton PR4 ....75 A8
Walton-le-D PR5 ....97 F5
Driver St 14 BB4 ....86 A7
Driving Gate BB4 ....106 A1
Dronsfield Rd FY7 ....198 F4
Drovers Way LA6 ....240 B7
Drovers Wlk LA3 ....212 F7
Druids Cl BL7 ....47 D3
Drumacre La E PR4 ....75 D6
Drumacre La W PR4 ....75 A6
Drumhead Rd PR6 ....61 D2
Drummersdale La L40 ....24 D7
Drummond Ave FY3 ....130 F7
Drybread La PR3 ....178 C2
Dryburgh Ave FY3 ....130 F3
Dryden Gr BB6 ....124 C4
Dryden Rd FY7 ....199 A4
Dryden St
6 Clayton-le-M BB5 ....124 F3
Padiham BB12 ....126 E7
Dryfield La BL6 ....32 A5
Duchess Ct FY2 ....152 B3
Duchess Dr FY2 ....152 B3
Duchess St BB3 ....81 F7
Duchy Ave PR2 ....118 B4
Ducie Pl PR1 ....118 F1
Duck St 2 Clitheroe BB7 .166 F8
Smallwood Hey PR3 ....201 A7
Wray LA2 ....238 D6
Duckett St 3 BB11 ....127 E6
Ducketts La PR3 ....159 B8
Duckshaw Rd BB3 ....64 F6
Duckworth Cl PR3 ....181 D3
Duckworth Dr PR3 ....181 D3
Duckworth Hall BB5 ....103 A2
Duckworth Hall Brow
BB5 ....103 A1
Duckworth Hill La BB5 ..103 B1
Duckworth La
Rawtenstall BB4 ....68 E8
Tarleton PR4 ....56 F8
Duckworth St
Barrowford BB9 ....170 D2
Blackburn BB2 ....101 D3
3 Bury BL9 ....33 A4
Church BB5 ....103 E6
Darwen BB3 ....81 F2
Duddle La PR5 ....97 D2
Duddon Ave Darwen BB3 ..81 E3
Fleetwood FY7 ....198 D2
Maghull L31 ....5 F2
Duddon Cl LA3 ....217 F3
Dudley Ave
Blackpool FY2 ....152 D1
Oswaldtwistle BB5 ....103 C4
Dudley Cl PR4 ....95 A1
Dudley St Brierfield BB9 .148 C5
Colne BB8 ....171 F5
Morecambe LA4 ....217 C4
Duerden St BB9 ....148 D7
Duffins Cl OL12 ....52 D3
Dugdale Ct FY4 ....110 F5
Dugdale La BB7,BD23 ....235 F1
Dugdale Rd BB12 ....127 C7
Dugdale St BB11 ....128 A5
Dugdales Cl FY4 ....111 E7
Dugie St BL0 ....50 B7
Duke Ave PR8 ....35 C4
Duke of Sussex St BB2 ...81 B8
Duke St
Bamber Bridge PR5 ....77 E7
Blackburn BB2 ....101 D5
Blackpool FY1 ....130 B1
Brierfield BB10 ....148 F3
Burton in L LA6 ....242 C3
Chorley PR7 ....43 C6
Clayton-le-M BB5 ....125 A2
Colne BB8 ....171 D4
Colne,Cotton Tree BB8 ....172 B5
Formby L37 ....11 F2
Great Harwood BB6 ....124 B5
Heysham LA3 ....212 E7
High Bentham LA2 ....239 D8
Lancaster LA1 ....218 C1
Oswaldtwistle BB5 ....103 D3
Preston PR1 ....97 B7
Ramsbottom BL0 ....50 A4
Rawtenstall BB4 ....69 E8
Rochdale OL12 ....52 F1
Southport PR8 ....35 B5
Duke St Prim Sch PR7 ...43 C6
Duke's Wood La WN8 ....9 D3
Dukes Brow
Blackburn BB2 ....101 C6
Great Harwood BB6 ....124 B5
Dukes Ct BB2 ....101 B6
Dukes Dr BB3 ....82 F1
Dukes Mdw PR2 ....117 A5
Dukes Way L37 ....11 F2
Dulas Gn L32 ....1 A1
Dulas Rd L32 ....1 A1
Dumb Tom's La LA6 ....242 E1
Dumbarton Cl 2 FY4 ....111 A6
Dumbarton Rd LA1 ....215 A7
Dumfries Cl FY2 ....152 F5
Dunald Mill La LA2,LA6 .237 B6
Dunbar Cl FY4 ....111 A6
Dunbar Cres PR8 ....21 F8
Dunbar Dr Fulwood PR2 ..117 D4
2 Heysham LA3 ....212 E7
Dunbar Rd Fulwood PR2 ..116 F3
Southport PR8 ....34 F1
Duncan Ave FY2 ....152 C6
Duncan Cl
Brownside BB10 ....128 F5
Lytham St Anne's FY8 ....110 D1
Duncan Pl FY7 ....198 E4
Duncan St Burnley BB12 ..127 A5
Horwich BL6 ....32 C3
Duncroft Cl BB7 ....189 E2
Dundas St BB8 ....171 C4
Dundee Cl OL10 ....33 F1
Dundee Dr BB1 ....102 A4
Dundee La BL0 ....50 B6
Dundee St LA1 ....215 A7
Dunderdale Ave BB9 ....148 C7
Dunderdale St PR3 ....140 B7
Dundonald St PR1 ....97 D8
Dundonnell Rd BB9 ....171 A1
Dunedin Rd BL8 ....49 F2
Dunelt Ct 2 FY1 ....130 C2
Dunelt Rd FY1 ....130 D2
Dunes Ave FY4 ....110 B5
Dunes Dr L37 ....11 C4
Dunes Ho FY8 ....89 F5
Dungeon La WN8 ....18 C7
Dunham Dr PR6 ....61 C6
Dunkeld St 5 LA1 ....215 A7
Dunkenhalgh Way
Church BB5 ....103 E7
Clayton-le-M BB5 ....124 E1
Dunkenshaw Cres LA1 ...215 B2
Dunkirk Ave
Carnforth LA5 ....221 E8
Fulwood PR2 ....117 C3
Dunkirk La Leyland PR26 ..59 C8
New Longton PR26 ....76 A1
Dunkirk Mews PR25 ....59 D8
Dunkirk Rd PR8 ....34 F2
Dunlin Ave LA3 ....212 F5
Dunlin Cl FY5 ....176 A5
Dunlin Dr FY8 ....90 E7
Dunlop Ave PR8 ....21 C2
Dunmail Ave 1 FY3 ....130 F2
Dunmore St PR1 ....97 B8
Dunnock La PR4 ....116 F4
Dunnockshaw Community Woodland Trail*
BB11 ....106 E6
Dunny Shop Ave BB5 ...104 A4
Dunoon Cl PR2 ....116 F4
Dunoon Dr BB1 ....102 D3
Dunoon St BB11 ....127 D5
Dunrobin Dr PR7 ....60 D1
Dunscar Dr PR6 ....61 E1
Dunsop Cl
3 Bamber Bridge PR5 ....77 F8
1 Blackpool FY1 ....130 D1
Dunsop Ct 2 FY1 ....130 D1
Dunsop Gdns LA3 ....217 F2
Dunsop Rd PR2 ....118 D4
Dunsop St BB1 ....101 F7
Dunster Ave BB5 ....103 C5
Dunster Gr BB7 ....166 C6
Dunster Rd PR8 ....21 E8
Dunvegan Cl 3 FY4 ....111 A6
Durban Ct FY5 ....175 C4
Durban Gr BB11 ....127 E4
Durham Ave
Burnley BB12 ....127 B7
Cleveleys FY5 ....175 E3
Lancaster LA1 ....215 A4
Lytham St Anne's FY8 ....89 E7
Durham Cl Blackburn BB1 .101 F4
Leyland PR25 ....59 E7
Morecambe LA3 ....217 B2
Durham Dr
Oswaldtwistle BB5 ....103 F3
Ramsbottom BL0 ....50 B3
Wilpshire BB1 ....122 F6
Durham Gr 1 PR3 ....181 B7
Durham Rd
Blackpool FY1 ....130 D5
Darwen BB3 ....81 F2
Wilpshire BB1 ....122 F7
Durham St
Accrington BB5 ....104 D7
Skelmersdale WN8 ....17 D2
Durley Rd FY1 ....130 D2
Durn St 1 OL14 ....109 A1
Dutch Barn Cl PR7 ....61 B2
Dutton Ct 1 FY3 ....130 D5
Dutton Lee Cotts PR3 ...142 A7
Dutton Rd FY3 ....130 D5
Dutton St 15 BB5 ....104 C6
Duttonfield Cl PR26 ....76 E3
Duttons Way BB1 ....102 D1
Duxbury Cl L31 ....5 E3
Duxbury Dr BL9 ....33 C2
Duxbury Hall Rd PR7 ....43 E3
Duxbury Ho 8 PR6 ....43 D7
Duxbury Jubilee Pk*
PR7 ....43 D3
Duxbury St Darwen BB3 ...65 B6
Earby BB18 ....197 C2
Dye House La 6 LA1 ....214 F8
Dyer St PR4 ....113 F5
Dyers La L39 ....15 E4
Dyke La PR3 ....201 A3
Dyke Nook BB7 ....166 F6
Dykes La LA5 ....225 F2
Dymock Rd PR1 ....118 D1
Dymock Rd N PR1 ....118 D1
Dyneley Ave BB10 ....128 F4
Dyneley Rd BB1 ....102 C7
Dyson St BB2 ....101 F2

E

Eachill Gdns BB1 ....103 B8
Eachill Rd 2 BB1 ....124 B1
Eager La L31 ....5 B8
Eagle Brow Cl FY5 ....176 B4
Eagle St Accrington BB5 ..104 B5
Blackburn BB1 ....102 C4
2 Nelson BB9 ....170 F1
Oswaldtwistle BB5 ....103 C2
Eagles The FY6 ....153 E5
Eagley Bank OL12 ....71 E6
Eagley Rd BB9 ....148 C4
Ealand Chase BL6 ....31 F3
Ealing Gr PR6 ....61 F3
Eamont Ave PR9 ....54 B5
Eamont Pl FY7 ....198 D2
Eanam BB1 ....101 F5
Eanam Old Rd BB1 ....101 F5
Earby Lead Mining Mus*
BB18 ....197 B2
Earby Rd BB18 ....194 F8
Earby Springfield Prim Sch
BB18 ....197 C1
Earcroft Way BB3 ....81 E5
Eardley Rd LA3 ....212 E8
Earhart Cl WN8 ....9 E8
Earl Rd BL0 ....50 B6
Earl St
Barnoldswick BB18 ....196 C2
Blackburn BB1 ....101 E6
Burnley BB10 ....128 B8
Clayton-le-M BB5 ....124 F2
Colne BB8 ....171 D4
Great Harwood BB6 ....124 B5
Lancaster LA1 ....218 D1
11 Nelson BB9 ....170 F1
Preston PR1 ....96 F8
Ramsbottom BL0 ....50 D6
Earlesdon Ave BB18 ....196 F1
Earlham St BB18 ....197 C2
Earls Ave PR5 ....77 E8
Earls Dr BB3 ....82 E1
Earls Way PR7 ....60 D2
Earlsway FY3 ....131 D5
Earlswood WN8 ....18 E1
Earnsdale Ave BB3 ....81 D2
Earnsdale Cl BB3 ....81 E2
Earnsdale Rd BB3 ....81 E3
Earnshaw Ave OL12 ....52 E3
Earnshaw Dr PR25 ....76 D1
Earnshaw Rd OL13 ....87 F3
Earnshaw Row 18 OL13 ...87 F3
Easby Cl L37 ....12 A2
Easdale Ave LA4 ....217 E5
Easedale Cl
Burnley BB12 ....127 B8

Easedale Cl *continued*
Hest Bank LA5 . . . . .220 F2
Easedale Dr PR8 . . . . .21 B4
Easington LA1 . . . . .218 A2
Easington Cres FY3 . . . . .131 B8
East Ave BB18 . . . . .196 B2
East Bank
2 Barrowford BB9 . . . . . .170 D4
Water BB4 . . . . .107 A1
East Bank Ave BB4 . . . . . . .85 B2
East Bank Rd FY8 . . . . . . .89 E5
East Beach FY8 . . . . .91 C3
East Boothroyden FY1 . .130 B8
East Cecil St FY8 . . . . .91 A3
East Chorley Business Ctr 3
PR6 . . . . .43 D8
East Cliff PR1 . . . . .96 F6
East Cliff Rd PR1 . . . . .96 F6
East Cliffe FY8 . . . . .91 C3
East Cres BB5 . . . . .104 B8
East Croft BB9 . . . . .171 B2
East Ct FY5 . . . . .175 D5
East Dene WN8 . . . . .27 B2
East End St BB8 . . . . .171 C4
East Gate BB4 . . . . .85 B3
East Gate Cl FY8 . . . . . . .110 C4
East Hills St 21 BB18 . . . .196 B2
East Holme FY8 . . . . .91 C4
East La Galgate LA2 . . . . . .211 B6
Maghull L29 . . . . .4 B2
East Lancashire Rd BB1 .122 F3
East Lancashire Rly*
Ramsbottom BL0 . . . . . . .50 C5
* Ramsbottom BL0 . . . . .50 C5
East Lodge Pl BB10 . . . . .128 E1
East Mead Blackpool FY3 .130 F3
Ormskirk L39 . . . . .15 B2
East Meade L31 . . . . .5 C2
East Mount WN5 . . . . .10 F6
East Par
19 Barnoldswick BB18 . . . .196 B2
17 Rawtenstall BB4 . . . . . . .86 A3
East Park Ave
Blackburn BB1 . . . . .101 D7
Darwen BB3 . . . . .64 F8
East Park Ct BB1 . . . . . . .101 D6
East Park Dr FY3 . . . . . . .131 A5
East Park Rd BB1 . . . . . . .101 D6
East Rd Fulwood PR2 . . . . .118 A3
Lancaster LA1 . . . . .215 A8
Maghull L31 . . . . .5 F1
East Sq PR4 . . . . .95 A1
East St Bamber Bridge PR5 . .77 E7
Blackburn BB2 . . . . .101 C3
Blackburn,Feniscowles BB2 .80 D8
Brierfield BB9 . . . . .148 C5
Edenfield BL0 . . . . .68 D4
Hapton BB12 . . . . .126 C4
Haslingden BB4 . . . . .68 A7
Leyland PR25 . . . . .77 B1
Leyland PR25 . . . . .77 B2
Morecambe LA3 . . . . .216 E4
10 Nelson BB9 . . . . .170 D1
Padiham BB12 . . . . .146 C1
13 Preston PR1 . . . . .97 A8
Rawtenstall BB4 . . . . .85 F5
Southport PR9 . . . . .35 D7
East Terr PR7 . . . . .60 D4
East Topping St 3 FY1 . . .130 B5
East View Bacup OL13 . . . . .87 F2
3 Bamber Bridge PR5 . . . . .77 A7
Fulwood PR2 . . . . .118 F5
9 Galgate LA2 . . . . .211 A4
Grimsargh PR2 . . . . .139 B1
Grindleton BB7 . . . . .190 B7
Pendleton BB7 . . . . .167 B4
Preston PR1 . . . . .97 A8
9 Preston,Frenchwood
PR5 . . . . .97 C6
Ramsbottom BL0 . . . . .50 C3
Ramsbottom,Stubbins BL0 . .68 C1
Read BB12 . . . . .145 D2
Rising Bridge BB5 . . . . .85 A8
Trawden BB8 . . . . .172 C2
Winmarleigh PR3 . . . . .203 F6
East View Ct LA1 . . . . . . .218 B3
East View Terr
Abbey Village PR6 . . . . .80 B3
14 Barnoldswick BB18 . . . .196 B2
East Ward Com Prim Sch
BL9 . . . . .33 B2
East Way PR6 . . . . .43 D8
East Wlk BL7 . . . . .47 D2
Eastbank Ave FY4 . . . . . . .111 A7
Eastbank St PR8 . . . . .35 B6
Eastbank Street Sq 9
PR8 . . . . .35 B7
Eastbourne Cl PR2 . . . . . .116 F5
Eastbourne Rd
Blackpool FY4 . . . . .110 B6
Southport PR8 . . . . .35 A3
Eastcliff LA2 . . . . .237 F5
Eastcott Cl BB2 . . . . .82 A8
Eastern Ave BB10 . . . . . . .148 C1
Eastfield Dr Longton PR4 . .95 A1
West Bradford BB7 . . . . . . .189 F6
Eastgate Accrington BB5 . .104 C6
Fulwood PR2 . . . . .117 E4
Morecambe LA3 . . . . .217 E2
Ribchester PR3 . . . . .141 E4
Whitworth OL12 . . . . .52 C7
Eastham Hall Cvn Pk FY8 .91 E6
Eastham Pl BB11 . . . . .128 B6
Eastham St Burnley BB10 .128 B5
Clitheroe BB7 . . . . .189 E1
Eastham St *continued*
Lancaster LA1 . . . . .215 A7
Preston PR1 . . . . .117 E1
Eastlands Heysham LA3 . .213 A7
Leyland PR26 . . . . .59 C7
Eastleigh WN8 . . . . .18 D1
Eastmoor Dr BB7 . . . . . . .166 F7
Easton Cl PR2 . . . . .118 D6
Eastpines Dr FY5 . . . . . . .152 F8
Eastside FY4 . . . . .110 F8
Eastway Freckleton PR4 . . . .93 A6
Fulwood PR2 . . . . .118 B6
Maghull L31 . . . . .5 E1
Eastway Bsns Village
PR2 . . . . .118 B8
Eastwood Ave
Blackpool FY3 . . . . .130 E8
2 Fleetwood FY7 . . . . .198 F3
Eastwood Cl 6 BL9 . . . . . .33 B2
Eastwood Cres BB4 . . . . . .86 C2
Eastwood Rd PR25 . . . . . . .76 F1
Eastwood St
Barnoldswick BB18 . . . . . .196 C3
2 Blackburn BB1 . . . . .102 A6
Rawtenstall BB4 . . . . .86 C2
Eastwood Terr BB18 . . . . .196 C3
Eaton Ave FY1 . . . . .130 C1
Eaton Ct FY8 . . . . .89 F6
Eaton Pl PR4 . . . . .113 F5
Eaton Way FY6 . . . . .131 E8
Eaves Ave BB11 . . . . .127 D2
Eaves Cl BB5 . . . . .125 F1
Eaves Green La PR3 . . . . .138 F8
Eaves Green Rd PR7 . . . . .43 B5
Eaves La Chorley PR6 . . . . .43 E8
Cuddy Hill PR4 . . . . .136 D7
Fulwood PR2 . . . . .117 E3
Eaves Lane Hospl PR6 . . . .43 E8
Eaves Rd FY8 . . . . .111 A1
Eaves St FY1 . . . . .130 B7
Eavesdale WN8 . . . . .9 E8
Evesham Cl PR5 . . . . .97 A1
Eaveswood Cl PR5 . . . . . . .97 E1
Ebenezer Terr BB7 . . . . . .144 B4
Ebony St 11 BB1 . . . . . . .102 A7
Ebor Lo PR8 . . . . .35 A5
Ebor St BB10 . . . . .148 B2
Eccles Rd L37 . . . . .11 D1
Eccles St Accrington BB5 .104 B7
Blackburn BB2 . . . . .101 E3
Preston PR1 . . . . .118 C1
Ramsbottom BL0 . . . . .50 B6
Eccles's La L40 . . . . .27 B7
Ecclesgate Rd FY4 . . . . . .111 A5
Eccleshill Cotts BB3 . . . . .82 C4
Eccleshill Gdns BB3 . . . . .82 C4
Eccleshill Rd BB3 . . . . . . .81 F6
Eccleshill St 1 BB12 . . . .126 C8
Eccleston Prim Sch PR7 . . .41 B6
Eccleston Rd FY1 . . . . . . .130 D1
Eckersley Cl BB2 . . . . .81 D8
Eclipse Rd BB2 . . . . .80 D8
Ecroyd Rd PR2 . . . . .117 C2
Ecroyd St Leyland PR25 . . . .77 A1
Nelson BB9 . . . . .148 C8
Edale Ave BB4 . . . . .85 C2
Edale Cl PR25 . . . . .60 A7
Edale Ct PR1 . . . . .117 F1
Edale Dr WN6 . . . . .29 E2
Eddington Rd FY8 . . . . .90 B4
Eddleston Cl FY3 . . . . . . .131 D5
Edelston Rd 5 FY1 . . . . . .130 C6
Eden Ave Edenfield BL0 . . . .68 D3
Fleetwood FY7 . . . . .198 D2
Lytham St Anne's FY8 . . . . . .90 E3
Morecambe LA4 . . . . .217 F5
Southport PR9 . . . . .53 F3
Eden Cl BB9 . . . . .170 D4
Eden Ct BL0 . . . . .68 D2
Eden Gdns PR3 . . . . .140 B8
Eden Gr LA5 . . . . .221 B6
Eden Hall PR1 . . . . .117 E1
Eden La BL0 . . . . .68 D2
Eden Mount Way LA5 . . . .223 F2
Eden Pk Blackburn BB2 . . .101 A8
Lancaster LA1 . . . . .214 F4
Eden St Accrington BB5 . . .104 A5
Blackburn BB1 . . . . .102 A5
9 Blackpool FY1 . . . . .130 C6
Edenfield BL0 . . . . .68 D2
Leyland PR25 . . . . .60 A8
Edenfield PR4 . . . . .74 F4
Edenfield Ave FY6 . . . . . .153 F2
Edenfield CE Prim Sch
BL0 . . . . .68 D4
Edenfield Cl PR8 . . . . .35 E3
Edenfield Rd
Ramsbottom OL11,OL12 . . . .51 E4
Rochdale OL11,OL12 . . . . . . .52 B1
Edenfield St OL11,OL12 . . .52 C1
Edenhurst WN8 . . . . .9 E8
Edenhurst Apartments
BB4 . . . . .68 D8
Edenhurst Cl L37 . . . . .11 C2
Edenhurst Dr L37 . . . . .11 C2
Edensor Terr BB3 . . . . .81 F2
Edenvale Ave FY2 . . . . . . .152 B4
Edenvale Cres LA1 . . . . . .218 C3
Edenvale Rd LA1 . . . . .218 C3
Edenway PR2 . . . . .117 D7
Edgar St Accrington BB5 . .104 B6
Huncoat BB5 . . . . .125 E2
Nelson BB9 . . . . .170 F2
16 Ramsbottom BL0 . . . . . . .50 B5
Edgar St W 17 BL0 . . . . . .50 B5
Edge End BB6 . . . . .124 B5
Edge End Ave BB9 . . . . . .148 D6
Edge End High Sch BB9 .148 D6
Edge End La
Brierfield BB9 . . . . .148 D6
Great Harwood BB6 . . . . . .124 B6
Edge End Rd BB6 . . . . . . .124 B5
Edge End Terr BB2 . . . . . . .80 B3
Edge Gate La PR6 . . . . .63 A6
Edge Hall Rd WN5 . . . . .10 E5
Edge Hill Coll PR7 . . . . . . .43 A8
Edge Hill Univ Coll L39 . . . .16 A3
Edge La Bacup OL13 . . . . . .71 C8
Barnoldswick BB18 . . . . . .231 F1
Edgworth BL7 . . . . .48 A8
Rawtenstall BB4 . . . . .86 D3
Edge Yate La BB4 . . . . .86 B5
Edgecott Cl LA3 . . . . .213 A7
Edgefield PR7 . . . . .61 B2
Edgefield Ct FY3 . . . . .131 B8
Edgehill Cl PR2 . . . . .117 D4
Edgehill Cres PR25 . . . . . . .76 E2
Edgehill Dr PR2 . . . . .117 D4
Edgeley Ct 1 BB12 . . . . . .127 D7
Edgemoor Cl OL12 . . . . . . .71 E5
Edgeside BB6 . . . . .124 B5
Edgeside La BB4 . . . . .86 F2
Edgeware Rd BB2 . . . . . . .101 C6
Edgeway Pl 3 FY5 . . . . . .176 C1
Edgeway Rd FY4 . . . . .110 E5
Edgeworth Vale BL7 . . . . . .48 E6
Edgley Ct PR4 . . . . .95 E2
Edgley Dr L39 . . . . .16 A5
Edgworth Gr BB10 . . . . . .128 C6
Edgworth Views BL7 . . . . .48 D8
Edinburgh Cl PR25 . . . . . . .77 C1
Edinburgh Dr BB5 . . . . . .103 F3
Edinburgh Rd Formby L37 . .11 E1
Haslingden BB4 . . . . .84 F1
Edisford Prim Sch BB7 . . .166 C7
Edisford Rd
Clitheroe BB7 . . . . .166 C8
Waddington BB7 . . . . .189 B4
Edison St BB3 . . . . .81 F1
Edith St
Barnoldswick BB18 . . . . . .196 B3
Blackburn BB1 . . . . .102 A4
Nelson BB9 . . . . .148 F8
Shuttleworth BL0 . . . . .50 E8
Edleston Lodge 2 PR2 . . .118 F4
Edleston St BB5 . . . . .103 F4
Edmondsen Pl 4 FY7 . . . .198 F2
Edmondson St BB18 . . . . .196 B3
Edmondson's La BD23 . . .197 F8
Edmonton Dr BB2 . . . . . . .101 A8
Edmonton Pl FY2 . . . . . . .152 F3
Edmund Gennings Ct
BB7 . . . . .190 D5
Edmund St
5 Accrington BB5 . . . . . . .104 C5
Blackburn BB2 . . . . .81 D7
Burnley BB10 . . . . .148 B1
Darwen BB3 . . . . .82 B1
3 Preston PR1 . . . . .97 B8
Edmundson St
Blackburn BB2 . . . . .101 C5
3 Church BB5 . . . . .103 E6
Edward Cl PR4 . . . . .57 A5
Edward Ct 9 BB5 . . . . . . .103 E6
Edward Sq 10 PR1 . . . . . .118 A1
Edward St
Accrington BB5 . . . . .104 E1
13 Bacup OL13 . . . . .88 A3
Bamber Bridge PR5 . . . . . . .77 E8
Barnoldswick BB18 . . . . . .196 C3
Blackpool FY1 . . . . .130 B5
Burnley BB11 . . . . .128 A6
3 Carnforth LA5 . . . . .223 D2
Chorley PR6 . . . . .43 D7
8 Church BB5 . . . . .103 E6
Darwen BB3 . . . . .82 A2
8 Earby BB18 . . . . .197 B2
7 Great Harwood BB6 . . . .124 C5
Haslingden BB4 . . . . .85 B6
Horwich BL6 . . . . .32 A3
Lancaster LA1 . . . . .215 A8
2 Leyland PR25 . . . . .60 A8
Lytham St Anne's FY8 . . . . . .89 F7
Morecambe LA4 . . . . .217 A5
Nelson BB9 . . . . .170 F2
Preston PR1 . . . . .96 F8
Rawtenstall BB4 . . . . .86 A8
4 Rishton BB1 . . . . .124 B1
Thornton FY5 . . . . .176 B4
Walton-le-D PR5 . . . . .97 C5
Whitworth OL12 . . . . .71 D2
Edward VII Quay PR2 . . . . .96 B7
Edwell Ave FY4 . . . . .110 D8
Edwin Waugh Gdns OL12 .52 D3
Edwinstowe Rd FY8 . . . . . .90 D6
Egan St PR1 . . . . .97 A8
Egbert St PR1 . . . . .118 A1
Egerton WN8 . . . . .9 D8
Egerton Gr PR7 . . . . .43 B6
Egerton Lodge BL7 . . . . . . .47 E1
Egerton Prim Sch BL7 . . . .47 D3
Egerton Rd Belmont BL7 . . .46 E4
Blackpool FY1 . . . . .130 B7
Leyland PR25 . . . . .76 F2
Preston PR2 . . . . .117 B1
Egerton Vale BL7 . . . . .47 D2
Egremont Ave FY5 . . . . . . .175 D5
Egypt Mount BB4 . . . . .85 D2
Egypt Terr 3 BB4 . . . . . . .85 E2
Eider Cl FY5 . . . . .175 F5
Eidsforth La PR3 . . . . . . .226 A1
Eidsforth Rd LA4 . . . . . . .217 B6
Eight Acre Ave BB7 . . . . .145 F8
Eight Acre La Formby L37 . .12 B6
Yealand Redmayne LA5 . . .225 E4
Eildon Dr FY6 . . . . .153 D1
Elaine Ave FY4 . . . . .130 F1
Elbow La L37 . . . . .11 F3
Elbow St PR7 . . . . .43 C7
Elbut La BL9 . . . . .33 F5
Elcho St PR1 . . . . .118 A2
Elder Ave L40 . . . . .25 F4
Elder Cl Clayton Green PR6 .78 C2
Fulwood PR2 . . . . .118 D6
Warton PR4 . . . . .92 E6
Elder Ct BB5 . . . . .104 E8
Elder St BB9 . . . . .170 F2
Elderberry Cl FY5 . . . . . . .175 F5
Elderbrook Cl PR4 . . . . . . .73 E4
Elderwood Ave FY5 . . . . .153 B7
Eldon Ct FY8 . . . . .89 F7
Eldon Gr LA3 . . . . .212 F7
Eldon Ho PR6 . . . . .43 D7
Eldon Prim Sch PR1 . . . . .117 E2
Eldon Rd BB1 . . . . .101 D7
Eldon St Chorley PR6 . . . . . .43 D7
Preston PR1,PR2 . . . . .117 D2
Eldons Croft PR8 . . . . .21 D5
Eldwick St BB10 . . . . .148 C1
Eleanor St Blackburn BB1 .101 F5
3 Nelson BB9 . . . . .170 E1
Electricity St BB5 . . . . . . .104 B6
Elgar Cl BB2 . . . . .102 A2
Elgin Cres BB11 . . . . .127 D4
Elgin Pl FY3 . . . . .131 A7
Elgin St 4 Lancaster LA1 .215 A7
Preston PR1 . . . . .118 A2
Elijah St 4 PR1 . . . . .97 D8
Elim Ct 4 FY8 . . . . .91 C3
Elim Gdns BB2 . . . . .101 C1
Elim Pl BB2 . . . . .101 C1
Elim View BB10 . . . . .148 D2
Eliza St Burnley BB10 . . . .128 B5
Ramsbottom BL0 . . . . .50 D6
Elizabeth Ave PR8 . . . . . . .21 E6
Elizabeth Cl FY3 . . . . .131 D5
Elizabeth Ct
Blackpool FY3 . . . . .130 D6
9 Lancaster LA1 . . . . .214 F7
Poulton-le-F FY6 . . . . .153 D3
Elizabeth Dr BB4 . . . . .68 A8
Elizabeth Ho BB3 . . . . .82 B1
Elizabeth Sq 8 PR1 . . . . .118 A1
Elizabeth St
Accrington BB5 . . . . .103 F5
Blackburn BB1 . . . . .101 F5
Blackpool FY1 . . . . .130 C6
Burnley BB11 . . . . .128 A5
Edenfield BL0 . . . . .68 D3
9 Fleetwood FY7 . . . . .199 B5
Nelson BB9 . . . . .170 E1
Padiham BB12 . . . . .126 C7
Preston PR1 . . . . .96 F8
Whitewell Bottom BB4 . . . . .86 F4
Elker Cotts BB7 . . . . .143 F4
Elker La BB7 . . . . .143 F5
Elker Mews BB7 . . . . .143 F3
Elkfield Dr FY3 . . . . .153 A1
Elkin Rd LA4 . . . . .217 D5
Elland Pl FY1 . . . . .130 B1
Elland Rd BB9 . . . . .148 C6
Ellel Hall Gdns LA2 . . . . .210 F3
Ellel St John the Evangelist
CE Prim Sch LA2 . . . . . .211 A3
Ellen Ct PR1 . . . . .117 F2
Ellen St Bamber Bridge PR5 .97 E1
Darwen BB3 . . . . .65 A7
11 Nelson BB9 . . . . .148 D8
Preston PR1 . . . . .117 E1
Preston PR1 . . . . .117 F2
Ellenrod Dr OL12 . . . . .52 A2
Ellenrod La OL12 . . . . .52 A2
Ellenshaw Cl Darwen BB3 . .82 B1
Rochdale OL12 . . . . .52 A2
Eller Brook Cl PR6 . . . . . . .43 F1
Eller Brook Ho L39 . . . . . . .15 E6
Ellerbeck Ave PR2 . . . . . .118 E5
Ellerbeck Cl BB10 . . . . . . .148 E3
Ellerbeck Rd
Accrington BB5 . . . . .104 B7
Cleveleys FY5 . . . . .175 C2
Darwen BB3 . . . . .82 B1
Ellerbrook Dr L40 . . . . .25 F3
Ellerbrook Way L39 . . . . . .15 E6
Ellerigg La LA6 . . . . .243 A6
Ellershaw Ho 12 LA1 . . . .218 D2
Ellerslie Rd PR2 . . . . .117 B1
Ellesmere Ave Colne BB8 .171 F5
Thornton FY5 . . . . .176 D1
Ellesmere Gr LA4 . . . . . . .217 A3
Ellesmere Rd
Blackpool FY4 . . . . .130 E1
Darwen BB3 . . . . .81 E3
Morecambe LA4 . . . . .216 F4
Elletson St FY6 . . . . .153 D4
Elliott Ave BB3 . . . . .65 B6
Elliott Cl PR1 . . . . .117 E2
Elliott Gdns WN6 . . . . .19 E7
Elliott St Burnley BB10 . . .128 C5
Preston PR1 . . . . .117 E1
Preston PR1 . . . . .117 E2
Elliott Wlk PR1 . . . . .117 E2
Ellis Dr LA4 . . . . .217 E6
Ellis St
Barnoldswick BB18 . . . . . .196 B2
1 Burnley BB11 . . . . .127 E5
19 Ramsbottom BL0 . . . . . . .50 B5
Ellisland FY4 . . . . .131 C1
Ellison Fold BB5 . . . . .124 E3
Ellison Fold La BB3 . . . . . .82 C1
Ellison Fold Terr BB3 . . . . .82 B1
Ellison St Accrington BB5 .104 B6
Darwen BB3 . . . . .82 A2
Ellwood Ave
Lancaster LA1 . . . . .218 E4
Morecambe LA3 . . . . .217 C2
Ellwood Ct LA3 . . . . .217 D2
Ellwood Gr LA3 . . . . .217 C2
Elm Ave Blackpool FY3 . . . .130 E5
Galgate LA2 . . . . .210 F4
Poulton-le-F FY6 . . . . .153 D3
Preston PR2 . . . . .117 A2
Warton PR4 . . . . .92 D6
Elm Brow PR3 . . . . .162 C4
Elm Cl Barnoldswick BB18 .196 A1
Haslingden BB4 . . . . .85 B3
Rishton BB1 . . . . .103 B8
Salterforth BB18 . . . . .194 E8
Elm Ct Poulton-le-F FY6 . . .153 D3
Skelmersdale WN8 . . . . .17 E1
Elm Dr
3 Bamber Bridge PR5 . . . . .97 F1
Formby L37 . . . . .11 D1
Elm Gr Chorley PR6 . . . . . . .61 E2
Clayton-le-W PR25 . . . . .77 D3
Darwen BB3 . . . . .82 B3
Fulwood PR2 . . . . .118 E2
6 Horwich BL6 . . . . .32 E1
Kirkham PR4 . . . . .114 B7
Morecambe LA4 . . . . .217 E7
Skelmersdale WN8 . . . . .17 E1
Elm Mill BB10 . . . . .128 A8
Elm Park Dr PR8 . . . . .21 E5
Elm Pl L39 . . . . .15 E4
Elm Rd Burscough L40 . . . . .25 E3
Southport PR8 . . . . .35 B4
Elm St 7 Bacup OL13 . . . . .88 A3
Blackburn BB1 . . . . .102 A7
Burnley BB10 . . . . .128 A8
Bury BL9 . . . . .33 B2
Colne BB8 . . . . .171 E6
Edenfield BL0 . . . . .68 E3
Fleetwood FY7 . . . . .199 A4
Great Harwood BB6 . . . . . .124 C4
Haslingden BB4 . . . . .85 B3
9 Nelson BB9 . . . . .170 E1
Ramsbottom BL0 . . . . .50 D6
Rawtenstall BB4 . . . . .86 A3
Rochdale OL12 . . . . .52 F1
Whitworth OL12 . . . . .71 D2
Elm Tree Gr BB6 . . . . . . .143 C5
Elmbank Ave FY5 . . . . . . .152 C7
Elmcroft La L38 . . . . .3 A3
Elmdale Cl L37 . . . . .11 D2
Elmer's Gn WN8 . . . . .18 D2
Elmer's Green La WN8 . . . .18 C4
Elmers Wood Rd WN8 . . . .18 D2
Elmfield Dr PR5 . . . . .78 C6
Elmfield Hall Flats BB5 . .103 F7
Elmfield St BB5 . . . . .103 F7
Elmhurst Rd FY8 . . . . .90 B8
Elmpark Gate OL12 . . . . . . .52 B3
Elmpark Gr OL12 . . . . .52 B3
Elmpark Vale OL12 . . . . . . .52 B3
Elmpark View OL12 . . . . . .52 B3
Elmpark Way OL12 . . . . . . .52 B3
Elmridge WN8 . . . . .9 D8
Elmridge Cres FY2 . . . . . .152 F3
Elms Ave Cleveleys FY5 . . .175 E2
Lytham St Anne's FY8 . . . . . .90 E3
Elms Ct LA4 . . . . .217 E7
Elms Dr Morecambe LA4 . .217 E7
Wrea Green PR4 . . . . .113 B4
Elms Rd LA4 . . . . .217 E7
Elms Sch PR1 . . . . .118 A3
Elms The
Clayton Green PR6 . . . . .78 C1
Maghull L31 . . . . .5 D3
Southport PR8 . . . . .35 C5
Southport,Birkdale PR8 . . . . .34 F6
Elmsdale Cl LA1 . . . . .218 C2
Elmsfield Pk L39 . . . . .6 A6
Elmside Cl FY5 . . . . .176 D2
Elmslack Ct LA5 . . . . .224 C4
Elmslack La LA5 . . . . .224 C4
Elmsley St PR1 . . . . .117 E2
Elmslie Gdns FY3 . . . . . . .130 E3
Elmstead WN8 . . . . .9 D8
Elmswood Cl FY8 . . . . .90 F4
Elmwood Chorley PR7 . . . . .61 B1
Longridge PR3 . . . . .140 A8
Skelmersdale WN8 . . . . .18 C3
Elmwood Ave
1 Leyland PR25 . . . . .76 E1
Preesall FY6 . . . . .200 B4
Elmwood Cl BB5 . . . . .104 D6
Elmwood Ct PR4 . . . . .132 F2
Elmwood Dr
Higher Penwortham PR1 . . . .96 B4
Thornton FY5 . . . . .176 C1
Elmwood Gdns LA1 . . . . . .215 A2
Elmwood St BB11 . . . . . . .127 D5
Elsby Ave FY5 . . . . .153 C8
Elsie St 10 BL0 . . . . .50 A4
Elsinore Cl FY7 . . . . .198 F5
Elslack La BD23 . . . . .197 F7
Elson Rd L37 . . . . .11 D1
Elston Ave FY3 . . . . .131 A8
Elston Gn PR2 . . . . .139 E1
Elston La PR2 . . . . .119 F7
Elston Lodge 7 PR2 . . . . .118 F4
Elswick WN8 . . . . .9 C8
Elswick Gdns BB2 . . . . . . .121 D3
Elswick Gn PR9 . . . . .54 A5
Elswick Ind Pk PR4 . . . . .156 A1
Elswick Lodge BB2 . . . . . .121 E3
Elswick Pl Blackpool FY4 . .110 E5
Lytham St Anne's FY8 . . . . . .90 B8
Elswick Rd Leyland PR25 . . .59 D8
Preston PR2 . . . . .116 E1
Southport PR9 . . . . .53 F4

Elswick St BB3 82 B1
Elsworth Cl L37 2 C8
Elterwater FY6 199 E5
Elterwater Pl
Blackpool FY3 131 C2
Lancaster LA1 218 E1
Eltham Ct FY3 153 B1
Elton Rd BB1,BB4 83 B5
Elton St 3 PR2 117 C1
Elvaston Rd FY6 153 C6
Elvington Rd L38 3 A2
Elwood Grange FY8 89 C8
Ely Cl Darwen BB3 82 C1
Wilpshire BB1 122 F6
Ely Mews PR9 54 A2
Embankment Rd BL7 48 C5
Emerald Ave BB1 122 F2
Emerald Cl FY5 152 F7
Emerald Cotts BL8 49 F3
Emerald St BB1 122 F2
Emerson Ave FY4 110 D7
Emerson Cl L38 3 A4
Emerson Rd PR1 118 D2
Emerson St LA1 215 A4
Emesgate La LA5 224 C3
Emily St
Bamber Bridge PR5 77 A8
Blackburn BB1 102 A6
Burnley BB11 128 A4
Emlsett Rd PR5 97 F3
Emma St BB5 103 F6
Emmanuel Christian Sch OL12 52 D1
Emmanuel Holcombe CE Prim Sch BL8 50 A6
Emmanuel Rd PR9 53 F2
Emmanuel St PR1,PR2 117 E2
Emmaus Rd LA3 212 F6
Emmett St Horwich BL6 32 B3
Preston PR1 117 F1
Emmott Ct BB8 172 E6
Emmott La BB8 172 D6
Emnie La PR26,PR25 59 C7
Empire Gr 2 FY3 130 D7
Empire Ho BB5 104 B6
Empire St BB6 124 D6
Emporium The 7 BB7 166 E8
Empress Ave PR2 117 E4
Empress Cl L31 5 B1
Empress Dr FY2 152 B1
Empress St
Accrington BB5 103 F6
Blackburn BB3 81 F7
Colne BB8 171 E5
Empress Way PR7 60 E2
End St BB8 171 B4
Endcliffe Rd LA4 217 C5
Endeavour Cl PR2 96 B7
Enderley Ct FY5 176 C1
Ending Rake OL12 52 C4
Endsleigh Gdns FY4 110 E6
Endsleigh Gr LA1 218 A3
Enfield Cl Eccleston PR7 41 C5
Huncoat BB5 125 E2
Enfield Rd
Accrington BB5 125 D2
Blackpool FY1 130 C7
Engine La L37 3 E8
England Ave
Blackburn BB2 81 D8
Blackpool FY2 152 C4
English Martyrs' Pl PR1 117 F2
English Martyrs' RC Prim Sch PR1 117 E1
Ennerdale WN8 9 D8
Ennerdale Ave
Blackburn BB1 102 C3
Fleetwood FY7 198 C1
Maghull L31 5 E2
Morecambe LA4 217 D4
Ennerdale Cl
Clitheroe BB7 166 C7
Formby L37 11 D3
Forton PR3 207 B3
Knott End-on-S FY6 199 F6
Lancaster LA1 218 F2
Leyland PR25 60 A7
Oswaldtwistle BB5 103 D5
Ennerdale Dr
Ormskirk L39 15 B2
Walton-le-D PR5 97 E5
Ennerdale Rd
Blackpool FY4 131 C1
Burnley BB10 128 E5
Chorley PR7 43 A6
Clitheroe BB7 166 C7
Formby L37 11 E3
Longridge PR3 139 F5
Ennismore St BB10 148 C1
Enoch Brow BB2 80 C8
Ensign Ct FY8 110 C4
Enstone WN8 18 D1
Enterprise Ct BB5 125 D1
Enterprise Dr PR26 77 A4
Enterprise Way
Fleetwood FY7 176 A6
Nelson BB8 170 F3
Enterprise Workshops
Kirkby L33 1 B1
Southport PR9 36 A6
Entwisle Rd BB5 104 B8
Entwistle Hall La BL7 48 B8
Entwistle St BB3 82 A1
Entwistle Sta BL7 48 B8
Ephraim St PR1 97 C7
Epping Ave BB5 125 B1
Epping Cl FY2 152 E5
Epping Pl PR6 43 D8
Epsom Cl PR6 61 F4
Epsom Croft PR6 31 B7
Epsom Gr L33 1 A6
Epsom Rd FY5 152 F8
Epsom Way BB5 104 D5
Epworth St BB3 65 B6
Equity St BB3 65 A8
Erdington Rd FY1 130 C3
Eric Morecambe Ho 9 LA4 217 F4
Ericson Dr PR8 35 B5
Erith Gr FY2 152 C5
Ermine Cl BB2 82 A8
Ermine Pl LA3 217 E3
Ernest St Bacup OL13 71 C8
6 Church BB5 103 E6
Clayton-le-M BB5 124 F1
Cornholme OL14 109 C1
Ernlouen Cl BB2 81 A8
Erskine Rd PR6 61 E1
Escar St 9 BB11 127 F5
Escott Gdns 11 BB10 128 A8
Escowbeck Ho LA2 237 B3
Esher Pond PR2 117 C6
Eshton Terr BB7 166 E7
Esk Ave Edenfield BL0 68 D5
Fleetwood FY7 198 D2
Eskbank WN8 9 C8
Eskbrook WN8 18 C1
Eskdale WN8 9 B8
Eskdale Ave
Fleetwood FY7 198 D1
Ormskirk L39 15 C2
Eskdale Cl Blackpool FY4 130 F1
Brierfield BB10 148 B4
Formby L37 11 D2
Fulwood PR2 117 F8
Eskdale Cres BB2 80 E8
Eskdale Ct FY5 175 D1
Eskdale Dr Formby L37 11 D2
Kirkham PR4 114 A7
Maghull L31 5 E2
Eskdale Gdns BB12 146 C2
Eskdale Gr FY6 199 F6
Eskdale Pl LA4 217 D4
Eskdale Rd Leyland PR25 60 C7
Longridge PR3 139 F6
Eskew La LA2 239 B8
Eskham Cl PR4 113 E6
Eskrigge Cl 4 LA1 218 D4
Eskrigge La LA2 238 A8
Esp La BB18 231 F1
Esplanade
Knott End-on-S FY6 199 D6
Preston PR1 97 B5
Southport PR8 34 F7
Esplanade Mews FY6 199 E5
Esplanade The
Fleetwood FY7 199 A5
Rishton BB1 103 A8
Essex Ave Burnley BB12 127 B7
Heywood OL10 33 E1
Essex Cl BB2 101 D3
Essex Pl FY2 152 F2
Essex Rd
3 Morecambe LA4 217 F4
4 Rishton BB1 124 A1
Southport PR8 22 A8
Standish WN1 30 B1
Essex St Accrington BB5 104 D6
Barnoldswick BB18 196 B2
Colne BB8 171 E4
Darwen BB3 82 C1
Horwich BL6 32 D1
Nelson BB9 170 E1
Preston PR1 118 A1
Essie Terr BB18 196 B1
Essington Ave LA4 217 A4
Est Bank Rd BL0 50 A3
Esther St BB1 102 C5
Esthwaite Gdns LA1 218 F1
Ethel St
Barnoldswick BB18 196 C2
Whitworth OL12 71 D2
Ethersall Rd BB9 148 E6
Eton Ave BB5 104 C7
Eton Cl BB12 126 E6
Eton Ct PR9 53 C1
Eton Pk PR2 118 C5
Eton Way WN5 10 F8
Ettington Dr PR8 21 A5
Ettrick Ave FY7 198 D3
Europa Dr PR26 77 A4
Europa Way LA1 214 C8
Euston Gr LA4 217 B5
Euston Rd LA4 217 B5
Euston St PR1 96 E7
Euxton Balshaw La Sta PR7 60 D1
Euxton CE Prim Sch PR7 60 C2
Euxton Hall Ct PR7 60 C2
Euxton Hall Gdns PR7 60 C1
Euxton Hall Hospl PR7 60 C1
Euxton Hall Mews PR7 60 C2
Euxton La Chorley PR7 61 B3
Euxton PR7 60 E4
Euxton St Mary's RC Prim Sch PR7 60 C3
Evans St Burnley BB11 127 F4
Horwich BL6 32 D4
Preston PR2 117 D1
Evanstone Cl 5 BL6 32 B3
Eve St BB9 171 A2
Evelyn Rd BB3 81 E5
Evelyn St BB10 148 A1
Evenwood WN8 18 D1
Evenwood Ct WN8 18 C1
Everard Cl L40 23 F7
Everard Rd PR8 35 D4
Everest Cl FY8 111 A1
Everest Ct 2 PR4 113 F6
Everest Dr FY2 152 C5
Everest Rd FY8 111 A2
Evergreen Ave PR25 60 A7
Evergreen Cl PR7 43 B5
Evergreens The
Blackburn BB2 80 F8
Cottam PR4 116 E4
Formby L37 11 D4
Eversham Cl PR9 55 A5
Eversholt Cl BB12 147 D7
Eversleigh Ave FY5 176 A3
Eversleigh St PR1 117 E1
Eversley WN8 18 D1
Everton BB2 102 A1
Everton Rd
Blackpool FY4 110 C6
Southport PR8 35 A4
Everton St BB3 81 F1
Every St Brierfield BB9 148 B6
Burnley BB11 127 E5
Nelson BB9 148 D8
Ramsbottom BL0 50 D6
Evesham Ave PR1 96 E2
Evesham Cl
5 Accrington BB5 104 A7
Blackpool FY5 152 E7
Heysham LA3 213 A6
Hutton PR4 95 C1
Evesham Manor PR9 55 A6
Evesham Rd
Lytham St Anne's FY8 90 A5
Normoss FY3 131 B7
Evington WN8 18 D1
Ewell Cl PR6 61 F4
Ewood BB2 101 D1
Ewood Cvn Site BB2 101 D1
Ewood La BB4 68 C7
Ewood Park (Blackburn Rovers FC) BB2 81 D8
Exchange St
Accrington BB5 103 F5
18 Blackburn BB1 101 E5
Blackpool FY1 130 B6
Colne BB8 171 D4
Darwen BB3 82 A2
Edenfield BL0 68 D3
Exchange The 2 BB8 171 D5
Exe St PR1 118 B2
Exeter Ave LA1 215 B6
Exeter Dr FY5 176 A2
Exeter Pl 2 PR2 116 E2
Exeter St Blackburn BB2 101 D2
3 Blackpool FY4 130 C1
Exmoor Cl PR9 54 B6
Exmouth St BB11 128 A5
Exton St BB9 148 A5
Extwistle Rd BB10 129 B7
Extwistle Sq BB10 128 E5
Extwistle St
Burnley BB10 128 B8
Nelson BB9 148 D7
Eyes La Bretherton PR26 57 E3
Newburgh WN8 27 A3

F

Factory Brow
Blackrod BL6 31 D3
Scorton PR3 204 E6
Factory Hill Horwich BL6 32 D4
5 Lancaster LA1 218 E1
Factory La Adlington PR6 31 B8
Barrowford BB9 170 D4
Middleworth Green PR1 96 F3
17 Padiham BB12 146 C1
Factory St BL0 50 C7
Fair Elms LA1 214 D7
Fair Haven Ct 2 FY8 90 D4
Fair Hill BB4 68 A7
Fair Oak Cl PR2 118 F3
Fair View OL13 71 C8
Fair View Cres OL13 88 B3
Fair View Rd BB11 128 B5
Fair Way FY6 177 C7
Fairacres WN6 29 B1
Fairbairn Ave BB12 127 C8
Fairbairn St BL6 32 B3
Fairbank Gr LA4 217 A3
Fairbank Wlk BB4 106 A2
Fairburn WN8 18 B3
Fairclough Rd
Accrington BB5 104 A3
Thornton FY5 176 A3
Fairfax Ave FY2 152 E5
Fairfax Cl PR3 181 D6
Fairfax Pl PR5 97 D2
Fairfax Rd PR2 118 E4
Fairfield PR3 181 C8
Fairfield Ave
Newchurch BB4 86 F2
Normoss FY3 131 B7
Poulton-le-F FY6 153 D3
Fairfield Cl Carnforth LA5 223 E1
Clitheroe BB7 166 C7
Lancaster LA1 214 E8
Ormskirk L39 15 E7
Fairfield Com Prim Sch BL9 33 D3
Fairfield Ct
Fleetwood FY7 198 F2
Poulton-le-F FY6 153 D4
Fairfield Dr
Brierfield BB10 148 C3
Bury BL9 33 D3
Fairfield Dr *continued*
Clitheroe BB7 166 C7
Ormskirk L39 15 E7
Preston PR2 117 B2
Fairfield General Hospl BL9 33 E4
Fairfield Gr LA3 216 E2
Fairfield Rd
Blackpool FY1 130 C8
Fulwood PR2 118 A4
Lancaster LA1 214 E8
Leyland PR25 59 F8
Morecambe LA3 216 E2
Nelson BB9 149 B8
Poulton-le-F FY6 131 F7
Southport PR8 21 C5
Fairfield St
Accrington BB5 103 F4
5 Bamber Bridge PR5 77 B7
Fairham Ave 6 PR1 96 D2
Fairhaven WN8 18 C3
Fairhaven Ave FY7 175 D7
Fairhaven Cl 6 FY5 176 D1
Fairhaven La FY8 89 E5
Fairhaven Lake* FY8 90 C3
Fairhaven Rd
Blackburn BB2 101 F1
Leyland PR25 76 D1
Lytham St Anne's FY8 89 F5
Middleforth Green PR1 96 E5
Southport PR9 54 B4
Fairhaven Way LA4 217 D5
Fairheath Rd LA2 239 B4
Fairhill Terr BB4 68 A7
Fairholme Rd BB11 128 B3
Fairholmes Cl 1 FY5 176 B3
Fairholmes Ct 2 FY5 176 B3
Fairholmes Way FY5 176 B3
Fairhope Ave
Lancaster LA1 218 C3
Morecambe LA4 217 F6
Fairhope Ct BB2 101 C6
Fairhurst Ave WN6 29 D3
Fairhurst Ct FY5 175 D3
Fairhurst St FY1 130 C6
Fairhurst's Dr WN8 27 B2
Fairlawn Rd FY8 90 F3
Fairlea Ave LA4 217 F6
Fairlie WN8 18 C3
Fairmont Dr FY6 177 D2
Fairsnape Ave PR3 140 B7
Fairsnape Dr PR3 181 B6
Fairsnape Rd FY8 91 D4
Fairstead WN8 18 C3
Fairthorn Wlk L33 1 A3
Fairview Ave FY8 90 A7
Fairview Cl PR4 74 F5
Fairview Dr Adlington PR6 30 F8
Adlington PR6 44 A1
Fairway Chorley PR7 61 C2
Fleetwood FY7 198 C1
Higher Penwortham PR1 96 B6
Poulton-le-F FY6 153 A2
Southport PR8 53 C2
Whitworth OL12 52 C7
Fairway Gdns FY6 199 D5
Fairway Rd FY4 110 E8
Fairways Fulwood PR2 118 A6
Horwich BL6 32 C3
Lytham St Anne's FY8 90 A6
Fairways Ave PR3 137 C3
Fairways Ct Formby L37 11 C5
Wilpshire BB1 122 F5
Fairways Dr BB11 127 E2
Fairways The WN8 18 D3
Fairweather Ct BB12 146 D1
Fairwinds Ave PR4 73 D4
Falcon Ave BB3 81 E3
Falcon Cl Blackburn BB1 101 D8
Bury BL9 33 B4
Falcon Ct BB5 124 F2
Falcon Dr FY6 153 B2
Falcon St PR1 118 B2
Falinge Fold OL12 52 D1
Falinge Park High Sch OL12 52 D1
Falinge Rd OL12 52 E1
Falkirk Ave FY2 152 C6
Falkland WN8 18 C3
Falkland Ave FY4 130 F2
Falkland Rd PR8 35 D5
Falkland St PR1 96 F7
Falkus Ct 6 FY6 153 D3
Fall Barn Rd BB4 86 B2
Fall Kirk LA2 240 F1
Fallbarn Cres BB4 86 A1
Fallbarn Rd BB4 86 B2
Fallowfield Cl PR4 113 E6
Fallowfield Dr
Burnley BB12 127 D8
Rochdale OL12 52 D2
Fallowfield Rd FY8 90 C6
Falmouth Ave
Fleetwood FY7 175 C8
Haslingden BB4 85 C2
Falmouth Rd FY1 130 C2
Falshaw Dr BL9 50 E1
Falstone Ave BL0 50 C4
Far Croft PR5 97 A1
Far East View 16 BB18 196 B2
Far Field PR1 96 D3
Far La PR1 96 C2
Far Moor La LA1 215 C8
Far Nook PR6 61 B7
Faraday Ave BB7 166 D8
Faraday Dr PR2 118 C7
Faraday Rise OL12 52 B1
Faraday St BB12 127 D7
Faraday Way FY2,FY6 153 A6
Fareham Cl
Bamber Bridge PR5 97 F3
Fulwood PR2 118 A4
Fareham Dr PR9 55 A5
Farfield Dr BB3 81 F6
Farholme La OL13 70 D8
Faringdon Ave FY4 110 E5
Farington Ave PR25 59 D7
Farington Gate PR25 77 B2
Farington Prim Sch PR25 77 B3
Farington Rd PR5,PR26 77 A6
Farington St Paul's CE Prim Sch PR26 76 F7
Farleton Cl LA5 223 C5
Farleton Ct 3 LA1 218 D4
Farleton Old Rd LA2 238 A5
Farley La Roby Mill WN8 19 A3
Skelmersdale WN8 18 F3
Farm Ave Adlington PR6 31 A8
Bacup OL13 87 F4
Farm Cl Southport PR9 36 A8
Thornton FY5 176 B2
Farm House Cl
Blackburn BB1 102 C4
Lucas Green PR6 61 C6
Farm Meadow Rd WN5 10 E5
Farmdale Dr L31 5 E1
Farmdale Rd LA1 215 B5
Farmend Cl PR4 75 B8
Farmer Parr's Animal World (Mus)* FY7 175 F7
Farmer's Row BB2 81 B7
Farnborough Rd PR8 21 F8
Farnborough Road Inf & Jun Schs PR8 22 A8
Farnell Pl FY4 110 D6
Farnham Way FY6 153 C5
Farnlea Dr LA4 217 E5
Farnworth Rd FY5 176 D1
Faroes Cl BB2 101 F1
Farrer Ave LA1 211 B7
Farrer St BB9 148 C7
Farrier Rd L33 1 A2
Farriers Fold 4 LA3 212 F7
Farriers Yd LA2 237 C3
Farringdon Cl PR1 118 F1
Farringdon Cres PR1 118 F1
Farringdon La PR2 118 F3
Farringdon Pl PR1 118 F1
Farrington Cl
1 Blackburn BB2 101 C1
Burnley BB11 127 C3
Farrington Ct BB11 127 C3
Farrington Dr L39 15 E6
Farrington Pl BB11 127 C3
Farrington Rd BB11 127 B3
Farrington St PR7 43 C8
Farthings The PR7 60 F1
Faulkner Cl PR8 21 C6
Faulkner Gdns PR8 21 C6
Faulkner's La PR3 207 B1
Favordale Rd BB8 172 A5
Fawcett WN8 18 B3
Fawcett Cl BB2 101 D3
Fawcett Rd L31 5 D3
Fayles Gr FY4 131 A1
Fazackerley St PR2 117 C1
Fazakerley St 13 PR7 43 C8
Fearn Dene 2 OL12 52 B2
Fearnhead Ave BL6 32 B5
Fearnlea Cl 1 OL12 52 B2
Fearns Com Sports Coll OL13 87 A1
Fearns Moss BB4,OL13 87 A1
Fecitt Brow BB1 102 D4
Fecitt Rd BB2 101 B6
Federation St BB18 196 A3
Feilden Pl BB2 80 D8
Feilden St BB2 101 D5
Feildens Farm La BB2 121 B3
Felgate Brow FY3 130 E5
Felix St BB11 128 B7
Fell Brow PR3 140 B6
Fell Cl 5 PR5 77 F8
Fell End Cvn Pk LA7 225 E8
Fell Rd Casterton LA6 243 C2
Morecambe LA4 217 F4
Waddington BB7 189 A6
Fell View Brierfield BB10 148 D3
Caton LA2 237 C3
Chorley PR6 43 E6
Garstang PR3 181 C8
Grimsargh PR2 139 C2
Southport PR9 54 D6
Weir OL13 88 A8
West Bradford BB7 189 D7
Whalley BB7 144 A7
Fell View Cl PR3 181 C8
Fell Way FY6 177 D7
Fellborough Lodge 5 FY8 90 A8
Fellery St PR7 43 C8
Fellfoot Lodge PR2 119 A4
Fellfoot Rd LA6 243 A3
Fellgate LA3 217 E2
Fells View BB7 144 A4
Fellside Cl BL8 49 F1
Fellside View LA3 212 F7
Fellstone Vale PR6 80 A1
Fellstone View PR6 80 A1
Fellway Cl 7 PR5 77 C8
Felstead WN8 18 B2
Felstead St PR1 97 D8
Felton Way PR4 74 F3

Feltons WN8 .18 B2
Fenber Ave FY4 .110 C7
Fencegate BB12 .147 C7
Fengrove PR4 .75 A8
Fenham Carr La LA1 .215 C7
Feniscliffe Dr BB2 .101 A2
Feniscowles Prim Sch
BB2 .80 C8
Fennel Cl FY2 .152 F4
Fenney Ct WN8 .18 C1
Fennyfold Terr BB12 .126 C6
Fensway PR4 .95 D2
Fenton Ave BB18 .196 D3
Fenton Rd Blackpool FY1 .130 C6
Fulwood PR2 .118 C4
Fenton St LA1 .214 E8
Fenwick St BB11 .127 D3
Ferguson Gdns OL12 .52 F3
Ferguson Rd FY1 .130 E2
Ferguson St BB2 .81 D7
Fermor Rd Becconsall PR4 .73 E1
Preston PR1 .118 F1
Fern Ave BB5 .103 F3
Fern Bank Carnforth LA5 .223 D1
Chorley PR6 .61 D3
Lancaster LA1 .215 A5
Maghull L31 .5 E1
Nelson BB9 .148 E7
Fern Breck Cotts FY6 .200 A2
Fern Cl
[2] Bamber Bridge PR5 .77 B8
Skelmersdale WN8 .17 E1
Fern Ct FY7 .198 C1
Fern Gore Ave BB5 .104 A3
Fern Gr FY1 .130 C3
Fern Hill La OL12 .52 A3
Fern Isle Cl OL12 .52 B6
Fern Lea Bolton-le-S LA5 .221 A4
Nelson BB9 .148 E8
Fern Lea St BB4 .69 D8
Fern Mdw PR6 .78 C2
Fern Rd BB11 .127 E4
Fern St Bacup OL13 .87 F3
Colne BB8 .171 F6
Newchurch BB4 .86 F1
Ramsbottom BL0 .50 D7
Fern Terr BB4 .85 A3
Fernbank Ave BB18 .196 A3
Fernbank Ct BB9 .148 E7
Ferncliffe Dr LA3 .216 D2
Ferndale
[4] Blackburn BB1 .102 A6
Skelmersdale WN8 .18 C2
Ferndale Ave FY4 .110 D7
Ferndale Cl
Freckleton PR4 .93 D7
Leyland PR25 .60 B7
Thornton FY5 .176 C2
Ferndale Dr WN6 .19 E7
Ferndale St BB10 .128 C8
Ferngrove BL9 .33 B4
Fernhill Ave OL13 .70 E8
Fernhill Cl OL13 .70 E8
Fernhill Cres [1] OL13 .70 E8
Fernhill Dr OL13 .70 E8
Fernhill Gr [2] OL13 .70 E8
Fernhill Pk OL13 .70 E8
Fernhill Way [4] OL13 .70 E8
Fernhills BL7 .47 E2
Fernhurst Ave FY4 .130 D1
Fernhurst Gate L39 .15 B1
Fernhurst St BB2 .81 D8
Fernlea Ave
Barnoldswick BB18 .196 B2
Oswaldtwistle BB5 .104 A3
Fernlea Cl BB2 .81 B8
Fernlea Dr BB5 .124 F4
Fernleigh PR26 .59 A8
Fernleigh Cl FY2 .152 D4
Fernley Rd PR8 .35 A5
Ferns The Bacup OL13 .88 A1
Bamber Bridge PR5 .97 C3
Preston PR2 .117 C2
Fernside Way OL12 .52 A1
Fernstone Cl BL6 .32 A3
Fernview Dr BL0 .50 A1
Fernville Terr [9] OL13 .70 D8
Fernwood Ave FY5 .153 B8
Fernwood Cl FY8 .90 E4
Ferny Knoll Rd WA11 .8 F4
Fernyhalgh Ct PR2 .118 D6
Fernyhalgh Gdns PR2 .118 D6
Fernyhalgh Gr PR2 .118 D6
Fernyhalgh La PR2 .118 D7
Fernyhalgh Pl PR2 .118 D6
Ferrier Bank PR4 .92 D5
Ferrier Cl [1] BB1 .102 C5
Ferry Rd PR2 .95 F8
Ferry Side La PR9 .54 C5
Ferry View Ct FY7 .199 C5
Ffrances Pas [31] LA1 .214 F8
Fiddler's La Chipping PR3 .184 F4
Clayton Green PR6 .78 B2
Fidler La PR26 .76 F5
Field Cl L40 .25 F3
Field Edge La PR3 .201 E5
Field Maple Dr PR2 .118 F3
Field Rd LA3 .212 D6
Field St Blackburn BB2 .101 B2
Blackpool FY1 .130 C2
Padiham BB12 .126 C7
Skelmersdale WN8 .17 D2
Field Top OL13 .88 A7
Field Wlk L39 .16 B5
Fielden St Burnley BB11 .127 D5
Fielden St *continued*
Chorley PR6 .43 E8
[5] Leyland PR25 .76 D1
Fieldfare Cl
Middleworth Green PR1 .96 E3
Thornton FY5 .176 A5
Fieldfare Ct PR7 .42 F5
Fieldhouse Ave FY5 .176 D2
Fieldhouse Ind Est OL12 .52 F2
Fieldhouse Rd OL12 .52 F2
Fieldhouse Sch OL12 .52 F1
Fielding Cres BB2 .101 A1
Fielding La
Great Harwood BB6 .124 B5
Oswaldtwistle BB5 .103 E3
Fielding Pl PR6 .31 B8
Fielding Rd FY1 .130 D8
Fielding St BB1 .124 C1
Fieldings Bldgs [9] BB4 .85 E2
Fieldings The L31 .5 B4
Fieldlands PR8 .36 A2
Fields End BB6 .123 C8
Fields Rd BB4 .85 C1
Fields The PR7 .41 B7
Fieldsend LA3 .213 A7
Fieldside Ave PR7 .60 C1
Fieldside Cl PR5 .97 C3
Fieldview WN8 .10 A7
Fieldway FY8 .110 E2
Fife Cl PR6 .43 E6
Fife St Accrington BB5 .104 A4
Barrowford BB9 .170 C1
Fifth Ave Blackpool FY4 .110 C7
Burnley BB10 .148 B3
Bury BL9 .33 D4
Filberts Cl PR2 .117 C3
Filberts The PR2 .117 C3
File St PR7 .43 C7
Filey Pl Blackpool FY1 .130 B6
Fulwood PR2 .117 A4
Filey Rd FY8 .111 A1
Filton Gr LA3 .217 E3
Finch Cl BB1 .101 E6
Finch La
Appley Bridge WN6 .28 B1
Cottam PR4 .116 E4
Finch Mill Ave WN6 .19 D7
Finch St [5] BB3 .81 F2
Finch's Cotts [6] PR1 .96 E4
Finches The FY6 .153 B2
Finchley Rd FY1 .130 B8
Findon WN8 .18 C2
Fine Jane's Way PR9 .36 B8
Finney Park Dr PR2 .95 D8
Finnington Cotts BB2 .80 A6
Finnington La BB2 .80 A6
Finsbury Ave
Blackpool FY1 .130 D2
Lytham St Anne's FY8 .90 B4
Finsbury Pl BB2 .81 D8
Finsley Gate BB11 .128 A5
Finsley St BB10 .148 E3
Finsley View BB10 .148 F3
Fir Cl FY7 .198 C2
Fir Cotes L31 .5 E1
Fir Ct BB5 .104 E8
Fir Gr Blackpool FY1 .130 E2
Warton PR4 .92 D6
Fir Grove Rd [11] BB11 .128 B4
Fir St Burnley BB10 .128 B5
Bury BL9 .33 A2
Haslingden BB4 .85 B3
Nelson BB9 .148 F8
Ramsbottom BL0 .50 D7
Southport PR8 .35 F6
Fir Tree Ave PR2 .117 B4
Fir Tree Cl Hest Bank LA5 .220 F2
Much Hoole PR4 .74 E3
Skelmersdale WN8 .9 D7
Fir Tree La Haskayne L39 .14 F3
Ormskirk L39 .15 A2
Fir Tree Pl FY5 .152 F8
Fir Tree Way [3] BL6 .32 E1
Fir Trees Ave
Bamber Bridge PR5 .77 A8
Fulwood PR2 .119 A4
Fir Trees Cl BB9 .149 A8
Fir Trees Cres [1] PR5 .77 A8
Fir Trees Gr BB12 .146 E5
Fir Trees La BB12 .146 E5
Fir Trees Pl PR2 .118 F4
Fir Trees Rd PR5 .97 A1
Firbank PR7 .60 C2
Firbank Ave PR4 .57 A7
Firbank Rd LA1 .218 E1
Firbeck WN8 .18 C1
Fircroft WN6 .29 A2
Firfield Cl PR4 .113 E5
Firs Cl L37 .11 D5
Firs Cres L37 .11 D5
Firs La L39 .14 E3
Firs Link L37 .11 D4
Firshill Cl FY5 .153 B8
First Ave Blackpool FY4 .110 C7
Church BB5 .104 A8
Clifton PR4 .115 C1
Poulton-le-F FY6 .153 E3
Preesall Park FY6 .200 C1
Preston PR2 .117 A2
West Bradford BB7 .189 D7
Wrea Green PR4 .113 B4
First Terr LA3 .209 B5
Firswood Cl FY8 .90 E4
Firswood Rd L40,WN8 .17 C3
Firtree Cl PR7 .43 C3
Firtrees Dr BB2 .80 F8
Firwood WN8 .18 D3
Firwood Cl PR3 .140 A8
Firwood La PR5 .99 B5
Fish House La PR3 .185 B5
Fish La L40 .38 B2
Fish Rake La BL0,BB4 .68 E6
Fisher Dr Orrell WN5 .10 E7
Southport PR9 .35 F7
Fisher St FY1 .130 C6
Fisher's La FY4 .111 A5
Fisher's Slack La FY6 .155 B2
Fishergate PR1 .96 F7
Fishergate Ct [12] PR1 .96 E7
Fishergate Ctr PR1 .96 F7
Fishergate Hill PR1 .96 E6
Fishergate Wlk [7] PR1 .96 F7
Fishermans Cl L37 .11 E6
Fishermans Reach PR4 .113 D4
Fishmoor Dr BB2 .81 F8
Fishwick La PR6 .79 B1
Fishwick Par PR1 .97 D8
Fishwick Prim Sch PR1 .118 E1
Fishwick Rd PR1 .97 C8
Fishwick View PR1 .97 D8
Fitchfield PR1 .96 F2
Fitzgerald St PR1 .118 C1
Fitzroy Rd FY2 .152 D3
Fitzroy St PR1 .96 E7
Five Acres PR26 .76 E4
Five Ashes La LA2 .210 F7
Five Lane Ends
Hampson Green LA2 .207 D8
Preesall FY6 .200 A2
Singleton FY6 .154 D4
Flag La Bamber Bridge PR1 .96 F1
Bretherton PR26 .58 A5
Runshaw Moor PR26,PR7 .59 D4
Flag St OL13 .70 E8
Flagg La PR6 .43 F5
Flakefleet Ave FY7 .198 E1
Flamstead WN8 .18 C1
Flare Rd LA3 .212 D6
Flash La L40 .39 B4
Flat La LA5 .225 E3
Flatfield Way L31 .5 E1
Flatman's La L39 .13 E1
Flats Ret Pk The PR5 .97 C5
Flats The Chorley PR7 .43 B6
Kirkham PR4 .114 B4
[3] Kirkham PR4 .114 B5
Flax Cl BB4 .68 A8
Flax La L40 .25 F2
Flax Moss Cl BB4 .68 A8
Flax St [8] BL0 .50 A4
Flaxfield Rd L37 .12 A3
Flaxfield Way PR4 .114 A5
Flaxfields L40 .25 F3
Flaxton WN8 .18 C1
Fleet La LA2 .238 A8
Fleet St Blackpool FY1 .130 C4
Chorley PR7 .43 C7
Horwich BL6 .32 D3
Longridge PR3 .140 A7
Lytham St Anne's FY8 .89 D8
Nelson BB9 .170 E1
[4] Preston PR1 .96 F7
Fleet Street La PR3 .141 A6
Fleet Wlk [5] BB11 .128 A6
Fleetgreen LA1 .218 C3
Fleetwood Charles Saer Com Prim Sch FY7 .198 D3
Fleetwood Chaucer Com Prim Sch FY7 .199 A4
Fleetwood Cl
Blackburn BB2 .101 F1
Southport PR9 .53 F3
Fleetwood Cres PR9 .55 A6
Fleetwood Ct PR9 .53 D1
Fleetwood Dr PR9 .55 A6
Fleetwood Flakefleet Prim Sch FY7 .198 E2
Fleetwood High Sch
FY7 .198 D2
Fleetwood Hospl FY7 .199 B5
Fleetwood Old Rd PR4 .133 E3
Fleetwood Rd
Blackpool FY5 .152 D7
Burnley BB10 .148 C2
Carleton FY6 .153 B5
Esprick PR4 .133 D5
Fleetwood FY7 .175 E8
Kirkham PR4 .113 F7
Padiham BB12 .126 D8
Southport PR9 .53 E3
Fleetwood Rd N FY5 .176 B3
Fleetwood Rd S FY5 .153 B7
Fleetwood Sh & L Village
FY7 .199 A3
Fleetwood St
[6] Leyland PR25 .77 B2
Preston PR2 .117 D1
Fleming Ho [8] LA1 .218 D2
Fleming Sq
Blackburn BB2 .101 E4
Longridge PR3 .140 B7
Flensburg Way PR26 .76 D4
Fletcher Ave PR4 .57 A6
Fletcher Rd Preston PR1 .118 C1
Rishton BB1 .103 A8
Fletcher St
Blackburn BB2 .101 D3
Bury BL9 .33 A2
Nelson BB9 .148 F7
Fletcher's Dr L40 .25 E4
Flett St PR2 .117 C1
Fletton Cl OL12 .52 E2
Fletton Mews OL12 .52 E2
Flimby WN8 .18 D1
Flimby Cl BB2 .81 F8
Flintoff Way PR1 .118 B3
Flintron Brow LA2 .233 A2
Flip Rd BB4 .85 A2
Flockton Ct [9] BL6 .32 B4
Flordon WN8 .18 D2
Florence Ave
Burnley BB11 .127 C4
Warton PR4 .92 D5
Florence Pl [1] BB1 .102 A6
Florence St
Blackburn BB1 .102 A6
Blackpool FY4 .111 A6
Burnley BB11 .127 C5
[1] Church BB5 .103 E6
Flower Fields PR3 .181 D2
Flower Scar Rd OL14 .88 E6
Flowerfield PR4 .116 E6
Flowers Cl BB2 .81 D7
Floyd Rd PR2 .118 E3
Floyer St PR1 .97 B7
Fluke Hall La PR3 .201 B8
Fold BB9 .170 E5
Fold Gdns OL12 .52 B4
Fold House Cvn Pk PR3 .201 D4
Fold The Rawtenstall BB4 .86 A2
Thornton-in-C BD23 .197 B5
Fold View BL7 .47 E1
Folds BL6 .31 C3
Folds St BB12 .127 F8
Foldside PR4 .93 C7
Folkestone Cl
Cleveleys FY5 .175 F4
Warton PR4 .92 E7
Folkestone Rd
Lytham St Anne's FY8 .89 F8
Southport PR8 .35 F3
Folly La Barnoldswick BB8 .193 F7
Lancaster LA1,LA2 .218 B4
Folly Terr BB4 .86 B8
Folly Wlk [20] OL12 .52 F1
Fontwell Cl WN6 .29 F1
Fooden La BB7 .230 E4
Foot Mill Cres OL12 .52 D2
Foot Wood Cres OL12 .52 D2
Footeran La LA5 .225 E3
Forbes Ct BB11 .127 A3
Ford La Goosnargh PR3 .160 F2
Silverdale LA5 .224 E5
Ford St Barrowford BB9 .170 E4
Burnley BB10 .148 B1
Lancaster LA1 .218 B1
Fordham Cl PR8 .35 E3
Fordside Ave BB5 .124 E4
Fordstone Ave FY6 .200 A4
Fordway Ave FY3 .130 F6
Fore St BB3 .81 F7
Foregate PR2 .117 E4
Foreside BB9 .170 E5
Forest Ave BB12 .147 E8
Forest Bank BB4 .86 A7
Forest Bank Rd BB4 .86 A7
Forest Becks Brow BB7 .230 D6
Forest Brook Ho PR2 .117 F3
Forest Cl PR5 .97 C3
Forest Dr
Lytham St Anne's FY8 .90 F4
Shevington Moor WN6 .29 A2
Skelmersdale WN8 .18 C3
Forest Fold WN6 .19 E6
Forest Gate
Blackpool FY3 .130 E5
Morecambe LA3 .217 E2
Forest Gr PR3 .137 B8
Forest Ho BB9 .148 D7
Forest Holme Cl BB4 .87 A7
Forest La BB9 .170 B2
Forest Pk LA1 .214 C7
Forest Rd PR8 .35 D6
Forest St Burnley BB11 .128 B6
Forest Holme BB4 .87 A7
Nelson BB9 .170 D1
Forest View
[14] Barrowford BB9 .170 D3
Brierfield BB9 .148 A5
Rochdale OL12 .52 D2
Forest Way PR2 .117 F6
Forester Dr BB12 .147 D8
Forester's Bldgs [9]
BB18 .196 B2
Foresters Hall [12] PR1 .96 F8
Forestry Houses BB7 .228 C5
Forestway PR25 .59 F8
Forfar Gr BB11 .127 D3
Forfar St BB11 .127 D3
Forge Cl L40 .16 E4
Forge Cnr BB7 .144 C5
Forge La PR3 .181 E8
Forge St [3] OL13 .87 F2
Forges St PR25 .77 A1
Forgewood Cl LA2 .219 E6
Forgewood Dr LA2 .219 D6
Formby Ave FY7 .175 D7
Formby Bridge L37 .11 E2
Formby Bsns Pk L37 .12 B3
Formby By-Pass
Formby L37 .12 B5
Hightown L37,L38 .3 B8
Formby Cl BB2 .81 F8
Formby Cres PR4 .74 F8
Formby Fields L37 .12 A2
Formby Gdns L37 .11 F4
Formby High Sch L37 .11 E4
Formby La Formby L37 .12 B2
Haskayne L39 .14 E2
Formby Pl PR2 .116 E2
Formby Point Cvn Pk
L37 .11 B1
Formby Rd FY8 .110 F1
Formby St L37 .11 E2
Formby Sta L37 .11 E2
Forrest Ct [4] FY3 .130 E8
Forrest St BB1 .102 A5
Forrester Cl PR25 .76 E1
Forrestside BB2 .81 D7
Forshaw Ave
Blackpool FY3 .130 F8
Lytham St Anne's FY8 .89 D8
Forshaw Cl [6] FY7 .198 F2
Forshaw Rd [3] PR1 .96 D2
Forsythia Dr PR6 .78 B4
Fort Ave PR3 .141 D3
Fort St Accrington BB5 .104 B6
Blackburn BB1 .102 A5
[11] Clayton-le-M BB5 .124 F3
Clitheroe BB7 .166 D7
Read BB12 .145 D2
Fort Street Ind Est BB1 .102 A6
Forton Primary Sch
PR3 .207 B3
Forton Rd [8] PR2 .116 E1
Forty Acre La PR3 .163 B5
Forward Ind Est PR25 .76 E2
Foscote Rd L33 .1 A4
Fossdale Moss PR26 .76 C1
Fosse Bank Ct BB2 .82 A8
Fosse Cl BB1,BB2 .82 A8
Fosse Ct LA3 .217 E3
Foster Croft PR1 .96 C6
Foster Ct Bury BL9 .33 D4
Chorley PR6 .61 E1
Foster Rd
Barnoldswick BB18 .196 A3
Formby L37 .11 D2
Foster St Accrington BB5 .104 C7
Chorley PR6 .61 E1
Fosterfield Pl PR6 .61 E1
Fosters Cl PR9 .36 B8
Fosters Green Rd WN8 .18 D3
Fothergill St [1] BB8 .171 C5
Foul La PR8,PR9 .36 A5
Fouldrey Ave FY6 .153 F5
Foulds Cl BB8 .171 C3
Foulds Rd BB8 .172 B3
Foulds Terr BB8 .172 C2
Foulridge Wharf* BB8 .194 D2
Foundary Gdns LA5 .223 D3
Foundry La Halton LA2 .219 A7
Halton LA2 .219 B6
Foundry St [1] Bacup OL13 .87 F2
Blackburn BB2 .101 D4
[3] Burnley BB11 .127 F6
[15] Chorley PR7 .43 C8
[23] Darwen BB3 .82 A1
Haslingden BB4 .85 B2
Rawtenstall BB4 .85 F1
Fountain Pl BB5 .104 B5
Fountain Sq [3] BB9 .170 D3
Fountain St
Accrington BB5 .104 A5
Barnoldswick BB18 .196 C2
Bury BL9 .33 A2
Colne BB8 .171 D4
Darwen BB3 .65 A8
Nelson BB9 .170 E1
Fountain St N [12] BL9 .33 A3
Fountains Ave
Blackburn BB1 .102 B8
Read BB12 .145 D1
Fountains Cl PR7 .43 D5
Fountains Reach PR5 .97 D1
Fountains The
Barrowford BB9 .170 D3
Ormskirk L39 .15 E6
Fountains Way
Formby L37 .12 B2
Oswaldtwistle BB5 .103 B5
Four Acre La PR3 .162 E5
Four Lane Ends
Barley BB7 .192 B2
Blackpool FY3 .131 A6
Bretherton PR26 .58 A7
Burton in L LA2 .242 C1
Carleton FY6 .153 B5
Charnock Richard PR7 .42 C4
Clitheroe BB7 .167 A6
Dolphinholme LA2 .226 A8
Gregson Lane PR5 .98 D2
Halsall L39 .23 D3
Halton LA2 .218 F7
Heapey PR6 .62 C4
Morecambe LA3 .216 D1
Simonstone BB12 .145 F4
Thornton FY5 .176 E1
Wray LA2 .238 E4
Four Lane Ends Rd OL13 .70 B8
Four Oaks Rd PR5 .78 B7
Fouracre BB2 .121 E2
Fourfields PR5 .97 E2
Fourth Ave Blackpool FY4 .110 C7
Bury BL9 .33 D4
Fowler Ave PR26 .77 B6
Fowler Cl PR5 .99 C2
Fowler Height Cl BB2 .81 B7
Fowler Hill La PR3 .204 B5
Fowler Ind Pk BL6 .32 C2
Fowler La Farington PR26 .76 F6
Leyland PR5,PR26 .77 B5
Fowler St PR2 .117 D3
Fox Gr LA3 .216 E3
Fox Ind Est [2] FY2 .152 E1
Fox La Coupe Green PR5 .98 E3
Leyland PR25 .59 E7
Fox Lane Ends PR4 .113 A5
Fox St Accrington BB5 .104 B6
Clitheroe BB7 .189 E1
Horwich BL6 .32 C2
Padiham BB12 .126 F6

Fox St *continued*
Preston PR1 .....96 F7
Foxcote PR7 .....61 C2
Foxcroft BB12 .....127 D8
Foxdale Ave FY3 .....130 D7
Foxdale Cl Bacup OL13 .....88 A1
Edgworth BL7 .....48 E7
Southport PR8 .....35 E3
Foxdale Gr PR1 .....118 D3
Foxdale Pl LA1 .....218 C2
Foxen Dole La BB12 .....147 A5
Foxes Farmhouse FY6 .....131 E7
Foxes Terr PR3 .....157 C7
Foxfield Ave LA4 .....217 C3
Foxfield Cl BB5 .....103 D4
Foxfield Dr BB4 .....86 F4
Foxfields FY6 .....177 C8
Foxfold WN8 .....18 D3
Foxglove Ave L40 .....25 F4
Foxglove Cl
Hesketh Bank PR4 .....73 E4
Standish WN6 .....29 D2
Walton Summit PR5 .....78 B8
Foxglove Ct OL12 .....52 D3
Foxglove Dr Bury BL9 .....33 D3
Lucas Green PR6 .....61 C5
Foxglove Way PR4 .....93 D7
Foxhall Rd FY1 .....130 B3
Foxhall Sq 8 FY1 .....130 B3
Foxhill Bank Brow BB5 .....103 E5
Foxhill Cl L37 .....11 C3
Foxhill Dr BB4 .....86 F4
Foxhill Terr BB5 .....103 E4
Foxhole Rd Chorley PR7 .....42 F8
Euxton PR7 .....60 F1
Foxholes Rd Horwich BL6 .....32 D4
Morecambe LA4 .....217 D6
Foxhouse La L31 .....5 F1
Foxhouse St BB2 .....101 C5
Foxstones Cres BB2 .....81 A8
Foxstones La BB10 .....129 B2
Foxwell Cl BB4 .....85 C2
Foxwood Chase BB5 .....104 E8
Foxwood Cl WN5 .....10 E5
Foxwood Dr PR4 .....113 E5
Foxwood The PR7 .....42 C1
Frailey Cl PR8 .....21 C4
France St Blackburn BB2 .....101 D4
Church BB5 .....103 E6
Frances St 3 BB3 .....81 F2
Francis Ave BB9 .....170 E5
Francis St Blackburn BB2 .....101 B1
Blackpool FY1 .....130 B6
Burnley BB10 .....148 A1
3 Clayton-le-M BB5 .....124 F3
Colne BB8 .....171 B3
Preston PR2 .....117 C1
Frank St
4 Accrington BB5 .....125 A1
Barnoldswick BB18 .....196 B2
Preston PR1 .....117 F1
Frankland Ho 15 LA1 .....218 D2
Franklands PR4 .....95 A1
Franklands Dr PR2 .....119 A5
Franklands Fold PR4 .....75 A8
Franklin Ainsworth Ho 2
BB6 .....124 C5
Franklin Rd BB2 .....101 B3
Franklin St
2 Burnley BB12 .....127 C6
Clitheroe BB7 .....166 D7
27 Darwen BB3 .....82 A1
Lancaster LA1 .....214 F5
Fraser Ave PR1 .....96 E5
Fraser St Accrington BB5 .....104 A4
Burnley BB10 .....148 B1
Frazer Gr 13 FY4 .....130 B1
Freckleton CE Prim Sch
PR4 .....93 C7
Freckleton Ct FY8 .....91 C3
Freckleton Dr L33 .....1 A5
Freckleton Rd
Kirkham PR4 .....114 B3
Southport PR9 .....53 F4
Freckleton St
Blackburn BB2 .....101 E4
Blackpool FY1 .....130 C3
Kirkham PR4 .....114 B4
2 Lytham St Anne's FY8 .....91 C3
Freckleton Strike Lane Prim Sch PR4 .....93 B8
Frederick Row BB1 .....102 B5
Frederick St
Accrington BB5 .....104 A6
Barnoldswick BB18 .....196 A3
6 Blackburn BB2 .....101 E3
2 Blackpool FY4 .....110 D8
Chorley PR6 .....43 E7
Darwen BB3 .....82 A2
Oswaldtwistle BB5 .....103 E4
12 Ramsbottom BL0 .....50 B5
Fredora Ave FY3 .....131 A2
Free La BB4 .....68 A6
Free Trade St 16 BB11 .....127 F6
Freeholds La
Waddington BB7 .....188 F6
Waddington BB7 .....188 F7
Freeholds Rd OL12 .....71 E6
Freeholds Terr OL12 .....71 E6
Freeman's La PR7 .....42 E3
Freemantle Ave FY4 .....110 B4
Freetown Bsns Pk 11
BL9 .....33 A4
Freightway LA3 .....217 E2
French Cl BB2 .....101 B4
French Rd BB2 .....101 B4
Frenchwood Ave
Lytham St Anne's FY8 .....90 F3
Frenchwood Ave *continued*
Preston PR1 .....97 B6
Frenchwood Com Prim Sch
PR1 .....97 B6
Frenchwood Knoll PR1 .....97 B6
Frenchwood St 4 PR1 .....97 A6
Freshfield Ave BB5 .....124 E3
Freshfield Ct L37 .....11 E4
Freshfield Cvn Pk L37 .....11 B6
Freshfield Prim Sch L37 .....12 A4
Freshfield Rd L37 .....11 E4
Freshfield Sta L37 .....11 E5
Freshfields PR2 .....116 D3
Friar St 24 LA1 .....214 F8
Friar's Moss Rd LA2 .....232 A8
Friar's Pas 23 LA1 .....214 F8
Friargate Horwich BL6 .....32 C4
Preston PR1 .....96 F8
Friargate Wlk 6 PR1 .....96 F7
Friars The PR2 .....117 E4
Friars Wlk L37 .....12 B2
Friary Cl PR4 .....114 C4
Friday St PR6 .....43 D8
Frieldhurst Rd OL14 .....109 C1
Frinton Gr FY2 .....152 E6
Frith's Ct PR5 .....98 F1
Friths Ave PR5 .....98 E1
Frobisher Dr FY8 .....110 D1
Frog La L40 .....26 D3
Frome St PR1 .....118 D1
Froom St PR6 .....43 F8
Fry St BB9 .....148 F8
Fryent Cl BL6 .....31 D2
Fryer Cl PR1 .....96 D1
Fulford Ave 1 PR2 .....116 C1
Fulham St BB9 .....170 F2
Full View BB2 .....81 B8
Fullers Terr OL13 .....87 F1
Fulmar Cres LA3 .....212 F5
Fulmar Terr BB5 .....103 E3
Fulmars The FY6 .....153 B2
Fulshaw Rd PR2 .....117 B2
Fulwood & Cadley Prim Sch
PR2 .....117 D4
Fulwood Ave
Becconsall PR4 .....73 F1
Blackpool FY3 .....130 F8
Southport PR8 .....35 D4
Fulwood Dr LA4 .....217 F6
Fulwood Hall Hospl
PR2 .....118 C5
Fulwood Hall La PR2 .....118 B4
Fulwood High Sch & Arts Coll
PR2 .....117 D6
Fulwood Hts PR2 .....118 C5
Fulwood Row PR2 .....118 E6
Funchal Ave L37 .....11 D1
Furlong Cres FY3 .....153 A1
Furlong Gn FY5 .....153 E8
Furlong La FY6 .....153 D5
Furness Ave
Blackburn BB1 .....102 B8
Fleetwood FY7 .....199 D1
Formby L37 .....11 F3
Lancaster LA1 .....211 B7
Normoss FY3 .....131 A8
Ormskirk L39 .....15 E4
Read BB12 .....145 D1
Furness Cl Chorley PR7 .....43 D5
Southport PR8 .....21 B3
Furness Ct 3 FY3 .....131 A8
Furness Dr
High Bentham LA2 .....239 D8
Poulton-le-F FY6 .....154 A3
Furness Rd LA3 .....216 D2
Furness St
7 Burnley BB10 .....148 B1
3 Lancaster LA1 .....218 B1
Furnessford Rd LA2 .....239 A6
Furnival Dr L40 .....25 D4
Further Ends Rd PR4 .....93 B6
Further Field PR5 .....78 A8
Further Heights Rd 1
OL12 .....52 F1
Further La BB2,PR5 .....100 A8
Further Wilworth BB1 .....122 E2
Furthergate BB1 .....102 B5
Furthergate Ind Est
BB1 .....102 B5
Fushetts La LA2 .....239 D8
Futura Pk BL6 .....32 C1
Fylde Ave Lancaster LA1 .....211 B7
Leyland PR26 .....76 E4
Fylde Coast Hospl FY3 .....130 F7
Fylde Ct FY6 .....199 D5
Fylde Rd
Lytham St Anne's FY8 .....90 D5
Poulton-le-F FY6 .....153 E4
Preston PR1,PR2 .....117 D1
Southport PR9 .....54 B4
Fylde Road Ind Est PR1 .....117 D1
Fylde St Kirkham PR4 .....114 A4
Preston PR1 .....96 E8
Fylde View Cl FY6 .....153 D2

G

Gabbot St PR7 .....31 A7
Gable Mews L37 .....12 A1
Gable The LA6 .....240 B7
Gables Pl LA4 .....217 D5
Gables The PR4 .....116 E4
Gadfield St 2 BB3 .....65 B8
Gadsby St FY1 .....130 B2
Gage St 32 LA1 .....214 F8
Gaghills Rd BB4 .....86 F1
Gaghills Terr 3 BB4 .....86 F1
Gainsborough Ave
Bamber Bridge PR5 .....77 A7
Blackburn BB2 .....101 C6
Burnley BB11 .....127 F3
Morecambe LA4 .....217 D6
Gainsborough Rd
Blackpool FY1 .....130 D4
Ramsbottom BL0 .....50 B1
Southport PR8 .....34 E3
Gaisgill Ave LA4 .....217 B3
Gait Barrows Nature Reserve* LA7 .....225 A7
Gale St OL12 .....52 F3
Gales La L40 .....40 A3
Galgate Silk Mills Ind Est
LA2 .....211 B4
Gall La OL14 .....109 C3
Galleries The 1 BB9 .....148 E8
Gallery The L37 .....11 F3
Galligreaves St BB2 .....101 D3
Galligreaves Way BB2 .....101 D3
Galloway Cl 2 OL10 .....33 F1
Galloway Cres FY2 .....152 F5
Galloway Dr WN8 .....10 B6
Galloway Rd FY7 .....198 F5
Gallows La PR3 .....142 A6
Galway Ave FY2 .....152 D3
Gamble Rd FY5 .....176 B4
Gambleside Cl BB4 .....106 A1
Game St BB6 .....124 C5
Gamull La PR2 .....118 F5
Gandy La OL12 .....52 D4
Gannow Bsns Pk BB12 .....127 B6
Gannow La BB12 .....127 C6
Gantley Ave WN5 .....10 D3
Gantley Cres WN5 .....10 D3
Gantley Rd WN5 .....10 D4
Ganton Cl PR8 .....35 E3
Ganton Ct PR1 .....96 A6
Garbett St BB5 .....104 A4
Garden Ave PR4 .....113 B4
Garden City BL0 .....50 A2
Garden Cl FY3 .....131 A2
Garden Pl LA6 .....240 C7
Garden Row OL12 .....52 D2
Garden St
Abbey Village PR6 .....80 C2
Accrington BB5 .....104 B7
11 Bacup OL13 .....70 C8
1 Bamber Bridge PR5 .....77 B7
6 Barnoldswick BB18 .....196 B2
Blackburn BB2 .....101 C4
Brierfield BB9 .....148 B5
Colne BB8 .....171 D4
Great Harwood BB6 .....124 C4
Higham BB12 .....146 F5
Kirkham PR4 .....114 A4
Lytham St Anne's FY8 .....89 E6
Nelson BB9 .....148 E8
Oswaldtwistle BB5 .....103 D4
Padiham BB12 .....146 C1
Preston PR1 .....96 F7
Ramsbottom BL0 .....50 C6
Ramsbottom,Brooksbottoms
BL0 .....50 C3
Garden Terr
17 Blackpool FY4 .....130 B1
Chorley PR7 .....61 C1
Heysham LA3 .....213 A2
Garden Vale Bsns Ctr 1
BB8 .....171 B4
Garden View Pl 1 FY4 .....130 E1
Garden Wlk
Cleveleys FY5 .....175 D5
Preston PR2 .....117 B1
Gardeners Mews 10
FY1 .....130 C7
Gardeners Row BB7 .....145 F7
Gardeners View L33 .....1 A6
Gardenia Cl PR6 .....78 B4
Gardens Gr LA4 .....217 A4
Gardens The Halton LA2 .....219 B6
Turton Bottoms BL7 .....48 D4
Gardiners Pl WN8 .....8 E8
Gardner Arc LA3 .....216 E4
Gardner Bldgs LA3 .....216 E4
Gardner Rd Formby L37 .....12 B4
Lancaster LA1 .....218 D2
Morecambe LA3 .....216 E3
Warton LA5 .....223 D5
Gardner St 18 PR1 .....96 F8
Gardner's La PR3 .....182 D3
Garfield Ave LA1 .....214 D7
Garfield Ct FY3 .....131 C2
Garfield Dr LA4 .....217 F4
Garfield St
Accrington BB5 .....104 D5
8 Cornholme OL14 .....109 C1
Fleetwood FY7 .....199 B5
Garfield Terr PR6 .....61 D2
Garland Gr 2 FY7 .....198 D3
Garner Ave BB2 .....81 D7
Garnet Cl 4 FY5 .....152 F7
Garnet St 3 LA1 .....215 A8
Garnett Gn L39 .....15 D4
Garnett Pl WN8 .....9 A7
Garnett Rd BB7 .....166 C7
Garnett St
Barrowford BB9 .....170 D2
Darwen BB3 .....82 B1
Morecambe LA4 .....217 B6
Ramsbottom BL0 .....50 B5
Garrick Gr FY3 .....130 E7
Garrick Par PR8 .....35 A6
Garrick St BB9 .....170 F2
Garrison Rd PR2 .....118 B3
Gars End LA2 .....238 D6
Gars The LA2 .....238 D6
Garsdale Ave BB10 .....148 B4
Garsdale Cl PR5 .....97 E5
Garsdale Rd PR2 .....118 E4
Garsden Ave BB1 .....102 E3
Garstang Cl FY6 .....153 C3
Garstang Com Prim Sch
PR3 .....181 C8
Garstang High Sch PR3 .....181 D5
Garstang New Rd FY6 .....154 E3
Garstang Rd
Bilsborrow PR3 .....159 A4
Bowgreave PR3 .....181 D4
Catterall PR3 .....181 E1
Chipping PR3 .....185 C2
Cockerham LA2,PR3 .....206 E2
Fulwood PR1,PR2,PR3 .....117 E5
Kirkham PR4 .....113 F6
Little Eccleston PR3,FY6 .....155 D5
Newsham PR3 .....137 B4
Singleton FY6 .....154 C3
Southport PR9 .....54 A5
St Michael's on W PR3 .....157 C7
Stake Pool PR3 .....202 B3
Garstang Rd E FY6 .....153 E3
Garstang Rd N PR4 .....113 F7
Garstang Rd S PR4 .....113 F6
Garstang Rd W FY3,FY6 .....153 B2
Garstang St BB3 .....82 A2
Garstang St Thomas' CE Prim Sch PR3 .....181 B6
Garston St BL9 .....33 A4
Garstone Croft PR2 .....117 D6
Garswood Cl
Brierfield BB12 .....147 F2
Maghull L31 .....5 E3
Garth Edge OL12 .....71 E6
Garton Ave FY4 .....110 D6
Gas Field Rd LA3 .....212 E2
Gas House La LA2 .....239 D8
Gas St Adlington PR7 .....31 A6
Bacup OL13 .....87 F2
8 Burnley BB11 .....127 F6
Haslingden BB4 .....84 F1
Longridge PR3 .....140 A8
Gas Terr PR25 .....77 B2
Gaskell Cl LA5 .....224 C3
Gaskell Cres FY5 .....176 A2
Gaskell Ho LA1 .....218 C4
Gaskell Rd PR1 .....96 E5
Gaskell St PR6 .....43 E8
Gate Ho PR1 .....96 E7
Gate St BB1 .....102 A5
Gatefield Ct BB11 .....128 A4
Gategill Gr WN5 .....10 D3
Gateland BB18 .....194 D8
Gates La L29 .....4 C1
Gatesgarth Ave PR2 .....117 F7
Gateside Ct 2 FY3 .....131 A8
Gateside Dr FY3 .....130 F8
Gateway Cl FY5 .....153 D7
Gathurst La WN6 .....19 F5
Gathurst Rd
Fulwood PR2 .....117 C2
Orrell WN5 .....10 E8
Gaulter's La FY6 .....200 C4
Gaw Hill La L39 .....15 B3
Gaw Hill View L39 .....15 B3
Gawthorpe Edge BB12 .....126 F8
Gawthorpe Hall* BB12 .....146 F1
Gawthorpe Rd BB12 .....127 D7
Gawthorpe St 18 BB12 .....146 C1
Gawthorpe View BB12 .....146 F5
Gaydon Way FY5 .....152 E7
Gaylands La BB18 .....197 C2
Gayle Way 1 BB5 .....103 F4
Gaythorne Ave PR1 .....97 F8
Geddes St BB2 .....100 F2
Geldof Dr FY1 .....130 C8
General St FY1 .....130 B6
Geneva Rd PR2 .....118 C4
Genoa St BB11 .....127 C4
Geoffrey Lodge 13 PR2 .....118 F4
Geoffrey St Bury BL9 .....33 A4
Chorley PR6 .....61 D1
Preston PR1 .....97 C8
Ramsbottom BL0 .....50 A4
George Ave
Blackpool FY4 .....130 F1
Great Harwood BB6 .....124 B4
George Dr PR8 .....21 E5
George La BB12 .....145 C2
George Rd BL0 .....50 B5
George St Accrington BB5 .....103 F4
4 Bacup OL13 .....70 C8
Barnoldswick BB18 .....196 C4
Blackburn BB2 .....101 E4
Blackpool FY1 .....130 C6
Burnley BB11 .....127 F5
Chorley PR7 .....43 C7
13 Clayton-le-M BB5 .....124 F3
Clitheroe BB7 .....166 D6
Darwen BB3 .....82 A2
1 Earby BB18 .....197 B1
Great Harwood BB6 .....124 C5
Haslingden BB4 .....85 B3
Horwich BL6 .....32 C3
3 Lancaster LA1 .....214 F7
Leyland PR25 .....77 B2
Longridge PR3 .....140 A8
11 Lytham St Anne's FY8 .....91 B3
Morecambe LA4 .....217 C5
Oswaldtwistle BB5 .....103 E5
Preston PR1 .....97 B7
Rishton BB1 .....124 B1
Whalley BB7 .....144 C5
Whitworth OL12 .....52 C8
George St W BB2 .....101 D4
George Terr WN5 .....10 D5
George's La Banks PR9 .....55 A7
Horwich BL6 .....32 E5
George's Rd PR1 .....96 F7
George's Row 2 BB4 .....69 F8
Georgian Pl L37 .....11 E1
Gerald Ct 4 BB11 .....128 B4
Gerard Way L33 .....1 A2
German La
Bolton Green PR7 .....42 D7
1 Coppull PR7 .....42 E1
Gerrard Pl WN8 .....8 F7
Gerrard St Lancaster LA1 .....214 D7
Preston PR1 .....96 E7
Gerrard's Fold PR6 .....80 B2
Gerrard's Terr FY6 .....153 C4
Gertrude St Nelson BB9 .....171 A2
Shawforth OL12 .....71 E6
Ghants La FY6 .....177 E2
Ghyll La BB18 .....196 E4
Ghyll Mdws BB18 .....196 D4
Giant Axe (Lancaster FC)
LA1 .....214 E8
Gib Hey La PR3 .....161 F7
Gib Hill La BB4 .....106 B2
Gib Hill Rd BB9 .....171 B1
Gib La Blackburn BB2 .....81 A7
Hoghton PR5 .....99 C3
Gibfield Rd BB8 .....171 A3
Gibfield Sch BB8 .....171 B2
Gibraltar Rd PR4 .....132 E5
Gibraltar St BB2 .....101 B6
Gibson St BB9 .....170 F2
Giddygate La L31 .....6 B1
Gidlow Ave PR6 .....31 A7
Gilbert Pl L40 .....25 B4
Gilbert St Brierfield BB10 .....148 E2
4 Chorley PR7 .....43 C6
Ramsbottom BL0 .....68 C1
Rawtenstall BB4 .....86 D1
Gilbertson Rd PR7 .....43 E2
Gildabrook Rd FY4 .....110 D5
Gilderdale Ct 2 FY8 .....91 C4
Gildow St 1 PR1 .....96 E8
Giles St Clitheroe BB7 .....166 E7
Nelson BB9 .....170 E1
Gilescroft Ave L33 .....1 A4
Gilett Farm Cvn Pk FY4 .....111 F5
Gilhouse Ave PR2 .....116 C1
Gill Ct FY4 .....110 B5
Gill La PR4 .....75 C5
Gill Nook PR4 .....75 A5
Gill St Burnley BB12 .....127 E6
Colne BB8 .....171 B3
Nelson BB9 .....170 D1
Gillcroft PR7 .....41 B7
Giller Cl PR1 .....96 F2
Giller Dr PR1 .....96 F2
Giller Fold 1 PR1 .....96 F2
Gillett St 6 PR1 .....118 C1
Gillhead Brow LA2 .....242 D1
Gillians BB18 .....194 B8
Gillians La BB18 .....194 B8
Gillibrand Cl PR1 .....96 C1
Gillibrand Ho PR7 .....61 C2
Gillibrand Prim Sch PR7 .....43 B6
Gillibrand St Chorley PR7 .....43 C7
Darwen BB3 .....81 F3
Walton-le-D PR5 .....97 D5
Gillibrand Wlks PR7 .....43 C7
Gillibrands Rd WN8 .....9 A7
Gillies St Accrington BB5 .....104 C6
Blackburn BB2 .....101 F3
Gillison Cl LA6 .....241 C2
Gillow Ave LA1 .....211 B7
Gillow Ct LA1 .....214 F5
Gillow Pk PR3 .....155 F6
Gillow Rd PR4 .....113 F5
Gills Croft BB7 .....167 A7
Gilpin Ave L31 .....5 E2
Gilpin Cl 2 LA1 .....218 A2
Gilstead Ave LA3 .....213 A8
Gin Bow PR7 .....43 D6
Gin Croft La BL0 .....68 E4
Gingham Brow BL6 .....32 E4
Girvan Gr BB11 .....127 D5
Girvan Wlk 1 OL10 .....33 F1
Gisburn Ave FY8 .....90 C6
Gisburn Gr Blackpool FY3 .....130 E7
Burnley BB10 .....128 D5
Gisburn Old Rd
Barnoldswick BB7,BB9 .....193 C7
Foulridge BB9 .....193 E4
Gisburn Prim Sch BB7 .....231 B3
Gisburn Rd
Barnoldswick BB18 .....196 A3
Barrowford BB9 .....170 E5
Bolton-by-B BB7 .....230 C4
Fulwood PR2 .....118 E4
Gisburn Road Prim Sch
BB18 .....196 B2
Gisburn St
Barnoldswick BB18 .....196 B3
Blackburn BB2 .....101 C4
Gisburne Park Hospl
BB7 .....231 B4
Gladden Pl WN8 .....8 E8
Glade The Blackburn BB2 .....81 D6
Morecambe LA4 .....217 E5
Glades The FY8 .....91 C4
Gladeswood Rd L33 .....1 B1
Gladeway FY5 .....153 D7
Gladstone Cres OL13 .....88 A2
Gladstone Rd PR9 .....35 F6
Gladstone St Bacup OL13 .....88 A2
Blackburn BB1 .....102 B6

Gladstone St *continued*
Blackpool FY4 130 C1
Bury BL9 33 B3
2 Cornholme OL14 109 B1
Great Harwood BB6 124 C5
Gladstone Terr
Abbey Village PR6 80 C1
16 Barrowford BB9 170 D3
Blackburn BB2 100 F1
3 Lancaster LA1 218 E1
Trawden BB8 172 B4
Gladstone Way 4 FY5 175 F1
Glaisdale Dr PR8 35 F3
Glamis Dr Chorley PR7 43 B8
Southport PR9 54 B3
Glamis Rd PR25 60 C8
Glamorgan Gr BB12 127 A7
Glangarry 7 FY8 91 C3
Glasson Cl BB2 101 F1
Glastonbury Ave FY1 130 E2
Gleb Mews PR4 115 D2
Glebe Cl Accrington BB5 104 B5
Burton-in-K LA6 240 C7
Fulwood PR2 117 F4
Maghull L31 5 B1
Standish WN6 29 F1
Glebe Cotts BB4 85 A6
Glebe Ct 20 LA1 215 A8
Glebe La Banks PR9 55 A7
Kirkham PR4 114 C4
Glebe Pl PR8 35 B7
Glebe Rd Skelmersdale WN8 9 A8
Standish WN6 29 F1
Glebe St Burnley BB11 128 B4
Great Harwood BB6 124 C5
Glebe The PR26 59 B8
Glebelands PR4 57 A5
Gledhill Way BL7 48 A1
Gledstone View BB18 196 A3
Glegside Rd L33 1 A2
Glen Cottage (Youth Hostel) BB18 197 D2
Glen Cres OL13 70 A8
Glen Dr WN6 19 E8
Glen Eldon Rd FY8 89 E7
Glen Garth BB18 196 D3
Glen Gdns OL12 52 F2
Glen Gr PR2 118 F5
Glen Park Dr PR4 73 D4
Glen Rd BB4 69 F8
Glen Royd 1 OL12 52 C1
Glen Sq BB11 127 F2
Glen St Bacup OL13 70 E8
Blackpool FY3 130 E4
Burnley BB11 127 E6
Colne BB8 171 D6
Ramsbottom BL0 50 B7
Glen The Blackburn BB2 81 D6
Caton LA2 237 C3
Fulwood PR2 118 F2
Knott End-on-S FY6 199 E4
Glen Top OL13 70 A8
Glen View PR3 141 B8
Glen View Ave LA3 212 E6
Glen View Cres LA3 212 E6
Glen View Dr LA3 212 E6
Glen View Rd BB11 127 E2
Glen View St 1 OL14 109 B1
Glen Way BB9 148 B6
Glenapp Ave FY4 111 A6
Glenarden Ave FY5 152 F8
Glenavon Dr OL12 52 D3
Glenbeck Cl BL6 32 D1
Glenborough Ave OL13 70 C8
Glenbrook Cl BB2 117 A6
Glenburn High Sch WN8 9 B8
Glenburn Rd WN8 18 A1
Glencarron Cl BB3 65 F8
Glencoe Ave
Blackpool FY3 153 A1
Hoddlesden BB3 82 E1
Glencoe Cl OL10 33 F1
Glencourse Dr PR2 118 D5
Glencoyne Dr PR9 54 B5
Glencroft PR7 60 C3
Glencross Pl FY4 110 E7
Glendale Ave PR5 97 C1
Glendale Cl
Blackpool FY2 152 F5
Burnley BB11 128 A3
Leyland PR25 60 B7
Poulton-le-F FY6 153 C3
Glendale Cres PR5 97 C1
Glendale Dr BB2 121 E2
Glendale Gr
Fulwood PR2 118 D2
Kirkby L33 1 A5
Glendale Way L37 11 F2
Glenden Foot OL12 52 D2
Glendene Pk BB1 122 E5
Glendor Rd BB10 128 E5
Gleneagles Ave BB3 82 E1
Gleneagles Ct PR4 114 B4
Gleneagles Dr
Brockhall Village BB6 143 C6
Euxton PR7 60 D4
Fulwood PR2 117 B7
Higher Penwortham PR1 96 A6
Morecambe LA4 217 D6
Southport PR8 21 C3
Gleneagles Way 1 BL0 50 B5
Glenfield Ave FY2 152 E6
Glenfield Cl BB1 102 B7
Glenfield Cvn Site PR3 201 C5
Glenfield Park Ind Est
Blackburn BB1 102 B7
Nelson BB9 171 A1
Glenfield Rd BB9 171 A1
Glengreave Ave BB1 122 E3
Glenholme Gdns FY6 153 C2
Glenluce Cres BB1 102 D3
Glenluce Dr PR1 97 F8
Glenmarsh Way L37 12 B3
Glenmere Cres FY5 152 C7
Glenmore PR6 78 A3
Glenmore Ave FY5 176 B2
Glenmore Cl BB5 104 E2
Glenmore Rd BL0 49 F2
Glenpark Dr PR9 54 B4
Glenrose Terr PR8 35 A5
Glenroy Ave BB8 171 D6
Glenroyd Cl FY3 130 E3
Glenroyd Dr L40 25 E4
Glenshiels Ave BB3 65 E8
Glenside WN6 28 B2
Glentworth Rd E LA4 217 D3
Glentworth Rd W LA4 217 C3
Glenview Cl PR2 119 A3
Glenview Ct PR2 119 A3
Glenway PR1 96 C4
Glenwood St 3 FY3 130 D5
Global Way BB3 82 A5
Globe La BL7 47 D3
Globe Mill 7 BB4 86 F2
Glossop Cl FY2 152 C6
Gloucester Ave
Accrington BB5 104 A7
Blackpool FY1 130 D4
8 Clayton-le-M BB5 124 F3
Cleveleys FY5 175 D3
Horwich BL6 32 D2
Lancaster LA1 215 A4
Leyland PR25 77 C3
Gloucester Ct
5 Blackpool FY1 130 D4
Horwich BL6 32 D2
Gloucester Dr LA3 216 E3
Gloucester Rd
Blackburn BB1 102 D5
Chorley PR7 43 C6
Lytham St Anne's FY8 90 D4
Rishton BB1 103 A8
Southport PR8 34 F5
Glover Cl PR26 58 F6
Glover Rd PR7 29 D7
Glover St Horwich BL6 32 B4
Preston PR1 97 A7
Glover's Ct 23 PR1 97 A7
Glynn St BB5 103 F7
Godiva St BB10 148 A1
Godley St BB11 128 B6
Godwin Ave 7 FY3 130 E3
Goe La PR4 93 B6
Goit St Blackburn BB2 101 C2
Newchurch BB4 86 F1
Goitside BB9 170 E1
Golbourne St PR1 118 B1
Goldacre La BB6 124 A7
Goldburn Cl PR2 116 F6
Golden Hill 9 PR25 77 B2
Golden Hill La PR25 76 F2
Golden Hill PRU PR25 76 E2
Golden Way PR1 96 C3
Goldfield Ave BB10 128 F6
Goldfinch Dr BL9 33 C4
Goldfinch St PR1 118 B1
Goldhey St 13 BB1 102 A7
Goldsboro Ave FY3 130 F3
Goldshaw Cl BB12 169 C3
Goldstone Dr FY5 152 F7
Golf Rd L37 11 E5
Golf View PR2 117 A6
Golgotha Rd LA1 215 A6
Golgotha Village LA1 215 B7
Gonder La PR3 182 E3
Gooch St BL6 32 C2
Good Shaw Fold Cl BB4 106 A2
Good St PR1 96 E7
Goodall Cl BB18 197 B2
Goodenber Cres 15 LA2 239 D8
Goodenber Rd LA2 239 D8
Goodshaw Ave
Blackburn BB1 122 E1
Goodshaw Chapel BB4 106 A1
Goodshaw Ave N BB4 106 A2
Goodshaw Chapel* BB4 106 B1
Goodshaw Cl BB1 101 E8
Goodshaw Fold Rd BB4 105 F2
Goodshaw La
Accrington BB5 105 C1
Goodshaw Chapel BB4 106 B2
Goodwood Ave
Blackpool FY2 152 D1
Fulwood PR2 117 F7
Slyne LA2 218 D8
Goodwood Ct LA1 215 B4
Goodwood Rd LA1 215 B4
Goose Cote Hill BL7 47 E1
Goose Foot Cl PR5 99 D7
Goose Foot Cott PR5 99 D4
Goose Foot La PR5 99 C6
Goose Green Ave PR7 42 F1
Goose Green La BB8 172 B2
Goose Hill St 13 OL13 87 F3
Goose House La BB3 82 A3
Goose Lane Cotts PR3 185 E1
Goosebutts La BB7 166 F7
Gooselands BD24 236 F6
Gooseleach La BB12 145 E1
Goosnargh La PR3 138 B7
Goosnargh Whitechapel Prim Sch PR3 160 D7
Gordale Cl
Barnoldswick BB18 196 A2
Blackpool FY4 111 A8
Gordon Ave
Accrington BB5 104 A4
Maghull L31 5 C3
Southport PR9 53 C1
Thornton FY5 176 B2
Gordon Ho 11 PR9 35 C8
Gordon Rd
Fleetwood FY7 198 F3
Lytham St Anne's FY8 90 D4
8 Nelson BB9 170 D1
Gordon St Bacup OL13 87 F4
14 Blackpool FY4 130 B1
Burnley BB12 127 F7
Chorley PR6 43 D7
Church BB5 103 E5
Clayton-le-M BB5 125 A2
Colne BB8 171 F5
Darwen BB3 82 A3
Preston PR1 117 E1
Rawtenstall BB4 85 F2
Southport PR9 35 C8
Worsthorne BB10 129 B6
Gordon Terr 1 LA1 215 A5
Gordon Way OL10 33 F1
Gordonstoun Cres WN5 10 F7
Gordonstoun Pl
Blackburn BB2 101 C3
8 Thornton FY5 176 A2
Gore Cl BL9 33 C1
Gore Dr L39 15 E3
Gores La L37 11 F5
Gores Rd L33 1 C1
Goring St PR7 43 D7
Gornall's Bldgs 7 BB4 85 E2
Gorple Gn BB10 129 B5
Gorple Rd BB10 129 D5
Gorple St BB10 148 E3
Gorrell Cl BB12 169 D2
Gorse Ave FY5 175 F3
Gorse Bank BL9 33 C3
Gorse Cl
Great Knowley PR6 61 E5
Tarleton PR4 57 A6
Gorse Gr Fulwood PR2 118 E3
Haslingden BB4 68 A8
Longton PR4 95 A1
Gorse La PR4 56 D5
Gorse Rd Blackburn BB2 101 B5
Blackpool FY3 130 E4
Gorse St BB1 102 B6
Gorse Way L37 11 C4
Gorsefield L37 12 A6
Gorsewood Rd PR25 76 E1
Gorsey Brow WN6 29 B2
Gorsey La Banks PR9 55 C7
Haskayne L39 13 B7
Hightown L38 3 B2
Mawdesley L40 40 C1
Gorsey Pl WN8 9 B7
Gorst La L40,PR9 25 A6
Gorsuch La L39,L40 23 D4
Gorton Fold BL6 32 C3
Gorton St FY1 130 C6
Gosforth Rd
Blackpool FY2 152 C1
Southport PR9 35 F8
Gough La
Clayton Brook PR5 78 C5
Walton Summit PR5 78 B6
Goulding Ave PR25 77 B1
Goulding St PR7 43 D6
Gowans La PR6 79 A8
Gower Ct PR26 76 D3
Gower Gdns L40 25 F3
Gower Gr PR4 75 A5
Goyt St FY8 89 F7
Grab La LA1 215 C7
Graburn Rd L37 11 F4
Gracamy Ave PR4 92 D5
Grace St BL6 32 B3
Gradwell St 2 PR1 96 E8
Grafton Ave
Accrington BB5 104 E2
Brierfield BB10 148 B5
Grafton Ct 3 Chorley PR7 43 B5
12 Darwen BB3 81 F2
Grafton Dr PR8 21 A5
Grafton Pl LA3 216 E3
Grafton Rd Fulwood PR2 118 F4
Morecambe LA3 216 E3
Grafton St Adlington PR7 30 F6
Blackburn BB2 101 D2
Blackpool FY1 130 C7
Clitheroe BB7 166 F8
Nelson BB9 170 F1
Preston PR1 96 E6
Grafton Terr 11 BB3 81 F2
Grafton Villas OL13 87 F1
Graham Ave
Appley Bridge WN6 28 C2
Bamber Bridge PR5 77 C8
Graham Rd PR3 204 C2
Graham St
Hoddlesden BB3 82 F1
Lancaster LA1 214 F6
Morecambe LA4 217 A5
1 Padiham BB12 126 D7
4 Preston PR1 118 B1
Grampian Way FY8 91 D5
Granary The FY5 176 A2
Granby Ave FY3 130 E8
Granby Cl PR9 53 F3
Granby St BB12 127 D6
Grand Manor Dr FY8 90 D7
Grane Pk BB4 85 A2
Grane Rd BB4 84 C2
Grane St BB4 85 B2
Grange Ave
Barrowford BB9 170 F5
Fulwood PR2 118 F4
Fulwood PR2 119 A4
Great Harwood BB6 124 C6
Rawtenstall BB4 86 B3
Southport PR9 35 E8
Thornton FY5 176 B2
Grange Cl
Great Harwood BB6 124 C6
Hoghton PR5 99 B4
Knott End-on-S FY6 199 F6
Oswaldtwistle BB5 104 A3
Rawtenstall BB4 86 B2
Grange Cres BB4 86 A2
Grange Ct 13 FY1 130 C7
Grange Dr Coppull PR7 29 D8
Coupe Green PR5 98 E4
Euxton PR7 60 C4
Grange Farm Cotts PR4 93 E5
Grange Gdns FY6 153 D2
Grange La
Accrington BB5 104 C5
Formby L37 11 E5
Hutton PR4 94 D3
Newton-w-S PR4 114 F2
Stalmine FY6 177 B7
Grange Park Cl PR1 96 A6
Grange Park Way BB4 84 F1
Grange Pl PR2 118 F4
Grange Rd Blackburn BB2 101 B2
Blackpool FY3 130 F7
Edgworth BL7 48 C1
Elswick PR4 155 F1
Fleetwood FY7 198 D3
Fulwood PR2 117 C3
Hambleton FY6 177 D1
Hightown L38 2 E6
Holme Chapel BB10 108 A7
Leyland PR25 76 D2
Lytham St Anne's FY8 89 E7
Rawtenstall BB4 86 B2
Singleton FY6 155 A3
Southport PR9 35 E7
Whitworth OL12 71 D3
Grange St
Accrington BB5 104 C5
Barnoldswick BB18 196 A3
Burnley BB11 127 E5
Clayton-le-M BB5 124 E3
Morecambe LA4 217 E6
2 Rawtenstall BB4 86 A2
Grange Terr 19 BB4 86 A3
Grange The Arnside LA5 224 A8
Cottam PR4 116 E5
Edgworth BL7 48 E5
Lytham St Anne's FY8 90 E3
Southport PR9 54 C3
Wilpshire BB1 122 F5
Grange View
Carnforth LA5 223 D3
Hest Bank LA5 220 F3
Grange View Rd LA6 221 F6
Grangefield PR4 94 F1
Granings The PR4 116 D6
Granny's Bay FY8 90 C3
Grant Cl LA1 214 D7
Grant Dr PR4 75 A5
Grant Mews BL0 50 B7
Grant Rd BB2 101 B3
Grant St Accrington BB5 104 A6
Burnley BB11 127 E5
Grantham Cl PR8 35 A1
Grantham Rd
5 Blackpool FY1 130 C7
Southport PR8 35 A1
Weeton Camp PR4 132 E6
Grantham St BB2 101 B2
Granton Cl L37 11 E3
Granton Wlk PR2 117 A4
Grants La BL0 50 C6
Granville Ave
Becconsall PR4 73 E2
Maghull L31 5 C2
Granville Cl L39 6 B8
Granville Ct Chorley PR6 61 E1
Southport PR9 53 D1
Granville Gdns BB5 104 D3
Granville Pk L39 6 C8
Granville Pk W L39 6 B8
Granville Rd
Accrington BB5 104 D3
Blackburn BB2 101 B5
Blackpool FY1 130 D5
Brierfield BB9 148 C6
Chorley PR6 61 E1
Darwen BB3 64 F8
Great Harwood BB6 124 D6
Lancaster LA1 218 C3
Morecambe LA3 216 E3
Southport PR8 34 D4
Granville St Adlington PR6 31 A7
Brierfield BB10 148 F2
14 Burnley BB10 128 A8
Colne BB8 171 E5
Haslingden BB4 68 A7
Grape La PR26 58 C1
Grasmere Ave
Blackburn BB1 122 C1
3 Fleetwood FY7 198 E4
Leyland PR25 77 A3
Orrell WN5 10 F8
Padiham BB12 146 C1
Skelmersdale WN8 10 B7
Grasmere Ave *continued*
Thornton FY5 176 B2
Grasmere Cl
Accrington,Hillock Vale BB5 104 E8
Bamber Bridge PR5 97 D2
Colne BB8 172 A5
Euxton PR7 60 E1
Fulwood PR2 118 C4
8 High Bentham LA2 239 D8
Rishton BB1 124 A1
Grasmere Dr 9 LA2 239 D8
Grasmere Gr
Longridge PR3 139 F5
Whittle-le-W PR6 61 B7
Grasmere Rd
Blackpool FY1 130 D2
Formby L37 11 D3
Haslingden BB4 68 C8
Hightown L38 3 A4
Knott End-on-S FY6 199 F6
Lancaster LA1 215 A8
Lytham St Anne's FY8 110 E1
Maghull L31 5 D2
Morecambe LA4 217 E6
Grasmere St
Burnley BB10 148 A2
10 Rochdale OL12 52 F1
Grasmere Terr
Bacup OL13 87 F4
Chorley PR7 43 B5
Grassington Dr
Brierfield BB10 148 D3
Bury BL9 33 D1
Grassington Pl 4 FY5 152 F8
Grassington Rd FY8 90 C7
Gratton Pl WN8 9 A8
Grave-Yard La L39 7 A6
Gravel Cl PR9 54 F5
Gravel La Banks PR9 54 F5
Banks PR9 55 B3
Gravel The PR4 55 F2
Graver Weir Terr BB4 107 A1
Graving Dock Rd FY8 91 D4
Gravners Field FY5 176 D2
Grayrigg Dr LA4 217 B3
Grays Pl LA3 216 E2
Great Arley Sch FY5 176 B3
Great Avenham St 3 PR1 97 A6
Great Bolton St BB2 101 E3
Great Close La BD23, BD24 236 D6
Great Croft Cl BB18 196 A3
Great Eaves Rd BL0 50 C7
Great Eccleston Copp CE Prim Sch PR3 156 A3
Great Flatt OL12 52 B1
Great George St
Colne BB8 171 D5
Preston PR1 118 A1
Great Gill PR4 75 A5
Great Greens La PR5 78 C5
Great Hanover St PR1 118 A1
Great Harwood Prim Sch BB6 124 B5
Great Hay PR4 74 E2
Great Hey PR4 74 E2
Great House Barn Rivington* BL6 31 F8
Great John St 20 LA1 214 F8
Great Lee OL12 52 D3
Great Lee Wlk OL12 52 D2
Great Mdw
Bamber Bridge PR5 77 A8
Chorley PR7 61 A2
Great Shaw St PR1 96 F8
Great Stone of Fourstones* LA2 239 D5
Great Stones Cl BL7 47 E2
Great Townley St PR1 97 D8
Great Tunstead PR4 75 A7
Great Wood Cl PR7 42 F6
Great Wood Prim Sch LA4 217 E5
Greave Cl Bacup OL13 88 B3
Rawtenstall BB4 86 A4
Greave Clough Cl 9 OL13 88 A3
Greave Clough Dr OL13 88 B3
Greave Cres 10 OL13 88 A3
Greave Rd OL13 88 B3
Greave Terr OL13 88 B3
Greaves Cl
Appley Bridge WN6 19 F8
Banks PR9 55 A6
Greaves Ct 3 LA1 215 A5
Greaves Dr LA1 214 F6
Greaves Hall Ave PR9 55 A5
Greaves Mdw PR1 96 E2
Greaves Mead LA1 214 F5
Greaves Rd LA1 214 F6
Greaves St
Great Harwood BB6 124 C4
Haslingden BB4 84 F2
9 Preston PR1 97 A7
Greaves The LA1 215 A6
Greaves-Town La PR2 116 E1
Grebe Cl FY3 131 B7
Grebe Wharf 2 LA1 218 E1
Green Acre PR3 138 D6
Green Acres PR4 93 C7
Green Ave FY4 110 C6
Green Bank
5 Bacup OL13 70 D8
Barnoldswick BB18 196 D4
Green Bank Bsns Pk BB1 102 C7

Green Bridge N BB4 . . . . . .69 E7
Green Bridge S BB4 . . . . . .69 E7
Green Brook Cl BL9 . . . . . .33 A4
Green Cl BB11 . . . . .127 E2
Green Close Pk BB2 . . . .101 C2
Green Dick's La PR3 . . . .200 E5
Green Dr
Bamber Bridge PR5 . . . . .97 C1
Barton PR3 . . . . .137 B8
Cleveleys FY5 . . . . .175 C5
Clitheroe BB7 . . . . .190 A2
Fulwood PR2 . . . . .117 E7
Higher Penwortham PR1 . . . .96 B5
Lytham St Anne's FY8 . . . . . .91 C5
Poulton-le-F FY6 . . . . .131 E8
Green End PR5 . . . . .99 E7
Green End Ave BB18 . . . .197 B2
Green End Barn BB18 . . .197 B1
Green End Cl 12 OL13 . . . .88 A3
Green End Rd BB18 . . . . .197 B1
Green Gate Fulwood PR2 .117 C3
Hutton PR4 . . . . .95 C1
Green Haworth CE Prim Sch
BB5 . . . . .104 B1
Green Head Cotts 6
LA2 . . . . .239 B8
Green Hey
Lytham St Anne's FY8 . . . . . .91 D4
Much Hoole PR4 . . . . .74 E3
Green Heys Dr L31 . . . . .5 F1
Green Hill OL13 . . . . .88 A1
Green Hill La LA2,LA6 . . .237 B6
Green Hill Rd OL13 . . . . . . .88 A1
Green Howarth View
BB5 . . . . .104 A3
Green La Banks PR9 . . . . . .55 C4
Bilsborrow PR3 . . . . .159 B2
Bispham Green L40 . . . . .27 B7
Blackburn BB2 . . . . .101 A1
Bretherton PR26 . . . . .58 C7
Chipping PR3 . . . . .185 F3
Coppull PR7 . . . . .30 A8
Cowan Bridge LA6 . . . . . . .242 B6
Downham BB7 . . . . .191 B6
Farington PR26 . . . . .76 E7
Formby L37 . . . . .11 F5
Freckleton PR4 . . . . .93 B6
Garstang PR3 . . . . .181 A7
Grindleton BB7 . . . . .190 A7
Halton LA2 . . . . .219 F8
Holmes PR4 . . . . .56 C4
Horton BD23 . . . . .231 E5
Horwich BL6 . . . . .32 B5
Kingsfold PR4 . . . . .96 C1
Lancaster LA1,LA2 . . . . . . .218 E6
Lancaster,Bailrigg LA1,
LA2 . . . . .211 A7
Longridge PR3 . . . . .140 B8
Maghull L31 . . . . .5 A2
Maghull L31 . . . . .5 C1
Morecambe LA3 . . . . .217 B2
Ormskirk L39 . . . . .15 E6
Orrell WN5 . . . . .10 D3
Padiham BB12 . . . . .126 C8
Preesall FY6 . . . . .200 C2
Riley Green PR5 . . . . .79 E8
Samlesbury Bottoms PR5 . . .99 B7
Skelmersdale L40 . . . . .18 A6
Sollom PR4 . . . . .56 D1
Standish WN6 . . . . .29 D1
Woodsfold PR4 . . . . .135 E6
Green La E PR3 . . . . .204 C2
Green La The L40 . . . . .25 F4
Green La W
Freckleton PR4 . . . . .93 B5
Garstang PR3 . . . . .204 B1
Green Lane Ave L39 . . . . . .15 E6
Green Link L31 . . . . .5 B2
Green Mdw BB8 . . . . .172 B2
Green Meadow La FY6 . . .177 C1
Green Mount BB6 . . . . . . .144 D8
Green Nook La PR3 . . . . .139 F6
Green Oak Pl FY5 . . . . . . .153 A8
Green Park Ct BB7 . . . . . .144 D8
Green Park Dr L31 . . . . .5 B1
Green Park Prim Sch L31 . . .5 B2
Green Pk BB7 . . . . .144 C5
Green Pl PR5 . . . . .78 A6
Green Rd BB8 . . . . .171 D4
Green Ridge Cl BB9 . . . . .148 D5
Green Row BB3 . . . . .81 B6
Green St Adlington PR6 . . . .31 B8
12 Barnoldswick BB18 . . . . .196 B2
Burnley BB10 . . . . .148 B1
Chorley PR7 . . . . .43 A5
Darwen BB3 . . . . .82 A1
Edenfield BL0 . . . . .68 E3
Great Harwood BB6 . . . . . . .124 B5
Lancaster LA1 . . . . .218 E1
Lytham St Anne's FY8 . . . . . .91 A3
Morecambe LA4 . . . . .217 B6
Oswaldtwistle BB5 . . . . . . .103 C2
Padiham BB12 . . . . .126 C7
Rawtenstall BB4 . . . . .86 A3
Green St E 17 BB3 . . . . . . .82 A1
Green The Adlington PR6 . . .43 F2
Bispham Green L40 . . . . .27 B8
Bolton-le-S LA5 . . . . .221 B5
Churchtown PR3 . . . . .181 A2
Colne BB8 . . . . .171 F6
5 Darwen BB3 . . . . .82 A1
Eccleston PR7 . . . . .41 C6
Fulwood PR2 . . . . .118 F2
Hesketh Bank PR4 . . . . .73 E3
Nelson BB9 . . . . .171 B2
Parbold WN8 . . . . .27 B2
Ramsbottom BL8 . . . . .49 F1
Silverdale LA5 . . . . .224 D2
Green The *continued*
Weeton PR4 . . . . .132 F2
Wrea Green PR4 . . . . .113 B3
Green Way 4 FY4 . . . . . . .110 F7
Green Wlk Blackrod BL6 . . .31 D1
Earby BB18 . . . . .197 A1
Southport PR8 . . . . .21 D5
Green's La Haskayne L31 . .14 C1
Maghull L31 . . . . .5 C8
Stalmine FY6 . . . . .177 F7
Greenacre Blackburn BB3 . .81 F6
Westhead L40 . . . . .16 E4
Greenacre Cl BL0 . . . . .50 E7
Greenacre Ct LA1 . . . . . . .215 B3
Greenacre Pk LA2 . . . . . .220 E2
Greenacre Rd LA2 . . . . . .220 E2
Greenacre St BB7 . . . . . . .166 E7
Greenacres Chorley PR7 . . .43 C5
Edgworth BL7 . . . . .48 E6
Fulwood PR2 . . . . .117 B7
Read BB12 . . . . .145 D2
Greenacres Ave PR4 . . . .114 A4
Greenacres Dr PR3 . . . . .181 D6
Greenacres The PR4 . . . . .95 D2
Greenbank
4 Horwich BL6 . . . . .32 D1
Ormskirk L39 . . . . .15 C2
Poulton-le-F FY6 . . . . .153 E3
Whitworth OL12 . . . . .52 C5
Greenbank Ave
Maghull L31 . . . . .5 C3
Orrell WN5 . . . . .10 D3
Preston PR1 . . . . .117 D2
Greenbank Dr
Fence BB12 . . . . .147 E8
Southport PR8 . . . . .34 E2
Greenbank High Sch PR8 .34 E1
Greenbank Pk BB4 . . . . . . .86 B2
Greenbank Pl PR1 . . . . . .117 E1
Greenbank Rd
Blackburn BB1 . . . . .102 B6
Middleworth Green PR1 . . . .96 E4
Rochdale OL12 . . . . .52 F2
Greenbank Sch OL12 . . . . . .52 F1
Greenbank St
Preston PR1 . . . . .117 D2
Preston PR1 . . . . .117 E1
Rawtenstall BB4 . . . . .86 B2
Greenbank Terr BB3 . . . . . .81 F6
Greenbank Way BB1 . . . .102 C6
Greenbanks FY2 . . . . .152 F3
Greenbarn Way BL6 . . . . . .31 D1
Greenberfield La BB18 . .196 C4
Greenbriar Cl FY3 . . . . . .152 F1
Greenbrook Cl BB12 . . . .126 F6
Greenbrook Rd BB12 . . . .126 F6
Greenbrook St 6 BL9 . . . .33 A4
Greencliffe La BB10 . . . . .129 A1
Greencroft PR1 . . . . .96 D3
Greendale Ave BB4 . . . . . .86 E2
Greendale Cl
Fleetwood FY7 . . . . .198 C2
Southward Bottom BB10 . . .108 A7
Greendale Dr LA5 . . . . . .223 D3
Greendale Mews 1
PR2 . . . . .116 E2
Greendale View BB7 . . . .190 B8
Greenfield Ave
Chatburn BB7 . . . . .190 D5
Clitheroe BB7 . . . . .166 C8
Parbold WN8 . . . . .27 B2
Greenfield Cl PR9 . . . . . . .54 A3
Greenfield Ct 2 LA1 . . . .215 A7
Greenfield Dr PR5 . . . . . . .77 A8
Greenfield Gdns 1 BB4 . . .85 B2
Greenfield Ho 18 LA1 . . .215 A8
Greenfield La PR3 . . . . . .161 A6
Greenfield Park (Cvn Pk)
PR4 . . . . .93 F8
Greenfield Rd
Adlington PR6 . . . . .31 A8
Blackpool FY5 . . . . .152 E8
Burnley BB10 . . . . .128 D4
Chorley PR6 . . . . .43 E8
Colne BB8 . . . . .171 A4
Colne BB8 . . . . .171 D4
Fleetwood FY7 . . . . .198 F2
Southport PR8 . . . . .36 C1
Greenfield St Darwen BB3 .65 C6
Haslingden BB4 . . . . .85 B3
12 Lancaster LA1 . . . . .215 A8
Rawtenstall BB4 . . . . .86 A3
Greenfield Terr
3 Cornholme OL14 . . . . . . .109 A1
Oswaldtwistle BB5 . . . . . . .103 A1
Greenfield View BB3 . . . . .82 A7
Greenfield Way PR2 . . . . .117 B5
Greenfields Blackburn BB2 .81 D7
Caton LA2 . . . . .237 C3
Hesketh Bank PR4 . . . . .73 D4
Greenfields Cres PR4 . . . .113 E6
Greenfinch Ct FY3 . . . . . .131 B6
Greenfold Dr BB4 . . . . . . .106 A2
Greenfoot 5 LA2 . . . . . . .239 B8
Greenfoot La LA2 . . . . . .239 D8
Greenford Cl WN5 . . . . . . .10 D6
Greenford Rd PR8 . . . . . . .21 C4
Greengate FY5 . . . . .176 D2
Greengate Cl 6 BB12 . . . .127 D7
Greengate La LA5 . . . . . .221 C8
Greenhalgh La
Adlington PR6 . . . . .31 B8
Greenhalgh PR4 . . . . .133 D4
Greenhall Cl PR3 . . . . . . .181 D6
Greenham Ave L33 . . . . .1 A6
Greenhaven WN8 . . . . .10 B7
Greenhead Ave BB1 . . . . .102 B7
Greenhead La BB12 . . . . .147 D5
Greenhey Pl WN8 . . . . .8 F8
Greenheys Ave FY6 . . . . .153 B4
Greenheys Cres BL8 . . . . . .49 F1
Greenhill BB6 . . . . .124 B5
Greenhill Ave PR4 . . . . . .114 A6
Greenhill Pl 2 FY1 . . . . .130 C6
Greenholme Ave LA4 . . . .217 B3
Greenhurst Cl BB2 . . . . . .101 D4
Greenings La PR9 . . . . .37 C3
Greenland Ave WN6 . . . . . .29 E1
Greenland La PR6 . . . . . . .31 D5
Greenlands Cres PR2 . . .118 E3
Greenlea Cl WN5 . . . . .10 D5
Greenlea Dr LA4 . . . . .217 D5
Greenloon's Dr L37 . . . . . .11 C3
Greenloon's Wlk L37 . . . . .11 C2
Greenmead Cl PR4 . . . . . .116 E5
Greenmoor La PR3 . . . . . .141 B7
Greenmount Ave
1 Kirkham PR4 . . . . .114 A5
1 Thornton FY5 . . . . .176 A3
Greenmount Cl BL8 . . . . . .49 F2
Greenmount Dr BL8 . . . . . .49 F2
Greenmount Prim Sch
BL8 . . . . .49 F2
Greenock Cl BB11 . . . . . . .127 D4
Greenock Dr OL10 . . . . . . .33 F1
Greenock St BB11 . . . . . .127 D4
Greenpark Cl BL8 . . . . .49 F1
Greens Arms Rd BB3,BL7 .47 E7
Greens La Bacup OL13 . . . .88 A3
Bacup,Nun Hills OL13 . . . . . .70 D7
Haslingden BB4 . . . . .68 C7
Greens The OL12 . . . . .71 C1
Greenset Cl LA1 . . . . .218 C4
Greenside Cottam PR4 . . .116 D4
Euxton PR7 . . . . .60 C3
Ribchester PR3 . . . . .141 E3
Greenside Ave
Blackburn BB2 . . . . .81 A8
Preston PR2 . . . . .116 C1
Greenside Cl
Hawkshaw BL8 . . . . .49 B3
Kirkby L33 . . . . .1 A6
Greenside Dr BL8 . . . . .49 F1
Greenside Gdns PR26 . . . . .59 B7
Greenslate Ave WN6 . . . . .19 E8
Greenslate Ct WN5 . . . . . . .10 E3
Greenslate Rd WN5 . . . . . .10 E3
Greensnook La OL13 . . . . .88 A3
Greensnook Mews 5
OL13 . . . . .88 A3
Greensnook Terr 1
OL13 . . . . .88 A3
Greenstone Ave BL6 . . . . . .32 B3
Greensward Cl WN6 . . . . . .29 B1
Greensway PR3 . . . . .137 C3
Greenthorn Cres PR2 . . . .119 A2
Greenthorne Cl BL7 . . . . . .48 E7
Greenthorne Terr 2 BB3 . .65 A8
Greenvale WN6 . . . . .19 F4
Greenville Dr L31 . . . . .5 C1
Greenwater Ct 7 LA1 . . .218 D2
Greenway Catterall PR3 . .181 D3
Eccleston PR7 . . . . .41 B7
Fulwood PR2 . . . . .117 D7
Higher Penwortham PR1 . . . .96 B4
Horwich BL6 . . . . .32 F3
Greenway Ave WN8 . . . . . . .9 B8
Greenway Cl WN8 . . . . .17 E2
Greenway Ho FY6 . . . . . . .153 E3
Greenway Mews BL0 . . . . . .50 C4
Greenway St BB3 . . . . .81 F3
Greenways Becconsall PR4 .73 F1
Lytham St Anne's FY8 . . . . . .90 B6
Orrell WN5 . . . . .10 D3
Over Kellet LA6 . . . . .237 B8
Greenwich Dr FY8 . . . . . . .90 D5
Greenwood PR5 . . . . .78 B4
Greenwood Ave
Blackpool FY1 . . . . .130 E2
Hest Bank LA5 . . . . .220 F2
Horwich BL6 . . . . .32 D1
Greenwood Cl
Lytham St Anne's FY8 . . . . . .90 E4
Ormskirk L39 . . . . .15 C1
Greenwood Cres LA5 . . . .220 F2
Greenwood Ct PR25 . . . . . .77 A1
Greenwood Dr LA5 . . . . . .220 F2
Greenwood Gdns PR8 . . . . .35 A5
Greenwood La BL6 . . . . . . .32 E1
Greenwood Rd WN6 . . . . . .29 E2
Greenwood St
1 Bamber Bridge PR5 . . . . . .97 E1
Preston PR1 . . . . .97 B7
Greenwood The BB2 . . . . . .81 D7
Greetby Hill L39,L40 . . . . .16 A6
Greetby Pl WN8 . . . . .9 A8
Greg Ho 13 LA1 . . . . .218 D2
Gregareth Cl 5 LA1 . . . . .218 A2
Gregory Ave FY2 . . . . . . .152 C5
Gregory Fold BB4 . . . . .68 A7
Gregory La L39 . . . . .23 B3
Gregory Mdw PR3 . . . . . .181 B7
Gregory Pl FY8 . . . . .91 A3
Gregory's Ct LA1 . . . . . . .215 A4
Gregson Cl 5 FY4 . . . . . .110 F7
Gregson Dr 3 FY7 . . . . . .198 F2
Gregson La
7 Blackburn BB2 . . . . .101 D5
Gregson Lane PR5 . . . . .98 E1
Higher Walton PR5 . . . . .98 C2
Gregson Rd LA1 . . . . .215 A7
Gregson St Darwen BB3 . . . .65 A8
Lytham St Anne's FY8 . . . . . .91 A3
Gregson Way PR2 . . . . . . .118 B5
Gregson's Ave L37 . . . . . . .11 E5
Grenada Cl BB3 . . . . .81 F6
Grenfell Ave FY3 . . . . . . .130 E7
Grenville Ave
Bamber Bridge PR5 . . . . .97 D2
Lytham St Anne's FY8 . . . . .110 E1
Gresham Rd FY5 . . . . .175 D1
Gresham St BB4 . . . . .86 F1
Gresley Ave BL6 . . . . .32 B3
Gresley Ct LA1 . . . . .214 F6
Gresley Pl FY2 . . . . .152 E2
Gressingham Dr LA1 . . . .215 A4
Gressingham Ho 3 LA1 . .215 A3
Gressingham Wlk LA1 . . .215 B3
Greta Heath LA6 . . . . .242 C3
Greta Pl Fleetwood FY7 . . .198 D3
Lancaster LA1 . . . . .218 C2
Gretdale Ave FY8 . . . . .89 E8
Gretna Cres FY5 . . . . .152 D8
Gretna Rd BB1 . . . . .122 F1
Gretna Wlk BB1 . . . . .122 F1
Grey Heights View PR6 . . .43 E8
Grey St Barrowford BB9 . . .170 D3
Burnley BB10 . . . . .128 A8
Greyfriars Ave PR2 . . . . .117 D5
Greyfriars Cres PR2 . . . . .117 D5
Greyfriars Dr PR1 . . . . . . .96 C5
Greyfriars Rd PR8 . . . . . . .21 B6
Greyhound Bridge Rd
LA1 . . . . .218 D1
Greystock Ave PR2 . . . . .117 E6
Greystock Cl PR5 . . . . .78 B8
Greystock Pl PR2 . . . . . . .117 E6
Greystoke Ave BB2 . . . . . . .80 E8
Greystoke Ct FY4 . . . . . . .110 B5
Greystoke Pl FY4 . . . . . . .110 B5
Greystokes L39 . . . . .15 D2
Greystonegill La LA2 . . . .239 F7
Greystones PR26 . . . . .76 B1
Greystones Dr BB12 . . . . .147 E8
Greythwaite Ct LA1 . . . . .214 D6
Greywood Ave BL9 . . . . . . .33 B2
Griffin Cl Burnley BB11 . . .127 B5
Bury BL9 . . . . .33 B4
Huncoat BB5 . . . . .125 F1
Griffin Park Prim Sch
BB2 . . . . .101 B3
Griffin St BB2 . . . . .101 B3
Griffiths Dr PR9 . . . . .35 F8
Griffon Ho PR9 . . . . .53 F2
Grime St Chorley PR7 . . . . .43 D6
Darwen BB3 . . . . .81 F2
7 Ramsbottom BL0 . . . . .50 A4
Grimeford La BL6,PR6 . . . .31 C5
Grimeford Mill PR6 . . . . . . .31 D6
Grimeshaw La LA1 . . . . . .219 B3
Grimrod Pl WN8 . . . . .9 A7
Grimsargh St 10 PR1 . . . .118 D1
Grimsargh St Michaels CE
Sch PR2 . . . . .139 C1
Grimshaw Green La L40,
WN8 . . . . .27 C6
Grimshaw La L39 . . . . .15 E7
Grimshaw Pk BB2 . . . . . . .101 F3
Grimshaw Rd WN8 . . . . .9 D8
Grimshaw Ret Pk BB2 . . .101 F3
Grimshaw St
Accrington BB5 . . . . .104 A5
6 Barrowford BB9 . . . . . . .170 D4
Burnley BB11 . . . . .128 A5
5 Church BB5 . . . . .103 E6
2 Clayton-le-M BB5 . . . . . .124 F2
Darwen BB3 . . . . .65 B7
Great Harwood BB6 . . . . . . .124 C5
Preston PR1 . . . . .97 A7
Grindlestone Ct PR3 . . . . .138 E6
Grindlestone Hirst BB8 . . .171 C3
Grindleton Brow BB7 . . . .190 B7
Grindleton CE Prim Sch
BB7 . . . . .190 C8
Grindleton Cl FY3 . . . . . . .131 B8
Grindleton Gr BB10 . . . . .128 D5
Grindleton Rd
1 Blackburn BB2 . . . . .101 C4
Grindleton BB7 . . . . .190 B7
West Bradford BB7 . . . . . . .189 F6
Gringley Rd LA4 . . . . .217 C3
Grinstead Cl PR8 . . . . .34 F1
Grisedale Ave BB1 . . . . . .102 C2
Grisedale Cl L37 . . . . .11 E3
Grisedale Dr BB12 . . . . . .127 B8
Grisedale Pl PR7 . . . . .43 B5
Gristlehurst La BL9 . . . . . .33 F5
Gritstone Cl LA1 . . . . . . .215 D8
Grizedale Ave
Garstang PR3 . . . . .181 B7
Lancaster LA1 . . . . .211 B7
Poulton-le-F FY6 . . . . .153 C3
Grizedale Cl
Clayton-le-M BB5 . . . . .124 E2
Fulwood PR2 . . . . .118 F2
Grizedale Cres PR2 . . . . . .119 A2
Grizedale Ct
Blackpool FY3 . . . . .130 E5
8 Thornton FY5 . . . . .176 B3
Grizedale Pl
Fulwood PR2 . . . . .118 F2
Morecambe LA3 . . . . .216 E1
Grizedale Rd
Blackpool FY4 . . . . .131 C1
Lancaster LA1 . . . . .218 F2
Grosvenor Cl PR8 . . . . .34 E3
Grosvenor Ct
Carnforth LA5 . . . . .223 C1
Cleveleys FY5 . . . . .175 C2
6 Lytham St Anne's FY8 . . . .90 A8
Southport PR8 . . . . .34 E4
Grosvenor Gdns PR8 . . . . . .34 F3
Grosvenor Ho PR9 . . . . .36 A6
Grosvenor Lodge BB1 . . .122 F6
Grosvenor Mews PR4 . . .114 B4
Grosvenor Park Prim Sch
LA3 . . . . .217 F2
Grosvenor Pl
Carnforth LA5 . . . . .223 C1
Preston PR2 . . . . .117 B2
Southport PR8 . . . . .34 F3
Grosvenor Rd
Carnforth LA5 . . . . .223 D1
Chorley PR7 . . . . .43 B6
Morecambe LA3 . . . . .216 D3
Southport PR8 . . . . .34 E4
Grosvenor St
Blackpool FY1 . . . . .130 C5
Burnley BB12 . . . . .127 F7
Colne BB8 . . . . .171 F5
Lytham St Anne's FY8 . . . . . .91 C3
Preston PR1 . . . . .97 B7
Grosvenor Way
5 Blackburn BB1 . . . . .101 E5
Horwich BL6 . . . . .32 C3
Groundwork Countryside
Ctr* BB4 . . . . .85 E1
Grouse St OL12 . . . . .52 F1
Grove Ave Adlington PR6 . . .31 A7
Longton PR4 . . . . .74 F8
Grove Cres PR6 . . . . .31 A7
Grove Ct Lancaster LA1 . . .214 F6
Oswaldtwistle BB5 . . . . . . .103 C3
Grove La BB12 . . . . .146 E1
Grove Mead L31 . . . . .5 F1
Grove Mill PR7 . . . . .41 C5
Grove Pk Ormskirk L39 . . . .15 F7
Southport PR9 . . . . .35 F8
Grove Rd Preston PR5 . . . . .97 C6
Skelmersdale WN8 . . . . .10 C8
Grove St Accrington BB5 . .104 A6
Bacup OL13 . . . . .88 A3
12 Bamber Bridge PR5 . . . . .77 F8
Barrowford BB9 . . . . .170 D3
Blackburn BB2 . . . . .101 E2
4 Burnley BB11 . . . . .127 D5
Bury BL9 . . . . .33 C3
Earby BB18 . . . . .197 B2
Leyland PR25 . . . . .59 D8
Lytham St Anne's FY8 . . . . . .89 F7
Morecambe LA4 . . . . .216 F4
Nelson BB9 . . . . .148 E8
Oswaldtwistle BB5 . . . . . . .103 D3
Southport PR8 . . . . .35 A4
Grove Terr PR8 . . . . .35 A5
Grove The
Appley Bridge WN6 . . . . .28 C2
Bilsborrow PR3 . . . . .159 A5
4 Burnley BB12 . . . . .127 B6
Carnforth LA5 . . . . .223 B1
Chipping PR3 . . . . .185 D4
Chorley PR7 . . . . .61 C2
Cleveleys FY5 . . . . .175 E3
Clitheroe BB7 . . . . .189 F1
Higher Penwortham PR1 . . . .96 B4
Lancaster LA1 . . . . .215 A7
Ormskirk L39 . . . . .6 C7
Oswaldtwistle BB5 . . . . . . .103 E5
Preston PR2 . . . . .117 B1
Rufford L40 . . . . .39 A3
Whalley BB7 . . . . .144 C5
Grovewood PR8 . . . . .34 E5
Grovewood Dr WN6 . . . . . .19 E8
Grovewood Ho PR7 . . . . . . .61 C2
Grundy Cl Bury BL9 . . . . . . .33 A1
Southport PR8 . . . . .35 E5
Grundy La BL9 . . . . .33 A1
Grundy Mews FY4 . . . . . . .110 C7
Grundy St 7 PR25 . . . . .77 B2
Grundy's La PR7 . . . . .43 D1
Guardian Cl PR2 . . . . .118 A4
Gubberford La PR3 . . . . . .204 D4
Guernsey Ave
Blackburn BB2 . . . . .101 F1
Leyland PR7 . . . . .60 F6
Guide La BB12 . . . . .147 A7
Guide Rd PR4 . . . . .73 E6
Guild Hall Arc 5 PR1 . . . . .97 A7
Guild Park Hosp PR3 . . . . .138 F5
Guild Row 7 PR1 . . . . .97 A7
Guild Way PR1 . . . . .96 D7
Guildford Ave
Blackpool FY2 . . . . .152 D6
Great Knowley PR6 . . . . .61 E4
Guildford Rd
29 Preston PR1 . . . . .97 A7
Southport PR8 . . . . .35 B2
Guildford Way FY6 . . . . . .153 C6
Guildhall St PR1 . . . . .96 F7
Guilford St BB9 . . . . .148 B5
Guinea Hall Cl PR9 . . . . . . .55 A5
Guinea Hall La PR9 . . . . . . .55 A5
Guinea Hall Mews PR9 . . . .55 A5
Gulf La LA2,PR3 . . . . .202 D7
Gummers Howe Wlk
LA5 . . . . .221 E8
Gurney St BB2 . . . . .101 B3
Gutter La BL0 . . . . .50 B7
Guy St BB12 . . . . .146 C1
Guys Ind Est L40 . . . . .25 B2
Guys Thatched Hamlet (Craft
Ctr)* PR3 . . . . .158 F3
Guysyke BB8 . . . . .171 C4
Gynn Ave FY1 . . . . .130 B8
Gynn Sq FY1 . . . . .130 B8

H

Habergham Dr BB12 126 F8
Habergham High Sch BB12 127 A7
Habergham St 19 BB12 146 C1
Hackensall Rd FY6 199 E5
Hacking Cl BB6 143 C1
Hacking Dr PR3 139 F5
Hacking St Bury BL9 33 A2
Darwen BB3 81 F1
5 Nelson BB9 170 F2
Hacklands Ave PR2 116 C1
Haddings La BB12 147 A8
Haddon Ct FY2 152 C5
Haddon Pl PR2 117 D3
Haddon Rd FY2 152 C5
Hadlee Terr LA1 218 B1
Hadleigh Rd FY6 153 C6
Hadrian Rd LA3 217 E3
Hadstock Ave L37 11 D1
Hagg La PR3 156 C8
Hagg St BB8 171 C4
Haig Ave Lancaster LA1 214 D8
Leyland PR25 76 F1
Preston PR2 117 D2
Southport PR8 35 E5
Tarleton PR4 57 A7
Haig Rd FY1 130 B1
Haigh Cl PR7 43 A7
Haigh Cres Chorley PR7 43 B7
Maghull L31 5 C4
Haigh Ct PR8 35 F6
Haigh Hall Cl BL0 50 B4
Haighton Ct PR2 118 A7
Haighton Dr PR2 118 E6
Haighton Green La PR2 138 E2
Hail St BL0 50 A4
Hala Cres LA1 215 A3
Hala Gr LA1 215 A3
Hala Hill LA1 215 B3
Hala Rd LA1 215 A3
Hala Sq LA1 215 A3
Halcyon Cl 6 OL12 52 B2
Haldane Rd BB3 81 E4
Haldane St BB10 148 B2
Halden Rd LA3 216 E3
Hale Carr Gr LA3 216 E1
Hale Carr La LA3 216 E1
Hale St BB11 128 A4
Hales Rushes Rd PR3 178 C4
Half Acre PR5 77 A8
Half Acre La BL6 31 C2
Halford Pl FY5 152 E7
Halfpenny La
Andertons Mill PR7 41 B3
Longridge PR3 139 F8
Halifax Rd Brierfield BB9 148 C5
Lane Bottom BB10 149 D3
Nelson BB9,BB10 148 E5
Southport PR8 21 C5
Halifax St FY3 130 F3
Hall Ave FY4 130 C1
Hall Brow Cl L39 16 B4
Hall Carr La PR4 74 D6
Hall Carr Mill Cotts BB4 86 B2
Hall Carr Rd BB4 86 A1
Hall Cl Caton LA2 237 B3
Rawtenstall BB4 86 A6
Hall Coppice The BL7 47 E1
Hall Croft PR4 95 D2
Hall Dr Caton LA2 237 B3
Heysham LA3 213 A2
Morecambe LA4 217 E4
Hall Fold OL12 52 C8
Hall Garth Gdns LA6 240 B1
Hall Gate PR7 61 A2
Hall Gate La FY6 177 C8
Hall Gdns OL12 52 C2
Hall Gn WN8 10 B7
Hall Gr LA3 213 A2
Hall Greaves Cl LA3 209 D8
Hall Green Cl WN8 10 B7
Hall Green La L40,PR7 41 A3
Hall Hill BB7 228 D1
Hall Hill St 4 BB12 146 C1
Hall La Appley Bridge WN6 28 D2
Bickerstaffe L39 7 E4
Bispham Green L40,WN8 27 A6
Bracewell BD23 231 F3
Great Eccleston PR3 156 C4
Ince Blundell L38 3 F3
Kirkby L33 1 A8
Leyland PR25 76 F2
Longton PR4 74 E7
Maghull L31 5 B7
Mawdesley L40 40 D3
Orrell WN5 10 F4
Rivington BL6 45 A2
Royal Oak L33,L39 7 B1
Skelmersdale L40 17 A6
St Michael's on W PR3 157 E6
Hall Mdws BB8 172 C3
Hall More Cvn Pk LA7 225 E7
Hall Park Ave BB10 128 F4
Hall Park Ctr FY8 90 F4
Hall Park Dr FY8 90 E6
Hall Pk Haslingden BB4 85 A6
Lancaster LA1 214 F4
Hall Rd Bescar L40 23 F6
Bescar L40 24 B6
Fulwood PR2 117 E5
Middleworth Green PR1 96 E3
Hall Rd *continued*
Trawden BB8 172 B3
Hall St Bacup OL13 87 F3
Blackburn BB2 101 E2
Burnley BB11 128 A6
Clitheroe BB7 166 E7
Colne BB8 171 D4
Haslingden BB4 85 B2
Morecambe LA4 217 B6
Preston PR2 117 C1
Ramsbottom BL0 50 C2
12 Rawtenstall BB4 86 A3
Southport PR9 35 C7
Whitworth OL12 52 B8
Whitworth OL12 52 C8
Worsthorne BB10 129 A5
Hall's Cotts FY4 111 A6
Hallam Cres BB9 149 A8
Hallam La LA3 213 A2
Hallam Rd BB9 149 A8
Hallam St 11 BB5 125 A1
Hallam Way FY4 111 E7
Hallbridge Gdns WN8 10 B8
Hallcroft WN8 18 C2
Halley Rd BB3 81 E3
Halley St OL13 88 A7
Hallfield Rd BB6 124 D6
Hallgate Hill BB7 229 B4
Halliwell Cres PR4 95 E1
Halliwell Ct 7 PR7 43 C7
Halliwell Hts PR5 97 F3
Halliwell La PR6 61 C4
Halliwell Pl 8 PR7 43 C7
Halliwell St
Accrington BB5 104 E2
Chorley PR7 43 C7
Hallmoor Cl L39 15 E2
Hallows Cl PR3 157 C6
Hallows Farm Ave OL12 52 D2
Hallows St BB10 148 A2
Hallsall Dr LA4 217 F6
Hallsalls Sq PR3 156 B5
Hallwell St BB10 128 A8
Hallwood Cl BB10 148 B4
Hallwood Rd PR7 43 A5
Halmot Ct 3 BB4 86 E1
Halmote Ave BB12 146 F5
Halsall Bldgs 6 PR9 35 C8
Halsall Ct L39 15 D6
Halsall Hall L39 23 B1
Halsall Hall Dr L39 23 B1
Halsall La Formby L37 11 F3
Haskayne L39 14 D6
Ormskirk L39 15 D6
Halsall Manor Ct L39 23 B1
Halsall Rd Halsall L39 23 C2
Southport PR8 22 A8
Halsbury St PR1 97 B6
Halstead Cl BB9 170 D4
Halstead La BB9 170 D4
Halstead Rd PR2 118 E5
Halstead St Burnley BB11 127 F5
Bury BL9 33 A4
Worsthorne BB10 129 A6
Halstead Wlk BL9 33 A5
Halton Ave
Clayton-le-W PR25 77 D1
Cleveleys FY5 175 E4
Halton Chase L40 16 E4
Halton Ct LA4 217 B3
Halton Gdns
Blackpool FY4 110 F8
Cleveleys FY5 175 F4
Halton Pl Fulwood PR2 118 F4
Longridge PR3 140 B8
Halton Rd Lancaster LA1 218 E4
Maghull L31 5 D3
Nether Kellet LA6 221 E5
Halton St PR4 132 E6
Hambledon Dr 6 PR1 96 E2
Hambledon St 10 BB12 126 D8
Hambledon Terr
Higham BB12 146 F6
2 Padiham BB12 126 F7
Hambledon View
Padiham BB12 126 F7
Read BB12 145 D1
Hambleton Cl PR4 94 F1
Hambleton Cvn Pk FY6 177 D4
Hambleton Prim Sch FY6 177 D2
Hameldon App BB11 127 D5
Hameldon Ave BB5 104 E2
Hameldon Cl BB11 126 C2
Hameldon Rd
Goodshaw Chapel BB4 106 A2
Hapton BB11 126 D2
Hameldon View BB6 124 D5
Hamer Ave
Blackburn BB1 102 D5
Goodshaw Chapel BB4 106 A1
Hamer Rd PR2 117 D3
Hamer St 18 Darwen BB3 65 A8
Ramsbottom BL0 50 B2
Rawtenstall BB4 86 A2
Hamerswood Dr PR3 181 D2
Hamilton Ct
6 Blackpool FY1 130 B4
8 Lytham St Anne's FY8 91 D4
Hamilton Dr LA1 218 A3
Hamilton Gr PR2 118 E3
Hamilton Rd
Barrowford BB9 170 C1
Chorley PR7 43 C7
Fulwood PR2 118 D4
Morecambe LA4 218 A6
Nelson BB8 171 A2
Hamilton St BB2 101 D2
Hamilton Way OL10 33 E1
Hamlet Cl BB2 101 C3
Hamlet Gr PR4 134 F4
Hamlet Rd FY7 198 F4
Hamlet The Adlington PR7 43 F1
Lytham St Anne's FY8 110 F2
Hammer Terr BL0 50 C3
Hammerton Gn 17 OL13 87 F3
Hammerton Hall Cl LA1 218 C4
Hammerton Hall La LA1 218 C4
Hammerton Pl FY3 131 A8
Hammerton St
Bacup OL13 87 F4
Burnley BB11 127 F5
Hammond Ave OL13 70 D8
Hammond Ct PR1 117 E1
Hammond Dr BB12 145 C2
Hammond Rd L33 1 C3
Hammond St Nelson BB9 148 F7
Preston PR1 117 E1
Preston PR1 117 E2
Preston PR1 117 F2
Hammond's Row 17 PR1 97 A8
Hampden Ave BB3 65 B7
Hampden Rd PR25 77 A2
Hampden St
6 Burnley BB11 128 B4
Hapton BB12 126 C4
Hampsfell Dr LA4 217 B3
Hampshire Cl BB1 123 A7
Hampshire Pl FY4 110 F6
Hampshire Rd
Bamber Bridge PR5 97 E3
Rishton BB1 124 A1
Hampson Ave PR25 77 D1
Hampson Cotts LA2 211 B1
Hampson Gr FY6 200 A4
Hampson La LA2 211 C1
Hampson St BL6 32 B4
Hampson Terr PR3 156 C5
Hampstead Cl FY8 90 E6
Hampstead Mews 3 FY1 130 C7
Hampstead Rd
Fulwood PR2 118 D2
Standish WN6 29 D1
Hampton Cl PR7 43 B8
Hampton Ct FY8 90 C8
Hampton Pl FY5 175 E3
Hampton Rd
Blackpool FY4 110 C8
Formby L37 11 E1
Morecambe LA3 216 E3
Southport PR8 35 C5
Hampton St PR2 117 C2
Hamptons The FY6 153 D1
Hanbury St PR2 117 C1
Hancock St BB2 101 C3
Hand La L40 40 F5
Handbridge The PR2 117 E5
Handel St OL12 52 B8
Handley Rd 4 FY1 130 C6
Handsworth Ct 4 FY1 130 C7
Handsworth Rd FY1 130 C7
Handsworth Wlk PR8 35 F3
Hanging Green La LA2 220 E1
Hanley Cl FY6 177 C7
Hanmer Pl 3 LA1 215 A6
Hannah St
Accrington BB5 104 B5
15 Bacup OL13 88 A3
Darwen BB3 65 B8
Hanover Cres FY2 152 C5
Hanover St Colne BB8 171 D5
Morecambe LA4 217 B5
4 Preston PR1 117 F1
Hansby Cl WN8 9 E8
Hanson Bldgs 5 BB12 126 C8
Hanson St Adlington PR7 30 F6
Great Harwood BB6 124 C4
Rishton BB1 124 C1
Hanstock Cl WN5 10 E5
Hants La L39 15 E6
Happy Mount Ct LA4 217 F7
Happy Mount Dr LA4 217 E7
Hapton CE Methodist Prim Sch BB11 126 C4
Hapton Rd BB12 126 C7
Hapton St
7 Padiham BB12 126 D8
Thornton FY5 176 B4
Hapton Sta BB11 126 C4
Hapton Way BB4 106 A2
Harbour Ave PR4 92 E6
Harbour Cl 11 FY7 198 F2
Harbour Ho 7 FY8 91 D4
Harbour La Brinscall PR6 62 D7
Edgworth BL7 48 D5
Warton PR4 92 E6
Harbour Trad Est 13 FY7 198 F2
Harbour Way FY7 199 B3
Harbury Ave PR8 21 A4
Harcles Dr BL0 50 B2
Harcourt Mews 12 BL6 32 B4
Harcourt Rd
Accrington BB5 104 D3
Blackburn BB2 101 C6
Blackpool FY4 110 D8
Lancaster LA1 218 C3
Harcourt St
14 Bacup OL13 87 F3
2 Burnley BB11 127 D5
Preston PR1 117 E1
Hard Knott Rise LA5 221 E8
Hardacre La
Lucas Green PR6 61 C5
Rimington BB7 231 B2
Hardacre St L39 15 F6
Hardaker Ct 1 FY8 89 E6
Hardcastle Rd PR2 117 E3
Harden Rd BB18 195 A6
Hardhorn Ct FY6 153 D3
Hardhorn Rd FY6 153 D2
Hardhorn Way FY6 153 D2
Harding Rd L40 25 D4
Harding St PR6 31 B8
Hardlands Ave 4 LA4 217 F4
Hardman Ave
Rawtenstall BB4 86 A1
Rawtenstall,Hugh Mill BB4 69 A8
Hardman Cl
Blackburn BB1 102 F4
Rawtenstall BB4 69 F7
Hardman Dr BB4 69 F7
Hardman St
Blackburn BB2 101 C3
3 Blackpool FY1 130 C6
Hardman Terr OL13 70 D8
Hardman Way 24 BB3 82 A1
Hardsough Fold BL0 68 C5
Hardsough La BL0 68 D5
Hardwen Ave 7 PR2 116 C1
Hardwicke Ho 10 LA1 214 E8
Hardwicke St 4 PR1 97 A8
Hardy Ave
Barnoldswick BB18 196 A3
Brierfield BB9 148 B6
Hardy Cl PR2 95 F8
Hardy Ct 13 BB9 148 E8
Hardy Dr PR7 43 A7
Hardy St Blackburn BB1 122 F1
Brierfield BB9 148 B6
Hare Clough Cl BB2 101 F3
Hare Runs Ho LA1 218 D3
Harebell Cl Blackburn BB2 80 D8
Formby L37 11 F1
Rochdale OL12 52 D3
Hareden Brook Cl BB1 101 F3
Hareden Cl 4 PR5 77 F8
Hareden Rd PR2 118 F2
Harefield Rise BB12 127 D7
Hareholme La BB4 86 D2
Hares La PR8 36 D1
Harestone Ave PR7 43 A5
Harewood PR7 61 B2
Harewood Ave
Blackpool FY3 153 A1
Lancaster LA1 215 A3
Morecambe LA3 216 E2
Simonstone BB12 145 E2
Southport PR8 21 C6
Harewood Cl FY6 153 C5
Harewood Rd PR1 118 C2
Hargate Ave OL12 52 A2
Hargate Cl BL9 50 C2
Hargate Rd FY5 176 C2
Hargher St BB11 127 D5
Hargreaves Ave PR25 60 B8
Hargreaves Ct
Clitheroe BB7 166 C7
Fulwood PR2 116 F4
Whitewell Bottom BB4 86 F6
Hargreaves Dr BB4 85 F2
Hargreaves Fold La BB4 87 A7
Hargreaves La 2 BB2 101 E3
Hargreaves Rd BB5 103 C4
Hargreaves St
9 Accrington BB5 104 C5
Brierfield BB10 148 F3
14 Burnley BB11 127 F6
Colne BB8 171 B4
Haslingden BB4 85 B3
Hoddlesden BB3 82 F1
Nelson BB9 148 C7
Southport PR8 35 C6
Thornton FY5 176 B3
Whitewell Bottom BB4 86 E5
Hargrove Ave
Burnley BB12 127 D7
Padiham BB12 146 C1
Harington Cl L37 11 D3
Harington Gn L37 11 D3
Harington Rd L37 11 D4
Harland St PR2 117 D3
Harland Way OL12 52 B2
Harlech Ave FY1 130 D1
Harlech Cl BB4 85 B1
Harlech Dr Leyland PR25 77 C1
Oswaldtwistle BB5 103 C4
Harlech Gr FY5 176 D2
Harleston Rd L33 1 A3
Harleston Wlk L33 1 A3
Harley Bank LA2 239 C8
Harley Cl LA2 239 C8
Harley Rd FY3 130 E4
Harley St BB12 127 C6
Harling Rd PR1 118 D1
Harling St BB12 127 B6
Harold Ave
8 Blackpool FY4 111 A6
Burnley BB11 127 C4
Harold St Burnley BB11 127 D5
Colne BB8 171 C4
Harold Terr PR5 77 A8
Harper St BB18 196 A3
Harper's La PR6 61 D1
Harperley PR7 61 B2
Harpers La BB12 147 D8
Harridge Ave OL12 52 C3
Harridge La L39,L40 24 A1
Harridge St OL12 52 C3
Harridge The OL12 52 C3
Harrier Ct LA1 214 E8
Harrier Dr Blackburn BB1 101 D8
Skelmersdale WN8 9 E8
Harriet St BB11 127 E5
Harrington Ave FY4 110 B5
Harrington Rd
Chorley PR7 43 B8
Morecambe LA3 216 E3
Harrington St
Accrington BB5 125 A1
Preston PR1 117 F1
Harris Ave FY1 130 D1
Harris Cl OL10 33 E1
Harris Ct 2 BB7 166 E8
Harris Ctr PR2 117 E5
Harris Mus & Art Gallery* PR1 97 A7
Harris Prim Sch PR2 117 B7
Harris Rd WN6 29 B3
Harris St Fleetwood FY7 199 A4
2 Preston PR1 97 A7
Harrison Ave FY5 176 B2
Harrison Cres
Blackrod BL6 31 C3
Morecambe LA3 216 D1
Harrison Dr BB8 171 C6
Harrison La PR4 96 B2
Harrison Rd Adlington PR7 31 A6
Chorley PR7 43 C6
Fulwood PR2 117 E6
Harrison St Bacup OL13 71 B8
Barnoldswick BB18 196 C1
Blackburn BB2 101 D4
Blackpool FY1 130 C3
Brierfield BB10 148 F2
5 Cornholme OL14 109 B1
Horwich BL6 32 B4
Ramsbottom BL0 50 C7
Harrison Terr BB7 190 B8
Harrison Trading Est PR1 118 C1
Harrock La L40,WN6 27 F6
Harrock Rd PR25 77 D1
Harrod Dr PR8 34 E3
Harrogate Cres BB10 148 D2
Harrogate Rd FY8 90 C7
Harrogate Way PR9 54 C6
Harrop Pl PR2 118 E4
Harrow Ave
Accrington BB5 104 C7
Fleetwood FY7 198 F3
Harrow Cl Orrell WN5 10 F8
Padiham BB12 126 E6
Harrow Dr BB1 102 B3
Harrow Gr LA4 217 F4
Harrow Pl Blackpool FY4 110 A5
Lytham St Anne's FY8 90 E5
Harrow St BB5 103 E4
Harrow Stiles La OL13 107 E1
Harrowdale Pk LA2 219 D7
Harrowside FY4 110 B6
Harrowside Brow 3 FY4 110 B6
Harrowside W FY4 110 A5
Harry Potts Way BB10 128 B5
Harry St Barrowford BB9 170 D3
Salterforth BB18 194 D7
Harsnips WN8 18 C2
Harswell Cl WN5 10 E5
Hart St Blackburn BB1 101 F4
Burnley BB11 128 A6
Southport PR8 35 E6
Hart's Houses BL6 32 D5
Hart's La WN8 9 F8
Hartford Ave FY1 130 D2
Hartington Rd
Brinscall PR6 63 A8
Darwen BB3 81 E4
Preston PR1 96 D7
Hartington St
Brierfield BB9 148 B5
Colne,Cotton Tree BB8 172 B5
Lancaster LA1 215 B8
Rishton BB1 124 A1
Hartland WN8 18 C2
Hartland Ave PR9 54 B5
Hartlands Cl BB10 148 D3
Hartley Ave BB5 104 A3
Hartley Cres PR8 34 F2
Hartley Dr BB9 149 A7
Hartley Gdns BB8 172 C6
Hartley Homes BB8 172 C6
Hartley Rd PR8 34 F2
Hartley St
3 Blackburn BB1 101 E6
2 Burnley BB11 127 C5
Colne BB8 171 D5
Earby BB18 197 B1
Great Harwood BB6 124 D6
2 Haslingden BB4 85 B3
Horwich BL6 32 B3
Nelson BB9 148 E7
2 Oswaldtwistle BB5 103 E4
Rochdale OL12 52 B1
Hartleys Terr BB8 171 E4
Hartmann St BB5 104 A6
Hartshead WN8 18 C2
Hartwood Gn PR6 61 C3
Hartwood Rd PR9 35 D7
Harvest Dr PR6 61 C6
Harvesters Fold PR4 134 F4
Harvey Longworth Ct BB4 106 A1
Harvey St 14 Nelson BB9 170 E1
Oswaldtwistle BB5 103 D4
Harvington Dr PR8 21 B5
Harwich Rd FY8 111 A1
Harwin Cl OL12 52 D3
Harwood Ave FY8 89 E8
Harwood Cl FY6 177 C7
Harwood Gate BB1 102 B6

Harwood La BB6 ....124 E6
Harwood New Rd BB6 ...124 E6
Harwood Rd Rishton BB1 .124 A2
Wilpshire BB1 ....123 D4
Harwood St
14 Blackburn,Cob Wall BB1 ....102 A7
Blackburn,Green Bank BB1 ....102 B6
Darwen BB3 ....81 E2
Harwood's La BB3 ....82 E1
Hasbury Dr FY5 ....176 C2
Hasgill Ct LA1 ....218 C1
Haskoll St BL6 ....32 D1
Haslam Ct 1 BB10 ....148 B1
Haslam Dr L39 ....15 D7
Haslam St BL9 ....33 A4
Haslemere Ave 6 FY3 ...130 E3
Haslemere Ind Est PR25 ..76 F3
Haslingden Broadway Prim Sch BB4 ....68 C8
Haslingden Grane (Trail)* BB4 ....84 A2
Haslingden High Sch BB4 ....68 B8
Haslingden Old Rd
Blackburn BB1,BB5 ....102 E3
Rawtenstall BB4 ....85 E2
Haslingden Prim Sch BB4 ....85 B2
Haslingden Rd
Blackburn BB1,BB2 ....102 B2
Oswaldtwistle BB5 ....83 D7
Rawtenstall BB4 ....85 E2
Haslingden St James CE Prim Sch BB4 ....85 B3
Haslow Pl FY3 ....130 F7
Hassall Dr PR4 ....156 A1
Hassett Cl PR1 ....96 E6
Hastings Ave
Blackpool FY2 ....152 E5
Warton PR4 ....92 E7
Hastings Cl
Blackburn BB1 ....102 C4
Thornton FY5 ....176 C1
Hastings Pl FY8 ....91 A3
Hastings Rd Kirkham PR4 .114 B2
Lancaster LA1 ....214 F5
Leyland PR25 ....77 B2
Preston PR2 ....117 B1
Southport PR8 ....34 E1
Thornton FY5 ....176 C1
Hastings The LA1 ....214 F5
Haston Lee Ave BB1 ....122 F3
Hasty Brow Rd LA2 ....218 B6
Hatfield Ave
Fleetwood FY7 ....198 F3
Morecambe LA4 ....217 F6
Hatfield Cl FY5 ....176 C2
Hatfield Ct LA4 ....217 F6
Hatfield Gdns 2 FY7 ....198 E2
Hatfield Mews 2 FY7 ...198 F2
Hatfield Rd
Accrington BB5 ....104 D7
Fulwood PR2 ....118 E3
Southport PR8 ....21 C6
Hatfield Wlk 1 FY7 ....198 E2
Hathaway FY4 ....110 E8
Hathaway Fold 4 BB12 .126 D7
Hathaway Rd
Fleetwood FY7 ....198 E4
Lancaster LA1 ....218 C3
Hatlex Dr LA2 ....220 E2
Hatlex Hill LA2 ....220 E2
Hatlex La LA2 ....220 E2
Hattersley St BB11 ....127 E6
Hatton St PR7 ....30 F6
Haugh Ave BB12 ....145 E2
Haulgh St BB10 ....148 B2
Haunders La PR4 ....74 B1
Havelock Cl BB2 ....101 D3
Havelock Rd
Bamber Bridge PR5 ....77 E7
Middleforth Green PR1 ....96 E5
Havelock St
Blackburn BB2 ....101 C2
5 Blackpool FY1 ....130 B4
Burnley BB12 ....127 B6
Lancaster LA1 ....215 A6
Oswaldtwistle BB5 ....103 D3
11 Padiham BB12 ....146 C1
Preston PR1 ....117 D2
Preston PR1 ....117 E2
Preston PR1 ....117 F2
Haven Brow L39 ....6 C8
Haven Rd FY8 ....91 C3
Haven Sch FY5 ....175 E4
Haven St BB10 ....128 C5
Haven Wlk L31 ....5 C4
Havenbrook Gr BL0 ....50 A3
Haverbreaks Pl LA1 ....214 E6
Haverbreaks Rd LA1 ....214 E5
Haverholt Cl BB8 ....171 C5
Haverholt Rd BB8 ....171 C5
Haverthwaite Ave LA3 ....212 F7
Havre Pk BB18 ....196 C2
Hawarden Ave LA4 ....217 C5
Hawarden Rd 1 PR1 ....118 E1
Hawarden St BB9 ....148 E7
Hawes Dr BB8 ....171 F6
Hawes Side La FY4 ....110 E8
Hawes Side Prim Sch FY4 ....110 E7
Hawes Terr BB10 ....148 B2
Hawesside St PR9 ....35 C7
Haweswater Ave PR7 ....43 B6
Haweswater Gr L31 ....5 F2
Haweswater Pl 3 LA4 ....217 E4
Haweswater Rd 1 BB5 .125 D1
Hawick Gr OL10 ....33 E1
Hawk Cl BL9 ....33 B4
Hawk St Burnley BB11 ....128 A6
Carnforth LA5 ....223 E2
Hawker Dr WN8 ....9 E8
Hawkeshead Cl BB2 ....101 B4
Hawkhurst Ave PR2 ....117 D6
Hawkhurst Cres PR2 ....117 D6
Hawkhurst Rd
Middleforth Green PR1 ....96 E5
Preston PR1 ....118 B1
Hawking Pl FY2 ....152 F5
Hawkins Cl PR1 ....117 E1
Hawkins St
Blackburn BB2 ....101 B2
Preston PR1 ....117 E1
Hawks Gr BB4 ....86 A1
Hawksbury Dr PR1 ....96 D2
Hawksclough WN8 ....18 D2
Hawkshaw Ave BB3 ....81 E3
Hawkshaw Bank Rd BB1 ....101 D8
Hawkshaw La BL8 ....49 B5
Hawkshaw St BL6 ....32 B3
Hawkshead PR1 ....96 E3
Hawkshead Ave PR7 ....60 D1
Hawkshead Cl L31 ....5 E2
Hawkshead Dr LA4 ....217 C3
Hawkshead Rd
Fulwood PR2 ....118 E5
Knott End-on-S FY6 ....199 F6
Hawkshead St
Blackburn BB2 ....101 B4
Southport PR8,PR9 ....35 D7
Hawkshead Terr FY4 ....111 D8
Hawksheath Cl BL7 ....47 E1
Hawksley St BL6 ....32 D2
Hawkstone Cl
Huncoat BB5 ....125 F1
Thornton FY5 ....153 D8
Hawkstone Ct LA4 ....217 F6
Hawkswood PR7 ....41 B6
Hawkswood Gdns BB9 ....148 A4
Hawksworth Ave LA3 ....216 E2
Hawksworth Cl L37 ....12 A6
Hawksworth Dr L37 ....12 A6
Hawksworth Gr LA3 ....216 D2
Hawksworth Rd BB5 ....104 B8
Hawley Gn OL12 ....52 D2
Hawley St Colne BB8 ....171 C4
Colne,Cotton Tree BB8 ....172 C5
Haworth Art Gallery* BB5 ....104 D3
Haworth Ave
Accrington BB5 ....104 D3
Ramsbottom BL0 ....50 A2
Rawtenstall BB4 ....85 F2
Haworth Dr OL13 ....70 C8
Haworth St
Accrington BB5 ....125 B1
Edgworth BL7 ....48 D5
Oswaldtwistle BB5 ....103 E4
Rishton BB1 ....124 B1
Haws Ave LA5 ....223 D1
Haws Hill LA5 ....223 D1
Hawthorn Ave Caton LA2 .237 C3
Darwen BB3 ....82 C2
Edenfield BL0 ....68 D2
Fleetwood FY7 ....175 E8
Orrell WN5 ....10 F6
Oswaldtwistle BB5 ....103 F3
Ramsbottom BL0 ....50 A2
Hawthorn Bank BB5 ....125 A3
Hawthorn Cl Caton LA2 ..237 C3
Kirkham PR4 ....113 E6
Langho BB6 ....123 D8
Leyland PR26 ....76 D2
New Longton PR4 ....76 A7
Whalley BB7 ....144 A7
Hawthorn Cres
Preston PR2 ....116 D1
Skelmersdale WN8 ....17 E1
Hawthorn Dr BB1 ....103 B8
Hawthorn Gdns BB5 ....125 A3
Hawthorn Rd Bacup OL13 ..88 A2
Blackpool FY1 ....130 C7
Bolton-le-S LA5 ....221 A6
Fulwood PR2 ....118 E2
Morecambe LA4 ....217 F4
Hawthorne Ave
Brierfield BB10 ....148 C5
Garstang PR3 ....181 B8
Higher Walton PR5 ....98 C3
Horwich BL6 ....32 E1
Newton-w-S PR4 ....114 F3
Hawthorne Cl
Barrowford BB9 ....170 B1
Clayton Green PR6 ....78 B3
Nelson BB9 ....149 B8
Hawthorne Cres L37 ....12 A2
Hawthorne Dr BB18 ....196 C4
Hawthorne Gr
17 Barrowford BB9 ....170 D3
Carleton FY6 ....153 B5
Southport PR9 ....35 F7
Hawthorne Ind Pk BB7 ..190 A1
Hawthorne Lea FY5 ....153 C8
Hawthorne Mdws BB4 ..106 A1
Hawthorne Pl BB7 ....189 E1
Hawthorne Rd
Burnley BB11 ....127 F4
Thornton FY5 ....153 C8
Hawthorne St BB1 ....101 F8
Hawthorne Terr BB8 ....194 E1
Hawthornes The L40 ....39 B3
Hawthorns Jun Sch BB1 ....101 F8
Hawthorns The
Bilsborrow PR3 ....159 A5
Eccleston PR7 ....41 B7
Fulwood PR2 ....117 F6
Lancaster LA1 ....215 A2
Lytham St Anne's FY8 ....110 F2
Newburgh WN8 ....27 A1
1 Newchurch BB4 ....86 F1
Wilpshire BB1 ....122 F6
Woodplumpton PR4 ....136 E2
Haxey Wlk BL6 ....31 F3
Haydock Ave PR25 ....60 A8
Haydock Gr LA3 ....216 D1
Haydock La BL7 ....48 B1
Haydock Rd LA1 ....215 B3
Haydock Sq 1 BB6 ....124 C5
Haydock St
6 Bamber Bridge PR5 ....97 E2
3 Blackburn BB1 ....122 E1
Burnley BB10 ....148 C1
Haydocks La PR4 ....116 D5
Haydon Ave PR5 ....77 A7
Hayfell Ave LA4 ....217 C3
Hayfell Cres LA2 ....220 D1
Hayfell Gr LA2 ....220 D1
Hayfield BB2 ....101 A7
Hayfield Ave
Blackpool FY2 ....152 E2
Gregson Lane PR5 ....98 E1
Poulton-le-F FY6 ....153 E3
Hayfield Cl
Gregson Lane PR5 ....98 E1
Ramsbottom BL8 ....49 F1
Hayfield Rd L39 ....15 E7
Hayfields BB18 ....194 E8
Hayhurst Cl BB7 ....144 C6
Hayhurst Farm Terr BB7 ....166 F7
Hayhurst Rd BB7 ....144 C6
Hayhurst St BB7 ....166 F7
Haylemere Ct PR8 ....34 E5
Hayling Pl PR2 ....117 A4
Haylot Dr LA2 ....219 D7
Haylot Sq 9 LA1 ....215 A8
Haymans Gn L31 ....5 E1
Haymarket FY8 ....90 B6
Haymarket Lodge PR9 ....53 D1
Hayshaw Mews PR3 ....207 D3
Haysworth St PR1 ....117 F2
Hayward Gr WN6 ....29 D2
Haywood Cl
Accrington BB5 ....104 B8
Fulwood PR2 ....118 A8
Haywood Rd BB5 ....104 B8
Hazel Ave
Bamber Bridge PR5 ....98 A1
Bury BL9 ....33 B2
Clayton-le-M BB5 ....124 F2
Darwen BB3 ....82 B2
Fleetwood FY7 ....175 F8
Ramsbottom BL0 ....50 B1
Hazel Bank 2 LA1 ....212 F7
Hazel Cl
Bamber Bridge PR5 ....97 F1
Blackburn BB2 ....101 C4
Higher Penwortham PR1 ....96 B3
Knott End-on-S FY6 ....199 F6
Hazel Coppice PR2 ....116 E3
Hazel Ct Fulwood PR2 ....117 E7
Ormskirk L39 ....15 E5
Hazel Dene BB7 ....189 E6
Hazel Gr Bacup OL13 ....88 B3
Bamber Bridge PR5 ....98 A1
Blackburn BB1 ....102 F5
Blackpool FY3 ....130 E5
Chorley PR6 ....61 C3
Clayton-le-M BB5 ....125 A2
Clitheroe BB7 ....166 C7
Fulwood PR2 ....119 A4
Lancaster LA1 ....214 D8
Longridge PR3 ....140 B8
Rawtenstall BB4 ....85 F4
Southport PR8 ....35 E7
Tarleton PR4 ....56 F8
Hazel Hall La BL0 ....50 B1
Hazel La WN8 ....18 B4
Hazel Mount BL7 ....47 E2
Hazel St Ramsbottom BL0 ..50 A4
Rising Bridge BB5 ....85 A8
Hazelbank Gdns L37 ....11 E5
Hazeldene Ave 2 BB4 ....85 B2
Hazeldene Rd FY7 ....198 F2
Hazelhead La PR3 ....204 E2
Hazelhurst Cl BL0 ....50 B4
Hazelhurst Com Prim Sch BL0 ....50 A4
Hazelhurst Dr PR3 ....181 A7
Hazelhurst Lodge 12 PR2 ....118 F4
Hazelhurst Rd PR2 ....119 A2
Hazelmere Rd
Fulwood PR2 ....117 D8
Preston PR2 ....117 A1
Hazelmoor BB1 ....122 E6
Hazelmount Ave LA5 ....223 D3
Hazelmount Cres LA5 ....223 D3
Hazelmount Dr LA5 ....223 C3
Hazelrigg La LA2 ....211 C7
Hazels The Coppull PR7 ....42 E1
Wilpshire BB1 ....122 E6
Hazelwood
Silverdale LA5 ....224 C2
Southport PR8 ....34 F1
Hazelwood Ave L40 ....25 E4
Hazelwood Cl
Blackburn BB1 ....123 A1
Leyland PR25 ....76 E1
Hazelwood Dr
Hesketh Bank PR4 ....73 E4
Morecambe LA4 ....217 F6
Hazelwood Gdns LA1 ....215 A2
Hazelwood Rd BB9 ....149 A8
Hazlehurst Cl L37 ....11 C2
Hazlewood Cl FY5 ....176 A2
Head Dyke La PR3 ....201 C3
Headbolt La Halsall PR8 ...22 A4
Kirkby L33 ....1 A5
Headfort Cl FY2 ....152 D2
Headingley Cl BB5 ....125 F1
Headingly Ave WN8 ....17 C1
Headlands St OL12 ....52 E1
Headlands The LA3 ....212 D7
Headley Rd PR25 ....76 E1
Headroomgate Rd FY8 ...89 F8
Heads La BB18 ....195 B6
Heald Brow BB18 ....196 A4
Heald Cl Rochdale OL12 ....52 C3
Weir OL13 ....88 A8
Heald Croft PR3 ....181 D6
Heald Dr OL12 ....52 C3
Heald House Rd PR25 ....60 C7
Heald La OL13 ....88 A8
Heald Rd BB10,BB12 ....148 A2
Heald St Blackpool FY3 ...130 D6
6 Chorley PR6 ....43 E8
Healdwood Cl BB12 ....147 F3
Healdwood Dr BB12 ....147 F3
Healey Ave OL12 ....52 D4
Healey Ct BB11 ....127 F5
Healey Dell Cotts OL12 ...52 B4
Healey Dell Nature Reserve* OL12 ....52 B4
Healey Gr OL12 ....52 C5
Healey Hall Farm OL12 ...52 C4
Healey Hall Mews OL12 ..52 C4
Healey La OL12 ....52 E3
Healey Mount BB11 ....127 F4
Healey Prim Sch OL12 ....52 E3
Healey Row BB11 ....127 F5
Healey St FY3 ....130 D7
Healey Stones OL12 ....52 E4
Healey Wood Rd BB11 ...127 F4
Heaning Ave
Accrington BB5 ....104 D8
Blackburn BB1 ....102 D4
Heanor Dr PR8 ....35 F3
Heap Bridge Village Prim Sch BL9 ....33 D1
Heap Brow BL9 ....33 D1
Heap Clough BB4 ....84 C3
Heap Ct PR9 ....35 E8
Heap St Brierfield BB9 ....148 A5
Burnley BB10 ....148 B1
Bury BL9 ....33 D1
Rawtenstall BB4 ....86 A8
Worsthorne BB10 ....129 B6
Heapey Fold La PR6 ....44 C7
Heapey Ho PR6 ....62 A3
Heapey Rd PR6 ....61 F2
Heapfold 4 OL12 ....52 B2
Heaplands BL8 ....49 F1
Heapworth Ave BL0 ....50 B6
Heartwood Cl BB2 ....101 A8
Heasandford Ind Est
Burnley BB10 ....128 D8
Burnley BB10 ....148 D2
Heasandford Prim Sch BB10 ....128 B8
Heath Ave BL0 ....50 B1
Heath Gr LA3 ....212 E6
Heath Hill Dr OL13 ....70 C8
Heath St BB10 ....128 B8
Heathbourne Rd OL13 ....70 C8
Heather Bank
Burnley BB11 ....127 C4
Rawtenstall BB4 ....68 F8
Heather Brow BB18 ....197 D2
Heather Cl Brierfield BB9 .148 D4
Burscough L40 ....25 E4
Chorley PR6 ....43 E8
Formby L37 ....12 B5
Haslingden BB4 ....68 A8
Horwich BL6 ....32 B4
Southport PR8 ....21 D2
Thornton FY5 ....176 B1
Heather Gr PR2 ....118 E3
Heather Lea Dr PR6 ....62 F8
Heatherfield BL7 ....48 E6
Heatherfield Pl PR2 ....117 C1
Heatherlands
Haslingden BB4 ....68 A6
Millgate OL12 ....71 D4
Heatherlea Cl WN8 ....10 C7
Heatherlea Rd BB12 ....147 D7
Heatherleigh PR26 ....76 D3
Heatherleigh Gdns BB2 ..81 D6
Heathers The
Clayton Brook PR5 ....78 C4
Knott End-on-S FY6 ....199 F5
Heatherside Rd BL0 ....50 C7
Heatherway PR2 ....118 E6
Heatherways L37 ....12 A6
Heathey La L39,PR8 ....23 A7
Heathfield PR6 ....43 F1
Heathfield Ave OL13 ....70 C8
Heathfield Cl L37 ....12 A6
Heathfield Dr PR2 ....118 E4
Heathfield Pk BB2 ....100 F6
Heathfield Rd Bacup OL13 .70 C8
Fleetwood FY7 ....198 E2
Southport PR8 ....21 F6
Heathfoot Ave LA3 ....212 E6
Heathfoot Dr LA3 ....212 E6
Heathgate Fence BB12 ....147 D8
Skelmersdale WN8 ....18 C2
Heathland WN8 ....10 B7
Heathrow Pl PR7 ....43 A7
Heathway PR2 ....117 F5
Heathway Ave FY3 ....130 E6
Heathy La L39 ....13 B8
Heatley Cl BB2 ....101 D3
Heatley St PR1 ....96 F8
Heaton Bottom Rd LA3 ..213 E5
Heaton Cl
Bamber Bridge PR5 ....97 D4
Burscough L40 ....25 D4
Carleton FY6 ....153 C5
Morecambe LA3 ....217 E3
Skelmersdale WN8 ....10 A7
Thornton FY5 ....153 C8
Heaton Ho LA1 ....214 F5
Heaton Mount Ave PR2 ..117 F7
Heaton Pl PR1 ....118 E1
Heaton Rd Lancaster LA1 .214 F5
Lytham St Anne's FY8 ....90 A8
Heaton St
3 Blackburn BB2 ....101 E4
Leyland PR25 ....76 E2
Standish WN6 ....29 E1
Heatons Bridge Rd L40 ..24 D3
Heaviley Gr BL6 ....32 A5
Hebden Ave FY1 ....130 D1
Heber St BB11 ....106 B4
Hebrew Rd BB10 ....128 A8
Hebrew Sq 12 BB10 ....128 A8
Heckenhurst Ave BB10 ..129 A6
Hector Rd BB3 ....81 E5
Hedge Row PR4 ....113 B3
Hedge Rows OL12 ....71 C1
Hedgerow The BB2 ....101 A8
Hedgerows Rd PR26 ....59 A8
Heeley Rd FY8 ....89 E8
Height Barn La OL13 ....71 A8
Height Croft BB9 ....148 E5
Height La PR3 ....161 F7
Height Side La BB4 ....86 B7
Heights Ave OL12 ....52 E2
Heights Cl OL12 ....52 E2
Heights Cotts BB5 ....104 F4
Heights Ct OL12 ....52 E1
Heights La OL12 ....52 E1
Heights Rd BB9 ....148 D6
Heights The BL6 ....32 D1
Heightside Ave BB4 ....86 E2
Heightside Mews BB4 ....86 E2
Helen's Cl FY4 ....110 E6
Helena St BB10 ....128 B5
Helks Brow LA2 ....239 B2
Hellifield PR2 ....117 F7
Hellifield Rd
Bolton-by-B BB7 ....230 E5
Gisburn BB7 ....231 C4
Helm Cl BB11 ....127 D2
Helmcroft 5 BB4 ....85 A1
Helmcroft Ct 1 BB4 ....85 B1
Helmn Way BB9 ....170 F2
Helmsdale WN8 ....18 C2
Helmsdale Cl BL0 ....50 A4
Helmsdale Rd
Blackpool FY4 ....110 F7
Nelson BB9 ....171 A1
Helmshore Prim Sch BB4 ....68 A7
Helmshore Rd
Haslingden BB4 ....68 A7
Ramsbottom BL8,BB4 ....68 A3
Helmshore Textile Mus* BB4 ....67 F8
Helmside Ave LA4 ....217 C3
Helmsley Gn 2 PR25 ....77 B1
Helston Cl Burnley BB11 ..127 B4
Southport PR9 ....54 B5
Helton Cl BB9 ....170 D4
Helvellyn Dr BB12 ....127 C8
Hemingway FY4 ....110 D8
Hemingway Pl 1 BB9 ....148 F8
Hemp St OL13 ....87 F1
Hempshaw Ave BB4 ....106 A2
Henderson Rd
Fleetwood FY7 ....198 F2
Weeton Camp PR4 ....132 E6
Henderson St PR1 ....117 E2
Hendon Pl PR2 ....116 E2
Hendon Rd BB9 ....148 F8
Hendriff Pl 4 OL12 ....52 F1
Hendry La BB2 ....81 D7
Henfield Cl BB5 ....125 A3
Henley Ave FY5 ....175 D2
Henley Ct
7 Blackpool FY2 ....152 E1
Southport PR9 ....53 E1
Henley Dr PR9 ....53 F1
Henley Mews LA3 ....216 E3
Henley St 9 OL12 ....52 F1
Hennel Ho PR5 ....97 C4
Hennel La
Bamber Bridge PR5 ....97 B2
Bamber Bridge PR5 ....97 C3
Bamber Bridge PR5 ....97 C4
Henrietta St Bacup OL13 ...87 F2
Blackburn BB2 ....101 C5
Preston PR1 ....97 B8
Henrietta Street Ind Est 2 OL13 ....87 F2
Henry Gdns BB9 ....148 B5
Henry St Accrington BB5 ..104 D3
Bank Lane BL0 ....50 D7
Blackpool FY1 ....130 C2
Church BB5 ....103 F6
Clayton-le-M BB5 ....125 A2

Henry St *continued*
Colne BB8 .....171 C4
Lancaster LA1 .....214 F7
Lytham St Anne's FY8 .....91 A3
2 Nelson BB9 .....170 D1
Rawtenstall BB4 .....85 F2
Rishton BB1 .....124 B1
Henry Whalley St BB2 .....101 A2
Henson Ave FY4 .....110 E6
Henthorn Cl 4 BB7 .....166 D7
Henthorn Rd BB7 .....166 C6
Henthorne St 1 FY1 .....130 C6
Henwick Hall Ave BL0 .....50 B4
Herbert St Bacup OL13 .....70 D8
Blackburn BB2 .....101 D2
Burnley BB11 .....127 E5
Horwich BL6 .....32 B4
Leyland PR25 .....77 A1
Padiham BB12 .....126 D7
Preston PR1 .....118 B1
Hereford Ave
8 Blackpool FY3 .....130 E3
Burnley BB12 .....127 B7
Garstang PR3 .....181 B8
Hereford Cl BB5 .....104 B7
Hereford Dr BB7 .....166 F7
Hereford Gr Cottam PR4 .....116 D5
Skelmersdale WN8 .....10 B6
Hereford Rd
Blackburn BB1 .....102 C5
Nelson BB8,BB9 .....171 A2
Southport PR9 .....35 F7
Hereford St BB9 .....148 C8
Herevale Hall Dr BL0 .....50 B4
Heriot Cl 8 FY5 .....175 F1
Heritage The PR25 .....76 F3
Heritage Way
Cleveleys FY5 .....175 F1
Tarleton PR4 .....57 A5
Herkomer Ave BB11 .....127 E2
Herlebeck Rise LA1 .....218 F2
Hermitage Cl WN6 .....19 E7
Hermitage St BB1,BB5 .....124 C1
Hermitage The FY5 .....175 F2
Hermitage Way FY8 .....90 D6
Hermon Rd FY5 .....175 E1
Hermon St 2 PR1 .....118 C1
Hern Ave PR5 .....77 A8
Heron Cl Blackburn BB1 .....101 D8
Cleveleys FY5 .....175 F5
Heron Ct BB11 .....127 C5
Heron Dr LA4 .....217 C3
Heron Way Blackpool FY3 .....131 B6
Kirkham PR4 .....114 B2
Oswaldtwistle BB5 .....103 E3
Herons Ct L31 .....5 B4
Herons Reach BL0 .....68 B4
Herons Wharf WN6 .....19 D7
Heronsyke LA1 .....218 D4
Herring Arm Rd FY7 .....199 A2
Herschel Ave BB12 .....127 C8
Herschell St
2 Blackburn BB2 .....101 B1
Preston PR1 .....97 B6
Hertford St BB2 .....101 C2
Hesketh Ave Banks PR9 .....55 A6
Blackpool FY2 .....152 B4
Hesketh Cl Darwen BB3 .....65 C6
Fulwood PR2 .....118 E1
Hesketh Ct Blackpool FY2 .....152 B4
Great Harwood BB6 .....124 E6
Hesketh Dr Maghull L31 .....5 F1
Rufford L40 .....39 A3
Shevington Moor WN6 .....29 A2
Southport PR9 .....53 F1
Hesketh Gn L40 .....39 B4
Hesketh La Becconsall PR4 .....73 F1
Hesketh Lane PR3 .....162 D7
Tarleton PR4 .....57 A7
Hesketh Links Ct PR9 .....53 E2
Hesketh Lodge L37 .....11 E3
Hesketh Manor PR9 .....53 E2
Hesketh Pl FY7 .....199 B5
Hesketh Rd Burscough L40 .....25 D4
Fulwood PR2 .....118 E1
Heysham LA3 .....212 E8
Longridge PR3 .....140 A8
Lytham St Anne's FY8 .....111 A1
Southport PR9 .....53 D2
Hesketh St
Great Harwood BB6 .....124 C5
Preston PR2 .....117 C1
Hesketh-with-Becconsall All Saints CE Sch PR4 .....73 E4
Heskin Cl L31 .....5 D4
Heskin Hall Ct L39 .....15 D8
Heskin La L39 .....15 D8
Heskin Pemberton's CE Prim Sch CE Prim Sch PR7 .....41 E2
Hesley La BD24 .....236 E6
Hessam Hts LA3 .....212 F5
Hesse St 1 BB3 .....65 A8
Hest Bank La LA2 .....218 C7
Hest Bank Rd LA4 .....217 E6
Hester Cl L38 .....2 F4
Hestham Ave LA4 .....217 B4
Hestham Cres LA4 .....217 B4
Hestham Dr LA4 .....217 B4
Hestham Par LA4 .....217 B4
Hetherington Pl FY2 .....152 E2
Hetton Lea BB9 .....170 C3
Heversham WN8 .....18 C2
Heversham Ave PR2 .....117 F7
Heversham Cl
Lancaster LA1 .....215 B3
Heversham Cl *continued*
Morecambe LA4 .....217 C3
Hewart Dr BL9 .....33 C3
Hewart St BB12 .....127 A7
Hewitt Bsns Pk WN5 .....10 E4
Hewitt Cl PR4 .....95 E1
Hewitt St 8 PR25 .....77 B2
Hewlett Ave PR7 .....42 D1
Hewlett Ct BL8 .....50 A1
Hewlett St PR7 .....42 D1
Hewngate PR5 .....98 E1
Hexham Ave FY5 .....175 E4
Hexham Cl BB5 .....104 E3
Hexham Rd LA4 .....217 F5
Hey Bottom La OL12 .....52 F6
Hey End PR4 .....75 F8
Hey Head Ave BB4 .....70 A8
Hey House Mews BL8 .....49 F4
Hey St BB9 .....170 E1
Heycrofts View BL0 .....68 E3
Heydon Cl L37 .....11 D1
Heyes Rd WN5 .....10 E6
Heyes St WN6 .....19 C7
Heyes The PR6 .....78 B2
Heyescroft L39 .....7 D6
Heyfold Gdns BB3 .....81 F3
Heyhead St BB9 .....148 C5
Heyhouses BB7 .....146 A8
Heyhouses Ct FY8 .....90 B8
Heyhouses Endowed CE Inf Sch FY8 .....89 F7
Heyhouses Endowed CE Jun Sch FY8 .....89 F8
Heyhouses La FY8 .....90 C7
Heyhurst Rd BB2 .....101 D5
Heymoor Ave BB6 .....124 D6
Heys BB5 .....103 D3
Heys Ave 5 BB4 .....85 A3
Heys Cl Blackburn BB2 .....81 C7
Rawtenstall BB4 .....86 C1
Heys Ct Blackburn BB2 .....81 C8
Oswaldtwistle BB5 .....103 E3
Heys La
Barley Green BB12 .....169 D5
Blackburn BB2,BB3 .....81 C7
Darwen BB3 .....81 F2
Great Harwood BB6 .....124 E5
Oswaldtwistle BB5 .....103 E3
Heys Lane Ind Est BB6 .....124 E5
Heys St Bacup OL13 .....87 F1
Haslingden BB4 .....85 A3
Rawtenstall BB4 .....86 C1
Thornton FY5 .....176 B3
Heys The Coppull PR7 .....42 F2
Parbold WN8 .....27 C3
Southport PR8 .....34 D4
Heysham Ave LA3 .....212 F8
Heysham Bsns Pk LA3 .....212 E2
Heysham Cres BB2 .....101 F1
Heysham Hall Dr LA3 .....212 E6
Heysham Hall Gr LA3 .....212 E7
Heysham High Sch LA3 .....216 F3
Heysham Mossgate Rd LA3 .....212 F7
Heysham Nuclear Power Sta Nature Reserve* LA3 .....212 D4
Heysham Pk LA3 .....212 E7
Heysham Port Sta LA3 .....212 C5
Heysham Rd
4 Heysham LA3 .....212 E7
Morecambe LA3 .....216 D2
Southport PR9 .....35 F7
Heysham St 2 PR1 .....117 E1
Heywood Cl L37 .....11 E3
Heywood Com High Sch OL10 .....33 E1
Heywood Rd PR2 .....116 E2
Heywood St
1 Blackpool FY1 .....130 B4
Bury BL9 .....33 A1
Great Harwood BB6 .....124 C4
Heyworth Ave BB2 .....81 C7
Hibbert Terr LA1 .....214 F3
Hibson Rd Nelson BB9 .....148 D8
Nelson,Little Marsden BB9 .....148 D7
Hic Bibi La PR7 .....29 E6
Hick's Terr 5 BB1 .....124 B1
Hickory St BB1 .....101 F7
Hickson Ave L31 .....5 C3
Hidings Court La LA4 .....217 B4
Hiers House La BB8 .....171 B5
Higgin St Burnley BB10 .....128 B5
Colne BB8 .....171 D5
Worsthorne BB10 .....129 B5
Higgin's La L40 .....25 C4
High Bank PR6 .....62 A3
High Bank Cres BB3 .....65 A7
High Banks L31 .....5 C3
High Barn La OL12 .....71 C3
High Bentham Bsns Pk LA2 .....239 D7
High Bentham Prim Sch LA2 .....239 D8
High Cl BB12 .....126 E6
High Cop PR6 .....78 F4
High Crag Ct LA5 .....223 E6
High Ct LA4 .....217 F5
High Fold BB18 .....195 A6
High Gate FY7 .....198 D3
High Gate La FY6 .....177 A6
High Gn PR25 .....76 F7
High La Bickerstaffe L39 .....7 C8
Laneshaw Bridge BD22 .....174 A8
Ormskirk L39,L40 .....16 A8
Salterforth BB18 .....194 C5
High Legh FY8 .....90 C3
High Mdw PR5 .....97 B2
High Moor La WN6 .....28 B4
High Moss L39 .....15 E3
High Mount Ct 2 LA1 .....214 F7
High Mount Ho 1 LA1 .....214 F7
High Park Pl PR9 .....36 A8
High Park Rd PR9 .....36 A8
High Peak Rd OL12 .....52 C6
High Rd Halton LA2 .....219 C7
Lowgill LA2 .....239 C5
High St Accrington BB5 .....104 B4
Belmont BL7 .....46 C4
Blackburn BB1 .....101 E5
Blackpool FY1 .....130 B6
Brierfield BB9 .....148 B5
Burton in L LA6 .....242 C3
Chapeltown BL7 .....48 C4
10 Chorley PR7 .....43 C8
Clitheroe BB7 .....166 B8
Colne BB8 .....171 E5
Darwen BB3 .....82 A1
Elswick PR4 .....155 F1
Fleetwood FY7 .....199 B4
Garstang PR3 .....181 C7
Great Eccleston PR3 .....156 B5
Haslingden BB4 .....85 B4
Horwich BL6 .....32 B4
Lancaster LA1 .....214 F7
Mawdesley L40 .....40 B1
Nelson BB9 .....148 D7
Oswaldtwistle BB5 .....103 F3
Padiham BB12 .....146 D1
14 Preston PR1 .....97 A8
Rishton BB1 .....124 B1
Skelmersdale WN8 .....17 E1
Standish WN6 .....29 E1
Higham Gr FY3 .....130 F2
Higham Hall Rd BB12 .....146 F5
Higham Rd BB12 .....146 C3
Higham Side Rd PR4 .....135 C6
Higham St BB12 .....146 D1
Highbank BB1 .....122 F1
Highbank Ave FY4 .....111 A8
Highbank Hotel 7 PR2 .....117 C1
Highbury Ave
Blackpool FY3 .....130 E8
Fleetwood FY7 .....198 F3
Highbury Gate PR4 .....156 A2
Highbury Pl BB1 .....101 D6
Highbury Rd FY8 .....110 E1
Highbury Rd E FY8 .....110 E1
Highbury Rd W FY8 .....110 D1
Highcroft 17 LA2 .....239 D8
Highcroft Ave FY2 .....152 E5
Highcroft Way OL12 .....52 F4
Highcross Ave FY6 .....131 D8
Highcross Hill FY6 .....131 D8
Highcross Rd FY6 .....153 D1
Highdale LA3 .....213 A7
Higher Antley St BB5 .....104 A5
Higher Audley St BB1 .....101 F4
Higher Austin's BL6 .....32 F1
Higher Bank Rd PR2 .....117 F3
Higher Bank St
Blackburn BB2 .....101 B6
Withnell PR6 .....80 A1
Higher Barn BL6 .....32 F3
Higher Barn St 2 BB1 .....102 A5
Higher Blackthorn OL13 .....87 F4
Higher Bold Venture BB3 .....65 A6
Higher Booths La BB4 .....106 A1
Higher Change Villas OL13 .....88 B4
Higher Chapel La BB7 .....230 A1
Higher Church St BB3 .....82 B1
Higher Cockcroft 14 BB1 .....101 E5
Higher Commons La BB2 .....121 C4
Higher Compley Cvn Pk FY6 .....153 C2
Higher Croft
Kingsfold PR1 .....96 C2
2 Kingsfold PR1 .....96 D2
Higher Croft Cotts BB3 .....81 F8
Higher Croft Rd BB2,BB3 .....81 F8
Higher Cross Row 8 OL13 .....87 F3
Higher Cswy BB9 .....170 D3
Higher Dunscar BL7 .....47 E1
Higher Eanam BB1 .....102 A5
Higher Feniscowles La BB2 .....80 B8
Higher Field BB6 .....123 C8
Higher Firs Dr BB5 .....125 A3
Higher Fold La BL0 .....50 E7
Higher Furlong PR4 .....74 F6
Higher Gate BB5 .....125 F1
Higher Gate Rd BB5 .....125 F1
Higher Gn FY6 .....153 E3
Higher Greenfield PR2 .....117 B5
Higher Heys BB5 .....103 E3
Higher Hill BB3 .....80 F2
Higher House Cl BB2 .....81 A7
Higher House La PR6 .....62 B2
Higher Knowles BL6 .....32 E2
Higher La Haslingden BB4 .....85 B4
Holmes PR4 .....56 C3
Salterforth BB18 .....194 B7
Scorton PR3 .....204 F4
Skelmersdale,Dalton WN8 .....18 C7
Skelmersdale,Up Holland WN8 .....10 C7
Higher Lawrence St 14 BB3 .....81 F2
Higher London Terr BB3 .....82 B2
Higher Mdw PR25 .....77 E1
Higher Mill St BB4 .....86 A3
Higher Moor Cotts FY2 .....152 F2
Higher Moor Rd FY3 .....153 A2
Higher Moss La L37 .....13 A2
Higher Moulding BL9 .....33 E5
Higher Park Rd BB18 .....194 C8
Higher Peel St 8 BB5 .....103 D3
Higher Perry St BB3 .....82 B2
Higher Ramsgreave Rd BB1 .....122 C3
Higher Rd
Knowle Green PR3 .....163 B3
Longridge PR3 .....162 E2
Tosside BD23 .....236 C5
Higher Reedley Rd BB9, BB10 .....148 D5
Higher Row BL9 .....33 B3
Higher Saxifield BB10 .....148 E3
Higher South St BB3 .....82 A1
Higher Summerseat BL0 .....50 B2
Higher Syke LA2 .....233 C2
Higher Tentre BB11 .....128 B5
Higher View WN8 .....10 C6
Higher Walton CE Prim Sch PR5 .....98 C3
Higher Walton Mill PR5 .....98 B4
Higher Walton Rd PR5 .....97 E4
Higher Waterside BB3 .....82 E3
Higher Witton Rd BB2 .....101 B4
Highergate Cl BB5 .....125 F2
Highfield Bacup OL13 .....87 F2
Brinscall PR6 .....62 F8
Great Harwood BB6 .....124 B5
Rawtenstall BB4 .....86 A7
Highfield Ave
Bamber Bridge PR5 .....97 C1
Brierfield BB10 .....148 B3
Foulridge BB8 .....194 E1
Fulwood PR2 .....118 C4
Inskip PR4 .....135 C8
Leyland PR25 .....77 C3
Highfield Cl Adlington PR6 .....31 A7
Clifton PR4 .....115 C1
Oswaldtwistle BB5 .....103 F3
Tarleton PR4 .....57 A5
Highfield Cres
5 Barrowford BB9 .....170 D3
Morecambe LA4 .....216 F4
Nelson BB9 .....170 E3
Highfield Ct BB4 .....85 A2
Highfield Dr
Fulwood PR2 .....117 E8
Hest Bank LA2 .....220 D1
Kingsfold PR1 .....96 D2
Longridge PR3 .....140 B6
Longton PR4 .....74 F6
Highfield Gdns BB2 .....101 E2
Highfield Gr PR5 .....97 C2
Highfield High Sch FY4 .....110 E6
Highfield Ind Est PR7 .....61 D2
Highfield La L40 .....24 D7
Highfield Mews BB3 .....65 B8
Highfield Pk
Haslingden BB4 .....85 A1
Maghull L31 .....5 F1
Highfield Prim Sch PR6 .....43 E8
Highfield Priory Sch PR2 .....118 F5
Highfield Rd
Adlington PR6 .....31 A7
Blackburn BB2 .....101 E3
Blackpool FY4 .....110 E6
Blackrod BL6 .....31 E1
Carnforth LA5 .....221 E8
Clitheroe BB7 .....166 F7
Croston PR26 .....58 D2
Darwen BB3 .....82 B1
1 Earby BB18 .....197 B2
Edenfield BL0 .....68 D3
Ormskirk L39 .....15 E7
Rawtenstall BB4 .....86 D1
5 Rishton BB1 .....124 A1
Southport PR9 .....54 B3
Highfield Rd N
Adlington PR6 .....31 A8
Chorley PR7 .....61 C2
Highfield Rd S PR7 .....61 C1
Highfield St
4 Darwen BB3 .....65 B8
Haslingden BB4 .....85 A2
Highfield Terr LA2 .....239 C8
Highfurlong Sch FY3 .....153 A2
Highgale Gdns PR5 .....77 C7
Highgate Blackpool FY4 .....110 D5
Goosnargh PR3 .....138 D6
Higher Penwortham PR1 .....96 B5
Nelson BB9 .....148 D7
Highgate Ave PR2 .....117 E4
Highgate Cl Fulwood PR2 .....117 F4
Newton-w-S PR4 .....114 F3
Highgate Cres WN6 .....19 E7
Highgate La Warton PR4 .....92 E6
Whitworth OL12 .....52 C5
Highgate Pl FY8 .....90 D6
Highgate Rd Maghull L31 .....5 D3
Skelmersdale WN8 .....10 B7
Highgrove Ave PR7 .....41 F3
Highgrove Cl LA4 .....217 A4
Highgrove Ct PR26 .....58 F8
Highland Ave PR1 .....96 B4
Highland Brow LA2 .....211 A4
Highland Dr PR7 .....60 E6
Highland Lo WN6 .....29 D1
Highland Rd BL6 .....32 E1
Highmeadow WN8 .....10 A6
Highmoor BB9 .....148 F6
Highmoor Pk BB7 .....166 F8
Highrigg Dr PR3 .....137 F1
Highsands Ave L40 .....39 A3
Hightown BB4 .....86 E4
Hightown Rd BB4 .....86 F4
Hightown Sta L38 .....3 A4
Highways Ave PR7 .....60 D1
Highwoods Pk BB6 .....143 B5
Higson St BB2 .....101 D5
Hilary Ave FY2 .....152 C5
Hilary St BB10 .....148 A1
Hilbre Cl PR9 .....53 F1
Hilbre Dr PR9 .....53 F1
Hilderstone La LA5 .....240 A7
Hildrop Rd 7 BB9 .....170 F1
Hill Cl WN6 .....19 E8
Hill Cres PR4 .....115 A2
Hill Crest OL13 .....87 D1
Hill Crest Ave
Burnley BB10 .....128 F4
Fulwood PR2 .....117 E8
Hill Croft
Clayton Green PR6 .....78 A2
Kirkham PR4 .....114 B5
Hill End La BB4 .....86 C1
Hill Field Croft PR3 .....204 C1
Hill Hos 16 BB3 .....65 A8
Hill House Fold La WN6 .....28 C5
Hill House La
Jack Green PR6 .....79 A7
Wrightington WN6 .....28 C5
Hill La Blackrod BL6 .....31 C2
Colne BB8 .....172 C7
Nether Kellet LA6 .....221 F4
Hill Pl BB9 .....148 D6
Hill Rd
Higher Penwortham PR1 .....96 C5
Lancaster LA1 .....218 D3
Leyland PR25 .....77 C1
Hill Rd S PR1 .....96 D3
Hill Rise Haslingden BB4 .....85 C1
1 Ramsbottom BL0 .....50 A4
Hill Rise View L39 .....15 A1
Hill Side LA1 .....214 E8
Hill St Accrington BB5 .....104 C5
Barnoldswick BB18 .....196 C2
Blackburn BB1 .....102 B5
Blackpool FY4 .....130 B1
Brierfield BB9 .....148 B5
Carnforth LA5 .....223 D1
3 Church BB5 .....125 A1
Colne BB8 .....171 D4
Fence BB9 .....147 F6
Oswaldtwistle BB5 .....103 D5
Padiham BB12 .....126 C8
Preston PR1 .....96 F8
Ramsbottom BL9 .....50 C3
Rawtenstall BB4 .....86 A7
Southport PR9 .....35 B7
Hill Top Barrowford BB9 .....170 D4
Colne,Cotton Tree BB8 .....172 C4
Foulridge BB8 .....194 C2
Longridge PR3 .....162 D2
New Longton PR4 .....76 A6
Trawden BB8 .....172 B2
Hill Top Cl Freckleton PR4 .....93 D7
Yealand Redmayne LA5 .....225 E4
Hill Top La Earby BB18 .....197 A2
Whittle-le-W PR6 .....61 D8
Hill View Beverley BB9 .....170 E7
7 Blackburn BB1 .....122 E1
2 Rawtenstall BB4 .....85 F1
Hill View Dr PR7 .....29 D8
Hill View Rd PR3 .....204 C1
Hill Wlk PR25 .....77 A2
Hillam La LA2 .....206 B7
Hillary Cres L31 .....5 D1
Hillary Ct L37 .....11 E2
Hillbrook Rd PR25 .....76 F2
Hillcliffe FY8 .....89 E5
Hillcrest Maghull L31 .....5 F1
Skelmersdale WN8 .....9 B8
Hillcrest Ave
Bolton-le-S LA5 .....221 A5
Fulwood PR2 .....117 A4
Longridge PR3 .....140 A7
Hillcrest Cl PR4 .....57 A8
Hillcrest Dr Bescar L40 .....23 F7
Longridge PR3 .....140 A7
Tarleton PR4 .....57 A8
Hillcrest Rd
Blackburn BB2 .....100 F2
Blackpool FY4 .....110 B4
Langho BB6 .....123 C8
Ormskirk L39 .....15 E6
Hillcroft Fulwood PR2 .....117 C7
High Bentham LA2 .....239 D7
Hilldean WN8 .....10 C8
Hillingdon Rd BB10 .....148 D3
Hillingdon Rd N BB10 .....148 D3
Hillkirk Dr OL12 .....52 C3
Hillmount Ave LA3 .....212 F8
Hillock Cl L40 .....24 A7
Hillock La Bescar L40 .....24 A7
Skelmersdale WN8 .....18 D7
Warton PR4 .....92 E8
Hillocks The PR26 .....58 B1
Hillpark Ave
Fulwood PR2 .....117 D4
Gregson Lane PR5 .....98 D1
Hills Ct 2 LA1 .....218 D1
Hills The PR2 .....119 C7
Hillsborough Ave BB9 .....148 D5
Hillsea Ave LA3 .....212 F8
Hillside Burnley BB11 .....127 D3
Tarleton PR4 .....57 A6
Hillside Ave
Blackburn BB1 .....102 C4
Blackrod BL6 .....31 E1
Brierfield BB10 .....148 C5
15 Darwen BB3 .....65 A8
Egerton BL7 .....48 B1

Hillside Ave *continued*
Farington PR26 76 F7
Fulwood PR2 117 D4
Hill Dale WN8 27 D5
Horwich BL6 32 C4
Kirkham PR4 114 C5
Ormskirk L39 15 D3
Preesall FY6 200 B4
Hillside Cl Blackburn BB1 102 C4
Blackpool FY3 130 E6
Brierfield BB9 148 C5
Burnley BB11 127 D2
Clitheroe BB7 166 E6
Euxton PR7 60 C1
Goodshaw Chapel BB4 106 A1
Great Harwood BB6 124 C6
Thornton FY5 153 D8
Hillside Com Prim Sch
WN8 9 D8
Hillside Cres Horwich BL6 32 C4
Weir OL13 87 F7
Whittle-le-W PR6 61 C8
Hillside Ct L39 15 D3
Hillside Dr Newchurch BB4 86 E2
Stalmine FY6 177 C7
West Bradford BB7 189 F6
Hillside Gdns BB3 65 A7
Hillside Rd
Haslingden BB4 85 C3
Low Bentham LA2 239 C8
2 Preston PR1 97 C6
Ramsbottom BL0 50 A5
Southport PR8 34 E1
Hillside Sch PR3 140 D7
Hillside Sta PR8 34 E1
Hillside View BB9 148 C5
Hillside Way OL12 71 C1
Hillside Wlk
Blackburn BB1 102 C4
Rochdale OL12 52 D4
Hillstone Ave OL12 52 D4
Hillstone Cl BL8 49 F2
Hillsview Rd PR8 21 C4
Hilltop OL12 52 C5
Hilltop Dr BB4 68 C7
Hilltop Wlk L39 15 C3
Hillview Rd PR4 114 A6
Hillview Short Stay Sch
BB11 127 D5
Hillylaid Rd FY5 176 D2
Hilmont Terr BB1 101 F7
Hilmore Rd LA4 217 A5
Hilstone La FY2 152 D1
Hilton Ave
6 Blackpool FY1 130 B1
Horwich BL6 32 A3
Lytham St Anne's FY8 90 C6
Hilton Ct FY8 89 E5
Hilton Rd BB3 65 B8
Hilton St BB3 65 A8
Hilton's Brow PR6 79 B4
Hinchley Gn L31 5 B1
Hind St Burnley BB10 148 B2
4 Preston PR1 96 E6
Hind's Head Ave WN6 28 F6
Hindburn Ave L31 5 F2
Hindburn Pl 2 LA1 218 C2
Hinde St LA1 218 E1
Hindle Fold La BB6 124 C6
Hindle St Accrington BB5 104 B6
Bacup OL13 70 D8
Darwen BB3 81 F2
Haslingden BB4 85 B3
Hindley Beech 1 L31 5 C2
Hindley Cl PR2 118 C7
Hindley Ct 3 BB9 170 C1
Hindley St 5 PR7 43 C6
Hinton St BB10 128 B5
Hippings La BB4 86 F1
Hippings Meth Prim Sch
BB5 103 E3
Hippings Vale BB5 103 D4
Hippings Way BB7 189 E2
Hirst St 5 Burnley BB11 128 B4
6 Cornholme OL14 109 B1
Padiham BB12 146 C1
Hoarstones Ave BB12 147 D7
Hob Gn BB2 121 F2
Hob La BL7 48 C7
Hobart Pl FY5 152 F8
Hobart St BB11 128 B6
Hobberley Dr WN8 9 E8
Hobbs La PR3 183 A4
Hobcross La L40 26 A2
Hobson St BB4 85 F4
Hobson's La LA6 240 C2
Hockley Pl FY3 130 F7
Hodder Ave
Blackpool FY1 130 D1
Chorley PR7 43 B5
Fleetwood FY7 198 D2
Maghull L31 5 F2
Morecambe LA3 217 F3
Hodder Bridge Ct BB7 165 B7
Hodder Brook PR2 119 A3
Hodder Cl
6 Bamber Bridge PR5 77 F8
Fleetwood FY7 198 C2
Hodder Ct BB7 165 C4
Hodder Dr BB7 189 D7
Hodder Gr Clitheroe BB7 166 C7
Darwen BB3 81 E4
Hodder Pl Blackburn BB1 101 F6
Lancaster LA1 215 B5
Lytham St Anne's FY8 90 C7
Hodder St
Accrington BB5 104 D6
1 Blackburn BB1 101 E6
Hodder St *continued*
Brierfield BB10 148 C3
Longridge PR3 140 B7
Hodder Way FY6 153 D2
Hoddlesden Fold BB3 82 F1
Hoddlesden Rd BB3 82 E1
Hoddlesden St Paul's CE Prim Sch BB3 82 F1
Hodge Bank Bsn Pk
BB9 170 D2
Hodge Brow BL6 44 F4
Hodge La BB18 194 B8
Hodge St PR8 35 B7
Hodgefield BB7 144 A4
Hodgson Ave PR4 93 A5
Hodgson High Sch Tech Coll
FY6 153 F3
Hodgson Pl FY6 153 D2
Hodgson Rd FY1 130 C8
Hodgson St Darwen BB3 82 B1
3 Oswaldtwistle BB5 103 E4
Hodson St
Bamber Bridge PR5 97 E1
Southport PR8 35 C6
Hogarth Ave BB11 127 F3
Hogarth Cres PR4 134 F4
Hogg's La PR7 43 E5
Hoggs Hill La L37 11 F1
Hoghton Ave OL13 71 A8
Hoghton Cl LA1 214 D6
Hoghton Gr PR9 35 C8
Hoghton La PR5 98 D3
Hoghton Pl 3 PR9 35 B7
Hoghton Rd Leyland PR25 76 D1
Longridge PR3 140 C7
Hoghton St
8 Bamber Bridge PR5 77 A8
Southport PR9 35 C7
Hoghton Twr* PR5 99 E1
Hoghton View PR1 97 C6
Holbeck Ave
Blackpool FY4 110 F8
Morecambe LA4 217 F4
Rochdale OL12 52 D4
Holbeck St BB10 148 A1
Holborn Dr L39 15 C3
Holborn Hill L39 15 C4
Holcombe Brook Prim Sch
BL0 50 A2
Holcombe Ct BL0 49 F2
Holcombe Dr BB10 128 B6
Holcombe Gr PR6 61 E1
Holcombe Lee BL0 50 A4
Holcombe Mews BL0 49 F3
Holcombe Old Rd BL8,
BL0 50 A5
Holcombe Prec BL0 49 F3
Holcombe Rd
Blackpool FY2 152 E1
Haslingden BB4 67 F8
Ramsbottom BL8 49 F2
Holcombe Village BL8 50 A6
Holcroft Pl FY8 90 F4
Holden Ave Bury BL9 33 E4
Ramsbottom BL0 50 A5
Holden Cl BB9 170 C1
Holden Fold BB3 82 B3
Holden La BB7 230 B5
Holden Pl BB4 84 F1
Holden Rd Brierfield BB9 148 A5
Brierfield,Reedley BB10 148 B3
Holden St Accrington BB5 104 B5
Adlington PR7 30 F7
Belthorn BB1 82 F6
Blackburn BB2 101 C4
Burnley BB11 127 F5
Clitheroe BB7 166 F8
Holden Way LA1 214 F5
Holden Wood Dr BB4 84 F1
Hole House La BB7 235 E2
Hole House St BB1 102 C5
Holgate FY4 110 F6
Holgate Dr WN5 10 E6
Holgate St
Brierfield BB10 148 F3
Great Harwood BB6 124 C5
Holgates Cvn Pk LA5 224 B5
Holhouse La BL8 49 F2
Holker Bsns Ctr 2 BB8 171 B4
Holker Cl Coupe Green PR5 98 E3
Lancaster LA1 214 D6
Holker La PR26 59 B4
Holker St Colne BB8 171 B4
Darwen BB3 65 B8
Holland Ave
Bamber Bridge PR5 97 E2
Rawtenstall BB4 85 F3
Holland Bsns Pk L40 17 C4
Holland Ct WN8 9 D2
Holland House Ct PR5 97 E3
Holland House Rd PR5 97 F3
Holland Lodge 4 PR2 118 F4
Holland Moor Prim Sch
WN8 9 E7
Holland Moss WN8 9 A5
Holland Pl BB9 170 E2
Holland Rd PR2 117 C1
Holland St
Accrington BB5 103 F6
Blackburn BB1 101 D6
3 Burnley BB12 126 B8
Holland's La WN8 17 A1
Holliers Cl L31 5 E1
Hollies Cl Blackburn BB2 80 F8
Catterall PR3 181 D2
Hollies Rd BB1 123 A7
Hollies The PR8 34 F6
Hollin Bank BB9 148 B6
Hollin Bridge St BB2 101 D2
Hollin Cl BB4 86 F4
Hollin Gr BB4 86 A4
Hollin Hall BB8 172 C1
Hollin Hill BB11 128 B3
Hollin La Knowley PR6 62 C2
Rawtenstall BB4 86 A4
Hollin Mill St BB9 148 B6
Hollin St BB2 101 C2
Hollin Way
Rawtenstall,Constable Lee
BB4 86 A4
Rawtenstall,Rush Bed BB4 86 A6
Hollingreave Dr BB4 86 A5
Hollingreave Rd BB11 128 A4
Hollings PR4 75 F7
Hollington St BB8 172 B5
Hollinhead Cres PR2 117 B4
Hollinhurst Ave PR1 96 C6
Hollinhurst Brow LA2 239 C2
Hollinhurst View BB12 146 F5
Hollins Ave BB10 128 F4
Hollins Cl Accrington BB5 104 C4
Hoghton PR5 99 C3
Hollins Ct 1 BB18 196 B3
Hollins Gr PR2 117 B3
Hollins Grove St BB3 81 F3
Hollins Hill PR3 207 C2
Hollins La
Accrington BB5 104 D3
Edenfield BL0 68 E2
Hollins Lane PR3 207 C2
Runshaw Moor PR26 59 C4
Silverdale LA5 224 D1
Hollins Rd
Barnoldswick BB18 196 A2
Darwen BB3 81 F4
Nelson BB9 171 A2
Preston PR1 118 B2
Hollins Tech Coll The
BB5 104 D2
Hollinshead St PR7 43 C8
Hollinshead Terr BB3 64 B7
Hollinview Cl BB4 86 A5
Hollinwood Dr BB4 86 A5
Hollow Gill Brow BD23,
BD24 236 F5
Hollowbrook Way 4
OL12 52 D2
Hollowell La BL6 32 D1
Hollowford La L40 26 D2
Hollowforth La PR4 136 E5
Hollowhead Ave BB1 122 F5
Hollowhead Cl BB1 122 F5
Hollowhead La BB1 123 A5
Hollowrane LA6 240 C7
Holly Ave BB4 85 C1
Holly Bank
Accrington BB5 104 C4
Edgworth BL7 48 B7
Fulwood PR2 117 C5
Warton LA5 223 D5
Holly Cl Clayton Green PR6 78 B2
Skelmersdale WN8 17 E1
Thornton FY5 176 C3
Westhead L40 16 E4
Holly Cres PR7 42 E2
Holly Ct BB1 101 F7
Holly Fold La L39,WA11 8 E3
Holly Gr Longridge PR3 140 A8
Tarleton PR4 57 A7
Holly Ho 8 BB11 128 B5
Holly La Ormskirk L39 15 B4
Rufford L40 39 C3
Skelmersdale L39,WA11 8 E4
Holly Mews FY8 110 F2
Holly Mount BB4 68 A7
Holly Mount RC Prim Sch
BL8 49 D1
Holly Pl PR5 78 B6
Holly Rd Blackpool FY1 152 C1
Thornton FY5 176 B3
Holly St Blackburn BB1 101 F7
Burnley BB10 128 B5
Bury BL9 33 A2
Nelson BB9 148 F8
Oswaldtwistle BB5 103 D4
Ramsbottom BL0 50 C3
Holly Terr BB1 101 F8
Holly Tree Cl BB3 65 A6
Holly Tree Way BB2 80 F8
Holly Wlk LA1 214 D8
Hollybank Cl PR2 116 F5
Hollybrook Rd PR8 35 A5
Hollytree Cl BB4 85 F5
Hollywood Ave
Blackpool FY3 130 E5
Higher Penwortham PR1 96 C3
Hollywood Gr FY7 198 F4
Holman St 5 PR1 118 C1
Holmbrook Cl BB2 81 F8
Holmby St BB10 148 B2
Holmdale Ave PR9 54 C4
Holme Ave FY7 175 D8
Holme Bank BB4 85 F1
Holme Cl BB18 195 A7
Holme Cres BB8 172 B3
Holme End BB12 147 F4
Holme Hill BB7 189 E2
Holme House Rd OL14 109 C1
Holme La Caton LA2 237 C3
Haslingden BB4 68 D8
Rawtenstall BB4 68 E8
Holme Lea BB5 124 F4
Holme Mills Ind Est LA6 240 B8
Holme Pk LA2 239 D7
Holme Rd
Bamber Bridge PR5 77 E8
Holme Rd *continued*
Burnley BB12 127 E7
Clayton-le-M BB5 124 E4
Higher Penwortham PR1,
PR2 96 C7
Holme Slack Com Prim Sch
PR1 118 C3
Holme Slack La PR1 118 C3
Holme St Accrington BB5 104 C6
Bacup OL13 70 D8
Barrowford BB9 170 D2
Colne,Cotton Tree BB8 172 B5
Darwen BB3 65 A8
Nelson BB9 148 E8
Holme Terr Nelson BB9 148 C8
Rawtenstall BB4 68 D8
Holme The
Calder Vale PR3 182 E8
Rawtenstall BB4 68 E8
Holme Vale BB4 68 A6
Holmebrook Dr BL6 32 D1
Holmefield Ave FY5 175 E2
Holmefield Cl FY5 175 E2
Holmefield Ct 8 BB9 170 D3
Holmefield Gdns 15
BB9 170 D3
Holmefield Gr 1 L31 5 C1
Holmefield Rd
Knott End-on-S FY6 199 E5
Lytham St Anne's FY8 90 A7
Holmehouse Lodge 15
PR2 118 F4
Holmes Ct Fulwood PR1 117 E3
Garstang PR3 181 C8
Holmes Dr OL13 87 F4
Holmes La OL13 87 F3
Holmes Mdw 3 PR26 76 B1
Holmes Rd FY5 176 B3
Holmes Sq 7 BB11 128 B5
Holmes St Burnley BB11 128 B5
Forest Holme BB4 87 A7
Padiham BB12 126 D8
Rawtenstall BB4 86 B3
Holmes Terr BB4 85 F5
Holmes The BB4 85 F5
Holmestrand Ave BB11 127 B4
Holmeswood PR4 114 A5
Holmeswood Cres PR3 137 B8
Holmeswood Meth Sch
L40 38 C6
Holmeswood Pk BB4 68 E8
Holmeswood Rd L40 38 D6
Holmfield Cres 2 PR2 116 D1
Holmfield Pk L37 11 D4
Holmfield Rd
Blackpool FY2 152 B2
Fulwood PR2 118 A4
Holmrook Rd PR1 118 B1
Holmsley St BB10 128 B5
Holmwood Cl L37 11 D3
Holmwood Gdns L37 11 D4
Holsands Cl PR2 118 E6
Holst Gdns BB2 102 A1
Holstein Ave OL12 52 D4
Holstein St PR1 97 A8
Holt Ave PR7 42 F2
Holt Brow PR25 60 A6
Holt Coppice L39 6 A7
Holt La PR6 78 E3
Holt Mill Rd BB4 69 D8
Holt Sq BB9 170 E5
Holt St Orrell WN5 10 D5
Ramsbottom BL0 50 D6
9 Rawtenstall BB4 69 E8
Rishton BB1 124 C1
Whitworth OL12 71 C1
Holt St W BL0 50 B5
Holt's Terr OL12 52 E2
Holts La FY6 153 F2
Holy Cross RC High Sch
PR7 43 C4
Holy Family RC Prim Sch
Blackpool FY1 130 C8
Fulwood PR2 116 F4
Southport PR9 35 E7
Warton PR4 92 E6
Holy Saviour RC Prim Sch
BB9 170 E2
Holy Souls RC Prim Sch
BB1 122 E1
Holy Trinity CE Prim Sch
Burnley BB11 127 E5
Formby L37 11 F3
Southport PR9 35 C8
Holy Trinity RC Prim Sch
BB9 148 C5
Holy Trinity Sch BB3 82 A1
Holy Trinity Stacksteads CE Prim Sch OL13 70 C8
Holyoake Ave FY2 152 E1
Holyoake St
Burnley BB12 127 A6
2 Cornholme OL14 109 A1
Home Breeze Ho 1
LA4 217 E6
Home Farm Cl LA2 238 D6
Home Farm Mews PR26 58 D1
Home Field PR3 181 C8
Homeacre Ave BB7 145 F8
Homechase Ho PR8 34 F4
Homefylde Ho 4 FY3 130 E3
Homelinks Ho FY8 90 D3
Homer Ave PR4 56 F7
Homer St 1 BB11 127 C5
Homesands Ho PR9 35 D8
Homestead PR5 78 B4
Homestead Cl 4 PR25 76 D1
Homestead Dr FY7 198 E1
Homestead The 9 FY8 91 A3
Homestead Way FY7 198 E1
Homewood Ave LA4 217 F6
Homfray Ave LA3 217 E3
Homfray Gr LA3 217 E3
Honey Hole BB2 101 E2
Honey Holme La BB10 107 F7
Honey Moor Dr FY5 176 B4
Honeypot La FY6 154 D4
Honeysuckle Cl PR6 61 B5
Honeysuckle Gr PR4 73 E4
Honeysuckle Pl FY2 152 F6
Honeysuckle Row PR2 118 E2
Honeysuckle Way OL12 52 D3
Honeywood Cl BL0 50 A3
Honister Ave FY3 130 F2
Honister Cl 6 FY7 198 D3
Honister Rd
Brierfield BB10 148 B3
Lancaster LA1 218 F2
Honister Sq FY8 110 F2
Honiton Ave BB2 81 C8
Honiton Way PR4 116 F6
Hoo Hill Ind Est FY3 130 E8
Hoo Hill La FY3 130 E8
Hood St 4 BB5 104 C6
Hoodhouse St BB11 127 E4
Hookwood Ave FY5 175 D1
Hoole La Banks PR9 55 A6
Nateby PR3 180 B5
Hoole St Michael CE Prim Sch PR4 74 C1
Hools La PR3 201 A5
Hope Cl FY5 176 B4
Hope La PR3 162 E5
Hope Sq PR9 35 D7
Hope St Accrington BB5 104 B5
Adlington PR6 31 B8
Bacup OL13 87 F4
Blackburn BB2 101 D5
Brierfield BB9 148 B5
Chorley PR7 61 C1
Darwen BB3 81 F1
Great Harwood BB6 124 C4
Haslingden BB4 85 B2
Horwich BL6 32 B4
Lancaster LA1 215 A7
Lytham St Anne's FY8 90 A7
Morecambe LA4 217 C4
Nelson BB9 148 D8
12 Padiham BB12 126 D8
4 Preston PR1 96 F8
Ramsbottom BL0 50 B5
Rawtenstall BB4 86 C1
Southport PR9 35 C7
Worsthorne BB10 129 B6
Hope St N BL6 32 B5
Hope Terr
10 Bamber Bridge PR5 77 A8
Blackburn BB2 101 C6
Hopkinson St BB8 172 B3
Hopkinson Terr BB8 172 C3
Hopton Rd FY1 130 B2
Hopwood Ave BL6 32 C4
Hopwood St
Accrington BB5 104 B4
4 Bamber Bridge PR5 77 E8
Bamber Bridge PR5 77 F7
Blackburn BB2 101 E3
8 Burnley BB11 127 E6
Preston PR1 97 A8
Horace St 7 BB12 127 D6
Horden Rake BB2 80 E7
Horden View BB2 80 E7
Hordley St BB12 127 A6
Horeb Cl 5 BB12 126 D7
Hornbeam Cl PR1 96 B3
Hornby Ave
Fleetwood FY7 175 D8
Fulwood PR2 118 E4
Hornby Bank Hornby LA2 238 B8
Nether Kellet LA6 221 F5
Hornby Croft PR26 59 B8
Hornby Ct
4 Blackburn BB2 101 C4
Kirkham PR4 114 B4
Lancaster LA1 218 C4
Hornby Dr Lancaster LA1 215 A4
Newton-w-S PR4 114 F2
Hornby Hall Cl LA2 238 B7
Hornby High Sch LA2 238 B7
Hornby La PR4 156 F2
Hornby Park Ct 1 FY3 130 D4
Hornby Rd Blackpool FY1 130 C4
Caton LA2 237 C3
Chorley PR6 43 E6
Longridge PR3 140 B8
Lytham St Anne's FY8 89 E5
Southport PR9 54 A4
Wray LA2 238 D1
Wray LA2 238 D6
Hornby St Burnley BB11 128 A5
Oswaldtwistle BB5 103 E3
Hornby Terr LA4 217 C6
Hornby's La
Hale Nook PR3 178 A5
Moss Edge PR3 178 D6
Hornchurch Dr PR7 43 A7
Horncliffe Cl BB4 68 E8
Horncliffe Hts BB9 148 E5
Horncliffe Rd FY4 110 B6
Horncliffe View BB4 60 B8
Horne St BB5 104 C7
Horning Cres BB10 148 D2
Horns La PR3 161 B3

Hornsea Cl Fulwood PR2 117 A4
Thornton FY5 176 D2
Hornsey Ave FY8 110 B4
Horridge Fold BL7 47 E3
Horrobin Fold BL7 48 C2
Horrobin La
Chapeltown BL7 48 C2
Rivington PR6,BL6 44 E1
Horrocks Fold PR4 74 E3
Horrocks Rd BL7 48 D6
Horrocksford Way LA1 214 D6
Horse Park La PR3 202 A5
Horsebridge Rd FY3 131 B8
Horsefield Ave OL12 52 C6
Horses Health Farm*
BD24 236 F6
Horsfall Ave 2 FY8 91 A3
Horsfall Cl BB5 104 B7
Horsfield Cl BB8 171 F5
Horton Ave BB10 148 B3
Horton Lodge BD23 231 E4
Horwich Bsns Pk BL6 32 B2
Horwich Heritage Ctr*
BL6 32 C4
Horwich Parish CE Prim Sch
BL6 32 C4
Hoscar Moss Rd L40 26 D3
Hoscar Sta L40 26 D4
Hospital Cotts PR3 140 F6
Hosticle La LA6 241 C7
Hothersall La PR3 140 D4
Hough La PR25 77 A1
Houghclough La PR3 184 F1
Houghton Ave 6 FY4 110 D8
Houghton Cl
Lytham St Anne's FY8 110 F2
Middleforth Green PR1 96 C3
Houghton Ct Halton LA2 219 C7
7 Thornton FY5 176 B3
Houghton La WN6 19 F6
Houghton Rd PR1 96 C3
Houghton St 8 PR6 43 D8
Houghton's La WN8 18 C1
Houghtons Rd WN8 18 B3
Houldsworth Rd PR2 117 E3
Hounds Hill 2 FY1 130 B4
Hounds Hill Ctr FY1 130 B5
Houseman Pl FY4 110 E7
Hove Ave FY7 175 C8
Hove Cl BL8 49 F1
Hove Rd FY8 89 F6
Howard Brook Ho PR1 118 F1
Howard Cl
Accrington BB5 103 F5
Lytham St Anne's FY8 110 E1
Maghull L31 5 F1
Howard Ct PR9 53 D1
Howard Dr PR4 56 F7
Howard Mews LA5 223 C1
Howard Rd PR7 43 C5
Howard St Blackpool FY1 130 C6
Burnley BB11 127 D5
Nelson BB9 148 C8
Rishton BB1 124 A1
26 Rochdale OL12 52 F1
Howards La WN5 10 F7
Howarth Ave BB5 103 F7
Howarth Cres FY6 153 E3
Howarth Rd PR2 117 D3
Howarth's St BB4 87 A8
Howden Hts FY6 153 B3
Howe Ave FY4 110 E8
Howe Croft BB7 166 F8
Howe Dr BL0 50 B2
Howe Gr PR7 43 A7
Howe Wlk 4 BB11 128 A6
Howells Cl L31 5 D2
Howgill Ave LA1 218 E4
Howgill Cl BB9 148 F6
Howgill La BB7 231 C1
Howgill Way FY8 91 D5
Howgills The PR2 118 A7
Howick CE Prim Sch PR1 95 F3
Howick Cross La PR1 95 E5
Howick Moor La PR1 96 A3
Howick Park Ave PR1 95 F4
Howick Park Cl PR1 95 F4
Howick Park Dr PR1 95 F4
Howick Row PR2 95 D5
Howorth Cl BB11 128 A3
Howorth Rd BB11 128 A3
Howsin St BB10 148 A1
Hoylake Cl PR2 117 B6
Hoyle Ave FY8 110 F2
Hoyle Bottom BB5 103 E1
Hoyle St Bacup OL13 70 E8
Rising Bridge BB5 85 A8
Whitworth OL12 71 D3
Hoyles La PR4 116 D6
Hozier St BB1 102 C5
Hubert Pl LA1 214 D8
Hubie St BB12 127 F7
Huck La FY8 91 E7
Hud Hey Ind Est BB4 85 B5
Hud Hey Rd BB4 85 B5
Hud Rake BB4 85 B4
Hudcar La BL9 33 A4
Hudson Ct PR5 78 C8
Hudson Pl BB2 101 B8
Hudson Rd FY1 130 D2
Hudson St
Accrington BB5 104 C4
Brierfield BB9 148 B5
Burnley BB11 127 D5
6 Cornholme OL14 109 C1

Hudson St *continued*
9 Preston PR1 97 A7
Hufling Ct 8 BB11 128 B4
Hufling La BB11 128 B4
Hugh Barn La PR4 75 F7
Hugh Bsns Pk BB4 69 E8
Hugh La PR26 76 D3
Hugh Rake BB4 85 F6
Hughes Ave BL6 32 A4
Hughes Cl 11 BL9 33 A3
Hughes Gr FY2 152 E1
Hughes St BB11 128 A5
Hull Rd FY1 130 B4
Hull St Burnley BB11 128 B5
Preston PR2 96 C8
Hullet Cl WN6 19 E8
Hulme Ave FY5 176 C2
Hulme St PR8 35 A7
Hulmes Bridge Bsns Ctr
L39 23 D2
Hulton Dr BB9 148 E6
Humber Ave 2 FY3 130 E8
Humber Sq BB10 148 C2
Humber St PR3 140 A7
Humblescough La PR3 180 D5
Humphrey St BB9 148 B6
Huncoat Ind Est BB5 125 C1
Huncoat Ind Pk BB5 125 D1
Huncoat Sta BB5 125 E2
Hundred End La PR4,PR9 72 F1
Hungerford Rd FY8 89 F5
Hunslet St Burnley BB11 128 B6
Nelson BB9 148 F7
Hunstanton Cl PR7 60 D5
Hunt Fold Dr BL8 49 F1
Hunt Rd L31 5 D1
Hunt St 2 PR1 96 D7
Hunter Ave PR4 57 A6
Hunter Rd PR4 114 B2
Hunter St Brierfield BB9 148 B5
Carnforth LA5 223 D2
Hunter's La PR4 56 B3
Hunters Chase WN5 10 E1
Hunters Dr BB12 127 D8
Hunters Fold PR4 75 A5
Hunters Gate LA1 214 E5
Hunters Gn BL0 49 F3
Hunters Lodge
Bamber Bridge PR5 97 D3
Blackburn BB2 100 F1
Hunters Rd PR25 77 D1
Hunting Hill Cvn Pk
LA5 223 C1
Hunting Hill Rd LA5 223 B1
Huntingdon Ct 5 PR9 54 A2
Huntingdon Gr L31 5 C4
Huntingdon Hall Rd
PR3 164 A2
Huntingdon Rd FY5 175 C1
Huntington Dr BB3 65 A7
Huntley Ave 4 FY3 130 E7
Huntley Cl LA4 217 E5
Huntley La PR5 120 E1
Huntley Mount Rd BL9 33 B3
Huntley St BL9 33 B3
Huntly Way OL10 33 E1
Huntroyde Ave BB12 126 B8
Huntroyde Cl 2 BB12 127 D7
Hunts Field PR6 78 C2
Huntsmans Chase PR4 114 F6
Hurlston Ave WN8 9 C8
Hurlston Dr L39 15 E7
Hurlston Hall Country Cvn Pk
L40 24 C2
Hurlston La L40 24 C1
Hurn Gr PR7 43 A7
Hurst Brook PR7 42 F1
Hurst Cres BB4 86 B3
Hurst Gn L40 40 C2
Hurst La BB4 86 B3
Hurst Pk PR1 96 C4
Hurst St BL9 33 A2
Hurst's La L39 7 B2
Hurstdene Cl FY6 153 F3
Hurstead St BB5 104 E1
Hurstleigh Dr LA3 213 A7
Hurstleigh Hts FY5 176 E2
Hurstmere Ave FY4 110 E8
Hurstway PR2 117 D7
Hurstway Cl PR2 117 D7
Hurstwood L37 11 E5
Hurstwood Ave
Blackburn BB2 101 A1
Burnley BB10 128 D5
Hurstwood Dr FY2 152 D2
Hurstwood Ent Pk BB4 85 A2
Hurstwood Gdns BB9 148 D4
Hurstwood La BB10 129 B4
Hurtley St BB10 128 A8
Hut La PR6 44 B3
Hutch Bank Rd BB4 84 F2
Hutchinson Ct BB3 82 A2
Hutchinson St 4 BB2 101 E3
Hutton CE Gram Sch
PR4 95 D2
Hutton Cl LA6 240 C7
Hutton Cres LA4 217 A4
Hutton Ct WN8 17 D1
Hutton Dr BB12 127 E7
Hutton Gdns LA5 223 C4
Hutton Gr LA4 217 A4
Hutton Hall Ave PR4 95 E1
Hutton Rd WN8 17 D1
Hutton St Blackburn BB1 102 B5
Standish WN1 30 A3
Hutton Way
5 Lancaster LA1 218 B1

Hutton Way *continued*
Ormskirk L39 15 E5
Huyton Rd PR6,PR7 31 A6
Huyton Terr PR6 31 B6
Hyacinth Cl BB4 67 F8
Hyatt Cres WN6 29 C3
Hyde Rd Blackpool FY1 130 B2
Morecambe LA4 217 F4
Hydeaway Ct LA4 217 B4
Hygiene BB5 124 E2
Hynd Brook Ho BB5 104 A5
Hyndburn Bridge BB5 124 F5
Hyndburn Cl
Carnforth LA5 223 F2
Morecambe LA3 217 F3
Hyndburn Dr BB3 81 D4
Hyndburn Park Prim Sch
BB5 104 A6
Hyndburn Rd
Accrington BB5 104 A6
Church BB5 103 F6
Great Harwood BB6 124 F5
Hyndburn St BB5 103 F6
Hyning Rd LA5 223 E8
Hynings The BB6 124 B6
Hythe Cl Blackburn BB1 102 C4
Southport PR8 35 E3

I

Ibbison Ct FY1 130 C3
Icconhurst Cl BB5 104 E2
Ice St BB1 101 E7
Iddesleigh Rd 3 PR1 118 E1
Iddon Ct 6 FY1 130 C6
Idlewood Pl FY5 152 F8
Idstone Cl BB2 82 A8
Ightenhill Cty Prim Sch
BB12 127 C6
Ightenhill Park La BB12 127 C8
Ightenhill Pk Mews 1
BB12 127 C7
Ightenhill St BB12 146 C1
Ilex Mill BB4 86 A2
Ilford Rd FY4 130 E1
Ilkley Ave
Lytham St Anne's FY8 90 C6
Southport PR9 54 C6
Ilkley Gr FY5 152 E8
Illawalla The FY5 153 E6
Illingworth Rd PR1 118 E1
Ilway PR5 97 E3
Imperial Gdns BB9 148 D8
Imperial St 2 FY1 130 B7
Ince Cres L37 11 D3
Ince La PR7 41 C6
Inchfield
Skelmersdale WN8 18 B2
Worsthorne BB10 129 B6
India Mill Bsns Ctr 4
BB3 65 A8
India St Accrington BB5 103 F6
Darwen BB3 65 B8
Ramsbottom BL0 50 C3
Industrial Cotts 10 BB4 69 F8
Industrial Pl 4 OL13 87 F2
Industrial St Bacup OL13 88 A2
Ramsbottom BL0 68 C1
Industry Rd 8 OL12 52 F1
Industry St Darwen BB3 82 B2
Whitworth OL12 71 D2
Infant St 11 BB5 104 C6
Infirmary Cl BB2 101 D2
Infirmary Rd BB2 101 D2
Infirmary St BB2 101 E2
Ing Dene Ave BB8 171 B4
Ing Dene Cl BB8 171 B4
Ingersol Rd BL6 32 E1
Ingfield Terr OL14 109 C1
Ingham Brow BL6 32 F4
Ingham St
Barrowford BB9 170 D3
Bury BL9 33 A1
Padiham BB12 146 D1
Inglby Cl BB1 102 D5
Ingle Cl 5 PR6 61 D1
Ingle Head PR2 117 D6
Ingle Nook BB10 128 F4
Ingle View LA6 242 C3
Ingleborough Dr BB18 196 A2
Ingleborough Rd LA1 218 B3
Ingleborough View
Brinscall PR6 63 A8
Carnforth LA5 221 E8
14 High Bentham LA2 239 D8
Hornby LA2 238 B6
Ingleborough Way PR25 77 C2
Ingleby Cl Cleveleys FY5 175 F5
Standish WN6 29 D2
Inglehurst Rd BB11 127 B5
Inglenook Cl 7 FY5 175 F1
Ingleton Ave FY2 152 F4
Ingleton Cl BB5 104 D5
Ingleton Dr LA1 215 A4
Ingleton Ho 2 LA1 215 A3
Ingleton Rd Fulwood PR2 118 E4
Southport PR8 35 E3
Ingleway FY5 175 F3
Ingleway Ave FY3 130 F6
Inglewhite WN8 18 A2
Inglewhite Fold 2
BB12 126 D7
Inglewhite Rd PR3 161 C3
Inglewood Cl Bury BL9 33 C4
Fleetwood FY7 198 C1
Warton PR4 92 D6
Inglewood Gr FY2 152 E5

Ingol Com Prim Sch
PR2 116 F4
Ingol Gdns FY6 177 C2
Ingol Gr FY6 177 C2
Ingol La FY6 177 D2
Ingot St PR1 96 D8
Ingram WN8 18 B1
Ings Ave
Barnoldswick BB18 196 B3
Rochdale OL12 52 B2
Ings La OL12 52 C2
Ingthorpe Ave FY2 152 D5
Inkerman Rd PR4 132 F6
Inkerman St Bacup OL13 88 A2
Blackburn BB1 101 E6
9 Padiham BB12 126 C8
Preston PR2 117 D2
12 Rochdale OL12 52 F1
Inner Prom FY8 90 B3
Innes Sch OL12 52 C1
Inskip WN8 18 A2
Inskip Ct WN8 18 B2
Inskip Pl Blackpool FY4 110 E5
Lytham St Anne's FY8 90 A8
Inskip Rd Leyland PR25 76 D2
Preston PR2 116 E1
Southport PR9 54 A4
Wharles PR4 135 A5
Inskip St BB12 126 C8
Inskip St Peter's CE Sch
PR4 135 B8
Institute St BB12 126 D8
Intack Cvn Pk LA6 237 A7
Intack La BB2 121 B2
Intack Prim Sch BB1 102 D5
Intack Rd PR4 75 B8
Intake Cres BB8 171 F6
Intake La Maghull L39 4 E8
Skelmersdale L39 8 B2
Interlink Express Stadium
(Accrington Stanley FC)
BB5 104 B8
Inver Rd FY2 152 D3
Inverness Rd BB3 64 F8
Ipswich Pl FY5 175 C2
Ipswich Rd PR2 118 D2
Ireby Rd LA6 242 C3
Irene Pl BB2 101 B5
Irene St BB10 128 C5
Iris St BL0 50 B6
Iron St Blackburn BB2 101 E3
Horwich BL6 32 C2
Irongate PR5 77 C8
Ironside Cl PR2 118 B4
Irton Rd PR9 35 E8
Irvin Ave PR9 54 C5
Irvin St PR1 118 B1
Irvine St 8 BB9 170 F2
Irving Cl FY2 152 F5
Irving Pl BB2 101 B5
Irving St PR9 53 B1
Irwell WN8 18 A3
Irwell Ho 10 BB4 69 E8
Irwell Rd WN5 10 F7
Irwell St 7 Bacup OL13 87 F2
Burnley BB12 127 A6
Longridge PR3 140 B7
Longridge PR3 140 B8
Lytham St Anne's FY8 89 F7
Ramsbottom BL0 50 C6
Irwell Terr 12 OL13 87 F2
Irwell Vale Rd BB4 68 C6
Irwell Vale Sta BL0 68 C5
Isa St 5 BL0 50 A4
Isabella St Longridge PR3 140 A8
Rochdale OL12 52 F2
Isherwood Fold BL7 48 D7
Isherwood St
Blackburn BB2 101 D1
1 Preston PR1 118 B1
Preston PR1 118 C1
Islamic Coll Jamea Al
Kauthar LA1 214 F5
Island Cotts BL9 50 C2
Island La PR3 203 B3
Islay Rd FY8 90 E6
Isle of Man BB1 122 E4
Isle of Man St BB4 87 A7
Isleworth Dr PR7 43 B7
Islington BB2 101 E3
Islington Cl BB10 148 D3
Ivan St BB10 148 B2
Ivegate Colne BB8 171 D5
Foulridge BB8 194 E1
Ivinson Rd BB3 82 B3
Ivory St 1 BB12 127 C6
Ivy Ave Blackpool FY4 110 E5
Haslingden BB4 85 C3
Ivy Bank PR2 118 D6
Ivy Cl Clayton-le-W PR25 77 E2
Ring o'Bells L40 26 A3
Ivy Cotts
11 Rawtenstall BB4 69 F8
Tockholes BB3 80 F3
Ivy Gdns FY5 176 A4
Ivy Gr 2 BB4 86 A3
Ivy House Cl PR5 78 B7
Ivy St Blackburn BB2 101 E2
Burnley BB10 148 B1
Nelson BB8 171 A2
Ramsbottom BL0 49 F3
1 Rawtenstall BB4 69 F8
Southport PR8 35 D6
Ivy Terr BB3 65 B6
Ivybridge WN8 18 B2
Ivydale WN8 18 B2

J

j2 Bsns Pk BL9 33 C2

J

Jack La BD23 236 F4
Jack Walker Way BB2 81 D7
Jackdaw Rd BL8 49 F2
Jacks Key Dr BB3 65 C5
Jacksmere La L40,PR8 23 B8
Jackson Cl Haskayne L39 13 F5
Lancaster LA1 214 C7
Jackson Heights Rd BB1 83 B4
Jackson Rd
2 Chorley PR7 43 A5
1 Leyland PR25 76 D1
Jackson St
8 Bamber Bridge PR5 77 F8
Blackpool FY3 130 E7
6 Burnley BB10 128 A8
Chorley PR7 43 D6
5 Clayton-le-M BB5 124 F3
Jackson Terr LA5 223 D3
Jackson's Banks Rd
BB2 120 E6
Jackson's Common La
L40 24 B1
Jackson's La L40 27 E7
Jacob St BB5 104 C5
Jacob's La PR4 115 A7
Jacson St 3 PR1 97 A7
Jade Cl L33 1 A3
Jagoe Mews BB18 197 A1
Jagoe Rd BB18 197 A1
James Ave Blackpool FY4 130 F1
Great Harwood BB6 124 B5
James Pl Coppull PR7 29 E8
Standish WN6 29 D2
James Sq WN6 29 D2
James St Bacup OL13 70 B7
Bamber Bridge PR5 97 E1
Barnoldswick BB18 196 B1
4 Barrowford BB9 170 D4
Belthorn BB1 82 F6
Blackburn BB1 101 E5
Burnley BB10 148 A1
Bury BL9 33 A1
12 Clayton-le-M BB5 124 F3
Colne BB8 171 E4
1 Darwen BB3 82 A1
Earby BB18 197 B1
Egerton BL7 47 D3
Great Harwood BB6 124 B5
Haslingden BB4 85 A2
Horwich BL6 31 F3
Huncoat BB5 125 E2
30 Lancaster LA1 214 F8
Morecambe LA4 217 C5
Oswaldtwistle BB5 103 D3
Preston PR1 97 B7
Rawtenstall BB4 86 A2
Rishton BB1 124 C1
Salterforth BB18 194 D7
Whitworth OL12 71 D2
James St W 6 BB3 82 A1
Jameson Rd FY7 199 A1
Jameson St 2 FY1 130 C3
Jameston Rise 14 BL6 32 B4
Jane La Catforth PR4 135 E5
Leyland PR26 76 A3
Jane St OL12 71 E6
Jane's Brook Rd PR8 35 E4
Jane's Mdw PR4 57 A5
Janice Dr PR2 117 D7
Janine Cl LA4 217 A4
Jannat Cl BB5 104 B5
Jarrett Rd L33 1 A4
Jarrett Wlk L33 1 A4
Jarvis St OL12 52 F1
Jasmine Rd PR5 97 A3
Jason Ct FY8 89 D7
Jasper St BB1 122 F1
Jefferson Cl LA1 214 D7
Jefferson Way OL12 52 F3
Jeffrey Ave PR3 140 B7
Jeffrey Hill Cl PR2 119 C7
Jeffrey Sq FY1 130 D3
Jellicoe Cl FY8 110 E1
Jem Gate FY5 152 D8
Jemmett St PR1 117 E2
Jenny La Blackpool FY4 111 C7
Higher Wheelton PR6 79 C1
Jenny Nook LA3 213 A7
Jenny St BB9 148 D6
Jensen Cl LA1 214 E6
Jensen Dr FY4 112 A6
Jepheys Pl 17 OL12 52 F1
Jepheys St OL12 52 F1
Jepp Hill 3 BB18 196 B2
Jepps Ave PR3 137 B7
Jepps La PR3 137 B8
Jepson St 9 BB3 65 A8
Jepson Way FY4 110 F4
Jericho Rd BL9 33 E4
Jersey Ave FY2 152 E2
Jersey Fold PR7 60 E6
Jersey St BB2 101 B1
Jervis Cl FY8 110 D1
Jesmond Ave FY4 110 B7
Jesmond Ct FY8 89 F8
Jesmond Gr LA4 217 D3
Jessel St BB2 101 B2
Jesson Way LA5 223 C1
Jevington Way LA3 213 A7
Jewel Holme BB9 148 A5

Jib Hill Cotts BB10 ......148 D2
Jinny La BB12 ....169 E4
Jobling St BB8 ....171 B3
Jockey St BB11 ....127 C5
Joe Connolly Way 2
BB4 ....69 E8
Joe La PR3 ....181 D2
John Cross CE Prim Sch
PR3 ....159 A4
John Henry St OL12 ......71 D4
John Hill St 3 FY4 ......130 F2
John Kay Ct LA1 ....218 B3
John o' Gaunt St 15
BB12 ....146 C1
John St
2 Bamber Bridge PR5 .....97 E1
Barnoldswick BB18 ....196 B1
Barrowford BB9 ....170 E4
Blackpool FY1 ....130 B2
Brierfield BB9 ....148 B6
4 Carnforth LA5 ....223 D2
Church BB5 ....103 E7
Clayton-le-M BB5 ....124 F3
Colne BB8 ....171 C4
Coppull PR7 ....42 E1
Darwen BB3 ....81 F2
Earby BB18 ....197 B1
5 Galgate LA2 ....211 A4
Haslingden BB4 ....85 B3
Leyland PR25 ....77 A1
Newchurch BB4 ....86 F1
Oswaldtwistle BB5 ....103 D3
Thornton FY5 ....176 B4
Whitworth OL12 ....71 D2
John Wall Ct 8 BB7 ....166 D8
John William St 7 PR1 ..97 C8
Johnny Barn Cl BB4 ......86 D2
Johnny Barn Cotts BB4 ..86 D2
Johns Wood Cl PR7 ......42 F6
Johnson Cl
Carnforth LA5 ....223 C1
Lancaster LA1 ....214 C7
Johnson New Rd BB3 ....82 E2
Johnson Rd
Blackpool FY4 ....130 F2
Waterside BB3 ....82 D4
Johnson St PR9 ....35 B8
Johnson's Meanygate
PR4 ....56 D7
Johnspool PR2 ....117 C6
Johnston Cl BB2 ....101 C5
Johnston St BB2 ....101 C5
Johnsville Ave FY4 ......110 E7
Joiner's Row BB2 ....101 E3
Joiners Alley 10 BB6 ....124 C5
Jolly Tar La PR7 ....30 B7
Jonathan Cl BB4 ....68 A8
Jones St BL6 ....32 B4
Jones' Gr FY7 ....199 B5
Jones's Yd LA6 ....240 B7
Joseph St
Barrowford BB9 ....170 D2
Darwen BB3 ....82 B1
3 Rochdale OL12 ....52 D2
Joy Pl OL12 ....52 F2
Joy St Ramsbottom BL0 ....50 B6
Rochdale OL12 ....52 F2
Joyce Ave FY4 ....130 F2
Jubilee Almshouses
PR26 ....58 B1
Jubilee Ave Ormskirk L39 ..15 F6
Orrell WN5 ....10 D4
Preesall FY6 ....200 A4
Preston PR2 ....116 D1
Jubilee Bldgs 19 LA2 ...239 D8
Jubilee Cl Darwen BB3 ....82 D1
Haslingden BB4 ....85 A1
Jubilee Ct
1 Haslingden BB4 ....85 A1
11 Lancaster LA1 ....214 E8
Jubilee Cts PR25 ....59 E8
Jubilee Dr Cleveleys FY5 .175 C4
Skelmersdale WN8 ....8 E8
Jubilee La FY4 ....111 B5
Jubilee La N FY4 ....111 B6
Jubilee Pl PR6 ....61 D1
Jubilee Rd
9 Bamber Bridge PR5 .....77 A8
Church BB5 ....103 F7
Formby L37 ....11 D1
Haslingden BB4 ....85 A1
Walmer Bridge PR4 ....74 F4
Jubilee St
Accrington BB5 ....125 A1
Blackburn BB1 ....101 E4
Brierfield BB10 ....148 F3
Darwen BB3 ....82 A1
Oswaldtwistle BB5 ....103 E4
Read BB12 ....145 D2
Jubilee Terr Clifton PR4 ..115 C1
Freckleton PR4 ....93 C7
Goosnargh PR3 ....138 D5
Langho BB6 ....143 D1
Jubilee Trad Est PR1 ....117 E1
Jubilee Way Croston PR26 .58 B3
Lytham St Anne's FY8 ......90 C8
Jud Falls BB7 ....165 A3
Judd Holmes La PR3 ....162 D7
Jude St BB9 ....148 D8
Judeland PR7 ....61 A2
Judge Fields BB8 ....171 D6
Judges Lodgings Mus*
LA1 ....214 E8
Judith St OL12 ....52 C3
Julia Mews 5 BL6 ....32 B4
Julia St BL6 ....32 B4
July St 17 BB1 ....102 A4
Jumbles Beck BL7 ....48 D4
Jumbles Ctry Pk* BL7 ....48 D2
Jumps La OL14 ....109 E1
Junction La L40 ....25 E3
Junction Rd Preston PR2 ..96 D7
Rainford Junction WA11 .....8 F1
Junction St
Brierfield BB9 ....148 B6
Burnley BB12 ....127 E6
Burnley,Whittlefield BB12 ..127 E7
Colne BB8 ....171 A3
Darwen BB3 ....65 B7
Junction Terr PR7 ....60 C5
June Ave FY4 ....131 A1
June St 16 BB1 ....102 A4
June's Wlk PR4 ....75 A5
Juniper Cl FY6 ....200 A5
Juniper Croft PR6 ....78 A1
Juniper Ct BB5 ....104 E8
Juniper St 6 BB1 ....102 A7
Juno St BB9 ....170 F2
Jutland St PR1 ....97 A8

K

Kairnryan Cl FY2 ....152 F5
Kale Gr L33 ....1 A5
Kaley La BB7 ....190 E5
Kane St PR2 ....117 C1
Kate St 3 BL0 ....50 B6
Kateholm OL13 ....88 A7
Kay Brow BL0 ....50 C6
Kay Fold Lodge BB1 ....122 D2
Kay Gdns BB11 ....128 B5
Kay St Blackburn BB2 ....101 E3
Blackpool FY1 ....130 B4
Brierfield BB9 ....148 B5
Bury BL9 ....33 A3
Chapeltown BL7 ....48 C4
Clitheroe BB7 ....166 D6
Darwen BB3 ....82 B1
3 Oswaldtwistle BB5 ....103 D3
1 Padiham BB12 ....146 D1
1 Preston PR1 ....96 E7
Ramsbottom BL0,BL9 ....50 C3
Rawtenstall BB4 ....86 A2
Kaymar Ind Est PR1 ......97 C7
Kayswell Rd LA4 ....217 F5
Kearsley Ave PR4 ....57 A6
Keasden Ave FY4 ....110 D7
Keasden Rd BB7 ....235 E6
Keating Ct 3 FY7 ....199 A3
Keats Ave Bolton-le-S LA5 .221 A5
Longshaw WN5 ....10 D1
Rochdale OL12 ....52 A1
Warton PR4 ....92 E6
Keats Cl Accrington BB5 ..104 E2
Colne BB8 ....171 D6
Eccleston PR7 ....41 D5
Thornton FY5 ....176 A2
Keats Fold 3 BB12 ......126 F7
Keats Rd BL8 ....49 F2
Keats Terr PR8 ....35 F6
Keats Way PR4 ....116 D4
Kebs Rd OL14 ....109 D3
Keele Cl FY5 ....176 A2
Keele Wlk BB1 ....101 F4
Keen Cl PR4 ....95 E2
Keeper's Hey FY5 ....176 A4
Keeper's La PR3 ....204 F1
Keepers Gate FY8 ....90 D7
Keepers Wood Way PR7 ..42 F6
Keer Bank 1 LA1 ....218 A2
Keer Holme La LA6 .....240 E4
Keighley Ave BB8 ....171 D6
Keighley Rd Colne BB8 ..171 F5
Laneshaw Bridge BB8 .....172 D6
Trawden BB8 ....172 C4
Keirby Wlk BB11 ....128 A6
Keith Gr FY5 ....175 D1
Keith St BB12 ....127 C6
Kelbrook Dr BB11 ....127 E3
Kelbrook Prim Sch
BB18 ....195 A6
Kelbrook Rd BB18 ....194 E7
Kelk Beck Cl L31 ....5 F2
Kellet Acre 4 PR5 ....77 A7
Kellet Ave PR25 ....77 D1
Kellet Ct 1 LA1 ....214 E8
Kellet La
Bolton-le-S LA5,LA2 ......221 C3
Borwick LA6 ....240 B3
Walton Summit PR5 ....78 B7
Kellet Rd Carnforth LA5 ...223 E1
Over Kellet LA6 ....240 A1
Kellet Road Ind Est LA5 .223 F1
Kellett St 8 PR7 ....43 C8
Kelmarsh Cl FY3 ....131 B2
Kelne Ho 7 LA1 ....214 E8
Kelsall Ave BB1 ....102 B8
Kelsey St LA1 ....214 E8
Kelso Ave FY5 ....175 D1
Kelsons Ave FY5 ....176 C2
Kelswick Dr BB9 ....148 E6
Kelverdale Rd FY5 ......152 F8
Kelvin Rd FY5 ....152 D6
Kelvin St BB3 ....81 F1
Kelwood Ave BL9 ....33 D5
Kem Mill La PR6 ....61 B8
Kemble Cl BL6 ....32 B5
Kemp Ct BB1 ....122 F3
Kemp St FY7 ....199 B4
Kemple View BB7 ....166 D6
Kempton Ave FY3 ....130 E3
Kempton Park Fold PR8 ..35 F3
Kempton Rd LA1 ....215 B4
Kempton Rise BB1 ......101 F3
Kenbury Cl L33 ....1 A4
Kenbury Rd L33 ....1 A4
Kendal Ave
Barrowford BB9 ....170 D4
Blackpool FY3 ....153 A1
Cleveleys FY5 ....175 D4
Kendal Cl WA11 ....8 F2
Kendal Dr Maghull L31 .....5 E2
Morecambe LA4 ....217 F4
Rainford Junction WA11 .....8 F2
Kendal Rd
Lytham St Anne's FY8 .....110 D1
Ramsbottom BL0 ....50 A2
Kendal Rd W BL0 ....49 F2
Kendal Row BB1 ....82 F6
Kendal St Blackburn BB1 ..101 E6
Clitheroe BB7 ....189 F1
5 Nelson BB9 ....170 D1
Preston PR1 ....96 E8
Kendal Way PR8 ....21 B3
Kendall Cl BB2 ....81 D8
Kenilworth Ave FY7 .....198 E3
Kenilworth Cl BB12 .....126 E8
Kenilworth Ct FY8 ....89 F6
Kenilworth Dr
Clitheroe BB7 ....166 C6
Earby BB18 ....195 A8
Kenilworth Gdns FY4 ...110 B7
Kenilworth Pl
Fleetwood FY7 ....198 E3
Lancaster LA1 ....215 A5
Kenilworth Rd
Lytham St Anne's FY8 ......89 F6
Morecambe LA3 ....217 C3
Southport PR8 ....21 B4
Kenlis Rd PR3 ....181 F4
Kenmay Way L33 ....1 A3
Kenmure Pl PR1 ....117 F2
Kennedy Cl LA1 ....214 D6
Kennedy Ho FY1 ....130 B1
Kennelwood Ave L33 ......1 A3
Kennet Dr PR2 ....117 F8
Kennett Dr PR25 ....77 B2
Kennington Prim Sch
PR2 ....118 A4
Kennington Rd PR2 .....118 A4
Kensington Ave PR1 ......96 B6
Kensington Cl BL8 ....50 A1
Kensington Ct Formby L37 .12 A3
Morecambe LA4 ....217 E6
Kensington Dr BL6 ....32 D3
Kensington Gdns PR5 ....97 C1
Kensington Ho LA1 ......214 F5
Kensington Ind Pk PR9 ...35 C6
Kensington Pl BB11 .....127 D4
Kensington Rd
Blackpool FY3 ....130 E4
Chorley PR7 ....43 B7
Cleveleys FY5 ....175 C3
Formby L37 ....11 E1
Lancaster LA1 ....214 F5
Lytham St Anne's FY8 ......90 D4
Morecambe LA4 ....217 B5
Southport PR9 ....35 C6
Kensington St BB9 ......148 C7
Kent Ave
2 Bamber Bridge PR5 .....97 D3
Cleveleys FY5 ....175 E4
Formby L37 ....12 A1
Kent Ct BB9 ....170 D4
Kent Dr Blackburn BB1 ...102 E4
Clayton-le-W PR25 ....77 D1
Kent Ho LA1 ....214 F7
Kent Rd Blackpool FY1 ...130 C3
Formby L37 ....12 A1
Southport PR8 ....35 A4
Kent St Blackburn BB1 ....101 F4
Burnley BB12 ....127 F7
Fleetwood FY7 ....199 B5
3 Lancaster LA1 ....218 D2
Preston PR1 ....117 F2
Kent Way LA3 ....217 F3
Kent Wlk BB4 ....68 A8
Kent's Cl PR4 ....113 E7
Kentmere Ave
Bamber Bridge PR5 ....97 E1
Leyland PR25 ....77 A3
Kentmere Cl
Burnley BB12 ....127 B8
5 Fleetwood FY7 ....198 D3
Kentmere Dr
4 Blackburn BB2 ....80 E8
Blackpool FY4 ....131 C1
Longton PR4 ....75 B8
Kentmere Gr 1 LA4 ....217 D4
Kentmere Rd LA1 ....218 E1
Kenton Cl L37 ....11 F6
Kenwood Ave LA4 ....217 A4
Kenworthys Flats PR8 ....35 B8
Kenwyn Ave FY3 ....130 E3
Kenyon La Dinckley BB6 ..142 F4
Whittle-le-W PR6 ....61 F7
Kenyon Rd
Morecambe LA4 ....217 F5
Nelson BB9 ....148 B7
Standish WN6 ....29 D2
Kenyon St
6 Accrington BB5 ....104 C6
Bacup OL13 ....71 B8
Blackburn BB1 ....102 C6
Bury BL9 ....33 A3
Ramsbottom BL0 ....50 C6
Rawtenstall BB4 ....86 A3
Kenyon's La L37 ....12 A3
Kenyons La L31 ....5 E3
Kenyons Lodge L31 ....5 E3
Keppel Pl BB11 ....127 E6
Kepple La PR3 ....181 B6
Kerenhappuch St 5 BL0 ..50 B5
Kerfoot's La WN8 ....8 C8
Kerr Pl PR1 ....96 D8
Kershaw Cl 6 BB4 ....86 A7
Kershaw St 8 Bacup OL13 .87 F2
Bury BL9 ....33 A2
Chorley PR6 ....61 E1
Church BB5 ....103 E7
Kerslake Way L38 ....3 A4
Kerslea Ave FY3 ....131 D8
Kerton Row PR8 ....34 F4
Keston Gr FY4 ....110 C5
Kestor La PR3 ....140 A7
Kestrel Cl Blackburn BB1 .101 D8
Cleveleys FY5 ....175 F5
Knowley PR6 ....62 A3
Kestrel Ct PR9 ....35 D7
Kestrel Dr Bury BL9 ....33 B4
Darwen BB3 ....81 D3
Kestrel Mews WN8 ....18 C4
Kestrel Pk WN8 ....18 C4
Kestrel Terr BB5 ....103 E3
Keswick Cl
Accrington BB5 ....125 D1
Maghull L31 ....5 E2
Southport PR8 ....21 C3
Keswick Ct LA1 ....218 F1
Keswick Dr BB2 ....80 E8
Keswick Gr Heysham LA3 .212 E5
Knott End-on-S FY6 ......199 F5
Keswick Rd
Blackpool FY1 ....130 C3
Burnley BB10 ....148 B2
Lancaster LA1 ....218 F1
Lytham St Anne's FY8 ......89 E8
Keswick Way WA11 ....8 F2
Keswick Wlk LA1 ....218 F1
Kettering Rd PR8 ....21 B5
Kevin Ave FY6 ....153 F5
Kevin Gr LA3 ....213 D1
Kew Gdns
Higher Penwortham PR1 ....96 B5
Leyland PR25 ....77 B3
Kew Gr FY5 ....175 D1
Kew House Dr PR8 ....36 A2
Kew Rd Formby L37 ....11 D1
Nelson BB9 ....170 F2
Southport PR8 ....35 B3
Kew Ret Pk PR9 ....36 A4
Kew Woods Prim Sch
PR8 ....35 F3
Key View BB3 ....65 C5
Keynsham Gr BB12 ......127 D7
Khyber St BB8 ....171 C4
Kibble Cres BB10 ....148 C3
Kibble Gr BB9 ....148 D4
Kibboth Crew BL0 ....50 B7
Kidbrooke Ave FY4 ......110 B4
Kidder St BB2 ....81 D8
Kiddlington Cl PR5 ....77 D8
Kiddrow La BB12 ....127 A7
Kidsgrove PR2 ....116 F5
Kielder Ct 3 FY8 ....91 C4
Kielder Dr BB12 ....127 E7
Kilbane St FY7 ....198 F1
Kilburn Rd WN5 ....10 C5
Kilcrash La PR3 ....180 D7
Kildale Cl L31 ....5 C2
Kildare Ave FY5 ....176 A4
Kildare Rd FY2 ....152 D3
Kilgrimol Gdns FY8 .....110 C1
Kilkerran Cl PR6 ....43 D8
Killer St 1 BL0 ....50 C6
Killiard La BB2 ....100 E5
Killingbeck Cl L40 ....25 D4
Killington St BB10 ......148 C2
Killingworth Mews 5
BL6 ....32 D1
Killon St BL9 ....33 A1
Kilmory Pl FY2 ....152 F5
Kilmuir Cl PR2 ....118 C5
Kiln Bank OL12 ....71 C2
Kiln Bank La OL12 ....71 C2
Kiln Cl BB7 ....190 A2
Kiln Croft PR6 ....78 B3
Kiln Ct 1 LA1 ....218 D1
Kiln Hill BB12 ....146 F6
Kiln House Way BB5 ....104 A3
Kiln La Hambleton FY6 ....177 B2
Paythorne BB7 ....231 C6
Rimington BB7 ....230 F2
Skelmersdale WN8 ....17 E1
Wray LA2 ....238 D6
Kiln St Nelson BB9 ....148 D8
Ramsbottom BL0 ....50 B5
Kiln Terr 8 OL13 ....70 D8
Kiln Wlk OL12 ....52 E2
Kilnbank Ave LA4 ....217 A5
Kilngate PR5 ....97 C3
Kilnhouse La FY8 ....111 A1
Kilns The BB11 ....128 B3
Kilruddery Rd PR1 ....96 E5
Kilsby Cl PR5 ....97 E3
Kilworth Ht PR2 ....117 C5
Kimberley Ave FY4 ......110 D5
Kimberley Cl BB10 ......148 F3
Kimberley Rd PR2 ....117 C2
Kimberley St Bacup OL13 ..70 A7
Brierfield BB10 ....148 F3
Coppull PR7 ....42 E1
Kimberly Cl PR4 ....93 B6
Kimble Cl BL8 ....49 F2
Kime St BB12 ....127 C6
Kincardine Ave 7 FY4 ...111 A6
Kincraig Pl FY2 ....152 F6
Kincraig Prim Sch FY2 ..152 F6
Kincraig Rd FY2 ....152 F5
Kindonan Ave 6 FY4 ....111 A6
King Edward Ave
Blackpool FY2 ....152 B1
Lytham St Anne's FY8 ......90 A4
King Edward St BB5 ....103 C3
King Edward Terr BB9 ..170 D2
King Edward VII & Queen Mary Schs FY8 ....90 B4
King George Ave FY2 ....152 B1
King George Ct 19 OL13 ..87 F3
King George V Coll PR8 ..35 E5
King Henry Mews BB7 ..230 D3
King La BB7 ....166 E8
King St Accrington BB5 ...104 B6
5 Bacup OL13 ....87 F2
6 Bamber Bridge PR5 .....77 B7
Barnoldswick BB18 ....196 B2
Blackburn BB2 ....101 D4
Blackpool FY1 ....130 C5
Brierfield BB9 ....148 A5
Brierfield,Harle Syke BB10 .148 F3
Carnforth LA5 ....223 D1
Chorley PR7 ....43 D6
5 Clayton-le-M BB5 .....124 F2
Clitheroe BB7 ....166 E8
Colne BB8 ....171 E5
Fleetwood FY7 ....199 A4
15 Great Harwood BB6 ...124 C5
Haslingden BB4 ....85 B4
High Bentham LA2 ....239 D8
Horwich BL6 ....32 A4
Lancaster LA1 ....214 F8
Leyland PR25 ....77 A1
Longridge PR3 ....140 B7
Morecambe LA4 ....217 B5
Padiham BB12 ....126 C8
Ramsbottom BL0 ....50 C6
Rawtenstall BB4 ....69 E8
Southport PR8 ....35 A6
Whalley BB7 ....144 C5
Whitworth OL12 ....71 D3
King Street Terr BB9 ....148 A5
King William St BB1 .....101 E5
King's Bridge Cl 4 BB2 ..101 B1
King's Bridge St BB2 ....101 B1
King's Cl FY6 ....153 E3
King's Cres LA3 ....216 E3
King's Croft PR5 ....97 D5
King's Cswy BB9 ....148 E5
King's Dr LA5 ....223 E1
King's Highway
Accrington BB5 ....105 B2
Huncoat BB5 ....104 F8
King's Rd Accrington BB5 .104 B7
Blackburn BB2 ....101 B1
Lytham St Anne's FY8 ......89 E5
King's Sq FY1 ....130 C5
King's Wlk FY5 ....175 D5
Kingcraig Ct FY2 ....152 F4
Kingfisher Bank BB11 ...127 C4
Kingfisher Cl
Blackburn BB1 ....101 E8
Chorley PR7 ....42 F5
Kingfisher Ct Maghull L31 ...5 B4
Oswaldtwistle BB5 ....103 E3
Southport PR9 ....35 D8
Kingfisher Ctr Bacup OL13 .70 E8
10 Rawtenstall BB4 ....86 A3
Kingfisher Dr Bury BL9 ....33 B4
Poulton-le-F FY6 ....153 B2
Kingfisher Mews FY6 ...153 B2
Kingfisher Pk WN8 ....18 C4
Kingfisher St PR1 ....118 B1
Kings Arc 37 LA1 ....214 F8
Kings Arms Cl 34 LA1 ...214 F8
Kings Ave BB4 ....86 A1
Kings Cl L37 ....11 E2
Kings Cres PR25 ....77 A1
Kings Ct Fleetwood FY7 ..199 B4
Leyland PR25 ....77 A1
Kings Dr Fulwood PR2 ...117 D5
Hoddlesden BB3 ....82 F1
Padiham BB12 ....126 E6
Kings Hey Dr PR9 ....53 F1
Kings Lea PR7 ....30 F8
Kings Mdw PR8 ....21 D3
Kings Meadow Prim Sch
PR8 ....21 D3
Kings Rd Cleveleys FY5 ...175 C2
Formby L37 ....11 E2
Kingsacre PR3 ....181 A3
Kingsbarn Cl PR2 ....118 D6
Kingsbridge Cl PR1 ......96 E2
Kingsbridge Wharfe
BB2 ....101 B1
Kingsbury Cl PR8 ....21 B4
Kingsbury Ct WN8 ....18 C4
Kingsbury Pl BB10 ......148 D3
Kingsbury Sch
Ormskirk L39 ....15 E5
Skelmersdale WN8 ....17 D1
Kingscote Dr FY3 ....130 E7
Kingsdale Ave
Brierfield BB10 ....148 C3
Fulwood PR2 ....118 D5
Morecambe LA3 ....216 E1
Kingsdale Cl Leyland PR25 .60 B6
Walton-le-D PR5 ....97 F5
Kingsdale Rd LA1 ....214 D7
Kingsfold Christian Sch The
PR4 ....73 E2
Kingsfold Dr PR1 ....96 D2
Kingsfold Prim Sch PR1 ..96 D2
Kingshaven Dr PR1 ......96 E2
Kingshotte Gdns BB9 ...170 C3

Kingsland Gr
Blackpool FY1 .... 130 D3
12 Burnley BB11 .... 128 B4
Kingsland Rd BB11 ...... 128 B4
Kingsley Ave BB12 ...... 126 E7
Kingsley Cl Blackburn BB2 . 80 D7
Church BB5 .... 103 F7
Maghull L31 .... 5 C5
Thornton FY5 .... 176 A3
Kingsley Ct 5 FY1 ...... 130 C4
Kingsley Dr PR7 .... 43 A5
Kingsley Rd
Blackpool FY3 .... 131 B2
Cottam PR4 .... 116 E6
Laneshaw Bridge BB8 .... 172 D6
Kingsley St BB9 .... 170 F2
Kingsmead
Blackburn BB1 .... 102 D4
Chorley PR7 .... 43 C5
Kingsmede FY4 .... 110 E6
Kingsmere Ave FY8 ...... 110 F1
Kingsmill Ave BB7 ...... 144 A8
Kingsmuir Ave PR2 ...... 118 D4
Kingsmuir Cl LA3 ...... 212 E7
Kingston Ave
Accrington BB5 .... 104 A4
Blackpool FY4 .... 110 C5
Kingston Cl FY6 .... 199 F6
Kingston Cres
Haslingden BB4 .... 68 A7
Southport PR9 .... 54 C5
Kingston Dr FY8 .... 90 D6
Kingston Mews 4 FY5 .. 176 B3
Kingston Pl BB3 .... 81 F7
Kingsway Accrington BB5 . 104 A8
Bamber Bridge PR5 .... 77 E8
Blackburn BB3 .... 82 A7
Blackpool FY4 .... 110 C7
Burnley BB11 .... 128 A6
Cleveleys FY5 .... 175 C2
Euxton PR7 .... 60 E2
Great Harwood BB6 .... 124 F6
Hapton BB11 .... 126 C3
Heysham LA3 .... 213 A8
Higher Penwortham PR1 .... 96 B6
Huncoat BB5 .... 125 F1
Lancaster LA1 .... 218 E1
Leyland PR25 .... 59 E7
Lytham St Anne's FY8 ...... 90 C4
Preston PR2 .... 116 F2
Southport PR8 .... 35 A7
Kingsway Ave PR3 ...... 137 C3
Kingsway Ct
2 Lytham St Anne's FY8 ... 90 C4
Morecambe LA3 .... 216 E1
Kingsway Sports Ctr
LA1 .... 218 E1
Kingsway W PR1 .... 96 B6
Kingswood Cl FY8 .... 90 E4
Kingswood Coll L40 ...... 24 A6
Kingswood Pk PR8 ...... 34 F5
Kingswood Rd PR25 ...... 77 A2
Kingswood St 6 PR1 ...... 96 E7
Kinloch Way L39 .... 15 D6
Kinnerton Pl FY5 ...... 152 F8
Kinross Cl Blackburn BB1 . 102 A4
1 Ramsbottom BL0 .... 50 A2
Kinross Cres FY4 ...... 131 A1
Kinross St BB11 .... 127 D4
Kinross Wlk 7 BB1 ...... 102 A4
Kintbury Rd FY8 .... 89 F4
Kintour Rd FY8 .... 90 E6
Kintyre Cl FY4 .... 110 F7
Kintyre Way LA3 ...... 212 E7
Kipling Dr FY3 .... 131 B2
Kipling Pl BB6 .... 124 B4
Kirby Dr PR4 .... 93 B6
Kirby Rd Blackburn BB2 .. 101 D1
Blackpool FY1 .... 130 B2
Nelson BB9 .... 148 B8
Kirby's Cotts L39 .... 6 B3
Kirk Ave BB7 .... 166 C8
Kirk Head PR4 .... 74 E2
Kirk Hill Rd BB4 .... 85 C3
Kirk Ho BB5 .... 103 E6
Kirk Rd BB5 .... 103 E7
Kirk View BB4 .... 87 A1
Kirkbeck Cl LA2 ...... 237 D3
Kirkby Ave
Clayton-le-W PR25 .... 77 E1
Cleveleys FY5 .... 175 E4
Kirkby Bank Rd L33 ...... 1 C2
Kirkby Lonsdale Rd
LA2 .... 219 D7
Kirkby Lonsdale Rd
Caton LA2,LA6 .... 237 B6
Over Kellet LA6 .... 240 B1
Kirkdale Ave
Lytham St Anne's FY8 ...... 89 F7
Newchurch BB4 .... 86 E1
Kirkdale Cl BB3 .... 65 C6
Kirkdale Gdns WN8 ...... 10 A7
Kirkdale Rd BB6 .... 123 C8
Kirkdene Ave BB8 ...... 194 D1
Kirkdene Mews BB8 .... 194 D1
Kirkes Rd LA1 .... 215 A7
Kirkfell Dr BB12 .... 127 C8
Kirkfield PR3 .... 185 D3
Kirkgate Burnley BB11 .... 128 B4
Kirkham PR4 .... 114 B4
Kirkgate La LA6 .... 240 B4
Kirkham & Wesham Prim Sch
PR4 .... 113 F5
Kirkham & Wesham Sta
PR4 .... 113 F6
Kirkham Ave FY1 .... 130 E2
Kirkham By-Pass PR4 ... 114 B4
Kirkham Cl PR25 .... 76 D1
Kirkham Gram Jun Sch
PR4 .... 113 F4
Kirkham Gram Sch PR4 .... 113 F5
Kirkham Mus* PR4 ...... 114 A5
Kirkham Rd
Freckleton PR4 .... 93 B8
Kirkham PR4 .... 114 E6
Southport PR9 .... 54 A4
Weeton PR4 .... 132 F2
Kirkham St PR1 .... 96 E8
Kirkham Trad Pk PR4 .... 114 B4
Kirkhill Ave BB4 .... 85 C3
Kirklake Bank L37 ...... 11 C2
Kirklake Rd L37 .... 11 D2
Kirkland & Catterall St Helen's CE Prim Sch
PR3 .... 181 A2
Kirkland Pl PR2 .... 95 E8
Kirklands Chipping PR3 ... 185 E3
Hest Bank LA2 .... 220 E1
Kirklands Rd LA6 ...... 237 B8
Kirklees Rd PR8 .... 34 F1
Kirkmoor Cl BB7 .... 189 D1
Kirkmoor Rd BB7 ...... 166 E8
Kirkstall Ave
Blackpool FY1 .... 130 E2
Read BB12 .... 145 D1
Kirkstall Cl PR7 .... 43 D5
Kirkstall Dr
Barnoldswick BB18 ...... 196 D3
Chorley PR7 .... 43 D5
Formby L37 .... 12 B2
Kirkstall Rd Chorley PR7 ... 43 D5
Southport PR8 .... 34 F2
Kirkstone Ave
Blackburn BB2 .... 80 E8
Fleetwood FY7 .... 198 D1
Kirkstone Dr
Blackpool FY5 .... 152 C7
Morecambe LA4 .... 217 D5
Kirkstone Rd FY8 ...... 110 D1
Kirton Cres FY8 .... 90 C6
Kirton Pl FY5 .... 175 E1
Kit Brow La LA2 .... 211 D6
Kittiwake Cl 13 FY5 ...... 175 F1
Kittiwake Rd PR6 .... 62 A3
Kittlingborne Brow PR5 ... 98 A3
Kitty La FY4 .... 111 B4
Knacks La OL12 .... 52 A5
Knaresboro Ave FY3 ...... 130 F3
Knaresborough Cl FY6 .. 153 D5
Knebworth Cl PR6 ...... 78 C2
Knight Cres BB3 .... 82 A6
Knighton Ave BB2 ...... 101 C8
Knights Cl FY5 .... 175 F1
Knightsbrdige Cl PR4 ... 113 E6
Knightsbridge Ave
Blackpool FY4 .... 110 D6
Colne BB8 .... 171 B5
Knightsbridge Cl
Kirkham PR4 .... 113 E6
2 Lytham St Anne's FY8 ... 90 D6
Knightsbridge Ct PR9 ...... 53 D1
Knightscliffe Cres WN6 ... 19 D6
Knitting Row La PR3 ... 178 A3
Knob Hall Gdns PR9 ...... 53 F3
Knob Hall La PR9 .... 53 F3
Knoll La PR4 .... 75 A4
Knoll The LA2 .... 218 C8
Knot Acre PR4 .... 76 A8
Knot La
Newsholme BB7,BD23 .... 231 D5
Walton-le-D PR5 .... 97 F5
Knott Hill OL12 .... 71 D6
Knott Hill St OL12 .... 71 E6
Knott La LA5 .... 224 A8
Knott St BB3 .... 82 A1
Knotts Brow BL7 .... 48 F4
Knotts Dr BB8 .... 171 C3
Knotts La
Bolton-by-B BB7,BD23 .... 230 B8
Colne BB8 .... 171 D3
Padiham BB12 .... 126 E6
Knotts Mount BB8 ...... 171 C3
Knowe Hill Cres LA1 .... 215 B3
Knowl Cl BL0 .... 50 C4
Knowl Gap Ave BB4 ...... 85 A1
Knowl Mdw BB4 .... 68 A6
Knowle Ave
Blackpool FY2 .... 152 C1
Cleveleys FY5 .... 175 E2
Southport PR8 .... 21 C6
Knowle La BB3 .... 82 A3
Knowle The FY2 .... 152 C2
Knowles Brow BB7 ...... 165 B3
Knowles Rd FY8 .... 89 E7
Knowles St
1 Chorley PR7 .... 43 C6
Preston PR1 .... 97 D8
Rishton BB1 .... 124 B1
Knowlesly Mdws BB3 ...... 65 C6
Knowlesly Rd BB3 .... 65 B6
Knowley Brow PR6 .... 61 E2
Knowlmere St BB5 ...... 104 B7
Knowlys Ave LA3 .... 212 F8
Knowlys Cres 4 LA3 ...... 212 F8
Knowlys Dr 3 LA3 ...... 212 F8
Knowlys Gr LA3 .... 212 F8
Knowlys Rd LA3 .... 212 E8
Knowsley Ave
Blackpool FY3 .... 130 E3
Leyland PR25 .... 77 C4
Knowsley Cl
Gregson Lane PR5 .... 98 F2
Lancaster LA1 .... 214 D6
Knowsley Cres
Shawforth OL12 .... 71 E6
Thornton FY5 .... 176 C2
Weeton PR4 .... 132 E2
Knowsley Dr PR5 .... 98 F2
Knowsley Gate FY7 ...... 198 D4
Knowsley Gr 6 BL6 ...... 32 D1
Knowsley Ind Pk L33 ...... 1 C2
Knowsley La Edgworth BL7 . 66 E4
Rivington PR6 .... 44 E4
Knowsley Park Way BB4 .. 68 B8
Knowsley Rd
Haslingden BB4 .... 68 B8
Leyland PR25 .... 60 C8
Ormskirk L39 .... 15 F5
Southport PR9 .... 53 C1
Wilpshire BB1 .... 122 F5
Knowsley Rd Ind Est BB4 . 68 B8
Knowsley Rd W BB1 .... 122 E5
Knowsley Road Ind Est
BB4 .... 85 B1
Knowsley St
3 Colne BB8 .... 171 D4
31 Preston PR1 .... 97 A7
Knox Gr FY1 .... 130 D3
Knunck Knowles Dr
BB7 .... 189 E1
Knutsford Rd FY3 ...... 131 B2
Knutsford Wlk L31 .... 5 D4
Knuzden Brook BB1 .... 102 D4
Korea Rd PR2 .... 118 B4
Kumara Cres FY4 ...... 131 B1
Kyan St BB10 .... 148 B2
Kylbarrow La LA5 ...... 225 F2
Kylemore Ave FY2 ...... 152 D3
Kytson Cl 1 FY1 .... 130 D7

L

Laburnam Cotts PR3 .... 201 E5
Laburnum Ave
Bamber Bridge PR5 .... 77 B8
Lytham St Anne's FY8 ...... 91 B5
Laburnum Cl
Burnley BB11 .... 127 D3
Preston PR1 .... 118 C3
Laburnum Dr
Fulwood PR2 .... 117 D8
Oswaldtwistle BB5 ...... 103 F3
Skelmersdale WN8 .... 17 D1
Laburnum Gr
Burscough Bridge L40 ...... 25 E6
Horwich BL6 .... 32 E1
Lancaster LA1 .... 214 D8
Maghull L31 .... 5 F1
Southport PR8 .... 35 F7
Laburnum Pk LA5 ...... 221 C8
Laburnum Rd
Blackburn BB1 .... 102 A8
Chorley PR6 .... 61 D3
Haslingden BB4 .... 68 A7
2 Lancaster LA1 .... 218 D2
Laburnum St
6 Blackpool FY3 .... 130 D7
Haslingden BB4 .... 85 A3
Lacey Ct 19 BB4 .... 85 B3
Lachman Rd BB8 .... 172 B3
Lacy Ave PR1 .... 96 E2
Ladbrooke Gr BB11 ...... 127 E2
Lade End LA3 .... 212 E8
Ladies Row PR4 .... 134 F4
Ladies Wlk LA1 .... 218 E2
Ladies Wlk Ind Est LA1 .. 218 E2
Lady Acre PR5 .... 78 A8
Lady Alice's Dr L40 ...... 16 E8
Lady Anne Cl L40 .... 24 B7
Lady Cl BB3 .... 82 A6
Lady Crosse Dr PR6 ...... 61 C7
Lady Green Ct L38 .... 3 E3
Lady Green La L38 .... 3 D4
Lady Hartley Ct BB8 .... 172 D6
Lady Hey Cres PR2 ...... 116 C1
Lady Pl PR5 .... 97 E4
Lady St PR1 .... 96 F8
Lady Well Dr PR2 ...... 118 C7
Lady's Wlk L40 .... 16 C6
Ladybank Ave PR2 ...... 118 D7
Ladybower La FY6 ...... 153 B3
Ladyman St 9 PR1 ...... 96 E7
Ladysmith Ave BL9 ...... 33 A5
Ladysmith Rd PR2 ...... 117 C2
Ladywell St PR1 .... 96 E8
Lafford La WN8 .... 19 C2
Lagonda Dr
Blackpool FY4 .... 111 F6
Peel Hill FY4 .... 112 A6
Lagonda Way FY4 ...... 111 F6
Laidley's Wlk FY7 ...... 198 E5
Lairgill Row LA2 .... 239 E8
Laister Ct 7 LA4 .... 217 E6
Laithbutts La LA6 ...... 221 F5
Laithe St Burnley BB11 ... 127 F4
Colne BB8 .... 171 C4
Lake Ave LA4 .... 216 F4
Lake Gr LA4 .... 216 F4
Lake Point FY8 .... 90 D3
Lake Rd
Lytham St Anne's FY8 ...... 90 C4
Morecambe LA3 .... 216 F3
Lake Rd N FY8 .... 90 C4
Lake Side Cotts WN1 ...... 30 C1
Lake View BL7 .... 46 C5
Lake View Rd BB8 ...... 171 D7
Lakeber Ave LA2 .... 239 D8
Lakeber Cl 11 LA2 ...... 239 D8
Lakeber Dr 13 LA2 ...... 239 D8
Lakeland Cl
Billington BB7 .... 144 A3
Forton PR3 .... 207 B3
Lakeland Dr BB7 .... 144 A8
Lakeland Gdns PR7 ...... 43 A5
Lakeland Ho LA4 .... 217 E7
Lakeland Way BB12 ...... 127 B8
Lakes Dr WN5 .... 10 E6
Lakeside Ave WN5 .... 10 E3
Lakeside Ct PR9 .... 53 C1
Lakeview Ct PR9 .... 35 B8
Lakeway FY3 .... 130 F6
Lakewood Ave FY5 ...... 175 D1
Lamaleach Dr PR4 .... 93 A6
Lamb Row BB7 .... 145 E7
Lamb's La PR3 .... 201 A4
Lambert Cl PR2 .... 118 E3
Lambert Rd Fulwood PR2 . 118 E3
Lancaster LA1 .... 218 C3
Lambert St BB8 .... 172 C2
Lamberts Mill Footwear Mus* BB4 .... 86 B2
Lambeth Cl
Blackburn BB1 .... 102 A4
Horwich BL6 .... 32 D3
Lambeth Ct PR2 .... 117 E5
Lambeth St
Blackburn BB1 .... 102 A4
Colne BB8 .... 172 B5
Lambing Clough La BB7 . 142 E7
Lambourne WN8 .... 18 B4
Lambridge Cl LA4 ...... 217 B3
Lambs Hill Cl 7 FY5 .... 176 D1
Lambs Rd FY5 .... 153 D8
Lambshear La L31 .... 5 C4
Lambton Gates BB4 ...... 86 C2
Lamlash Rd BB1 .... 102 D4
Lammack Prim Sch
BB1 .... 122 C1
Lammack Rd BB1 .... 101 C8
Lamour Pl 4 FY7 .... 198 D3
Lanark Ave FY2 .... 152 C6
Lanark Cl OL10 .... 33 F1
Lanark St BB11 .... 127 D4
Lancambe Ct LA1 ...... 218 A2
Lancashire Ambulance Service HQ PR3 .... 137 C1
Lancashire Coll PR7 ...... 43 A8
Lancashire Constabulary HQ
PR4 .... 95 E1
Lancashire Enterprise Bsns Pk PR26 .... 77 A4
Lancashire Fire & Rescue HQ
PR2 .... 117 D8
Lancashire Rd PR26 ...... 77 A4
Lancashire St LA4 ...... 216 E4
Lancaster & Lakeland Nuffield Hospl The
LA1 .... 215 A7
Lancaster & Morecambe Coll
LA1 .... 217 F3
Lancaster & Morecambe Coll (Annexe) LA4 .... 217 B5
Lancaster Ave
Accrington BB5 .... 104 B7
Clayton-le-W PR25 .... 77 E1
Great Eccleston PR3 ...... 156 C5
Haslingden BB4 .... 68 B8
Horwich BL6 .... 32 D2
Lytham St Anne's FY8 ...... 89 F4
Ramsbottom BL0 .... 50 A4
Thornton FY5 .... 176 C2
Lancaster Castle* LA1 .. 214 E8
Lancaster Christ Church CE Prim Sch LA1 .... 215 B8
Lancaster Cl
Adlington PR6 .... 31 B7
Great Eccleston PR3 ...... 156 C5
Knott End-on-S FY6 ...... 199 F5
Maghull L31 .... 5 F1
Southport PR8 .... 34 E4
Lancaster Cres WN8 ...... 17 E1
Lancaster Ct Chorley PR7 .. 61 C2
Parbold WN8 .... 27 C2
Lancaster Dallas Road Comm Prim Sch LA1 .... 214 E7
Lancaster Dr Banks PR9 ... 54 F5
Brinscall PR6 .... 62 E8
Clayton-le-M BB5 .... 125 A3
Clitheroe BB7 .... 166 C7
Padiham BB12 .... 126 D6
Lancaster Gate Banks PR9 . 54 F5
Fleetwood FY7 .... 198 D4
14 Lancaster LA1 .... 214 F8
Nelson BB9 .... 148 D7
Lancaster Gdns PR8 ...... 34 E4
Lancaster Girls' Gram Sch
LA1 .... 214 E7
Lancaster Ho
28 Preston PR1 .... 97 A7
Southport PR8 .... 34 E4
Lancaster L Pk* LA1 .... 215 B6
Lancaster La
Clayton-le-W PR25 .... 77 E2
Parbold WN8 .... 27 C3
Lancaster Lane Sch
PR25 .... 77 D1
Lancaster Maritime Mus*
LA1 .... 218 C1
Lancaster Moor Hospl
LA1 .... 215 D8
Lancaster Pl
Adlington PR6 .... 31 A8
Blackburn BB2 .... 101 B5
Lancaster Rd
Blackpool FY3 .... 131 A3
Carnforth LA5 .... 221 B7
Caton LA2 .... 237 B3
Lancaster Rd *continued*
Cockerham LA2 .... 206 C6
Fisher's Row PR3 .... 201 E5
Formby L37 .... 11 E1
Garstang PR3 .... 204 C1
Hornby LA2 .... 238 B7
Knott End-on-S FY6 ...... 199 F5
Lancaster LA3 .... 213 D3
Morecambe LA4 .... 217 C5
Morecambe,Torrisholme
LA4 .... 217 F4
Moss Edge PR3 .... 178 E6
Preesall FY6 .... 200 C3
Preston PR1 .... 96 F8
Preston PR1 .... 97 A8
Ratten Row PR3 .... 156 A8
Slyne LA2 .... 218 D6
Southport PR8 .... 34 E4
Lancaster Rd N PR1 .... 117 F1
Lancaster Road Prim Sch
LA4 .... 217 D4
Lancaster Royal Gram Sch
LA1 .... 215 A8
Lancaster Royal Gram Sch (Annexe) LA1 .... 215 B7
Lancaster St
Blackburn BB2 .... 101 C4
Colne BB8 .... 171 D5
Coppull PR7 .... 42 F1
Oswaldtwistle BB5 ...... 103 C3
Lancaster Sta LA1 ...... 214 E8
Lancaster Way 16 PR1 .... 97 A8
Lancastergate PR25 ...... 59 F8
Lanchester Ct PR25 ...... 59 D6
Lanchester Gdns BB6 ... 143 C6
Lancia Cres FY4 .... 112 A6
Lancing Pl BB2 .... 101 C3
Land End L31 .... 6 C1
Land Gate OL12 .... 71 F5
Land La New Longton PR4 .. 75 D5
Southport PR9 .... 54 D4
Landcrest Cl PR4 .... 114 B2
Landing La BB7 .... 229 F4
Landless St BB9 .... 148 A5
Landseer Ave FY2 ...... 152 C4
Landseer Cl BB11 ...... 127 E3
Landseer St PR1 .... 118 C1
Landsmoor Dr PR4 ...... 95 A1
Lane Bottom BB18 ...... 194 B8
Lane End BB11 .... 126 C2
Lane End La OL13 .... 88 A1
Lane End Rd OL13 .... 71 A8
Lane Ends Brierfield BB9 . 148 D6
Longridge PR3 .... 140 F8
Rivington PR6 .... 44 D4
Lane Ends Ct 2 FY4 .... 130 E1
Lane Foot Brow LA2 .... 239 D4
Lane Head LA2 .... 238 D6
Lane Head La OL13 ...... 87 F3
Lane Ho BB8 .... 172 C1
Lane House Cl BB2 ...... 81 B8
Lane Side OL13 .... 88 A4
Lane Side Terr BB5 ...... 125 D6
Lane The Carleton FY6 .... 153 A3
Sunderland LA3 .... 209 A5
Lane Top
Colne,Cotton Tree BB8 .... 172 C5
Fence BB12 .... 147 D7
Lanedale PR4 .... 75 A8
Lanefield Dr FY5 .... 175 C4
Laneshaw Bridge Prim Sch
BB8 .... 172 E6
Laneshaw Cl BB3 .... 81 E4
Laneside Altham BB5 .... 125 D6
Great Harwood BB6 ...... 124 A6
Laneside Ave
Accrington BB5 .... 104 B8
Higham BB12 .... 146 F6
Laneside Ho 5 BB4 ...... 85 B2
Laneside Rd BB4 .... 85 C2
Lang St Accrington BB5 .... 104 A6
Blackpool FY1 .... 130 C6
Langber End La LA6 .... 242 F1
Langcliffe Rd PR2 ...... 118 E4
Langdale LA2 .... 237 C3
Langdale Ave
Clitheroe BB7 .... 166 C7
Croston PR26 .... 58 B3
Formby L37 .... 11 D2
Hesketh Bank PR4 .... 73 D4
Rawtenstall BB4 .... 85 E2
Langdale Cl
3 Accrington BB5 .... 125 D1
Bamber Bridge PR5 .... 97 D1
Blackburn BB2 .... 80 E8
Formby L37 .... 11 D2
Freckleton PR4 .... 93 A6
Thornton FY5 .... 176 B2
Langdale Cres PR2 ...... 118 E3
Langdale Ct
Cleveleys FY5 .... 175 F1
3 Fleetwood FY7 .... 198 E2
4 Garstang PR3 .... 181 B7
Higher Penwortham PR1 .... 96 C4
Langdale Dr
Burscough L40 .... 25 E4
Maghull L31 .... 5 E2
Langdale Gdns PR8 ...... 34 F1
Langdale Gr PR6 .... 61 B7
Langdale Pl
1 Blackpool FY4 .... 131 C1
Lancaster LA1 .... 218 E2
Langdale Rd
Blackburn BB2 .... 80 E8
Blackpool FY4 .... 131 C1
Carnforth LA5 .... 221 E8
Fulwood PR2 .... 118 E3
Lancaster LA1 .... 218 E2

Langdale Rd continued
Leyland PR25 60 B6
Longridge PR3 139 F5
Lytham St Anne's FY8 110 D1
Morecambe LA4 217 D5
Padiham BB12 146 C2
Langdale Rise BB8 171 F6
Langden Brook Mews LA3 217 F2
Langden Brook Sq BB1 102 A3
Langden Cres PR5 77 F8
Langden Dr PR2 119 A3
Langden Fold PR2 139 D1
Langdon Way FY2 152 E2
Langfield BB10 129 B6
Langfield Ave FY4 110 C5
Langfield Cl PR2 117 F8
Langford St BB5 104 E1
Langham Ave BB5 104 B8
Langham Rd
Blackburn BB1 101 D7
Standish WN6 29 D1
Langham St BB12 127 B6
Langho St BB2 101 C1
Langho Sta BB6 143 C1
Langho Woods BB6 143 C5
Langholm Cl 6 PR25 76 D1
Langholme Cl BB9 170 C1
Langholme Rd PR1 96 B4
Langholme St BB9 148 E6
Langholme Way OL10 33 F1
Langley Cl Hightown L38 2 F2
Standish WN6 29 E2
Langley Ct L40 25 B5
Langley La PR3 137 F6
Langley Pl L40 25 B4
Langley Rd Burscough L40 25 B4
Lancaster LA1 215 A7
Langport Cl PR2 117 F8
Langridge Way LA4 217 B3
Langroyd Rd BB8 171 E6
Langsford Cl BB18 196 C2
Langshaw Dr BB7 166 F6
Langshaw La LA2 211 D5
Langstone Cl BL6 32 B3
Langthwaite Rd LA1,LA2 215 E5
Langton Ave WN6 29 E1
Langton Brow
Eccleston PR7 41 D5
Longridge PR3 140 B7
Langton Cl Blackburn BB2 81 C7
Eccleston PR7 41 D5
Lancaster LA1 218 E4
Leyland PR26 59 C8
Langton Pl WN6 29 E1
Langton Rd PR4 114 A5
Langton St PR1 96 D7
Langtree WN8 18 B3
Langtree La Elswick PR4 155 F2
Standish WN6 29 D3
Langwood FY7 198 E2
Langwood La WA11 9 C1
Langwyth Rd BB10 129 E5
Lansborough Cl PR26 59 B8
Lansbury Pl 3 BB9 170 F2
Lansdown Hill PR2 117 C7
Lansdown Rd PR4 114 A7
Lansdowne Cl
Burnley BB11 127 F4
Ramsbottom BL0 50 B5
Lansdowne Gr LA4 217 E7
Lansdowne Pl 1 FY1 130 B6
Lansdowne Rd
Burnley BB11 127 E4
Lytham St Anne's FY8 90 D5
Morecambe LA4 217 E7
Southport PR8 35 E6
Lansdowne St BB2 101 B3
Lansil Ind Est LA1 218 E3
Lansil Way LA1 218 E3
Lansil Wlk LA1 218 E3
Lanterns The FY6 153 D4
Lapford Cres L33 1 A4
Lapford Wlk L33 1 A4
Lappet Gr PR4 116 E5
Lapwing Row FY8 90 E7
Lapwings The FY6 153 B2
Larbreck Ave PR4 156 A1
Larbreck Hall Cvn Pk PR3 155 C5
Larbreck Rd FY3 130 E7
Larch Ave PR6 61 E2
Larch Cl Blackburn BB2 80 F8
Freckleton PR4 93 A5
Knott End-on-S FY6 200 A5
Rawtenstall BB4 68 F8
Skelmersdale WN8 17 E1
Larch Dr PR6 62 F7
Larch Gate PR5 98 E2
Larch Gr
Bamber Bridge PR5 97 F1
Garstang PR3 181 C8
Lancaster LA1 214 D8
Larch Rd BB5 103 F3
Larch St Blackburn BB1 102 A7
Burnley BB12 127 C7
Bury BL9 33 B2
Nelson BB9 148 F8
Southport PR8 35 E6
Larch Way L37 11 D4
Larches Ave PR2 116 F1
Larches La PR2 116 E1
Larches The BB1 101 F7
Larchgate PR2 118 C7
Larchway PR3 140 B8
Larchwood
Higher Penwortham PR1 96 B4
Lancaster LA1 215 B4
Larchwood continued
Preston PR2 116 E1
Larchwood Cl FY8 90 F4
Larchwood Cres PR25 76 E1
Largs Rd BB1 102 C3
Lark Ave 3 PR1 96 E4
Lark Cl FY3 131 B3
Lark Ct FY7 198 D1
Lark Hill Blackburn BB1 101 F6
Higher Walton PR5 98 B3
Rawtenstall BB4 86 A3
Lark Hill Pl OL12 52 E1
Lark St 4 Burnley BB12 127 C7
Colne BB8 171 E6
Darwen BB3 65 B5
Larkfield PR7 41 B6
Larkfield Cl BL8 49 F1
Larkfield Ct PR9 54 A3
Larkfield La PR9 54 A3
Larkfield Prim Sch PR9 54 A3
Larkhill
Brockhall Village BB6 143 C5
Skelmersdale WN8 18 B4
Larkhill Ave BB10 148 C5
Larkhill Gr L38 2 F3
Larkhill La L37 11 C4
Larkhill Rd PR1 97 B7
Larkhill St Blackpool FY1 130 C6
Preston PR1 97 B7
Larkholme Ave FY7 198 E1
Larkholme La FY7 198 E1
Larkholme Par FY7 198 D1
Larkholme Prim Sch FY7 175 D8
Larkspur Cl Blackburn BB2 80 D8
3 Southport PR8 35 D6
Last Drop Village The* BL7 48 A1
Latham Ave
9 Blackpool FY3 130 E3
Ormskirk L39 16 A5
Latham Cres PR4 57 A6
Latham Rd BL6 31 C3
Latham Row BL6 32 F3
Latham St Burnley BB10 148 B1
Preston PR1 97 A6
Lathom Ave
Morecambe LA4 217 D4
Parbold WN8 27 B3
Lathom Cl L40 25 E4
Lathom Dr L31 5 E3
Lathom Gr LA4 217 D4
Lathom High Sch WN8 17 F3
Lathom La L40 16 C7
Lathom Rd Bickerstaffe L39 7 F8
Southport PR9 53 C1
Lathom St 8 BL9 33 A4
Lathom St James CE Prim Sch L40 16 E4
Lathom Way PR3 181 D6
Latimer Cl 2 WN5 10 F7
Latimer Dr PR4 75 F7
Lauderdale Ave FY5 175 D1
Lauderdale Cres 1 PR2 118 F4
Lauderdale Rd PR2 118 F4
Lauderdale St PR1 96 E6
Laund Gate BB12 147 D8
Laund Gr BB5 104 D3
Laund Hey View BB4 85 B1
Laund La Haslingden BB4 85 C3
Ollerton Fold PR6 79 E4
Laund Rd BB5 104 D3
Laund St BB4 85 F4
Laund The PR26 76 A1
Laundry Rd N FY4 111 A5
Laura St BL0 50 C2
Laurel Ave Blackpool FY1 130 E2
Burscough Bridge L40 25 E6
Darwen BB3 82 B2
Euxton PR7 60 B3
Fleetwood FY7 175 F8
Lytham St Anne's FY8 91 B5
Laurel Bank LA1 214 D7
Laurel Bank Ave PR2 117 C3
Laurel Bank Terr BB2 80 B7
Laurel Dr
Skelmersdale WN8 17 F2
Thornton FY5 153 B8
Laurel Gr PR8 35 E7
Laurel St 4 Bacup OL13 87 F3
Burnley BB11 128 B4
3 Bury BL9 33 B2
10 Preston PR1 97 A7
Laurels The Coppull PR7 42 F3
Kirkham PR4 113 D4
Poulton-le-F FY6 153 F3
Laureston Ave LA3 212 F6
Laurie Pl 2 OL12 52 F1
Laurier Ave 3 FY4 110 C6
Laurier Rd BB10 148 B2
Lauriston Cl 4 FY4 111 A6
Lavender Cl PR2 118 C6
Lavender Gr PR7 43 C5
Lavender Hill BB4 68 F8
Lavender Way FY6 199 F5
Laverick Rd LA2 237 A5
Laverton Cl BL9 33 E1
Laverton Rd FY8 90 A4
Law St Cornholme OL14 109 B1
Newchurch BB4 86 F1
Lawley Rd BB2 101 A5
Lawn Ct 2 FY1 130 D4
Lawn St BB10 128 A8
Lawn Tennis Ct FY4 110 D5
Lawns Ave WN5 10 C5
Lawns The PR9 53 F2
Lawnsdale Cvn Pk FY8 112 E1
Lawnswood Ave
Lancaster LA1 215 A3
Poulton-le-F FY6 153 C2
Lawnswood Cres FY3 131 C2
Lawnswood Dr LA3 217 C2
Lawnwood Ave PR7 43 A5
Lawrence Ave
Bamber Bridge PR5 97 D2
Burnley BB11 127 C4
Burnley BB11 127 C5
Lytham St Anne's FY8 90 A6
Preston PR1 97 B5
Simonstone BB12 145 E2
Lawrence Cl OL12 52 A1
Lawrence La PR7 41 C7
Lawrence Rd Chorley PR7 43 B7
Higher Penwortham PR1 96 B5
Lawrence Row 4 FY7 199 A4
Lawrence St
Blackburn BB2 101 C4
12 Blackpool FY4 130 B1
Fulwood PR2 117 D3
Padiham BB12 146 D1
Whitewell Bottom BB4 86 F4
Lawrie Ave BL0 50 B5
Lawson Cl LA1 214 F3
Lawson Gdns LA2 218 C8
Lawson Pl LA2 218 C8
Lawson Rd Blackpool FY3 131 A3
Horwich BL6 32 C4
Lytham St Anne's FY8 111 A2
Lawson St 3 Chorley PR6 43 E7
Preston PR1 96 F8
Rawtenstall BB4 86 A8
Southport PR9 36 A7
Lawsons Ct 4 FY5 176 C1
Lawsons Rd FY5 176 C2
Lawswood Formby L37 11 E5
6 Thornton FY5 176 C1
Lawton Cl PR6 79 B1
Laxey Gr PR1 118 D3
Laxey Rd BB2 101 E1
Laycock Gate FY3 130 D6
Layton Prim Sch FY3 130 E8
Layton Rd Blackpool FY3 130 E6
Preston PR2 116 E1
Layton Sta FY2 152 E1
Lazenby Ave FY7 198 C2
Lea Bank BB4 86 D2
Lea Com Prim Sch PR2 116 D1
Lea Cres L39 15 F7
Lea Ct L39 15 E7
Lea Dr BB2 81 E6
Lea La Cottam PR4 116 B5
Gressingham LA2 237 F8
Heysham LA3 212 E6
Lea Mount Dr BL9 33 D4
Lea Neeld's Endowed CE Prim Sch PR4 116 C4
Lea Rd Lucas Green PR6 61 C5
Preston PR2,PR4 116 D3
Lea St Mary's RC Primary Sch PR4 115 F2
Lea Way Cl FY5 153 D7
Leach Cres FY8 110 F2
Leach La FY8 110 E1
Leach Pl PR5 78 B8
Leach St Blackburn BB2 101 E2
Colne BB8 171 C4
Leaches Rd BL0 50 D8
Leachfield Cl 2 LA2 211 A4
Leachfield Ind Est PR3 204 B1
Leachfield Rd LA2 210 F4
Leacroft BB3 82 A6
Lead Mines Clough* PR6 45 A7
Leadale PR2 116 D2
Leadale Cl WN6 29 D1
Leadale Gn PR25 76 E1
Leadale Rd PR25 76 E1
Leaford Ave FY3 130 E8
Leafy Cl PR25 60 B7
Leagram Cres PR2 119 A3
Leamington Ave
Baldingstone BL9 50 E1
Burnley BB10 148 C1
Southport PR8 21 D5
Leamington Rd
Blackburn BB2 101 B6
Blackpool FY1 130 D5
Lytham St Anne's FY8 89 F6
Morecambe LA4 217 D3
Southport PR8 21 D5
Leamington St BB9 148 E7
Leander Gdns FY6 153 D2
Leapers View LA6 237 B8
Leaside Cl OL12 52 D2
Leathercote PR3 181 C6
Leathwood L31 5 E1
Leavengreave Ct OL12 71 D4
Leaver St BB12 127 A5
Leaverholme Cl BB10 108 A7
Leavesley Rd FY1 130 D8
Lebanon St BB10 128 C5
Leck Ho 11 LA1 215 A3
Leck St Peter's CE Prim Sch LA6 242 B7
Leckhampton Rd FY1 130 B8
Leckonby St PR3 156 B5
Ledburn WN8 18 B3
Ledbury Ave FY8 90 B5
Ledbury Rd FY3 131 B7
Ledson Gr L39 6 B7
Lee Brook Cl BB4 86 A4
Lee Gr BB10 128 F4
Lee Green St 3 BB10 128 A8
Lee La Bispham Green L40 27 C7
Great Harwood BB1 124 B3
Lee La continued
Horwich BL6 32 B4
Whittlestone Head BL7 66 B2
Lee Rd Bacup OL13 70 E8
Blackpool FY4 111 B8
Nelson BB9 170 F2
Lee St Accrington BB5 104 C6
Bacup OL13 87 F2
Barrowford BB9 170 D3
Longridge PR3 140 A7
Rawtenstall BB4 86 A4
Burnley BB10 128 A8
Lee View OL13 88 B1
Lee's St OL13 71 C8
Leebrook Rd BB4 85 F4
Leech House La LA2 211 A5
Leeds Cl 15 BB1 102 A4
Leeds Rd Blackpool FY1 130 D5
4 Nelson BB9 148 E8
Nelson BB9 170 F1
Leehouse Dr FY6 131 D8
Leek St PR1 97 E8
Leeming La LA6 242 C3
Lees Cotts BL7 48 C2
Lees Ct LA3 212 E7
Lees La WN8 18 E7
Lees Rd Adlington PR6 31 B8
Kirkby L33 1 B2
Lees The BB10 108 A7
Leesands Cl PR2 118 E5
Leeson Ave PR7 42 D4
Leeswood WN8 18 B3
Leet Rd BB12 146 F5
Leeward Cl BB3 81 F6
Leeward Rd PR2 95 F8
Legh La PR4 56 B4
Leicester Ave
Cleveleys FY5 175 E3
Garstang PR3 181 B7
Horwich BL6 32 A3
Leicester Gate FY5 175 E3
Leicester Lodge 3 PR2 118 F4
Leicester Rd
Blackburn BB1 102 C5
Blackpool FY1 130 D5
Preston PR1 118 A1
Leicester St PR9 35 B8
Leigh Brow PR5 97 B2
Leigh Pk BB11 126 C3
Leigh Row PR7 43 C7
Leighton Ave
Fleetwood FY7 198 D3
Maghull L31 5 D2
Leighton Ct LA4 217 A3
Leighton Dr LA1 214 D7
Leighton Hall* LA5 225 C1
Leighton Moss Nature Reserve* LA5 225 A3
Leighton Moss Visitor Ctr* LA5 224 F2
Leighton St PR1 96 E8
Leinster Rd LA1 215 A5
Leisure Lakes Cvn Pk PR4 55 E1
Leith Ave FY5 175 D2
Lemon Tree Ct FY8 110 B4
Lemonius St BB5 104 C4
Lench Rd BB4 69 D8
Lench St BB4 69 F8
Lenches Fold BB8 171 D4
Lenches Rd BB8 171 D3
Lendel Cl L37 11 E3
Lennon St 3 PR7 43 C7
Lennox Ct FY4 110 D6
Lennox Gate FY4 110 D7
Lennox Rd OL14 109 A1
Lennox St 18 Preston PR1 97 A7
Worsthorne BB10 129 A6
Lennox Wlk OL10 33 F1
Lenton Ave L37 11 D4
Lentworth Ave FY2 152 D5
Lentworth Dr LA1 215 A4
Lentworth Ho 5 LA1 215 A3
Leo Case Ct 5 PR1 97 D8
Leonard St
Barnoldswick BB18 196 B2
Nelson BB9 148 E7
Leonard Terr BB3 82 E3
Leopold Gr FY1 130 B5
Leopold Rd BB2 101 B6
Leopold St BB8 171 B4
Leopold Way BB2 82 A8
Lesley Rd PR8 35 E7
Leslie Ave Caton LA2 237 C3
Thornton FY5 176 C2
Letchworth Dr PR7 43 B6
Letchworth Pl 2 PR7 43 B6
Letcliffe Ctry Pk* BB18 194 B8
Lethbridge Rd PR8 35 D5
Letitia St BL6 32 A3
Levant St BB12 126 C7
Leven Ave FY7 198 D3
Leven Gr BB3 81 E4
Leven St BB11 128 B4
Levens Cl Banks PR9 55 A5
Blackburn BB2 81 F8
Lancaster LA1 214 D7
Poulton-le-F FY6 131 E8
Levens Ct LA3 216 E2
Levens Dr
Clayton-le-W PR25 77 D2
Morecambe LA3 216 E2
Poulton-le-F FY6 153 D1
Levens Gr FY1 130 D3
Levens St 12 PR1 118 D1
Levens Way LA5 224 C3
Levensgarth Ave PR2 117 F8
Lever Cl BB2 100 F7
Lever House La PR25 77 C2
Lever House Prim Sch PR25 77 C3
Lever Park Ave BL6 32 B5
Lever Park Sch BL6 32 C3
Lever St Blackpool FY3 130 E4
16 Ramsbottom BL0 50 C6
Rawtenstall BB4 86 B2
Levine Ave FY4 131 A1
Lewis Cl PR7 30 E6
Lewis Ct PR9 35 D8
Lewis Dr OL10 33 F1
Lewis St BB6 124 D5
Lewis Textile Mus* BB1 101 E5
Lewtas St FY1 130 B6
Lewth La PR4 136 B5
Lex St PR1 97 C8
Lexton Dr PR9 54 B3
Ley Ct LA1 214 D8
Ley St BB5 104 E2
Leybourne Ave PR8 21 F7
Leyburn Ave
Blackpool FY2 152 C5
Fleetwood FY7 198 E2
Leyburn Cl
Accrington BB5 104 E5
Fulwood PR2 118 E5
Leyburn Rd Blackburn BB2 81 C7
Lancaster LA1 218 D3
Leycester Dr LA1 218 A3
Leyfield PR1 96 E2
Leyfield Cl FY3 153 A1
Leyfield Rd PR25 59 F8
Leyland Cl Southport PR9 54 E5
Trawden BB8 172 B3
Leyland La Leyland PR25 76 D2
Runshaw Moor PR26,PR25 59 D4
Leyland Meth Inf Sch PR25 77 B1
Leyland Meth Jun Sch PR25 77 B1
Leyland Rd Burnley BB11 128 B6
Middleworth Green PR1 96 E3
Southport PR9 53 C1
Leyland St BB5 103 F5
Leyland St Andrew's CE Inf Sch PR25 59 F8
Leyland St James CE Prim Sch PR26 59 B8
Leyland St Mary's RC Prim Sch PR25 76 F1
Leyland St Mary's RC Tech Coll PR25 59 E7
Leyland Sta PR25 77 B2
Leyland Way Leyland PR25 77 C1
Ormskirk L39 15 F6
Leylands The FY8 90 F2
Leys Cl Elswick PR4 156 A1
Wiswell BB7 144 F8
Leys Rd FY2 152 D1
Leyster St LA4 217 C5
Leyton Ave PR25 59 D7
Leyton St OL12 52 F2
Libby La PR3 201 C6
Library Ave LA1 211 B7
Library Mews FY4 110 E7
Library Rd PR6 78 B4
Library St Chorley PR7 43 C7
Church BB5 103 E6
15 Preston PR1 97 A7
Lichen Cl PR7 42 D4
Lichfield Ave LA4 217 D6
Lichfield Rd
Blackpool FY1 130 C8
Chorley PR7 43 C6
Preston PR2 116 F2
Liddesdale Rd BB9 171 B2
Liddington Cl BB2 82 A8
Liddington Hall Dr BL0 50 B4
Lidget Ave PR2 116 C1
Lidgett BB8 172 A5
Lidum Park Ind Est FY8 91 E5
Liege Rd 4 PR25 60 A8
Lifeboat Pl 13 FY7 199 B5
Lifeboat Rd L37 11 B1
Lifton Rd L33 1 A2
Liggard Ct FY8 91 C4
Lightbown Ave FY3 130 E3
Lightbown Cotts BB3 81 E2
Lightbown St BB3 82 A3
Lightburne Ave FY8 89 F5
Lightfoot Cl PR2 117 D8
Lightfoot Green La PR4 117 B8
Lightfoot La PR2,PR4 117 B7
Lighthorne Dr PR8 21 A4
Lighthouse Cl 4 FY7 199 B5
Lighthurst Ave PR7 43 C6
Lighthurst La PR7 43 D5
Lightwood Ave
2 Blackpool FY4 130 C1
Lytham St Anne's FY8 90 D3
Lilac Ave
1 Blackpool FY1 130 D2
Haslingden BB4 85 B3
Kingsfold PR1 96 F2
Lytham St Anne's FY8 91 B5
Southport PR8 21 D2
Lilac Cl PR4 92 D5
Lilac Cres PR4 134 F4
Lilac Gr Abbey Village PR6 80 C2
Clitheroe BB7 166 C7
Darwen BB3 82 B3
Knott End-on-S FY6 199 E5
Preston PR1 118 C3

Lilac Gr *continued*
Skelmersdale WN8 17 E1
Lilac Rd BB1 102 A8
Lilac St BB8 171 F6
Lilac Terr 3 OL13 70 D8
Lilacs The FY6 153 F3
Lilburn Cl BL0 50 C4
Lilford Cl PR4 57 A5
Lilford Rd BB1 101 D6
Lily Gr Lancaster LA1 215 A5
Preston PR1 118 C3
Lily St 16 Bacup OL13 87 F2
Blackpool FY1 130 C5
Darwen BB3 82 B1
Nelson BB9 148 F6
Lima Rd FY8 90 B6
Lima St BL9 33 B3
Limbrick
21 Blackburn BB1 101 E5
Blackburn BB1 101 E6
Limbrick Cl PR6 43 E7
Lime Ave Galgate LA2 211 A4
Kirkham PR4 114 B4
Oswaldtwistle BB5 103 D2
Lime Chase PR2 117 C8
Lime Cl PR1 96 B4
Lime Ct WN8 17 E1
Lime Gr Blackpool FY2 152 E2
Chorley PR7 43 C5
Garstang PR3 181 B8
Lancaster LA1 214 D8
Longridge PR3 140 A8
Lytham St Anne's FY8 89 D8
Poulton-le-F FY6 153 E2
Preston PR2 116 F2
Ramsbottom BL0 50 D7
Skelmersdale WN8 17 E1
Thornton FY5 176 C1
Lime Rd Accrington BB5 104 C7
Haslingden BB4 85 C3
Lime St Blackburn BB1 101 E6
Clitheroe BB7 189 F1
Colne BB8 171 E6
Great Harwood BB6 124 C6
Nelson BB9 148 C8
Southport PR8 35 E6
Lime Tree Gr BB4 86 A4
Lime Tree Way L37 11 C2
Limebrest Ave FY5 153 D8
Limechase Cl 9 FY4 111 A6
Limefield BB2 101 B5
Limefield Ave
Brierfield BB9 148 C6
Whalley BB7 144 C6
Limefield Ct BB2 101 B5
Limefield Dr WN8 9 E7
Limefield St BB5 104 D5
Limerick Rd FY2 152 D3
Limers Gate
Rochdale OL12 52 F5
Sharneyford OL14 88 E4
Limers La BB6 124 A6
Limes Ave Darwen BB3 65 A8
Euxton PR7 60 C4
Morecambe LA3 216 E3
Limestone Trail* BB10 108 E6
Limewood Cl
Accrington BB5 104 D6
Haslingden BB4 68 A7
Limey La BB11 106 E6
Limont Rd PR8 21 D5
Lina St BB5 103 F6
Linacre La L37 4 B7
Linadale Ave 4 FY5 176 B2
Linaker Dr L39 14 B8
Linaker Prim Sch PR8 35 B5
Linaker St PR8 35 B5
Linby St BB10 128 B5
Lincoln Ave
Cleveleys FY5 175 E3
Fleetwood FY7 198 E3
Lincoln Chase PR2 116 C1
Lincoln Cl Blackburn BB1 102 B4
Morecambe LA4 217 D3
Lincoln Ct
1 Accrington BB5 104 A7
Blackpool FY1 130 C4
Lincoln Ho 7 PR1 97 B7
Lincoln Pk BB7 190 A1
Lincoln Pl BB4 85 A3
Lincoln Rd
Blackburn BB1 102 B4
Blackpool FY1 130 C5
Earby BB18 197 B2
Lancaster LA1 214 E7
Southport PR8 35 A1
Lincoln St Burnley BB11 128 A4
Cornholme OL14 109 B1
3 Haslingden BB4 85 A3
Preston PR1 118 B1
Lincoln Way
Clitheroe BB7 190 A2
Garstang PR3 181 B7
Lincoln Wlk PR1 118 B1
Lindadale Ave BB5 104 A3
Lindadale Cl BB5 104 A3
Lindale Ave PR2 139 E1
Lindale Cres BB10 148 A2
Lindale Gdns FY4 110 E6
Lindale Rd Fulwood PR2 118 A4
Longridge PR3 139 F5
Lindbeck Ct FY4 111 C8
Lindbeck Rd FY4 131 C1
Lindbergh Ave LA1 214 E4
Lindel La FY6 200 B2
Lindel Rd FY7 198 F2
Linden Ave
Blackburn BB1 101 D6
Cleveleys FY5 175 F3
Orrell WN5 10 E6
Ramsbottom BL0 50 D6
Linden Cl
Bamber Bridge PR5 97 B1
Barrowford BB9 170 B1
Cleveleys FY5 175 F2
Edenfield BL0 68 D2
Linden Cres BB3 82 C2
Linden Ct 7 Earby BB18 197 B1
Orrell WN5 10 E6
Linden Dr
Bamber Bridge PR5 97 B1
Clitheroe BB7 166 F7
Linden Fold PR4 156 A1
Linden Gn FY5 175 F2
Linden Gr Chorley PR6 61 D3
Fulwood PR2 118 E3
Garstang PR3 181 C8
Orrell WN5 10 E6
Linden Lea Blackburn BB2 80 F8
Rawtenstall BB4 68 F8
Linden Mews FY8 110 F2
Linden Pl FY2 152 E3
Linden Rd Colne BB8 171 D5
Earby BB18 197 B1
Linden St BB10 128 B5
Linden Wlk WN5 10 E6
Lindens WN8 18 B4
Lindens The FY6 200 B4
Linderbreck La FY6 131 E8
Lindeth Cl
Nether Kellet LA6 221 F6
Silverdale LA5 224 C2
Lindeth Gdns 8 LA1 218 D3
Lindeth Rd LA5 224 C2
Lindholme WN8 18 C3
Lindisfarne Ave BB2 101 F1
Lindisfarne Cl BB12 127 E7
Lindle Ave PR4 95 E2
Lindle Cl PR4 95 E2
Lindle Cres PR4 95 E2
Lindle La PR4 96 A2
Lindley Ave WN5 10 C5
Lindley Croft FY5 176 E2
Lindley Dr WN8 27 C3
Lindley St
Bamber Bridge PR5 77 B8
Blackburn BB2 101 B2
Lindon Park Rd BB4 68 C7
Lindow Cl 13 LA1 214 F7
Lindow Sq LA1 214 E7
Lindow St LA1 214 F7
Lindred Rd BB9 148 B7
Lindsay Ave
Blackpool FY3 130 E3
Leyland PR25 77 B1
Lytham St Anne's FY8 90 B6
Poulton-le-F FY6 153 D2
Lindsay Ct Blackpool FY8 110 B4
Morecambe LA3 217 C2
Lindsay Dr PR7 43 A7
Lindsay Pk BB10 128 F5
Lindsay St Burnley BB11 128 A6
Horwich BL6 32 D1
Lindsey Ho 2 BB5 104 A7
Linedred La BB9 148 B7
Lines St LA4 217 B5
Linfield Terr FY4 110 E6
Lingart La PR3 204 D1
Lingdales L37 12 B5
Lingfield Ave BB7 166 E6
Lingfield Cl LA1 215 B3
Lingfield Ct BB2 80 C8
Lingfield Rd FY7 198 F2
Lingfield Way BB2 80 D8
Linghaw La LA2 239 F8
Lingmoor Dr BB12 127 A8
Lingmoor Rd LA1 218 F1
Lingwell Cl PR6 61 C5
Link 59 Bsns Pk BB7 190 A2
Links Ave PR9 53 F3
Links Ct FY8 89 E5
Links Dr LA2 239 D8
Links Field PR2 117 C3
Links Gate Fulwood PR2 117 C3
Lytham St Anne's FY8 90 A6
Thornton FY5 153 D7
Links La BB2 80 C8
Links Lodge FY8 90 A6
Links Rd Blackpool FY1 130 C8
Higher Penwortham PR1 96 B6
Kirkby L32 1 A1
Knott End-on-S FY6 199 D5
Lytham St Anne's FY8 89 E5
Links The FY5 175 C4
Links View FY8 90 C5
Linkside Ave BB9 149 B8
Linley Gr BL0 50 A2
Linnet Cl FY3 131 B6
Linnet Dr BL9 33 B4
Linnet La FY8 90 E7
Linnet St PR1 118 B2
Linslade Cres L33 1 A4
Linton Ave LA3 216 D1
Linton Dr BB11 127 D3
Linton Gdns BB9 170 C3
Linton Gr PR1 96 B5
Linton St PR2 117 D3
Lion Ct 11 BB5 103 E6
Lion La BL6 31 C2
Lion St BB5 103 E6
Lionel St BB12 127 C6
Lions Ct 1 FY8 91 D4
Lions Dr BB1 102 D1
Liptrott Rd PR7 43 A5
Lisbon Dr Burnley BB11 127 E5
Darwen BB3 82 C1
Lisbon St 17 OL12 52 C1
Lismore Pk PR8 34 E4
Lister Croft BD23 197 A5
Lister Gr LA3 212 F8
Lister St Accrington BB5 104 A6
3 Blackburn BB2 101 E3
Lister Well Rd BB18 194 A6
Litchford Ho BB4 86 C2
Little Acre Longton PR4 75 A8
Thornton FY5 153 D8
Little Banks Cl PR5 78 B6
Little Brewery La L37 11 F6
Little Carr La PR7 43 D5
Little Cl Leyland PR26 76 E3
Middleforth Green PR1 96 C3
Little Coppins La FY6 153 E1
Little Digmoor Prim Sch
WN8 9 B6
Little Fell La LA2 215 E3
Little Fell Rd LA1,LA2 215 F6
Little Flatt OL12 52 B1
Little Hey La L37 12 B4
Little Hoole Prim Sch
PR4 75 A5
Little La Banks PR9 55 B7
Longridge PR3 140 A7
Southport PR9 54 B1
Little Meadow La L40 39 D4
Little Moor BB7 166 E6
Little Moor Clough BL7 47 E2
Little Moor View BB7 166 E6
Little Peel St 8 BB2 101 D5
Little Poulton La FY6 153 F4
Little Queen St BB8 171 C4
Little Scotland BL6 31 B2
Little St BB5 104 A6
Little Stones Rd BL7 47 E2
Little Toms La BB10 148 D3
Little Tongues La FY6 200 B4
Little Twining PR4 75 A7
Littledale Ave LA3 213 A8
Littledale Mews LA2 218 F6
Littledale Rd
Crossgill LA2 237 E1
Quernmore LA2 232 C8
Littlemoor Cl BB7 146 A8
Littlemoor Ho BB7 146 A7
Littlemoor Rd BB7 166 E7
Littleton Gr WN6 29 E2
Littleton Manor PR9 55 A5
Littlewood FY7 198 E3
Littondale Gdns BB2 80 D7
Liverpool Ave PR8 21 D5
Liverpool New Rd PR4 74 F5
Liverpool Old Rd
Much Hoole PR4 74 C1
Much Hoole PR4 74 E3
Sollom PR4 57 B2
Southport PR8 21 C1
Walmer Bridge PR4 74 F5
Liverpool Rd
Bickerstaffe L39 7 C5
Blackpool FY1 130 D5
Burnley BB12 127 A6
Formby L37 12 A1
Higher Penwortham PR1 96 B5
Hightown L37 3 A8
Longton PR4 74 F7
Maghull L31 5 D4
Much Hoole PR4 74 D2
Ormskirk L39 15 B2
Preston PR1 96 D6
Preston,Hutton PR1,PR4 95 F3
Royal Oak L39 6 F4
Rufford L40 39 C5
Skelmersdale WN8 8 C8
Sollom PR4 57 A3
Southport PR8 21 F8
Liverpool Rd N
Burscough Bridge L40 25 E5
Maghull L31 5 C2
Liverpool Rd S
Burscough L40 25 D2
Maghull L31 5 C1
Livesey Branch Rd BB2 81 D8
Livesey Fold PR6 80 A1
Livesey Hall Cl BB2 100 E1
Livesey St
11 Lytham St Anne's FY8 91 A3
Padiham BB12 126 C8
Preston PR1 97 B7
Rishton BB1 124 B2
Livesley's La
Great Altcar L37 12 F2
Haskayne L37 13 A2
Livet Ave FY4 110 D7
Livingstone Rd
Accrington BB5 104 B8
Blackburn BB2 101 B4
Blackpool FY1 130 C4
Livingstone St BB9 148 B5
Livingstone Wlk BB9 148 B6
Lloyd Cl Lancaster LA1 218 B1
12 Nelson BB9 148 E8
Lloyd St Darwen BB3 81 F3
Whitworth OL12 71 C1
Lloyd Wlk 11 BB9 148 E8
Lloyd's Ave LA4 217 A4
Lobden Cres OL12 52 D8
Lochinch Cl FY4 111 A6
Lochinver Gr 7 OL10 33 F1
Lock Gate BB4 85 C1
Lock La PR4 57 B2
Lock St 10 BB5 103 E4
Locka La
Gressingham LA6 240 F3
Lancaster LA1 218 D4
Locke Ind Est 1 BL6 32 B3
Lockerbie Ave FY5 152 D8
Lockfield Dr BB18 196 C4
Lockhart Rd PR1 117 F2
Lockhurst Ave FY5 152 F8
Lockside BB2 101 D2
Lockside Rd PR2 95 F8
Lockwood Ave FY6 153 D4
Lockyer Ave BB12 127 B7
Locomotion Ind Est BL6 32 B2
Lodge Bank Brinscall PR6 62 F7
Horwich BL6 31 F3
Lodge Bank Est BL6 31 F3
Lodge Cl
2 Bamber Bridge PR5 97 F1
Blackpool FY5 152 C7
Freckleton PR4 93 B7
Lodge Ct Blackpool FY5 152 C7
Inskip PR4 157 B1
Staining FY3 131 D5
Lodge La Bacup OL13 87 F1
Clifton PR4 115 D1
Elswick PR4 156 B1
Farington PR26 76 E6
Lytham St Anne's FY8 91 F5
Melling LA2 241 D1
Rainford Junction L39,WA11 8 D1
Singleton FY6 154 D2
Lodge Mill La BL0 69 A1
Lodge Rd Catterall PR3 182 A1
Orrell WN5 10 E4
Lodge St Accrington BB5 104 C7
Lancaster LA1 214 F8
Preston PR1 96 E8
Ramsbottom BL0 50 C6
Shuttleworth BL0 50 E8
Lodge The FY8 90 E7
Lodge View
Farington PR26 76 E7
Longridge PR3 140 A6
Lodge Wood Cl PR7 43 A6
Lodges Ct 6 LA4 217 E6
Lodges Gr LA4 217 E6
Lodgeside BB5 124 F3
Lodgings The PR2 118 C5
Lodore Rd FY4 110 C6
Lofthouse Way FY7 199 A4
Loftos Ave FY4 110 D8
Logwood St BB1 101 F7
Lois Pl BB2 101 C5
Lomas La BB4 68 F8
Lomax Cl BB6 124 D6
Lomax Sq BB6 124 D5
Lomax St 7 Bury BL9 33 A3
Darwen BB3 82 A2
Great Harwood BB6 124 C5
Ramsbottom BL8 49 F1
Rochdale OL12 52 F1
Lomeshaye Bsns Village
BB9 148 C8
Lomeshaye Ind Est BB9 148 B7
Lomeshaye Jun Sch
BB9 148 C8
Lomeshaye Pl BB9 148 C8
Lomeshaye Rd BB9 148 D7
Lomeshaye Way BB9 148 C8
Lomond Ave
Blackpool FY3 130 F2
Lytham St Anne's FY8 90 B5
Lomond Cl PR7 60 D4
Lomond Gdns BB2 100 F1
London La PR8 22 D8
London Rd
Blackburn BB1 101 E6
Blackpool FY3 130 D6
Preston PR1 97 C6
London Sq 2 PR8 35 B7
London St Fleetwood FY7 199 B4
Southport PR8,PR9 35 B7
London Terr BB3 82 B2
London Way PR5 97 C3
London Wlk BB1 101 E6
Londonderry Rd LA3 212 E5
Long Acre Cl LA5 221 C8
Long Acre Pl FY8 91 A4
Long Barn Brow PR5 99 E2
Long Barn Row PR5 99 E2
Long Bldg BB7 230 C1
Long Butts PR1 96 D2
Long Cl Clitheroe BB7 190 A2
Leyland PR26 59 A8
Long Copse PR7 60 F1
Long Croft Barton PR3 137 B8
Longton PR4 95 A1
Long Croft Mdw PR7 61 B2
Long Cswy BB7 231 B2
Long Cswy The BB10 108 D7
Long Dales La Caton LA6 237 A6
Over Kellet LA6 237 A7
Long Gn BB18 197 C2
Long Hey La BB1,BB3 83 A2
Long Heys or Back La
WN8 18 F5
Long Ing La BB18 196 C2
Long La Abbeystead LA2 232 F1
Banks PR9 55 B6
Bickerstaffe L39 7 B7
Chorley PR6 44 B4
Laneshaw Bridge BB8 172 D7
Low Bentham LA2 239 B7
Maghull L29 4 B1
Oakenclough PR3 226 B1
Ormskirk L39 6 F8
Pleasington BB2 100 B2
Quernmore LA2 232 A5
Long La *continued*
Skelmersdale WN8 9 E3
Street PR3 226 B5
Tockholes BB3 81 A3
Long Lane End LA2 211 E7
Long Level LA6 241 F8
Long Lover La BB7 192 C8
Long Marsh La LA1 218 B1
Long Mdw Chorley PR7 43 A5
Colne BB8 172 A5
Kirkham PR4 113 E5
Mellor Brook BB2 121 B2
Much Hoole PR4 74 F4
Long Meanygate PR9 37 C7
Long Moss PR26 59 A8
Long Moss La PR4 76 A6
Long Moss Mdws PR4 75 F6
Long Row Blackburn BB2 122 B2
Calder Vale PR3 182 E8
Long Wham La PR4 75 D1
Longacre
Clayton Brook PR5 78 C5
Longton PR4 74 F8
Southport PR9 53 F3
Longacres Dr OL12 71 D2
Longacres La OL12 71 D2
Longber La LA6 242 B3
Longbrook Ave PR5 97 E1
Longcliffe Dr PR8 21 C4
Longcroft Cotts BL9 50 F1
Longfield Formby L37 12 B5
Fulwood PR2 117 F8
Higher Penwortham PR1 96 B4
Longfield Ave Coppull PR7 42 E2
Poulton-le-F FY6 153 D4
Longfield Ct BB18 196 B1
Longfield Dr LA5 221 C8
Longfield Manor PR7 43 A5
Longfield Pl FY6 153 D4
Longfield Terr BB10 107 E8
Longfold Maghull L31 5 E1
Mere Brow PR4 55 F2
Longford Ave FY2 152 E5
Longford Rd PR8 35 A2
Longhey WN8 18 C4
Longholme Rd 9 BB4 86 A2
Longhouse La FY6 131 D8
Longlands Ave LA3 212 E8
Longlands Cres LA3 212 F8
Longlands La LA3 212 E7
Longlands Rd LA1 218 C3
Longley Cl PR2 117 F8
Longley La PR3 160 B2
Longmeadow La
Heysham LA3 213 A7
Thornton FY5 176 C3
Longmeanygate
Leyland PR26 76 D2
Leyland,Midge Hall PR26 76 A2
Longmere Cres LA5 221 C8
Longmire Way LA4 217 A5
Longmoor La PR3 180 E6
Longridge Ave FY4 110 E5
Longridge CE Prim Sch
PR3 140 A7
Longridge Community Hospl
PR3 140 A7
Longridge Cty Prim Sch
PR3 139 F8
Longridge Dr OL10 33 F2
Longridge Fell Forest Wlk
(E)* BB7 164 F6
Longridge Fell Forest Wlk
(W)* PR3 164 A4
Longridge Heath BB9 148 D4
Longridge High Sch
PR3 140 A6
Longridge Lodge 14
PR2 118 F4
Longridge Rd
Hesketh Lane PR3 162 D6
Hurst Green BB7,PR3 142 D8
Longridge PR3 162 B3
Red Scar PR2 119 B6
Longroyd Rd BB18 197 B1
Longsands Com Prim Sch
PR2 118 D5
Longsands La PR2 118 E6
Longshaw Ave WN5 10 E1
Longshaw Cl
Longshaw WN5 10 E1
Rufford L40 39 A5
Longshaw Comm WN5 10 E1
Longshaw Inf Sch BB2 81 E8
Longshaw Jun Sch BB2 101 E1
Longshaw La BB2 101 D2
Longshaw Old Rd WN5 10 E1
Longshaw St BB2 101 D1
Longsight Ave
Accrington,Hillock Vale
BB5 104 E8
Clitheroe BB7 189 F1
Longsight Rd
Langho BB6 143 B2
Langho BB6 143 D2
Osbaldeston BB1,BB2 121 E4
Ramsbottom BL0 50 A2
Longstock Hall CP Sch
Avondale Unit PR5 77 B8
Longstock Hall Moor Hey Sch
PR5 97 A1
Longton Ave FY5 176 B2
Longton Brickcroft Nature
Reserve* PR4 74 F6
Longton Brickcroft Visitor
Ctr* PR4 74 F7
Longton Bsns Pk PR4 74 E4
Longton By-Pass PR4 75 C6

Longton Cl BB1 .....102 C5
Longton Ct PR8 .....21 C5
Longton Dr Formby L37 ...12 A6
Morecambe LA4 .....217 E4
Longton Prim Sch PR4 ...75 A8
Longton Rd
Blackpool FY1 .....130 C5
Burnley BB12 .....127 E8
Longton St
Blackburn BB1 .....102 C5
Chorley PR6 .....43 E8
Longton's Cotts LA6 ....240 B1
Longtons La BD23 .....236 B3
Longway FY4 .....110 F8
Longwood Cl FY8 .....90 E4
Longworth Ave
Blackrod BL6 .....31 C3
Burnley BB10 .....128 D6
Coppull PR7 .....42 F2
Longworth Clough BL7 ...47 D2
Longworth La BL7 .....47 C2
Longworth Rd
Billington BB7 .....144 B4
Egerton BL7 .....47 B3
Horwich BL6 .....32 C4
Longworth Rd N BL7 .....46 D5
Longworth St
5 Bamber Bridge PR5 .....97 E2
Chorley PR7 .....43 B6
Preston PR1 .....118 C1
Lonmore PR5 .....97 D3
Lonsdale Ave
Fleetwood FY7 .....198 E3
Lancaster LA1 .....211 B7
Morecambe LA4 .....217 E4
Ormskirk L39 .....15 F7
Lonsdale Cl PR25 .....60 A6
Lonsdale Cres 3 FY7 ...198 E3
Lonsdale Dr PR26 .....58 B3
Lonsdale Gdns 4 BB9 ...170 D3
Lonsdale Gr LA4 .....217 E4
Lonsdale Mews 5 PR5 ....77 A8
Lonsdale Pl LA1 .....215 A5
Lonsdale Rd
Blackpool FY1 .....130 B2
Formby L37 .....11 F3
Hest Bank LA2 .....220 D1
Morecambe LA4 .....217 E4
Preston PR1 .....118 C1
Southport PR8 .....35 D4
Lonsdale St
Accrington BB5 .....103 F5
Burnley BB12 .....127 C7
Nelson BB9 .....170 F1
Lord Ave OL13 .....87 C1
Lord Nelson Wharf PR2 ...96 B8
Lord Sefton Way L37 .....12 E2
Lord Sq BB1 .....101 E5
Lord St Accrington BB5 ...104 B6
Bacup OL13 .....87 F2
Blackburn BB2 .....101 E5
Blackpool FY1 .....130 B6
Brierfield BB9 .....148 B5
Burscough Bridge L40 .....25 E5
Bury BL9 .....33 A2
Bury,Heap Bridge BL9 .....33 C1
Chorley PR6 .....43 D7
Clayton Green PR6 .....78 C1
Colne BB8 .....171 C5
Darwen BB3 .....82 A2
Eccleston PR7 .....41 C5
Fleetwood FY7 .....199 B4
Great Harwood BB6 .....124 C4
Horwich BL6 .....32 B4
Lancaster LA1 .....218 D1
Lytham St Anne's FY8 .....89 E7
Morecambe LA4 .....217 B6
Oswaldtwistle BB5 .....103 E4
Preston PR1 .....97 A8
Rawtenstall BB4 .....86 A2
Rawtenstall,Crawshawbooth BB4 .....86 A7
Rishton BB1 .....124 B1
Southport PR8,PR9 .....35 B7
Lord St W
12 Blackburn BB2 .....101 E5
Southport PR8 .....35 A6
Lord Street Mall 10 BB1 .101 E5
Lord Street Prim Sch
BL6 .....32 B4
Lord Street Sch BB8 .....171 C5
Lord's Ave PR5 .....77 B7
Lord's Close Rd LA2 ....239 E2
Lord's Cres BB3 .....82 A6
Lord's La Kingsfold PR1 ...96 E1
Longridge PR3 .....162 B2
Lord's Lot Rd
Capernwray LA6 .....240 D1
Over Kellet LA6 .....240 C1
Lord's Wlk PR1 .....97 A8
Lords Croft PR6 .....78 A2
Lordsgate Dr L40 .....25 E3
Lordsgate La L40 .....25 C2
Lordsome Rd LA3 .....216 E2
Lorne Rd FY2 .....152 D2
Lorne St Chorley PR7 .....43 C7
Darwen BB3 .....81 F2
Lytham St Anne's FY8 .....91 D4
Lorne Way OL10 .....33 F1
Lorraine Ave PR2 .....117 E3
Lorton Cl Burnley BB12 ...127 B8
Fulwood PR2 .....117 F6
Lostock Gdns FY4 .....110 E6
Lostock Hall Com High Sch
PR5 .....97 C1
Lostock Hall Com Prim Sch
PR5 .....97 B1
Lostock Hall Sta PR5 .....77 B8
Lostock La PR5 .....77 D7
Lostock Mdw PR6 .....78 A1
Lostock Rd PR26 .....58 C3
Lostock Sq PR5 .....77 B7
Lostock View PR5 .....77 B7
Lothersdale Cl BB10 ....148 D3
Lothian Ave FY7 .....198 D3
Lothian Pl FY2 .....152 E5
Lottice La BB5,BB1 .....103 A1
Lotus Dr FY4 .....112 A6
Loud Bridge Back La
PR3 .....161 D8
Loud Bridge Rd PR3 .....161 D7
Loughlin Dr L33 .....1 A5
Loughrigg Cl BB12 .....127 B7
Loughrigg Terr FY4 .....131 C1
Louie Pollard Cres BB6 .124 D6
Louis St BL0 .....68 D5
Louis William St BB1 .....82 D8
Louise St FY1 .....130 B3
Loupsfell Dr LA4 .....217 C4
Lourdes Ave PR5 .....97 A1
Louvain St BB18 .....196 A3
Lovat Rd PR1 .....117 F2
Love Clough Rd BB4 ....105 F2
Love La BL0 .....68 E1
Loveclough Pk BB4 .....106 A3
Lovely Hall La BB1 .....122 D7
Low Bank BB12 .....126 E6
Low Bentham Com Prim Sch
LA2 .....239 B8
Low Bentham Rd LA2 ...239 C8
Low Croft PR3 .....137 B2
Low Fold BB18 .....195 A6
Low Gn PR25 .....76 F1
Low Hill BB3 .....65 A6
Low La Leck LA6 .....242 B7
Morecambe LA4 .....217 F5
Low Mill LA2 .....237 B3
Low Moor La BB18 .....196 B1
Low Moor Rd FY2 .....152 E3
Low Rd Halton LA2 .....219 E7
Heysham LA3 .....213 A2
Low St LA6 .....242 C3
Lowcroft
High Bentham LA2 .....239 E8
Skelmersdale WN8 .....18 C3
Lowcross Rd FY6 .....153 E2
Lowe View BB4 .....87 A1
Lowe's La WN8 .....17 F8
Lower Alt Rd L38 .....2 F4
Lower Antley St BB5 ...103 F5
Lower Ashworth Cl BB2 .101 C4
Lower Audley Ind Est
BB2 .....101 F3
Lower Audley St BB1,
BB2 .....101 F4
Lower Bank Rd PR2 .....117 F3
Lower Bank St PR6 .....80 A1
Lower Barn St BB3 .....65 C7
Lower Barnes St BB5 ...124 E4
Lower Burgh Rd PR7 .....43 A4
Lower Burgh Way PR7 ....43 B4
Lower Carr La L37 .....4 B7
Lower Chapel La BB7 ...190 B8
Lower Clough St BB9 ...170 D2
Lower Clowes BB4 .....68 E8
Lower Clowes Rd BB4 .....68 E8
Lower Cockcroft 13
BB2 .....101 E5
Lower Copthurst La PR6 ..61 E7
Lower Cribden Ave BB4 ..85 D2
Lower Croft 1 PR1 .....96 D2
Lower Croft St 3 BB18 ..197 B2
Lower Cross St 26 BB3 ...82 A1
Lower Darwen Prim Sch
BB3 .....82 A6
Lower East Ave BB18 ....196 B3
Lower Eccleshill Rd BB3 .82 A5
Lower Field PR26 .....76 F6
Lower Gate Rd BB5 .....125 F2
Lower Gn
Poulton-le-F FY6 .....153 E3
3 Rochdale OL12 .....52 C1
Lower Greenfield PR2 ...117 B5
Lower Hazel Cl BB2 .....101 C4
Lower Iley PR4 .....95 A1
Lower Hill BB3 .....80 F2
Lower Hill Dr PR6 .....44 A1
Lower Hollin Bank St
BB2 .....101 D2
Lower House Gn BB4 .....87 A8
Lower House Rd PR26 .....59 D8
Lower La Freckleton PR4 ...93 D7
Haslingden BB4 .....85 B4
Kirkham PR4 .....114 C1
Longridge PR3 .....140 B7
Lower Laithe Cotts BB9 .170 C2
Lower Laithe Dr BB9 ....170 C3
Lower Lune St 7 FY7 ...199 B5
Lower Makinson Fold 2
BL6 .....32 D1
Lower Manor La BB12 ...147 F2
Lower Mdw BL7 .....48 D6
Lower Mead BL7 .....47 F1
Lower Mead Dr BB12 ...147 F2
Lower North Ave BB18 ..196 B2
Lower Park St BB18 ....196 C2
Lower Parrock Rd BB9 ..170 C1
Lower Philips Rd BB1 ...102 C8
Lower Prom
Southport PR8 .....35 A7
Southport PR8 .....35 B8
Lower Rd Longridge PR3 ..140 E7
Shuttleworth BL0 .....50 E8
Lower Ridge Cl BB10 ....128 B6
Lower Rook St BB18 ....196 C2
Lower Rosegrove La
BB12 .....127 A5
Lower School St 6
BB8 .....171 D4
Lower Tentre BB11 .....128 B5
Lower Timber Hill La
BB11 .....128 A2
Lower Waterside Farm Cotts
BB3 .....82 E3
Lower West Ave BB18 ...196 B2
Lower Wilworth BB1 ....122 E1
Lower Wlk FY2 .....152 C7
Lowerfield BB6 .....123 C8
Lowerfields BB12 .....126 F6
Lowerfold BB6 .....124 C6
Lowerfold Cl OL12 .....52 C4
Lowerfold Cres OL12 .....52 C4
Lowerfold Dr OL12 .....52 C4
Lowerfold Rd BB6 .....124 C6
Lowerfold Way OL12 .....52 C4
Lowergate BB7 .....166 E8
Lowerhouse Cres BB12 .127 A6
Lowerhouse Fold BB12 ..127 A6
Lowerhouse Jun Sch
BB12 .....127 A6
Lowerhouse La
Burnley,Rose Grove BB12 ..127 B6
Padiham BB12 .....126 F6
Lowes Ct
3 Blackpool FY1 .....130 B1
5 Thornton FY5 .....176 B3
Lowes Gn L37 .....12 B3
Lowes Rd BL9 .....33 A6
Lowesby Cl PR5 .....97 E3
Loweswater Cl BB5 .....104 F8
Loweswater Cres BB12 ..127 B8
Loweswater Dr 5 LA4 ...217 D4
Lowesway Blackpool FY4 ..110 F8
6 Thornton FY5 .....176 B3
Lowfield Cl PR4 .....114 F2
Lowfield Rd FY4 .....110 F7
Lowgill La LA2 .....239 C3
Lowick Cl PR5 .....98 E4
Lowick Dr FY6 .....153 D1
Lowland Way FY2 .....152 F6
Lowlands Rd
Bolton-le-S LA5 .....221 A5
Morecambe LA4 .....217 C4
Lowndes St PR1 .....117 E2
Lowood Gr PR2 .....116 D1
Lowood Lodge 7 FY8 ....91 A3
Lowood Pl BB2 .....101 A6
Lowrey Terr FY1 .....130 B2
Lowry Cl PR5 .....77 A7
Lowry Hill La L40 .....26 B2
Lowstead Pl FY4 .....110 E6
Lowstern Cl BL7 .....47 E1
Lowther Ave
Blackpool FY2 .....152 B2
Maghull L31 .....5 F2
Morecambe LA3 .....217 E3
Lowther Cres PR26 .....76 D2
Lowther Ct Blackpool FY2 .152 B2
5 Lytham St Anne's FY8 ...91 A3
Lowther Dr PR26 .....76 D3
Lowther La BB8 .....194 D1
Lowther Pl BB1 .....102 A8
Lowther Rd
Fleetwood FY7 .....198 F4
Lancaster LA1 .....218 F1
Lowther St Colne BB8 ....171 E6
Nelson BB9 .....148 C8
Preston PR2 .....117 C1
Lowther Terr
Appley Bridge WN6 .....19 C8
Lytham St Anne's FY8 .....91 A3
Lowthian St 25 PR1 .....96 F8
Lowthorpe Cres PR1 ....118 B2
Lowthorpe Pl PR1 .....118 B2
Lowthorpe Rd PR1 .....118 B2
Lowthwaite Dr BB9 .....148 E6
Lowton Rd FY8 .....90 A8
Loxham Gdns FY4 .....110 D6
Loxley Gdns BB12 .....126 F6
Loxley Gn PR2 .....118 C6
Loxley Pl FY5 .....152 E7
Loxley Pl E FY5 .....152 F7
Loxley Rd PR8 .....35 D4
Loxwood Cl PR5 .....97 A3
Loynd St
11 Great Harwood BB6 ...124 C5
Ramsbottom BL0 .....50 D6
Loyne Pk LA6 .....241 D7
Loyne Sch The LA1 .....218 B2
Lubbock St BB12 .....127 C6
Lucas Ave PR7 .....42 D8
Lucas La E PR6 .....61 C6
Lucas La W PR6 .....61 C5
Lucas St BL9 .....33 A3
Lucerne Cl PR2 .....118 C4
Lucerne Rd PR2 .....118 C4
Lucy St Barrowford BB9 ..170 D3
Lancaster LA1 .....214 F8
Morecambe LA4 .....217 B6
Ludlow WN8 .....18 C4
Ludlow Dr L39 .....15 D7
Ludlow Gr FY2 .....152 F2
Ludlow St WN6 .....29 D3
Luke St 17 OL13 .....70 C8
Lulworth WN8 .....18 C4
Lulworth Ave
Blackpool FY3 .....131 A3
Preston PR2 .....117 D2
Lulworth Lodge PR8 .....34 F5
Lulworth Pl PR5 .....97 D2
Lulworth Rd
Fulwood PR2 .....118 A4
Southport PR8 .....34 F5
Lumb Carr Ave BL0,BL8 ...50 A4
Lumb Carr Rd BL0,BL8 ...50 A4
Lumb Cotts BL0 .....68 B4
Lumb Holes La BB4 .....69 E7
Lumb La BB4 .....86 F4
Lumb Scar 9 OL13 .....87 F2
Lund St Blackburn BB2 ...101 C4
2 Preston PR1 .....97 A8
Lunds Cl L40 .....16 E4
Lunds La PR4 .....74 D1
Lune Ave L31 .....5 E2
Lune Cl PR4 .....114 C5
Lune Dr Clayton-le-W PR25 .77 E2
Morecambe LA3 .....217 F3
Lune Gr FY1 .....130 C3
Lune Ho
5 Lancaster LA1 .....218 D1
Lancaster,Abraham Heights
LA1 .....214 F7
Lune Ind Est LA1 .....214 C8
Lune Rd Fleetwood FY7 ...198 F4
Lancaster LA1 .....218 B1
Lune Sq LA1 .....218 D1
Lune St Colne BB8 .....171 E4
Lancaster LA1 .....218 D1
Longridge PR3 .....140 B8
Padiham BB12 .....126 D8
Preston PR1 .....96 F7
Lune Terr LA1 .....218 D1
Lune Valley LA1 .....218 F4
Lune View FY6 .....199 E6
Lune View Cvn Pk LA2 ..219 C6
Lunedale Ave FY1 .....130 C1
Lunesdale Cl FY8 .....90 C7
Lunesdale Ct
Butt Yeats LA2 .....238 B6
Lancaster LA1 .....218 F1
Lunesdale Dr PR3 .....207 B3
Lunesdale Rd 2 PR4 ....114 A5
Lunesdale Terr LA2 .....237 E4
Lunesdale View LA2 ....219 D7
Luneside LA1 .....214 C8
Lunt La L29 .....4 D1
Lunt Rd L29 .....4 C1
Lupin Cl Accrington BB5 ..104 A7
Lucas Green PR6 .....61 B5
Lupin Rd BB5 .....104 B7
Lupton Dr BB9 .....170 D4
Lupton Pl LA1 .....218 B3
Lupton St PR7 .....43 C6
Lutner St BB11 .....128 A5
Luton Rd Cleveleys FY5 ...175 E1
Preston PR2 .....116 F2
Lutwidge Ave PR1 .....118 C1
Lyceum Ave 3 FY3 .....130 D4
Lychfield Dr PR5 .....77 E7
Lychgate 21 PR1 .....97 A8
Lydd Gr PR7 .....43 A7
Lyddesdale Ave FY5 ....152 D8
Lydgate Brierfield BB10 ..148 E2
Chorley PR7 .....43 A5
Lydia St BB5 .....104 B4
Lydiate La
Bilsborrow PR3 .....159 C6
Leyland PR25 .....77 C4
Newtown PR7 .....59 B1
Lydiate Lane End PR7 ....59 B2
Lydiate Prim Sch L31 .....5 C4
Lydiate Station Rd L31 ....4 E5
Lydric Ave PR5 .....98 E2
Lyelake La L40 .....16 F2
Lymbridge Dr BL6 .....31 D1
Lyme Gr FY6 .....199 E5
Lymm Ave LA1 .....218 A3
Lyncroft Cres FY3 .....130 E7
Lyndale WN8 .....18 B4
Lyndale Ave
Bamber Bridge PR5 .....97 C2
Haslingden BB4 .....85 B2
Wilpshire BB1 .....123 A7
Lyndale Cl Leyland PR25 ...60 B6
Rawtenstall BB4 .....86 A7
Wilpshire BB1 .....123 A7
Lyndale Ct FY7 .....199 B5
Lyndale Cvn Site FY4 ....111 F6
Lyndale Gr PR5 .....97 C2
Lyndale Rd BB11 .....126 C3
Lyndale Terr BB7 .....231 B3
Lynden Ave LA4 .....217 E5
Lyndeth Cl PR2 .....118 E6
Lyndhurst Maghull L31 .....5 D1
Skelmersdale WN8 .....18 B4
Lyndhurst Ave
Blackburn BB1 .....102 E5
Blackpool FY4 .....130 D1
Lyndhurst Dr PR2 .....116 E2
Lyndhurst Gr BB6 .....124 E6
Lyndhurst Rd
Blackburn BB2 .....101 E2
Burnley BB10 .....128 C5
Darwen BB3 .....81 F3
Southport PR8 .....35 B2
Lyndon Ave BB6 .....124 E6
Lyndon Ct BB6 .....124 E6
Lyndon Ho BB6 .....124 F6
Lynfield Rd BB6 .....124 E6
Lynn Gr 6 FY1 .....130 B7
Lynn Pl PR2 .....118 D2
Lynslack Terr LA5 .....224 B8
Lynthorpe Rd
Blackburn BB2 .....101 E2
Nelson BB9 .....171 A1
Lynton Ave
Blackpool FY4 .....110 D8
Leyland PR25 .....60 C8
Lynton Ct FY7 .....175 C8
Lynton Dr PR8 .....34 E1
Lynton Rd Accrington BB5 .103 F4
Lynton Rd continued
Southport PR8 .....34 E1
Lynwood Ave
Blackpool FY3 .....130 E8
Clayton-le-M BB5 .....124 F4
Darwen BB3 .....81 E4
Grimsargh PR2 .....139 C2
Ormskirk L39 .....15 C3
Lynwood Cl
Clayton-le-M BB5 .....124 F4
Colne BB8 .....171 D7
Darwen BB3 .....81 E3
Skelmersdale WN8 .....9 D7
Whalley BB7 .....144 A7
Lynwood Dr FY6 .....177 C7
Lynwood End L39 .....15 C3
Lynwood Rd
Blackburn BB2 .....101 B6
Huncoat BB5 .....125 E2
Lyons La PR6 .....43 D7
Lyons La S PR7 .....43 D7
Lyons Rd PR8 .....35 A5
Lystra Ct FY8 .....89 F5
Lyth Rd LA1 .....218 F2
Lythall Ave FY8 .....91 D4
Lytham CE Prim Sch FY8 .91 B4
Lytham Cl Fulwood PR2 ..117 D3
Lancaster LA1 .....215 C7
Lytham Ct PR7 .....60 D4
Lytham Hall* FY8 .....90 F4
Lytham Hall Park Prim Sch
FY8 .....90 F3
Lytham Heritage Ctr*
FY8 .....91 B3
Lytham Lifeboat Mus*
FY8 .....91 C2
Lytham Rd Blackburn BB2 .101 F1
Blackpool FY1,FY4 .....110 C6
Brierfield BB10 .....148 C2
Freckleton PR4 .....93 B6
Fulwood PR2 .....117 D3
Saltcotes,Moss Side FY8 ...112 E1
Southport PR9 .....54 A4
Warton FY8,PR4 .....92 D5
Lytham St Chorley PR6 ....43 E7
Rochdale OL12 .....52 E3
Lytham St Anne's High Tech
Coll FY8 .....90 C5
Lytham St Anne's Local
Nature Reserve* FY8 ..110 B1
Lytham St Annes Way
FY8 .....90 D7
Lytham Sta FY8 .....91 A3
Lytham Windmill (Mus)*
FY8 .....91 C2
Lythcoe Ave PR2 .....117 C4
Lythe Fell Ave LA2 .....219 D7
Lythe Fell Rd LA2 .....234 F8
Lythe La LA2 .....239 E2
Lytles Cl L37 .....12 A2
Lytton St BB12 .....126 F7

M

Maaruig Cvn Pk FY6 ....200 A6
Mabel Ct FY4 .....110 B8
Mabel St Colne BB8 .....171 F5
2 Rochdale OL12 .....52 D2
Maberry Cl WN6 .....19 D7
Macaulay St BB11 .....127 C5
Macauley Ave FY4 .....110 F8
Macbeth Rd FY7 .....198 E4
Mackay Croft 4 PR6 .....43 D8
Mackenzie Cl 5 PR6 .....43 D8
Maclaren Cl FY3 .....131 D5
Macleod St BB9 .....148 D8
Maddy St 2 PR1 .....96 D8
Madeley Gdns OL12 .....52 C1
Maden Rd OL13 .....87 F2
Maden St BB5 .....103 E6
Maden Way OL13 .....87 F2
Madison Ave
Blackpool FY2 .....152 B5
Hest Bank LA5 .....220 E2
Madryn Ave L33 .....1 A2
Maesbrook Cl PR9 .....55 B5
Mafeking Ave BL9 .....33 A5
Mafeking Rd PR2 .....117 C2
Magdalen Ave FY5 .....175 D1
Maggots Nook Rd WA11 ...9 A1
Maghull Homes The L31 ...5 B1
Maghull La L31 .....6 B1
Maghull Smallholdings Est
L31 .....5 F3
Magnolia Cl PR2 .....118 C6
Magnolia Dr PR25 .....77 E2
Magnolia Rd PR1 .....96 B3
Magpie Cl BB11 .....127 C5
Maharishi School of the Age
of Enlightenment L40 ...18 A5
Maida Vale FY5 .....152 D8
Maiden Cl Rawtenstall BB4 .69 F8
Skelmersdale WN8 .....17 C2
Maiden St BB4 .....85 B6
Main Ave LA3 .....212 F3
Main Cl LA3 .....209 D8
Main Dr FY6 .....153 E2
Main Rd Bolton-le-S LA5 ..221 B5
Galgate LA2 .....211 A3
Hest Bank LA2 .....220 F1
Nether Kellet LA6 .....221 F5
Main Sprit Weind PR1 ....97 A7
Main St Bolton-by-B BB7 ..230 D4
Burton-in-K LA6 .....240 B7

Main St *continued*
Cockerham LA2 .... 206 D4
Downham BB7 .... 191 B5
Gisburn BB7 .... 231 C3
Grindleton BB7 .... 190 B8
Heysham LA3 .... 212 E8
High Bentham LA2 .... 239 D8
Hornby LA2 .... 238 B7
Kelbrook BB18 .... 195 A6
Lancaster LA1 .... 218 D2
Low Bentham LA2 .... 239 B8
Overton LA3 .... 209 D8
Rathmell BD24 .... 236 F6
Warton LA5 .... 223 D5
Whittington LA6 .... 241 D7
Wray LA2 .... 238 D6
Mains La
Bispham Green L40 .... 27 A6
Poulton-le-F FY6 .... 154 B4
Mainway LA1 .... 218 D2
Mairscough La L39 .... 14 B1
Maitland Ave FY5 .... 175 D1
Maitland Cl 5 PR1 .... 97 C8
Maitland Pl BB4 .... 86 A1
Maitland St
18 Bacup OL13 .... 87 F2
4 Preston PR1 .... 97 C8
1 Preston PR1 .... 97 D8
Majestic Bldgs 24 BB18 .... 196 B2
Majestic Mews WN5 .... 10 D5
Major St Accrington BB5 .... 104 B4
Ramsbottom BL0 .... 50 B6
Rawtenstall BB4 .... 86 A7
Makinson Ave BL6 .... 32 E1
Makinson La BL6 .... 32 F4
Makinsons Row 11 LA2 .... 211 A4
Malcolm Pl FY7 .... 198 E4
Malcolm St PR1 .... 118 D1
Malden St PR25 .... 77 A1
Maldern Ave FY6 .... 153 C5
Maldon Pl PR2 .... 118 D2
Malham Ave
5 Accrington BB5 .... 103 F4
Blackpool FY4 .... 110 D8
Malham Cl Lancaster LA1 .... 218 B3
Southport PR8 .... 35 E3
Malham Gdns BB1 .... 101 F3
Malham Pl PR2 .... 118 E4
Malham Rd BB10 .... 148 D3
Malham View Cl BB18 .... 196 A1
Malham Wend BB9 .... 170 C3
Malkin Cl BB9 .... 170 E8
Malkin La BB7 .... 165 F6
Mall The Burnley BB11 .... 128 A6
Fulwood PR2 .... 118 E2
Lytham St Anne's FY8 .... 90 C7
Mallard Cl Heysham LA3 .... 212 F5
Leyland PR25 .... 59 D8
Ormskirk L39 .... 15 C2
Thornton FY5 .... 176 A4
Mallard Ct Blackpool FY3 .... 131 B6
Lancaster LA1 .... 214 E8
Mallard Dr BL6 .... 32 A3
Mallard Ho L31 .... 5 B4
Mallard Pl BB5 .... 103 D3
Mallards The PR9 .... 54 C3
Mallards Wlk PR5 .... 78 A5
Mallee Ave PR9 .... 54 A3
Mallee Cres PR9 .... 54 A3
Malley La PR4 .... 136 C8
Mallom Ave PR7 .... 60 E1
Mallory Ave L31 .... 5 B4
Mallow Wlk LA3 .... 217 B2
Mallowdale FY5 .... 176 A4
Mallowdale Ave LA3 .... 213 A8
Mallowdale Rd LA1 .... 218 B2
Malt Kiln Brow PR3 .... 185 E4
Malt Kiln Gr PR3 .... 156 A5
Malt St BB5 .... 104 B7
Maltby Pl 2 FY4 .... 130 F2
Malthouse Bsns Ctr L39 .... 15 E6
Malthouse Ct
Ormskirk L39 .... 15 E6
3 Preston PR2 .... 117 D1
Malthouse The 4 PR2 .... 117 D1
Malthouse Way PR1 .... 96 D3
Maltings The Longton PR4 .... 74 F8
Middleworth Green PR1 .... 96 D4
Thornton FY5 .... 176 A4
Whittington LA6 .... 241 D7
Maltkiln La
Bispham Green L40,WN8 .... 27 C7
Ormskirk L39 .... 6 E8
Malton Dr PR5 .... 77 A7
Malvern Ave
Blackburn BB2 .... 101 D1
Blackpool FY1 .... 130 D2
Lancaster LA1 .... 215 A6
Oswaldtwistle BB5 .... 103 E3
Padiham BB12 .... 126 D6
Preston PR1 .... 97 B6
Stalmine FY6 .... 177 C7
Malvern Cl
6 Accrington BB5 .... 104 A7
Bamber Bridge PR5 .... 77 C8
Horwich BL6 .... 32 C5
Malvern Ct
6 Nelson BB9 .... 148 F8
Southport PR8 .... 35 A6
Malvern Gdns PR8 .... 35 A6
Malvern Rd
Lytham St Anne's FY8 .... 90 D5
Nelson BB9 .... 171 A1
Preston PR1 .... 97 B6
Malvern St Preston PR1 .... 97 B5
Malvern St *continued*
Standish WN6 .... 29 D3
Malvern Way BB4 .... 68 A7
Manby Cl PR5 .... 98 E3
Manchester Mill Ind Est
PR1 .... 97 C8
Manchester Rd
Accrington BB5 .... 104 D3
Barnoldswick BB18 .... 196 B1
Blackpool FY3 .... 130 D6
Blackrod BL6 .... 31 E1
Burnley BB11 .... 127 E3
Clow Bridge BB11 .... 106 D6
Hapton BB11,BB12 .... 126 C4
Haslingden BB4 .... 85 B2
Haslingden,Ewood Bridge
BB4 .... 68 D7
Nelson BB9 .... 148 D7
Preston PR1 .... 97 B7
Ramsbottom BL0,BL9 .... 50 E4
Southport PR9 .... 35 C7
Mancknols St BB9 .... 149 A7
Mancknols Walton Cottage Homes BB9 .... 149 B8
Mandela Ct BB1 .... 101 E6
Mandeville Rd PR8 .... 21 B5
Mandeville Terr BL8 .... 49 B2
Manfield WN8 .... 18 A3
Mangholes BB4 .... 85 B7
Manion Ave L31 .... 5 B5
Manion Cl L31 .... 5 B5
Manitoba Cl BB2 .... 101 B8
Manley Cl BL9 .... 50 C2
Manner Sutton St BB1 .... 101 F5
Manning Rd
4 Preston PR1 .... 118 E1
Southport PR8 .... 35 E6
Manor Ave Burscough L40 .... 25 D2
Fulwood PR2 .... 118 B4
Higher Penwortham PR1 .... 96 B4
Ribchester PR3 .... 141 D3
Slyne LA2 .... 218 C8
Manor Brook 1 BB5 .... 104 C6
Manor Cl Burton in L LA6 .... 242 C3
Coupe Green PR5 .... 98 F3
Slyne LA2 .... 218 C8
Manor Cres
Burscough L40 .... 25 D2
Slyne LA2 .... 218 D8
Manor Ct
11 Blackpool FY1 .... 130 C7
3 Blackpool,Hawes Side
FY4 .... 130 E1
Caton LA2 .... 237 D4
Fulwood PR2 .... 117 B7
4 Southport PR9 .... 54 A2
Manor Ctyd LA3 .... 212 E8
Manor Dr Burscough L40 .... 25 D2
Cleveleys FY5 .... 175 D3
Kirkham PR4 .... 114 C4
Slyne LA2 .... 218 C8
Manor Farm LA6 .... 241 D7
Manor Fields BB7 .... 144 C5
Manor Gdns L40 .... 25 D2
Manor Gr
Higher Penwortham PR1 .... 96 A4
Morecambe LA3 .... 216 F2
Skelmersdale WN8 .... 17 F1
Manor House Cl
Leyland PR26 .... 59 B8
Maghull L31 .... 5 C1
Manor House Cotts BB3 .... 65 E8
Manor House Cres PR1 .... 118 B3
Manor House Dr WN8 .... 9 E3
Manor House La PR1 .... 118 C3
Manor House Park Flats
FY5 .... 175 C3
Manor La Hest Bank LA2 .... 220 F1
Higher Penwortham PR1 .... 96 B4
Manor Lodge L37 .... 11 E4
Manor Mews FY6 .... 153 E4
Manor Pk PR2 .... 118 C4
Manor Pl BB5 .... 103 F7
Manor Rd Blackburn BB2 .... 101 B5
Blackpool FY1 .... 130 D4
Burnley BB12 .... 127 B7
Burscough L40 .... 25 D2
Clayton Green PR6 .... 78 B3
Clitheroe BB7 .... 166 D7
Colne BB8 .... 171 E7
Darwen BB3 .... 64 F8
Fleetwood FY7 .... 198 E4
Garstang PR3 .... 204 C1
Horwich BL6 .... 32 D4
Inskip PR4 .... 135 C8
Shevington WN6 .... 19 F6
Slyne LA2 .... 218 D8
Southport PR9 .... 54 A2
Whalley BB7 .... 144 C5
Wrea Green PR4 .... 113 B4
Manor St Accrington BB5 .... 104 D7
Bacup OL13 .... 87 F1
Bury BL9 .... 33 A2
Nelson BB9 .... 148 F8
Ramsbottom BL0 .... 50 B7
Manor Way Coppull PR7 .... 29 D8
Wrea Green PR4 .... 113 B3
Manor Wood
Fleetwood FY7 .... 198 E4
Kirkham PR4 .... 114 B7
Manorcroft PR4 .... 74 F8
Manse Ave WN6 .... 28 F5
Mansell Way BL6 .... 32 D1
Mansergh St BB10 .... 148 C2
Mansfield Ave BL0 .... 50 B2
Mansfield Cres BB9 .... 148 C6
Mansfield Dr PR5 .... 98 E3
Mansfield Gr BB9 .... 148 C6
Mansfield High Sch
BB9 .... 148 B6
Mansfield Rd FY3 .... 130 D8
Mansion House Bldgs 2
BB4 .... 86 A7
Mansion St S BB5 .... 104 D6
Manston Gr PR7 .... 43 A7
Manx Jane's La PR9 .... 54 A4
Manxman Rd BB2 .... 101 F1
Many Brooks Ho PR5 .... 98 E1
Maple Ave Blackpool FY3 .... 130 D5
Brinscall PR6 .... 62 F7
Burscough L40 .... 25 E4
7 Bury BL9 .... 33 B2
6 Clitheroe BB7 .... 166 D7
Fleetwood FY7 .... 175 F8
Haslingden BB4 .... 85 C3
Horwich BL6 .... 32 E1
Morecambe LA3 .... 216 E2
Thornton FY5 .... 153 C8
Maple Bank BB10 .... 128 C7
Maple Cl Formby L37 .... 11 C1
Newton-w-S PR4 .... 114 F2
Whalley BB7 .... 144 D6
Wilpshire BB1 .... 122 E6
Maple Cres
8 Preston PR1 .... 96 E7
Rishton BB1 .... 103 B8
Maple Ct
Clayton-le-W PR25 .... 77 D3
Garstang PR3 .... 204 C1
Maple Dr
Bamber Bridge PR5 .... 97 F1
Oswaldtwistle BB5 .... 103 F3
Poulton-le-F FY6 .... 153 E2
Maple Gr Chorley PR6 .... 61 D3
Fulwood PR2 .... 119 A4
Grimsargh PR2 .... 139 D1
Higher Penwortham PR1 .... 96 B4
Lancaster LA1 .... 214 D8
Ramsbottom BL0 .... 50 D6
Warton PR4 .... 92 D6
Maple Rd PR3 .... 204 C1
Maple St Blackburn BB1 .... 102 A7
Clayton-le-M BB5 .... 124 F1
Great Harwood BB6 .... 124 D6
3 Rishton BB1 .... 124 B1
Southport PR8 .... 35 E6
Maplebank 3 PR2 .... 116 C1
Maples The PR26 .... 58 F6
Maplewood
Skelmersdale WN8 .... 18 A4
Southport PR9 .... 53 F2
Maplewood Ave FY6 .... 200 A5
Maplewood Cl
Chorley PR7 .... 43 E6
Leyland PR25 .... 59 E8
Lytham St Anne's FY8 .... 90 F4
Maplewood Dr FY5 .... 152 C8
Maplewood Gdns LA1 .... 215 A2
Marabou Dr BB3 .... 81 E3
Marathon Pl PR26 .... 76 C3
Marble Ave 5 FY5 .... 152 F7
Marble Ct BB5 .... 103 E4
Marble Pl PR8 .... 35 B7
Marble Pl Sh Ctr PR8 .... 35 B7
Marble St BB5 .... 103 E4
March St BB12 .... 127 F8
Marchbank Rd WN8 .... 17 D1
Marchwood Rd FY3 .... 131 B8
Marcroft Ave FY4 .... 110 E7
Mardale Ave
Blackpool FY4 .... 131 C1
Morecambe LA4 .... 217 D5
Mardale Cl PR8 .... 21 B4
Mardale Cres PR25 .... 60 B7
Mardale Rd
1 Lancaster LA1 .... 218 E1
Longridge PR3 .... 139 F5
Preston PR1 .... 119 A1
Maresfield Rd PR1 .... 96 E5
Margaret Rd PR1 .... 96 E4
Margaret St
Blackburn BB1 .... 102 D4
Oswaldtwistle BB5 .... 103 C2
1 Preston PR1 .... 97 A8
Rawtenstall BB4 .... 85 F4
Margate Ave FY4 .... 110 E6
Margate Rd Fulwood PR2 .... 117 A4
Lytham St Anne's FY8 .... 89 F8
Maria Ct 9 BB11 .... 128 B4
Maria Sq BL7 .... 46 D4
Maria St BB3 .... 65 B6
Marians Dr L39 .... 15 E7
Maricourt Ave BB1 .... 102 D5
Marilyn Ave 4 PR5 .... 77 B8
Marina Ave
2 Blackpool FY1 .... 130 D2
Poulton-le-F FY3 .... 131 D8
Marina Cl PR5 .... 97 A1
Marina Dr
Bamber Bridge PR5 .... 97 A1
Fulwood PR2 .... 117 E7
Marina Gr PR5 .... 97 A1
Marina Mews FY7 .... 199 B3
Marina Rd L37 .... 11 F1
Marine Ave BB11 .... 127 C4
Marine Ct LA3 .... 216 E4
Marine Dr Hest Bank LA2 .... 220 D1
Lytham St Anne's FY8 .... 90 D3
Southport PR8 .... 34 E7
Southport,Marshside PR8,
PR9 .... 53 D4
Marine Gate Mans PR9 .... 35 B8
Marine Ind Ctr FY8 .... 91 D4
Marine Par
Fleetwood FY7 .... 198 C1
Southport PR8 .... 35 A8
Marine Rd E LA4 .... 217 C6
Marine Rd W LA3,LA4 .... 216 F4
Marine Road Central
LA4 .... 217 A5
Mariners Cl FY7 .... 198 E1
Mariners Way PR2 .... 96 B8
Marino Cl FY5 .... 153 D8
Maritime Ct PR8 .... 35 B7
Maritime St FY7 .... 198 F2
Maritime Way PR2 .... 95 F7
Mark Cl PR1 .... 96 F1
Mark Rd L38 .... 2 F4
Mark Sq PR4 .... 57 A6
Mark St Bacup OL13 .... 70 C8
Burnley BB10 .... 148 B1
Mark's Ave PR26 .... 76 E5
Markazul Uloom Sch
BB2 .... 101 F2
Market Ave 2 BB1 .... 101 E5
Market Chambers BL0 .... 50 C7
Market Cross 5 L39 .... 15 E5
Market Ho PR7 .... 31 A6
Market Pl Adlington PR7 .... 31 A7
12 Chorley PR7 .... 43 C8
3 Clitheroe BB7 .... 166 E8
10 Colne BB8 .... 171 E5
Edenfield BL0 .... 68 D3
Garstang PR3 .... 181 C7
Longridge PR3 .... 140 B7
4 Poulton-le-F FY6 .... 153 D3
Ramsbottom BL0 .... 50 C7
Standish WN6 .... 29 E1
Market Sq Burnley BB11 .... 128 A6
4 Kirkham PR4 .... 114 B5
10 Lancaster LA1 .... 214 F8
Lytham St Anne's FY8 .... 91 A3
Nelson BB9 .... 148 D8
Market St Adlington PR7 .... 31 A6
Bacup OL13 .... 87 F2
7 Barnoldswick BB18 .... 196 B2
Blackpool FY1 .... 130 B5
Carnforth LA5 .... 223 D2
Chorley PR7 .... 43 C7
Church BB5 .... 103 E5
Colne BB8 .... 171 E5
Darwen BB3 .... 82 A1
Edenfield BL0 .... 68 D4
Hambleton FY6 .... 177 C2
Kirkham PR4 .... 113 F6
Lancaster LA1 .... 214 F8
Millgate OL12,OL13 .... 71 D4
Morecambe LA4 .... 217 A5
9 Nelson BB9 .... 148 D8
Preston PR1 .... 96 F8
5 Rawtenstall BB4 .... 69 F8
Southport PR8 .... 35 B7
Standish WN6 .... 29 E1
Whitworth OL12 .... 52 C6
Market St W PR1 .... 96 F8
Market Street La 7
BB2 .... 101 E4
Market Way
8 Blackburn BB1 .... 101 E5
6 Ormskirk L39 .... 15 E5
Market Wlk PR7 .... 43 C8
Marketgate 28 LA1 .... 214 F8
Markham Dr PR8 .... 35 E2
Markham Rd BB2 .... 101 B3
Markham St PR2 .... 117 C1
Markland St
3 Preston PR1 .... 96 E7
6 Ramsbottom BL0 .... 50 C6
Marklands Rd BL6 .... 32 E5
Markross St BB4 .... 86 A2
Marl Ave PR1 .... 96 B4
Marl Cop PR26 .... 58 A6
Marl Croft PR1 .... 96 D2
Marl Gr WN5 .... 10 D4
Marl Hill Cres PR2 .... 119 A2
Marl Pits BB4 .... 86 B3
Marl Rd L33 .... 1 C3
Marland WN8 .... 18 A4
Marlboro Rd FY3 .... 130 E4
Marlborough WN8 .... 18 A4
Marlborough Ave
Cleveleys FY5 .... 175 D5
Maghull L31 .... 5 D3
Warton PR4 .... 92 D6
Marlborough Cl
Ramsbottom BL0 .... 50 C3
Whitworth OL12 .... 52 C7
Marlborough Ct WN8 .... 18 A4
Marlborough Dr
Bamber Bridge PR5 .... 97 D3
Fulwood PR2 .... 117 D7
Marlborough Gdns 5
PR9 .... 35 C8
Marlborough Rd
Accrington BB5 .... 104 C7
Lytham St Anne's FY8 .... 110 E1
Morecambe LA3 .... 216 E3
Southport PR9 .... 35 C7
Marlborough St
Burnley BB11 .... 128 A4
Chorley PR6 .... 61 E1
14 Rochdale OL12 .... 52 C1
Marled Hey BL7 .... 48 D5
Marles Ct BB10 .... 128 B8
Marlfield PR4 .... 74 F4
Marlfield Cl PR2 .... 116 F5
Marlhill Rd FY3 .... 131 B8
Marlin St 7 BB9 .... 170 F2
Marlow Ct PR7 .... 30 F6
Marlowe Ave
Accrington BB5 .... 104 E2
Padiham BB12 .... 126 F7
Marlowe Cres BB6 .... 124 B4
Marlton Rd BB2 .... 101 D1
Marlton Way LA1 .... 214 E6
Marmaduke Cotts LA6 .... 241 D4
Marple Cl WN6 .... 29 B2
Marquis Cl BB3 .... 81 F7
Marquis Dr PR4 .... 93 C7
Marquis St PR4 .... 113 F5
Marron Cl PR25 .... 59 E8
Mars St BL7 .... 48 E6
Marsden Cl PR7 .... 41 B7
Marsden Com Prim Sch
BB9 .... 148 D7
Marsden Cres BB9 .... 149 A8
Marsden Ct BB10 .... 148 C3
Marsden Dr BB9 .... 148 D6
Marsden Gr BB9 .... 148 C5
Marsden Hall Rd BB9 .... 149 A8
Marsden Hall Rd N BB9 .... 171 B1
Marsden Hall Road S
BB9 .... 149 A8
Marsden Height Cl BB9 .... 148 F5
Marsden Mall 5 BB9 .... 148 E8
Marsden Pl BB9 .... 149 A8
Marsden Rd
Blackpool FY4 .... 110 D8
Brierfield BB10 .... 148 C3
Southport PR9 .... 35 E7
Marsden Sq BB4 .... 85 B4
Marsden St
Accrington BB5 .... 104 B4
Blackburn BB2 .... 101 B2
6 Haslingden BB4 .... 85 A3
Kirkham PR4 .... 114 B5
Marset Cl OL12 .... 52 A1
Marsett Pl PR2 .... 118 E5
Marsh Brows L37 .... 11 E2
Marsh Cl LA2 .... 206 B4
Marsh Cres LA4 .... 217 F4
Marsh Ct 2 FY5 .... 176 A2
Marsh Dr PR4 .... 93 D7
Marsh Gate BB3 .... 82 D1
Marsh Gates PR4 .... 93 D7
Marsh Hos LA2 .... 206 B4
Marsh House La BB3 .... 82 C1
Marsh La Brindle PR6 .... 79 B5
Cockerham LA2 .... 206 B4
Glasson LA2 .... 209 D3
Hambleton FY6 .... 177 C1
Ince Blundell L37,L38 .... 3 E6
Longton PR4 .... 74 D8
Ormskirk L40 .... 24 D1
Preston PR1 .... 96 F7
5 Preston PR1 .... 96 F8
Withnell Fold PR6 .... 79 A4
Marsh Mill Thornton FY5 .... 176 B2
* Thornton FY5 .... 176 B2
Marsh Moss La L40 .... 25 C7
Marsh Rd Banks PR9 .... 72 D1
Hesketh Bank PR4 .... 73 F4
Thornton FY5 .... 176 A2
Marsh St Blackburn BB1 .... 101 E6
Horwich BL6 .... 32 A4
4 Lancaster LA1 .... 218 B1
Marsh Terr BB3 .... 82 A2
Marsh View PR4 .... 114 F2
Marsh Way Clitheroe BB7 .... 189 F2
Kingsfold PR1 .... 96 C2
Marshall Ave BB5 .... 125 F2
Marshall Gr PR2 .... 117 A4
Marshall's Brow PR1 .... 96 E3
Marshall's Cl Maghull L31 .... 5 C4
5 Middleworth Green PR1 .... 96 E4
Marshallsay L37 .... 12 A2
Marsham Cl PR3 .... 181 D6
Marsham Gr BB3 .... 82 C1
Marshaw Pl PR3 .... 181 A6
Marshaw Rd LA1 .... 218 B2
Marshdale Rd FY4 .... 110 F7
Marshes La The PR4 .... 38 A8
Marshside Nature Reserve*
PR9 .... 53 E5
Marshside Prim Sch PR9 .... 54 A5
Marshside Rd PR9 .... 53 F4
Marston Cl PR2 .... 117 C7
Marston Cres L38 .... 3 A2
Marston Moor PR2 .... 117 C7
Mart La L40 .... 25 E5
Martholme Ave BB5 .... 125 A3
Martholme Cl BB6 .... 124 D6
Martholme La BB6 .... 124 F8
Martin Ave FY8 .... 110 C4
Martin Croft Rd BB4 .... 85 A5
Martin Dr BB3 .... 65 C6
Martin Field Rd PR1 .... 96 E2
Martin La
Drummersdale L40 .... 24 E6
Rochdale OL12 .... 52 B1
Martin Mere* L40 .... 38 B1
Martin St Burnley BB10 .... 148 B1
Bury BL9 .... 33 D3
Turton Bottoms BL7 .... 48 D4
Martin Top La BB7 .... 192 C7
Martindale Cl BB1 .... 102 C2
Martindales The PR6 .... 78 B3
Martinfield PR2 .... 117 F8
Martinfields BB10 .... 148 C4
Martinique Dr BB3 .... 81 F6
Martins Ave PR7 .... 43 E2
Martins La WN8 .... 9 D7
Martland Ave WN6 .... 19 F5
Marton Dr Blackpool FY4 .... 110 D8
Burnley BB11 .... 127 E3
Morecambe LA4 .... 217 F6
Marton Fold FY4 .... 111 A4
Marton Mere Cvn Pk
FY3,FY4 .... 131 C2
Marton Pl LA4 .... 217 F6
Marton Prim Sch FY4 .... 110 F7
Marton Rd PR2 .... 95 F8

Marton St 4 LA1 214 F7
Marton View FY3 130 E4
Marton Wlk 4 BB3 65 B6
Marwick Cl WN6 29 D2
Mary Ave PR8 21 E6
Mary Brown Cotts BB7 190 C8
Mary St Blackburn BB1 102 A4
5 Burnley BB10 128 B5
Carnforth LA5 223 D3
Colne BB8 171 C4
Lancaster LA1 214 F8
Ramsbottom BL0 50 B5
Rishton BB1 124 B1
Mary St E BL6 32 B4
Mary St W Horwich BL6 32 A4
Longridge PR3 140 A8
Mary Towneley Fold
BB10 128 C4
Marybank Cl PR2 118 C5
Maryland Cl LA5 224 D2
Masefield Ave
Padiham BB12 126 E7
Thornton FY5 176 A3
Masefield Cl
Brockhall Village BB6 143 B5
Great Harwood BB6 124 B4
Masefield Pl PR5 97 D2
Mason Cl PR4 93 C6
Mason Hill View PR2 118 A4
Mason House Cres PR2 117 A5
Mason Row BL7 47 E2
Mason St
7 Accrington BB5 104 C6
Bury BL9 33 A2
Chorley PR6 61 E2
Colne BB8 171 D5
Egerton BL7 47 E1
Horwich BL6 32 B3
Oswaldtwistle BB5 103 D3
Masonfield PR5 78 B5
Masonfield Cres LA1 215 D7
Masongill Fell La LA6 242 E7
Masons Ct 1 FY7 198 E3
Masons Way 8 BB18 196 B3
Masonwood PR2 118 A6
Massam's La L37 11 F6
Massey Croft OL12 52 C8
Massey La BB9 148 A5
Massey St Brierfield BB9 148 A4
Burnley BB11 128 A6
Bury BL9 33 B3
Masterson Ave BB12 145 D2
Matcham Ct 11 FY1 130 B5
Matchmoor La BL6 32 F4
Mather Ave BB5 104 B8
Mather St FY3 130 D7
Mathias Ct LA4 217 B6
Matlock Ave PR8 35 B4
Matlock Cl PR8 35 B4
Matlock Cres PR8 35 B4
Matlock Gr BB10 148 C2
Matlock Pl PR2 117 A5
Matlock Rd PR8 35 B4
Matlock St 13 BB3 81 F2
Matrix Pk PR7 60 D7
Matterdale Rd PR25 60 B7
Matthew Cl BB8 171 E4
Matthew St BB2 101 B2
Matthews Ct FY4 110 D7
Matthias St LA4 217 B6
Mattock Cres LA4 217 F5
Maud St Barrowford BB9 170 D2
Chorley PR7 43 B6
Maudland Bank PR1 96 E8
Maudland Rd
Blackpool FY1 130 C2
Preston PR1 96 E8
Maudsley St
Accrington BB5 104 C6
Blackburn BB1 101 F5
Maureen Ave 3 PR5 77 B8
Maurice Gr FY2 152 E1
Maurice St BB9 148 D8
Mavis Dr PR7 42 E2
Mavis Rd BB2 101 A5
Mawdesley St Peter's CE
Prim Sch L40 40 C3
Mawdsley Cl L37 12 B3
Mawdsley Terr L39 15 F7
Maxwell Gr FY2 152 E2
Maxwell St BL9 33 B3
May Bell Ave FY5 175 F3
May La Bilsborrow PR3 159 C8
Claughton PR3 182 E1
May St Barrowford BB9 170 D2
Blackburn BB1 102 A4
Edgworth BL7 48 E6
Nelson BB9 170 F2
May Terr BB7 144 A4
Maybank Cl PR9 54 A1
Maybury Ave BB12 127 B7
Maybury Cl 21 BL0 50 B5
Maycroft Ave FY6 153 B5
Mayfair BL6 32 D3
Mayfair Cl Haslingden BB4 68 A7
Hightown L38 2 F2
Lytham St Anne's FY8 90 D6
Mayfair Cres BB1 122 F5
Mayfair Ct PR9 53 D1
Mayfair Dr FY5 153 C8
Mayfair Gdns 5 FY5 176 C1
Mayfair Rd Blackpool FY1 130 E2
Burnley BB10 128 E5
Nelson BB9 171 A1
Mayfayre Ave L31 5 B5
Mayfield Darwen BB3 65 B7
Woodsfold PR4 135 E6
Mayfield Ave
Adlington PR6 31 A7
Bamber Bridge PR5 77 C8
Blackpool FY4 110 C5
Clitheroe BB7 166 F7
Formby L37 11 C1
Fulwood PR2 117 A5
Fulwood PR2 117 B4
Haslingden BB4 85 A1
5 Kirkham PR4 114 A5
Lancaster LA1 218 C3
Oswaldtwistle BB5 103 F4
Thornton FY5 176 A4
Mayfield Cl BL0 50 A2
Mayfield Ct L37 11 F5
Mayfield Dr LA4 217 E6
Mayfield Fold BB11 128 B3
Mayfield Gdns BB5 103 F4
Mayfield Pl 10 FY7 198 F2
Mayfield Prim Sch FY8 89 E8
Mayfield Rd
Blackburn BB1 122 E3
8 Chorley PR6 61 D1
High Bentham LA2 239 D7
Leyland PR25 60 A7
Lytham St Anne's FY8 89 E8
Preston PR2 117 B1
Ramsbottom BL0 50 A2
Skelmersdale WN8 10 B7
Mayfield Sch PR7 43 C6
Mayfield St BB2 101 E3
Mayflower Ave PR1 96 A3
Mayflower Cotts WN1 30 C1
Mayflower Gr PR3 181 E1
Mayflower Ind Est L37 12 A1
Mayflower St BB2 101 B2
Mayhall Ct L31 5 D2
Maylands Pl BB9 170 C3
Maylands Sq LA4 217 C4
Maynard St PR1,PR2 117 D2
Mayo Dr PR4 57 A6
Mayor Ave FY1 130 C2
Maypark PR5 78 A5
Mayson St BB1 101 E4
Maytree Wlk WN8 18 B4
Mayville Rd BB9 148 B6
McCall Cl PR4 113 A3
McDonald Rd LA3 212 D5
McKenzie St PR5 77 F8
Mead Ave PR25 60 B8
Meadow Ave
Fleetwood FY7 198 E1
Knott End-on-S FY6 200 A6
Southport PR8 35 C4
Meadow Bank
Kingsfold PR1 96 C3
Maghull L31 5 B2
3 Ormskirk L39 15 F5
Meadow Bank Ave
BB10 148 B5
Meadow Bank Cotts BB4 85 E3
Meadow Bank Mews 2
BB9 170 F2
Meadow Bank Rd 15
BB9 148 D8
Meadow Brook Ho 1
PR1 118 A1
Meadow Brow PR9 54 D5
Meadow Cl
Billington BB7 144 A3
Blackpool FY2 152 D2
Brierfield BB10 148 C4
Clifton PR4 115 D2
Foulridge BB8 194 D1
Huncoat BB5 125 F1
Skelmersdale WN8 9 D7
Westhead L40 16 E4
Wrea Green PR4 113 B3
Meadow Clough WN8 18 B4
Meadow Cotts OL12 71 D3
Meadow Court Rd LA4 217 C3
Meadow Cr PR4 113 F6
Meadow Cres FY6 153 A3
Meadow Croft
Nether Kellet LA6 221 F4
West Bradford BB7 189 E5
Meadow Ct
11 Oswaldtwistle BB5 103 E4
Preston PR1 96 E6
Treales PR4 135 A1
Meadow Dr
Bolton-le-S LA5 221 A5
Ormskirk L39 15 C2
Warton PR4 92 C5
Meadow Field PR1 96 E2
Meadow Gate BB3 82 B2
Meadow Gdns BB1 124 B1
Meadow Head Ave OL12 52 D6
Meadow Head Cl BB2 101 A1
Meadow Head La
Longton PR4 74 F7
Tockholes BB3 81 B4
Meadow Ho 7 PR1 97 A8
Meadow La
Clayton Brook PR5 78 B4
Croston PR26 57 E1
Hesketh Bank PR4 73 F4
Hoscar L40 26 C6
Knott End-on-S FY6 199 F4
Lytham St Anne's FY8 91 E4
Maghull L31 5 F1
Rufford L40 39 D3
Southport PR8 21 D3
Meadow Pk Galgate LA2 210 F4
Garstang PR3 204 C1
Haslingden BL0 68 C4
Kirkham PR4 113 E6
Staining FY3 131 D5
Meadow Pk *continued*
Tarleton PR4 57 B6
Meadow Reach PR1 96 B2
Meadow Rise BB2 81 A8
Meadow St
Accrington BB5 104 C6
Adlington PR7 31 A6
Barnoldswick BB18 196 A4
17 Burnley BB11 127 F6
Darwen BB3 65 B6
Great Harwood BB6 124 C4
Lancaster LA1 214 D8
Leyland PR25 77 A1
Padiham BB12 146 C1
Preston PR1 97 A8
Wheelton PR6 62 A7
Meadow Terr BB3 81 E5
Meadow Vale
Blackburn BB2 81 E6
Leyland PR26 59 A8
Meadow View
Adlington PR6 30 F8
Clitheroe BB7 166 C8
Farleton LA2 238 A6
Great Plumpton PR4 112 F7
Lancaster LA1 218 B3
Rochdale OL12 52 A1
Southport PR8 35 D4
Meadow Way
Arkholme LA6 241 B3
Bacup OL13 87 F2
Barnoldswick BB18 196 D4
Blackrod BL6 31 E1
Coppull PR7 29 D8
Edgworth BL7 48 E6
Garstang PR3 204 C2
Ramsbottom BL9 50 C2
Meadoway
Accrington BB5 104 A7
Longton PR4 74 F8
Tarleton PR4 57 A5
Meadowbarn Cl PR4 116 E5
Meadowbridge Cl L40 16 E4
Meadowbrook
Blackpool FY3 131 C2
Burscough L40 25 D2
Meadowbrook Cl BL9 33 C4
Meadowcroft
Blackburn BB3 82 A6
Euxton PR7 60 B3
Formby L37 11 F2
Lytham St Anne's FY8 111 A1
Skelmersdale WN8 18 B4
Meadowcroft Ave
Catterall PR3 181 D3
Cleveleys FY5 175 E2
Hambleton FY6 177 C1
Meadowcroft Bsns Pk
PR4 96 B1
Meadowcroft Cl BB4 86 A5
Meadowcroft Gr LA3 216 E1
Meadowcroft Rd PR25 59 D7
Meadowfield
Fulwood PR2 117 F8
Halton LA2 219 C7
Skelmersdale WN8 10 A7
Meadowfield Cl
Halton LA2 219 C7
Whalley BB7 144 A7
Meadowfields BB2 81 D7
Meadowhead Cty Inf Sch
BB2 101 B1
Meadowhead Jun Sch
BB2 81 B8
Meadowland Cl PR26 76 E3
Meadowlands
Charnock Richard PR7 42 D4
Clitheroe BB7 166 C8
Meadows Ave Bacup OL13 87 F4
Cleveleys FY5 175 F2
Haslingden BB4 85 C2
Meadows Cl LA5 225 E4
Meadows Dr BB4 106 A1
Meadows The
Arnside LA5 224 C8
Bamber Bridge PR5 97 F3
Billington BB7 144 A4
Burnley BB12 127 D8
Cleveleys FY5 175 F2
Colne BB8 171 D6
Darwen BB3 81 E5
Elswick PR4 155 F1
Heskin Green PR7 41 E2
Hollins Lane PR3 207 C2
2 Leyland PR26 76 B1
3 Maghull L31 5 D1
Oswaldtwistle BB5 103 F3
Whitworth OL12 71 C1
Yealand Redmayne LA5 225 E3
Meadowside
Claughton LA2 237 F5
Croston PR26 58 A2
Grindleton BB7 190 C8
Lancaster LA1 214 F7
Walmer Bridge PR4 75 A5
Meadowside Ave BB5 124 E3
Meadowside Dr PR5 98 E1
Meadowside Rd LA4 217 B3
Meads Rd PR2 117 B1
Meadup Ct LA3 217 A2
Meadway Becconsall PR4 73 F2
Blackpool FY4 130 F1
Clayton Green PR6 78 B3
Higher Penwortham PR1 96 A5
Padiham BB12 126 B7
Ramsbottom BL0 68 C1
Skelmersdale WN8 18 A4
Meadway Cl BL6 32 D3
Meagles La PR3,PR4 155 E3
Mealhouse La 6 PR7 43 C8
Mealrigg La LA6 241 A7
Meanwood Ave FY4 110 F7
Meanwood Brow 15
OL12 52 C1
Meanwood Prim Sch
OL12 52 C1
Meanygate PR5 97 E1
Mearbeck Pl 6 LA1 218 B2
Mearley Brook Fold
BB7 166 F7
Mearley Rd PR2 118 E4
Mearley St BB7 166 E7
Mearley Syke BB7 166 F8
Mearsbeck LA3 216 E3
Meath Rd PR1 96 D6
Mede The PR4 114 B3
Medina Cl BB5 104 B5
Medlar Cl PR4 113 E6
Medlar Ct PR4 114 A6
Medlar Gate PR4 114 A6
Medlar La PR4 133 E4
Medlar-with-Wesham CE
Prim Sch PR4 113 F6
Medley St OL12 52 F1
Medlock Ave FY7 198 D2
Medlock Pl FY7 198 D2
Medway PR2 117 F6
Medway Ave FY7 175 D8
Medway Cl PR5 97 B1
Medway Dr BL6 32 D3
Medway Ho 6 PR1 97 D8
Meeting House La LA1 214 E8
Meins Croft BB2 101 A6
Meins Rd BB2 100 F6
Melba Rd PR2 118 E3
Melbert Ave PR2 117 C3
Melbourne Ave
Blackpool FY5 152 F7
Fleetwood FY7 175 E8
Melbourne Cl BL6 32 C3
Melbourne Ct 1 FY5 152 F8
Melbourne Gr BL6 32 C3
Melbourne Rd 11 LA1 215 A8
Melbourne St
6 Accrington BB5 125 A1
7 Darwen BB3 65 B6
2 Newchurch BB4 86 F1
Oswaldtwistle BB5 103 D3
Padiham BB12 126 D7
19 Preston PR1 96 F8
Melbreck WN8 18 A4
Melbury Dr BL6 32 F1
Meldon Grange LA3 213 A8
Meldon Rd LA3 213 A7
Meldreth Cl L37 11 C1
Melford Cl PR6 61 F3
Melford Dr WN5 10 D3
Melfort Cl BB2 100 F1
Melia Cl BB4 85 F2
Melita St 6 BB3 65 B8
Melling Brow LA6 241 C2
Melling Ct 3 Colne BB8 171 C5
Morecambe LA4 217 A3
Melling Ho 4 LA1 215 A3
Melling Mews PR3 181 C8
Melling Rd Hornby LA2 238 B7
Southport PR9 35 E7
Melling St 17 PR1 96 F8
Melling St Wilfrid CE Prim
Sch LA6 241 D2
Melling's La FY8 111 A1
Mellings Ave WN5 10 E1
Mellings Fold 3 PR1 97 C6
Mellings Wood FY8 111 A1
Mellishaw La LA3 217 D1
Mellor Brow BB2 121 D2
Mellor Cl Burnley BB11 127 D3
Standish WN6 29 E2
Mellor Ct PR3 140 B7
Mellor La BB2 121 F3
Mellor Pl 6 PR1 97 B7
Mellor Rd Kirkham PR4 114 A5
Leyland PR25 76 D2
Mellwood Ave FY3 152 F1
Melrose Ave
Blackpool FY3 130 E8
Burnley BB11 127 D4
Fulwood PR2 118 C5
Morecambe LA4 217 C5
Oswaldtwistle BB5 103 F3
Southport PR9 54 B5
Melrose Gdns PR26 58 C2
Melrose St 10 Darwen BB3 81 F2
Lancaster LA1 215 A7
Ramsbottom BL0 50 B2
Melrose Terr OL13 88 A7
Melrose Way PR7 43 D5
Melton Gr FY8 90 E3
Melton Pl Blackpool FY5 152 C8
Leyland PR25 77 B1
Melville Ave
Barnoldswick BB18 196 A3
Darwen BB3 65 A7
Melville Dr BB2 101 D5
Melville Gdns BB3 65 A8
Melville Rd
Blackpool FY2 152 C4
Heysham LA3 212 E5
Melville St Burnley BB10 148 C1
Darwen BB3 65 A8
Melvin Ho PR9 35 B8
Memorial Gdns PR3 159 A4
Memory Cl PR4 93 B7
Menai Dr PR2 117 D7
Mendip Cl Horwich BL6 32 C5
Lytham St Anne's FY8 91 E5
Mendip Rd PR25 77 D1
Menivale Cl PR9 54 B5
Meols Cl L37 11 E2
Meols Cop High Sch PR8 35 F5
Meols Cop Rd PR8,PR9 35 F4
Meols Cop Ret Pk PR9 36 A4
Meols Cop Sta PR9 35 F7
Meols Ct PR9 55 A6
Meolsgate Ave PR4 57 A7
Mercer Cres BB4 68 A8
Mercer Ct Adlington PR7 43 F1
Maghull L31 5 A3
Mercer Dr BB6 124 E6
Mercer Ho 5 BB5 125 A1
Mercer Rd PR5 97 A1
Mercer St
16 Clayton-le-M BB5 124 F3
Great Harwood BB6 124 D5
1 Padiham BB12 126 F7
Preston PR1 97 C8
Mercer's La L39 7 B4
Merchants Ho 4 BB1 101 F4
Merchants Landing BB1 101 F3
Merchants Quay 1 BB1 101 F3
Merclesden Ave BB9 171 B1
Mercury Way WN8 9 E7
Mere Ave
Burscough Bridge L40 25 E6
Fleetwood FY7 198 D1
Mere Brook FY3 131 E5
Mere Brow La PR4 56 A2
Mere Cl Broughton PR3 137 C3
Skelmersdale WN8 17 F2
Mere Ct Burnley BB11 127 B4
Burscough Bridge L40 25 E5
Mere Fold PR7 42 D3
Mere La Banks PR9 55 A2
Holmeswood PR4 38 A7
Rufford L40 38 E3
Mere Park Ct FY3 131 A2
Mere Rd Blackpool FY3 130 D5
Formby L37 11 D2
Mere Sands Wood Nature
Reserve* L40 38 F4
Meredith St BB9 148 E7
Merefell Rd LA5 221 A6
Merefield PR7 61 A1
Merefield Sch PR8 21 B4
Merefold BL6 31 F3
Mereland Cl WN5 10 E6
Mereland Rd FY3 131 A2
Merepark Dr PR9 54 B4
Meres Way PR8 35 B2
Mereside Cl PR4 74 F7
Mereside Prim Sch FY4 131 C1
Merewood WN8 18 A4
Meriden Cl PR8 21 B5
Merlecrest Dr PR4 57 A8
Merlewood BL0 68 E3
Merlewood Ave PR9 54 B3
Merlin Cl PR6 62 A3
Merlin Ct BB5 103 D3
Merlin Dr BB5 103 D3
Merlin Gr Leyland PR25 59 C8
Padiham BB12 126 E6
Merlin Rd BB2 101 B6
Merlyn Rd FY5 175 E1
Merrick Ave PR1 97 F8
Merrilox Ave L31 5 D3
Merry Trees La PR4 116 E5
Merryburn Cl PR2 118 A4
Merscar La L40 24 D6
Mersey Ave Darwen BB3 81 D3
Formby L37 11 E6
Maghull L31 5 F2
Mersey Rd Blackpool FY4 110 B8
Fleetwood FY7 198 F4
Orrell WN5 10 F7
Mersey St Bacup OL13 88 A1
Burnley BB12 127 A6
Longridge PR3 140 B8
Preston PR2 96 C8
Merton Ave PR2 117 F6
Merton Gr PR6 61 F3
Merton St Burnley BB12 127 F7
4 Nelson BB9 170 D1
Messenger St BB9 149 A7
Meta St BB2 101 E2
Metcalf Dr BB5 125 D6
Metcalfe Cl BB2 81 D8
Metcalfe St BB12 127 B5
Mete St PR1 97 D8
Methuen Ave
Coupe Green PR5 98 E3
Fulwood PR2 117 E6
Methuen Cl PR5 98 E3
Methuen Dr PR5 98 F3
Metropolitan Bsns Pk
FY3 131 B2
Metropolitan Dr FY3 131 B2
Mettle Cote OL13 88 A1
Mewith La LA2 239 C6
Mews The 1 Darwen BB3 65 C7
Lancaster LA1 215 B6
Morecambe LA4 217 E5
1 Padiham BB12 146 C1
Southport PR8 35 A5
Mexford Ave FY2 130 D8
Meyler Ave FY3 130 E8
Michael Pl LA4 217 D5
Michael Wife La BL0 68 F3
Michael's La L39 22 C3
Michaels Cl L37 11 E3
Michaelson Ave LA4 217 E4
Mickering La L39 6 C5

Mickleden Ave PR2 117 F7
Mickleden Rd FY4 131 C1
Micklefield Ct 2 PR25 76 D1
Micklegate FY5 152 C7
Micklehurst Cres BB11 127 D2
Mickleton Dr PR8 21 A5
Middle Hey PR4 74 E3
Middle Hill OL12 52 F4
Middle Holly Rd PR3 204 C8
Middle La LA2 211 A6
Middle Meanygate PR4 56 C7
Middle Moss La
Great Altcar L37 12 F3
Haskayne L37 13 A2
Middle St Blackpool FY1 130 B3
Colne BB8 171 C4
Lancaster LA1 214 F8
Whitworth OL12 71 D1
Middle Turn BL7 48 D7
Middle Withins La L37,L38 4 A7
Middlecot Cl WN5 10 E5
Middlefield PR26 59 A8
Middleforth Gn PR1 96 E4
Middleforth Ind Est 4
PR1 96 E4
Middlegate LA3 217 E2
Middlegate Gn BB4 106 A1
Middlesex Ave BB12 127 B7
Middleton Ave FY7 198 D1
Middleton Dr BB9 170 E6
Middleton Rd
Heysham LA3 212 E5
Heysham,Middleton LA3 213 B2
Middleton Way LA3 212 F6
Middlewood WN8 18 A4
Middlewood Cl
Eccleston PR7 41 C6
Ormskirk L39 6 C7
Middlewood Dr L39 6 C7
Middlewood Rd L39 6 C7
Midfield BB6 123 C8
Midge Hall La Bescar PR9 37 C3
Leyland PR4,PR5 75 F4
Midgeland Rd FY4 111 B5
Midgeland Terr FY4 111 C5
Midgery La PR2 118 B7
Midgley St BB8 171 E4
Midhurst Dr PR8 21 B4
Midland St
12 Accrington BB5 104 C5
Nelson BB9 170 E1
Midland Terr LA5 223 D3
Midsummer St BB2 101 C5
Midville Pl 15 BB3 82 A1
Milbanke Ave PR4 114 A5
Milbeck Cl PR3 139 F5
Milbourne Rd BL9 33 A6
Milbourne St FY1 130 C5
Milbrook Cl BB11 127 B5
Milburn Ave FY5 175 F5
Mildred Cl FY5 176 A3
Mile End Cl BB8 194 D1
Mile End Row BB2 101 B6
Mile Rd FY6 155 A1
Mile Stone Mdw PR7 60 D4
Miles Ave OL13 70 D8
Miles La WN6 19 E6
Miles St PR1 117 F2
Miles Wlk PR1 117 E2
Milestone Mdw PR7 60 D4
Milestone Pl LA2 237 C3
Miletas Pl FY8 90 C4
Milford Ave FY2 152 D1
Milford Cl L37 11 C1
Milford St Colne BB8 171 C5
6 Rochdale OL12 52 F1
Milk St BL0 50 B5
Milking La BB3 82 A6
Milking Stile La LA1 214 D8
Mill Bank WN6 19 D7
Mill Brook PR3 181 D3
Mill Brook Pl BB7 166 D1
Mill Brow Haskayne L39 14 A7
Lowgill LA2 239 B2
Mill Brow Rd BB18 197 C2
Mill Cl PR4 135 C8
Mill Cotts BB3 82 F3
Mill Ct PR3 140 B8
Mill Dam Cl L40 25 C2
Mill Dam La L40 16 D8
Mill Entrance BB5 124 F2
Mill Field
Clayton-le-M BB5 124 F4
Parbold WN8 27 C1
Mill Gap St 17 BB3 65 A8
Mill Gate Fulwood PR2 117 D3
15 Rawtenstall BB4 86 A3
Mill Gdns 6 LA2 239 D8
Mill Gn BB8 171 D4
Mill Haven PR2 117 D3
Mill Hey Ave FY6 153 E1
Mill Hey La L40 39 C3
Mill Hill
Oswaldtwistle BB5 103 E4
Preston PR1 96 E8
Mill Hill Bridge St BB2 101 B2
Mill Hill Cotts BL6 44 F1
Mill Hill Gr LA3 213 A2
Mill Hill La BB11 126 B3
Mill Hill St BB2 101 B2
Mill Hill Sta BB2 101 B2
Mill Ho 19 LA1 215 A8
Mill Ho Mews 17 LA1 215 A8
Mill House La Brindle PR6 78 F8
Longridge PR3 141 A8
Mill House View WN8 10 C7
Mill La Appley Bridge WN6 19 D7
Bacup OL13 88 B3
Becconsall PR4 73 F2
Blackburn BB2 101 E4
Bolton Green PR7 42 A8
Bolton Green PR7 60 A1
Bolton-le-S LA5 221 A6
Burscough L40 25 E4
Carnforth LA5 223 D4
Caton LA2 237 B3
Clayton Green PR6 78 C1
Coppull PR7 42 E2
Darwen BB3 64 A5
Earby BB18 197 D2
Eccleston PR7 41 C5
Elswick PR4 156 B1
Fleetwood FY7 199 B4
Fulwood PR2 117 C4
Gisburn BB7 231 B4
Goosnargh PR3 138 E6
Great Harwood BB6 125 A6
Halton LA2 219 D6
Hambleton FY6 177 E1
Haskayne L39 14 F1
Hesketh Lane PR3 162 C8
Heskin Green PR7 42 A2
Horwich BL6 32 D4
Leyland PR25 59 D8
Leyland,Earnshaw Bridge
PR26 76 E3
Low Bentham LA2 239 C7
Parbold WN8 27 C1
Skelmersdale WN8 17 F2
Skelmersdale,Up Holland
WN8 10 A8
Southport PR9 54 A1
Staining FY3 131 D5
Stalmine FY6 177 D7
Waddington BB7 189 A8
Walton-le-D PR5 97 D5
Warton PR4 92 F6
Wrea Green PR4 113 A3
Mill Lane Cres PR9 54 A1
Mill Lane Ind Est BB7 231 B3
Mill Leat Cl WN8 27 C2
Mill Leat Mews WN8 27 C2
Mill Nook OL12 52 F3
Mill Rd Orrell WN5 10 D5
Southport PR8 21 D5
Mill Row BB4 85 F5
Mill St Accrington BB5 104 F1
Adlington PR6 31 B8
Bacup OL13 87 F3
Barnoldswick BB18 196 A2
Barrowford BB9 170 D4
Church BB5 103 F6
Clayton-le-M BB5 124 F2
4 Coppull PR7 42 E1
Great Harwood BB6 124 C5
Haslingden BB4 85 B5
Lancaster LA1 215 A8
Leyland PR25 77 B3
Leyland,Seven Stars PR25 59 D8
Nelson BB9 148 A7
Ormskirk L39 15 F5
Oswaldtwistle BB5 103 D3
Padiham BB12 126 C8
Preesall FY6 200 B3
Preston PR1 96 D8
Ramsbottom BL0 50 A4
Southport PR8 35 C6
West Bradford BB7 189 E5
Wheelton PR6 62 A7
Mill The Leyland PR26 76 D2
Preston PR1 96 F8
Mill View PR4 93 B7
Mill View Ct L39 7 E6
Mill Wood Cl PR6 79 C3
Mill Yd BL9 33 A3
Millar Barn La BB4 69 F8
Millar's Pace PR9 54 B5
Millbank Fulwood PR2 117 C3
4 Preston PR1 97 B8
Millbank Brow L40 25 F3
Millbank La L31,L39 5 F3
Millbrook BB12 147 E8
Millbrook Cl
Skelmersdale WN8 17 E2
Wheelton PR6 62 A7
Millbrook Ct BB7 189 E5
Millbrook Mews 1 FY8 91 C3
Millbrook Row PR6 44 B1
Millbrook St BB3 81 F7
Millbrook Way PR1 96 C3
Millcombe Way PR5 97 E3
Millcroft Chorley PR7 61 A2
Fulwood PR2 117 D4
Millcroft Ave WN5 10 D5
Milldyke Cl FY4 110 F6
Millenium Ct FY8 110 B4
Miller Ave PR6 80 B2
Miller Cl BB5 103 C5
Miller Cres FY6 154 E1
Miller Ct
14 Lancaster LA1 218 D2
Lancaster,Haverbreaks
LA1 214 E5
Miller Field PR2 116 E3
Miller Fold Ave BB5 104 B3
Miller Ho 4 PR1 97 A7
Miller La Catforth PR4 135 E4
Cottam PR4 116 E5
Miller Rd PR1,PR2 118 E2
Miller St
4 Blackpool FY1 130 B1
11 Preston PR1 97 C8
Ramsbottom BL9 50 C2
Miller's Brow PR3 207 E3
Millers Cl FY8 90 D7
Millers Ct L39 15 F5
Millers Nook WN8 10 B7
Millersdale Cl FY5 153 E7
Millersgate PR4 116 E4
Millet Terr BL9 33 E7
Millett St BL0 50 D7
Millfield Cl PR4 92 F6
Millfield High Sch FY5 153 C8
Millfield Rd
Blackpool FY4 110 F6
Chorley PR7 61 C1
Millfold OL12 71 D2
Millgate OL7 47 D2
Millgate Rd 18 BB4 86 A3
Millgate Terr OL12 71 E5
Millgreen Cl WN8 10 A7
Millham St BB1 101 E6
Millholme Dr LA2 239 D7
Millhouse Lo PR8 21 D5
Millhouse St BL0 50 E8
Millington Ave FY4 110 E8
Millom Ave FY2 152 D4
Millom Cl FY7 175 C8
Millrace Ct 5 LA1 218 D2
Millrose Cl WN8 17 F2
Mills St OL12 71 D1
Millstone Ct 3 LA1 218 D3
Millthorne Ave BB7 166 D7
Millthorne Ho 9 BB7 166 D8
Millwood Cl BB2 101 A1
Millwood Glade PR7 61 B1
Millwood Rd PR5 97 B3
Milman Cl L39 15 D3
Milne St BL0 68 C5
Milner Rd Darwen BB3 81 E4
Lytham St Anne's FY8 90 E4
Milner St Burnley BB10 128 A8
Preston PR1 118 A2
Whitworth OL12 52 C8
Whitworth OL12 71 C1
Milnshaw Gdns BB5 104 B7
Milnshaw La BB5 104 B6
Milnthorpe Ave FY5 175 D5
Milton Ave Blackpool FY3 130 F5
Clitheroe BB7 189 E1
2 Thornton FY5 176 A3
Milton Cl
Bamber Bridge PR5 97 D2
Darwen BB3 82 C1
Great Harwood BB6 124 B4
Haslingden BB4 68 A7
Milton Cres Kirkham PR4 114 A5
Poulton-le-F FY6 131 D8
Milton Ct PR7 42 E1
Milton Dr L39 16 A4
Milton Gr
Barnoldswick BB18 196 A3
Longshaw WN5 10 D1
Orrell WN5 10 F6
Milton Rd Colne BB8 171 D5
Coppull PR7 29 E8
Milton St
3 Barrowford BB9 170 D4
1 Blackburn BB1 102 A5
Brierfield BB9 148 B5
Brierfield,Harle Syke BB10 148 F3
Clayton-le-M BB5 124 F3
Fleetwood FY7 199 A4
Nelson BB9 170 D1
Oswaldtwistle BB5 103 E4
Padiham BB12 126 E7
Ramsbottom BL0 50 B6
Southport PR9 36 A7
Milton Terr PR6 61 D2
Milton Way L31 5 B1
Mimosa Cl PR7 61 A3
Mimosa Rd PR2 118 E2
Mincing La BB2 101 E4
Minden Rd PR4 132 E5
Minehead Ave BB10 148 D2
Minerva Rd LA1 214 C8
Minnie St OL12 71 D2
Minnie Terr BB2 101 C6
Minor St 13 BB4 86 A7
Minstead Ave L33 1 A2
Minster Cres BB3 65 C8
Minster Dr LA3 217 B2
Minster Pk FY4 116 E5
Minstrel Wlk FY6 153 D4
Mint Ave BB9 170 D4
Mint St BL0 68 C2
Mintholme Ave PR5 98 E2
Mintor Rd L33 1 A2
Mire Ash Brow BB2 121 D1
Mire Ridge BB8 172 A3
Mirfield Gr 11 FY4 130 D1
Miry La WN8 27 D2
Mission Cotts L40 26 B8
Mission The BB8 172 C6
Mitcham Rd FY4 111 B8
Mitchell St Burnley BB12 127 C6
Clitheroe BB7 166 D7
4 Colne BB8 171 D5
Mitella St BB10 128 C5
Mitre St BB11 127 E6
Mitten's La L37 12 A4
Mitten's La L37 12 B3
Mitton Ave
Barrowford BB9 170 F6
Rawtenstall BB4 86 A4
Mitton Cl Blackburn BB2 101 C1
Heywood OL10 33 F2
Mitton Dr PR2 119 A3
Mitton Gr BB10 128 D5
Mitton Hos BB9 170 F6
Mitton Rd
Great Mitton BB7 165 F2
Whalley BB7 144 B7
Mitton St BB1 101 F7
Mizpah St BB10 128 C5
Mizzy Rd OL12 52 F1
Moira Cres PR2 118 F4
Moleside Cl BB5 104 D6
Mollington Rd BB2 101 B7
Molly Wood La BB11 126 F5
Molyneux Ct 18 PR1 97 A8
Molyneux Dr FY4 110 D7
Molyneux Pl FY8 91 A4
Molyneux Rd L39 6 C7
Mona Pl PR1 96 E8
Mona Rd BB2 101 E1
Monarch Cres FY8 90 B8
Monarch St BB5 103 E4
Money Close La LA3 212 D4
Moneyclose Gr LA3 212 D5
Monk Hall St BB10 128 A7
Monk St Accrington BB5 104 A6
2 Clitheroe BB7 166 D7
Monk's La FY6 200 A1
Monkroyd Ave BB18 196 A2
Monkroyd Rd BB8 172 F7
Monks Carr La L37,L38 4 A6
Monks Cl L37 12 A1
Monks Dr Formby L37 12 A1
Longridge PR3 140 A6
Withnell PR6 80 A1
Monks Gate FY8 90 D7
Monks La L40 25 D7
Monks Wlk PR1 96 C6
Monkswell Ave LA5 221 A5
Monkswell Dr LA5 221 A5
Monkswood Ave LA4 217 E5
Monmouth Ct PR2 116 F3
Monmouth Rd BB1 102 C5
Monmouth St
5 Burnley BB12 127 D6
Colne BB8 172 A5
Monroe Dr 3 FY7 198 D3
Montagu Mews L37 11 E5
Montagu Rd L37 11 E5
Montague Cl BB2 101 D4
Montague Rd BB11 127 E5
Montague St
Blackburn BB2 101 D5
Blackpool FY4 110 B8
Brierfield BB9 148 B5
4 Clitheroe BB7 166 D8
Colne BB8 171 E6
Montcliffe Cotts BL6 32 E5
Montcliffe Rd PR6 61 E1
Monteagle Dr LA2 238 B7
Monteagle Sq LA2 238 B7
Montfield Hey BB9 148 A5
Montford Ct BB12 147 F6
Montford Rd BB9 147 F6
Montgomery Ave PR9 36 B6
Montgomery Cl BB5 104 E2
Montgomery Gr BB12 127 C7
Montgomery High Sch
FY2 152 D5
Montgomery St 7 PR5 77 F8
Monthall Rise LA1 218 F1
Montjoly St PR1 97 C7
Monton Rd BB3 81 E4
Montpelier Ave FY2 152 C5
Montreal Ave FY1 130 D4
Montreal Rd BB2 101 C8
Montrose Ave
Blackpool FY1 130 C3
Ramsbottom BL0 50 A2
Montrose Cl PR6 43 E6
Montrose Cres LA3 212 E7
Montrose Dr PR9 53 F1
Montrose St
Blackburn BB2 101 C3
Brierfield BB9 148 B6
Burnley BB11 127 F4
Montrose Terr 17 BB18 196 B2
Moody La L40 40 E1
Moody St 5 WN6 29 E1
Moon Ave 7 FY1 130 B2
Moon Bay Wharf LA3 212 D6
Moon St PR5 77 E8
Moons Acre LA2 239 D8
Moor Ave
Appley Bridge WN6 19 E8
Higher Penwortham PR1 96 A4
Moor Cl Darwen BB3 65 D8
Lancaster LA1 215 A8
Southport PR8 21 D2
Moor Close La LA6 240 B1
Moor Dr WN8 9 D7
Moor Edge BB7 144 B6
Moor End Prim Sch
BB5 103 D4
Moor Field
New Longton PR4 76 A7
Whalley BB7 144 B6
Moor Gate 14 LA1 215 A8
Moor Hall La PR4 114 F4
Moor Hall St PR1 117 E2
Moor Hey Cotts PR26 58 A6
Moor La
Billington BB6,BB7 144 B2
Butt Yeats LA2 238 C5
Clitheroe BB7 166 E8
Darwen BB3 82 B3
Haslingden BB4 84 F6
Hutton PR4 95 D1
Ince Blundell L38,L23 3 E2
Lancaster LA1 215 A8
Langho BB6 123 E8
Maghull L29 4 D1
Moor La *continued*
Padiham BB12 146 C1
Preston PR1 117 F1
Salterforth BB18 194 C6
Southport PR8 21 C2
Waddington BB7 229 D2
West Bradford BB7 189 D7
Whalley BB7 144 B6
Wiswell BB7 144 F7
Moor Nook Com Prim Sch
PR2 119 A3
Moor Park Ave
Blackpool FY2 152 E4
Preston PR1 118 A2
Moor Park High Sch
PR1 118 A2
Moor Park Inf & Jun Sch
FY2 152 E3
Moor Platt Cl BL6 32 F3
Moor Rd
Barber's Moor PR26 58 D3
Chorley PR7 43 B5
Haslingden BB4 67 F5
Orrell WN5 10 E6
Ramsbottom BL8 50 A6
Rivington PR6 44 E7
Moor Side La BB7 144 F8
Moor St Clayton-le-M BB5 124 F3
Kirkham PR4 114 A5
33 Lancaster LA1 214 F8
Ormskirk L39 15 F5
Moor View Bacup OL13 88 A4
Bacup,Brandwood OL13 70 B7
Rawtenstall BB4 69 F6
Salterforth BB18 194 E8
Moor Way BL8 49 C3
Moorbottom Rd BL8 49 E5
Moorbrook Sch PR2 117 E3
Moorbrook St PR1 117 E1
Moorcroft Blackburn BB3 82 A6
Broughton PR3 137 B2
Edenfield BL0 68 D2
Moorcroft Cres PR2 118 D3
Moore Dr BB12 146 F5
Moore St Blackpool FY4 130 B1
Colne BB8 171 C5
Nelson BB9 148 F7
Padiham BB12 126 F7
Preston PR1 97 C7
Moore Tree Dr FY4 111 A8
Moorend BB7 166 F7
Moores La WN6 29 D2
Moorfield BL7 48 D6
Moorfield Ave
Accrington,Hillock Vale
BB5 104 F8
Blackburn BB1 122 E3
Blackpool FY3 130 E6
Carleton FY6 153 B4
Moorfield Cl
Clayton-le-M BB5 125 B3
Fulwood PR2 117 E8
Preston PR1 96 A2
Moorfield Dr
Clayton-le-M BB5 125 B3
Fulwood PR2 118 E3
Lytham St Anne's FY8 91 A4
Moorfield Ind Est BB5 125 B3
Moorfield La L40 24 C3
Moorfield Pl 3 OL12 52 F1
Moorfield Rd PR25 59 C8
Moorfield Sch PR1 118 A3
Moorfield Way BB5 125 B3
Moorfields Blackpool FY2 152 F4
Chorley PR6 61 E1
Moorfields Ave PR2 117 E8
Moorgate Accrington BB5 104 B2
Blackpool FY4 110 F6
Bury BL9 33 A3
Fulwood PR2 117 F5
Ormskirk L39 15 E4
Moorgate Gdns 2 BB2 101 C1
Moorgate La BB6 143 A5
Moorgate Rd BB18 196 A1
Moorgate Ret Pk 13 BL9 33 A3
Moorgate St BB2 101 C1
Moorhead Gdns PR4 92 E7
Moorhead High Sch
BB5 104 A7
Moorhead St 2 BB8 171 C5
Moorhen Pl 14 FY5 175 F1
Moorhey Cres
Higher Penwortham PR1 96 B5
Walton Summit PR5 78 A8
Moorhey Dr PR1 96 B5
Moorhouse Ave BB5 104 A4
Moorhouse Cl BB5 104 A4
Moorhouse St
Accrington BB5 104 A4
1 Blackpool FY1 130 B7
Burnley BB11 127 C5
Moorhouses L38 2 F3
Moorings The
Burnley BB12 127 E7
4 Chorley PR6 43 E8
Hest Bank LA2 220 D1
Maghull L31 5 B4
Moorland Ave
Blackburn BB2 80 D7
Clitheroe BB7 189 F3
Darwen BB3 81 D2
Earby BB18 197 C1
Fulwood PR2 118 D4
Poulton-le-F FY6 153 E4
Whitworth OL12 52 C7
Moorland Cl BB9 170 F6
Moorland Cres
Clitheroe BB7 189 F2

Moorland Cres *continued*
Fulwood PR2 118 D4
Whitworth OL12 52 C7
Moorland Dr
Brierfield BB9 148 D4
Horwich BL6 32 F3
Moorland Gate PR6 43 F6
Moorland Gdns FY6 153 E4
Moorland Rd
Blackburn BB2 81 C7
Burnley BB11 127 F3
Clitheroe BB7 189 F2
Langho BB6 143 C1
Lytham St Anne's FY8 90 A7
Poulton-le-F FY6 153 F4
Moorland Rise BB4 85 C2
Moorland Sch Ltd BB7 189 E3
Moorland St OL12 52 E1
Moorland Terr OL12 52 A1
Moorland View BB9 148 E6
Moorlands PR1 117 E3
Moorlands Gr LA3 216 E3
Moorlands Terr OL13 88 A1
Moorlands The OL13 88 A8
Moorlands View BL0 68 D5
Moorside Melling LA6 241 D2
Wharles PR4 134 D3
Moorside Ave
Blackburn BB1 102 D4
Brierfield BB9 148 D4
Fulwood PR2 118 F3
Horwich BL6 32 C4
Moorside Cl LA6 241 D2
Moorside Com Prim Sch
WN8 9 E7
Moorside Cres OL13 88 A4
Moorside Dr
Clayton-le-M BB5 125 A2
Preston PR1 96 B2
Moorside La PR4 136 C4
Moorside Prim Sch LA1 215 B4
Moorside Rd Caton LA2 237 D3
Edgworth BL7 66 D1
Moorsview BL0 50 B6
Moorthorpe Cl BB3 65 A6
Moorview Cl BB10 148 E2
Moorview Ct 2 FY4 110 F7
Moorway FY6 153 F4
Moray Cl BL0 50 A4
Morecambe Bay Com Prim Sch LA4 217 B5
Morecambe Bay Nature Reserve (RSPB)* LA5 220 D5
Morecambe High Sch
LA4 217 C6
Morecambe Rd
Blackburn BB2 101 F1
Lancaster LA3,LA1 218 A2
Morecambe Rd Sch LA3 217 F3
Morecambe St E LA4 217 B6
Morecambe St W LA4 217 B6
Morecambe Sta LA4 217 A5
Moresby Ave FY3 131 B7
Moreton Dr
Poulton-le-F FY6 153 D2
Staining FY3 131 D5
Moreton Gn 2 LA3 212 F7
Moreton Pk BB7 144 E2
Moreton St BB5 104 B6
Morewood Dr LA6 240 C7
Morland Ave
Bamber Bridge PR5 77 A7
Kirkham PR4 113 F7
Morley Ave BB2 101 A1
Morley Cl LA1 218 C3
Morley Croft PR26 76 E3
Morley La PR3 202 A5
Morley Rd Blackpool FY4 130 E1
Lancaster LA1 218 C3
Southport PR9 35 E8
Morley St 1 BB12 126 D8
Morningside LA1 214 E7
Mornington Ct PR1 118 F1
Mornington Rd
Adlington PR6 31 B8
Higher Penwortham PR1 96 B5
Lytham St Anne's FY8 91 E4
Preston PR1 118 F1
Southport PR9 35 C7
Morris Cl PR25 60 A8
Morris Cres PR2 118 D2
Morris Ct PR2 118 D2
Morris Hey L39 23 D3
Morris Rd Chorley PR6 61 E1
Fulwood PR2 118 D2
Skelmersdale WN8 10 A7
Morrison St PR6 61 D2
Morse St BB10 128 D5
Morston Ave FY2 152 E1
Mort St BL6 32 B4
Mortimer Gr LA3 213 A8
Morton St 22 BB1 101 E5
Morven Gr PR8 35 E7
Moscow Mill St BB5 103 E5
Mosedale Dr BB12 127 B8
Moseley Ave BB18 196 F1
Moseley Cl BB11 128 A2
Moseley Rd BB11 128 A3
Mosley Ave BL0 50 B2
Mosley St
Barnoldswick BB18 196 B2
Blackburn BB2 101 E2
4 Leyland PR25 77 A1
Nelson BB9 148 D8
Preston PR1 97 C8
Southport PR8 35 B4
Mosman Pl BB9 170 C3
Moss Acre Rd PR1 96 E2
Moss Ave Orrell WN5 10 D3
Preston PR2 117 A2
Moss Bank Coppull PR7 42 E1
Ormskirk L39 15 D2
Moss Bank Ct L39 15 D2
Moss Bank Pl FY4 110 F8
Moss Bridge L40 26 C3
Moss Bridge La L40 26 C2
Moss Bridge Pk PR5 77 C8
Moss Cl Chorley PR6 43 E8
Haslingden BB4 68 A8
Moss Cotts L40 17 A3
Moss Delph La L39 15 C1
Moss Dr BL6 32 F3
Moss Edge Cotts FY8 111 A2
Moss Edge La
Blackpool FY4 111 A3
Lytham St Anne's FY8 111 B2
Moss End Way L33 1 D3
Moss Fold Rd BB3 81 E5
Moss Gate BB1 102 B6
Moss Gdns PR8 35 C2
Moss Gn L37 12 B4
Moss Hall La FY8 90 E7
Moss Hall Rd
Accrington BB5 104 C8
Bury BL9 33 D1
Moss Hey La PR4 56 A3
Moss House La
Great Plumpton PR4 112 C7
Much Hoole PR4 75 B2
Stake Pool PR3 202 A4
Stalmine FY6 177 D8
Moss House Rd
Blackpool FY4 111 A6
Broughton PR4 137 B2
Moss La
Appley Bridge WN6 28 E3
Bamber Bridge PR5 77 B8
Banks PR9 55 D6
Becconsall PR4 73 C1
Bickerstaffe L39 7 F2
Blackburn BB1,BB5 102 F3
Blackrod BL6 31 F2
Bretherton PR26 58 C8
Burscough L40 26 A7
Catforth PR4 135 D5
Chipping PR3 186 A1
Clayton-le-W PR25 77 D2
Coppull PR7 42 E1
Croston PR5 40 A8
Duncombe PR3 158 D2
Farington PR26 76 D5
Formby L37,L39 12 E5
Garstang PR3 181 B7
Glasson LA2 209 E1
Hambleton FY6 177 D1
Hightown L38,L23 3 C2
Holme Mills LA5 240 A8
Inskip PR4 157 B3
Kingsfold PR1 96 E1
Kirkby,Northwood L33 1 B3
Leyland PR25 77 C2
Lucas Green PR6 61 D5
Maghull L31 5 E2
Maghull,Lydiate L31 5 D5
Morecambe LA4 217 A5
New Longton PR4 75 E7
Silverdale LA5 224 F5
Skelmersdale WN8 8 F6
Southport PR9 36 C8
St Michael's on W PR3 157 B8
Walmer Bridge PR4 75 C4
Wymott PR26 58 F5
Moss La E PR4 115 A8
Moss La W PR4 114 F7
Moss Lane View WN8 8 F6
Moss Lea PR4 57 A7
Moss Nook
Burscough Bridge L40 25 E6
Ormskirk L39 15 C2
Moss Pl LA1 218 E4
Moss Rd Lancaster LA3 213 E7
Orrell WN5 10 D3
Southport PR8 35 C2
Moss Side
Barnoldswick BB18 196 C2
Formby L37 12 B4
Moss Side La
Hale Nook FR6,PR3 178 C7
Lane Heads PR3 156 E5
Mere Brow PR4 55 F4
Stalmine FY6 177 E7
Wrea Green PR4 113 A3
Moss Side Prim Sch
PR26 76 B1
Moss Side St OL12 71 E5
Moss Side Sta FY8 112 D1
Moss Side Way PR26 59 C8
Moss St
Bamber Bridge PR5 77 B8
Blackburn BB1 102 A6
7 Clitheroe BB7 166 D8
Great Harwood BB6 124 C4
Preston PR1 96 E8
Ramsbottom BL9 50 D2
Moss Terr PR6 61 E5
Moss View Maghull L31 5 F1
Ormskirk L39 15 E4
Southport PR8 21 E5
Moss Way 3 FY4 110 F7
Moss Wood Cl PR7 43 A6
Mossbank 7 BB1 102 A6
Mossbourne Rd FY6 153 C2
Mossbrook Dr PR4 116 F5
Mossdale 6 BB1 102 A6
Mossdale Ave PR2 118 D4
Mossfield Cl
Bamber Bridge PR5 77 B8
Bury BL9 33 B3
Mossfield Rd PR6 43 E8
Mossfields WN6 28 F6
Mossgate Cty Prim Sch
Heysham LA3 212 F8
Morecambe LA3 216 E1
Mossgiel Ave PR8 21 B5
Mosshill Cl L31 5 C3
Mosslands PR25 76 D1
Mosslawn Rd L32 1 A1
Mosslea Dr PR3 137 B8
Mossom La FY5 152 D7
Mossway PR4 75 F7
Mossy Lea Fold WN6 29 A3
Mossy Lea Rd WN6 28 F5
Mostyn Ave BB18 197 B1
Mostyn St BB3 81 E4
Motherwell Cres PR8 35 F3
Mottram Cl PR6 61 C5
Mottram Mews 7 BL6 32 B4
Mottram St BL6 32 B4
Moulden Brow BB2 80 B7
Moulding Cl BB2 101 B4
Mounsey Rd PR5 77 F8
Mount Ave
Lancaster LA1 218 D3
Morecambe LA4 217 F7
Rawtenstall BB4 69 F8
Mount Carmel RC High Sch
BB5 104 A4
Mount Carmel Sch L39 15 D2
Mount Cres Orrell WN5 10 F6
Over Town BB10 108 A8
Mount Gdns LA4 217 E7
Mount House Cl L37 12 B5
Mount House Rd L37 12 B5
Mount La Burnley BB10 128 F1
Over Town BB10 108 A8
Shore OL14 109 C3
Mount Pleasant
Adlington PR6 31 A8
Arnside LA5 224 C8
16 Bacup OL13 70 C8
Blackburn BB1 101 F5
Brinscall PR6 63 A8
Chatburn BB7 190 D5
Edgworth BL7 48 D5
High Bentham LA2 239 D8
Nangreaves BL9 50 F3
Nelson BB10 149 C6
7 Preston PR1 96 F8
Rawtenstall BB4 85 E2
Sabden BB7 146 A7
Slaidburn BB7 229 B7
Sollom PR4 57 A3
Whittle-le-W PR6 61 C8
Worsthorne BB10 129 A5
Mount Pleasant La LA5 221 B5
Mount Pleasant Prim Sch
BB5 124 F2
Mount Pleasant St
3 Burnley BB11 127 F5
Cornholme OL14 109 A1
3 Horwich BL6 32 D1
6 Oswaldtwistle BB5 103 E4
Mount Rd Burnley BB11 127 F4
Fleetwood FY7 199 A5
Mount St Accrington BB5 104 B4
18 Barrowford BB9 170 D3
Blackpool FY1 130 B6
Brierfield BB9 148 B5
Clayton-le-M BB5 125 A2
Fleetwood FY7 199 A4
Great Harwood BB6 124 C6
Horwich BL6 32 D2
Preston PR1 96 F7
Ramsbottom BL0 50 B6
Rawtenstall BB4 85 E2
Southport PR9 35 D7
Mount St James BB1 102 F4
Mount Terr BB4 86 A2
Mount The
Blackburn BB2 101 C6
Skelmersdale WN8 9 B8
Mount Trinity 3 BB1 101 F5
Mount Zion Ct OL14 109 A1
Mountain Ash OL12 52 B3
Mountain Ash Cl OL12 52 B3
Mountain La BB5 104 C4
Mountain Rd PR7 29 E8
Mountbatten Cl PR2 96 B7
Mountbatten Rd PR7 43 B6
Mountfield Ct WN5 10 F7
Mountside Cl OL12 52 F2
Mountside View OL12 52 D3
Mountwood WN8 18 A4
Mountwood Lo PR8 21 C5
Mowbray Ave BB2 101 F2
Mowbray Dr
Blackpool FY3 152 F1
Burton-in-K LA6 240 C7
Mowbray Pl 1 FY7 198 E4
Mowbray Rd FY7 198 E4
Mowbreck Ct PR4 114 A6
Mowbreck La PR4 114 B7
Mowbrick La LA2 220 D1
Mowgrain View 2 OL13 87 F3
Muirfield PR1 96 A6
Muirfield Cl Euxton PR7 60 D4
Fulwood PR2 117 B6
Muirfield Dr PR8 21 C4
Mulberry Ave PR1 96 A3
Mulberry Cl PR4 115 C1
Mulberry Cotts 10 LA2 211 A4
Mulberry Ct 1 BL6 32 D1
Mulberry La LA1 215 A2
Mulberry Mews
Blackpool FY2 152 F6
5 Kirkham PR4 114 B5
Mulberry St BB1 102 B5
Mulberry Wlk 3 BB1 102 B5
Mulgrave Ave PR2 117 A1
Mullion Cl PR9 54 B5
Muncaster Rd PR1 117 F2
Munro Ave WN5 10 E6
Munro Cres PR2 118 E3
Munster Ave FY2 152 D3
Murchison Gr FY5 175 E1
Murdock Ave PR2 117 D2
Murdock St BB2 101 B4
Murray Ave PR26 76 E5
Murray St Burnley BB10 148 B1
Leyland PR25 77 B1
Preston PR1 117 E1
Musbury Cres BB4 86 A1
Musbury Mews BB4 84 F1
Musbury Rd BB4 67 F7
Musbury View BB4 84 F1
Musden Ave BB4 68 A7
Museum of Lancashire*
PR1 97 B8
Museum St 19 BB1 101 E5
Myers St
Barnoldswick BB18 196 B1
Burnley BB10 128 A8
Myerscough Ave
Blackpool FY4 110 F5
Lytham St Anne's FY8 89 D8
Myerscough Coll PR3 158 D5
Myerscough Hall Dr
PR3 158 E5
Myerscough Planks
PR3 159 A2
Myerscough Smithy Rd
BB2 120 E4
Myndon St LA1 218 D3
Myra Ave LA4 217 C4
Myra Rd FY8 90 B4
Myrtle Ave Blackpool FY3 130 D5
Burnley BB11 127 D4
Cleveleys FY5 175 F5
Poulton-le-F FY6 153 E5
Myrtle Bank Rd
9 Bacup OL13 87 F3
Blackburn BB2 81 C8
Myrtle Cotts OL13 88 A2
Myrtle Dr PR4 114 C4
Myrtle Gdns BL9 33 B2
Myrtle Gr
1 Barnoldswick BB18 196 C2
Burnley BB10 128 F4
Haslingden BB4 85 A1
Morecambe LA3 216 F3
Southport PR9 35 E7
Myrtle St N BL9 33 B2
Myrtle St S 8 BL9 33 B2
Mystic Mews 8 L39 15 E5
Mythop Ave FY8 91 C4
Mythop Cl 1 FY8 91 C4
Mythop Ct FY4 131 D1
Mythop Pl PR2 116 F1
Mythop Rd
Lytham St Anne's FY8 91 C4
Weeton FY4,PR4 132 C2
Mythop Village FY4 131 F2
Mytton St BB12 126 D8
Mytton View BB7 166 D7

N

Naarian Ct BB1 101 F7
Nab La Blackburn BB2 101 D5
Oswaldtwistle BB5 103 B4
Nab Rd PR6 61 E1
Nab View BB7 144 A4
Nab Wood Dr PR7 43 A6
Nab's Head La PR5 99 E8
Nabbs Fold BL8 49 F3
Nabbs Way BL8 50 A1
Naburn Dr WN5 10 E5
Nairn Ave WN8 18 B5
Nairn Cl Blackpool FY4 111 A7
Standish WN6 29 D1
Nairne St BB11 127 D5
Nancy St BB3 82 B1
Nansen Rd
Blackburn BB2 101 B3
Fleetwood FY7 199 A3
Nantwich Ave OL12 52 F3
Napier Ave Blackpool FY4 110 B6
Tarleton PR4 56 F8
Napier Cl FY8 110 E1
Napier St
6 Accrington BB5 104 C5
Nelson BB9 148 E7
Napier Terr PR8 35 A5
Naples Rd BB3 82 C1
Naptha La PR4 76 C6
Narcissus Ave BB4 68 A8
Nares Rd BB2 101 B3
Nares St PR2 117 C1
Narrow Croft Rd L39 15 B1
Narrow La Leyland PR5 75 F2
Ormskirk L39 15 B1
Narrow Lane (Clieves Hills)
L39 14 E6
Narrow Moss La L39,L40 15 E8
Narrowgates Cotts
BB12 169 C5
Narvik Ave BB11 127 B4
Nasmyth St BL6 32 C3
Nateby Ave FY4 110 E5
Nateby Cl Longridge PR3 139 F8
Nateby Cl *continued*
Lytham St Anne's FY8 90 B7
Nateby Crossing La
PR3 181 A8
Nateby Ct 2 FY4 110 B6
Nateby Hall La PR3 203 F1
Nateby Pl PR2 116 F1
Nateby Prim Sch PR3 180 C6
National Football Mus The*
PR1 118 B2
Nave Cl BB3 82 C1
Navena Ave FY7 198 E2
Navigation Bsns Village
PR2 96 A8
Navigation Ho 6 BB1 101 F3
Navigation Way
Blackburn BB1 101 F3
1 Fleetwood FY7 199 A3
Preston PR2 96 A7
Naylor's Terr BL7 46 C5
Naylorfarm Ave WN6 19 F5
Naze Ct Freckleton PR4 93 B6
4 Newchurch BB4 86 E1
Naze La PR4 93 B6
Naze La E PR4 93 C5
Naze Lane Ind Est PR4 93 C4
Naze Rd BB4 86 E1
Naze View Ave 4 BB4 86 F2
Neales Fold PR9 54 D5
Neapsands Cl PR2 118 D5
Near Mdw PR6 78 C3
Neargates PR7 42 D3
Neath Cl
Bamber Bridge PR5 97 E3
Blackburn BB1 101 E7
Ned's La
Smallwood Hey PR3 201 A5
Stalmine FY6 177 D5
Neddy Hill LA6 240 B7
Neddy La BB7 144 A4
Nedens Gr L31 5 C3
Nedens La L31 5 C3
Needham Ave LA4 217 A3
Needham Rise LA4 217 A3
Needham Way WN8 18 B5
Needless Hall La BD23 231 E7
Nell Carrs BL0 50 E8
Nell La PR5 77 E4
Nell's La L39 5 F5
Nelson & Colne Coll
Barrowford BB9 170 D2
Colne BB8 171 A5
Colne BB8 171 D5
Nelson Ave PR25 77 B1
Nelson Cres PR2 116 D2
Nelson Ct Fleetwood FY7 198 F3
Preston PR2 95 E8
Southport PR8 34 F4
Nelson Dr PR2 116 D2
Nelson Gdns PR4 135 C8
Nelson Rd
2 Blackpool FY1 130 B2
Brierfield BB10 149 A4
Chorley PR7 43 C7
Fleetwood FY7 198 F3
Nelson Sq BB11 127 F5
Nelson St Accrington BB5 104 C5
Bacup OL13 71 C8
3 Bamber Bridge PR5 77 E8
Clitheroe BB7 166 B8
7 Colne BB8 171 D5
1 Darwen BB3 81 F2
Great Harwood BB6 124 D6
Horwich BL6 32 D3
7 Kirkham PR4 113 F5
Lancaster LA1 214 F8
Lytham St Anne's FY8 91 D3
Morecambe LA4 217 A5
Southport PR8 35 A6
Nelson Sta BB9 148 E8
Nelson Terr Church BB5 103 F6
Preston PR1 96 D8
Nelson Way PR2 95 E8
Nene Cl PR25 60 B7
Neps La BB7 231 C6
Neptune St BB11 127 F6
Neptune Way BB3 82 B6
Nesswood Ave FY4 110 E6
Neston St PR1 97 E8
Nether Beck LA6 240 A2
Nether Kellet Com Prim Sch
LA6 221 E4
Nether Kellet Rd LA6 237 B8
Nether View LA2 241 E1
Netherby St BB11 127 E4
Netherfield Cl BB12 127 D7
Netherfield Gdns 9
BB9 148 E8
Netherfield Rd BB9 148 E8
Netherheys Cl BB8 171 B5
Netherlands Rd LA4 217 C4
Netherley Rd PR7 29 E8
Netherton Ho 13 BB6 124 C5
Nethertown Cl BB7 144 B6
Netherwood Gdns BB6 143 B5
Netherwood Rd BB10 128 D7
Netherwood St BB10 148 E2
Nethway Ave FY3 130 F6
Netley Ave OL12 52 F3
Network 65 Bsns Pk
BB11 126 F4
Neverstitch Cl WN8 17 F2
Neverstitch Rd WN8 17 D2
Nevett St PR1 97 D8
Nevill St PR8 35 B7

Neville Ave FY5 175 E1
Neville Dr FY5 153 B8
Neville St PR3 140 A7
Nevy Fold Ave BL6 32 F3
New Acres Carnforth LA5 223 F2
Newburgh WN8 27 A1
New Bank Rd BB2 101 B6
New Barn BB4 68 B6
New Barn La BB4 69 A8
New Bath St BB8 171 E6
New Bonny St FY1 130 B4
New Briggs Fold BL7 47 E2
New Brown St 17 BB9 170 D1
New Brunswick St BL6 32 B3
New Bury Cl BB5 103 C3
New Century Apartments
BL0 50 C7
New Chapel La BL6 32 F2
New Chapel St BB2 101 B2
New Church Cl 14 BB5 124 F3
New Church Ho 6 FY1 130 C4
New Church Mews 5
BB10 148 B1
New Cock Yd 25 PR1 97 A7
New Court Dr BL7 47 E3
New Court Way L39 15 F5
New Cswy L37,L38 3 B8
New Cut Cl PR8 22 A8
New Cut La L39,PR8 22 D6
New Fold WN5 10 C4
New Foul La PR8 36 A4
New Garden Fields BB4 87 A7
New Garden St 1 BB2 101 E3
New Ground Ct BB10 148 C3
New Hague BB18 194 F3
New Hall Ave FY4 111 B5
New Hall Ave N FY4 111 B6
New Hall Dr PR8 36 C1
New Hall Hey Bsns Pk
BB4 85 F1
New Hall Hey Rd BB4 85 F1
New Hall La PR1 97 C8
New Hall Rd BL9 33 E4
New Hall St BB10,BB12 148 A1
New Hey La PR4 114 E5
New House La PR3 203 F3
New House St BB8 171 E5
New Inn Yd LA4 217 B6
New La
Burscough Bridge L40 25 B6
Burton-in-K LA6 240 B7
Duncombe PR3 158 F8
Eagland Hill PR3 179 D7
Great Mitton BB7 165 E6
Haskayne L39 13 E3
Middleworth Green PR1 96 E3
Newtown PR7 59 A1
Ormskirk L39 15 E2
Oswaldtwistle BB5 103 C2
Smallwood Hey PR3 201 B2
Southport PR9 54 E3
Tarleton PR4 56 D6
Thornton FY5 153 C7
New Lane Head PR26 59 A2
New Lane Pace PR9 55 B8
New Lane Sta L40 25 B7
New Line OL13 71 B8
New Line Ind Est OL13 71 A8
New Links Ave PR2 117 A6
New Longton All Saints CE
Prim Sch PR4 75 F7
New Market St
15 Blackburn BB1 101 E5
Chorley PR7 43 C8
Clitheroe BB7 166 E8
Colne BB8 171 D5
New Market The FY1 130 B1
New Meadow Cl BB1 82 A8
New Meadow La L37 3 F8
New Miles La WN6 19 F5
New Mill St
Blackburn BB1 101 F6
Eccleston PR7 41 C6
New Moss La PR6 61 C5
New Oxford St BB8 171 E6
New Palace Ct BB12 127 B7
New Park St 2 BB2 101 D5
New Pastures 4 PR5 77 C8
New Plough Yd BB6 124 D5
New Quay Rd LA1 214 B8
New Rd Adlington PR6 31 D8
Bamber Bridge PR5 97 B1
Blackpool FY8 110 B4
Burnley BB11 128 B2
Coppull PR7 42 F3
Croston PR5 40 B7
Earby BB18 197 B2
Formby L37 12 A5
Ingleton LA6 242 F4
Lancaster LA1 214 F8
Newchurch BB4 86 F2
Rufford L40 39 B3
Silverdale LA5 224 F1
Staynall FY6 177 B4
Warton LA5 223 A6
Whitworth OL12 71 B1
New Rough Hey PR2 116 F6
New Row Altham BB5 125 E6
Trawden BB8 172 C4
New Row Cotts PR3 163 D1
New Scotland Rd BB9 170 E1
New St Blackrod BL6 31 D2
Brinscall PR6 62 F8
2 Burnley BB12 126 B8
Carnforth LA5 223 D2
New St *continued*
Caton LA2 237 D3
Colne BB8 171 B3
Eccleston PR7 41 C6
Halton LA2 219 C6
Haskayne L39 14 B8
14 Haslingden BB4 85 B3
Lancaster LA1 214 F8
Mawdesley L40 40 C2
Morecambe LA4 217 A5
Nelson BB9 170 F1
Rochdale OL12 52 E2
New Summerseat House Sch
BL0 50 B2
New Taylor Fold BB10 148 F3
New Way Royal Oak L39 7 C2
Whitworth OL12 71 C1
New Wellington Cl BB2 101 C1
New Wellington Gdns
BB2 101 C1
New Wellington St BB2 101 C1
Newark Pl Fulwood PR2 117 D8
4 Preston PR2 116 E2
Newark Rd OL12 52 F3
Newark Sq OL12 52 F3
Newark St BB5 103 F5
Newarth La PR4 73 E3
Newbeck Cl BL6 32 D1
Newbigging Ave 5 BB4 86 F2
Newburgh CE Prim Sch
WN8 27 A1
Newburn Cl WN8 18 B5
Newbury Ave 3 FY4 110 D8
Newbury Cl PR2 117 C8
Newbury Gn PR2 117 C8
Newbury Rd
Lytham St Anne's FY8 90 A4
Skelmersdale WN8 18 B5
Newby Ave
Fleetwood FY7 198 D1
Poulton-le-F FY6 153 D1
Newby Back La BB7 231 A1
Newby Cl Burnley BB11 127 E2
Southport PR8 21 B3
Newby Ct L37 11 F3
Newby Dr
Clayton-le-W PR25 77 E2
Lancaster LA1 218 D3
Skelmersdale WN8 18 B5
Newby La BB7 192 B8
Newby Pl Blackpool FY4 131 B1
Fulwood PR2 118 D4
Newby Rd BB5 104 E8
Newcastle Ave
Blackpool FY3 130 D4
Cleveleys FY5 175 F4
Newcastle St BB2 101 C3
Newchurch CE Prim Sch
BB4 86 E1
Newchurch Cl BB2 101 F2
Newchurch Old Rd OL13 87 E1
Newchurch Rd
Bacup OL13 70 C8
Rawtenstall BB4 86 C2
Newcombe Rd BL0 50 B2
Newcroft LA5 223 E6
Newfield Ct FY8 89 F6
Newfield Dr
Blackburn BB1,BB2 82 A8
Nelson BB9 148 E8
Newfield Rd PR5 78 A7
Newfield Sch BB1 82 B8
Newgate Fulwood PR2 117 E4
Morecambe LA3 217 E2
Newgate Ave WN6 19 E8
Newgate La PR4 76 C8
Newgate Rd WN8 9 F7
Newhaven Dr PR3 181 D2
Newhouse Rd
Accrington BB5 125 D1
Blackpool FY4 130 F2
Newington Ave BB1 122 F3
Newlands PR7 41 C6
Newlands Ave
Blackpool FY3 130 F2
Burscough L40 25 F4
Clitheroe BB7 166 C7
Higher Penwortham PR1 96 B5
Lancaster LA1 215 B5
Rochdale OL12 52 F3
Newlands Cl
5 Blackburn BB2 80 E8
Rochdale OL12 52 F3
Newlands Rd
Lancaster LA1 215 C5
Lytham St Anne's FY8 90 C5
Morecambe LA4 217 C4
Quernmore LA1 215 E6
Newlands Way FY6 153 C1
Newlyn Ave
Blackpool FY4 110 E5
Maghull L31 5 E1
Newlyn Ct FY4 110 E5
Newlyn Dr WN8 9 D7
Newlyn Pl PR2 116 F5
Newman Gr FY5 175 E5
Newman Rd 2 FY1 130 D8
Newman St BB10 148 B1
Newmarket Ave LA1 215 B3
Newmarket St LA4 217 E7
Newport Ct PR2 116 F3
Newport St BB9 170 E1
News La WA11 8 F2
Newsham Hall La PR4 136 F3
Newsham Pl LA1 215 A5
Newsham Rd LA1 215 A5
Newsham St 1 PR2 117 D1
Newsome St PR25 77 A1
Newstead Dr WN8 18 B5
Newstet Rd L33 1 C2
Newthorn BB5 104 A1
Newton Ave
Poulton-le-F FY6 153 C2
Preston PR1 98 A8
Newton Bluecoat CE Prim
Sch PR4 115 A2
Newton Cl Freckleton PR4 93 C7
Leyland PR26 59 B8
Newton Ct PR2 117 B1
Newton Dr
Accrington BB5 104 D3
Blackpool FY3 130 E5
Holme Chapel BB10 108 A7
Ramsbottom BL8 50 A1
Skelmersdale WN8 18 B5
Newton Dr E FY3 131 B7
Newton Gr FY5 153 D7
Newton Hall Holiday Ctr
FY3 131 C6
Newton Ho PR1 97 A8
Newton Pl FY3 131 A7
Newton Rd
Lytham St Anne's FY8 90 A7
Preston PR2 117 B2
Newton St Blackburn BB1 102 B5
Burnley BB12 127 C7
Clitheroe BB7 166 D7
Darwen BB3 82 B2
Oswaldtwistle BB5 103 C5
2 Preston PR1 97 B8
Southport PR9 36 A7
Newton Terr LA1 218 E3
Newtown BB18 196 B2
Newtown St BB8 171 E5
Nib La PR1 76 E8
Nichol St PR7 61 C1
Nicholas St
Brierfield BB10 148 E3
Burnley BB11 128 A5
Colne BB8 171 C4
Darwen BB3 81 F1
Nicholl Ct FY8 89 D6
Nicholl St 1 BB10 128 A8
Nicholson Cres LA4 217 D5
Nick Hilton's La PR6 44 D3
Nickey La BB2 121 F2
Nickleton Brow PR6 44 C2
Nickson Weind PR3 181 C7
Nicksons La FY6 200 B4
Nicola Cl OL13 88 A7
Nightfield La BB2 120 F6
Nightingale Cl
Blackburn BB1 102 B1
Whalley BB7 144 A7
Nightingale Cres 4
BB11 127 C5
Nightingale Dr FY6 153 B2
Nightingale Rd BL6 31 C3
Nightingale St PR6 31 A8
Nile Cl PR2 95 E8
Nile St 5 Lancaster LA1 214 F8
12 Nelson BB9 170 D1
Preston PR1 97 A7
Nimes St PR1 97 D8
Nine Elms PR2 117 C6
Nineteen Acre La LA5 225 F4
Nineveh St 12 BB8 171 E5
Nipe La WN8 9 B5
Nithside FY4 131 C1
Niton Cl BB4 85 C1
Nixon La PR26 59 A8
Nixon's La PR8 21 E7
Nixons Ct PR26 58 F8
Nixons La WN8 9 D7
Noble St 13 Darwen BB3 65 A8
Great Harwood BB6 124 C4
Rishton BB1 124 B1
Noblett Ct 9 FY7 198 F2
Noblett St BB1 101 F5
Noel Gate L39 15 B1
Noel Jones Ct FY8 89 E7
Noel Rd LA1 218 C3
Noel Sq PR2 118 E1
Noels Villa PR3 138 E4
Noggarth Rd BB12 169 F2
Nolan St PR8 35 C5
Nook Cotts PR3 180 C6
Nook Cres PR2 139 C1
Nook Croft BB18 197 C2
Nook Farm Ave OL12 52 F3
Nook Field PR3 138 D6
Nook Glade PR2 139 C1
Nook La
Bamber Bridge PR5 77 D6
Blackburn BB2 100 F1
Churchtown PR3 181 A3
Mawdesley L40 40 E5
Oswaldtwistle BB5 103 B2
Nook Terr Blackburn BB2 101 A1
1 Rochdale OL12 52 F3
Nook The
Appley Bridge WN6 19 E7
Bolton-le-S LA5 221 A4
Staining FY3 131 D5
Nookdales Cotts LA6 242 F1
Nookfield PR26 76 A1
Nookfield Cl FY8 91 A4
Nooklands PR2 117 E4
Noon Sun St OL12 52 F1
Noor St PR1 118 A1
Nora St BB9 170 D3
Norbreck Cl BB2 81 F8
Norbreck Ct FY5 152 C6
Norbreck Dr PR2 116 E1
Norbreck Prim Sch FY5 152 D8
Norbreck Rd FY5 152 C7
Norburn Cres L37 11 F2
Norbury Cl PR9 54 C5
Norcliffe Rd FY2 152 C5
Norcote Lodge L37 11 E4
Norcross Brow PR6 63 B8
Norcross La FY5 153 A7
Norcross Pl PR2 116 F1
Norden Ct
Great Harwood BB6 124 E5
1 Rishton BB1 124 B1
Norden High Sch BB1 124 A2
Norden View BB1 124 A2
Norfield L39 15 F5
Norfolk Ave
Blackpool FY2 152 B3
Burnley BB12 127 B7
Cleveleys FY5 175 E3
Morecambe LA3 216 E2
Padiham BB12 126 D6
Norfolk Cl
7 Clayton-le-M BB5 124 F3
Leyland PR25 59 E7
Norfolk Gr
Accrington BB5 104 A7
Southport PR8 34 F1
Norfolk Rd
Bamber Bridge PR5 97 D4
Blackpool FY3 131 A2
Longshaw WN5 10 E1
Lytham St Anne's FY8 91 C5
Preston PR1 118 A1
Southport PR8 34 F1
Norfolk St
Accrington BB5 104 D7
Blackburn BB2 101 C2
Colne BB8 171 E5
Darwen BB3 82 B1
Lancaster LA1 218 D2
Nelson BB9 170 D1
Rishton BB1 124 A1
Norham Cl BB12 127 E7
Norkeed Rd FY5 152 C7
Norland Dr LA3 212 F8
Norman Cl FY5 175 F1
Norman Rd BB5 103 C5
Norman St
Blackburn BB2 101 C3
Burnley BB10 128 A7
Bury BL9 33 B4
Normandie Ave FY2 152 D3
Normandy Rd PR4 137 B3
Normanhurst L39 16 A4
Normington Cl L31 5 C4
Normoss Ave FY3 131 A7
Normoss Rd FY3 131 C7
Norris House Dr L39 6 C8
Norris St 3 Chorley PR7 43 C6
Darwen BB3 82 B1
Fulwood PR2 117 D3
Preston PR1 117 E2
Norris Way L37 12 B3
Norse Cotts PR26 57 E6
North Albert St 12 FY7 199 B5
North Albion St FY7 199 A4
North Ave
Barnoldswick BB18 196 B2
Blackpool FY3 130 D7
Ramsbottom BL8 49 F1
North Bank Ave BB1 122 E1
North Church St FY7 199 B5
North Cliff St 6 PR1 96 E6
North Cliffe Sch BB6 124 B6
North Clifton St 7 FY8 91 B3
North Cres FY8 89 E6
North Croft PR3 181 C8
North Ct Blackpool FY5 152 E8
Cleveleys FY5 175 D5
North Dr
Appley Bridge WN6 28 C2
Blackpool FY5 152 D6
Cleveleys FY5 175 E2
Inskip PR4 157 C1
Kirkham PR4 113 F6
Lancaster LA1 211 B8
North Dunes L38 2 F4
North East Ave PR6 63 A8
North East Dr LA1 211 B8
North End Football Gd
(Preston North End FC)
PR1 118 B2
North End La L38 3 A6
North Gr 1 PR5 77 C8
North Highfield PR2 118 E6
North Ho 10 PR8 35 B7
North Houses La FY8 111 D1
North Leach Dr PR8 21 A5
North Meade L31 5 C2
North Meadowside PR4 75 A6
North Mersey Bsns Ctr
L33 1 D4
North Moor La L39 23 E2
North Moss La L37 12 D7
North Nook La PR3 183 E3
North Par 7 BB18 196 B3
North Park Ave BB9 170 C1
North Park Dr FY3 130 F5
North Perimeter Rd L33 1 D4
North Prom FY8 89 D7
North Quarry Bsns Pk
WN6 28 D2
North Rd Blackburn BB1 102 C3
Bretherton PR26 58 B7
Carnforth LA5 223 E2
Lancaster LA1 214 F8
Preston PR1 117 F1
Rawtenstall BB4 86 C2
Southport PR9 54 C4
North Ribble St 7 PR5 97 C6
North Road Prim Sch
LA5 223 D1
North Spine LA1 211 B8
North Sq Blackpool FY3 130 D6
Cleveleys FY5 175 D5
North St
Barnoldswick BB18 196 B1
Brierfield BB10 148 F3
Burnley BB10 148 A1
Chorley PR7 61 D2
2 Clitheroe BB7 189 F1
Colne BB8 171 E6
Fleetwood FY7 199 B5
Hapton BB12 126 C5
Haslingden BB4 85 C1
Morecambe LA4 217 B5
14 Nelson BB9 170 D1
Newchurch BB4 86 E1
Padiham BB12 146 C1
Preston PR1 96 F8
Ramsbottom BL0 68 C2
Rawtenstall BB4 86 A2
Southport PR9 35 C8
Water BB4 87 A8
Whitworth OL12 71 C1
North Syke Ave PR2 116 C1
North Union View PR5 76 F8
North Vale PR6 43 F1
North Valley Rd BB8 171 D5
North Valley Ret Pk
BB8 171 D5
North View Kirkham PR4 113 F5
Ramsbottom BL0 50 B2
Ramsbottom,Strongstry BL0 68 C2
Rawtenstall BB4 86 A8
Whitworth OL12 71 D1
North View Cl PR3 156 C5
North Warton St FY8 91 C3
North West Dr LA1 211 A8
Northall PR4 74 E2
Northam Cl PR9 54 A5
Northbrook Gdns PR25 76 E1
Northbrook Prim Sch
PR25 76 F1
Northbrook Rd PR25 76 F1
Northcliffe BB6 124 B6
Northcote Rd
Langho BB6 143 C3
Preston PR1 96 D7
Northcote St Darwen BB3 65 B6
4 Haslingden BB4 85 B2
8 Leyland PR25 77 A1
Northdene WN8 27 B2
Northenden Rd PR7 42 E1
Northern Ave PR4 74 E2
Northern Prim Sch OL13 87 F6
Northern Terr LA5 224 F5
Northfield
Skelmersdale WN8 18 B4
Southport PR9 53 C1
Northfield Ave FY1 130 B8
Northfield Cl L33 1 A4
Northfield Rd
Blackburn BB1 101 E7
Rising Bridge BB5 85 A8
Northfleet Ave FY7 198 E2
Northfold Com Prim Sch
FY5 175 E4
Northgate Blackburn BB2 101 E5
Blackpool FY2 152 C4
Goosnargh PR3 138 D6
Leyland PR25 77 B2
Lytham St Anne's FY8 89 D6
Morecambe LA3 217 E2
Whitworth OL12 52 C7
Northgate Cl BL6 32 C1
Northgate Dr PR6 61 E2
Northlands Fulwood PR2 117 E6
Leyland PR26 59 C7
Northleach Ave 2 PR1 96 F2
Northside PR7 60 C3
Northumberland Ave
Blackpool FY2 152 B1
Cleveleys FY5 175 F5
Northumberland Cl BB3 65 C6
Northumberland St
2 Chorley PR7 43 D7
Morecambe LA4 217 A5
Northway Broughton PR3 137 C3
Fleetwood FY7 198 D1
Fulwood PR2 117 D7
Maghull L31,L39 5 E4
Ormskirk L39 15 A1
Skelmersdale WN8 18 B2
Northway Prim Sch L31 5 E3
Northways WN6 29 D2
Northwood Cl
Burnley BB12 127 D7
Lytham St Anne's FY8 90 E4
Northwood Way FY6 153 D2
Norton Ave LA3 216 D3
Norton Ct FY8 89 F4
Norton Dr LA3 216 E2
Norton Gr LA3 216 D2
Norton Pl LA3 216 D2
Norton Rd Garstang PR3 204 C2
Morecambe LA3 216 D2
Rochdale OL12 52 F3
Norton St 1 BB12 126 C4
Norton Vale FY5 176 D2
Norway Ho 11 BB8 171 D5
Norwich Pl
Blackpool FY2 152 D5
33 Preston PR1 97 A7
Norwich St BB1 101 F7
Norwood Ave
Becconsall PR4 73 F2
Blackburn BB2 101 E2

Norwood Ave *continued*
Blackpool FY3 .... 130 E8
Southport PR9 .... 35 E7
Norwood Cl PR6 .... 31 A8
Norwood Cres PR9 .... 35 E7
Norwood Ct 13 LA1 .... 215 A8
Norwood Cty Prim Sch
PR9 .... 35 E7
Norwood Dr LA4 .... 217 F3
Norwood Gdns PR9 .... 35 F7
Norwood Rd
Lytham St Anne's FY8 .... 89 C8
Southport PR8,PR9 .... 35 F6
Notre Dame Gdns BB1 .... 102 A6
Nottingham Rd PR1 .... 118 A1
Nottingham St BB1 .... 102 A4
Novak Pl 6 LA4 .... 217 F4
Nowell Gr BB12 .... 145 D2
Nowell St 17 BB6 .... 124 C5
Noyna Ave BB8 .... 194 E1
Noyna Rd BB8 .... 194 E1
Noyna St BB8 .... 171 E6
Noyna View BB8 .... 171 E7
Nun's St LA1 .... 215 A8
Nurseries The Formby L37 .... 12 A2
Hesketh Bank PR4 .... 73 E3
Nursery Ave L39 .... 16 A6
Nursery Cl Coppull PR7 .... 42 E4
Leyland PR25 .... 59 F8
Nursery Dr Becconsall PR4 .... 73 F1
Formby L37 .... 11 F2
Nursery La PR4 .... 75 E8
Nursery Nook BB3 .... 82 D5
Nursery Rd L31 .... 5 C4
Nuthall Rd PR8 .... 35 F3
Nuttall Ave
Great Harwood BB6 .... 124 C4
Horwich BL6 .... 32 A3
Nuttall Cl BL0 .... 50 C5
Nuttall Hall Cotts BL0 .... 50 D5
Nuttall Hall Rd BL0 .... 50 D5
Nuttall La BL0 .... 50 C4
Nuttall Rd Blackpool FY1 .... 130 D2
Ramsbottom BL0 .... 50 D4
Nuttall St Accrington BB5 .... 104 C5
Bacup OL13 .... 88 B3
Blackburn BB2 .... 101 D1
Blackburn,Ewood BB2 .... 81 D8
7 Burnley BB11 .... 128 B4
Bury BL9 .... 33 A1
Rawtenstall BB4 .... 86 B3
Nuttall St Mews 3 BB5 .... 104 C5
Nutter Cres BB12 .... 146 F5
Nutter Rd Accrington BB5 .... 104 C7
Cleveleys FY5 .... 175 D3
2 Preston PR1 .... 96 E7

O

O'Hagan Ct BB9 .... 148 B6
Oak Ave Blackpool FY4 .... 110 D8
Euxton PR7 .... 60 D3
Galgate LA2 .... 210 F4
Higher Penwortham PR1 .... 96 B3
9 Horwich BL6 .... 32 E1
Kirkham PR4 .... 114 B4
Longridge PR3 .... 140 A7
Morecambe LA4 .... 217 F6
Ormskirk L39 .... 15 D4
Ramsbottom BL0 .... 50 A2
Rising Bridge BB5 .... 85 A8
Thornton FY5 .... 153 C8
Oak Bank Accrington BB5 .... 125 D2
Gregson Lane PR5 .... 98 E1
Oak Cl Barrow BB7 .... 166 D1
Millgate OL12 .... 71 D4
Rishton BB1 .... 103 B8
Oak Cres WN8 .... 17 D1
Oak Croft PR6 .... 78 B2
Oak Dr Burscough L40 .... 25 F3
Chorley PR6 .... 61 C3
Freckleton PR4 .... 93 A5
Halton LA2 .... 219 D7
Oak Gates BL7 .... 47 E1
Oak Gn L39 .... 15 F5
Oak Gr Darwen BB3 .... 82 B2
Garstang PR3 .... 181 C7
New Longton PR4 .... 76 A6
Oak Hill Cl BB5 .... 104 C4
Oak La Accrington BB5 .... 104 D5
Newton-w-S PR4 .... 114 F2
Oak Rd PR3 .... 181 B8
Oak Ridge BB7 .... 189 D7
Oak St Accrington BB5 .... 104 C5
Bacup OL13 .... 88 A3
Blackburn BB1 .... 101 F7
Brierfield BB9 .... 148 B6
Burnley BB12 .... 127 C6
Clayton-le-M BB5 .... 124 F1
Clow Bridge BB11 .... 106 B4
Colne BB8 .... 171 F6
Fleetwood FY7 .... 199 A4
Great Harwood BB6 .... 124 C6
Millgate OL12 .... 71 D5
2 Nelson BB9 .... 170 E1
Oswaldtwistle BB5 .... 103 D3
Preston PR1 .... 97 A7
Ramsbottom BL0 .... 50 B5
Southport PR8 .... 35 E6
Oak Terr BB18 .... 196 C3
Oak Tree Ct WN8 .... 18 D3
Oak Tree Dr PR4 .... 113 E4
Oak View Leyland PR25 .... 76 E2
Millgate OL12 .... 71 D2
Oakdene Ave BB5 .... 125 E1
Oaken Bank BB10 .... 148 E3
Oaken Cl OL13 .... 88 B3
Oakenclough Cotts PR3 .... 226 C2
Oakenclough Rd
Bacup OL13 .... 88 B3
Bleasdale PR3 .... 183 F4
Oakeneaves Ave BB11 .... 127 D2
Oakengate PR2 .... 118 C7
Oakengates WN6 .... 29 F1
Oakenhead Cl PR3 .... 160 D7
Oakenhead St PR1 .... 118 E1
Oakenhead Wood Old Rd
BB4 .... 85 E3
Oakenhurst Rd BB2 .... 101 D4
Oakenshaw Ave OL12 .... 52 C6
Oakenshaw View OL12 .... 52 C6
Oakfield Fulwood PR2 .... 117 F7
Preston PR2 .... 117 B1
Oakfield Ave
Barnoldswick BB18 .... 196 A3
Clayton-le-M BB5 .... 124 E3
Huncoat BB5 .... 125 E1
Oakfield Cl BL6 .... 32 F2
Oakfield Cres BB5 .... 103 F4
Oakfield Dr Formby L37 .... 11 D4
Leyland PR26 .... 59 B8
Oakfield House Sch
PR4 .... 115 C5
Oakfield Rd
Blackburn BB2 .... 81 D7
Hightown L38 .... 2 F2
Oakfields L39 .... 16 A5
Oakford Cl PR9 .... 55 B5
Oakgate Cl PR4 .... 56 F5
Oakgrove FY4 .... 110 D6
Oakham Ct 12 PR1 .... 97 A7
Oakhill Cl L31 .... 5 D2
Oakhill Coll BB7 .... 144 D6
Oakhill Cottage La L31 .... 5 D4
Oakhill Dr L31 .... 5 D4
Oakhill Rd L31 .... 5 D3
Oakhurst Ave BB5 .... 125 E1
Oakland Ave FY5 .... 152 D6
Oakland Glen PR5 .... 97 A3
Oakland St
4 Bamber Bridge PR5 .... 97 E1
Nelson BB9 .... 148 E8
Oaklands Ave
Barrowford BB9 .... 170 D3
Tarleton PR4 .... 57 A7
Oaklands Ct LA1 .... 214 C5
Oaklands Dr
Higher Penwortham PR1 .... 96 A4
Rawtenstall BB4 .... 85 E2
Oaklands Gr PR2 .... 116 F1
Oaklands Rd BL0 .... 68 D2
Oaklands Terr BB1 .... 101 F7
Oaklea WN6 .... 29 A2
Oakleaf Cl PR3 .... 138 C6
Oakleaf Ct FY5 .... 175 D4
Oakleaf Way FY4 .... 131 D1
Oaklee Gr L33 .... 1 A4
Oakleigh WN8 .... 9 D2
Oakleigh Terr 8 OL14 .... 109 B1
Oakley Rd
Morecambe LA3 .... 216 D2
Rawtenstall BB4 .... 85 F2
Oakley St BB4 .... 85 E2
Oakmere PR6 .... 78 C3
Oakmere Ave PR6 .... 79 D2
Oakmere Cl BB2 .... 81 D6
Oakmoor Ave FY2 .... 152 E4
Oakridge Cl PR2 .... 117 F7
Oaks Bar BB1 .... 122 C8
Oaks Brow BB1 .... 122 C7
Oaks The
Bamber Bridge PR5 .... 97 B3
Chorley PR7 .... 43 B4
Leyland PR26 .... 59 A7
Poulton-le-F FY6 .... 153 D4
Southport PR8 .... 34 F6
St Michael's on W PR3 .... 157 C7
Oaksfield BB3 .... 81 E5
Oakshaw Dr OL12 .... 52 A1
Oakshott Pl PR5 .... 78 B7
Oaktree Ave
Clayton-le-W PR25 .... 77 D4
Fulwood PR2 .... 117 A4
Oaktree Cl PR2 .... 117 A4
Oakville Rd LA3 .... 212 E5
Oakway PR3 .... 140 A8
Oakwood WN8 .... 18 D3
Oakwood Ave
Bamber Bridge PR5 .... 97 C4
Blackburn BB1 .... 123 B1
Lytham St Anne's FY8 .... 90 E4
Shevington WN6 .... 19 F5
Southport PR8 .... 21 D6
Oakwood Cl
Blackpool FY4 .... 110 F4
Brierfield BB10 .... 148 D3
Darwen BB3 .... 81 E5
Thornton FY5 .... 176 D2
Oakwood Dr
Fulwood PR2 .... 117 D8
Southport PR8 .... 21 E5
Oakwood Gdns LA1 .... 215 A2
Oakwood Gr LA5 .... 220 F2
Oakwood Rd
Accrington BB5 .... 104 D3
Chorley PR7 .... 43 B6
Coppull PR7 .... 42 F2
Oakwood View PR7 .... 43 B4
Oakworth Ave PR2 .... 118 F5
Oasis Cl L40 .... 39 B3
Oasis Wildlife Ctr* LA7 .... 225 F8
Oat St BB12 .... 126 D7
Oban Cres PR1 .... 118 D3
Oban Ct PR2 .... 139 D1
Oban Dr BB1 .... 102 C3
Oban Pl FY2 .... 152 E6
Oban St BB10 .... 128 C8
Observatory Rd BB2 .... 102 A2
Occupation La
Singleton FY6 .... 154 D4
Stalmine FY6 .... 177 C7
Ocean Bvd FY4 .... 110 A7
Ocean Ct FY6 .... 199 D5
Ocean Way FY5 .... 175 C3
Odell Way PR5 .... 97 E3
Off Botanic Rd PR9 .... 54 A1
Off Mount Pleasant St 7
BB5 .... 103 E4
Offerton St BL6 .... 32 A3
Ogden Cl BB4 .... 68 A7
Ogden Dr BB4 .... 68 A7
Old Acre L38 .... 2 F3
Old Back La BB7 .... 144 F7
Old Bank La
Blackburn BB1,BB2 .... 102 B2
Blackburn BB2 .... 102 A2
Old Bank St 4 BB2 .... 101 E4
Old Boundary Way L39 .... 15 F6
Old Bridge La FY6 .... 154 B7
Old Bridge Way PR6 .... 61 D1
Old Buckley La PR3 .... 141 D7
Old Carr Mill St BB4 .... 85 B5
Old Chapel The BB1 .... 124 B1
Old Clitheroe Rd PR3 .... 163 E3
Old Cock Yd PR1 .... 97 A7
Old Croft PR2 .... 117 D8
Old Dawber's La PR7 .... 60 B1
Old Engine Ho The 12
BL0 .... 50 C6
Old Engine La
Ramsbottom BL0 .... 50 D6
Skelmersdale WN8 .... 17 C2
Old Farmside BB2 .... 81 D7
Old Forge FY8 .... 90 D7
Old Gates Dr BB2 .... 80 F8
Old Gn BL8 .... 49 F1
Old Greaves Town La
PR2 .... 116 E1
Old Greenwood La BL6 .... 32 D1
Old Ground St 8 BL0 .... 50 C6
Old Hall Bsns Pk PR9 .... 36 A5
Old Hall Cl
Bamber Bridge PR5 .... 77 E8
7 Morecambe LA4 .... 217 F4
Roughlee BB9 .... 170 B5
Old Hall Dr
Bamber Bridge PR5 .... 77 E8
Huncoat BB5 .... 125 F1
Old Hall La
Charnock Green PR7 .... 42 B6
Pleasington BB2 .... 100 C2
Old Hall Pk PR3 .... 137 E3
Old Hall Sq BB10 .... 129 A5
Old Hall St BB10 .... 128 A8
Old Hey Croft 5 PR1 .... 96 D2
Old Hive PR3 .... 185 D4
Old House La FY4 .... 111 D7
Old Kiln OL13 .... 70 D8
Old La Bispham Green L40 .... 27 D8
Earby BB18 .... 197 B2
Formby L37 .... 11 F6
Haskayne L39 .... 13 E3
Horwich BL6 .... 32 F2
Kelbrook BB18 .... 194 F4
Maghull L31 .... 5 E4
Salterforth BB18 .... 194 B5
Shawforth OL12,OL13 .... 71 E6
Old Lancaster La PR2 .... 117 D1
Old Lancaster Rd PR3 .... 181 B2
Old Langho Rd BB6 .... 143 C5
Old Laund St BB12 .... 147 E8
Old Links Cl PR9 .... 36 B8
Old Lodge La PR3 .... 159 A8
Old Lord's Cres BL6 .... 32 B5
Old Lostock La PR5 .... 77 E7
Old Mains La FY6 .... 153 F6
Old Market Ct LA4 .... 217 B6
Old Meadow Ct 3 FY3 .... 130 E3
Old Meadow La 2 FY3 .... 130 E3
Old Meadows Rd OL13 .... 88 A5
Old Mill Ct PR4 .... 74 F5
Old Mill Dr BB8 .... 171 F4
Old Mill Hill L39 .... 15 D3
Old Mill La Formby L37 .... 11 F4
Hill Dale L40 .... 27 F6
Old Mill St BB1 .... 101 F6
Old Mill Terr PR6 .... 61 E1
Old Mill The PR5 .... 97 F2
Old Millstones PR1 .... 96 D7
Old Moor Rd LA2 .... 238 F8
Old Moss La L39 .... 13 C5
Old Nab Rd BB6 .... 123 E8
Old Oak Gdns PR5 .... 97 A2
Old Oliver La BD24 .... 236 C6
Old Orch PR2 .... 117 D5
Old Park La PR9 .... 36 A8
Old Parsonage La BB12 .... 126 B8
Old Penny Gdns LA4 .... 217 E4
Old Pepper La WN6 .... 29 B2
Old Pope La PR4 .... 76 B8
Old Prescot Cl L31 .... 6 C2
Old Quarry La BL7 .... 47 F1
Old Raike BD23 .... 236 C4
Old Rake BL6 .... 32 E5
Old Rd BD23 .... 197 C6
Old Rectory Gn L39 .... 6 A7
Old Rectory The LA2 .... 206 C5
Old Roman Rd BB12,BB7 .... 145 A3
Old Rough La L33 .... 1 A2
Old Row Barrow BB7 .... 166 D1
Kirkham PR4 .... 114 B4
4 Rawtenstall BB4 .... 85 E2
Old Sawmill The BD24 .... 236 E7
Old Sch Mews 8 BB4 .... 85 B3
Old School Cl PR26 .... 59 A8
Old School Dr PR4 .... 75 B8
Old School Ho The
Blackburn BB1 .... 82 D8
Higher Walton PR5 .... 98 B3
Old School La
Adlington PR7 .... 30 E5
Bamber Bridge PR5 .... 77 C6
Euxton PR7 .... 60 D3
Tockholes BB3 .... 80 F2
Old School Mews 12
OL13 .... 70 C8
Old School Row 3
BB12 .... 127 B6
Old School The LA2 .... 219 C6
Old St BB4 .... 86 F1
Old Station Cl PR2 .... 139 D1
Old Station Ct 8 BB7 .... 166 E8
Old Stone Trough La
BB18 .... 195 A5
Old Swan Cl BL7 .... 47 E2
Old Tom's La FY6 .... 177 E8
Old Town Cl WN8 .... 8 D8
Old Town Ct L37 .... 11 E4
Old Town Hall Mews
LA4 .... 217 B6
Old Town La L37 .... 11 E4
Old Town Way WN8 .... 8 D8
Old Trafford Cvn Pk
LA3 .... 212 F4
Old Trafford Pk LA3 .... 213 A4
Old Tram Rd
Bamber Bridge PR5 .... 77 F7
Preston PR1,PR5 .... 97 A4
Old Vicarage PR1 .... 97 A8
Old Vicarage Ct FY8 .... 89 F5
Old Vicarage Rd BL6 .... 32 F3
Old Will's La BL6 .... 32 B6
Old Worden Ave PR7 .... 60 E7
Oldbury Pl FY5 .... 152 F8
Olde Stoneheath Ct PR6 .... 44 B4
Oldfield 7 Kingsfold PR1 .... 96 D2
Much Hoole PR4 .... 74 F4
Oldfield Ave
Blackpool FY2 .... 152 C4
Darwen BB3 .... 81 E3
Oldfield Carr La FY6 .... 153 E1
Oldfield Cl FY6 .... 153 E1
Oldfield Cres FY6 .... 153 E3
Oldfield Rd PR5 .... 78 A7
Oldham St Burnley BB11 .... 127 F4
Morecambe LA4 .... 217 B6
Olivant St BB12 .... 127 C7
Olive Bank BB6 .... 143 D1
Olive Cl PR6 .... 61 C5
Olive Gr Blackpool FY3 .... 130 E5
Skelmersdale WN8 .... 17 E1
Southport PR8 .... 35 E7
Warton PR4 .... 92 D6
Olive La BB3 .... 82 B2
Olive Rd LA1 .... 218 D2
Olive St OL13 .... 70 E8
Olive Terr BB4 .... 85 F5
Oliver Ct FY6 .... 199 E5
Oliver Pl LA5 .... 223 E2
Oliver St 10 OL13 .... 70 C8
Oliver's Pl PR2 .... 118 B8
Olivers Pl PR2 .... 118 A8
Oliverson's CE Prim Sch
PR3 .... 138 D6
Ollerton La PR6 .... 79 E4
Ollerton La End PR6 .... 79 E3
Ollerton Rd FY8 .... 90 D5
Ollerton St PR6 .... 44 A1
Ollerton Terr PR6 .... 79 E3
Olympia St BB10 .... 128 C5
Olympic Way FY4 .... 111 C8
Omerod St BB4 .... 87 A8
Omrod Pl 1 FY1 .... 130 B2
Onchan Dr OL13 .... 88 B1
Onchan Rd BB2 .... 101 E1
One Ash Cl OL12 .... 52 F2
Onslow Cres PR8 .... 35 A2
Onslow Rd FY3 .... 130 F7
Ontario Cl BB2 .... 101 A8
Oozebooth Terr BB1 .... 101 E7
Oozehead La BB2 .... 101 B5
Opal Cl 6 FY5 .... 152 F7
Opal St BB1 .... 122 F2
Openshaw Dr BB1 .... 101 E8
Openshaw St BL9 .... 33 A1
Oporto Cl BB11 .... 127 E5
Oram Rd PR5 .... 78 F8
Oram St BL9 .... 33 A4
Orange St BB5 .... 104 B8
Orchard Ave
Blackpool FY4 .... 110 C6
Bolton-le-S LA5 .... 221 A6
New Longton PR4 .... 76 A7
Poulton-le-F FY6 .... 153 E1
Orchard Bridge 6 BB11 .... 127 F6
Orchard Cl Becconsall PR4 .... 73 F3
Blackburn BB2 .... 81 D6
Euxton PR7 .... 60 D3
Freckleton PR4 .... 93 A6
Fulwood PR2 .... 117 A5
Silverdale LA5 .... 224 B2
Slyne LA2 .... 218 D8
Thornton FY5 .... 176 B4
Wrea Green PR4 .... 113 B3
Orchard Croft 2 PR5 .... 77 A8
Orchard Ct Fulwood PR2 .... 117 D5
Maghull L31 .... 5 F1
Orchard Dr
Fleetwood FY7 .... 198 E1
Lucas Green PR6 .... 61 C5
Oswaldtwistle BB5 .... 103 F5
Orchard End PR3 .... 156 C5
Orchard Grange PR1 .... 96 A5
Orchard La
Lancaster LA1 .... 214 D7
Longton PR4 .... 74 F8
Southport PR8 .... 21 D4
Orchard Lo L39 .... 15 F6
Orchard Mill Dr PR26 .... 58 B2
Orchard Pl PR4 .... 74 E3
Orchard Rd FY8 .... 89 E6
Orchard St
5 Barnoldswick BB18 .... 196 B2
Great Harwood BB6 .... 124 C4
1 Leyland PR25 .... 77 B1
26 Preston PR1 .... 96 F8
Orchard The
Burnley BB11 .... 127 C4
Clitheroe BB7 .... 189 E2
Croston PR26 .... 58 C3
Kirkham PR4 .... 114 E6
Little Eccleston PR3 .... 156 A5
Ormskirk L39 .... 15 D5
Warton PR4 .... 92 E6
Woodplumpton PR4 .... 136 E1
Wray LA2 .... 238 D6
Orchard View L39 .... 15 D1
Orchard Wlk
Grimsargh PR2 .... 139 C2
Ramsbottom BL8 .... 49 F1
Orchards The
Barnoldswick BB18 .... 196 C3
Carleton FY6 .... 153 B5
Orrell WN5 .... 10 E5
Overton LA3 .... 209 D8
Southport PR8 .... 21 D4
Orchid Cl WN8 .... 10 B6
Orchid Way OL12 .... 52 D3
Ord Ave FY4 .... 130 F1
Ord Rd PR2 .... 117 C2
Orders La PR4 .... 114 A4
Ordnance St BB1 .... 102 A5
Oregon Ave FY3 .... 130 E8
Oriole Cl 9 BB1 .... 101 F6
Orion Bldgs 1 FY5 .... 175 D2
Orkney Cl BB1 .... 102 D3
Orkney Rd 1 FY1 .... 130 C2
Orme Ho L39 .... 16 A5
Orme St 1 FY1 .... 130 C3
Ormerod Bldgs 1 OL13 .... 70 D8
Ormerod Rd BB10,BB11 .... 128 B7
Ormerod St
Accrington BB5 .... 104 B5
Burnley BB11 .... 128 A5
Colne BB8 .... 171 C4
Haslingden BB4,BB5 .... 85 B7
5 Nelson BB9 .... 148 F8
Rawtenstall BB4 .... 86 A2
Thornton FY5 .... 176 B4
Worsthorne BB10 .... 129 A5
Ormerod Terr
Barrow BB6 .... 144 D8
Foulridge BB8 .... 194 E1
Ormond Ave
Blackpool FY1 .... 130 B8
Westhead L40 .... 16 E4
Ormond St BL9 .... 33 A3
Ormonde Cres L33 .... 1 A2
Ormont Ave FY5 .... 175 E2
Ormrod St BL9 .... 33 A2
Ormrods The BL9 .... 33 F5
Orms Way L37 .... 11 E3
Ormsby Cl WN6 .... 29 E2
Ormskirk & District General
Hospl L39 .... 16 A4
Ormskirk Asmall Prim Sch
L39 .... 15 D6
Ormskirk Bsns Pk L39 .... 15 F6
Ormskirk CE Prim Sch
L39 .... 16 A6
Ormskirk Coll L39 .... 15 E5
Ormskirk Lathom Park CE
Prim Sch L40 .... 17 A8
Ormskirk Old Rd L39 .... 7 F7
Ormskirk Rd
Bickerstaffe L39 .... 7 E7
Preston PR1 .... 97 A8
Rainford Junction WA11 .... 8 D1
Skelmersdale,Chapel House
WN8 .... 17 C1
Skelmersdale,Tanhouse WN8 .... 9 D7
Skelmersdale,Up Holland
WN8 .... 10 A7
Ormskirk Sch
Ormskirk L39 .... 15 F4
Ormskirk L39 .... 16 B5
Ormskirk St Anne's RC Prim
Sch L39 .... 15 E4
Ormskirk Sta L39 .... 15 F5
Ormskirk West End Prim Sch
L39 .... 15 E7
Ormston Ave BL6 .... 32 C5
Orpen Ave BB11 .... 127 F3
Orpington Sq BB10 .... 148 C3
Orrell Cl 3 PR25 .... 76 D1
Orrell Gdns WN5 .... 10 F6
Orrell Hill La L38 .... 3 C4
Orrell Holgate Prim Sch
WN5 .... 10 E5
Orrell La L40 .... 25 D5
Orrell Newfold Com Prim Sch
WN5 .... 10 D4
Orrell Rd WN5 .... 10 E7
Orrell RU FC WN5 .... 10 E5
Orrell Sta WN5 .... 10 E4
Orrell Water Pk* WN5 .... 10 E4

Orrest Rd PR1 119 A1
Orton Ct BB9 170 D4
Orwell Cl L37 11 D1
Osbaldeston La BB2 121 D5
Osbert Croft PR4 95 A1
Osborne Ave FY5 175 F1
Osborne Cres LA3 216 F3
Osborne Dr PR6 78 C2
Osborne Gr
Cleveleys FY5 175 D5
Morecambe LA4 217 A3
Osborne Rd
Bamber Bridge PR5 97 D3
Blackburn BB2 101 B6
Blackpool FY4 110 B8
Cleveleys FY5 175 D5
Formby L37 11 E1
Lytham St Anne's FY8 89 F5
Morecambe LA3,LA4 216 F3
Southport PR8 21 B6
Osborne St 11 PR1 96 E7
Osborne Terr Bacup OL13 70 D8
Darwen BB3 81 E2
1 Rawtenstall BB4 85 E2
Spen Brook BB12 169 D2
Whitewell Bottom BB4 86 F4
Osborne Way BB4 85 A1
Osbourne Way PR1 118 A1
Oscar St 4 FY4 130 F2
Oslo Rd BB11 127 B5
Osprey Cl Blackburn BB1 101 D8
Knowley PR6 62 A3
Oswald Rd
Lytham St Anne's FY8 91 D4
Preston PR2 117 C1
Oswald St
Accrington BB5 104 D6
Blackburn BB1 101 E6
Burnley BB12 127 F8
Oswaldtwistle BB5 103 D3
Rishton BB1 124 C2
Oswaldtwistle Mills Shopping Village* BB5 103 E4
Otley Rd FY8 90 B7
Ottawa Cl BB2 101 A8
Otterburn Cl FY3 153 B1
Otterburn Gr BB10 128 D6
Otterburn Rd BB2 81 C7
Otters Cl PR2 118 F2
Ottershaw Gdns BB1 101 E8
Ottery Cl PR9 54 A5
Otway St PR1 117 E2
Oulton Cl L31 5 B4
Our Lady & St Anselm's RC Prim Sch OL12 71 D2
Our Lady & St Edward's RC Prim Sch PR2 117 D8
Our Lady & St Gerard's RC Prim Sch PR5 77 A8
Our Lady & St Hubert's RC Prim Sch BB6 124 E6
Our Lady & St John RC Arts Coll BB1 102 C3
Our Lady & St Paul's RC Prim Sch OL10 33 F1
Our Lady Of Compassion RC Prim Sch L37 12 A3
Our Lady of Lourdes RC Prim Sch
Carnforth LA5 223 E1
Southport PR8 35 A1
Our Lady of Perpetual Succour RC Prim Sch BB2 81 E8
Our Lady of the Assumption RC Prim Sch FY4 110 F5
Our Lady Queen of Peace RC High Sch WN8 17 F4
Our Lady Star of the Sea RC Prim Sch FY8 89 F6
Our Lady's RC High Sch
Fulwood PR2 117 C4
Lancaster LA1 218 D1
Ousby Ave LA3 217 B2
Ousby Rd LA3 217 B2
Ouseburn Rd BB2 81 C8
Ousle Rock BB12 169 E2
Out La PR26 58 C2
Out Moss La LA4 217 B4
Out Rawcliffe CE Prim Sch PR3 178 F2
Outer Prom FY7 198 E5
Outgate Rd PR4 116 D4
Outlet La L31,L39 6 F1
Outlook The L38 2 F4
Outram Ho PR5 97 D1
Outram La 2 BB1 122 E1
Outram Way PR5 77 E8
Outterside St PR7 31 A6
Outwood Rd BB11 128 B4
Oval The Burnley BB11 127 C3
Shevington WN6 19 F5
Ovangle Rd LA3 217 F2
Over Hos BL7 48 B6
Over Town BB10 129 A1
Overdale Gr FY3 131 A8
Overdell Dr OL12 52 C4
Overfield Way OL12 52 F2
Overshores Rd BL7 48 B8
Overton Rd PR2 95 E8
Overton St Helen's CE Sch LA3 213 D1
Ovington Dr PR8 35 E3
Owen Ave L39 15 F6
Owen Ct BB5 124 F3
Owen Rd LA1 218 D2
Owen St Accrington BB5 104 C7
Burnley BB12 127 A5
Darwen BB3 82 A3
Preston PR1 97 B8
Owen's La L39 13 E2
Owen's Row BL6 32 C3
Owens St PR6 43 E7
Owlet Hall Rd BB3 81 E2
Owsten Ct BL6 31 F3
Owtram St 2 PR1 97 C8
Ox Hey BB5 124 F4
Ox Hey Ave PR2 116 C1
Ox Hey Cl BL0 50 C7
Ox St 15 BL0 50 B5
Oxcliffe Ave LA3 216 D1
Oxcliffe Gr LA3 216 D1
Oxcliffe New Farm Caravans LA3 216 F1
Oxcliffe Rd LA3 216 F2
Oxendale Rd FY5 176 D2
Oxenholme Ave FY5 175 D4
Oxenhurst Rd FY3 131 A8
Oxford Ave BB5 125 A3
Oxford Cl Blackburn BB1 101 F4
Padiham BB12 126 D6
Oxford Ct
4 Lytham St Anne's FY8 90 D4
Southport PR8 34 F4
Oxford Dr Blackburn BB1 102 E4
Kirkham PR4 114 C4
Oxford Gdns PR8 34 E4
Oxford Pl
9 Burnley BB11 128 B5
Lancaster LA1 218 C3
Oxford Rd
Bamber Bridge PR5 77 F8
Blackpool FY1 130 D5
Burnley BB11 128 B5
Cleveleys FY5 175 D3
Fleetwood FY7 198 E3
Fulwood PR2 117 D4
Lytham St Anne's FY8 89 E8
Lytham St Anne's,Ansdell FY8 90 D4
Nelson BB9 171 A2
Orrell WN5 10 F8
Skelmersdale WN8 17 E1
Southport PR8 34 E4
Oxford St Accrington BB5 104 B6
Adlington PR7 31 A6
Brierfield BB9 148 B5
Bury BL9 33 A1
Carnforth LA5 223 D1
9 Chorley PR7 43 C7
Colne BB8 171 E5
Darwen BB3 81 F4
Lancaster LA1 218 D3
Morecambe LA4 217 B6
Preston PR1 97 A6
Oxford Way
Fleetwood FY7 198 E3
Rochdale OL12 52 E2
Oxhey Cl BB10 128 F6
Oxheys Ct 2 PR1 117 E2
Oxheys Ind Est PR1 117 D2
Oxheys St PR1 117 D2
Oxhill Pl FY5 152 F7
Oxhouse Rd WN5 10 D4
Oxley Cl PR4 113 F5
Oxley Rd PR1 118 D1
Oxley Rd N PR1 118 D1
Oystercatcher Gate FY8 90 E7

P

Paa La BB7 231 C7
Packet La LA5 221 A4
Pad Cote La BD22 174 A8
Paddington Ave PR3 157 C7
Paddington Barn PR3 157 C7
Paddock Ave PR26 59 A8
Paddock Dr FY3 131 C2
Paddock La BB1 102 D4
Paddock Rd WN8 9 C5
Paddock St 9 BB5 103 E4
Paddock The
Blackburn BB2 101 A8
Carleton FY6 153 C5
Formby L37 12 A5
Fulwood PR2 118 A6
4 Kingsfold PR1 96 E2
Ormskirk L39 15 C3
Oswaldtwistle BB5 103 E4
Ramsbottom BL0 50 B7
Rufford L40 39 C4
Sawley BB7 230 C1
Southport PR8 21 C4
Thornton FY5 153 B8
Padgate Pl BB11 127 B4
Padiham Gawthorpe High Sch BB12 126 E8
Padiham Green CE Prim Sch BB12 126 C8
Padiham Prim Sch BB12 126 D8
Padiham Prim Sch Annexe BB12 126 E8
Padiham Rd
Burnley BB12 127 E6
Burnley,Whittlefield BB12 127 C7
3 Burnley,Whittlefield BB12 127 D6
Padiham BB12 126 F7
Sabden BB7 146 A7
Padstow Cl PR9 54 A5
Padway PR1 96 D2
Page Ct L37 11 F3
Pagefield Cres BB7 167 A7
Pages Ct PR5 77 B7
Paignton Rd BB1 101 D7
Painley Cl FY8 91 A4
Painter Wood BB7 144 B4
Paisley St BB11 127 D5
Palace Ct LA3 216 E4
Palace Gdns BB12 127 B7
Palace Rd PR8 34 E5
Palace St Burnley BB12 127 C7
Bury BL9 33 A2
Palais Bldgs 3 L40 25 E5
Palatine Ave LA1 215 A5
Palatine Cl FY3 131 C6
Palatine High Sch FY4 110 C8
Palatine Rd
Blackburn BB2 101 C5
Blackpool FY1 130 C4
Cleveleys FY5 175 D4
Southport PR8 34 F5
Palatine Sq BB11 127 E5
Palatine St 10 BL0 50 C6
Paley Rd 1 PR1 96 D7
Palfrey Cl FY6 153 B6
Pall Mall Blackburn BB2 100 E5
Chorley PR7 43 C6
Palladium Bldgs 7 FY1 130 B1
Palm Ct WN8 17 E2
Palm Dr FY6 153 B6
Palm Gr PR8 35 E6
Palm St Blackburn BB1 102 A7
5 Burnley BB11 127 D5
Palma St 4 OL14 109 B1
Palmaston Cl LA1 214 E6
Palmer Ave FY1 130 C2
Palmer Gr 3 LA4 217 E6
Palmer St BB1 101 D6
Palmerston Cl BL0 50 C4
Palmerston Rd PR9 35 F6
Palmerston St BB12 126 D7
Palmetto View FY8 90 D7
Pankhurst Cl BB1 102 B1
Pansy St N BB5 104 B7
Pansy St S BB5 104 B7
Panton St BL6 32 D1
Parade The LA5 223 B1
Paradise Cl PR6 61 C8
Paradise La
1 Blackburn BB2 101 E4
Formby L37 12 A6
Leyland PR26 76 B1
Paradise St
Accrington BB5 104 B5
Barrowford BB9 170 E5
Blackburn BB1 101 D4
11 Burnley BB11 127 F6
Great Knowley PR6 61 F3
2 Newchurch BB4 86 F2
Ramsbottom BL0 50 C7
Paradise Terr 2 BB2 101 E4
Paragon Way LA1 214 C8
Parbold Cl Blackpool FY3 152 F1
Burscough L40 25 E3
Parbold Douglas CE Prim Sch WN8 27 D3
Parbold Hill WN8 27 E2
Parbold Our Lady & All Saints RC Prim Sch WN8 27 C2
Parbold Sta WN8 27 C2
Pardoe Cl PR4 73 E3
Pardoe Ct L40 25 F3
Paris BB1 122 E4
Parish St 11 BB12 126 C8
Park Ave
Barnoldswick BB18 196 B1
Barrowford BB9 170 C1
Blackburn BB1 101 D6
Burnley BB11 127 E4
Chatburn BB7 190 D5
Clitheroe BB7 189 E1
Euxton PR7 60 D2
Fleetwood FY7 198 F3
Formby L37 11 F1
Great Harwood BB6 124 D6
Haslingden BB4 85 B1
Lancaster LA1 215 B7
Longshaw WN5 10 E1
Lytham St Anne's FY8 90 E3
Maghull L31 5 D3
Much Hoole PR4 74 E2
New Longton PR4 75 F8
Ormskirk L39 15 E5
Preston PR1 118 B2
Ramsbottom BL0 50 D6
Salterforth BB18 194 E8
Southport PR9 35 E8
Park Bridge Rd BB10 128 D3
Park Brow Dr L32 1 A1
Park Cl Formby L37 2 E8
Fulwood PR2 118 D3
Middleworth Green PR1 96 D4
Parbold WN8 27 D3
Park Cotts BB8 150 D7
Park Cres Accrington BB5 104 A4
Bacup OL13 70 F8
Blackburn BB2 101 C6
Haskayne L39 13 F4
Haslingden BB4 85 C1
Morecambe LA4 217 E7
Southport PR9 53 D1
Stalmine FY6 177 C8
Park Ct LA1 214 F3
Park Dr Brierfield BB9 148 C5
Nelson BB9 148 F7
Preston PR2 116 D1
Park Farm Cl PR4 74 F8
Park Farm Rd BB2 80 D8
Park Gate Rd BB1 142 D1
Park Hall L Ctr PR7 42 A4
Park Hall Rd PR7 41 F3
Park Head BB7 144 F2
Park Hey Dr WN6 19 E7
Park High Sch BB8 171 F6
Park Hill
Barnoldswick BB18 196 C1
21 Rochdale OL12 52 F1
Park Hill Rd PR3 181 C7
Park Ho
4 Lancaster LA1 218 D1
Longridge PR3 140 A7
Park House La LA2 239 A5
Park La Brierfield BB9 148 C5
Caton LA2 237 B5
Galgate LA2 211 A6
Garstang PR3 204 A4
Great Harwood BB6 124 D6
Holmes PR4 56 B2
Horwich BL6 32 D3
Kirkham PR4 114 A7
Maghull L31 5 F3
Middleworth Green PR1 96 E3
Oswaldtwistle BB5 103 E3
Preesall FY6 200 B3
Wennington LA2 238 E8
Park Lane Dr L31 6 B2
Park Lee Hospl BB2 101 E2
Park Lee Rd BB2 101 E2
Park Link L39 15 B1
Park Mews BB7 231 B3
Park Mill Pl PR1 118 A1
Park Pl Blackburn BB2 101 B3
Blackburn,Feniscowles BB2 80 D7
24 Preston PR1 97 A7
Walton-le-D PR5 97 E4
Park Prim Sch
Colne BB8 171 F5
Skelmersdale WN8 17 E1
Park Rd Accrington BB5 104 A6
Adlington PR7 30 F6
Bacup OL13 87 F1
Barnoldswick BB18 196 B1
Blackburn BB2 101 E3
Blackpool FY1 130 D3
Burnley BB10 128 E1
Chorley PR7 43 C8
Coppull PR7 42 E1
Darwen BB3 65 B6
Edgworth BL7 48 E5
Formby L37 11 E1
Fulwood PR2 118 A4
Gisburn BB7 231 B3
Great Harwood BB6 124 D5
Haslingden BB4 67 F7
Kirkham PR4 113 F4
Lancaster LA1 215 A8
Leyland PR25 60 A7
Longshaw WN5 10 F1
Lytham St Anne's FY8 89 E6
Mellor Brook BB2,PR5 121 A1
Middleworth Green PR1 96 D4
Newchurch BB4 86 F1
Ormskirk L39 15 E5
Padiham BB12 126 C8
Poulton-le-F FY6 153 E4
Ramsbottom BL0 49 F3
Rishton BB1 124 C1
Silverdale LA5 224 D4
Southport PR9 35 D8
Thornton FY5 176 B1
Park Rd W PR9 53 C1
Park Road Ind Est OL13 87 F1
Park Sch FY3 130 E4
Park Side BB18 195 A8
Park Sq LA1 215 A8
Park St Accrington BB5 104 C6
Barnoldswick BB18 196 B1
Barrowford BB9 170 D4
Chorley PR7 61 C1
Clitheroe BB7 166 E7
Eccleston PR7 41 C6
Great Harwood BB6 124 D5
Haslingden BB4 85 B3
Haslingden,Bridge End BB4 67 F7
Lytham St Anne's FY8 91 B3
Morecambe LA4 217 E6
Park Stone Rd PR3 137 C3
Park Street E BB9 170 E4
Park Terr Blackburn BB1 101 D7
Great Harwood BB6 124 D6
Park View
Accrington BB5 104 A7
Carnforth LA5 223 D3
Gisburn BB7 231 B3
Middleworth Green PR1 96 D4
Newchurch BB4 86 F1
Padiham BB12 126 C8
Park View Ave PR2 117 B2
Park View Cl BB9 148 B7
Park View Ct 2 FY4 110 C6
Park View Rd FY8 91 B4
Park View Terr
Abbey Village PR6 80 C1
Salterforth BB18 194 D7
Park Wall Rd L29,L38 4 B2
Park Way Colne BB8 171 C6
Formby L37 11 F1
Middleworth Green PR1 96 D4
Park Wlk PR2 118 A4
Park Wood Dr BB4 85 E2
Parkbourn L31 6 A2
Parkbourn Dr L31 6 A2
Parkbourn N L31 6 A2
Parkbourn Sq L31 6 A2
Parkdale Gdns BB2 81 D6
Parke Mews PR6 79 C3
Parke Rd PR6 62 E8
Parker Ave BB7 166 E6
Parker Cres L39 15 F7
Parker La Burnley BB11 128 A5
New Longton PR4 76 C6
Parker St
Accrington,Higher Baxenden BB5 104 E2
Accrington,Hillock Vale BB5 104 E8
3 Blackpool FY1 130 C5
Brierfield BB10 148 F3
Burnley BB11 128 A6
Bury BL9 33 A2
Chorley PR7 61 C1
Colne BB8 171 C5
Lancaster LA1 215 A8
11 Nelson BB9 170 F2
Preston PR2 117 D2
Rishton BB1 124 C2
Parker Terr BB7 231 B3
Parkers Fold PR3 181 C2
Parkers Wood Cl PR7 43 A6
Parkes Way BB2 81 D7
Parkfield Ave PR2 117 B2
Parkfield Cl Leyland PR26 59 C8
Ormskirk L39 15 C4
5 Preston PR2 116 C1
Parkfield Cres 6 PR2 116 C1
Parkfield Dr
Lancaster LA1 215 A6
Preston PR2 95 C8
Parkfield Gr L31 5 C1
Parkfield View PR2 95 C8
Parkgate PR3 138 D5
Parkgate Dr
Lancaster LA1 215 C7
Leyland PR25 59 F7
Parkhead La PR3 182 A8
Parkhill Gr OL14 109 A1
Parkinson Fold BB4 68 C6
Parkinson La PR3 162 B8
Parkinson St
Blackburn BB2 101 C2
Burnley BB11 128 A4
Foulridge BB8 194 D1
Haslingden BB4 85 A3
Parkinson Way 1 FY4 130 C1
Parkland Cl FY5 175 C1
Parkland Gr LA3 216 E2
Parkland View BB11 127 E2
Parklands
Skelmersdale WN8 18 D2
Southport PR9 35 E8
Parklands Ave PR1 96 A4
Parklands Cl PR1 96 A4
Parklands Dr PR2 117 E8
Parklands Gr PR2 117 E8
Parklands High Sch PR7 43 A8
Parklands The PR3 181 D3
Parklands Way BB2 81 B8
Parks The LA4 217 E7
Parkside Morecambe LA4 217 C3
Preston,Holme Slack PR1 118 B3
Preston,Lea PR2 116 D2
Whitworth OL12 71 D2
Parkside Ave PR7 43 C8
Parkside Cl 12 OL14 109 B1
Parkside Cres WN5 10 F6
Parkside Ct
Morecambe LA4 217 C3
Southport PR9 53 D1
Parkside Dr PR6 61 B6
Parkside La PR3 181 A7
Parkside Rd
Cornholme OL14 109 B1
Lytham St Anne's FY8 90 A7
Nelson BB9 149 B8
Parkside View FY5 176 A4
Parkstone Ave
Carleton FY6 153 B5
Thornton FY5 153 D8
Parksway FY6 199 D5
Parkthorn Rd PR2 95 C8
Parkview Cl LA4 217 B3
Parkview Flats FY8 89 D6
Parkway Blackpool FY3 131 A6
Shevington Moor WN6 29 A2
Parkwood BL7 47 D2
Parkwood Ave BB12 127 D7
Parkwood Ct BB4 85 E2
Parkwood Mews 1 BB9 170 F2
Parliament St
Burnley BB11 128 B5
11 Colne BB8 171 E5
19 Darwen BB3 82 A1
Lancaster LA1 218 D1
Morecambe LA3 216 E4
Skelmersdale WN8 10 C7
Parlick Ave PR3 140 B7
Parlick Rd Fulwood PR2 119 A2
Garstang PR3 181 B6
Parr Cottage Cl PR7 41 C7
Parr La PR7 41 C7
Parr's La L39 15 D1
Parramatta St 8 BB4 86 A2
Parrock Cl PR1 96 E3
Parrock Par BB4 86 A7
Parrock Rd BB9 170 C2
Parrock St
Barnoldswick BB18 196 B2
19 Nelson BB9 170 E1
9 Rawtenstall BB4 86 A7
Parrox Fold FY6 200 A5
Parrox La PR4 114 E2
Parrys Way FY6 153 E4
Parsley Cl FY2 152 F3
Parson La BB7 166 E8

Parson's Brow 4 PR7 43 C7
Parson's Bullough Rd
PR6,BL6 44 E5
Parsonage Ave PR3 141 D3
Parsonage Brow WN8 10 A8
Parsonage Cl 3 Bury BL9 33 A2
Morecambe LA3 217 C2
Skelmersdale WN8 10 A7
Parsonage Cotts 9 BB7 166 E8
Parsonage Dr BB9 148 C5
Parsonage Gdns PR4 57 A5
Parsonage La PR3 185 C1
Parsonage Rd BB1 123 A4
Parsonage St Bury BL9 33 A3
2 Church BB5 103 E5
Colne BB8 171 C4
Part St PR8 35 B6
Parth St BL9 33 D1
Partnership Way BB1 102 D2
Partridge Ave FY5 176 A4
Partridge Dr BB5 104 F1
Partridge Hill 4 BB12 146 D1
Partridge Hill St 5
BB12 146 D1
Passmonds Cres OL11,
OL12 52 B1
Past La Lane Ends BB7 230 A5
Lane Ends BB7 230 A7
Pasture Cl
Barnoldswick BB18 196 C4
Burnley BB11 127 E3
Pasture Dr Bonds PR3 181 D6
Foulridge BB8 194 D1
Pasture Field FY6 153 B6
Pasture Field Cl PR26 76 C1
Pasture Gr BB7 144 A7
Pasture La
Barrowford BB9 170 C5
Hest Bank LA5 220 E4
Pasturegate BB11 127 E3
Pasturegate Ave BB11 127 E4
Pasturelands BB4 106 A1
Pasturelands Dr BB7 144 A3
Pastures The
Blackburn BB2 101 A8
Grimsargh PR2 139 D1
Southport PR9 54 D5
Paterson St BB2 101 E3
Pathfinders Dr LA1 214 E4
Patience St 11 OL12 52 C1
Patmos St BL0 50 D6
Paton St OL12 52 D3
Patrick Ave BB12 145 D2
Patrick Cres BB4 86 C2
Patten St Blackburn BB1 102 C5
Colne BB8 171 D4
Preston PR1 96 F8
Patterdale Ave
Blackburn BB1 102 C3
Blackpool FY3 130 F2
Fleetwood FY7 198 D1
Oswaldtwistle BB5 103 D5
Thornton FY5 176 B3
Patterdale Cl
Brierfield BB10 148 C4
Southport PR8 21 B3
Patterdale Cres L31 5 E2
Patterdale Rd LA1 218 F1
Patterson Ct 8 FY8 91 C3
Pattison Cl OL12 52 D3
Paul's La Hambleton FY6 177 C2
Southport PR9 53 F3
Paulhan St BB10 148 B2
Pavey Cl FY4 110 F8
Pavilion Cl OL12 52 F2
Pavilion View PR26 58 B2
Pavilions The
Blackpool FY4 110 D4
Preston PR2 96 C7
Paxton Pl WN8 9 C4
Paxton St BB5 104 B6
Paynter Cl Barrow BB7 166 D1
Clayton-le-M BB5 125 A2
Paythorne Ave BB10 128 D5
Paythorne Cl FY3 153 B1
Peabody St BB3 82 A2
Peace Pl FY5 176 B4
Peace St BB11 127 D5
Peacehaven WN8 17 E1
Peachtree Cl PR2 118 D6
Peacock Cres LA2 220 E1
Peacock Dr PR3 204 D1
Peacock Hall Rd PR25 59 D7
Peacock Hill Cl PR2 119 C7
Peacock La LA2 220 E1
Peahall La PR3 202 A4
Pear Ave BL9 33 C3
Pear Pl 16 OL14 109 B1
Pear St 17 OL14 109 B1
Pear Tree Ave PR7 42 F3
Pear Tree Cl 2 PR5 97 E2
Pear Tree Cres PR5 97 E2
Pear Tree Croft PR4 75 A8
Pear Tree Ctyd PR4 115 E2
Pear Tree La PR7 60 E3
Pear Tree Rd PR6 78 B3
Pear Tree Sch PR4 114 A5
Pear Tree St 7 PR5 97 E2
Pearfield PR25 77 A2
Pearl Ave 6 FY2 152 E1
Pearl Brook Ind Est 4
BL6 32 B3
Pearl St Accrington BB5 103 F5
Blackburn BB1 122 F1
Pearson St
Blackburn BB2 101 D4
Bury BL9 33 B3
Peart St BB10 148 B2
Peartree Rd PR26 58 B3
Pebble Ct FY5 175 C3
Pechell St 5 PR2 117 C1
Pedder Ave LA3 213 C1
Pedder Dr LA3 213 D1
Pedder Gr LA3 213 D1
Pedder La FY6 177 B1
Pedder Rd LA3 213 C1
Pedder St
Morecambe LA4 217 A5
Preston PR2 96 E8
Pedder's La
Blackpool FY4 110 D7
Preston PR2 117 A1
Pedders Gr PR2 96 A8
Pedders La PR2 96 A8
Pedders Way PR2 96 A8
Peebles Gr BB11 127 D3
Peel Ave Blackpool FY3 130 D7
Heysham LA3 212 E6
Lancaster LA1 218 D2
Ramsbottom BL0 50 A5
Peel Bank Rd BB5 103 B4
Peel Brow BL0 50 D6
Peel Brow Sch BL0 50 D6
Peel Cl BB2 81 E8
Peel Cres LA1 214 D8
Peel Dr OL13 88 B1
Peel Gdns BB8 171 C5
Peel Hall Rd BL0 50 B2
Peel Hall St PR1 118 B1
Peel Hill FY4 111 E7
Peel Ho LA1 218 C1
Peel Mount
Blackburn BB1 102 F4
Ramsbottom BL0 50 A4
Peel Mount Cl BB1 102 F4
Peel Park Ave
Accrington BB5 104 D7
Clitheroe BB7 166 F7
Peel Park Cl
Accrington BB5 104 D7
Clitheroe BB7 166 F7
Peel Park Prim Sch
BB5 104 D7
Peel Pl BB9 170 F6
Peel Rd Blackpool FY4 111 F4
Colne BB8 171 B4
Fleetwood FY7 198 F3
Skelmersdale WN8 9 E5
Peel St Accrington BB5 104 C6
Adlington PR6 31 B8
Blackburn BB2 101 C2
Chorley PR7 43 C7
Clitheroe BB7 166 E8
Haslingden BB4 85 A3
6 Oswaldtwistle BB5 103 D3
Padiham BB12 126 D8
Preston PR2 96 E8
Rawtenstall BB4 86 C2
Southport PR8 35 F6
Peel Twr* BL8 49 F5
Peel Wlk L31 5 B2
Peerart Ct BB8 171 C4
Peers Clough Rd BB4 86 F7
Peet Ave L39 15 D4
Peet's La PR9 54 A1
Peg Way PR4 92 F6
Peg's La FY8 91 B8
Pegbank La LA6 241 A8
Pelham Ave 3 FY3 130 E8
Pelham St 3 BB1 102 A6
Pemberton Dr LA4 217 F5
Pemberton Pl LA4 217 F5
Pemberton St BB1 122 E1
Pembroke Ave
Blackpool FY2 152 B3
Morecambe LA4 217 D6
Pembroke Cl BL6 32 A4
Pembroke Ct
Blackpool FY2 152 B3
13 Darwen BB3 82 A1
14 Rochdale OL12 52 F1
Pembroke Pl Chorley PR7 43 B6
Leyland PR25 60 A8
Pembroke Rd FY8 90 D4
Pembroke St
Accrington BB5 104 D6
Bacup OL13 87 F1
Blackburn BB2 101 E3
11 Burnley BB10 148 B1
Pembury Ave PR1 96 F3
Pen-y-ghent Way BB18 196 A2
Penarth Ct PR2 116 F3
Pendle Ave Bacup OL13 88 A3
Chatburn BB7 190 E5
Clayton-le-M BB5 124 F4
Lancaster LA1 211 B6
Pendle Bridge BB12 147 F3
Pendle Cl Bacup OL13 88 A2
Blackpool FY3 152 F1
Pendle Comm Hospl
BB9 170 E1
Pendle Ct
Barnoldswick BB18 196 C3
5 Clitheroe BB7 166 F8
Kirkham PR4 114 A6
Longridge PR3 140 A7
Skelmersdale WN8 9 D3
Pendle Dr Blackburn BB2 101 F2
Horwich BL6 32 C5
Ormskirk L39 16 A6
Whalley BB7 144 A7
Pendle Fields BB12 147 D7
Pendle Heritage Ctr*
BB9 170 E4
Pendle Hill Cl PR2 119 C7
Pendle Ho BB1 101 F5
Pendle Ind Est BB9 148 F7
Pendle Pl
Lytham St Anne's FY8 91 C4
Skelmersdale WN8 9 D4
Pendle Rd Brierfield BB9 148 A5
Clayton-le-W PR25 77 D1
Clitheroe BB7 167 A7
Downham BB7 191 D3
Great Harwood BB6 124 F6
Lancaster LA1 218 B3
Pendle Row BB12 169 C5
Pendle St Accrington BB5 104 A5
Barrowford BB9 170 C3
Blackburn BB1 102 A5
Nelson BB9 170 D1
Padiham BB12 126 D8
Pendle St E BB7 145 F7
Pendle St W BB7 145 F7
Pendle Terr BB7 191 E8
Pendle Trad Est BB7 190 C4
Pendle View
Barley BB12 169 C6
Brockhall Village BB6 143 C6
Clayton-le-M BB5 125 A3
Foulridge BB8 194 E1
Grindleton BB7 190 B7
Higham BB12 146 F6
Huncoat BB5 125 F2
West Bradford BB7 189 D7
Pendle Way
Burnley BB12 127 E6
7 Nelson BB9 148 E8
Pendlebury Cl PR4 75 B8
Pendlehurst St BB11 127 E4
Pendlemist View BB8 171 C3
Pendleside BB9 148 B8
Pendleside Cl BB7 145 F7
Pendleton Ave
Accrington BB5 103 F4
Rawtenstall BB4 86 A4
Pendleton Rd
Pendleton BB7 167 A2
Wiswell BB7 144 F8
Penfold L31 5 E1
Pengarth Rd BL6 32 C4
Penguin St PR1 118 B2
Penhale Cl LA3 212 E6
Penhale Ct LA3 212 E6
Penhale Gdns LA3 212 E6
Penhill Cl 4 FY2 130 D8
Penistone St 6 BB12 127 D6
Penketh Pl WN8 9 C5
Penn St BL6 32 C3
Pennine Ave PR7 60 D1
Pennine Cl
8 Blackpool FY1 130 C4
Horwich BL6 32 C5
Pennine Cres BB9 148 C5
Pennine Gdns PR3 181 A7
Pennine Gr BB12 146 C2
Pennine Pl WN8 9 B6
Pennine Rd Bacup OL13 88 A2
Chorley PR6 43 E8
Horwich BL6 32 C5
Pennine View
Dolphinholme LA2 226 A8
Fleetwood FY7 199 B4
Glasson LA2 209 E4
Great Eccleston PR3 156 C5
Kirkham PR4 114 C5
Morecambe LA4 217 B4
Pennine Way
Barnoldswick BB18 196 A2
Brierfield BB9 148 C5
Great Eccleston PR3 156 C5
Stalmine FY6 177 D7
Pennines The PR2 118 A7
Pennington Ave L39 15 E6
Pennington Ct
Heysham LA3 212 E6
Ormskirk L39 15 F6
Pennington La WN2 30 E1
Penny House La BB5 104 C7
Penny St Blackburn BB1 101 F5
Lancaster LA1 214 F7
3 Preston PR1 97 A8
Penny Stone Rd LA2 219 C7
Pennyfarthing La 7
FY5 176 A2
Pennystone Rd FY2 152 B4
Penrhos Ave FY7 198 E1
Penrhyn Rd LA1 218 A2
Penrith Ave
Cleveleys FY5 175 D4
Heysham LA3 212 F8
Southport PR8 21 C3
Penrith Cres Colne BB8 171 B3
Maghull L31 5 E2
Penrith Rd BB8 171 A3
Penrod Way LA3 212 D5
Penrose Ave FY4 130 F1
Penrose Pl WN8 9 E4
Penshaw Cl 6 BB1 122 F1
Penswick Ave FY5 175 E1
Pentland Rd L33 1 A4
Penwell Fold WN8 9 E8
Penwortham Broad Oak Prim
Sch PR1 96 C2
Penwortham Brow PR1 96 C6
Penwortham Ct PR1 96 D4
Penwortham Girls' High Sch
PR1 96 C5
Penwortham Hall Gdns
PR1 96 E3
Penwortham Middleforth CE
Prim Sch PR1 96 D3
Penwortham Prim Sch
PR1 96 A5
Penwortham St Teresa's RC
Prim Sch PR1 96 A5
Penwortham Way
Farington PR26,PR4 76 D7
Kingsfold PR1 96 C1
Penzance St BB2 101 B2
Peplow Rd LA3 213 A8
Pepper La WN6 29 B3
Perch Pool La PR9 36 F4
Percival Ct 2 PR8 35 A6
Percival St
Accrington BB5 103 F5
Blackburn BB1 101 F7
Darwen BB3 81 F3
Percy Rd LA1 214 F6
Percy St Accrington BB5 104 D6
Blackburn BB2 101 B2
Blackpool FY1 130 C7
Bury BL9 33 B3
9 Chorley PR7 43 D7
Colne BB8 171 E6
Fleetwood FY7 198 F4
Nelson BB9 148 E7
Oswaldtwistle BB5 103 B5
Preston PR1 97 A8
Ramsbottom BL0 50 B5
Shawforth OL12 71 E6
Peregrine Dr BB3 81 D3
Peregrine Pl PR25 76 D2
Peridot Cl BB1 122 F2
Perimeter Rd L33 1 E2
Peronne Cres BB1 102 D5
Perpignan Way 16 LA1 214 F8
Perry St BB3 82 B2
Perryn Pl WN6 29 F1
Pershore Gdns FY3 131 B8
Pershore Gr PR8 21 A4
Pershore Rd FY8 90 B5
Persia St BB5 103 F6
Perth Cl FY5 152 F7
Perth St Accrington BB5 104 B4
Blackburn BB2 101 C3
Burnley BB11 127 D5
Lancaster LA1 215 A7
8 Nelson BB9 170 F1
Perthshire Gr PR7 60 F6
Peter Birtwistle Cl BB8 171 E5
Peter Grime Row BB5 125 F2
Peter La LA5 225 E1
Peter Martin St 3 BL6 32 B4
Peter St
9 Barrowford BB9 170 D4
Blackburn BB1 102 A6
Blackpool FY1 130 D5
Chorley PR7 43 C8
Colne BB8 171 E4
5 Lancaster LA1 214 F7
Rawtenstall BB4 86 A2
Peterfield Rd 1 PR1 96 E2
Peterhouse Sch PR9 54 B3
Peters Ave L40 25 E4
Petersan Ct PR6 61 C3
Petersbottom La LA2 239 E4
Petre Cres BB1 103 B8
Petre Rd BB5 124 F2
Petrel Cl BB1 101 D8
Petunia Cl PR25 77 E2
Petworth Rd PR8 21 B6
Pharos Ct 8 FY7 199 B5
Pharos Gr 2 FY7 199 B5
Pharos Pl FY7 199 B5
Pharos St FY7 199 B5
Pheasant Wood Dr FY5 175 F5
Pheasantford Gn BB10 128 B8
Pheasantford St BB10 128 B8
Philip Ave PR4 114 B4
Philip Dr PR8 21 F6
Philip St
Barnoldswick BB18 196 B2
Darwen BB3 82 B1
Philips Rd Blackburn BB1 102 B8
Weir OL13 88 A7
Phillip St FY4 130 F2
Phillip's Cl L37 11 F2
Phillip's La L37 11 F2
Phillips La BB8 171 B3
Phillipstown BB4 86 E4
Phoenix St
8 Lancaster LA1 218 D1
Rochdale OL12 52 C1
Phoenix Way BB11 127 C5
Phyllis St OL12 52 B1
Physics Ave LA1 211 B7
Piazza The LA1 215 C7
Piccadilly LA1 214 F3
Piccadilly Cl LA1 214 F3
Piccadilly Gr LA1 214 F3
Piccadilly Rd BB11 127 E5
Piccadilly Sq 2 BB11 127 E5
Piccadilly St BB4 85 B3
Pickard Cl BB18 196 D4
Pickard St LA1 214 F6
Pickering Cl FY8 90 B7
Pickering Fold BB1 82 B7
Pickering St BB9 148 B5
Pickerings The 2 PR5 77 C8
Pickles Dr L40 25 D4
Pickles St BB12 127 D7
Pickmere Ave FY4 110 E8
Pickmere Cl FY5 176 A4
Pickthorn Cl LA1 218 B4
Pickup Fold 3 BB3 65 C7
Pickup Fold Rd BB3 65 C7
Pickup Rd DD1 103 A8
Pickup St Accrington BB5 103 F5
11 Bacup OL13 87 F2
Blackburn BB1 102 A5
Clayton-le-M BB5 124 F3
Picton St BB2 81 B8
Pier Ct FY8 89 D7
Pier Ho 3 BB1 101 F3
Pier St FY1 130 B3
Pierce Cl Lancaster LA1 214 D7
Padiham BB12 146 C1
Piercefield Ct L37 12 A5
Piercefield Rd L37 11 F5
Piercy Higher Mount
BB4 86 F3
Piercy Mdw BB4 86 F3
Piercy Mount BB4 86 F3
Piercy Rd BB4 86 F3
Piercy Terr BB4 86 F3
Pierpoint Il FY8 89 D7
Pierston Ave FY2 152 C1
Pike Ct FY7 198 C2
Pike View BL6 32 D4
Pikelaw Pl WN8 9 C5
Pikestone Ct 9 PR6 43 E8
Pilgrim St BB9 148 F6
Pilkington Dr BB5 125 A3
Pilkington Rd PR8 35 D5
Pilkington St
6 Blackburn BB1 101 E4
14 Ramsbottom BL0 50 B5
Pilling Ave
Accrington BB5 104 E2
Lytham St Anne's FY8 90 C7
Pilling Cl Chorley PR7 43 D6
Southport PR9 53 F5
Pilling Cres FY3 131 A8
Pilling Ct FY3 153 A1
Pilling Field BL7 47 E1
Pilling La Chorley PR7 43 D6
Maghull L31 5 A5
Pilling Lane FY6 200 B7
Pilling Pl WN8 9 C5
Pilling St Haslingden BB4 85 B6
3 Rawtenstall BB4 69 F8
Pilling St John's CE Prim Sch
PR3 201 C6
Pilmuir Rd BB2 101 E1
Pilot St BB5 104 B7
Pimbo La WN8 9 F3
Pimbo Rd WN8 9 C5
Pimhole Rd BL9 33 B2
Pimlico BB7 189 F3
Pimlico Link Rd BB7 190 C2
Pimlico Rd BB7 189 F2
Pinch Clough Rd BB4 86 F5
Pincock Brow PR7 42 C8
Pincock St PR7 42 C8
Pinder Cl BB7 189 B4
Pinder St BB9 170 F2
Pine Ave Blackpool FY1 130 E2
Much Hoole PR4 74 D4
Ormskirk L39 15 F7
Pine Cl Fulwood PR2 118 F4
Halton LA2 219 C6
Newburgh WN8 27 A1
Rishton BB1 103 B8
Skelmersdale WN8 17 F1
Pine Cres
Oswaldtwistle BB5 103 F3
Poulton-le-F FY6 153 E2
Pine Crest L39 15 B2
Pine Dr L39 15 F6
Pine Gr Chorley PR6 61 D3
Clitheroe BB7 166 D7
Garstang PR3 204 C1
Ormskirk L39 15 F7
Southport PR9 35 D7
Pine Lake* LA6 240 A3
Pine St Bacup OL13 88 A1
Blackburn BB1 102 A7
Burnley BB11 128 B5
Bury BL9 33 B2
Darwen BB3 65 B8
Haslingden BB4 85 C3
Lancaster LA1 218 C1
Morecambe LA4 217 C4
Nelson BB9 148 F8
Pine St N BL9 33 B3
Pine St S BL9 33 B2
Pine Way PR4 114 B7
Pine Wlks PR2 116 C1
Pines Cl PR5 78 C4
Pines The Leyland PR26 59 A8
Southport PR8 34 F6
Pineway PR2 117 C4
Pinewood Blackburn BB2 80 F8
Skelmersdale WN8 18 D3
Pinewood Ave
Blackpool FY2 152 E4
Broughton PR3 137 C3
Caton LA2 237 C3
Formby L37 11 D1
Hest Bank LA5 220 F2
Knott End-on-S FY6 200 A5
Morecambe LA4 217 F6
Thornton FY5 153 B7
Pinewood Cl Formby L37 11 D2
Lancaster LA2 214 E2
Southport PR8 36 C1
Pinewood Cotts 1 LA2 239 D8
Pinewood Cres
Leyland PR25 59 E8
Lytham St Anne's FY8 90 D4
Orrell WN5 10 E6
Ramsbottom BL0 50 B2
Pinewood Dr
Accrington BB5 104 E6
Nelson BB9 149 A7
Pinfold Barrowford BB9 170 E5

Pinfold *continued*
Longton PR4 ....75 A8
Pinfold Cl Fulwood PR2 ...118 E5
Southport PR8 ....21 B3
Pinfold La Inskip PR4 ....157 C2
Lancaster LA1 ....218 D2
Longridge PR3 ....140 B4
Pinfold L40 ....23 F3
Southport PR8 ....21 B3
Pinfold Pl
5 Kirkham PR4 ....113 F5
Nelson BB9 ....171 B1
Skelmersdale WN8 ....9 D4
Pinfold Prim Sch L40 ....24 A3
Pinfold St PR1 ....97 E8
Pingle Croft PR6 ....78 A2
Pingwood La L33 ....1 A5
Pink Pl BB2 ....101 B3
Pink St BB12 ....127 C6
Pinnacle Dr BL7 ....47 E2
Pinner La BB4 ....85 F7
Pinners Cl BL0 ....50 B7
Pintail Cl Moss Side PR26 ..76 A1
5 Rochdale OL12 ....52 B2
Pintail Way FY8 ....90 E7
Pioneer Cl BL6 ....32 C4
Pioneer St BL6 ....32 C4
Piper Cotts LA4 ....217 C3
Piper Lea BB4 ....87 A1
Piper's La LA6 ....240 C8
Pippin Bank OL13 ....87 F1
Pippin St Burscough L40 ....25 A2
Thorpe Green PR6 ....78 E5
Pit Hey Pl WN8 ....9 C5
Pitt St Lancaster LA1 ....214 F8
11 Padiham BB12 ....126 D8
Preston PR1 ....96 E7
Southport PR9 ....35 F6
Pittman Ct PR2 ....118 B8
Pittman Way PR2 ....118 C7
Pitts House La PR9 ....36 B8
Pittsdale Ave FY3 ....131 A2
Pitville St BB3 ....81 F3
Place The FY1 ....130 B7
Place-de-Criel 12 BB9 ....148 D8
Plain Pl BB2 ....101 E3
Plainmoor Dr FY5 ....152 F7
Plane St Bacup OL13 ....87 F4
Blackburn BB1 ....102 A7
Plane Tree Cl BB11 ....127 D3
Plane Tree Rd 7 BB1 ....102 A7
Planet Earth Ctr (Obsy & Planetarium)* OL14 ....88 F4
Plant St
Oswaldtwistle BB5 ....103 D3
Preston PR2 ....117 C1
Plantain Wlk LA3 ....217 B2
Plantation Ave
Arnside LA5 ....224 C8
Knott End-on-S FY6 ....199 E5
Plantation Gr LA5 ....224 C8
Plantation La LA2 ....232 D1
Plantation Rd
Accrington BB5 ....104 E6
Blackburn BB2 ....101 B1
Burscough L40 ....25 B4
Edgworth BL7 ....48 F7
Plantation Sq BB5 ....104 D6
Plantation St
Accrington BB5 ....104 D6
Bacup OL13 ....70 C8
Burnley BB10 ....128 A7
6 Nelson BB9 ....170 F1
Rawtenstall BB4 ....86 B2
Plantation The BD23 ....236 B3
Plantation View
Bacup OL13 ....87 F6
Ramsbottom BL0 ....50 C3
Platt Cl BB5 ....104 A5
Platt La WN1 ....30 B3
Platt St FY1 ....130 C6
Platten Gr LA4 ....217 C5
Platts La L40 ....25 D2
Platts Lane Ind Est L40 ....25 D2
Pleasant Gr FY5 ....176 B2
Pleasant Pl 4 BB11 ....127 F5
Pleasant St
Blackpool FY1 ....130 B7
Haslingden BB4 ....85 B3
3 Lytham St Anne's FY8 ....91 B3
Pleasant View
Bacup OL13 ....70 C7
15 Barnoldswick BB18 ....196 B2
Blackpool FY4 ....111 A4
Coppull PR7 ....42 F2
Earby BB18 ....197 C1
Hoddlesden BB3 ....82 F1
Leyland PR26 ....76 C3
Newchurch BB4 ....86 F1
Tockholes BB3 ....81 A1
Withnell PR6 ....80 A1
Pleasington Ave PR3 ....181 D6
Pleasington Cl
Blackburn BB2 ....101 B4
Blackpool FY4 ....111 A8
Pleasington Gr BB10 ....128 D5
Pleasington La BB2 ....80 C8
Pleasington Nature Reserve* BB2 ....100 D3
Pleasington Rd BB2 ....100 C1
Pleasington St BB2 ....101 B4
Pleasington Sta BB2 ....100 C1
Pleasureland* PR8 ....34 F7
Pleck Farm Ave BB1 ....101 E8
Pleck Pl FY6 ....153 B6
Pleck Rd BB5 ....104 C6
Pleckgate Fold BB1 ....122 E1
Pleckgate High Sch BB1 ....122 D1
Pleckgate Rd BB1 ....122 E1
Plessington Ct PR3 ....140 A7
Plevna Rd PR1 ....97 C8
Plex La L39 ....14 C5
Plex Moss La L39 ....13 D8
Plock Gn PR7 ....43 C5
Plough La L40 ....17 A4
Ploughlands The 2 PR2 ....116 E1
Plover Cl FY5 ....176 A5
Plover Dr Bury BL9 ....33 B4
Heysham LA3 ....212 F5
Plover St Burnley BB12 ....127 D6
Preston PR1 ....118 B1
Plover View 2 BB12 ....127 D6
Plovers Way FY3 ....131 B6
Plox Brow PR4 ....57 A6
Plumbe St BB11 ....128 A5
Plumpton Ave FY4 ....110 F5
Plumpton Field PR4 ....136 E2
Plumpton La
Great Plumpton PR4 ....112 E7
Halsall L39 ....22 E2
Plumpton Rd PR2 ....117 C2
Plumtree Cl PR2 ....118 C6
Plunge Rd BL0 ....68 E3
Plungington Rd PR1,PR2 ..117 E2
Plymouth Ave FY7 ....175 C8
Plymouth Gr PR6 ....43 E8
Plymouth Rd FY2,FY3 ....152 E1
Poachers Trail FY8 ....90 D7
Poachers Way FY5 ....176 A4
Pochard Pl 5 FY5 ....175 F1
Pocklington St BB5 ....104 D2
Poets' Rd BB12 ....126 F7
Pointer Ct LA1 ....214 F6
Pointer Gr LA2 ....219 D7
Pointer The LA1 ....214 F6
Poland St BB5 ....103 F5
Pole La BB3 ....65 C8
Pole St Preston PR1 ....97 A8
Standish WN6 ....29 E1
Polefield PR2 ....117 E7
Police St BB3 ....82 A1
Police Yd 18 LA2 ....239 D8
Pollard Pl LA1 ....218 E4
Pollard Row BB12 ....169 F1
Pollard St
Accrington BB5 ....104 C7
Burnley BB11 ....127 D5
4 Nelson BB9 ....170 E1
6 Preston PR1 ....96 E8
Pollards La BL9 ....50 C2
Pollux Gate FY8 ....90 C4
Polly Gn OL12 ....52 F3
Polperro Dr PR4 ....93 A6
Pomfret St
Blackburn BB2 ....101 D3
Burnley BB11 ....127 E6
Pompian Brow PR26 ....57 E6
Pond Cl PR4 ....57 A5
Pond Gdns FY6 ....153 B6
Pond St LA5 ....223 D2
Pond Terr LA5 ....223 D2
Pont St BB9 ....148 D7
Pontville Residential Sch L39 ....15 D3
Pool Ct FY7 ....198 D1
Pool Foot La FY6 ....154 E4
Pool Hey La PR8,PR9 ....36 B3
Pool House Com Prim Sch PR2 ....117 A6
Pool House Ct PR2 ....117 A6
Pool House La PR2 ....117 A5
Pool La PR4 ....93 A4
Pool St PR9 ....54 D5
Poole Rd PR2 ....118 A4
Poole St BB1 ....102 C5
Poolhill Cl FY5 ....152 E7
Poolside Wlk PR9 ....54 C4
Poot Hall OL12 ....52 F3
Pope La Fulwood PR2 ....119 A3
Kingsfold PR1 ....96 C2
White Stake PR4 ....76 B8
Pope Wlk PR1 ....96 D3
Poplar Ave
Bamber Bridge PR5 ....97 F1
Blackpool FY3 ....130 D5
Bury BL9 ....33 B3
Euxton PR7 ....60 C4
Great Harwood BB6 ....124 D6
Horwich BL6 ....32 E1
Kirkham PR4 ....114 A4
Longton PR4 ....75 B8
Poulton-le-F FY6 ....153 E2
4 Rochdale OL12 ....52 C1
Warton PR4 ....92 D6
Poplar Bank PR9 ....53 D1
Poplar Cl
Bamber Bridge PR5 ....97 F1
Oswaldtwistle BB5 ....103 F3
Rishton BB1 ....103 B8
Poplar Ct FY8 ....89 E5
Poplar Dr Coppull PR7 ....42 F1
Freckleton PR4 ....93 A5
Higher Penwortham PR1 ....96 C5
Longridge PR3 ....140 A8
Skelmersdale WN8 ....17 F1
Poplar Gr
Bamber Bridge PR5 ....97 F1
Fulwood PR2 ....119 A4
Ramsbottom BL0 ....50 D7
Poplar St Blackburn BB1 ....101 F7
2 Blackburn BB1 ....102 A7
Poplar St *continued*
Chorley PR7 ....43 D6
Haslingden BB4 ....85 B3
Nelson BB9 ....170 F1
Southport PR8 ....35 E6
Poplar Terr BB4 ....85 F6
Poplars The Adlington PR7 .30 F6
Burscough L40 ....25 E2
Poppy Ave PR6 ....61 D2
Poppy Cl PR8 ....35 B2
Poppy La L39 ....16 B1
Poppyfield PR4 ....116 F6
Poppyfields PR4 ....73 E4
Porritt Ave LA1 ....214 D8
Porritt St Bury BL9 ....33 A4
Bury BL9 ....33 B4
Porritt Way BL0 ....50 C7
Port Royal Ave LA1 ....214 C8
Port Way Heysham LA3 ....212 D5
Preston PR2 ....96 C7
Portal Gr BB12 ....127 B6
Porter Pl 2 PR1 ....97 A6
Porter St Accrington BB5 ..103 F5
Preston PR1 ....118 B1
Porter St E 4 PR4 ....113 F6
Porters Row FY6 ....177 C7
Portfield Bar BB7 ....144 F3
Portfield La BB6 ....144 F3
Portfield Rd BB7 ....144 E4
Porthcawl Ct PR2 ....116 F3
Portland Cotts PR6 ....62 D8
Portland Ct FY4 ....111 A1
Portland Dr LA3 ....217 B2
Portland Ind Est 12 BL9 ....33 A4
Portland Pl BL6 ....32 C3
Portland Rd
Blackpool FY1 ....130 D4
Langho BB6 ....123 C8
Portland St
Accrington BB5 ....104 A6
Barrowford BB9 ....170 D3
Blackburn BB2 ....101 C3
Bury BL9 ....33 A4
1 Chorley PR6 ....43 D8
Colne BB8 ....171 F5
Darwen BB3 ....65 B6
Lancaster LA1 ....214 F7
Nelson BB9 ....148 D8
Preston PR1 ....96 D7
Southport PR8 ....35 B5
Portman St PR1 ....118 B1
Portree Cl PR2 ....118 C5
Portree Cres BB1 ....102 D3
Portree Rd FY2 ....152 E5
Portsmouth Ave BB10 ....148 E2
Portsmouth Cl 7 FY5 ....175 F4
Portsmouth Dr PR6 ....43 E8
Portway FY2 ....152 E6
Post Horse La LA2 ....238 B7
Post La PR4 ....92 F6
Post Office Ave 1 PR9 ....35 B7
Post Office Bldgs 18 BB18 ....196 B2
Post Office Row
St Michael's on W PR3 ....157 C7
Tunstall LA6 ....241 D4
Westhouse LA6 ....242 E4
Post Office Yd 8 BB8 ....171 E5
Postern Gate Rd LA2 ....232 A8
Pot Gn BL0 ....50 A3
Pot House La Darwen BB3 .82 C3
Oswaldtwistle BB5 ....103 F2
Potter La
Coupe Green PR5 ....98 D5
Samlesbury PR5 ....119 E2
Potter Pl WN8 ....9 D5
Potter St 5 BL9 ....33 A3
Poulton Ave
Accrington BB5 ....104 A8
Lytham St Anne's FY8 ....90 B8
Poulton Cres PR5 ....98 D3
Poulton Ct PR9 ....35 F7
Poulton Dr FY6 ....153 F3
Poulton Gdns FY6 ....153 F3
Poulton Gr 3 FY7 ....199 A4
Poulton Old Rd FY3 ....152 F1
Poulton Rd
Blackpool FY3 ....130 E8
Carleton FY6 ....153 C5
Fleetwood FY7 ....198 F4
Morecambe LA4 ....217 B5
Southport PR9 ....35 F7
Poulton Sq LA4 ....217 B6
Poulton St
Fleetwood FY7 ....199 A4
Kirkham PR4 ....114 B5
Preston PR2 ....117 C1
Poulton-le-Fylde Sta FY6 ....153 D4
Poulton-le-Sands CE Prim Sch LA4 ....217 B6
Powder House La LA1, LA4 ....218 A4
Powderworks La L31 ....6 C3
Powell Ave FY4 ....110 D8
Powell St
Barnoldswick BB18 ....196 B3
Burnley BB11 ....127 E4
Darwen BB3 ....82 A2
Powis Dr PR4 ....57 A8
Powis Rd PR2 ....96 B8
Powys Cl BB4 ....85 B1
Poynter St 4 PR1 ....118 C1
Poynton St BL9 ....33 A1
Prairie Cres BB10 ....148 B2
Pratt St BB10 ....148 B1
Preesall Cl
Lytham St Anne's FY8 ....90 B7
Preesall Cl *continued*
Preston PR2 ....116 E1
Southport PR9 ....53 F4
Preesall Fleetwood's Charity CE Prim Sch FY6 ....200 B3
Preesall Mill Ind Est FY6 ....200 B2
Preesall Moss La FY6 ....200 D2
Preesall Rd PR2 ....116 E1
Preese Gdns PR4 ....156 A1
Premier Bsns Pk BB6 ....124 D6
Premier Way FY6 ....153 F3
Prenton Gdns FY5 ....153 A7
Prescot Cl BL9 ....33 A1
Prescot Gn L39 ....15 D3
Prescot Pl Blackpool FY3 .131 A2
Thornton FY5 ....176 C2
Prescot Rd L31,L39 ....6 D6
Prescott Ave L40 ....39 A3
Prescott Rd WN8 ....9 F4
Prescott St BB10 ....128 C5
Presfield Sch PR9 ....54 A3
Press Rd FY8 ....89 D8
Prestbury Ave
Blackpool FY4 ....110 C5
Southport PR8 ....21 B5
Prestbury Cl BL9 ....33 A1
Prestbury Dr LA3 ....217 B2
Preston Beck BB18 ....197 B2
Preston Coll Winckley Building PR1 ....96 F7
Preston Coll, Fulwood Campus PR2 ....117 F5
Preston College, Park Campus PR1 ....117 F2
Preston Ent Ctr 5 PR1 ..117 F1
Preston Grange Prim Sch PR2 ....119 A4
Preston Greenlands Com Prim Sch PR2 ....118 E3
Preston Lancaster New Rd PR3 ....181 B4
Preston Lancaster Old Rd PR3 ....181 D2
Preston Lancaster Rd
Bilsborrow PR3 ....159 A6
Cabus PR3 ....204 C5
Forton LA2,PR3 ....207 C5
Galgate LA2 ....211 A5
Preston Muslim Girls Sec Sch PR1 ....118 B1
Preston New Rd
Blackburn BB2 ....101 B5
Blackpool FY3,FY4 ....131 C2
Clifton PR4 ....94 C7
Freckleton PR4 ....93 D7
Little Plumpton PR4 ....112 C6
Mellor Brook BB2,PR5 ....120 D1
Samlesbury PR2,PR5 ....119 E1
Southport PR9 ....54 B4
Preston Nook PR7 ....41 C5
Preston Old Rd
Blackburn BB2 ....80 D8
Blackpool FY3 ....131 A2
Clifton PR4 ....115 C1
Freckleton PR4 ....93 C6
Preston Rd
Charnock Richard PR7 ....42 C4
Chorley PR6,PR7 ....61 C2
Clayton Brook PR5,PR6,PR7 .78 B4
Grimsargh PR2,PR3 ....139 E2
Inskip PR4 ....135 D7
Leyland PR25 ....77 B2
Longridge PR3 ....140 A5
Longridge PR3 ....140 E6
Lucas Green PR6 ....61 C4
Lytham St Anne's FY8 ....91 D4
Ribchester PR3 ....141 B5
Southport PR9 ....35 E8
Standish PR7,WN6 ....29 D5
Preston St Carnforth LA5 .223 D2
1 Chorley PR6 ....61 D1
Darwen BB3 ....81 F3
Fleetwood FY7 ....199 B4
Kirkham PR4 ....114 B5
16 Rochdale OL12 ....52 C1
Preston Sta PR1 ....96 E7
Prestwich St BB11 ....127 E5
Prestwood Pl WN8 ....9 F4
Pretoria St 2 OL12 ....52 C1
Price Cl LA1 ....218 C3
Price St 9 Blackpool FY1 .130 B1
Bury BL9 ....33 A1
Prickshaw OL12 ....52 B6
Prickshaw La OL12 ....52 B6
Priestfield Ave BB8 ....171 B5
Priesthouse Cl L37 ....12 A3
Priesthouse La L37 ....12 A3
Priestfield FY5 ....153 A7
Priestley Nook 4 BB5 ....104 C5
Primet Bridge BB8 ....171 C4
Primet Bsns Ctr 4 BB8 ....171 B4
Primet High Sch BB8 ....171 B3
Primet Hill BB8 ....171 C4
Primet Hts BB8 ....171 B3
Primet Prim Sch BB8 ....171 B3
Primet St BB8 ....171 C4
Primrose Ave FY4 ....110 D6
Primrose Bank
1 Bacup OL13 ....70 C8
Blackburn BB1 ....101 F6
Blackpool FY2 ....152 F6
Primrose Cl
Blackburn BB2 ....101 B2
Formby L37 ....12 B5
Hesketh Bank PR4 ....73 E4
Southport PR9 ....54 C6
Primrose Cotts
Calder Vale PR3 ....182 E7
Middleton LA3 ....213 A2
Primrose Ct
1 Blackburn BB1 ....101 F5
6 Lancaster LA1 ....215 A7
Morecambe LA4 ....217 B5
Primrose Dr
2 Blackburn BB1 ....101 F5
Bury BL9 ....33 D4
Primrose Gr PR1 ....118 C3
Primrose Hill Colne BB8 ..171 F5
Mellor BB1,BB2 ....122 A3
3 Preston PR1 ....97 B7
Primrose Hill Prim Sch PR7 ....60 B4
Primrose Hill Rd PR7 ....60 B4
Primrose Hill Sch BB10 ..148 D2
Primrose La Preston PR1 .118 C3
Standish WN6 ....29 D2
Primrose Rd
Clitheroe BB7 ....166 D6
Preston PR1 ....118 C3
Primrose Row PR7 ....59 F1
Primrose St
Accrington BB5 ....104 A4
9 Bacup OL13 ....70 C8
Brierfield BB9 ....148 B5
Burnley BB10 ....148 C1
Chorley PR6 ....43 D8
Clitheroe BB7 ....166 D7
Darwen BB3 ....65 B8
Lancaster LA1 ....215 A7
6 Morecambe LA4 ....217 B5
Primrose Terr
Blackburn BB2 ....101 B2
Blackpool FY4 ....111 A4
1 Darwen BB3 ....65 B8
Langho BB6 ....143 C1
Primrose Way
Carleton FY6 ....153 B6
Church BB5 ....103 E7
Primula Dr BB3 ....82 A7
Prince Ave LA5 ....223 E1
Prince Charles Gdns PR8 .34 F4
Prince Lee Mdws BB3 ....65 B8
Prince St Bacup OL13 ....71 D7
11 Burnley BB11 ....127 E5
Darwen BB3 ....81 F1
Ramsbottom BL0 ....50 C6
Prince's Pk WN6 ....19 F4
Prince's Rd PR5 ....97 E5
Prince's St BB2 ....101 D4
Princes Cres LA4 ....217 E7
Princes Ct
Higher Penwortham PR1 ....96 B6
Lytham St Anne's FY8 ....89 D7
Princes Dr PR2 ....117 E6
Princes Gdns LA4 ....217 E5
Princes Rd
Higher Penwortham PR1 ....96 B6
Lytham St Anne's FY8 ....90 D4
Princes Reach PR2 ....96 A7
Princes St Rishton BB1 ..124 B1
Southport PR8 ....35 A6
Princes Way
Cleveleys FY5 ....175 C1
Fleetwood FY7 ....198 D3
Princess Alexandra Way LA3 ....212 D5
Princess Ave
Clitheroe BB7 ....189 F1
Kirkham PR4 ....113 F6
Lancaster LA1 ....214 F6
Poulton-le-F FY6 ....153 D3
Princess Ct
5 Blackpool FY1 ....130 B3
4 Morecambe LA4 ....217 E6
Princess Gate PR9 ....53 F2
Princess Gdns BB2 ....80 C7
Princess Par FY1 ....130 B6
Princess Rd Adlington PR6 .31 B8
Cleveleys FY5 ....175 C2
Princess St
Accrington BB5 ....103 F6
17 Bacup OL13 ....87 F2
10 Bamber Bridge PR5 ....77 F8
2 Bamber Bridge,Lostock Hall PR5 ....77 B7
Blackburn BB2 ....101 C2
Blackpool FY1 ....130 B3
Burnley BB12 ....126 B8
Chorley PR7 ....43 D6
4 Church BB5 ....103 E6
Colne BB8 ....171 C4
Great Harwood BB6 ....124 D5
Haslingden BB4 ....85 B2
Leyland PR25 ....77 B1
Nelson BB9 ....148 D7
Preston PR1 ....97 B7
27 Rochdale OL12 ....52 F1
Whalley BB7 ....144 C5
Whitworth OL12 ....52 C8
Princess Way
Burnley BB12 ....127 F7
Euxton PR7 ....60 E2
Princeway FY4 ....110 C7
Pringle Bank LA5 ....223 D6
Pringle Ct PR3 ....181 C7
Pringle St BB1 ....102 A3
Pringle Wood PR3 ....137 C2
Prinny Hill Rd BB4 ....85 A3
Printer's Ct BL7 ....48 D4
Printers Fold BB12 ....126 E6
Printshop La BB3 ....65 A6
Prior's Cl BB2 ....101 A6
Prior's Oak Cotts PR1 ....96 C6
Priors Wlk BB7 ....230 C1

Priorsgate LA3 ....217 C2
Priorswood Pl WN8 ....9 F4
Priory Cl Blackburn BB1 ..102 E4
Burscough L40 ....25 D5
Formby L37 ....12 B2
Higher Penwortham PR1 ....96 C6
6 Lancaster LA1 ....214 E8
Leyland PR25 ....77 C2
Morecambe LA3 ....217 C2
Newchurch BB4 ....86 E2
Pleasington BB2 ....100 C2
Tarleton PR4 ....57 A6
Priory Cres PR1 ....96 C6
Priory Ct
7 Blackpool FY1 ....130 C5
Burnley BB11 ....128 B2
Lytham St Anne's FY8 ....89 E7
Priory Dr BB3 ....65 C8
Priory Gate FY4 ....110 C5
Priory Gdns PR8 ....34 F4
Priory Gr L39 ....15 D4
Priory Grange
Darwen BB3 ....65 C8
Southport PR8 ....35 A4
Priory La
Higher Penwortham PR1 ....96 C6
Hornby LA2 ....238 B7
Priory Mews
Lytham St Anne's FY8 ....90 D7
Southport PR8 ....34 F6
Priory Nook WN8 ....10 C7
Priory Pl BB3 ....65 C8
Priory Rd WN8 ....10 C7
Priory St 5 Nelson BB9 ..170 F1
Preston PR2 ....96 D8
Priory Tech Coll PR1 ....96 A5
Priory Way BB18 ....196 A2
Priory Wlk 6 LA1 ....215 A8
Pritchard St
Blackburn BB2 ....101 E2
Burnley BB11 ....127 E5
Private La BB4 ....68 C8
Procter Moss Rd
Lower Green Bank LA2 ....232 B3
Quernmore LA2 ....215 D1
Procter St BB2 ....101 F3
Procter's Brow LA2 ....239 B5
Proctor Cl BB9 ....148 F5
Proctor Rd L37 ....11 C4
Progress Ave BB1 ....102 A7
Progress Bsns Pk PR4 ..114 A4
Progress Ct FY3 ....131 B8
Progress Rd BB9 ....170 F3
Progress St Chorley PR6 ..43 E8
Darwen BB3 ....82 B1
Progress Way FY4 ....111 B6
Promenade Ainsdale PR8 ..20 F6
Blackpool FY1,FY4 ....130 D5
Blackpool,Bispham FY2 ....152 B6
Cleveleys FY5 ....175 C5
Southport PR8,PR9 ....35 B8
Promenade N FY5 ....175 C3
Promenade Rd FY7 ....199 A5
Promenade S FY5 ....175 C2
Prospect Ave
Bamber Bridge PR5 ....77 B8
Darwen BB3 ....81 E2
Hest Bank LA2 ....220 E1
Prospect Bldgs 5 BB9 ..148 D8
Prospect Ct PR3 ....140 B6
Prospect Dr LA2 ....220 E1
Prospect Farm Cvn Pk
BB8 ....171 D3
Prospect Gdns BB3 ....81 E2
Prospect Gr LA4 ....217 C4
Prospect Hill
Haslingden BB4 ....85 A2
4 Rawtenstall BB4 ....86 A3
Prospect Pl
7 Middleworth Green PR1 ..96 E4
Preston PR2 ....117 B1
Skelmersdale WN8 ....9 F5
Prospect Rd BB4 ....86 A3
Prospect St
Great Harwood BB6 ....124 D5
Lancaster LA1 ....215 A7
Newchurch BB4 ....86 F1
Prospect Terr Bacup OL13 ..70 E7
10 Barrowford BB9 ....170 D4
Belthorn BB1 ....82 F6
Brinscall PR6 ....63 A8
Clow Bridge BB11 ....106 B4
Huncoat BB5 ....125 E2
Newchurch BB4 ....86 F1
Prospect View
Bamber Bridge PR5 ....77 A7
9 Rawtenstall BB4 ....86 A3
Provence Ave BB6 ....143 C6
Providence St BB1 ....102 A8
Prudy Hill FY6 ....153 D4
Prunella Dr BB3 ....82 A7
Pudding La OL14 ....109 C2
Pudding Pie Nook La
PR3 ....137 F4
Puddle House La FY6 ..131 F8
Pudsey Rd OL14 ....109 B2
Pump House La PR26 ....58 F6
Pump St Blackburn BB2 ..101 D4
Burnley BB11 ....127 E6
Clitheroe BB7 ....166 D8
Preston PR1 ....97 A8
Punnell's La L31 ....4 F5
Punstock Rd BB3 ....81 F1
Purbeck Dr BL6 ....32 F1
Pye Busk LA2 ....239 E8
Pye Busk Cl LA2 ....239 E8
Pye's Cotts L39 ....5 E7
Pygon's Hill La L31 ....5 D6

Q

Quaile Holme Rd FY6 ..199 D5
Quaker Brook La PR5 ..99 A3
Quaker La BB3 ....82 A2
Quakerfields BB3 ....82 A2
Quakers Terr WN6 ....29 D3
Quakers View BB9 ....148 A5
Quakers' Pl WN6 ....29 E1
Quality Row BB7 ....164 E1
Quarlton Dr BL8 ....49 B3
Quarry Bank
Garstang PR3 ....181 C6
Haslingden BB4 ....84 F1
Quarry Bank St 3 BB12 .127 C7
Quarry Dr L39 ....15 C1
Quarry Farm Ct BB7 ....190 D5
Quarry Hill OL12 ....52 E3
Quarry Hill Nature Reserve*
BB9 ....148 F6
Quarry Mount L39 ....16 A6
Quarry Mount Mews
LA1 ....215 A7
Quarry Rd Brinscall PR6 ..62 F7
Caton LA2 ....237 E3
Chorley PR6 ....43 E6
Halton LA2 ....219 C6
Lancaster LA1 ....215 A7
Quarry St
13 Accrington BB5 ....104 C5
Bacup OL13 ....88 A2
Blackburn BB1 ....101 F5
Hapton BB11 ....126 C2
Padiham BB12 ....146 D1
Ramsbottom BL0 ....50 D6
Rochdale OL12 ....52 E1
Shawforth OL12 ....71 E6
Quarrybank 3 FY5 ....152 F8
Quarryside Dr L33 ....1 A3
Quay W FY8 ....89 E5
Quayle Ave FY4 ....110 E8
Quayside
5 Blackburn BB1 ....101 F4
Fleetwood FY7 ....199 B3
Quebec Ave FY2 ....152 E3
Quebec Rd BB2 ....101 B8
Queen Anne St
4 Haslingden BB4 ....85 A3
Southport PR8 ....35 B7
Queen Elizabeth Cres
BB5 ....104 D5
Queen Elizabeth Ct LA4 .217 A5
Queen Elizabeth's Gram Sch
BB2 ....101 C6
Queen Elizabeth's Gram Sch
(Annexe) BB2 ....101 D6
Queen Ho BB4 ....86 D1
Queen Mary Ave FY8 ....90 A5
Queen Mary Sch FY8 ....90 A4
Queen Mary Terr BB7 ..144 B7
Queen Sq LA1 ....214 F7
Queen St
12 Accrington BB5 ....104 C6
Bacup OL13 ....87 F2
5 Bacup,Stacksteads OL13 .70 C8
4 Bamber Bridge PR5 ....77 B7
Barnoldswick BB18 ....196 B1
Barrowford BB9 ....170 D4
Blackpool FY1 ....130 B6
Brierfield BB10 ....148 F2
Burnley BB11 ....127 F5
Bury BL9 ....33 A2
Carnforth LA5 ....223 D1
Clayton-le-M BB5 ....124 F3
Clitheroe BB7 ....166 C8
Colne BB8 ....171 C4
Darwen BB3 ....81 F2
Fleetwood FY7 ....199 A4
Great Harwood BB6 ....124 D5
Hoddlesden BB3 ....82 F1
Horwich BL6 ....32 B3
Lancaster LA1 ....214 F7
Lytham St Anne's FY8 ....91 A3
Morecambe LA4 ....217 B5
Nelson BB9 ....170 E1
Ormskirk L39 ....15 E4
Oswaldtwistle BB5 ....103 E4
Padiham BB12 ....126 C8
Preston PR1 ....97 B7
Ramsbottom BL0 ....50 B6
Rawtenstall BB4 ....86 A2
Whalley BB7 ....144 C5
Queen St E 3 PR7 ....43 D6
Queen Street Mill*
BB10 ....148 F2
Queen Vera Rd 4 FY1 ..130 B5
Queen Victoria Hospl
LA4 ....217 B5
Queen Victoria Rd
Blackpool FY1 ....130 C2
Burnley BB10 ....148 B1
Queen Victoria St BB2 ..101 B2
Queen's Cl Clitheroe BB7 .166 E7
Poulton-le-F FY6 ....153 E3
Queen's Cres PR4 ....114 B4
Queen's Ct FY2 ....152 B2
Queen's Dr Carnforth LA5 .223 E1
Oswaldtwistle BB5 ....103 F3
Queen's Gr PR7 ....43 C8
Queen's Lancashire
Regiment Mus The*
PR2 ....118 D4
Queen's Lancashire Way
BB11 ....127 F6
Queen's Park Hospl
BB2 ....102 A2
Queen's Park Rd
Blackburn BB1 ....102 A3
Burnley BB10 ....128 C7
Queen's Park Tech Coll
BB1 ....102 C2
Queen's Prom FY2 ....152 B5
Queen's Rd
Accrington BB5 ....104 C7
Blackburn BB1 ....102 B3
Burnley BB10 ....148 B2
Chorley PR7 ....43 C8
Darwen BB3 ....65 B6
Formby L37 ....11 D2
Fulwood PR2 ....117 E3
Lytham St Anne's FY8 ....89 F5
Walton-le-D PR5 ....97 E4
Queen's Sq
Hoddlesden BB3 ....82 F1
Poulton-le-F FY6 ....153 D3
7 Rawtenstall BB4 ....86 A2
Queen's Terr
3 Bacup OL13 ....70 E8
Blackburn BB2 ....101 B1
Fleetwood FY7 ....199 C5
Queens Ave L37 ....11 E5
Queens Croft L37 ....11 D2
Queens Ct Fulwood PR2 ..117 E3
Ormskirk L39 ....15 E4
Queens Ctyd 7 PR9 ....35 C8
Queens Dr Fulwood PR2 ..117 D6
Longridge PR3 ....140 A7
Morecambe LA4 ....217 E6
Staining FY3 ....131 E5
Queens Drive Prim Sch
PR2 ....117 D5
Queens Garth BD23 ....197 B5
Queens Gn L39 ....13 F5
Queens Jubilee Nature
Trail* PR8 ....34 E5
Queens Pl Kirkham PR4 ..113 F7
Ramsbottom BL9 ....50 C2
Queens Rd Clitheroe BB7 .166 E7
Orrell WN5 ....10 C5
Southport PR9 ....35 C8
Queens Rd W BB5 ....104 A7
Queens Ret Pk PR1 ....97 B7
Queens Sq 1 FY1 ....130 B5
Queens Wlk FY5 ....175 D4
Queensberry Rd BB11 ..127 E5
Queensborough Rd BB5 .104 B7
Queensbury Rd FY5 ....175 C2
Queenscourt Ave PR1 ....96 E2
Queenscourt Hospice
PR8 ....35 F4
Queensdale Cl PR5 ....97 E4
Queensgate Chorley PR7 ..43 B7
Nelson BB9 ....148 D7
Queensway
Bamber Bridge PR5 ....97 E1
Blackburn BB2 ....81 A8
Blackpool FY4 ....110 C7
Brinscall PR6 ....62 F8
Church BB5 ....103 F7
Clitheroe BB7 ....166 E7
Euxton PR7 ....60 E2
Higher Penwortham PR1 ....96 B6
Leyland PR25 ....59 E7
Lytham St Anne's FY4,FY8 .111 B2
Newchurch BB4 ....86 E1
Poulton-le-F FY6 ....153 D3
Preston PR2 ....116 F2
Shevington WN6 ....19 F4
Waddington BB7 ....189 B4
Warton PR4 ....92 E7
Queensway Cl PR1 ....96 B6
Queensway Ct FY8 ....111 A1
Queensway Ind Est FY8 ..111 A2
Quernmore Ave FY3 ....131 A3
Quernmore Brow LA2 ..232 B5
Quernmore CE Prim Sch
LA2 ....232 A7
Quernmore Dr
Glasson LA2 ....209 E4
Kelbrook BB18 ....195 A5
Quernmore Ind Est PR4 ..93 C6
Quernmore Rd
Caton LA2 ....237 B2
Kirkby L33 ....1 A3
Lancaster LA1,LA2 ....215 D7
Quernmore Wlk L33 ....1 A3
Quillet The LA5 ....224 F3
Quin St PR25 ....77 A1
Quinton Cl PR8 ....21 A4

R

Rabbit La Burscough L40 ..24 F4
Cow Ark BB7 ....187 F6
Raby Sq LA4 ....217 B6
Raby St
4 Morecambe LA4 ....217 B5
1 Rawtenstall BB4 ....86 A2
Radburn Brow PR6 ....78 B3
Radburn Cl PR6 ....78 B3
Radcliffe Ct BB12 ....127 A6
Radcliffe Rd FY7 ....198 F2
Radeclyffe St BB7 ....189 E1
Radfield Ave 14 BB3 ....65 A8
Radfield Head BB3 ....64 F8
Radfield Rd BB3 ....64 F8
Radford Bank Gdns 12
BB3 ....65 A8
Radford Gdns BB3 ....65 A7
Radford St BB3 ....65 A8
Radley Ave FY3 ....130 E8
Radnor Ave
Burnley BB12 ....127 A7
Radnor Ave *continued*
Cleveleys FY5 ....175 F1
Radnor Cl BB5 ....103 C4
Radnor Dr PR9 ....53 F3
Radnor St Accrington BB5 .104 B7
5 Preston PR1 ....96 E8
Radway Cl FY5 ....152 F7
Radworth Cres FY4 ....131 B1
Raeburn Ave BB11 ....127 E3
Raedale Ave BB10 ....148 B4
Raeside Ct FY8 ....90 A4
Raglan Rd Burnley BB11 ..127 E5
Morecambe LA3 ....216 E3
Raglan St 8 Colne BB8 ....171 D4
4 Nelson BB9 ....148 D8
Preston PR2 ....117 D2
Raikes Hill 2 FY1 ....130 C5
Raikes Hill Dr LA2 ....218 C8
Raikes Mews 6 FY1 ....130 C5
Raikes Par FY1 ....130 C5
Raikes Rd
Great Eccleston PR3 ....156 C5
Preston PR1 ....118 C1
Thornton FY5 ....153 E8
Rail Cl WA11 ....8 F2
Railgate OL13 ....71 C8
Railton Ave BB2 ....81 A8
Railway App L39 ....15 F5
Railway Ave PR9 ....54 F5
Railway Cotts Coppull PR7 .42 F1
Preston PR4 ....116 C3
Salwick PR4 ....115 C4
Railway Crossing La
LA1 ....214 C5
Railway Gr 5 BB1 ....102 A7
Railway Path L39 ....15 E4
Railway Pl LA2 ....209 F5
Railway Rd
Adlington PR6,PR7 ....31 A7
Blackburn BB1 ....101 E5
Brinscall PR6 ....63 A8
Chorley PR6 ....61 D1
Darwen BB3 ....82 A1
Haslingden BB4 ....85 B4
Ormskirk L39 ....15 F5
Skelmersdale WN8 ....8 E8
Railway St Bacup OL13 ....70 B8
23 Barnoldswick BB18 ....196 B2
Brierfield BB9 ....148 B5
Burnley BB11 ....127 F7
Chorley PR7 ....43 D7
Foulridge BB8 ....194 D1
Lancaster LA1 ....214 F6
Leyland PR25 ....77 B2
Nelson BB9 ....148 E7
Ramsbottom BL0 ....50 C6
Ramsbottom,Summerseat
BL0,BL9 ....50 C2
Southport PR8 ....35 B5
Railway Terr
Brierfield BB9 ....148 B5
Entwistle BL7 ....48 B8
Great Harwood BB6 ....124 C4
10 Kirkham PR4 ....113 F6
Rawtenstall BB4 ....85 F1
Simonstone BB12 ....125 E8
Southport PR8 ....35 A5
Railway View
5 Accrington BB5 ....104 C6
Billington BB7 ....144 B4
Blackburn BB2 ....101 B2
Brierfield BB9 ....148 B6
Croston PR26 ....58 A2
3 Darwen BB3 ....65 B8
Railway View Ave BB7 ..189 E1
Railway View Rd BB7 ..189 E1
Rainford Junc WA11 ....8 F2
Rainford Rd L39,WA11 ....8 C4
Rainhall Cres BB18 ....196 D3
Rainhall Rd BB18 ....196 B2
Rake 4 BL0 ....50 B6
Rake Fold BL0 ....50 A6
Rake Foot BB4 ....85 B3
Rake La PR4 ....92 D5
Rake The LA2 ....232 E1
Rake Top OL12 ....52 C1
Rake Top Ave BB12 ....146 F6
Rakehead La OL13 ....70 B8
Rakehouse Brow LA2 ..232 F2
Rakes Bridge BB3 ....82 A7
Rakes House Rd BB9 ....170 F2
Rakes La BD23 ....231 F5
Rakes Rd LA2 ....237 E4
Raleigh Ave FY4 ....110 B5
Raleigh Cl FY8 ....110 D1
Raleigh Rd PR2 ....117 E6
Raleigh St BB12 ....126 E7
Ralph St BB5 ....104 C8
Ralph's Wife's La PR9 ....54 E6
Ramparts The LA1 ....218 E2
Ramper Gate FY5 ....175 D2
Rams Clough La BB5 ....84 A8
Ramsay Cl FY8 ....110 D1
Ramsay Ct FY6 ....199 D5
Ramsbottom Cottage Hospl
BL0 ....50 C5
Ramsbottom Heritage Ctr*
BL0 ....50 B7
Ramsbottom La BL0 ....50 C7
Ramsbottom Rd
Hawkshaw BL8,BL7 ....49 A3
Horwich BL6 ....32 C3
Ramsbottom St BB5 ....104 B7
Ramsbottom Sta BL0 ....50 C6
Ramsbottom Stubbins Prim
Sch BL0 ....68 D1
Ramsden St LA5 ....223 D2
Ramsey Ave Bacup OL13 ..88 A1
Ramsey Ave *continued*
Blackpool FY3 ....130 D7
Preston PR1 ....118 D3
Ramsey Gr BB10 ....148 C2
Ramsey Rd BB2 ....101 D1
Ramsgate Cl PR4 ....92 E7
Ramsgate Rd FY8 ....90 A8
Ramsgreave & Wilpshire Sta
BB1 ....122 F4
Ramsgreave Ave BB1 ..122 D2
Ramsgreave Dr BB1 ....122 D1
Ramsgreave Rd BB1 ....122 E4
Ramshill Ave FY6 ....153 B5
Ramson Ct LA3 ....217 B2
Ranaldsway PR25 ....59 D8
Randal St BB1 ....101 E6
Randall St 10 BB10 ....148 B1
Randolph St 21 BB1 ....102 A4
Ranelagh Dr PR8 ....21 F7
Range High Sch L37 ....2 C8
Ranger St BB5 ....104 B5
Rangeway Ave FY4 ....110 C7
Ranglet Rd PR5 ....78 B7
Rangletts Ave PR7 ....43 C6
Ranglit Ave PR2 ....116 C1
Rankin Ave PR4 ....73 F2
Rankin Cl BB18 ....196 C2
Rankin Dr BB3 ....82 E1
Ranlea Ave LA4 ....218 A6
Ranleigh Dr WN8 ....27 A1
Rannoch Dr BB2 ....100 F1
Ranslett Ct L37 ....12 A3
Rantreefold Rd LA2 ....239 C4
Rapley La PR4 ....136 A8
Ratcliffe Fold 5 BB4 ....85 B3
Ratcliffe St Darwen BB3 ..65 B8
10 Haslingden BB4 ....85 B3
Ratcliffe Wharf La PR3 ..207 B1
Rathbone Rd L38 ....2 F4
Rathlyn Ave FY3 ....130 E7
Rathmell CE Prim Sch
BD24 ....236 E7
Rathmell Cl FY3 ....153 B1
Rathmill Sike BB7 ....230 B1
Rathmore Cres PR9 ....54 B3
Ratten La PR4 ....95 D3
Raven Ave BB4 ....68 A7
Raven Cl PR7 ....42 F5
Raven Croft BB4 ....68 B8
Raven Meols La L37 ....11 F2
Raven Moels Hills Nature
Reserve* L37 ....2 B7
Raven Oak La BB10 ....129 B5
Raven Pk BB4 ....68 B8
Raven Rd BB2 ....101 B5
Raven St 3 Nelson BB9 ..170 F1
Preston PR1 ....118 C1
Raven's Cl FY3 ....131 B7
Ravendale Cl OL12 ....52 A1
Ravenglass Ave L31 ....5 D2
Ravenglass Cl
Blackburn BB2 ....102 A1
Blackpool FY4 ....110 E7
Kirkham PR4 ....114 A7
Ravenhead Dr WN8 ....10 A7
Ravenhead Way WN8 ....9 F6
Ravenhill Dr PR7 ....61 C1
Ravens Cl LA1 ....218 C3
Ravens Close Brow LA2 ..241 F1
Ravens Gr BB10 ....148 C4
Ravens The L37 ....11 F2
Ravens Wood BB2 ....101 B5
Ravenscroft L37 ....11 F2
Ravenscroft Ave L39 ....15 E4
Ravenscroft Cl BB1 ....123 A1
Ravenscroft Way BB18 ..196 C3
Ravensthorpe PR7 ....61 A1
Ravenswing Ave BB2 ..101 B7
Ravenswood
Fulwood PR2 ....118 E2
Great Harwood BB6 ....124 B6
Ravenswood Ave FY3 ..131 B7
Ravenwood Ave FY4 ..110 D5
Rawcliffe Dr PR2 ....95 E8
Rawcliffe Rd
12 Chorley PR7 ....43 C7
Ratten Row PR3 ....156 C7
Rawcliffe St
Blackpool FY4 ....110 B8
Burnley BB11 ....128 A6
Rawlinson Ct PR9 ....35 D8
Rawlinson Gr PR9 ....53 F1
Rawlinson La PR6 ....43 E1
Rawlinson Rd PR9 ....53 E1
Rawlinson St
1 Darwen BB3 ....65 B6
16 Horwich BL6 ....32 B4
5 Kirkham PR4 ....113 F6
Raws St BB11 ....128 A6
Rawson Ave BB5 ....104 A4
Rawson St 12 BB10 ....148 B1
Rawsons Rake BL0,BL8 ..50 A6
Rawsthorne Ave
Edenfield BL0 ....68 D2
Haslingden BB4 ....85 B2
Rawstorne Cl PR4 ....93 A6
Rawstorne Cres PR4 ....95 E1
Rawstorne Rd PR1 ....96 B5
Rawstorne St BB2 ....101 C4
Rawstron St OL12 ....71 C1
Rawtenstall Balladen Com
Prim Sch BB4 ....68 F8
Rawtenstall Cribden House
Com Specl Sch BB4 ....85 E1
Rawtenstall Rd BB4 ....85 C1

Rawtenstall Sta BB4 ......85 F1
Rawtenstall Water Prim Sch BB4 ......87 A8
Rawtenstall Waterfoot Prim Sch BB4 ......69 F8
Rawthey Rd 5 LA1 ......218 B2
Ray La PR3 ......181 F4
Raybourne Ave FY6 ......153 C3
Raygill Ave BB11 ......127 D3
Raygill Pl 3 LA1 ......218 B2
Raylees BL0 ......50 C4
Raymond Ave FY2 ......130 D8
Raynor St BB2 ......101 D5
Rays Dr LA1 ......214 F3
Read St 2 BB5 ......125 A1
Read St John's CE Prim Sch BB12 ......145 D2
Read's Ave FY1 ......130 C4
Reading Cl 14 BB1 ......102 A4
Reads Ct 7 FY1 ......130 C4
Reaney Ave 3 FY4 ......110 E7
Rear West Lodge FY6 ......177 C1
Record St BB18 ......196 B1
Rectory Cl Chorley PR7 ......43 C8
Croston PR26 ......58 C2
Darwen BB3 ......65 C8
Newchurch BB4 ......86 E1
Tarleton PR4 ......57 A5
Rectory Gdns LA2 ......206 C5
Rectory Hill BL9 ......33 D4
Rectory La Bury BL9 ......33 D4
Standish WN1,WN6 ......30 A1
Rectory Paddock LA2 ......219 C6
Rectory Rd Blackpool FY4 ......130 E1
Burnley BB12 ......127 F7
Southport PR9 ......54 A1
Red Bank Rd FY2 ......152 C4
Red Barnes L37 ......11 F5
Red Bridge La LA5 ......224 F4
Red Cat La L40 ......25 E7
Red Court Cvn Pk LA5 ......223 D1
Red Cross St 5 PR1 ......96 E7
Red Delph La WA11 ......8 D1
Red Fold L39 ......15 C2
Red House La PR7 ......41 B6
Red La Colne BB8 ......171 B7
Eccleston PR7 ......41 E6
Red Lees Ave BB10 ......128 F4
Red Lees Rd BB10 ......129 A2
Red Lion Cl 2 L31 ......5 C1
Red Lion Sh Ctr L31 ......5 C1
Red Lion St
Burnley BB11 ......128 A5
Earby BB18 ......197 C2
Red Marsh Dr FY5 ......176 C3
Red Marsh Ind Est FY5 ......176 C3
Red Rake BB1 ......101 C7
Red Rose Ct BB2 ......101 D4
Red Rose Lodge FY4 ......130 F1
Red Sands L39 ......15 D3
Red Scar Ind Est PR2 ......119 B5
Red Scar St BB8 ......171 C4
Red Shell La BB1,BB5 ......83 B7
Red Spar Rd BB10 ......148 D3
Redcar Ave Cleveleys FY5 ......175 F5
Fulwood PR2 ......117 A4
Redcar Cl PR8 ......35 F3
Redcar Rd Blackpool FY1 ......130 B8
Lancaster LA1 ......215 B3
Redcliffe Gdns L39 ......15 E3
Redcross St OL12 ......52 F1
Redcross St N OL12 ......52 F1
Rede Ave FY7 ......198 C2
Redearth Rd BB3 ......65 A8
Redearth St BB3 ......65 A8
Redeswood Ave FY5 ......152 E8
Redfearn Wood OL12 ......52 B2
Redgate Formby L37 ......12 A2
Ormskirk L39 ......15 D5
Redgate Cl BB11 ......128 B3
Redgate Dr L37 ......12 B2
Redgate Prim Sch L37 ......12 A2
Redhill PR4 ......95 C1
Redhill Gr PR6 ......61 E3
Redhills Dr PR8 ......35 F3
Redisher Cl BL0 ......49 F3
Redisher Croft BL0 ......49 F3
Redisher La BL8 ......49 E3
Redlam BB2 ......101 B3
Redlam Brow BB2 ......101 C3
Redman Rd BB10 ......148 B4
Redmayne Dr LA5 ......223 F2
Redmayne St 3 PR1 ......97 D8
Redness Cl BB9 ......148 E6
Redruth Dr
Carnforth LA5 ......223 C1
Crag Bank LA5 ......221 C8
Redruth St BB12 ......127 D6
Redsands Dr PR2 ......118 D5
Redstart Pl 12 FY5 ......175 F1
Redvers Rd BB3 ......81 E5
Redvers St Burnley BB10 ......148 B1
Lancaster LA1 ......214 D8
Redvers Terr FY1 ......130 B8
Redwing Ave
1 Cleveleys FY5 ......175 F4
Great Harwood BB6 ......124 B6
Redwing Rd BL8 ......49 F2
Redwood Ave
Leyland PR25 ......76 E1
Maghull L31 ......5 C3
Redwood Chase PR4 ......113 E4
Redwood Cl
Blackpool FY4 ......110 C4
Rochdale OL12 ......52 B3
Redwood Dr Chorley PR7 ......43 D6
Longridge PR3 ......140 A8
Morecambe LA4 ......217 E5
Ormskirk L39 ......15 D4
Rawtenstall BB4 ......68 F8
Redwood Gdns FY5 ......176 E2
Redwood Hts LA1 ......215 C7
Reed Row BB8 ......171 D3
Reed St Bacup OL13 ......88 A3
Burnley BB11 ......128 A4
Reedfield Brierfield BB10 ......148 C4
Clayton Brook PR5 ......78 C4
Reedfield Pl PR5 ......78 A6
Reedley Dr
Brierfield BB10 ......148 C4
Brierfield,Reedley BB10 ......148 B4
Reedley Farm Cl BB10 ......148 B5
Reedley Gr BB10 ......148 B3
Reedley Prim Sch BB10 ......148 C4
Reedley Rd BB9,BB10 ......148 C5
Reedmace Wlk LA3 ......217 B2
Reeds Brow WA11 ......9 C1
Reeds Cl BB4 ......86 A6
Reeds La BB4 ......86 A6
Reeds The Lancaster LA1 ......218 C1
Ormskirk L39 ......15 D6
Reedsholme Cl BB4 ......86 A6
Reedy Acre Pl FY8 ......90 F4
Reedy Moor Terr BB8 ......194 C1
Reedyford Cott BB9 ......170 D2
Reedyford Rd BB9 ......170 E2
Reedymoor La BB8 ......194 C1
Reeford Gr BB7 ......166 D7
Rees Pk L40 ......25 F3
Reeth Way 3 BB5 ......103 F4
Reeval Cl BB18 ......197 C2
Reeveswood PR7 ......41 B6
Regal Ave FY4 ......110 E6
Regal Ct PR8 ......21 D5
Regal Terr 5 LA1 ......218 D3
Regency Ave PR5 ......77 D8
Regency Cl Kirkham PR4 ......113 E5
Whalley BB7 ......144 A7
Regency Gdns
Blackpool FY2 ......152 D2
Southport PR8 ......34 E4
Regent Ave Colne BB8 ......171 E6
Lytham St Anne's FY8 ......90 D6
Regent Cl Padiham BB12 ......126 C7
Southport PR8 ......34 F4
Regent Ct
4 Blackpool FY1 ......130 B6
Fulwood PR2 ......117 E5
Lytham St Anne's FY8 ......89 D8
2 Southport PR9 ......35 C8
Regent Dr PR2 ......117 D4
Regent Gr PR2 ......117 E5
Regent Mews PR8 ......34 F4
Regent Park Ave LA3, LA4 ......216 F3
Regent Park Gr LA4 ......217 A4
Regent Pk PR2 ......117 E5
Regent Pl BB9 ......170 E2
Regent Rd
Bamber Bridge PR5 ......97 D4
Blackpool FY1 ......130 C5
Chorley PR7 ......43 C7
Church BB5 ......103 F7
6 Leyland PR25 ......77 A1
Morecambe LA3 ......216 F3
Southport PR8 ......34 F4
Regent Rd E FY1 ......130 C5
Regent St Bacup OL13 ......88 A2
Blackburn BB1 ......101 E5
Brierfield BB9 ......148 B5
Coppull PR7 ......42 E1
Haslingden BB4 ......85 B3
Lancaster LA1 ......214 E7
Longridge PR3 ......140 A7
Nelson BB9 ......170 F2
Preston PR1 ......96 F6
Ramsbottom BL0 ......50 A4
Rochdale OL12 ......52 F1
Waddington BB7 ......189 B4
Regents Cl BB2 ......100 C2
Regents Terr FY6 ......153 E3
Regents View BB1 ......122 E1
Regents Way PR7 ......60 D2
Regentsway 6 PR5 ......77 E8
Reginald St BB8 ......171 C5
Reigate PR6 ......61 F3
Reiver Rd PR26 ......76 C3
Renacres Hall Hospl L39 ......23 B5
Renacres La L39 ......23 B5
Rendel St BB12 ......127 C7
Rendsburg Way 15 LA1 ......214 F8
Renfrey Cl L39 ......15 E8
Rennie Cl PR3 ......181 D6
Rennie Ct LA1 ......214 E5
Rennie St BB10 ......128 C5
Renshaw Dr
Bamber Bridge PR5 ......97 E2
Bury BL9 ......33 C3
Renshaw St 8 BB10 ......148 B1
Renwick Ave FY4 ......110 D8
Repton Ave
Blackpool FY1 ......130 C8
Morecambe LA4 ......217 F4
Reservoir Rd FY5 ......176 C3
Reservoir St
Burnley BB11 ......127 F4
Darwen BB3 ......81 F1
Reta Dr FY5 ......176 A3
Retford Rd L33 ......1 A2
Revidge Rd BB1,BB2 ......101 C7
Revoe Prim Sch FY1 ......130 C3
Revoe St FY1 ......130 C3
Rewe Cl BB2 ......81 C8
Rexington Bldgs BB11 ......127 C4
Reynolds St
Burnley BB11 ......127 E3
Lancaster LA1 ......218 C1
Rhoda St BB9 ......170 F1
Rhoden Rd Leyland PR26 ......76 C1
Oswaldtwistle BB5 ......103 D2
Rhodes Ave
Blackburn BB1 ......101 D8
Haslingden BB4 ......68 A7
Rhodesway PR5 ......98 E2
Rhuddlan Cl BB4 ......85 B1
Rhuddlan Gdns FY5 ......176 D2
Rhyddings High Sch BB5 ......103 E4
Rhyddings High Sch (Annexe) BB5 ......103 E5
Rhyddings St BB5 ......103 E4
Rhyddings The BL9 ......33 E7
Rhyl Ave BB1 ......101 E7
Rhyl St FY7 ......199 B5
Ribble Ave
Brierfield BB10 ......148 C2
Darwen BB3 ......81 E4
Freckleton PR4 ......93 A6
Great Harwood BB6 ......124 E6
Grindleton BB7 ......190 B7
Maghull L31 ......5 E2
Southport PR9 ......54 C4
Whalley BB7 ......144 A7
Ribble Bank PR1 ......96 B6
Ribble Bank St PR1 ......96 E7
Ribble Brook Ho PR1 ......117 F1
Ribble Bsns Pk BB1 ......102 B8
Ribble Cl Freckleton PR4 ......93 A6
Middleworth Green PR1 ......96 E4
3 Preston PR1 ......96 E6
Withnell PR6 ......80 A1
Ribble Cres Kirkham PR4 ......114 B5
5 Preston PR5 ......97 C6
Ribble Ct 2 PR1 ......96 D6
Ribble Discovery Ctr* FY8 ......90 C3
Ribble Dr Baldingstone BL9 ......50 F1
Hesketh Bank PR4 ......73 E4
West Bradford BB7 ......189 D7
Ribble Hall PR1 ......117 F1
Ribble Ho Blackburn BB1 ......101 F5
11 Preston PR1 ......97 D8
Ribble La BB7 ......190 D6
Ribble Lodge 10 FY8 ......91 A3
Ribble Rd Blackpool FY1 ......130 C4
Fleetwood FY7 ......198 F4
Leyland PR25 ......59 D8
Shevington Moor WN6 ......29 B2
Ribble St Bacup OL13 ......71 A8
Blackburn BB1 ......101 E6
Lytham St Anne's FY8 ......89 D6
Padiham BB12 ......126 D8
Preston PR1 ......96 E7
Ribble View BB7 ......189 F4
Ribble View Cl PR4 ......92 F6
Ribble Way BB7 ......166 C8
Ribblesdale Ave
Accrington BB5 ......104 B8
Clitheroe BB7 ......189 E2
Wilpshire BB1 ......123 A7
Ribblesdale Cl
Blackpool FY4 ......111 A8
Kirkham PR4 ......114 A5
Ribblesdale Ct
Gisburn BB7 ......231 B3
5 Morecambe LA4 ......217 B5
Ribblesdale Dr
Forton PR3 ......207 B3
Grimsargh PR2 ......139 C1
Ribblesdale High Sch Technology Coll BB7 ......166 E7
Ribblesdale Pl
Barrowford BB9 ......170 E6
Blackburn BB2 ......101 C5
Chorley PR7 ......43 B7
Preston PR1 ......96 F6
Ribblesdale Rd PR3 ......141 E3
Ribblesdale St BB10 ......128 B8
Ribblesdale View BB7 ......190 E5
Ribbleside Cvn Pk PR3 ......142 A4
Ribbleton Ave PR2 ......118 E2
Ribbleton Avenue Inf Sch PR1 ......118 D2
Ribbleton Avenue Meth Jun Sch PR1 ......118 D2
Ribbleton Dr BB5 ......104 C8
Ribbleton Gr BB7 ......144 A7
Ribbleton Hall Cres 2 PR2 ......118 F3
Ribbleton Hall Dr PR2 ......118 F3
Ribbleton Hall High Sch PR2 ......118 F3
Ribbleton Hospl PR2 ......118 F2
Ribbleton La PR1 ......118 C1
Ribbleton Pl 6 PR1 ......97 B8
Ribbleton St 9 PR1 ......97 B8
Ribby Ave Kirkham PR4 ......113 F5
Wrea Green PR4 ......113 C4
Ribby Pl Blackpool FY4 ......131 B1
Preston PR2 ......116 F1
Ribby Rd Kirkham PR4 ......113 F4
Wrea Green PR4 ......113 C4
Ribby-with-Wrea CE Prim Sch PR4 ......113 B4
Ribchester Ave
Blackpool FY4 ......131 B1
Burnley BB10 ......128 D5
Ribchester Rd
Copster Green BB1 ......142 A1
Dinckley BB6,PR3 ......142 C4
Lytham St Anne's FY8 ......91 D4
Ribchester Rd *continued*
Wilpshire BB1 ......122 E6
Ribchester Roman Bath Ho* PR3 ......141 E3
Ribchester St Wilfrid's CE Prim Sch PR3 ......141 E3
Ribchester Way BB9 ......148 D4
Rice Gr FY1 ......130 D8
Richard Burch St 2 BL9 ......33 A3
Richard Durning's Endowed Prim Sch L40 ......27 D7
Richard St Brierfield BB9 ......148 B5
Burnley BB11 ......128 B5
Shuttleworth BL0 ......50 E7
Weir OL13 ......88 A7
Richard Thornton's CE Prim Sch LA6 ......242 B3
Richard's St 7 PR4 ......113 F6
Richard's Way FY8 ......110 E2
Richards Rd WN6 ......29 B3
Richards Way 3 FY5 ......175 F1
Richards Wlk 7 LA1 ......218 B1
Richardson Cl PR4 ......93 C6
Richardson St FY1 ......130 B4
Richmond Ave
Accrington BB5 ......104 B5
Barnoldswick BB18 ......196 A3
Burnley BB10 ......128 F4
Burscough L40 ......25 E3
Cleveleys FY5 ......175 E2
Haslingden BB4 ......85 C2
Lancaster LA1 ......218 D4
Morecambe LA4 ......217 D4
Wrea Green PR4 ......113 B3
Richmond Cl Brinscall PR6 ......62 E8
Hightown L38 ......2 F2
Richmond Cres BB1 ......102 E5
Richmond Ct
8 Blackpool FY1 ......130 B7
Burscough L40 ......25 E3
Chorley PR7 ......43 C6
Leyland PR26 ......76 B1
Richmond Gr L31 ......5 E3
Richmond Hill 23 BB1 ......101 E5
Richmond Hill La PR3 ......207 D2
Richmond Hill St BB5 ......104 B5
Richmond Ho Chorley PR7 ......43 C6
9 Lancaster LA1 ......218 D3
11 Preston PR1 ......97 A7
Richmond Ind Est BB5 ......104 B5
Richmond Mews L40 ......25 E3
Richmond Pk BB3 ......82 A2
Richmond Rd
Accrington BB5 ......104 A4
Barnoldswick BB18 ......196 A3
Barrowford BB9 ......170 C1
Blackpool FY1 ......130 B7
Chorley PR6 ......43 E6
Eccleston PR7 ......41 C7
Lytham St Anne's FY8 ......89 E6
Southport PR8 ......34 F2
Richmond St
Accrington BB5 ......104 A5
Accrington BB5 ......104 B5
Burnley BB11 ......127 E5
Horwich BL6 ......32 B3
2 Preston PR1 ......97 B7
Richmond Terr
17 Blackburn BB1 ......101 E5
Clitheroe BB7 ......166 D7
Darwen BB3 ......82 A2
Rickard Rd BB9 ......148 E6
Ridding La BB7 ......144 B5
Riddings Ave BB10 ......128 F6
Riddings La BB7 ......144 C6
Riddiough Ct OL12 ......52 C8
Ridehalgh La BB10 ......149 F2
Ridehalgh St BB8 ......171 B3
Ridge Ave BB10 ......128 D6
Ridge Cl PR9 ......54 C5
Ridge Ct Burnley BB10 ......128 C7
Longridge PR3 ......140 C8
Ridge Gr LA3 ......212 F8
Ridge La Lancaster LA1 ......218 E1
Lancaster,Ridge LA1 ......219 A2
Roughlee BB12 ......169 F4
Ridge Prim Sch LA1 ......218 F1
Ridge Rd Burnley BB11 ......128 B6
Chorley PR6 ......43 E7
Ridge Row BB10 ......128 D6
Ridge Sq LA1 ......218 F1
Ridge St
Barnoldswick BB18 ......196 B2
Lancaster LA1 ......218 E1
Ridge Way PR1 ......96 E4
Ridgeford Gdns PR2 ......117 D5
Ridgemont PR2 ......117 C6
Ridgeway
Barrowford BB9 ......170 C3
Barrowford BB9 ......170 D3
Great Harwood BB6 ......124 B6
Ridgeway Ave BB2 ......82 A8
Ridgeway Dr Maghull L31 ......5 E3
Thornton FY5 ......153 D8
Ridgeway The
Fleetwood FY7 ......198 D3
Nelson BB9 ......148 D7
Ridgeways BB4 ......85 C2
Ridgmont Cl BL6 ......32 F3
Ridgmont Dr BL6 ......32 F3
Ridgway BL6 ......31 C2
Ridgway Ct FY8 ......90 A7
Ridgwood Ave FY3 ......130 E5
Riding Barn St BB5 ......103 F7
Riding Cl BB18 ......196 C2
Riding Head La BL0 ......50 F8
Riding La L39 ......13 E4
Riding St Burnley BB11 ......127 E5
Riding St *continued*
Preston PR1 ......117 F1
Southport PR8 ......35 B6
Ridings The
Burnley BB12 ......127 D8
Lucas Green PR6 ......61 C6
Southport PR9 ......54 A3
Ridley La
Barber's Moor PR26 ......58 D3
Maghull L31 ......5 D1
Mawdesley L40 ......40 F2
Ridley Rd PR2 ......117 C2
Ridley St 2 FY3 ......130 D5
Rifle St BB4 ......85 B2
Rigby Ave BL6 ......31 C2
Rigby Cl PR4 ......93 C6
Rigby Rd Blackpool FY1 ......130 B3
Maghull L31 ......5 B3
Rigby St Colne BB8 ......171 C5
Nelson BB9 ......148 D8
Preston PR1 ......97 C8
Rigg Ho 10 LA1 ......218 D2
Rigg La Quernmore LA2 ......232 B7
Whitechapel PR3 ......184 B1
Rigg St BB9 ......148 E8
Riley Ave FY8 ......89 F5
Riley Cl PR25 ......60 A8
Riley Ct FY8 ......89 F4
Riley Green Switch Rd BB2,PR5 ......79 F7
Riley St Accrington BB5 ......104 B4
Bacup OL13 ......87 F5
Brierfield BB9 ......148 B5
Burnley BB11 ......128 B4
Earby BB18 ......197 B2
Rimington Ave
Accrington BB5 ......104 A3
Burnley BB10 ......128 D5
Colne BB8 ......171 C6
Rimington Cl BB2 ......101 F2
Rimington Cvn Pk BB7 ......231 B1
Rimington La BB7 ......191 D7
Rimington Pl
Lytham St Anne's FY8 ......90 B6
Nelson BB9 ......171 B1
Rimmer Gn PR8 ......36 D1
Rimmer's Ave Formby L37 ......11 E6
Southport PR8 ......35 B6
Ring Dyke Way FY8 ......91 A4
Ring Lows La OL12 ......52 F4
Ring O'Bells La L40 ......26 B2
Ring Way PR1 ......96 F7
Rings St BB4 ......106 A2
Ringstone Cres BB9 ......149 B8
Ringstones La LA2 ......239 D4
Ringtail Ct L40 ......25 B4
Ringtail Ind Est L40 ......25 B2
Ringtail Pl L40 ......25 B4
Ringtail Rd L40 ......25 B4
Rington Ave FY6 ......153 B6
Ringway Chorley PR7 ......43 A7
Cleveleys FY5 ......175 E4
Ringwood Ave BL0 ......50 A4
Ringwood Cl
Accrington BB5 ......125 B1
Lytham St Anne's FY8 ......90 F3
Ringwood Rd PR1 ......118 C2
Ripley Cl L31 ......5 E1
Ripley Ct LA1 ......214 F6
Ripley Dr FY8 ......90 B6
Ripley St Thomas' CE High Sch LA1 ......214 F6
Ripon Ave 1 LA1 ......218 D4
Ripon Brook PR1 ......118 F1
Ripon Cl Cleveleys FY5 ......175 E5
Great Eccleston PR3 ......156 C5
Southport PR8 ......35 F3
Ripon Hall Ave BL0 ......50 B4
Ripon Pl LA3 ......212 E6
Ripon Rd Blackpool FY1 ......130 D4
Lytham St Anne's FY8 ......90 D5
Oswaldtwistle BB5 ......103 C5
Ripon St Blackburn BB1 ......102 B4
Nelson BB9 ......148 D7
Preston PR1 ......117 E2
Ripon Terr PR1 ......118 F1
Rise The LA5 ......221 B6
Risedale Dr PR3 ......140 B7
Risedale Gr BB2 ......81 A7
Rishton Meth Prim Sch BB1 ......124 B1
Rishton Rd
Clayton-le-M BB5 ......124 E3
Wilpshire BB1 ......123 C5
Rishton St FY1 ......130 C4
Rishton Sta BB1 ......103 A8
Rising Bridge Rd BB4, BB5 ......85 A7
Ritherham Ave FY5 ......175 D3
River Bank Terr BB5 ......125 E6
River Cl L37 ......12 B1
River Dr BB12 ......126 D8
River Hts PR5 ......77 C8
River Lea Gdns BB7 ......166 F8
River Par PR1 ......96 D6
River Rd FY5 ......176 E3
River St Bacup OL13 ......87 F1
Blackburn BB1 ......101 F4
Colne BB8 ......171 D4
Darwen BB3 ......81 F2
Lancaster LA1 ......218 C1
Preston PR1 ......96 E7
Ramsbottom BL0 ......50 C6
Trawden BB8 ......172 C3
River View Glasson LA2 ......209 E5
Tarleton PR4 ......57 A8
River Way BB9 ......170 D4
Rivermead Ct PR3 ......204 C1

Rivermead Dr PR3 181 C8
Rivermeade PR8 35 D4
Rivers Edge The OL12 71 C1
Rivers St WN5 10 E6
Rivers View Fold LA2 226 A8
Riversedge Rd PR25 59 C8
Riversgate FY7 198 F4
Riverside
Bamber Bridge PR5 77 E7
Clitheroe BB7 166 B8
Hightown L38 2 F4
Preston PR1 96 E5
Riverside Ave PR26 76 E4
Riverside Cl Halton LA2 219 C6
Leyland PR26 76 E4
Riverside Cres PR26 58 A2
Riverside Ct OL12 71 D4
Riverside Cvn Site PR9 55 D3
Riverside Dr
Hambleton FY6 177 B1
Ramsbottom BL0 50 B2
Riverside Fold BB12 169 E5
Riverside Ind Est BB5 124 D2
Riverside Ind Pk PR3 181 C2
Riverside Lofts LA1 218 C1
Riverside Mews BB4 86 F4
Riverside Mill 3 BB8 171 B4
Riverside Park Ind Est LA1 218 F4
Riverside Pk BB4 86 F4
Riverside Rd PR1 96 E5
Riverside Terr 4 BB18 197 B1
Riverside View BB5 124 E4
Riverside Wlk BB4 68 A7
Riversleigh Ave
Blackpool FY1 152 C1
Lytham St Anne's FY8 90 E3
Riversleigh Ct FY8 90 E3
Riversway Blackpool FY3 130 F6
4 Lancaster LA1 218 D2
Poulton-le-F FY6 153 F5
Preston PR2,PR4 95 D8
Riversway Bsns Village PR2 96 A8
Riversway Dr BB3 81 F6
Riversway Enterprise Workshops PR2 95 E8
Riversway Managed Workshops PR2 95 F8
Riversway Motor Pk PR2 95 D7
Riverview Ct LA4 217 B3
Riverway Cl PR5 77 D8
Rivington & Blackrod High Sch BL6 32 B6
Rivington & Blackrod High Sch (Annexe) BL6 32 B4
Rivington Ave
Adlington PR6 31 B7
Blackpool FY2 152 D5
Rivington Cl
Poulton-le-F FY6 153 D3
Southport PR8 35 A3
Tarleton PR4 56 F8
Rivington Ctry Pk* BL6 32 A8
Rivington Dr
Burscough L40 25 E3
Skelmersdale WN8 10 C7
Rivington Hall Cl BL0 50 C4
Rivington Ho 2 BL6 32 B4
Rivington La
Adlington PR6 31 D6
Horwich BL6 32 A7
Rivington BL6 44 F1
Rivington Park Ind Sch BL6 44 F1
Rivington Pl PR7 29 D6
Rivington Prim Sch BL6 44 F1
Rivington Rd
Belmont BL6,BL7 46 B4
Chorley PR6 61 E1
Rivington St
Blackburn BB1 102 B4
Blackrod BL6 31 D2
Rochdale OL12 52 F1
Rivington View PR6 61 E1
Rixton Gr FY5 176 B4
Roach Bridge Cotts PR5 98 E6
Roach Rd PR5 99 B4
Roach St BL9 33 C1
Road La OL12 52 D4
Robbin's Bridge L31 5 E5
Robert St Accrington BB5 104 C7
Barnoldswick BB18 196 B2
Blackburn BB2 101 E3
Colne BB8 171 E5
15 Darwen BB3 81 F2
Great Harwood BB6 124 D6
43 Lancaster LA1 214 F8
Newchurch BB4 86 F2
Oswaldtwistle BB5 103 D3
Ramsbottom BL0 68 C1
Roberts Ct Leyland PR25 59 F8
Warton LA5 223 D6
Roberts St 2 Chorley PR7 43 C7
Nelson BB9 148 F8
7 Rawtenstall BB4 86 A3
Robertson Ct FY7 198 F1
Robin Bank Rd BB3 82 A2
Robin Cl PR7 42 D3
Robin Croft LA2 241 A1
Robin Hey PR26 76 B1
Robin Hill Dr WN6 29 B2
Robin Hill La WN6 29 C3
Robin Hood La WN6 28 B3
Robin House La BB10 149 C4
Robin La
High Bentham LA2 239 D8
Hill Dale WN8 27 C5
Robin La continued
Rimington BB7 231 B1
Robin Rd BL0 50 B2
Robin St PR1 118 D1
Robins Cl FY6 153 A4
Robins La Blackpool FY6 153 A4
Carleton FY6 153 A6
Robinson Ct BB18 196 A3
Robinson La BB9,BB10, BB12 148 A4
Robinson St
Blackburn BB1 102 B7
Burnley BB10 128 A8
Chatburn BB7 190 E5
Colne BB8 171 C5
Foulridge BB8 194 D1
Fulwood PR2 117 D3
18 Horwich BL6 32 B4
Robson St BB9 148 B6
Robson Way FY3 153 A2
Roby Mill WN8 19 B3
Roby Mill CE Prim Sch WN8 19 B3
Rochdale Infmy OL12 52 F1
Rochdale Old Rd BL9 33 D4
Rochdale Rd Bacup OL13 88 A1
Bury BL9 33 B2
Edenfield BL0 68 F2
Ramsbottom BL0,BL9 51 B7
Rochester Ave
Cleveleys FY5 175 F4
Morecambe LA4 217 D3
Rochester Cl OL13 88 A7
Rochester Dr BB10 148 C3
Rochford Ave FY5 175 E1
Rock Bridge Fold BB4 86 E5
Rock Brow PR3 163 B7
Rock Fold BL7 47 F1
Rock Gdns PR5 99 B3
Rock Hall Rd BB4 85 B3
Rock La Burnley BB11 128 B3
Tockholes BB3 81 A3
Trawden BB8 172 C3
Rock m' Jock LA2 237 B3
Rock St Accrington BB5 104 E2
Clitheroe BB7 166 E8
18 Haslingden BB4 85 B3
Horwich BL6 32 B3
Shuttleworth BL0 50 E7
Thornton FY5 176 B4
Rock Terr Egerton BL7 47 F1
Pendleton BB7 167 B4
11 Rawtenstall BB4 86 A7
Rock Villa Rd PR6 61 C8
Rock Water (Bird Conservation Ctr)* BB10 129 C2
Rockburgh Cres PR4 75 A5
Rockcliffe Ave OL13 87 E1
Rockcliffe Dr OL13 87 E1
Rockcliffe Rd OL13 87 F1
Rockcliffe St 5 BB4 86 A3
Rockcliffe Villas OL13 70 E8
Rockfield Gdns 2 L31 5 C2
Rockfield Rd BB5 104 D6
Rockfield St BB2 101 E3
Rockhaven Ave BL6 32 C4
Rockingham Rd FY2 152 D3
Rockliffe La OL13 88 A1
Rockliffe Rd OL13 87 F1
Rockliffe St BB2 101 E2
Rockville BB9 170 E5
Rockville Ave FY5 152 F8
Rockwood Cl BB10 148 E3
Roddlesworth La PR6 63 E8
Roddlesworth Nature Trail* BB3 64 B8
Roddlesworth Vistor Ctr* BB3 64 B8
Rodhill La BB7 230 B3
Rodney Ave FY8 110 E1
Rodney St Blackburn BB2 101 C3
3 Preston PR1 96 F8
Rodwell Wlk FY3 130 F8
Roe Greave Rd BB5 103 D3
Roe Hey Dr PR7 42 F2
Roe La PR9 35 E8
Roe Lee Park Prim Sch BB1 122 F2
Roe Lee Pk BB1 122 F2
Roe St OL12 52 C1
Roe-Park Mews PR9 35 E8
Roebuck Cl BB2 101 D3
Roebuck Prim Sch PR2 117 D2
Roebuck St PR2 117 C2
Roeburn Dr LA3 217 F2
Roeburn Pl LA1 218 C2
Roeburn Terr LA2 238 D6
Roeburndale Cres LA3 213 A8
Roedean Ave LA4 217 F4
Roedean Cl Maghull L31 5 D2
12 Thornton FY5 176 A2
Roehampton Cl 11 FY5 176 A2
Rogerley Cl FY8 91 A4
Rogersfield BB6 123 B8
Rolleston Rd BB2 101 B4
Roman Cres LA2 237 C3
Roman Mus* PR3 141 E3
Roman Rd
Blackburn BB1,BB2 82 B8
Preston PR1 97 B7
Whittlestone Head BB3 66 A4
Roman Way
Cleveleys FY5 175 F1
Clitheroe BB7 167 A8
Kirkham PR4 114 C4
Red Scar PR2 119 C6
Roman Way Ind Est PR2 119 C6
Rome Ave BB11 127 C4
Romford Rd PR1 118 C2
Romford St 2 BB12 127 C7
Romiley Dr WN8 17 F2
Romney Ave
Barrowford BB9 170 D3
Blackpool FY4 130 D1
Burnley BB11 127 E3
Fleetwood FY7 198 E3
Romney St BB9 148 D7
Romney Wlk BB1 102 C4
Romsey Ave L37 12 B2
Ronald St Blackburn BB1 102 C5
Burnley BB12 127 A5
Ronaldsway Nelson BB9 171 B2
Preston PR1 118 D3
Ronaldsway Cl OL13 88 B1
Ronbury Cl 1 BB9 170 C1
Roney St BB2 101 C5
Ronwood Cl PR4 155 F1
Ronwood Ct PR2 96 B8
Roocroft Sq BL6 31 C2
Roods The LA5 223 E6
Rook Hill Rd OL13 70 B8
Rook St
Barnoldswick BB18 196 B2
Colne BB8 171 D5
Nelson BB9 170 E1
Preston PR1 118 B1
3 Ramsbottom BL0 50 C6
Rookery Ave WN6 19 E8
Rookery Cl Chorley PR7 43 A6
Kingsfold PR1 96 F2
Rookery Dr PR1 96 F2
Rookery Rd
Barnoldswick BB18 196 C3
Southport PR9 53 F1
Rookwood PR7 41 B6
Rookwood Ave PR7 61 C2
Rooley Moor Rd
Bacup OL12,OL13 70 C4
Rochdale,Shawfield OL12 52 A3
Rochdale,Spotland Fold OL12 52 C1
Rooley St OL12 52 C1
Rooley View OL13 87 E1
Roosevelt Ave LA1 214 D7
Roots La PR4 135 E2
Rope Wlk PR3 181 C7
Ropefield Way OL12 52 E3
Rosary Ave FY4 130 E1
Roscoe Ave FY5 176 D2
Roscoe Lowe Brow PR6 31 D7
Rose Acre La LA5 225 F2
Rose Ave Blackpool FY1 130 D2
Burnley BB11 127 E4
Fulwood PR2 117 C3
Rose Bank Lancaster LA1 215 A5
Rawtenstall BB4 86 A3
Rose Bank St OL13 87 F3
Rose Cl PR25 77 E2
Rose Cotts
Low Bentham LA2 239 B8
Preesall FY6 200 C3
Rose Cres
Skelmersdale WN8 17 E1
Southport PR8 21 C2
Rose Ct 1 FY7 198 F4
Rose Fold
Middleworth Green PR1 96 D4
Thornton FY5 176 B4
Rose Fold Cotts PR1 96 D4
Rose Gdns PR4 73 E4
Rose Gr LA2 210 F4
Rose Grove Sta BB11 127 B5
Rose Hill Euxton PR7 60 C4
Ramsbottom BL0 50 B6
Southport PR8,PR9 35 D6
Rose Hill Ave BB1 102 A4
Rose Hill Rd BB2 100 C1
Rose Hill St Bacup OL13 87 F2
Darwen BB3 65 B8
Rawtenstall BB4 106 A1
Rose Hill Terr 7 BB3 65 B8
Rose La PR1 118 C3
Rose Lea PR2 118 D6
Rose Mount BB4 86 F1
Rose Pl Accrington BB5 104 B4
Ormskirk L39 15 D2
Rose St Accrington BB5 104 B4
Bacup OL13 87 F2
7 Blackburn BB2 101 E3
Darwen BB3 82 B1
Leyland PR25 77 B3
Morecambe LA4 217 B6
Newchurch BB4 86 E2
14 Preston PR1 97 A7
Rose Terr PR2 117 B2
Rose Vale St BB4 86 B2
Roseacre FY4 110 C5
Roseacre Cl BB4 86 F4
Roseacre Dr PR4 156 A1
Roseacre Pl
Lytham St Anne's FY8 90 B8
5 Preston PR2 116 E1
Roseacre Prim Sch FY4 110 C5
Roseacre Rd PR4 134 D6
Rosebank
Clayton-le-M BB5 125 A3
Edenfield BL0 68 D1
2 Preston PR2 116 C1
Rosebank Ave 3 FY4 110 C5
Rosebay Ave BB2 80 D8
Rosebay Cl L37 12 A3
Roseberry Ave PR4 116 E5
Roseberry Cl BL0 50 C3
Rosebery Ave
Blackpool FY4 110 B6
Lancaster LA1 215 A5
Lytham St Anne's FY8 90 B4
Morecambe LA4 217 C4
Rosebery St
Burnley BB10 148 B2
Cornholme OL14 109 B1
Southport PR9 36 A6
Rosecroft Cl L39 15 E6
Rosedale Ave
Blackpool FY4 131 A2
Heysham LA3 213 A8
Rosedale St BB4 85 F5
Rosedene LA2 218 D7
Rosedene Cl PR4 116 E5
Rosefinch Way FY3 131 B3
Rosegarth LA2 218 D7
Rosegrove Cvn Pk FY6 200 A6
Rosegrove Inf Sch BB12 127 A6
Rosegrove La BB11 127 B5
Rosehill Ave
Burnley BB11 127 E4
12 Nelson BB9 170 F1
Rosehill Bsns Pk 1 PR9 35 D6
Rosehill Com Inf Sch BB11 127 F3
Rosehill Dr L39 15 C2
Rosehill Jun Sch BB11 127 E3
Rosehill Mans L39 15 C2
Rosehill Mt BB11 127 E4
Rosehill Rd Burnley BB11 127 F3
Nelson BB8 171 A2
Roseland Ave BB9 148 C6
Roseland Cl L31 5 B4
Roselea Dr PR9 54 C4
Roselyn Ave FY4 110 C5
Rosemary Ave
Blackpool FY4 110 C5
Cleveleys FY5 175 F3
Rosemary Ct Formby L37 11 F3
1 Kingsfold PR1 96 C2
Rosemary La Formby L37 11 F3
Haskayne L39 14 B4
8 Lancaster LA1 214 F8
Swillbrook PR4 136 A1
Rosemeade Ave PR5 77 B8
Rosemede Ave FY4 130 F2
Rosemount OL13 88 A4
Rosemount Ave
Barnoldswick BB18 196 A3
Burnley BB11 127 E4
Knott End-on-S FY6 200 A5
Rosendale Cl OL13 88 B3
Rosendale Cres OL13 88 B3
Roseway Blackpool FY4 110 C5
Lytham St Anne's FY8 90 B6
Poulton-le-F FY6 153 C3
Preston PR2 117 A1
Rosewood Cottam PR4 116 E5
Southport PR9 53 F2
Rosewood Ave
Blackburn BB1 101 F8
Burnley BB11 127 E3
Haslingden BB4 85 C3
Higher Walton PR5 98 C3
Rosewood Cl Chorley PR7 43 D6
Lytham St Anne's FY8 90 E4
1 Thornton FY5 176 D1
Rosewood Dr Chorley PR7 43 E6
Higher Walton PR5 98 B3
Roshaw PR2 139 C1
Rosklyn Rd PR6 43 E7
Rosley St BB8 172 B5
Ross St Brierfield BB9 148 B5
Darwen BB3 65 A6
Rossall Cl
Coupe Green PR5 98 E3
Fleetwood FY7 175 D8
Padiham BB12 126 D6
Rossall Ct Cleveleys FY5 175 C5
Fleetwood FY7 198 E3
Rossall Dr PR2 117 C4
Rossall Gate FY7 175 C8
Rossall Gdns FY5 175 D4
Rossall Grange La FY7 198 D3
Rossall Hospl FY7 175 C8
Rossall La FY7 175 E7
Rossall Rd Blackpool FY3 130 D7
Chorley PR6 61 E1
Cleveleys FY5 175 D3
Fulwood PR2 117 C4
Lancaster LA1 218 A2
Lytham St Anne's FY8 90 D4
Rossall Sch FY7 175 C6
Rossall St PR2 117 C1
Rossall Terr BB2 101 E1
Rossendale Ave
Burnley BB11 127 E2
Lancaster LA1 211 B8
Morecambe LA4 217 C6
Rossendale Ave N FY5 176 B2
Rossendale Ave S FY5 176 B1
Rossendale General Hospl BB4 85 D2
Rossendale Mus* BB4 85 E2
Rossendale Rd
Burnley BB11 127 C3
Lytham St Anne's FY8 90 A7
Rossendale Sch BL0 51 A7
Rosser Ct 18 BB9 148 E8
Rossett Ave FY4 131 C1
Rossetti Ave BB11 127 F3
Rossington Ave FY2 152 E5
Rosslyn Ave FY6 200 A6
Rosslyn Cres FY6 200 B5
Rosslyn Cres E FY6 200 B5
Rossmoyne Rd LA1 215 A4
Rostle Top Rd 6 BB18 197 B1
Rostrevor Cl 4 PR26 76 B1
Rostron Cres L37 11 E1
Rostron Rd BL0 50 B6
Rostron's Bldgs BB4 86 D1
Rothay Ave FY7 198 D2
Rothbury Pl FY8 91 C4
Rotherhead Cl BL6 31 F2
Rotherwick Ave PR7 43 B7
Rothesay Cres LA3 212 D5
Rothesay Rd
Blackburn BB1 102 D3
Brierfield BB9 148 C6
Heysham LA3 212 D5
Rothley Ave PR8 21 A4
Rothsay Rd LA3 212 E5
Rothwell Ave BB5 104 C4
Rothwell Cl L39 15 D5
Rothwell Cres PR2 118 F4
Rothwell Ct PR25 77 A2
Rothwell Dr
Fleetwood FY7 198 D3
Ormskirk L39 15 B2
Southport PR8 21 A4
Rothwell Lodge 5 PR2 118 F4
Rothwell Rd PR6 31 B7
Rothwell St BL0 50 B6
Rotten Row Caton LA2 237 D3
Southport PR8 34 F6
Rough Hey Gate BB5 103 F2
Rough Hey Ind Est PR2 119 B7
Rough Hey Pl PR2 119 B7
Rough Hey Rd PR2 119 B7
Rough Heys BB5 104 A2
Rough Heys La FY4 110 E7
Rough Hill La BL9 33 E4
Rough Lea Rd FY5 175 D2
Rough Lee Rd BB5 104 C4
Roughlee CE Prim Sch BB12 169 F4
Roughlee Gr BB10 128 D5
Roughlee Old Hall BB9 170 A5
Roughlee St BB9 170 D2
Roughlee Terr BB11 106 B4
Roughwood Dr L33 1 A4
Round Acre
Bamber Bridge PR1 97 A1
Nab's Head PR5 99 E7
Round Barn BL7 66 B3
Round Hill Pl BB10 128 E1
Round Mdw PR26 76 C1
Round Meade The L31 5 C2
Round Wood PR1 96 C7
Roundel St BB10 148 B2
Roundell Rd BB18 196 C3
Roundhay FY4 110 F8
Roundhill La BB4 85 A7
Roundhill Rd BB4,BB5 84 E6
Roundhill View BB5 85 A8
Roundhouse The 44 LA1 214 F8
Roundway FY7 175 C8
Roundway Down PR2 117 C7
Roundway The L38 2 F3
Roundwood Ave BB10 148 A4
Row The Heapey PR6 62 D3
Silverdale LA5 224 E3
Rowan Ave Fulwood PR2 119 A4
2 Horwich BL6 32 E1
Oswaldtwistle BB5 103 D2
Rowan Bank LA2 219 C7
Rowan Cl Blackburn BB1 123 B1
Bonds PR3 181 D6
Burscough Bridge L40 25 F6
Higher Penwortham PR1 96 B3
Rochdale OL12 52 B3
Rowan Croft PR6 78 B1
Rowan Dr BL9 33 B3
Rowan Gr Burnley BB10 128 C6
Chorley PR6 61 C3
Rowan La WN8 18 B4
Rowan Tree Cl BB5 104 D7
Rowangate PR2 118 C7
Rowans The Adlington PR6 31 A8
Aughton L39 6 A7
Poulton-le-F FY6 153 A2
Rowberrow Cl PR2 118 D6
Rowen Pk BB2 101 B8
Rowland Ave BB9 149 A8
Rowland Cl FY5 175 F2
Rowland La FY5 175 F2
Rowland St BB5 104 A5
Rowlands Rd BL9 50 D2
Rowley La BB10 128 D6
Rowley Trad Est FY8 89 D7
Rowntree Ave FY7 198 F3
Roworth Cl PR5 97 E3
Rowsley Rd FY8 89 D7
Rowton Heath PR2 117 C7
Roxburgh Rd FY4 111 A6
Roxton Cl BL6 32 B5
Roy St OL14 109 A1
Royal Albert Cotts LA1 214 E4
Royal Ave Blackpool FY3 130 F3
Fulwood PR2 117 E6
Kirkham PR4 114 B4
Leyland PR25 59 E7
Royal Bank Rd FY3 130 E3
Royal Beach Ct FY8 89 D7
Royal Birkdale Golf Club The PR8 34 D2
Royal Brook Ho 7 PR1 118 A1
Royal Cl L37 12 A1
Royal Cres L37 12 A1

Royal Cross Prim Sch
PR2 116 E1
Royal Ct Brierfield BB10 148 F3
11 Lancaster LA1 214 F7
Royal Dr PR2 117 D3
Royal Fold LA3 212 E8
Royal Gdns BL0 50 A3
Royal Lancaster Infmy
LA1 214 F7
Royal Lytham & St Anne's
Golf Course FY8 90 B5
Royal Oak Ave BB1 122 E1
Royal Oak Bldgs 16 FY4 130 B1
Royal Oak Cotts BB9 170 B4
Royal Oak Mdw LA2 238 B8
Royal Pl FY8 90 C8
Royal Preston Hospl The
PR2 117 F6
Royal Rd LA4 217 C6
Royal Terr PR8 35 A7
Royal Troon Ct PR4 114 A4
Royal Umpire Cvn Pk
PR26 58 E2
Royalty Ave PR4 96 A1
Royalty Gdns PR4 76 A8
Royalty La PR4 76 A8
Royalty Mall LA4 217 A5
Royds Ave
Accrington BB5 104 C3
Morecambe LA3 216 D2
Royds Gr LA3 216 D1
Royds Rd OL13 70 A7
Royds St Accrington BB5 104 C4
Bury BL9 33 D4
Lytham St Anne's FY8 89 E5
Royle Rd
4 Burnley BB12 127 F6
Burnley BB12 127 F7
Chorley PR7 43 C8
Royle St 1 FY1 130 B1
Roylen Ave FY6 153 B5
Royles Brook Cl 9 FY5 176 B3
Royles Ct FY5 176 B2
Roynton Rd BL6 32 B7
Royshaw Ave BB1 101 E8
Royshaw Cl BB1 101 E8
Royston Cl BL8 49 F1
Royston Rd FY6 153 F5
Royton Dr PR6 61 C5
Ruby St Blackburn BB1 122 F2
Ramsbottom BL0,BL9 50 C3
Rudd St BB4 85 A3
Ruddington Rd PR8 35 E2
Rudman St OL12 52 E2
Rudyard Ave WN6 29 E2
Rudyard Dr BB3 65 D8
Rudyard Pl Blackpool FY3 130 F7
Lytham St Anne's FY8 89 E8
Ruecroft Cl WN6 19 D8
Ruff La L39,L40 16 B4
Rufford Ave L31 5 E3
Rufford CE Sch L40 39 B4
Rufford Cl PR7 43 B3
Rufford Cotts L40 38 C6
Rufford Dr PR9 54 F5
Rufford New Hall L40 39 B5
Rufford Park La L40 39 A5
Rufford Rd
Bispham Green L40 39 F1
Lytham St Anne's FY8 90 D5
Southport PR9 54 C4
Rufford Sta L40 39 D4
Rufus St PR1 118 C2
Rugby Ave BB5 104 C7
Rugby Dr WN5 10 F8
Rugby St 9 FY4 130 D1
Rumley's Fold BB11 127 E2
Runcorn Ave FY2 152 F2
Rundle Rd PR2 117 D3
Runnel The L39 23 B1
Runnymede Ave FY5 175 D2
Runriggs The FY5 176 B1
Runshaw Ave WN6 19 E8
Runshaw Coll PR7 60 E4
Runshaw Hall PR7 60 A5
Runshaw Hall La PR7 60 A5
Runshaw La Euxton PR7 60 B3
Runshaw Moor PR7 59 E3
Runshaw Sixth Form Coll
PR25 60 B6
Rupert St Carnforth LA5 223 D3
Nelson BB9 148 C7
Rochdale OL12 52 C1
Rush Hey Bank BB11 107 D8
Rushbed Cotts BB4 86 A6
Rushbed Dr BB4 86 A6
Rushden Rd L32 1 A1
Rushes Farm Cl BB5 103 C4
Rushey Cl BB4 86 A6
Rushley Dr LA2 220 D1
Rushley Way LA2 220 D1
Rushmoor Cl BB4 106 A1
Rushton Ave BB18 197 B1
Rushton Cl BB9 171 B2
Rushton St 5 Bacup OL13 70 E8
Barrowford BB9 170 D3
Great Harwood BB6 124 B4
Rushworth Bldgs OL13 70 C8
Rushworth St E 6 BB10 148 B1
Rushy Field BB5 124 F5
Rushy Hey PR5 77 A7
Rushy Hill View 19 OL12 52 C1
Ruskin Ave
9 Blackpool FY1 130 B2
Colne BB8 171 D6
Ruskin Ave *continued*
Leyland PR25 77 A1
Oswaldtwistle BB5 103 C5
Padiham BB12 126 E7
Thornton FY5 176 A3
Ruskin Cl PR4 56 F6
Ruskin Dr LA4 217 E6
Ruskin Gr Bolton-le-S LA5 221 A5
Hapton BB11 126 C4
Ruskin Ho LA1 218 C4
Ruskin Pl BB9 170 F2
Ruskin Rd Freckleton PR4 93 B6
2 Lancaster LA1 218 D3
Ruskin St Burnley BB10 148 A2
Preston PR1 97 B6
Rusland Ave FY4 131 D1
Rusland Dr PR5 98 E4
Ruslands Gdns LA4 217 C4
Russell Ave
Blackpool FY5 152 D8
Colne BB8 171 E6
Leyland PR25 60 C8
Preston PR1 98 A8
Southport PR9 36 A7
Russell Ct Burnley BB11 128 B4
Lytham St Anne's FY8 89 F6
Southport PR9 54 B4
Russell Dr LA4 218 A4
Russell Mews 40 LA1 214 F8
Russell Pl BB6 124 B5
Russell Rd Carnforth LA5 223 E1
Southport PR9 36 A6
Russell Sq PR6 61 D1
Russell Sq W 6 PR6 61 D1
Russell St
Accrington BB5 104 C5
Bacup OL13 87 F4
Blackburn BB2 101 E3
39 Lancaster LA1 214 F8
6 Nelson BB9 148 D8
Russell Terr BB12 126 D7
Russia St BB5 103 F6
Ruth St Edenfield BL0 68 D2
Whitworth OL12 71 D1
Rutherford Pl FY8 110 B4
Ruthin Cl BB1 101 E7
Ruthin Ct PR2 116 F3
Ruthin Dr FY5 176 D2
Rutland Ave
1 Bamber Bridge PR5 97 D3
Blackburn BB1 102 E4
Burnley BB12 127 A6
Cleveleys FY5 175 E3
Fleetwood FY7 198 F3
Freckleton PR4 93 C7
Lancaster LA1 215 A5
Poulton-le-F FY6 153 C3
Rutland Cl
Clayton-le-M BB5 124 F3
Garstang PR3 181 B8
Rutland Cres L39 15 E7
Rutland Ct FY8 90 D5
Rutland Pl 8 BB12 126 D7
Rutland Rd
Lytham St Anne's FY8 90 D5
Southport PR8 35 D5
Rutland St
Accrington BB5 103 F5
Blackburn BB2 101 B3
Colne BB8 171 F5
1 Nelson BB9 170 F1
Preston PR1 97 C8
Rutland Wlk BB4 68 A8
Ryan Cl PR25 76 E1
Ryburn Ave
Blackburn BB2 101 B6
Blackpool FY4 130 E1
Ryburn Rd L39 15 E4
Rycliffe St BB12 146 C1
Rydal Ave
Bamber Bridge PR5 97 D2
Blackpool FY1 130 C3
Darwen BB3 65 A8
Fleetwood FY7 198 E4
Formby L37 11 D3
Freckleton PR4 93 A6
Kingsfold PR1 96 C3
5 Orrell WN5 10 F7
Poulton-le-F FY6 153 D3
Thornton FY5 176 B1
Rydal Cl
5 Accrington BB5 125 D1
Blackrod BL6 31 C3
Brierfield BB10 148 C4
Fulwood PR2 118 C4
Padiham BB12 146 C1
Rydal Ct LA4 217 B5
Rydal Gr
Knott End-on-S FY6 199 F6
Morecambe LA3 216 D2
Rydal Mount BB1 82 F6
Rydal Pl Chatburn BB7 190 C3
Chorley PR7 43 C6
Colne BB8 172 A5
Rydal Rd Blackburn BB1 102 A7
Hambleton FY6 177 C2
Haslingden BB4 68 C8
Hest Bank LA5 220 F4
Lancaster LA1 215 A8
Lytham St Anne's FY8 89 E8
Morecambe LA3 216 D2
Preston PR1 118 D2
Rydal St BB10 148 A2
Ryddingwood PR1 96 B6
Ryde Cl BB4 85 C1
Ryden Ave Cleveleys FY5 175 D3
Leyland PR25 77 C1
Ryden Rd BB1 122 D6
Ryder Cl L39 15 C2
Ryder Cres Ormskirk L39 15 C1
Southport PR8 21 E7
Ryding Cl PR26 76 E3
Ryding's La PR9 55 D8
Rydinge The L37 12 A6
Rydings The BB6 143 A1
Rye Gdns BB2 81 D6
Rye Gr 3 BB12 126 D7
Rye Moss La L37 4 B8
Rye St PR1 118 A1
Ryecroft PR6 62 A7
Ryecroft Ave FY6 177 C1
Ryecroft La BL7 46 C5
Ryecroft Pl FY6 177 C2
Ryefield PR6 62 A7
Ryefield Ave
Haslingden BB4 85 B2
Kingsfold PR1 96 D2
Ryefield Ave W BB4 85 B2
Ryefield Pl BB4 85 B2
Ryeground La L37 12 A5
Ryeheys Rd FY8 89 E8
Ryelands Cres PR2 95 E8
Ryelands Prim Sch LA1 218 B2
Ryelands Rd LA1 218 C2
Ryknild Way LA3 217 F3
Ryland Ave FY6 153 C3
Rylands Rd PR7 43 B7
Rylands St BB10 148 B1
Ryldon Pl FY4 131 A2
Rylstone Dr
Barnoldswick BB18 196 A2
Morecambe LA3 216 D1
Rymers Gn L37 11 E4
Ryscar Way FY2 152 F6
Rysdale Cres LA4 217 C4
Ryson Ave FY4 130 F1

S

Sabden Brook Ct BB7 146 A8
Sabden Pl FY8 90 C7
Sabden Prim Sch BB7 145 F8
Sabden Rd Higham BB12 146 F6
Padiham BB12 146 B4
Whalley BB7 145 A4
Sabden Wlk BB2 101 F2
Saccary La BB1,BB2 122 A4
Sackville Gdns BB9 148 A5
Sackville St
Barnoldswick BB18 196 B1
Blackpool FY4 110 C6
Brierfield BB9 148 B5
10 Burnley BB11 127 F5
6 Bury BL9 33 A3
Chorley PR6 43 E7
Nelson BB9 148 F7
Sacred Heart RC Prim Sch
Blackburn BB2 101 B6
Chorley PR6 43 E7
Church BB5 103 F6
Colne BB8 171 D7
Preston PR2 117 C1
Thornton FY5 176 B3
Saddle Lodge 11 PR2 118 F4
Saddler Nook La LA6 241 C8
Saddlers Mews 5 BB7 166 E8
Sadler St 3 BB5 103 E5
Sadlers Row FY8 90 D7
Saer Cl FY7 198 D3
Saffron Cl 4 BB9 170 C1
Sagar Dr PR4 93 A6
Sagar Fold Colne BB8 171 F5
Ormskirk L39 6 D8
Sagar Holme Terr BB4 86 E5
Sagar La OL14 109 D3
Sagar St Eccleston PR7 41 C6
Nelson BB9 148 E8
Sage Cl FY2 152 F3
Sage Ct PR1 96 C2
Sage La PR1 118 B3
Sahara Fold 1 BB1 102 A7
SS John Fisher & Thomas
More RC High Sch
BB8 171 B2
SS Peter & Paul RC Prim Sch
L40 40 F2
St Aidan's Ave
Blackburn BB2 101 D2
Darwen BB3 65 B8
St Aidan's CE Prim Sch
Bamber Bridge PR5 97 F1
Blackburn BB2 101 C2
St Aidan's CE Tech Coll
FY6 200 B3
St Aidan's Cl BB2 101 C1
St Aidan's Rd 8 PR5 97 E2
St Aidans Pk 9 PR5 97 E2
St Alban's Ct 2 BB1 101 F6
St Alban's Pl PR7 43 D5
St Alban's RC Prim Sch
BB1 101 F6
St Alban's Rd
Blackpool FY1 130 D4
Darwen BB3 81 E4
Lytham St Anne's FY8 89 F7
St Albans Rd
Morecambe LA4 217 F6
Rishton BB1 103 A8
St Ambrose Terr 5 PR25 77 B2
St Andrew's Ave
Cleveleys FY5 175 D2
Preston PR2 117 B2
St Andrew's CE Prim Sch
Oswaldtwistle BB5 103 D4
Preston PR2 117 B1
St Andrew's CE Prim Sch
continued
Ramsbottom BL0 50 B5
St Andrew's Cl
Leyland PR25 60 A7
Oswaldtwistle BB5 103 D4
Ramsbottom BL0 50 C4
St Andrew's Ct FY5 175 D2
St Andrew's Ct 1 BB5 103 D3
St Andrew's Pl
Blackburn BB1 101 D6
Southport PR8 35 B6
St Andrew's Rd PR1 118 A2
St Andrew's Rd N FY8 89 E7
St Andrew's Rd S FY8 89 F6
St Andrew's St
Blackburn BB1 101 D6
4 Burnley BB10 148 B1
St Andrews Cl
Colne BB8 171 C3
Euxton PR7 60 D4
Lancaster LA1 215 C8
St Andrews Ct FY8 89 E7
St Andrews Gr LA4 217 D6
St Andrews Maghull CE Prim
Sch L31 5 D1
St Andrews Rd BB6 143 C6
St Andrews Way PR25 60 A8
St Ann's Ct BB7 166 B8
St Ann's Sq BB7 166 C8
St Ann's St 5 BB2 101 E3
St Anne & St Joseph's RC
Prim Sch BB5 104 D5
St Anne's Ave LA4 217 F5
St Anne's CE Prim Sch
BB4 86 F3
St Anne's Cl Caton LA2 237 C3
Formby L37 11 F6
St Anne's Coll Gram Sch &
Jun Sch FY8 89 E5
St Anne's Cres BB4 86 F3
St Anne's Ct WN6 19 F5
St Anne's Dr BB12 147 D7
St Anne's on-the-sea Sta
FY8 89 E7
St Anne's Path L37 11 F6
St Anne's Pl 18 LA1 214 F8
St Anne's Pleasure Island
Family Fun Pk* FY8 89 E5
St Anne's RC Prim Sch
Blackburn BB2 101 D4
Leyland PR25 59 D8
St Anne's RC Sch PR4 113 A6
St Anne's Rd Formby L37 11 F6
Leyland PR25 77 C3
Ormskirk L39 15 D4
St Anne's Rd E FY8 89 F7
St Anne's Rd W FY8 89 E6
St Anne's St
Padiham BB12 126 C7
Preston PR1 118 A2
St Anne's Way BB12 147 D7
St Annes Cl
5 Blackburn BB1 101 F3
4 Church BB5 103 E5
St Annes Ct FY4 130 C1
St Annes Rd
Blackpool FY4 110 D7
4 Chorley PR6 43 E7
Great Eccleston PR3 156 C5
Horwich BL6 32 C4
Southport PR9 53 F4
St Anthony's Cl PR2 117 C4
St Anthony's Cres PR2 117 C4
St Anthony's Dr PR2 117 C4
St Anthony's Pl 7 FY1 130 C7
St Anthony's RC Prim Sch
PR2 117 C4
St Anthony's Rd PR1 118 A2
St Anthonys Pl PR4 114 A4
St Antony's RC Prim Sch
BB1 102 C3
St Augustine of Canterbury
RC Prim Sch BB12 127 B6
St Augustine's RC High Sch
Billington BB7 144 A4
St Augustine's RC Prim Sch
PR1 97 A7
St Austell Dr BL8 49 F2
St Austell Pl LA5 221 C8
St Austin's Pl PR1 97 A7
St Austin's Rd PR1 97 A7
St Barnabas St
Blackburn BB2 101 C5
2 Darwen BB3 65 B6
St Barnabas' & St Paul's CE
Prim Sch BB2 101 D5
St Barnabas' Pl PR1 118 A1
St Bartholomew's CE Prim
Sch OL12 52 C8
St Bartholomew's Parish CE
Sch BB6 124 C6
St Bede's Ave FY1 130 B1
St Bede's RC High Sch
Blackburn BB2 81 A8
Lytham St Anne's FY8 91 C4
Ormskirk L39 15 D4
St Bedes Cl L39 15 D3
St Bee's Cl BB2 101 F1
St Benet's Cl PR5 97 D1
St Bernadette's RC Prim Sch
FY2 152 D5
St Bernadettes RC Prim Sch
LA1 215 B4
St Bernard Ave FY3 130 F7
St Bernard's RC Prim Sch
PR2 116 C1
St Bernard's Rd FY6 199 E6
St Brides Cl BL6 32 A4
St Catherine Cl FY3 153 B1
St Catherine's CE Prim Sch
BL6 32 A3
St Catherine's Dr PR2 117 C4
St Catherine's RC Prim Sch
PR25 77 C2
St Catherines Cl 4 PR25 77 C2
St Catherines Ct 26 LA1 214 F8
St Catherines Way PR5 77 C7
St Cecilia St BB6 124 D5
St Cecilia's RC High Sch
PR3 140 A6
St Celia's Way LA4 217 E6
St Chad's Ave BB7 190 D5
St Chad's CE Prim Sch
FY6 153 D3
St Chad's Dr LA1 218 B3
St Chad's RC Prim Sch
PR6 61 F6
St Chad's Rd
Blackpool FY1 130 B2
Preston PR1 118 C1
St Chads Cl FY6 153 D2
St Charles' RC Sch BB1 124 B1
St Charles' Rd BB1 124 B1
St Christines Ave PR25 77 C4
St Christopher's CE High Sch
BB5 104 A7
St Christopher's Rd
PR1 118 A2
St Christopher's Way
LA4 217 D6
St Clair Dr PR9 54 A1
St Clair Rd BL8 49 F3
St Clare's RC Prim Sch
PR2 117 F7
St Clares Ave PR2 118 A6
St Clement St
Blackburn BB1 102 B4
Blackburn BB1 102 B5
St Clement's Ave FY3 130 E5
St Clements Ave PR5 77 C3
St Clements Cl 3 BB1 102 B4
St Clements Ct BB9 170 C3
St Crispin Way BB4 85 A2
St Cuthbert St BB10 148 C2
St Cuthbert's CE Prim Sch
Darwen BB3 81 E3
Halsall L39 23 B1
St Cuthbert's Cl
Fulwood PR2 117 D3
1 Lytham St Anne's FY8 91 A3
3 Southport PR9 54 A2
St Cuthbert's Ct 6 FY8 91 A3
St Cuthbert's RC Prim Sch
FY4 110 C8
St Cuthbert's Rd
Bamber Bridge PR5 97 A1
Preston PR1 118 A2
Southport PR9 54 A2
St Cuthberts Cl BB3 81 E3
St David's Ave
Blackburn BB2 80 E7
Cleveleys FY5 175 D2
St David's Gr FY8 89 D8
St David's Rd
Leyland PR25 77 C2
Preston PR1 118 A2
St David's Rd N FY8 89 D8
St David's Rd S FY8 89 F6
St David's Wood BB5 104 D7
St Deny's Croft 3 BB7 189 E1
St Edmund Hall Cl BL0 50 C4
St Edmund's RC Prim Sch
WN8 17 F1
St Edmund's Rd FY4 130 E1
St Edmund's St BB6 124 D5
St Edward's RC Prim Sch
BB3 81 E4
St Frances Cl 4 BB1 101 F3
St Francis CE Prim Sch
BB2 100 F1
St Francis Cl PR2 118 A7
St Francis RC Prim Sch
PR3 161 A2
St Francis' Rd BB2 101 A2
St Gabriel Cl WN8 19 C3
St Gabriel's Ave BB1 122 F3
St Gabriel's CE Prim Sch
BB1 122 E2
St George Ct FY1 130 D6
St George's Ave
Blackburn BB2 101 B1
Cleveleys FY5 175 D2
Lytham St Anne's FY8 89 E7
St George's CE High Sch
FY4 111 A8
St George's CE Prim Sch
PR7 43 E5
St George's La
Cleveleys FY5 175 D2
Lytham St Anne's FY8 89 E6
St George's Pl PR9 35 B7
St George's Quay LA1 218 C1
St George's Rd
Blackpool FY4 110 C6
Formby L37 11 E4
Hightown L38 2 F5
Lytham St Anne's FY8 89 E6
Preston PR1 118 A2
St George's Sh Ctr PR1 96 F7
St George's Sq FY8 89 D7
St George's St PR7 43 C7
St George's Terr BB4 70 A6
St Georges Cl BB8 171 C3
St Georges Pk PR4 113 E6
St Georges Rd BB9 148 F7

St Georges Terr BB3 81 F1
St Gerrard's Rd PR5 97 A1
St Giles St 7 BB12 146 C1
St Giles Terr 6 BB12 146 C1
St Gregory Rd PR1 118 B2
St Gregory's Pl PR7 43 C5
St Gregory's RC Prim Sch
Chorley PR7 43 C5
Maghull L31 5 C4
Preston PR1 118 B3
St Helen's Cl PR3 181 A2
St Helen's Rd
Clayton Green PR6 78 C1
Overton LA3 209 E8
St Helens Cl BB5 103 F3
St Helens Rd L39 16 A2
St Helens Well PR4 57 A5
St Helier Cl BB2 81 C8
St Helier's Pl PR3 137 A7
St Heliers Rd FY1 130 C1
St Hilda's CE Prim Sch
FY6 153 B5
St Hilda's Cl PR7 43 C4
St Hilda's RC Girls' High Sch
BB11 127 C3
St Hilda's Rd FY8 89 D8
St Hilda's Way PR7 43 C4
St Hubert's Rd BB6 124 C4
St Hubert's St BB6 124 D5
St Ignatius' Pl 6 PR1 97 A8
St Ignatius' RC Prim Sch
PR1 97 A8
St Ignatius' Sq 5 PR1 97 A8
St Ives Ave Blackpool FY1 130 E3
Freckleton PR4 93 A6
St Ives Cres PR2 117 A4
St Ives Rd BB1 102 D4
St Jame's CE Prim Sch
BB3 82 B2
St Jame's Terr PR5 99 E7
St James CE Prim Sch
BB3 82 A7
St James Cl
Bamber Bridge PR5 77 B8
Church BB5 103 E7
3 Haslingden BB4 85 B3
Ormskirk L40 16 C3
St James Ct
1 Bamber Bridge PR5 77 B8
Blackburn BB1 101 E7
Heysham LA3 212 E7
9 Lancaster LA1 214 E8
Standish WN6 29 D2
St James Ho BB5 104 B5
St James Lodge
Leyland PR26 59 B8
Lytham St Anne's FY8 90 A5
St James Mews BB5 103 E7
St James Pl
4 Padiham BB12 126 D8
Southport PR8 35 B5
St James RC Sch WN8 18 B4
St James Rd
Blackpool FY4 110 C6
Church BB5 103 E7
St James Row BB4 86 A3
St James Sq 15 OL13 87 F3
St James St Bacup OL13 87 F2
Brierfield BB9 148 B5
1 Rawtenstall BB4 86 A3
Southport PR8 35 B6
St James' CE Prim Sch
BB1 101 E7
St James' Cres BB3 82 B2
St James' Lanehead CE Prim
Sch BB10 148 D2
St James' RC Prim Sch
WN5 10 D4
St James' Rd
10 Barnoldswick BB18 196 B2
Orrell WN5 10 D4
St James' Sq 11 BB18 196 B2
St James' St
Accrington BB5 104 B5
Blackburn BB2 101 C1
Rawtenstall,Waterfoot BB4 69 E8
St James's CE Prim Sch
BB7 166 E7
St James's Dr LA6 240 B7
St James's Gdns PR26 59 B8
St James's La 6 BB11 128 A6
St James's Pl
Blackburn BB1 101 E7
9 Chorley PR6 43 E7
St James's Rd
Blackburn BB1 101 E7
Preston PR1 117 F2
St James's Row 13 BB11 127 F6
St James's St
Burnley BB11 127 F6
8 Chorley PR6 43 E7
Clitheroe BB7 166 E7
Burnley BB11 128 A6
St James-the-Less RC Prim
Sch BB4 85 F3
St Jerome's RC Prim Sch
L37 11 C3
St John Ave FY7 198 D2
St John Bosco RC Prim Sch
L31 5 B2
St John RC Jun Sch
BB10 148 C3
St John Rigby RC Sixth Form
Coll WN5 19 F2
St John Southworth RC Prim
Sch BB9 148 D7
St John St Bacup OL13 87 F3
Colne BB8 171 E5
St John St *continued*
Horwich BL6 32 B3
St John Stone RC Prim Sch
PR8 21 D2
St John the Baptist RC Prim
Sch BB12 126 C7
St John Vianney RC Prim Sch
FY1 130 E2
St John with St Augustine CE
Prim Sch BB5 104 C7
St John with St Michael CE
Prim Sch OL12 71 E5
St John's Ave Darwen BB3 65 B8
Morecambe LA3 216 E2
Poulton-le-F FY6 153 E5
Silverdale LA5 224 C3
Thornton FY5 176 D1
St John's CE Meth Prim Sch
PR6 62 E7
St John's CE Prim Sch
Blackpool FY1 130 C5
Great Harwood BB6 124 C4
Higham BB12 147 A6
Nelson BB9 149 B8
Southport PR9 54 C5
St John's Cl
Accrington BB5 104 E2
5 Rawtenstall BB4 86 A7
Read BB12 145 D2
St John's Ct
5 Bacup OL13 87 F3
8 Blackpool FY1 130 C5
6 Burnley BB12 127 C6
6 Lytham St Anne's FY8 91 C3
St John's Gn PR25 76 E1
St John's Gr
Morecambe LA3 216 E2
Silverdale LA5 224 C3
St John's Pl Nelson BB9 149 A8
16 Preston PR1 97 A7
St John's RC Inf Sch
BB10 148 B1
St John's RC Prim Sch
Burscough L40 25 E2
Poulton-le-F FY6 153 E4
St John's Rd
5 Burnley BB12 127 C6
Morecambe LA3 216 D2
Padiham BB12 126 C7
Southport PR8 34 F1
Walton-le-D PR5 97 D5
St John's Sh Ctr PR1 97 A8
St John's St Darwen BB3 65 B8
Great Harwood BB6 124 C4
Lytham St Anne's FY8 91 C3
Rawtenstall BB4 69 F8
St John's Stonefold CE Prim
Sch BB5 85 A7
St John's Terr LA3 217 C2
St Johns Ave
Kirkham PR4 113 F4
Smallwood Hey PR3 201 C5
St Johns Cl PR6 61 B7
St Johns Ct Fulwood PR3 137 F1
Southport PR8 21 D4
St Johns RC Prim Sch
WN8 18 C1
St Johns Wood FY8 90 E3
St Joseph & St Bede RC Prim
Sch BL9 33 B4
St Joseph's Con Ctr WN8 19 B2
St Joseph's RC High Sch &
Sports Coll BL6 32 E1
St Joseph's RC Inf Sch
PR6 61 D1
St Joseph's RC Prim Sch
Adlington PR6 31 B8
Bacup OL13 87 D1
Barnoldswick BB18 196 B3
Chorley PR6 61 D2
Darwen BB3 65 A8
Gregson Lane PR5 98 E1
Hurst Green BB7 164 F1
Kirkham PR4 113 F7
Lancaster LA1 218 D3
Preston PR1 118 C1
Ramsbottom BL0 50 B6
Withnell PR6 80 A1
St Joseph's RC Prim Sch
Wrightington WN6 29 A3
St Joseph's Terr 1 PR1 118 C1
St Josephs Cl FY3 130 E5
St Josephs Pl PR6 61 D1
St Josephs Prep Sch
BB12 127 A8
St Jude's Ave PR5 97 D1
St Judes Ave PR25 77 C4
St Katherines Dr BL6 31 C3
St Kentigern's RC Prim Sch
FY3 130 D5
St Kitts Cl BB3 81 E6
St Laurence's CE Prim Sch
PR7 61 C1
St Lawrence Ave BB2 101 B8
St Lawrence St BB6 124 C5
St Lawrence's Ave PR3 137 B8
St Leger Ct 11 BB5 104 C5
St Leonard Ct 6 LA1 218 E1
St Leonard's Ave BL6 32 F1
St Leonard's CE Prim Sch
Bamber Bridge PR5 97 C4
Padiham BB12 146 C1
St Leonard's CE Sch
BB6 143 E2
St Leonard's Cl PR2 117 A3
St Leonard's Ct FY8 89 D8
St Leonard's Gate LA1 214 F8
St Leonard's Rd FY3 131 A3
St Leonard's Rd E FY8 89 E8
St Leonard's Rd W FY8 89 D8
St Leonard's St 8 BB12 146 C1
St Leonards CE Prim Sch
BB2 121 A5
St Louis Ave FY3 130 F7
St Lucia Cl BB3 81 F6
St Luke & St Philip's CE Prim
Sch BB2 101 D3
St Luke's Bldg 2 PR8 35 D6
St Luke's CE Prim Sch
Formby L37 11 D1
Lancaster LA1 218 D3
Slyne LA2 218 C8
St Luke's Church Rd L37,
L38 2 C8
St Luke's Ct 1 FY4 110 C6
St Luke's Dr Formby L37 11 C2
Orrell WN5 10 E4
St Luke's Gr PR9 35 E7
St Luke's Pl 9 PR1 118 C1
St Luke's RC Prim Sch
WN8 9 E6
St Luke's Rd
Blackpool FY4 110 C6
Southport PR9 35 D7
St Lukes Ct 2 LA1 214 E8
St Margaret's CE Prim Sch
LA2 238 B7
St Margaret's Ct
1 Blackburn BB1 102 B5
1 Fleetwood FY7 199 A4
St Margaret's Gdns
BB11 126 C4
St Margaret's Rd
Bolton-le-S LA5 221 B6
1 Leyland PR25 77 C2
Morecambe LA4 217 D6
St Margarets Cl PR2 117 A4
St Margarets Way BB1 102 B5
St Maria Goretti RC Prim Sch
PR2 118 F5
St Marie's RC Prim Sch
L33 1 A3
St Maries RC Prim Sch
Standish WN6 29 E2
St Mark's CE Prim Sch
Bury BL9 33 A4
Scarisbrick L40 23 D7
St Mark's Pl
Blackburn BB2 101 B4
1 Blackpool FY3 130 E8
St Mark's Pl E 5 PR1 96 D8
St Mark's Pl W 4 PR1 96 D8
St Mark's Rd
Blackburn BB2 101 B4
Preston PR1 96 D8
St Marks RC Prim Sch
WN8 9 E8
St Marlow Ave 1 PR25 77 C3
St Martin's Coll LA1 215 B6
St Martin's Ct FY5 175 F2
St Martin's Dr BB2 80 D8
St Martin's Rd
Blackpool FY4 110 C6
Lancaster LA1 215 A7
Preston PR1 118 A2
St Martins Cl FY6 153 B5
St Mary & St Michael RC
Prim Sch PR3 181 C6
St Mary CE Prim Sch
BB2 121 D2
St Mary Cl FY3 153 B1
St Mary Magdalen's CE Prim
Sch BB5 104 B7
St Mary Magdalen's RC Prim
Sch PR1 96 E4
St Mary Magdalene's RC Prim
Sch BB12 127 D8
St Mary's & St Andrews RC
Prim Sch PR3 137 A5
St Mary's & St Benedicts RC
Prim Sch PR5 97 E1
St Mary's & St Joseph's RC
Prim Sch BB1 101 F3
St Mary's Ave
Bamber Bridge PR5 97 D1
Barnoldswick BB18 196 D3
St Mary's CE Prim Sch
Eccleston PR7 41 C6
Hawkshaw BL8 49 C2
Spen Brook BB12 169 C3
St Mary's Cl PR5 97 D1
St Mary's Coll BB1 101 E7
St Mary's Ct
Clayton-le-M BB5 124 F2
Mellor BB2 121 E2
Preston PR1 97 B8
Rawtenstall BB4 85 F2
St Mary's Dr BB6 143 D1
St Mary's Gate
Burnley BB11 128 B5
Euxton PR7 60 C3
St Mary's Gdns
Mellor BB2 121 E2
Southport PR8 21 F7
St Mary's Par LA1 214 E8
St Mary's Rawtenstall CE
Prim Sch BB4 85 F3
St Mary's RC Coll FY3 130 F7
St Mary's RC Prim Sch
Accrington BB5 103 F4
Bacup OL13 88 B2
Burnley BB10 128 B6
Chipping PR3 185 E3
Chorley PR7 43 A7
Claughton PR3 182 D1
Clayton-le-M BB5 124 F3
St Mary's RC Prim Sch *continued*
Fleetwood FY7 199 A5
Great Eccleston PR3 156 B5
Haslingden BB4 85 C2
Horwich BL6 32 D2
Morecambe LA4 217 C6
Osbaldeston BB2 121 D4
Sabden BB7 145 F7
St Mary's RC Prim Sch
Scarisbrick L40 24 A7
St Mary's RC Sch BB6 143 C1
St Mary's Rd
Bamber Bridge PR5 97 E1
Great Eccleston PR3 156 B5
Heysham LA3 212 E8
St Mary's St
4 Clitheroe BB7 189 E1
Nelson BB9 148 C8
Preston PR1 97 B8
St Mary's St N 7 PR1 97 B8
St Mary's Terr 6 BB4 86 A2
St Mary's Way BB4 86 A2
St Mary's Wlk 16 PR7 43 C8
St Marys Cl
Blackburn BB1 102 B5
Longridge PR3 140 A8
8 Preston PR1 97 C8
St Marys Wharfe BB1 101 F3
St Matthew St BB11 127 E5
St Matthew's CE Prim Sch
BB1 101 F4
St Matthew's CE Sch
PR1 97 D8
St Matthew's Ct 9
BB11 127 E5
St Matthew's RC Prim Sch
WN8 9 D7
St Michael & All Angels CE
Prim Sch BB8 171 E8
St Michael & St John's RC
Prim Sch BB7 166 E8
St Michael Rd L39 5 F7
St Michael with St John CE
Prim Sch BB1 101 E6
St Michael's CE High Sch
PR7 61 C1
St Michael's CE Prim Sch
PR4 114 B5
St Michael's Cl
Blackburn BB2 80 E7
Bolton-le-S LA5 221 A4
Chorley PR7 61 B1
Southport PR9 53 F3
St Michael's Cres LA5 221 A4
St Michael's Ct
Barrowford BB9 170 C2
1 Blackburn BB1 101 F6
St Michael's Gr
Bolton-le-S LA5 221 A4
Morecambe LA4 217 C4
St Michael's La LA5 221 A4
St Michael's Pl
Bolton-le-S LA5 221 A4
Newsham PR3 137 B5
St Michael's Rd
Duncombe PR3 158 D4
4 Leyland PR25 77 C3
Preston PR1 118 A2
St Michael's St BB1 101 F7
St Michael's Terr PR26 58 B2
St Michael's-on-Wyre CE
Prim Sch PR3 157 C6
St Michaels Cl PR2 117 D3
St Michaels Pk L39 6 A7
St Michaels Rd
Blackpool FY2 152 D3
Kirkham PR4 114 C5
St Mildred's Way LA3 212 E6
St Monica's Way FY4 131 D1
St Nicholas Arcs 13 LA1 214 F8
St Nicholas Cres LA5 221 B6
St Nicholas Gr PR4 113 B4
St Nicholas La LA5 221 A6
St Nicholas Rd
Blackpool FY4 111 B5
Church BB5 103 F7
St Nicholas' Ave BB7 145 F8
St Nicholas' CE Prim Sch
Blackpool FY4 111 A4
Church BB5 103 F7
St Ogg's Rd LA4 217 C3
St Oswald Ho LA1 215 A6
St Oswald St LA1 215 A6
St Oswald's CE Prim Sch
BB1 102 E4
St Oswald's Cl
Blackburn BB1 102 E4
Preston PR1 118 C2
St Oswald's RC Prim Sch
Accrington BB5 104 A3
Longton PR4 75 B8
St Oswald's RC Prim Sch
Coppull PR7 29 D8
St Oswald's Rd BB1 102 E4
St Patrick's Pl PR5 97 E4
St Patrick's RC Prim Sch
Heysham LA3 213 A8
Southport PR9 54 A2
Walton-le-D PR5 97 E4
St Patrick's Rd N FY8 89 E7
St Patrick's Rd S FY8 89 F6
St Patrick's Wlk LA3 212 E7
St Paul's Ave
Blackburn BB2 101 D5
Lytham St Anne's FY8 90 B4
Preston PR1 118 A1
St Paul's CE Prim Sch
Adlington PR6 31 A7
Bury BL9 33 B4
Nelson BB9 148 D6
Oswaldtwistle BB5 103 E4
Ramsbottom BL0 50 C6
St Paul's Cl Adlington PR6 31 A8
Clitheroe BB7 166 C8
St Paul's Constable Lee CE
Prim Sch BB4 86 A4
St Paul's Ct
5 Burnley BB11 127 F5
12 Oswaldtwistle BB5 103 E4
10 Preston PR1 97 A8
St Paul's Dr Caton LA2 237 D3
Lancaster LA1 214 F5
St Paul's Pas PR8 35 A6
St Paul's RC Prim Sch
BB2 80 D8
St Paul's Rd
Blackpool FY1 130 B8
Lancaster LA1 214 F5
Nelson BB9 148 E6
Preston PR1 118 A1
1 Rishton BB1 124 A1
St Paul's Sq Preston PR1 97 A8
Southport PR8 35 A6
St Paul's St
Blackburn BB2 101 D5
Bury BL9 33 A3
Clitheroe BB7 166 C8
Oswaldtwistle BB5 103 E4
4 Ramsbottom BL0 50 C6
Southport PR8 35 A6
St Paul's Terr
Clitheroe BB7 166 C8
Hoddlesden BB3 82 E2
St Paul's Villas BL9 33 A3
St Paul's Wlk 4 FY8 90 C4
St Pauls Cl PR26 76 F7
St Pauls Mans 4 PR8 35 A6
St Peter & St Paul's CE Prim
Sch BB1 124 A2
St Peter St
Blackburn BB2 101 E4
2 Rishton BB1 124 A1
St Peter's Ave Formby L37 11 D4
Haslingden BB4 85 B2
St Peter's CE Prim Sch
Accrington BB5 104 A2
Burnley BB11 128 A6
Chorley PR6 61 E2
Formby L37 12 A5
Fulwood PR2 117 F7
Heysham LA3 212 E7
St Peter's Cl Darwen BB3 65 B8
Formby L37 11 D4
Salesbury BB1 122 D6
St Peter's Pl
Fleetwood FY7 199 B4
7 Haslingden BB4 85 B2
St Peter's RC Cath*
LA1 215 A8
St Peter's RC High Sch
WN5 10 F7
St Peter's RC Prim Sch
Blackburn BB2 101 B2
Lytham St Anne's FY8 91 C5
Newchurch BB4 86 E2
St Peter's Rd
Lancaster LA1 215 A8
Newchurch BB4 86 E2
Southport PR8 35 A3
St Peter's Sq 8 PR1 96 E8
St Peter's St Chorley PR6 61 E1
1 Preston PR1 96 F8
St Peters Mews 16 LA1 215 A8
St Philip St BB10 148 A1
St Philip's CE Prim Sch
Nelson BB9 148 E8
Southport PR8 35 C5
St Philip's Ct BB2 101 C3
St Philip's Rd PR1 118 A2
St Philip's St
Blackburn BB2 101 B3
13 Nelson BB9 170 E1
St Pius X Prep Sch PR2 117 E4
St Richards RC Prim Sch
WN8 17 D1
St Saviour's Cl PR5 77 F7
St Saviour's Com Prim Sch
OL13 71 A8
St Saviours Ct OL13 87 F1
St Silas's CE Prim Sch
BB2 101 B6
St Silas's Rd BB2 101 B6
St Stephen's Ave
8 Blackburn BB1 102 A7
Blackpool FY2 152 B2
St Stephen's CE Inf Sch
BB1 102 B7
St Stephen's CE Jun Sch
BB1 102 B7
St Stephen's CE Prim Sch
Burnley BB11 128 B4
Preston PR1 96 E6
St Stephen's Rd
9 Blackburn BB1 102 A7
Hightown L38 2 F4
Preston PR1 118 B2
Standish WN6 29 C1
St Stephen's St 2 BB11 128 B4
St Stephens Way BB8 171 F6
St Stephens Rd PR4 113 F4

St Stephens' CE Prim Sch PR9 55 A5
St Teresa's Ave FY5 175 D1
St Teresa's RC Prim Sch
Cleveleys FY5 175 D1
Preston PR1 118 E1
Southport PR8 35 A4
Up Holland WN8 19 B1
St Theodore's RC Sports Coll & Sixth Form BB10 128 B7
St Theresa's Dr PR2 117 C4
St Theresas Cl [2] PR4 114 B5
St Thomas CE Prim Sch
Blackburn BB1 102 B5
Maghull L31 5 D4
St Thomas Cl
Blackpool FY3 153 B1
Haslingden BB4 68 A7
St Thomas Ct [4] BL9 33 A2
St Thomas More Wlk LA1 214 D8
St Thomas Rd PR4 114 A4
St Thomas St BB1 102 B4
St Thomas the Martyr CE Prim Sch WN8 10 B7
St Thomas' CE Prim Sch
Bury BL9 33 B1
Lytham St Anne's FY8 89 F6
St Thomas' Pl PR1 117 F1
St Thomas' Rd
Lytham St Anne's FY8 89 F6
Preston PR1 118 A2
St Thomas' St PR1 117 F1
St Thomas's Ct WN8 10 C7
St Thomas's Rd
Chorley PR7 43 C8
Rawtenstall BB4 86 A7
St Thomas's Sq [4] PR7 43 C8
St Veronica's RC Prim Sch BB4 68 B7
St Vincent Ave FY1 130 E3
St Vincent's RC Prim Sch OL12 52 A1
St Vincent's Way PR8 35 A4
St Vincents Cl BB3 81 F6
St Vincents Rd PR2 117 F5
St Walburga's Rd FY3 130 F7
St Walburge Ave PR2 96 E8
St Walburges Gdns [8] PR2 96 D8
St Wilfred's Dr OL12 52 D4
St Wilfrid St [3] PR1 96 F7
St Wilfrid's CE High Sch & Tech Coll BB2 101 D3
St Wilfrid's CE Prim Sch LA2 219 C7
St Wilfrid's Pk LA2 219 C7
St Wilfrid's Pl WN6 29 F1
St Wilfrid's RC Prim Sch PR3 140 A8
St Wilfrid's Rd WN6 29 F1
St Wilfrid's Terr PR3 140 A7
St Wilfrid's Way [6] WN6 29 E1
St Williams RC Prim Sch PR3 201 E4
St Wulstan's RC Prim Sch
Fleetwood FY7 198 E3
Great Harwood BB6 124 C5
Salcombe Ave FY2 152 F2
Salcombe Dr PR9 54 A5
Salcombe Rd FY8 110 C1
Salem Mews LA3 212 E8
Salem St BB4 85 B3
Salerno St BB11 127 C4
Sales's La BL9 51 B3
Salesbury CE Prim Sch BB1 122 D7
Salesbury View BB1 122 F4
Salford BB1 101 E5
Salford Ct PR8 21 C5
Salford Rd Galgate LA2 211 A3
Southport PR8 21 C5
Salford St BL9 33 A4
Salisbury Ave FY6 199 E5
Salisbury Cl LA3 217 B2
Salisbury Ct
Knott End-on-S FY6 199 E5
Lancaster LA1 214 D8
Salisbury Rd
Blackpool FY1 130 D4
Brinscall PR6 62 F8
Darwen BB3 81 E3
Horwich BL6 32 F1
Lancaster LA1 214 D8
Preston PR1 96 D7
Salisbury St
[3] Chorley PR7 43 D7
Colne BB8 171 E5
Great Harwood BB6 124 E6
[15] Haslingden BB4 85 B3
[5] Preston PR1 118 D1
Southport PR9 36 A6
Sallowfields WN5 10 D5
Sally's La PR9 54 B2
Salmesbury Ave FY2 152 E2
Salmon St PR1 97 C7
Salmons Leap PR4 113 E4
Salmsbury Hall Cl BL0 50 C4
Salop Ave FY2 152 C4
Salt Aire Sports Ctr LA1 218 A1
Salt Ayre La
Lancaster LA1 218 B1
Morecambe LA1 217 F1
Salt Marsh Cl FY6 177 B1
Salt Marsh La FY6 177 B1
Salt Pit La L40 40 F3
Saltash Rd FY5 176 B5
Saltburn St BB12 127 B6
Saltcotes Pl FY8 91 D4
Saltcotes Rd FY8 91 D7
Salter Fell Rd LA1 218 B2
Salter St PR1 117 F1
Salterford La BB10 129 A4
Salterforth La
Barnoldswick BB18 196 E2
Salterforth BB18 194 D7
Salterforth Prim Sch BB18 194 D8
Salterforth Rd BB18 197 A1
Salthill Ind Est BB7 190 A2
Salthill Rd BB7 189 F1
Salthill View BB7 189 F1
Salthouse Ave FY1 130 C3
Saltpit La L31 5 E1
Salus St BB10 148 C1
Salwick Ave FY2 152 D5
Salwick Cl PR9 53 F5
Salwick Pl
Lytham St Anne's FY8 90 A8
Preston PR2 116 E1
Salwick Rd PR4 135 B3
Salwick Sta PR4 115 C5
Sambourn Fold PR8 21 A5
Samlesbury Aerodrome BB2,PR5 120 F3
Samlesbury CE Prim Sch PR5 119 D1
Samlesbury Hall* PR5 120 E2
Samuel St Bury BL9 33 A3
Preston PR1 97 D8
Sanctuary The [5] FY4 110 C5
Sand Beds La BL0,BB4 69 B5
Sand La LA5 223 C4
Sandbank Cotts OL12 71 C2
Sandbank Gdns OL12 71 C2
Sandbeds La LA2 238 A8
Sandbrook Gdns WN5 10 D5
Sandbrook Rd Orrell WN5 10 C5
Southport PR8 21 D4
Sandbrook Way PR8 21 C3
Sandcastle (L Pool)* FY4 110 A8
Sanderling Cl
Cleveleys FY5 152 F8
Lytham St Anne's FY8 90 E7
Sanderling Rd L33 1 A3
Sanders Gr LA4 217 A4
Sanderson La PR7 28 A8
Sanderson St [9] BL9 33 A3
Sandersons Way FY4 110 F8
Sandfield [4] FY5 176 A2
Sandfield Cotts L39 15 D2
Sandfield Ho [6] LA1 215 A3
Sandfield Pk L39 15 D2
Sandfield Rd OL13 88 A1
Sandfield St [11] PR25 77 B1
Sandford Dr L31 5 D2
Sandford Rd WN5 10 C5
Sandgate Blackpool FY4 110 D5
Chorley PR7 43 D5
Lytham St Anne's FY8 89 C7
Sandham St [7] PR6 43 D8
Sandhams Way FY4 111 D8
Sandheys Dr PR9 53 F1
Sandhill St BB3 65 B5
Sandhills L38 2 F3
Sandhills Ave FY4 110 B5
Sandhills Cl BB18 194 E8
Sandholme La PR3 182 A4
Sandholme Villas BB18 197 A1
Sandhurst Ave
Blackpool FY2 152 C5
Lytham St Anne's FY8 89 E7
Sandhurst Cl Formby L37 11 C1
[9] Kirkham PR4 113 F5
Sandhurst Ct FY8 89 D6
Sandhurst Grange FY8 89 E7
Sandhurst St BB11 128 B6
Sandhurst Way L31 5 B5
Sandicroft Ave FY6 177 C1
Sandicroft Pl FY6 200 B4
Sandicroft Rd FY1 152 C1
Sandilands Gr L38 2 F3
Sandiway Ct PR9 35 E8
Sandiway Dr BB10 148 F3
Sandiways L31 5 E1
Sandiways Cl FY5 153 C8
Sandon Pl FY4 110 C4
Sandon Rd PR8 34 F1
Sandon St Blackburn BB2 101 C3
Darwen BB3 82 B2
Sandon Terr BB2 101 C3
Sandown Cl PR4 113 E5
Sandown Ct
[30] Preston PR1 97 A7
[1] Southport PR9 35 C8
Sandown Rd
Haslingden BB4 85 C2
Lancaster LA1 215 B3
Thornton FY5 176 B1
Sandpiper Cl
[8] Blackburn BB1 101 F6
Normoss FY3 131 B6
Sandpiper Ct FY5 175 C2
Sandpiper Pl [10] FY5 175 F1
Sandpiper Sq [5] BB11 127 C5
Sandridge Ave PR7 43 B7
Sandridge Pl FY4 110 B4
Sandringham Ave
Leyland PR25 77 C1
Thornton FY5 176 B1
Sandringham Cl
Adlington PR7 30 E6
[5] Barrowford BB9 170 C1
Blackburn BB1 122 E1
Tarleton PR4 57 A6
Whalley BB7 144 A7
Sandringham Ct
Lytham St Anne's FY8 90 D4
Morecambe LA4 217 A4
Southport PR8 35 B8
Sandringham Dr
Brinscall PR6 62 F8
Ramsbottom BL8 50 A1
Sandringham Gr [2] BB4 85 A1
Sandringham Lodge [2] FY5 175 D2
Sandringham Park Dr PR4 76 A8
Sandringham Rd
Bamber Bridge PR5 97 D3
Chorley PR7 43 B8
Darwen BB3 81 E4
Eccleston PR7 41 C7
Formby L37 11 E1
Horwich BL6 32 E2
Lytham St Anne's FY8 90 A5
Morecambe LA4 217 A4
Southport PR8 34 E3
Southport,Ainsdale PR8 21 C5
Sandringham Way PR4 116 E6
Sands Cl BB1 124 B2
Sands Rd BB1 124 B2
Sands The BB7 144 C5
Sands Way FY1 130 C3
Sandsdale Ave PR2 118 C5
Sandside Dr LA4 217 C3
Sandwell Ave FY5 176 C2
Sandwich Cl BB1 102 C4
Sandwick Cl PR2 117 E7
Sandy Bank Rd BL7 48 D5
Sandy Brook Ho PR2 117 F7
Sandy Cl FY5 175 C3
Sandy Gate La PR4 137 B2
Sandy La Accrington BB5 104 E5
Adlington PR7 30 F6
Barrowford BB9 170 D2
Bispham Green L40 39 F2
Blackburn BB3 81 E6
Blackpool FY4 111 A4
Brindle PR5,PR6 79 C6
Brinscall PR6 62 E8
Clayton Green PR6 78 C3
Fleetwood FY7 175 D7
Hambleton FY6 177 C1
Hightown L38 3 A3
Holmeswood L40 38 D5
Holmeswood L40 38 E5
Leyland PR25 60 A8
Lower Bartle PR4 116 D7
Maghull,Holt Green L39 6 B6
Maghull,Lydiate L31 5 C5
Mawdesley L40 40 A1
Newburgh WN8 26 F1
Ormskirk L40 16 D7
Orrell WN5 10 D4
Out Rawcliffe PR3 178 F1
Pleasington BB2 100 C2
Preesall FY6 200 B4
Skelmersdale WN8 17 D1
Sollom L40 39 A8
Thorpe Green PR6 78 E4
Sandy La Ctr WN8 17 D1
Sandy Pl [7] PR25 60 A8
Sandy Way L40 38 D4
Sandybeds Cl BB5 104 D2
Sandybrook Cl PR2 118 E5
Sandycroft PR2 118 F2
Sandyfields PR4 116 E6
Sandyforth Ave FY5 176 B3
Sandyforth La PR4 117 A8
Sandygate BB11 127 F6
Sandyhall La BB9 170 A2
Sandylands Arc LA3 216 D3
Sandylands Com Prim Sch LA3 216 E3
Sandylands Prom LA3 216 D3
Sanfield Cl L39 15 E6
Sangara Dr BB3 81 F7
Sangness Dr PR8 35 E3
Sansbury Cres BB9 171 A2
Santon Cl PR4 114 A7
Sanvino Ave PR8 21 D5
Sapphire St BB1 122 F1
Sarah La PR26 57 F5
Sarah St Bacup OL13 71 C8
Darwen BB3 82 B1
Edenfield BL0 68 E3
Sarahs Fold FY6 177 C7
Sark Gdns BB2 101 F1
Sarmatian Fold PR3 141 D3
Sarscow La PR26 58 E2
Saswick Ct PR4 134 B7
Saul St PR1 96 F8
Saul's Dr LA5 224 A8
Saunder Bank BB11 128 A5
Saunder Height La BB4 86 E3
Saunders Cl BB4 86 A7
Saunders Mews PR7 43 C3
Saunders Rd BB2 101 C5
Saunders St PR9 53 C1
Saunders' La Hutton PR4 95 D2
New Longton PR4 95 E1
Savick Ave PR2 116 D1
Savick Cl PR5 77 F8
Savick Ct PR2 117 D4
Savick Rd PR2 117 D4
Savick Way PR2 116 E3
Saville Ave FY6 153 B6
Saville Rd Blackpool FY1 130 C1
Maghull L31 5 C3
Saville St PR7 43 C5
Savon Hook L37 12 B1
Savoy Ave LA3 217 C3
Savoy St Accrington BB5 103 F5
[4] Preston PR1 96 E7
Sawdon Ave PR8 35 E3
Sawley Abbey* BB7 230 C1
Sawley Ave
Accrington BB5 104 D7
Blackpool FY4 110 D5
Lytham St Anne's FY8 90 C6
Read BB12 145 D1
Sawley Cl BB3 65 C8
Sawley Cres PR2 118 F2
Sawley Dr BB6 124 E6
Sawley Rd Chatburn BB7 190 E6
Grindleton BB7 190 C8
Sawley BB7 230 C1
Sawmills Ind Est FY1 130 D6
Sawrey Ct BB5 124 E2
Sawthorpe Wlk FY6 153 B3
Sawyer St [5] OL12 52 F1
Saxby Gr FY4 130 F1
Saxenholme PR8 34 F5
Saxifield St BB10 148 E3
Saxon Cl
Oswaldtwistle BB5 103 C5
Thornton FY5 153 C8
Saxon Hey PR2 117 C3
Saxon Hts LA3 212 F5
Saxon Lodge PR8 34 F5
Saxon Rd PR8 34 F5
Saxon St BB10 128 A7
Scafell Ave LA4 217 D5
Scafell Cl BB12 127 C8
Scafell Rd Lancaster LA1 218 E2
Lytham St Anne's FY8 111 A2
Scaffold La L38 3 D4
Scaitcliffe St BB5 104 B5
Scale Farm Rd LA1 218 A2
Scale Hall La
Lancaster LA1 218 B2
Newton-w-S PR4 115 A2
Scar End Cl OL13 88 A8
Scar St BB2 101 B3
Scarborough Rd
Blackburn BB2 102 A1
Lytham St Anne's FY8 111 A1
Scargill Rd LA5,LA6 221 F1
Scarisbrick Ave
Parbold WN8 27 C2
Southport PR8 35 A7
Scarisbrick Cl L31 5 E3
Scarisbrick Ct PR8 35 C6
Scarisbrick New Rd PR8 35 D5
Scarisbrick Pk L40 24 A6
Scarisbrick St
Ormskirk L39 15 E6
Southport PR9 35 B7
Scarlet St PR6 43 E7
Scarlett Dr PR4 95 F2
Scarlett St BB11 127 E5
Scarr Dr OL12 52 F3
Scarr La BB2 101 A6
Scarr Terr OL12 71 D2
Scarsdale Ave FY4 110 C5
Scarth Hill La L39 16 A2
Scarth Hill Mans L39 15 E2
Scarth La BB12 126 B5
Scarth Pk WN8 9 C7
Scawfell Rd PR7 43 B5
Sceptre Way PR5 78 B6
Schleswig St PR1 97 A8
Schleswig Way PR26 59 C7
Schofield Ave FY3 131 B7
Schofield Cl BB4 85 F2
Schofield Rd BB4 85 F2
Schofield St Darwen BB3 81 F2
Haslingden BB4 68 A6
[3] Rawtenstall BB4 69 E8
Schola Green La
Morecambe LA4 217 B4
Morecambe LA4 217 B5
Scholars Ct FY8 89 E5
Scholars Gn PR2 116 C1
Scholefield Ave BB9 148 E5
Scholefield La BB9 148 F5
Scholes Bank BL6 32 A5
Scholes St BB3 81 F2
Scholey Head La BB10 108 A8
School Ave L37 11 F3
School Brow PR6 61 B7
School Cl Ormskirk L39 15 C1
Southport PR8 35 B2
School Ct Egerton BL7 47 E2
Ramsbottom BL0 68 D2
School Field PR5 78 B5
School Fields BB18 197 B3
School Hillocks Cotts [4] PR5 77 A8
School Ho The BB10 148 D2
School House Gn L39 15 F5
School House Gr L40 25 D5
School House La BB5 104 B1
School House Mews [7] PR6 43 E7
School La
Bamber Bridge PR5 97 F2
Blackburn BB1 82 D8
Brinscall PR6 62 E8
Burnley BB11 128 A7
Burscough Bridge L40 25 F5
Catforth PR4 136 A4
Earby BB18 197 B2
Edgworth BL7 48 D8
Euxton PR7 60 D3
School La *continued*
Farington PR5 76 F7
Formby L37 11 F3
Forton LA2,PR3 207 B3
Freckleton PR4 93 C7
Hammerton Mere BB7 235 E3
Haskayne L39 13 F4
Inskip PR4 157 D1
Kirkham PR4 114 B5
Laneshaw Bridge BB8 172 E6
Leyland PR25 77 A1
Leyland,Moss Side PR26 59 A8
Longton PR4 75 A8
Lytham St Anne's FY8 91 A3
Maghull L31 6 A1
Mawdesley L40 40 C1
Mereclough BB10 129 A1
Newton-w-S PR4 115 A2
Ollerton Fold PR6 79 F4
Out Rawcliffe PR3 178 F2
Pilling PR3 201 C6
Preesall FY6 200 B3
Roby Mill WN8 19 B3
Simonstone BB12 145 F1
Skelmersdale,Chapel House WN8 17 E1
Skelmersdale,Up Holland WN5,WN8 10 C7
Standish WN6 29 D1
Westhead L40 16 E3
Winmarleigh PR3 203 F6
Wray LA2 238 D6
School Rd Blackpool FY4 111 B5
Heysham LA3 212 E7
Hightown L38 2 F4
Thornton FY5 153 C8
School St Accrington BB5 104 B6
Bacup OL13 70 B8
Bamber Bridge PR5 97 F2
Bury BL9 33 B1
Colne BB8 171 D4
Darwen BB3 82 A1
Great Harwood BB6 124 C4
Horwich BL6 32 C3
Kelbrook BB18 195 A6
Leyland PR25 77 B2
Nelson BB9 148 C8
Preston PR1 96 E7
Ramsbottom BL0 50 B5
Rawtenstall BB4 86 A8
Rishton BB1 124 B1
Walmer Bridge PR4 74 F5
Whitewell Bottom BB4 86 F4
School Terr
Salterforth BB18 194 D8
Whitworth OL12 71 D1
School View BL7 48 D8
School Villas LA2 211 B5
Schoolfold PR4 73 E4
Schoolhouse Fold BB11 126 C3
Schoolhouse La LA2 219 D7
Schwartzman Dr PR9 55 A6
Scorton Ave FY3 130 F7
Scorton CE Prim Sch PR3 204 E6
Scorton Hall Pk PR3 204 E6
Scorton Ho LA1 215 A2
Scotch Green La PR3 160 A6
Scotforth Ct [1] LA1 215 A3
Scotforth Rd
Lancaster LA1 215 A4
Preston PR1 97 C8
Scotforth St Paul's CE Prim Sch LA1 215 A4
Scotland Bank Terr BB2 81 C8
Scotland La BL9 33 D8
Scotland Pl [11] BL0 50 C6
Scotland Rd
Carnforth LA5 223 E3
[8] Nelson BB9 148 D8
[15] Nelson BB9 170 D1
Scotshaw Brook Ind Est BB3 81 E7
Scotswood Ave FY4 110 D6
Scott Ave Accrington BB5 104 E2
Morecambe LA4 216 F3
Simonstone BB12 145 E2
Scott Cl Blackpool FY4 110 F8
Maghull L31 5 D1
Oswaldtwistle BB5 103 D5
Scott Dr L39 15 F7
Scott Gr LA4 217 A4
Scott Laithe La BB7 230 E3
Scott Mews FY4 110 F8
Scott Park Rd BB11 127 E4
Scott Rd LA3 216 F3
Scott St Clayton-le-M BB5 124 F3
Nelson BB9 170 D1
Padiham BB12 126 F7
Southport PR9 36 A7
Scott's Terr BB11 127 D6
Scott's Wood PR2 117 D7
Scout Rd Edenfield BL0 69 A2
Egerton BL7 47 B1
Newchurch BB4 86 F3
Scow Croft La PR6 62 D4
Scowcroft Dr LA4 217 E5
Scriffen La LA2 211 D3
Scudamore Cres [6] FY4 130 D1
Sea View Lancaster LA1 215 A5
Longridge PR3 161 D2
Walmer Bridge PR4 74 F5
Sea View Cl LA2 218 B8
Sea View Dr LA2 218 B8
Sea Wall FY7 198 C3
Seabank Rd
Fleetwood FY7 199 A5
Southport PR9 35 B8

Spring La *continued*
Haslingden BB4 .85 B4
Nab's Head PR5 .99 C8
Spring Mdw PR25 .77 E1
Spring Mdws
Clayton-le-M BB5 .125 A3
Darwen BB3 .65 D7
Spring Pl Colne BB8 .171 D5
Whitworth OL12 .71 D3
Spring Rd WN5 .10 F8
Spring Row BB8 .172 C6
Spring Side Millgate OL12 .71 D4
Rawtenstall BB4 .69 F6
Spring Side Cotts BL7 .47 A2
Spring St Accrington BB5 .103 F4
Bacup OL13 .87 F1
Bank Lane BL0 .50 D7
[1] Cornholme OL14 .109 C1
Horwich BL6 .32 B4
[6] Leyland PR25 .77 B1
Nelson BB9 .148 C7
[5] Oswaldtwistle BB5 .103 E4
Ramsbottom BL0 .50 B6
Rawtenstall BB4 .86 A8
Rishton BB1 .124 B2
Spring Terr
[7] Bacup OL13 .70 D8
Goodshaw Chapel BB4 .105 F2
Langho BB6 .143 D1
Oswaldtwistle BB5 .103 D4
Rochdale OL12 .52 A1
Spring Terr S [5] BB4 .85 E2
Spring Vale PR3 .207 B3
Spring Vale Garden Village BB3 .65 C6
Spring Vale Rd BB3 .65 B7
Spring View
Blackburn BB2 .101 C5
Over Town BB10 .108 A8
Spring Villas [18] OL14 .109 B1
Spring Wood Nature Trail* BB7 .144 E5
Spring Wood St BL0 .50 B7
Spring Yd [5] BB8 .171 D5
Springbank BB9 .170 E5
Springbank Ave FY5 .176 C2
Springbank Gdns BB4 .105 F2
Springbrook Ave FY5 .152 F8
Springburn Cl BL6 .32 D1
Springcroft [1] PR25 .77 C3
Springdale Rd BB6 .123 C8
Springfield Blacko BB9 .170 D8
High Bentham LA2 .239 E8
Springfield Ave
Accrington BB5 .103 F4
Bacup OL13 .88 A3
Blackburn BB2 .100 E1
Earby BB18 .197 C1
Kirkham PR4 .113 E5
Springfield Bank BB11 .128 B5
Springfield Cl
Burscough L40 .25 D2
Formby L37 .11 C2
Whalley BB7 .144 D6
Springfield Com Prim Sch BB10 .128 B5
Springfield Cres LA2 .239 E8
Springfield Ct [1] FY3 .130 E3
Springfield Dr
Newchurch BB4 .86 E1
Thornton FY5 .176 B4
Springfield Flats [7] BB3 .65 A8
Springfield Gdns
Nether Kellet LA6 .221 F5
Scorton PR3 .204 E6
Springfield Mews [2] BB5 .103 D3
Springfield Rd
Adlington PR6 .31 A8
Blackpool FY1 .130 B6
Burnley BB11 .128 A4
Burnley BB11 .128 B5
[1] Chorley PR7 .43 C8
Coppull PR7 .29 E8
Great Harwood BB6 .124 B4
Horwich BL6 .32 D1
Leyland PR25 .59 D7
Lytham St Anne's FY8 .89 E6
Maghull L39 .5 F6
Nelson BB9 .148 E6
[4] Ramsbottom BL0 .50 A2
Rawtenstall BB4 .86 B3
Springfield Rd N PR7 .29 E8
Springfield St
Blackburn BB2 .101 B3
Darwen BB3 .65 A8
Lancaster LA1 .214 F7
Morecambe LA4 .216 F4
Oswaldtwistle BB5 .103 D4
Preston PR1 .117 E1
Springfield Terr
Adlington PR6 .31 D8
Blackburn BB2 .101 A1
Fleetwood FY7 .176 A6
Springfield View BB11 .106 C5
Springhill Ave OL13 .70 D8
Springhill Villas OL13 .70 D8
Springmount BB18 .197 C2
Springmount Dr WN8 .27 C5
Springs Cres PR6 .61 E5
Springs Mews PR6 .61 E6
Springs Rd Chorley PR6 .61 D2
Longridge PR3 .140 B8
Springsands Cl PR2 .118 E5
Springthorpe St [5] BB3 .65 B6
Springvale BB5 .103 F4
Springvale Bsns Pk BB3 .65 B6
Springwater Ave BL0 .50 A3
Springwood Cl PR5 .97 A3
Springwood Dr
Chorley PR7 .43 E5
Rufford L40 .39 A5
Springwood Rd BB10 .128 E5
Springwood Terr OL14 .109 B1
Sprodley Dr WN6 .28 B2
Spruce Ave Bury BL9 .33 B2
Lancaster LA1 .214 F4
Spruce Cl PR2 .118 C7
Spruce Ct BB5 .104 E8
Spruce St BL0 .50 B5
Spruce Way L37 .11 C3
Sprucewood Cl BB5 .104 D6
Spurrier St PR26 .77 A4
Spymers Croft L37 .12 A6
Square House La PR9 .55 C6
Square La Burscough L40 .25 E3
Catforth PR4 .135 F4
Square St BL0 .50 C6
Square The
Blackpool FY3 .131 A2
Brinscall PR6 .62 F7
Burton-in-K LA6 .240 B7
Cleveleys FY5 .175 D5
Cumeragh Village PR3 .138 F5
Great Eccleston PR3 .156 B5
[1] Leyland PR25 .77 B2
Scorton PR3 .204 E6
Waddington BB7 .189 B4
Walton-le-D PR5 .97 F5
Whalley BB7 .144 C5
Worsthorne BB10 .129 B5
Squire Rd BB9 .148 F8
Squire's Gate Rd PR2 .117 C3
Squires Cl PR5 .98 E2
Squires Ct
[7] Blackpool FY4 .110 C5
[10] Lytham St Anne's FY8 .91 B3
Squires Gate Ind Est FY4 .110 E4
Squires Gate La FY4 .110 D5
Squires Gate Sta FY8 .110 B4
Squires Rd PR1 .96 C6
Squires Wood PR2 .118 D6
Squirrel Fold PR2 .118 F2
Squirrel Gn L37 .11 C5
Squirrel La BL6 .32 A4
Squirrel's Chase PR5 .77 A7
Squirrels Chase PR4 .115 D1
Squirrels Cl BB5 .104 E8
Stable Cl Gisburn BB7 .231 B3
Kirkham PR4 .114 A6
Stable La PR6 .62 A7
Stable Yd PR3 .201 E5
Stables Cl BB4 .86 A6
Stables The Leyland PR7 .60 A5
Whalley BB7 .144 B8
Whitworth OL12 .71 C1
Stack Croft PR6 .78 A2
Stack La OL13 .71 B8
Stackhouses The [2] BB11 .128 A6
Stadium Ave FY4 .110 E5
Staffa Cres BB1 .102 D4
Stafford Ave FY6 .153 D1
Stafford Cl PR4 .156 A1
Stafford Moreton Way L31 .5 D1
Stafford Rd
[11] Preston PR1 .118 A1
Southport PR8 .35 A1
Stafford St Burnley BB10 .128 A7
Darwen BB3 .81 F4
Nelson BB9 .149 A8
Skelmersdale WN8 .17 D1
Staghills Rd BB4 .86 D1
Stainburn Cl WN6 .19 E6
Stainforth Ave FY2 .152 E5
Staining Ave PR2 .95 F8
Staining CE Prim Sch FY3 .131 D5
Staining Old Rd FY3,FY6 .131 D7
Staining Rd FY3 .131 C6
Staining Rd W FY3 .131 D5
Staining Rise FY3 .131 E5
Stainton Dr BB12 .127 E8
Stainton Gr [1] LA4 .217 E4
Stakepool Dr PR3 .201 E4
Stakes Hall Pl BB2 .101 C2
Stalls Rd LA3 .212 F2
Stalmine Ctry Pk FY6 .177 D5
Stalmine Hall Pk FY6 .177 C8
Stalmine Prim Sch FY6 .177 D7
Stamford Ave FY4 .110 D7
Stamford Ct FY8 .89 D8
Stamford Dr PR6 .61 C5
Stamford Pl [3] BB7 .189 F1
Stamford Rd
Skelmersdale WN8 .17 D2
Southport PR8 .35 B2
Stanagate PR4 .115 C1
Stanah Gdns FY5 .176 E2
Stanah Prim Sch FY5 .176 D1
Stanah Rd FY5 .176 E2
Stanalee La PR3 .160 B8
Stanbury Cl
Brierfield BB10 .148 E2
Bury BL9 .33 D1
Stanbury Dr BB10 .148 E2
Stancliffe St BB2 .101 C3
Standen Hall Cl BB10 .148 E3
Standen Hall Dr BB10 .148 D3
Standen Rd BB7 .166 F7
Standen Road Bglws BB7 .166 F7
Standhouse La L39 .15 C2
Standing Stone La BB8, BB9 .194 A2
Standish Com High Sch WN6 .29 C2
Standish Ctr The [4] WN6 .29 E1
Standish St
Burnley BB11 .128 A6
Chorley PR7 .43 D7
Standish St Wilfred's CE Prim Sch WN6 .29 F1
Standridge Clough La BB18 .197 D1
Standroyd Dr BB8 .172 A5
Standroyd Rd BB8 .172 A5
Stanedge Cl BL0 .50 C4
Stanford Gdns BB2 .102 A1
Stanford Hall Cres BL0 .50 B4
Stang Top Rd BB9 .169 F6
Stangate L31 .5 B2
Stanhill La BB5 .103 C4
Stanhill Rd BB1,BB5 .102 F4
Stanhill St BB5 .103 C3
Stanhope Ave LA3 .217 E3
Stanhope Ct LA3 .217 F3
Stanhope Rd [1] FY1 .130 C7
Stanhope St
Burnley BB12 .127 F7
Darwen BB3 .82 A2
Preston PR1 .117 E2
Stanier Pl BL6 .32 C2
Stanifield Cl PR25 .77 B3
Stanifield La PR5,PR25 .77 C5
Stankelt Rd LA5 .224 C2
Stanlawe Rd L37 .11 E6
Stanley Ave
Cleveleys FY5 .175 E2
Hutton PR4 .95 D2
Leyland PR25 .77 C4
Middleforth Green PR1 .96 E5
Poulton-le-F FY6 .153 D3
Southport PR8 .34 F3
Stanley Cl PR3 .140 B7
Stanley Croft PR4 .137 B3
Stanley Ct
Accrington BB5 .104 D7
Burscough Bridge L40 .25 E5
Chipping PR3 .185 E3
Kirkham PR4 .114 B4
Stanley Dr Darwen BB3 .65 B5
Hornby LA2 .238 B7
Stanley Fold PR5 .76 F8
Stanley Gate
Fleetwood FY7 .198 D3
Mellor BB2 .121 E2
Stanley Gr
Higher Penwortham PR1 .96 A5
Horwich BL6 .32 D1
Stanley High Sch PR9 .53 F4
Stanley Ho PR1 .96 E7
Stanley Mount [6] OL13 .87 F3
Stanley Park Cl FY3 .130 F3
Stanley Pl [9] Chorley PR7 .43 C8
Lancaster LA1 .214 D8
Preston PR1 .96 E7
Stanley Prim & Inf Sch FY3 .131 B2
Stanley Range BB2 .101 B1
Stanley Rd Blackpool FY1 .130 C4
Fleetwood FY7 .198 F3
Formby L37 .11 E6
Kirkham PR4 .113 F7
Leyland PR25 .77 C4
Lytham St Anne's FY8 .90 D3
Morecambe LA3 .216 E3
Skelmersdale WN8 .10 B7
Stanley St
Accrington BB5 .104 D6
Bacup OL13 .87 F4
Blackburn BB1 .102 B6
Brierfield BB9 .148 B6
[6] Burnley BB11 .127 F5
Carnforth LA5 .223 D1
Colne BB8 .171 D5
Kirkham PR4 .114 B4
[10] Leyland PR25 .77 B1
Longridge PR3 .140 A8
Morecambe LA4 .217 B6
Nelson BB9 .148 D8
Ormskirk L39 .15 F5
Oswaldtwistle BB5 .103 D3
Preston PR1 .97 B8
Ramsbottom BL0 .50 B5
Rochdale OL12 .52 E1
Southport PR9 .35 B8
Stanley Terr PR1 .96 E7
Stanley Villas PR5 .99 B4
Stanley Way WN8 .17 E3
Stanleyfield Cl PR1 .118 A1
Stanleyfield Rd PR1 .118 A1
Stanmere Ct BL8 .49 B3
Stanmore Ave FY4 .110 F6
Stanmore Dr LA1 .214 E5
Stannanought Rd WN8 .18 E2
Stanner Lodge FY8 .110 F2
Stanning Cl PR25 .59 E8
Stanrose Cl BL7 .47 E1
Stansfeld St BB2 .101 C3
Stansfield Ave L31 .5 F1
Stansfield Cl [7] BB9 .170 D4
Stansfield Rd BB4 .69 E8
Stansfield St
[2] Bacup OL13 .70 C8
Blackpool FY1 .130 C1
Burnley BB11 .127 B5
[6] Darwen BB3 .65 A8
Nelson BB9 .148 E8
Stansfield Terr [14] OL14 .109 B1
Stansford Ct PR1 .96 D4
Stansted Rd PR7 .43 A7
Stansy Ave LA3 .216 E1
Stanthorpe Wlk BB10 .148 A1
Stanworth Brow PR6 .80 A5
Stanworth Rd BB9 .148 D8
Stanworth St BB10 .129 B5
Stanworth Terr PR6 .80 B4
Stanzaker Hall Dr PR3 .158 D7
Stapleton Rd L37 .11 D1
Star Bank OL13 .70 D7
Star La BL6 .31 F3
Star St Accrington BB5 .103 F5
Darwen BB3 .82 B1
Starbeck Ave FY4 .130 D1
Starfield Cl FY8 .91 A4
Starkie St
[6] Blackburn BB1 .101 F5
Burnley BB11 .127 E5
Darwen BB3 .65 B8
[12] Leyland PR25 .77 B1
Preston PR1 .96 F6
Starr Gate FY4 .110 B4
Starrgate Dr PR2 .116 E1
Startifants La PR3 .184 F4
Startifants Lane End PR3 .185 A5
Startley Nook PR4 .76 B6
States Rd FY8 .90 B6
Statham Rd WN8 .17 D3
Statham Way L39 .15 E4
Station App
[1] Burscough Bridge L40 .25 E5
Ormskirk L39 .15 F5
Station Ave WN5 .10 D5
Station Bldgs LA5 .223 D2
Station Brow PR25 .77 B2
Station Cl Rishton BB1 .103 A8
Wilpshire BB1 .122 F4
Station Cotts LA6 .241 D2
Station Ct LA2 .238 B7
Station La
Burton-in-K LA6 .240 B7
Nateby PR3 .203 B1
Newsham PR3 .137 A5
Scorton PR3 .204 D7
Station Par OL14 .108 F1
Station Rd Adlington PR7 .31 A6
Bamber Bridge PR5 .77 E8
Banks PR9 .54 F5
Barnoldswick BB18 .196 B2
Blackpool FY4 .110 B8
Blackrod BL6 .31 E1
Chapeltown BL7 .48 C4
Clitheroe BB7 .166 E8
Coppull PR7 .42 F1
[3] Cornholme OL14 .109 C1
Croston PR26 .58 B3
Fleetwood FY7 .199 A4
Foulridge BB8 .194 D1
Great Harwood BB6 .124 D5
Halton LA2 .219 C6
Haskayne L39 .13 E7
Haslingden BB4 .85 B4
Haslingden,Bridge End BB4 .68 A7
Hesketh Bank PR4 .73 F3
Hest Bank LA2 .220 D1
High Bentham LA2 .239 D7
Hoghton PR5 .99 B2
Holme Mills LA6 .240 B8
Hornby LA2 .238 B7
Huncoat BB5 .125 E2
[2] Kirkham PR4 .113 F5
Lancaster LA1 .214 E8
Lytham St Anne's FY8 .91 B3
Maghull L31 .5 A6
Morecambe LA4 .217 B5
New Longton PR4 .75 F8
Ormskirk L39 .15 F6
Padiham BB12 .126 C8
Parbold WN8 .27 C2
Poulton-le-F FY6 .153 E4
Ramsbottom BL8 .49 F1
Rimington BB7 .191 E8
Rishton BB1 .124 A1
Rufford L40 .39 D4
Salwick PR4 .115 C4
Singleton FY6 .132 C8
Southport PR8 .21 C5
Thornton FY5 .176 D1
Walmer Bridge PR4 .74 D4
Whalley BB7 .144 C5
Whitworth OL12 .71 D3
Whitworth,Broadley OL12 .52 C5
Wrea Green PR4 .113 B4
Station Road Ind Est BB6 .124 E5
Station Sq FY8 .91 A3
Station Terr
Abbey Village PR6 .80 C2
Blackpool FY4 .110 B8
Station View BB6 .143 D1
Station Way
Garstang PR3 .181 C8
Hornby LA2 .238 B7
Staunton St LA5 .223 D3
Staveley Ave L40 .25 E4
Staveley Gr FY7 .198 D2
Staveley Pl PR2 .116 E2
Staveley Rd
Skelmersdale WN8 .17 E3
Southport PR8 .21 D4
Staynall La FY6 .177 B4
Stead St BL0 .50 C6
Sted Terr BB1 .101 E6
Steeley La PR6 .43 D7
Steeple View PR2 .96 D8
Steer St BB10 .148 B1
Steeton Rd FY3 .153 B1
Stefano Rd [1] PR1 .97 C8
Steiner St BB5 .104 A6
Steiner's La BB5 .103 E7
Step Row OL13 .87 F5
Stephen St
Blackburn BB2 .101 B2
Lytham St Anne's FY8 .89 E7
Stephendale Ave PR5 .78 B8
Stephens Gr LA3 .209 D8
Stephenson Dr BB12 .127 C7
Stephenson St
[2] Chorley PR6 .43 E7
Horwich BL6 .32 B2
Stephenson Way L37 .12 C3
Sterling Pl [3] OL10 .33 F1
Sterndale Ave WN6 .29 E2
Stevenson Ave [2] PR25 .77 C3
Stevenson St E BB5 .104 A5
Stevenson St W BB5 .103 F5
Steward Ave LA1 .215 B5
Stewart Cl LA5 .224 B8
Stewart Ct [9] LA1 .218 D2
Stewart St Blackburn BB2 .81 D8
Burnley BB11 .128 B4
[11] Preston PR1 .96 D8
Stiles Ave PR4 .95 C1
Stiles The L39 .15 E5
Stirling Cl Chorley PR6 .43 E7
Clitheroe BB7 .166 C6
[1] Leyland PR25 .77 C1
Stirling Ct
[8] Blackpool FY1 .130 D7
Lane Bottom BB10 .149 B4
Southport PR9 .54 A2
Stirling Dr BB1 .101 F4
Stirling Rd Blackpool FY3 .130 D7
Lancaster LA1 .215 A7
Stirling St BB2 .101 B1
Stock Cl OL12 .52 E2
Stockbridge Cotts BB7 .164 E3
Stockbridge Dr BB12 .126 E8
Stockbridge Rd BB12 .126 D7
Stockclough La BB2 .80 D6
Stockdale Cres PR5 .77 F8
Stockdove Way FY5 .175 E3
Stockdove Wood FY5 .175 E3
Stockholm St BB11 .127 B5
Stockley Cres L39 .7 E6
Stockley Dr WN6 .19 E8
Stockpit Rd L33 .1 D2
Stocks Cl PR6 .79 B1
Stocks Ct
Heskin Green PR7 .41 E3
[5] Poulton-le-F FY6 .153 D3
Stocks La
Barnoldswick BB7 .193 A7
Carleton FY6 .153 A3
Heskin Green PR7 .41 E3
Stocks Lane End PR3 .181 D2
Stocks Park Dr BL6 .32 C3
Stocks Rd PR2 .117 C2
Stocks Resr & Gisburn Forest Walks* BB7 .235 E3
Stocks St [7] PR1 .96 E8
Stocksgate OL12 .52 B2
Stockwood Cl BB2 .101 A8
Stockydale Rd FY4 .111 A6
Stoke Ave FY1 .130 D2
Stokes Hall Ave PR25 .60 A8
Stone Bridge La BB5 .103 E3
Stone Cl BL0 .50 A4
Stone Croft PR1 .96 D2
Stone Cross Gdns PR3 .181 D2
Stone Edge Rd BB9 .170 E6
Stone Edge View BB9 .170 E6
Stone Fold BB5 .85 B8
Stone Hall La WN8 .19 A5
Stone Hill Dr BB1 .123 A1
Stone Hill La OL12 .52 A2
Stone Holme Terr BB4 .86 A8
Stone Mill Cotts BL7 .48 D4
Stone Moor Bottom BB12 .126 C6
Stone Pits BL0 .68 E3
Stone Row Head LA1 .215 C8
Stone St Haslingden BB4 .84 F2
Rawtenstall BB4 .69 F8
Stonebarn Dr L31 .5 C3
Stonebridge Cl [6] PR5 .77 C8
Stonebridge Terr PR3 .140 A7
Stonechat Cl FY3 .131 B6
Stonecroft BB9 .170 E6
Stonecroft Rd PR25 .59 D7
Stonecrop WN6 .28 D2
Stonefield Longton PR4 .74 F8
Middleworth Green PR1 .96 E4
Stonefield Cotts BB2 .100 B2
Stonefold Ave PR4 .95 C1
Stonegate Fold PR6 .44 B1
Stonehill Cres OL12 .32 A3
Stonehill Dr OL12 .52 B3
Stonehill Rd OL12 .52 B3
Stoneholme Ind Est BB4 .86 A8
Stoneholme Rd BB4 .86 A8
Stonehouse Gn PR6 .78 B3
Stoneleigh Cl PR8 .21 C4
Stoneleigh Ct LA5 .224 C3
Stones Bank Rd BL7 .47 B5
Stones La PR3 .181 E3
Stoneway Rd FY5 .175 E1
Stonewell [17] LA1 .214 F8
Stoney Bank Rd BB10 .107 C2
Stoney Brow WN8 .19 B1
Stoney Butts PR2 .95 D8
Stoney Croft Dr LA5 .223 E6

Stoney Ct BB8 .194 E1
Stoney Holt PR25 .77 E1
Stoney La Adlington PR7 .30 E4
Bamber Bridge PR5 .77 C6
Foulridge BB8 .194 E1
Freckleton PR4 .93 B5
Galgate LA2 .211 B3
Hambleton FY6 .177 C2
Longridge PR3 .161 C7
Parbold WN6,WN8 .27 E4
Stoney St BB11 .128 B4
Stoneycroft BB10 .129 A5
Morecambe LA4 .217 D6
Stoneycroft Ave BL6 .32 D4
Stoneycroft Cl BL6 .32 D5
Stoneygate Cleveleys FY5 .175 F1
17 Preston PR1 .97 A7
Stoneygate La WN6 .28 B2
Stoneyholme Cty Prim Sch
BB12 .127 F8
Stoneyhurst Ave
Burnley BB10 .128 D5
Thornton FY5 .153 D8
Stoneyhurst Ht BB9 .148 D4
Stoneyroyd OL12 .71 D1
Stonor Rd PR7 .30 F7
Stony Bank PR6 .79 A6
Stony Croft Pl 2 FY4 .110 C5
Stony Fold Brow BB3 .64 A5
Stony Hill Ave FY4 .110 C5
Stony La Cockerham PR3 .206 F2
Hollins Lane PR3 .207 D3
Shore OL14 .109 E2
Stonybutts 9 BB1 .101 E5
Stonycroft Ave FY4 .110 C5
Stonygate La PR3 .141 D6
Stonyhurst PR7 .43 C4
Stonyhurst Cl
Blackburn BB2 .101 D4
Padiham BB12 .126 E6
Stonyhurst Coll BB7 .165 A3
Stonyhurst Coll Gdns*
BB7 .165 A2
Stonyhurst Rd BB2 .101 D4
Stoop St BB11 .127 C5
Stoopes Hill BB18 .197 C2
Stoops Fold BB2 .121 E2
Stoops La BB7 .191 F8
Stopes Brow BB1,BB3 .82 A7
Stopford Ave FY2 .152 E2
Stopford Ct 1 BB5 .124 F3
Stopgate La L33 .1 C7
Stopper La BB7 .192 B7
Store St Blackburn BB3 .82 A7
17 Haslingden BB4 .85 B3
Horwich BL6 .32 C4
Storey Ave LA1 .214 D8
Storey Hall LA1 .214 E5
Storey Inst (Coll of F Ed)
LA1 .214 E8
Stork Cl FY5 .175 F1
Stork St BB3 .65 D8
Storrs La LA5 .225 B4
Storwood Cl WN5 .10 E5
Stott St 1 Nelson BB9 .148 D8
Rochdale OL12 .52 F1
Stour Lodge PR2 .117 C6
Stourton Rd PR8 .21 C4
Stourton St BB1 .124 A2
Stout St BB2 .101 D4
Strait La LA2 .232 F1
Straits BB5 .103 E4
Straits La BB12 .145 D2
Straits The PR5 .99 B2
Strand Rd PR1 .96 D7
Strand St W PR2 .96 C8
Strand The Blackpool FY1 .130 B6
Fleetwood FY7 .175 D8
Horwich BL6 .32 D3
Strands Farm Ct LA2 .238 B7
Strang St 9 BL0 .50 C6
Strange St BB11 .128 B4
Stransdale Cl 5 PR3 .181 B7
Stratfield Pl 5 PR25 .77 B1
Stratford Cl
Lancaster LA1 .218 C3
Southport PR8 .21 A6
Stratford Dr PR2 .117 D4
Stratford Pl
Blackpool FY1 .130 E2
2 Fleetwood FY7 .198 E4
Stratford Rd Chorley PR6 .43 D8
Lytham St Anne's FY8 .90 B7
Stratford Way
7 Accrington BB5 .104 A7
Colne BB8 .171 F5
Strathaven Pl 6 OL10 .33 F1
Strathclyde Rd BB1 .102 A4
Strathdale FY4 .110 F7
Strathmore Cl BL0 .50 C4
Strathmore Gr PR7 .43 B7
Strathmore Rd PR2 .117 E3
Strathyre Cl FY2 .152 F5
Stratton Ct BB9 .148 E6
Stratton Gr BL6 .32 B5
Strawberry Bank 1
BB1 .101 D5
Strawberry Fields PR7 .61 B3
Strawberry Mews 1
LA3 .212 F8
Streatly Wlk BB2 .82 A8
Street The PR6 .44 E3
Strellas La LA5 .221 C1
Stretford Pl OL12 .52 E3
Stretton Ave FY4 .110 E8
Stretton Dr PR9 .35 F8
Stretton Rd BL0 .50 A2
Strickens La PR3 .182 C6
Strickland Dr LA4 .217 E5
Strickland's La FY6 .177 D6
Stricklands La PR1 .96 E4
Strike La PR4 .93 B8
Strine The L40,PR4 .57 A1
Stromness Gr 4 OL10 .33 F1
Strongstry Rd BL0 .68 C2
Stronsay Pl FY2 .152 F6
Stroyan St BB10 .128 C5
Strutt St 2 PR1 .118 B1
Stryands PR4 .95 C1
Stuart Ave Bacup OL13 .70 D8
Morecambe LA4 .217 D6
Stuart Cl 14 Darwen BB3 .82 A1
Fulwood PR2 .118 E3
Stuart Pl FY3 .153 A1
Stuart Rd Fulwood PR2 .118 E3
Thornton FY5 .176 C2
Stuart St Accrington BB5 .104 B7
5 Barnoldswick BB18 .196 C2
Stubbins La Catterall PR3 .181 F2
Ramsbottom BL0 .50 C8
Sabden BB7 .146 A7
Stubbins St BL0 .68 C1
Stubbins Vale Cvn Pk
BB7 .146 A7
Stubbins Vale Rd BL0 .68 C1
Stubbins Vale Terr BL0 .68 B1
Stubbylee La OL13 .70 F8
Stubley Holme 5 OL14 .109 A1
Stubley La OL14 .109 B1
Studfold PR7 .61 B2
Studholme Ave PR1 .96 E2
Studholme Cl 8 PR1 .96 E2
Studholme Cres PR1 .96 E2
Studley Ct PR9 .53 D1
Stump Cross La BB7 .230 F5
Stump Hall Rd BB12 .146 F7
Stump La PR6 .43 D8
Stunstead Cotts BB8 .172 C2
Stunstead Rd BB8 .172 C3
Sturgess Cl L39 .15 F7
Sturminster Cl 5 PR1 .96 E2
Styan St FY7 .199 A4
Stydd La PR3 .141 E4
Sudell Ave L31 .5 F2
Sudell Cl BB3 .82 C1
Sudell Cross 20 BB1 .101 E5
Sudell La L31,L39 .5 E6
Sudell Prim Sch BB3 .82 B1
Sudell Rd BB3 .82 B1
Sudellside St BB3 .82 B1
Suffolk Ave BB12 .127 A6
Suffolk Cl PR25 .59 E6
Suffolk Rd Blackpool FY3 .131 A2
Preston PR1 .118 A1
Southport PR8 .22 A8
Suffolk St BB2 .101 C2
Sugar Stubbs La PR9 .55 C4
Sugham La LA3 .212 F8
Sulby Cl PR8 .34 F3
Sulby Dr Fulwood PR2 .118 F5
Lancaster LA1 .214 F6
Sulby Gr Fulwood PR2 .119 A5
Morecambe LA4 .217 E6
Sulby Rd BB2 .101 E1
Sullivan Dr BB2 .102 A1
Sullom Side La PR3 .182 C5
Sullom View PR3 .181 C6
Sultan St BB5 .104 D7
Sulyard St LA1 .214 F8
Summer St Horwich BL6 .32 B4
Nelson BB9 .148 C7
Skelmersdale WN8 .18 A4
Summer Trees Ave PR2 .116 D3
Summerdale Dr BL0 .50 B2
Summerer Gr PR4 .132 F6
Summerfield
Leyland PR25 .76 F3
Thornton-in-C BD23 .197 A5
Summerfield Cl PR5 .97 B2
Summerfield Dr LA2 .218 C7
Summerfields Coppull PR7 .29 F7
Lytham St Anne's FY8 .89 C8
Summerhill LA2 .239 D7
Summerseat La BL0 .50 A2
Summerseat Meth Prim Sch
BL9 .50 D2
Summerseat Sta BL9 .50 C2
Summersgill Rd LA1 .218 B2
Summerton Wlk BB3 .82 A2
Summerville 4 FY4 .110 C6
Summerville Ave FY3 .131 E5
Summerville Wlk 4
BB2 .101 D5
Summerwood Cl FY2 .152 D1
Summerwood La
Halsall L39 .23 C1
Haskayne L39 .14 D8
Summit Cl OL10 .33 F4
Summit Dr PR4 .93 C6
Summit St OL10 .33 F3
Summit The BD23 .197 A5
Summit Works BB11 .127 E2
Sumner Ave L39 .13 F4
Sumner Rd L37 .11 F3
Sumner St Blackburn BB2 .101 E3
Leyland PR25 .77 A1
Sumner's La PR5 .40 A7
Sumners Barn PR2 .118 E6
Sumpter Croft PR1 .96 E2
Sumpter Ct 3 PR1 .96 F2
Sun St Colne BB8 .171 E5
Lancaster LA1 .214 F8
Nelson BB9 .148 C8
Oswaldtwistle BB5 .103 E4
Sun St *continued*
Ramsbottom BL0 .50 B7
Sun Terr 7 OL14 .109 B1
Sunacre Ct LA3 .216 E3
Sunbank Cl OL12 .52 D2
Sunbury Ave PR1 .96 D3
Sunbury Dr PR8 .21 B4
Suncliffe Rd BB9 .148 D4
Suncourt PR8 .34 F6
Sunderland Ave
Cleveleys FY5 .175 F4
Hambleton FY6 .177 D2
Sunderland Dr LA3 .217 A2
Sunderland St BB12 .127 B6
Sunfield Cl FY4 .111 A7
Sunnindale Ave BB4 .87 A1
Sunningdale PR4 .137 B3
Sunningdale Ave
Blackpool FY4 .131 A2
Fleetwood FY7 .175 D7
Hest Bank LA2 .220 D1
Sunningdale Cl PR4 .114 A4
Sunningdale Cres LA2 .220 D1
Sunningdale Ct FY8 .90 A6
Sunningdale Dr FY5 .153 D8
Sunningdale Gdns
Brierfield BB10 .148 D3
Formby L37 .11 E3
Sunningdale Pl PR4 .135 C8
Sunny Bank Kirkham PR4 .113 F5
Middleworth Green PR1 .96 F3
Sunny Bank Ave
Blackpool FY2 .152 C4
Newton-w-S PR4 .115 A2
Sunny Bank Cl BB4 .68 A6
Sunny Bank Cotts BB4 .67 F5
Sunny Bank Mill 6 PR4 .113 F5
Sunny Bank Rd
Blackburn BB2 .101 E1
Haslingden BB4 .68 A6
Sunny Bank Sch BB11 .127 E4
Sunny Bank Terr 3
OL14 .109 B1
Sunny Bower Cl BB1 .123 B1
Sunny Bower Rd BB1 .123 B1
Sunny Brow PR7 .43 A2
Sunny Dr WN5 .10 F6
Sunny Lea St BB4 .85 F5
Sunny Rd PR9 .54 A2
Sunny View PR6 .80 C2
Sunnybank Dr BB5 .103 C2
Sunnybank Rd LA5 .221 A5
Sunnybank St
Darwen BB3 .82 A1
8 Haslingden BB4 .85 A3
Sunnycliff Ret Pk LA3 .217 D1
Sunnyfield Ave
Morecambe LA4 .217 E6
Southward Bottom BB10 .108 A8
Sunnyfield La BB3 .66 A8
Sunnyfields L39 .16 A5
Sunnyhill PR2 .118 C5
Sunnyhill Cl BB3 .81 D2
Sunnyhurst BB3 .81 D1
Sunnyhurst Ave FY4 .110 D6
Sunnyhurst Cl BB3 .81 D2
Sunnyhurst La BB3 .81 D2
Sunnyhurst Rd BB2 .101 D4
Sunnyhurst Wood Visitor
Ctr* BB3 .81 D2
Sunnymede Dr L31 .5 D3
Sunnymede Sch PR8 .34 F6
Sunnymede Vale BL0 .50 A3
Sunnymere Dr BB3 .81 E2
Sunnyside
5 High Bentham LA2 .239 D8
Ormskirk L39 .6 C7
Southport PR8 .34 F3
Sunnyside Ave
Billington BB7 .144 B4
1 Blackburn BB2 .80 E8
Ribchester PR3 .141 D3
Warton PR4 .92 E6
Wilpshire BB1 .123 A7
Sunnyside Camp Site
LA3 .217 A2
Sunnyside Cl
Freckleton PR4 .93 B7
Lancaster LA1 .214 E7
Rawtenstall BB4 .86 A6
Sunnyside Ct PR9 .53 C1
Sunnyside Cvn Pk PR3 .158 F5
Sunnyside La LA1 .214 E7
Sunnyside Terr FY6 .200 C3
Sunset Cl L33 .1 A5
Super St BB5 .124 E4
Surgeon's Ct PR1 .96 F7
Surrey Ave Burnley BB12 .127 B7
Darwen BB3 .81 F3
Surrey Cl PR9 .54 C5
Surrey Rd
Barrowford BB9 .170 D2
Blackburn BB1 .102 D5
Surrey St Accrington BB5 .104 D6
Preston PR1 .97 C8
Sussex Ave BL9 .33 E1
Sussex Cl Church BB5 .103 F7
Standish WN1 .30 B1
Sussex Dr Blackburn BB1 .102 A4
Garstang PR3 .181 B7
Haslingden BB4 .68 B8
Sussex Rd Blackpool FY3 .130 E6
Rishton BB1 .102 F8
Southport PR8,PR9 .35 D6
Sussex St
25 Barnoldswick BB18 .196 B2
Burnley BB11 .128 B4
1 Nelson BB9 .170 E1
Sussex St *continued*
Preston PR1 .118 A1
Sussex Wlk 10 BB1 .102 A4
Sutch La L40 .26 B5
Sutcliffe St Bacup OL13 .71 C8
Brierfield BB10 .148 F3
18 Burnley BB11 .127 F6
7 Chorley PR7 .43 D7
Sutcliffe Terr BB1 .82 F6
Sutherland Cl BB1 .123 A7
Sutherland Rd
Blackpool FY1 .130 C8
Heywood OL10 .33 F1
Sutherland St BB8 .171 C4
Sutherland View 2 FY1 .130 C7
Sutton Ave
Brierfield BB10 .148 D2
Tarleton PR4 .57 A8
Sutton Cres BB5 .125 F1
Sutton Dr PR2 .95 D8
Sutton Gr PR6 .61 F4
Sutton La Adlington PR6 .31 B8
Tarleton PR4 .56 F5
Sutton Pl FY1 .130 C4
Sutton Rd L37 .11 E1
Sutton St Blackburn BB2 .80 D8
Weeton Camp PR4 .132 E6
Sutton's La L37 .12 E3
Swain St OL12 .52 E1
Swainbank St BB11 .128 B5
Swaine St BB9 .148 C8
Swainson St
11 Blackpool FY1 .130 C6
Lytham St Anne's FY8 .90 F3
Swainstead Raike BD24 .236 E8
Swaledale LA2 .211 B4
Swaledale Ave BB10 .148 B4
Swalegate L31 .5 C2
Swallow Ave 1 PR1 .96 E4
Swallow Cl Blackpool FY3 .131 B2
Thornton FY5 .176 A4
Swallow Ct PR6 .78 C1
Swallow Dr
Blackburn BB1 .101 E6
Bury BL9 .33 B4
Swallow Field PR4 .74 E3
Swallow Pk 6 BB11 .127 C5
Swallow Wharf 8 LA1 .218 E1
Swallowfields
Blackburn BB1 .101 E8
Cottam PR4 .116 E5
Swallowfold PR2 .139 D1
Swan Alley 2 L39 .15 E5
Swan Delph L39 .15 C2
Swan Dr FY5 .175 F1
Swan Farm Cl BB3 .81 F7
Swan La L39 .5 F6
Swan Mdw BB7 .189 D1
Swan Rd BL8 .49 F2
Swan St Blackburn BB2 .101 E3
Darwen BB3 .65 B6
Preston PR1 .97 C8
Swan Yd 1 LA1 .215 A7
Swanage Ave FY4 .110 B6
Swanage Rd BB10 .148 C1
Swanfield Ct BB8 .172 A5
Swanfield Terr BB8 .172 A5
Swanpool La L39 .15 C2
Swansea St PR2 .96 C8
Swansey La PR6 .78 C1
Swarbrick Ave PR2 .139 D1
Swarbrick Cl FY1 .130 D7
Swarbrick Ct PR3 .140 B7
Swarbrick St PR4 .114 A4
Sweet Briar Cl OL12 .52 E2
Sweet Briar La OL12 .52 E2
Sweetclough Dr BB12 .126 F6
Swift Cl Blackburn BB1 .101 F5
Blackpool FY3 .131 B3
Swift Gdns LA3 .212 F5
Swift's Fold WN8 .8 D8
Swilkin La FY6 .177 E6
Swill Brook La 1 PR1 .97 C6
Swinburn Gr WN5 .10 D1
Swinburne Cl BB5 .104 E2
Swinden Hall Rd BB9 .170 E2
Swinden La BB8 .171 A2
Swindon Ave 7 FY4 .110 D8
Swindon St BB11 .127 D5
Swinglehurst Cotts PR3 .185 E3
Swinglehurst La PR3 .185 E3
Swinless St BB10 .128 B8
Swinshaw Cl BB4 .106 A2
Swinside PR4 .116 D4
Swiss St BB5 .103 F6
Swithemby St BL6 .32 A4
Sword Meanygate PR4 .56 C6
Sycamore Ave
Blackpool FY4 .110 F5
Burnley BB12 .127 B7
Euxton PR7 .60 D3
Garstang PR3 .181 B8
Nelson BB9 .149 A8
Sycamore Bglws BB7 .231 C3
Sycamore Cl
Blackburn BB1 .101 F8
Burnley BB12 .127 C6
Fulwood PR2 .118 C6
Mawdesley L40 .40 C2
Rishton BB1 .103 B8
Sycamore Cres
Caton LA2 .237 C3
Clayton-le-M BB5 .125 A5
1 Rawtenstall BB4 .85 F1
Sycamore Ct PR7 .43 B5
Sycamore Dr
Kirkham PR4 .113 D4
Middleworth Green PR1 .96 E3
Sycamore Dr *continued*
1 Skelmersdale WN8 .17 E2
Sycamore Gdns
Foulridge BB8 .194 D1
Heysham LA3 .212 E6
Sycamore Gr
Accrington BB5 .104 E3
Darwen BB3 .82 B2
Formby L37 .11 C1
Lancaster LA1 .214 D8
Sycamore Rd
Bilsborrow PR3 .159 A5
Blackburn BB1 .101 F8
Caton LA2 .237 C3
Chorley PR6 .61 D2
Fulwood PR2 .118 E2
Sycamore Rise
Brierfield BB9 .148 D5
Foulridge BB8 .194 D1
Sycamore Trad Est FY4 .110 F5
Sycamore Way BB18 .196 A1
Sycamore Wlk 1 BL6 .32 E1
Syd Brook La PR5,L40 .40 E7
Sydenham Terr OL12 .52 D3
Sydney Ave BB7 .144 D5
Sydney St Accrington BB5 .104 C6
1 Burnley BB11 .127 F6
Clayton-le-M BB5 .125 A1
Darwen BB3 .65 B7
Hoddlesden BB3 .82 F1
Lytham St Anne's FY8 .89 F6
Sydney Terr BB8 .172 C3
Syke Hill 13 PR1 .97 A7
Syke House La PR3 .160 E4
Syke La OL12 .52 F4
Syke Rd OL12 .52 F4
Syke Side Dr BB5 .125 E6
Syke St PR1 .97 A7
Sykefield BB9 .148 A5
Sykelands Ave LA2 .219 D7
Sykelands Gr LA2 .219 D7
Sykes Cl BB18 .194 E8
Sykes St BL9 .33 A3
Sylvan Dr BB11 .127 B4
Sylvan Gr PR5 .98 A2
Sylvan Pl LA3 .212 E6
Sylvancroft PR2 .117 A5
Sylvester St LA1 .214 E7
Symonds Rd PR2 .117 E3

T

Tabby Nook PR4 .55 F2
Tabby's Nook
Newburgh WN8 .27 A1
Skelmersdale WN8 .18 A8
Taberner Cl WN6 .29 F1
Tabley La PR4 .116 E7
Tabor St BB12 .127 D6
Tadema Gr BB11 .127 F2
Tadlow Cl L37 .11 C1
Tag Croft PR2 .116 F5
Tag Farm Ct PR2 .116 F5
Tag La PR2 .117 A4
Talaton Cl PR9 .54 A5
Talbot Ave 4 BB5 .124 F2
Talbot Cl Clitheroe BB7 .166 F7
Rawtenstall BB4 .68 E8
Talbot Ct
11 Blackpool FY4 .130 B1
3 Lytham St Anne's FY8 .90 A8
Talbot Dr Brierfield BB10 .148 F2
Euxton PR7 .60 D2
Southport PR8 .35 B6
Talbot Gr BL9 .33 A6
Talbot Ho PR7 .61 C2
Talbot Rd Accrington BB5 .104 A8
Blackpool FY1,FY3 .130 C6
Leyland PR25 .76 E2
Lytham St Anne's FY8 .91 C4
Middleforth Green PR1 .96 E5
Preston PR1 .96 D7
Talbot Row 2 PR7 .60 D1
Talbot Sq FY1 .130 B5
Talbot St Brierfield BB10 .148 F2
Burnley BB11 .128 B6
Chipping PR3 .185 E3
Chorley PR6 .61 E1
Colne BB8 .171 D6
Fulwood PR2 .117 D4
Rishton BB1 .124 C1
Southport PR8 .35 A6
Talbot Terr 1 FY8 .91 B3
Tall Trees LA1 .218 D4
Tamar Cl PR25 .60 B7
Tamar St PR1 .97 E8
Tamneys The WN8 .17 F1
Tan Hill Dr LA1 .218 D3
Tan House Cl WN8 .27 C3
Tan House La WN8 .27 C2
Tan Pit Cotts WN8 .19 C4
Tan Yard La PR3 .140 C8
Tan Yd PR3 .140 C8
Tancaster WN8 .17 E1
Tanfield Nook WN8 .27 C2
Tanfields WN8 .17 F1
Tanglewood PR2 .118 B5
Tanhouse 6 LA2 .211 A4
Tanhouse La PR6 .61 F6
Tanhouse Rd WN8 .9 E7
Tanner Barn BB5 .85 B7
Tanner St 15 BB11 .127 F6
Tanners Croft 5 BL0 .50 B6
Tanners St BL0 .50 B6
Tanners Way FY8 .90 D7
Tannersmith La L40 .40 F5
Tanpits La LA6 .240 B7

Tanpits Rd BB5 103 F6
Tansley Ave PR7 42 D1
Tansley Cl BL6 32 C2
Tansy La PR3 206 F4
Tanterton Hall Rd PR2 117 A6
Tanyard Cl PR7 42 D1
Tape St 2 BL0 50 B6
Taper St BL0 50 B6
Tapestry St BB2 101 D1
Tarbert Cres BB1 102 D4
Tarbet St LA1 215 A7
Tardy Gate Trad Ctr PR5 77 A8
Tarleton Ave BB11 128 B4
Tarleton Com Prim Sch PR4 56 F8
Tarleton High Sch PR4 57 A7
Tarleton Holy Trinity CE Prim Sch PR4 57 A5
Tarleton Lodge FY8 89 F4
Tarleton Mere Brow CE Prim Sch PR4 55 F2
Tarleton Rd PR9 36 A8
Tarleton St BB11 128 B4
Tarlscough La L40 38 D1
Tarlswood WN8 17 F1
Tarn Ave BB5 124 F4
Tarn Brook Cl BB5 125 F1
Tarn Brow L39 15 C3
Tarn Cl PR1 95 F4
Tarn Cotts LA5 221 C6
Tarn Ct FY7 198 D1
Tarn Hows Cl 1 PR7 43 B5
Tarn La LA6 240 B6
Tarn Rd Formby L37 11 D3
Thornton FY5 153 D7
Tarnacre Hall Bsns Pk PR3 180 D1
Tarnacre Hall Mews PR3 180 D1
Tarnacre La PR3 180 E2
Tarnacre View PR3 181 C6
Tarnbeck Dr L40 40 D2
Tarnbrick Ave PR4 93 C7
Tarnbrook Cl
Carnforth LA5 223 C1
Hest Bank LA5 220 F2
Tarnbrook Cotts PR3 201 E5
Tarnbrook Dr FY3 131 A7
Tarnbrook Rd
5 Heysham LA3 212 F8
2 Lancaster LA1 218 B2
Tarnside FY4 131 B1
Tarnside Rd WN5 10 E6
Tarnsyke Rd LA1 218 B2
Tarnwater La LA2 210 E7
Tarnway Ave FY5 153 D8
Tarradale PR4 94 F1
Tarragon Dr FY2 152 F4
Tarry Barn La BB7 167 A3
Tarvin Cl Brierfield BB10 148 F3
Southport PR9 54 D5
Tasker St 13 BB5 104 C6
Taskers Croft BB7 144 F8
Tatham Ct FY7 198 C1
Tatham Fells CE Prim Sch LA2 239 C4
Tattersall Sq BB4 86 F3
Tattersall St
5 Blackburn BB2 101 E4
Haslingden BB4 85 B6
Oswaldtwistle BB5 103 D4
2 Padiham BB12 126 D8
Tatton St BB8 171 B3
Tauheedul-Islam Girls' High Sch BB1 101 E6
Taunton Rd BB2 101 B5
Taunton St
8 Blackpool FY4 130 D1
Preston PR1 118 D1
Tavistock Dr PR8 21 B6
Tavistock St BB9 170 F1
Tawd Rd WN8 9 C8
Tay St Burnley BB11 127 D5
3 Preston PR1 96 D6
Taybank Ave FY4 110 D7
Taydale Cotts BB10 148 E3
Taylor Ave Newchurch BB4 86 F2
Ormskirk L39 16 A5
Taylor Cl BB2 101 C3
Taylor Ct BB4 85 A3
Taylor Gr LA4 217 F6
Taylor Holme Ind Est OL13 70 B8
Taylor St
Barnoldswick BB18 196 A2
Blackburn BB2 101 D3
Brierfield BB9 148 B6
Burnley BB10 128 A8
Bury BL9 33 A3
Chorley PR7 43 B5
Clitheroe BB7 166 F8
Darwen BB3 65 A8
Haslingden BB4 85 B6
2 Horwich BL6 32 B3
Preston PR1 96 D6
6 Rawtenstall BB4 86 A3
Rochdale OL12 52 F1
Skelmersdale WN8 17 C1
Whitworth OL12 52 D8
Taylor St W BB5 104 B6
Taylor's Bldgs BB6 143 D1
Taylor's Ind Est PR3 201 E5
Taylor's La
Fisher's Row PR3 201 D6
Holmes PR4 56 D3
Taylor's Meanygate PR4 56 A7
Taylors Cl FY6 153 C5
Taylors Pl 18 OL12 52 F1
Taymouth Rd 5 FY4 111 A6
Taywood Cl FY6 153 F4
Taywood Rd FY5 176 A4
Teak St BL9 33 B2
Teal Cl Blackburn BB1 101 D8
Leyland PR25 59 D7
Ormskirk L39 15 C2
Thornton FY5 176 A4
Teal Ct FY3 131 B6
Teal La FY8 90 E7
Teanlowe Ctr FY6 153 D3
Tears La WN8 17 F8
Teasel Wlk LA3 217 B2
Tebay Ave Cleveleys FY5 175 D4
Kirkham PR4 114 C5
Tebay Cl L31 5 F2
Tebay Ct LA1 218 C4
Tedder Ave Burnley BB12 127 B6
Southport PR9 36 A7
Teenadore Ave 1 FY4 110 E7
Tees Ct FY7 198 D2
Tees St PR1 118 C2
Teesdale 8 LA2 211 A4
Teesdale Ave FY2 130 D8
Teil Gn PR2 118 E6
Telford St Burnley BB12 127 C7
Horwich BL6 32 D2
Telletholme Ind Est L40 25 B3
Temperance St 8 PR6 43 E8
Temperance Terr OL13 87 F1
Temple Cl 2 BB1 102 B4
Temple Ct 10 PR1 96 F7
Temple Dr BB1 102 B4
Temple St
10 Blackpool FY1 130 B5
Burnley BB11 128 B5
Colne BB8 171 E6
Nelson BB9 148 F8
Temple Way PR6 61 D3
Templegate Cl WN6 29 F2
Templemartin 2 WN8 17 F2
Templeton Cl BB3 82 A2
Ten Row LA2 209 E5
Tenby 2 WN8 17 E2
Tenby Cl BB1 101 E7
Tenby Gr 6 OL12 52 C1
Tenby Rd 7 PR1 97 A6
Tenby St OL12 52 C1
Tennis St BB10 128 A8
Tennyson Ave
Chorley PR7 43 C6
Lytham St Anne's FY8 91 D4
Oswaldtwistle BB5 103 C4
Padiham BB12 126 E7
Read BB12 145 D2
Thornton FY5 176 A3
Warton PR4 92 D6
Tennyson Cl LA5 221 A5
Tennyson Dr
Longshaw WN5 10 D1
Ormskirk L39 15 D6
Tennyson Mill Ct PR1 118 D1
Tennyson Pl
Bamber Bridge PR5 97 D2
Great Harwood BB6 124 B4
Tennyson Rd
Blackpool FY3 130 F7
Colne BB8 171 D5
Fleetwood FY7 199 A4
Preston PR1 118 D1
Tennyson St
Brierfield BB10 148 F3
Burnley BB11 127 D5
6 Hapton BB12 126 C4
Tensing Ave FY2 152 D5
Tensing Rd L31 5 D1
Tenterfield St
23 Preston PR1 96 F8
6 Rawtenstall BB4 69 F8
Tenterheads BB4 69 F7
Terance Rd 2 FY4 110 E8
Tern Gr LA3 212 F5
Terra Cotta Bldgs BB4 107 A1
Terrace Row BB7 144 C4
Terrace St PR1 118 C1
Terrace The 7 LA2 239 B8
Terry St BB9 171 A2
Tetbury Cl 6 BB2 80 E8
Teven St 5 PR5 97 E1
Teversham WN8 17 F2
Teviot 4 WN8 17 E2
Teviot Ave FY7 198 D3
Tewkesbury 3 WN8 17 E2
Tewkesbury Ave FY4 110 D5
Tewkesbury Cl BB5 104 E3
Tewkesbury Dr FY8 91 D5
Tewkesbury St BB2 101 B1
Thames Ave BB10 148 C3
Thames Dr WN5 10 F7
Thames Ho 8 PR1 97 D8
Thames Prim Sch FY4 110 B7
Thames Rd FY4 110 B7
Thames St PR4 114 F2
Thane Row BB11 107 D7
Thanet WN8 17 F2
Thanet Lee Cl BB10 128 E1
Thealby Cl WN8 17 E2
Theatre St PR1 96 F7
Thelma St BL0 50 B6
Thermdale Cl 3 PR3 181 B7
Thetis Rd LA1 214 C8
Thickrash Brow LA2 239 D7
Third Ave Blackpool FY4 110 C7
Bury BL9 33 D4
Preesall Park FY6 200 C1
Thirlemere Ct LA1 218 F1
Thirlmere Ave
Burnley BB10 148 A2
Thirlmere Ave *continued*
Carleton FY6 153 C4
Colne BB8 171 F6
Fleetwood FY7 198 C1
Formby L37 12 A2
Haslingden BB4 68 C8
Horwich BL6 32 C2
1 Orrell WN5 10 F7
Padiham BB12 146 C2
Skelmersdale WN8 10 B7
Thirlmere Cl
2 Accrington BB5 125 D1
Adlington PR6 31 B8
6 Blackburn BB1 101 F6
Knott End-on-S FY6 199 F6
Longton PR4 75 B8
Maghull L31 5 E2
Thirlmere Dr Darwen BB3 82 C2
Longridge PR3 139 F5
Morecambe LA4 217 A4
Southport PR8 21 B3
Withnell Fold PR6 79 D2
Thirlmere Gr LA4 217 B4
Thirlmere Rd
Blackpool FY4 110 C7
Blackrod BL6 31 C3
Burnley BB10 128 E5
Chorley PR7 43 B6
Hightown L38 3 A4
Lancaster LA1 218 F2
Preston PR1 118 F1
Thirlmere Way BB4 106 A1
Thirsk WN8 17 E2
Thirsk Ave FY8 90 B7
Thirsk Gr FY1 130 D2
Thirsk Rd LA1 215 B4
Thistle Break LA3 213 A7
Thistle Cl Chorley PR6 43 E8
Cleveleys FY5 175 F5
Hesketh Bank PR4 73 E4
Thistle Ct L40 25 F6
Thistle St 15 OL13 87 F2
Thistlecroft PR2 117 A5
Thistlemount Ave BB4 86 F1
Thistleton Mews 3 PR9 35 C8
Thistleton Rd Preston PR2 95 E8
Thistleton PR4 155 C1
Thomas Gr LA4 217 B5
Thomas St
Blackburn BB2 101 D4
Brierfield BB9 148 A5
Burnley BB11 128 A5
Colne BB8 171 C4
2 Cornholme OL14 109 C1
7 Haslingden BB4 85 A3
Nelson BB9 148 E7
7 Oswaldtwistle BB5 103 D3
4 Preston PR1 97 B7
Whitworth OL12 71 D2
Thomas Weind PR3 181 C7
Thomason Fold BL7 48 D6
Thompson Ave L39 16 B5
Thompson Dr BL9 33 C3
Thompson St
Blackburn BB2 101 C4
Darwen BB3 65 B7
Horwich BL6 32 A3
8 Kirkham PR4 113 F6
Padiham BB12 126 D7
Preston PR1 118 D1
Thompson Street Ind Est BB2 101 C4
Thonock Rd LA4 217 D3
Thorburn Dr OL12 52 B7
Thorn Bank OL13 88 A2
Thorn Cres OL13 88 A2
Thorn Dr OL13 88 A2
Thorn Gdns OL13 88 A2
Thorn Gr Blackpool FY1 130 E2
Colne BB8 171 F6
Thorn Hill Cl BB1 102 A5
Thorn La PR3 140 B2
Thorn St Bacup OL13 88 A2
Burnley BB10 128 A8
Clitheroe BB7 166 D8
Great Harwood BB6 124 D6
Preston PR1 118 C1
Ramsbottom BL0 50 C3
Rawtenstall BB4 85 F5
Sabden BB7 146 A7
Thorn View BL9 33 C3
Thornbank FY3 131 B7
Thornbank Dr PR3 181 D2
Thornbeck Ave L38 2 F3
Thornber 1 WN8 17 F2
Thornber Ct BB10 148 C1
Thornber Gr FY1 130 D3
Thornber St BB2 101 C3
Thornbridge Ave L40 25 E3
Thornbury WN8 17 F2
Thornby 3 WN8 17 F2
Thorncliffe Dr BB3 65 D8
Thorndale 4 WN8 17 F2
Thorne St BB9 171 A2
Thorney Bank St 7 BB11 127 F5
Thorneybank Ind Est BB11 126 C2
Thorneycroft Cl FY6 153 B5
Thorneyholme RC Prim Sch BB7 228 C5
Thorneyholme Rd BB5 104 C8
Thorneyholme Sq BB12 169 E5
Thorneylea OL12 71 D1
Thornfield Lancaster LA1 214 F5
Much Hoole PR4 74 E3
Thornfield Ave
Fulwood PR2 118 F3
Thornfield Ave *continued*
Longridge PR3 140 A8
Newchurch BB4 86 E1
8 Rawtenstall BB4 69 F8
Thornton FY5 153 D8
Thornfield Cvn Pk FY3 131 D5
Thorngate PR1 96 B4
Thorngate Cl PR1 96 B4
Thornham Ct FY3 130 E5
Thornhill L39 6 B8
Thornhill Ave
Knott End-on-S FY6 200 A5
Rishton BB1 103 A8
Thornhill Cl
Blackpool FY4 110 F5
Ormskirk L39 6 B8
Thornhill Rd Chorley PR6 61 E2
Leyland PR25 59 D8
Ramsbottom BL0 50 A1
Thornhill St BB12 127 A6
Thornlea Dr OL12 52 B2
Thornleigh Cl 10 FY5 176 A2
Thornleigh Dr LA6 240 C7
Thornley Ave BB1 102 C6
Thornley Pl PR2 119 A3
Thornley Rd PR2 119 A3
Thornpark Dr 3 PR2 116 D1
Thorns Ave LA2 220 D1
Thorns The L31 5 B2
Thornthwaite Rd PR4 116 D4
Thornton WN8 17 F2
Thornton Ave
Fulwood PR2 117 B4
Lytham St Anne's FY8 90 B8
Morecambe LA4 217 C6
Thornton Cl
Accrington BB5 104 A8
Blackburn BB2 81 F8
Rufford L40 39 C4
Thornton Cleveleys Baines Endowed Prim Sch FY5 176 C1
Thornton Cleveleys Burn Naze Prim Sch FY5 176 B3
Thornton Cleveleys Manor Beach Prim Sch FY5 175 D3
Thornton Cleveleys Red Marsh Sch FY5 176 B3
Thornton Cleveleys Royles Brook Prim Sch FY5 176 A2
Thornton Cres
Burnley BB10 128 E5
Morecambe LA4 217 C5
Thornton Ctr FY5 176 C1
Thornton Dr
Coupe Green PR5 98 D4
Leyland PR26 76 E4
Thornton Gate FY5 175 D4
Thornton Gr LA4 217 C5
Thornton Hall Mews FY5 153 E7
Thornton Hts BD23 197 A5
Thornton in Craven Com Prim Sch BD23 197 B6
Thornton La Ingleton LA6 242 F5
Morecambe LA4 217 C6
Thornton Manor Ct BD23 197 A5
Thornton Pl FY5 176 A4
Thornton Rd
Burnley BB10 128 E5
Morecambe LA4 217 C6
Southport PR9 35 F7
Thorntrees Ave
Newsham PR3 137 B5
Preston PR2 116 D1
Thornway Ave FY5 153 D8
Thornwood WN8 17 F2
Thornwood Cl
5 Blackburn BB1 122 E1
Lytham St Anne's FY8 90 E4
Thornylea BB2 81 D7
Thorough Way PR3 203 E7
Thoroughfare The LA5 223 D5
Thoroughgood Cl L40 25 D2
Thorpe WN8 17 F2
Thorpe Ave LA4 217 F4
Thorpe Cl PR1 117 F1
Thorpe St BL0 50 B5
Thrang Brow La LA5 225 C6
Threagill La LA5 223 F5
Three Lane Ends PR6 62 C4
Three Nooks PR5 78 C5
Three Oaks Cl L40 26 B2
Three Point Bsns Pk BB4 85 A2
Three Pools PR9 54 C3
Three Rivers Woodland Pk BB7 189 D7
Three Tuns La L37 11 F3
Three Turns PR3 142 A8
Threefields PR2 117 A5
Threlfall PR7 60 F2
Threlfall Rd FY1 130 D1
Threlfall St 1 PR2 117 C1
Threlfall's La PR9 53 F2
Threshers Ct PR3 207 C2
Threshfield Ave LA3 212 F8
Thrimby Ct LA4 217 B4
Thrimby Pl LA4 217 B4
Thropps La PR4 75 D6
Throstle Cl BB12 128 A7
Throstle Gr LA2 218 D8
Throstle Mill OL13 87 F2
Throstle Nest La PR3 203 C4
Throstle St
Blackburn BB2 101 C4
7 Nelson BB9 170 E1
Throstle Way 1 FY5 175 F1
Throstle Wlk LA2 218 D8
Throup Pl BB9 170 E2
Thrum Fold OL12 52 D3
Thrum Hall La
Rochdale OL12 52 D3
Rochdale OL12 52 E3
Thrush Dr BL9 33 B4
Thrush St OL12 52 C1
Thrushgill Dr LA2 219 D7
Thurcroft Dr WN8 17 E2
Thurland Ct LA4 217 A3
Thurland Mill Cotts LA6 241 D3
Thurnham Glasson Christ Church CE Prim Sch LA2 209 E4
Thurnham Mews 7 LA1 214 F7
Thurnham Rd PR2 95 E8
Thurnham St LA1 214 F7
Thursby Ave FY4 110 D6
Thursby Cl PR8 21 B3
Thursby Pl 13 BB9 170 F2
Thursby Rd Burnley BB10 148 C1
Nelson BB9 170 F2
Thursby Sq BB10 128 A8
Thursden Ave BB10 148 F3
Thursden Pl BB9 171 B1
Thursfield Ave FY4 110 E8
Thursfield Rd BB10 128 B5
Thursford Gr BL6 31 D1
Thursgill Ave LA4 217 C3
Thurston WN8 17 E2
Thurston Rd PR25 77 A1
Thurston St BB11 128 B6
Thwaite Brow La LA5 221 B6
Thwaite La LA2 239 C5
Thwaites Ave BB2 121 E2
Thwaites Cl BB1 102 D2
Thwaites Rd BB5 103 C4
Thwaites St BB5 103 C3
Thyme Cl FY2 152 F3
Tib St 18 BL0 50 B5
Tiber Ave BB11 127 C4
Tiber St PR1 97 B7
Tibicar Dr E LA3 216 D1
Tibicar Dr W LA3 216 D1
Tiger The PR25 76 D2
Tilbury Gr WN6 19 D7
Tilcroft WN8 17 E2
Timber Brook PR7 61 A2
Timber St
Accrington BB5 104 C5
Bacup OL13 87 F1
Brierfield BB9 148 B6
Timberhurst BL9 33 D2
Timbrills Ave BB7 145 F8
Timms Cl L37 11 F5
Timms La L37 11 F5
Tincklers La PR7 41 A6
Tinedale View BB12 146 D1
Tinker's La LA2 226 B7
Tinkerfield PR2 117 E7
Tinklers La BB7 229 E7
Tinline St BL9 33 A2
Tinniswood PR2 117 B1
Tinsley Ave PR8 35 E3
Tinsley's La
Out Rawcliffe PR3 178 D4
Southport PR8 36 A1
Tintagel WN8 17 E2
Tintagell Cl BB2 80 C7
Tintern Ave Chorley PR7 43 D5
Rochdale OL12 52 E2
Tintern Cl
Accrington BB5 104 E2
Read BB12 145 D1
Tintern Cres BB1 102 B8
Tintern Dr L37 12 B2
Tippet Cl BB2 102 A1
Titan Way PR26 76 B2
Tithe Barn La
Knowley PR6 62 A4
Runshaw Moor PR25,PR7 59 F5
Scorton PR3 204 E5
Tithebarn Gate FY6 153 D4
Tithebarn Hill LA2 209 E5
Tithebarn Pl FY6 153 D4
Tithebarn Rd PR8 35 E6
Tithebarn St
Poulton-le-F FY6 153 D4
6 Preston PR1 97 A7
Preston PR1 97 A8
Skelmersdale WN8 10 B7
Tittrington Brow BB7 229 C2
Tiverton Ave WN8 17 E2
Tiverton Cl PR2 117 F8
Tiverton Dr Blackburn BB2 81 C8
Brierfield BB10 148 F3
Tockholes CE Prim Sch BB3 81 A3
Tockholes Rd Darwen BB3 81 F2
Tockholes BB3 81 A3
Tod Holes La BD23 236 E4
Todd Carr Rd BB4 86 F1
Todd Hall Rd BB4 84 F4
Todd La N PR5 97 C2
Todd La S PR5 77 C8
Todd's La PR9 55 A6
Todmorden Old Rd OL13 88 B5
Todmorden Rd
Bacup OL13 88 B4
Burnley BB11 128 B3
Cockden BB10 149 B1
Lytham St Anne's FY8 89 C8
Toll Bar Bsns Pk OL13 70 C8
Toll Bar Cres LA1 214 F3

Toll Bar Ct LA6 240 C7
Tollgate PR1 96 E4
Tollgate Cres L40 25 C2
Tollgate Rd L40 25 B3
Tolsey Dr PR4 95 D2
Tom Benson Way PR2, PR4 116 F4
Tom La BB4 86 F2
Tomlinson Rd
Heysham LA3 212 F6
Leyland PR25 76 F2
Preston PR2 117 C2
Tomlinson St BL6 32 B3
Tonacliffe Prim Sch OL12 52 C6
Tonacliffe Rd OL12 52 C6
Tonacliffe Terr OL12 52 C7
Tonacliffe Way OL12 52 C6
Tong End OL12 71 C2
Tong Ho 20 OL13 88 A3
Tong La Bacup OL13 88 B2
Whitworth OL12 71 D1
Tongbarn WN8 17 E2
Tongues La FY6 200 C6
Tontine WN5 10 C5
Tontine Rd WN5,WN8 10 C6
Tontine St BB1 101 E5
Toogood La WN6 28 D6
Tootell St PR7 43 B6
Tootle La L40 39 A3
Tootle Rd PR3 140 B8
Top Acre PR4 95 C1
Top Acre Rd WN8 9 C7
Top Barn La BB4 86 E1
Top Locks L40 26 A4
Top o' th' Croft BB2 81 D8
Top of Fawna Rd PR3 163 D1
Top Of Heap OL10 33 F2
Top of Wallsuches BL6 32 F4
Top Row BB7 145 F8
Topaz St BB1 122 F2
Topaz Way PR6 43 E6
Topiary Gdns PR3 181 D4
Topping Fold Rd BL9 33 C3
Topping St Blackpool FY1 130 B5
Bury BL9 33 A3
Toppings The PR3 181 C6
Tor Ave BL8 49 F2
Tor End Rd BB4 67 F6
Tor Hey Mews BL8 49 F2
Tor View Haslingden BB4 85 C1
Rawtenstall BB4 86 A1
Tor View Rd BB4 85 C1
Tor View Sch BB4 68 D8
Torcross Cl PR9 54 A5
Tormore Cl PR6 62 A3
Toronto Ave
Blackpool FY2 152 E3
Fleetwood FY7 198 E2
Toronto Rd BB2 101 C8
Torquay Ave
Blackpool FY3 131 A2
Brierfield BB10 148 D2
Torra Barn Cl BL7 47 E3
Torrentum Ct FY5 176 C1
Torridon Cl BB2 100 F1
Torrisholme Cty Prim Sch LA4 217 F5
Torrisholme Rd LA1 218 B3
Torrisholme Sq 8 LA4 217 F4
Torside Gr FY6 153 B3
Torsway Ave FY3 130 F6
Torver Cl BB12 127 B8
Totnes Cl FY6 153 C5
Totnes Dr PR9 54 A5
Tottenham Rd BB3 81 F6
Tottington Rd BL7,BL8 48 F2
Tottleworth BB6 124 C3
Tottleworth Rd BB1 124 C2
Toulmin Cl PR3 181 D2
Tow Scar Rd LA6 242 F6
Towbreck Gdns FY6 131 E8
Tower Ave Lancaster LA1 211 B7
Ramsbottom BL0 50 A5
Tower Bldgs 10 PR9 35 C8
Tower Cl FY5 176 A4
Tower Cotts 3 LA3 212 E7
Tower Ct Chapeltown BL7 48 C4
Lancaster LA1 214 F7
Tower Dene Prep Sch PR9 53 F2
Tower End L37 11 C5
Tower Gn PR2 117 F7
Tower Hill Clitheroe BB7 189 F1
Ormskirk L39 16 A5
Tower Hill Rd WN8 10 B6
Tower La PR2 117 F7
Tower Nook WN8 10 A5
Tower Rd Blackburn BB2 100 E2
Darwen BB3 65 B8
Tower St 13 Bacup OL13 87 F2
Blackpool FY1 130 B5
Chapeltown BL7 48 C4
Cornholme OL14 109 A1
Oswaldtwistle BB5 103 C5
Tower View Belthorn BB1 83 A5
Blackpool FY2 152 D2
Blackrod BL6 31 C3
Darwen BB3 82 C1
Higher Penwortham PR1 96 C7
Towers Ave L31 5 C2
Towers Ct BB2 101 D3
Town Brook Ho 5 PR1 117 E1
Town Brow PR25 77 F2
Town End
Bolton-le-S LA5 221 A3
Kirkham PR4 114 A5
Slaidburn BB7 229 C7
3 Thornton FY5 176 A2
Town End Cl L39 15 D4
Town Gate BB6 124 C5
Town Green Ct L39 6 C8
Town Green La L39 6 C8
Town Green Sta L39 6 C8
Town Hall Sq 8 BB6 124 C5
Town Hall St
16 Blackburn BB2 101 E5
9 Great Harwood BB6 124 C5
Town Head BB18 196 A1
Town Hill Bank BB12 146 D1
Town House Rd BB9 149 B8
Town La Coppull PR7 42 C1
Heskin Green PR7 41 C2
Much Hoole PR4 74 D1
Southport PR8 35 E3
Whittle-le-W PR6 61 D6
Town Lane (Kew) PR8 35 E3
Town Rd PR26 58 B2
Town View BB1 101 F4
Town Wlk BB1 101 F4
Towneley Ave
Blackpool FY4 110 E8
Huncoat BB5 125 F2
Towneley Cl LA1 214 D7
Towneley Hall (Art Gal & Mus)* BB11 128 C2
Towneley High Sch BB11 128 C4
Towneley Ho PR3 140 A7
Towneley Par PR3 140 A7
Towneley Rd PR3 140 A7
Towneley Rd W PR3 140 A7
Towneley St BB10 148 B1
Townfield Ave BB10 128 F6
Townfield Cl PR4 74 F7
Townfield La LA2 218 C7
Townfields 1 BB11 128 B5
Towngate Eccleston PR7 41 B7
Foulridge BB8 194 D1
Leyland PR25 59 F7
Leyland PR25 60 A8
Leyland PR25 77 A1
Townhouse Sch BB9 171 C1
Townlea Cl PR1 96 A3
Townley La PR1 95 D4
Townley St Brierfield BB9 148 B5
Brierfield,Harle Syke BB10 148 F3
Chorley PR6 43 D7
Colne BB8 171 E6
Morecambe LA4 217 B6
Townsend St
Haslingden BB4 85 A3
Rawtenstall BB4 69 F8
Townsfield LA5 224 C4
Townshill Wlk PR4 114 A6
Townsley St BB9 148 E6
Townsmoor Ret Pk 8 BB2 101 E3
Townsway PR5 77 C8
Towpath Wlk 2 LA5 223 D1
Toxhead Cl BL6 32 A3
Toy & Teddy Bear Mus of Childhood* FY8 89 D7
Tracks La WN5 10 D3
Trafalgar Cl PR2 117 D3
Trafalgar Ct PR8 34 F3
Trafalgar Mall 3 BB9 148 E8
Trafalgar Rd
Blackpool FY1 130 B2
Lancaster LA1 215 A6
Southport PR8 34 E3
Trafalgar St
Burnley BB11 127 F5
Chorley PR6 61 C1
Lytham St Anne's FY8 89 F7
Trafalgar Wharf PR2 96 B8
Trafford Gdns BB7 166 D1
Trafford St PR1 117 E2
Tramway La PR5 78 B6
Tranmere Ave LA3 216 D1
Tranmere Cres LA3 216 D1
Tranmere Rd FY4 130 E1
Tranmoor PR4 74 F6
Trans Brittania Enterprise Est BB11 127 B3
Trap Hill L37 11 C2
Trapp La BB12 145 F2
Trash La Rimington BB7 231 B1
Tockholes BB3 81 B2
Travellers Ct BB7 231 C3
Travers Lodge 8 PR2 118 F4
Travers Pl PR2 96 C8
Travers St BL6 32 D1
Travis St BB10 128 A8
Trawden Cl BB5 104 C4
Trawden Cres PR2 118 E4
Trawden Forest Prim Sch BB8 172 C2
Trawden Rd BB8 172 B4
Traylen Way OL12 52 A1
Treales CE Prim Sch PR4 134 E2
Treales Rd PR4 115 B6
Trecastle Rd L33 1 A4
Tredgold St BL6 32 C2
Treen Cl PR9 54 B6
Treesdale Cl PR8 34 F4
Treetop Villas PR9 53 F4
Treetops Ave BL0 50 A3
Trefoil Cl FY5 176 A5
Tremellen St BB5 104 A6
Trengrove St 7 OL12 52 C1
Trent Ave L31 5 F2
Trent Cl
Burscough Bridge L40 25 F5
Morecambe LA3 217 F2
Trent Rd Blackpool FY4 110 B7
Nelson BB9 149 A8
Trent St Longridge PR3 139 F7
Lytham St Anne's FY8 91 D3
Tresco Cl BB2 101 B1
Tretower Way FY5 176 D2
Trevarrick Ct BL6 32 E2
Trevelyan Dr WN5 10 D1
Trevor Cl BB1 101 F7
Trevor Rd Burscough L40 25 E4
Southport PR8 21 C4
Triangle The
Accrington,Hillock Vale BB5 104 E8
Fulwood PR2 117 E4
Trigg La PR6 62 D5
Trigge Ho PR7 61 C2
Trillium Way BB3 82 A7
Trinity & St Michael's CE Prim Sch PR26 58 C2
Trinity Cl Brierfield BB9 148 C5
Freckleton PR4 93 B7
Padiham BB12 126 D6
Trinity Ct 3 BB1 101 F6
Trinity Fold 20 PR1 96 F8
Trinity Gdns
Southport PR8 35 A6
Thornton FY5 176 A3
Trinity Gn BL0 50 B2
Trinity Mews PR9 35 C7
Trinity Pl 24 PR1 96 F8
Trinity Rd PR7 43 B7
Trinity Sch WN8 17 F1
Trinity St 15 Bacup OL13 70 C8
Blackburn BB1 101 F6
Oswaldtwistle BB5 103 D3
Trinity Student Village PR1 96 F8
Trinity Twrs 6 BB11 127 E6
Trinity Wlks PR4 57 A5
Trinket La LA2 238 E6
Tristan Ave PR4 75 A5
Troon Ave Blackburn BB1 102 C3
Thornton FY5 153 D8
Troon Cl PR7 60 D4
Troon Ct PR1 96 A6
Trough of Bowland* BB7 227 F7
Trough Rd BB7 228 B5
Troughton Cres 1 FY4 110 E8
Trout Beck BB5 124 F4
Trout St 8 Burnley BB10 128 A8
Preston PR1 97 C7
Troutbeck Ave
Fleetwood FY7 198 D2
Forton PR3 207 B3
Maghull L31 5 E2
Troutbeck Cl
Burnley BB12 127 B8
Hawkshaw BL8 49 B2
Troutbeck Cres FY4 111 D8
Troutbeck Dr BL0 50 C7
Troutbeck Pl PR2 118 E5
Troutbeck Rd Chorley PR7 43 B5
Lancaster LA1 218 E1
Lytham St Anne's FY8 110 D1
Trower St PR1 97 B6
Troy St BB1 101 F7
Trumacar Com Prim Sch LA3 212 E5
Trumacar La LA3 212 E5
Trumacar Terr LA3 212 E5
Truman Ave LA1 214 C7
Trumley Ct LA3 217 A2
Trundle Pie La L39 14 C6
Trunnah Gdns FY5 176 B3
Trunnah Rd FY5 176 B3
Truro Ave PR9 54 B5
Truro Pl 8 PR1 118 D1
Truro St 7 FY4 130 D1
Truscott Rd L40 25 D4
Tucker Hill BB7 189 E1
Tucker's Hill Brow WN2 31 B1
Tudor Ave Preston PR1 118 F1
Preston,Lea PR2 116 D1
Tudor Cl Carleton FY6 153 A4
1 Cleveleys FY5 175 F1
Darwen BB3 82 A2
Langho BB6 143 D1
Preston PR2 116 D1
Tudor Croft PR5 77 C7
Tudor Ct
Lytham St Anne's FY8 89 D8
Ormskirk L39 15 F6
Tudor Dr PR4 114 B2
Tudor Gate FY8 90 B8
Tudor Gdns L38 2 F4
Tudor Gr 2 LA4 217 E6
Tudor Mans PR8 34 F6
Tudor Pl FY4 110 B6
Tudor Rd
Lytham St Anne's FY8 89 D8
Southport PR8 21 B6
Tuer St PR25 76 F2
Tulip Gr OL12 52 E3
Tulketh Ave PR2 117 B1
Tulketh Brow PR2 117 C1
Tulketh Com Sports Coll PR2 117 B4
Tulketh Cres PR2 117 C1
Tulketh Rd PR2 117 B1
Tulketh St PR8 35 B7
Tunbridge Pl 7 PR1 118 D1
Tunbridge St 4 PR1 118 D1
Tunbrook Ave PR2 139 E1
Tunley Holme PR5 78 C5
Tunley La WN6 28 E5
Tunley Moss WN6 28 E4
Tunnel St Burnley BB12 127 D6
5 Darwen BB3 65 C7
Tunstall Dr BB5 125 B1
Tunstall Ho 10 LA1 215 A3
Tunstall St LA4 217 A5
Tunstead Ave BB12 125 E8
Tunstead Cres OL13 87 C1
Tunstead La Bacup OL13 70 B8
Rawtenstall BB4,OL13 87 B1
Tunstead Mill Terr 3 OL13 70 B8
Tunstead Rd OL13 87 C1
Tunstill Fold BB12 169 F1
Tunstill St BB10 148 B1
Turbary Rd LA6 242 E7
Turbary The PR2 117 C3
Turf Mdw BB4 106 A2
Turf Moor Football Gd (Burnley FC) BB10 128 B6
Turf St BB11 128 B6
Turflands PR26 58 B1
Turkey Red Ind Est BB5 84 F8
Turkey St Accrington BB5 104 D7
Out Rawcliffe PR3 178 A1
Turks Head Yd 22 PR1 97 A7
Turn La BB3 64 F8
Turn Rd BL0 50 E8
Turnacre L37 12 B6
Turnberry WN8 17 D2
Turnberry Ave FY5 153 D8
Turnberry Cl
Kirkham PR4 114 A4
Morecambe LA4 217 D6
Turnberry Way PR9 54 D5
Turnbridge Rd L31 5 C3
Turnbury Cl PR7 60 D4
Turncroft Rd BB3 65 B8
Turner Ave PR5 77 A7
Turner Fold BB12 145 D3
Turner Rd BB9 148 B8
Turner St 3 Bacup OL13 70 C8
4 Barnoldswick BB18 196 C2
Clitheroe BB7 166 E7
3 Preston PR1 118 A1
Rochdale OL12 52 E1
Turner's Pl OL12 52 E3
Turnerford Cl BL7 47 E1
Turney Crook Mews 9 BB8 171 D5
Turnfield PR2 116 F6
Turning La PR8 36 A1
Turnpike BB4 86 F1
Turnpike Fold LA2 218 D5
Turnpike Gr BB5 103 C5
Turnpike Rd L39 15 A2
Turnpike The PR2 117 D6
Turnstone FY3 131 B6
Turpin Green La PR25 77 B1
Turstall Cotts LA2 237 B3
Turton & Edgworth CE/Methodist Prim Sch BL7 48 D5
Turton Belmont Com Prim Sch BL7 46 C5
Turton Dr PR6 61 E1
Turton Gr BB10 128 D6
Turton Hollow Rd BB4 86 A8
Turton Rd BL8 49 B1
Turton Twr* BL7 48 C3
Tuscan Ave BB11 127 C5
Tuscany Gr BB6 143 C6
Tuson Croft PR4 74 F8
Tuson Dr PR2 96 E8
Tuson Ho 2 PR1 96 E2
Tustin Ct PR1 96 C8
Tuxbury Dr FY5 153 D8
Tuxford Ct 1 FY8 90 D6
Tuxford Rd FY8 90 C6
Tweed St Blackburn BB2 81 D8
4 High Bentham LA2 239 D8
6 Lytham St Anne's FY8 89 E6
Nelson BB9 149 A8
Tweed Street Ct 3 LA2 239 D8
Tweedys Ct PR3 185 C4
Twemlow Par
Heysham LA3 212 F8
Morecambe LA3 216 D1
Twenty Acre La PR4 75 B1
Twickenham Pl 4 FY8 90 D6
Twig La L31 5 E1
Twin Lakes Ind Est PR26 58 A3
Twine Wlk LA6 242 C3
Twinegate OL12 52 E3
Twist Moor La PR6 63 B8
Twistfield Cl PR8 34 F5
Twiston La BB7 191 D5
Twitter La BB7 189 A3
Two Acre La PR1 96 C1
Two Brooks La BL8 49 B2
Two Gates Dr BB3 82 B2
Two Gates Wlk BB3 82 B2
Two Laws Rd BD22 174 C1
Two Saints Pl L39 15 E5
Twyford Cl L31 5 E1
Twyn Ghyll Cvn Site BB7 231 B6
Tyldesley Rd FY1 130 B3
Tyne Ave 4 FY3 130 D4
Tyne Cl FY5 175 E5
Tyne St
1 Bamber Bridge PR5 97 F1
4 Preston PR1 96 D6
Tynedale Pl FY3 153 A1
Tynedale Rd FY3 153 B1
Tynwald Rd BB2 101 E1
Tyrer Rd L39 15 F7
Tyrer's Ave L31 5 B5
Tyrers Cl L37 11 F2
Tyrone Ave FY2 152 D2
Tyseley Gr BB18 197 A1
Tythebarn St BB3 82 B1

U

Udale Pl 1 LA1 218 C2
Uggle La LA1 214 F3
Uldale Cl Nelson BB9 148 E6
Southport PR8 21 D3
Ullswater Ave
Accrington BB5 125 D1
Fleetwood FY7 175 D8
Morecambe LA4 217 D4
Orrell WN5 10 F7
Rochdale OL12 52 C1
Thornton FY5 176 B1
Ullswater Cl
Blackburn BB1 101 F6
Hambleton FY6 177 C2
3 Rishton BB1 124 A1
Ullswater Cres
Carnforth LA5 221 E8
Thornton FY5 176 B1
Ullswater Rd
Blackpool FY4 110 C7
Burnley BB10 128 F5
Chorley PR7 43 B6
Fulwood PR2 118 C4
Lancaster LA1 215 A8
Ullswater Way BB4 106 A1
Ulnes Walton La PR26 59 A6
Ulpha Cl BB12 127 B8
Ulster Rd LA1 215 B5
Ulster St BB11 127 D5
Ulverston Cl
Blackburn BB2 102 A1
Maghull L31 5 E2
Ulverston Cres FY8 90 C7
Ulverston Dr BB1 124 A1
Under Billinge La BB2 100 F4
Underbank Cl 3 OL13 87 F3
Underbank Ho 1 OL13 87 F3
Underbank Rd
Haslingden BB4 84 F3
Rising Bridge BB5 85 A7
Thornton FY5 176 F1
Underbank Way 2 BB4 85 A3
Underley St BB10 148 C3
Underwood PR2 117 C3
Unicon Pk BB4 84 F3
Union Ct 13 OL13 70 C8
Union La PR3 178 C7
Union Pas 6 PR4 114 A5
Union Rd
Oswaldtwistle BB5 103 D3
Rawtenstall BB4 85 D2
Union St Accrington BB5 104 B6
Bacup OL13 87 F2
Bacup,Stacksteads OL13 70 C8
Blackburn BB2 101 E3
Brierfield BB9 148 B5
Chorley PR7 43 C8
Clitheroe BB7 166 C8
Colne BB8 171 E5
Darwen BB3 82 A1
Egerton BL7 47 D2
Haslingden BB4 85 A3
Morecambe LA4 217 A5
10 Preston PR1 96 F8
Ramsbottom BL0 50 C6
Rawtenstall BB4 86 A3
Southport PR9 35 C8
Whittle-le-W PR6 61 C8
Whitworth OL12 52 C8
Union Terr
Clow Bridge BB4 106 A4
Rawtenstall BB4 86 B2
Unit Rd PR8 21 D5
Unity St
3 Barnoldswick BB18 196 C2
Blackburn BB2 101 E2
Kelbrook BB18 195 A6
Unity Trad Est BB2 101 D4
Unity Way BB4 85 F3
Univ of Central Lancashire PR1 96 E8
Univ of Central Lancashire Avenham Bldg PR1 97 A6
Univ of Lancaster LA1 211 B7
Unsworth Ave FY6 200 A4
Unsworth St OL13 70 D7
Up Brooks BB7 190 A1
Up Holland High Sch WN5 10 C4
Up-Brooks Ind Est BB7 190 A1
Upholland Rd WN5 10 D2
Upholland Sta WN8 9 F4
Uplands Chase PR2 117 B6
Uplands Dr BB12 147 D7
Upper Ashmount BB4 86 C1
Upper Aughton Rd PR8 35 B4
Upper Cliffe (Bersham Dr) BB6 124 C6
Upper George St 23 OL12 52 F1
Upper Hill Way BB18 194 B7
Upper Lune St FY7 199 B5
Upper Mead BL7 47 F1
Upper Westby St FY8 91 A3
Upphall La LA6 240 C4
Uppingham WN8 17 D1
Uppingham Dr BL0 50 B7
Upton Ave PR8 21 B6

Upton Barn L31 5 C2
Upwood Cl FY2 152 E5
Urban View PR6 62 F8
Ushers Mdw LA1 214 E7
Usk Ave FY5 176 D2

V

Vale Ave BL6 32 A3
Vale Cl WN6 19 E8
Vale Coppice Horwich BL6 32 A3
Ramsbottom BL0 50 C3
Vale Cotts BL6 31 F2
Vale Cres PR8 21 C2
Vale Croft WN8 10 A6
Vale Ct BB5 125 F1
Vale Gr L32 1 A1
Vale House Cl BB7 144 C5
Vale La L40 17 F5
Vale Rd LA1 218 C3
Vale Royal PR4 114 C5
Vale St Bacup OL13 88 A3
Blackburn BB2 101 E2
Darwen BB3 81 F2
Haslingden BB4 85 B4
Turton Bottoms BL7 48 D4
Vale Terr Calder Vale PR3 182 E8
Newchurch BB4 86 F3
Vale The
Appley Bridge WN6 19 D8
Fulwood PR2 117 F5
Valentia Rd FY2 152 D3
Valentines La PR2,PR4 116 E4
Valentines Mdw PR4 116 E4
Valeway Ave FY5 152 D8
Valiants Shireworld Equestrian Ctr PR3 179 A2
Valley Cl BB9 171 A1
Valley Ctr The 4 BB4 86 A2
Valley Dr
Barnoldswick BB18 196 D4
Padiham BB12 126 D8
Valley Gdns
2 Earby BB18 197 B2
Padiham BB11 126 F4
Valley Mill Ct BB8 172 E6
Valley Rd
Barnoldswick BB18 196 C2
Earby BB18 197 B2
Higher Penwortham PR1 96 D5
Hoghton PR5 99 F3
Longridge PR3 140 C7
Wilpshire BB1 122 F5
Valley St BB11 127 B4
Valley Terr BB12 145 E1
Valley View
Bamber Bridge PR5 97 A3
Chorley PR6 43 E7
Fulwood PR2 118 A4
Millgate OL12 71 D4
Valligates BB1 102 B7
Vance Rd FY1 130 B4
Vancouver Cres BB2 101 C8
Vandyck Ave BB11 127 E2
Vardon Rd BB2 101 B2
Varley St Colne BB8 171 F6
2 Darwen BB3 82 A1
Preston PR1 118 A2
Varlian Cl L40 16 C3
Vaughan Cl L37 11 D4
Vaughan Rd PR8 35 B4
Vaughan St BB9 148 F7
Vauxhall St BB2 101 B3
Vauze Ave BL6 31 D1
Vauze House Cl BL6 31 D2
Veevers St Brierfield BB9 148 A6
7 Burnley BB11 127 F6
Padiham BB12 126 D8
Velvet St BB2 81 D8
Venables Ave BB8 171 F6
Venice Ave BB11 127 C4
Venice St BB11 127 D5
Ventnor Pl PR2 117 A4
Ventnor Rd
Blackpool FY4 110 B6
1 Chorley PR7 43 B6
Haslingden BB4 85 C1
Venture Ct BB5 125 D5
Venture Rd FY7 176 A6
Venture St 19 OL13 88 A3
Verax St OL13 87 F1
Verbena Cl BB3 82 A7
Verbena Dr FY6 199 F6
Vermont Gr FY5 152 E8
Verna St 15 BL0 50 C6
Vernon Ave
Blackpool FY3 130 E3
Warton PR4 92 E6
Vernon Cres LA2 211 A3
Vernon Ct
4 Galgate LA2 211 A4
Southport PR8 35 D5
Vernon Lodge FY8 89 F5
Vernon Pk 3 LA2 211 A4
Vernon Rd
Laneshaw Bridge BB8 172 D6
Lytham St Anne's FY8 110 E1
Ramsbottom BL8 50 A1
Southport PR9 36 A8
Vernon St Blackburn BB2 101 E4
Darwen BB3 82 B1
Nelson BB9 148 E7
Preston PR1 117 F1
Verona Ave BB11 127 C5
Verona Ct 6 FY5 176 A2
Veronica St BB3 81 E4
Verulam Rd PR9 54 B3
Vesta St 6 BL0 50 B6
Vevey St PR25 77 A1
Viaduct Rd PR5 99 F2
Vicar La LA6 241 C2
Vicar St
5 Blackburn BB1 101 F5
Great Harwood BB6 124 C4
Vicarage Ave
5 Burnley BB12 126 B8
Caton LA2 237 C3
Cleveleys FY5 175 D3
Vicarage Cl Adlington PR6 31 A8
Burton-in-K LA6 240 C7
Euxton PR7 60 D3
Formby L37 11 D4
Fulwood PR2 117 F4
Lytham St Anne's FY8 89 F7
Morecambe LA3 217 C2
Ormskirk L40 16 B3
Wrea Green PR4 113 B4
Vicarage Dr BB3 65 C8
Vicarage Fold BB7 144 F7
Vicarage Gdns L40 25 D4
Vicarage La
Accrington BB5 104 E1
Banks PR9 54 F7
Blackpool FY4 130 E1
Burton-in-K LA6 240 C7
Churchtown PR3 181 A2
Fulwood PR2 117 F4
Newton-w-S PR4 115 A3
Ormskirk L40 16 C3
Samlesbury PR5 119 E1
Wilpshire BB1 122 F6
Rawtenstall BB4 85 F2
Vicarage Rd
Barnoldswick BB18 196 C3
Blackrod BL6 31 D2
Formby L37 11 D4
Kelbrook BB18 195 A6
Nelson BB9 148 D7
Orrell WN5 10 D4
Poulton-le-F FY6 153 E3
Vicarage Rd W BL6 31 C2
Vicarage St 3 PR6 61 D1
Vicarage Wlk L39 15 E5
Vicarsfields Rd PR25 60 A7
Viceroy Ct 3 PR8 35 A6
Vickers Dr WN8 9 E8
Victor Ave LA4 217 E6
Victoria Apartments 20 BB12 146 C1
Victoria Ave
Accrington BB5 104 D2
2 Blackburn BB2 80 E8
Brierfield BB9 148 B6
Chatburn BB7 190 E5
Lancaster LA1 214 F5
Victoria Bldgs
Darwen BB3 82 E3
Formby L37 11 E5
8 Low Bentham LA2 239 B8
1 Preston PR1 96 F7
Victoria Bridge Rd PR8 35 C6
Victoria Bsns & Ind Ctr BB5 104 B4
Victoria Cl BB7 144 A7
Victoria Cross 4 BB1 101 E6
Victoria Ct
7 Blackburn BB1 101 E5
Broughton PR3 137 C2
Chatburn BB7 190 D5
Croston PR26 58 B3
Fulwood PR2 117 E3
Horwich BL6 32 C3
Padiham BB12 126 E7
Southport PR8 34 F4
Victoria Dr BB4 85 D2
Victoria Gdns BB9 170 C2
Victoria Hospl FY3 131 A5
Victoria Lodge BB12 145 D2
Victoria Mans PR2 96 A7
Victoria Mews
7 Clitheroe BB7 166 D7
Morecambe LA4 217 C6
Victoria Par
Morecambe LA4 217 C6
Preston PR2 117 B1
7 Rawtenstall BB4 69 E8
Victoria Park Ave
Leyland PR25 59 D7
Preston PR2 116 D1
Victoria Park Dr PR2 116 D1
Victoria Park Miniature Rly* PR8 34 E5
Victoria Pk WN8 17 C1
Victoria Pl Halton LA2 219 C6
6 Lancaster LA1 214 F7
Victoria Quay PR2 96 A7
Victoria Rd
Barnoldswick BB18 196 C2
Earby BB18 197 B2
Formby L37 11 D5
Fulwood PR2 118 A4
Horwich BL6 32 C2
Ince Blundell L38 3 E3
Kirkham PR4 113 F5
Lytham St Anne's FY8 89 F5
Ormskirk L39 15 C2
Padiham BB12 126 E7
Pleasington BB2 100 C1
Poulton-le-F FY6 153 E4
Preston PR5 97 D5
Victoria Rd E FY5 176 B1
Victoria Rd W FY5 175 E2
Victoria Sq FY5 175 D2
Victoria St
Accrington BB5 104 B5
Victoria St *continued*
13 Bacup OL13 70 D8
Bamber Bridge PR5 77 B8
Barrowford BB9 170 D3
25 Blackburn BB1 101 E5
Blackpool FY1 130 B5
Blackrod BL6 31 D2
1 Burnley BB11 127 F5
Burscough Bridge L40 25 E5
Carnforth LA5 223 D1
Chorley PR7 43 D7
Church BB5 103 E6
Clayton-le-M BB5 124 F2
Clayton-le-M BB5 124 F3
Clitheroe BB7 166 D7
9 Cornholme OL14 109 C1
22 Darwen BB3 82 A1
7 Earby BB18 197 B2
Fleetwood FY7 199 B5
Great Harwood BB6 124 D5
Haslingden BB4 85 A3
Longridge PR3 140 A7
Lytham St Anne's FY8 91 C3
Morecambe LA4 217 A5
Nelson BB9 148 D8
Oswaldtwistle BB5 103 D3
Preston PR1 117 E1
Ramsbottom BL0 50 B6
Rawtenstall BB4 86 C1
Rawtenstall,Waterfoot BB4 69 E8
Rishton BB1 124 B1
22 Rochdale OL12 52 F1
Southport PR8 35 B8
Wheelton PR6 62 A7
Whitworth OL12 52 C8
Victoria Terr
Abbey Village PR6 80 B2
12 Bamber Bridge PR5 77 A8
Billington BB7 144 A4
Calder Vale PR3 182 E8
2 Chorley PR6 61 D1
Glasson LA2 209 F5
5 Leyland PR25 60 A8
Mellor Brook BB2 121 C3
Tockholes BB3 80 F2
Wheelton PR6 62 A7
Victoria Way Formby L37 11 D5
Rawtenstall BB4 86 C2
Southport PR8 34 F7
Victoria Wharf LA1 218 C1
Victoria Works Ind Est BB11 127 B5
Victory Ave PR9 36 A7
Victory Cl BB9 148 E8
Victory Ctr The 2 BB9 148 E8
Victory Rd FY1 130 C6
Victory Wharf PR2 96 B8
View Rd BB3 81 E5
View St PR7 41 C7
Villiers Cl BB7 144 C6
Viking Cl PR8 35 A4
Viking Way LA3 212 F5
Villa Way PR3 181 C6
Village Cl WN8 8 D8
Village Croft PR7 60 D3
Village Dr PR2 118 F2
Village Green La PR2 116 F6
Village Way
Blackpool FY2 152 D5
Hightown L38 2 F4
Skelmersdale WN8 8 D8
Villas Ct LA1 214 E7
Villas Rd L31 6 B2
Villas The PR4 116 E5
Villiers Ct PR1 117 E2
Villiers St Burnley BB11 127 C5
Bury BL9 33 A3
Padiham BB12 126 D7
Preston PR1 117 D2
Preston PR1 117 E2
Vincent Ct BB2 81 D8
Vincent Rd BB9 148 F8
Vincent St Blackburn BB2 81 D8
Colne BB8 171 F6
8 Lancaster LA1 215 A7
Vincit St BB10 128 C8
Vine Ct FY2 152 C1
Vine St Accrington BB5 104 A6
Brierfield BB9 148 B5
Chorley PR7 61 C1
Lancaster LA1 214 F6
Oswaldtwistle BB5 103 C3
Preston PR1 96 D8
Ramsbottom BL0 50 A4
Vinery The PR4 75 F8
Viola Cl WN6 29 D2
Violet St BB10 148 A1
Virginia Ave L31 5 D3
Virginia Gr L31 5 C3
Virginia St PR8 35 C6
Viscount Ave BB3 82 A6
Viscount Dr LA1 214 E1
Vivary Way BB8 171 B5
Vivian Dr PR8 35 A2
Vulcan Rd PR4 114 B1
Vulcan St 4 Nelson BB9 170 F1
Southport PR9 35 C7

W

Wackersall Rd BB8 171 B3
Waddington & West Bradford CE Prim Sch BB7 189 C5
Waddington Ave BB10 128 D6
Waddington Ct FY8 90 C6
Waddington Hospl (Almshouses) BB7 189 B5
Waddington Rd
Accrington BB5 104 D6
Clitheroe BB7 189 E1
Fulwood PR2 119 A2
Lytham St Anne's FY8 90 C7
West Bradford BB7 189 D5
Waddington St
Earby BB18 197 B2
3 Padiham BB12 126 D8
Waddow Gn BB7 166 C8
Waddow Gr BB7 189 C4
Waddow View BB7 189 B4
Wade Brook Rd PR26 58 F6
Wade St BB12 146 D1
Wades Croft PR4 93 C6
Wades Ct FY3 152 F1
Wadham Rd PR1 97 B6
Wagon Rd LA2,PR3 226 B8
Waidshouse Cl BB9 148 E6
Waidshouse Rd BB9 148 E6
Wain Ct BB2 101 B4
Waingap Cres OL12 52 D8
Waingap Rise OL12 52 F4
Waingap View OL12 52 D7
Waingate Grimsargh PR2 139 C1
Rawtenstall BB4 86 B3
Waingate Cl BB4 86 B3
Waingate Ct PR2 139 C1
Waingate La BB4 86 B3
Waingate Rd BB4 86 B3
Waitholme La LA5 240 A7
Wakefield Ave LA4 217 D6
Wakefield Dr LA1 215 A4
Wakefield Rd FY2 152 E4
Walden Rd BB1 122 F4
Waldon St PR1 97 E8
Waldron WN8 8 D8
Wales Rd BB4 86 F1
Wales Terr BB4 86 F1
Walesby Pl FY8 90 D5
Walgarth Dr PR7 43 B7
Walk Mill Pl BB10 128 E1
Walk The
Hesketh Bank PR4 73 C4
Southport PR8 35 A5
Walkdale PR4 95 D2
Walkden Barn Cotts BB5 103 A1
Walkden St 28 OL12 52 F1
Walker Ave BB5 104 A4
Walker Cl L37 11 F2
Walker Gr LA3 212 F7
Walker La PR2 117 B6
Walker Office Pk BB1 82 C8
Walker Park Ind Est BB1 82 C7
Walker Pl PR1 97 B7
Walker Rd BB1 82 C7
Walker St Blackburn BB1 101 F4
Blackpool FY1 130 B6
Clitheroe BB7 166 F8
Preston PR1 96 F8
Walker Way FY5 176 B4
Walkers Hill FY4 111 A7
Walkers Ind Est LA3 212 F3
Wall La PR3 155 E5
Wall St Blackpool FY1 130 C7
Newchurch BB4 86 E2
Wallace Hartley Mews 1 BB8 171 D5
Wallace La PR3 207 C4
Wallbank Dr OL12 52 C7
Wallbrook Ave WN5 10 D1
Wallcroft St WN8 8 E8
Walled Garden The PR6 61 B6
Wallend Rd PR2 95 D7
Waller Ave FY2 152 C5
Waller Hill BB8 194 D1
Walletts Rd PR7 43 B6
Wallhurst Cl BB10 129 B5
Walling's La LA5 224 B4
Wallstreams Ct BB10 129 B5
Wallstreams La BB10 129 B5
Wallsuches BL6 32 F4
Walmer Ct PR8 34 F4
Walmer Gn PR4 74 F5
Walmer Rd
Lytham St Anne's FY8 89 F8
Southport PR8 35 A3
Walmersley Old Rd BL9 50 F2
Walmersley Rd BL9 50 E2
Walmsgate BB18 196 B2
Walmsley Ave BB1 103 B8
Walmsley Bridge La
Bilsborrow PR3 159 E8
Claughton PR3 182 E1
Walmsley Brow BB7 144 B4
Walmsley CE Prim Sch BL7 47 E1
Walmsley Cl Church BB5 103 E6
Garstang PR3 181 C7
Walmsley Ct BB5 124 F1
Walmsley St Darwen BB3 82 B2
Fleetwood FY7 199 A4
18 Great Harwood BB6 124 C5
Rishton BB1 124 B1
Walney Gdns BB2 101 F1
Walney Pl FY3 131 A7
Walnut Ave Bury BL9 33 C3
Haslingden BB4 85 C3
Walnut Cl PR1 96 B3
Walnut St Bacup OL13 87 F3
Blackburn BB1 101 F7
3 Blackburn BB1 102 A7
Southport PR8 35 C4
Walpole Ave FY4 110 B5
Walpole St
Blackburn BB1 101 F4
9 Burnley BB10 148 B1
Walro Mews PR9 54 A3
Walsden Gr BB10 128 C6
Walsh Fold BL7 48 D2
Walsh St Blackburn BB2 101 E2
Horwich BL6 32 B4
Walshaw High Sch BB10 148 D1
Walshaw La BB10 148 D2
Walshaw St BB10 128 B8
Walter Ave FY8 111 A2
Walter Pl FY8 111 A2
Walter Robinson Ct FY3 130 D6
Walter St Accrington BB5 104 B6
Blackburn BB1 102 A4
Blackburn BB1 102 B4
Brierfield BB9 148 B5
Darwen BB3 65 B5
Huncoat BB5 125 E2
Oswaldtwistle BB5 103 D3
Walter Street Prim Sch BB9 148 B5
Waltham Ave FY4 110 D5
Waltham Cl BB5 104 E3
Waltham Ct LA2 219 C7
Walthew Gn WN8 19 C3
Waltho Ave L31 5 E1
Walton Ave
Higher Penwortham PR1 96 B3
Morecambe LA4 217 F5
Walton Cl OL13 88 A1
Walton Cottage Homes BB9 171 A1
Walton Cres BB2 102 A1
Walton Gn PR5 97 C4
Walton Gr LA4 217 F5
Walton High Sch BB9 171 A2
Walton La BB9 171 A1
Walton St Accrington BB5 125 A1
Adlington PR7 31 A6
Barrowford BB9 170 E4
Colne BB8 171 D4
8 Nelson BB9 170 E1
Southport PR9 35 C8
Walton Summit Rd PR5 78 A7
Walton View PR1 97 D8
Walton's Par PR1 96 E7
Walton-le-Dale Com Prim Sch PR5 97 D2
Walton-le-Dale High Sch PR5 97 F2
Walverden Ave 4 FY4 110 D8
Walverden Cres 3 BB9 148 F8
Walverden Prim Sch BB9 148 F8
Walverden Rd
Brierfield BB9 148 D5
Lane Bottom BB10 149 B4
Walverden Terr BB9 148 F7
Wanes Blades Rd L40 26 E5
Wanishar La L39 14 A5
Wansbeck Ave FY7 198 D2
Wansbeck Ho FY7 198 D2
Wansfell Rd BB7 166 C7
Wanstead Cres FY4 130 E1
Wanstead St PR1 97 E8
Warbreck Ct FY2 152 B1
Warbreck Dr FY2 152 B2
Warbreck Hill Rd FY2 152 D1
Warburton Bldgs BB4 84 F1
Warburton St BB4 84 F1
Warbury St PR1 118 E1
Warcock La OL13 88 B3
Ward Ave Cleveleys FY5 175 D3
Formby L37 11 D2
Oswaldtwistle BB5 103 C3
Ward Green Cross PR3 141 A7
Ward Green La PR3 141 A7
Ward St
Bamber Bridge PR5 77 B7
Belmont BL7 46 C5
5 Blackpool FY1 130 B1
Burnley BB11 127 E6
Chorley PR6 43 E7
Great Harwood BB6 124 C5
Kirkham PR4 114 A4
Ward's End PR1 97 A7
Warde St 10 BB9 148 E8
Wardle Ct PR6 61 C6
Wardle Dr FY5 175 F3
Wardle St OL13 70 D8
Wardley's La FY6 177 A3
Wareham Cl BB5 125 B1
Wareham Rd FY3 152 F1
Wareham St BB1 102 A7
Warehouse La BB8 194 D1
Waring Dr FY5 176 A2
Warings The
Heskin Green PR7 41 E4
Nelson BB9 148 E6
Warkworth Terr 10 OL13 88 A3
Warley Ave LA3 217 E4
Warley Dr LA3 217 E4
Warley Rd FY1 130 C8
Warley Wise La BB8 195 F3
Warmden Ave BB5 104 E3
Warmden Gdns BB1 102 A7
Warne Pl LA1 218 B1
Warner Rd PR1 118 D1
Warner St
Accrington BB5 104 C5
Haslingden BB4 85 B3
Warpers Moss Cl L40 25 F5
Warpers Moss La L40 26 A5
Warren Ave N FY7 198 F4

Warren Ave S FY7 198 F4
Warren Cl LA2 218 C8
Warren Ct PR8 34 E5
Warren Dr Bacup OL13 71 C8
Barrowford BB9 170 C3
Blackpool FY5 152 E7
Slyne LA2 218 C8
Warren Fold BB7 142 F8
Warren Gn L37 11 D3
Warren Gr Blackpool FY5 152 E8
Heysham LA3 212 E5
Warren Rd Heysham LA3 212 E5
Southport PR9 36 A8
Warren St FY7 199 B4
Warren The
Blackburn BB2 101 A7
Fulwood PR2 118 E6
Warrenhouse Rd L33 1 B4
Warrenhurst Ho 1 FY7 198 F3
Warrenhurst Rd FY7 199 A4
Warrenside Cl BB1 123 A4
Warrington St BB1 102 A8
Warrington Terr BB6 144 D8
Warth La Ingleton LA6 242 F2
Rawtenstall BB4 69 E8
Warton Archbishop Hutton's Prim Sch LA5 223 D5
Warton Ave LA3 212 E6
Warton Crag Nature Reserve* LA5 223 C6
Warton Old Rectory* LA5 223 D5
Warton Pl PR7 43 A8
Warton Rd LA5 223 D2
Warton St
Lytham St Anne's FY8 91 C3
2 Preston PR1 96 E6
Wartonwood View 1 LA5 223 D1
Warwick Ave
Accrington BB5 104 B7
Clayton-le-M BB5 124 F3
Cleveleys FY5 175 F4
Darwen BB3 81 E3
Lancaster LA1 215 A5
Morecambe LA4 217 F6
Warwick Cl Church BB5 103 F7
Fulwood PR2 117 E4
Ramsbottom BL8 50 A1
Southport PR8 35 B4
Warwick Dr
Barnoldswick BB18 196 F1
Brierfield BB9 148 D5
Clitheroe BB7 189 F2
Padiham BB12 126 D7
Warwick Ho 10 PR1 97 A6
Warwick Pl
Fleetwood FY7 199 A5
Normoss FY3 131 B8
Warwick Rd
Bamber Bridge PR5 97 D4
Blackpool FY3 130 D7
Eccleston PR7 41 C7
Leyland PR25 59 E7
Lytham St Anne's FY8 89 F6
Warwick St Adlington PR7 30 F6
Church BB5 103 F7
Haslingden BB4 85 B3
Longridge PR3 140 A8
Nelson BB9 148 E7
Preston PR1 96 F8
Southport PR8 35 B4
Wasdale Ave
Blackburn BB1 102 C3
Maghull L31 5 F2
Wasdale Cl Leyland PR25 60 B6
Padiham BB12 146 C1
Wasdale Gr PR3 139 F5
Wasdale Rd FY4 111 A8
Wash La BL9 33 B2
Washbrook Cl BB7 166 D1
Washbrook Way L39 15 E4
Washburn Ct LA3 217 F2
Washington Ave
Blackpool FY2 152 E2
3 Morecambe LA4 217 B5
Washington Cl LA1 214 D7
Washington Ct FY2 152 E2
Washington Dr LA5 223 E6
Washington Hall Fire Brigade Training Ctr PR7 60 F2
Washington La PR7 60 F2
Washington St BB5 104 C6
Waste La LA2 226 C7
Wastwater Dr 4 LA4 217 E4
Watchyard La L37 12 A4
Water Fold BB4 87 A8
Water Head PR2 117 B3
Water La Edenfield BL0 68 D2
Preston PR2 117 D1
Southport PR9 54 D5
Water Mdws BB2 81 D7
Water St
9 Accrington BB5 104 C6
Adlington PR7 31 A6
1 Bamber Bridge PR5 97 F2
Brindle PR6 78 F5
Chorley PR7 61 C1
Clayton-le-M BB5 124 F5
1 Colne BB8 171 E5
Earby BB18 197 B2
Egerton BL7 47 D2
Great Harwood BB6 124 C5
Hapton BB12 126 C4
Lancaster LA1 218 D1
Water St *continued*
Nelson BB9 148 E8
8 Ramsbottom BL0 50 B5
Rawtenstall BB4 86 A8
Ribchester PR3 141 E3
Whitworth OL12 52 C8
Worsthorne BB10 129 B5
Water's Edge PR2 116 F3
Waterbarn La OL13 70 B8
Waterbarn St BB10 148 B1
Waterdale FY2 152 E5
Waterfall Mills BB2 101 B2
Waterfall Terr BL7 46 C5
Waterfield Ave BB3 65 B6
Waterfold Bsns Pk BL9 33 B1
Waterfold La BL9 33 C1
Waterfoot Ave
Blackpool FY3 130 E6
Southport PR8 21 B3
Waterfoot Bsns Ctr 6 BB4 86 F2
Waterford Cl
Adlington PR6 44 A1
Fulwood PR2 118 C5
Waterford St BB9 170 F1
Waterfront 2 BB1 101 F3
Waterfront Marine & Ind Est FY8 91 E3
Waterhead Cres FY5 152 C6
Waterhouse Gn PR6 61 B7
Waterhouse Nook PR7, BL6 31 A5
Watering Pool La PR5 97 B1
Waterleat Glade FY6 131 E8
Waterloo Cl BB2 81 B8
Waterloo Prim Sch FY4 130 D1
Waterloo Rd
Blackpool FY4 130 D1
Burnley BB11 128 B4
Burnley BB11 128 B5
Clitheroe BB7 166 F8
Kelbrook BB18 195 A6
Preston PR2 117 C1
Southport PR8 34 E2
Waterloo St
Accrington BB5 125 A1
Chorley PR7 61 C1
Waterloo Terr PR2 117 C1
Watermans Cl BL6 32 C4
Watermede WN5 10 E3
Waters Edge
3 Blackburn BB1 101 F4
Whalley BB7 144 C4
Waters Edge Gn PR3 181 C6
Waters Reach
Cleveleys FY5 175 C3
Lytham St Anne's FY8 90 D3
Waterside Blackpool FY2 152 D2
Lancaster LA1 218 D1
Waterside Cl PR3 181 B7
Waterside Ind Est BB8 171 E4
Waterside Mews BB12 126 D8
Waterside Pl LA4 217 B3
Waterside Rd Colne BB8 171 D4
Haslingden BB4 85 A2
Ramsbottom BL0,BL8,BL9 50 C3
Waterside Terr
10 Bacup OL13 87 F3
Waterside BB3 82 E3
Waterslack Rd LA5 224 E6
Waterworks Cotts L39 6 F4
Waterworks Rd L39 16 A6
Watery Gate La PR3,PR4 156 D3
Watery La Darwen BB3 65 B6
Garstang PR3 204 E1
Lancaster LA1 218 B3
Preston PR2 96 B8
Preston,Fishwick PR1 97 E7
Watery Lane Ind Est BB3 65 B6
Watford St 5 BB1 101 E6
Watkin La PR5 77 B7
Watkin Rd PR6 61 B8
Watkins Cl BB9 148 C4
Watling Cl LA3 217 E3
Watling Gate BB6 143 C6
Watling St BL8 49 A1
Watling Street Rd
Fulwood PR2 118 B3
Fulwood,Brookfield PR2 118 E5
Watson Ct FY4 110 D7
Watson Gdns OL12 52 D2
Watson Rd FY4 110 C7
Watson St Blackburn BB2 101 B2
8 Oswaldtwistle BB5 103 E4
Watt St Burnley BB12 127 C7
Sabden BB7 145 F7
Watton Beck Cl L31 5 F2
Watts Cl L33 1 A4
Watts St BL6 32 C2
Wavell Ave PR9 36 B7
Wavell Cl Accrington BB5 104 F1
Southport PR9 36 B7
Wavell St BB12 127 C6
Waverledge Bsns Pk BB6 124 B4
Waverledge Rd BB6 124 B4
Waverledge St BB6 124 C4
Waverley WN8 17 D1
Waverley Ave
Blackpool FY1 130 C8
Fleetwood FY7 198 D3
Waverley Cl
Brierfield BB9 148 D4
Read BB12 145 D1
Waverley Dr
New Longton PR4 75 F7
Tarleton PR4 57 A6
Waverley Gdns PR2 118 E2
Waverley Pl BB2 101 B5
Waverley Rd
Accrington BB5 104 E3
Blackburn BB1 102 F4
Preston PR1 118 D1
Wilpshire BB1 122 E4
Waverley St
1 Burnley BB11 127 E6
Southport PR8 35 A7
Waxy La PR4 93 C7
Way Gate FY5 175 D5
Way The LA3 217 F3
Wayfarers Arc PR8 35 B7
Wayman Rd FY3 130 D6
Wayoh Croft BL7 48 D6
Wayside FY6 199 D5
Weald The PR4 116 D5
Weasel La BB3 81 B2
Weatherhill Cres BB9 148 E5
Weaver Ave L40 25 F5
Weaver's Brow PR6 43 F5
Weaver's Croft BB7 144 A4
Weavers Cl FY8 90 D7
Weavers Ct BB8 172 B2
Webb St BL6 32 C3
Webber Ct BB11 127 A3
Webber Rd L33 1 C1
Weber St BB4 86 D1
Webster Ave FY4 110 E7
Webster Gdns PR4 75 A4
Webster Gr LA4 218 A6
Webster St PR2 117 C1
Wedgewood Rd BB5 125 F1
Wedgwood Ct FY8 90 A7
Weeton Ave
Blackpool FY4 110 E5
Cleveleys FY5 175 D3
Lytham St Anne's FY8 90 A8
Weeton Pl 4 PR2 116 E1
Weeton Prim Sch PR4 132 E6
Weeton Rd
Great Plumpton PR4 112 F7
Kirkham PR4 113 F7
Kirkham,Weeton PR4 113 C8
Weeton PR4 132 F2
Weeton Camp FY6,PR4 132 E7
Weeton St Michael's CE Prim Sch PR4 132 E1
Weets View BB18 196 C3
Weind The PR3 156 B5
Weir La OL13 88 A7
Weir St BB2 101 E4
Weirden Cl PR1 96 C1
Welbeck Ave
Blackburn BB1 102 B8
Blackpool FY4 130 E1
Fleetwood FY7 198 F3
Welbeck Gdns FY7 198 F3
Welbeck Ho 4 FY7 198 F4
Welbeck Rd PR8 35 A4
Welbeck Terr PR8 35 A4
Welbourne WN8 17 D1
Welburn Cl WN5 10 E5
Welburn Wlk FY5 176 D2
Welbury Cl 5 BB18 197 B2
Weld Ave PR7 43 C5
Weld Blundell Ave L31 5 B5
Weld Dr L37 11 D4
Weld Par PR8 34 F4
Weld Rd PR8 34 F5
Weldale PR8 34 F4
Weldbank La PR7 43 C5
Weldbank St PR7 43 C5
Weldon Dr L39 15 F4
Weldon St BB11 127 E5
Well Ct Clitheroe BB7 189 F1
3 Standish WN6 29 E1
Well Field BB5 125 A2
Well Fold BB7 166 F8
Well Head BB8 172 B4
Well Head Rd BB12 169 A3
Well La Brinscall PR6 62 F7
Haskayne L39 13 E6
Little Eccleston PR3 155 D6
Warton LA5 223 E5
Yealand Redmayne LA5 225 E3
Well Orch PR5 78 B5
Well St Burnley BB12 126 B8
Newchurch BB4 86 F3
Rishton BB1 124 B2
Well St N BL0 68 C2
Well St W 6 BL0 50 B5
Well Terr 1 BB7 189 F1
Welland Cl FY2 152 E4
Wellbrow Dr PR3 140 B8
Wellbrow Terr OL12 52 D2
Wellcross Rd WN8 10 B6
Wellesley St BB12 126 F6
Wellfield PR4 94 F1
Wellfield Ave PR25 76 F1
Wellfield Bsns Pk PR1 96 D8
Wellfield Dr BB12 127 D7
Wellfield High Sch PR25 76 F1
Wellfield La L40 16 C3
Wellfield Methodist & Anglican Church Sch BB12 127 D8
Wellfield Rd
Bamber Bridge PR5 77 A7
Blackburn BB2 101 C6
Preston PR1 96 D8
Wellgate BB7 166 F8
Wellhouse Rd BB18 196 B2
Wellhouse Sq 20 BB18 196 B2
Wellhouse St BB18 196 B2
Wellington Ave PR25 60 B8
Wellington Cl WN8 9 E8
Wellington Ct
7 Accrington BB5 104 C5
3 Burnley BB10 128 B5
Wellington Fold 3 BB3 82 A1
Wellington Mews BL7 48 D4
Wellington Pl PR5 97 D2
Wellington Rd
Blackburn BB2 101 C3
Blackpool FY1 130 B2
Lancaster LA1 215 A5
Preston PR2 117 C1
Turton Bottoms BL7 48 D4
Wellington St
Accrington BB5 104 C5
Barnoldswick BB18 196 B1
Chorley PR7 61 C1
Clayton-le-M BB5 124 F2
Great Harwood BB6 124 C4
Kirkham PR4 113 F5
Lytham St Anne's FY8 91 D3
16 Nelson BB9 170 D1
Preston PR1 96 D8
19 Rochdale OL12 52 F1
1 Southport PR8 35 A6
Wellington Street St Johns BB1 101 D6
Wellington Terr LA4 217 B5
Wellogate Gdns FY4 110 D6
Wellow Pl FY8 90 C6
Wells Cl Morecambe LA3 217 B2
Thornton FY5 176 A2
Wells Fold Cl PR6 78 C1
Wells St Haslingden BB4 85 B3
9 Preston PR1 118 D1
Welsby Rd PR25 59 D8
Welwyn Ave PR8 21 E6
Welwyn Pl FY5 175 E1
Wembley Ave
Blackpool FY3 130 E8
Higher Penwortham PR1 96 B5
Poulton-le-F FY6 153 E3
Wembley Ct PR1 96 B5
Wembley Rd FY5 176 B4
Wemyss Cl 1 LA3 212 E7
Wendover Rd FY6 153 A6
Wenlock Cl BL6 32 C6
Wenning Ave
High Bentham LA2 239 D7
Maghull L31 5 E2
Wenning Ct LA3 217 F2
Wenning Pl LA1 218 C2
Wenning St BB9 148 F7
Wennington Hall Sch LA2 241 E1
Wennington Rd
Southport PR9 35 F7
Wray LA2 238 D6
Wennington Sta LA2 238 E8
Wensley Ave FY7 198 E1
Wensley Bsns Pk BB2 101 B4
Wensley Cl BB11 127 E3
Wensley Dr
Accrington BB5 104 D5
Lancaster LA1 218 D3
Wensley Fold CE Prim Sch BB2 101 B5
Wensley Pl PR2 118 D4
Wensley Rd BB2 101 B4
Wensleydale Ave FY3 131 A7
Wensleydale Cl
Maghull L31 5 B2
Thornton FY5 153 D8
Wentcliffe Dr BB18 197 B1
Wentworth Ave
Fleetwood FY7 175 D7
Inskip PR4 135 C8
Wentworth Cl
Higher Penwortham PR1 96 A6
Southport PR8 21 C4
Wentworth Cres LA3 217 B2
Wentworth Ct PR4 114 B4
Wentworth Dr
Broughton PR3 137 C3
Euxton PR7 60 D4
Lancaster LA1 215 C7
Thornton FY5 153 D8
Wentworth Mews FY8 90 A6
Wentworth Pl PR3 137 C3
Werneth Cl PR1 96 F1
Wescoe Cl WN5 10 E5
Wesham Cross PR4 113 F7
Wesham Hall Cl PR4 114 A6
Wesham Hall Rd PR4 114 A6
Wesham Park Hospl PR4 113 F7
Wesley Cl LA2 239 D8
Wesley Ct
3 Fleetwood FY7 199 B5
16 Great Harwood BB6 124 C5
Wesley Dr LA3 212 F7
Wesley Gr 5 BB12 127 D7
Wesley Mews FY4 111 A7
Wesley Pl Bacup OL13 87 E1
Higham BB12 146 F6
Wesley St Accrington BB5 103 F6
Bamber Bridge PR5 77 F8
Blackburn BB1 101 F7
Brierfield BB9 148 B6
Oswaldtwistle BB5 103 E5
8 Padiham BB12 126 D8
Sabden BB7 145 F8
Southport PR8 35 B7
Wesley Terr OL13 88 A7
Wesleyan Row BB7 166 E8
Wessex Cl
Accrington,Hillock Vale BB5 104 F8
Standish WN1 30 B1
West Ave
Barnoldswick BB18 196 B2
Fulwood PR2 117 A6
West Bank PR7 43 C8
West Bank Ave FY8 90 E3
West Beach FY8 91 A2
West Bourne BB4 68 A8
West Bradford Rd
Clitheroe BB7 189 F4
Grindleton BB7 190 A6
Waddington BB7 189 C5
West Bridge L31 5 C1
West Cliff PR1 96 E6
West Cliff Terr PR1 96 E6
West Cliffe FY8 91 C3
West Close Ave BB12 146 F5
West Close Rd BB18 196 B3
West Craven High Tech Coll BB18 196 C1
West Cres
Accrington BB5 104 B8
Broughton PR3 137 C3
West Ct FY5 175 C5
West Dene WN8 27 B2
West Dr Clayton-le-W PR25 77 D3
Cleveleys FY5 175 E3
Inskip PR4 135 C8
Kirkham PR4 113 E7
Lancaster LA1 218 B2
Whalley BB7 144 A7
West Dr W FY5 175 D3
West End
Great Eccleston PR3 156 A5
Higher Penwortham PR1 96 B6
West End Bsns Pk BB5 103 B5
West End La PR4 92 B5
West End Prim Sch
Morecambe LA3 216 F4
Oswaldtwistle BB5 103 C5
West End Rd LA4 217 A4
West End Terr PR8 35 A7
West Exchange St 7 BB8 171 D4
West Field Rd BB18 196 A4
West Gate FY7 198 D4
West Gdns 1 OL13 70 B8
West Gillibrands Ind Est WN8 8 E8
West Hall La LA6 241 C7
West Hill BB9 170 D4
West Ing La BD23 231 D5
West La Downham BB7 191 A4
Formby L37 11 F6
West Lancashire Light Rly* PR4 73 F2
West Leigh Rd BB1 101 C8
West Lodge FY6 177 C1
West Mdw PR2 116 E3
West Meade L31 5 B2
West Moss La FY8 111 E1
West Mount WN5 10 F6
West Paddock PR25 59 E8
West Park Ave PR2 116 F2
West Park Dr FY3 130 E4
West Park La PR2 117 A2
West Park Rd BB2 101 C6
West Pennine Bsns Pk OL13 87 F5
West Pk PR9 53 D1
West Rd Fulwood PR2 117 F3
Lancaster LA1 214 E8
Thornton FY5 176 C3
West Sq PR4 75 A8
West St 9 Blackpool FY1 130 B5
Burnley BB10 128 C8
Chorley PR7 43 C7
Colne BB8 171 E4
Great Harwood BB6 124 C4
Lancaster LA1 214 F5
Morecambe LA3 216 E4
7 Nelson BB9 170 D1
Padiham BB12 126 B8
7 Ramsbottom BL0 50 B5
Rawtenstall BB4 69 E8
Southport PR8 35 A7
West Strand PR1 96 D8
West Street Com Prim Sch BB8 171 E4
West View Bacup OL13 70 B8
Bamber Bridge PR5 77 E7
Blackburn BB2 101 B4
Blackpool FY1 130 C3
Carnforth LA5 223 D3
Clitheroe BB7 166 D7
Darwen BB3 82 B3
Elswick PR4 155 F1
Garstang PR3 181 C7
Glasson LA2 209 E5
Grindleton BB7 190 B8
Haslingden BB4 85 B4
Haslingden,Bridge End BB4 68 A7
Hollins Lane PR3 207 D2
Kirkham PR4 113 F7
Longton PR4 75 A8
4 Newchurch BB4 86 F1
1 Ormskirk L39 15 F5
Oswaldtwistle BB5 103 E4
Over Town BB10 108 A8
Parbold WN8 27 C2
Preston PR1 118 C2
Ramsbottom BL0 68 C2
Waddington BB7 189 B4
Wheelton PR6 62 A7
West View Ave 8 FY1 130 B2
West View Pl BB2 101 B6
West View Rd
Morecambe LA4 217 A5
Whitewell Bottom BB4 86 F5

West View Terr
Billington BB7 144 A4
Padiham BB12 126 C7
1 Preston PR1 96 D8
Tockholes BB3 81 A2
West Way Chorley PR7 61 A2
Fleetwood FY7 175 D8
West Wing L40 17 B7
West Wlk BL7 47 D2
Westbank Ave FY4 111 A7
Westboro Cl LA3 216 D1
Westbourne Ave
Blackpool FY1 130 C1
Burnley BB11 127 D3
Wrea Green PR4 113 B3
Westbourne Ave S
BB11 127 E3
Westbourne Ct FY6 199 D5
Westbourne Dr LA1 214 D7
Westbourne Gdns PR8 34 D4
Westbourne Pl LA1 214 D8
Westbourne Rd
Chorley PR7 43 B6
Cleveleys FY5 175 D5
Heysham LA3 213 A2
Knott End-on-S FY6 199 D5
Lancaster LA1 214 D7
Southport PR8 34 D4
Warton LA5 223 C4
Westbrook Cres PR2 117 A3
Westbury Cl
Blackpool FY5 152 C7
Brierfield BB10 148 E2
Westbury Gdns BB1 102 C4
Westby Ave FY4 110 E5
Westby Cl FY4 111 D7
Westby Ct FY6 153 D2
Westby Gr FY7 199 B5
Westby Pl PR2 116 F1
Westby Rd
Lytham St Anne's FY8 89 E8
Westby PR4 112 E5
Westby St FY8 91 B3
Westby Way FY6 153 D2
Westcliff Prim Sch FY5 152 C5
Westcliffe BB6 124 B6
Westcliffe Dr
Blackpool FY3 130 E8
Morecambe LA3 217 A2
Westcliffe Rd PR8 34 F5
Westcliffe Wlk BB9 148 E7
Westcote St 6 BB3 65 B6
Westcroft PR4 74 E3
Westend Ave PR7 42 D1
Westerdale Dr PR9 55 B5
Westerlong PR2 116 D1
Western Ave BB11 127 E4
Western Ct OL13 70 B8
Western Dr PR25 76 D2
Western Rd OL13 70 C8
Westfield
Bamber Bridge PR5 77 A8
1 Nelson BB9 170 D1
Westfield Ave
Blackpool FY3 153 A1
Fleetwood FY7 198 E2
Normoss FY3 131 B7
Read BB12 145 D1
Westfield Cl BB7 144 A7
Westfield Ct FY5 176 B4
Westfield Dr
Bolton-le-S LA5 221 A6
Fulwood PR2 118 E4
Gregson Lane PR5 98 D1
Leyland PR25 76 E1
Warton PR4 92 F5
West Bradford BB7 189 E6
Westfield Gr LA4 217 A4
Westfield Rd FY1 130 D1
Westfields PR26 58 A2
Westgate
Barnoldswick BB18 196 A1
Burnley BB11 127 E6
Fulwood PR2 117 D5
Leyland PR25 59 F8
Morecambe LA3,LA4 217 C3
Read BB12 145 C1
Skelmersdale WN8 8 D8
Whitworth OL12 52 B7
Westgate Ave
Morecambe LA3 217 B2
Ramsbottom BL0 50 A2
Westgate Cl OL12 52 B7
Westgate Dr WN5 10 D5
Westgate La LA6 242 E5
Westgate Park Rd LA4 217 C3
Westgate Prim Sch LA4 217 B3
Westgate Rd FY8 110 C4
Westgate Trad Ctr 2
BB11 127 F6
Westham St LA1 215 A7
Westhaven PR9 35 D8
Westhaven Cres L39 15 C1
Westhead Ave L33 1 A1
Westhead Cl L33 1 A1
Westhead Rd PR26 58 B2
Westhead Wlk
1 Fleetwood FY7 198 F2
Kirkby L33 1 A1
Westholme Ct PR9 53 C1
Westholme Lower Sch
BB2 101 D6
Westholme Sch
Blackburn BB2 100 E6
Blackburn BB2 101 A6
Westhoughton Rd PR6,
PR7 43 F1
Westland Ave BB3 64 F8
Westlands PR26 59 C7
Westlands Ct FY5 153 B8
Westleigh Rd PR2 116 F1
Westminster Ave LA4 126 F4
Westminster Cl
Accrington BB5 104 E3
Darwen BB3 81 E3
Morecambe LA3 217 B2
Read BB12 145 D1
Westminster Dr PR8 21 A4
Westminster Pl
Eccleston PR7 41 A8
Hutton PR4 95 D1
Westminster Rd
Blackpool FY1 130 C8
Chorley PR7 43 C7
Darwen BB3 81 E3
Morecambe LA3,LA4 216 E3
Westmoor Gr LA3 212 E5
Westmoreland Rd PR8 35 D5
Westmoreland St BB9 148 C8
Westmorland Ave
Blackpool FY1 130 D3
Cleveleys FY5 175 D4
Westmorland Cl
Darwen BB3 65 C6
Higher Penwortham PR1 96 B4
Leyland PR25 59 E7
Westmorland St BB11 127 D5
Weston Pl 4 FY1 130 D1
Weston St 9 PR2 96 D8
Westover Ave LA5 223 E5
Westover Cl L31 5 C1
Westover Gr LA5 223 E5
Westover Rd Maghull L31 5 C1
Warton LA5 223 E5
Westover St LA4 217 B5
Westridge Ct PR9 35 D8
Westside FY4 110 F8
Westway Burnley BB11 127 D6
Freckleton PR4 93 A6
Fulwood PR2 118 A4
Hightown L38 2 F4
Maghull L31 5 C2
Westway Ct PR2 118 B4
Westway Sch BB12 127 F8
Westwell Gr 2 FY1 130 C4
Westwell Rd 4 PR6 61 D1
Westwell St Darwen BB3 81 E4
14 Great Harwood BB6 124 C5
Westwood Ave
Blackpool FY3 130 E4
2 Fleetwood FY7 198 E3
Poulton-le-F FY6 153 E3
Rishton BB1 124 A1
Westwood Cl PR8 35 E3
Westwood Ct BB1 102 A6
Westwood Mews FY8 91 A3
Westwood Prim Sch PR5 78 C4
Westwood Rd
Burnley BB12 127 C8
Clayton Brook PR5,PR6 78 C4
Leyland PR25 77 A2
Lytham St Anne's FY8 91 A3
Westwood St BB5 104 B7
Wetherall St PR2 117 D1
Wetherby Ave FY4 110 D5
Wetherfield Cl LA1 218 E4
Weymouth Rd FY3 130 F3
Weythorne Dr BL9 33 F4
Whalley Abbey* BB7 144 B5
Whalley Banks BB2 101 D4
Whalley Banks Trad Est
BB2 101 D4
Whalley CE Prim Sch
BB7 144 C5
Whalley Cres Darwen BB3 82 B1
Staining FY3 131 E5
Whalley Dr Formby L37 12 A2
Ormskirk L39 6 D8
Rawtenstall BB4 86 A4
Whalley Gdns OL12 52 B1
Whalley Ind Pk BB7 144 D8
Whalley La FY4 111 A8
Whalley New Rd BB1 122 F1
Whalley Old Rd
Billington BB6,BB7 144 B3
Blackburn BB1 102 A7
Sunny Bower BB1 123 B1
Whalley Pl FY8 90 B6
Whalley Range BB1 101 F6
Whalley Rd
Accrington BB5 104 B7
Bank Lane BL0 50 E7
Barrow BB7 166 D2
Billington BB6,BB7 143 F3
Burnley BB12 126 B8
Clayton-le-M BB5,BB6 124 F5
Clitheroe BB7 166 D5
Heskin Green PR7 41 D4
Hurst Green BB7 165 B1
Lancaster LA1 218 D4
Langho BB6 143 D1
Langho BB6 143 D2
Mellor Brook BB2 121 C3
Read BB12 145 C1
Rochdale OL12 52 B1
Sabden BB7 145 D6
Turner Green BB2,PR5 120 C2
Wilpshire BB1,BB6 123 B7
Whalley St
3 Bamber Bridge PR5 97 F2
Blackburn BB1 101 E6
Burnley BB10 148 A1
5 Chorley PR7 43 C7
5 Clitheroe BB7 166 D8
Whalley Sta BB7 144 B6
Whalley Terr BB3 81 B6
Whalleys Rd WN8 18 B5
Wham Bottom La OL12 52 D4
Wham Brook Cl BB5 103 B5
Wham Hey PR4 76 A7
Wham La
New Longton PR4 76 A7
Walmer Bridge PR4 75 D4
Whams La LA2 207 D7
Wharf Ho 7 BB2 101 B1
Wharf St Blackburn BB1 101 F5
Lytham St Anne's FY8 91 C3
Rishton BB1 124 C1
Wharfdale Ave BB10 148 B4
Wharfe Ct LA3 217 F3
Wharfedale
Blackpool FY4 110 F7
Galgate LA2 211 B4
Wharfedale Ave
Fulwood PR2 118 E5
Thornton FY5 176 B3
Wharfedale Cl
Blackburn BB2 80 D7
Leyland PR25 60 A7
Wharfedale Ct FY6 153 C3
Wharfedale Rd LA1 214 D8
Wharton Ave FY5 176 D1
Whave's La PR6 79 D4
Wheat La L40 26 A4
Wheat St Accrington BB5 104 A6
Padiham BB12 126 D7
Wheatacre WN8 8 E8
Wheatcroft Ave BB12 147 D8
Wheatfield PR26 59 A8
Wheatfield Cl 1 FY5 152 F7
Wheatfield Ct 8 LA1 214 E8
Wheatfield St
Lancaster LA1 214 E8
Rishton BB1 124 B2
Wheathead La BB9 170 B8
Wheatholme St BB4 86 B2
Wheatlands Cres FY3 131 C2
Wheatley Cl
3 Burnley BB12 127 D7
Fence BB12 147 D7
Wheatley Dr PR3 140 B8
Wheatley Gr BB9 170 C3
Wheatley Lane Prim Sch
BB12 147 E8
Wheatley Lane Rd
Barrowford BB9 170 B2
Fence BB12 147 E8
Wheatsheaf Ave PR3 140 A7
Wheatsheaf Wlk
4 Ormskirk L39 15 E5
Standish WN6 29 D1
Wheel La PR3 201 A6
Wheelton La PR25 77 A3
Wheelwright Cl BB7 231 D3
Wheelwrights Wharf L40 23 F4
Whelan Cl BB2 81 D7
Whernside FY4 110 F7
Whernside Cl BB18 196 A2
Whernside Cres PR2 118 D5
Whernside Gr LA5 223 F2
Whernside Rd LA1 218 B3
Whernside Way PR25 77 C1
Whewell Row BB5 103 C5
Whimberry Cl 1 PR6 43 E8
Whimbrel Dr FY5 176 A4
Whin Ave LA5 221 B6
Whin Dr LA5 221 B6
Whin Gr LA5 221 B6
Whin La PR3 155 B8
Whinberry Ave BB4 86 A1
Whinbrick Cotts PR4 113 B6
Whincroft BB11 127 E2
Whinfell Dr LA1 215 A3
Whinfield Ave
7 Chorley PR6 61 D1
Fleetwood FY7 198 E2
Whinfield La PR2 96 A8
Whinfield Pl
Blackburn BB2 101 A6
Preston PR2 96 A8
Whinfield St 9 BB5 125 A1
Whinney Brow PR3 207 C3
Whinney Heys Rd FY3 131 A6
Whinney Hill Rd BB5 125 C1
Whinney La
Blackburn BB2 101 C8
Euxton PR7 60 E3
Langho BB6 143 D1
Mellor BB2 122 B2
Whinneyfield La PR4 136 D2
Whinny La
Knott End-on-S FY6 199 E4
Waddington BB7 188 E6
Whinnysty La LA3 216 D1
Whinpark Ave FY3 131 A6
Whins Ave BB7 145 E7
Whins La Read BB12 145 E3
Wheelton PR6 62 A8
Whins The BB7 145 E7
Whinsands Cl PR2 118 D5
Whinsfell View LA4 217 B5
Whipp Ave BB7 166 D7
Whitaker Gn 8 BB4 85 E2
Whitaker St BB5 104 B7
Whitbarrow Sq 8 LA1 215 A8
Whitburn WN8 17 D1
Whitburn Rd L33 1 A4
Whitby Ave Fulwood PR2 116 F5
Southport PR9 54 D6
Whitby Dr BB2 102 A1
Whitby Pl PR2 116 F5
Whitby Rd
Lytham St Anne's FY8 111 A1
Morecambe LA4 217 C5
White Acre Rd BB5 104 E2
White Ash Est BB5 103 D4
White Ash La BB5 103 D3
White Ash Sch BB5 103 C4
White Birk Cl BL8 49 F2
White Bull St 4 BB12 127 C6
White Carr La Bury BL9 51 A1
Cleveleys FY5 153 A8
Hollins Lane PR3 207 E4
Treales PR4 134 C2
White Cross Ind Est LA1 214 F7
White Cross St LA1 214 F7
White Gate Fold PR7 42 E3
White Gr BB8 171 C6
White Hill Cl OL12 52 D4
White Horse Cl BL6 32 C5
White Horse La PR3 158 E1
White Hough Outdoor
Education Ctr BB12 169 E5
White House La
Bescar L40 37 C1
Lane Heads PR3 156 E4
White Lea PR3 204 C1
White Lee Ave BB8 172 C2
White Lee La PR3 183 C2
White Leys Cl BB18 196 F1
White Lund Ave LA3 217 C2
White Lund Rd LA3 217 C2
White Lund Trad Est
LA3 217 D2
White Mdw PR2 116 E3
White Moss La FY6 177 E4
White Moss Rd WN8 8 C7
White Moss Rd S WN8 8 D7
White Rd BB2 101 B6
White St 2 Burnley BB12 127 B6
Colne BB8 171 B4
White Walls Cl BB8 171 A3
Whiteacre WN6 29 A2
Whiteacre La BB6 144 E8
Whitebeam Cl
Cleveleys FY5 175 F5
Higher Penwortham PR1 96 B3
Whitebeck La LA6 240 B4
Whitebirk Dr BB1 102 C8
Whitebirk Ind Est BB1 102 B8
Whitebirk Rd BB1 102 D5
Whitecoats Dr FY8 91 D4
Whitecrest Ave 3 FY5 175 F4
Whitecroft Ave 8 BB4 85 B2
Whitecroft Cl BB4 85 B2
Whitecroft La BB2 121 E2
Whitecroft Mdws BB4 85 B2
Whitecroft View BB5 104 E2
Whitefield Cl Hightown L38 2 F2
Rufford L40 39 C3
Whitefield Inf Sch BB9 148 C8
Whitefield Mdw 5 PR5 97 F1
Whitefield Pl LA3 217 C2
Whitefield Prim Sch PR1 96 A4
Whitefield Rd PR1 96 A4
Whitefield Rd E PR1 96 B4
Whitefield Rd W PR1 96 A4
Whitefield St BB12 126 C4
Whitefield Terr BB11 128 B3
Whitefriar Cl PR2 117 A5
Whitegate LA3 217 D3
Whitegate Cl BB12 126 E7
Whitegate Dr FY3 130 E3
Whitegate Gdns BB12 126 E7
Whitegate Lodge 5
FY1 130 E3
Whitehalgh La BB6 143 C1
Whitehall Ave WN6 19 E8
Whitehall Ct 3 FY8 89 E6
Whitehall La Blackrod BL6 31 D3
Grindleton BB7 230 A1
Whitehall Rd
Blackburn BB2 101 B7
Darwen BB3 65 A5
Whitehall St Darwen BB3 65 B5
Nelson BB9 170 F1
Rochdale OL12 52 F1
Whitehaven Cl
Blackburn BB2 102 A1
Southport PR8 21 B3
Whitehaven St 7 BB11 127 E5
Whitehead Cl FY3 131 D5
Whitehead Dr PR26 76 E3
Whitehead St
Blackburn BB2 101 C5
21 Rawtenstall BB4 86 A3
Whitehey WN8 8 E8
Whitehey Rd WN8 8 E8
Whitehill Rd FY4 111 E6
Whiteholme Dr FY6 153 B6
Whiteholme Pl 3 PR2 116 E1
Whiteholme Rd FY5 152 F7
Whitehough Pl BB9 171 B1
Whitehouse Ave L37 12 A3
Whitehouse La L37 12 A3
Whiteledge Rd WN8 9 B6
Whitelees Way FY6 153 D3
Whitelens Ave 4 PR2 116 C1
Whiteley Ave BB2 101 A1
Whiteley St BB4 85 C1
Whiteleys La L40 16 D2
Whitelow Rd BL0 50 E5
Whitely Gr L33 1 A6
Whitemoor Rd BB8 194 C2
Whitemoss OL12 52 B2
Whitemoss Ave FY3 131 B7
Whitendale 10 LA1 218 A2
Whitendale Cres BB1 102 A3
Whitendale Dr
Bamber Bridge PR5 77 F8
Hest Bank LA5 220 F2
Whitendale Hall PR1 117 F1
Whitepits La LA2 239 D5
Whiterails Dr L39 15 D6
Whiterails Mews L39 15 D6
Whiteray Rd 9 LA1 218 B2
Whiteside Fold OL12 52 A1
Whiteside St 7 FY1 130 C6
Whiteside Way FY5 175 E3
Whitestock WN8 8 E8
Whitethorn Cl PR6 78 A2
Whitethorn Mews FY8 111 A2
Whitethorn Sq 4 PR2 116 D1
Whitethorne Mews FY5 153 C8
Whitewalls Dr BB8 171 A4
Whitewalls Ind Est
Colne BB8 171 A3
Nelson BB9 170 F2
Whitewell Cl PR3 181 D3
Whitewell Dr BB7 166 C7
Whitewell Pl 11 BB1 101 F6
Whitewell Rd BB5 104 D8
Whitewell Vale BB4 86 F2
Whitewood Cl FY8 90 E4
Whitley Ave
4 Blackpool FY3 130 D5
Cleveleys FY5 175 E5
Whitley Rd WN8 19 D3
Whitmoor Cl 7 LA4 217 B5
Whitmore Dr PR2 119 A2
Whitmore Gr PR2 119 A2
Whitmore Pl PR2 119 A2
Whitstone Dr WN8 9 D7
Whittaker Ave FY3 130 E7
Whittaker Cl BB12 127 B8
Whittaker St BB2 101 C5
Whittakers La BB7 189 F8
Whittam Ave FY4 130 E1
Whittam Cres BB7 144 B6
Whittam Ct BB10 129 B6
Whittam Rd Chorley PR7 43 B5
Whalley BB7 144 B6
Whittam St BB11 127 F5
Whitters La PR3 203 D2
Whittingham Dr BL0 50 C3
Whittingham La
Goosnargh PR3 138 C5
Grimsargh PR2 139 B2
Whittingham Rd PR3 139 F7
Whittle Cl BB7 189 F1
Whittle Dr L39 15 E7
Whittle Gn PR4 136 E3
Whittle Hill Egerton BL7 47 E3
Woodplumpton PR4 136 E3
Whittle La WN6,WN8 27 F4
Whittle Pk PR6 78 B2
Whittle St Haslingden BB4 85 A2
Rawtenstall BB4 86 A3
Whittle-le-Woods CE Prim
Sch PR6 61 B8
Whittlefield Prim Sch
BB12 127 D7
Whittles St OL13 71 B8
Whitton Mews 6 BL6 32 B4
Whittycroft Ave BB9 170 E6
Whittycroft Dr BB9 170 E6
Whitwell Ave 4 FY4 110 C5
Whitwell Cl WN6 29 D2
Whitwell Gdns BL6 32 B5
Whitworth Com High Sch
OL12 52 C8
Whitworth Dr PR7 43 A7
Whitworth Rake OL12 52 D8
Whitworth Rd OL12 52 F2
Whitworth Sq OL12 52 D8
Whitworth St Horwich BL6 32 C2
Kirkham PR4 113 F6
Whitworth Water Ski Ctr*
OL12 71 C2
Whitworth Way BB18 196 C4
Wholesome La
Bescar PR9 37 E3
New Longton PR4 75 E5
Whytha Rd BB7 192 D6
Wicken Tree Row BB12 145 F3
Wickentree Holt OL12 52 A1
Wickliffe St 9 BB9 170 F1
Wicklow Ave FY8 91 E5
Wicks Cres L37 11 C4
Wicks Gdns L37 11 D3
Wicks Gn L37 11 C3
Wicks Green Cl L37 11 C3
Wicks La L37 11 D3
Wickworth St BB9 149 A7
Widford Wlk BL6 31 E1
Widgeon Cl 5 FY5 175 F4
Widow Hill Rd BB10 148 D1
Wigan La
Adlington PR7,WN1 30 D7
Chorley PR7 43 E2
Wigan Rd
Bamber Bridge PR5 77 E7
Euxton PR7,PR25 60 C5
Ormskirk L39 16 A5
Skelmersdale WN8 8 F8
Westhead L40 16 E4
Wigeon Row FY8 90 E7
Wiggins La L40 38 B6
Wight Moss Way PR8 35 D3
Wignall St 8 PR1 118 C1
Wignalls Mdw L38 2 F3
Wigston Cl PR8 21 B4
Wigton Ave PR25 59 D7
Wilbraham St PR1 118 C1
Wilcove WN8 17 F1
Wild La FY4 111 D4
Wilderswood Ave BL6 32 C4

Wilderswood Cl PR6 78 C2
Wilderswood Ct BL6 32 D4
Wilding's La FY8 90 B8
Wildman St
3 Blackpool FY3 130 D7
Preston PR1 117 E2
Wildoaks Dr FY5 153 D8
Wilds Pl BL0 50 B5
Wildwood Cl BL0 50 A4
Wilfield St 7 BB11 127 E6
Wilford St FY3 130 E7
Wilfred Dr BL9 33 B4
Wilfred St BB5 104 C4
Wilkie Ave BB11 127 E2
Wilkin Sq 6 BB7 166 E8
Wilkinson Ave FY3 130 E4
Wilkinson Mount 6 BB18 197 B2
Wilkinson St
Bamber Bridge PR5 77 B8
Barrowford BB9 170 C2
Clow Bridge BB11 106 B4
Haslingden BB4 85 B4
Higham BB12 146 F5
Nelson BB9 148 E7
Wilkinson Way FY6 199 F5
Willacy La PR4 135 E3
Willacy Par LA3 216 E2
Willard Ave WN5 10 D3
Willaston Ave BB9 170 E8
Willey La LA2 206 D6
William Griffiths Ct BB2 101 B2
William Henry St 6 PR1 97 C8
William Herbert St 13 BB1 101 F6
William Hopwood St 8 BB1 102 A4
William St
Accrington BB5 104 C7
Bacup OL13 71 C8
11 Bamber Bridge PR5 77 A8
Blackburn BB2 101 E2
3 Blackpool FY3 130 E7
Brierfield BB9 148 B6
Carnforth LA5 223 D3
Clayton-le-M BB5 125 A1
Colne BB8 171 E4
11 Darwen BB3 82 A1
5 Earby BB18 197 B1
Horwich BL6 32 A3
17 Nelson BB9 170 E1
Ramsbottom BL0 68 C1
Whitworth OL12 71 C1
William Thompson Rec Ctr BB11 128 A5
William Young Cl PR1 118 C2
Williams Ave LA4 218 A6
Williams Dr BB2 102 A1
Williams La PR2 118 C7
Williams Pl 2 BB9 148 F8
Williams Rd BB10 128 B8
Williamson Park Butterfly Ho* LA1 215 B7
Williamson Rd LA1 215 A8
Willis Rd BB2 101 A2
Willis St 6 BB11 127 E5
Willoughby Ave FY5 175 D2
Willoughby St 6 BB1 101 E6
Willow Ave BB4 86 A4
Willow Bank
Bilsborrow PR3 159 A5
Darwen BB3 65 A6
Willow Bank La BB3 81 F1
Willow Brook
Accrington BB5 104 B6
Shirdley Hill L39 23 A6
Willow Chase PR4 113 D4
Willow Cl Adlington PR6 31 B8
Bamber Bridge PR5 77 A8
Barrowford BB9 170 B1
Clayton-le-M BB5 124 E3
Forton PR3 207 B3
Freckleton PR4 93 A5
Gregson Lane PR5 98 E1
Higher Penwortham PR1 96 A4
Thornton FY5 176 D1
Willow Coppice PR2 116 E3
Willow Cres
Burscough Bridge L40 25 F6
Clayton-le-W PR25 77 D3
Fulwood PR2 118 E2
Willow Ct
Poulton-le-F FY6 154 A3
Standish WN6 29 E2
5 Thornton FY5 176 D1
Willow Dr Barrow BB6 144 D8
Charnock Richard PR7 42 D3
Freckleton PR4 93 A5
Garstang PR3 204 C1
Nelson BB9 149 A8
Poulton-le-F FY6 131 D8
Skelmersdale WN8 17 E1
Wrea Green PR4 113 C4
Willow End L40 25 F4
Willow Field PR6 78 C3
Willow Field Chase PR5 99 B2
Willow Gn
2 Ormskirk L39 15 F5
Preston PR2 96 A8
Rufford L40 39 A3
Willow Gr Blackpool FY3 153 A1
Formby L37 11 F4
Goosnargh PR3 138 D6
Hambleton FY6 177 B2
Willow Gr continued
Lancaster LA1 215 B8
Morecambe LA4 217 F6
Southport PR9 35 E7
West Bradford BB7 189 D7
Willow Hey
Skelmersdale WN8 17 F1
Tarleton PR4 57 A7
Willow Ho PR8 35 A5
Willow La LA1 214 C7
Willow Lane Com Prim Sch LA1 214 D8
Willow Lodge FY8 90 C7
Willow Mill LA2 237 C3
Willow Mount BB1 122 F3
Willow Pk BB5 103 C2
Willow Pl PR4 155 F1
Willow Rd Chorley PR6 61 E2
Wymott PR26 58 F6
Willow St Accrington BB5 104 B6
Blackburn BB1 102 A7
Burnley BB12 127 E6
Bury BL9 33 B2
Clayton-le-M BB5 124 E3
Darwen BB3 81 F1
Fleetwood FY7 199 A4
Great Harwood BB6 124 C4
Haslingden BB4 85 B3
Rawtenstall BB4 69 E8
Willow Tree Ave
Broughton PR3 137 D3
Rawtenstall BB4 85 E2
Willow Tree Cres PR25 76 D1
Willow Tree Gdns 3 FY5 176 D1
Willow Trees Dr BB1 122 C1
Willow Way PR4 75 F7
Willow Wlk WN8 18 B4
Willow-Dale FY5 176 D1
Willowbank Ave FY4 110 E6
Willowbank Cotts PR26 58 B2
Willowbank Ct FY6 153 B5
Willowcroft Dr FY6 177 B1
Willowdene FY5 175 E1
Willowfield Rd LA3 213 A7
Willowgrove Pk FY6 200 B4
Willowhey PR9 53 F4
Willowmead Pk FY8 112 F2
Willowmead Way OL12 52 A2
Willows Ave
Cleveleys FY5 175 E1
Lytham St Anne's FY8 90 E3
Willows La
Accrington BB5 104 A3
Kirkham PR4 113 F5
Willows Park La PR3 140 B8
Willows RC Prim Sch The PR4 113 F5
Willows The Chorley PR7 43 B4
Coppull PR7 29 E8
Kirkham PR4 113 E4
Lytham St Anne's FY8 90 E3
Mawdesley L40 40 C2
Mellor Brook BB2 121 C3
Southport PR8 34 F6
Whitworth OL12 52 C5
Wills Ave L31 5 C2
Willshaw Rd FY2 152 B1
Wilmar Rd PR25 77 C2
Wilmcote Gr PR8 21 B4
Wilmore Cl BB8 171 C5
Wilmot Rd PR2 118 E3
Wilpshire Banks BB1 122 F4
Wilpshire Rd BB1 123 E4
Wilsham Rd WN5 10 E5
Wilson Cl PR4 57 A7
Wilson Dr PR4 155 F1
Wilson Fold BB12 127 B6
Wilson Fold Ave BL6 32 F1
Wilson Gr LA3 212 E8
Wilson Sq FY5 152 D7
Wilson St Blackburn BB2 101 D2
Bury BL9 33 A1
Clitheroe BB7 166 E7
Foulridge BB8 194 D1
Horwich BL6 32 A4
Wilson's Endowed CE Prim Sch LA6 237 B8
Wilton Cl Blackburn BB2 100 F8
Lancaster LA1 218 E4
Wilton Ct BB2 100 F7
Wilton Gr PR1 96 A4
Wilton Par FY1 130 B7
Wilton Pl 3 PR25 77 B1
Wilton St
Barrowford BB9 170 D3
Brierfield BB9 148 B5
Burnley BB10 148 B1
Wiltshire Ave BB12 127 B7
Wiltshire Dr BB4 68 B8
Wiltshire Mews PR4 116 D5
Wilvere Ct FY5 152 C7
Wilvere Dr FY5 152 C8
Wilworth Cres BB1 122 E2
Wimberley Banks BB1 101 F7
Wimberley Gdns 7 BB1 101 E6
Wimberley Pl 8 BB1 101 E6
Wimberley St BB1 101 E7
Wimbledon Ave FY5 152 D7
Wimbledon Ct FY5 152 D6
Wimborne FY8 89 F5
Wimborne Cl BL6 32 F1
Wimbourne Pl FY4 110 B6
Wimbrick Cl L39 15 D4
Wimbrick Cres L39 15 D3
Winchcombe Rd FY5 152 E7
Winchester Ave
Accrington BB5 104 C7
Winchester Ave continued
5 Blackpool FY4 130 D1
Chorley PR7 43 E4
Lancaster LA1 215 B5
Morecambe LA4 217 D6
Winchester Cl
Morecambe LA3 217 B2
4 Orrell WN5 10 F7
Winchester Dr FY6 153 B6
Winchester Rd
Longshaw WN5 10 D2
Padiham BB12 126 D6
Winchester St BB1 102 A3
Winchester Way 2 PR3 181 B7
Winckley Ct 11 PR1 96 F7
Winckley Rd
Clayton-le-M BB5 124 F2
Preston PR1 96 E6
Winckley Sq PR1 96 F7
Winckley St 9 PR1 96 F7
Winder Garth LA6 240 B1
Winder La PR3 207 B2
Windermere Ave
Accrington BB5 125 D1
Burnley BB10 148 A2
Clitheroe BB7 166 C7
Colne BB8 171 F6
Fleetwood FY7 175 D8
Leyland PR25 77 A3
Morecambe LA4 217 D4
Windermere Cl 4 BB1 101 F6
Windermere Cres PR8 21 C3
Windermere Ct 4 LA4 217 D4
Windermere Dr
Adlington PR6 44 B1
Darwen BB3 82 C3
Maghull L31 5 E2
Rainford Junction WA11 8 F2
Ramsbottom BL0 50 C7
Rishton BB1 124 A1
Windermere Ho PR1 96 B4
Windermere Rd
Bacup OL13 88 A3
Blackpool FY4 110 C8
Bolton-le-S LA5 221 A4
Carnforth LA5 221 E8
5 Chorley PR6 43 E7
Fulwood PR2 118 C4
Hightown L38 3 A4
Lancaster LA1 215 B8
Orrell WN5 10 F8
Padiham BB12 146 C2
Preston PR1 119 A1
Windermere Sq FY8 110 F2
Windfield Cl L33 1 A6
Windflower Dr PR25 77 E3
Windgate Much Hoole PR4 74 E2
Skelmersdale WN8 17 F1
Tarleton PR4 57 B5
Windgate Fold PR4 57 A5
Windham Pl LA1 218 A3
Windholme 6 LA1 218 A2
Windle Ash L31 5 C2
Windle Cl FY4 110 B4
Windmill Animal Farm* L40 38 B4
Windmill Ave
Kirkham PR4 114 C4
Ormskirk L39 15 F5
Windmill Cl FY3 131 E5
Windmill Ct 9 LA1 215 A3
Windmill Cvn Site FY4 111 E8
Windmill Ho
Blackpool FY4 110 F6
Southport PR9 53 F2
Windmill Hts WN8 10 A8
Windmill La PR6 79 B7
Windmill Pl FY4 110 F6
Windmill Rd WN8 9 F7
Windmill St LA1 214 D8
Windmill View PR4 114 A6
Windrows WN8 17 F1
Windrush Ave BL0 50 A2
Windrush The OL12 52 C4
Windsor Ave
Adlington PR7 30 F6
Blackpool FY4 110 B8
Church BB5 104 A8
Clitheroe BB7 166 C7
Fulwood PR2 117 B2
Haslingden BB4 85 A1
Lancaster LA1 215 B5
Longridge PR3 139 F7
Middleforth Green PR1 96 C3
Morecambe LA4 217 A3
New Longton PR4 96 A1
Newchurch BB4 86 E1
Thornton FY5 176 B2
Windsor Cl
Blackburn BB1 102 B3
Burscough L40 25 E3
Chorley PR7 43 B7
Leyland PR25 59 D7
Ramsbottom BL8 50 A1
Read BB12 145 D2
Windsor Ct
Poulton-le-F FY6 153 E3
Southport PR8 34 E4
Windsor Dr Brinscall PR6 62 E8
Fulwood PR2 117 D6
Horwich BL6 32 E2
Windsor Gdns PR3 181 B7
Windsor Gr LA4 217 A4
Windsor Lodge 3 FY8 90 D4
Windsor Pl
Barnoldswick BB18 196 D3
1 Fleetwood FY7 199 B5
Windsor Rd
Bamber Bridge PR5 97 D3
Blackburn BB2 101 B6
Blackburn,Knuzden Brook BB1 102 E4
Chorley PR7 43 B7
Darwen BB3 81 F3
Eccleston PR7 41 C7
Formby L37 11 F1
Garstang PR3 181 B7
Great Harwood BB6 124 D5
Lytham St Anne's FY8 90 A5
Lytham St Anne's,Ansdell FY8 90 D4
5 Maghull L31 5 C1
Morecambe LA3 216 F3
Normoss FY3 131 B7
Skelmersdale WN8 10 A8
Southport PR9 35 D7
Windsor St
Accrington BB5 104 C6
Burnley BB12 127 C6
Colne BB8 171 E5
Nelson BB9 149 A7
Windsor Terr FY7 199 B5
Windward Cl BB3 81 F6
Windy Bank BB8 171 E5
Windy Harbour Holiday Ctr FY6 154 F5
Windy Harbour Rd
Singleton FY6 155 A4
Southport PR8 21 E7
Windy Hill LA2 239 E8
Windy St PR3 185 E3
Windyhill 36 LA1 214 F8
Winery La PR5 97 C5
Winewall La BB8 172 C5
Winewall Rd BB8 172 B5
Wingate Ave
Blackpool FY5 152 D7
Morecambe LA4 217 C4
Wingate Pl FY5 152 D8
Wingate Wlk L33 1 A3
Wingate-Saul Rd LA1 214 E7
Wingates 2 PR1 96 C3
Wingrove Rd FY7 198 F2
Winifred Ave BL9 33 F4
Winifred La L39 6 B8
Winifred St
Blackpool FY1 130 B4
Ramsbottom BL0 50 B5
Rochdale OL12 52 B1
Winmarleigh CE Prim Sch PR3 203 E5
Winmarleigh Rd
Lancaster LA1 215 A2
Preston PR2 117 B1
Winmarleigh St 3 BB1 102 C5
Winmarleigh Wlk BB1 102 C4
Winmoss Dr L33 1 A5
Winnipeg Cl BB2 101 B8
Winnipeg Pl FY2 152 E3
Winscar Wlk FY6 153 B3
Winsford Cres FY5 152 C8
Winsford Wlk BB11 127 B5
Winslow Ave FY6 153 B5
Winslow Cl 7 PR1 96 E2
Winsor Ave PR25 60 B8
Winstanley Coll WN5 10 F3
Winstanley Gr 1 FY1 130 C5
Winstanley Rd Orrell WN5 10 F3
Skelmersdale WN8 8 F8
Winster Cl PR5 98 E4
Winster Ct BB5 124 E2
Winster Pk LA1 218 A2
Winster Pl FY4 131 D1
Winster Wlk LA1 218 A2
Winsters The WN8 17 F1
Winston Ave
Cleveleys FY5 175 F2
Lytham St Anne's FY8 90 B6
Winston Cres PR8 35 E2
Winston Rd BB1 101 D7
Winter Gardens Arc LA4 217 A5
Winter Hey La BL6 32 B3
Winter Hill Cl PR2 119 C7
Winterburn Rd BB2 81 C7
Winterley Dr BB5 125 E1
Winterton Rd BB3 82 A2
Winthorpe Ave LA4 217 D3
Winton Ave
Blackpool FY4 131 A1
Fulwood PR2 117 F6
Winton Gn BL6 32 F1
Winward Ho FY8 89 E5
Wiseman Cl LA4 217 C4
Wiseman St BB11 127 F6
Wisp Hill Gr LA2 219 D6
Wisteria Dr BB3 82 B7
Wiswell Cl
Brierfield BB10 148 E2
Rawtenstall BB4 86 A4
Wiswell La BB7 144 D6
Wiswell Shay BB7 144 E7
Witham Cl WN6 29 D1
Witham Rd WN8 17 D1
Withens Rd L31 5 D3
Withers St BB1 101 F4
Witherslack Cl LA4 217 B3
Withgill Piggery Cotts BB7 165 E6
Within Gr BB5 104 D8
Withington La PR7 41 E2
Withins Field L38 2 F3
Withins La L37 4 A7
Withnell Fold PR6 79 C2
Withnell Fold Old Rd PR6 79 E1
Withnell Fold Prim Sch PR6 79 C3
Withnell Gr PR6 61 E1
Withnell Rd FY4 110 B8
Withy Ct PR2 117 E3
Withy Grove Cl PR5 97 F1
Withy Grove Cres PR5 97 F1
Withy Grove Rd PR5 97 F1
Withy Par PR2 117 E4
Withy Trees Ave PR5 97 F1
Withy Trees Cl PR5 97 F1
Witney Ave BB2 80 E8
Wittlewood Dr BB5 125 B1
Witton Ave FY7 198 E1
Witton Ctry Pk* BB2 100 F4
Witton Ctry Pk Visitors Ctr* BB2 100 F3
Witton Gr FY7 198 E1
Witton Par BB2 101 C3
Witton Park High Sch BB2 101 A4
Witton St PR1 97 B8
Woborrow Rd LA3 212 E8
Woburn Cl BB5 104 E3
Woburn Gn PR25 77 B2
Woburn Rd FY1 130 C7
Woburn Way PR3 181 D2
Wold The PR6 62 A3
Wolfenden Gn BB4 69 F8
Wollaton Dr PR8 35 F3
Wolseley Cl PR25 60 A8
Wolseley Pl 20 PR1 97 A7
Wolseley Rd PR1 96 E5
Wolseley St
Blackburn BB2 101 D1
Lancaster LA1 215 A8
Wolsey Cl FY5 175 E3
Wolsley Rd
Blackpool FY1 130 B1
Fleetwood FY7 198 F4
Wolverton WN8 8 F8
Wolverton Ave FY2 152 B2
Wood Bank
Haslingden BB4 67 F6
Kingsfold PR1 96 C3
Wood Cl BB9 170 A5
Wood Clough Platts BB9 148 A5
Wood End
Brierfield BB12 147 F3
Kingsfold PR1 96 C1
Wood End Rd PR6 78 B2
Wood Gn Kirkham PR4 114 B7
Leyland PR25 76 E2
Wood Green Dr FY5 152 F8
Wood Hey Gr OL12 52 F4
Wood House La BB7 229 A8
Wood La Edenfield BL0 68 D2
Haskayne L37,L39 13 D1
Heskin Green PR7 41 E3
Hoscar L40 26 E5
Mawdesley L40 40 D5
Parbold WN8 27 D2
Wrightington Bar PR7,WN6 28 E8
Wood Lark Dr PR7 42 F5
Wood Lea Bank 9 BB4 69 F8
Wood Lea Rd BB4 69 F8
Wood Nook 1 BB4 86 A7
Wood Park Rd FY1 130 E1
Wood Road La BL8,BL9 50 C1
Wood St Blackpool FY1 130 B5
Brierfield BB9 148 B5
Burnley BB10 128 A8
Church BB5 103 E5
Colne BB8 171 E4
Darwen BB3 81 F1
Fleetwood FY7 175 E8
Great Harwood BB6 124 E5
Hapton BB12 126 C4
Horwich BL6 32 C3
1 Lancaster LA1 214 F8
Lytham St Anne's FY8 89 E6
Poulton-le-F FY6 154 A3
Ramsbottom BL0 50 B5
Wood Street Livesey Fold 9 BB3 81 F2
Wood Terr BB7 190 E5
Wood View
Blackburn BB2 100 F1
Burton in L LA6 242 C3
Wood View La FY6 177 C7
Wood's Brow PR3 141 B6
Wood's La PR3 180 A6
Woodacre Rd PR2 119 A2
Woodale Laithe BB9 170 C3
Woodbank Ave BB3 81 E2
Woodbank Ct 3 FY5 152 F7
Woodbine Gdns BB12 127 C7
Woodbine Rd
Blackburn BB2 101 B6
Burnley BB12 127 C6
Woodbine Terr OL14 109 B1
Woodbridge Gdns OL12 52 C2
Woodburn Cl BB2 101 A8
Woodbury Ave
Blackburn BB2 101 D2
Fence BB12 147 D7
Woodcock Cl FY5 176 A5
Woodcock Est PR5 77 B6
Woodcock Fold PR7 41 C7
Woodcock Hill Rd BB2 100 B3
Woodcote Cl L33 1 A4
Woodcourt Ave BB11 127 D3
Woodcrest BB1 122 F5
Woodcroft
Appley Bridge WN6 19 E6

Woodcroft continued
Skelmersdale WN8 8 F8
Woodcroft Ave BB4 85 F5
Woodcroft Cl PR1 96 C2
Woodcroft St BB4 85 F5
Woodfall PR7 61 B2
Woodfield PR5 78 C6
Woodfield Ave
Accrington BB5 104 D3
3 Blackpool FY1 130 B2
Rochdale OL12 52 E2
Woodfield Ct FY5 176 B1
Woodfield Rd
Blackpool FY1 130 B2
Chorley PR7 61 C1
Ormskirk L39 15 D3
Thornton FY5 176 D1
Woodfield Terr BB9 148 C5
Woodfield View BB7 144 C5
Woodfields
Hurst Green BB7 165 B3
Simonstone BB12 145 E3
Woodfold PR1 96 B3
Woodfold Cl BB2 121 C3
Woodfold La PR3 204 C5
Woodfold Park Farm
BB2 100 B8
Woodfold Pl BB2 101 B5
Woodford Copse PR7 43 A7
Woodgate LA3 217 F2
Woodgate Ave BL9 33 D4
Woodgate Hill Rd
Bury BL9 33 C3
Bury,Woodgate Hill BL9 33 D4
Woodgates Rd BB2 100 F5
Woodgrove Rd BB11 128 B3
Woodhall Cres PR5 98 E4
Woodhall Gdns FY6 177 C2
Woodhart La PR7 41 C5
Woodhead Cl
Ramsbottom BL0 50 C4
Rawtenstall BB4 87 A2
Woodhead Rd BB12 145 D2
Woodhey High Sch BL0 50 A3
Woodhey Rd BL0 50 A3
Woodhill Ave LA4 217 A3
Woodhill Cl LA4 217 A3
Woodhill La LA4 217 A4
Woodhouse Rd FY5 153 E8
Woodhurst Dr WN6 29 D1
Woodland Ave
Bacup OL13 87 F5
Bescar L40 23 F7
Thornton FY5 176 B2
Woodland Cl
Hambleton FY6 177 D1
Wrea Green PR4 113 B3
Woodland Cres FY6 200 A6
Woodland Dr
Clayton-le-M BB5 124 F5
Poulton-le-F FY6 153 E1
Standish WN6 29 E2
Woodland Gr
Blackpool FY3 130 E4
Egerton BL7 47 D2
Higher Penwortham PR1 96 B5
Woodland Pl BB3 81 F7
Woodland Rd OL12 52 C2
Woodland Terr OL13 87 F4
Woodland View
Bacup OL13 87 F4
Brinscall PR6 62 F7
Great Harwood BB6 124 C6
Woodlands Ave
Bamber Bridge PR5 98 A2
Blackburn BB2 100 E1
Fulwood PR2 118 E2
Kingsfold PR1 96 E2
8 Kirkham PR4 113 F5
Woodlands Cl Formby L37 11 D2
Newton-w-S PR4 114 F3
Ormskirk L39 16 A4
Rawtenstall BB4 86 D1
Southport PR9 35 D8
Woodlands Com Prim Sch
WN8 18 C2
Woodlands Cres PR3 137 B5
Woodlands Ct 5 FY8 90 D4
Woodlands Dr
Fulwood PR2 117 E8
Kirkham PR4 114 B7
Leyland PR25 76 F1
Morecambe LA3 216 E2
Shevington WN6 19 F4
Silverdale LA5 224 C4
Warton PR4 92 C5
West Bradford BB7 189 D7
Whalley BB7 144 C5
Woodlands Gr
Darwen BB3 81 D2
Grimsargh PR2 139 E1
Morecambe LA3 216 E2
Padiham BB12 146 B1
Woodlands Mdw PR7 43 C3
Woodlands Pk BB7 144 C5
Woodlands Prim Sch
L37 11 D3
Woodlands Rd
Edenfield BL0 68 D2
Formby L37 11 D3
Lancaster LA1 218 E4
Lytham St Anne's FY8 90 D4
Nelson BB9 148 F8
Woodlands Sch PR2 118 E2
Woodlands Specl Sch
FY3 130 E4
Woodlands The
Brockhall Village BB6 143 C6

Woodlands The continued
Garstang PR3 181 B8
6 Preston PR2 116 E1
Southport PR8 21 C5
Woodlands View LA6 237 B8
Woodlands Way
Longton PR4 74 F8
Newsham PR3 137 B5
Woodlea Chase BB3 65 C3
Woodlea Cl PR9 54 D5
Woodlea Gdns BB9 148 D5
Woodlea Jun Sch PR25 59 F8
Woodlea Rd
Blackburn BB1 102 B4
Leyland PR25 59 F8
Woodlee Rd PR4 73 F2
Woodleigh Cl L31 5 B5
Woodley Ave
Accrington BB5 104 C4
Thornton FY5 176 D1
Woodley Park Rd WN8 18 B4
Woodman La LA6 241 F6
Woodmancote PR7 61 B2
Woodmoss La PR8,L40 36 E2
Woodnook Prim Sch
BB5 104 C4
Woodnook Rd WN6 19 E8
Woodpecker Hill 3
BB11 127 C5
Woodplumpton La PR3 137 C2
Woodplumpton Rd
Burnley BB11 127 F1
Fulwood PR2 117 C3
Woodplumpton PR4 136 E2
Woodplumpton,Moor Side
PR4 136 D4
Woodplumpton St Anne's CE
Prim Sch PR4 136 D2
Woodridge Ave FY5 152 C8
Woodrow WN8 8 E8
Woodrow Dr WN8 27 A1
Woodroyd Dr BL9 33 C3
Woodruff Cl FY5 175 F5
Woodrush LA4 217 F6
Woods Brow BB2 120 D5
Woods Cl L39 14 A4
Woods Gn PR1 96 E6
Woods La PR3,PR4 135 E8
Woodsend Cl BB2 82 A8
Woodside Chorley PR7 43 E4
Euxton PR7 60 C3
Haslingden BB4 85 C1
Leyland PR25 77 C4
Woodside Ave
Clayton Green PR6 78 B1
Fulwood,Cadley PR2 117 E4
Fulwood,Ribbleton PR2 118 E3
New Longton PR4 75 F7
Rishton BB1 102 F8
Southport PR8 21 B3
Woodside Cl
Huncoat BB5 125 F1
Skelmersdale WN8 10 C8
Woodside Cres BB4 86 D1
Woodside Dr
Blackpool FY3 131 A5
Ramsbottom BL0 50 A5
Woodside Gr BB2 81 A8
Woodside Rd
Accrington,Hillock Vale
BB5 104 E8
Huncoat BB5 125 F1
Simonstone BB12 145 E2
Woodside Terr BB9 148 C8
Woodsley St BB12 127 B5
Woodstock Ave FY5 153 C8
Woodstock Cl 8 PR5 77 C8
Woodstock Cres BB2 80 E8
Woodstock Dr PR8 21 F8
Woodstock Gdns FY4 110 B7
Woodstock St 12 OL12 52 C1
Woodtop 1 BB11 127 D5
Woodvale Darwen BB3 81 F1
Leyland PR26 59 A8
Woodvale Ct PR9 55 A5
Woodvale Rd
Clayton Green PR6 78 B3
Southport PR8 21 E2
Woodville Rd
Adlington PR6 43 F1
Blackburn BB1 102 A7
Brierfield BB9 148 C6
2 Chorley PR7 43 C8
Kingsfold PR1 96 D2
Woodville Rd W 5 PR1 96 C2
Woodville St
Lancaster LA1 215 A8
Leyland PR25 77 B2
Woodville Terr
Darwen BB3 65 B6
Lytham St Anne's FY8 90 F3
Woodward Rd L33 1 D4
Woodway PR2 117 C4
Woodwell La LA5 224 C1
Wookey Cl PR2 118 D6
Wooley La BB5 104 F2
Woolman Rd FY1 130 C4
Woolpack BB8 171 E3
Woolwich St BB1 102 B5
Woone La BB7 166 D7
Worcester Ave
4 Accrington BB5 104 A7
Garstang PR3 181 B8
Lancaster LA1 215 B5
Leyland PR25 60 B8
Worcester Gdns PR4 116 D5
Worcester Pl PR7 43 E3

Worcester Rd
Blackburn BB1 102 C5
Blackpool FY3 131 A3
Worden Cl PR25 59 F7
Worden High Sch PR25 76 E1
Worden La PR25 60 A7
Worden Rd PR2 117 D3
Wordsworth Ave
Blackpool FY3 131 B2
Bolton-le-S LA5 221 A5
Longshaw WN5 10 D1
5 Lytham St Anne's FY8 91 D4
Orrell WN5 10 F6
Padiham BB12 126 E7
Thornton FY5 176 A2
Warton PR4 92 E6
Wordsworth Cl
Ormskirk L39 15 D6
Oswaldtwistle BB5 103 C4
Wordsworth Ct 1 FY8 90 C4
Wordsworth Dr BB6 124 B4
Wordsworth Gdns BB3 82 B1
Wordsworth Ho LA1 218 C4
Wordsworth Pl PR5 97 D2
Wordsworth Rd
Accrington BB5 104 A4
Colne BB8 171 D5
Wordsworth St
Brierfield BB10 148 F2
Burnley BB12 127 C6
5 Hapton BB12 126 C4
Wordsworth Terr PR6 61 D2
Workshop Rd LA3 212 F2
Worrall St 1 OL12 52 D2
Worsicks Cotts FY6 154 E1
Worsley Ave FY4 110 C7
Worsley Cl FY6 199 E5
Worsley Ct 18 BB5 103 E4
Worsley Rd FY8 90 C5
Worsley St
Accrington BB5 104 D4
Rising Bridge BB5 85 A8
Worsten Ave BB2 101 C1
Worsthorne Prim Sch
BB10 129 A6
Worston Cl
Accrington BB5 103 F4
Rawtenstall BB4 86 A4
Worston La BB6 124 F6
Worston Pl BB2 101 C5
Worswick Cres 3 BB4 86 A2
Worthalls Rd BB12 145 D1
Worthing Cl PR8 34 F3
Worthing Rd PR2 117 A4
Worthington Rd FY4 111 B4
Worthy St PR6 43 E7
Wraith St BB3 65 A8
Wray Cres
Wrea Green PR4 113 C4
Wymott PR26 58 F6
Wray Ct LA1 218 C4
Wray Gr FY5 152 D8
Wray with Botton Prim Sch
LA2 238 D6
Wraywood Ct FY7 198 C1
Wren Ave PR1 96 E5
Wren Cl Carleton FY6 153 A4
Thornton FY5 153 D8
Wren Dr BL9 33 B4
Wren Gr FY3 130 E2
Wren St Burnley BB12 127 C6
Nelson BB9 148 F8
Preston PR1 118 B2
Wrennalls La PR7 41 B5
Wright St Chorley PR6 43 E8
Horwich BL6 32 B4
6 Kirkham PR4 113 F6
Southport PR9 35 C7
Weir OL13 88 A7
Wright St W 4 BL6 32 B4
Wrightington Bar WN6 28 E8
Wrightington Hospl
WN6 28 D2
Wrightington Mossy Lea Prim
Sch WN6 28 F6
Wrights Fold PR25 60 C8
Wrights Terr PR8 35 B3
Wrigleys Cl L37 11 F5
Wrigleys La L37 11 F5
Written Stone La PR3 162 E1
Wroxham Cl BB10 148 D2
Wroxton Cl FY5 152 F7
Wycherley Rd OL12 52 B2
Wychnor PR2 117 B7
Wycollar Cl BB5 104 C4
Wycollar Dr BB2 101 A6
Wycollar Rd BB2 101 B6
Wycoller Ave BB10 128 D5
Wycoller Country Pk*
BB8 173 B3
Wycombe Ave FY4 110 B6
Wyfordby Ave BB2 101 A7
Wyke Cop Rd PR8,PR9 36 D2
Wyke La PR8,PR9 36 E6
Wyke Wood La PR9 36 F7
Wykeham Gr OL12 52 B1
Wykeham Rd FY8 91 B4
Wyllin Rd L33 1 A2
Wymundsley PR7 61 A2
Wyndene Cl PR3 140 C8
Wyndene Gr PR4 93 B6
Wyndham Gdns FY4 110 D6
Wyndham Pl LA4 217 F6
Wynfield PR5 97 F2
Wynnstay Ave L31 5 D3
Wynnwood Ave 1 FY1 130 D8
Wynotham St BB10 148 C1
Wyre Ave PR4 114 B5

Wyre Bank PR3 157 B6
Wyre Cl
Great Eccleston PR3 156 C5
Morecambe LA3 217 F2
Wyre Cres BB3 81 D4
Wyre Ct Fleetwood FY7 198 E3
Poulton-le-F FY6 154 A3
Wyre Estuary Ctry Pk*
FY5 176 E3
Wyre Gr FY1 130 C3
Wyre Ho LA1 214 F7
Wyre La PR3 204 D1
Wyre Rd FY5 153 F6
Wyre Side Cl PR3 181 C8
Wyre St Fleetwood FY7 198 F3
Kirkham PR4 113 F6
Lytham St Anne's FY8 90 A7
Padiham BB12 126 D8
Preston PR2 117 C1
Wyre Vale Cvn Pk PR3 204 B1
Wyre View FY6 199 E5
Wyredale Ct FY7 198 F3
Wyredale Rd FY8 89 C8
Wyrefields FY6 154 A3
Wyresdale Ave
Accrington BB5 104 A8
Blackpool FY2 152 D4
Morecambe LA3 216 E1
Poulton-le-F FY6 153 C3
Southport PR8 35 D4
Wyresdale Cres
Fulwood PR2 118 D4
Glasson LA2 209 E4
Scorton PR3 204 E7
Wyresdale Ct LA1 215 B7
Wyresdale Dr PR25 60 B6
Wyresdale Gdns LA1 215 B7
Wyresdale Rd
Knott End-on-S FY6 199 D5
Lancaster LA1 215 B6
Quernmore LA2 232 A6
Wyreside PR3 155 E8
Wyreside Dr FY6 177 B2
Wyreside Ecology & Visitor
Ctr* FY5 176 E3
Wyreside Hall LA2 226 B7
Wytham St 6 BB12 126 D7
Wythburn Ave BB2 80 E8
Wythburn Cl BB12 127 B8
Wythorpe Croft LA4 217 B4
Wyvern Way FY6 153 C5

Y

Yardley Ctr L33 1 C1
Yardley Rd L33 1 C1
Yare St 7 BB4 69 F8
Yarlside La BD23 231 E4
Yarm Pl BB11 128 A6
Yarmouth Ave BB4 85 C2
Yarraville St BB4 86 A2
Yarrow Ave L31 5 F2
Yarrow Cl Croston PR26 58 B2
Withnell PR6 80 A1
Yarrow Gate PR7 43 E6
Yarrow Gr BL6 32 B4
Yarrow Mill PR6 43 E6
Yarrow Pl PR25 59 D8
Yarrow Rd Chorley PR6 43 E6
Leyland PR25 59 D8
Yarrow Valley Pk PR7 43 A2
Yarrow Wlk LA3 217 B2
Yarwood St BL9 33 A2
Yates Fold BB2 101 F2
Yates St Blackpool FY1 130 B6
Chorley PR7 43 B5
Yeadon WN8 18 B1
Yeadon Gr PR7 43 A7
Yeadon Way FY4 110 D7
Yealand Ave LA3 212 F6
Yealand CE Prim Sch
LA5 225 E3
Yealand Dr LA1 215 A4
Yealand Gr LA5 223 E2
Yealand Rd LA5 225 E2
Yeargate Ind Est BL9 33 D2
Yellow Hall BB18 195 A5
Yellow House La PR8 35 B6
Yenham La LA3 213 E1
Yerburgh Rd BB2 121 E2
Yew Ct FY7 198 C1
Yew Gn PR4 114 B7
Yew St 10 Blackburn BB1 102 A7
2 Bury BL9 33 C3
Yew Tree Ave Euxton PR7 60 C4
Grimsargh PR2 139 C2
Yew Tree Cl
Garstang PR3 181 B8
Newton-w-S PR4 114 F3
Wilpshire BB1 122 E6
Yew Tree Dr
Blackburn BB2 122 B1
Low Bentham LA2 239 C8
Oswaldtwistle BB5 103 F3
Yew Tree Gdns
Silverdale LA5 224 C2
Stalmine FY6 177 C8
Yew Tree Gr BB4 68 F8
Yew Tree Rd
Blackpool FY3 153 A1
Ormskirk L39 15 E7
Yewbarrow Cl BB12 147 C1
Yewdale WN8 18 A1
Yewdale Ave LA3 212 F6
Yewlands Ave
4 Bamber Bridge PR5 97 F1
Fulwood PR2 117 E6

Yewlands Ave continued
Heskin Green PR7 41 F3
3 Leyland PR25 77 A1
Yewlands Cres PR2 117 E6
Yewlands Dr
Brierfield BB10 148 B3
Fulwood PR2 117 E6
Garstang PR3 204 C1
2 Leyland PR25 77 A1
Yewtree Ave PR2 119 A4
Yewtree Cl PR7 43 C3
Yewtree Gr PR5 77 A7
York Ave Cleveleys FY5 175 D2
Fleetwood FY7 198 E3
Fulwood PR2 117 E4
Haslingden BB4 68 B8
Southport PR8 35 A5
York Cl
4 Bamber Bridge PR5 97 D3
Clayton-le-M BB5 124 F3
Formby L37 11 F6
Leyland PR25 59 E7
York Cres BB1 122 F3
York Dr
Great Eccleston PR3 156 C5
Kirkham PR4 114 B2
Ramsbottom BL0 50 A4
York Fields BB18 196 B1
York Gdns PR8 35 A5
York Gr PR3 181 B7
York Ho Lancaster LA1 215 A5
27 Preston PR1 97 A7
York La BB6 123 D8
York Pl Accrington BB5 104 B7
Adlington PR6 31 A8
Morecambe LA4 217 C5
York Rd Blackpool FY2 152 B4
Formby L37 12 A3
Lancaster LA1 215 A5
Langho BB1,BB6 123 D6
Lytham St Anne's FY8 89 F5
Southport PR8 34 F4
York St Accrington BB5 104 B7
Bacup OL13 87 F5
Barnoldswick BB18 196 B2
Blackburn BB2 101 E3
Blackpool FY1 130 B3
Bury BL9 33 A2
Chorley PR7 43 D7
Church BB5 103 E6
Clitheroe BB7 189 F1
Colne BB8 171 F5
Great Harwood BB6 124 D5
Nelson BB9 148 F8
Oswaldtwistle BB5 103 C3
Rawtenstall BB4 86 A7
Rishton BB1 124 A1
York Terr Blackburn BB2 80 D8
4 Southport PR9 35 C8
York View BB3 81 B6
Yorke St 2 BB11 127 F5
Yorkshire St
Accrington BB5 104 C4
16 Bacup OL13 87 F3
Blackpool FY1 130 B3
Burnley BB11 128 B6
Huncoat BB5 125 E2
16 Nelson BB9 148 E8
Yorkshire St E LA4 216 F4
Yorkshire St W LA3 216 E4
Young Ave PR25 77 C1
Young St Blackburn BB2 101 B2
Ramsbottom BL0 50 B6

Z

Zama St 9 BL0 50 A4
Zebudah St BB2 101 C2
Zetland St Preston PR1 97 C7
Southport PR9 35 D7
Zion Rd BB1 102 A8
Zion St Bacup OL13 88 A3
Colne BB8 171 D4

Notes

Using the Ordnance Survey National Grid

Any feature in this atlas can be given a unique reference to help you find the same feature on other Ordnance Survey maps of the area, or to help someone else locate you if they do not have a Street Atlas.

The grid squares in this atlas match the Ordnance Survey National Grid and are at 500 metre intervals. The small figures at the bottom and sides of every other grid line are the National Grid kilometre values (**00** to **99** km) and are repeated across the country every 100 km (see left).

To give a unique National Grid reference you need to locate where in the country you are. The country is divided into 100 km squares with each square given a unique two-letter reference. Use the administrative map to determine in which 100 km square a particular page of this atlas falls.

The bold letters and numbers between each grid line (**A** to **F**, **1** to **8**) are for use within a specific Street Atlas only, and when used with the page number, are a convenient way of referencing these grid squares.

***Example** The railway bridge over DARLEY GREEN RD in grid square B1*

Step 1: Identify the two-letter reference, in this example the page is in **SP**

Step 2: Identify the 1 km square in which the railway bridge falls. Use the figures in the southwest corner of this square: Eastings **17**, Northings **74**. This gives a unique reference: **SP 17 74**, accurate to 1 km.

Step 3: To give a more precise reference accurate to 100 m you need to estimate how many tenths along and how many tenths up this 1 km square the feature is (to help with this the 1 km square is divided into four 500 m squares). This makes the bridge about **8** tenths along and about **1** tenth up from the southwest corner.

This gives a unique reference: **SP 178 741**, accurate to 100 m.

Eastings (read from left to right along the bottom) come before Northings (read from bottom to top). If you have trouble remembering say to yourself "Along the hall, THEN up the stairs"!

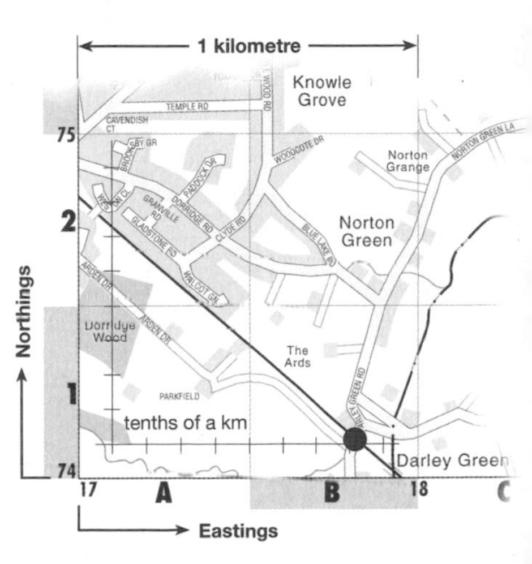

Addresses

Name and Address	Telephone	Page	Grid reference

Name and Address	Telephone	Page	Grid reference